HEINRICH HIMMLER

HEINRICH
HIMMLER

PETER LONGERICH

TRANSLATED BY

JEREMY NOAKES

AND

LESLEY SHARPE

OXFORD
UNIVERSITY PRESS

OXFORD
UNIVERSITY PRESS

Great Clarendon Street, Oxford OX2 6DP

Oxford University Press is a department of the University of Oxford.
It furthers the University's objective of excellence in research, scholarship,
and education by publishing worldwide in

Oxford New York

Auckland Cape Town Dar es Salaam Hong Kong Karachi
Kuala Lumpur Madrid Melbourne Mexico City Nairobi
New Delhi Shanghai Taipei Toronto

With offices in

Argentina Austria Brazil Chile Czech Republic France Greece
Guatemala Hungary Italy Japan Poland Portugal Singapore
South Korea Switzerland Thailand Turkey Ukraine Vietnam

Oxford is a registered trade mark of Oxford University Press
in the UK and in certain other countries

Published in the United States
by Oxford University Press Inc., New York

British Library Cataloguing in Publication Data

Data available

Library of Congress Cataloging in Publication Data

Data available

Typeset by SPI Publisher Services, Pondicherry, India
Printed in Great Britain
on acid-free paper by
Clays Ltd, St Ives plc

ISBN 978-0-19-959232-6

1 3 5 7 9 10 8 6 4 2

Acknowledgements

This book was written, with interruptions from other publications, over the last ten years and in various places: in London and Munich, in Washington, Frankfurt, and Essen, as well as almost everywhere I spent time during those years.

First and foremost, I should like to thank my colleagues and students at Royal Holloway College, University of London, who were once again willing to enable me to complete this work by generously allowing me periods of research. A series of research institutes gave me vital support by granting scholarships and visiting fellowships that provided the opportunity to discuss my work with others: the Center for Advanced Holocaust Studies at the US Holocaust Memorial Museum, the Fritz Bauer Institute in Frankfurt, and the Cultural Studies Institute in Essen.

In addition, in the last few years I have had the opportunity of presenting my work as it developed at a number of universities, in particular Freiburg, Stanford, Exeter, Oxford, and London (German History Seminar), also at the Villa Ten Hompel in Münster, at the Wewelsburg Documentation Centre, and at the Imperial War Museum.

I was also able to have intensive discussions about Himmler's personality with a group of psychoanalysts in Hamburg and a circle of psychotherapists in Cologne; the discussions with both groups made a distinct and lasting impact on my work on Himmler. I should like to thank all those who took part in these gatherings: Christiane Adam, Sabine Brückner-Jungjohann, Petra Demleux-Morawietz, Gundula Fromm, Beata Hammerich, Ulrich Knocke, Dr Bärbel Kreidt, Rita Krull-Wittkopf, Johannes Pfäfflin, Dr Peter Pogany-Wnendt, Erda Siebert, Dirk Sieveking, Dr Bernd Sonntag, and Matthias Wellershoff.

Dr Andreas Kunz, director of the branch of the Federal Archive in Ludwigsburg, drew my attention to the memoirs of Colonel Eismann, Himmler's military colleague on the staff of the Army Group Vistula. Mrs Christa Schmeisser, in the head administrative office of the Bavarian

Archives, obtained for me a transcription of Himmler's diaries and part of his correspondence. Mr Alois Schmidmeier helped me to decipher a number of shorthand passages in Himmler's letters. I am grateful to him as well as to all the staff of all the various archives and institutions that have supported my work.

P.L

Munich and London

July 2008

Contents

IV. INTO WAR: AMBITION AND DISAPPOINTMENT

V. THE GREATER GERMANIC REICH:
LIVING-SPACE AND ETHNIC MURDER

VI. DOWNFALL IN STAGES

Note on Sources

The primary sources for this biography are scattered across archives in several countries. Thus there are personal documents of Himmler's in the Bundesarchiv [Federal Archive] in Koblenz, in the Hoover Library in Stanford, California, and in the Special Archive in Moscow. Margarethe Himmler's diary, which provides insights into their marriage, and several family photograph albums have for some years been accessible to researchers in the US Holocaust Museum in Washington, DC. Some of Himmler's private papers are in the hands of various individuals and are continually being offered for sale in auction houses. It is, however, extremely unlikely that further material of Himmler's will come to light that provides significant insights into his political actions.

The Bundesarchiv in Berlin contains over 4,000 files of the Personal Staff of the Reichsführer-SS and varying quantities of material from the SS main offices. The collection of the personal files of SS leaders in the former Berlin Document Center (now part of the Bundesarchiv, Berlin) not only contains valuable information about their careers but, in some cases, substantial correspondence with Himmler and his personal staff. I have used several hundred of these files for this book.

The Munich archives proved very productive for Himmler's early years. The files of the Nazi Party's Reich propaganda headquarters in the Bundesarchiv, Berlin contain extensive correspondence of Himmler, who ran this office from 1926 to 1930 as its deputy head.

Finally, his activities are revealed in the files of a large number of other institutions, for example in those of the Foreign Ministry, which are held in its political archive in Berlin, in the documents of military agencies (Bundesarchiv, Freiburg), in those of various party and state agencies (Bundesarchiv, Berlin), but also in the files of British institutions, which are in the Public Record Office in London [now the National Archives].

As far as possible I have consulted the original documents in the relevant archives. However, I was obliged to make a few exceptions: in some cases

I have used copies of SS files from the Bundesarchiv in Berlin, which are available in the National Archives in Washington, DC, and used their reference numbers because trying to access these files in Berlin proved too time-consuming. In a number of cases I have also used copies of documents I was able to make during a lengthy stay in Yad Vashem in 1995–6. The originals are held in other archives.

The most important of the published sources is *Heinrich Himmler's Office Diary 1941/42*, which was edited by eight German historians. In an exemplary pioneering project, covering the particularly critical years 1941–2, they combined Himmler's hitherto undiscovered appointment notes, which were held in the Moscow Special Archive, with the Himmler calendars which were already available, and drew upon the Reichsführer's correspondence contained in various collections of files in order to provide a context for the diary entries. In the process they have provided an indispensable source.

Among other important published Himmler documents are the collection of speeches edited by Bradley Smith and Agnes F. Peterson and the very well-chosen collection of Himmler letters edited by Helmuth Heiber, which are in some cases absurd and in others shocking.

Since their publication in 1952 the memoirs of his masseur, Felix Kersten, *Totenkopf und Treue* (translated as *The Kersten Memoirs 1940–1945* (1956)), based on so-called diaries, have been a popular source for works on Himmler. According to the author, under his soothing hands the Reichsführer spoke freely about his views and plans. In some cases Kersten's accounts of Himmler's comments correspond remarkably closely to other reports of his views, for example in respect of his attitude to homosexuality (pp. 67 ff.) or on the theme of the 'rebirth of the clan' (pp. 191 ff.); but, on the other hand, they also contain fanciful exaggerations, as for example when he attributes to Himmler remarks about alleged 'studs' (*Zeugungshelfer*) in the Spring of Life (*Lebensborn*) homes (pp. 230 ff.). And Kersten's assertion that through his influence on Himmler he had managed to prevent the blowing up of the Zuidersee dyke and so saved large parts of Holland from being flooded (pp. 329 ff.) has long been disproved. Moreover, now that it is possible to compare his dates with those in the *Office Diary* a large number of discrepancies have emerged. In short, therefore, Kersten's book cannot in the strict sense be regarded as a reliable source.

There are a number of previous biographies of Himmler, in particular *Himmler: The Evil Genius of the Third Reich* by Willi Frischauer from 1953, Heinrich Fraenkel's and Roger Manvell's *Heinrich Himmler* from 1965, and Peter Padfield's *Himmler: Reichsführer SS* from 1990. These books use only a fraction of the primary sources on Himmler that are now available and, in view of the substantial research into the SS that has occurred in the meantime, must be regarded as completely out of date.

In 1970 Bradley Smith published a biography of the young Himmler (*Heinrich Himmler 1906–1926*) on the basis of his diaries. It is still very readable and provides important insights into the development of Himmler's personality. Josef Ackermann's *Heinrich Himmler as Ideologue*, published in 1970, is still considered a very sound work on this topic; also, Frank-Lothar Kroll's *Utopia as Ideology*, published a few years ago, is a substantial study of this subject.

In 2005 Katrin Himmler, a great-niece of Heinrich Himmler, gave an account of the Himmler family from her perspective and based to some extent on family tradition. *The Himmler Brothers* contains above all important material on the biographies of his brothers and their relationship to Heinrich.

Richard Breitman's study *The Architect of the 'Final Solution'* from 1991, dealing with Himmler's role in the extermination of the Jews, is largely restricted to the war years. Breitman has the merit above all of being the first person to have systematically studied the various Himmler office diaries available in Washington and placed them in the context of his correspondence. This has produced significant new insights into Himmler's activities during the war.

Breitman's main thesis, however, that Himmler had committed himself at an early stage—that is, at the turn of the year 1940/1—to murdering the European Jews is unconvincing and has not succeeded in winning support from fellow scholars. In contrast to Breitman this biography attempts to place Himmler's 'Jewish policy' in the context of his other activities; this procedure leads to very different results.

On the question of the persecution of the Jews this book has been able to make use of the very substantial literature that has appeared in the meantime. I should mention in this context—without claiming it to be a comprehensive list—the names of Götz Aly, Christopher Browning, Christian Gerlach, Raul Hilberg, Dieter Pohl, and Thomas Sandkühler. I should also refer to the fact that, as far as the Holocaust is concerned, this book is based on my earlier works on this topic.

However, during the past two decades not only Jewish persecution but numerous other aspects of the history of the SS and police apparatus have been the subject of a vast number of research studies. I have endeavoured to make use of this substantial research for this biography, and indeed without it this book could not have been written. Among these works, to name only a small selection, are those concerning the police by George C. Browder, Robert Gellately, Eric A. Johnson, and Patrick Wagner; those concerning general aspects of the concentration camps by Karin Orth and Johannes Tuchel; the studies of Martin Cüppers, Ralf Ogorreck, and Andrej Angrick on the Einsatzgruppen and other murder units, which substantially supplement the 'classic' works by Helmut Krausnick and Karl-Heinz Wilhelm. In addition, there are various contributions dealing with particular groups of victims: Michael Zimmermann's and Günther Lewy's books on the persecution of the Gypsies, and the contributions of Helmut Neuberger on the Freemasons, of Burkhard Jellonek on the homosexuals, of Detlef Garbe on the Jehovah's Witnesses, and of Wolfgang Dierker on the persecution of the churches.

Moreover, in the last few years substantial works have been written describing and analysing the activities of individual SS main offices and particular parts of the SS. Among these are, in particular, Torsten Querg's dissertation on the SD's foreign espionage, Michael Wildt's book on the Reich Security Main Office, Isabel Heinemann's book on the Race and Settlement Main Office, Jan Erik Schulze's and Michael Allen's studies of the Business and Administration Main Office, Bianca Vieregge's analysis of the SS and police's judicial system, Hermann Kaienburg's detailed account of the SS's business sector, and Gudrun Schwarz's study of the role of women in the SS. These works supplement older studies of other parts of the SS, for example the books by George H. Stein and Bernd Wegner on the Waffen-SS, Michael Kater's on the Ahnenerbe (which has still not been superseded), and Georg Lilienthal's study of the Spring of Life (*Lebensborn*) organization.

By integrating biography and structural history this book offers a new perspective by which the history of the SS, which in recent years has fragmented into its individual parts, can be reintegrated. In this way it represents an attempt to continue the work begun in the earlier general histories of the SS by Heinz Höhne (*The Order of the Death's Head: The Story of Hitler's SS*, published in 1969) and by Robert Lewis Koehl (*The Black Corps*, published in 1983).

Glossary of Terms

TABLE OF SS OFFICERS' RANKS

	British Army	US Army
SS-Oberstgruppenführer	General	General
SS-Obergruppenführer	Lieutenant-General	Lieutenant-General
SS-Gruppenführer	Major-General	Major-General
SS-Brigadeführer	Brigadier	Brigadier-General
SS-Oberführer	Senior Colonel	Senior Colonel
SS-Standartenführer	Colonel	Colonel
SS-Obersturmbannführer	Lieutenant-Colonel	Lieutenant-Colonel
SS-Sturmbannführer	Major	Major
SS Hauptsturmführer	Captain	Captain
SS-Obersturmführer	Lieutenant	First Lieutenant
SS-Untersturmführer	Second Lieutenant	Second Lieutenant

OFFICIAL TITLES/ SS–CONTROLLED ORGANIZATIONS/ABBREVIATIONS

Abschnitt	An SS district
Bürgermeister	Mayor of a town and, depending on its size, responsible either to the Landrat or to the Regierungspräsident but with certain autonomous powers under the principle of 'self-administration' (*Selbstverwaltung*)
BVP	Bavarian People's Party
County administrator	(Landrat) civil-service official in charge of a district roughly the size of an English rural district council and subordinate to the Regierungspräsident
District governor	(Regierungspräsident) civil-service official in charge of a district roughly the size of an average English county

EWZ	Einwanderer Zentralstelle, Łódź (Central Office for Immigration), the central office for organizing the settlement of repatriated ethnic Germans
Gauleiter	Head of a Nazi Party Gau, a district the size of a large city or a province
Gestapa	Geheimes Staatspolizeiamt (Secret State Police Office), the headquarters in Berlin of the secret state police (Gestapo)
Gestapo	Geheime Staatspolizei (the secret state (political) police)
HSSPF	Höhere SS- und Polizeiführer (Higher SS and Police Leader); senior SS official in charge of the SS and police in a large region
IKL	Inspektion der Konzentrationslager (Concentration Camp Inspector(ate))
KL/KZ	Konzentrationslager (concentration camp)
KPD	Kommunistische Partei Deutschlands (German Communist Party)
Kripo	Kriminalpolizei (the Criminal Police Department), a state organization
Lebensborn	Spring of Life organization, founded in 1936 by the SS to look after the racially and eugenically acceptable expectant mothers of illegitimate children, particularly of SS members, before and after birth by providing clinics and thereby to encourage such births
NSDAP	Nationalsozialistische Deutsche Arbeiterpartei (National Socialist German Workers Party = the Nazi Party)
Oberabschnitt	An SS district larger than an Abschnitt
Oberbürgermeister	Mayor of a large city and directly responsible to the Interior Ministry but with certain autonomous powers under the principle of 'self-administration' (*Selbstverwaltung*)
OKH	Oberkommando des Heeres (Army High Command)
OKW	Oberkommando der Wehrmacht (Armed Forces High Command)
Old Reich	(Altreich) Germany in its pre-1938 borders
Ostland	The Baltic States and Byelorussia (White Russia)
Ostmark	(Eastern March) the official title for Austria
Provincial governor	(Oberpräsident) the official in charge of a Prussian province, in the Third Reich usually also a Gauleiter
Reich Governor	(Reichsstatthalter) the most senior official in a federal state (Land), a new post introduced in 1933 and normally held by a Gauleiter
RFSS	Reichsführer-SS

RKF   Reichskommissar(iat) fur die Festigung deutschen Volkstums
                     (Reich Commissar[iat] for the Consolidation of the Ethnic
                     German Nation), Himmler's official post and office
                     coordinating all resettlement programmes, initially confined
                     to Poland, but eventually extended to the whole of German-
                     occupied Europe

RSHA   Reichssicherheitshauptamt (the Reich Security Main Office),
                     established in 1939 to bring the Security Police (Gestapo and
                     Kripo) and SD under one roof

RuSHA   Rasse- und Siedlungshauptamt (Race and Settlement
                     Main Office); this organized the racial assessment of
                     individuals and communities prior to their acceptance into
                     SS organizations and, where it was considered desirable, prior
                     to their resettlement, deportation, or extermination. It also
                     organized the resettlement of communities throughout
                     Europe

SA   Sturmabteilung (lit. Storm Department = stormtroopers)

SD   Sicherheitsdienst (Security Service), Nazi party organization
                     established by the SS in 1931 as an intelligence operation.
                     Originally partly a kind of ideological think-tank for
                     gathering information on and developing policy towards
                     Nazism's ideological opponents, it began to acquire
                     executive functions in the late 1930s

Selbstschutz   Auxiliary force of ethnic Germans in Poland

Sipo   Sicherheitspolizei (Security police), an amalgamation in 1936
                     of the Gestapo and Criminal police, though the two retained
                     distinct organizations

SPD   Sozialdemokratische Partei Deutchlands (German Social
                     Democratic Party)

SS   Schutzstaffel (Protection squad)

SSPF   SS- und Polizeiführer (SS and Police Leader)

Stapo   Gestapo

State Secretary   (Staatssekretär) the most senior permanent civil-service
                     official in a ministry

UWZ   Umwandererzentralstelle (Central Office for Resettlement),
                     the office that handled the deportation of 'ethnic aliens' prior
                     to the resettlement of ethnic Germans in their place

VDA   Volksbund für das Deutschtum im Ausland (National League
                     for Germans Abroad)

Verfügungstruppe   Special Duty troops, the military organization of the SS, the
                     precursor of the Waffen-SS

völkisch   Term dating from *c.*1900 denoting an ideology and
                        movement that stressed the importance of ethnicity in
                        determining national identity and considered that human
                        mentalities and behaviour and national cultures were largely
                        shaped by race/ethnicity ('blood') and that there was a
                        qualitative hierarchy of ethnicities. These beliefs were usually
                        accompanied by anti-Semitism

Volkssturm   A home guard established 25 September 1944

VoMi   Volksdeutsche Mittelstelle (Coordination Centre for Ethnic
                        German Resettlement), the central office for coordinating
                        the SS resettlement programme in eastern Europe

Waffen-SS   Armed SS, the military organization of the SS

WVHA   Wirtschafts- und Verwaltungshauptamt (Business and
                        Administration Main Office), the department responsible for
                        organizing the economic activities of the SS

z. b.V.   (*zur besonderen Verwendung*) 'for special assignment'

Abbreviations

ADAP	*Akten zur deutschen auswärtigen Politik 1938–1945*
AP Lodz	Archivum Panstwowe Łódź
ATB	Arbeitstagebuch Himmler (BAK, NL 1126)
BAB	Bundesarchiv, Abt. Berlin
BADH	Bundesarchiv, Abt. Dahlwitz-Hoppegarten
BAK	Bundesarchiv, Abt. Koblenz
BAM	Bundesarchiv/Militärarchiv, Freiburg
BHStA	Bayerisches Hauptstaatsarchiv, München
CDJC	Centre de Documentation Juive Contemporaine
DVA	Deutsche Versuchsanstalt für Ernährung und Verpflegung
EM	Ereignismeldungen UdSSR (BAK, R 58/214–221)
GstA	Geheimes Staatsarchiv, Berlin
IfZ	Institut für Zeitgeschichte, München
IMT	*International Military Tribunal*
KAM	Kriegsarchiv München
KTB	Kdostab
RFSS	Kriegstagebuch Kommandostab Reichsführer-SS
KTB	Pol. Btl. Kriegstagebuch Polizeibataillon
Leseliste	Leseliste Himmler (BAK, NL 1126/9)
LG	Landgericht
MbliV	*Ministerialblatt für die preußische innere Verwaltung*
NARA	US National Archives and Records Administration, Washington, DC
NLA, StA	Bückeburg Niedersächsisches Landesarchiv, Staatsarchiv Bückeburg
OA Moskau	Osobyi Archiv Moskva (Special Archive Moscow)
PAA	Politisches Archiv des Auswärtigen Amtes, Berlin
PrGS	*Preußische Gesetzsammlung*
PRO	Public Record Office, London [now the National Archives]
RFSSuChdDtPol	Reichsführer-SS und Chef der Deutschen Polizei
RGBl	*Reichsgesetzblatt*

RMBliV	*Ministerialblatt des Reichs- und Preußischen Ministeriums des Innern*
RVBl	*Reichsverwaltungsblatt*
StAMarburg	Staatsarchiv Marburg
StAMünchen	Staatsarchiv München
StAnw München	Staatsanwaltschaft München
TB	Tagebuch Himmler (BAK, NL 1126)
USHMM	US Holocaust Memorial Museum, Washington, DC
VF	Verfügungstruppe
VOGG	*Verordnungsblatt für das Generalgouvernement*
YIVO	Institute for Jewish Research, New York
YV	Yad Vashem, Jerusalem
ZStA Potsdam	Zentrales Staatsarchiv Potsdam
ZStL	Zentrale Stelle Ludwigsburg

Picture Credits

Archiv für Kunst und Geschichte, Berlin
Ills. 1, 7, 8, 12, 17, 30, 32
Bildarchiv Preußischer Kulturbesitz, Berlin
Ills. 4, 14, 16, 20, 24, 28
Bilderdienst Süddeutscher Verlag, München
Ills. 9, 10, 11, 21
Ullstein Bild, Berlin
Ills. 3, 6, 13, 18, 19, 31
US Holocaust Memorial Museum, Washington, DC
Ills. 2, 5, 15, 22, 23, 25, 26, 27, 29

The views and opinions associated with these photographs and the context within which they have been published do not reflect the views or principles of the Holocaust Memorial Museum nor does the publishing of these pictures imply that the Museum shares these views and opinions. The publisher and author apologize for any errors or omissions in the above list. If contacted they will be pleased to rectify these at the earliest opportunity.

Prologue

On the afternoon of 23 May 1945, more than two weeks after the German surrender, a group of about twenty suspects—German civilians and soldiers—who had been rounded up two days previously, were brought into the British forces' 31st Civilian Interrogation Camp near Lüneburg.[1]

Captain Selvester, the duty officer, began the routine interrogation of the prisoners: the men were brought individually into his office, where he took down their personal details and questioned them. He had been at work for some time when he heard from the sentries that three of the prisoners waiting outside his office were causing trouble by demanding to be seen immediately. This was extremely unusual. Selvester knew from experience that most prisoners would do anything to avoid drawing attention to themselves.

His curiosity aroused, Selvester ordered the three prisoners to be brought in. Thereupon a fairly short, ill-looking man in shabby civilian clothing entered his office, followed closely by two taller men of distinctly military bearing dressed half in civilian, half in military clothing. All three were under suspicion of belonging to the Secret Field Police. Selvester sent the two taller men out again in order to take a closer look at the shorter one, who was clearly in charge. The man removed a black patch covering his right eye, put on a pair of horn-rimmed spectacles, and introduced himself calmly as the person his outward appearance unmistakably indicated: Heinrich Himmler, the former Reichsführer-SS and Chief of the German Police, Commander of the Reserve Army of the German Wehrmacht, and Reich Minister of the Interior.

Selvester immediately sent for the most senior interrogation officer, Captain Smith, and, in order to be quite sure, both demanded a specimen signature from Himmler. At first Himmler refused, clearly suspecting the men were after a souvenir, but agreed in the end on condition that the paper was destroyed as soon as his signature had been compared with a copy kept in the camp.

After this Selvester himself set about searching the prisoner. First of all, he discovered documents in the name of Heinrich Hitzinger, Wehrmacht sergeant. In Himmler's jacket he then came upon a small tin with a glass phial containing a colourless liquid. Recognizing that it was a suicide capsule, Selvester asked Himmler as innocently as he could what was in the phial. The reply came that it was medicine to treat stomach cramps. When a second identical tin was found in Himmler's clothing Selvester was forced to conclude that his prisoner still had a further capsule hidden on or inside his person.

Himmler was therefore subjected to a minute examination that included all orifices, though the most likely and most dangerous hiding-place, his mouth, was carefully omitted. Instead, Selvester then ordered cheese sandwiches and tea, both of which Himmler was happy to accept without removing any suspicious object from his mouth. He did, however, refuse to put on the items of British uniform offered to him in place of his confiscated clothing, fearing most likely that the intention was to take photographs of him for use as propaganda.

So now he was sitting in his underclothes and draped in a blanket facing the British officers. It was established that the two men accompanying him were Obersturmbannführer Werner Grothmann, the SS leader's adjutant, and another member of his staff, Sturmbannführer Heinz Macher.

Towards evening a more senior secret-service officer arrived and began to interrogate Himmler. Meanwhile, the British began deliberating how they could retrieve intact the capsule presumed to be in Himmler's mouth. Military doctors were asked if drugs could be used to render him unconscious but this was rejected as too risky.[2]

The interrogation was brought to a temporary close towards midnight. Himmler was taken to the headquarters of the Second British Army in Lüneburg. The whole time he had been in Camp 31 Himmler had appeared cooperative, from time to time positively jovial, and willing to answer the British officers' questions, or at least that was Selvester's impression. Though at first he had seemed unwell, he had visibly recovered after being given something to eat and the chance to wash.

Once in Lüneburg Himmler was subjected to a thorough medical examination, in the course of which the doctor, Captain Wells, discovered in

Himmler's mouth, which he was reluctant to open, a blue-tipped object. As Wells attempted to remove this foreign body, Himmler jerked his head to one side to avoid him. He bit into the capsule and collapsed. After fifteen minutes all further attempts to remove the remains of the poison from his mouth and to revive him were abandoned. Closer inspection revealed that the poison was cyanide.[3]

Three days after his death Himmler's body was buried. Only a British officer and three sergeants who had dug the grave were present. There was no religious ceremony and the place of burial was unmarked.[4]

Himmler's behaviour during his final days is full of contradictions. Unlike other prominent Nazis he had not taken his own life in the last days of the war but rather gone into hiding, although in such an amateurish manner that he and those with him were bound to be caught at some point. When he fell into Allied hands he made sure they knew who he was and yet then evaded responsibility through suicide. The fact that he acted in this way and not in accordance with the virtues of an SS officer he perpetually preached—which included taking responsibility, in however crude a form, for one's own actions—was to disillusion his men deeply and result in the posthumous reputation of the Reichsführer-SS remaining largely negative even among his former adherents. In the post-war years no Himmler legend was waiting to be born.

In May 1945 Himmler had simply been absorbed into the flood of millions of refugees and soldiers. His end appears as puzzling as his career in the service of National Socialism. How could such a banal personality attain such a historically unique position of power? How could the son of a prosperous Bavarian Catholic public servant become the organizer of a system of mass murder spanning the whole of Europe?

The aim of this biography is to penetrate as far as possible the mystery of this man's personality and the motives underlying his monstrous deeds. To succeed in this, however, it is necessary to go beyond the established pattern of political biography and take into account quite literally the whole of Himmler's life in its separate stages and its various spheres of activity, including the non-political ones.

Such a comprehensive biographical approach allows us to reconstruct the development of this personality, its essential character traits and typical behaviour patterns in its formative years, which extend into the start of

Himmler's political career, and thereby to gain insights that will illuminate his later life. This method makes it altogether possible to explain what motivated this 'young man from a good family' to join the radical right-wing splinter party, the National Socialist German Workers' Party (NSDAP), in the mid-1920s, and what impelled someone who was fairly weak physically and nondescript in appearance to develop the protection squad (*Schutzstaffel*) he commanded into the martial SS and steer it on a course of selecting only the racially perfect. His personality also allows us to draw conclusions about what moved Himmler in the following years to stick stubbornly to his post in spite of defeats and frustrations, and to work consistently to build up a power structure that exercised decisive control over the territory under German domination. As far as the unprecedented crimes he organized are concerned, his own justification of them is indissolubly bound up with his biography, with his notion of 'decency', which on closer inspection turns out to be no more than a label for petit-bourgeois double standards.

A Himmler biography can, however, achieve much more. For if we build up a biographically coherent picture, with both chronological and synoptic analysis, of the diverse activities for which Himmler, as Reichs-führer-SS, Chief of the German Police, Reich Commissar for the Consolidation of the Ethnic German Nation, Reich Minister of the Interior, and Commander of the Reserve Army, was responsible, we are in a position to recognize that the individual fields of political activity for which Himmler was responsible were much more strongly interlinked than is commonly supposed. In addition, surprising coincidences of timing come to light that have not been recognized in research to date.

Research up to now on the history of the SS and Nazi Party structures has concentrated above all on the reconstruction of the mass crimes carried out by the SS (with the Holocaust clearly the main focus of attention), as well as on its various spheres of action. Thus, repression, racial extermination, the Waffen-SS, settlement and ethnic policies, espionage, and so on were considered primarily as a series of separate pillars of the SS empire. Yet if an explanation is sought for what held this exceptionally heterogeneous apparatus together and for how it came, in the course of time, to seek more and more tasks, to extend its areas of activity, and, on several occasions, to redefine itself, then the focus must be turned onto the life story of the man at its head. For Himmler was to redefine the role of the SS repeatedly, in clearly distinguishable phases of its existence.

From the small bodyguard unit he took over in 1929 he created in a very short time a paramilitary organization with elite pretensions sworn to serve the top Party leadership. In 1933/4 he was able to to propel himself relatively quickly up to the rank of Reich Chief of the Political Police. From this position he developed a comprehensive plan for the management of the whole of the police force which, after Hitler had appointed him Chief of the German Police, he intended to amalgamate with the SS to form a state protection corps (*Staatsschutzkorps*) to provide comprehensive internal security.

When at the end of the 1930s the so-called Third Reich began to expand, he set new targets; alongside settlement and racial selection of the population in territories identified for 'Germanization', he expanded the Waffen-SS and played a role in the policy of repression in the occupied territories. From 1941 onwards he introduced a policy of systematic mass murder based on racial criteria. In his eyes this was the first step towards setting up a qualitatively new, racially based power structure—the Greater Germanic Reich.

At the end of 1942, however, the regime went on the defensive and Himmler changed his emphasis once again. Now he concentrated entirely on guaranteeing 'security' within the area still under Nazi rule, and until the end of the war all the internally enforceable methods of violence of the Nazi state were united in his person.

This evidence suggests that Himmler's actual strength consisted in re-drawing every two or three years the master plans for his sphere of power, on the basis of which interdependent tasks, aligned with the overall policy of the regime and justifiable in terms of both power politics and ideology, were allocated to the individual parts of this heterogeneous power con-glomerate. By these means he responded to the increasing political radicali-zation of the Nazi regime and simultaneously gave that process decisive impetus.

This ability Himmler had to connect ideology and power politics in a most efficient way, by creating a continuous stream of new and wide-ranging tasks for his SS, makes one thing clear above all: the biographical approach offers the only adequate way of grasping and explaining the history of the SS in all its facets. Without the man at its head this heteroge-neous organization, constantly expanding and growing more radical, cannot be investigated in a way that is thorough and complete.

Added to this is the recognition that Himmler's personal predilections, aversions, and diverse quirks were deeply ingrained in the organization and leadership of the SS and actually played a formative role in its structure. This is, for instance, true of Himmler's idiosyncratic notion of personnel management, which included surveillance of the private lives of his men and in many respects is reminiscent of the behaviour of a strict and solicitous father figure. It is true also of his attempt to establish an SS cult that fitted entirely the Germanophile tendencies of this Catholic dissident. The state protection corps, into which Himmler wanted to develop the SS, offered him in many respects a form of self-protection, a cover organization behind which he could act out his personal desires and hide his own weaknesses.

Himmler as Reichsführer-SS was precisely not someone who exercised a political function or held an office with a stable group of powers, but rather in the course of time he created for himself from the diverse tasks allotted to him by the Führer a unique position of power that was completely geared to him as an individual. Leading the SS, ensuring its internal cohesion and its future viability, became in fact his whole life.

The more Himmler carried over his personal maxims into his leadership of the SS, and the more he and his office grew together, the more he disappeared as a private individual behind the function of Reichsführer-SS. While a variety of sources (in particular diaries and letters) provide us with a relatively large quantity of information about the private Himmler up to the start of the 1930s, such personal documents become ever rarer with the increase in his range of powers and in the claims his professional duties made on him. Himmler had hardly any private life any more. Although we have a large number of official documents at our disposal, in which Himmler's personality—his characteristic style, his resentments, predilections, and prejudices—clearly emerges, the purely biographical method, in spite of such evidence, comes up against its limits at the latest in the mid-1930s. It would also be presumptuous—as well as completely erroneous historiographically—to attempt to explain the actions of Heinrich Himmler as Reichsführer-SS first and foremost on the basis of his life. The history of National Socialism cannot be reduced to the intersecting careers of a number of leading Nazis.

Instead, what we have here is an effective combination of biography and structural history; if increasing weight is given in the course of our protagonist's life to structural history, this methodological and narrative shift of emphasis is the logical consequence of the process described here of office and individual becoming indistinguishable. The biographical element nevertheless remains significant in the description of every phase of Himmler's life. For in National Socialism the exercise of political power was quite simply inextricably linked to the biographies of leading Nazi functionaries. In the case of Heinrich Himmler this is true to an exceptional degree.

PART
I

Himmler's Early Years

I

Childhood and Youth

In 1980, a few weeks before his death, the German writer Alfred Andersch concluded work on an autobiographical 'school story'. The story describes a Greek lesson at the Wittelsbach Grammar School in Munich that took place fifty-two years before the story was published. Its model is the last Greek lesson Andersch experienced at this school in 1928.

The drama begins when 'Rex', the school's strict and universally feared headmaster, appears on a surprise visit to the class. First there is an argument between Rex and a very self-confident pupil from an aristocratic family that quickly escalates and ends with the headmaster telling the disobedient pupil, who will not submit to his authority, that he is expelled. But this was only the prelude: now Rex summons the hero of the story, whom Andersch calls Franz Kien, to the blackboard. Not only does he parade with positive pleasure the boy's pathetic knowledge of Greek, but with every trick of his trade—sarcasm, malice, meanness of spirit—he demolishes Kien-Andersch. He too is obliged to leave the school.

'Rex', it is revealed, was in fact called Himmler, and Andersch gave the story the title 'The Father of a Murderer'.

Andersch's 'school story' is a plausible attempt to understand the phenomenon that was Himmler: The career of a mass murderer, it is suggested here, is the result of a father–son conflict, in the course of which Heinrich Himmler becomes a radical right-wing revolutionary, rebelling against his overly strict father and turning into his 'mortal enemy'. Andersch asks if it was not inevitable that, 'as a result of "natural determinism"' (defined as the obvious rules of psychology, the laws of conflict between one generation and the next, and the paradoxical consequences of family tradition) 'such a father would produce such a son?' Andersch conceded that he had no definitive answer to this question.

After the advance publication of Andersch's story in the *Süddeutsche Zeitung* numerous letters appeared in the newspaper from readers who had known Gebhard Himmler personally. They do not paint an unambiguous picture: He is described as 'the kind of person who grovels to his superiors while oppressing his inferiors', but also as a 'vigorous person of high intellect who commanded respect'.[1]

Otto Gritschneder, a well-known Munich lawyer, who in numerous publications has criticized the Bavarian judicial system under National Socialism, recalled his former teacher Gebhard Himmler 'as Rex the just (and justice is of course very important to pupils), honestly striving to communicate to our young minds the culture and history of our native country and our continent'. Furthermore, Gritschneder had sat in the same classroom as Andersch. According to his account, Andersch had simply been a bad pupil and the decision to put an end to his career at the Wittelsbach Grammar School had been entirely reasonable.[2]

The Himmlers and their son Heinrich

As the son of a low-ranking Protestant civil servant, Gebhard Himmler, Heinrich Himmler's father, was a classic case of upward social mobility. Born in 1809, his father Johann Himmler, who came from a family of peasants and artisans from Ansbach and was himself trained as a weaver, had in the course of a varied career in the Bavarian military and police worked his way up to the rank of 'brigadier' (the police equivalent of sergeant). After his retirement in 1862 he had been employed up to his death in 1872 in the district administration of Lindau. A few months after his move to Lindau Johann Himmler, now 53, married Agathe Rosina Kiene, who was twenty-four years his junior, a Catholic and the daughter of a clockmaker from Bregenz.[3]

In 1865 the couple had a son, Gebhard. When he was 7 years old his father died. His mother brought him up a Catholic, and it was probably due to her influence that he owed that energy and commitment that helped him succeed in rising socially from his petit-bourgeois background to the professional middle class. In 1884 he began to study at Munich University, specializing in German literature and classical languages and graduating in 1888.[4] He went on to spend some time in St Petersburg, where at that point there was a relatively large German colony. There he was employed as a private tutor in the house of the honorary consul Freiherr von Lamezan.[5] Lamezan's friendship with the Bavarian Prince Regent Luitpold created contacts at the Bavarian court. Gebhard Himmler returned to Bavaria and tried to establish himself as a grammar-school teacher. From 1890 he taught first on a temporary basis at the Munich Grammar School, but from 1894 onwards he enjoyed the rare privilege of being appointed by Prince Arnulf of Wittelsbach, a brother of the Prince Regent and of the later King Ludwig III of Bavaria, as private tutor to his son Heinrich.[6] After completing this task successfully, in 1897 Gebhard Himmler was given a permanent position as a teacher at the long-established Wilhelm Grammar School in Munich.[7]

His new position enabled him finally to establish a family. In 1897 he married Anna Maria Heyder, the daughter of a Munich businessman. At the time they married she was 31, a year younger than her husband; she too had lost her father, who was 55 when she was born, at the age of 6.[8] It is thought she brought a not-inconsiderable fortune to the marriage.[9]

Heinrich, who was born on 7 October 1900, was the second child of this union, after Gebhard, who was born in July 1898. It was a great honour for the Himmlers that Prince Heinrich, then 16 years old, agreed to Gebhard Himmler's request that he be the child's godfather. Though the prince was ninth in line to the Wittelsbach crown and thus unlikely to succeed, his role as godparent strengthened the family's link to the court, and for the future of the ambitious Himmlers this was enormously important.[10] The youngest addition to the Himmler family was naturally named after his influential godfather; Luitpold, the name of the Prince Regent, was chosen for his second Christian name. Ludwig, the name of the Bavarian king who had died in 1886, had been selected for the eldest son's second Christian name. In 1905 Heinrich's younger brother Ernst was born.

It is clear that the Himmlers succeeded in their efforts to create an ordered life characterized by regular habits, hard work, and religious observance, as was typical of comfortably off families of state officials in Munich around 1900. While the mother devoted herself to the household and the welfare of the children, the father not only immersed himself in his career as a grammar-school teacher but tried also to give his sons as far as possible the benefit of his pedagogic skills.[11]

Central to this education was the transmission of a solid cultural canon, comprising in particular classical literature and sound knowledge of history and of Greek and Latin. The strong emphasis the father placed on acquainting his sons with social conventions and manners presumably also betrays the lack of confidence of someone who came from modest circumstances. It went without saying that religious belief and active participation in church life were part of the children's upbringing; Anna Himmler in particular attached so much importance to establishing their Catholic faith that their father felt he must warn against taking such things too far.[12]

As a father he exercised his authority not through being unapproachable or through overbearing strictness but rather through patient efforts with his sons; they were subject to a system of rules and prohibitions, while their father monitored their obedience precisely and at times pedantically. His strictness was designed to have a lasting effect and seems to have been altogether compatible with kindness, love, and affection.[13] In addition he spent a considerable part of his free time on his stamp collection, introducing his sons to this hobby as well. He also taught them stenography; a large part of the family correspondence is written in shorthand.[14]

Himmler's father kept a particular check on his children's successes at school and encouraged them to use the school holidays to consolidate what they had been taught. When his eldest son Gebhard lost more than half of his first school year through various illnesses, his father made great efforts not only to make up for what the boy had missed but to make him top of the class by the end of the second school year.[15] In addition, both parents paid attention to 'suitable friendships' for their offspring, preferably with children from Munich's upper middle classes.

Gebhard Himmler's pedantry, to which his great-niece has drawn attention, emerged in a particularly blatant form in 1910 when he was getting ready to embark on a journey to Greece—without his family. Gebhard made comprehensive preparations for the eventuality of his not returning alive. He wrote a long farewell letter to every member of the family, containing detailed advice on their future lives and numerous practical pointers on how to deal with everyday problems. He commended to his son Gebhard a veritable catalogue of virtues, calling on him to be 'hard-working, dutiful, and morally upright' and enjoining him to become 'a conscientious, religious man with a German outlook'. These words exactly reflect the maxims by which he brought up his three sons.[16] Unfortunately his letter to Heinrich has not survived. What becomes clear from these letters is that Himmler wanted his sons to go to university and gain their doctorate, though not in philology or theology. They were not to become officers either.

In those years before the First World War the Himmlers lived in apartments in favoured but by no means exclusive areas.[17] They employed a maid and were clearly free from financial worries. They kept up extensive contacts with numerous family members and had a relatively large circle of acquaintances.[18] The link to Prince Heinrich was maintained, and he took a lively interest in the progress of his godson and in how the Himmlers were faring. It was a warm relationship, as is shown by the preserved correspondence between Gebhard and the prince; at Christmas the Himmlers regularly received a visit from the prince and his mother, who after the death of her husband Prince Arnulf took the name Princess Arnulf.[19]

Solidly conservative, monarchist, Catholic, economically secure and culturally traditional, the Himmlers lived in a milieu that stood in stark contrast to the widespread reputation enjoyed by turn-of-the-century Munich as being the metropolis of a self-consciously modern culture, an art-loving, tolerant, and lively city. In fact cultural modernism and political liberalism in Munich had been in retreat since 1900. From the turn of the century the liberal city administration and Bavarian state ministry had found themselves increasingly under pressure from the Catholic-conservative Centre Party, which protested in particular against 'immorality' and against unconventional cultural trends, and specifically against the bohemian artistic world of the Schwabing district. In line with this stance of uncompromising rejection in the field of cultural politics, the Himmlers' world was largely untouched by the works of a Thomas or Heinrich Mann, by the Blaue Reiter artists, the Schwabing cabaret scene, or art nouveau.[20]

In 1902 the family moved temporarily to Passau, where Gebhard Himmler had been appointed to a post at the grammar school.[21] In February 1903 the 2-year-old Heinrich fell ill with a lung complaint, so his mother took the children for a few months to Wolfegg, a village in the Allgäu, as a cure for the illness. There was serious danger of Heinrich contracting tuberculosis, at that time the most common cause of infant death. When Heinrich's health was improving they returned to Passau; yet it is clear that the parents were anxious about the usual childhood diseases, which, as Heinrich was already severely weakened, threatened to have severe, perhaps fatal, results.[22]

In 1904 the family moved back to Munich, where Gebhard Himmler, who had in the meantime been promoted to the post of grammar-school professor,★ took up a position at the Ludwig Grammar School. Again the Himmlers moved into an apartment, this time in Amalienstrasse 86,

★ *Translators' note*: senior academic teacher.

immediately behind the university.[23] This was the start of a difficult time for Heinrich: not only did his brother, who had started school in September 1904, fall ill with a series of infections und thus replace Heinrich as the focus of his parents' care and attention, but Anna Himmler was facing a further pregnancy. In December 1905 Ernst was born, and Heinrich saw his parents' attention being directed primarily towards his younger brother.[24]

Heinrich was now in the complex position of the middle son, trapped between the model of the superior big brother and the solicitous care focused on little Ernst. In this situation, in which he perhaps feared being sidelined in the family, his illnesses became not only periods of suffering but also the chance to recapture his parents' interest. This experience is possibly at the root of his later psychosomatic complaints. Towards his younger brother he began to develop a certain good-natured condescension.[25]

In 1906 Heinrich started school at the cathedral school on Salvatorplatz in the city centre (and not at the school in Amalienstrasse which was the proper school for children from his district). Yet even here he was at first unlucky. Like his brother before him, in his first school year he missed a total of 150 school days through various infections such as coughs, measles, mumps, and above all pneumonia. With the help of a private tutor he caught up with the schoolwork he had missed,[26] but the fact that his parents, and in particular his father, had high expectations of him may well have combined with the new family dynamic created by his younger brother to put him under pressure—the more so because, in spite of good marks, he did not do as well as his elder brother. Only when he moved to the school in Amalienstrasse did his situation seem to ease. Heinrich was a good pupil there and also made friends with some of his classmates.[27]

The long summer holidays, which the family mostly spent in the foothills of the Bavarian Alps, were undoubtedly the most exciting time of the year. There were visits to places of interest, walks, boat trips, and other leisure activities. In 1910, on holiday in Lenggries, his father gave Heinrich the task of keeping a diary about their stay that summer. He wrote the first entry himself to show his son what to do. He continued to read and correct the boy's entries and saw to it that in the years following he wrote similar holiday diaries.[28]

It is hardly surprising that these holiday diaries resemble school exercises and basically do no more than list the activities. For instance, in 1911 Heinrich provided a running record of how many times he had gone swimming: the total was thirty-seven times.[29] This terse recounting of the

Ill. 1. Gebhard and Anna Himmler (seated) with their three children, Heinrich (left), Ernst (middle), and Gebhard (right), in 1906.

events of each day was something Heinrich continued with after his father had stopped checking the diaries. Paternal monitoring was replaced by self-monitoring.[30]

In 1910 Heinrich moved to the Wilhelm Grammar School, where his father had taught up to 1902.[31] At this time the boy was slightly built and relatively short. He had a sickly constitution, he was frequently unwell, and his whole appearance was delicate. The spectacles he was obliged to wear all the time dominated his round, still decidedly childish face. His receding chin reinforced this impression.

When one of his former fellow pupils, Wolfgang Hallgarten (he had fled from the Nazis to the United States and meanwhile become one of the leading American historians of Germany), discovered decades later that the future 'man of terror' had actually been the classmate whom everyone called 'Himmler', he simply refused at first to believe the irrefutable fact. Too great was the contrast between the Reichsführer-SS and that 'child of hardly average height, who was unusually pale and physically very awkward, with hair cut fairly short and even then a pair of gold-rimmed glasses on his slightly pointed nose', and who was frequently seen with 'a half-embarrassed, half-malicious smile on his face'. According to Hallgarten, Himmler had been a model pupil, liked by all the teachers; amongst the boys he had been regarded as a swot and been only moderately popular. Hallgarten had a particularly clear memory of the unhappy figure Himmler cut, much to the amusement of his fellows, in gymnastics. Hatred of the Jews, Hallgarten went on to say, was not something Himmler was at all associated with at that time; on the other hand, he said he remembered Heinrich's radically anti-French outlook.[32]

In 1913 Professor Himmler took over as deputy head of the grammar school in Landshut. This enabled the family to move into a house with a garden.[33] Fortunately a Munich friend, Falk Zipperer, also moved with his family to Landshut, where his stepfather, Ferdinand von Pracher, had become head of the district administration, from the Himmlers' point of view an ideal family background for their son's best friend. The friendship was to be lasting: in 1937, on the occasion of his friend's wedding, Himmler gave a lunch party;[34] in 1938 he accepted him into the SS, and in 1940 Zipperer, who had in the meantime gained his second doctorate in legal history, published an essay in a Festschrift for Himmler's fortieth birthday.[35] In 1944, when Himmler was getting ready for his last Christmas, Zipperer's wife, Liselotte, was noted down for a present.[36]

Another friendship that lasted to the end of the Second World War was with Karl Gebhard, three years older than Himmler. The two boys met in Landshut. Gebhard became a doctor and was later director of a sanatorium in Hohenlychen in the Berlin area that, as we shall see, was to play a special role in Himmler's life.[37] Heinrich also remained friends with Edi and Luisa Hager, whose father was a senior museums and galleries administrator.[38] On this evidence Heinrich was not at all a lone wolf, even if his classmates may have considered him a model pupil, a swot, and a weakling. His attainments during his time at school in Landshut, which lasted until 1919, were in fact above average. In religious education and history he was always graded 'very good' and in languages he was judged 'very good' to 'good'; his weakest subject was physics, for which one year he was given only 'satisfactory'. A school report from 1913/14 reads: 'An apparently very able student who by tireless hard work, burning ambition and very lively participation achieved the best results in the class. His conduct was exemplary.'[39]

Youth in wartime

Into this well-ordered world, just as the family was enjoying the summer of 1914 in picturesque Tittmoning on the German–Austrian border, burst the news of the crisis precipitated by the murder of the heir to the Austrian throne on 28 June in Sarajevo, which culminated in the outbreak of the First World War.

Heinrich's diary entries, in which the alarming news is recorded along-side the usual notes on his everyday activities, reflect the atmosphere of these decisive days and the sudden termination of the holiday idyll. For 29 July we read: 'Gebhard's birthday. *Outbreak of war between Austria and Serbia.* Excursion to Lake Waging.' The announcement of the outbreak of war is underlined in red. The entries for the next two days, which clearly concerned the programme of activities, are rubbed out and over the top, again in red, is written the sentence: '*Proclamation of a state of war*'. And now political and military events moved centre stage:

1. VIII. *Germany mobilizes* 2nd army corps. Even the Landsturm [territorials].
2. VIII. Played in the garden in the morning. Afternoon as well. 7.30 *Germany declares war on Russia.*

3. VIII. *Attacks on the French and Russian borders. Planes and spies.* We are packing up right away.

The Himmlers hurried back to Landshut. The abrupt end to the holiday was to mark the end of an era.

From now on military events, which at first went very well for Germany, dominate Heinrich's diary entries; for example, the entry for 23 August:

German Crown Prince's victory north of Metz (Longeville). Prince Heinrich wrote to father. During the attack on the French dragoons he was slightly wounded. Germany gives a dignified response to Japan's ultimatum. Germans in Ghent. Played the piano. [. . .] The Bavarians are said to have been very brave in yesterday's battle. In particular our 16ers are supposed to have put up an excellent fight with their bayonets. There are flags out all over town. The French and Belgians must have been surprised to be beaten so quickly. Territorial 1st Regiment has been called up. Namur is besieged. 8000 Russians taken prisoner at Gumbinnen.

And the next day he noted with excitement:

Pursuing the French has brought the army of the Bavarian Crown Prince rich pickings (prisoners, standards, and 150 guns). The 21st army corps has marched into Luneville. The Crown Prince's army is also still pursuing the enemy (advancing towards Longwy). Duke Albrecht of Württemberg beat a French army that was advancing across the Semois. The enemy is pursued and booty taken: Prisoners, generals, guns, standards. Our troops advance to the west of the Meuse towards Maubeuge. An English cavalry brigade is there and is beaten, really beaten! Hurray!

Every day he went to the offices of the local newspaper, where the latest news telegrams were displayed:

27. VIII. [. . .] Afternoon, went to see the telegrams. Prince Luitpold of Bavaria, the heir to the throne, has died of a throat infection in Berchtesgaden. The light cruiser, the Magdeburg, ran aground in fog at Odensholm [Osmussaar] in the Gulf of Finnland and could not be refloated. [. . .] The cruiser was scuttled. 85 men are missing, some are dead or wounded, another was picked up by a German torpedo boat. The worried philistines of Landshut are now hanging their heads, spreading dreadful rumours, and fearing that they will be massacred by the Cossacks. Today the first sizeable list of Bavarian army casualties was published.

28. VIII. [. . .] English army beaten.. [. . .] Now we are making terrific progress. I'm as happy at these victories as the English and French are no doubt annoyed at them, and the annoyance will be considerable. Falk and I would really like to fight right now ourselves. It's clear that the good old Germans and their loyal allies the Austrians are not afraid of a world full of enemies.

Seemingly those around him did not share that view to the same extent, as he records in a critical tone on 27 August: 'Generally speaking there is no particular enthusiasm in Lower Bavaria among the people at home. When the mobilization was announced in the old town everyone apparently started blubbing. I would have expected that least of all of the Lower Bavarians. They are usually so ready for a fight. A wounded soldier says the same. Often really dreadful and stupid rumours go round, all invented by people.'

On 6 September he noted that the people of Landshut were 'as mindless and fearful as ever. When they heard, as they thought, the news of the troops' retreat near Paris they all got diarrhoea and their hearts went into their boots. It's terrible how rumours fly about.'

On 30 August he observed, with contempt for the people in the town and compassion for the enemy captives, how a transport of French wounded was cared for at the station: 'The whole station was full of inquisitive Landshuters who became abusive and even violent when the seriously wounded French soldiers (who must be worse off than our wounded, because they're prisoners) were given water and bread.' He clearly regarded the Russians somewhat differently, as an entry from 4 September reveals: 'There are 90,000 Russians captured in East Prussia, not 70,000. (They multiply like vermin.)'

In spite of the war the Himmlers went on a summer holiday as usual in 1915, this time to Burghausen. Their arrival at the station in Mühldorf revived Heinrich's memories of the start of the war a year before. Although the jubilant patriotism of the first phase of the war was now over, he could not help having vivid recollections of the previous summer, 'when we stood at about the same time on the platform, doing army drill. It was 6 August when we came back from Tittmoning. A few days later they went off cheerfully to war. How many of them are alive today?'[40]

Everything connected with war and the military fascinated him. When in September 1915 his brother, who was two years older, had the opportunity to accompany his parents on a visit to wounded soldiers Heinrich acknowledged in his diary how much he envied him.[41] At the beginning of 1915 the Army Reserve (*Landwehr*) had created trenches and dugouts that Heinrich's class went to see. Heinrich was impressed: They are sketched and described in his diary.[42]

In July 1915 his brother Gebhard reached the age of 17 and joined the Territorials (*Landsturm*) and so could be counted as belonging to the military reserve. Heinrich commented longingly: 'If only I were old enough, I'd be out there like a shot.'[43] But as he was 14 at the outbreak of war Himmler was part of the so-called war youth generation: too young to be sent to the front as soldiers and yet old enough to follow the military and political events closely from the start, and also marked by the experience of having endured all the phases of the war as a collective national effort.[44]

In the early phase of the war in particular Heinrich and his friends tried to create through play some kind of access to the 'normality' of the war, which was to last for four years.[45] Sometimes in his diary the boundaries between war as a game and the real war become blurred: 'Played in the garden with Falk. 1000 Russians captured by our troops east of the Vistula. Austrians advance', he noted on 26 August 1914. Three days later: 'Played at sword-fighting with Falk. This time with 40 army corps and Russia, France and Belgium against Germany and Austria. The game is very interesting. Victory over the Russians in East Prussia (50,000 prisoners).'

From Easter to autumn 1915 he was a member of the Cadet Corps (*Jugendwehr*), where he and his classmates were given the preliminaries of military training. He was noted as showing 'commendable enthusiasm'.[46] 'To the Cadet Corps in the afternoon. Practice was pretty poor. I was lying for about quarter of an hour in a fairly wet field. It didn't do me any harm, though,' he noted in his diary.[47]

Heinrich began to complain of stomach pains, an ailment he suffered from to the end of his life.[48] He tried to overcome his physical weakness through sport. In his diary there is a reference to daily training with dumb-bells.[49] In February 1917 he became a member of the Landshut gymnastics club.[50]

Meanwhile the war began to affect the Himmlers' everyday life. Restrictions on the supply of food and important commodities became increasingly evident. In November 1916 the government introduced the Patriotic Auxiliary Service, which committed every German male aged between 17 and 60 who was not already in military service to make himself available for important war work. In the same month the news reached the Himmlers that Heinrich's godfather Prince Heinrich had been killed in Romania; he was only 32 years old. The Himmlers mourned not only a significant family friend but also the fact that their privileged access to the court, which had always held out the most alluring prospects for the three sons' future, was now irrevocably lost.[51]

In 1917 his elder brother's year group was called up into the armed forces: Gebhard had been in the Territorials for two years and in May 1917 he joined the 16th Bavarian Infantry Regiment in Passau, where he completed the first stage of officer training.[52] Falk Zipperer also left the grammar school in April 1917 and began officer training.[53]

Heinrich, who had been continuing his pre-military training since October 1915 in the Landshut Cadet Corps, wanted to take the same course.[54] In the summer of 1917, probably as a result of pressure from his son, Himmler's father began to make extensive efforts to get him accepted as a candidate for officer training with one of the Bavarian regiments. He successfully enlisted the help of the chamberlain to Princess Arnulf, the mother of the dead Prince Heinrich, and amongst other things he intervened to support Heinrich's application for the exclusive 1st and 2nd Infantry Regiments. His efforts were in vain, however, as the lists of applicants were already too long.[55] In the course of his correspondence with the military authorities Himmler's father was called upon to respond to the question of whether his son was considering becoming a professional army officer. 'My son Heinrich has a strong desire to be an infantry officer by profession', was his clear answer.[56]

Shortly before the start of the new school year—he had spent the usual summer holiday in Bad Tölz—Heinrich surprised everyone by leaving the grammar school. Up to that point he had completed seven years at the school. His last report indicated that he was a good, though not an excellent, pupil.[57] His leaving was evidently motivated by his fear of being conscripted while still at school, along with his cohort, before he had succeeded in gaining a post as an officer candidate in a first-class regiment. He was successful in his application to the Regensburg city administration for the patriotic auxiliary service: in October 1917 he was set to work in the war welfare office, an organization for the care of surviving relatives of fallen soldiers. After six weeks he put an end to this interlude and went back to the grammar school, after the schools ministry had made it clear in a directive that his age-group of pupils would not yet be conscripted.[58]

Heinrich the soldier

On 23 December he received the surprising news that the 11th Infantry Regiment would accept him as an officer candidate. Yet again the chamberlain already mentioned had been pulling strings: Himmler's father's contacts at court had, after all, finally been effective.[59] Heinrich left school and on

2 January began his training with the reserve battalion of the 11th Regiment at a camp near Regensburg.[60]

He proudly signed one of his first letters to his parents with the Latin tag 'Miles Heinrich', Heinrich the soldier, and the brand-new warrior expressed his manliness amongst other things by taking up smoking.[61] In contrast to this masculine pose, his almost daily letters to his parents in fact reveal the considerable difficulties he had in adjusting to the world of the military. Heinrich was homesick. He complained about the poor accommodation and wretched food, though on most evenings he could supplement this by going to pubs. He asked constantly for more frequent replies to his letters, for food, clean clothes, and other such things that would make his life in the barracks easier.[62] If his requests were not immediately fulfilled (he did after all receive seven parcels from home in the first five weeks of his military career[63]) he reacted in a hurt manner: 'Dearest parents! Today again I have got nothing from you. That's mean.'[64] After a few weeks he got used to the new life and the complaints in his letters became less frequent. Yet the correspondence shows how much he was still reliant on close contact with his parents.[65]

From the middle of February 1918 he regularly received leave to spend most weekends at home. By contrast, his brother Gebhard was sent in April 1918 to the western front and took part in heavy fighting in which there were severe losses.[66] Heinrich, however, became petulant if he got no mail from home for a few days: 'Dear Mother! Thank you so much for your news (which I did not get). It's so horrid of you not to write again.'[67] When the Regensburg training was coming to an end he hoped that he too would be sent to the front, but to his disappointment he learned that he was to be sent on a further training course. 'You could have saved your tears', he wrote to his mother, who had been viewing the prospect of a second son at the front with anxiety. 'Don't rejoice too soon, though. Things can change again just as quickly.'[68] On 15 June he continued his training just 40 kilometres from Landshut, in Freising. He was still able to spend most weekends at home.[69]

In his letters he described daily life in the military as before, but he now coped with it considerably better, as his lapidary descriptions show: 'We are given excellent treatment. This afternoon we bathed. [...] The food is very good.'[70] As before, problems with the food and reports about his changeable health are prominent;[71] his hunger for the many 'lovely little parcels'[72] from Landshut, for which he always sent a thank-you letter ('the cake was terrific!'[73]), never seemed to abate. Yet as the correspondence shows, his obvious need for the affection and love of his parents could not really be satisfied. Although he tried, after initial difficulties, to present himself to his parents in a manly, adult, and soldierly light (and he was certainly also impressed by the example of his elder brother, who was, after all, at the very same time in immediate mortal danger at the front), his letters continued to demand their lively participation in his everyday concerns and their permanent support in dealing with them.

In August he began to long for the end of the Freising course: 'The Freising course is getting more and more rotten and strict: oh well, we'll make a reasonable job of it, even if we're not brilliant', he wrote home.[74] Even after finishing this course[75] he was not, as he expected, sent to the front but had to complete a further course: he was ordered to Bamberg to begin a special two-week training in the use of heavy machine-guns on 15 September.[76] Even though it was becoming clear on the western front how critical the German military situation was after the failure of their spring offensive, the German army continued to give its officers extremely thorough training. Or was it that Heinrich's superiors thought he was simply not mature enough to be sent to the front as an officer cadet?

At the beginning of October the Bamberg course was over, and after a week's leave he had to go back to Regensburg to help, amongst other things, with the training of recruits.[77] Heinrich took a pessimistic view of the general situation: 'I now see the political future as terribly black, completely black', he wrote on 16 October to his parents. Like many others, he now regarded revolution as inevitable.[78]

Even so, Heinrich was determined to prove himself in action, and wrote an enthusiastic letter home saying he had met a lieutenant who had offered to transfer him to the front.[79] But that never happened, for in view of the political turbulence that was erupting at the beginning of November the company destined for the front was disbanded. He experienced the overthrow of the political regime and the end of the war in Landshut: on 7 November revolution broke out in Munich and the Bavarian king abdicated. On 9 November the revolutionary Council of the People's Deputies set itself up in Berlin and Kaiser Wilhelm II fled to Holland. On 11 November the new government signed the armistice, and in so doing conceded the defeat of the German Reich.

At the end of November Heinrich returned to his unit in Regensburg in the hope that the army would complete the training of the cohort of ensigns born in 1900. At first, however, he worked with his cousin Ludwig Zahler, who had in the meantime been promoted to lieutenant, on the demobbing of the regiment. Both rented rooms in Regensburg.[80] Heinrich also began to prepare for his Abitur.*[81] In Regensburg he became a sympathizer of the Bavarian People's Party (BVP), which had been founded in November 1918 by leading politicians of the Bavarian Centre Party. Heinrich contacted one of Gebhard's former classmates who was now active in the local Regensburg BVP party organization, and also called on his father to work for the new party.[82]

His brother Gebhard, meanwhile promoted to lieutenant and decorated with the Iron Cross, had returned uninjured from the front at the beginning of December. Heinrich, on the other hand, was forced to recognize a little while later that there was no longer any chance that he could continue his military career. In December 1918 he learned that all ensigns of his cohort were to be discharged from the army.[83] On 18 December he was demobbed and returned to Landshut.[84] The fact that he neither saw action at the front nor became an officer was to him a serious failure. Throughout his life he was to hold to the view that he had been prevented from following his true calling, that of an officer.

---

* *Translators' note*: Grammar-school leaving examination.

2

The Student of Agriculture

B ack in Landshut Himmler's first priority was to finish his grammar-school education. Up to that point he had successfully completed seven years; thanks to a special ruling he could make up the remaining time required for his school-leaving certificate by joining a special class for those who had done war service. The teacher in charge of this programme turned out to be none other than Himmler's father, who treated the group with his habitual strictness and pedantry, showing no favouritism at all towards his son.[1]

Heinrich's closest friend at this time was Falk Zipperer, who had come back from the war and also joined the special class. The two friends spent a great deal of time writing poems. Whereas Zipperer was talented and even published a series of verses, Himmler's were on the clumsy side.[2]

Meanwhile political conditions in Bavaria were becoming more tense. On 21 February Kurt Eisner, the leader of the German Independent Social Democratic Party (USPD) in Bavaria, who as a result of the revolution had become Prime Minister, was shot by an extreme right-wing officer. In the following weeks an increasingly sharp polarization emerged between the coalition government elected by the state assembly under the new Prime Minister Johannes Hoffmann and the radical left-wing soviet movement, which was particularly strong in Munich. Finally, in Munich on 7 April the Left proclaimed the creation of a soviet republic and Hoffmann's government fled from the city and retreated to Bamberg. The USPD left the Bavarian government. In northern Bavaria Reich army units and Free Corps (armed groups of volunteers made up of anti-revolutionary and anti-democratic returning soldiers) prepared to capture the capital of the new Bavarian republic.[3]

Heinrich again gave practical support to the Bavarian People's Party, if only for a short time, as his correspondence with the Regensburg party office shows.[4] At the end of April he joined the Landshut Free Corps and also the reserve company of the Oberland Free Corps. This Free Corps had only just been founded by Rudolf von Sebottendorf, chairman of the extreme right-wing Thule Society, and came into being with the support of Hoffmann's government in order to defeat the Munich soviet republic. Heinrich does not, however, seem to have taken part in the bloody battles that took place at the beginning of May.[5] Even so he remained a further two months in the Oberland Free Corps, taking a post in the supplementary company[6] and hoping still to be able to make a career as an officer. At any rate, the government had opened up the prospect of members of the Free Corps being taken into the Reichswehr. But when in August Free Corps units were adopted into the Reichswehr Oberland was not amongst them.

Initial difficulties

In July 1919 Heinrich Himmler, in accordance with a further special ruling for those who had done war service, received his school-leaving certificate, without ever having had to undergo the actual examination. In most subjects his mark was 'very good' and only in maths and physics did he have to make do with 'good'.[7] As a military career in the Reichswehr seemed increasingly improbable, he made the surprising decision to study agriculture at the Technical University in Munich. At first sight this choice of career is hard to reconcile with the status-conscious, socially ambitious Himmlers and their aspirations as members of the professional middle class, the more so because the family was based in the town and had no links to landowners who might have offered their son a post such as steward of an estate. On the contrary, the imminent and extensive dissolution of the old officer corps made it likely that numerous disbanded officers, as well as the new generation of sons of the nobility who would in the past have gone into the army, would now enter agriculture.

Precisely this circumstance most likely accounts for Himmler's decision, however: at the agricultural faculty he hoped he would be in the company of former officers, who, although forced to prepare for a means of earning a living, regarded their studies first and foremost as a way of filling in the time with like-minded people until the outbreak of a fresh war or a civil war. Here Heinrich could immerse himself fully in the milieu of reserve officers and paramilitary activities, in order if possible still to realize his actual aim, namely a career in the military. The general uncertainty that prevailed in the immediate post-war period may have encouraged Himmler's parents to judge his decision pragmatically. They did, after all, also accept the decision of Gebhard and Ernst to study engineering.

In the summer of 1919 Himmler's father was appointed headmaster of the grammar school in Ingolstadt, and the family managed to find a small estate nearby where Himmler was to gain the one-year's practical experience he needed for acceptance on his course of study. On 1 August 1919 he began the one-year placement on the estate of Economic Councillor Winter in Oberhaunstadt. Work on the farm consisted of a twelve-hour day, six days a week; Himmler had Sunday off but still had to work early in the morning with the livestock. From his letters to his parents[8] and the 'work diary' he immediately began it is clear that he found the unaccustomed hard physical labour difficult, but that 'Heinrich agricola', as he signed one of his letters, was also proud of what he achieved. Thus he noted on 26 August: 'Morning, swept the grain drying-floor, unloaded 3½ loads of barley on my own.' And on 29 August he recorded: 'Afternoon loaded sacks of rye onto a wagon. 105 sacks weighing 2 hundredweight each. 3 loads of barley.' As during his time with the military he was still provided with extra rations, clean clothes, and various other things by his parents.

His hope that his exertions would strengthen his weak constitution[9] was, however, soon dashed: on the second weekend he was already ill in bed, and after less than five weeks of his placement he became seriously ill. In the Ingolstadt hospital he was suspected of having paratyphoid fever and he was kept there for three weeks. During that time his family moved to Ingolstadt.[10] On 25 September he travelled to Munich to see the former family doctor, Dr Quenstedt, who according to Heinrich came to the following diagnosis: 'Enlarged heart. Not significant, but he should take a break for a year and study.'[11]

During the idleness forced on him by his illness Heinrich read voraciously. While still in hospital he began to compile a list of books he intended to read, noting for the months of September and October (after leaving hospital he went back to live with his parents) a total of twenty-eight works.[12]

He devoured half-a-dozen volumes of Jules Verne along with predominantly historical fiction, for example three books by Maximilian Schmidt, the writer of popular Bavarian tales. Goethe's *Faust* formed part of his reading, also Thomas Mann's novel *Royal Highness*, the only work of modern German literature in this period that was to be found on his list and one that he immediately disliked.[13] On the other hand, he found the two volumes of *Ossian*, a collection of ancient Celtic bardic poetry edited by the teacher and writer James Macpherson in 1762/3, to be 'interesting'. Allegedly collected in the Scottish highlands, the songs were in fact a forgery, the work of the editor himself. Whether Himmler was aware of this when reading must remain a mystery; whatever the case, this type of romantic heroic saga suited his taste exactly.[14]

Towards the end of his period of illness he turned to political reading-matter. He read a polemic against the Freemasons that was widely read in its day, written by Friedrich Wichtl, a member of the Austrian National Assembly, who set about creating an ethnic (*völkisch*) stereotype out of the negative image of the Freemasons prevalent above all in Catholic circles during the First World War.[15] Wichtl claimed that, among other things, Freemasonry was strongly influenced by the Jews, was aiming for world revolution, and was overwhelmingly to blame for the World War. Himmler agreed and commented: 'A book that sheds light on everything and tells us who we have to fight first.' It remains an open question whether this challenge was directed at the Freemasons or at the Jews allegedly concealed behind them. Shortly before this he had read the first eight volumes of *Pro-Palestine*, publications edited by the German Committee for the Promotion of the Jewish Settlement of Palestine, and thus had engaged with Zionist literature, though he made no comments on this reading.[16]

First semester in Munich

On 14 October he travelled to Munich for a further examination by Dr Quenstedt. With regard to his heart 'nothing out of the ordinary' was discovered.[17] There was now nothing to prevent his beginning his studies: on 18 October 1919 he registered at the Technical University.[18]

Heinrich Himmler was a disciplined and conscientious student, and his health stabilized right away.[19] At first he shared a room for a few weeks with his brother Gebhard and then rented a furnished room very close to the Technical University at Amalienstrasse 28.[20] He quickly adopted a particular rhythm in his everyday life. He took his meals very close to his lodgings at the home of Frau Loritz, the widow of a professional singer, who together with her two daughters provided meals for students.[21] He mostly spent the evenings there and the rest of his free time he spent with friends, of whom we shall hear more. He also frequently paid formal visits to acquaintances of his parents—apparently not only out of politeness or on his parents' account but because he enjoyed such social occasions.

He made several visits to Privy Councillor von Lossow, a family friend, who, as Himmler noted, showed himself to be immensely kind.[22] On occasion he also visited the home of Professor Rauschmeyer, with whose daughter Mariele he was later to become friends.[23] He was a particularly frequent guest at the Hagers, his main interest being their daughter Luisa, whom he had known for years. He visited friends and acquaintances who were ill as a matter of course.[24]

In November he became a member of the 'Apollo' fraternity, in which his father was one of the 'old boys'. Apollo was a duelling fraternity, in other words, a place where traditional fencing was cultivated. 'At 2.30 went to the pub, where there were 5 duels. [...] At least it strengthens the nerves and you learn how to take being wounded.'[25] The 'pub' (*Kneipe*), as the meetings of the members were known in the fraternity's jargon,[26] was of course linked to increased consumption of alcohol; 'It was very jolly. I drank 8 glasses of wine. At 12.30 we went home on the train. Most of us were tipsy, so it was very funny. I got a few of the brothers back to their digs. In bed at 2 a.m.'[27]

While conducting this social life Himmler continued to be a practising Catholic, who went to mass and confession and took communion.[28] In his diary we find entries such as: 'God will come to my aid.'[29] The Christmas Eve mass he attended in 1919 with his family in Ingolstadt made a very deep impression on him; 'We were standing at the front in the choir and the solemn mass was a powerful experience. The church reaches people through its imposing ritual and God through a sweet and simple child.'[30]

Like many students at the Technical University, Himmler was a member of the League of War Veterans,[31] and in addition involved himself in the Territorial army: he joined the 14th Alarm Company of the 21st Rifle Brigade,[32] a Reichswehr reserve unit, and took part in practice alerts and shooting exercises. After the defeat of the soviet republic in May, Munich had developed into the centre for counter-revolutionary activities. The Free Corps and paramilitary organizations of the political Right, which arose to resist revolution, were still in existence; they had extensive stockpiles of weapons at their disposal and worked closely with the Reichswehr.

On a number of occasions Heinrich had good reasons for believing that 'actions' would occur and he urgently wished to be involved. Thus, immediately before 9 November 1919, the first anniversary of the revolution, he expected the military to be deployed but then nothing happened.[33] In December 1919 a putsch seemed to be in the offing; his unit was put on standby, but again nothing happened: 'Went at half past 3 with Lu [Ludwig Zahler] to the alarm call. Out to the Pioneers' barracks. Guns delivered but nothing more was done. Perhaps something more will happen this year.'[34] The feeling of being a soldier gave him deep satisfaction: 'Lectures till 10, then put on the king's coat again. I am after all a soldier and will remain so.'[35] Another entry reads: 'Today I have another day in uniform. It's what I enjoy wearing most every time.'[36]

On 16 January he learned that Count Arco, the former lieutenant who, on 21 February 1919, had murdered the serving Bavarian Prime Minister Kurt Eisner in the street, had been condemned to death.[37] The death sentence provoked outrage among those on the political Right. The students at the Technical University took part in the protests—but they did not want to stop there. With support from military circles an initiative was planned to free the prisoner and possibly begin a putsch. Himmler already had a part to play in this. Concerning the day after the verdict he noted in his diary: 'Put on my uniform. At 8 there was a big meeting of all the students in the university's main lecture hall to bring about a pardon for Arco. It was a brilliant patriotic meeting. A deputation was sent off. Captain St., Lieutenant St., Lieutenant B., and I were in the Turkish barracks★.' There the deputation was met by like-minded officers. 'Lieutenant St. arranged everything with a captain. The whole thing would have worked wonderfully. Back at the university at 11, where at 12.30 the news arrived that the sentence had been commuted to imprisonment. However pleased we were, we were equally sorry that the business passed off so uneventfully. Oh well, there will be another time. But people have seen how tremendous Germany's universities are.'[38] In other words, the Technical University in Munich was not just a place for studying. He told his mother: 'The ministers knew all right why they commuted Arco's sentence. If they hadn't they would have had to answer for it. We were all ready and were actually sorry that everything went off so quietly. [. . .] But it will happen one of these days.'[39] Letters to his parents reveal that during the Kapp putsch, which was

★ *Translators' note*: Barracks in Türkenstrasse.

started by Free Corps units in Berlin, he was alerted and took part at night in a motorized military patrol through Munich.[40]

When in spring 1920 the Allies compelled the German government to disband the reserve units of the Reichswehr, Himmler immediately transferred to the newly founded Residents' Reserve (*Einwohnerwehr*), which had been created by the Bavarian government in order to circumvent the Allied ban.[41] He also joined the Freiweg Rifle Club, an organization with a similarly paramilitary background.[42] His activities in these areas had further practical advantages: he used the discounted rail-tickets reserved for the military that he could claim as a member of the 14th Alarm Company for his weekend visits to his parents.[43]

All the same, his diaries contain relatively little about the political events of these months. The reason for this may be that at this time his basic political attitudes were established and he moved in a milieu in which these beliefs were largely shared. In the elections for the General Student Committee (AStA), the students' representative body, he voted for the candidates from the right-wing German National People's Party.[44] He also attended student political meetings.[45] The anti-Prussian tirades of one priest at the New Year sermon displeased him[46]—Himmler was no Bavarian separatist but saw himself as a German nationalist. An established component of this set of views was also a conventional, as yet not racially based, anti-Semitism.[47]

At the end of 1919 he was, however, caught up in a serious conflict of conscience. In the circles he belonged to of students who 'bore arms' a lively debate was being conducted about whether Jewish students were eligible to fight duels; in other words, whether Jews might be admitted as members of duelling fraternities (in fact at this time basically no fraternity still accepted Jews) or whether, by the same token, it was permissible to duel with Jewish students. It was a question of honour, in essence a question of whether Jewish students were capable of being equally valuable members of the student body, with equal rights.

Within the German student body, a significant portion of which leaned sharply to the right, there was at this time a strong tendency to mark themselves off from their Jewish fellow students and in fact to deny that these were truly German; or to put it more precisely, to base the definition of 'German' on ethnic criteria. Behind the debate surrounding the so-called duelling question there was therefore an attempt on the part of extreme right-wing students to enforce ethnic criteria throughout the network of student fraternities. The German-speaking fraternities in Austria had already denied Jews duelling status as a matter of principle in the 1890s, and after the end of the First World War radically anti-Semitic students attempted to establish this principle throughout the fraternities. As a result Catholic members of fraternities experienced a fundamental conflict, as Catholic student organizations for reasons of principle resisted the marginalization of students of Jewish descent: though they were to a considerable extent also anti-Semitic in outlook, they explained their hostility to the Jews primarily on religious and cultural grounds rather than on racial ones.[48]

'After dinner I had a conversation [...] about Jewishness, questions of honour and so on. A very interesting discussion. I was thinking about it on the way home. I think I am heading for conflict with my religion', Himmler noted in his diary, revealing that although he sympathized with racial anti-Semitism he could not yet make up his mind to adopt fully a radical anti-Semitic position. 'Whatever happens,' the diary goes on, 'I shall always love God and pray to him, and belong to the Catholic church and defend it, even if I should be excluded from it.'[49] Three days later he and Ludwig Zahler had a discussion, again about 'the principles of fencing, matters of honour, the Church etc.'.

At a Christmas celebration at which a cleric made a speech that, in Himmler's view, was 'a right old sermon', his 'inner conflicts of faith' assailed him 'as never before'. Again and again the 'fencing matter' reared its head, but then for the time being the crisis was past: 'In the evening I prayed, although even before that I had more or less got over it. God will show me the way in all my doubts.'[50]

'A heart in conflict and turmoil'

Himmler's circle of friends in Munich consisted above all of Falk Zipperer and Ludwig Zahler, though the latter's friendship with Heinrich's brother Gebhard was closer. Even so, Heinrich spent much time with Ludwig and the two frequently had long discussions: 'Ludwig came home with me and we looked at books together in my room and talked. He is a good man and a brother to Gebhard and me.'[51] Falk, however, was in Heinrich's eyes 'a really nice, good friend and a great man of genius'.[52] Their shared interest in writing poetry still bound them together. A popular ballad they jointly wrote for a charitable cause was even performed for friends.[53] 'We began at

4.30, see programme. Everything went off brilliantly', he noted with satisfaction. 'The last number, when Lu and Käthe danced in rococo costumes, was charming. Then we had sandwiches and cakes. Then there was dancing.' Himmler had attended a class to overcome his initial clumsiness.[54] 'All the ladies were very nice, particularly Käthe, Mopperl, Friedl. Later Mr Küfner even poured schnapps. Lu and I chinked glasses (Cheers brother, we'll always stick together). Then more dancing. After that forfeits with lots of kisses. At about 1.30 we went home. I am very satisfied with the evening. Lu and I can also be satisfied.'[55]

As a 19-year-old Heinrich also developed a considerable interest in two girls in his circle. At first he took a fancy to Luisa Hager, whom he had known since their shared childhood and admired for some time. The two corresponded and Himmler paid a striking number of visits to the family.[56] The discovery that she too was a devout and practising Catholic filled him with enthusiasm. When he learned from an acquaintance that 'sweet, well-behaved Luisa goes to communion every day', it was 'the nicest thing that's happened to me all week'.[57] And yet he did not make any real progress; as he repeatedly stated, Luisa did not 'come out of her shell'.[58] She was 'really nice,' he noted after an evening spent with her and friends, 'but all the same not in the way I would like'.[59] He discussed the matter at length with Gebhard: 'If sweet young things knew how they worried us, they would no doubt try not to.'[60]

But he was also captivated by Maja, one of Frau Loritz's daughters and Ludwig Zahler's girlfriend. He confessed to being 'happy to be able to call this marvellous girl my friend'.[61] On a November evening he spent once more with Frau Loritz, 'I talked the whole time with Fräulein Maja about religion and so forth. She told me a lot about her life. I think I have now found a sister.'[62]

The friends saw each other often, went to concerts[63] and to the theatre[64] together, visited museums,[65] enjoyed the ice rink,[66] and made music.[67] In spite of the continuing tension of the political situation, economic problems, and food shortages the Munich students' daily lives were relatively untroubled and pleasant. Heinrich recorded memorable moments in his diary: 'Lectures began today. In the evening we sat together, arm in arm, until midnight.'[68] The following day his mood was sombre: 'In the evening we were in the room at the back. I was terribly serious and downcast. I think very difficult times are on the way, or is that not what these things mean?' And he noted the thought that was to liberate him from his depressive mood: 'I'm looking forward to the fight, when I shall wear the king's coat again.' The evening then continued very harmoniously:

First Maja sang 'Women's love and pain'. She sang the songs with tears in her eyes. Ludwig doesn't, I think, understand his darling girl. But I am not sure even of that for I don't know him well enough. Later Gebhard and Käthe played the piano. Ludwig and I sat together in an armchair and Mariele and Maja sat on the floor leaning against us. We all embraced each other, partly out of love and partly out of brotherly and sisterly friendship. It was an evening I shall never forget.[69]

His affection for Maja did not remain simply brotherly, and Heinrich's relationship with Ludwig, her boyfriend, became ever more complicated. 'I understand Ludwig less and less. Poor Maja', he wrote on 5 November in his diary: 'I am sorry for him and even more for Maja, who is nice. Human beings are miserable creatures. The saying is really true: restless is the heart till it rests on Thee, O God. How powerless one is, unable to do anything.' Heinrich was lovesick. He was engulfed by 'oppressive thoughts and inner conflicts', but his friends were not to notice anything.[70] He intended 'to be a friend to my friends, do my duty, work, battle with myself, and never let it happen that I lose control of myself,' as the high-flown language of his diary puts it.[71]

His efforts never to lose control over himself were put seriously to the test in the middle of November at an 'evening of hypnotism' at the Loritz home, when he fended off the invited hypnotist 'with all his powers of resistance'. Maja had a different experience: 'He had poor, sweet Maja completely in his power. I was sorry to see her that way. I could have strangled the brute in cold blood.'[72] The first plans to leave Munich behind and to move as a settler to the east emerged: 'At the moment I don't know for whom I am working. I work because it is my duty, because I find peace in work and I am working for my ideal of German womanhood, and with that ideal I will live out my life in the east, far from the beauty of Germany. I will struggle to make my way there as a German.'[73] Heinrich began to learn Russian.[74] Then once more the right way for him seemed to be to prove himself in 'war and struggle': 'Gebhard, Lu, and I talked for a long time about how good it would have been if we had stayed in the army. Together in the field and so on. Perhaps I wouldn't be here any more, one fighting spirit less. But I do not want to become weak and will never lose control of myself. In a few years perhaps I will have a chance to fight and to struggle and I'm looking forward to the war of liberation and will join up as long as I can move a muscle.'[75]

The diary entries about time spent with Maja, mostly in their circle of friends, became more numerous. They read and played music together, had profound discussions about life, sometimes sat together hand in hand and parted with a kiss.[76] In November, however, he was shocked to learn that Maja would be leaving Munich in January.[77] At the end of November, after he had again had the opportunity to say a few words to her, he made the resolution: 'Tomorrow I must know where I stand, for this situation is awful.' The next day he did in fact meet her again, but did not manage to clarify matters as he had hoped: 'After dinner until about 10.30 I helped Maja with her arithmetic. She was always thanking me profusely. Then home . . .'[78]

Again he wanted to plunge into battle: ' . . . if only I had dangers to face, and could risk my life and fight, that would be ecstasy. Oh human beings, with their affections, their indeterminable longing, their hearts in conflict and turmoil, are pathetic creatures. And yet I am proud to fight this battle and am determined not to be defeated.'[79] At the same time he noticed a growing distance on Maja's part: 'I don't know if I am only imagining it or if it really is so. Maja did not behave to me as she has done up to now. Went home at 1.'[80] Now he began to take a negative view of his chances with the object of his adoration.[81]

On 5 December, the night before St Nicholas's Day, he was pleased about a gift he took to be from Maja: 'Found a little St Nicholas basket at home. Gebhard found a golden hair on it. I think it's dear Maja's doing. I have kept the hair.' Three days later, however, he knew the truth: 'The St Nicholas presents recently came from Frl. Wahnschaffe, by the way. That shows how stupid a man in love is.' What could he do? He made a decision: 'Today I distanced myself inwardly from everything and now am relying on myself alone. If I don't find the girl whose qualities match mine and who loves me I shall just go to Russia alone.'[82]

The next day he wrote in his diary about Maja: 'I hope I see her again when I'm here the year after next, when she has been a year in the country. And I hope that by then this lovely personality has become more settled and mature and has won through. She has a Faustian temperament.'[83] The old year ended with resolutions for the new one: 'Then we played music together and drank punch. What will the new year bring? Whatever it is, with God's grace I intend to use it to become more mature and to continue to climb the path towards greater self-knowledge.'[84]

But only a few days later he was again in 'a terribly serious mood'.[85] There were highly unpleasant confrontations with his brother Gebhard and Ludwig Zahler, for he was obviously getting on their nerves: 'Ludwig told me I was touchy and he's certainly right in part. But not entirely.'[86] He was annoyed by Maja's behaviour after she ignored him at one of the evenings at the Loritz home, and he complained, full of self-pity (and probably completely without justification as far as Maja's alleged feelings for him were concerned): 'My experience with her and with Luisa is: "It's hard to think of anyone more heartless than many girls are who've once loved you."'[87]

Alongside his heartache, in this period his growing sexual curiosity is also apparent in the diary. With Ludwig and Gebhard he discussed 'the old topic of "Woman and whore"'.[88] In November he noted that 'in Odeonsplatz a whore tried to attach herself to us'—'unsuccessfully, of course', as he quickly added, but he admitted to himself: 'It's a very interesting thing, though.'[89] In December 1919 he discussed Wedekind's play *Wetterstein Palace*, in which sexual entanglements play an important role, with a fellow fraternity member who also recounted relevant experiences from his war service: 'I must say though that it wasn't just smut but something I was genuinely interested in, something a mature person must be thoroughly informed about.'[90] In March 1920 he reacted with deep agitation and disgust to a book about a love affair between a young priest and a 14-year-old boy: 'Sunday, 7.3.1920. 10.30 in the evening in a terrible mood. Munich—strange. The idealization of a homosexual man.—Ghastly pictures.'[91]

At the end of January and beginning of February 1920 a dose of flu kept him in bed, and he recorded with extreme precision what care his friends took of him and how much emotional support, which he clearly desperately needed, they gave him: 'Käthe always brought me my meals. Lu visited every day, sometimes twice. Schorschl also visited once. They are truly good, dear people and above all good friends. Käthl was like a sister. Lu is a brother to me. Friedl sent me an egg and always lots of greetings. She is a good sort [...].'[92]

Even so, taken as a whole the experiences of this first Munich period were very sobering for him. It is therefore not surprising that his favourite place was at home with his parents: 'There's just nowhere as nice as home.'

With them—and in letters—he engaged in quite detailed discussions about the things on his mind. 'In the evening went for a walk with Father. We talked a lot. About Luisa, about my Russian problem (mainly with Mother), about the political and economic future etc.'[93] At home 'I'm just a cheerful boy without any cares, but on leaving my parents' house I'm changed back again'.[94] His relationship with his father ('dear Dad') was harmonious for long stretches, though matters on which he clashed with his parents arose repeatedly; for example, a serious crisis was to develop in April 1921.[95]

As a perusal of the very detailed diary entries from his first semester in Munich makes abundantly clear, Heinrich Himmler had distinct problems in his personal relationships. Not only was he inexperienced and shy with girls, which was a function of his age, he was also uncertain in general about what he should and could expect of other people in his personal relations. He found it very difficult to judge the emotional attitudes of others and to respond to them appropriately. He simply did not know how to strike the right note in his behaviour with other people.

Psychologists would analyse this in terms of the consequences of an attachment disorder.[96] People who suffer from this kind of dysfunction acquired in early childhood frequently tend, while growing up and as adults, to attach very high expectations to personal relationships, though they cannot define these expectations precisely, and as a result they cannot be fulfilled. The consequence is a sense of frustration and the desire for more signs of affection. People with this problem are prone to feeling constantly exploited. From time to time they unload their feelings in outbursts of rage that others find difficult to comprehend, and then develop strategies to help them approach others which are often perceived as ingratiating. Often, however, they learn to conceal their emotional immaturity by means of particular behavioural techniques, and up to a certain point to compensate for it in their dealings with others.

As the letters from Himmler's period in the army have already made clear, he did in fact struggle with insatiable longings for affection and care—at first from his mother in particular and then in relation to his circle of friends. He tried to get close to others but always had the sense that he had not really succeeded. He made an effort always to be helpful and then was annoyed with himself because he feared he had made a fool of himself. He also had the experience of his behaviour towards others, though well intentioned, being seen by them as inappropriate and provoking mystified or defensive reactions.

It must be said that he made great efforts to compensate for these weaknesses. He was helped by a fundamental character trait, evident from his earliest childhood: his constant exercise of will-power and self-control. It became second nature to him to hold himself in check and avoid emotion as far as possible. In addition, he hoped that by rigorous self-discipline he would acquire that level of self-assurance that would allow him to disguise his emotional immaturity in dealing with personal relationships. This is the context in which the strict regime he applied to his contacts with people has to be seen: the enforced good behaviour, the routine visits, the conversational strategies, and finally the huge emphasis he placed on regular exchanges of letters and gifts. For his relations with others he needed a framework in which he could operate.

His habit of regarding and referring to himself as a 'soldier' can be interpreted as part of these strenuous efforts to gain control of himself and be recognized by others. As a member of the generation that grew to adulthood during the war, Himmler belonged to a cohort of middle-class young men who experienced the military defeat and revolution as the decisive events of their lives. For them the events of 1918/19 represented an existential challenge, demanding the response of a fundamentally new orientation geared to overcoming the defeat as an internal and external reality: this was to be achieved by a changed attitude to life and new way of living.

Thus, as Ulrich Herbert in particular has demonstrated, in those years a way of living emerged amongst those who became adults during the war that can be summed up in the words: sobriety, distance, severity, and rationality.[97] Himmler's determined struggle to conceal his relationship problems by means of strict observance of social formalities and rules for daily life, and to avoid and control emotion, was also matched, therefore, by a desire to live up to the demands of his contemporaries. This he could do much more easily as a Territorial soldier than in his everyday life as a student from a comfortable background. The world of the military, with its organization of every last detail, met his need for rules and control, and in view of the tendency in this masculine world to suppress emotion his difficulties in forming attachments must have appeared as a positive virtue. Herein lies the biographical key to his enthusiasm for the military and, after a career as an officer was denied him, for his later engagement in the paramilitary movement.

According to psychologists, the origins of attachment disorder go back to early childhood, to a lack of affection and mirroring on the part of the mother. What the cause was in Himmler's case can only be the subject of speculation. Possibly his brother's frequent illnesses were a factor, and perhaps also competition developed between Himmler and his younger brother and he fell into the classic role of the middle child who feels neglected. Whatever the causes of his difficult interpersonal relations, they remained a problem for him throughout his life.

The fruits of reading

The emotional upheavals of his first semester from October 1919 to March 1920 also made an impact on his reading list. A total of fourteen titles are listed, but politics and popular philosophy appeared only peripherally; a book on the Freemasons seemed to him too uncritical,[98] whereas he was gripped by Walter Flex's 'Poems and Thoughts from the Battlefield', which appeared under the title *The Great Feast*, because the book 'uses a poet's imagination to reproduce very convincingly and well the thoughts one has as a soldier'.[99]

At this time his main reading was novels and stories chiefly concerned with love, erotic attraction, and the battle of the sexes. He thought Georges Rodenbach's gloomy novel *Bruges-la-Morte* 'psychologically very good'. It tells of a man who continues to feel tied to his dead wife and murders his lover when she wants to take the wife's place. This reading-matter apparently suited Himmler's depressed mood in November.[100] He finished Ludwig Finckh's folksy novel *The Rose Doctor* (1906), putting it down with a feeling of 'satisfaction such as I have not felt for a long time'. His view was that it was 'a hymn of praise, and a justified one, to women'.[101] At the end of the winter semester he started on *Diary of a Lost Soul*, a bestseller about the fate of a girl who falls into prostitution. It was a book, as Himmler noted—clearly impressed—'that offers insight into dreadful human tragedies and makes one look at many a whore with very different eyes.'[102]

He read Ibsen's *A Doll's House* with great interest, and it challenged him to reach a conclusion about the causes of this marital tragedy: 'It is her fault, for allowing herself to be turned into a doll', adding 'in part' in modification of this verdict. He went on, however, to make a further point: 'She can never require her husband to sacrifice his honour.' Helmer, the husband, is to blame because, 'in cowardly fashion, he abandons his wife when she is in need, and afterwards acts as if something had happened.'[103] The fact that

Nora leads the life of a doll deprived of adult status is, according to Himmler, her own fault; the fact that her husband might have something to do with it is an idea that never even crossed his mind. The question of emancipation, the central problem of the play, which was after all already forty years old at the time, was clearly completely foreign to him. He did not know what to do with Nora, a woman breaking out of marital subservience; his still very adolescent concept of women—and this is shown by his responses to his reading—was instead dominated by the contrasting images of the ideal woman and the whore. Apart from that, the play strengthened him in the notion that a husband must above all protect his wife—though only as far as his 'honour' permitted it. He could hardly have provided a more telling example of his complete incomprehension of the debate about marriage as an equal partnership that was being conducted with increased intensity at the beginning of the Weimar Republic.

In the spring and summer of 1920 two anti-Semitic titles can be found on his list. It is clear that he was looking for an answer to the 'Jewish question', which as a result of the debate on duelling at the end of 1919 was a matter he too wanted to resolve. In April he read Artur Dinter's extraordinarily successful novel *The Sin against Blood*, to which he reacted with both approval and scepticism: 'A book that gives a startlingly clear introduction to the Jewish question and makes one approach this subject extremely warily but also investigate the sources on which the novel is based. For the middle way is probably the right one. The author is, I think, somewhat rabid in his hatred of the Jews.—The novel, with its anti-Semitic lectures, is written purely to push a particular line.'[104] Friedrich Spielhagen's *Ultimo*, by contrast, met with his complete approval.[105] On the evidence of his reading-list, the 'Jewish question' did not loom large in his interests again until 1922. In 1920, however, he was clearly not yet prepared to subscribe unequivocally to a radically anti-Semitic viewpoint.

In May 1920 he chanced upon a book that helped him to transform his lack of sexual experience and success with girls into true virtue. The work in question was Hans Wegener's sex-education book of 1906, *Young Men Like Us*, which focuses on the 'sexual problem of educated young men before marriage'.[106] Wegener warned about masturbation, prostitution, and sexual relations outside marriage, as well as preaching sexual abstinence in general before marriage. By contrast with many contemporary publications, however, he was not content to demand sexual abstinence on the grounds of possible health-risks, but rather he appealed first and foremost to the young man's honour and strength of will: chastity is here declared to be the essence of masculinity, correctly understood.

The central admonition is to maintain 'chivalrous reverence for a pure woman'.[107] Such a 'responsible' attitude, it is argued, permits friendly, platonic relationships with women:

Good, so let us trample our animal nature underfoot and with senses under control seek the friendship of such women. They will not withhold it and it will enrich our personal lives. It will restore to us in a purer form what we offered up, and if we were pure it will immerse us in greater purity. It will increase our strength in our battle with ourselves and we will be dubbed knights, pledged our whole lives to protect women. Until we have found the woman to whom we wish to belong for life, friendly relations with women are positively necessary.[108]

These words were balm to Himmler's bruised soul. In positive euphoria he decided to make Wegener's advice his own maxim. In his reading-list he drew the satisfied conclusion: 'A book containing the highest ideals. Demanding, but achievable. And I have achieved them already.—Probably the finest book of its kind that I have read.'[109]

Agricultural work experience

After the first two semesters in Munich Himmler had to carry out an agricultural work placement. Although we do not know much about Himmler's second semester, as there are no diary notes for the summer semester of 1920, we may assume nevertheless that the compulsory period in the country provided him with a welcome escape from Munich, where circumstances had become difficult. Relatives of the Loritz family, the Rehrls from Fridolfing in Upper Bavaria, had offered him a placement on their estate, and he embarked on the year ahead with great expectations, as he wrote to his father: 'a good diet' and work on the land will strengthen him physically, will in fact 'steel' him. He hopes also that 'his nerves and soul can find repose in nature and in the seriousness and jollity of the agricultural calling and way of life'.[110] By buying a motorbike he aimed to be mobile in his remote rural location.[111]

He arrived in Fridolfing on 7 September, and his letters to his parents show that he launched himself body and soul into the unaccustomed work.[112] His accommodation and food were good and he got to know the family. Right away he formed a friendship with the owner of the estate, Alois Rehrl, ten years his senior, that was to last for decades.[113] The two went hunting together; Himmler visited agricultural shows and went on a variety of excursions and tours of the mountains,[114] became a member of the German Touring Club and the Alpine Society,[115] and also took a lively part in country organizations and traditional festivities.[116] He even joined the Residents' Militia.[117] He attended church regularly,[118] and in his free time also enjoyed visiting acquaintances who lived nearby.[119] Throughout the placement he was in very close contact with his parents; his mother went on supplying him with numerous parcels,[120] while he in turn produced minute calculations to account for how he had spent the pocket money they paid him.[121] 'I promise always to strive to be a good man and remain so', he vowed to his father in a letter on the latter's fifty-sixth birthday.[122]

Himmler's reading at this time focused on further Ibsen plays, which he thought somewhat too 'realistic' but which made an 'uncommonly true' impression.[123] In *Love's Comedy* he saw 'the mendacity and social mores of love' pilloried.[124] He also liked the fact that in *Pillars of Society* we see 'the dishonesty and the deception on which society is built'; he was, however, above all impressed with 'how the good in society emerges through individual characters and still wins through'.[125] His motto that self-control and exercise of the will make it possible to master any situation is confirmed by Ibsen, whose drama about Pastor Brand, who destroys himself and others by his inflexibility, was for him, 'as far as morality and discipline of the will are concerned one of the best and most perfect dramas I know. It is a book that deals with the will, morality and life without compromises.'[126]

At the same time he devoured novels in which he saw representations of his ideal woman—*Poor Margarethe* by Enrica von Handel-Mazzetti for example, or Agnes Günther's *The Saint and the Fool*.[127] He also enjoyed books about the Nordic-Germanic heroes. Verner von Heidenstam's novel about the Swedish king Charles XII impressed him as the 'story of an iron man, who with his mind and will inspired a people up to the last day of his life and led each of these brave men on to be heroes—A man sorely needed in our time'.[128] When he read Felix Dahm's monumental novel about the Goths, *A Battle for Rome*, he was totally enthused by the 'gripping and vividly written story of a splendid, fine and truly Germanic people'; 'the perfidious Latins and feminine intrigues' could make one 'weep', however.[129]

Rudolph Stratz's novel *Light from the East*, about a nobleman of German descent in Estonia during the First World War opened up to him in 'blindingly clear' light a new perspective on the 'terrifying east'. 'If anyone wants to visualize the future', this is a book he has to read. 'It sheds light on the changing migrations in the east, the power and the inner strength of the Germanic peoples in the Baltic region, and about our own strength and weakness.'[130]

He was also impressed with Ernst Zahn's *Women of Tannö*. In the novel the inhabitants of a village make the decision to have no more children in order to avoid passing on haemophilia, which is prevalent in the community, to the next generation. Himmler commented: 'The fight against the power of the blood. How this battle is fought. From the most noble silence to the point of succumbing. An excellent novel.'[131]

He read various historical books, preferring those that chimed with his nationalism. He found an edition of speeches made in 1848 to the Frankfurt Parliament interesting principally because of 'analogies with the present-day revolution'.[132] In August 1920 he was reading about the 'Wars of Liberation' against Napoleon[133] and the First World War; a commemorative volume for German officers who were prisoners of war he devoured within a few days. He considered it a 'monument to Germans' emotional, intellectual and all-round competence [. . .] that edifies, elevates and is bound to inspire respect for what is essentially German'.[134]

At the turn of 1920/1 five novels of Conrad von Bolanden followed in quick succession. The author was a Catholic priest who, under a pseudonym, wrote historical works that were in equal measure aimed at a popular audience and written from a consistently Catholic perspective. It is clear from Himmler's comments that he did not adopt this standpoint uncritically. He particularly disliked Bolanden's anti-Protestant attitude, for he himself regarded it as a blessing that the confessional rift was being healed.[135] He was also sceptical about whether, from his 'purely Catholic' standpoint, Bolanden had taken a sufficiently comprehensive view of the causes of the French Revolution.[136] On the other hand he reacted enthusiastically to his polemic against the Freemasons; the fact that it was based on conventional Christian, rather than völkisch, arguments clearly did not concern him.[137]

When the work placement in Fridolfing came to an end in August 1921 he returned, strengthened in body and in self-confidence, to Ingolstadt, where he completed a further two-month placement at an engineering works. At the start of the winter semester of 1921/2 he resumed his studies at the Technical University in Munich.[138]

3

Struggle and Renunciation

Himmler resumed his studies at the beginning of November 1921. He found a room at No. 9 Briennerstrasse conveniently close to the Technical University, to the University (where he also attended lectures), and to the State Library.[1]

Unlike during his first year of study, he now usually had his meals in his lodgings. His contacts with the Loritz family, which during his first stay in Munich had been an important fixed point in his life, were now reduced to irregular visits. Since his old friend Ludwig Zahler had in the meantime become engaged to Käthe Loritz, which on occasion was to put a great strain on his friendship with Käthe, Heinrich was quite glad that this new arrangement enabled him, when necessary, to avoid encountering his friend's fiancée.[2]

Himmler had still not succeeded in establishing his independence from his parents; indeed, he does not appear even to have made a serious attempt to do so. He made numerous purchases for his father[3] and received in turn regular parcels of food and clothing from his parents.[4] 'Good old Mummy sends me lots of goodies', the 21-year-old gratefully noted in his diary at the beginning of 1922.[5] His correspondence with Ingolstadt was always as regular as before and Himmler, in his role as the conscientious son, continued to list all his tasks in minute detail,[6] portraying himself as a keen student. He was 'doing what was required'.[7] Apart from that, he plunged into student social life with his typical commitment. He sang in the church choir,[8] revived his regular social contacts, particularly with acquaintances of his parents,[9] and took an active part in the General Student Committee (AStA), the student representative body of the Munich Technical University. He was a candidate in the AStA elections at the end of 1921 and his tenth place on the fraternity students' list won him a seat.[10]

He spent most of his spare time involved in the activities of his fraternity, the League of Apollo. From early afternoon onwards he was frequently to be found in his fraternity fencing-room. However, he does not appear to have found the fencing exercises, to which he devoted himself so assiduously, at all easy.[11] He had to wait a long time for his first official duel, which had to be carried out in accordance with strict rules and which would qualify him to become a full member of his fraternity.

Nevertheless, he took part enthusiastically in the activities of the fraternity, which were dominated by complicated rules of honour and procedure involving endless debates about disciplinary matters and relations with other student fraternities.[12] He conscientiously visited sick and wounded members of the fraternity in hospital,[13] exploited the opportunity of getting to know the 'old boys' of the fraternity,[14] some of whom were influential figures, and enjoyed hospitality and assistance from other members, for example when travelling.[15]

Despite this selfless commitment, he did not receive the recognition from his fellow students that he was seeking. In November 1921 his application to be made an officer was rejected, 'because it's believed that the fencing would not be in good hands and, in any case, I would be liable to be prevented by my father from performing the role'.[16] He does not appear to have been aware of the fact that, as a relatively recent member and without having taken part in a duel, he had applied for a post for which he was entirely unsuitable.

In February 1922 he applied for the office of 'Fuchsmajor' (who was responsible for the supervision of the new members), but once again without success. 'On the one hand, I was hurt that I wasn't elected,' he confided to his diary, 'but on the other hand, it's very good. I've got more time. I haven't cultivated people and so I'm not well liked. Why?— Because friendly types make comments about me because of my fencing and because I talk too much.'[17]

When the elected candidate declined to serve Himmler proposed himself for the post to two fellow fraternity members, but again in vain. 'I shall never mention the matter again', he promised in his diary.[18] Evidently he was annoyed at his own behaviour, which his fellow fraternity members must have considered very importunate. His attempt in July 1922 to win the support of the League for an important change in the statutes also met with no success. When, at the end of the night-time session, the vote was called he found himself in the minority. He noted stubbornly: 'Defeated according to the rules, but morally in the majority.'[19]

This student had a full, indeed an overfull, diary of events to get through. Apart from various student and paramilitary activities, he was a member of several associations[20] and liked going to cafés, pubs, and dance venues;[21] he also went to the cinema[22] and accepted numerous private invitations. He was continually meeting acquaintances in the university district and evidently spent a lot of time 'rabbiting on', as he noted in his diary.[23] But, however hard he tried, he failed to achieve the popularity he yearned for.

'I have to struggle': the young Himmler and the opposite sex

He also had little success in his relationships with women. While his brother Gebhard had a steady girlfriend and his best friend, Ludwig Zahler, a fiancée, Himmler had to face the fact that, as far as love and sex were concerned, he was getting nowhere.

It was not that he lacked interest. His diaries, especially during his second stay in Munich, reveal an increasingly active interest in the most varied aspects of sex and every conceivable problem that could arise in relations with the opposite sex, an interest that, on occasion, could be described as obsessive. There are numerous descriptions of women in his diary, often chance acquaintances or objects of desire observed from afar. At a concert in February, for example, the pianist, 'a pretty woman', 'provoked all sorts of thoughts'. The relaxed atmosphere of the Munich Carnival also aroused his fantasy. At a Carnival party 'Zipfchen', a 'true Rhinelander', made a great impression on him. 'Of course we used the familiar "Du" form the whole evening . She was a sweet girl, 19 years old with a childlike quality, and yet a mature woman with a hot-blooded temperament, easy going and rash and yet not bad (as she herself said). We got on marvellously.'[24] Another Carnival acquaintance 'had quite a bosom'.[25] The girlfriend of a former comrade from the Landshut Free Corps period was 'certainly a good girl. But sexy.' When he took her home after an evening spent together because his acquaintance had to catch a train, he reflected: 'I think I could've had her.' But 'home to bed'.[26]

Conversations with his friend Ludwig Zahler, often on long evening walks, helped Himmler to calm his surging passions. In January, he noted, they had 'a long talk until 11 o'clock about sexual questions, abstinence, sexual performance'.[27] Two days later the pair talked about adultery, and

two weeks later the whole gamut of issues was discussed: 'sexual intercourse, contraception, abortion, the attitude of the individual and of the
state. Lu's attitude very laid back.'

Himmler, by contrast, had moral inhibitions. After a Carnival party he
noted:

Only got home at 2 o'clock. Walked with Lu. We spoke about the dangers of such
things. I have known what it's like to be lying together in pairs next to each other,
side by side. One gets into a passion where one has to summon up all one's powers
of control. The girls are then so far gone they no longer know what they're doing.
It's the burning unconscious yearning of the whole individual for the liberation of a
terribly strong natural instinct. That's why it's so dangerous for men and such a
responsibility. One could do what one wants with girls and yet one has enough to
do with controlling oneself. I feel really sorry for girls.[28]

After another, in his eyes, wild Carnival party he vowed to moderate his
behaviour: 'But it's terrible how hot one gets on such occasions. Look at
Mariele. She can't help it, but one has to be sorry for girls. One can't be
too careful. 11.15 went home with Lu. Talked about it. To bed at 1
o'clock.'

In spring 1922 Ludwig was replaced by a new companion with whom to
discuss sex. Alphons, the son of his landlady, Frau Wolff, was in Himmler's
eyes 'a ladykiller. But he doesn't go the whole way.' Alphons even let him
read letters from a girlfriend. 'I find it interesting from a psychological point
of view. One ought to get to know these kinds of people too.'[29] In the end
Himmler became Alphons's 'ghost-writer' and composed his replies not
only to his girlfriend ('a deep, romantic, hot-blooded, but good girl'[30]), but
also to another acquaintance, a cabaret dancer called Fiffi.

Himmler seized the opportunity to attend one of her performances with
Alphons, though they both told Frau Wolff that they were going elsewhere:
'Supposedly in Annast. I am, after all, the virtuous youth. But none the less
anyone ought to realize what we're up to.' Fiffi revealed herself to be 'a very
decent girl'.

Dancing for her is an art form in which she's completely absorbed. Terrific taste.
I got on with her really well. I talked about her dances and the others, and about her
costumes. She doesn't mind one expressing an opinion. She's about 18 years old, a
cute charming little thing, a virgin and good. She willingly accepts Alphons's
caresses, but only at the end, at the front door, does she give him a kiss as well[31]
[. . .] It would be a great shame if this girl got into the wrong hands.

But a few months later this 'charming little thing' provoked his displeasure: 'Smoked and chatted with Alphons. Fiffi has written an impertinent letter and returned his (our) letters.'[32]

Himmler preferred to look for an elevated kind of woman, an ideal female, the kind of woman who acquired an ever more prominent place in his thoughts and for whom, as was his firm intention, he wished to save himself. Käthe, Frau Loritz's daughter, who was unfortunately already engaged to his best friend Ludwig Zahler, fulfilled all the preconditions for this role. One Sunday evening, in January 1922, he was alone with her in the Loritz flat. The atmosphere was tense:

Little Käthe sat on the sofa; she was wearing a grey dress that she'd made herself and which really suited her. I sat opposite her in the armchair [. . .] We got on really well. We talked about lots of examples of egoism, jealousy, etc., about Theo, the nice Rehrls, about a lot of things, a lot of intimate things as one does between friends. Little Käthe was very sweet. In this way I was able to tell her a lot and this time we definitely got close. Naturally, whether it will last remains to be seen. But we have formed an intimate bond [. . .] I went home very contented. It was a nice and worthwhile evening.[33]

In June 1922 he met an Ingolstadt acquaintance on the train. 'She has a large landholding with a lot of livestock. A straightforward, often boyish, but I think, sweet and lively girl. It's the same as usual: I would need only to make the first move, but I can't flirt and I can't commit myself now—if I don't definitely feel this is "the one".'[34]

Himmler kept creating situations that he felt were erotic and which aroused his fantasy, while at the same time insisting to himself that he must refrain from taking advantage of them. Himmler believed in sexual abstinence, not only because he believed he ought to wait for 'the right one', but also because he considered he was on the brink of deciding on his future and so could not enter into any binding commitment. In a short time he hoped he would either be going off to war as an officer or on a journey to a far-off land as a settler.

'Talked about women,' he wrote after a Carnival party about a conversation with Ludwig,

and how on evenings like these a few hours can bring one close to other people. The memory of such times is among the purest and finest one can experience. They are moments when one would like to kneel down and give thanks for what one is blest with. I shall always be grateful to those two sweet girls. I would not like to call it love but for a few hours we were fond of each other and the lovely memory of it will last forever. Only one notices how one thirsts for love and yet how difficult and what a responsibility it is to make a choice and a commitment.—Then one gets to thinking, if only we could get involved in some more conflicts, war, mobilisation—I am looking forward to my duel.[35]

The repression of the subject of sexuality through the invocation of masculinity, heroism, and violence, and his self-imposed conviction that, predestined to be a solitary fighter and hero, he could not enter into any emotional commitments, form a constant refrain in his diary entries: 'I am in such a strange mood. Melancholy, yearning for love, awaiting the future. Yet wanting to be free to go abroad and because of the coming war, and sad that the past is already gone [...] Read. Exhausted. Bed.'[36] And on the occasion of Gebhard's engagement we read: 'Another of our group of two years ago has gone. Commitment to a woman forms a powerful bond. For thou shalt leave father and mother and cleave to thy wife. I am glad that once again two people so close to me have found happiness. But for me— struggle.'[37]

In May 1922 he visited friends in the country. As a prude, Himmler considered they were rather too permissive; he was shocked at their 3-year-old daughter, who ran around naked indoors in the evenings: 'Irmgard ran about naked before being put to bed. I don't think it's at all right at three, an age when children are supposed to be taught modesty.'[38]

His time with the family clearly provoked him so much so that he wrote at greater length on it in his diary:

She is a thoroughly nice, very competent, sweet but very tough-minded creature with an unserious way of looking at life and particular moral rules. He is a very skilled doctor and also a very decent chap. His wife can be very headstrong, and he has trained her well [. . .] He can be egotistic when he needs to be but he is a patriot and all in all a proper man.—The fact is, there are two kinds of people: there are those (and I count myself among them) who are profound and strict, and who are necessary in the national community but who in my firm view come to grief if they do not marry or get engaged when they're young, for the animalistic side of human nature is too powerful in us. Perhaps in our case the fall is a much greater one.— And then there are the more superficial people, a type to which whole nations belong; they are passionate, with a simpler way of looking at life without as a result getting bogged down in wickedness, who, whether married or single, charm, flirt, kiss, copulate, without seeing any more to it—as it is human and quite simply nice.—The two of them belong to this type of person. But I like them and they like me and by and large I like all these Rhinelanders and Austrians. They are all superficial but straightforward and honest.—But in my heart I cannot believe in their type even if, as now, the temptation is often strong.[39]

The masculine world, defined by a combative spirit and military demeanour, in which he spent a large part of his free time, the fencing sessions and evenings for the male membership of the Apollo fraternity, and the paramilitary scene he belonged to in Munich offered him a certain support and refuge amidst all the confusion. He was therefore all the more unsettled when, in March 1922, a fellow student lent him Hans Blüher's book on *The Role of Eroticism in Masculine Society*. This was a work much discussed at the time, the author of which puts forward the theory that the cohesiveness of movements defined by masculinity, such as the youth movement and the military, is explicable only on the basis of strong homoerotic attachments. It was precisely these attachments, which must be judged entirely positively, that made the members of these organizations capable of the highest achievements.

Himmler was shocked, as his diary indicates: 'Read some of the book. It's gripping and deeply disturbing. One feels like asking what the purpose of life is, but it does have one.—Tea. Study. Dinner. Read some more. [...] Exercises. 10.30 bed, restless night.'[40] Impressed, he noted in his reading-list: 'This man certainly penetrated to immense depths into the erotic in human beings and has grasped it on a psychological and philosophical level. Yet, for my liking, he goes in for too much bombastic philosophy in order to make some things convincing and to dress them up in scholarly language.' One thing, however, was plain to him: 'That there has to be a masculine society is clear. But I'm doubtful whether that can be labelled as an expression of the erotic. At any rate, pure pederasty is the aberration of a degenerate individual, as it's so contrary to nature.'[41]

Himmler's defence mechanism against women who had at first definitely aroused his erotic interest, his abrupt smothering of erotic ideas by means of fantasies of violence, but also his alarm when suddenly confronted by the homoerotic aspect of the world of male organizations are all phenomena associated with the basic attributes of the 'soldierly man' of those post-war years, and were widespread in the Munich milieu in which Himmler moved. In the 1970s, in his study *Male Fantasies*, which has since become a classic, Klaus Theweleit analysed the typical defensive behaviour of these men towards women on the basis of memoirs and novels from the milieu of the Free Corps. According to Theweleit: 'Any move "towards a woman" is stopped abruptly and produces images and thoughts connected to violent actions. The notion of "woman" is linked to the notion of "violence".'[42] The Free Corps fighters—and the young men who took them as their model in the paramilitary movements of the time—were basically in a world without women. In order to control and suppress their urges they had acquired a 'body armour'; physical union was experienced only in the bloody ecstasy of conflict or in their fantasies of conflict.

The image of the ideal woman, untouchable and desexualized, invoked by Himmler after he first came across it in the sex-education manual by Wegener is similarly typical of its time and milieu. Theweleit has described it in the form of the 'white nurse' who appears either as a mother or as a sister figure; for him she is 'the epitome of the avoidance of all erotic/threatening femininity. She guarantees the continued existence of the sister incest taboo and the link to a super-sensuous caring mother figure.'[43] Even Himmler got carried away when he met the sister of a seriously ill fellow student, who was looking after him: 'These girls are like that; they surrender themselves to the pleasure of love, but can show exceptional and supremely noble love; indeed that's usually the case.'[44]

War, struggle, renunciation—these three things intoxicated him, but the war still did not come and so, during his second stay in Munich, Himmler continued to pursue the idea of emigrating. But even this was more a case of castles in the air, a flight from the reality of post-war Germany, than of concrete plans.

At first Turkey attracted him; a Turkish student friend told him about the country and people: 'People are given as much land as they can cultivate. The population is supposed to be very willing and good-hearted, but one has to spare their feelings.'[45] Then, after a lecture at the League of German officers (General von der Goltz was speaking about the Baltic region and 'Eastern European issues'), he noted that he now knew 'more certainly than ever that if there's another eastern campaign I'll join it. The east is the most important thing for us. The west is liable to die. In the east we must fight and settle.'[46]

The next day he cut out a newspaper article about the possibilities of emigration to Peru: 'Where will I end up. Spain, Turkey, the Baltic, Russia, Peru? I often think about it. In two years I'll not be in Germany any more, God willing, unless there is fighting, war and I'm a soldier.'[47] In January he took a brief shine to Georgia, and asked himself again: 'Where will I end up, which woman will I love and will love me?'[48] A few weeks later, in conversation with his mentor Rehrl, he came back to the subject of Turkey: 'It would not cost much to build a mill on the Khabur.'[49]

Running parallel to this, his efforts to embark on a career as an officer proved fruitless, although his redoubled attempts since the beginning of 1922 to establish contacts with officers of the Reichswehr—at the beginning of December 1921 he had finally received his accreditation as an ensign[50]— and his activities throughout that year in the paramilitary scene in Munich resulted in his becoming more closely linked to potential leaders of a putsch. At a meeting of the Freiweg Rifle Club, for example, he had an important encounter: 'Was at the Rifle Club's evening at the Arzberg cellar—things are happening there again. Captain Röhm and Major Angerer were there too, very friendly.'[51]

Frustration

After only a few months in Munich he felt as frustrated as he had done during his first year of study. The confidence he had gained in Fridolfing that he would be able to show a new face to the world had dissipated. In his diary the self-reproaches mount up: he is simply incapable of keeping his mouth shut, a 'miserable chatterer'.[52] This is his 'worst failing'.[53] 'It may be human but it shouldn't happen.'[54] He constantly observed himself in his relations with other people to check if he was showing the necessary self-confidence—and usually the result, from his perspective, turned out to be unsatisfactory. 'My behaviour still lacks the distinguished self-assurance that I should like to have', he noted in November 1921.[55] While visiting Princess Arnulf, the mother of his late godfather, he had, as he realized afterwards, forgotten 'to ask after her health'; even so: 'Apart from the leave-taking my conduct was fairly assured.'[56]

Himmler at times regarded himself as a thoroughly unfortunate character, a clumsy buffoon. Dressed up as an Arab at a big Carnival party at the Loritz home, which had been decorated as a 'harem', he noted laconically: 'Loritz offered guests a colossal amount, beginning with cocoa, which I spilt all over my trousers.'[57] His lapidary description of a dance attended by members of his Apollo fraternity was unintentionally comic: 'All of us Apollonites were sitting at a table with our ladies. I hadn't brought one.'[58] On a visit to friends in the country he had to put up with mockery from the woman of the house: 'In particular, she poked fun at me when I said I had never chatted up girls and so forth, and called me a eunuch.'[59] Moreover, he had continual problems with his stomach, particularly when he had been up late the previous night. Because of his problems his fraternity gave him permission not to drink beer.[60]

Himmler showed distinct feelings of inferiority provoked by the repeated experience of not getting the emotional support he expected from other people. His attachment disorder kept resulting in his being left with a vague sense of emptiness after encounters with people who were actually close to him. After a visit by his mother to Munich, which culminated in coffee and cakes at the Loritz home ('Mrs Loritz, Lu, Kätherle, Aunt Zahler, Mariele, Pepperl, Aunt Hermine, Paula, Mother, Gebhard, and me'), he became 'very monosyllabic' at the end. In the evening he took stock:

Ill. 2. Himmler with his family and his fiancée Margarete Boden; on the left Heinrich's elder brother Gebhard with his wife Mathilde; standing behind Margarete to the right is Heinrich's younger brother Ernst. The dejection suggested by Heinrich's posture is no accident, for he often felt misunderstood by his family. Margarete shared this feeling.

The upshot of these past days. I'm someone who comes out with empty phrases and talks too much and I have no energy. Did no work. Mother and everyone very kind but on edge, particularly Gebhard. And empty conversation with Gebhard and Paula. Laughter, joking, that's all.—I could be unhappy but as far as they're concerned I'm a cheery chap who makes jokes and takes care of everything, Heini'll see to it. I like them but there is no intellectual or emotional contact between us.[61]

Even writing his diary occasionally turned into an 'exercise of the will'.[62] In a mood of depression he expressed it even more negatively: 'I'm such a weak-willed person that I am not even writing my diary.'[63] There was increasing evidence of difficulties in his relationships with others. In particular his relationship with Käthe, the more elevated woman he dreamt of and his friend Zahler's fiancée, went through several crises. As early as November the tensions were building up. Käthe reproached him with

despising women completely and seeing them as unimportant in every sphere, whereas there were in fact areas where women were in control.—I have never taken that view. I am only opposed to female vanity wanting to be in charge in areas where women have no ability. A woman is loved by a proper man in three ways.— As a beloved child who has to be told off and also perhaps punished because it is unreasonable, who is protected and cared for because it is delicate and weak and because it is so much loved.—Then as a wife and as a loyal and understanding comrade, who helps one with the battles of life, standing faithfully at one's side without restricting her husband and his intellect or constraining them.—And as a goddess whose feet one must kiss, who through her feminine wisdom and childlike purity and sanctity gives one strength to endure in the hardest struggles and at moments of contemplation gives one something of the divine.[64]

At the beginning of December 1921 open conflict broke out: 'A remark of mine caused a row this afternoon. The same old story. Everything I say provokes people. It is not Lu's fault, she's not blaming him. I'm the one who's supposed to be at fault. She says she doesn't understand Lu. You women don't understand any of us. She says I'm trying to take Lu away from her and so on. A lot of crying.' Himmler assumed Frau Loritz was behind the fuss, and decided: 'I'm going to break with Frau Loritz and Käthe for quite a time. We'll observe the social formalities but nothing more. If she's in trouble she will always find in me the same loyal friend as two years ago. In that case I will behave to her as though nothing had happened and look for no thanks.' And in general: 'I think too much of myself to play the fool to feminine caprice, that's why I've broken with her.

It's not easy, though, and when I look back I still can't understand it.' Hardly had he admitted this than he was challenging himself: 'But in the end I must be consistent. I intend to work on myself every day and train myself, for I still have so many deficiencies.'[65]

Although in January he had a discussion with Käthe on the sofa to clear the air, in March the fragile peace was finally over. Zahler had told him that she was reproaching him for having 'attached himself at a ball to an aristocratic woman in order to make good contacts'—in Himmler's view 'the egoism and jealousy of an injured woman'. 'Now there are mountains between us.'[66]

Arguments with his fellow students are hinted at in his diaries at various points. The 21-year-old complains in a highly condescending tone about the 'lack of interest and maturity of the young post-war generation of students', by which he means those who, unlike him, had done no military service.[67] The aim of 'every man should be to be an upright, straightforward, just man, who never shirks his duty or is fearful, and that is difficult'.[68] Himmler tried to get over the crisis by imposing a programme of discipline on himself, of which regular ju-jitsu exercises formed a part.[69]

Above all, however, he fantasized about a heroic future for himself, in comparison with which the tribulations of the present were insignificant. It was no accident that at the end of May 1922 he began a new diary with a poem taken from Wilhelm Meister's *The Register of Judah's Guilt*:

> Even if they run you through
> Stand your ground and fight
> Abandon hope of your survival
> But not the banner for
> Others will hold it high
> As they lay you in your grave
> And will win through to the salvation
> That was your inspiration.[70]

Student days come to an end

Himmler's increasingly brusque and disengaged manner may well also have been caused by the anxiety aroused in him by the thought of the approaching diploma exams. He was pursued by his parents' recurring concerns about the range of his activities in Munich, most of which were not related to his studies. On the occasions when he put in a burst of work, it was above all the thought of his father that oppressed him: 'Ambition because of the old man.'[71]

At times he was overcome by a wave of panic. 'One could get very worried at the thought of exams, study and time, study and being thorough. It's all so interesting but there's so little time.'[72] A few weeks later he lapsed into melancholy: 'Brooded about how time flies. The nice, blissful student days already soon over. I could weep.'[73] He was, however, successful in gaining advantages for himself, for the contacts among the academic staff that he had built up as an AStA representative proved useful. 'Dr Niklas is immensely obliging. I told him I didn't attend the lecture series. I am to tell him that in the exam and he will question me on the work placement.'[74]

To complete a programme of study in agricultural sciences the Technical University in Munich in its examination regulations scheduled a minimum of six semesters. Himmler had, however, taken advantage of a dispensation for those with war service, according to which he had been allowed to sit parts of the preliminary examination after only two semesters, in other words, during his work placement. By this means he was able to shorten his course to four semesters. In his submission he claimed to have been a member of the Free Corps from April to July 1919, and that 'as a result of over-exertion in the army' he had 'developed a dilatation of the heart'.[75] In reality, as he confessed in a discussion with one of his professors, the premature completion was 'not legal', but he got away with it.[76]

On 23 March 1922 he completed the last part of the preliminary examination and so was halfway towards passing the final examination. The semester was finished; Himmler went for a few days to Fridolfing, in order to boost his reserves of energy.[77] In May he visited friends in a village near Landshut and at the end of the month finally returned to Munich for his last semester of study.

The fact that in spring 1922 his father took up the post of headmaster at the long-established Wittelsbach Grammar School in Munich signified for Himmler that, at least to some extent, he was again under his father's watchful gaze. Until Frau Himmler also moved to Munich in the autumn Gebhard Himmler was alone and spent a relatively large amount of time with his son. At the end of May Himmler suddenly realized that his father's proximity could very easily lead to problems: 'Suddenly Father arrived all het up and in a terrible mood and reproached me etc.—Had something to eat. My good mood was completely destroyed and shattered; won't it be just great when we are together all the time; it'll be diabolical for us and for our parents, and yet they're such trifling things [that cause the rows].'

On the whole, however, the relationship between father and son developed harmoniously. The two met frequently for meals, chatted about this and that, and on one occasion even went together to a political event.[78] They were in agreement as far as their fundamental convictions were concerned, and Himmler even initiated his father into the mysteries of his paramilitary activities.[79]

Politicization

In the diary entries for 1922 there is an increasing number of references to discussion of the 'Jewish question'. The contexts in which these references occur indicate the wide range of issues which Himmler believed relevant to this topic. Thus, at the beginning of February he discussed with his friend Ludwig Zahler 'the Jewish question, capitalism, Stinnes, capital, and the power of money';[80] in March he talked with a fellow student about 'land reform, degeneracy, homosexuality, Jewish question'.[81]

At the beginning of 1922 his reading-list once more contained two anti-Semitic works. Himmler found confirmation of his anti-Jewish attitude above all in *The Register of Judah's Guilt*, the work by Wilhelm Meister already referred to.[82] He found Houston Stewart Chamberlain's *Race and Nation*, which he read shortly afterwards, convincing above all because its anti-Semitism was 'objective and not full of hate'.[83] This indicates that he saw the 'mob' anti-Semitism, which was relatively widespread during the post-war years and found expression in insults and acts of violence against Jews, as unacceptably vulgar. Instead, Himmler preferred 'objective' reasons for his anti-Semitic attitude and, unlike during the arguments about whether Jewish fellow students were eligible to duel, he was increasingly adopting racial theory, which appeared to provide the intellectual basis for such an approach.

From the beginning of 1922 onwards his diary contains an increasing number of negative characterizations of Jews. A fellow student is described as 'a pushy chap with a marked Jewish appearance'.[84] 'A lot of Jews hang out' in a particular pub. Wolfgang Hallgarten, the organizer of a protest demonstration of democratic students and a former classmate, is referred to as 'a Jew boy', a 'Jewish rascal'.[85] However, his diary shows that, despite his prejudice, he still tries to differentiate among the Jews he meets. In January, for example, he visited a lawyer on behalf of his father and noted: 'Extremely amiable and friendly. He can't disguise the fact that he's a Jew. When it comes to it he may be a very good person, but this type is in the blood of these people. He spoke a lot about society, acquaintances, and contacts. At the end, he said that he would be very glad to be of assistance to me. I've got a lot of fellow fraternity members, but all the same.—He didn't fight in the war because of problems with his heart.'[86] However, from summer onwards there was an increasing number of negative descriptions of, as well as dismissive remarks about, Jews, while he began to see himself not merely as 'Aryan', but as a 'true Aryan'.[87]

Himmler's increasing anti-Semitism coincided with the phase in the summer of 1922 when he became seriously politicized. While he had been very interested in politics since the end of the war and had made no bones about his hostility to the Left and his sympathies for the nationalist Right, now, in the early summer of 1922, he came out into the open with his views: he became actively involved with the radical Right.

This move was prompted by the murder of Walther Rathenau on 24 June. For the Right, the Reich Foreign Minister embodied the hated Weimar Republic like no other figure. He was attacked as the main representative of the 'policy of fulfilment' of the Versailles treaty, and his active engagement in support of democracy was seen as treason, particularly in view of his social origins as a member of the Wilhelmine upper-middle class. Moreover, the fact that he was a Jew made him the target of continual anti-Semitic attacks. And now a radical right-wing terrorist group in Berlin had taken action.

The German public responded to the assassination with dismay and bitterness, and it led to the formation of a broad front of opposition to the anti-Republican Right. On 21 July the Reichstag responded to the murder by passing a 'Law for the Protection of the Republic', which considerably facilitated the prosecution of political crimes and made a significant encroachment on the responsibilities of the federal states. The Bavarian government refused to implement the law and, on 24 July, issued its own 'Decree for the Protection of the Constitution of the Republic'. The competing legislation led to a serious crisis in relations between Bavaria and the Reich, which, after difficult negotiations, was resolved on 11 August.

Radical right-wing elements, in particular the Nazi Party, made full use of this crisis for their propaganda. Because of his willingness to compromise, the Prime Minister of Bavaria, Baron von Lerchenfeld, was a particular target of criticism. Hardly anyone on the political Right in Bavaria could avoid becoming affected by the politicization that developed as a result of these conflicts. The dividing-line now ran between the moderate Bavarian conservatives, who were united in the Bavarian People's Party (BVP) and supported the Lerchenfeld government on the one hand, and the right wing of the party under the former Bavarian Prime Minister Gustav von Kahr, the German Nationalists (who had adopted the name 'Bavarian Middle Party' in Bavaria), as well as various radical leagues and groups, to which the Nazis in particular belonged, on the other. These latter forces had embarked on a course of fundamental opposition to the Weimar Republic and, with growing determination, advocated the violent overthrow of the constitution. This alliance came to an end only with the so-called Hitler putsch of November 1923.[88]

It would be quite wrong, on the basis of this political constellation, to interpret Himmler's radicalization as a break with the conservative views of his parents, an interpretation which is put forward, for example, in Andersch's account of Himmler's father as a schoolmaster, 'The Father of a Murderer'. For, during these months, many Bavarian conservatives tended to contemplate radical political solutions. This undermines the argument that Himmler's involvement with the radical Right should be understood as a rebellion against his parents. It is clear from his diary, for example, that initially father and son attended political meetings together.

On 14 June they attended a meeting of the 'German Emergency League against the Disgrace of the Blacks' in the Zirkuskrone hall. The League attacked the deployment of French colonial soldiers in the occupied Rhineland, which was denounced as a national humiliation. According to the report in the newspaper *Münchner Neueste Nachrichten*, the main speaker, Privy Councillor Dr Stehle, described 'the occupation of the Rhineland by coloureds as a bestially conceived crime that aims to crush us as a race and finally destroy us'. After the meeting the excited crowd began a protest march, which was dispersed by the police.[89] Himmler noted in his diary: 'Quite a lot of people. All shouted: "Revenge". Very impressive. But I've already taken part in more enjoyable and more exciting events of this kind.'

On the following day he held forth in a pub, once again accompanied by his father. His diary entry conveys a good impression of the topics that were covered that evening: 'Talked with the landlord's family, solid types of the old sort, about the past, the war, the Revolution, the Jews, the hate campaign against officers, the revolutionary period in Bavaria, the liberation, the present situation, meat prices, increasing economic hardship, desire for the return of the monarchy and a future, economic distress, unemployment, struggle, occupation, war.' His father and his old acquaintance Kastl shared the view, as did many of the Munich middle class, that they were facing big changes and a major political settling of accounts. 'Father had spoken to Dr. Kastl, who shared these views. Once the first pebble starts to roll then everything will follow like an avalanche. Any day now, we may be confronted with great events.'

A few days later, in the wake of the attack on Rathenau, the political situation became critical. Himmler fully supported the murder: 'Rathenau's been shot. I'm glad. Uncle Ernst is too. He was a scoundrel, but an able one, otherwise we would never have got rid of him. I'm convinced that what he did he didn't do for Germany.'[90] However, two days after the assassination Himmler was no doubt astonished to discover that among his circle he was almost alone in holding this opinion. 'Meal. The majority condemned the murder. Rathenau is a martyr. Oh blinded nation!'[91] 'Käthe hasn't got a good word to say about the right-wing parties', while his father was 'concerned about the political situation'.[92] On the following Saturday he met an acquaintance at the Loritzes and had 'an unpleasant conversation [. . .] about Rathenau and suchlike (What a great man he was. Anyone who belonged to a secret organization—death penalty.) The women of course were shocked. Home.'[93]

On 28 June he took part in a demonstration in the Königsplatz against the 'war guilt lie'. It was a big protest meeting 'against the Allied powers and the Versailles Treaty'. He was evidently disappointed by the indecisive stance of his fraternity: 'Of course our club was useless; we went with the Technical University. The whole of the Königsplatz was jam-packed, definitely more than 60,000 people. A nice dignified occasion without any violence or rash acts. A boy held up a black, red, and white flag (the police captain didn't see it; it carries a three-month prison sentence). We sang the "Watch on the Rhine", "O Noble Germany", the "Flag Song", the "Musketeer", etc.–it was terrific. Home again. Had tea.'

The following day—five days after the assassination—he confided secretively to his diary: 'The identity of Rathenau's murderers is known—the C Organization. Awful if it all comes out.' The Consul Organization, which carried out paramilitary activities from its Munich base with the support of the Bavarian government, belonged to the same milieu in which Himmler now felt relatively confident through his membership of the Freiweg Rifle Club and his acquaintanceship with Ernst Röhm (the central figure in these circles) and other officers. While staying with his parents in Ingolstadt at the beginning of June Himmler had already learned details through an acquaintance of secret rearmament activities in Bavaria: 'Willi Wagner told us various things about what's going on etc. (training, weapon smuggling).'[94] Evidently such information was quite freely available in 'nationalist' circles. However, it can no longer be established whether Himmler knew more than the rumours that were circulating among his acquaintances.

On 3 July he had nothing but contempt for 'a meeting of the democratic students with the Reich Republican League to protest against the Black-White-Red terror in the Munich institutions of higher education', which his former classmate Wolfgang Hallgarten had helped organize. In his view there could be no talk of terror. When, a few days later, he visited Health Councillor Dr Kastl, at the request of his father, he learnt that 'I've been asked to collect signatures for a Reich Black-White-Red League to support a campaign for the reintroduction of the black, white, and red flag. Agreed of course. Home. Dinner.'[95]

He immediately began eagerly to collect signatures from among his large circle of acquaintances, not only from his fellow students but also from members of the Freiweg Rifle Club: '8 o'clock Arzbergkeller. "Freiweg" evening. Collected moderate number of signatures.' But there was more going on that evening, as he added, once again in a secretive manner: 'Talked about various things with Lieutenants Harrach and Obermeier and offered my services for special tasks.'[96] In Himmler's view, the decisive confrontation with the Republican forces appeared to be imminent, and he had the impression that he was going to play an important role in it.

On 17 June Himmler's duel finally took place, the long-awaited initiation ceremony of his duelling fraternity. His diary states:

I invited Alphons. Mine was the third duel. I wasn't at all excited. I stood my ground well and my fencing technique was good. My opponent was Herr Senner from the Alemanni fraternity. He kept playing tricks. I was cut five times, as I discovered later. I was taken out after the thirteenth bout. Old boy Herr Reichl from Passau put in the stitches, 5 stitches, 1 bandage. I didn't even flinch. Distl stood by me as an old comrade. My mentor, Fasching, came to my duel specially.

Klement Kiermeier, Alemannia, from Fridolfing had brought Sepp Haartan, Bader, and Jäger along with him. I also watched Brunner's duel. Naturally my head ached.

Himmler's father, from whom he had expected a dressing-down because of the fresh wounds in his face, reacted calmly: 'Went to see father. Daddy laughed and was relaxed about it.'[97]

Himmler's radicalization must have been encouraged by the fact that, as will have become clear to him in the course of these months, his plans for the future were built on sand. His hopes of a career as an officer were misplaced, and the alternative of completing a degree in politics (*Staatswissenschaften*) was to prove equally illusory. Himmler had already applied to the Politics faculty of Munich University in May 1922. In June 1922 he received the news from the dean that his previous agricultural studies would count towards his degree and that he would be exempted from paying student fees. This appeared to ensure the continuation of his student life in Munich: 'So I can stay here for the winter semester, that's marvellous, and my parents will be pleased.'[98] Himmler's father was initially fully in agreement with his son's continuing his studies, but warned him not to get further involved with his fraternity, but to concentrate entirely on work. 'Next year I'm supposed to devote myself solely to scholarship.'[99] He had already discussed plans for a doctorate some months before.[100] Dr Heinrich Himmler—this achievement, with his agricultural studies properly integrated into an academic education, would fulfil his parents' expectations of him.

However, in September 1922 Himmler was not preparing for the new semester but instead found himself in a badly paid office-job. It is not clear exactly what led to his change of mind. But between June and September he must have experienced a profound sense of disillusionment. This was probably caused by the awareness—presumably communicated in the first instance by his father—that in a time of galloping inflation the Himmlers' family income was insufficient to pay for all three sons to study simultaneously.[101]

In fact, in the early summer of 1922 inflation reached a critical stage. The cost of living had steadily increased since the previous summer: in June 1921—after a year of relative stability—it had been eleven times higher than before the war. Now, in June 1922, it had already gone up to forty times the pre-war level: '200 grams of sausage now costs RM 9. That's terrible. Where's it all going to end?'[102] Himmler noted in his diary. But that was to be by no means the highest point of the inflation. Prices doubled between June and August 1922 and between August and December they tripled again.[103]

Civil-service salaries could not keep pace with these price-rises. Although they had been continually increased since 1918, this had been done so slowly that these increases could cover only around 25–40 per cent of the continually rising cost of living.[104] Even if it is assumed that a bourgeois family, such as that of grammar-school headmaster Himmler, could make savings in its living expenses and could fall back on financial reserves, such reserves would eventually be exhausted. After years of inflation they would be getting close to the poverty line.

In 1922 the Himmler family had evidently reached that point, and his parents had to make it clear to their son Heinrich that they had exhausted their ability to finance his studies.[105] As a result, Himmler lost the sense of material security and freedom from worries that had characterized his life up until then. His parents no longer appeared to offer him the secure support on which he could always count if his expansive and nebulous plans should fail. The university was no longer the waiting-room in which one could comfortably mark time until the hoped-for clarification of the political situation, in the company of a circle of like-minded people. Instead, agriculture would have to become the basis for his employment, and that in the most difficult economic circumstances. Evidently it was only at this point, in the summer of 1922, that the reality of post-war Germany finally caught up with the young Himmler. Until then, in his plans for the future he had taken no account either of the political circumstances or of economic parameters, but instead had indulged in vague illusions.

Now the dreaming was over. It was time for the 22-year-old to find his bearings. He took his final exams at the end of the summer semester of 1922. The overall grade of his agricultural diploma was 'good'.[106] He was relatively successful in his search for a post. He was appointed assistant administrator in an artificial fertilizer factory, the Stickstoff-Land-GmbH in Schleissheim near Munich. Once again he had benefited from family connections: the brother of a former colleague of his father's had a senior position in the factory.[107] He remained in this job from 1 September 1922 until the end of September 1923. According to his reference from the firm, during this period he had 'taken an active part particularly in the setting up and assessment of various basic fertilization experiments'.[108]

Unfortunately we do not know how Himmler felt about this activity, how he organized his new life, and why he left the firm after a year, because no diaries have survived for the period from the beginning of July 1922 until February 1924. That is all the more unfortunate because it was precisely during this period that the event occurred that was to prompt his fundamental decision to make politics his profession: his participation in the putsch attempt of November 1923.

The path to the Hitler putsch

In the summer of 1923 the Weimar Republic stumbled into the most serious crisis it had faced hitherto. In January France had used the excuse of delays in Germany's delivery of reparations to occupy the Ruhr, prompting the Reich government under Wilhelm Cuno to call upon the local population to carry out passive resistance. There were strikes and a loss of production, the Ruhr was economically isolated, and the depreciation of the Reichsmark, which had already reached catastrophic proportions, went completely out of control. In August a new Reich government was formed under Gustav Stresemann, which included the German People's Party (DVP), the Centre Party, the German Democratic Party (DDP), and the Social Democratic Party (SPD) in a grand coalition. On 24 September the Stresemann government ceased the passive resistance against the Ruhr occupation.[109]

While, since the autumn, the Socialist governments in Thuringia and Saxony had been cooperating ever more closely with the Communist Party (KPD) and had begun to establish armed units, in Bavaria the seriousness of the crisis resulted in a further radicalization of the Right. In September 1923 the Storm Troop (SA) of the Nazi Party, the Free Corps unit Oberland, and the Reichsflagge, the paramilitary league led by Röhm, of which Himmler had in the meantime become a member, established the Deutsche Kampfbund or German Combat League. At the end of the month Röhm succeeded in securing the leadership of this formation for Hitler. However, behind the scenes the real strong-man was General Erich Ludendorff, the former Quartermaster-General of the imperial army and head of the Supreme Army Command.

The Bavarian government, however, responded by declaring a state of emergency and appointing Gustav Ritter von Kahr, who had been Prime

Minister during the years 1920–1, as 'General State Commissioner', in other words, as an emergency dictator. In view of the new situation, the Reichsflagge declared its support for von Kahr, whereupon Röhm, together with a section of the membership, established—*nomen est omen*—the Reichskriegsflagge (the Reich War Flag), an organization which Himmler also joined.

The Reich government in turn responded to the state of emergency in Bavaria by declaring a state of emergency in the Reich as a whole. Faced with this conflict, Otto von Lossow, the commander of the Reichswehr troops stationed in Bavaria, declined to follow orders from Berlin and was relieved of his command. The Bavarian government reacted by reinstating him and placing his troops under their authority. In doing so, the so-called triumvirate of von Kahr, von Lossow, and the chief of the state police, Hans Ritter von Seisser, found themselves involved in an open confrontation with the Reich, while in Bavaria they were opposed by the Kampfbund led by Hitler and Ludendorff.

The Kampfbund wanted to declare a Ludendorff–Hitler dictatorship in Munich and then set out with all available forces on an armed march against Berlin. On the way they intended to overthrow the Socialist governments in central Germany. Kahr was also contemplating a takeover in the Reich, but in the form of a peaceful *coup d'état* supported by the dominant right-wing conservative circles in north Germany, who counted on the support of the Reichswehr. This faced the Kampfbund with a dilemma. It could not simply join von Kahr if it did not wish to be marginalized, and yet it was too weak to act on its own.

There was an additional problem. On the northern border of Bavaria the (now 'Bavarian') Reichswehr had set about establishing a paramilitary border defence force against the Socialist governments in Saxony and Thuringia, with the aid of various combat leagues. The Kampfbund was involved in this operation, and in the process had had to subordinate itself to the Reichswehr leadership.

However, in October the Reich government ordered troops to march into central Germany, with the result that the excuse that a border defence was needed was no longer valid. In addition, with its announcement of a currency reform the Reich government had begun to win back public trust.

At the beginning of November, therefore, the Kampfbund was coming under increasing pressure to take action. The danger was that the triumvirate would come to terms with Berlin, and so the window of opportunity

Ill. 3. Himmler as the flag-bearer of the Reichskriegsflagge on 9 November 1923. The world of the paramilitaries enabled Himmler to escape from the upsetting experiences which he kept having in civilian life. It was here that he found an environment in which he could to some extent cope with his personal difficulties.

for a putsch was beginning to close. It was in this situation that the Kampfbund adopted the plan of seizing the initiative for a putsch themselves and dragging the forces around von Kahr along with them.

A rally announced by the triumvirate, to be held on the evening of 8 November 1923 in the Bürgerbräukeller, appeared to offer a favourable opportunity. Hitler, in the company of armed supporters, forced his way into the meeting, declared the Bavarian government deposed, announced that he was taking over as the head of a provisional national government, and forced Kahr, von Lossow, and von Seisser to join him. The subsequent history of the Hitler putsch is well known: early the following morning the three members of the triumvirate distanced themselves from these events and ordered the police and the Reichswehr to move against the putschists. The Hitler–Ludendorff supporters made a further attempt to gain control of the city centre, but the putsch was finally brought to an end at the Feldherrnhalle, when the police fired on them.[110]

In fact, the marchers had been aiming to get as far as the army headquarters in Ludwigstrasse, where Röhm and his Reichskriegsflagge were holding out. On the morning after the putsch, therefore, the citizens of Munich were confronted with a very unusual scene: the army headquarters, the former War Ministry, was cordoned off by Reichskriegsflagge members, and these putschists were in turn surrounded by troops loyal to the government. Behind the barbed-wire barricade was a young ensign, who on that day had the honour of carrying the flag of the paramilitary Reichskriegsflagge: Heinrich Himmler, son of the well-known headmaster of the Wittelsbach Grammar School. Here too the confrontation between the putschists and the forces of the state had led to bloodshed. After shots were fired from the building the besiegers returned fire, and two of the putschists were killed.[111] But, despite this incident, during the course of the day the Reichskriegsflagge and the Reichswehr came to an amicable arrangement. The Reichskriegsflagge departed peacefully and its members including Himmler, the flag-bearer, were not arrested.

With this unsuccessful putsch the attempt by the radical Right to force the conservatives to join them in a common front and get rid of the Republic had for the time being failed. It was to be almost ten years before a second alliance between right-wing radicals and right-wing conservatives achieved rather more success.

4

A New Start in Lower Bavaria

After the unsuccessful putsch attempt Himmler was facing personal and political bankruptcy. Five years after the end of the war he was neither an officer nor a colonial settler in a faraway land, but instead an unemployed agronomist unsuccessfully looking for a job.[1] His hopes of securing political change by force had been dashed by the crushing of the putsch. The more the economic and political situation stabilized, the more hopeless the völkisch cause appeared.

Nevertheless, Himmler continued to work for the banned Nazi Party, which had gone underground. According to various hints in his diary, during the months after the putsch he performed various clandestine services as a courier.[2] In mid-February he visited Röhm in Stadelheim prison: 'we had an excellent and fairly frank talk [...] I had brought him a *Grossdeutsche Zeitung* and some oranges, which he was very pleased with. He hasn't lost his good sense of humour and is still our good old Captain Röhm.'[3]

In the same month Himmler, who was once again living with his parents,[4] began to take on the role of a Nazi agitator in provincial Lower Bavaria, an area that was familiar to him from his childhood. He tried his hand at journalism, contributing a political piece for the *Langquaider Zeitung* with the title: 'A Letter from Munich'. Evidently, this 'Letter from Munich' was intended to be the forerunner of a series that would appear regularly and provide moral support for the Langquaid comrades, for there was a group of active Nazis in the town.[5] Whether he was able to realize this plan can, however, no longer be established.

His first 'Letter from Munich' was also published in the *Rottenburger Anzeiger*, a newspaper that appeared in the neighbouring county town.[6] The editor described the article in an introductory sentence as a contribution from 'völkisch circles'. The 'Letter' was written in Bavarian dialect and in a cunningly naive, conversational tone. Himmler had evidently taken Ludwig Thoma's 'Filser' letters as his model, namely the letters of a fictitious Bavarian parliamentary deputy written in Bavarian dialect.

Himmler, who used the appropriate pseudonym 'Heinz Deutsch', began his article with a little sarcastic prologue:

Writing letters was without a doubt easier to do in the old days than it is nowadays. There wasn't as much to report as there is now but then it wasn't so dangerous to do so. It's really not that simple. I hardly dare to think anything because I have so many thoughts that the police wouldn't like and I talk only to people who are in danger of ending up in Landsberg jail. So I shall put barbed wire round my brain and try to write in a tame, 'bourgeois' way.

This was followed by a fictitious conversation between Deutsch-Himmler and an evidently complacent Bavarian in a railway compartment, a gentleman with hat-size 61, a drooping moustache, well fed, and preoccupied with consuming some sausages:

'Yup, the French are on their way out. If the conference doesn't finish them then their currency will. Look how the franc's fallen' (he spoke just like a donkey neighing). 'The French'll go back of their own accord; they can't afford to go on.' 'Ah ha', I said, disappointedly. 'Wait and see. I reckon you'll have to wait till you're an old man for that to happen.' 'Yup, if the conference doesn't finish them then their currency will', repeated my philistine.

After Himmler-Deutsch has guided the conversation towards various topics, the article ends quite abruptly with a rather martial-sounding sentence: 'A German poet once said: "He who does not put his life on the line will never gain his life." Nowadays, people in Germany think that one can speculate for one's life with currency and shares. But the day will come when the Reich that Bismarck cemented together with blood and iron and is now falling apart through money will be revived once more with blood and iron. And that's when we'll come into our own.'

Himmler also made speeches. On the day when his article appeared in the *Rottenburger Anzeiger* Himmler spoke on behalf of the National Socialist Freedom Movement in the Lower Bavarian town of Kehlheim: 'Into the meeting, large hall, very full. Dr Rutz [a Nazi from Munich] was the main speaker, then there was an interval. I spoke about the workers being subject to stock-exchange capital, about food prices, wages, and what we ourselves should be doing about it. The meeting was definitely a success.' On the same evening there was another meeting in a nearby venue: 'Peasants and communists in the pub. First Dr Rutz, then me. Talked only about workers' issues. Rutz's and my speeches bordered on National Bolshevism. The main topic was the Jewish question.'[7] On the next day he spoke to peasants in Rohr, as he thought, 'quite well'. He noted that at the end of the meeting there was an incident involving a 'Jewish hop-merchant': 'Afterwards, I think the peasants gave him a good hiding.'[8]

Himmler saw himself very much in the role of a self-sacrificing party worker: 'We often stayed in the pub canvassing people until 2.45 in the morning. This service we're performing for the nation, for this disappointed, often badly treated and mistrustful nation, is really tough and hard going. They're scared stiff of war and death.'[9]

On 26 February 1924, a day after Himmler's speech in Rohr, the trial of the 9 November 1923 putschists began in Munich. Himmler had been questioned by the prosecutor about his role in the failed attempt to storm the army headquarters, but there was insufficient evidence to prosecute. In the course of the trial the defence proposed calling him as a witness but, as it turned out, he did not have to appear.[10]

Himmler was still contemplating the possibility of emigration. His Turkish student friend, with whom he had already discussed plans for emigration in 1921 and with whom he still corresponded, offered to arrange a position for him as an estate manager in western Anatolia.[11] In fact Himmler made some enquiries about this possibility of emigrating;[12] unfortunately, one is inclined to say, he could not summon up the courage to take the plunge. The Caucasus was another possibility under consideration, but was then quickly dropped ('Bolshevik rule, division of the land, nothing doing').[13] The same thing happened with Italy; a friend who lived in Milan could not, when contacted, offer him much hope. This acquaintance suggested, presumably with the aim of consoling him, that the only thing suitable for him would be 'a colonial-type job', perhaps in the Ukraine or in Persia, for 'in the final analysis, as an ordinary estate manager you would have the prospect of getting something in Germany anyway'.[14]

Himmler had, of course, already considered this possibility; but he had been forced to come to the sobering conclusion that his job prospects in agriculture were slim. At the beginning of November 1924, in response to his enquiry,[15] the Reich Association of Academically Educated Farmers informed him that his chances of getting a senior position in estate administration were virtually nil. The only conceivable vacancies would be as a deputy administrator or as an assistant on a trial farm.

Crisis

Himmler was not prepared to admit the failure of his plans for his personal, professional, and political life and increasingly came to adopt the role of an outsider who had been failed by other people. It was not he who was following the wrong course of action but those around him.

This perception applied to both his personal and his political life. His irritability and opinionated arrogance, which during the previous years had become increasingly evident and had more than once got him into difficulties, now became more marked and were fatally combined with his already well-known tendency to interfere in other people's affairs.

This was particularly apparent in the way in which Heinrich intervened in the engagement of his brother Gebhard during 1923–4. This episode demonstrates how frustrated he had become after the failed putsch, but it also shows how this failure had made him increasingly and blatantly aggressive, something which those closest to him were now to experience in a most dramatic fashion.

In November 1921 Gebhard had become engaged to Paula Stölzle, the daughter of a banker from Weilheim. From the start Himmler had certain reservations about the engagement.[16] After 'searching for a long time' he had chosen as his engagement present a gift that barely concealed his ambivalent feelings: Agnes Günther's novel *The Saint and the Fool*.[17]

When tensions emerged in the relationship during 1923—Gebhard accused Paula of being too friendly towards another man—Himmler acted as intermediary at the request of his brother. However, he interpreted his role rather differently from how Gebhard envisaged it.[18] He wrote a letter to Paula in which he reminded her that a man must have 'the assurance from his fiancée that she will not be unfaithful to him with a single word, a look, a touch, or a thought, even if he spends years away from her and they never see each other and often don't hear from each other for a long time, which might well be the case during the war years that are soon to come'. But Paula had failed this test 'dismally'. If her marriage was to be a happy one then she must be 'kept on a tight rein with *barbaric* strictness'. Since she was not 'strict and harsh' with herself and his brother was 'too good for you and has too little knowledge of human nature', someone else would have to undertake this task. It is no surprise that he felt it 'incumbent upon myself to do this'.[19] Paula's response was friendly but firm; she told him to mind his own business.[20]

Himmler, however, could not get over this incident, which he regarded as a matter of family honour. Some months later he heard another tale about Paula which prompted him to urge his parents to end the engagement.[21] It was only after he had been successful in this initiative that he approached his brother directly in 'the Paula matter', and 'spoke to him frankly about breaking off the engagement and told him what I thought of her in no uncertain terms'. During this conversation he learnt from Gebhard that Paula 'had already lost her innocence and was herself largely to blame'. He was surprised by how calmly Gebhard had taken it: 'Gebhard hasn't taken the whole thing (the breaking off of the engagement) to heart, but has completely come to terms with it. It's as if he has no soul; he shakes if off like a poodle. Our conversation lasted until half past ten. Read the paper. Slept. What a way to waste one's time.'[22]

When Gebhard informed Paula and her parents in writing of his wish to break off the engagement,[23] Paula, who in the meantime had come to the conclusion that marrying Gebhard would not be a good idea, replied accusing her ex-fiancé of 'allowing Heinrich to come between us and to tell me what to do'. She found it incomprehensible how 'your brother, who is two years younger than you, can have the nerve to think that he's entitled, for your sake and based on his experience of life, to tell me how to live my life'. She had found it very insulting.[24]

But Himmler was not prepared to let the matter rest. In March 1924, when the engagement had already been broken off, he hired a private detective to collect damaging material on Paula and in this way dug up some worthless small-town gossip.[25] Moreover, without Gerhard's knowledge he made enquiries about his brother's ex-fiancée from his acquaintances in Weilheim, only for the eventuality that the matter should have further repercussions, as he assured his informants. In the event of that happening he wanted to possess 'material' detrimental to the Stölzle family.[26]

With the 'Paula matter' Himmler's obsession with interfering in other people's private affairs and his almost voyeuristic interest in collecting details about their lives had reached a temporary high point. However, shortly afterwards he also alienated close friends with his didactic, totally humour-less, and arrogant manner. This is documented in a letter from May 1924 to his friends Friedl and Hugo, whose hospitality he had been happy to enjoy only a few months earlier.[27] The banal cause of the break was a postcard, which Friedl had sent to Himmler's mother three days earlier, in which she had asked Gebhard and Heinrich to advise Hugo, as they had promised to do, about the planned purchase of a car. Himmler could not stand the friendly ironic tone of this card:

We consider the style adopted in the card to my mother dated 20.5.24, which we received on the morning of the 22.5.24, to be decidedly hurtful to Gebhard and myself and therefore rather inappropriate. To start with, I find the first phrase 'in my hour of need' to be at the very least totally inappropriate. To speak of 'need' because one has not received a reply for three days in a matter concerning a car is at least an exaggeration. Evidently Friedl has no idea what need is! And then to write 'if neither of your two sons can be bothered'. I hope that you and Friedl are convinced that I am grateful to you for your generous hospitality and for the friendship that you have shown me up until now [sic] and that I am not expressing my gratitude for reasons of convention (I don't recognize them) but from inner conviction.

Deeply hurt, he continued:

I also believe that you will remember that I told you that you could rely on me in any situation, even and particularly if there should be a real need. I also believe I can say that I have always responded to small requests from you as if I was doing it for myself. So even if Friedl did not trust Gebhard, although that would be completely unjustified, she should have had enough trust in me to be sure that I wouldn't have let this matter go by the board.

Himmler also let his friends know to whose influence he attributed the insulting card: it could only be an act of revenge by Paula Stölzle, who, so he suspected, was stirring up hostility to him among his circle of friends! She was also the target of his warning that one should not get on the wrong side of him. He could, when forced to, 'behave very differently', and would 'not stop until the opponent concerned had been excluded from all moral and respectable society'. Evidently completely unaware of his impertinence, Himmler had the effrontery to end his letter with an appeal for sympathy: 'Unfortunately, I'm still here. Things are taking a terribly long time. This waiting for weeks on end is getting on my nerves. And these weeks that one is wasting in waiting later on could have turned out to be useful.'[28]

However, Himmler did receive some acknowledgment of his stance as a solitary hero and unappreciated pioneer of the völkisch cause. In June 1924 he received a letter from a female friend, which she had written more than six months before, a few days after the putsch, but had not sent off. Himmler admired this young woman, Maria Rauschmayer, the daughter of a Munich professor and colleague of his father's, who was working on her doctoral dissertation in the summer of 1924.[29] Mariele had already appeared several times in his diary as 'an exceptionally clever girl with a strong and honourable character who deserves the greatest respect' and who was admirably patriotic.[30]

Maria Rauschmayer wrote to Himmler as someone who shared her political views. She wanted to inform him about the events taking place and the political mood in Munich; she shared his anger and disappointment at Kahr's 'betrayal'; she wanted to encourage and support him in his political stance. But the letter also reveals sympathy and admiration that was deeply felt. Rauschmayer described her feelings on that 9 November when she encountered Himmler in front of the besieged army headquarters, the former Bavarian War Ministry:

In front of the War Min. troops of the Reichskriegsflagge. Heinrich Himmler in the vanguard, the flag on his shoulder, one could really see how secure the flag felt and how proud he was of it. I go up to him, unable to speak a word. But within me I can feel welling up the words

> Be proud: I am carrying the flag!
> Be free of care: I am carrying the flag!
> Be fond of me: I am carrying the flag!

In all my life I have never given a firmer handshake for I knew that he felt the same as me: for years unable to think of anything but Germany, Germany, Germany.

She concluded: 'This letter is for my friend Heinrich Himmler. It is intended as a small gesture indicating my deep gratitude and loyal acknowledgment of a deed which, for a few hours, once again gave one reason to hope. The letter has been written during the hours of deep disappointment and depression that followed.'[31]

In August he received another letter from her, a glowing declaration of belief in their common cause: 'For years to be able to think of nothing else, to work for it for years; Nation and Fatherland as the grandest cause is like a prayer emerging from one's innermost being.' She herself, however, did not wish to play an active part in the völkisch movement, and her reason for not doing so will have met with Himmler's full approval: 'You are a combat group, who want to clear a swamp, and marsh-goblins and swamp-witches are so revolting that I don't want to have anything to do with them. My view of the ideal German woman is to be at your side as a comrade and then to be with you after the fight.' She wrote that, shortly beforehand, she had responded to a request to form a völkisch women's group as follows:

Get yourself some kind of wake-up apparatus and awaken the best girls that you can find in Germany to the need to remain pure German women—so that the men, who nowadays have no time for it, will know where to get their wives from. But that is a small matter, for nowadays the struggle for survival is more difficult for women than for men. The result is that some get married who would have provided the best material, but who are still too young to be able to wait—and maybe to wait in vain.[32]

Himmler kept these two letters in his private papers. Unlike Paula, who, measured against his ideal, had so clearly failed, 'Mariele' had reinforced his fantasy of the ideal woman, who would reserve herself for the solitary, celibate fighter. Bearing in mind how central his commitment to this image of womanhood was for Himmler's self-image as a man, a soldier, a political activist, and as a self-styled Teuton, one can guess how important Maria Rauschmayer's encouragement would have been to him, particularly at a time when he felt anything but secure.

In search of a world-view

Himmler's reading from the period 1923–4 shows that he was trying to find a 'world-view' in the broadest sense that would provide him with a solid foundation for his life. It is striking that he tried to integrate the most important elements of radical right-wing ideology, which are increasingly apparent in his thinking—anti-Semitism, extreme nationalism, racism, hostility to democracy—into a far more comprehensive world-view, cobbled together from the most varied sources.

He distanced himself more and more from Roman Catholicism. Instead, he became increasingly preoccupied with works that, in his view, dealt with occult phenomena in a serious 'scholarly' way; for example, a book about 'Astrology, Hypnosis, Spiritualism, Telepathy',[33] topics which, at the peak of the inflation and during the subsequent period of upheaval, were generally in vogue.[34] In 1925 he was to read a book about the power of pendulums,[35] and in the same year he approached an astrologer with a request for four horoscopes.[36]

He was impressed by an account of the Pyramid of Cheops—'history built and written in stone and a representation of the universe, which a genius has written in the form of this pyramid'—since it showed 'a range of knowledge that we conceited people of culture have long ago lost and even now have not recovered to the same extent'.[37]

During January and February 1923 he read a book on Spiritualism, and commented in his notes that it had convinced him that Spiritualism was true. Thus, Himmler assumed that it was possible to communicate with the souls of the dead.[38] Already, in May 1921, he had read a book twice within a short time which claimed to prove there was life after death; despite being somewhat sceptical, he was inclined to believe the evidence put forward. 'The transmigration of souls', he noted at the end of his commentary on it.[39] It was a topic that was also to preoccupy him after he became Reichsführer-SS (RFSS).

In December 1923 he began reading Ernst Renan's *The Life of Jesus*, and approved of its anti-Jewish interpretation of the Son of God. This allowed him to overlook the fact that some things in the book were 'certainly not right'. At least Renan illuminated 'many matters that have been kept secret from us'.[40] In February 1924 he perused Ernst Haeckel's *The Riddle of the World* but completely rejected its monist world-view; 'the motley collection of unproven attacks on and denials of a personal God' were 'absolutely disgusting'.[41] Thus, despite his growing doubts about Catholic teachings, he had not yet broken with his God.

In addition, from 1923 onwards he was keen on anti-Semitic literature. He was, however, disappointed by a book on the German criminal *argot* (*Mauscheldeutsch*), since the author was 'evidently someone patronized by Jews and in any event not a Jew-hater'.[42] By contrast, the *Handbook on the Jewish Question* published by Theodor Fritsch, who since the 1880s had been one of the most important German anti-Semites, met with his approval: 'it shocks even someone who knows the score.'[43] Shortly afterwards he read *The False God: Evidence against Jehovah*, by the same author. Evidently Fritsch provided him with backing for his existing scepticism about the Old Testament. 'One suddenly begins to understand things that one couldn't grasp as a child about what quite a lot of biblical stories are worth. And, as is the case with all these books, comes to appreciate the terrible scourge and danger of religion by which we are being suffocated.'[44]

In February, during a visit to his friends Friedl and Hugo Höfle, he read two novels combining an anti-Semitic leitmotif with erotic themes, which he thoroughly enjoyed.[45] During a train journey in September 1924 he devoured a pamphlet of the anti-Semitic Ethnic German Defence and Resistance League (Deutschvölkische Schutz und Trutz Bund), which was totally in accordance with his views.[46]

And finally he came across *In the Power of Dark Forces* by a certain Gotthard Baron von der Osten-Sacken. This book, which first appeared in 1924, was a classic example of a shift from anti-Semitism to paranoia. Himmler clearly saw this, and yet it did not detract from the author's plausibility in his eyes, as is plain from his notes: 'Description of the Jewish system which is designed to condemn people to a moral death. It's conceivable that there's a persecution complex involved in all this to a certain degree. But the system undoubtedly exists and the Jews operate it.'[47]

There are also a whole series of anti-Jesuit works on his reading list. After reading the first book, he noted, in November 1923: 'It's becoming increasingly clear to me that expelling the Jesuits was one of the best and most sensible things Bismarck ever did.'[48] According to his notes, the 'influence of this powerful order' was also reflected in the novel *The Sadist in a Priest's Cassock*, which he read a few months later.[49]

In May 1924 *The Guilt of the Ultramontanists: A Reckoning with the Centre Party* provided, as far as he was concerned, 'a new and fearful insight into an enemy workshop. One gets really bitter when one reads all about it. What have we done to these people that they won't let us live? And that's even more true now. We want to be Germans and to fight to be so against all our enemies.' And yet he claimed that his criticism was not directed at the Christian religion as such. 'What enemies of the faith and of the Christian religion of love these people are.'[50] His comment on another anti-Jesuit pamphlet, which dealt with the 'black hangmen of the German people, who've been exposed', is particularly revealing: for him the 'ultramontane question' was 'definitely a secondary issue and the Jewish question the primary one, and not the other way round'.[51]

After the unsuccessful putsch he got to know Hitler through two books, and noted in his reading-list: 'He is a truly great man and above all a genuine and pure one. His speeches are marvellous examples of Germanness and Aryanness.'[52] This is in fact the first occasion on which Hitler's name appears in Himmler's surviving writings—his diary, correspondence, and reading-list. He was not one of those Nazi supporters who were attracted by the 'Führer's' charisma; instead, he became politically involved primarily in the context of the general preparations for a putsch that were being carried out by right-wing paramilitary organizations in the years 1922/3. If he had a political hero at this time it was Röhm, not Hitler.

It is clear from his reading-list for the years 1923–4 that his interest in 'Teutonic' topics not only endured but increased.[53] Above all, in September 1923 he began reading the trilogy of novels by Werner Jansen published between 1916 and 1920. These were popular adventure stories in the form of versions of the *Nibelungenlied* and other sagas. Jansen had tried to transform these sagas into Teutonic-German myths, and infused them with racist and Teutonic clichés. The result was a kind of Karl May★ for Teutonic enthusiasts and, above all, young readers.

To begin with, a few weeks after his participation in the Hitler putsch Himmler embarked on *The Book of Loyalty*. He was bowled over; 'One of the most magnificent and most German books I've ever read. He deals with the issue of German loyalty marvellously and provides a really true view of the state and the nation. Hagen is an ideal character.'[54] He had acquired a copy of the *Nibelungenlied* even before he had finished reading this 'Nibelungen novel'. 'Its immortal language, depth, and Germanness reflect an eternal beauty', he commented in his reading-list.[55] Almost a year later he read Jansen's *Book of Passion*, which he enjoyed just as much: '...I really feel that I belong to these Teutons, but that at the moment I'm very much alone in feeling this.'[56] Again, reading this novel prompted him to study an original source. He got hold of Tacitus' *Germania* and commented: 'What a marvellous picture of how pure and noble our ancestors were. That's how we should be again, or at least some us.'[57] A few weeks later he read Jansen's version of the *Gudrun* saga, and once more was swept away: 'It's the noble song of the Nordic woman. That is the ideal of which we Germans dream in our youth, for which we as men are prepared to die and in which we still believe', even if, he regretfully noted, 'one is so often disappointed'.[58] He was never to find his Gudrun, but when, in 1929, he came to select a name for his daughter, the choice was not a difficult one.

Apart from Jensen's novels, Hans Günther's treatment of 'the heroic ideal', which appeared under the title *Knight, Death, and Devil*, also had a crucial influence on Himmler's notion of 'Germanic heroism'. He read the book twice in the course of 1924, and noted briefly and pointedly: 'A book that expresses in wise and carefully considered words and sentences what I have felt and thought since I began to think.'[59] Germanic mythology,

★ *Translators' note*: Karl May (1842–1912) was a popular novelist specializing in Wild West stories.

reinforced by all sorts of occult ideas, evidently became for him a kind of substitute religion.

The rural agitator

In the summer of 1924 Himmler took the fateful decision to adopt the role of political activist as his profession and the true purpose of his life. He began to work for the Lower Bavarian Nazi Gregor Strasser, a post which he appears to have acquired as a result of his involvement with the NSDAP in Lower Bavaria.[60]

Born in 1892, Strasser was a pharmacist in Landshut, one of the main towns of Lower Bavaria, and had held the rank of first lieutenant in the First World War. For some years he had been one of the leading Nazis in the region and had taken part in the Hitler putsch, for which he had been placed on remand. However, he was a candidate for the Völkisch Bloc, which was acting as a substitute for the banned Nazi Party in the Bavarian state elections of 6 April and 4 May (in the Palatinate). The Völkisch Bloc received 17.4 per cent of the vote (as much as the Social Democrats). Strasser was elected, released from prison, and took over the leadership of the Völkisch Bloc in the Bavarian parliament. Nowhere else in the Reich was the extreme Right so well represented in parliament. In the Reichstag elections of December 1924 Strasser also won a seat, this time as a candidate of the National Socialist Freedom Movement (Nationalsozialistische Frei-heitsbewegung), a combined völkisch and Nazi grouping; as a Reichstag deputy he resigned his seat in Bavaria.

As a supporter of a 'German Socialism', Strasser advocated views different from those of Hitler, particularly on social and economic issues. He de-manded the 'nationalization' of land and of the means of production, and within the NSDAP represented a decidedly anti-capitalist stance.[61] His main task now consisted in trying to build up the party in north Germany. For this reason alone he spent little time in Bavaria, his old power-base, where Himmler now took over the office and dealt with party matters in Lower Bavaria more or less independently.[62]

During this period Himmler alternated between despondency and a determination to keep going. In August 1924 he wrote to his acquaintance in Milan (in response to a discouraging letter about the job prospects in Italy):

As you can see, I'm still here. I've got a terrific lot to do. I have to run the whole organization in Lower Bavaria and to build it up in every way. I don't have any time for myself and answering a letter promptly is out of the question. I'm very much enjoying the organizational work, for which I'm entirely responsible, and things would be great if one could look forward to victory or prepare for a struggle for freedom in the near future. As it is, it involves a lot of self-denial by us racists [*Völkische*]; it's work that will never bear visible fruit in the near future. One always has to bear in mind that the fruits of this work will be gathered only in later years and at the moment we may well be fighting a losing battle [. . .]

But we few are continuing with this work without wavering [. . .] Because one has to say to oneself if we don't do this work, which has got to be done, this sowing of the German idea, then no one will do it and then, in years to come, when the time is ripe, nothing will happen because nothing has been sown. It is selfless service for the great idea and a great cause, for which of course we shall never receive recognition and do not expect to receive it.[63]

In fact the conditions for agitation in favour of the Nazi cause in Lower Bavaria were, all things considered, not bad. For example, in the Reichstag election of December 1924 the Völkisch Bloc received 10 per cent of the vote in Landshut and became the third-strongest party after the BVP and the SPD; this exceeded the overall election results gained by the candidates of various Nazi groupings in Bavaria (5.1 per cent) and the Reich (3 per cent).[64]

In December 1924 Hitler was released from Landsberg prison, and in February 1925 he re-founded the Nazi Party (the ban on the party had been lifted after Hitler had promised the Bavarian prime minister to obey the law). Himmler in Landshut now had the task of bringing the Lower Bavarian Nazis, whom Strasser had gathered under the flag of the National Socialist Freedom Movement,[65] over to the NSDAP.

However, this did not occur without conflict. In July 1925 Nazi Party headquarters complained to Strasser that not a single membership form, on which the Lower Bavarian Nazis were obliged to sign up for the NSDAP, had reached Munich, let alone any subscriptions.[66] So in August Himmler travelled to Munich to discuss the organizational details of the transfer of almost 1,000 Lower Bavarian Hitler supporters, organized in twenty-five local branches, to the new NSDAP. However, he warned the headquarters beforehand that he would not deal with Max Amann (at that point head of the party publishing-house, the Eher Verlag), with whom he had had a confrontation on his previous visit six months earlier. He signed his letter, as was usual for the racists at the time, with 'A True German Greeting of Hail (*treudeutschem Heilgruß*).'[67]

Himmler's fussiness about his personal dignity, and the lack of charm he showed in his personal manners, were not the only reasons for the tensions between the Munich headquarters and the Landshut office. Contrary to what he had said in his letter to his Milan acquaintance, Himmler had difficulty in coping with Landshut party business. He kept failing to meet the deadlines given him by Munich headquarters. He generally excused himself by referring to permanent overwork and speeches he had delivered outside the area.[68]

It took until the spring of 1926 before all the membership forms, which were supposed to have been filled in during the summer of 1925, were finally sent in, and the submission of the subscriptions, 10 pfennigs per member per month, to Munich was equally slow. Himmler evidently could cope only by responding to the increasingly urgent reminders from head-quarters with an explanation in terms of local culture: 'The long delay, particularly in Landshut, really has less to do with people's indifference and more to do with their dislike of making any written or formal statement, something that is particularly prevalent in Lower Bavaria.'[69] In addition, there were political differences. For example, on one occasion headquarters wanted to know why the founder of the Nazi Party, Anton Drexler, who was now *persona non grata*, had been allowed to speak at a party meeting in Landshut.[70]

At least Himmler could count it as a success that the Munich headquarters had officially recognized the Landshut office,[71] and had recognized the *Kurier für Niederbayern* (with a circulation of 4,000 copies) as the party's official local newspaper.[72] In his activity report to the Gau rally of the Lower Bavarian NSDAP on 2 May 1926 in Landshut he produced a set of meticulously prepared figures: in the course of slightly more than six months 340 letters had been received and 480 letters and cards sent; no fewer than 2,131 items of propaganda material were distributed 'in the form of special editions, copies of *Weltkampf*, *Nationalsozialistische Briefe*, leaflets, other newspapers, and pamphlets'.[73] This account cannot, however, dis-guise the fact that Himmler was not, in the first instance, a pedantic and industrious party bureaucrat, who directed the party's activities from his desk in Landshut. On the contrary, he saw his job above all as continually to travel round the Gau and look after the local branches. Thus, between mid-November 1925 and the beginning of May 1926 he spoke at twenty-seven meetings throughout the Gau of Lower Bavaria (this made him the most active party speaker in the Gau) as well as at twenty meetings outside the Gau, not just in Bavaria but also in Westphalia and north Germany, in the Hamburg area, in Schleswig-Holstein, and Mecklenburg.

His speaking activities were, of course, given extensive coverage in the *Kurier von Niederbayern*, the party newspaper edited by Himmler. In his role as an energetic rural agitator he dealt mainly with day-to-day political issues: he attacked the Dawes Plan (the 1924 adjustment by the Germans and the Allies of the reparations imposed by the Versailles Treaty),[74] justified the Nazis' support for compensation for the former royal families,[75] and strongly criticized the Treaty of Locarno.[76] However, his comments on day-to-day politics were saturated with völkisch ideology and implied more general political positions. Anti-Semitism formed a leitmotif in his speeches; he expatiated on 'dark Jewish conspiracies', spoke on the theme of 'Jews and Bolshevism' and on the 'Dangers posed by Jewry'.[77]

On 9 October 1924 he published a rabidly anti-Semitic article in his party newspaper. 'Newspapers, the telegraph and the telephone, inventions of the German and Aryan spirit,' were now, he explained to his readers, being used 'in the service of the Jewish drive for world supremacy'. And now 'the newest invention [...] the wireless transmitter', which as 'radio entertainment could be a means of education for the improvement of a whole nation and as such of huge benefit to the state and the nation', was 'without exception in the hands of Jewish businesses'. As a result 'of course only purely Jewish Talmudic productions of trite pseudo-culture or shamelessly corrupted products of the German spirit are broadcast to the world'. In May and June 1925, seemingly prompted by having just read an exposé ('a marvellous book'), he concentrated in particular on Freemasonry, or rather on the alleged close relationship between Freemasons and Jews. Moreover, in the book he had come across a historical elite which in his opinion represented a model, the warrior caste of the Hindus: 'we must be the Kshatriya caste. That will be our salvation.'[78] But those were private thoughts which he did not reveal to the Lower Bavarian peasants. However, in his speeches he did admit that as a model of organization the hated Freemasons were not to be despised. Thus, in a speech in Dingolfing in May 1925, 'On the Character and Goals of the Freeemasons', he 'repeatedly emphasized that we National Socialists could learn much from this organization, each part of which is highly efficient, and so long as we fail to awaken the same sense of duty in ourselves we shall never achieve our goal'.[79]

Himmler also repeatedly dealt with agricultural issues in this predominantly agrarian district of Lower Bavaria, these being only too obvious given the agrarian crisis that began in 1925–6. Many peasants had become heavily indebted during the preceding years and now found themselves faced with falling prices. On 15 April 1926, for example, the *Kurier* reported on a meeting of the Plattling NSDAP local branch in which 'Herr Dipl.-Ag. Party comrade Himmler from Landshut spoke about the collapse of German agriculture'. According to the *Kurier*, numerous farmers had attended from the surrounding villages, who 'listened with bated breath to the speaker's clear and lively observations'. Himmler had larded his thoroughly anti-Semitic speech with numerous references to agrarian issues, which were intended to demonstrate his expertise in the subject. He related 'the terrible suffering of our nation since 1918', he described 'the systematic stifling and muzzling of every profession, and now their last representative, the peasantry, was about to succumb to international stock-exchange Jewry'. Mercilessly he castigated 'the so-called peasant leadership, whether they are called Heim or Kühler, Schlittenbauer or Gandorfer, since they're all slaves of Jewish loan capital'. The former employee of the Schleissheim nitrogen-fertilizer plant referred to the 'disastrous influence of the artificial fertilizer syndicates' as well as the no less fateful role of the grain exchange, 'which dictates prices to the peasant so that, despite the heavy burdens and taxes, he can hardly recoup the costs of production, with the result that he is forced to sell plots of land at knock-down prices or to take on loans from Jewish banks on crippling conditions'. According to Himmler, the only salvation lay in 'at last getting to know who our real common enemy is, and in the indomitable will to take on this enemy together'; all 'those of German stock must join together in a socially aware national community with the election slogan "the common weal before self-interest" and establish a new state based on National Socialism under the banner of the swastika'.[80]

At the same time Himmler published a piece in the *Nationalsozialistische Briefe* in which he expressed very similar views: 'the monopolistic position of the artificial fertilizer concerns' allegedly bore the primary responsibility for the high production costs which, together with cheap imports, the high price of credit, and 'Jewish' speculation in land, would lead to the collapse of

German agriculture.[81] He repeated the same arguments in an article which appeared in the *Kurier von Niederbayern* in July 1926.[82]

Himmler was also fond of impressing his listeners with wide-ranging historical observations. In a speech in Geisenhausen on 12 September 1925, for example, he explained 'the more significant links between the paths taken by German and Jewish politics'. He began, according to the *Kurier*, 'with, so to speak, the earliest years of German history [...] then briefly touched on the intellectual characteristics of our neighbouring states [...] then discussed the Jesuits, the Reformation, the peasantry [...] and explained the more profound causes of the Thirty Years War', and then finally, in dealing with 'the noble and far-sighted policies of Bismarck', reached the climax of his speech.[83] On 19 November 1925 in Landshut, 'in a speech lasting two hours [...] he described the paths followed by Jewish politics in Spain, France, England, and Germany from the Middle Ages until today'.[84] It can also be shown that, from autumn 1925 onwards, Himmler increasingly referred to the idea of 'National Socialism', in other words the political slogan of his mentor, Gregor Strasser.[85] Sometimes these rhetorical efforts met with immediate success. According to a report in the *Kurier*, 'following a short speech by party comrade Himmler on 20 November 1924 in the village of Astorf, a new local branch of the Völkisch Bloc was founded and joined by all twenty-four of the men present'. A local branch was also founded in Malgersdorf at the end of November after Himmler had spoken about 'The Coming Reichstag Elections'.[86]

On 9 March 1926, according to a party member from Dingolfing, 'Party comrade Himmler' had 'once again agreed to favour us with a talk'. The remark of the reporter to the effect that Himmler 'had developed [*sic*] into an excellent speaker with a profound intellect, wide knowledge, and logical eloquence' suggests that he may have felt less 'gratified' on the occasion of previous talks by Himmler.[87] In any event, the reports in the *Kurier* show that the frequency of his speeches increased sharply after the spring of 1925, that the individual branches requested his presence more often, and that he now also increasingly spoke outside the Gau area. 'Party comrade Himmler made a major impression', according to a *Kurier* report on a speech he gave in Siegen at the beginning of April 1925. According to the article, the trip to southern Westphalia was a real triumph: 'His success was even greater in Niederscheiden, Weidenau, and Eisern, where Party comrade Himmler also spoke. Let's hope we shall soon see the return of this fresh and ardent canvasser for our great ideas. Hail!'[88]

One topic was noticeable for its absence from all these speeches: Adolf Hitler. That is all the more remarkable given that, during the years 1925–6, and based on his reputation as a 'martyr' of the failed putsch, Hitler was busy constructing a real Führer cult round himself and using this systematically to create a dictatorial position for himself within the NSDAP and to enlarge the mass basis of the party. Himmler's more matter-of-fact and somewhat distanced approach to Hitler was probably influenced by his mentor Strasser, who saw in Hitler primarily a useful front-man for 'National Socialism', but was by no means prepared to let himself be carried away by the wave of Führer worship. After Himmler had gradually waded through the first volume of *Mein Kampf* during the course of 1925–7, he noted rather tersely: 'There is a lot of truth in it.' But he also commented critically: 'The first chapters on his youth contain a number of weaknesses.'[89] He read the second volume of Hitler's work in December 1927, and agreed above all with the passages concerning 'the difference in value between the various human races'. He mentioned Hitler's comment, referring to Socialist functionaries whom he considered responsible for Germany's defeat, that 'twelve or fifteen thousand of these Hebrew corrupters of the nation ought to have been gassed' during the war.[90] There is no evidence, however, that he was at all enthusiastic about the book; the second volume does not even appear in his reading-list, which he otherwise kept very carefully. Himmler does not appear to have had the typical revivalist type experience that would have drawn him into a charismatic relationship with Hitler.

Considering Himmler's extensive speechifying and travel, it is not surprising that he rather neglected his bureaucratic duties in the Landshut party office. He was probably happy to put up with this failing: dealing with matters on the spot and keeping in constant contact with the people 'outside' seemed to him more important. Moreover, he needed time for his paramilitary activities, which he still kept up in Landshut. This time the organization was called the 'William Tell Shooting and Hiking League', a successor organization to the Landshut Free Corps, founded in 1919, of which he had already been a member in that year.

In January 1926 the Tell Shooting and Hiking League aroused the interest of the police. The Nazi Party office in Landshut, Himmler's place of work, was under observation and, when he left the building around midday on 12 January, the criminal police waiting outside requested him to accompany them to the police-station for an interrogation.

According to Himmler's statement to the police, the purpose of the Tell League was 'the physical and mental training and further education of young people through hiking and rifle shooting'. They did not possess military weapons. The subsequent search of Himmler's lodgings and the lodgings of a retired Major Mahler produced written material belonging to the latter indicating that the previous summer the League had held exercises in which members had been armed with infantry weapons. However, Himmler brazenly maintained that weapons had not been used and that the assumption was 'pure speculation' on the part of the police. A Reichswehr first lieutenant turned up, who confirmed this statement.[91] The investigations appear not to have been pursued; the authorities evidently had no interest in investigating paramilitary activities backed by the Reichswehr.

Himmler was now 26 years of age and, despite his largely independent activity in Landshut, was generally regarded in the party as the 'young man' who worked for Gregor Strasser. In April 1926 a visitor arrived from the Rhineland. Party comrade Joseph Goebbels made a series of speeches in Lower Bavaria accompanied by Himmler. 'In Landshut: Himmler: a good chap, very intelligent', Goebbels noted patronizingly in his diary.[92]

5

The Party Functionary

In September 1926 Gregor Strasser became propaganda chief of the NSDAP. This appointment was evidently part of an internal party arrangement to resolve finally the conflict between the Party headquarters and the more 'left'-inclined 'Working Group of North-West German Gauleiters of the NSDAP' that had been going on since 1925. The most important representatives of the 'north-west German' line were given significant posts in the party and were thereby neutralized as a potential core of internal opposition. This was after they had been outmanoeuvred by Hitler at a meeting of party leaders in Bamberg in February 1926. Apart from Strasser, who may be regarded as the mentor of the working group, Joseph Goebbels, who went to Berlin as Gauleiter in October 1926, and Franz Pfeffer von Salomon, who took over the leadership of the storm troopers (SA) on 1 November and soon renamed himself Franz von Pfeffer, were also rewarded in this way.[1] Himmler accompanied Strasser to Munich as his deputy.[2] At the end of January 1927 Strasser informed the party leadership that he had also appointed Himmler his deputy as Gauleiter of Lower Bavaria.[3]

In the first years after its re-founding the NSDAP was a small and politically insignificant splinter group of right-wing radicals on the furthest edge of the political spectrum and received fewer votes in elections than the Nazis had achieved under other names during 1924. However, the Nazi Party was the only right-radical group that operated throughout the Reich and, unlike the others, had a more or less unified organizational structure.

In addition to propaganda, the Munich headquarters, which Himmler joined in the summer of 1926, had a number of departments. There was the Reich Management Department headed by the then 27-year-old Philipp Bouhler, a First World War officer and failed German literature student.[4] However, Bouhler increasingly had to relinquish responsibilities to the Reich Organization Department, which was set up in July 1926 under the retired Lieutenant-General Bruno Heinemann, who was also head of the party's Investigation and Conciliation Committee. Gregor Strasser was to replace Heinemann as head of the Reich Organization in 1928. As Reich Treasurer, Franz Xaver Schwarz had been responsible for the party's finances since 1925. Schwarz, who was considered honest and efficient, was to retain this position until the end of the so-called Third Reich in 1945. To begin with, a trainee schoolteacher, Hermann Schneider, acted as Party Secretary until he was replaced by Karl Fiehler, a low-ranking local government official.[5] And, finally, as chief of the SA, Franz von Pfeffer was a member of the party leadership from the end of 1926.[6] Max Amann, with whom Himmler had crossed swords the previous year, was closely linked with the party leadership; Hitler's former sergeant from his Regiment No. 12 was responsible for the party's publishing house, the Eher Verlag.

Apart from the politically ambitious Strasser and the SA chief von Pfeffer, who was politically aware and, in seeing the SA as a paramilitary league, wanted as far as possible to maintain its autonomy, the party leadership was largely composed of people with limited leadership potential who as a rule concentrated on their specific tasks. In doing so, however, they could, as was the case with Himmler, work largely independently, covered by the authority of the party leader; the individual heads of department were authorized by Hitler to act in his name vis-à-vis the party organizations in their particular spheres of operation.

This arrangement reflected Hitler's style of leadership and his aim, if possible, to avoid getting involved in the numerous arguments, struggles over competence, and rivalries which went on within the party and instead to await their conclusion from afar. In this way he succeeded in avoiding having his leadership aura, the Führer principle, degraded by the day-to-day conflicts within the party. Moreover, Hitler, who during these years was travelling extensively in order to win support for the party, spent comparatively little time at party headquarters and was difficult to reach, even for his closest colleagues.[7] His correspondence was mainly dealt with by his faithful private secretary Rudolf Hess, who was, however, regarded by many as a strange person.

Since Himmler and the other functionaries in the party headquarters always used Hitler's authority to back their instructions, they did everything they could to secure his position vis-à-vis the party comrades outside. This was clearly, from Hitler's point of view, a further positive aspect of his working methods. Himmler had exceptional freedom of action because the propaganda chief, Strasser, was frequently engaged in party activities elsewhere through the responsibilities imposed by his seat in the Reichstag and as one of the foremost party agitators.[8] When Strasser was appointed head of the Reich Party Organization in January 1928 and Hitler provisionally, though in fact only nominally, took over the role of Reich Propaganda Chief himself, Himmler increased his freedom of action still further.

Himmler was mainly concerned with organizational matters: he conducted the correspondence with the local branches, sent them propaganda material, assessed propaganda suggestions from party comrades, requested reports, and so on. In the process he endeavoured above all to unify the party's various propaganda activities and to bring them under the control of party headquarters. For this purpose, from 1926 onwards a series of numbered 'Instructions and Announcements'[9] appeared in party newspapers which unmistakably bore Himmler's signature, as did the pamphlet *Propaganda* issued in spring 1928, in which practical suggestions were given for the organization of the party's propaganda.[10]

In addition, he was responsible, together with the various Gau headquarters, for coordinating the deployment of party speakers throughout the Reich. Naturally, he paid particular attention to the preparation of the—as he put it in his correspondence—'Hitler meetings', which were still the most important means of propaganda for the party. While he was often not in a position to meet the requests of the local branches for Hitler to come and speak, particularly since the latter was careful only to make a limited number of speeches, nevertheless he could not resist sending out to the local branches 'Directives for Meetings involving the Party Leader' and also questionnaires for the preparation of the, often long-awaited, speech.[11] The demand of local party organizations for other speakers could often not be met because of a lack of attractive party speakers capable of being deployed outside their home territory.

In particular, Himmler endeavoured to use his role as deputy Reich Propaganda Chief to construct a comprehensive, internal party reporting service. Over two full sides of the pamphlet he listed thirteen different types of report which had to be regularly sent in by the local branches, insisting that 'failure to keep to the deadlines will result in a stern warning and, where necessary, be reported to the Führer'.[12] Among the things to report were: 'all Jews living in the area of the local branch or Gau, including if possible Jews who have been baptized, with exact details of name, age, occupation, and domicile. This report is necessary for us to be able at last to produce an

accurate statistical breakdown of the number of Jews in the population.'
Also, they were to provide details of all Freemasons, the names of the locally
'most vicious opponents', all 'the known addresses of Germans living
abroad', all cases of the 'mistreatment of, attacks on, and terrorist acts against
party comrades that have been committed by opponents in the respective
district or Gau since the founding of the party', and 'all sentences of
imprisonment or fines imposed on party comrades on the basis of political
interrogations or charges'. Finally, 'where necessary' further reports on
other topics should be submitted, which Himmler did not omit to list in
detail. The pamphlet documents Himmler's pedantry and his obsessive need
to exercise control, as well as his megalomania, for such a reporting and data
system—had the Gaus and local branches actually obeyed his instructions—
would have swamped the Reich headquarters's ability to cope.

Apart from his other activities, Himmler was continually on the move.
His office diaries from this period show that he not only visited Upper
Bavaria and the Gau of Lower Bavaria, but made numerous trips to other
parts of Germany. In January 1927, for example, he spent some time in
Thuringia, where a state election was due; at the beginning of February he
travelled to Westphalia and at the end of April to the Ruhr; in May he spent
time in Mecklenburg because of the state election there; and on the way
back he stopped off in Potsdam and in Chemnitz; in the second half of June
he was in various parts of north Germany, on 14 July in Vienna, in mid-
October in Hesse, and so it went on uninterrupted.[13]

In the course of these journeys he played an active role as a party speaker;
on average he spoke more than once a week at internal party meetings or
made public speeches. In doing so he continued to use the anti-capitalist
rhetoric of his mentor Strasser, as is clear from a speech in Potsdam on
13 October 1926: 'In the course of history periods of capitalism and
socialism alternate with one another; capitalism is the unnatural, socialism
the natural economic system.' He went on to outline the alleged alternation
of 'socialist' and 'capitalist' phases of German history. He placed the Peasant
Wars, the epoch of Frederick the Great, as well as the reforms of Freiherr
vom Stein under the heading of 'socialism'; again and again such attempts at
reform had been blocked by capitalism:

Capitalism has once again taken over the throne. Nowadays people are no longer
interested in whether someone's an honest chap, but just in how much money he
has. People don't ask where the money has come from, but whether he's got it.

Capitalism seizes control of machinery, the most noble invention of mankind, and uses it to enslave people. This causes people to long for freedom and this longing for freedom expresses itself in the workers' class struggle. The German bourgeoisie don't understand that and so we get the Socialists' struggle going on till 1918.

Himmler even went so far as to suggest there was broad agreement between the Nazi and communist visions of the future: 'The National Socialists and the Red Front have the same aspirations. The Jews falsified the Revolution in the form of Marxism and that failed to bring fulfilment. Why, is not the issue today. So, there's still a longing for Socialism.'[14]

This link that was emerging between Himmler's anti-capitalist and anti-Semitic rhetoric was evident in other speeches. Thus, in a speech made in the Munich district of Neuhausen in October 1926 he was quoted by the police report as saying: 'It's not true when people claim that the Jews manage to get on in the world because they're clever. If the NSDAP committed perjury and behaved as ruthlessly and brutally as the Jews do then it would have made more progress long ago.'[15] In April 1927 the police reported on a speech he made to the Nazi branch in Regensburg as follows:

The Jews have used capitalism for their own ends and in their struggle for power they understand very well how to play off 'Internationalism' against the nations. Internationalism neutralizes the importance of the individual nations and aims at enslaving all the workers of the world. There's only one way of avoiding this fate: to unite all the German workers on the basis of nationalism in order to introduce a socialist regime. Our aim is to establish a powerful, nationalist, socialist, German workers' party.[16]

A few weeks after Himmler had taken up his new post there were state elections in Saxony in which, with a vote of 1.6 per cent, the NSDAP fared much worse than its followers had expected; a few months before, in June, it had gained only 1.7 per cent in the state election in Mecklenburg-Schwerin. Party comrades blamed this lack of electoral success on the incompetence of party headquarters; this represented a challenge for the recently appointed deputy Propaganda Chief. At the end of 1926 the hopes of the membership were focused on the Thuringian state elections to be held in January 1927. A certain Fritz Schusnus, who was appointed campaign manager by the Thuringian party leadership, wrote to Munich in October: 'If the organization of the election campaign in Mecklenburg and Saxony had been handled differently the result wouldn't have been so disappointing. We would never recover if we had an election result in

Thuringia like those in Saxony and Mecklenburg. I would, therefore, like to request Reich headquarters to move heaven and earth to make sure that we don't have the same confusion and lack of direction here as they had in Saxony.'[17] However, Himmler could not do much to help; he told Schusnus that they did not possess substantial sums of money and that there was no point in launching a major campaign in December.[18] In the event, the party could consider the 3.5 per cent that the NSDAP won in the state election in January as only a very modest success.

Appointed campaign manager for the next state election in Mecklenburg-Schwerin, which took place on 22 May 1927, Himmler approached the task systematically, as was his wont. He saw his main task as being to cover the state with a dense net of meetings with Nazi speakers. The available sources show that his methodical approach ended up being rather schematic: 'I class speakers' spoke at total of sixty-three meetings, 'II class speakers' at fifty, 'those of III class quality' had to cover around 300 meetings in smaller locations.[19] However, his splendid plan was in danger of collapsing because Himmler was prepared to launch the campaign only when the Mecklenburg membership had proved that they had fulfilled the official requirements for participation in the election. One month before the election Himmler demanded 'a report' from the party members in the north within a few days, to the effect that they had paid the obligatory deposit of 3,000 Reich marks officially required for permission to submit a party list and that the requisite list supported by 3,000 signatures had been officially certified. Himmler insisted categorically that, in the event that these had not occurred within the deadline, 'we shall not participate in the election'.[20]

The Gau leadership in Mecklenburg-Lübeck was somewhat put out by this curt tone. Those responsible insisted on starting the campaign without waiting for a green light from Munich.[21] One of the leading Mecklenburg party members wrote to Himmler that his idea of limiting the campaign to the last fourteen days was 'nonsense'. It would be much more sensible to extend the campaign to cover the last three weeks, although that was no longer feasible. But that was the fault of party headquarters in Munich, namely Himmler's. The party officials in Parchim in Mecklenburg were on edge: 'It would have been possible if the Munich headquarters hadn't adopted such an absurdly bureaucratic attitude. Forgive me the harsh words, but it's the truth. What on earth does Reich headquarters think of the Mecklenburg Gau leader? In my view, if the Gau leader reports that he's collected the 3,000 Reich marks and 3,000 signatures then party headquarters ought to believe him! After all, the Gau leader isn't a fool or a misbehaving child who is telling a lie! For Reich headquarters to demand official police confirmation for the Gau leader's statements just shows the most incredible lack of trust.' They told him they had got in touch with Hitler's secretary, Hess, directly and arranged not to make the start of the election campaign dependent on the official confirmation of the handing in of the election list.[22]

Himmler, who had been bypassed in this manner, was not prepared to accept these accusations. With a mixture of self-opinionatedness and patronizing irony, and referring to the highest authority in the party, he responded in point eighteen of a long letter concerning the deployment of speakers in Mecklenburg:

It is not a revelation to me that it would be more sensible to carry out propaganda long before the start of an election campaign, indeed I am well aware of the fact. However, if I am responsible for something then I have to take other matters into consideration. The Gau can just about manage an election campaign of fourteen days' duration. We all know very well what would be nice and ideal. But we have to deal with what is. We are going to stick with a propaganda campaign during the last fourteen days. I should like to add that I have discussed this 'nonsense' with Herr Hitler and Herr Hitler has approved this 'nonsense'.

Moreover, he pointed out that his request for a report on the signatures and the deposit had been prompted by 'Herr Hitler himself'. If, for example, some of the signatures had not been recognized by the authorities, then 'a vast apparatus involving huge costs would have been set in motion for nothing. It is right and proper that you should be thinking of the interests of your Gau. But it is also right and proper that those outside the Gau should take a broader view. This should not be seen in any way as a lack of trust.'[23]

The Mecklenburg election campaign reached a critical stage when, just before the date of the election, it became known that Hitler would not be available to speak at meetings. On 18 May, four days before the election, Himmler informed the party members in Mecklenburg of the decision in a manner which indicates that, to put it mildly, a great deal of discontent had built up among the membership: 'However, as National Socialists we know that Hitler would not have cancelled unless he had had a very good reason for doing so [. . .] It would be unscrupulous and cowardly if, as a result of this, a branch leader permitted a bad and mutinous mood to develop or even sat on his hands. There can be no place in a National Socialist organization for the words "impossible" or "we can't".[24] In fact, instead of the planned 400 meetings, the Mecklenburg Nazis held only 106. The election result was disastrous for the party: 5,611 votes or 1.8 per cent.[25] The NSDAP did not take part in the elections in tiny Mecklenburg-Strelitz held in July of the same year; however, the German-Völkisch Freedom Movement won 5 per cent of the vote.

In Hamburg, in February 1927, the NSDAP received only a meagre 2.2 per cent of the vote. Himmler's period as Reich Propaganda Chief also covered the Reichstag election defeat of 1928 when the party gained only 2.8 per cent of the vote (in December 1924, when Hitler was in prison, it was 3 per cent). The state elections in Prussia and in a number of other states, which were held on the same day, produced similarly depressing results. However, it was encouraging that the party achieved relatively good results in a number of rural districts. The party leadership which, primarily under Strasser's influence, until then had focused above all on trying to win over the urban working class from the Socialist parties, now switched to a tactic in which rural areas assumed greater importance. This naturally suited Himmler, with his diploma in agriculture, for he had also campaigned among the peasants of Lower Bavaria during the years 1924–6.

Accordingly, in December he drafted a new plan for concentrating propaganda in particular regions. For this purpose he evidently reverted to a tactic that he had developed for the Mecklenburg state election of May 1927 but had not been able fully to put into practice. He informed the various Gau headquarters that they were intending to cover every region from time to time with 'large-scale propaganda actions'. For this purpose 70 to 100 meetings would be held in a Gau within a period of seven to ten days, and there would also be a propaganda week with special propaganda evenings for the SA, for the Hitler Youth, and for the press. The Reich Propaganda Department would be in overall charge. They had already planned propaganda actions in the 'Eastern March' (as Austria was referred to in völkisch circles) in January 1929, in Halle-Merseburg in February, and in Saxony in March 1929.[26]

The plan was characteristic of Himmler's schematic approach. Moreover, Himmler's ideas once again far exceeded the practical possibilities open to the party: given their limited organizational capabilities, most Gaus were simply not in a position to carry out such elaborate campaigns.[27] The shortage of speakers who could be deployed outside their home districts was also a serious obstacle. For this reason Himmler advocated transforming the correspondence courses for party speakers, which the Thuringian Gauleiter Fritz Reinhardt had been organizing since 1926, into an official 'NSDAP Speakers' College'. Reinhardt was the proprietor of a college for commercial correspondence courses.[28] In fact, Himmler's proposal for 'large-scale propaganda actions' contained ideas that were taken up a short time later by the Nazi Party, when it had the necessary organizational resources. Nazi propaganda targeted at particular regions, which was to reach a hitherto exceptional intensity in rural areas, became characteristic of the NSDAP during the years 1930–3.[29]

However, it was not only the discrepancy between Himmler's elaborate planning coupled with his insistence on exercising control and the poorly developed party apparatus in the provinces that prevented the deputy Propaganda Chief from becoming a popular figure in the NSDAP. He was not helped by his overbearing and arrogant manner in dealing with subordinates, which had already become apparent in connection with the Mecklenburg election campaign. Typical of this was his refusal, allegedly on the grounds of permanent work pressure, to behave in a friendly manner. His letters from this period are marked by an impersonal style, the lack of the slightest signs of politeness, and by the reduction of the content to brief pieces of information and instructions. He frequently requested a reply 'by return of post'[30] and 'an immediate response',[31] or stated, 'I decisively reject [...] the tone of your letter'.[32] He would not tolerate any opposition. Reprimands were common. For example, in April 1927 he wrote to the Hersbrück local branch: 'I must say that we here were astonished at how a local branch of the NSDAP could think of requesting a talk by someone who isn't a Party member. I would like to refer you to the Propaganda Memorandum and suggest that you read it, as one would expect of the secretary of a local branch. You will then see that it is stated on page 9 that meetings can be held only by members of the party.'[33] Also in April 1927 he advised the Hof branch urgently to hold a 'German Day': 'I recommend you read pages 34 and 35 of the Propaganda Memorandum, which you were obliged to order.'[34] When a party sympathizer wrote that he wished the party would engage in less 'bashing around blindly', Himmler replied in August 1928: 'You might have spared yourself the final sentence, because we know what we have to do and we know very well who and what we have to bash.'[35]

In July 1927 he requested a party member in Stettin to report on internal matters in the local party 'on his word of honour', which he explained as follows: 'You have to include everything you know about the goings-on in Stettin.' And: 'As an SS leader you must have enough discipline in you to carry out an order without asking about the whys and the wherefores. If your report has not arrived within eight days I shall see to it that you are excluded from the SS and initiate further steps.'[36]

It was typical of him to make it clear that enquiries were basically superfluous and, in view of his being permanently under pressure of work, represented an unnecessary burden: '1. I have received your letter of 8 inst. 2. Even if you overwhelm me with letters I still cannot give you any more speakers, since I do not have any more. What is more, you are imposing a burden on our work here. With Greetings and Hail . . .'[37] If he was dealing with prominent party members, however, he could not be more obsequious. Thus, in marked contrast to his normal impersonal style, his letters to Franz Ritter von Epp are always addressed to 'The most respected Herr General', and instead of the usual brief 'with German greetings', he signs off with extreme servility: 'With German greetings I am, Herr General, your most humble servant.'[38]

Himmler also got used to justifying his decisions where possible by claiming that they had been reached while carrying out Hitler's instructions or in consultation with other members of the Reich Party leadership: 'If I am properly to fulfil the Führer's instructions to allocate the election meetings and to provide properly for all the areas where major campaigns are being conducted, then every local branch must ensure that it obeys the Führer's orders.'[39] In February 1927 he rejected the request of the Aschaffenburg branch to hold a German Day, and added: 'This decision is final and has been reached in agreement with all the members of the Reich Party leadership.'[40]

Himmler reacted particularly aggressively to a request from the *West-deutscher Beobachter*, a party newspaper that appeared in Cologne. A few days previously the paper had asked for 'the twenty-five points of the party programme to be sent as quickly as possible in the enclosed format'.[41] Himmler had misunderstood the request and assumed that the people in Cologne did not know their own programme. The members in Cologne were, of course, familiar with its contents; what they wanted from Munich was a particular format, which could be used in order to publish the programme in the paper. This misunderstanding produced a classic overreaction from Himmler:

We have never before come across such an incredible request from the editors of a newspaper recognized by the party [. . .] I suggest that you look in your membership card and also get the Rhineland Gau leadership office to let you have *Leaflet No. 1: The 25 Points*, and you should acquaint yourself with *The 25 Points* by Party comrade Alfred Rosenberg, as well as issue No. 1 of the *National Socialist Library* by Gottfried Feder, in which you will find the other 13 points that you do not yet know. Apart from that, I should like to say that with us SA members who do not know it are thrown out.[42]

The party members associated with the *Westdeutscher Beobachter* were shocked and felt very insulted. They regretted that Himmler's letter 'could have been written at all', since such a response was not 'calculated to create or encourage a relationship of trust between party comrades'. The author of the letter went on:

If I wanted to play your game I might perhaps ask you the question: when did you first become aware of the NSDAP's programme? I have known it since spring 1922 and really have no need to feel ashamed of my services to the NSDAP. You, as a member of the Reich leadership, when you are writing to party comrades who have been active in and made great sacrifices for our movement—and I count myself among their number—should take special care to refrain from using methods that may be appropriate for dealing with a Marxist muckraker and bigwig.[43]

Himmler justified himself, as usual, by hiding behind his colleagues in the party leadership: 'I have shown your letter to several members of the Reich leadership before replying to it. I am by no means alone in the view I hold.' He claimed that, apart from him, 'two other gentlemen in party headquarters have come to the conclusion that you do not know the points or at least the explanations of the points'.[44]

Himmler's unsuccessful and yet all the more contentious activity for party headquarters raises the question: why did his party career not come to an end in the 1920s? Why did none of the numerous conflicts in which he was involved lead to his dismissal from the party leadership?

The fact that he was able to hold on to his position will have had much to do with his skill at fitting in with the power structure of this 'Führer-dominated' party, and at not making enemies, at any rate at party-leadership level. During these years there was antagonism between the Munich leadership and party members in the provinces, which found expression in frequent conflicts. What held the party together was the charisma of the party leader, in other words, Hitler's ability continually to convince party members in the provinces that their exceptional talents would in the end help the party to victory.

So long as, in his conflicts with party members in the provinces, Himmler appealed to the authority of the party leader or to the 'gentlemen' in party headquarters, he could be reasonably sure that, in the final analysis, he would get the backing of Hitler and his colleagues. Hitler's style of leadership, which was to let Himmler and the other functionaries in party headquarters operate largely independently, had the result, as already indicated, that their position was essentially dependent on Hitler's role as the absolute leader remaining intact. Hitler was, in turn, loyal to his colleagues. If he had continually intervened to correct Himmler's approach or criticized him vis-à-vis the party rank-and-file, his own authority might have suffered. In addition, in Gregor Strasser Himmler had an important mentor in party headquarters, from whom he could count on additional support.

Although he now belonged to the more intimate leadership staff around Hitler, it cannot be said that Himmler's personal relations with Hitler at this juncture were particularly close. Their meetings on a personal level were probably few and far between, and when Hitler had meetings with his people they soon turned into his long-winded monologues.[45] It is significant that there are no records of Himmler, even at a later period, reminiscing about common experiences with Hitler during the 'time of struggle'. The deputy Reich Propaganda Chief was, in the final analysis, an insignificant party functionary working for the party leader, whom Hitler clearly kept at arm's length.

Agricultural expert of the NSDAP and member of the Artamanen movement

During this period Himmler also acted as the party's agricultural expert. In this function he developed agrarian ideas, which he described as 'a völkisch peasant policy'. The structural crisis in agriculture, which he had analysed in previous years and linked with anti-Semitic propaganda, was to be combated through a programme of settlement, particularly in eastern Germany; in his eyes this would also represent a contribution towards the regeneration of the German 'national body' and towards the 'recovery of its military morale'.[46]

The development of Himmler's ideas for a 'völkisch peasant policy' was directly linked to his involvement with the 'Artamanen', which can be traced from 1928. The Artamanen movement had been in existence since 1924; in 1928 it became more organized and from then onwards called itself the Artam League. It was a völkisch youth league, which had initially seen its main task as being to send groups of young people ('Artamanen groups') to estates in eastern Germany, in order to replace Polish seasonal workers. The idea behind the project was to reconnect urban young people with the soil through hard work on the land, and thereby, at the same time, help to secure the 'ethnic German [völkisch] frontier'. According to the league, at the end of the 1920s there were 2,000 young people involved in this agricultural project. This badly paid and self-sacrificial work, regarded as voluntary labour service, was regarded by the league as its first step towards playing an active role in the 'internal colonization' of eastern Germany; for this purpose it organized its own settlement projects. In addition, within its ranks the league encouraged the idea of the 'Ostlandfahrt', the 'journey to the East Land'; in other words, these settlement activities were by no means to be confined to German territory.[47]

The league, which was a strong supporter of the ideology of 'blood and soil', was also anti-Slav, anti-urban, and anti-Semitic. Thus, from the start there was a close ideological affinity with Nazism, and a large number of Artamanen were in fact members of the Nazi Party. In 1937, for example, Friedrich Schmidt, who was leader of the league from 1925 to 1927, became head of the Nazi Party's Main Indoctrination Department. His successor, Hans Holfelder, who was leader of the league from 1927 onwards, was also closely associated with the NSDAP,[48] and from September 1927 onwards he was Himmler's link with the Artam League.[49]

The league's principles matched Himmler's earlier enthusiasm for settlement in the east. Its model of how to live—a simple way of life, hard work, avoidance of nicotine and alcohol, sexual abstinence, adherence to Teutonic traditions—corresponded with the maxims that he himself followed. From 1928 onwards he acted as the Gau leader for Bavaria, a post in which he was confirmed in January 1929, only three weeks after his appointment as Reichsführer-SS (RFSS). The office of the Bavarian Gau was based within the building housing the NSDAP headquarters. Thus, Himmler was easily able to deal with the matters arising to do with the league. In fact there was only a very small organization in Bavaria, with about twenty members in all.[50] There is no record of Himmler having

played a very active part in the league; he can be shown as having participated only twice in events at the national level.[51] In fact his main role was to
act as the link between the Nazi leadership and Holfelder. His involvement
was very much 'at the behest of the party', as he later recalled.[52] For
example, he recommended party members to join the Artamanen[53] and
instigated the exclusion of those party members who had broken their work
contracts with the league.[54]

At the end of the 1920s the league became the scene of major disputes.
At the end of 1929 there was a disagreement between one group, who
wanted to focus above all on 'selection and settlement' and advocated a
bündisch way of life modelled on the organizations of the German youth
movement, and another group, whose members were more closely linked
to the NSDAP and favoured turning voluntary service on the land into
a labour service organization; they also advocated subordinating the
league to the Nazi Party. Himmler was definitely a member of the second
group, as is clear from a series of statements that he made in his role as
deputy Propaganda Chief. Thus, in 1928, commenting on romantic agrarian ideas, he wrote: 'internal colonization, cultivating heathland, horticulture—these are all forms of aid for declining, self-satisfied nations.
Advocating internal colonization to a nation as a way out of a crisis
simply means encouraging its cowardice.'[55] 'Settlement policy', he noted
succinctly in 1930, 'can only ever be pursued after one has achieved power,
never beforehand.'[56]

At a meeting of the Artamanen 'parliament' (*Reichsthing*) on 21 December
1929 the *bündisch* group passed a motion of no confidence in the league's
leadership, which was closely linked to the NSDAP; in response they were
immediately thrown out of the organization. Moreover, Friedrich Schmidt,
referred to above, imposed a further sanction: he read out a letter from
Himmler announcing that the group who had been defeated should also
consider themselves excluded from the Nazi Party. Himmler, who was not
present at the meeting, had evidently prepared this statement beforehand in
anticipation of the row.[57] After the split, those who had been excluded
established a new association called 'The Artamanen' and the NSDAP
appeared to lose interest in maintaining close links with the Artam League.
With the Nazi Party's establishment of an agrarian cadre, the 'Agrarian
Political Apparatus' headed by R. Walther Darré, in 1930 Himmler gave
up his involvement in agricultural matters and, apart from that, sought to
integrate the league into the Nazi Party.[58]

As the NSDAP's agricultural expert, for a short time in 1929 Himmler was responsible for editing *Der Bundschuh*, a weekly with the subtitle 'A Fighting Journal for the Awakening Peasantry'.[59] In the first issue, which appeared on 2 May 1929, Himmler explained to its readers why the paper's title was taken from the peasant revolts of the sixteenth century: 'Four hundred years ago, the Bundschuh flag was unfurled for the first time as the German peasants rebelled against personal servitude and the lack of national freedom, against oppression and exploitation, and rose up in support of a great and unified Reich and for the rights of the ordinary man. And so, once again, the Bundschuh is being unfurled at a time of crisis for German peasants.' The paper contained a mixture of practical information for its peasant readership and political and ideological contributions. There was a particular column devoted to the topic of 'Peasant and Jew'. In addition, it regularly published the announcements of the Artam League.

Looking at Himmler's role as the NSDAP's agrarian expert during these years, it is clear that, while on the one hand his views on agriculture were imbued with völkisch ideology, on the other, he did not allow himself to be carried away by agrarian notions that were romantically inspired. In his view, what was decisive for solving Germany's agricultural problems was the question of power: so long as the Nazi Party was not in control of Germany there was no point in trying to provide Germany with a new agrarian structure through settlement. Thus, to begin with, all efforts in this direction must be integrated into the party's propaganda.

From 'lonely freebooter' to husband and father

In the late summer of 1927 Himmler made a fateful acquaintanceship: he met Margarete Boden, his future wife. The date 12 September was specially marked out in his pocket diary; perhaps this was the day on which he saw Margarete for the first time. If this assumption is correct, they met in the town of Sulzbach in Bavaria, where Himmler was staying during one of his numerous speechifying trips.[60] In view of what we know about Himmler's ideal woman, we should not be surprised by Margarete's occupation: she was a nurse. The couple at once began a lively correspondence.[61] *Her* letters have survived; *his* may also have done but are not available to researchers.[62] In any event, Himmler soon opened a special file for Margarete's letters; he always scrupulously noted the date and time of their receipt.[63]

He provided her with papers and newspaper cuttings and accounts of his travels in the service of the movement.[64] She was concerned about the dangers and burdens involved: 'So you managed to get out of Brunswick all right, despite the fact that there was a fight. It's sad that it always has to come to this, and not only for those involved.'[65] And on the following day she wrote: 'Oh no -do you really have to speak 20 times in these 20 meetings? It would be awful. And you've got to go on doing this till Christmas.'[66] She repeatedly asked him about his health.[67] In November the correspondence became more personal. After Himmler had hinted that he had been a bit disappointed by her last letter, Margarete replied: 'Frankly, I thought you would be pleased at getting two letters in such a short space of time.'[68] So why was he disappointed? Margarete kept probing, but evidently Himmler did not want to pursue the matter.[69]

It is already clear from these first letters that Margarete Boden was an embittered woman: 'Your letters always refer to my "mistrust" and my wish to give it all up. You're right. I have lost faith in humanity, above all in men's honesty and sincerity in their relations with women. Believe me, that's worse than if one were just mistrustful. I'm really afraid of believing in the truth of words.'[70] Nevertheless, she was prepared to take the acquaintanceship further. They agreed to meet in Berlin.[71]

During this meeting, which occurred in December, Himmler appears to have abandoned his dogged commitment to remaining celibate. After his Berlin visit they addressed one another in the familiar 'Du' form. Now her letters were addressed to: 'My dear, beloved', 'My dear silly fool', or 'Silly fool and beloved'.[72] When she finally asked how she should address him in her letters,[73] Himmler suggested for the sake of simplicity 'Heini', which is what he had been called as a young boy. 'What shall we call the "bigger" boy now? Something else?' she replied mischievously.[74]

In this first phase of their relationship, still committed to his role as 'a soldierly man', Himmler portrayed himself as a 'freebooter' (*Landsknecht*), and told her (as is clear from her letter): 'We freebooters should really remain solitary and ostracized.'[75] However, the 'freebooter' was quite ready to confess his weaknesses. Thus, he complained to her about his continuing 'submissiveness' to his parents. 'Surely you don't think your "submissiveness" is noticeable at home?', she wrote back. 'In the first place it's not in your character to change, at least not in a way that would be obvious. Secondly, it wouldn't be a nice thing to do. Give in sometimes, my silly fool, but only if you yourself think you should.'[76]

He also did not deny his dislike of big cities, indeed his fear of the metropolis. She replied by making gentle fun of him: 'You needn't be frightened of big cities. I shall do my very best to protect you.'[77] She regularly asked him about his stomach problems, which he was to complain about during the coming months, and enquired anxiously about the results of his visits to the doctor: 'Did you go and see Uncle Doctor?'[78] From her letters it appears that Himmler believed his stomach pains were psychosomatic and attributed them to his constant attempts to discipline and control himself—to be 'good and decent', as he put it. He remarked to her that he would like once in a while to be allowed 'not to be good and decent', as a kind of therapy.[79]

Himmler also appears to have admitted to her the issues he had with his outward appearance, for his rather insignificant and weak chin did not accord with his soldierly image of himself. 'Why have you got your hand in front of your face?' she commented about a photo he had sent her. 'Did you want to cover up your chin?'[80]

She quickly began to have doubts about the emotional basis of this new relationship: did he feel her deep affection as a burden? Did he doubt whether her love for him was as strong as his love for her?

My love, which will last for ever, should never be a burden to you, that is to say, never become too 'much'. But you are convinced that I haven't reached the right degree of affection because I just could not help saying when asked what I feel in my heart of hearts. Whether that feeling is still there I leave to you to sense, to feel. You write, 'Whatever happens I will always feel the same towards you and love you always', and, in spite of what you go on to say, that's severe [. . .]. I cannot possibly think that you really feel I might not love you as much as you love me.[81]

When she confessed to fearing that her love might be a burden to him, he troubled her by asking if he perhaps wrote to her too often. Did that mean, she wrote back, that he did not *want* to write to her so often?[82]

Margarete Boden was an independent woman, who was very competent in her chosen profession and who, in her work environment, as head of nursing at a small private clinic in which she was a partner, behaved in an assured manner: 'On rereading your letter I have just noticed that you wrote "small". You'll have to make that up to me. Anyway, it's not true and you wouldn't say that if you saw me in my clinic . . .'[83] Yet this professional confidence concealed a deep insecurity.

The approaching end-of-year festivities provoked gloomy thoughts in her. 'I dread Christmas for it is a festival of peace and yet what an awful year it was. The autumn was lovely, though, and it gave me faith in human beings again. I can believe and trust once more [...] Now I have to go across to the festivities. If only they were over, for I so dislike being the "matron".'[84] The day before New Year's Eve she wrote: 'Tomorrow is the dreadful day when everyone is having a party and I must be alone. It really is awful. You see what a terribly discontented creature I am, wanting everything to suit me.'[85] She began the New Year full of pessimism.[86]

Ill. 4. Heinrich Himmler in a photograph taken by Heinrich Hoffmann around 1930. Himmler covered his chin even for Hitler's personal photographer.

From the start the relationship between the two had its difficulties: 'Love without pain and worry is something I can't imagine', she wrote.[87] And: 'You have no idea how utterly miserable I am. [...] Do you doubt my love? I can say with certainty that no other woman will love you as I love you.' And she added: 'You may understand me, you will understand me, if—no, because—you love me.'[88]

He spent the holiday with his parents; he clearly used the stay amongst other things to give his father a lecture on the tactics of street-fighting. 'What a good and "loving" son you are', she wrote back. 'People at home have most definitely not noticed any "submissiveness". You horrid boy. How can you do such a thing.'[89] Her political position tended to be moderate. She had little sympathy for his radicalism: 'Why do you reach for the dagger in such a bloodthirsty way?' she asked him. 'Being a conservative is after all a nice thing to be.'[90] And was the party not exploiting him? 'I can't understand how you can let the party get you down so much that you can't even write a letter. I'll bet the other esteemed gentlemen don't allow themselves to be so used. And I'm sure you're not getting any sleep any more [...] and the result is that you're getting ill and wretched. I'd like to know who gets any benefit from you then.'[91] Even to her he clearly made use of the claim of permanent overwork, which he always carried before him like a shield.

During the early months of 1928 the two met a number of times, for example in Bavaria in mid-January[92] and then in Berlin at the beginning of February,[93] at Easter in Berlin, and at Whitsun in Munich.[94] On several occasions in the days before they were due to meet she reminded him to bring with him the books of puzzles he loved so much—after all, they did not want to get bored![95]

Her letters are full of doubts about the possibilities of a future together. Without further explanation, for example, she wrote to him that a friend had 'advised her against marrying a man 7 years younger.'[96] Nevertheless she finally renounced her independence, though it was patently not easy for her, even if she tried to disguise the emerging conflicts somewhat through the mock-sulking, mischievous style of her letters. 'This poor little rascal of a woman is very sad because the wicked man won't allow her any work of her own. She wants to argue back and if she can't she'll look for pastures new.'[97] Conversely, she made it clear to him that the freedom of his bachelor existence would soon end: 'Cinema, theatre, you're a pleasure-loving man. Sweetheart, there'll be very little of that after we're married.

Ill. 5. Margarete Boden and Heinrich Himmler in the year they married. From the start they faced difficulties in establishing a life together.

You'd better take advantage of the opportunity while you can.'[98] When he sent her a letter setting out various matters in a numbered list, as was his custom, she rejected this manner of writing: 'Never again write 1.) 2.) 3.) like a typical bureaucrat.'[99]

She also feared she would be rejected by his parents.[100] She was simply unable to write them a letter: 'Sweetheart, I simply cannot write to them myself. My love, what heartache your relationship with me will bring you. I am so fearful of new people.'[101] In the eyes of the Himmler family she must be a terrible disappointment, she said: 'Sweetheart, how disappointed your sister-in-law will be by me. The fact is I'm so mistrustful and can never accept that people are well disposed towards me.'[102]

At the latest after their meeting in February 1928 it is clear that Heinrich Himmler and Margarete Boden had decided to marry.[103] She began the process of leaving the private clinic and asked for reimbursement of her share. The sum agreed upon was 12,000 Reich marks;[104] yet she obviously felt she had been fleeced by the director of the clinic: 'A Jew is always a

Jew! And the others are no better.'[105] More problems arose, however, when they established their joint household. They decided on a relatively inexpensive prefabricated wooden house, for which they acquired a plot of land in Waldtrudering near Munich.[106] They had to buy furniture and household goods, and Himmler planned to buy a car. At first he thought he could obtain a mortgage, but when he stopped responding to her constant requests for information[107] it was clear that this plan would not be realized. They now had to make do with Marga's 12,000 marks; she repeatedly complained that his demands were too great and that he spent too much.[108] In the end the house was entered under her name in the land register.[109]

The car she favoured buying was the Hanomag and not the more expensive Dixi that he wanted: 'The cheapest Dixi costs 2,595 marks from Eisenach, which will certainly bring it up to 3,000 marks. Sweetheart, that's too expensive. I wish we would settle for the Hanomag.'[110] Himmler got his way, however: they bought a Dixi, although in fact he had no driving licence. She constantly impressed on him that he must get one: 'Sweetheart, why do we want a car if nobody can drive.'[111] He actually passed the test on 27 June 1928.[112] They were married on 3 July.[113]

The newlyweds planned to supplement the meagre salary Himmler earned as a party functionary by selling agricultural products: they intended to make use of the garden and to begin some small-scale animal breeding. They got a dog. Himmler had, after all, a diploma in agriculture and was the agriculture specialist for the NSDAP. But production never really got properly under way. Himmler was constantly travelling, though Margarete kept him up to date about progress. The news was, however, mostly bad: 'The hens are not laying yet. The dog has been having its litter all day. The pig is eating.'[114] 'On Sunday the chicks arrived. Only 23 and 10 are dead already [...] They weren't hatched. I'll never do that again. The incubator is not working properly and uses too much oil. The turkeys and hens are laying well. Oh my dear, what is happening to me. The rabbits are not doing anything yet [...][115]—11 trees are completely dead. 8 pears and 3 apples.'[116]—'The hens are laying really badly. 2 eggs a day. It makes me so cross when I think we were intending to live off them and even start saving at Whitsun. Always bad luck. I am so careful, but the money is gone again right away.'[117]

On 8 August their only child was born. The little girl was baptized a Protestant and named Gudrun.[118] The enlargement of the family did not make the situation easier, as Margarete's complaints to him demonstrate: 'That awful dog Töhle keeps on barking, and so the baby can't sleep either.'[119] Nor were the animals thriving: 'The hens are laying very badly.'[120]

Promotions to head the SS

During this period Himmler also experienced a number of changes in his professional life. His appointment as 'Deputy Reichsführer-SS' in September 1927 was almost certainly largely due to the fact that he organized meetings for prominent party speakers. Since 1925 the party had been establishing a number of 'protection squads' (*Schutzstaffeln*) in its main centres of support and using the title SS. These were small groups of party activists who were primarily responsible for protecting big meetings and the public appearances of prominent party figures. Himmler's activity in the Reich propaganda headquarters involved responsibility for deploying 'individual SS units when planning public meetings'. To perform this role he was obliged to exercise certain command functions, that were now given formal recognition with his appointment as deputy Reichsführer-SS (under Erhart Heiden). In addition there was the fact that Himmler already had SS experience: he had been in command of the Lower Bavarian SS since 1926.[121]

In 1927 the SS was a very small formation. It had been founded in spring 1925. At that time Hitler had given his old supporter Julius Schreck the task of setting up a personal bodyguard, a 'staff-guard', which after a few weeks was renamed 'protection squad'. Similar formations had existed before the 1923 putsch. Hitler had already founded a staff-guard in March 1923, which had been replaced in May by a 'Stosstrupp [assault-group] Adolf Hitler' under Joseph Berchtold; almost all the members of the protection squad, including Schreck, had belonged to the Stosstrupp.[122] The uniforms of the new protection squads were borrowed from those of the old staff-guard or the Stosstrupp: in addition to the windcheaters worn by the SA, the members of these former organizations had worn black ski caps with a silver death's-head badge and swastika armbands edged with black. The protection squads continued this tradition: while they too wore brown shirts, which in the meantime had been adopted by the party, they also wore a black tie, a black cap with a death's head, a black, white, and red cockade, riding breeches, and swastika armbands.[123]

Ill. 6. Before the NSDAP achieved its breakthrough in September 1930 Himmler's role at Party Headquarters was more that of a faceless bureaucrat than anything else. Here he can be seen in a group of leading Nazis who had met together on 22 September in the Saxon spa town of Bad Elster. State elections were taking place on the same day.

In September 1925 Schreck had sent a circular to all Gau headquarters and independent local branches of the NSDAP requesting them to establish protection squads.[124] The 'function' of the protection squads, which was outlined in guidelines specially issued for the purpose, was to be 'the protection of the local meetings' of the NSDAP as well as to 'strengthen the personal protection of our leader Adolf Hitler in the event of his speaking there or in the neighbourhood of the local branch concerned'. The protection squads were to be 'neither a paramilitary organization nor a bunch of hangers-on, but rather small groups of men on whom our movement and our leader can rely. They must be people who are in a position to protect our meetings from troublemakers and our movement from "professional grousers". For members of the protection squad there must be no ifs and buts; they must observe our party discipline.' In addition they had the task of 'canvassing for and winning over' new members as well as subscribers and advertisers for the party newspaper, the *Völkischer Beobachter.*

Moreover, Schreck decreed in the same circular that the only people permitted to join the protection squads were party members between 23 and 25 years of age, who were fit and 'powerfully built'. 'They must be comrades who stand for the old motto, "all for one and one for all".' A protection squad should be composed of a leader and ten men or, in larger places, there could be more than ten men. They were to be subordinated to a high command to be established in party headquarters, and would 'finance themselves by collecting contributions'. Another version of the directives composed in a still more martial tone included further organizational details and emphasized the autonomy of the protection squads vis-à-vis other party organizations: 'Neither the local branch nor the Gau headquarters has the right to interfere in the internal organization of the local SS.' The protection squads were not 'a subsection of the SA, but are of equal status'.[125] However, at this point an SA did not exist; banned following the putsch attempt, Hitler delayed re-founding it until the end of 1926, since before doing so he wanted to secure the party's control over its strong-arm squad.[126]

In April 1926 Berchtold, the old leader of the Stosstrupp Adolf Hitler, who in the meantime had returned from Austria, took over leadership of the protection squads from Schreck. The main reason for Schreck's replacement was the opinion, which appears to have been widely held in party headquarters, that, as one SS man put it, 'Schreck does not have the requisite leadership qualities and organizational talent and also does not have the reputation that will ensure that the SS can become an elite troop within the movement'.[127]

Soon after his appointment Berchtold emphasized the SS's claim to elite status in a circular to the leaders of the protection squads. It allegedly brought together 'the best and most activist elements within our movement'; they were not concerned with numbers but 'solely with the inner worth of each individual'.[128] Moreover, at the party rally in 1926 Hitler handed over to Berchthold the 'blood flag', the swastika flag which had been carried in the failed putsch and which allegedly had been 'coloured by the blood of a fallen National Socialist'.[129] It was only at the end of 1926 that the SS was subordinated to the newly formed SA under von Pfeffer; as a result, Berchtold lost his independence but was given the title Reichsführer-SS.[130] In March 1927 Berchtold was replaced by his deputy, Erhard Heiden, to whom Himmler was now assigned as his deputy.[131]

Hardly anything is known about Himmler's role as deputy Reichsführer-SS. However, it is clear from the few remaining documents that, from the beginning, he did not content himself with his immediate task of deploying the protection squads to fit in with party headquarters' plans for meetings. Instead, he concentrated on reforming the SS's internal organization. In September 1927, directly after taking over his new function, he issued an 'Order No. I' to all protection squads, and made it clear that from now on the SS leadership would once again operate with a tough style of management, which for various reasons had not been the case during the previous weeks. This was followed by a series of instructions. Membership subscriptions and insurance premiums were to be paid promptly. He ordered the protection squads regularly to report on 'all political or other events of significance', and above all on the activities of their opponents, especially 'Freemasons and prominent Jewish figures'. They were informed that there were plans to set up a comprehensive intelligence service. Thus, with the help of the protection squads Himmler was endeavouring to create a special network of informants for the project which he had long been planning, namely for the party to set up its own intelligence service.

In addition, he regulated the weekly 'SS duties' down to the very last detail. Great emphasis was placed on 'drill manoeuvres', such as 'standing at attention, standing at ease, right and left turns', and the like. 'Appearances in public should differ in no respect from those of an army unit.' Members of the protection squads, Himmler insisted, should keep out of all internal disputes and should not participate in discussions during party meetings.[132] Also, their uniforms required further standardization; evidently the party rally had shown up flaws in this respect.[133]

In January 1929 Hitler relieved Heiden of his post, 'for family reasons', as the party's official statement put it, and appointed his successor with the following announcement: 'I hereby appoint the previous deputy Reichsführer-SS, Heinrich Himmler, to the post of Reichsführer-SS.' We have no further clues to explain either Heiden's dismissal or Himmler's appointment. Initially, Himmler retained his post in the Reich propaganda headquarters; the position of Reichsführer-SS could evidently still be carried out on the side.[134]

There is uncertainty about the numerical strength of the SS when Himmler took up his appointment. His own later statements differed. He mentioned variously 260, 280, 290, or 300 members,[135] the SS Guidance Booklets (SS-Leithefte) referred to 'exactly 270 men'.[136] These numbers were probably understated in order to emphasize Himmler's achievement in building up the force. A police report of 23 May 1929 refers to 1,402 members; an internal SA order of 3 May 1929 mentions 748 SS members in the 'official' SS units, in other words in those that were organized in accordance with the regulation requiring squads to consist of ten men.[137] However, such a rapid increase following Himmler's appointment is unlikely, as his initial organizational measures were designed more to achieve a cautious consolidation of the organization rather than a rapid expansion.[138]

Himmler's first test in his new function came with the NSDAP's Reich Party rally that took place in Nuremberg in September 1929. He dealt with the details in a special order of 6 July. Every SS man was obliged to take part in the rally. They had to get ready for 'the most strict duties' and devote the rest of the time before this high point in the party's calendar to carrying out drill manoeuvres: 'Immaculate marching in double columns (8 pairs side by side).' Himmler wanted to leave nothing to chance, and carefully organized his SS's journey to Nuremberg: 'Every SS leader will be responsible to me for ensuring that his squad brings with it a sufficient number of shoe and clothes brushes.' Considerately, he recommended that they should have had 'plenty of sleep beforehand', and reminded them 'most emphatically' of the 'ban on alcohol'.[139]

Shortly before the party rally he issued another order in which he once again demanded 'the strictest discipline', 'total commitment to doing one's duty', 'the greatest possible sense of manly honour', and for 'every instruction to be followed in the most exact and scrupulous manner'. To ensure strict punctuality, he insisted that 'on arrival in Nuremberg all watches are to be set according to the station clock'. In addition, he ordered that 'permission is required to drink liquids offered by the population or from water bottles during marches, since excessive drinking on an empty stomach or when overheated can lead to serious accidents'.[140] The SS put in a satisfactory performance in Nuremberg. The high point was the solemn ceremony in which the SS received the first ten 'Storm Flags'. This was followed by a propaganda march in which the SS marched as a single block behind a visibly proud Himmler.[141]

The new Reichsführer-SS soon found less and less time for his duties in the Reich Propaganda Department. Hitler had already offered Goebbels the post of Reich Propaganda Chief in place of Gregor Strasser.[142] Goebbels had recommended himself for this post through his performance as Berlin Gauleiter, where he had developed an effective style of propaganda. However, shortly after this offer had been made Goebbels came to suspect an intrigue by Otto Strasser (like his brother a member of the 'left' wing of the party), in which he might be being offered 'the appearance of power' in Munich in order to get rid of him as Gauleiter of Berlin.[143]

However, this suspicion did not last, and in November 1929 Goebbels discussed in detail with Himmler, who was to become his 'Famulus', how his takeover of the Reich Propaganda Department should be managed.[144] Goebbels's assessment of Himmler remained positive, but not without some doubts: 'I am working out with him the basis for our future cooperation over propaganda. He is a fine little man. Amiable but also vacillating. A Strasser product. But we'll sort it out.'[145]

During the following months Himmler kept Goebbels in touch with 'all sorts of goings on among the Munich camarilla', in other words, Hitler's entourage. 'Appalling', commented Goebbels on the 'terrible shambles and cliquishness down there'.[146] In March Himmler urged him to take over the Reich Propaganda Department, but Goebbels held back and continued to wait for the 'summons from Munich'. Hitler had to take the 'first step', otherwise: 'Götz v. Berlichingen'.*[147]

However, in April 1930 he finally agreed to go. The Propaganda Department was split into two sections: Fritz Reinhardt's speakers' college, and a Section II which Goebbels was in charge of.[148] He noted in his diary: 'In the evening a discussion with my secretary, Himmler. We very quickly came to an agreement.' In May he noted: 'he's not particularly clever, but hardworking and well-meaning.'[149] 'Himmler is fitting in very well',[150] he is 'getting to know the ropes',[151] but is still getting 'too bogged down in details'.[152]

---

* *Translators' note*: An allusion to Goethe's play of that name, containing the famous line: 'He can lick my arse!'

In fact the two of them had little time to get used to their new roles, for the Reichstag election of September 1930 was approaching. On 29 July Goebbels recorded the conclusion of the preparations: 'Yesterday, RPD: Finished dealing with propaganda. Final discussion with Himmler. From now on he can deal with it on his own. The foundations are laid. Anything that still has to be done is purely technical stuff.' At this point it must have been clear to him that after the election he would have to look for a new deputy, for the more the NSDAP expanded, the more the post of Reichs-führer-SS was becoming a full-time job. Moreover, the party had responded to Himmler's growing importance by allocating him a promising place on its electoral list for the Reichstag election.[153] And, in fact, after winning a seat in the Reichstag, he stepped down from the post of deputy Reich Propaganda Chief in mid-November.[154]

As the organizer of the party's propaganda, Himmler played a not-insignificant part in its remarkable success in the Reichstag election of 14 September 1930, in which it increased its share of the vote from 2.6 to 18.3 per cent. The victory represented a political earthquake, and resulted in what had hitherto been a splinter party becoming a significant power factor within German politics. However, as deputy to Goebbels, who patronized him, Himmler was too much in the propaganda chief's shadow to draw from this success significant advantages for his future career in the Nazi movement. He also failed to utilize his seat in the Reichstag. Although he was a member of the Reichstag until 1945, he never made a speech. And he carried out his functions within the party's parliamentary group with little enthusiasm.[155] When he falsely described the Liberal deputy, Theodor Heuss, as a Jew in a pamphlet entitled *The Reichstag*, published in the series NS-Bibliothek, he was forced to withdraw the accusation following strong protests.[156]

Nevertheless, gaining a Reichstag seat produced an important change in Himmler's circumstances: his Reichstag salary freed him at last from pressing financial worries. That he now possessed parliamentary immunity and was entitled to free rail travel were additional practical benefits. Above all, however, by giving up his position as deputy Propaganda Chief, he was able to concentrate on one thing. From now on Himmler had only one job, that of Reichsführer-SS.

6

Reichsführer-SS

Shortly after the Reichstag elections in September 1930, at which the NSDAP achieved its great breakthrough, the SS became involved in a serious crisis that had broken out in the Nazi movement as a result of the simmering conflict between the SA and the party leadership. The conflict had been provoked by the demand, put forward above all by the SA chief in eastern Germany, Walter Stennes, for SA leaders to be given promising seats on the party's electoral lists in the forthcoming elections. Confronted with the SA's failure to persuade the party leadership to accede to its demand, the SA's supreme commander, von Pfeffer, resigned on 12 August 1930.

The conflict escalated when Stennes then announced that the SA in the area for which he was responsible would cease cooperating with the party. In fact, by 30 August he was prepared to give way, but when an SS man was discovered eavesdropping on a meeting of SA leaders, all talk of compromise came to an end. On the very same day, SA storm troopers forced their way into the Berlin party headquarters, which was defended by an SS guard unit. A fight developed which had to be stopped by the police, who had been summoned by the SS.

Hitler now intervened, hurrying to Berlin and holding talks with the two adversaries. On 1 September he made a speech to the SA in which he announced that he himself was going to take over the leadership of both the SA and the SS. During the resultant jubilation he was able to secure a 'declaration of loyalty' from the assembled SA men.[1] Simultaneously, open conflict had also broken out between the party and the SA in Augsburg. Himmler and the leader of the Bavarian SS, Sepp Dietrich, travelled to Augsburg and were only just able to prevent the SA from demolishing party headquarters. There were similar conflicts in Dachau in October 1930 and Hanau in February 1931. In both cases the local party leadership had to be protected by the SS.[2]

In the course of this crisis the SS had projected itself to the party leadership as a totally loyal counterweight to the SA, or rather to the SA leadership. During the following years the SS leadership cultivated the notion that the SA storm troopers, who were at heart loyal and honourable men, were being incited against the party leadership by a corrupt and power-hungry clique, and that in the face of such a dangerous threat there was only one effective antidote, the SS. Summing up the Berlin incident eleven years later, Himmler claimed that 'the SA men were not in the least disappointed; the only people who were disappointed were Herr Pfeffer and his camarilla, who had envisaged the SA as a Free Corps under the protection of the NSDAP with which to play politics and, when necessary, to blackmail the Führer'.[3]

According to the official story, which the SS leadership put about a few years later, after the Stennes putsch Hitler coined the motto, 'Your honour means loyalty' ('Deine Ehre heißt Treue'), which subsequently became 'the most important guiding principle of every SS man'. That may or may not be true. But it is in any case significant that the moral precept chosen by the SS as its motto should refer to an internal party conflict which took place during the 'time of struggle'.[4]

SA and SS

At the end of 1930, only a few months after the Stennes crisis, it did look very much as if Himmler would succeed in removing the SS from their position of subordination to the SA. In an SS order of December 1930 he stated: 'The complete separation of the SS from the SA in terms of both organization and functions has been accomplished.' In fact, this 'complete separation' was to occur only after 30 June 1934; until then Himmler remained subordinate to the SA leadership, which Hitler reorganized towards the end of the year.[5] After Hitler had taken over personal command of both the SA and the SS at the beginning of September 1930, the day-to-day running of the SA was carried out by von Pfeffer's chief of staff, Otto Wagener.[6] At a meeting of SA leaders in Munich on 30 November 1930 Hitler announced the appointment of a new SA chief: Ernst Röhm, who had returned from a lengthy stay in Bolivia.

This appointment came as a surprise. It is true that Röhm had become a kind of patron of the SA during the years 1920 to 1923 when, as a captain in the Reichswehr, he was endeavouring to coordinate the activities of the various paramilitary leagues, and had been closely connected with the history of this organization. However, from the very beginning his interest had been focused on the SA's military potential. He saw it as a paramilitary league and not, as Hitler did, a unit whose main function was to serve the party. By integrating the SA into a military alliance, the Kampfbund, in the autumn of 1923, he had effectively put Hitler under pressure to launch the putsch of 9 November. Nevertheless, after his arrest Hitler had assigned Röhm the task of reorganizing the SA, and during 1924 the latter had once more tried to incorporate it into a large unified paramilitary organization, the Frontbann. When Hitler left Landsberg prison at the end of 1924 the irreconcilable differences between the two men came to the fore. Hitler had learnt from the experience of November 1923 that a militarization of the SA, as Röhm had pursued and continued to pursue it, was politically a cul-de-sac. Röhm had then left the SA and taken employment as a military adviser in Bolivia. There was no evidence that Röhm had revised his views on the role of SA in the meantime. Thus, even after his appointment he continued to hold views diametrically opposed to those of Hitler.[7]

It is therefore difficult to understand why Hitler chose Röhm. Basically, it was a concession to the rebelliously minded SA leaders, who, being mostly former army officers and Free Corps fighters like the old warrior Röhm himself, did not believe that the SA should be 'in the hands of a politician'. Instead, it should be 'in the hands of the leaders of its own units', as a participant in a meeting of SA leaders on 30 November 1930 put it in a memorandum.[8] In Röhm's favour was also the fact that, as a result of his absence abroad, he had not been involved in the factional struggles and, despite their differences of opinion, he maintained a good relationship with Hitler. Röhm took up his post at the beginning of 1931 under the 'Supreme SA Leader, Adolf Hitler'.

Contrary to the assumption that Himmler had expressed at the end of 1930, the SS remained subordinated to the SA. This was made unmistakably clear in the Order No. 1 signed by Röhm on 16 January 1931: 'On 14 January 1931, the Supreme SA Leader ordered that the Reichsführer of the SS should be subordinate to the Chief of Staff [of the SA].'[9] As we have seen, Himmler was an old acquaintance and comrade of Röhm's. The standard-bearer of the Reichskriegsflagge, Röhm's own paramilitary league, on 9 November 1923, had not let anything stop him from visiting

Röhm in Stadelheim prison after the abortive putsch. Also, Himmler had corresponded with Röhm during his Bolivian exile and had encouraged him in his decision to return to Germany.[10]

Full of pride, he had kept his old mentor in touch with the development of the SS and had not omitted to emphasize his earlier role in the Reichskriegsflagge: 'Many an SS leader has felt the benefit of the training I got from you', he wrote in November 1929. 'The boss has set us quite a target of recruiting several thousand men by the spring and so we've got to meet it.'[11] Röhm replied in March 1930: 'I would like to congratulate you above all for increasing the size of the SS. Knowing you as I do, I had no doubt that it was being led in the old spirit and along the lines of our old RKF.'[12]

It is unclear whether Himmler was yet aware of Röhm's homosexuality. He must have heard rumours about it, but may have rejected them as opposition propaganda. It was not until the summer of 1931 that the opposition press supplied clear evidence of his homosexual orientation. The publication of private letters of Röhm in March 1932 finally provided irrefutable proof.[13] At this point, however, Himmler probably calculated that he could exploit his superior's sexual orientation and the loose living of many SA men by contrasting it with the virtue and discipline characteristic of the SS. This is a point to which we shall return.

After his appointment Röhm immediately set about defining the relationship between the SA and SS. The Order No. 1 of 16 January, already referred to, stated: 'The tasks of the SA and the SS are distinct. Thus there should be no differences of opinion or friction between the two.' In future, the SS should be no larger than 10 per cent of the complement of the SA; the SA should not recruit from the SS and vice versa. Röhm's detailed instructions give an indication of where in practice the friction was likely to occur: 'In the event that both the SA and the SS are engaged on party duties, overall command shall be exercised by the highest-ranking and longest-serving SA or SS leader in uniform, so long as there is a unit present of which he is in command and the number of SA and SS units involved corresponds to the ratio of 1:10.' In the event that 'both the SA and the SS are engaged on party duties', the SA should be responsible for 'protecting the meeting'; 'the protection of the speaker, the political leaders, and the leaders present as guests shall be the responsibility of the SS'. In the case of marches the following regulation applied: 'The main task of the SA is to carry out propaganda marches; the SS has the task of manning the barriers and maintaining security (street patrols). In the case of marches where leaders take the salute, with the exception of those manning the barriers, the SS will march as a unit at the back of the SA column.' And, finally: 'All SA and SS leaders, political leaders, and party comrades are obliged to follow the orders of the SS when it is carrying out its duties.'[14]

The rapid growth of the SS required continual adjustments to the organization. Already in 1930 three SS Higher Command districts had been created, a kind of regional inspectorate from which the SS Abschnitte (sections or districts) would emerge.[15] Order No. 25 of 12 May 1931 introduced new titles for the units. From now on the SS no longer organized itself in brigades but in 'Standarten'; the Standarten were then divided into several 'Sturmbanns'.[16] In order to increase its flexibility, emphasis was placed on establishing 'motorized units'.[17] Moreover, Himmler professionalized the work of his staff, which by 1931 was already composed of five departments, by introducing rules of procedure.[18]

Whereas the SA recruited its members above all from the lower-middle and working classes, the SS mainly recruited from the 'better class of person'. There were, however, continual complaints that the SS was trying to recruit SA members. Thus, the General Inspector of the SA, for example, complained to Röhm about its 'uncomradely manner of recruitment'.[19] The rivalry between the two Nazi mass paramilitary organizations was also exacerbated by the fact that the SS projected itself as the much more disciplined of the two, and claimed to enjoy the particular trust of the party leadership.[20] According to an order issued by SS-Oberführer Sepp Dietrich in a self-confident tone, the SS had been 'bonded together from the most active elements in the party as a particularly reliable instrument of power in the hands of the supreme leader'. It was intended 'for those duties that go beyond the normal responsibilities and operations carried out by the SA', in particular, 'for the maintenance of order and security'.[21]

Above all, however, the SS was to be used again and again against the undisciplined SA. In particular, during the so-called second Stennes revolt of April 1931 the SS was employed as an internal party disciplinary force with which to tame the SA. Although it had apparently been settled, the conflict between the party's political leadership and the SA leadership, which had broken out for the first time in east Germany—Stennes's area of responsibility—in the late summer of 1930, had never really been resolved. In the winter of 1930–1, therefore, Stennes increasingly adopted an anti-parliamentary stance, which was inevitably liable to clash with Hitler's 'policy of legality'. Stennes's increasingly radical rhetoric ran the risk of provoking a ban on the party; this had been greatly facilitated by an emergency decree issued by the Reich President. In the light of this situation, Hitler dismissed Stennes at the beginning of April, which prompted the latter to declare that he was 'taking over' the party in Berlin and in the eastern provinces of Prussia. Stennes instructed the SA to occupy the party's offices in Berlin (they met with physical resistance from the SS). He was able to win over a section of the SA in his area of responsibility, but there was no general SA uprising. The Berlin party leadership quickly regained control of its offices. During the following weeks the SA leadership corps in north and east Germany was systematically purged of Stennes supporters; around 500 SA men had to leave.[22]

The structure and future responsibilities of the SS

Around two months later, in June 1931, Himmler gave a talk at a meeting of SS leaders on the subject of 'The Purposes and Aims of the SS, the Relationship between the SS, the SA, and the Political Formations'. It is the only surviving document from the 'time of struggle' which reveals Himmler's ideas for the future tasks and aims of the SS in a coherent manner.

After some introductory remarks on the 'traditions of the SS', Himmler concluded that while the SA were the 'regiments of the line', the SS were 'the guards', 'the Führer's last reserve [. . .] Whenever it comes to the last roll of the dice, in every nation it is the guards who prove decisive.' Since this was the role that Hitler had assigned to the SS, 'it has been set up for this purpose and everybody must go along with this [. . .] because it is an order from our leader and every order must be obeyed'. Himmler continued: 'The SS must become a force that includes the best human material that we still possess in Germany. The SS must be held together by the shared community of blood. It must be impossible for it to fall apart.' It was true that there were still 'blemishes', but nevertheless 'we are on the way to becoming a force that is better than a military unit, that is more disciplined than they are. Only when we can claim to compete with the best military unit shall we have earned the right to wear the death's-head badge, only then will we be the guards.' Only then, as Himmler put it later, would 'the old front-line soldiers want to support us, only then will they come over to us and at that moment the "Stahlhelm"* will be finished. There will be only one "League of Front-line Soldiers": the SS.'

---

* *Translators' note*: Himmler is referring here to the right-wing veterans' organization, the Stahlhelm ('Steel-Helmet') League of Front-line Soldiers.

In a central passage of the speech Himmler developed the idea of a final impending conflict between the 'Nordic nation' on the one side and 'Bolshevism' on the other:

Shall we, by filtering out the valuable blood through a process of selection, once again succeed in training and breeding a nation on a grand scale, a Nordic nation? Shall we once again succeed in settling this Nordic people in surrounding territory, turning them into peasants again and from this seedbed create a nation of 200 million? Then the earth will belong to us! But if Bolshevism is victorious then this will mean the extermination of the Nordic race, of the last valuable Nordic blood, and this devastation would mean the end of the earth.

According to Himmler, the SS would have a pioneering role to play in this final struggle:

We have been given the greatest and most magnificent task that a nation can be faced with. As far as the value of our blood and the numbers of our population are concerned we are dying out. We are called upon to establish foundations so that the next generation can make history, and if we create the right foundations it will be a great one. The best soldiers, the best Germans will come to us of their own accord, we will not need to seek them, if they see that the SS has been set up correctly, that the SS is really good.

What is remarkable about this major speech is the fact that Himmler assumed that his fantasy of the final struggle between 'the Nordic nation' and 'Bolshevism' would take place only in the 'next generation', and that he saw his own task as being above all to create the basis for this struggle for existence. Himmler saw the key to creating such an elite organization as being the selection of the 'racially best people':

An SSF [SS leader] will never keep someone with a typical Slav face in his unit for very long because so long as that person is in the troop or storm (*Sturm*), he will never get the troop or storm into a proper order. He will soon notice that there is no community of blood with the other comrades, who are of more Nordic descent. The passport photos that have to be submitted together with the application forms ensure that Reich headquarters can inspect the heads of the SS candidates. One only needs to try the experiment of admitting a Mongol to the SS; it's certain that he would be thrown out during the trial period. But so long as this Mongol is in the SS it will be impossible to create the spirit which is essential for the SS. The breaking-point will come when the racially pure person will stay the course whereas the racially impure will fall by the wayside.

Thus the selection must involve not only the careful inspection of the future SS leader but also include his family:

The Oberführer must take particular care with the selection of leaders. He must scrutinize the milieu and the family of the person whom he has envisaged appointing to a leadership position. A good and completely impeccable leader can never come from an inferior milieu; he will always have scruples and he will never have the decisiveness that an SSF must possess.

Finally, Himmler dealt with the role of the SS within the Nazi movement: 'We must be the best possible comrades of the SA and at the same time always provide models for them. We must always work the hardest and yet never talk about what we have achieved, for there is an old proverb that says: "He who talks a lot never achieves anything."' What was decisive was the recognition that the SS received from the political leadership for its reliability and loyalty: 'Not everybody likes us; we may be shoved into a corner after we have done our work; we must not expect any gratitude. But our leader knows that he can rely on his SS. We are his favourite and most valuable organization because we have never disappointed him.'[23]

In the same month, July 1931, Himmler issued 'Provisional Service Regulations for the Work of the SS', which spelled out the duties of SS members in detail. According to these, SS members had to assemble four times a month. They were expected to take part in monthly meetings of the local branches and once a month undertake a propaganda trip, while two further days in the month were to be devoted to actual 'SS duties'. These were to involve drill as well as ju–jitsu, which Himmler had practised in his student days with more or less enthusiasm.

Again, Himmler underlined the claim of the SS to elite status; it should not let itself descend to the level of petty local disputes: 'The SS never takes part in the discussion at membership meetings. Participation in membership meetings is for the purpose of indoctrinating SS members, who are not permitted to smoke or to leave the hall during the lecture.' Also, Himmler instructed that SS members were not allowed to get involved in the internal affairs of the SA.

The Service Regulations also laid down what songs all SS members were required to know by heart,[24] as well as the details of their uniform. The SS uniform was to consist of a brown shirt, SS armbands, a black tie, a party badge, a black cap with a death's-head badge, black trousers, black leather gaiters, black shoes with shoelaces or riding boots, as well as a black belt. The carrying or use of firearms was strictly forbidden and would result in dismissal from the SS and the party. Admission to the SS was to be governed by the 'strictest criteria'. The applicants had to be at least 1.70 metres tall and at least 23 years of age. In view of the fact that the SA consisted mainly of young men aged between 18 and 25, the higher age-threshold imposed for the SS underlined its claim to a special status.[25]

During the coming months the Service Regulations were augmented by numerous additional orders, for example to do with the organization of the staffs,[26] the establishment of marching bands,[27] and the medical examination of SS members.[28] In the end the SS leadership's obsession with detail went so far as to differentiate between six different types of order, each with its own distribution list, which were cascaded down over the SS organization throughout the country.[29]

In the summer of 1931 Himmler took another decision that was to have far-reaching consequences; he decided to set up a separate SS intelligence service. The person he chose for this task was Reinhard Heydrich. Heydrich had been dismissed from the Navy in April 1931 after he had broken off an engagement and been found guilty of dishonourable conduct by a naval court of honour.[30] He had got to know Himmler through SS-Gruppenführer Friedrich Karl Freiherr von Eberstein. After he had joined the Hamburg SS in July 1931 he was received by the Reichsführer-SS, who was impressed by Heydrich's former position as 'Nachrichtenoffizier' ('information officer'—not realizing at the time that Heydrich had been a signals, not an intelligence, officer). On 1 August 1931 Heydrich began his job as head of the new 'Ic Service', as the agency, using military jargon, was called.[31]

In a secret order of September 1931 Himmler defined the structure of an intelligence network that was to reach down to Standarte level.[32] To begin with, however, Heydrich was the only member of the organization. This changed only after the ban on the SA and SS in April 1932, when the intelligence service was provisionally camouflaged as the 'Press Information Service'. During the following months Heydrich succeeded not only in establishing a headquarters but also in recruiting colleagues throughout the Reich, who reported their observations to it independently of the Standarte reports. On 19 July 1932—the ban had been lifted in June—Himmler appointed Heydrich head of the Party's Security Service (SD) and ten days later promoted him to the rank of Standartenführer.[33]

The Nazi mass movement had been continually expanding since its great success in the Reichstag election of September 1930. It was now also continually making gains in state and local elections. It benefited above all from the fact that the Brüning government, which was backed by the Reich President's right to issue emergency decrees, failed to come up with adequate solutions to the political and economic crisis and thus kept providing the NSDAP with opportunities for attacking the 'system'.

Although dwarfed by its competitor, the SA, whose membership had risen from 88,000 to 260,000 between January and December 1931,[34] the SS had also grown significantly, although it still remained far behind the quota of 10 per cent of the SA which Röhm had fixed in January 1931 as the official ratio of SS to SA. On 1 January 1931 the SS contained 2,272 members, three months later 4,490, and in October Himmler noted that the membership of the SS now stood at 10,000 with another 3,000 candidate members.[35] At this point it was organized into thirty-nine Standarten, which were combined into eight Abschnitte.[36]

In his June 1931 speech to SS leaders, however, Himmler had emphasized that it was not so much a question of numbers, but rather the SS's elite character that was to be decisive for the task it had set itself as a racial avantgarde. Thus 'racial criteria' also had to play a part in admissions to the SS. During its initial years the Reichsführer-SS did in fact scrutinize every application himself, and in the process, as he told Wehrmacht officers in a speech in 1937, focused in particular on the applicant's photo, asking himself the question: 'Does the man's face reveal clear traces of foreign blood such as excessively protruding cheekbones, in other words, a case where ordinary people would say: he looks like a Mongol or a Slav?'[37] However, during the first months after the so-called seizure of power in 1933 the pressure to join the SS was so great that admission was more or less indiscriminate. It was only then that a systematic form of racial examination was introduced for admission to the organization in order to control the stream of applicants.

But it was not only the SS applicants themselves who were examined. At the end of 1931, with his 'Engagement and Marriage Order', Himmler insisted on the examination of the race and 'hereditary health' of the future wives of SS members.[38] The order began with the programmatic sentence: 'The SS is a band of German men of strictly Nordic origin, selected according to certain principles', and determined that, for the purpose of 'selecting and maintaining blood that is racially and genetically of high quality', from 1 January 1932 all SS members had to secure 'permission to marry'. Applications would be assessed by a new Racial Office, which would also start a 'clan book' (*Sippenbuch*) for every SS member.

Himmler was fully aware of the fact that his marriage order would meet with incomprehension, indeed ridicule, outside his organization. He even anticipated this reaction. Point no. 10 of the order stated: 'The SS is convinced that with this order it has taken a step of great significance. Derision, scorn, and incomprehension will not sway us; the future is ours!' Himmler referred to it twelve years later, and in a speech to the Wehrmacht admitted that the marriage order had been regarded 'at the time as ridiculous, as nonsense, as exaggerated, and had not been understood and had been rejected even by some in the ranks of the SS'.[39]

However, the marriage order was not simply a fad of Himmler's but an integral part of the SS's attempts to distinguish itself from the plebeian SA. The marriage order was meant to express the fact that within the SS there was a fundamentally different attitude to masculinity and the relationship between the sexes to that prevalent in the SA. The image of itself projected by the SA was of a bunch of tough-guys, who liked on occasion to get drunk, were not averse to a punch-up, had a relaxed attitude to sex (which included tolerating homosexuality in their own ranks), and in general lived without ties.[40] The SS man, on the other hand, was expected to be disciplined, to be reserved in manner, to be 'Aryan', and through his marriage to contribute to the improvement of the 'racial quality' of the German people.

As head of the new Racial Office[41] Himmler appointed SS-Standarten-führer Walther Darré, who was already responsible for propaganda within the SS.[42] As leader of the Nazi agricultural movement, Darré had contributed far more to the expansion of the NSDAP as a mass movement through his mobilization of the 'rural nation' than Himmler had done in his role as the desk officer within party headquarters responsible for agricultural questions. Indeed, he was seen as one of the coming men in the NSDAP.[43] This was attributable not only to his success in mobilizing support among the rural population, but also to the fact that he was one of the movement's keenest ideologists. In his works *The Peasantry as the Life Spring of the Nordic Race* and *A New Aristocracy from Blood and Soil* he had put forward the view that the German people needed to be 'nordified' through a systematic racial policy. Darré wanted to create a new aristocracy from the peasantry, or rather to re-create the 'Germanic aristocracy' that was rooted in the German people by establishing hereditary landholdings (*Hegehöfe*) and by the selection of the women who would marry into them on the basis of racial principles. The selection was to be carried out by so-called 'Breeding Wardens' (*Zucht-warte*).

There was much in common between the intellectual worlds of Himmler and Darré: Teutonic fantasies, hostility to Christianity (which Darré blamed for the decline of the Germanic aristocracy), and common membership of the Artamanen movement, and the two men were on friendly terms. With Darré's appointment to the Racial Office Himmler exposed the SS to the blood-and-soil ideology and mythologizing of 'the Teutons'. Himmler, who owed his career in the party not to original ideas but to his role as a functionary, would have had difficulty imposing these ideas on the SS as required beliefs. Darré, however, through his published works and his political success, was regarded as an authority, which is why Himmler tried to win him for the SS.

At first, however, all this remained purely symbolic. The SS began the actual 'selection' of the SS candidates and their future wives on a large scale only after 1933.[44] At the start of his career as Reichsführer-SS, and particularly in his immediate sphere of operation, Himmler evidently had other priorities.

Himmler's leadership corps

Like all of us Gruppenführer I owe to the confidence and generosity shown me by the Reichsführer-SS all that I now am. I not only owe him my high rank, but above all it is thanks to his great work and the training that he has put me through that I have developed into what I am now. To be able to serve him loyally and selflessly is not only an obvious duty but doing so gives me the greatest pleasure and the sense of being honoured.[45]

These sentences were written by Himmler's adjutant Karl Wolff in January 1939, for the tenth anniversary of Himmler's appointment as Reichsführer-SS. And, if one takes a look at the SS leadership corps of the early years, it is clear that Wolff was by no means the only one who owed the Reichsführer 'all that I now am'.

The SS leadership team before 1933 was recruited above all from the age cohort born between 1890 and 1900. Almost all of them had served as young soldiers in the World War, the majority since 1914 and most of them as officers, and then often served a few more years in a Free Corps, before being released into a civilian life in which the majority failed to find their feet and experienced that failure as a decline in their social status.

Wolff himself, born in 1900, had served in the exclusive guards regiment of the Grand Duke of Hesse and then joined the Free Corps, until he was discharged as a highly decorated lieutenant. At the beginning of the 1920s he initially trained as a banker and then, after various failed attempts, managed to get a position in advertising, eventually opening his own advertising agency in Munich. During the world depression this firm, which typically used his wife's noble family name in its title, got into serious difficulties. With his entry into the party and the SS in October 1931 this extremely status-conscious 31-year-old hoped he had found a career that would be appropriate for someone of his social standing.[46]

August Heissmeyer was born in 1897 and fought in the war from 1915 onwards, ending up as a lieutenant. His detailed curriculum vitae, which is preserved in his SS personal file, describes the chequered path of a typical post-war career. However, he presents this as if it were the result of his involvement with the 'movement': 'I began as a worker in the Marienthal woollen goods factory in Hamelin and then went to Göttingen in the summer of 1919 and attended a course in order to gain my Abitur. I was forced [*sic*] to interrupt my studies on account of the Kapp putsch.' Heissmeyer took part in the crushing of the left-wing uprising that had broken out in the aftermath of the putsch. But, 'when there was no further opportunity of participating in the struggle, I returned to Göttingen and passed my Abitur in October 1930 [...] I then began to study law and economics in Göttingen, Kiel, and then again in Göttingen [...] Compelled to leave the University as a result of the inflation, I went to work as a miner in Westphalia.' Here he was tempted to become a communist, but then changed his political views: 'I soon heard about Nazism and was swept away [...] In the autumn of 1922 I got a job in the Höchst chemical works as a blue-collar worker. In February 1923 I was put in charge of the safety section of the pesticides department.'

However, in April 1925 Heissmeyer was dismissed on the grounds of his political activity for the NSDAP. In the meantime he had married and had a son: 'I returned with the family to live with my parents-in-law in Hamelin. My attempts to get back to flying proved unsuccessful [...] I then returned to Göttingen to finish my studies with the help of my parents-in-law. However, things turned out differently because very soon, in October

1925, I took over command of the SA [. . .] When my father-in-law heard about my political activities he cut off my monthly allowance.'

Heissmeyer then had to cut down on his political involvement and concentrate on maintaining his family:

To begin with, I became a fruit-tree salesman. My family had been living apart from me for three years in Hamelin and I now brought them to live with me in Göttingen. When nobody wanted to buy any more trees, after about 1½ years I became a salesman for Siemens–Schuckert. But business collapsed because of the increasing shortage of money and the economic crisis. I then became a driving instructor in a driving school [. . .] in Göttingen where I worked from February to December 1931. In December 1930 I joined the Göttingen SS. By November 1931 I had succeeded in increasing its numbers from 18 to 600.

In December 1931 he was put in charge of Standarte 12 and 'moved to Brunswick, while my family had to stay behind in Göttingen for financial reasons'.[47] In October 1932 he took over Abschnitt XVII (Münster).

Kurt Wege, who was born in 1891, had been a soldier from 1911 onwards and was discharged in 1920 as a lieutenant. His subsequent career was chequered. To begin with he worked in farming and began a degree in agriculture, which he had to interrupt in 1923 because of the inflation. He then tried to get by as an unskilled worker, then as a cashier, and then as a clerk, but was repeatedly made redundant. In 1926 he once again became a student—'since I couldn't find suitable employment'—but then gave it up and instead did a correspondence course in bookkeeping. He earned his keep as a 'security official' with the Berlin Guard and Security Service, a private firm. 'But I had to give up this strenuous night work for health reasons.' He was appointed secretary of the National Transport League on a trial basis, but his 'appointment failed to be confirmed as a result of disagreements between the two chairmen. I also became ill as a result of my previous work as a security official.' Between 1927 and 1929 he worked as a salesman. In addition to his career problems, he suffered personal tragedy: his wife died in 1923 and Wege, who had two school-age children, went to live with his mother. In December 1929 he finally found permanent employment with the NSDAP Gau Berlin. From there he switched to the salaried position of an SS-Oberführer and leader of SS Abschnitt XIII (Stettin).[48]

Richard Hildebrandt, who was born in 1897, passed his Abitur in 1915, volunteered for military service, and was discharged from the army as a lieutenant in 1918. After the war he studied economics, languages, history, and art history, without finishing his degree in any of them. He then worked in banking and as a clerk in commerce and industry in various places. In spring 1928 he went to the United States, where he worked 'mainly in manual occupations (farming, horticulture, artisanal)'. In 1930 he returned to Germany. He had already joined the party in 1922, and on his return from the United States he again became actively involved and joined the SS in 1931, where he was appointed adjutant to Sepp Dietrich, the head of the Munich SS Abschnitt.[49]

Friedrich Wilhelm Krüger was born in 1894 as the son of an officer. He left grammar school without taking his Abitur, took part in the World War as an infantry officer and in various post-war military actions, and was discharged from the army in 1920 as a lieutenant. At first he tried his hand at bookselling, but lost his job in 1924 and switched to a management post in the Berlin waste-disposal department, from which he was also dismissed in 1928. He described his profession from now onwards as 'independent businessman'. Krüger also began a family in these economically difficult years. He married in 1923 and his first son was born in 1929. He joined the NSDAP at the end of 1929. In 1933 he was in temporary charge of SS Abschnitt III (Berlin), but then switched to the SA, where he was appointed to senior positions. In 1935, however, he was to return to the SS.[50]

Friedrich Jeckeln was born in 1895. He was unable to finish his mechanical-engineering degree because of the outbreak of the World War. He volunteered for the army and achieved the rank of lieutenant, and from 1917 onwards was a pilot in the Flying Corps. He married in 1918 and administered an estate that belonged to his father-in-law. However, they soon fell out with one another. Jeckeln concluded from the behaviour of his father-in-law that, as he told Himmler some years later, he must have married into a family of Jewish extraction. This notion (for which there was no evidence) resulted in his becoming increasingly alienated from his wife. From then onwards he spent a considerable amount of time with a group of former officers, among whom, as he admitted, he 'sometimes consumed a significant amount of alcohol'. Finally, he left the farm and he and his wife separated. During the following years he tried in vain to establish himself in another profession. He married for a second time, but got into considerable financial difficulties as a result of old debts owed to his father-in-law and the maintenance payments due to his first wife, and had to declare himself bankrupt. 'I felt a broken man and was financially ruined.

I couldn't find a job and get settled', as he subsequently put it when describing this period in his life to Himmler. It was while in this depressing personal situation that he joined the NSDAP in 1929, at the beginning of the economic crisis, and in the following year the SS. When his divorced wife once again complained to Himmler that her former husband was behind with maintenance payments, Jeckeln responded: 'Only when Germany is free will I be able to put right everything that has been brought about by the decline of our nation and fatherland.' Thus, for him the Nazi 'seizure of power' came as his salvation.[51]

Werner Lorenz was born in 1891 and went to a military cadet school. He joined the army in 1912 and became an officer in 1914. He described his career during the post-war period in his curriculum vitae as follows: 'After the war ended, his regiment was deployed on frontier guard duties; until June 1919 he commanded a squadron of his regiment. He was then discharged. Since 1929 actively involved in the NSDAP. Joined the Danzig SS in January 1930', which he subsequently built up. Significantly, his curriculum vitae does not mention his civilian life at all. In his SS personal file his occupation is given as 'soldier'.[52]

Kurt Wittje was born in January 1894 and, from June 1932 onwards, was leader of SS Abschnitt IX (Würzburg). He was one of the few high-ranking SS leaders who managed to get taken on by the Reichswehr as an officer during the 1920s. However, in 1928 he had to leave the army because of suspicions of homosexual activities, and joined the board of a limited company. He joined the SS in 1931; he wisely kept the reason for his discharge from the army to himself.[53]

The leaders of Abschnitt V (Essen), Karl Zech, Abschnitt X (Kiel), Paul Moder, and Abschnitt XVI (Zwickau), Heinrich Schmauser, all of them former army officers, had had to follow similar careers that they did not consider appropriate to their social standing, such as 'commercial employee, miner and mining official',[54] 'mail order manager, clerk',[55] or 'in banking'.[56]

Among the high-ranking SS leaders there are three who, in terms of their birth and personal circumstances, can definitely be described as upper class. Thus, on the basis of his birth Josias, Hereditary Prince of Waldeck and Pyrmont, was certainly an exception among the high-ranking SS leaders. Born in 1896, the prince had fought in the World War, was discharged from the army as a lieutenant, and had subsequently studied agriculture and economics at Munich University. It was there that he had got to know

Himmler.[57] In 1923 he broke off his studies without having graduated. To begin with, he was involved in the Jungdeutscher Orden, which he left in 1926. He joined the SS in November 1929, where, in September 1930, he became Himmler's adjutant and then his 'chief of staff'.[58] The leader of Abschnitt VI (Breslau), Udo von Woyrsch, who was born in 1895, had a full-time job managing his father's estate.[59] The later Munich police chief, Friedrich Karl Freiherr von Eberstein, who was born in 1894, became a factory owner in the 1920s after a standard military career as a cadet, war volunteer, army officer, and member of a Free Corps. He joined the SS in 1929, but was provisionally transferred to the SA, where he filled a number of high-ranking posts.[60]

Only three of the early high-ranking SS officers had not achieved the rank of officer in the military. Sepp Dietrich, who was born in 1892, came from a humble background and began his career in the hotel business. He was called up into the army in 1914, discharged as a sergeant in 1919, and then joined the Free Corps. Between 1920 and 1923 he worked for the Bavarian state police, and then, thanks to the head of the Munich NSDAP, Christian Weber, in the latter's petrol station. From 1925 onwards he was involved with the NSDAP; he joined the party and the SS in 1928. Two months later he had already become leader of the Munich SS Standarte and, in July 1929, SS-Oberführer for the whole of Bavaria. In July 1930, as Oberführer South, he took over responsibility for the SS throughout southern Germany. He was promoted to Gruppenführer in December 1931 and from February 1932 was in charge of Hitler's bodyguard, which was to operate from 1933 onwards as the staff guards at the Reich Chancellery and was to form the basis of the 'Leibstandarte'.[61]

Kurt Daluege, who was born in 1897 the son of a middle-ranking civil servant, served in the army from 1916 onwards, where, like Dietrich, he achieved the rank of sergeant. After the defeat he was involved in various paramilitary organizations and took part in confrontations with Polish militia. From 1921 onwards he studied at the Technical University in Berlin and graduated with a diploma in civil engineering. At the same time he was involved with radical right-wing organizations, and joined the NSDAP in 1923. To begin with he was active in the SA; indeed, he was the leader of the SA in Berlin–Brandenburg from 1926 to 1929. However, the fact that Walter Stennes was appointed SA-Oberführer for northern Germany instead of himself may have persuaded Daluege to accept Hitler's advice and transfer to the SS in the summer of 1930, where he took over the leadership of the Berlin SS. In this role Daluege was to play a decisive part in the party's internal surveillance of the unruly Berlin SA. In civilian life Daluege had succeeded in establishing a conventional middle-class existence for himself that was markedly different from the personal biographies of the other high-ranking SS leaders. He earned his living as a senior manager in the Berlin city department for refuse disposal, was married in 1926, and had three children.[62]

Among the former NCOs was Alfred Rodenbücher, who was leader of the SS Abschnitt XIV (Bremen) from October 1932 onwards. Born in 1900, he had joined the Navy in 1916 as a cabin boy and ultimately been promoted to the rank of chief petty officer. In 1930 he transferred from the Navy to the career of a low-ranking civil servant. His appointment to a leading position in the rapidly expanding SS offered him the prospect of a much more prestigious career.[63]

Rodenbücher, like Himmler, belonged to the so-called war youth generation, who, while being fully aware of and experiencing the effects of the war, had not actually been able to fight in it. Among this age cohort, which formed a definite minority within the SS leadership, was Fritz Weitzel, who was born in Frankfurt in 1904. An apprentice locksmith, Weitzel had at first been a member of the Socialist Workers' Youth organization, but then transferred his allegiance to the NSDAP in 1923. Soon after the founding of the SS in 1925 he took over its organization in Frankfurt. After being appointed to various different posts, at the end of 1930 he was made leader of the SS in the whole of western Germany. In 1930 he was also a successful candidate in the Reichstag election, which gave him financial security.[64] In 1927 Weitzel had been sentenced to a month's imprisonment for his involvement in an abortion case.[65] When a party member reported this to Himmler, he replied that he was fully aware of the circumstances and that he was of the 'opinion that Party comrade Weitzel's honour had not been affected or damaged in any way by the whole affair'. He would ignore any further 'letters of denunciation' in this matter.[66] In fact the sentence did not have any negative effect on Weitzel's career.

Wilhelm Rediess, who was born in 1900 in Heinsberg in the lower Rhine area, served a few months in the army from June 1918 but was not sent to the front. A qualified electrician, after his discharge from the army Rediess could not find employment in his trade. To begin with he worked as a trainee in agriculture, and then, between 1924 and 1928, after having undergone the appropriate training, was employed as a skilled mechanic in various firms. 'I became unemployed after the collapse of my firm as a result of the economic crisis', he noted in his curriculum vitae. After the occupation of the Rhineland by French troops in 1923 he joined the Völkisch-Social-Bloc, which later went over to the NSDAP en masse. In 1925 he became the leader of an SA Sturm in Düsseldorf. He joined the SS in 1930 and took over Abschnitt XI (Koblenz) on 1 January 1931.[67]

With a remarkable instinct Himmler had gathered round himself a group of men who, although they no more matched the high ideals of the SS than he did himself, were nevertheless men on whose loyalty he could rely. Many of them were dependent on him for their very material existence, a situation which, when necessary, he knew well how to exploit. This, then, was the team with which he set about building up his organization.

A mass organization in the making

At the end of 1931 Himmler gave orders that the regional structure of the SS should be changed to conform to that of the SA. He subordinated the SS Abschnitte to two Gruppenkommandos (one for south, the other for north Germany) and appointed Weitzel and Dietrich as their chiefs.[68] In the course of 1932 they were joined by further Gruppenkommandos—East, South-East, and West—out of which the Oberabschnitte later emerged. Below this level there was a continuing increase in the number of Abschnitte. In January 1932 Himmler ordered the creation of SS Flying Units separate from the NS Flying Corps, in order to attract those interested in flying and gliding to the SS.[69] In April 1932, when the paramilitary units (SA and SS) were temporarily banned, the SS contained more than 25,000 members; after the ban had been lifted in June there were already more than 41,000.[70] This meant that the SS had succeeded in reaching the 10 per-cent quota fixed by Röhm, indeed in slightly exceeding it. The whole organization was financed half by membership contributions and half by contributions from so-called sponsor members.[71]

In order to cope with these changes Himmler concentrated on consolidating the Munich headquarters. On 15 July 1932 he created an SS Administration Office (SS Verwaltungsamt) under a businessman, Gerhard Schneider. However, the 'Reich Finance Administration' under Paul Magnus Weickert was dissolved in October 1932. Weickert himself was dismissed from the SS, possibly on the grounds of embezzlement. This gave

Schneider the opportunity to expand the Administration Office, which was to fill a key position within the SS headquarters. However, in 1934 he too had to go because of embezzlement. The Weickert and Schneider cases were not the only errors of judgment that Himmler was to make in his appointment of key personnel.[72]

In addition to such organizational measures, Himmler tried to unify the SS's rapidly growing leadership corps in various other ways. For example, he arranged a special leadership course at the party's so-called Reich Leadership School in Munich, to run from 31 January to 20 February 1932.[73] For the first time dressed in his black uniform, which after the course was introduced into the SS generally in order to distinguish it from the brown shirts of the SA,[74] he used this opportunity to give several lectures which, according to his later adjutant, Karl Wolff, covered 'world revolution, the Jews, Freemasons, Christianity, and racial problems'.[75] In 1939, on the occasion of the tenth anniversary of Himmler's appointment, Wolff described the impression his first meeting with Himmler made on him: 'What impressed all those who had not yet met the Reichsführer-SS face to face was how, when marching slowly along the ranks, his clear eyes looked into our very souls. From this moment onwards he had succeeded in establishing the personal link that bound each one of us to his strong personality.'[76]

During a post-war interrogation by the Munich prosecutor's office, Wolff's memory of Himmler's appearance was rather different: 'By contrast, Himmler's appearance, pale and wearing a pince-nez, was rather disappointing. He lacked a strict military bearing and the self-confidence vis-à-vis an audience that one needs [. . .] If you talked to him one to one after his lectures his gleaming pince-nez no longer gave his eyes a distracting coldness and they could suddenly seem warm and even humorous.'[77]

It may not appear surprising that the description of Himmler's appearance that Wolff gave to the prosecutor differed from that in the piece celebrating his anniversary. Many of his contemporaries, however, noticed the different sides to Himmler's personality revealed in Wolff's descriptions—the coldness, the attempt to project authority, the insecurity which he endeavoured to disguise with informality and joviality. The contradiction between Himmler's claim to be a member of an elite and his attempt to project a soldierly presence and the reality of his average appearance was only underlined by the smart black uniform which he had now adopted. Even the fact that Himmler had tried to give himself a suitable image, with a very short military haircut and a moustache, could not disguise the 'pale, whey face,

Ill. 7. Himmler gained in self-confidence with his success in building up the SS. But he tried to conceal his continuing awkwardness in relations with other people by adopting an ostentatiously 'soldierly' bearing.

the receding chin and the blank expression' that 'Putzi' Hanfstaengel, Hitler's foreign-press chief, who for a time shared an office with Himmler, could remember so well.[78]

During a six-hour train journey that he shared with Himmler, Albert Krebs, a Nazi functionary from Hamburg, gained the impression of a man who was strenuously trying, through his self-presentation, to compensate for what he felt he lacked. According to Krebs: 'Himmler behaved coarsely and he showed off by adopting the manners of a freebooter and expressing anti-bourgeois views, although in doing so he was clearly only trying to disguise his innate insecurity and awkwardness.' However, what Krebs found really intolerable was the 'stupid and endless prattle that I had to listen to'. Never in his life had he heard 'such political rubbish served up in such a concentrated form and that from a man who had been to university and who was professionally engaged in politics'. Himmler's conversation had been 'a peculiar mixture of warlike bombast, the saloon-bar views of a petty bourgeois, and the enthusiastic prophecies of a sectarian preacher'.[79] Evidently Himmler's constant urge to express his views, for which he had continually criticized himself in his diaries, had not waned in the meantime. In fact the opposite was true, and, when combined with the self-confidence which he ostentatiously displayed, it clearly got on the nerves of those around him.

During the years 1929–32 a centrally directed and highly structured mass organization had been created from what had begun as a few dozen 'protection squads' (*Schutzstaffeln*), which were scattered across the whole of the Reich, consisting of no more than a few hundred men and function- ing mainly as bodyguards for Nazi leaders. This success was not primarily due to Himmler himself, but above all to the fact that, as a newly appointed Reichsführer-SS, in 1929–30 he found himself in the middle of an histori- cally unique process of political radicalization and mobilization, which worked in favour of the NSDAP. To begin with, his contribution lay essentially in creating organizational structures which made it possible to divert from the flood of hundreds of thousands of predominantly young men who wanted to join the SA a certain proportion into the SS, and at the same time to keep pace with this tremendous growth.

During these years Himmler demonstrated for the first time in his life real organizational talent. The strictly hierarchical structure into which he was integrated as Reichsführer-SS was evidently much more congenial to him than the more opaque situation that had confronted him as secretary of the Lower Bavarian Gau or as deputy Propaganda Chief. In those positions he continually had to mediate between the different views held by party headquarters and the rank and file, a role which he clearly found difficult. Moreover, he had also developed an—albeit vague—idea of how the SS should develop, which went far beyond the protection of NSDAP leaders and the provision of an internal party intelligence service. He envisaged an elite guard, associated with the idea of racial selection, which would have the utopian future task of reviving the 'Nordic race'. And he had recognized that, in order to strengthen its position within the Nazi movement, one thing was essential: absolute 'loyalty' to the party leadership, through which the SS could differentiate itself from the SA.

Himmler and the end of the Republic

Despite repeated electoral successes, the NSDAP did not succeed in forming a government. According to the Weimar Constitution, the Reich President was by no means obliged to appoint the leader of the largest party as Chancellor. On the contrary, the Constitution permitted him to rule without parliament, thanks to his power to issue emergency decrees. If a parliamentary majority opposed government policy, he could dissolve the legislature.

In the spring of 1932 it became clear that the Brüning government, which had hitherto been supported by Reich President Hindeburg's emergency decrees and by the SPD in parliament, was coming to an end. Of all things it turned out to be the ban on the SA and the SS, which Brüning had issued in April, that initiated the demise of his government. General Kurt von Schleicher, who had opposed the ban on 'military-political' grounds, spun a wide-ranging intrigue against the Chancellor, which eventually led to his fall.[80]

Von Schleicher made an agreement with Hitler behind the scenes: Hitler offered to support a new presidential government if the NSDAP's paramilitary organizations were once more allowed to operate freely and if new elections were held. In return, Schleicher did his best to undermine Brüning's position with Hindenburg. Hindenburg finally dismissed Brüning on 30 May 1932, and appointed Franz von Papen, an old friend of Schleicher's, as the new Reich Chancellor. Von Schleicher took on the post of Reich

Defence Minister. The Reichstag was dissolved in accordance with the agreement with Hitler, and new elections fixed for 31 July. The ban on the SA and SS was lifted punctually in mid-June to coincide with the start of the election campaign. On 20 July the Papen government replaced the Social Democrat-led government of Prussia with a 'Reich Commissar', and thereby removed one of the Weimar Republic's last defensive bastions.

In these elections the NSDAP achieved its greatest triumph hitherto; it won 37.4 per cent of the vote. After this success—the party had once again managed to double its vote compared with the previous election of September 1930—the NSDAP assumed that it was about to seize power. In east Germany Nazi activists stepped up their campaign of violence to produce a wave of terror. They were in the process of breaking with the party's 'policy of legality' and moving towards an open revolt against the state. On 1 August 1932, the day after the Reichstag election, the SA and SS launched a series of bomb attacks and assaults on the NSDAP's opponents in Königsberg. A communist city councillor was murdered, and the publisher of the Social Democrat newspaper *Königsberger Volkszeitung*, as well as the right-wing liberal former district governor (*Regierungspräsident*) of Königsberg and another communist functionary, were seriously injured. In the coming days this campaign of terror was extended to the whole of East Prussia and then to the province of Silesia, with further attacks and murders.[81]

There is clear evidence that it was Himmler who was primarily responsible for the Königsberg terror campaign and gave the orders to Waldemar Wappenhaus, the leader of the East Prussian Standarte. There is a letter in Wappenhaus's SS personal file dated 1938, in which, commenting to the SS's head of personnel on accusations that had been made against him, he referred to old 'services' he had rendered. After all, 'in 1932, as leader of the Königsberg Standarte', he had 'carried out the RFSS's order to finish off the communist chiefs' and, as a result, had suffered 'police persecution as a wanted man'.[82]

Wappenhaus's reference to the way in which orders were issued at the time is a rare document. Naturally, in the quasi-civil war situation of the years 1930–3 documents relating to political murders were not kept by the SS, and although after the takeover of power there was much talk of the 'heroic deeds' of the 'time of struggle', the unpleasant details of the terror campaigns of those days were concealed. In future Himmler too preferred to remain silent about his role in these violent political conflicts.

Violence meted out to political opponents, their 'elimination', was never a moral problem for Himmler. As we have seen, during his student days he had already played an active part in paramilitary organizations and come to terms with the idea of a civil war. He had been involved in an armed putsch. He regarded the post-war conflicts as merely an extension of the World War, for which he had prepared so thoroughly during his military service. As far as he was concerned, the Weimar Republic's years of stability were simply a short interlude in the struggle against 'Marxism', which had to be destroyed.

In August 1932, by taking vigorous measures, the police and judiciary managed once again to put a stop to the wave of violence launched by Nazi supporters in eastern Germany. It was against the background of these conflicts that, on 13 August, the decisive meeting took place between the election victor and the Reich President, at which—and that was the firm conviction of the Nazis—Hindenburg would offer Hitler the office of Reich Chancellor. The Reich President, however, merely asked Hitler to

Ill. 8. Himmler's election to the Reichstag in September 1930 gave him financial security and immunity from prosecution. However, as a parliamentarian he was almost invisible. After giving up the Reich Propaganda department to Goebbels, Himmler concentrated on his leadership of the SS. Re-elected in July 1932, he along with the other Nazi deputies, swore an oath of personal loyalty to Hitler on 29 August in the Hotel Kaiserhof in Berlin.

cooperate with the new government and, after the latter declined to do so, published a statement in which he publicly repudiated Hitler.[83]

From this point onwards the NSDAP came under increasing pressure. For years its supporters had been asked to make great sacrifices and been promised power in return, but now it appeared that, despite enormous electoral successes, the prospect of their taking over the government had receded into the far distance. The party leadership's 'tactic of legality' appeared to have failed. When, in the middle of September, the Reichstag was dissolved and the party once again found itself facing the rigours of an election, its supporters became disappointed and apathetic. This was particularly true of the SA, but also affected the otherwise so reliable and disciplined SS, which in any case during the second half of the year had seen, by comparison with the rapid growth of the preceding months, only a modest increase in membership.[84]

In September 1932 a number of internal reports on the mood in the SS reflect the mixed reactions within the organization. Thus Abschnitt IV (Brunswick) reported to headquarters that the 'dissolution of the Reichstag and the resultant delay in the seizure of power initially caused the SS to be somewhat depressed'. But 'belief in our final victory is unbroken [...] the troops are filled with a revolutionary spirit faithful to the National Socialist programme',[85] a sentence which implies a pointed criticism of the 'legal' tactics of the party leadership, which were precisely not 'revolutionary'.

The leader of SS-Gruppe East reported: 'the mood of the SS in my Group area is good and has by no means given way to depression.' However, the reporter then immediately qualified this statement by commenting: 'It is only economic worries that make it more difficult for individuals to perform the duties they have taken on; it is only their financial concerns that make them vulnerable to depression.'[86]

According to Gruppe South, the mood within the south German SS was 'normal'. However, 'our movement's failure to take power [...] has produced a certain amount of depression and insecurity'.[87] Gruppe South-East (Silesia) reported that in general the mood was 'good'; however, in some formations 'there is discontent because the political situation is uncertain'.[88] Gruppe West reported: 'the mood among the SS in Group West is very good, the SS's fighting spirit is revolutionary, belief in victory and in the Führer is unshakeable',[89] and, similarly, Abschnitt VII (Danzig) noted that 'the mood' was 'calm and confident'.[90]

The discontent in the SS hinted at here manifested itself among other things in increased tension with the SA, whose situation—they felt themselves cheated of their reward after years of 'commitment' to the movement—was almost desperate.[91] In the middle of December 1932 Röhm noted, in a confidential circular to the highest-ranking SA leaders and the Reichsführer-SS, that there had been an increase, 'recently to an alarming extent', in the number of 'complaints about a deterioration in the relationship between the SA and SS'. He, therefore, requested his Inspector-General, Curt von Ulrich, to call a meeting of the highest-ranking SA leaders with a delegation of SS led by Himmler. The date was fixed for 10 January 1933.[92]

However, by then the general political situation had long since changed. In the election of 6 November the Nazi Party suffered losses for the first time; it could secure only 33.1 per cent of the vote. Right-wing conservatives saw this result as a caesura: the NSDAP appeared to have passed the high-point of its success; now it ought to be possible to keep it under control within a coalition government.

At the beginning of December 1932 General von Schleicher succeeded in asserting his authority in a confrontation with von Papen. He made it clear to the cabinet that the Reichswehr would not be in a position to control the opposition forces of both Left and Right simultaneously. Thus, another way out of the crisis had to be found. When Hindenburg appointed him as von Papen's successor in a cabinet that was otherwise hardly altered, von Schleicher was convinced that he could come up with another solution. Claiming the need to give priority to a work-creation programme, the new Chancellor endeavoured to form a 'cross-party front' made up of trades unions, professional organizations, Reichswehr, and Nazis, calculating that he could split off the 'left' wing of the NSDAP around Gregor Strasser from the rest of the party.

Strasser did indeed enter discussions with von Schleicher on the matter, but in the process isolated himself from the rest of the Nazi leadership, finally resigning from all his party offices on 8 December. Although Strasser had thereby become *persona non grata* in the NSDAP, Himmler still maintained contact with him. Even as late as April 1933 he employed Strasser, who was now working as an estate agent, to sell his property in Waldtrudering.[93]

In the meantime von Papen, who was still highly regarded by Hindenburg, was working behind the scenes to construct a new government involving the Nazis. The notorious first meeting between him and Hitler took place on 4 January 1933 at the Cologne home of the banker Kurt Freiherr von Schroeder. Himmler was actively involved, and indeed played a significant role, in the ongoing negotiations. A few days later, on 10 January, Himmler, accompanied by Hitler's economic adviser Wilhelm Keppler, visited the Berlin businessman Joachim von Ribbentrop and, in Hitler's name, asked whether he could arrange another meeting. On 18 January the two met again in Ribbentrop's villa, where Hitler, Röhm, and Himmler lunched with von Papen. According to Ribbentrop, Hitler used this opportunity once more to request that he be given the Chancellorship. Von Papen declined the request on the grounds that Hindenburg would not accept it. In fact, he said that he himself wanted to become Chancellor, with Hitler's support. But Hitler was not interested.[94]

A few days later—in the meantime, Franz Seldte, the leader of the veterans' organization the Stahlhelm, had declared his support for Hitler—von Papen changed his mind and declared himself willing to let Hitler become Chancellor. It was largely under his influence that Hindenburg was also persuaded to change his mind. Hindenburg now informed von Schleicher that he was not prepared to protect him from the Reichstag majority by granting him another dissolution of parliament. This obliged von Schleicher to resign and paved the way for a Hitler–Papen government.

PART
II

Inside The Third Reich

7

The Takeover of the Political Police

On 30 January 1933 Hitler became Chancellor of a coalition government. Six months later the Nazis had taken control of the whole of the state apparatus, emasculated the Constitution, and become the dominant political force in almost every sphere of life. In brief, this process occurred in the following stages: the emergency decree of 28 February 1933 in response to the Reichstag fire, which suspended the most important civil rights enshrined in the Constitution; the victory of the Nazi-led coalition in the Reichstag election of 5 March; the Enabling Law of 24 March, which neutralized parliament and transferred legislative power to the government; the 'coordination' of the federal states; the elimination of the trades unions as well as of all political parties apart from the NSDAP; finally, the establishment of effective control over all interest groups, social organizations, and clubs right down to local level. By July 1933 the Nazis were in total command of the situation.

This takeover of power in stages was carried out by a clever combination of measures 'from above' and quasi-revolutionary 'actions' by the party's rank and file. But terror played a central role.[1] Its effects were devastating. Nevertheless, during this phase it was by no means organized in a uniform manner or carefully coordinated. It was only during the course of the so-called 'seizure of power' that the Nazis succeeded in constructing a terror apparatus, and it would take quite a time before they had created a uniform system covering the Reich as a whole. Himmler became the key figure in this process and, in the end, was able to establish his authority in the face of all his rivals and opponents.

Bavaria as the springboard

Essentially, the Nazis used the following political mechanisms to combat and terrorize their political opponents, and it was only gradually that they integrated them into a coordinated system: the takeover of the political police, its detachment from the regular police organization, and its utilization in the interests of the new regime; the appointment of SA and SS men as auxiliary police; the use of so-called 'protective custody', in other words, the indefinite internment of persons without due process,[2] as well as the establishment of numerous detention camps, in which the actual or alleged opponents of the new regime were subjected to unrestrained and arbitrary treatment. The whole situation was complicated by the fact that a power struggle developed within the various German states between the SA, SS, and the party's political organization over who was to control the various instruments of terror, a struggle that produced different results in each state.

Hermann Göring, the second-most powerful man in the Nazi Party, was appointed acting Minister of the Interior in Prussia, the largest German state. He used his position to take control of the police and, by removing the political police from the general police administration, he was able to create a 'Secret State Police' (*Geheime Staatspolizei* = Gestapo) for combating political opponents. On 22 February he began recruiting 'auxiliary police' from the ranks of the SA and SS. However, both organizations began at once to exploit the situation by assuming a quasi-police role independently of the police authorities and detaining tens of thousands of alleged or actual opponents. They held them in makeshift camps, which they operated either autonomously or acting for the state authorities, who had effectively transferred to the SA and SS responsibility for guarding these prisoners.[3]

Bavaria, the second-largest state, was the last to fall victim to the Nazi seizure of power. On 9 March Reich Minister of the Interior Wilhelm Frick appointed the retired Lieutenant-General Franz Ritter von Epp, who was one of the most prominent Nazis in the state, to be Reich Governor in Bavaria under the pretext that Heinrich Held's conservative government was incapable of maintaining order. The 'proof' for this assertion was provided by SA and SS units, whose rowdy demonstrations in Munich guaranteed the requisite disorder.[4] On the same evening as his appointment von Epp assigned to the Nazi Gauleiter of Upper Bavaria, Adolf Wagner, the post of acting Bavarian Interior Minister, and to Heinrich Himmler the post of acting Munich police chief. Department VI of police headquarters, which controlled the political police, and which during the Weimar Republic had been responsible for combating political extremism throughout Bavaria, was taken over by Heydrich, who immediately began to build it up as an effective base.[5]

Ill. 9. [The notice reads]:

Business closed by the police on account of profiteering.
Proprietor is in protective custody in Dachau
The Bavarian Political Police Commander
Signed: Himmler

With the SS camp at Dachau, Himmler, as chief of the political police in Bavaria, had created a model for the future system of Nazi concentration camps. Right from the start Himmler understood how to exploit the terror associated with Dachau with carefully targeted publicity. As early as spring 1933 there was no need to explain what was implied by a reference to Dachau.

On 12 March acting police chief Heinrich Himmler gave a press conference, at which he commented on the mass arrests that he had ordered
during the preceding days:

I have made quite extensive use of protective custody [. . .] I felt compelled to do
this because in many parts of the city there has been so much agitation that it has
been impossible for me to guarantee the safety of those particular individuals who
have provoked it. I must emphasize one point in particular: for us a citizen of the
Jewish faith is just as much a citizen as someone who is not of the Jewish faith and
his life and property are subject to the same protection. We make no distinction in
this respect.

Apart from that, he had decided to arrest all the leaders and functionaries of
the Communist Party (KPD) and of the Reichsbanner and the Iron Front
(i.e. the paramilitary units of the democratic parties and the trades unions).[6]
On 15 March, six days after Himmler's appointment as acting Munich
police chief, Wagner appointed him to be 'political adviser to the Interior
Ministry', thereby giving him effective responsibility for the political police
throughout the state.[7] Before the month was out Himmler had been
appointed commander of the Bavarian auxiliary political police. This appointment was in his capacity as Reichsführer-SS, which meant that he
could now appoint SS members to be auxiliary policemen; initially, a
maximum complement of 1,020 was envisaged.[8] On 1 April he was
officially appointed 'Commander of the Bavarian Political Police'. Himmler now controlled the political police, the auxiliary political police, and
'those concentration camps that already exist and those that are still to be
established' throughout the state of Bavaria.[9] Ten days later—in the meantime, Himmler had given up his post as Munich police chief to SA-
Obergruppenführer August Schneidhuber[10]—he was given responsibility
for all matters relating to protective custody.[11]
As a result of these appointments and assignments of responsibility
Himmler had accumulated a considerable amount of power within a very
short period of time. He was in charge of a special police force that had been
removed from the regular police structure. It was tightly organized, entirely
focused on combating political opponents, and permitted to deploy the SS
within its recently assigned area of responsibilities. He could arbitrarily put
people in protective custody in his concentration camps, who would then
be indefinitely subject to his whim. Above all, as commander of the political
police—and this was certainly one reason for his appointment—Himmler

represented an effective counterweight to the special commissars whom Röhm had appointed from the ranks of the SA in order to control the Bavarian administration. While it was true that the special commissars had police responsibilities, for which they had the SA auxiliary police at their disposal, Himmler could give directives to the SA special commissars in matters concerning the *political* police.[12]

On 15 March the political police had already begun to establish a camp for prisoners in protective custody in the grounds of an old gunpowder factory in the town of Dachau near Munich.[13] Himmler announced the measure on 20 March, justifying it on the grounds of 'state security'. No attention would be paid to 'petty objections', and there were plans for an establishment of 5,000 prisoners. Himmler announced brashly that enquiries to police headquarters about the length of protective custody simply held up the police unnecessarily. The result was that 'every enquiry would merely mean that the prisoner would have to spend an extra day in protective custody'.[14]

Initially the Dachau camp was guarded by a squad of Munich police. However, acting in his capacity as head of the Bavarian auxiliary political police, on 2 April Himmler ordered the camp to be handed over to the SS.[15] With this move Himmler had wangled for the SS a task that officially came under the remit of, and was financed by, the state. On 11 April the Munich police left the camp in which there were at the time over 200 prisoners. Immediately after taking over the camp the SS indulged in an orgy of violence which cost four Jewish prisoners their lives. There were further murders, with prisoners either dying from mistreatment or being shot.[16]

Subsequent investigations revealed that the camp commandant, Hilmar Wäckerle, had issued 'special regulations', according to which 'martial law' was to prevail in the camp. Indeed, there was a camp court over which he presided and which could even pass death sentences.[17] The indescribable conditions existing in Dachau not only became widely known,[18] but led to the Munich prosecutor's office becoming involved. In the course of his investigations the public prosecutor, Wintersberger, demanded from Himmler an explanation for four unaccountable deaths, and showed him, among other things, photographs of the disfigured corpses. The investigations came to nothing, but the affair did produce sufficient pressure to prompt von Epp to call a meeting attended by, among others, the Bavarian Ministers of Justice and the Interior, at which Himmler was obliged to agree to replace Wäckerle as commandant of Dachau.[19]

Himmler found a candidate to succeed him who at this moment was at the lowest point of his life, and who gratefully seized the chance offered him to make a new start. This was Theodor Eicke, the later Inspector of Concentration Camps and leader of the SS–Death's Head military units formed from concentration camp guards.[20] The appointment of Eicke, one of the first important ones made by Himmler following the seizure of power, is a classic example of his personnel policy. It involved recruiting failures who were turned into compliant subordinates by a mixture of strict discipline, gestures of concern for their welfare, and also the appearance of trust, as these offenders were assigned tasks that they had to carry out largely independently.

Born in 1892, Eicke was a military paymaster who, after his discharge from military service, had tried unsuccessfully to join the police several times and had finally ended up in charge of security at the IG Farben plant in Ludwigshafen. Having joined the party in 1928, in 1930 he was given the job of establishing the SS in Ludwigshafen, a task that resulted in his becoming an SS-Standartenführer the following year. In 1932 he was discovered constructing a bomb and arrested; IG Farben dismissed him without notice. According to his own account, the affair was the result of a trap set for him by the party's Palatinate Gau, with which he was permanently at odds, and this explanation is not totally implausible. Be that as it may, he was sentenced to two years' imprisonment. During a period of prison-leave granted on health grounds, he received an order from Himmler to escape to Italy. During his journey there he met the Reichsführer in Munich, who assured him of his goodwill and support and promoted him to the rank of Oberführer.

In February 1933 Eicke returned to Germany, assuming that under the new regime his punishment would be suspended. Shortly afterwards he once more became involved in serious internal party conflict. Himmler ordered him to come to Munich and gave him a dressing down on account of his behaviour. According to Eicke, he made him promise in future not to become involved in political matters or in those involving the SS.[21] However, on 21 March Eicke was arrested once more because he was considered guilty, possibly unjustly, of having been involved in an unauthorized action by the Ludwigshafen SS which had led to a confrontation with the police. After going on hunger strike he was transferred to a mental hospital in Würzburg, whereupon Himmler removed him from the list of the SS (a milder form of discharge than dismissal), on the grounds of his having broken his word of honour, although the Reichsführer acknowledged his 'poor health and nervous breakdown' as mitigating circumstances.[22]

During this period Eicke sent several letters appealing to Himmler, including one of eighteen sides justifying his position. The director of the clinic in which Eicke was held, Werner Heyde, told Himmler that in his view Eicke was not mentally unbalanced (a few years later Heyde was to provide Eicke, who was by then Inspector of Concentration Camps, with hereditary-biological assessments, and later on played a leading role in the 'euthanasia' murders).[23] Himmler responded by supporting Eicke's family with a gift of 200 Reich marks and requested Heyde to release Eicke from the hospital at Whitsun. He was intending 'to employ him in some way, if possible in a state post'.[24]

By appointing Eicke to be commandant of Dachau camp on 26 June, Himmler was effectively deploying someone as his tool who owed his rehabilitation entirely to him. Eicke was fully aware of the fact: 'If my Führer had not achieved power in Germany,' he wrote to Himmler in November 1933, 'I would have spent all my life going to prison and would never have been able to take up public office.'[25]

Eicke did not disappoint Himmler. Within a short time he had developed a type of regime in Dachau that differed markedly from that in the other concentration camps during the early Nazi years: the so-called Dachau model.[26] Among the essential elements of this system were: the sealing off of the camp from the outside world, in particular the determination to prevent escapes; the separation of the guards from the commandant's office; the introduction of work details for the prisoners; systematized use of force through the introduction of a uniform set of punishments, the 'Disciplinary and Punishment Code';[27] as well as strict discipline for the guards, who were subject to a specific disciplinary code.[28] The aim of creating the impression that the old arbitrary regime had now been replaced by one that was strict but nevertheless bound by certain rules was an additional aspect of this new system. In actual fact the camp was ruled by arbitrary terror; the prisoners lived in continual fear for their lives. Eicke was concerned above all to prevent arbitrary murders by the guards; the right to kill prisoners should be confined solely to the camp authorities.

The 'Disciplinary and Punishment Code' made it clear that within the camp any behaviour by a prisoner could be construed as encouragement to protest or mutiny, in other words, as a crime that carried the death penalty. It stated that anyone who 'makes political statements designed to encourage protest, or makes provocative speeches', anyone who 'collects, receives, buries, or passes on by word of mouth or in any other way information, whether true or false, designed for hostile propaganda, anyone who encourages others to flee or to commit a crime shall be hanged as an agitator by right of revolutionary law'. A prisoner who physically attacked a guard, encouraged another to mutiny, or 'who during a march or during work yells, shouts, agitates or holds speeches' would be 'shot on the spot as a mutineer' or hanged. Whereas under Eicke's predecessor there had been 'martial law', now the decision over life and death was no longer bound by a formal process, and in fact murders did not cease. However, as a result of the camp being sealed off, the improved discipline of the guards, and the systematization of terror, the murder cases could be more easily concealed, so that the judiciary could not find any justification for intervening. In general the murders were portrayed as suicide or as the prisoner having been shot while trying to escape.[29]

The commander of the political police, Heinrich Himmler, on whose authority the 'Disciplinary and Punishment Code' was explicitly based, was responsible for implementing this process of concealment. For it was Himmler who was obliged to inform the Bavarian Interior Ministry about the deaths in Dachau, and who confirmed the falsified accounts of suicide or 'attempts at flight'.[30] For this reason alone it is clear that Himmler was aware of the excesses and murders in Dachau. In other words, he knew that the image projected to the outside world of Dachau as a 'model camp' was a complete distortion of the facts. Himmler visited the camp on a number of occasions. In August 1933 Röhm joined him in inaugurating a memorial stone in memory of Horst Wessel, 'donated' by the prisoners,[31] and in January 1934, on the occasion of a party meeting, he invited the Reich Party leaders and the Gauleiters to look round the camp. In the course of these visits he was reassured that the camp authorities were capable of effectively maintaining the illusion that this was a normal and well-regulated prison camp. In March 1934 Himmler received a letter from the Bavarian Prime Minister, Ludwig Siebert, who had recently visited Dachau, in which he was explicitly congratulated on the conditions in this 'model prison camp'. The letter was published in the German press.[32]

Nevertheless, in December 1933 a series of unexplained deaths in Dachau was the subject of discussion at a meeting of the Bavarian cabinet. The cabinet had already discussed Himmler's performance as commander of the political police on a number of occasions.[33] At this meeting Reich Governor von Epp decided that the investigations into the deaths should not be shelved, as requested by Interior Minister Wagner, acting for Himmler,[34] but instead should be pursued with the full rigour of the law.[35] Thereupon Himmler appealed to Röhm for support. Röhm informed the civil servant in the Ministry of Justice assigned to the political police to deal with the matter that he intended to discuss the affair with Hitler.[36] Röhm and Himmler adopted delaying tactics which in the end proved successful. Nothing happened before the prosecutor involved in the case was transferred in the summer of 1934, and his successor then closed the case. In effect, Dachau had become *terra incognita* for the judiciary.[37]

During the first months of 1933 it was above all communists and Social Democrats who were arrested, several thousand people in all.[38] In June 1933, however, Himmler launched a special action directed against the conservative Bavarian People's Party (BVP), which involved the arrest of all the party's Reichstag and state parliamentary deputies with the exception of Count Eugen von Quadt, Economics Minister in the state government, and which was designed to force the party to dissolve itself.[39] After this had occurred and the BVP functionaries had been released, in August 1933 there were exactly 3,965 persons in protective custody in Bavaria, 2,420 of them in Dachau. Faced with von Epp's demand that he curb the use of protective custody, Himmler continually reduced the numbers. In June 1934 there were 2,204, of whom 1,517 were in Dachau camp.[40]

Himmler had needed only a year in which to construct a closed system consisting of the political police, the SS deployed as auxiliaries, and Dachau concentration camp, which he was able to seal off from any interference by the Bavarian state authorities. Towards the end of this year, a year that had been so successful for him, he began to focus on the political police in the other German states. To begin with, however, he cleverly gave a wide berth to the biggest state, Prussia, where the political police was directly subordinate to its powerful Prime Minister, Hermann Göring.

From state to state

Considering his clumsy behaviour in his previous party posts, Himmler displayed a surprising degree of diplomatic and political skill in the way in which he approached the expansion of his power basis outside Bavaria. In particular, his strategy of placing people he could trust in key positions or winning the loyalty of such persons by conferring on them SS rank proved successful. Himmler succeeded in creating the impression among the regional party bosses that by transferring the political police to the SS, which took the form of appointing Himmler as commander of the political police in the individual states, they were not giving up a decisive power base but rather securing the support of the SS. There was, however, another reason why the Nazi bosses in the federal states were so amenable to Himmler, namely, the continuing lack of discipline of the SA, even after Hitler had officially declared an end to the revolution in June 1933. Its demand for a 'second revolution', and the tensions with the political wing of the NSDAP that resulted from it, persuaded the new rulers in the states that it was in their interest to look for an ally. The fact that in recent years the SS had acquired the reputation of being a disciplined elite organization that was invariably loyal to the party leadership and at the same time completely ruthless in dealing with the enemies of Nazism played an important part in their decision. Its recent 'successes' in dealing with its opponents could be observed in the way Himmler had handled matters in Bavaria.[41] The fact that the SS had an organization that spanned the Reich and operated relatively effectively with its own intelligence service, the SD (*Sicherheitsdienst*), was an additional point in its favour. The SD provided Himmler with an intelligence operation controlling local informants and, by recruiting members of the political police into the SD, he created his own network. In fact, as we shall see, the SD was temporarily involved in a crisis in the summer of 1933. However, by the autumn, when Himmler began to be appointed chief of the political police in the various states, his intelligence service had begun to restore its position.

Himmler also benefited from the fact that in March 1933 the SS was in a position to establish, albeit only to a limited extent, armed units based in barracks. The first of these was a special 'staff guard' for the Führer's personal protection. This was established on 17 March on Hitler's orders by the head of his personal bodyguard, Sepp Dietrich, who had played an important role in the development of the SS in both north and south Germany. The unit, consisting of 120 men, was composed of members of the SA and SS and wore SS uniform. In the spring of 1933 it was assigned to the Prussian state police as an auxiliary police unit, renamed 'Sonderkommando Berlin z.b.V.' (for special assignments), and considerably enlarged. The Wehrmacht took over the military training of what had now become an 800-strong force. This was effectively a small private army which had been created unconstitutionally and illegally, made solely responsible to the Führer, and renamed 'Leibstandarte Adolf Hitler' ('Adolf Hitler's body-guard') during the party rally in September. Its special position was under-lined when, on 9 November, it swore allegiance to Hitler personally. Although Dietrich always emphasized the independence of his force from the Reich leadership of the SS, the Sonderkommando z.b.V. was not only used to protect the dictator but was also deployed to combat political opponents, and thereby contributed towards strengthening the position of the SS and its Reichsführer in the power struggle for control of the instruments of repression in the Reich capital.[42]

In the spring of 1934, in view of the impending conflict with the SA, Himmler succeeded in effectively integrating the force into the SS hier-archy.[43] In 1933 and 1934 further armed 'political units' were created on the initiative of the SS-Oberabschnitte in Munich, Ellwangen, Arolsen, Hamburg, and Wolterdingen.

The Free and Hansa City of Hamburg was the first state to offer to hand over its political police to Himmler. The details of how this happened provide remarkable insights into his tactics.[44] During the course of their seizure of power in Hamburg the Nazis had been unsuccessful in establish-ing a uniform apparatus of repression. Indeed, the opposite was true. As in many other places, there was strong rivalry among various individuals and cliques for control of the terror being exercised against political opponents. Control over the political police, which had been removed from the general police organization, changed hands several times. In addition, there was a Commando z.b.V. directly subordinate to the head of the uniformed police, which had been strengthened by SA auxiliary police, and which carried out arrests and raids to a large extent independently. It was notorious for its numerous illegal acts and bloody excesses. Political opponents were held in two camps, which were subordinate to the judiciary or rather the regular police. The Hamburg SD had been effectively neutralized by the Gauleiter, Karl Kaufmann.[45]

However, Himmler had a good relationship with Gauleiter Kaufmann; they had known each other since 1927 and used the familiar 'du' form of address. In 1933 Himmler made several visits to Hamburg, not only in order to strengthen his ties with Kaufmann but also presumably to make further contacts. Thus, from the start he had supported the appointment of Carl Vincent Krogmann as the senior mayor of Hamburg,[46] and some time during the summer of 1933 he offered Hans Nieland, who had been acting police chief since March 1933 and then became a senator, a high SS rank.[47] After Nieland moved to his Senate post he was replaced as police chief in May 1933 by Wilhelm Boltz, the leader of the Hamburg Naval SA. Boltz, who had the reputation within the SA of being elitist and ostentatiously distanced himself from the proletarian behaviour of the other brown-shirts, was another of Himmler's long-standing acquaintances.[48]

More important, however, was the fact that in October the Nazi leadership in Hamburg decided to appoint Bruno Streckenbach as chief of the political police. He was a member of the SS and another of Himmler's intimates.[49] Gauleiter Kaufmann received the rank of SS-Oberführer,[50] and his close associate, Georg Friedrich Ahrens, was admitted to the SS as a Standartenführer and made head of the local SD.[51] Streckenbach was also admitted to the SD.[52] As a result of these appointments, such a close-knit relationship between party leadership and SS had been established in Hamburg that the local party leadership could assume that the formal takeover of the political police by the SS on 24 November 1933 did not involve ceding any authority in this important area. Indeed, from now on the use of SS personnel for tasks of the local political police would be covered by the highest authority of the SS.

One of Streckenbach's first acts as Hamburg police chief was an official trip to Munich to study the Bavarian model.[53] It did not take him long to apply the example of a uniform system of repression developed there to Hamburg. Fuhlsbüttel prison, where political prisoners were incarcerated and where an SS unit imposed a frightful regime of sadistic brutality, was subordinated to the political police. The final responsibilities remaining with the prison authorities were removed in the summer of 1934.[54]

Himmler had achieved his goal through a combination of building up personal contacts, the wooing of important party figures by assigning them high SS ranks, and the targeted placing of SS members in key positions. He had even made use of the undisciplined behaviour of individual SS men or of whole units (as with the Hamburg SD or the SS Sturm deployed in Fuhlsbüttel) to create the impression that it was through his personal intervention and his appointment of the right people that 'orderly conditions' had been restored.

During these decisive months Himmler was continually on the move in order to find out what was going on in the various state capitals. In December 1933, a few weeks after his success in Hamburg, he was appointed political police chief in Lübeck and Mecklenburg. The exact circumstances of his appointment are not entirely clear. However, the assignment of the rank of SS-Brigadeführer to Friedrich Hildebrandt, the Reich Governor of the two states, in November 1933, together with the fact that Ludwig Obdach, who took over the Mecklenburg political police in November, had been received into the SS shortly beforehand, suggest that Himmler had followed the same tactics in these two northern states as he had in Hamburg.[55]

In Württemberg[56] Himmler had managed to persuade the Reich Governor, Wilhelm Murr, of the need to maintain a section of the SS auxiliary police as an armed force to be deployed for political purposes, in other words, as an armed unit housed in barracks. The fact that the Reich had promised to pay for this played a decisive part in Murr's decision.[57] The presence of this unit provided Himmler with an important power base in Württemberg. His contact man there was Walter Stahlecker, who had been appointed deputy political police chief in May 1933. However, in November he was transferred because he was permanently at odds with his superior, Hermann Mattheiss, who was a strong supporter of the SA.

On 9 December 1933 Himmler was appointed commander of the political police in Württemberg. The decisive reason for this is likely to have been his good relationship with Reich Governor Murr and the latter's desire to rationalize the expensive apparatus of the political police.[58] The fact that, from autumn 1933 onwards, the SS-Oberabschnitt South-West was being run by a dynamic individual based in Stuttgart, in the shape of Werner Best, is also likely to have played a role.[59] However, Himmler was able to secure complete control only in May 1934, when Stahlecker replaced his old boss, Mattheiss, as chief of the political police. Mattheiss was to fall victim to the so-called Röhm putsch on 30 June 1934; Stahlecker made his career in the security police, and in 1941 was appointed commander of Einsatzgruppe A operating in the Baltic states. Murr was granted the rank of SS-Gruppenführer on 9 September 1934.[60]

On 18 December 1933 Himmler took over the political police in Baden.[61] This move was supported not only by Hess in the name of Hitler, but also by the Gauleiter of Baden, Robert Wagner, and by the Baden Interior Minister, Karl Pflaumer, who was a member of the SS. Both of these men appear to have assumed that this would strengthen the position of the Baden political police vis-à-vis attempts by the Reich government to take it over.[62]

In Bremen, where Himmler had first got to know the leading party officials in May 1933, a major conflict erupted in November between the police chief, Theodor Laue, and the local SA, which was notorious for its thuggish behaviour. As a result of this disagreement, Röhm expelled Laue, who was an old SA member, from the brown-shirts, whereupon Laue sought Himmler's support. In fact, Himmler already had an important ally in Bremen in the shape of the chief of the local Gestapo, Erwin Schulz. Schulz had been a member of the political police before 1933 and had already served the SS as an informant. Having prepared the ground in Bremen, Himmler was able to secure his appointment as commander of the political police on 22 December, following brief negotiations with Reich Governor Carl Röver and the mayor Richard Markert.[63] On 5 January 1934 he was appointed commander of the political police in Oldenburg, of which Röver was also the Reich Governor,[64] and between the end of 1933 and the beginning of 1934 Himmler was equally successful in taking over the political police in Anhalt,[65] Hesse,[66] Thuringia,[67] and Saxony.[68]

Brunswick is another case in which it appears that Himmler managed to win over influential officials by assigning them ranks in the SS. His appointment as chief of the political police on 27 January by the Prime Minister, Dietrich Klagges, had the full support of the Reich Governor, Wilhelm Loeper. Loeper had already informed Himmler in December of his wish to be given a rank in the SS appropriate to his position; he was appointed SS-Gruppenführer in February 1934.[69] Klagges was appointed SS-Gruppenführer on the same day as Himmler's appointment as chief of the political police.[70] Himmler's appointment in Brunswick was particularly important because in the summer of 1933 there had been a major clash between Klagges and the SD. Himmler had resolved the issue through a 'tactical retreat',[71] and thereby avoided further tension with the Brunswick party leadership. In April 1934 the political police in Brunswick was taken over by the leader of the SS-Gruppe North-West and head of the Brunswick State Police Office, Friedrich Jeckeln, who enjoyed the confidence of both Himmler and Klagges.[72]

The only obstacles in Himmler's path were posed by the two tiny states of Lippe and Schaumburg-Lippe, where he came up against opposition from the Reich Governor, Alfred Meyer. It was not until April 1934 that he managed to take control of the political police in these states.[73]

Himmler's position as boss of a terror apparatus that was operating effectively in Bavaria and also as the head of the SS, an organization that covered the whole of Germany, enabled him to act as a counterweight to the SA. This will have played an important part in the decision of the various heads of the state governments to let him take over their political police forces. The growing conflict with the SA was increasingly replacing the combating of political opposition in the scale of priorities. The Reichsführer-SS was evidently believed to be capable of dealing with the SA and of coordinating the political police forces. At the beginning of 1934 Himmler had in fact established a 'Central Office' in Munich especially for this purpose.[74] It was also crucial that he never challenged the authority of the local party bosses. On the contrary, he swore unconditional loyalty to them.[75] And in a number of cases the regional leaders did indeed retain authority, at least during the early years, over 'their' political police forces, as can be shown for Baden, Brunswick, Hamburg, Saxony, and Hesse.[76] Himmler was not even in total control of the political police in Bavaria. He could not prevent the Munich police chief and high-ranking SA leader August Schneidhuber from removing control over the processing of political offences from the political police and transferring it back to police headquarters.[77]

If Himmler was already intending to take over the whole of the German police and the Third Reich's terror apparatus, then he was successful at concealing it. In fact there is no convincing evidence that this was his aim at the time.[78] Instead, it is entirely possible that at this point he did not intend to do more than unify the political police forces of the German states under his command and merge them with the SS.

The struggle to control the Prussian Gestapo

Himmler's strategy of gradually taking over as commander of the various state political police forces would have had little *political* effect if he had not succeeded in securing control of the political police in what was by far the largest German state, Prussia. For it was only by taking personal control of all the political police forces that he would be in a position to coordinate them, in other words, turn them into a uniform organization and subject them to central direction, as opposed to simply accumulating titles.

Prussia at this time was the scene of a particularly vicious, complex, and opaque struggle among various factions, each of which was bent on acquiring control over the apparatus of repression that was being constructed. For it was clear to all involved that what happened in Prussia would determine who in future would control the political police throughout the Reich. This is not the place to deal with the details of this struggle; what is important in this connection is how Himmler managed to exploit certain openings in order to further his appointment as Inspector of the Secret State Police (Gestapo).

The central figure in this power struggle was Hermann Göring, acting Prussian Minister of the Interior and, since April 1933, also Prussian Prime Minister. Göring did not rely on the traditional agency for controlling the political police, namely the police department in the Prussian Interior Ministry, but instead appointed the leader of SS-Gruppe East, Kurt Daluege (who during the years 1930–3 had played a major part in keeping control of the unruly east German SA) as Commissar z.b.V. (for special assignments) within the ministry. Although formally he had assigned him only minor responsibilities, in fact Göring intended Daluege to play the key role within the Prussian police apparatus.[79] His official responsibilities made him relatively independent of SS headquarters in Munich. Thus, despite his high rank in the SS hierarchy, Daluege was not, as one might at first assume, Himmler's Trojan horse within the ministry, but rather Göring's man. Indeed, in May 1933 Göring appointed him head of the police department in his ministry and in September gave him command of the Prussian police.[80]

However, Göring created another instrument for the special purpose of combating political opponents. He removed the political police, which up until then had been part of the criminal police, from the general police organization and subordinated it to a new Secret State Police Office (*Geheimes Staatspolizeiamt* = Gestapa), which came under his direct control. To head this new central state agency he appointed Rudolf Diels, who since 1931 had been responsible within the police department of the Prussian Interior Ministry for combating communism. In fact, this continuity of personnel was typical for this new special police department, which was staffed mainly by officials from the police and judiciary who had served under Weimar. In matters concerning the political police the Gestapa had the right to issue directives to the previous political police sections within the criminal police departments in the Prussian districts, which were now renamed State Police Offices (*Staatspolizeistellen* or *Stapostellen*). This provided the foundation for the development of the Gestapo (*Geheime Staatspolizei*, 'Secret State Police').

In practice it was to become clear that in Prussia, as in the other states led by top Nazis who in the meantime had been appointed as provincial governors (*Oberpräsidenten*), district governors (*Regierungspräsidenten*), and police chiefs, these party functionaries would exercise considerable influence over the regional police organizations. They resisted Göring's attempts at centralization with some measure of success.[81] Himmler, therefore, initially focused his attentions on the provinces. As had been the case with the other states, he aimed to infiltrate the Prussian political police by placing some of his men in the Gestapo organization or by appointing senior Gestapo officers to ranks within the SS, thereby securing their loyalty to him personally.[82]

Apart from utilizing such personal contacts, Himmler could exercise influence above all through the auxiliary police (*Hilfspolizei*), which Göring had established on 22 February 1933.[83] Within a few weeks, the 25,000 SA men, who together with 15,000 SS and 10,000 members of the Stahlhelm provided the bulk of the auxiliary police,[84] began to pose a problem. Their thuggish and arbitrary behaviour was threatening to undermine the authority of both the party and the state. In this situation Göring and Diels concluded that the SS was the most suitable instrument for keeping control of its old rival the SA, as had repeatedly been the case during the internal party conflicts of the early 1930s. At least it appeared to be the lesser of two evils. According to an edict issued by the Prussian Interior Ministry on 21 April 1933, auxiliary police duties involving the political police would in future be confined to the SS; the role of the SA auxiliary police would be limited to assisting the general police.[85] This meant that the Interior Ministry envisaged that the political police and the SS would be amalgamated to a certain extent, whereas the SA would have to restrict itself to duties such as cordoning off streets, providing security for major events, and suchlike.

The fact that in June 1933 the SA chief, Röhm, was appointed Commissar of the auxiliary police in Prussia, whereas Himmler was appointed Commissar of the auxiliary political police, was a further indication of the way things were going.[86] In fact Diels then informed Daluege that in future only applicants to the Gestapo who were members of the SS would be accepted, thereby overriding the formal provisions for Gestapo appointments.[87] Göring gave his retrospective approval for this.[88] Moreover, as the commander of the auxiliary police attached to the Gestapo, Himmler had his own liaison officer in the Gestapa in the shape of Untersturmführer Walter Sohst,[89] and he and Heydrich were able to place a number of other contacts in the Gestapo headquarters.[90]

On 2 August 1933, in the aftermath of Hitler's announcement of the end of the 'National Socialist revolution', Göring dissolved the auxiliary police and, on 1 October, Diels organized the SS auxiliaries who had been discharged into an SS Commando Gestapo under SS-Brigadeführer Max Henze. The commando took over the notorious informal prison in Columbia House and established its base there, physically separated from Gestapo headquarters in Prince Albrecht Palace. This provided Himmler with a unit within the Gestapo that could operate largely independently, and which, moreover, controlled a concentration camp that, while officially remaining under the authority of the state, was in fact completely subject to the arbitrary behaviour of the SS.[91] On the same day Himmler dismissed Daluege from his post as SS-Gruppenführer East, and appointed him head of a staff to be deployed for special assignments. Daluege had become tied in to Göring's police organization, and this step had the effect of removing his influence within the SS and, in particular, the possibility of his taking control of the SS personnel in Berlin.[92]

There was another unit operating independently in Berlin as auxiliary police with the task of combating political opponents and competitors. This was the so-called SS-Sonderkommando Berlin for special assignments, which consisted of members of the unit that Sepp Dietrich had formed to ensure Hitler's personal protection and which in September 1933 was to be transformed into the Leibstandarte Adolf Hitler.[93] Although Dietrich always stressed his complete independence vis-à-vis the SS Reich headquarters, in practice this force strengthened Himmler's position in the Reich capital.

By contrast, it soon became clear that the activities of the SD in Berlin were not particularly helpful. Although Heydrich had moved SD headquarters from Munich to Berlin following the Nazi takeover of power, in practice his new tasks in Bavaria prevented him from operating effectively. Moreover, the party's intelligence service, which at this stage may have had some thirty to forty members throughout the whole of the Reich, was still in its infancy. Above all, however, in the summer of 1933 the SD became involved in a serious crisis because, in the wake of its disputes with the party leadership in Hamburg and Brunswick referred to above, it was accused by leading party figures of interfering with the party's internal affairs. In response, during that same summer Heydrich moved SD headquarters back to Munich and reorganized it.[94]

Himmler now strengthened Heydrich's position by promoting him in July from chief of staff of the SD to head the service.[95] He also provided him with support by negotiating a deal with Rudolf Hess in the autumn by which in future the SD would intervene in internal party matters only with the latter's permission.[96] In return, Hess issued a party instruction on 13 November which announced that Hitler had expressly ordered that the SD should continue to operate, thereby refuting rumours to the contrary.[97] Four days earlier, on 9 November 1933, Himmler had raised the SD to the status of an Office (*Amt*) within the SS and promoted Heydrich to the rank of Brigadeführer.[98] Finally, Heydrich restructured the SD by establishing three operational departments—Home, Foreign, and Freemasons[99]— which by the beginning of 1934 were represented in all seven of the regional Oberabschnitte.[100] On 9 June 1934 Hess, acting in his role as the Führer's Deputy for party affairs, announced that in future the SD was to be the NSDAP's official intelligence service.[101]

The SD was far too much involved in its own problems, however, to be of any assistance to Himmler in Prussia. Moreover, Himmler suffered another setback. In the autumn of 1933 the Prussian Interior Ministry ordered the dissolution of the unauthorized SA camps. Himmler was, however, thwarted in his attempt to ensure that the prisoners released as a result should be handed over to the SS. Indeed, the numerous cases of mistreatment, murder, and assaults on the local population by SS guards in the big camps on the moors of the Emsland prompted the Interior Ministry to replace them with police. Yet paradoxically this ultimately turned out to work in favour of Himmler's Prussian ambitions. By having to replace the SS guards, the Prussian Interior Ministry had shown that its original concept of placing the SS concentration camp guards under state supervision was not viable. The lesson to be learnt from this episode was that one could not use SS terror in the camps as a deterrent while at the same time ensuring effective state supervision. Himmler's Bavarian model, which combined the political police and the concentration camps in the hands of the SS, appeared preferable.[102]

Himmler was able to benefit from the temporary breach between Göring and Diels that occurred in the autumn of 1933. Evidently prompted by Daluege, who considered Diels a traitor, Göring began a move against Diels, who promptly fled to Czechoslovakia. Göring fairly soon realized that he needed Diels's help in the struggle against the SA, particularly in view of the fact that the latter's successor, Paul Hinkler, proved completely incompetent in the post,[103] and so he persuaded him to return from exile. However, after taking up his post again in Berlin, Diels began to seek the support of the SD. In fact, even before his return Himmler had appointed him an SS-Standartenführer.[104]

But, in the final analysis, what was to prove decisive for Himmler's success in Prussia was the power struggle between Göring and Reich Interior Minister Wilhelm Frick.[105] While Göring reorganized the Prussian police, Himmler had managed to some extent to infiltrate the political police (Gestapo) in what was the largest German state. It was a force that was in the process of being created but had already acquired an autonomous status. At the same time, Frick was making considerable efforts to unify the whole police structure throughout the Reich and establish a national police headquarters to include the political police. Under his scheme it was unclear how much authority over the police the federal states would retain, and it was precisely this question that was the subject of negotiation between Frick and Göring in the spring and summer of 1933.

In fact, the planned amalgamation of the Reich and Prussian Interior Ministries provided Frick with a new opportunity to bring the Gestapo under his control.[106] Göring tried to prevent this from happening with the Second Gestapo Law of 30 November 1933, by removing the Gestapo from the control of the Prussian Interior Ministry, of which he was the acting head, and subordinating it to himself in his role as Prussian Prime Minister.[107] As a result, Diels, who now received the title of Inspector of the Gestapo, became the head of an agency that was not only (as a result of the law of April 1933) detached from the general police organization but was no longer subject to the authority of a departmental minister. Moreover, in March 1934 Göring completely removed the regional Gestapo offices from the rest of the police organization in Prussia.[108] The substantial autonomy attained by the political police in what was the largest German state, and the fact that it was no longer subject to effective control, must have encouraged the ambitious Himmler to regard it as an ideal base for his future operations. Göring was to prove the key to achieving his goal.

As early as the end of 1933 Himmler had begun to distance himself from his nominal superior, Röhm, and to move closer to Göring. At the beginning of 1934 he began to acquire compromising material on Diels from various sources, including Ludwig Grauert, the state secretary in the Prussian Interior Ministry, and Diels's colleague Hans Gisevius, but also from Nazi figures within the police apparatus (Daluege and Artur Nebe, an official within the Gestapa), as well as from the Berlin SD-Oberabschnitt East which had been reactivated under Heydrich's close associate Hermann Behrends.[109] While a few weeks earlier Himmler had supported Diels against Göring, he now plotted to remove the Gestapo chief.

In April 1934 Frick and Göring finally reached a compromise: Frick took over the Prussian Interior Ministry in addition to his role as Reich Interior Minister, thereby taking control of by far the largest police organization in the Reich (which was still headed by Daluege). He now sought to take over all the police forces in the rest of the Reich, which was liable to bring him into a direct confrontation with Himmler.

From the beginning of 1934 Frick and Göring had been trying to reduce the use of protective custody.[110] Among other things, they had used a meeting of the Reich Governors in March to try to achieve this.[111] In response, the Reich Governor of Bavaria, von Epp, and its Minister of Justice, Hans Frank, had taken further steps to cut down on protective custody but had met with opposition from the Interior Minister, Adolf Wagner, who supported Himmler.[112] In April Göring and Frick reached agreement on the introduction of uniform regulations for the use of protective custody.[113] Frick's directive implementing the agreement stated that the imposition of protective custody was the responsibility of the 'highest state authority' (that is, the Prussian Gestapa or the Bavarian political police). This meant that nobody could be taken into protective custody in Prussia without Göring's approval.

After this decisive safeguard had been put in place, both Frick and Göring believed they could risk handing over the political police throughout the Reich, including Prussia, to Himmler. It was not intended that Himmler should amalgamate the political police departments of the various states into a single organization, but rather that he should act as their combined leader. In this way it was assumed that his political position could be reduced to an acceptable level. This was, of course, a very formalistic approach, and it would not take Himmler long to transform his personal position of leadership into a real power base. Göring had insisted that Himmler should submit to him all important incoming and outgoing correspondence. But this turned out to be an inadequate means of controlling him, despite Himmler's eager promise to fulfil the request. It was naive to believe that Himmler could be appointed to a position of authority with a suitable organization at his command and then somehow be effectively supervised from outside.[114]

Thus Himmler's success in Prussia, which was to smooth his path to the takeover of the political police throughout the Reich, was due in part to his tactic of infiltration and of integrating key figures into the SS, in part to his diplomatic skills and his correct assessment of the interests and weaknesses of his opponents, in part to his ability to appear to subordinate himself to Göring, and, last but not least, to the fact that he did not reveal any further ambitions as far as the police were concerned. It appears that Himmler was trusted to provide the necessary coordination of the various police forces without using this function as a springboard to an unlimited expansion of his power.

All in all, Himmler had cleverly succeeded in utilizing the power struggles of his rivals for his own ends. The decisive factor was the threat the SA had either appeared to, or actually did, pose and which prompted Frick and Göring to end their dispute and include Himmler in their compromise settlement by granting him what appeared to be an appropriate post. An additional point was the fact that the leading Nazi politicians in the states preferred to see the political police in Himmler's hands rather than in Frick's, who, it was believed, would centralize it and integrate it once more into the general police organization in the form of a Reich political police force.

On 10 April 1934 Himmler was appointed 'Inspector of the Secret State Police in Prussia'. The intention was that Heydrich, acting as Himmler's deputy, should take over as head of the Secret Political Police Office (Gestapa), while Göring continued to remain officially head of the Secret State Police (Gestapo).[115]

While Himmler was focusing on securing his appointment as head of the political police departments of the federal states, he found himself confronted by a serious challenge created by the rapid expansion of the SS following the Nazi takeover of power. New members had poured into the SS in the weeks after 30 January 1933. In the spring of 1933 the number of SS members had already increased to 100,000, and after a temporary ban on the admission of new members between April and November 1933, the organization had more than doubled in size by the spring of the following year. Himmler later described this expansion as the 'most serious crisis that the SS has ever experienced'; it took three or four years to sort out the negative repercussions.[116] By 1935, according to his calculations, 60,000 members of the SS had had to be excluded.[117]

However, the number of sponsoring members or patrons also increased rapidly: from 13,217 to 167,272. These 'sponsors' (*fördernde Mitglieder* [*FM*]) were effectively honorary members, usually well-off individuals who paid regular contributions to the SS either out of sympathy or under intimidation. During the following year it had grown to 342,492, although subsequently there was a slight reduction, in particular on account of the ban on meetings issued in June 1934, which also banned the recruitment of patrons. Although the SS was financing itself predominantly from party subsidies (in reality taxes) by 1934 at the latest, the 'FM' funds' represented a significant sum. They increased from 204,000 Reich marks in 1932 to RM 4,285,000 in 1933 and RM 6,972,000 in 1934.[118]

In May 1933 Himmler had moved his command staff from Munich to Berlin. During these months the number of Standarten was doubled from 50 to 100; in the winter of 1933–4 Himmler introduced Oberabschnitte or regions, which replaced the previous combination of SS-Abschnitte (districts) into Gruppen (groups). The fact that in February 1934 Himmler moved his staff back to Munich[119] indicates what a turbulent life the Reichsführer-SS was leading during these months. On his return to Munich he restructured the SS headquarters, which in future consisted of three agencies: the SS Office (*Amt*) for general management, the SD Office, and the Race and Settlement Office, as well as his personal staff.[120]

It was also in February 1934 that Himmler appointed Oswald Pohl, a former naval paymaster born in 1892, as the new head of the SS administration. Himmler had been seeking a reliable and experienced administrator. Pohl's two predecessors, Paul Weickert and Gerhard Schneider, had been dismissed for embezzlement and excluded from the SS. Since the SS (as part of the SA) was receiving public subsidies from 1933 onwards and had to account for the use of this money, Himmler needed an expert who was familiar with the budgetary regulations of the public sector.[121]

Himmler had discussed with Pohl the possibility of his joining the SS leadership for the first time in May 1933 in Kiel. Two days after this meeting Pohl wrote Himmler a letter in which he explained his reasons for contemplating a change of career. According to Pohl, while he enjoyed being in the Navy, 'my professional life does not provide me with intellectual satisfaction or an outlet for my creative urges and my mania for work. I want to work and I can work until I collapse.'[122] Himmler liked him, and after a long interval, which was caused by the formalities of Pohl's departure from the Navy, on 12 February he appointed him head of Department IV (Administration) in the SS Office, backdated to 1 February.[123]

When Himmler took over the Prussian Gestapa in April 1934 he once again moved back to Berlin from Munich, taking Heydrich with him. The SS leadership then gradually followed and took up residence in the Prince Albrecht Palace. This building was to become the synonym for the secret police of the Nazi state.[124] The foundations for the terror system had been laid.

The 30 June and its consequences

Himmler had understood how to utilize the complicated and tense domestic political situation that existed in 1933–4 to secure control of the political police departments of the federal states. It was his services in the violent 'resolution' of this tangled situation that were to create the conditions for enabling the Reichsführer-SS to achieve a central position of power within the Nazi regime that was neither constantly challenged nor limited by other major Nazi figures.

Given the opaque domestic political constellation that existed at the time, the prehistory of 30 June is a complex one. It can briefly be summarized as follows: broadly speaking, there was a mood of discontent in the country. A year after the takeover of power the economic crisis had still not been solved: only about a third of the 6 million unemployed had found work. The results of the first elections to the 'Councils of Trust' in the factories had been so bad for the Nazis that they were never published. There was disappointment among the rural population because the inheritance law that had been introduced, with its regulations restricting the transfer of farms, had limited the opportunities for accessing credit, while the new marketing system introduced under the auspices of the 'Reich Food Estate', with its prescribed prices and compulsory measures, was felt to be unjust. Both Catholics and Protestants were disturbed by the regime's religious policies, and the 'bossy' behaviour of party functionaries was prompting an increasing number of complaints. There was not much left of the mood of optimism about a new start that had gripped a section of the population in 1933.[125]

Against the background of this tense situation the SA represented an additional dangerous source of discontent.[126] In the middle of 1934 the Nazi

Party's army consisted of around 4.5 million members, approximately nine times as many as there had been in January 1933. This huge increase was not only the result of the influx of new members after the seizure of power, but also, and above all, a consequence of the incorporation of right-wing paramilitary organizations such as the Stahlhelm.

Relying on this huge, albeit heterogeneous and relatively undisciplined, force, the SA leadership under Röhm now endeavoured to secure its own share of the Nazi state. It had at least managed to achieve the appointment of SA commissars to the state machine, to begin the arming of sections of the SA, as well as to secure the state financing of SA staffs. On 1 December 1933 Röhm had been appointed a Reich minister. However, despite these successes it was still unclear how this emerging SA empire was to be integrated into the new Nazi state. The SA leadership combined this unresolved claim to power with repeated and threatening demands for a 'second revolution'. During 1933–4 the rowdy behaviour of the SA, its numerous acts of violence and infringements of the law, which now that political opponents had been suppressed were directed mainly against the general public, were increasingly becoming a public nuisance and underlined the storm-troopers' aggressive potential.

Above all, however, Röhm posed a threat to the Reichswehr's role as the organization primarily responsible for the defence of the Reich. While initially there had been agreement between the Reichswehr and the SA that the latter would concentrate mainly on pre-military training and strengthening frontier defences, the SA leadership soon began planning to create an armed militia which, had these plans been realized, would have reduced the Reichswehr to a mere training organization within an SA people's army.

On 28 February 1934 Hitler made an announcement to the leadership of the SA and the Wehrmacht in which he rejected the SA's extensive military ambitions; he ordered it to reach an agreement with the Reichswehr that would restrict the SA to auxiliary military functions. Although Röhm signed the agreement, immediately after this event he made it clear to his leadership corps that he was by no means prepared to abide by it. And these statements were passed on to Hess.[127]

Meanwhile, conservatives were hoping that the conflict with the SA could be utilized to win back lost ground from the Nazis in the governing coalition and conceivably to reintroduce the monarchy following the anticipated demise of Hindenburg, who was 86 years old. These opponents were banking primarily on the Vice-Chancellor, von Papen.

At the beginning of 1934, the opponents of the SA—party, Gestapa, and Reichswehr—began to mobilize. Rudolf Diels, the head of the Prussian Gestapa, claimed in his memoirs to have been given the task by Hitler of collecting material against the SA. At the beginning of February the leadership of the Reichswehr gave identical instructions to their subordinates.[128] After Himmler and Heydrich had taken over the Gestapa in April the search for compromising material was evidently intensified.[129] The Reichswehr also began a propaganda campaign in April in which the army was proclaimed as the nation's 'sole bearer of arms', an obvious affront to the SA.[130]

In May the military agencies were once more instructed to report on breaches by the SA of the agreement reached in February.[131] In the same month the Gestapo and the Intelligence Department in the War Ministry began a loose cooperation, exchanging information about the SA.[132] Werner Best, who had been appointed head of the SD's organization in March, also concentrated on acquiring information about the SA in addition to his task of reorganizing and building up the SD headquarters, which at that time was still based in Munich.[133] At the same time, Röhm, who was not oblivious to these activities, gave instructions to collect material concerning 'activities hostile to the SA'.[134]

At the beginning of June a new situation began to emerge: Hindenburg, who was seriously ill, withdrew to his estate in East Prussia. This meant that the most important ally of the conservatives had become more or less incapable of action. On 11 May the NSDAP had already begun a major propaganda campaign against 'grumblers and carpers', which was now significantly intensified. The target was obvious: the party was focusing on its critics among the bourgeoisie. However, at the beginning of June a lengthy personal conversation had taken place between Hitler and Röhm, which the latter at least is likely to have taken as a sign of an easing of tension. He went off to a spa for a cure and ordered the SA to go 'on leave' for the month of July.[135]

The fact that nevertheless, in the middle of June, the situation became critical was not so much down to Röhm but was due rather to an initiative by von Papen. On 17 June he made a widely reported speech at the University of Marburg in which he sharply criticized the Nazis' arbitrary and terroristic rule. When the Propaganda Ministry blocked the distribution of the speech von Papen threatened Hitler that he would offer his resignation to the Reich

President. This had the effect of transforming his actions into a government crisis. For von Papen's resignation would have threatened the continuation of the coalition between the Nazis and the conservatives, and this might have prompted Hindenburg to galvanize himself and dismiss Hitler as Reich Chancellor. The regime was not yet sufficiently stable, however, to survive such a step without suffering damage.

Hitler solved the crisis by directing his actions not primarily against the conservatives but rather against the SA. He calculated that by neutralizing the SA leadership he would solve the combination of domestic political problems at one stroke: the mass of discontented SA men would lose their spokesmen, the threat of a 'second revolution' would have been removed, the issue of control over the armed forces would be resolved, the majority of the population would be relieved by the elimination of this source of trouble, and the alliance between the Nazis and the conservative elites would emerge strengthened from these events. Insofar as it could be portrayed as the crushing of an alleged coup, the conservatives would be prepared to tolerate the exclusion or even liquidation of a few conservative critics.

Thus, at the end of June 1934 the trap was closing on the SA leadership. Practical preparations for its elimination had already been made at the beginning of the month. Theodor Eicke, the commandant of Dachau, had carried out a practice deployment of SS troops in the Munich area. At the end of June the SS and SD Oberabschnitt commanders assembled in the Bavarian capital, where Himmler and Heydrich informed them that an SA revolt was about to happen; appropriate 'counter-measures' were then set in train.[136] There is evidence that the Reichswehr was making similar preparations to deal with this scenario.[137]

On 30 June Röhm and other high-ranking SA leaders were arrested at Bad Wiessee, where Röhm was staying on holiday. Similar arrests occurred in Silesia, Berlin, and other places. Around 150 to 200 people were executed: apart from numerous SA leaders, there were conservative politicians, notably the former Reich Chancellor, General von Schleicher, Vice-Chancellor von Papen's associates Herbert von Bose and Edgar Jung, as well as the former head of the police department in the Prussian Interior Ministry and leading representative of the Catholic lay organization Catholic Action, Erich Klausener. Moreover, a number of old scores were settled. Gustav Ritter von Kahr, who, while acting as Bavarian State Commissar, had prevented the Hitler putsch in November 1923; the publisher Fritz Gerlich, who was a strong critic of the Nazis; and Gregor Strasser, who had not been forgiven for his behind-the-scenes contacts with Schleicher in December 1932—all fell victim to the SS execution squads. There was at least one case of mistaken identity, namely the Munich music critic Eduard Schmidt, murdered because he was confused with someone with the same name.

In this conflict between the party, the party's army, the regular army, and the conservative elites Himmler, who as Reichsführer-SS was still subordinate to Röhm, had succeeded in joining the right side in time without compromising himself in any way. He had played a not-insignificant part in carrying out the 'action', without appearing to have intrigued against Röhm and his associates.

In the cases of Ernst Röhm and Gregor Strasser, Himmler had authorized the murder by his subordinates of the two men who had laid the foundations of his career and with whom he had had good personal relations. If Himmler had needed to demonstrate his absolute loyalty to Hitler, he had surely done so with his actions on 30 June 1934.[138]

The neutralization of the SA leadership represented a huge increase in Himmler's power. As Ulrich Herbert put it, his SS had emerged 'as a new power centre within the regime and as the real victor' of the 'Röhm affair'.[139] This was the main result of the sudden alteration that had occurred in the overall balance of power within the regime. Himmler's enormous political gain from the 30 June was in marked contrast to the subordinate role he had played in the power struggle that preceded the upheaval. Himmler's new role was evident above all in the changes that then occurred.

On 15 July the regulation that had already been issued by the Führer's Deputy, according to which the SD was declared the sole authorized intelligence service for the Party, came into effect. On 20 July Hitler ordered that the SS be removed from the SA's organization and that in future it should be autonomous, and he justified this move with specific reference to the 'great services' rendered by the SS 'in connection with the events of 30 June'.[140]

From June 1934 onwards the Leibstandarte and the armed political action squads (*politische Bereitschaften*) developed into the SS-Verfügungstruppe or Armed SS, the predecessor of the Waffen-SS. Eicke, who had been appointed Inspector of Concentration Camps and commander of the guard units on 4 July, was made responsible for supervising all the concentration

Ill. 10. Himmler enjoyed visiting the concentration camps he controlled, as in this case where he is photographed visiting Dachau in May 1935. Such visits also enabled him to convince groups of high-ranking visitors that the inmates were being subjected to a strict but fair regime. But in fact he was well informed about the reality of the prisoners' inhumane treatment and the numerous murders.

camps throughout the Reich, and began to create a second armed force (the Death's Head units) from the guards. A central office for coordinating the political police commanders of the federal states had already been created within the Gestapa in May, an important step towards the unification of the political police under Himmler. It could now begin to be developed into an effective instrument.[141]

Himmler's position was still not unchallenged, however. Frick continued to hold the view that the new instruments of repression, which the so-called Third Reich had created and transferred to Himmler—the autonomous Gestapo, the concentration camps that had been subordinated to it immediately after 30 June, as well as the practice of protective custody—were merely temporary phenomena which, after a general normalization of the situation had occurred, should once again be strictly subordinated to the state administration.[142]

Coming immediately after the emasculation of the SA, however, the timing for a move against this emerging concentration of power in Himmler's hands was exceptionally unfavourable, and Göring soon put an end to it. When Frick instructed the state governments no longer to cooperate with 'unofficial persons', that is to say, the SD, Göring immediately and brusquely rejected this as far as the sphere of the Gestapo was concerned, in other words for Prussia, and in doing so referred explicitly to the events of 30 June.[143] Himmler responded more cautiously and cooperatively. He issued an order restricting the cooperation of the SD with the Gestapo to the passing on of information. Moreover, the SD was forbidden to perform executive functions.[144]

Göring, for his part, began a move against Frick. In a message to the heads of the Stapo offices, the provincial governors, and district governors of 6 July 1934 he emphasized that the Gestapo was to remain 'an autonomous part of the internal administration' that he considered 'of great importance for the stability of the new state'. The heads of the Gestapo offices should operate closely with the district governors, but obey their directives only if there were no instructions to the contrary from the Gestapa or from him.[145] Frick, acting in his capacity as Reich Interior Minister, then responded by ordering that all state governments, as well as all provincial governors and district governors in Prussia, should send in monthly reports on the political situation, since the creation of a 'special political police' had by no means absolved them of their political responsibilities.[146] Göring conceded the point, and a few days later Frick too back-pedalled. He agreed to Göring's regulation of 6 July, since the latter had explained to him that it was a temporary measure.[147]

This meant that the Gestapo had succeeded in maintaining its position as an autonomous agency in the state of Prussia, while the district governors, as heads of the internal administration, were still permitted to send political situation reports to the Interior Ministry, so that in certain circumstances there could be a counterbalance to the reports of the Gestapo. It was only in 1936, after his appointment as Chief of the German Police, that Himmler was able to put an end to this dual system.

The abortive Vienna putsch

The 30 June 1934 was, however, also the starting-point for a painful defeat for the SS: the abortive Nazi putsch in Austria of July 1934, in which the SS played a major role.[148]

From the spring of 1933 onwards there had been tension between the authoritarian clerical regime of the Austrian Chancellor, Engelbert Dollfuss, and Nazi Germany. In May the Reich introduced the 'thousand-mark barrier', a fee of a thousand marks for a visa for those wishing to visit Austria. The following month Dollfuss banned the Austrian NSDAP. The response was a wave of terror attacks by Austrian Nazis, supported by Germany.

In July 1934 a group of Austrian Nazis, including the 'State Inspector' of the Austrian NSDAP, Theodor Habicht, and the leader of the local SA, Hermann Reschny, organized a putsch.[149] The aim was to arrest the members of the Dollfuss government during a cabinet meeting and to replace them with a new cabinet under a Nazi member, Anton Rintelen. Since the Dollfuss government had suspended parliament in 1933 and had issued a new constitution the following year, the putschists hoped that his government would not be regarded as legitimate, so that substantial sections of the police (who to a considerable extent had been infiltrated by the Nazis) and of the army would switch sides. The new cabinet would then secure Anschluss (unification) with the Reich.

Naturally, the Austrian Nazis were not operating on their own. On 22 July they had their plans approved by Hitler, as is clear from a note in his diary by Goebbels, who was present at the meeting: 'Austrian question. Will it succeed? I'm very sceptical.'[150] The success of the plan depended very much on the effectiveness of a Viennese SS unit, the SS–Standarte 89. This 'military Standarte', originally an SA formation, which consisted of active soldiers and police or those who had been dismissed for their political activities, had subordinated itself to Himmler in the spring of 1934 without the permission of the SA leadership, thereby creating much bad blood within the Austrian SA.[151] This action was now to come home to roost.

On 25 July a unit of the Standarte 89 occupied the Federal Chancellery on the Ballhausplatz, where the cabinet was meeting. However, since the plot had been betrayed, most of the ministers had managed to leave the building beforehand. A squad under the leadership of a former NCO of the Federal Army, Otto Planetta, was nevertheless able to seize the Federal Chancellor, Dollfuss. In circumstances that have never been explained, in the course of a struggle he was, however, seriously injured by two gunshot wounds and died three hours later, without receiving either the medical attention or spiritual support that he had requested.[152] The circumstances of the murder of Dollfuss in particular were to confirm the international image of the SS as an utterly inhumane and ruthless organization: SS members had violently, and under degrading conditions, brought about the agonizing death of the head of a sovereign state. Dollfuss, a controversial and decidedly right-wing politician, had become a martyr murdered by the SS.[153]

During the course of 25 July it became apparent that the security forces did not support the intended change of regime. The police, army, and paramilitary Heimwehr besieged the Chancellery, and that evening the putschists surrendered on the basis of an assurance that they could travel unhindered to Germany. In view of the murder of Dollfuss, however, the Austrian government did not feel itself bound by that assurance. Seven putschists, including Planetta, were condemned to death and executed.[154]

Nevertheless, numerous Nazis in the Austrian provinces, particularly in Carinthia and Styria, interpreted the events in Vienna as the signal for a general uprising. In a number of places fights broke out between SA, SS, other Nazi militias and the police and army, as well as the Heimwehr, which was called up as a 'defence force'. By the end of the month the forces of the state had managed to emerge as victors. A detailed analysis of these events has shown that one reason for the failure of the putsch was that the Nazis did not proceed in a coordinated fashion under a united leadership.[155] Hitler distanced himself from the affair and ordered the dissolution of the Austrian NSDAP.

The abortive coup had repercussions for years in the form of intrigues and mutual recriminations.[156] The mistrust between SS and SA that had turned into enmity as a result of the events of 30 June had contributed to the failure of the operation. Although the Austrian SA had promised the plotters its support in principle, the Viennese SA had failed to come to the assistance of their unpopular SS comrades, while for their part the putschists had ignored the SA in their preparations because its involvement would have undermined the autonomy of their actions.[157] A case was brought against Georg Reschny, the leader of the Austrian SA, before the Supreme Party

Court on the grounds of his alleged betrayal of the putsch, but was dropped at Himmler's request for fear of implicating other high-ranking party leaders.[158]

It was not until four years later, in April 1938, directly after the Anschluss with Austria, that Himmler ordered a thoroughgoing investigation of these events. The 'Reichsführer-SS's Historical Commission Concerning the Uprising of the Austrian National Socialists in July 1934', which was chaired by Heydrich, finally concluded that the SA leadership had regarded the takeover of the Standarte by the SS as 'a betrayal of the SA'.[159] 'The tension between a section of the SA leadership and the SS, which then emerged into the open in the Reich on 30 June 1934, also became evident in Austria. This also explains the attitude the SA leadership in Austria later adopted towards the plans for the uprising.'[160] However, the extent to which the SA bore actual blame for the collapse of the putsch attempt was understandably not discussed in detail in the report, and nor was it in the end assessed. Instead, betrayal, technical mistakes, and cock-ups were blamed for the failure. Significantly, the exact circumstances of Dollfuss's murder could also not (or were not intended to) be clarified.

8

From Inspector of
the Prussian Gestapo to Chief
of the German Police

I t was to take until the autumn of 1935 before Himmler had secured
control over the whole of the German police. During this second stage of
his accretion of power he benefited from the relatively unstable situation in
which the Nazi regime found itself at this time.

In the first place, there was the international situation. As a result of the
abortive putsch in Austria, Germany had provoked the enmity of Mussolini,
and the announcement of the introduction of national military service in
March 1935, as well as the military occupation of the Rhineland the
following year, both of which were clear breaches of the Versailles treaty,
inevitably prompted fears of foreign intervention. And yet the Third Reich
was not yet prepared for such conflicts. In addition, there were domestic
uncertainties. The year 1935 saw the regime involved in serious conflicts
with conservative elements and with the churches and, moreover, the
communist underground movement was still active. Thus, the Nazi leadership was concerned that its ambitious foreign-policy plans could be torpe-
doed by a collapse of the 'home front'. The '1918 complex', the fear of a
'stab in the back', was deeply rooted.[1]

It was against this background that, after a lot of to-ing and fro-ing,
Himmler was able to succeed in pushing through his policy of establishing
a uniform and permanent terror system that was outside the law and
covered the whole of the Reich. Himmler operated at various levels. In
the first place, he built up the armed SS units; secondly, he brought the
whole of the concentration camp system under his control and unified it;
thirdly, he strengthened and unified the Gestapo and introduced new

elements into the programme for combating political enemies; fourthly, he developed this programme into a comprehensive scheme for providing a 'general preventive anti-subversion system' (*Generalprevention*) covering the whole of society, thereby persuading Hitler to appoint him Chief of the German Police.

Since the SS continued to grow and its tasks continued to expand, it became necessary to carry out various organizational changes, and in fact, with his order of 14 December 1934, Himmler carried out a complete reorganization of the SS. In future the SS was divided into three sections: the SS-Verfügungstruppe, consisting of the armed political squads including the Leibstandarte; the SS concentration camp guards; and the General SS, to which all other members of the SS belonged.[2]

The militarized SS

The deployment of armed SS units to neutralize the SA leadership on 30 June 1934 had been in the interests of the Reichswehr leadership and had met with their approval. A further, albeit limited, expansion of the number of these units had also met with the approval of the military, provided that the monopoly of the Reichswehr as the 'nation's sole bearer of arms' was not seriously threatened. Thus, on 24 September 1934 the Reichswehr Ministry issued guidelines for the SS-Verfügungstruppe with reference to an order from Hitler. These agreed to the establishment of armed units—three regiments and an intelligence section—although initially only one battalion (the Leibstandarte) was to be created. Additional units with the aim of establishing a full division were established, but significantly only with the permission of the Reichswehr Ministry.

The edict demonstrates the Wehrmacht's intention of keeping the military ambitions of the SS within bounds. Basically, the SS was to be unarmed; the establishment of armed SS units was to be an exception and was intended to enable the SS to carry out certain domestic political tasks that the Führer might assign to it. The force would be under the command of the Reichsführer-SS; in wartime it would be at the disposal of the Wehrmacht.[3] The Wehrmacht endeavoured to restrict the training of the SS units and their wartime mobilization to such an extent that in any future war they would be able to play only a subordinate military role.[4]

However, of the total of three leadership academies that were planned, two were envisaged as officer academies, each with 250 training places. And the number of officer recruits to be trained in eight-month courses far exceeded the requirements of the Verfügungstruppe as laid down in the edict of 24 September.[5] If one also takes into account the fact that Himmler requested the Wehrmacht to give priority in its conscription programme to SS members who had not yet served in the armed services, and his declared intention of accepting only men into the SS who had done their military service, then it begins to become clear that in the long term Himmler wished to build up the General SS into a reserve troop for a much larger SS army.[6] Himmler tried to defuse immediate concerns that the Wehrmacht's monopoly of arms might be being undermined in private talks with the Reichswehr Minister, Werner von Blomberg, and his Chief of Staff, Ludwig Beck, which took place in October 1934.[7] Himmler insisted that the SS was not pursuing military goals like the SA; it was not intended to develop into a 'military organization alongside the Wehrmacht'. The SS's military training and organization were simply intended to underline its elite character. It is clear from the surviving records of the army leadership that these statements met with disbelief.[8]

Beck's guidelines for the cooperation of the army with the SS dated 18 December 1934 show that the Reichswehr leadership was trying as far as possible to establish control over the SS units. Thus, although it permitted the creation of two further units (Sappers and Intelligence), Himmler's pressing demand for the SS to have its own artillery was refused. In other words, the creation of a fully equipped division was to be delayed for as long as possible. And initially this negotiating strategy worked.[9] On 2 February 1935 Hitler decided that the Verfügungstruppe should be expanded and equipped to full division strength only in time of war.[10]

The new tasks and the reorganization involved considerably more work for SS headquarters. In January 1935, therefore, Himmler raised the three departments that he had established the previous year (SS Office, SD Office, and Race and Settlement Office) to the rank of Main Offices. The 'Staff of the Reichsführer-SS' remained as his personal instrument for exercising leadership.[11] On 1 June 1935, a few months after this reorganization, Himmler appointed Oswald Pohl, the head of the Administration office within the SD Main Office, to be 'Head of the SS Administration'. This meant that Pohl took over the supervision of the administrative department of the SD Main Office as well as that of the Race and Settlement Main

Office in addition to his existing job. In later years Pohl was to develop these responsibilities into a position of real power.[12]

However, Himmler's main focus during this period was on his struggle to retain and extend his control over the concentration camp system and the German police.

The centralization and unification of the concentration camp system

In May 1934, immediately after his appointment as Inspector of the Gestapa, Himmler had assigned the Dachau commandant, Eicke, the task of reorganizing the state concentration camps in Prussia. Even before the end of the month, Eicke had taken over the Lichtenburg camp in the Prussian province of Saxony and begun to reorganize it along the lines of Dachau. On 20 June he was officially appointed Inspector of Concentration Camps. Although he was formally subordinated to the SS Office, in practice he reported directly to Himmler.[13]

At the beginning of July 1934 Eicke, who had played a leading role in the murders of 30 June, took over the Oranienburg camp, which was under the authority of the SA, and closed it. A number of smaller camps were also closed.[14] Following on from this, he reorganized the Esterwegen camp, which Himmler had already taken over 'personally' on 20 June, along the lines of Dachau, replacing the SA guards with SS.[15] He followed the same course of action with the Sachsenburg camp in the federal state of Saxony, which was taken over in August.[16] Columbia House in Berlin, the 'house prison' of the Gestapa, which was run by an SS squad, was transferred to him in December 1934, and the small Sulza camp in Thuringia in April 1936.[17]

During 1935 Himmler was exceptionally successful, as will be shown in the next section, in countering all the attacks by the Interior and Justice Ministers on the brutal way in which protective custody was carried out in the camps. In the course of these disputes Himmler persuaded Hitler on 20 June to transform the concentration camp guards into a military force and to finance the camps and guards with Reich funds.[18] This meant that the first stage in the reorganization of the camps had been completed by mid-1935. At the same time, the number of prisoners had reached its lowest-ever level of around 3,000.

The self-confident Gestapo chief

On 11 October 1934 Himmler made a speech to the staff of the Secret State Police Office. He used the opportunity to remind them that he had spoken to a number of members of the Gestapo at the same venue shortly after 30 June. This had been 'the worst day that could happen to a soldier in his life'. For 'having to shoot one's own comrades, with whom one has stood shoulder to shoulder in the struggle for an ideal, in some cases for 8 or 10 years, and who have then let one down, is the most bitter experience that can or should happen to a person'. However, according to Himmler, 30 June had been an important test for the Gestapo.

Later on in his speech Himmler projected an image of himself as a strict but caring boss. If they had requests to make they should not put them in anonymous letters: 'You will always find my door open if you come to me with a request which you wish to make in connection with yourself or a colleague, which has something to do with official business, or whether it's a personal request because you have a problem as a result of a misfortune or some other mishap [...] I can put up with frankness and I will then help you or at least offer you advice in so far as it is in my power to do so.' That also applied to financial matters. Thus, he would try his best to negotiate any fringe benefits that had been promised from the responsible authorities. Himmler also used the speech for an attack on bureaucratic methods, which, by using examples, he made to appear ridiculous. Instead, they should work with 'military speed'. One of his demands was that all documents should be signed personally by the person responsible for them.

Finally, Himmler painted the picture of a humane secret police, a sort of service provider for internal security: 'The nation must be convinced that the most just agency in the new state, the one that is most correct, is the feared Secret State Police. The nation must believe that if someone is pulled in he has been justly pulled in; they must believe that in all other matters, if they don't harm the state, the members of the Secret State Police will behave in a friendly way, that they have warm hearts and an absolute sense of justice.' He exhorted his colleagues to receive visitors 'in a polite and friendly manner'. Nobody should be 'bawled out'. The Gestapo people should see themselves as 'facilitators', not 'dictators'. Himmler painted his colleagues the picture of an office climate that was positively idyllic: the following months should be used to strengthen comradeship and to achieve a 'cheerful willingness to get on with the work'. Moreover, the working day would be cut by one hour. But when necessary they must sometimes work longer. However, he was very happy to grant an extra free day at Christmas or on other occasions. He ended his speech with three 'Sieg Heils!'[19]

During the first months after 30 June Himmler, who was still only deputy head of the Gestapo, was primarily concerned to achieve the maximum possible room for manoeuvre vis-à-vis his boss, Göring. Reflecting on the performance of the Gestapo during the years 1933 to the beginning of 1935 in a speech made in 1936 in the presence of Göring, Himmler criticized it as 'unsatisfactory',[20] thereby revealing the difference in the goals of the two men. Whereas Himmler pressed for all bureaucratic obstacles and legal restrictions on the Gestapo to be removed in order to make it more efficient, after 30 June 1934 Göring was seeking ways through which he might be able to exercise some kind of control over Himmler's activities.

In June 1934 Göring's state secretary, Paul Körner, was still asking Himmler to provide a monthly list of all cases in which protective custody had been imposed for more than seven days. However, Himmler was dilatory in handling the request. While Göring did receive a list of protective-custody prisoners from the Gestapa in the summer of 1934 in connection with Hitler's amnesty of 7 August, there does not appear to have been any monthly reporting of the figures.[21]

In October Göring made a new attempt. He issued a set of instructions for the Secret State Police in which he listed in detail what rights he reserved to himself as head of the Secret Police: the issuing of 'general directives', the 'overall supervision of the agency's work', personnel matters involving higher-ranking officials, the framing of the budget, and not least, 'the supervision of the Inspector's performance and discipline'. It was particularly important that Göring insisted that these rights of supervision should be exercised by the Prussian State Ministry, in other words, by his office as Prime Minister. This would have subjected the Gestapa to effective bureaucratic control.[22] Moreover, the concentration camps were subordinated to Himmler in his role as head of the Gestapo and not, as Himmler had requested in August 1934, as Reichsführer-SS, since that would have meant that Göring would have lost all state control over the camps.

Ill. 11. On 20 April 1934 Göring appointed Himmler 'Inspector' of the Prussian Secret State Police Office (Gestapa). Although Göring officially retained control of the Secret State Police (Gestapo) in the largest German state, in fact Himmler was very quickly to succeed—above all as a result of the events of 30 June 1934—in evading this check on his power.

In the final analysis, however, Göring's attempt to secure control over Himmler in his new role proved impossible. As the responsible official in the State Ministry put it: 'We failed to subordinate the Secret State Police to its legally prescribed supervisory authority.' The Gestapa thwarted every attempt by the state bureaucracy to control the concentration camps, by failing to respond to requests and by submitting to the budgetary authorities a demand for a lump sum instead of detailing each item of proposed expenditure. As the State Ministry had meanwhile acquired a copy of the regulations for Esterwegen concentration camp, and Göring was therefore aware of the arbitrary terror regime practised in the camp, the state authorities were faced with the problem of whether, in view of their failure to exercise de facto control, they should continue to claim the right to supervise Himmler's empire, when this would mean, as the same official put it, that 'the Prime Minister as well as the State Ministry's desk official would share responsibility for the measures of the Secret State Police'.[23]

The result was that, only a few weeks after issuing his regulations, Göring changed tack. On 20 November 1934 he announced that in future his powers as head of the Gestapo would be exercised by Himmler. In those matters that he had reserved for himself the correspondence would be conducted under the heading 'Prussian Secret State Police: The Deputy Chief and Inspector'. Although he informed Himmler on the same day that he reserved the right 'to issue him with instructions in matters of fundamental importance or in individual cases',[24] this did not alter the fact that Himmler had emerged the victor in this power struggle.

Gestapo and SD

As has already been mentioned, after Himmler's and Heydrich's takeover of the Gestapa the SD headquarters was moved back to Berlin.[25] In January 1935 the SD Office (like the SS Race and Settlement Office) was raised to the status of a Main Office and divided into three departments: Administration and Organization (until 1935 under the direction of Werner Best, who then transferred to the Gestapa), Domestic Affairs (under Hermann Behrends), and Foreign Affairs (under Heinz Johst).[26]

During the years 1933–4 Himmler had regarded the SD primarily as an instrument with which to achieve his appointment as head of the political police departments of the federal states through internal party espionage and

the establishment of personal contacts. Now the Security Service acquired a
secret-police role complementary to that of the Gestapo. The number of
permanent staff had increased by the end of 1934 to 850, among them
numerous graduates and members of the intelligentsia.[27] The SD Domestic
Affairs Department not only kept tabs on the actual and construed opponents
of Nazism but also initiated systematic and comprehensive reporting on the
whole of society. The Foreign Department concentrated its efforts on building up an autonomous foreign intelligence organization. During its early years
the Foreign Department was still relatively small and appears to have been
insignificant. One focus of its activities was the potential to utilize the Sudeten
German minority for activities in Czechoslovakia.[28] However, if one bears in
mind the fact that in January 1934 Göring agreed with the Foreign Ministry's
proposal to ban the Gestapo from undertaking intelligence work abroad, then
one can reasonably interpret these activities as an attempt to use the SD to get
round this ban, which indeed could never be fully enforced.[29]

In fact, Himmler and Heydrich sought to achieve close links between the
Gestapo and the SD. For example, Heydrich demanded that all members of
the political police forces who were simultaneously members of the SS
should join the SD. From 1936 onwards this was also demanded of criminal
police officers. In fact the members of the SD formed a separate network
within the Gestapo so that, towards the end of the 1930s, a close intermesh-
ing of security police and SD was to emerge.[30]

On 4 July, immediately after the emasculation of the SA, Himmler had
issued guidelines for the cooperation of the political police and the SD.
According to Himmler, the SD, which had just been declared by Hess to be
the sole intelligence organization of the party, was 'to participate in the
carrying out of the duties of state security and represents an important
complement to those state agencies that have been assigned these tasks'.
As the 'rule for the clear separation of the spheres of operation', Himmler
laid down that the police agencies of the state should combat 'the enemies of
the Nazi state', while the SD should 'investigate the enemies of National
Socialist values and initiate their combating and countering by the police
authorities of the state'. Thus the SD was 'banned from undertaking any
executive actions'.[31]

In a set of 'Joint Service Instructions for the Political Police and the SD'
from 1935 or early 1936 Himmler reasserted these principles, and insisted on
close cooperation between the two organizations. Even if the SD could not
take executive action, 'as an auxiliary agency of the police' it was still to be

provided with internal information and to have access to documents. It could request the Gestapo to carry out searches, and conversely the political police could assign it intelligence tasks.[32]

At the same time, limits were imposed on the extent to which the SD could pry into internal party affairs. At the end of 1935 Heydrich ordered that in future 'investigations and the surveillance of party affairs' were to be banned 'throughout the Security Service', since various SD offices, 'particularly in small states and districts', had 'allowed themselves to become too involved in local affairs' and thus had not always been in a position 'to report objectively on alleged or actual irregularities within party agencies'.[33] However, the message for the SD, which had begun its life as a party intelligence agency, was clear: it must now concentrate above all on its new sphere of operations.

Gestapo and Reichswehr

Although there were tensions between the SS and the Reichswehr concerning the SS's armed units, during 1935 and 1936 Himmler and Heydrich were able to win the support of the army leadership for expanding the role of the Gestapo. When the Gestapa was set up it had also taken over the responsibility for combating civil espionage that had hitherto lain with the political police. The fact that the Gestapo now began to increase its activities in this area initially led to disagreements and conflict with military intelligence. At the end of 1934 relations between the Gestapo and the Reichswehr had reached a low point. Himmler, Göring, and Heydrich launched rumours to the effect that the Commander-in-Chief of the army, Werner von Fritsch, was planning a coup. In order to reduce the tension, on 3 January Hitler made a public declaration of loyalty to the army and, on 13 January, Himmler himself gave a speech to senior officers outlining the role of the SS with the aim of restoring confidence.[34]

At the beginning of 1935 the situation was also eased by the fact that military intelligence acquired a new head in the shape of Wilhelm Canaris, an acquaintance of Heydrich's. Unlike his predecessor, Conrad Patzig, who was an opponent of the SS, Canaris was relatively open to collaboration with the Gestapa.[35] As early as 17 January Heydrich and Canaris had made a written agreement demarcating the responsibilities between military intelligence and 'police intelligence'. These so-called 'ten commandments' laid down that the Gestapo would be responsible for counter-intelligence work in armament factories, frontier protection, and policing foreigners; the Gestapo then organized a separate frontier police force. Heydrich also reorganized Department III of the Gestapa, which was responsible for counter-intelligence, to take account of its new responsibilities. In the spring of 1935 he removed the section responsible for foreign intelligence from the department and assigned it to the department responsible for combating internal enemies, under an innocuous-sounding title. This avoided disputes over competencies with military intelligence and ensured that Göring's order that the Gestapo should not conduct espionage appeared to be being adhered to. At the beginning of 1936 Heydrich appointed his new head of organization, Werner Best, who was able to establish good relations with Canaris, to head up Department III.[36]

The agreement with Canaris also dealt with the role the SD was to play in counter-intelligence. It was now to be specifically responsible for 'intelligence cooperation' in the securing of armaments factories and in frontier intelligence activities, though without having executive powers; in other words, for the recruitment of informants. This was the first time that the SD had been recognized by an important state agency.[37]

While the SD was to derive profit from this cooperation in the long run, the Gestapo benefited immediately from working together with the Reichswehr. As early as January 1935 the Reichswehr Minister, Werner von Blomberg, sent a copy of the 'ten commandments' to the Reich Finance Minister with a request for financial support for the Gestapo's counter-intelligence work; his request was approved. Moreover, he asked Reich Minister of the Interior, Wilhelm Frick, to unify the Reich's counter-intelligence police operations. In July he described his ideas in more detail to Hitler: it was not simply a matter of 'creating a unified organization and direction for the political police in the Reich with official status with which the Reichswehr can deal and work', but of establishing a 'Reich political police force'. In this way Himmler had acquired an ally for his plan to create an official institution which could absorb the responsibility for the political forces of the federal states that had hitherto been simply embodied in his person.[38]

In December 1936 Canaris and Best reached a further agreement in the form of an extension to the 'ten commandments'. Among other things, this established the priority for military over civilian counter-intelligence, which represented a significant concession by the Gestapo to the armed forces.[39]

Protective custody and the Gestapo

Even after Himmler's takeover of the Gestapa, Frick continued to try to restrict the arbitrary handling of protective custody. In a letter to the Bavarian state government of 30 January 1935 the Reich Interior Minister complained about the large number of prisoners in protective custody in Bavaria, and emphasized the responsibility of the Bavarian Interior Minister, Adolf Wagner, for these events. Frick demanded that Wagner should continually scrutinize these cases of protective custody, as was the case in Prussia. On 20 February Himmler, who was brought in by Wagner, then secured a decision by the Führer which he minuted in the margin of Frick's letter of complaint: 'The prisoners are to remain in custody.'[40]

From the beginning of 1935 onwards, however, there was an increasing number of civil actions and investigations concerning cases of mistreatment in concentration camps.[41] According to Hans Gisevius, who at the time was a member of the police department in the Reich Interior Ministry, in the spring of 1935 Frick selected one of the most striking cases, namely, of a Nazi functionary who had been arrested for criticizing the conditions in the Papenburg concentration camp. According to Gisevius, Frick demanded that Himmler should order the immediate release of this man, and said that if the same thing happened again he would begin an action against Himmler for wrongful detention. But his threat proved completely ineffective.

Gisevius recalled another case, in which the lawyer representing the widow of Erich Klausener, the senior civil servant murdered on 30 June 1934, had been arrested by the Gestapo because, in order to represent the insurance claims of his client, he had had to dispute the official version that Klausener had committed suicide. He, Gisevius, had then prepared a report for Frick, which the latter had sent to Hitler. Himmler had recounted the affair at a meeting of Nazi leaders, who had subsequently criticized Frick for the way he had gone about things.

Himmler repeatedly managed to get senior figures to cover up for his arbitrary rule. His position was strengthened not least by the fact that on 2 May 1935 the highest Prussian administrative court decided that Gestapo measures were not subject to revision by the administrative courts.[42] Five days later, during a meeting in which complaints against mistreatment were being discussed, the Gestapa chief gave Hitler a letter from a former Dachau inmate to Eicke, expressing his gratitude for 'the good time he had had as a prisoner'.[43] Frick received support for his attempt to limit the arbitrary system in the concentration camps from the Reich Minister of Justice, Franz Gürtner. In a letter to Frick dated 14 May, Gürtner demanded that, while corporal punishment in the camps should not be abolished, it should be 'uniformly and clearly' regulated; arbitrary mistreatment and torture should be ended and brutal guards punished.[44]

At this time Himmler had already proposed a draft Gestapa law with which he aimed to confront his opponents with a fait accompli. It proposed that the Gestapa should be raised to the status of a Prussian ministry. As far as its responsibilities were concerned, the draft stated tersely: 'The head of the Secret State Police shall determine the particular matters that are to be transferred to the Secret State Police.'[45] However, Himmler's attempt to acquire such an extensive range of powers was rejected, not only by the Prussian Justice and Interior Ministries but by the whole of the Prussian cabinet.

The cabinet meeting of 27 June 1935, which was attended by Himmler, was also unanimous in taking the opportunity to restrict protective custody. The ministers decided that it was not permissible to prevent lawyers from representing prisoners in protective custody. Moreover, in future, protective custody should not be imposed for a specified period nor should it be imposed instead of a sentence of imprisonment. In addition, Frick informed his colleagues that the Interior Ministry was working on a draft law that would create a clear 'legal basis' for the measures of the Secret State Police. Thus, by taking the initiative at Reich level, Frick wanted to try to pre-empt Himmler's attempt to introduce a regulation for Prussia, and in this way to set limits to his terror system.[46]

Himmler gets his way

Himmler defended his position by spending the spring and summer of 1935 making strenuous efforts to prove that his radical methods were necessary and, moreover, efficient. In doing so he placed particular emphasis on the 'communist threat'.

By this time the Gestapo had already extensively researched the structures of the communist milieu. The local activists who were likely to engage in communist underground activity were often already well known and, thanks to its active recruitment of informants, the Secret State Police was often in a position to roll up regional communist networks at a stroke and carry out mass arrests. Between 1934 and 1935–6 the same process kept recurring in most of the KPD districts, that is to say, the communist networks would be destroyed, then after several months rebuilt, then destroyed again, and then rebuilt until gradually the reserves of communist resistance fighters were exhausted. Any underground activity that still took place in fact usually took place under the eyes of the Gestapo. It determined when the communist underground cells would be finally eliminated and, from 1935 onwards, carried out spectacular mass arrests, during which communists would be arrested 'as a preventive measure' without it having to be proved that they had actually taken part in resistance activities.[47] The 'communist threat' was thus a phenomenon that was largely under the control of the Gestapo, which put Himmler in the comfortable position of being able to produce 'successes' in the struggle against the communist underground whenever he needed to. In this way he could 'prove' three things: the continuing threat posed by the KPD, the watchfulness of his political police, as well as the need to extend the competence of the Gestapo in order to be ready to meet future threats.

As early as 28 March 1935 Himmler had sent Justice Minister Gürtner a detailed memorandum concerning the 'communist movement'. In this memorandum, which there is reason to believe was written by Best, he not only outlined the communist threat in the most sombre colours but also argued that it could not be effectively combated by using the methods of a liberal state. The author of the memorandum began with the general statement that in 'a liberal state' the police's hands were 'tied by formal laws'. The 'individualistic-liberal values, which asserted the rights of political prisoners, enabled them to behave towards the police in a particularly trucu-lent manner'. This was a very different matter under National Socialism:

Every individual is a member of the organism of the state [. . .] If he places himself outside the community and becomes a criminal, he becomes a pest to everybody and will be attacked by everybody, that is to say, by the state. In this struggle the state will be acting in self defence [. . .] The police are the arm and the eyes of the law. They must be the first to defend the security of the state under the conditions imposed by having to act in self defence. They cannot treat a criminal who ignores ethical and moral principles, who is excluding himself from the national commu-nity, according to aesthetic criteria. He must be made to feel that the state is just as ruthless in its treatment of him as he was intolerant towards the state.

It was thus essential, 'given the need to protect the state, really to get to grips with criminals during the course of police interrogation', and equally necessary 'for the authoritarian, National Socialist state to provide its executive agencies with the means to compel offenders to adopt another attitude towards it. To refer to the integrity of the person of an offender who has been arrested on the basis of evidence is to adopt a liberal perspective.' That was a clear justification of torture, even if Himmler emphasized in this memorandum that he had forbidden the political police to use any 'violence' during interrogations.

The 'communist movement in Germany', the memorandum continued, 'is continually growing. This is not so much the result of economic conditions as, above all, a consequence of the completely inadequate means for pursuing members of the movement'. Only when functionaries who had been arrested 'can be compelled by every means to reveal their meeting places, their illegal hideouts, etc.' would there be success in 'penetrating further into the communist organizations' and 'preventing' the illegal KPD 'from developing into a mass party'.[48]

The memorandum is an important piece of evidence pointing to a change in the way the Gestapo operated. Whereas hitherto the Gestapo had primarily responded to actual acts of resistance, now it was moving towards preventive actions against the whole of the communist milieu. In order to bolster his claim that the communist threat was ubiquitous Himmler now launched a wave of arrests covering the whole of the Reich.

To begin with, the five-man Central Executive of the KPD was arrested in March 1935.[49] In the same month the Gestapo netted 350 members in Saxony, 300 in Gau Halle-Merseburg, and 280 in Düsseldorf.[50] In the Ruhr, where the KPD had already been largely wiped out in 1934, further mass arrests took place in May 1935,[51] as well as in Cologne during June and July 1935.[52] In Hamburg the Gestapo began to carry out a major series of arrests in June 1935, and by the autumn around 1,000 communists had been caught.[53] In Chemnitz, Zwickau, and other central-German towns the Gestapo also carried out a wave of arrests in the spring and summer of 1935.[54] In Munich, where the KPD had been forming its third illegal leadership in Upper Bavaria since 1934,[55] the Gestapo had succeeded in penetrating so deeply into the organization that it could more or less direct the party's underground activities at will. In the summer and autumn of 1935, and during the following summer, the communist groups in the Bavarian capital were finally eliminated in the course of two series of mass arrests.[56]

On 12 July 1935, when the mass arrests were already in progress, Himmler ordered the first major action that was purely preventive in intention: the arrest of a thousand former KPD functionaries throughout the Reich. In fact, a far larger number of communists were to be taken into 'preventive custody' in the course of these mass arrests.[57] In addition, in the summer of 1935 Himmler ordered between 200 and 300 communists to be put in concentration camps as a reprisal for a shooting incident that took place between border police and alleged communist smugglers near the Czech border in Saxony.[58] In the course of 1935 a total of around 14,000 communist functionaries were arrested.[59]

In the end, the criticism that was directed at the arbitrary acts of the Gestapo and the cases of mistreatment in the concentration camps, in particular by conservatives, had no effect. It did, however, lead to the whole Gestapo being disciplined through its division into a hierarchy of levels, and its organization being tightened, more effectively controlled from its headquarters, and unified.[60] This was above all the work of Werner Best, who had been appointed Heydrich's deputy and head of the administrative department in the Gestapa at the beginning of 1935.[61]

In February 1936 Himmler was able finally to consolidate his position at the head of the Prussian Gestapa. On 10 February, after almost a year of consultations, the Prussian Gestapa Law was issued, which to large extent reflected his ideas.[62] The law concluded the development of the political police into an autonomous special government department along the lines that he had envisaged. There was no mention of the restrictions on protective custody which the cabinet had agreed the previous June. The decisive factor in this success was Hitler's very personal interest in this matter. Himmler, who was directly subordinated to him as Reichsführer-SS, provided Hitler with the guarantee of being able to move against anyone at any time he felt like it, as had happened on 30 June 1934. This could now be achieved through an organization that operated to perfection, was highly disciplined, and had been removed from the hierarchy of the internal administration but otherwise worked in accordance with the principles of the Prussian bureaucracy. A secret police that was integrated into the general police apparatus and internal administration, and which Hitler could only have deployed by involving the ministerial bureaucracy, would not have provided him with this capability. Thus, Himmler was the man who enabled Hitler actually to exercise his position as a dictator with, in principle, unlimited power through the deployment of state terror.

The fact that Himmler had succeeded in making protective custody, a form of imprisonment that had emerged at the time of the takeover of power and was by its very nature indeterminate and not subject to any legal supervision, into a permanent institution and to do so despite the protests of the Reich Ministries of the Interior and Justice, provided the real foundation for his position of power within the dictatorship. In the person of Himmler, an arbitrary prerogative state had succeeded in replacing a state that had operated according to the law and was bound by norms. However, for Himmler this turning-point represented merely the first stage in his career in the Third Reich.

'Phases in Our Struggle'

Himmler's attempts to free the political police from all irksome legal bonds, to make it more independent, and to protect it from outside interference coincided with a public campaign which Himmler's deputy, Heydrich, had launched in May 1935 with a series of articles in the SS journal, *Das Schwarze Korps*, with the title 'Phases in Our Struggle'.[63]

The basic idea for the series was that, following the destruction of all opposition organizations, the enemies of Nazism had by no means been defeated. The Nazi movement was, it was claimed, far too little aware of the fact that the real threat came from 'intellectual forces' who were maintaining the struggle against Nazism with undiminished energy. The 'driving forces behind this opposition [were] always the same: World Jewry, World Freemasonry, and a to a large extent politicized official priesthood' (Heydrich corrected himself in the next issue of *Das Schwarze Korps* to the effect that 'Freemasonry' was really simply 'a front organization for Jewry'). These forces, it was further claimed, generally operated in 'disguise' against Nazism, with so-called specialists within the state machine, who had allowed themselves to be 'coordinated' only for appearances' sake, playing a key role. This represented a massive attack on Himmler's opponents within the state administration, who were simply being labelled as enemies of Nazism. In this scenario 'Bolshevism', which had hitherto always been rated enemy number one, now appeared merely as a superficial phenomenon behind which the 'real' opponents were hiding. The state police, it was said, were incapable of dealing with these on their own. Instead, in this 'ideological struggle' the SS, as 'the ideological shock troops' of the Nazi movement, were called upon to play a role in the vanguard. In any event, the struggle would be fought without quarter given: 'If we are to look after our people we must treat our opponents harshly, even at the risk of sometimes hurting an individual opponent and of possibly being vilified by some, no doubt well-meaning, people as wild brutes.'

This series of articles marked the Gestapo's transition from the policy of destroying the communist underground organization to a much broader conception of pursuing 'its intellectual originators' and 'the brains behind the operation'. The four articles were directly linked to the systematic persecution of Catholic priests and lay brothers as well as with the so-called second anti-Semitic wave, which the party launched in the spring of 1935 and finally led to the issuing of the Nuremberg Laws in September of the same year.

In 1936 high-ranking SS functionaries repeatedly took up Heydrich's ideas and expanded on them.[64] Four points in particular were emphasized: first, in order to achieve success the struggle against their political enemies—Jews, Freemasons, politically active priests—must be pursued with foresight, comprehensively, and above all preventively;[65] secondly, the work of the political police must not be limited by legal restrictions;[66] thirdly, the Gestapo, the SD, and the General SS must be merged to form a 'State Protection Corps';[67] and fourthly, uncompromising harshness and ruthlessness were required in pursuit of these goals, a point to which Himmler kept returning.[68]

As early as in his speech to the German Peasants' Rally in Goslar, which was intended as a fundamental statement of his views, Himmler had emphasized that the SS would ensure 'that never again can a Jewish-Bolshevist revolution of subhumanity be initiated in Germany, the very heart of Europe, either from within or by outside emissaries. We shall act as a merciless sword of judgement on all these forces, of whose existence and activities we are well aware, on the day that they make even the slightest attempt—whether today, in decades, or in millennia.'[69]

In a speech on 5 March 1936 to the Prussian State Council, a body that Göring had created in 1933 as a replacement for the organization representing the Prussian provinces, which had been dissolved, Himmler emphasized once again his determination above all to be merciless and ruthless. At first he referred to the past dispute about the creation of an autonomous secret police, without disguising his satisfaction at having emerged as the victor of this conflict: 'And so in the course of 1934 we came to the point where,

with German decency but—and I believe I'm entitled to make this comment—totally underestimating our opponents, we almost completely
cleared the concentration camps and even contemplated whether we
couldn't dissolve the political police and integrate it completely into the
rest of the police, the criminal police, and into the general administration.'
At the time he himself had taken the 'opposite view' and 'urgently warned
against such ideas'. For 'the idea that the political struggle against our
opponents: Jewry, Bolshevism, Jewified world Freemasonry, and all the
forces that do not want a new, revived Germany is over, is in my view a
grave error, for Germany is right at the beginning of what may be a
centuries-long struggle, perhaps the decisive world struggle with these
forces of organized subhumanity.'

With this speech Himmler had for the first time discovered the useful
formula with which in future he was repeatedly to describe the conglomeration of enemies the SS saw itself confronted with. And in this context he
referred to his favourite topic of 'decency' (*Anständigkeit*), which he now
used in a most interesting way. The Reichsführer-SS considered it

as one of the greatest tasks of the German people to reassert the decency that is
fundamental to us in the way in which we conduct our struggles, and that our
conflicts, not only the physical and intellectual ones, but also those relating to
rational, human, official, departmental, and world political issues, whether in the
most mundane or in the most significant spheres, are pursued in an exemplary
manner. We must cultivate these values in all areas of life at home and outside
Germany vis-à-vis all those opponents who are worthy of this way of proceeding.

This did not apply, however, to the most dangerous opponents, to whom he
once again specifically denied the status of human beings with equal rights:

But it would be mad to apply this chivalrous attitude to Jewry and Bolshevism,
whose political methods involve amorality, deception, and mendacity and who, in
accordance with typical Jewish principles, consider the failure to destroy an opponent as weakness. Also to adopt a chivalrous form of combat towards a Jesuit, who
is engaged in a struggle for earthly power and who justifies lying in a way that is
incomprehensible to us through the theory of the 'reservatio mentalis', would be
virtually the equivalent of surrender [...] All in all, I should like to say that we
Germans must at last learn not to regard the Jews and Jewish-influenced organizations as human beings who are members of our species and as people who share our
way of thinking.

The Gestapo, Himmler continued, must 'combine the two elements'
through which Germany had become great: 'the military and the civil

service.'[70] However, what sounds like a peace-offering to the state bureau-cracy was perhaps intended only to disguise the fact that at this point the political scene had been set for the realization of a programme that inter-preted the concept of 'state protection' far more extensively than was suggested by the public statements of leading SS functionaries during the years 1935–6. The Reichsführer-SS was aiming to take over the whole of the German police and thereby to realize a concept of preventive repression, in which the struggle against political enemies was to go hand in hand with the elimination of the allegedly 'biological' roots of criminality.

In June 1935 Hitler approved Himmler's proposal to form the concentra-tion camp guards into a military unit.[71] On 18 October 1935 Himmler then managed to persuade Hitler that the German police needed to be reorga-nized, and secured the latter's agreement that he should take over the whole of the police. However, Himmler's appointment as 'Chief of the German Police' occurred only nine months after this decisive meeting, as before then lengthy negotiations had to take place with the Interior Ministry. In fact, from September 1935 Frick had been pursuing his own plans to establish a Reich police force and to reintegrate the Gestapo into the general police organization.[72]

One can reconstruct Himmler's line of argument from the notes he made of his meeting with Hitler on 18 October 1935.[73] At first he talked about the pursuit of political opponents, which at that time had already passed its peak. ('1. Treatment of the communists'). Then, under '2. Abortion', he discussed the dangers this allegedly posed for 'the whole nation' and the requisite police counter-measures. He used '3. Asocial elements' to consider how the tradi-tional range of police tasks could be expanded in the Third Reich. Finally, he dealt with the topic '4. Guard units', and under '5. Gestapo edict', opposed the attempts of Reich Interior Minister Frick to establish a Reich police force and reintegrate the Gestapo into the general police organization.[74]

Himmler achieved more in his meeting with Hitler than the takeover of the police. As is clear from a note that he made on the same day, Hitler also agreed to the creation of SS leadership colleges and discussed with him the possibility of 'internal unrest' and, in this context, the expansion of the armed SS units (SS-Verfügungstruppe).[75] Thus, the aim of amalgamating the SS and the police and their deployment under the auspices of a security concept that went far beyond conventional police tasks was beginning to emerge in outline. What this involved in detail Himmler would clarify only after his appointment to the new post of Reichsführer-SS and Chief of the German Police.

Only a few days later, on 21 October 1935, Hitler rejected Frick's proposal to take over the Reich Security Service, in other words, the small special unit responsible for the personal protection of the dictator and senior politicians of the regime. Hitler informed Frick that Himmler was formally responsible for the Reich Security Service; but in fact Hitler was himself in command, and in particular retained for himself the selection of its personnel. Frick's move could thus be interpreted as an attempt to restrict the dictator's room for manoeuvre in a sensitive area, an exceptionally clumsy one, given his ambitions vis-à-vis the police.[76]

Himmler, on the other hand, continued to exploit his advantage. On 1 November 1935 he had another meeting with Hitler. The Reich Justice Ministry had submitted complaints about the arbitrary nature of protective custody and the terror exercised in the concentration camps. Himmler succeeded in rebutting the accusations, and could subsequently curtly inform the Justice Minister that Hitler had expressly forbidden the employment of lawyers in cases of protective custody and, apart from that, saw no reason to intervene after being presented with a list of deaths in the concentration camps produced by the Justice Ministry. This was unnecessary in view of the 'exceptionally conscientious management of the concentration camps'.[77] In March 1936 the Justice Minister did manage to secure Himmler's agreement in principle to permit particular lawyers, who would be appointed in agreement with the Gestapo, to represent concentration camp prisoners. However, in the event the Gestapo prevented the implementation of this regulation by systematic stalling.[78] It is clear that for Himmler it was a matter of principle: prisoners in protective custody should on no account be able to claim the protection of the law. It was precisely the arbitrary character of concentration camp imprisonment that produced its deterrent effect, and it was on this fear that, in the final analysis, Himmler's power was based.

On 17 June 1936 Hitler finally appointed Himmler 'Reichsführer-SS and Chief of the German Police within the Reich Ministry of the Interior'.[79] The formula 'within the Reich Ministry of the Interior' proved in practice to be just as meaningless as the statement in the same law that Himmler was 'personally and directly' subordinate to the Reich Interior Minister. What was decisive was the fact that Frick had proved unable to integrate Himmler effectively into his ministry. In fact the opposite occurred; Himmler removed the police from the internal administration and took over the responsibility for it himself. What proved decisive was the linking together of the police and the SS. As Reichsführer-SS, Himmler was already directly subordinate to Hitler and, therefore, could always receive his orders directly from his 'Führer'. As Chief of the German Police, Himmler carefully evaded the Reich Interior Ministry by immediately creating two new Main Departments: the Security Police, comprising the Gestapo and the Criminal Police (Kripo) under Heydrich, and the Order Police under Daluege. These were hybrid organizations that anticipated the intended amalgamation of SS and police.[80]

On 20 September 1936 the Reich and Prussian Minister of the Interior issued an edict delegating to the Gestapa the duties of the political police commanders of the federal states, These were the duties that Himmler had hitherto carried out via the headquarters of the Police Commander based within the Gestapa. From now on they were to be exercised directly by the Secret State Police Office (Gestapa) itself.[81] This meant that the centralized secret Reich police force, which the Nazi leaders in the individual states had hoped to prevent, had finally come about. They now had to accept that their influence on the political police was minimal.[82]

9

The State Protection Corps

In a dictatorship the head of the police is assessed above all on the basis of how far he succeeds in neutralizing actual or alleged opponents of the regime. Thus, on the one hand, he will try to demonstrate the existence of such opponents by preparing reports on the threat they pose and, on the other, continually seek to document how such opponents have successfully been eliminated. However, he faces a certain dilemma in having to achieve a satisfactory balance in the relationship between threat and repression. If opponents are combated too successfully then the threat will decline and the police chief will thereby undermine his position in the long term; but if he paints the threat in too dark colours and thus reveals that, despite the measures of persecution, the threat is not declining but actually increasing, then he will simply demonstrate his incompetence. It is thus essential for him to achieve the right degree of both threat and its successful repression.

Applied to Himmler's position as Chief of the German Police in the 1930s, this process produced the following scenario: the Nazis' main opponents were the communists. From 1933 onwards the reports of the Gestapo and SD documented a continual growth in the communist threat and, as a result, an increase in the combating of the communist movement. As was suggested above, however, this trend could not continue indefinitely if the security police did not wish to jeopardize its work; on the other hand, from its point of view an end to the communist threat could not be desirable because it would remove an essential basis for its very existence.

There were two possible ways of escaping from this dilemma: an expansion of the range of opponents and the conception of 'preventive defence'. If the efforts of the security police were no longer concentrated primarily on defence against concrete threats and the exposure of acts of resistance that had already taken place, and instead focused on possible threats in the medium or long term, which could spring from a multiplicity of sources—or, to put it another way, on fictional threats—then the success of the security apparatus would be freed from its fatal dependence on concrete dangers. The work of the security police could then be portrayed as the result of far-sighted planning. In other words, the success of prevention as a strategy depended primarily on how convincing the security police was in depicting the future dangers.

With Hitler's fundamental agreement in the autumn of 1935 to his using a comprehensive concept of prevention as the basis for police work, Himmler had succeeded in taking the first step towards implementing this strategy. The transition to 'general prevention' then occurred on several levels.

In the first place, Himmler decided to reorientate the combating of the communist movement—explicitly in the light of a coming war—towards preventive measures, so that in future he could report both a reduction in communist activities and an increase in the number of communist prisoners. The combating of communism no longer needed to be justified in terms of communist acts of resistance, with the result that the embarrassment of repeated successes in this sphere being regarded in the final analysis as a sign of failure was avoided. The targets for this 'preventive' project were 'the brains behind the operation', 'troublemakers', and 'intellectual initiators'; and, by associating communism with other 'international' enemies, the increased persecution of Jews and priests who were critical of the regime could be construed within the same uniform conception of prevention. However, the substantial halt to the campaign against the churches in 1937 resulted in the repression increasingly being concentrated on the Jewish minority.

Secondly, Himmler extended the preventive task of combating opponents to all forms of opposition, even those that were harmless and unspecific. The spreading of rumours and jokes, public demonstration of discontent with the regime, statements of loyalty to the Christian churches, and so on allegedly threatened the internal unity of the nation, and so the security police, as the protector of the national community, had to intervene.

Thirdly, Himmler integrated the combating of criminality into the work of the security police by representing criminality as essentially a consequence of biological defects, which must be—preventively—eliminated. Fourthly, he set the security police the task of focusing on the 'national plagues' of abortion and homosexuality in order to ensure the German people's biological survival.

The transition to prevention resulted in a considerable extension and reorientation of traditional police work; in fact the police was integrated into a reformed apparatus of repression organized on the basis of a division of labour. The amalgamation of political repression and the combating of criminality was a logical consequence of the combination of the Gestapo and the criminal police (Kripo) to form the security police. While the restructured police continued to perform the executive functions as before, the provision of evidence of potential threats was primarily the task of the SD, which had intellectual ambitions and which was now closely linked with the state police. Moreover, the ideological indoctrination of the police, in particular the orientation of police work along biological lines, made the integration of SS and police appear sensible.

Thus Himmler succeeded in making the takeover of the whole of the police apparatus in 1936 appear not as a simple accumulation of power but as part of a much broader project, which involved a more far-reaching security concept: the amalgamation of the police and the SS. What Himmler envisaged was a state protection corps that would avert all potential threats to the nation and the 'Aryan race' as perceived by Nazi racial ideology.

On the occasion of his taking up his post as Chief of the German Police on 18 June 1936 Himmler made a speech in the courtyard of the Prussian Interior Ministry in which he justified the expansion of the police on the grounds of the need to be prepared for future conflicts with external enemies:

We are a country in the heart of Europe surrounded by open borders, surrounded by a world that is becoming more and more Bolshevized, and increasingly taken over by the Jew in his worst form, namely the tyranny of a totally destructive Bolshevism. To believe that this development is going to come to an end in a year's time, or in several years or even in decades, is culpably reckless and erroneous. We must assume that this struggle will last for generations, for it's the age-old struggle between humans and subhumans in its current new phase of the struggle between the Aryan peoples and Jewry and the organizational form Jewry has adopted of Bolshevism. I see my task as being to prepare the whole nation for this struggle by building up the police welded together with the order of the SS as the organization to protect the Reich at home just as the Wehrmacht provides protection against threats from abroad.[1]

This notion of Himmler's, the German police 'welded together with the order of the SS', was then adopted by Werner Best in an influential article in the journal of the Academy of German Law in order to explain that this concept of a 'state protection corps', which hitherto had been used for the amalgamation of the political police and the SS, had now acquired a new meaning. It now described the planned fusion of the SS and the whole of the police service.[2] The point that was being unambiguously made was that Himmler's appointment as Chief of the German Police did not mean that the Gestapo was being reintegrated into the general police apparatus but, on the contrary, marked the start of a development, in the course of which the police would be completely removed from the traditional administrative apparatus and be linked to the SS to form an entirely new type of 'state protection corps'.

A few months later Himmler went a step further, and proposed the final departure of the police from the principle of legality. Whereas in previous years he, together with Heydrich and Best, had demanded and achieved a special status for the political police unrestricted by 'legal norms', he now demanded that this should apply to the whole of the police.

Significantly, he announced his fundamental opposition to—indeed contempt for—the principle of legality at the inaugural session of the Committee for Police Law. He conceded that this might 'appear odd', given that the location of the meeting was the Academy for German Law, but he was by no means inclined—'you will appreciate that'—to make any concessions concerning his basic position, as became clear from his reminiscences about the first phase following the seizure of power: 'We National Socialists then set to work [. . .] not without justice, but possibly outside the law. Right from the start I took the view that it did not matter in the least if our actions were contrary to some clause in the law; in my work for the Führer and the nation I do what my conscience tells me is right and what is common sense.' Viewed from a völkisch standpoint, 'in every nation there must be certain things that can only be seen in a certain way, and whether seen by a cowherd or a minister, it would not be decent to regard them in any other way'.

On this occasion Himmler put forward another idea: 'We Germans,' he said, because of the particular development of the country, '[have] become obsessed with making rules', and 'through our rule-making with its strict regulations and discipline [have] produced two types, the civil servant and the soldier'. But the German police could not be 'simply civil servants or soldiers'; rather, they must develop 'a soldierly civil service'. Himmler had already advocated this fusion of soldier and civil servant as a future model for the Gestapo six months earlier in his speech to the Prussian state councillors in March. But now he gave this version a further twist. Himmler recommended the model of a soldierly civil service for the whole of the German police force. It would be 'given more and more training—and that will be the work of generations—and one day will share the spirit of the SS, an un-civil service-like and un-soldierly organization, that has been created in the spirit of an order based on blood and promoting family inheritance and which must develop over centuries, even millennia'.[3]

In March 1937 Himmler once more expressed his views about the tasks of the police in public. The occasion was a publication to mark the sixtieth birthday of Interior Minister Frick, Himmler's main opponent in his take-over of the police. Himmler used his article to stress once more, contrary to the views of Frick, who was rightly called by his biographer the 'legalist of the unjust state',[4] that as a matter of principle the activities of the police could not be described or restricted by law.

In Himmler's view, the police had to perform two main duties: '(a) the police must carry out the will of the leadership of the state and create and maintain the order that it wishes to establish. (b) The police must secure the German nation as an organic entity, its life force and its institutions, against destruction and subversion.' The powers of a police force that was set such tasks 'must not therefore be constrained by formal limits, because these limits would otherwise also stand in the way of it carrying out the tasks set by the state leadership'. Like the Wehrmacht, the police could act only on the orders of the leadership and not according to the law.

Himmler then dealt in detail with the functions of the order police (*Ordnungspolizei*) and security police (*Sicherheitspolizei*). While the first was mainly responsible for 'maintaining public order', the security police fundamentally had 'the defensive task of averting attacks from all those forces which in any way might weaken or destroy the health, the life force, and the effectiveness of the nation and the state'. The criminal police must concentrate on those people 'who, as a result of physical or intellectual degeneration, have removed themselves from the natural bonds of the national community and in the ruthless pursuit of their own personal interests have breached the regulations that have been instituted for the protection of the nation and the community'. The Secret State Police (*Geheime Staatspolizei*), on the other hand, was engaged in a 'continual struggle' against those who, 'as tools of the ideological and political enemies of the German people, are trying to undermine the unity of the German nation and to destroy its state power'.[5]

Ill. 12. Himmler addressing the Committee for Police Law. Among his attentive audience were (from l. to r.): Reinhard Heydrich, Hans Frank, Werner Best, and Kurt Daluege.

In his contribution to the celebratory volume Heydrich added an 'offensive' component to Himmler's envisaged 'defensive' role for the police: 'it has to be offensively investigating all opposition and combating it in order to pre-empt its destructive and subversive effects.' In particular, Heydrich made a close link between conventional crime and ideological and political threats to the so-called Third Reich: 'Subhumans threaten the health and life of the national body in two respects: as criminals they damage and undermine the community and they also act as tools and weapons for the plans of those powers hostile to the nation.' According to Heydrich, 'international, ideological, and intellectual opponents' utilized 'subhumanity, which is invariably bent on subversion and disorder, but also the supporters of their own political and ideological organizations, in other words Jewry, Freemasonry, and the politicized churches. Moreover, they utilize all those other groups in the German nation who, whether consciously or having been misled, support special interests that are detrimental to the German people (Legitimists, etc.).'[6]

In this description of the role of the security police everything had been thrown together: the struggle against crime, against 'subhumanity', against any kind of disorder, against Jews, Freemasons, and the churches. All these unpleasant manifestations were to be 'pre-emptively' dealt with. It could hardly be clearer that the preventive policy of the new police leadership was directed against a conglomeration of enemies of the state of the most varied stripe that was impossible to disentangle, and that whoever had the authority to define these enemies and to pursue them would effectively have unlimited power. Himmler and Heydrich were ultimately able to secure their demand that the activities of the police should not be limited by law. No codification of police duties in a new police legal code was ever produced. Up until 1945 the legal basis for the measures carried out by the police remained the Reichstag Fire Decree of 28 February 1933, which had suspended the fundamental rights of the Weimar Constitution. Thus the German police, which Himmler took over in 1936, acted under a permanent state of emergency.

In his public comments on the police at this time Himmler repeatedly emphasized the determination and 'toughness' of the Gestapo and the SS in dealing with enemies of the state. He admitted that this attitude had resulted in the SS being not exactly popular with the public, a fact that was not inconvenient for him, as it was, after all, part of a strategy of surrounding the Gestapo, SS, and concentration camps with an aura of terror. Already in November 1935 Himmler had admitted to the German Peasants' Rally that he knew that 'there are some people in Germany who feel sick when they see this black uniform; we understand that and do not expect that many people will like us. But all those whose hearts are true to Germany will and should respect us, and those who for some reason and at some time have a bad conscience about the Führer or the nation should fear us.'[7]

In a radio broadcast to mark German Police Day in January 1937 Himmler noted that he saw his main task as being 'to neutralize all malign opponents and enemies of the National Socialist state. Whether the opponent is communist or reactionary is irrelevant.' They would pursue 'disciples of Moscow' in just the same way as 'incorrigible reactionaries' or 'religious malcontents'. He knew, Himmler continued, that 'I and my colleagues have made a number of enemies as a result of the toughness with which we have carried out this task, and will go on making them. But I am convinced that it's better to be misunderstood by a few, to be hated by some opponents, but in the process to do what is necessary for Germany.'[8]

The picture painted by Himmler and leading SS functionaries of the police, and above all of the Gestapo, was sometimes underlined by such threatening gestures, but sometimes by the assurance that normal citizens had nothing to fear, that they would be treated fairly and justly, and, moreover, that the pursuit of opponents was being carried out in accordance with purely objective considerations. Himmler summed up this ambivalent public representation in his speech on the occasion of the 1937 German Police Day in the following formula: 'tough and implacable where necessary, understanding and generous where possible.'[9]

Since 1933 the Nazi regime had made no secret of its belief in a police force, or rather a secret police, operating ruthlessly against political opponents and criminals. The initial emphasis of this propaganda had been on the need effectively to eliminate communist or 'Marxist' opponents. During the mid-1930s the emphasis shifted towards asserting that the police in general, and the security police in particular, provided comprehensive protection for the national community by suppressing any oppositional activity that was 'hostile to the nation', and through its preventive measures ensured that crime was nipped in the bud. It publicly advocated the notion of 'police justice', in other words, the regime's practice of using the Gestapo to punish actual or alleged miscreants. At the same time, it tried to present the police as 'a friend and helpmate', as the official slogan put it, and to stress the high moral value of police work.

However, in numerous newspaper articles and publications, above all those marking German Police Day,[10] which was celebrated annually from 1934 onwards and from 1937 lasted for a whole week, one theme was stressed above all: the notion of an ever-present and all-knowing secret police; in short, a Gestapo myth was created.[11]

Gestapo and SD

According to Himmler, the police should show themselves to be 'understanding and generous', above all, as he put it in a speech to mark the 1937 German Police Day, because they had to rely on the 'active and sympathetic support of every German national comrade'.[12] He expressed his astonishment, however, at the extent of this 'cooperation' as it manifested itself in

the day-to-day operations of the police. Thus, in a speech on the Brocken*
to celebrate the summer solstice on 22 May 1936, he commented 'that
Germany is the biggest hotbed of gossip in the world. It's sometimes really
quite difficult to retain any respect for people when one keeps hearing how
they denounce each other, how they keep making idiots of themselves. In
Germany one doesn't need to have any agents; the people do all the
informing themselves.'[13]

Research into the Gestapo[14] appears at first glance to confirm this picture
of a society that kept watch on itself. Thus, in his study of the Düsseldorf
Gestapo Reinhard Mann came to the conclusion that only 15 per cent of the
cases that he examined[15] had been initiated by the Gestapo itself, whereas at
26 per cent denunciations stemming from the population played a relatively
large role. The American historian Eric A. Johnson also concluded that 24
per cent of cases taken up by the Gestapo in Krefeld were the result of
denunciations.[16]

If one looks at the particular groups of offences, however, a rather more
complex picture emerges. In the prosecution of cases of 'racial disgrace'
(sexual relations between 'Aryans' and Jews) and other inadmissible contacts
with Jews, as well as of so-called 'unpatriotic behaviour' (Heimtücke), in
other words, the spreading of rumours, jokes, and so on, the number of
denunciations was quite high, whereas in the case of the pursuit of political
opponents, homosexuals, as well as supporters of the major Christian
denominations and the Jehovah's Witnesses they played a comparatively
small role.[17] It is also important to note, as Johnson points out, that
denunciations mostly concerned minor offences, whereas in relation to
'real' opponents of the regime, in other words, cases which often had serious
consequences, they were much less frequent. Above all, even if denunciations were of considerable importance for the day-to-day work of the
Gestapo, in comparative terms the absolute numbers of cases of denunciation were relatively small. Thus, only a small percentage of the population
volunteered information to the Gestapo. Such cases should not be used to
draw more far-reaching conclusions about the state of 'German society'.[18]
Thus, although the Gestapo was dependent on the 'co-operation' of the
population in the pursuit of certain offences, such as the maintenance of
contacts with Jews, it would be wrong simply to accept Himmler's vision of
a society where 'the people do all the informing themselves'.

* Translators' note: The highest peak in the Harz mounatins.

In relation to the tasks it had been set and its reputation, the Gestapo's organization was relatively small. At the beginning of 1934 the Prussian Gestapo had approximately 1,700 employees, of whom around 700 were employed in the headquarters. In June 1935 the figure had risen to 2,700, with the number employed in headquarters remaining roughly the same. If one applies these figures to the Reich as a whole, then there were around 4,200 people employed in the political police in 1935, of whom around 10 per cent were female secretaries. Up until 1937 this number increased to around 7,000 employees.[19] Of the Gestapo employees who were employed in 1937, around three-quarters had worked in various parts of the police force, 5 per cent had been taken on from other state organizations (such as the judicial system), and 20 per cent were newly employed, in other words, mainly party supporters.[20]

The size of the Gestapo varied significantly from government district to government district. Thus, in 1937 the Gestapo office in Bielefeld controlled a district of more than 870,000 inhabitants with fifty-three officers, the one in Hildesheim had thirty officers controlling around 600,000 people, and the one in Chemnitz had fifty-five officers responsible for more than a million inhabitants.[21] However, one should not overlook the fact that the Gestapo had a relatively large number of informants. So-called 'trusties' headed a network of informants, which the Gestapo divided into various categories based on reliability and importance. Some of these informants were opponents who had been forced to cooperate with the regime, others were paid spies.[22]

In his new function Himmler unified the Gestapo apparatus throughout the Reich and gave it the same independence from the internal administration as he had already secured for it in Prussia. The heads of the Gestapo offices were supposed to act as 'desk officers' for political police matters for their state governments, and also to be bound by their instructions, but this applied only insofar as 'instructions to the contrary had not been issued by the Secret State Police Office'. And where there was disagreement, the Gestapa had the final decision as to whether the head of the district Gestapo office should obey the instructions of his state government or not. This rendered the 'inclusion' of the Gestapo in the internal state administration an absurdity.[23]

The SD, as the party's intelligence agency, was not directly affected by the takeover of the police by Himmler in June 1936 and the resultant reorganization. However, the fact that Heydrich, the head of the SD, was put in charge of the newly created Security Main Office, which was responsible for the security police, increased his potential for influence, even if he was still not permitted to take executive action as head of the SD.[24]

At the beginning of 1936 Heydrich had already reorganized the SD Main Office within the SS headquarters. Most important was the fact that the tasks of the Office of Domestic Affairs had been divided into 'ideological assessment' (initially under Hermann Behrends, then under Franz Alfred Six) and 'assessment of the domestic situation' (under Reinhard Höhn, later under Otto Ohlendorff). While the 'ideological assessment' concentrated on those groups that were seen as the main enemies of Nazism and so were divided into the sections: 'Freemasons', 'Jews', 'religious and political movements',[25] the 'assessment of the domestic situation' department set about constructing an elaborate system for information-gathering and reporting that went far beyond the surveillance of political opponents and was designed to cover the entire spectrum of life in the Third Reich. It was divided into three groups: Economics; Culture—Scholarship—Education—Ethnic issues; and Administration and the Law—Party and State—Higher Education and Students.

By issuing the so-called division-of-functions order, the 'Combined Order for the Security Service of the Reichsführer-SS and for the Secret State Police of the Head of the Main Office of the Security Police and SD', on 1 July 1937, Heydrich introduced a detailed demarcation of the functions of the two organizations.[26] The SD, in which in the meantime young committed intellectuals had acquired leadership positions establishing valuable contacts to the world of scholarship, and in a number of cases achieving academic careers,[27] was to be 'exclusively' responsible for the spheres of scholarship, ethnic matters and folklore, art, education, party and state, the constitution and administration, foreign affairs, Freemasonry, and clubs and societies; the Gestapo, on the other hand, was to be 'exclusively' responsible for 'Marxism, treason, émigrés'. As far as the churches, pacifism, Jewry, the right-wing movement, other groups hostile to the state, the economy, and the press were concerned, all 'general and fundamental issues were to be dealt with by the SD and all individual cases by the Gestapo'.

How, then, from 1936 onwards did the Gestapo carry out its role in practice? Statistics prepared by Reinhard Mann on the basis of the files of the Düsseldorf Gestapo for the whole period 1933 to 1945 show that 30 per cent of the cases investigated by the Gestapo concerned the pursuit of banned organizations, mainly the KPD and SPD (although this area of Gestapo activity more or less came to a halt during the war); 29 per cent of cases investigated dealt with publicly deviant behaviour, mainly criticisms of the regime; 17 per cent with other forms of deviant behaviour, such as the spreading of banned pamphlets or listening to enemy radio broadcasts; 12 per cent of the investigations involved conventional criminality.[28] In his study of the Düsseldorf office Johnson comes to the conclusion that the Gestapo's activities concentrated on three groups in particular: Jews, members of the Left, as well as opposition priests and members of sects. The control of other 'normal' Germans, with the exception of homosexuals, was relatively lax, and if they ever got caught up in a Gestapo investigation they were usually let off with a warning or a minor penalty.[29]

As time went on, however, the focus of its activity shifted. While up until 1935–6 the pursuit of communists had been the first priority, in the following years this group played a much-reduced role, and for a very simple reason: by 1936 the communist underground organization had been almost completely destroyed.[30] In 1935 the Gestapo had arrested around 14,000 communists, in 1936 11,678, and in 1938 8,068.[31] Himmler, however, made no bones about the fact that he intended to continue keeping the communist functionaries in the camps. For, as he put it in 1937, even if the KPD and its organizations had ceased to exist, in future 'a large number of members of our nation could keep becoming vulnerable to the poison of Bolshevism'.[32]

After the elimination of the communists, the Gestapo and the SD concentrated on the so-called 'wire-pullers', the intellectual opposition—Freemasons, Jews, and politicized priests—on whom Himmler, Heydrich, and Best had increasingly focused since 1935. Here too, however, there were significant differences in the way these groups were treated.

Freemasons

In the speeches he made during the 1930s Himmler invariably counted the Freemasons among the Nazis' arch-enemies and referred to them in the same breath as the Jews, the Bolsheviks, and the politicized priests.[33] However, the Reichsführer-SS, who since his youth had been a believer in the widespread conspiracy theories concerning the Freemasons, did not specify in these speeches what exactly the allegedly nefarious activity of the Freemasons consisted of.

In fact, in the meantime he must have come to the conclusion that the Freemasons posed no threat to the Nazi regime. This assessment was shared by the experts of the Gestapo and SD: for them, from the mid-1930s onwards, the combating of Freemasonry was no longer a priority. In 1935, in his influential series of articles in Das Schwarze Korps, 'Phases of Our Struggle', Heydrich demonstratively referred to Freemasonry as merely 'an auxiliary organization of Jewry' and therefore indicated that it was no longer regarded as a separate threat.[34]

Because of the Nazis' hostility to Freemasonry, most of the lodges had already dissolved themselves in 1933 or had been dissolved by the state governments.[35] By the summer of 1935 all the associations of Freemasons had been liquidated.[36] Former members of lodges were discriminated against in the Third Reich, for example, if they were employed in the public sector.[37] Moreover, as a matter of principle they were excluded from party membership, which automatically blocked their access to a wide range of privileged positions.[38] But there was no systematic persecution of Freemasons. What is more, the fact that someone was a Freemason or had previously been one did not generally justify the imposition of protective custody.

The dwindling significance of Freemasonry was reflected in the organizational arrangements of the Gestapo and SD. Whereas before 1933 the SD had kept a special register of Freemasons,[39] after its move to Berlin at the beginning of 1935 it established a 'Museum of Freemasonry' in which the items confiscated from the lodges, their libraries, and documents were collected together.[40] It was being signalled that the 'problem' now belonged to the past. At the beginning of 1936 the SD department originally specifically devoted to Freemasonry was amalgamated with the desk officers dealing with the Jews and church matters to form a main department responsible for 'Ideologies'.[41] From the summer of 1937 onwards the Gestapo no longer dealt with this topic. Under the order of 1 July 1937 dealing with the demarcation of functions referred to above, Freemasonry was allocated entirely to the SD.[42]

Jews

With the destruction of the communist underground appearing to be imminent, 'the Jews' were among those 'intellectual forces' referred to in Himmler's public speeches who were secretly intriguing against Nazism and who, from 1935 onwards, were increasingly to be the target of the SS leadership and the Gestapo. However, for the period before the November pogrom of 1938 it is impossible to find any lengthy anti-Semitic statements by Himmler. He mostly treated the question of the Jews cursorily and often in a stereotypical manner along with the other enemies, and without spending any time on them.[43]

It was only in his major speech to the Reich Peasant Rally in Goslar of November 1935—in other words, a few weeks after the issuing of the Nuremberg Laws—that he embarked on a comprehensive anti-Jewish polemic. Significantly, the speech was printed under the title 'The SS as an Anti-Bolshevik Combat Organization', thereby emphasizing the link between anti-Semitism and 'anti-Bolshevism'.

Himmler ranged very widely. He began by introducing the farmers gathered together in Goslar to the Persian Empire of Xerxes I (519–465 BC) in order to explain the moral perniciousness of the Jewish festival of Purim. Himmler reinterpreted the annual commemoration of the saving of the Persian Jews from a pogrom—Xerxes had ordered a mass slaughter of his Jewish enemies—as 'the radical destruction of an Aryan nation by Jewish-Bolshevik methods'. Then he described a series of similar 'tragedies' in which, however, one could in some cases only 'sense [. . .] that here our age-old enemy, the Jew, in some form or through one of his organizations had his bloody hands in the affair'. Himmler's list included: 'the tireless executioner's sword wielded at Cannstatt and Verden' (in other words, the mass killing of Alemannen in 746 by Karlmann and of the Saxons by Charlemagne in 782); the medieval and early modern witch trials ('We can visualize the fires burning at the stakes on which tens of thousands of the martyred and tortured bodies of mothers and girls of our nation burnt to ashes'); 'the courts of the Inquisition which depopulated Spain'; the Thirty Years War; the French Revolution ('a revolution organized solely by the order of Freemasons, this marvellous Jewish organization'); as well as the Russian Revolution of 1917.

When looking through his manuscript, Himmler may have had doubts about whether his arguments would stand up. The idea that Jewish string-pullers should have manipulated Charlemagne, the 'Slaughterer of the Saxons', of all people and should have conceived the Spanish Inquisition must have been hard to take, even for hard-line anti-Semites. Moreover, by referring to Persians, Spaniards, French, and Russians he had extended the list of those who had suffered from Jewish machinations so much that the central role of the Teutons as the 'victims' of the Jewish world conspiracy had become insufficiently clear. Thus, he asked his listeners not to succumb 'to excessive Aryan and German objectivity' by focusing on the details but rather to concentrate on 'the general point'.

During the first years of the Third Reich neither the Gestapo nor the SD played a prominent role in Jewish persecution. During this period the Jewish policy of the Nazi regime was initially driven decisively by the subtle interaction of party activists and state legislation. The party started 'actions' against the Jews, such as the boycott of 1 April 1933 and the riots of spring and summer 1935, or the pogrom of November 1938, to which the state bureaucracy then responded with measures in order further to restrict the lives of the Jewish minority. As far as the party was concerned, apart from the staff of the Führer's Deputy under Rudolf Hess and Martin Bormann, a key role was played by a number of particularly anti-Semitic Gauleiters (Goebbels in Berlin, Grohé in Cologne, Streicher in Nuremberg), while the state operations were controlled by the Reich Interior Ministry.

The role of the Gestapo in this sphere was above all to keep the activities of Jewish organizations under surveillance[44] and to carry out state measures. However, the Gestapo became increasingly unwilling to wait for laws or decrees, and began initiating such measures by issuing its own edicts. In January 1935, for example, the Gestapo ordered returning émigrés to be interned in 're-education camps', which effectively meant concentration camps, as was made clear in a regulation issued a few weeks later.[45] In February 1935 the Gestapa banned all events in which support was sought for Jews to remain in Germany.[46] Another example was the flag ban of February 1935, which forbade Jews to raise the swastika; it was not legally confirmed until September 1935 with the Reich Flag Law.[47]

Himmler's involvement in such bans varied. In July 1936, for example, he signed a directive that required requests for licences to run a pub to make it clear whether the applicant was a Jew,[48] and on 15 June 1936 he informed the state secretary in the Reich Interior Ministry, Hans Pfundtner, of Hitler's request that in future Jews should not be allowed to use German first names. However, the Interior Ministry did not act on this for another eighteen months.[49]

In general, Himmler left the implementation of anti-Jewish measures to Heydrich, who during the 1930s became the central figure in the Jewish policy of the Gestapo and SD. Heydrich's role was increased by the fact that Göring, in his position as head of the 'Raw Materials and Foreign Exchange

Staff' (the precursor of the Four Year Plan organization), assigned him the task of setting up a 'Foreign Exchange Search Office'. This new responsibility enabled Heydrich in future to move against Jews who were under 'suspicion of emigrating' on the grounds of alleged breaches of foreign-exchange regulations.[50] This appointment was the first of a whole series of responsibilities involving Jewish persecution which the Reich Marshall assigned to the head of the security police and SD during the coming years. This created two competing chains of command involving Jewish policy: Hitler–Himmler–Heydrich and Hitler–Göring–Heydrich. The Reichsführer-SS was thereby in danger of being excluded from the decision-making process in the event of his proving insufficiently active on the anti-Semitic front.

As far as Jewish persecution was concerned, both the Gestapo and the SD concentrated above all on encouraging emigration and preventing all attempts at 'assimilation' by German Jews. A Gestapa report of November 1934 formulated this as a programme, stating: 'it is the aim of the state police to encourage Zionism as much as possible and support its efforts at pursuing emigration.'[51] However, for this purpose it was necessary to know the numbers involved and who was to be supported. Thus, from 1935 onwards Gestapo offices recorded the names of Jews domiciled in their districts, a process that had been substantially concluded by 1939.[52]

Meanwhile, the SD's Jewish department had acquired a group of young, self-confident officials—Dieter Wisliceny, Herbert Hagen, Theodor Dannecker, and Adolf Eichmann—who, in the course of 1937, set about developing their own comprehensive version of Jewish policy. Their intention was to harmonize the various and sometimes conflicting aims of Jewish persecution—expulsion, forcing the Jews out of the economy and society, and plundering them. This group believed that its position as the brains trust for Jewish policy had been confirmed by Heydrich's 'functions order' of 1 July 1937, in which he had assigned all Jewish matters to the SD.[53]

From now on the SD increasingly involved itself in the practice of Jewish persecution, which was really the task of the Gestapo. When the German–Polish Agreement on Upper Silesia of 1922 came to an end in July 1937 and the Nazi regime could now apply the anti-Jewish legislation to this part of the country as well, Eichmann, who had been sent to Breslau a few weeks before, carried out vital preliminary work there.[54] After the so-called Anschluss with Austria this SD tactic of trying to acquire an executive role came to fruition with its assumption of auxiliary tasks for the Gestapo.[55]

The churches

Unlike in the case of the Jews, there was one group among those Himmler defined as enemies that aroused in him something akin to passion: Christians. And that was particularly the case when he was speaking to closed meetings of members of the SS, when he did not need to pay any attention to wider considerations of policy regarding the churches.

Thus, in 1938 he declared: 'Christian doctrine has been responsible for the destruction of every nation. A religion which (a) sees women as sinful, (b) marriage as the lesser evil—it is at least better than the alternative, such teaching is in the long run absolutely liable to bring every nation to the grave.' Christianity, according to Himmler, was 'the destroyer of every nation'.[56] On the occasion of the transfer of the expropriated headquarters of the Order of Teutonic Knights to the SS by the city of Vienna in 1939 he informed his listeners that he had 'the firm intention' 'thoroughly to break with' two developments that had had fatal repercussions for German history: 'in the first place, with a doctrine that in our view is wrong for Teutons, the fateful doctrine of an Asiatic Christianity, and secondly, with the squandering of blood [. . .] caused by the negation of the clan and the negation of the family.'[57]

He warned the Oberabschnitt leaders on 9 June 1942: 'We shall have to deal with Christianity in a much tougher way than hitherto. We must sort out this Christianity; it has plagued us throughout our history and weakened us in every conflict. If our generation doesn't do it then I believe it could go on for a long time. We must face up to the need to deal with it.'[58] Three months later, on 16 September 1942, in a speech to SS and police leaders in Hegewald, his Ukrainian summer headquarters, he described Christianity as 'a perverse ideology that is alien to life', because 'in a typically oriental way it equates women with sin and has regarded procreation as legitimate only if a priest has given his blessing; then it was just about all right. But—and this was the strongest moral impulse of the Catholic Church—every sexual act between a man and woman in which the object was not to have a child or in which it was prevented was declared a mortal sin.'[59]

For the sake of outward appearances, however, Himmler tried to create the impression that the SS was neutral in its attitude towards the Christian denominations. Thus, in January 1934 he expressed his displeasure at having read in a newspaper report that 'an SS formation has taken part in the enthronement of a state bishop'. Himmler described this as 'tasteless' and 'incorrect', since 'the SS members who had been ordered to participate would have been thereby exposed to moral conflict'. A 'politicization of religious life does not accord with our ideology. Even the appearance of it must be avoided at all costs.'[60] In October 1934 he insisted that clergy and, in March 1935, theology students must quit the SS.[61] In September 1935 he banned SS members from 'participating in leadership roles' in religious communities, in particular with the German Christians.[62] Himmler did not intend to reform Christianity in Nazi Germany; rather, he wanted to draw a clear dividing-line against Christian communities of any kind. In November 1937 he even went so far as to ban SS members in uniform from taking part in religious ceremonies.[63]

This policy of distancing himself set certain limits to attacks on the churches. In September 1934 Himmler issued an SS order 'strictly' banning 'any disturbance or any tactless behaviour during the religious ceremonies of all denominations'.[64] In October 1935 he reassured Hitler, who was evidently concerned about the well-known hostile attitude of the SS to the churches, that 'he valued highly peaceful relations between state and church'.[65] In July 1937 he noted in an SS order that he had had to expel a Platoon Leader (*Scharführer*) from the SS for 'a speech that was riddled with tactless remarks about Church matters'.[66] A month earlier, during a course of 'ideological indoctrination', he had banned 'any attacks on the person of Christ', since 'such attacks or the abuse of Christ as a Jew [are] unworthy of us' and 'definitely historically untrue'; which showed that he shared the notion of an 'Aryan Jesus' that was widespread in völkisch circles.[67] He also declined to attack Christianity publicly as 'Jewish-Roman'.[68] In 1941 he wrote to a corporal in the Wehrmacht, who wanted to become a theology student, that he was unable to grant his wish 'to remain a member of the SS as a theologian on principle'. The basic regulation had been passed in order to keep the SS 'out of the conflicts among the religious denominations'.[69]

The fact that the SS leadership did not demand that its members leave their churches, however much this was considered desirable, fitted in with this public image of neutrality vis-à-vis the churches. At the end of 1938 21.9 per cent of SS members described themselves, like Himmler, as 'believers in God' (*gottgläubig*); in other words, they did not belong to any Christian denomination. Significantly, the figure was 53.6 per cent for the armed SS formation, and in the case of the Death's Head units as much as 69 per cent.[70] Officially Himmler emphasized that he left it up to his members whether or not they belonged to a Christian denomination. In 1936 he advised the leader of the Düsseldorf Oberabschnitt, Fritz Weitzel, not to ask SS leaders during their indoctrination course to produce essays on the topic of 'How I Came to Leave the Church'. He considered that 'dangerous'; instead, he suggested 'Is Belief in God the Same Thing as Membership of a Religious Denomination?'[71] In February 1937 he told the Gruppenführer that he was strongly against forcing people to leave the church—it should not be made into a 'sport' within the SS.[72]

In 1937 he wrote to a pastor, in reply to a query: 'Every SS man is free to be a member of a church or not. It is a personal matter, which he has to answer for to God or his conscience.' SS men should not, however, be atheists, for 'that is the only world- or religious view that is not tolerated within the SS'.[73] 'I have nothing to do with denominations,' he told army officers in July 1944, 'I leave that to each individual. But I have never tolerated an atheist in the ranks of the SS. Every member has a deep faith in God, in what my ancestors called in their language Waralda, the ancient one, the one who is mightier than we are.'[74]

At the Gruppenführer meeting in November 1936 he stated that, in particular, they should not 'rip out from old people's hearts what they consider holy', and illustrated this with a personal example: 'My father [Gerhard Himmler had died that same year] was—in accordance with the tradition of our family—a convinced Christian, in his case a convinced Catholic. He knew my attitude very well. But we never discussed religion apart from a conversation about the political harmfulness and perniciousness of the Christian churches, about which we both agreed. I never challenged his viewpoint and he didn't mine.' He could 'sympathize' with someone who said: 'I've got to christen my child for the sake of my parents. By all means. Go ahead. One can't change 70-year-olds.'[75]

However, the anti-Christian remarks by Himmler quoted above, which were based on fundamental ideological considerations, indicate that his repeated comments about religious tolerance in the SS were purely tactical. When, at the end of 1940, he remarked in a speech that after the war he envisaged a 'clear and peaceful separation of church and state',[76] in fact he did not consider that to be the final goal of Nazi church policy; in reality he was bent on the destruction of Christianity, which was opposed to his biological-völkisch aims. But in this case the pure doctrine could not be implemented; despite various anti-church initiatives, the regime could never bring itself to make the removal of the Christian churches and Christian doctrine official policy. And so Himmler was obliged to be cautious.

During the first years of the regime the Gestapo and SD concentrated their surveillance and persecution measures against the churches above all on the Catholics. Although the Nazi state and the Vatican had made a Reich Concordat in July 1933, which guaranteed the existence of the Catholic Church, two years after the seizure of power the radical elements within the Nazi movement set about altering the status quo to their advantage. Apart from Hess and his chief of staff, Martin Bormann, above all Reichsleiter Alfred Rosenberg and Himmler were the key figures among these anti-church hardliners. As the elimination of the Christian churches was not opportune, their strategy in the medium term was to remove the privileged position of the churches as far as their status as public institutions was concerned. Reduced to the status of private institutions, the churches were to be gradually excluded from public life.

Himmler, however, was rarely involved publicly in the anti-church measures of the Gestapo and SD. He left this sphere largely to Heydrich, who was in full agreement with Himmler on church matters. Himmler's public caution was probably largely determined by his unwillingness to appear as a radical opponent of the churches and for the SS in general to be equated with anti-church fundamentalism. Ironically, between 1935 and 1941 the SD department dealing with church matters was headed by a former Catholic priest, Albert Hartl. Having joined the party in 1933, Hartl finally burnt his bridges in 1934 and joined the SD. Because of a denunciation his position within the church had become untenable.[77]

In 1935 the Nazi state began to target the Catholic religious orders with a wave of criminal trials, which were accompanied by a massive anti-church campaign in the press. The focus of the investigations was twofold: first, infringements of the currency laws (evidence was provided by the cross-frontier financial transactions made by various orders); secondly, alleged sexual misdemeanours involving members of the orders. The investigations concerning currency violations started at the beginning of 1935 and were systematically expanded in March 1935. The Gestapo and SD were actively involved, and utilized the searches of monasteries in particular to confiscate all sorts of material. The actual trials were prepared centrally by a special department of the Berlin prosecutor's office. The first trials took place in

May 1935. By the end of 1935 almost seventy priests and members of orders had been found guilty in thirty trials. Some trials continued into the war.[78]

The prosecuting authorities, however, considered that the cases of alleged sexual misdemeanours by Catholic priests and members of orders were of far greater propaganda value. From spring 1935 onwards the prosecuting authorities, the criminal police and the Gestapo, collected material concerning alleged homosexual activity, making extensive use of the material that had been confiscated in the cases involving currency offences.[79] In 1935 the Gestapo set up a special commando in its section dealing with cases of homosexuality.[80] The SD also became involved in these.[81] The comprehensive investigations led to a wave of trials, lasting, with a pause during the summer Olympics, until the summer of 1937. In the end there were 250 so-called 'morality trials', in which more than 200 members of Catholic orders, mostly laymen, were convicted.[82]

In addition, three more lines of attack on the churches emerged during the course of 1935. In the middle of that year the Nazi state restricted Catholic youth organizations to purely religious activities,[83] and through regulations issued by the Reich Press Chamber a large part of the Catholic press was eliminated during 1935–6.[84] Finally, the party began a campaign, initially in Bavaria but then in other states, which aimed at encouraging parents no longer to send their children to church schools (in which, although they were state schools, the churches had traditionally enjoyed a considerable amount of influence), but instead to 'community schools', in other words, state schools without a denominational ethos.[85] The Gestapo and SD also had a hand in these measures.

The surveillance of the Protestant Church was, by contrast, of secondary importance for the Gestapo and SD.[86] During 1935–6 the regime had initially attempted, with the help of loyal German Christians, to get control of the state churches and to establish a centralized Reich church regime. This, however, failed in the face of internal church opposition. There were major conflicts between the German Christians and the emerging opposition movement of the Confessing Church, which were resolved only by Hans Kerrl, who was appointed Reich Church minister in July 1935. There was a fundamental difference of viewpoint between Kerrl on the one hand, and Himmler and the anti-church hardliners on the other. Whereas Kerrl wished in the first instance to strengthen the German Christians, the hardliners considered this an unwarranted enhancement of the Christian elements. They wanted rather to distance themselves from all Christian groups.[87] The Gestapo and SD thus kept out of these church conflicts; instead, they tried to undermine Kerrl's position within the regime by tenacious intrigue, which was assisted not least by the gathering of information from Kerrl's ministry.[88] In any case, Himmler succeeded, together with Hess and the support of Goebbels among others, in preventing Kerrl's plans for the coordination of the Protestant Church.[89] 'Kerrl wants to conserve the Church, we want to liquidate it', noted Goebbels in February 1937, after a long conversation with Himmler and Wilhelm Stuckart on the eve of a discussion on the Obersalzberg about the churches issue. And he concluded that 'the differences between us are not just tactical but fundamental'.[90]

In July 1937 there was a change in the regime's policy towards the churches.[91] The papal encyclical *Mit brennender Sorge* ('With Burning Anxiety') removed all illusions that the Catholic Church would submit to the regime's church policies without a fight. And, as far as the Protestant Churches were concerned, the leadership of the regime had to recognize that the German Christians did not have the potential to coordinate the church from within. However, the impending shift to an expansionist foreign policy made it advisable to make peace on the home front. Therefore Hitler gradually withdrew from church policy. The fundamental reorientation of the relationship between the Nazi state and the churches sought by radical party elements was postponed. In view of this situation, the birthday gift Himmler presented to Hitler on 20 April was significant: he gave his Führer Otto Rahn's book *Lucifer's Courtiers*, a history of heretics, bound in the finest pigskin.[92]

The strategy of forcing the churches out of public life by a series of measures was continued, however. Thus, during the years 1937 to 1939 the Gestapo gradually banned the Catholic youth organizations, often on the basis of 'information' provided by the SD, because they had not adhered to the ban on taking part in non-religious activities. It refrained, however, from spectacular actions, a tactical move that was also evident when Himmler introduced further measures against Catholic institutions.[93] When, in April 1937, Kerrl's suggestion that the Catholic Young Men's Associations should be banned was passed on to Himmler, he told the security police to seek Hitler's opinion before taking action.[94]

In the autumn of 1937 Himmler got to see the internal minutes of the Fulda Conference of Catholic bishops for the first time, and so was informed about the proceedings of what was the highest-level committee of the German Catholic Church.[95] As a 'sign of close cooperation' he allowed

Heydrich to pass them on to Kerrl during a conference dealing with church matters at the beginning of November.[96] Apart from such individual successes, however, despite all their attempts, despite their spies and listening devices, the Gestapo and SD were poorly informed about the internal discussions being carried on at the top of the German Catholic Church.[97]

On the other hand, on Hitler's orders the Gestapo devoted a lot of attention to the Jehovah's Witnesses, the small faith community of so-called 'Serious Bible Students', who numbered approximately 35,000.[98] The Jehovah's Witnesses refused to take part in elections, to give the Hitler salute, to join Nazi organizations, or to perform military service.[99] All these things were incompatible with their strict religious commandments. The Bible Students were banned in Prussia[100] and dismissed from public service as early as June 1933.[101] But despite the ban the group continued their missionary work in several places.[102]

In the course of 1936 the Gestapo increased its persecution of the Jehovah's Witnesses, with torture being used during their interrogations.[103] The first nationwide wave of arrests took place in August and September 1936.[104] The Bible Students reorganized themselves in secret, and in December 1937 distributed leaflets in a number of places, but the subsequent comprehensive wave of arrests in practice led to the destruction of the whole organization. Since the Jehovah's Witnesses consistently refused to perform military service, they were persecuted particularly harshly during the war.[105]

In 1936, as part of his anti-church policy, Himmler gave the SD a 'special project' of a peculiar nature. This was the 'Special Witch Project' (*Hexen-Sonderauftrag*), with which Himmler endeavoured to find out the extent of witch-hunting in the past.[106] This was prompted by the public row caused by the 1935 German Peasant Calendar issued by the Reich Food Estate, controlled by Richard Walther Darré, who shared Himmler's views. This had referred to the 'nine million [...] fighters for justice, champions of the faith, heretics, and witches who had been murdered, tortured to death, and burnt' at the instigation of the Christian churches.[107] In his speech to the Goslar Peasants' Rally Himmler had alluded to the row that this had caused: 'We can visualize the fires burning at the stakes on which tens of thousands of the martyred and tortured bodies of mothers and girls of our nation burnt to ashes as a result of the witch trials.'[108] It is possible that he even believed one of his own ancestors had been burnt as a witch.[109]

In any event, Himmler considered it a unique opportunity to catalogue all the material dealing with the persecution of witches that was scattered in numerous archives in Germany, and use it to mount a propaganda campaign against the churches, calling them to account for their historical responsibility for this mass murder. A task of historical importance for the SS!

To begin with the task was given to the 'SS Literature Section' at the German Library in Leipzig, an offshoot of the SD, which from 1936 onwards had been supervised by its Central Department I, 3. After the establishment of the Reich Security Main Office in 1939 the H [Hexe] Special Project was transferred to the Department for Researching the Opposition under Franz Six. It had fourteen full-time employees, and this team set about systematically researching the extensive literature and examining every case of witch persecution in the German archives. The researches were carried out clandestinely and were continued until 1944. Their results were contained in 33,846 pages of data, which together formed a substantial 'Witch File'.

Himmler also commissioned the author Friedrich Norfolk, who was a full-time employee of Six's department, to write a historical novel on the subject of the persecution of witches, and also requested him to write 'a large number of shorter H[exen]-stories of 60 to 100 pages'.[110] Herbert Blank, a 'special prisoner of the RFSS' in Sachsenhausen on account of his work for Otto Strasser who was by profession an author of historical novels, was given the task of studying witch-trial records in his cell and of writing short stories on the basis of these.[111] A picture book and a film on the topic were also planned, as well as a serious academic series.[112]

In the end, however, this huge project was basically restricted to the gathering of material. There was no significant scholarly work done on the material and no substantial programme of publications. Whether this was because the people involved were not in a position (or not willing) to produce more, or whether Himmler found himself prevented from advancing the project on the grounds of church policy, is unclear.

The criminal police

In May 1944, in a speech to Wehrmacht generals, Himmler confessed:

In the past and right up to the present day I have done many things—I admit that quite openly—which were not permissible under the existing laws, but needed to be done on the basis of the laws of reason and common sense. Naturally, in some cases I had no authority under the law to arrest a criminal who had not committed an offence. The law laid down that I, acting as the police, had to wait until this man, who had already carried out three burglaries and maybe had killed two people in the process and had done his fifteen years in gaol, was caught in the act or had committed a new offence.[113]

By stating this principle of neutralizing the criminal before he could commit a crime, Himmler described with disarming logic the programme on which he embarked in 1936 to reorientate the criminal police (Kripo) towards a preventive form of combating crime, and in doing so he was guided by the utopian vision of a 'national community without criminals'.

With the issuing of the 'New Organization of the Criminal Police' on 20 September 1936 Himmler transferred to the Prussian State Criminal Police Department 'the practical direction of the police' in all the federal states. The logical next step of transforming this office into the Reich Criminal Police Department occurred on 15 July 1937. The existing criminal police apparatus was now controlled centrally as a Reich criminal police service, organized hierarchically, and unified through a system of regional and district criminal police departments.[114]

Many of the measures undertaken during Himmler's regime resulted in a modernization of the criminal police, such as had already been demanded by many experts since the 1920s. Training was unified and centralized, a leadership college was created for the security police as well as a criminal police college in the Charlottenburg district of Berlin.[115] So-called Reich centres were created in the Reich Criminal Police Department for each type of crime (capital crimes, burglary, counterfeiting, and so on), which concentrated above all on serial offences committed at the national level and on particularly serious cases. An 'Institute of Criminal Technology'[116] was set up and technical centres were established in the provinces for routine tasks. Considerable emphasis was placed on the efficient gathering and transmission of data.[117]

From 1937 on Himmler appointed Inspectors of the Security Police and SD throughout the Reich, the majority of whom belonged to the Gestapo and SD and were intended to increase the effectiveness of the two agencies.[118] However, the aim of amalgamating the criminal police and the Gestapo to form the security police was only partially realized. Although numerous criminal police officers were transferred to the Gestapo to deal with its shortage of experts in the detection of crime, there was neither a routine exchange of personnel between the two branches of the security police nor was there a single career track for the members of the security police. Instead, the two branches developed independent images and became rivals, a rivalry that was encouraged by Himmler in that he allowed both to pursue particular 'delinquents' such as homosexuals, 'asocials', and so-called 'racial offenders' in competition with one another. There is evidence for believing that in the process of this competition the more brutal methods of the Gestapo rubbed off on the Kripo.[119]

The unification, centralization, and modernization of the criminal police created the preconditions for shifting the focus of its work, as indicated, to the prevention of crime. In 1933 the regime had already introduced 'preventive custody' for repeat offenders. However, this measure had been restricted to a few hundred people who had to serve their time in concentration camps. At the beginning of 1937 Himmler decided considerably to increase the number of offenders under preventive custody. He told Wehrmacht officers in January that,

in view of the fact that I consider criminality in Germany is still far too high, I am going to lock up far more career criminals than hitherto after they have committed a few offences, say three or four, and then not let them out again. We, and particularly we with our sentimental humanitarian views and inadequate laws, can no longer justify letting these people loose on humanity, especially these murderers, people who commit robberies, car thefts etc., who cost us an arm and a leg to chase after them.[120]

A follow-up telex to the Prussian State Criminal Office of 23 February 1937 stated that 'the population was seriously disturbed' by 'robberies, systematic burglaries, and serious sex crimes', and Himmler ordered that 2,000 'unemployed professional and habitual criminals should be immediately arrested and confined in concentration camps'.[121] This action was carried out in March 1937, and 2,000 men with previous convictions were in fact arrested and confined in camps. The number of 'preventive prisoners' quintupled as a result of the action; preventive custody was no longer an exception but became routine.[122]

The action of March 1937 represented the prelude to the escalation of preventive criminal policy, which was also racially charged.[123] For the transition to the combating of crime through prevention was justified in biological terms. According to the most influential criminologists and their colleagues, who called themselves 'criminological biologists', criminality was above all genetically determined. Thus it was necessary to 'eliminate' those marginal social groups who had been made out to be the bearers of 'asocial' genes and who therefore had a tendency to criminality. The combating of criminality was thus a matter of race, and was placed in the service of Nazi ideology. At the beginning of 1938 a Central Office for Genealogical Research on Criminals was established in the Reich Criminal Police Department.[124]

The implementation of preventive criminal police action was based on the 'Fundamental Decree Concerning the Preventive Combating of Crime by the Police' issued by the Reich Interior Minister on 14 December 1937, which expressly referred to the results of research in criminal biology.[125] The preventive combating of crime was to be secured in two ways: first, through 'the systematic police surveillance' of those with previous convictions, for example through police restrictions on residence, bans on making contact, imposition of abstinence from alcohol, and so on; secondly through the extended use of 'preventive custody'. These measures were to be applied not only to those who had been legally convicted but also to people who had been deemed 'asocial'.[126]

While in January 1938 the criminal police prepared a major action to take thousands of 'asocials' into custody, Himmler ordered the Gestapo to take action independently against 'work-shy' persons, a further example of the way in which he put the Kripo under pressure through competition under the security police umbrella. He ordered the labour exchanges to report to the Gestapo all those who were able-bodied and who had twice rejected job offers, or had started work but then left it without good reason. The action lasted from 21 to 30 April and resulted in 2,000 more prisoners being sent to Buchenwald.[127]

The criminal police began its asocial operation ('Work-shy Reich') on 13 June. In a telex of 1 June 1938 Heydrich had ordered the regional Kripo offices within a week 'to take at least 200 male able-bodied persons (asocials)' into police preventive custody in their area. They should focus above all on tramps, beggars, 'Gypsies and people who are travelling around in a Gypsy-like way', and pimps, as well as 'persons who have committed many previous offences such as resisting arrest, bodily harm, affray, trespass, etc. and have thereby demonstrated that they are unwilling to fit in with the national community'.[128]

The decree of 1 June had justified the operation not simply on the grounds that 'criminality has its roots in the asocial', but also cited a second motive: the rigorous implementation of the Four Year Plan, which did not permit 'asocial people to evade work and thereby sabotage the Four Year Plan'. In fact the measure had been prompted by Himmler's Four-Year-Plan representative, Ulrich Greifelt; it belongs within the context of the compulsory transition from a labour market to a regime of 'labour deployment' in order thereby to alleviate the alarming labour shortage resulting from rearmament.[129] Significantly, the timing of the action coincided with the construction of production facilities in the concentration camps for which workers were required. Moreover, 'Work-shy Reich' may well have been intended to have a disciplining and intimidating effect on the whole workforce as an accompaniment to the introduction of civil conscription, which occurred on 22 June 1938.[130]

On 1 June Heydrich also ordered that in the same week 'all male Jews in each criminal police district who have been punished with a term of imprisonment of more than one month shall be taken into police preventive custody'. Obviously, the aim was thereby to associate part of the Jewish minority with the milieu of asocials and criminals, a trend that is also apparent in press propaganda during these weeks.[131]

The raids on 'asocial' marginal groups continued during the following months. At the end of 1938 12,921 people were in preventive custody and 3,231 persons were under systematic surveillance.[132] Although we do not possess reliable criminal statistics for the whole period from 1933 to 1945, there is nevertheless some evidence that the rate of criminality did in fact decline during the years after 1933. The rigorous combating of criminality, in particular the arrest of 'potential' offenders, will presumably have contributed to this. What was decisive, however, was the fact that with the ending of the world economic crisis the enormous increase in the rate of criminality during the years 1930–3 reverted to a normal level.[133]

In the course of the measures against 'asocials' the police also increasingly took action against the Gypsies. They belonged to the groups who, during the raids of 1938, became a particular target of the criminal police.[134] In previous years the Gypsies had already been subject to increased surveillance and discrimination by the authorities, and since 1935 the local governments of various big cities had begun to confine Gypsies in special closed camps.[135] From the mid-1930s onwards, however, the Nazi system had begun to place Gypsy persecution on a new foundation. The origins of the 'Gypsy plague' with regard to their alleged 'genetic roots' were now to be tackled and dealt with. Gypsies were particularly liable to fall victim to the sterilization measures introduced by the authorities. Marriage with 'those of German blood' was banned on the basis of both the Law for the Protection of German Blood and the Marriage Health Law.[136]

In autumn 1936 the Prussian State Criminal Police Office organized the centralization of Gypsy persecution—in the meantime the Reich Criminal Police Office had been created—and in 1938 a Reich Centre for the Combating of Gypsies was established.[137] By mid-1939 a criminal police organization reaching down to the local police authorities had been established for 'combating Gypsies'. The Reich Criminal Police Office worked closely together with the Research Centre for Racial Hygiene in the Reich Health Office, which since 1937 had been subjecting all the Gypsies living in the Reich—Sinti and Roma—to anthropological and genealogical examination. On the basis of this material the Research Centre produced 'expert' racial hygiene reports in which they developed an elaborate classification of 'ethnically pure' and 'half-caste' Gypsies.[138]

Based on this classification, on 8 December 1938 Himmler issued a fundamental order on the question of 'race'. He told the police authorities it was 'advisable to deal with the Gypsy question on the basis of race'. Experience had shown that 'the half-castes [were] mainly responsible for Gypsy criminality. On the other hand, it has been shown that the attempts to make the Gypsies settle in one place have been unsuccessful, particularly in the case of the racially pure ones, because of their urge to travel. Thus when it comes to the final solution of the Gypsy question it will be necessary to treat the racially pure Gypsies and the half-castes separately.' To facilitate this Himmler ordered the official registration of all Gypsies, half-caste Gypsies, and 'people who travel around in a Gypsy fashion' over 6 years of age.[139] In this way virtually the whole Sinti and Roma population of the Reich was subject to registration by the criminal police and individual examination by the Research Centre for Racial Hygiene.

In June 1939 Himmler ordered a special 'action' against the Gypsies in the Burgenland in Austria, where, as a result of a compulsory resettlement programme by the Habsburgs, around 8,000 Sinti and Roma were living. The Reich Criminal Police Office ordered preventive custody for 'work-shy and particularly asocial Gypsies or Gypsy half-castes in the Burgenland'. As a result, hundreds were sent to Dachau concentration camp.[140]

The fight against abortion and homosexuality

Apart from the pursuit of politically and ideologically defined enemies of Nazism—communists, Jews, Freemasons, Christians—and the preventive combating of crime, which was becoming increasingly part of 'labour deployment', during the years 1936–9 the Chief of the German Police was preoccupied above all with the regulation of sexual activity, that is to say, the fight against abortion and homosexuality.

Himmler made clear the extent of his commitment to this in January 1937 in a speech at the start of the German Police Day. This was a propaganda week in which the population was asked to support the work of the defenders of law and order under the motto: 'The Police are Your Friends and Helpers.' Himmler stated that 'homosexuality and the widespread practice of illegal abortion' were 'plagues', which 'would inevitably lead any nation into the abyss'. The police were, however, already involved in the 'merciless pursuit of these abominations'.[141] In the spring of 1937, at a workshop in Berlin, he declared that in future he would judge the effectiveness of the police according to their success in the fight against homosexuality and abortion.[142]

For Himmler the fight against these two 'plagues' was an important personal concern. He told the Council of Experts on Population and Racial Policy on 15 June 1937: 'I have actually spent days and nights pondering about these two matters, which are among those of greatest concern to me. For someone who is normal and decent it's not that easy to look into these things and try and explain them. I have asked myself the question: is this the reason why our nation is so morally debased and bad?'[143]

Himmler repeatedly reminded people that the consequences of the two 'plagues' for population policy were enormous. While in his speech to the Committee on Police Law in October 1936 he was unwilling to speculate on the number of abortions,[144] in February 1937 he gave the SS-Gruppenführer a figure of 500,000–800,000 per year.[145] In September of the same year he gave the Council of Experts on Population and Racial Policy a figure of 400,000,[146] and in September 1938 he boasted in a public address to the Organization of Germans Abroad that he had succeeded in reducing the number of abortions from 600,000–900,000 in 1932–3 to 400,000–500,000.[147] In February 1937 he estimated to the Gruppenführer that 350,000 women annually were becoming sterile as a result of abortions;[148]

in June he gave a figure of 100,000 victims to the Committee of Experts,[149] and in September 1938 spoke of 50,000.[150]

Thus Himmler was very free with his assessment of the numbers of abortions, depending on whether he was referring to the threat to population policy they posed or the successes that had been achieved in this sphere. He told the Committee of Experts that if they could succeed in saving 100,000 children annually from abortion then in thirty years they would have an army of 400,000 men, an estimate that he had already included in a memorandum to Hitler.[151]

Himmler's most detailed statement on homosexuality is contained in the speech that he made to the SS-Gruppenführer meeting on 18 February 1937 in Bad Tölz. Homosexuality, the dangers that it caused and the fight against it, was the main topic of this speech, which deserves to be quoted extensively because it reveals the extent of Himmler's homophobia.[152]

To begin with, Himmler reminded people that, on their seizure of power in 1933, the Nazis had been faced with around 2 million people who were members of 'homosexual associations'. By this Himmler meant a variety of organizations which had campaigned for the repeal of paragraph 175 of the Penal Code. He admitted that not all members of these organizations were 'actually homosexual themselves', but he estimated that one could reckon on there being between 1 million and 2 million homosexuals in Germany; indeed he even mentioned estimates of 4 million homosexual men. With a figure of 2 million homosexuals, he told the Gruppenführer, one could reckon on some 7 to 10 per cent of sexually mature men being homosexual. 'That means, if things stay the same, that our nation is going to be wiped out by this plague.' In addition, there were 2 million killed in the war, who could no longer reproduce, so that 'the lack of around 4 million men who were capable of reproducing' would 'disrupt Germany's sexual equilibrium'.

What was decisive, he preached to his listeners, was the fact that 'all matters involving sex [were] not private matters of the individual', but rather they affected 'the life and death of the nation, world power, and the [alternative of] becoming like the Swiss. The nation that has a lot of children can expect to become a world power and achieve world domination. A nation with good racial characteristics that has few children is heading for the grave; in 50 or 100 years it will be insignificant, in 200 or 500 it will have died out.'

Himmler then went on to paint a picture of the 'national plague' of homosexuality:

For hundreds of years, for thousands of years the Teutonic peoples and in particular the German people have been ruled by men. But as a result of homosexuality this male state is in the process of destroying itself. As far as the state is concerned, I consider the main error to be the fact that the state, the people's organization [the Reichstag?], the army, and whatever else you choose as examples of state institutions, all of them appoint people to posts, except in the case of human inadequacies, on the basis of performance.

But just as in the state and in the commercial world a male boss would always prefer a young, attractive woman as a typist, even if she were less efficient, to an older, less attractive but more efficient one, so there was the danger that a same-sex oriented boss would also make personnel decisions on the basis of erotic criteria. But if 'an erotic principle, a male–female sexual principle is introduced in the male state and is applied to the relations between one man and another', that 'will bring about the destruction of the state'.

Thus homosexuality, he concluded, 'undermines performance and any system based on performance and destroys the foundations of the state. In addition, homosexuals are psychologically sick to the core. They are soft; when it comes to the crunch they are invariably cowards. I believe that they can occasionally be brave in war but when it comes to civil courage they are the most cowardly people in existence.' Homosexuals were also pathological liars. And: 'In my experience [sic] homosexuality leads to a complete unsoundness of mind, I might almost say, craziness.' Homosexuals were liable to blackmail; they were characterized by an 'insatiable need to talk'—a characteristic which in his youth, it will be recalled, Himmler considered his worst weakness. But finally, and 'I have to speak from their perspective, although these people like to pretend that they love each other, there is in fact no loyalty involved in the love of one man for another, whereas in other circumstances men are normally loyal to each other'.

The conclusion was that it was vital to combat homosexuality, for otherwise 'it will be the end of Germany, the end of the Teutonic world'. The Teutons used to drown their 'Urnings' in bogs. 'Unfortunately, I must say, in our case that's no longer possible.' It was only in the SS that one could deal with it with the appropriate rigour. Himmler claimed that there were around eight to ten cases of homosexuality a year in the SS. Those involved—and in fact, according to secret SS statistics the number was considerable larger[153]—would, after they had been sentenced and had served their term, be 'taken to a concentration camp and shot while trying to escape'.

Himmler's long-winded statements show from his point of view what a threat homosexuality posed to his own identity and his notion of masculinity and order. It was a case of a confrontation between two utterly incompatible worlds: his own, which he associated with the set of values: man—masculinity—male friendship—loyalty—performance—state; and the other, which he associated with femininity, eroticism, unbridled sexuality, chaos, and downfall. In his view there was only one way of treating homosexuals who wanted to move unrecognized from this milieu into the political sphere, namely, as enemies of the state who had to be eliminated.

In the same speech Himmler also dealt with the causes of homosexuality in detail:

In my view there has been far too great a masculinization of our whole life, to the extent that we are militarizing absurd things, and are putting all our efforts into perfecting how people should present themselves in public, how disciplined they are and how well they pack their knapsacks. I think it's terrible when I see girls and women, above all girls, going around with a perfectly packed knapsack. It makes me sick. I think it's catastrophic when women's organizations, women's societies, women's clubs engage in areas of activity which undermine all feminine charm, all feminine dignity and grace. I think it's catastrophic—I'm speaking generally, because in fact it has nothing directly to do with us—when we stupid men want to turn women into logical thinkers, try and teach them everything conceivable, when we masculinize women so that in time the differences between the sexes, the polarity, will disappear. Then we've not far to go to homosexuality.

Then he really got going: 'If a boy who is in love with a girl is laughed at excessively and is not taken seriously and is called a softie and if he is told that chaps don't go around with girls then he won't. And then there'll only be friendships between men. Men will decide everything in the world and the next stage will be homosexuality.'

Himmler then referred to the work by Hans Blüher, *The Role of Eroticism in Male Society*, which he had read in 1922 and the basic ideas of which he evidently assumed were familiar to his audience:

Those are the ideas of Hans Blüher, which then claim 'the greatest form of love is not that between man and woman, for that produces children, and that's animalistic.

The greater form of love is the sublimated love between man and man. It's that that has produced the greatest achievements in world history' [. . .] That's the line that's now being served up to young people in an easily digestible form, young people who are already in what is really a very masculinized movement and who, as a result of being in male camps, have no opportunity of meeting girls. In my view we needn't be surprised that we have gone down the road towards homosexuality.

In the next section of his speech Himmler went on to apply the notion of 'an erotic male association' to one of his main opponents: Christianity. 'I'm convinced that the priesthood and the whole of Christianity basically amounts to an eroticized male society for the purpose of upholding and maintaining this 2,000-year-old Bolshevism.' One had to assume, Himmler continued, that while more than 50 per cent of the country clergy were not homosexual, in the monasteries the figure for homosexuality was 90 to 100 per cent:

But I hope that in four years' time we shall have proved that the majority of the organization of the church: its leadership, its priesthood, represents a homosexual, erotic male society, which on this basis has terrorized humanity for 1,800 years, has required from it large sacrifices of blood and in the past has issued sadistically perverse statements. I need only refer to the trials of witches and heretics.

The attitude which denigrates women is typically Christian, and we, as National Socialists, have adopted this kind of thinking right up to the present time—in some cases as solid heathens—without realizing it [. . .] I'm also aware of a certain tendency in our ranks to try to exclude women from all events and festivals. The same people complain that here or there women are clinging to the churches or have not been won over 100 per cent to National Socialism. But they shouldn't complain, given that they treat women as second-class human beings and above all keep them from participating in our internal activities [. . .]

It's up to us to be clear about the fact that our movement, our ideology will be able to survive if it's supported by women, for men grasp things with their reason, whereas women grasp everything with their emotions. The greatest sacrifices in the witch and heretic trials were made by German women and not by men. The clerics knew very well why they burnt 5,000–6,000 women because they were emotionally loyal to the old knowledge and the old doctrine and emotionally and instinctively were not prepared to abandon it, whereas the men, on the basis of logical thinking, had already come to terms with the fact: there's no point any more. We've been politically defeated. I give in. I'll let myself be baptized.

After this brief digression Himmler returned to his central theme: 'In my view there is too much masculinization in our whole movement, and this exaggerated masculinization provides fertile soil for homosexuality.' Then, on the basis of what he had been saying, Himmler made some suggestions to the Gruppenführer, gave some tips on how the two sexes could, so to speak, get to know one another:

In line with what I've indicated, please make sure that our men get a chance to dance with girls at the summer solstice. I think it's absolutely right that we should organize the occasional dance for new recruits in the wintertime, and we need to make sure that we invite the best girls rather than inferior ones and give SS men the chance to dance with the girls and enjoy themselves. I consider that important for one reason above all, namely, in order to make sure that no one is ever set on the wrong road towards homosexuality.

In the case of adolescents also, Himmler continued, they should make sure 'that boys of 16–17 meet girls at dancing classes, evening get-togethers, or in some other way. Experience has shown that it's at the age of 15–16 that boys are most vulnerable. If they fall for a dancing partner or get a girlfriend then they're OK, then they will no longer be at risk':

In fact we in Germany don't need to worry about bringing boys and girls together at too early an age and encouraging them to take part in sexual intercourse. No. Our climate, our race and nation, ensure that 16-year-old boys consider their relationships with girls as the purest and most ideal form of love. The moment they have fallen in love with a girl—and I must repeat this—then mutual mastur-bation with friends, male friendships, or friendships between boys of this sort of sexual nature are out of the question because they are ashamed of themselves in the eyes of their girlfriends. They have a personal bond.

In this speech Himmler was clearly referring above all to his own (slow) sexual development. Although he had been a keen participant in dancing classes and idolized numerous girls and young women and cultivated friend-ships with them, he had evidently not had intimate relations with the opposite sex until the age of 27. On the contrary, he had rejected close ties and sexual activity on the grounds that he had to save himself for a 'masculine' task. Moreover, he had spent his youth above all in organiza-tions notable for that overt masculinity that he now considered so danger-ous. And before that, he had had very close ties with the Catholic Church, whose priests he now described as being members of a 'homosexual erotic male association'.

Thus one can regard this speech as a more or less unconscious reflection on the 'threat' of the temptations of homosexuality to which he himself had been subject in the past. It was to a considerable extent self-criticism, a critical examination of the way in which, until his marriage in 1928, he had adopted the image of 'a soldierly man' or 'a solitary freebooter'. The fact that he eventually abandoned this image and redefined the SS as an 'order of clans (*Sippenorden*)' was, on the one hand, certainly a result of his need to create a distinct profile vis-à-vis the SA, which was indeed the target of his description of the dangerously excessive masculine tendencies in the Nazi movement. On the other hand, however, as is clear from his speech of February 1937, in retrospect Himmler considered that his move away from an exclusive ideal of masculinity rescued him from the homosexual temptations to which he was liable and which he had described so vividly in his speech. During the following months and years, Himmler acted upon the notion that one must protect youth from the dangers of homosexuality by permitting natural relations between the sexes. Later on he spoke out against the condemnation of sex before marriage and discrimination against illegitimate births.[154]

Himmler's homophobia not only determined his hostility to an excessive 'masculinizing' of the Nazi movement, it also dominated his views on the ways in which SS members should relate to one another; he wanted to avoid emotional relationships becoming too close, to eliminate feelings as far as possible. The SS should not be bound together by male friendships and Eros, but by sober comradeship and, above all, by 'soldierly' discipline. The Reichsführer-SS transferred his obsession with self-control to the male organization of the SS.

How, then, did the police pursuit of homosexuals work in practice? During the months after the murder of Röhm and his supporters the Gestapo and police had begun systematically to move against homosexuals.[155] This was facilitated by the strengthening of paragraph 175 of the Penal Code in June 1935.[156] With Himmler's takeover of the German police in June 1936 the measures were intensified. Already in October Himmler signed an order establishing a Reich Centre for the Combating of Homosexuality and Abortion, and issued detailed guidelines for the arrest of homosexuals.[157] Josef Meisinger, the head of the department, was also responsible for the special Gestapo desk, which Himmler had established in 1934 and which existed alongside the criminal police arrangments for the pursuit of homosexuals.[158] The Reich Centre had above all the task of registering particular categories of homosexual men who had come into conflict with the law. The aim was, on the one hand, to prevent homosexuals from 'penetrating' the party, the Wehrmacht, and the civil service, and on the other, to gather material that would compromise particular groups (Jews, Freemasons, leading representatives of the Weimar 'system'). By 1940 they had filled 42,000 cards.[159]

The number of sentences increased significantly from 1935 onwards as a result of these measures—from fewer than 4,000 in the years 1933–4 to over 22,000 in the period 1936–8—but these figures also show that the police and judiciary had no problem confronting the spectre of millions of homosexuals that Himmler had raised in his speech in Bad Tölz.[160] In March 1937, a few weeks after this speech, *Das Schwarze Korps* published an article clarifying the SS's official line on the matter. According to this it was necessary to differentiate: only 2 per cent of all homosexuals were 'really abnormal'; as far as the majority was concerned, it was a case of people who had been seduced and who, with the aid of work therapy, educational measures, and the threat of punishment could be weaned away from their vice. Even if the article marked the start of a campaign by *Das Schwarze Korps* against homosexuality, it had become clear that there was no intention on the part of the Reich leadership of the SS to criminalize millions of men.[161] Thus, in May 1937 Himmler announced to the working party of the criminal police referred to above that the vast majority of homosexuals could be transformed into 'normal men'.[162]

On a number of occasions the Chief of the German Police intervened directly in the pursuit of homosexuals. In March 1937, in the course of discussions about a new Penal Code, Himmler demanded that, as a matter of principle, in the case of breaches of the ban on homosexuality it should be possible to impose not just imprisonment but also penal servitude.[163] In October 1937 he surprisingly ordered that actors or artists should not be arrested for 'unnatural sexual relations' without his permission.[164] In May 1939 he instructed the Reich Criminal Police Office not to be too strict in their interpretation of the legally required voluntary principle when it came to the sterilization of homosexuals.[165]

During the Second World War the pursuit of homosexuals was no longer a priority for the security police. Although in July 1940 Himmler ordered that homosexuals who had seduced more than one partner should be taken into preventive custody,[166] the aim now was more to control the practice rather than persecute it. When, three years after his tirade of February 1937, Himmler came to talk about the topic again, in a speech to the Gauleiters and other high-level party functionaries, he appeared confident 'that we shall overcome this vice, this terminal illness for a nation. I believe I can say that our young people are no longer providing recruits for this vice, or not to such an extent. In general, our young people have largely given up this aberration, so that this vice, or let us say the recruitment to this vice, is coming to an end and the number of men who are falling for this vice has reduced.' In his view the group in question was 'still half a million strong'.[167]

Did Himmler really believe that within a matter of three years three-quarters of all homosexuals had given up this 'vice'? The fact that, only a few years after his homophobic panic attacks, Himmler could comment relatively calmly on the topic provides another example of his pragmatism. Since, during the war, the Gestapo and police could not devote much effort to it, he simply declared the problem solved, just as, at the end of the 1930s, he had already played down the number of abortions and, during the war, was to adjust his views on other matters of sexual policy to suit changed circumstances. Moreover, from his point of view Himmler had good reasons for no longer going out on a limb on the question of the pursuit of homosexuals. In 1938 he had falsely accused the Commander-in-Chief of the army, Werner von Fritsch, of homosexuality, and as a result had damaged his reputation with Hitler not inconsiderably, a point we shall return to.

Apparently it was only the SS and police who were to be excluded from the more lax attitude towards homosexuality. In November 1941 Hitler's 'Purification Edict' introduced the death penalty for such cases within the SS and police.[168] In the edict, which announced the new regulation, Himmler committed the members of the SS and police to act as 'pioneers in the fight to eliminate homosexuality among the German people'.[169] In practice, however, it became apparent that as a rule only a few death sentences were passed. Himmler examined such sentences very carefully and suspended a number of them.[170]

Himmler's behaviour in the case of Unterstumführer Otto Rahn is also significant. This writer, whose subject-matter—the search for the Holy Grail and the history of heretics —enjoyed Himmler's particular approval and who was personally aquainted with Himmler and had helped him in his research into his family history, in 1939 suddenly requested his discharge from the SS and shortly afterwards committed suicide. The reason for this action was clearly the fact that he could no longer conceal his homosexuality.

Himmler considered this a 'particularly tragic' case, as Rahn had done everything possible to make up for his 'failings' vis-à-vis the SS. Indeed,

Himmler had a notice signed by Wolff placed in *Das Schwarze Korps*, which described Rahn as 'a decent SS man'—in other words, an exoneration.[171] Himmler also ensured that Rahn's *Lucifer's Courtiers*, which he had given to Hitler in 1937 as a present in a special edition, was distributed to the SS as a gift (and like other works of Rahn) was even republished towards the end of the war.[172] This was despite opposition from Rosenberg's office, which made objections based on 'the personality of the deceased author'.[173]

Order police

Up until now we have dealt fairly extensively with the activities of the security police under Himmler's leadership. How did the much larger section of the police, the order police (*Ordnungpolizei*), develop during these years?

In June 1936 Himmler had already instructed Kurt Daluege, the chief of the Order Police Main Office, concerning the duties of his office. These involved, above all, responsibility for the Schutzpolizei (the uniformed police in the cities), the Gendarmerie (the equivalent formation in the rural districts), the traffic police, the local police (*Gemeindepolizei*), as well as various administrative matters involving the police such as in the sphere of trading standards and health supervision.[174]

On 1 September 1936 Himmler assigned Inspectors of the Order Police to the provincial governors in the Prussian provinces and to those Reich Governors whose headquarters were located where the commanders of the military districts were based; in general they performed supervisory functions. However, from 1937 onwards they were assigned to the new Higher SS and Police Leaders. In this role, as part of the process of Reich centralization, they contributed towards removing the police authorities, which had hitherto been subordinate to the state governments, from the responsibility of the regional administrations altogether.[175]

In 1935, as part of the rearmament programme, the so-called Landespolizei* was integrated into the Wehrmacht, with the result that the uniformed police lost approximately half its strength and was reduced from 104,000 to fewer than 49,000 officers. By 1938 the uniformed police—Schutzpolizei, Gendarmerie, and local police—had once more reached a

---

* *Translators' note*: The Landespolizei was a paramilitary police force housed in barracks.

total of 100,000 officers. Priority was given to former soldiers who had been discharged from the Wehrmacht after between two and five years' service.[176] Thus half the personnel with whom the uniformed police entered the war consisted of recent recruits, the majority of whom had military experience. This force was supplemented by approximately the same number of superficially trained police reservists.

While during the second half of the 1930s the order police was heavily involved in training its own recruits, at the same time it was assigned numerous new functions in the Nazi police state, including the control of prices, dealing with passports and identity cards—which were now much more strictly controlled—and recording details for the national register, in which the police wished to include all Germans. In addition, there was the need to provide security for the numerous large-scale events, parades, marches, and state receptions as well as cordoning-off manoeuvres and, last but not least, the supervision of defence matters. Large contingents of the order police were also involved in the annexations of Austria, the Sudetenland, and Czechoslovakia. Thousands of police remained in the occupied territories.[177]

In October 1936 Himmler integrated the Emergency Technical Assistance organization, which in the event of war, catastrophes, internal unrest, and the like was designed to ensure the continued functioning of essential services, into the police, and in June 1937 subordinated it to the Order Police Main Office.[178] The voluntary fire brigades, which contained around 1.5 million men, and the professional fire service in the big cities were combined to form a fire protection service and subordinated to a newly created Inspector of Fire Services attached to the Chief of the Order Police.[179] These were all measures intended to create a new central task for the police, namely, the guaranteeing of protection against air raids and the removal of bomb damage in the event of war.

Expansion of the concentration camps (KZs)

Between the summer of 1936 and the summer of 1937 Himmler dissolved the small protective custody camps—Esterwegen, Sachsenburg, Columbia House, Lichtenburg, and Sulza. Of the old camps only Dachau remained. Instead, the Inspectorate of Concentration Camps developed a new type of camp, of which the first to be built was Sachsenhausen near Berlin, the successor to the Esterwegen and Columbia House camps.[180]

The design of the camps was based on the principle of placing separate functional centres—the actual camp itself, the offices of the commandant, the guards' barracks, the residential building of the members of the commandant's staff—within a closed complex of buildings. In the words of Himmler, who inspected the camp at the end of 1936,[181] it was 'a completely new, modern, and contemporary concentration camp that was capable of being extended', which secured 'the Reich against enemies of the state in peacetime as well in the event of mobilization'.[182]

In the summer of 1937 the Concentration Camp Inspectorate established a second camp, Buchenwald, outside Weimar, after Himmler himself had personally inspected the site on the Ettersberg hill.[183] In addition, Dachau was considerably extended on Himmler's orders.[184] In May 1938 the Flossenbürg concentration camp was established in eastern Bavaria,[185] and in August 1938, after the Anschluss with Austria, Mauthausen was opened near Linz.[186] In the same month the Concentration Camp Inspectorate established its new headquarters in Oranienburg in the immediate vicinity of Sachsenhausen. In December 1938 work began on the Neuengamme camp near Hamburg, a sub-camp of Sachsenhausen that initially had the aim of reopening a brick factory that had been closed.[187] In May 1939 a female concentration camp was added at Ravensbrück.[188]

The expansion of the concentration camp system was clearly a preparatory measure for the outbreak of war. Already at the beginning of 1937 Himmler announced that 'in the event of war' one 'would have to lock up a considerable number of unreliable characters'.[189] In the light of this, the camp system was designed for 30,000 to 50,000 prisoners. The number of prisoners had already been slowly increasing from the end of 1936 onwards—at the turn of the year 1934–5 it had sunk to 3,000—and by the start of the war had reached 21,000. However, as a result of the mass arrests after the pogrom of November 1938 the number of prisoners had briefly amounted to over 50,000.[190]

As before, the decision over the confinement and release of prisoners was a matter for the Gestapo. Eicke's office was responsible for conditions in the camps. Basically, within the camps there was a strict division between the guards and the commandant's office, which consisted of the adjutant's office, the political department, the protective custody leader, and the camp doctor, as well as the administration.[191] Certain subordinate functions were delegated to—often criminal—prisoners, who in return received certain privileges. In this way the SS included a section of the prisoners as tools of their terror system. The prisoners received a prisoner's number, which had to be visible on their uniform. In the winter of 1938–9 it was decided to mark the prisoners with a uniform badge. Prisoners had to wear cloth triangles on their clothing, the colour of which indicated to which category they belonged: political prisoners, criminals, Jews, homosexuals, and so on.

According to Himmler, the inmates represented a real collection of oddities. 'None of them has been put there unjustly,' he declared to a group of Wehrmacht officers in January 1937. 'They are the dregs of criminality, of people who have taken the wrong path. There could be no better demonstration of the laws of heredity and race [...] There are people there with hydrocephalus, people who squint, people with deformities, half-Jews, a mass of racially inferior material.'[192] On 8 November 1937 he told the SS-Gruppenführer that 'we shall have to keep people with several previous convictions in the camps for many years, at least until they have got used to living an ordered life, and that doesn't mean becoming what we would consider to be decent people, but rather having had their will broken'. 'The 'Bolshevik leaders' could also not expect to be freed.[193]

But what was to be done with all these prisoners? In 1938 Himmler geared the KZ system towards pursuing new goals and fulfilling new tasks. He began increasingly to deploy the prisoners for work projects, with plants being established in the KZs. The new intake of prisoners in the KZs were now predominantly people who were labelled as being work-shy or asocial. In other words, the phase associated with the 'economization' of the KZs had begun.

The first notion of deploying KZ prisoners for labour tasks can be traced back to the turn of the year 1936–7.[194] The motive was not primarily economic; what was decisive was rather the fact that the growing labour shortage in the Reich inevitably made people consider the idea of utilizing KZ prisoners for labour projects (as had already happened with judicial prisoners). Had the SS not made any efforts in this direction the KZ prisoners would eventually have been taken over by the Labour Ministry.[195]

The large-scale employment of prisoners was prompted by cooperation with Albert Speer, who in January 1937 had been assigned by Hitler the job of rebuilding Berlin. Speer, however, was in danger of failing in this task because labour and building materials were in short supply as a result of the rearmament boom. In this situation Himmler offered Speer his assistance: KZ prisoners could provide the granite and bricks for Berlin's major buildings. Speer could finance the construction of brickworks and granite quarries from his budget. An agreement was signed on 1 July 1938, in other words, immediately after 10,000 people had been put in the camps as a result of the action 'Work-shy Reich'. Himmler's line of confining 'asocials' on the basis of 'general prevention on racial grounds' now seemed to have an economic pay-off as well.[196]

The upshot of the cooperation between Himmler and Speer was the creation, in April 1938, of a company, the German Earth and Stone Quarries Ltd. (Deutsche Erd- und Steinwerke GmbH). The company set about establishing three brickworks and two granite quarries in close proximity to concentration camps. The decisions concerning the location of the new Flossenbürg KZ and the extension to Dachau were determined largely by the fact that there were quarries in the immediate vicinity. The granite quarries would even prove profitable; this was not the case with the brickworks, which suffered from poor management.[197]

As was the case from the first days of Dachau concentration camp on, the prisoners in all the camps suffered under a cruel and arbitrary system. They were subjected to every conceivable form of chicanery, torture, and mistreatment. Punishment exercises; hours of standing for roll-calls, often in bad or icy weather; forced labour in work details, for example under marshy conditions until they were exhausted: all these were commonplace. Draconian punishments such as floggings on a punishment-block or solitary confinement in tiny cells with minimum food for weeks on end were imposed arbitrarily, and interrogations were carried out with the most brutal methods of torture. Moreover, the guards frequently murdered prisoners, such murders being either disguised as suicide or simply filed under the terse formula 'shot while trying to escape'. Being forced to live in an extremely confined space, inadequate and poor-quality food, and excessive hours of work of the most physically demanding kind also formed part of camp life.[198]

Himmler made a vigorous defence of the terror regime in the concentration camps, for example in an argument with the Justice Minister, Franz Gürtner, in the spring of 1938. In March 1938 Gürtner spoke to Himmler about the large number of prisoners who had been shot while 'trying to escape' from the concentration camps. Two months later he received a letter from Himmler.[199] To begin with, Himmler explained that after his conversation with Gürtner he had instructed Eicke 'to remind the Death's Head units once more that they should shoot only in the case of extreme emergencies', but in the meantime had come deeply to regret having taken this step. For, as he put it to the Justice Minister, he had been 'very shocked' by the result of his intervention. Only two days before, he himself had had to view the corpse of 'a fine 24-year-old SS man whose skull had been bashed in by two criminals with a shovel'. He was 'seriously upset by the idea that, as a result of excessive lenience, [. . .] now one of my decent men had lost his life'. As a result, he had reinstated the old instruction 'that, strictly in accordance with service regulations, after someone has been called upon three times [to halt] or in the event of a physical attack the [guards] should shoot without warning'. Moreover, he had mentioned the case to Hitler and had received his approval to hang one of the escaped prisoners, who had been caught in the meantime, in front of the assembled inmates. He informed Gürtner of this a fortnight later, and ordered the execution to be carried out.[200]

Himmler repeatedly used the opportunity to deal with the issue of conditions in the concentration camps in public, for example in his speech to Wehrmacht officers in January 1937:

The camps are surrounded with barbed wire, with an electrified fence. If anybody enters a banned zone or goes where he is not supposed to, he will be shot. If anybody makes even the slightest attempt to flee from his workplace, for example while working on a moor or on building a road, he will be shot. If anybody is impertinent or rebellious, and that sometimes happens, or at least is attempted, he will either be put in solitary confinement, in a dark cellar with bread and water or— please don't be shocked, I have applied the old Prussian penitentiary regulations of 1914–1918—he will in the worst cases receive twenty-five strokes. Claims by the foreign press that acts of cruelty, of sadism, occur are completely inconceivable.[201]

In a speech broadcast to mark German Police Day in January 1939 he said, among other things:

Imprisonment in a concentration camp is certainly, like any loss of personal freedom, a form of punishment and a strict measure. Tough new values, hard work, a regular life, exceptional residential and personal cleanliness, impeccable food, strict but just treatment, the requirement to relearn how to work and thereby to learn artisanal skills are all part of the educational process. The sign above these camps states: there is a way to freedom. Its milestones are: obedience, hard work, honesty, order, cleanliness, sobriety, truthfulness, self-sacrifice, and love of the fatherland.[202]

This 'doctrine' of the Reichsführer-SS' was prominently displayed in large letters above the assembly-ground of Sachsenhausen.[203]

Himmler made regular inspections of the camps: 'Every year I visit the camps myself,' he explained in January 1937, 'and arrive unannounced to have a look around.'[204] Walter Janka, who was imprisoned in KZ Sachsenburg for his communist activities, described in his memoirs such an inspection by Himmler in February 1935. However, this visit was not unannounced. Over three days and nights, 'everything had been swept, cleaned, and put in order'. Those prisoners who were going to be in the front row were given new prison uniforms. 'With a gesture that could have meant anything, Himmler, escorted by the commandant, strode up and down the ranks of the SS. Now and then he stopped and exchanged a few words. In front of the prisoners he increased his step and no words were exchanged with them. Himmler did not waste a single glance on the assembled prisoners.'

According to Janka's report, the Reichsführer later made a tour of the camp and in the process visited the bookbinder's workshop, in which Janka worked together with a number of other communist prisoners, and asked them some very awkward questions. For example, Himmler asked Janka whether he held the SS responsible for the death of his brother, who had allegedly hanged himself in a KZ in April 1933. Janka preferred not to answer.[205]

As confirmed by other prisoners, during such visits Himmler appears to have liked to present himself in the pose of the victor. On 30 September 1942, during a visit to Sachsenhausen KZ, for example, he encountered Herbert Blank, a 'special prisoner of the Reichsführer-SS'. Blank had been a leading member of the Combat Group of Revolutionary National Socialists, in other words, the group which, under the leadership of Otto Strasser, had split off from the Nazis in 1930. Blank recorded in an article published in 1948 that Himmler had advised him to 'get used to the idea' 'that I can never release you as long as you live'.[206] On a visit to Dachau in June 1938 Himmler insisted on being introduced to the 'prominent' Austrian prisoners individually.[207]

Himmler also liked giving guided tours of the camps. For example, in 1936 he took the members of the Friends of the Reichsführer-SS (a sponsors' organization) as well as the Reich leadership of the NSDAP and its Gauleiters round Dachau; in spring 1938 he took a large group of journalists round Sachsenhausen, and in the summer of 1938 Reich Interior Minister

Frick and high-ranking civil servants. In the following January he was present when Eicke and Pohl showed police chiefs round Sachsenhausen, and in the summer he arranged a further visit of the same camp for his circle of Friends; at the end of 1940 he was there to greet a delegation of ethnic German politicians from Alsace.[208]

The expansion of the armed units

With his appointment as Chief of the German Police Himmler's ambitions appeared to be entirely concentrated on internal security. This is the impression he tried to create with the Wehrmacht, in order not to arouse any suspicions in their minds concerning the further development of the SS's armed units.[209] On 1 October 1936 Himmler had established the Inspectorate of the Verfügungstruppe, which was subordinated to the SS Main Office, and appointed the commander of the leadership school in Brunswick, Paul Hausser, to head it.[210] Moreover, in the same year he combined existing units to create two new regiments in addition to the Leibstandarte, the SS-Standarten 'Deutschland' and 'Germania'. And then, following the so-called Anschluss with Austria, he established the Vienna Standarte, 'Der Führer'.[211] Furthermore, the expansion of the concentration camps led to the guard units of the KZs, the Death's Head units, being increasingly drawn into the militarization process. From 1937 onwards they were combined to form three Standarten and, after the Anschluss with Austria, were joined by an additional one.[212]

On 17 August 1938 Hitler issued an edict, which Himmler had seen and made alterations to in draft, regulating the basis on which the armed SS units were to operate and their relationship with the Wehrmacht.[213] Hitler determined that the armed units and the Death's Head units were neither part of the Wehrmacht nor of the police, but a 'standing armed force'. The Death's Head units were designed 'to solve special tasks of a police nature', while the armed units were to be at Hitler's 'exclusive disposal'. This description of the tasks of the armed units was much vaguer than the one given in 1934. At that time it had been established that the armed SS units were primarily to have domestic political functions, and that the Wehrmacht could call on them in time of war. As late as January 1937 Himmler had emphasized to Wehrmacht officers that he would assign elements of the police to the army in the event of a war, while the Death's

Head units would form an 'intervention force' distributed throughout the Reich.[214] However, in the same speech he had also stated that in a future war, in addition to the three fronts on land, sea, and in the air, there would be a fourth 'battlefield': 'the German homeland.'[215] Thus, in his view, in a future war it would be completely impossible to draw a sharp line separating domestic political security functions from military activity, and it was this view of the comprehensive nature of a future war that formed the basis for his vision of the special position of a state protection corps in the Third Reich.

Himmler used another occasion, an address to SS-Gruppenführer on 8 November 1938, to explain that, in his view, there was absolutely no contradiction between the internal security tasks of the SS and their engagement on the front line:

If I describe the overall task of the SS as being, together with the police [...] to guarantee Germany's internal security then this task can be carried out only if a section of the SS, this leadership corps, is prepared to stand and die at the front. If we didn't make any sacrifices and didn't fight at the front then we should have lost the moral authority to shoot down people at home who are trying to avoid their commitments and behaving as cowards. That is the function of the armed units, that is their glorious task—to be permitted to go the front.

Furthermore, Himmler announced his intention to have a whole army corps instead of the single division which he had been allocated. Evidently he was aiming to thwart the Wehrmacht's intention of using the armed SS as auxiliaries in a future war, distributed among the various fronts, and instead to lead his men into battle as a closed formation.[216]

Between January 1935 and December 1938 Himmler built up the armed units from a figure of barely 5,000 to over 14,000 men, and the Death's Head units from barely 2,000 to over 9,000.[217] He did this with some degree of finesse. When, during the mobilization for the occupation of the Sudetenland in autumn 1938, the SS armed units as well as some Death's Head formations were integrated into the army, Himmler recruited up to around 5,000 men into the SS as 'police reinforcements'. He retained 2,000 of these reservists in the Death's Head units and in 1939 recruited further reservists.[218]

The military character of the armed SS units was made very clear in a Führer edict of 18 May 1939. In it Hitler ordered that the existing units should be formed into a division, but also made it clear that this marked 'the end of the expansion of the Verfügungstruppe'. The edict also established a limit to the size of armed SS formations of 20,000 for the Verfügungstruppe, 14,000 for the Death's Head units, and 25,000 for the police reinforcements.[219] By the outbreak of war Himmler had brought the actual strength of the Verfügungstruppe up to around 18,000 men and that of the Death's Head units, including the police reinforcements, to over 22,000, which therefore remained slightly below the limit.[220]

Himmler clarified how he envisaged the deployment of the armed SS formations in the event of a war or civil war at a Gruppenführer meeting in Munich on 8 November 1938:

I have told the commander of the Standarte 'Deutschland' that I consider it right, and this also applies to the coming war, that SS men should never be taken prisoner. Before that can happen they should take their own lives. We shall also not take any prisoners. Future wars won't be skirmishes but rather life-and-death struggles between nations [. . .] However kind and decent we may want to be as individuals, we will be pitiless if it is a matter of preserving our nation from death. Then it doesn't matter if 1,000 inhabitants of a town have to be finished off. I will do it and I would expect you to carry it out as well.[221]

The amalgamation of SS and police

Himmler pursued his goal of amalgamating the SS and police to form a 'state protection corps' with great determination. We have already dealt with his ideological premises and the role he envisaged for it. The Reichsführer-SS and Chief of the German Police rapidly got to grips with the personnel and organizational issues involved. In 1937 Himmler created the post of Higher SS and Police Leader (HSSPF). The incumbents of the new post, which had been created specifically with reference to the mobilization for war, operated in future as his personal representatives in the regions, and were entitled to issue directives to the various branches of the SS and police within a military district in his name.[222] According to Himmler, this represented an important step towards 'uniting the SS and police to form a corps for the Führer's protection'.[223]

On 12 March 1938 the Reichsführer-SS made the first appointment: Obergruppenführer Friedrich Karl Freiherr von Eberstein, the commander of Oberabschnitt South and head of the police department in the Bavarian Interior Ministry, was appointed HSSPF in the Military Districts VII and

XIII.[224] Another wave of appointments followed in June 1938. However, the HSSPFs' responsibilities for the individual military districts, while at the same time being assigned to the regional state administrations, produced confusing chains of command.

Himmler's strategy of favouring SS leaders when filling posts in the police, and of admitting as many members of the police as possible to the SS, represented a further important element in his policy of trying to merge the two organizations. As part of this process the regulations for admission to the police were continually simplified.[225] Above all, he wished to emphasize the harmony that existed between the SS and police. Thus, during the party rally of 1938 a delegation of order police paraded demonstratively within the SS column.[226] Already in 1937 Himmler had granted the order police the right to wear the SS runes on their uniform.[227] Members of the security police who were simultaneously members of the SS were permitted to wear SS uniform while performing their duties.[228] During the war this privilege was extended to members of the security police who were not even members of the SS.[229]

Himmler also ensured that the procedure for the approval of SS marriages, on which there will be more below, also applied to members of the police.[230] Moreover, from 1937 onwards the police were integrated into the system of SS indoctrination that had been created by then.[231] Furthermore, the police were included in the 'Teutonic' rituals and celebrations typical of the SS. For example, on Himmler's orders the order police and security police, like the SS, replaced the traditional Christmas celebrations with 'Yule celebrations' on the day of the winter solstice.[232] Much more serious was the fact that, shortly after the start of the war, members of the SS and police were subjected to a special SS judicial system modelled on that of the Wehrmacht. In this way Himmler ensured that crimes or misdemeanours committed by police and SS men were dealt with within the SS and were not revealed to the outside world.[233]

Himmler regarded the fusion of SS and police as a moral imperative. In his radio broadcast on German Police Day in 1937 he expressed his conviction that the fact that 'they are rooted in the order of the SS, are bound by the strict rules of the SS [will] give German police officers the strength, with integrity and decency, to treat every case fairly, to be tough and uncompromising where necessary, to show understanding and magnanimity where possible and, in the process, despite all the filth and mean-spiritedness the police inevitably experience, to affirm the goodness and merits of the German people'.[234]

It is clear that Himmler's attempt to turn the SS and police into a solidly structured, uniform 'state protection corps' that could never be split up again was a response to political imperatives. It is equally clear, however, that political calculation was not the only motive for his designing his organization in the way he did. The organization and aims of the state protection corps were influenced by his phobias and prejudices, his fads and fancies, and his passions to an almost astonishing extent. His homophobia, for example, culminated in his making the pursuit of homosexuals one of the main tasks of the security police. There was his deep hostility to Christianity, his idealization of everything military, his control-freakery which, among other things, led him to attempt to withdraw the SS and police from the state's judicial system. What the Reichsführer-SS and Chief of the German Police defined as 'protection of the state' can just as easily be seen as Himmler protecting himself, and that in a dual sense: in terms of a defence against his personal fears, and as a protective shield behind which he could follow his own personal interests and aims. That applies particularly to the SS, which, unlike the police, was removed from the grasp and intervention of other state agencies. Here, as we shall now see, Himmler could implement his own peculiar ideas unimpeded.

PART III

The Order

IO

Ideology and Religious Cult

Between 1935 and 1937 there were about 200,000 members of the SS, and by the end of 1938, after the annexation of Austria, exactly 238,159, 95 per cent of whom belonged to the General SS. They came from all parts of society.[1] Compared with the population as a whole they were decidedly over-represented in commerce, in the field of health-care, in the public services, and among semi-skilled and unskilled workers; among skilled workers and members of the free professions they were slightly under-represented; in agriculture above all, however, they were distinctly under-represented. Only 10 per cent of SS members worked in agriculture; in the Reich in general the proportion was around 22 per cent. Thus the social profile of the SS tended towards that of a modern service industry, and it is difficult to reconcile that with the vision Himmler was continually conjuring up of an 'order' rooted in blood and soil.[2]

The Reichsführer-SS therefore regarded it as his main task to strengthen the unity of the SS, whose composition was in fact heterogeneous and which was expanding in several directions, in such a way as to secure the organization's long-term viability. In 1936, on the occasion of the annual meeting of Gruppenführer held at the commemorations of 9 November 1923, he made the following pronouncement on this problem:

I have often told you that I shall always strive to ensure that there are no false starts, and that, if at some time in the future there is weak leadership, there will be no gradual fragmentation, in the sense that first of all there'll be the General-SS, then the protection division; the third function will be a kind of police; the SD will be a kind of criminal or state police; the fifth branch will be an institute for ideological training and a research body—with the result that the order loses its unity and somehow disintegrates into its component parts.[3]

'The entire SS', as Himmler put it two years later on the same occasion, 'consists today of numerous branches, various kinds of troop formations and other kinds of institutions. All these things are splendid, but we must make an extraordinarily concerted and conscious effort to ensure that all these sections we have built up always retain a sense of being parts of a whole. [. . .] Everyone is first and foremost an SS man; after that he belongs to the General SS, the Verfügungstruppe [armed units], the Death's Head units, or the SD.' He therefore asked the Gruppenführer 'continually to impress on the men and their officer corps that they are only part of a whole and that they count only insofar as the whole counts'.[4] As Himmler once again made clear in an address delivered in September 1940, the Waffen-SS could 'endure only if the SS as a whole endures. If the whole corps really is an order which lives according to its own laws and understands that one part is unthinkable without all the others.'[5]

In the concept of the 'order' or, as he insisted, the 'clan order' (*Sippen-orden*) based on racial selection Himmler believed he had found the appropriate formula to capture the nature of the SS. In the *SS-Leithefte* (*SS Guidance Booklets*) of 1943 there is an attempt to refine the notion of the SS as an order. There we read: 'Within the context of a particular world-view an order is that close-knit community whose members surrender complete power over their lives to that world-view and all commit themselves willingly to following its precepts.' The similarity to Christian orders is no coincidence, the article says, and it is important to recognize that, in spite of the 'alien and wrong-headed philosophy of life' that Christian orders cultivate, they brought together 'people who wished to dedicate their lives to an idealistic and elevated goal'.[6]

Himmler's annual November speech of 1936 to the Gruppenführer contains the first mention of his idea of needing another ten years to secure the inner cohesiveness he was aiming for in the SS and police, an idea to which he returned several times the following year.[7] Indeed, in the eight-and-a-half years that remained to him as Reichsführer-SS his main focus was to be the internal integration of the SS. He went about this in a variety of ways: organizational measures; the development of a philosophy particular to the SS, created by his establishing a specific SS cult with attendant rituals, symbols, and 'sacred' sites; the propagation of a doctrine of virtue specific to the SS; and last but not least, a leadership style that was highly idiosyncratic and yet geared to the conduct of his subordinates.

★

The constant expansion of the SS forced Himmler repeatedly to adapt its command structures. In 1935 he had, as mentioned above, already promoted the three SS Section Offices (*Ämter*) to Main Offices (*Hauptämter*). Now he made further decisions.[8] In November 1936 he expanded the chief adjutant's office, headed by Karl Wolff, into the 'Personal Staff of the Reichsführer-SS'. Wolff was given the rank of 'Chief of Staff'.[9] The actual adjutancy, headed by Werner Grothmann, was now part of the Personal Staff, as were a Personal Department of the Reichsführer-SS (under Rudolf Brandt), a Chancellery of the Reichsführer-SS, and a gradually increasing number of departments and divisions that in part had a connecting function to the other Main Offices. When in 1939 the Personal Staff was declared a Main Office, Himmler named Wolff retroactively as Head of the Main Office, and in so doing underlined the particular position Wolff's post had acquired during the previous years.[10] In addition, a series of departmental heads in the SS Main Office were given posts in Himmler's Personal Staff and thus were visibly upgraded. For example, Pohl, head of the administrative department in the SS Main Office, was simultaneously 'administrative director' of the SS and the head of the medical department, and was given the title 'Reich Medical Officer SS'.[11]

On 9 November 1936 Himmler also redefined the role of the Oberabschnittsführer: now they were assigned to the three Main Offices (and no longer only to the office of the Reichsführer-SS and the SS Main Office), and thus had the task at regional level 'of safeguarding the unity of the SS order as a whole in accordance with the guidelines laid down by me', as Himmler put it. 'I expect of my Oberabschnittsführer that they will not regard this first and foremost as a boost to their power but rather that, as National Socialists and SS men, they will devote themselves to their new and wide-ranging task with a high degree of responsibility and with respect for the great and sometimes neglected achievements of the organizations— the Security Service and the Race and Settlement office—that are put under their direction.'[12]

The Race and Settlement Main Office under Walter Darré had since 1935 consisted of five departments: the Central Office, the Racial Office (where racial research was conducted), the Indoctrination Office, the Clan Office (responsible for the selection of applicants and permissions to marry), and the Settlement Office.[13] The actual headquarters for the SS leadership was the SS Main Office, originally responsible for leadership, administration, personnel administration, and the SS court. After 1933 it accumulated numerous new tasks, in particular responsibility for the armed SS units, concentration camps, border controls, and officer-training colleges (*Junkerschulen*). In August 1938 it acquired responsibility for indoctrination from the Race and Settlement Main Office.[14] At the beginning of 1939 the SS Main Office, after the relocation of the Court Office, already consisted of twelve departments.[15]

The SD headquarters under Heydrich, which in 1935 had been elevated to the status of a Main Office, retained its basic structure, and in ensuing years was also organized into three offices: Administration and Organization, Home, and Foreign.[16] In 1936 new additions were the two Main Offices of the security police (also under Heydrich) and the order police (under Daluege), a configuration that revealed the planned amalgamation of the SS and the police.

In April 1939 two further Main Offices were set up: Himmler named the administrative director of the SS, Oswald Pohl, as head of a new Main Office for Administration and Business, and in addition made him head of a Main Office for Budgeting and Buildings that he placed under the Reich Interior Ministry.[17] In reality both Main Offices under Pohl functioned as one unit that could act in its capacity as a state or as an SS institution. From 1 June 1939 the two corresponding units in the Personal Staff were made into two independent Main Offices, the Personnel Office and the Court Office.[18]

While in the mid-1930s the General SS was still almost 50 per cent financed from membership dues (an additional special contribution was levied on non-party members) and the payments of patrons, in 1939 Himmler succeeded in having the entire SS budget paid by the Reich Treasurer of the NSDAP, in effect, therefore, from state funds. According to the financial planning documents for 1935, the total SS budget amounted to *c.*15 million Reich marks. In 1936 it was a good 18 million and in 1937 and 1938 around 19 million.[19] In the mid-1930s, however, Himmler acquired a further source of finance, namely regular donations from an exclusive circle of entrepreneurs and managers from the German business world.

The prehistory of this 'Friends of the Reichsführer-SS' organization stretches back to the end of 1927, when the industrialist Wilhelm Keppler was asked by Hitler to assemble a consultative group on economic matters. Up to the takeover of power this relatively informal group had met three or four times. Their discussions did not, however, make any impact to speak of on the NSDAP programme. Keppler, Kurt Freiherr von Schröder, and other members of the circle had, on the other hand, played an important role in creating the contacts that led in late 1932 and early 1933 to soundings concerning a Hitler–von Papen government. Himmler knew Keppler at the latest from this period.[20]

After the takeover of power Hitler had made Keppler his economic adviser, though without creating for him a central role in the development of economic policy. The 'Keppler Circle' instead looked to the leadership of the SS. In March 1933 Himmler admitted the industrialist into the SS as a Standartenführer,[21] and soon the circle was called 'Friends of the Reichs-führer-SS'.[22] Meetings became more frequent, until from 1939 onwards they occurred almost once a month.[23] At the meetings there were lectures on political, economic, and cultural topics. Himmler, who determined the membership himself,[24] took part frequently in the meetings in the first years, giving lectures about police matters and ancestral research or taking the members on a tour of a concentration camp; in 1936, for example, they went to Dachau. In 1937 they were the guests of the Berlin police department.[25] After the outbreak of war Himmler's appearances at the meetings of his 'friends' grew less and less frequent, and from 1940 they evidently ceased altogether. Nevertheless, in December 1943 the Friends went on a three-day excursion from Berlin to Himmler's East Prussian military headquarters, where the Reichsführer informed his guests about the range of his responsibilities.[26]

In 1939 the Friends were thirty-six members strong. Among them, in addition to Keppler and Schröder, were leading representatives of German business such as Rudolf Bingel, the chief executive and chair of the board of Siemens–Schuckert, Heinrich Bütefisch, board member of IG Farben, Friedrich Flick, chief executive of Mitteldeutsche Stahlwerke, Karl Ritter von Halt, member of the board of the Deutsche Bank, and Hans Walz, managing director of Robert Bosch. In addition there were high-ranking representatives from the steel and machine-manufacturing industries, banking and insurance, and the shipping industry. Hermann Behrends and Oswald Pohl, as representatives of the SS, were also members, as was Carl Vincent Krogmann, the incumbent mayor of the city of Hamburg, as well as representatives of various ministries, the Reich Bank, and party administration.[27]

In 1936 Himmler appears to have asked the Friends to make donations to the SS for cultural and social purposes. The sum raised in 1936 is estimated at 600,000 Reich marks, and by 1939–40 rose to a good 1 million Reich marks per year.[28] The funds were clearly used for special tasks, for example, to fit out the Wewelsburg (of which more later), or to support projects of the Ahnenerbe (Ancestral Heritage) organization or the Lebensborn (Spring of Life) association. The Friends boosted the Reichsführer-SS's reputation in business circles and conversely opened up to its members the possibility of approaching one of the leading representatives of the regime with projects—or of making money through the extensive programme of Aryanization.[29]

Finally, Himmler's efforts to build up a comprehensive organization were completed by the founding of businesses owned by the SS. In addition to various workshops in concentration camps and the manufacture, developed since 1938, of construction materials (these have already been discussed[30]), in the 1930s Himmler supported a series of smaller businesses that served a wide variety of purposes. All these businesses were managed from the Personal Staff office.

One example was the Magdeburg publishing house Nordland, which specialized in bringing out ideologically relevant writings. Another was Anton Loibl, a private limited company founded in 1936, with the help of which Hitler's chauffeur, an acquaintance of Himmler's, developed the application of a patent for pedal-operated reflectors, which since 1937 had been mandatory for bicycles. A considerable part of the profit was diverted to the SS's 'academic research' organization, the Ahnenerbe, and to the Lebensborn association. In 1937 the private limited company Friedrich Franz Bauer was created as a way of enabling the man in question, a personal friend of Himmler, to disseminate his photographs.[31]

The Allach porcelain factory set up by Himmler in January 1936 had a peculiar position among the SS businesses. In addition to Karl Diebitsch, a kind of personal adviser to Himmler on matters of taste, who was brought into the Personal Staff as a specialist in art and design, three further SS members were involved as founders of the firm.[32] These four straw men were, however, forced to surrender their share of the business in October 1939 to Pohl, who incorporated it in German Economic Enterprises (*Deutsche Wirtschaftsbetriebe* = DWB).

Situated in the north of Munich, Allach saw itself not as an economic enterprise but as a 'state manufactory'.[33] Two-thirds of its production went to the SS, the police, and the Wehrmacht.[34] The SS benefited from large discounts, as a result of which the manufactory ran in the early years at a loss.[35] Himmler planned to make good the losses after the war with the help of profits from a large agricultural estate, and intended by this means to grant the Reichsführer-SS in perpetuity an 'unlimited right to make gifts' of the Allach products.[36] During the war he had the workforce replaced to a great extent by prisoners from Dachau concentration camp, which was nearby.[37]

The porcelain manufactory's range stretched in total to 240 models, all bearing the double *Sig* rune, the emblem of the SS—a grandiose collection of SS kitsch. 'Emblematic figures of the movement' such as the 'SS flag-bearer', as well as figurines of historical soldiers and of animals ('alsatian', 'rutting stag', 'young hare'), were available in porcelain, while the compulsory bust of the Führer, the Yule light (candle-holder) indispensable to the SS family, and 'Germanic' utensils such as vases and dishes could be obtained in pottery. In addition, and increasingly during the war, Allach produced everyday items for the Waffen-SS.[38]

The emerging conflict with 'Asia'

Although an ideology specific to the SS was to become the means of binding the organization together, before the outbreak of the Second World War statements from Himmler concerning the future goals of the SS were relatively rare. Apart from his programmatic speech at the NS Leaders Conference of 1931 there are in fact only three speeches in which he discussed the role of the SS in a future 'Third Reich' and fundamental ideological questions: his speech at the Reich Peasants' Rally of November 1935, which was also published under the title *The SS as an Anti-Bolshevik Fighting Force*; his lecture to a Wehrmacht course on national politics in January 1937; and finally, his speech of November 1938 to the SS-Gruppenführer.[39] There are also indications to be found in the indoctrination material over which Himmler exercised control, such as the *SS Guidance Booklets*.

If these speeches and materials are analysed more closely, it appears that an idea fundamental to Himmler's ideological outlook was that there existed a superior Nordic or Germanic race, which, as the leader of the 'white races' and thus also representative of humanity as a whole, was engaged in a millennia-long struggle with racially inferior opponents. The endpoint of this conflict would be a final clash between the racially superior—in other words the 'Germanic'—peoples, and their opponents, the inferior races, or to put it in drastic terms, a 'struggle between humans and subhumans'.[40] The rise of National Socialism under the leadership of the genius Hitler, the idea runs, opened up the historically unique opportunity to win this battle. If they should lose, the inexorable consequence would be the destruction of the Germanic—in other words, the white—race.

In public presentations of this idea Himmler identified Freemasons, communists, and Jews as dangerous enemies; within the SS he made it clear that he considered Christianity to be at least as dangerous. The Jews, who in Himmler's programmatic speech of 1931 had not even been mentioned, appeared in the changing guise of both string-pullers and the intellectual gurus of the enemy camp. Jews were both Freemasons and communists, and somehow or other they were also behind the intrigues of Christianity.[41] Because, however, the Jews were to blame for everything, they remained, even in Himmler's tirades, curiously insipid. By contrast, his rhetoric took flight when he was speaking against communists, homosexuals, and above all against Christianity.

At the beginning of the 1940s Himmler's concept of the enemy was decisively extended. He now favoured the view that the Teutons were engaged in a perpetual struggle with forces repeatedly thrusting forth from Asia to conquer Europe and destroy the Teutons: 'inevitably, like the swing of the pendulum.'[42] Himmler traced a line beginning with the Huns and stretching via the Magyars, the Mongols, Turks, and Tartars to the Soviet communists. In the final analysis it was the 'conflict between a Germanic Reich and subhumans'.[43]

In the process he was to stress again and again the alleged close symbiosis of communists and Jews, and develop the idea that 'Jewish Bolshevism' was attempting to mobilize the masses of the Asian continent against the 'Teutons'.[44] The fact that he repeatedly placed this Jewish-Bolshevik threat in a 'historical' context and presented it as the most recent manifestation of 'Asiatic' imperialism indicates an important shift in his vision of the world: the original arch-enemy 'the Jews' (whom he had always named in the 1930s in the same breath as the communists, Freemasons, and Jesuits), was now replaced by a much more encompassing enemy, the 'Asians'. It goes without saying that this vision of the enemy included 'the Jew'; as Himmler emphasized, the war was a racial war against 'Jewry and Asians'.[45] The change in Himmler's conception of the enemy is shown also by the fact that he no longer designated another important ideological enemy, Christianity, as the product of 'Jewish' influence, as he had done in the 1930s, but rather as a religion infected by 'Asian' elements. In 1944 these came together in the formulation 'purely Near Eastern Christianity, relayed by Jews'.[46] Himmler's anti-Semitism was therefore always an integral part of a colourful collage of hostile images.

First in 1938, but above all in the 1940s, a further change in his terminology can be observed: the future Reich that was to be established was no longer simply 'Germanic' but 'Greater Germanic' (*grossgermanisch*), in other words, it was to include 'related blood' from various European states and ethnic German minorities, take possession of extensive territories in eastern Europe, and, by expelling or exterminating the indigenous population, 'Germanize' them. Himmler conceived of this Greater Germanic Reich not as a Greater Germany extended by a few provinces but as an entirely new kind of supranational state organization created on a racial basis.[47] The historical analogy in his mind was that of the foundation of the Reich or Empire of 1871: just as Prussia had become a part of the German Empire, so the Greater German Reich would be absorbed into the Greater Germanic Reich.[48]

His vision of a final conflict with the Asian powers is probably to be found most distinctly in a speech he made on 16 September 1942 to the leaders of the SS at his Ukrainian headquarters at Hegewald. He warned his audience that, just as 'an Attila was born in this seething mass of millions of subhumans, in the same way suddenly in some coupling of two people the spark can be ignited' by means of which 'an Attila, a Genghis Khan, a Tamberlaine, a Stalin can emerge from lost traces of Nordic-Germanic-Aryan blood that is floating in this mass and which alone can give rise to powers of leadership and organization'. If, however, 'such a genius, such a dictator, such a Genghis Khan is born and simultaneously on the other side no Adolf Hitler is born', then 'things may turn out very badly for the white race'. There was only one way of successfully meeting this challenge: 'If you encounter any example of good blood somewhere in the east—and this is the first principle you must take note of—you can either win it over to your side or you must kill it. To leave it, on the other hand, so that tomorrow another leader emerges, whether of small, great, or indifferent stature, would be a crime against us all, for in the end only our own blood can defeat us.'[49]

Here a new idea comes into play: The greatest threat, in Himmler's view, no longer comes from an Asian–Bolshevik bloc under Jewish leadership but from Asian masses subordinated to strong leader figures, whose sudden emergence he could explain to himself only by positing the accidental breeding back of 'lost' 'Germanic' genes. On another occasion he claimed fancifully: 'Originally what probably happened was that we had a German-ic–Nordic ruling class who—and this is reported even by academic histor-ians—had assumed the position of lords or princes over some peoples in the east, in part at their request. They probably said, "Send us somebody for we cannot control ourselves and we want somebody to keep us in order".'[50] The more the Soviet Union proved itself to be at least a match for National Socialist Germany in the Second World War, the more clearly this idea crystallized in Himmler's utterances: Genghis Khan, Lenin, and Stalin became leaders with 'Aryan' roots.[51] Simultaneously—in 1942 Himmler had embarked on the 'Final Solution' of the Jewish question on a European scale—the Jews receded more and more as the principal enemy; in 1943 he was already referring to the Jewish question in the past tense.[52]

It has no doubt already become obvious that Himmler's politico-histori-cal ideology was a construct of the imagination that is almost impossible to analyse in detail on the basis of intellectual history. Not only was it inconsistent within itself and terminologically extremely vague, but in the course of time it also underwent significant changes that called into ques-tion its own foundations. The definition of the Germanic collective was dependent on a capriciously applied concept of race, and the hated ene-mies, the opponent, were described so imprecisely and were so closely linked that they were practically interchangeable and could be blamed for anything. At the end the Teutons were fighting a hostile leader class that was their own mirror-image. Himmler asked the Reich Peasants' Rally of 1935 to focus more on the 'line of argument as a totality', and that is the procedure that must be followed here if these ideas are to acquire any coherent meaning.

That does not, however, mean that there were no constants in his outlook. The restoration of some kind of 'Germanic' Reich that would colonize the east was without doubt one of them, as was his deep hostility towards the peoples settled in this east, towards Christianity, and towards the Jews. Yet these constants could be translated in very diverse ways into programmes of imperialist conquest and campaigns of annihilation.

It would therefore be wrong to assume that it was Himmler's priority to translate an ideological fixed programme into reality. Rather, he was first and foremost a highly flexible and adaptable politician who knew how to legitimize whatever policy he adopted by dressing it up with appropriate ideology. Or to put it another way, Himmler the politician wished to avoid being too hemmed in by Himmler the ideologue.[53]

Overcoming Christianity

In order to arm them for the forthcoming epochal conflict between 'humans and subhumans' Himmler wanted to direct the SS to one task above all: it was to act as the vanguard in overcoming Christianity and restoring a 'Germanic' way of living. As he understood it, this was the actual mission of his Schutzstaffel; it was to this task that it owed its identity and the justification for its existence.

Christianity seemed to him so dangerous because its sexual morality stood in opposition to the biological revolution he planned, and because the principle of Christian mercy contradicted his demand for unwavering severity in dealing with 'subhumans'.[54] Replacing Christian principles with 'Germanic' virtues was the precondition if they were to prevail against the 'subhumans' and secure the future.

In Himmler's concept the dual process of 'de-Christianization' and 'Germanization' was to impact on all aspects of life: custom and moral behaviour, in particular sexual morality; the legal system; the entire realm of culture; and the social order. This general revision of outdated values that Himmler aimed for corresponded strikingly to his own personal development. Not only did he blame the 'homosexual male order' of the Catholic Church and the prudery rooted in his Catholic upbringing for his own delayed sexual development and for what he subsequently was to call with shock the 'threat' of homosexual temptations. In the face of his gradually waning enthusiasm for his wife after ten years of marriage, towards the end of the 1930s, he also felt limited in his private needs by the dominant morality of Christian marriage. 'Germanic generosity' could be of use here. His reorientation towards 'Germanic' values also enabled him to create a moral system by which he could reject the humanitarian values he had grown up with, and which had obstructed the development of a ruthless policy of expanding living-space.

There is no doubt about Himmler's anti-communism and anti-Semitism, and he sought to destroy both groups without mercy. Yet he was basically much more interested in Christianity: the conflict with the Christian world in which he had grown up had truly existential significance for him, and by linking opposition to Christians with the idea of restoring the lost Germanic world he had set himself the overriding challenge of his life. A political consideration was also important: anti-Semitism and anti-communism were fundamental to National Socialism, both ideologically and in its political practice. The SS would be hard put to establish a distinctive profile in these areas. By linking de-Christianization with re-Germanization, Himmler had provided the SS with a goal and purpose all its own.

We have already seen that, in spite of his rejection of Christianity, Himmler set immense store by the fact that his men and he himself 'believed in God'.[55] What he said about his own 'belief in God' was, however, vague. In his speeches he occasionally referred to 'Waralda, the ancient (*das Uralte*)', but without deriving from that a concept of divinity to which he or the SS were committed. For example, in a speech to senior naval officers in 1943 he propounded the view that those who observed and understood the process of natural selection were 'believers in their innermost being'. 'They are believers because they recognize that above us is an infinite wisdom. The Teutons had a beautiful expression for it: Waralda, the ancient. We may dispute how it can be revered and how in earthly terms it can be broken down into cults and varieties.'[56]

Himmler was not willing to profess belief in public in Wotan or other Germanic deities. In secret, however, he thought about the question of whether it might not be possible to decipher such 'Germanic' ideas of divinity. In May 1940 he turned to Walter Wüst, the head of the Ahnenerbe, and asked him 'to research where in all of North-Germanic Aryan culture the concept of the lightning flash, the thunderbolt, Thor's hammer, or the hammer thrown or flying through the air appears. Also, where there are sculptures of a god holding an axe and appearing in a flash of lightning.' He requested him to collect 'all such evidence, whether in pictures, sculpture, writing, or legend', because he was convinced that in this case it was 'not natural thunder and lightning but rather a case of an earlier, highly developed weapon our forefathers had, possessed of course by only a few, namely by the Aesir, the gods, and presuming an extraordinary knowledge of electricity'.[57] The final remark about electricity indicates that Himmler believed this weapon had actually existed and had really been in the hands of god or godlike beings; had he been interested only in the depiction of the phenomenon of the thunderbolt he would not have needed to bother about the construction of the alleged weapon, and could have left it entirely to the imagination of the artist. Or had his enthusiasm made his thoughts run away with him? The fact that Wiligut (of whom we will hear more later), his adviser in all Germanic and occult questions, presented him with a plan to introduce a primitive Germanic religion in place of Christianity does indeed lend strength to the supposition that among his intimate associates Himmler pursued these ideas seriously.[58]

In general, however, Himmler's attitude to religious questions was characterized by his radically utilitarian outlook, indeed by unvarnished cynicism: if Christianity was harmful that was above all because it stood in the way of Himmler's intended demographic revolution. When, for example, during the war a volunteer division of Muslims was created for the Waffen-SS (see Ill. 31), he praised Islam as 'a religion that is both practical and appealing to soldiers', for it trained 'men for me in this division and promises them heaven if they have fought and fallen in battle'.[59]

He came to respect the Jehovah's Witnesses, tens of thousands of whom were imprisoned in his concentration camps as a result of their pacifist and anti-Nazi attitudes, because of their stubborn will to resist: 'If their fanaticism could be harnessed for Germany or a similar fanaticism be created in the nation as a whole in wartime, we would be stronger than we are today!'[60] They also lived frugal lives and were hard-working and honest. For that reason he not only employed them in his own household and in those of friends and SS families,[61] but expressed the view that precisely these qualities should be propagated among the suppressed nations in the east, where in addition the Jehovah's Witnesses' pacifism was extremely welcome to the Germans! In July 1944, in a long letter, Himmler therefore ordered the then-head of the Reich Security Main Office, Dr Ernst Kaltenbrunner, to export the religion to the occupied eastern territories (which by this time were no longer occupied): 'In the case of all Turkish peoples the Buddhist faith is suitable but for other nations the teachings of the Bible Students [Jehovah's Witnesses] are the appropriate ones.'[62]

For his own men too Himmler had a ready store of pragmatic solutions to existential questions. Answers to the question of human transience were not to be sought in the realm of religion but in the cult of ancestors he propagated. This practice of revering ancestors, in his view, strengthened each individual's consciousness of being linked to the continuum of succeeding generations; the transience of the individual was abolished in the immortality of the nation. At the meeting of Gruppenführer on the eve of the November 1938 commemoration of the Munich putsch he claimed that 'we shall be unconquerable and immortal as a nation, truly immortal as an

Aryan–Nordic race, if we hold firm by selection to the law of blood and, maintaining the cult of our ancestors, recognize the eternal cycle of all being and action and of every other kind of life in this world. A nation that preserves its ancestors will always have children; only nations without ancestors are childless.'[63]

The subsequent text of the speech shows, however, that Himmler not only equated immortality with the perpetuation of the Volk as a collective—a typically völkisch attitude—but that in his view immortality was also something an individual could experience: 'And however bitter death is for the moment—for it means taking leave—we know equally on the basis of the most ancient conviction of our blood that it is merely a move to another plane; for we have all seen each other somewhere before and by the same token will see one another in the next world.'[64]

Ill. 13. 'For us death has no terrors [. . .] The individual dies but even while he lives in his children his nation goes on after him', wrote Himmler in 1942 in a preface to a document from the SS Hauptamt giving instructions on the conduct of dignified 'SS obsequies'. The ceremony for Reinhard Heydrich—at which Himmler gave the eulogy—was conducted in the Reich Chancellery and was seen as exemplary. Heydrich had died after an assassination attempt.

Himmler also concerned himself intensively with the question of rein-carnation. He declared to the Gruppenführer in February 1937 that this 'was a question that could be discussed for hours'. He claimed to be personally neutral: 'I must say that this belief has as much in its favour as many other beliefs. This belief can no more be proved by the methods of exact science than Christianity, the teaching of Zarathustra, Confucius, and so on. But it has a big plus: a nation that has this belief in reincarnation, and reveres its ancestors and thus itself, always has children, and such a nation has eternal life.'[65]

On a personal level Himmler did in fact have very clear views on this matter, as is demonstrated by a letter he sent the same month to SS-Hauptsturmführer Eckhardt. Karl August Eckhardt, whose main occupation was that of Professor of Legal History, had shown Himmler a manuscript with the title 'Earthly Immortality', on which the Reichsführer-SS had commented very favourably. Himmler let Eckhardt know that his work was 'an immensely valuable contribution and a complete confirmation of what has been passed down orally over millennia, though, as in the case of all such things, it has not been recognized in academic studies'. He did want to see changes, however; he objected to Eckhardt's term 'transmigration of souls' and wished it to be replaced by 'rebirth in the clan and in the same blood'.[66] The revised manuscript was published as a book in 1937, and was distributed by Himmler to the SS in 1939 in a special edition.[67]

Naturally Eckhardt had responded to Himmler's comments when revis-ing the work. There was no more mention of transmigration of souls but of 'a belief in reincarnation' that was 'of Aryan origin'. In the foreword Eckhardt quoted one of Himmler's favourite writers, Werner Jansen; in his 'most profound book', the 'heroic song of Robert the Devil, Duke of Normandy', he named this heroic figure as the chief witness for his main thesis that the Teutons had believed in 'reincarnation'.

The cult of the Teutons

Himmler pursued vigorously the aim of making the SS the focus of a cult of the Teutons. In doing so he was not satisfied with laying bare the allegedly 'Germanic roots' of contemporary Germans and exhorting them to develop a cult of their ancestors. Rather, his purpose was to bring to light in a comprehensive new interpretation the supposedly

Germanic core of German history: it was the duty of National Socialism, he claimed, to lead the Germans back to their true Germanic identity. In this Himmler's thinking was not primarily historical but racial: what distinguished Germanic-German history in his eyes was the fact that it was shaped by people with constant, genetically determined dispositions and abilities and thus could be regarded not as a historical continuum but as a stable world.[68]

In endeavouring to create a Germanic myth special to the SS Himmler was above all concerned to reveal the pre-Christian world of the Teutons as exemplary and their Christianization as a fatal mistake, indeed as a crime, and so by stripping away the layers behind the façade of an imposed Christianity to show the true Germanic core of medieval history. Admittedly none of these topics was new: at the latest since the beginning of the nineteenth century Germanic myth and enthusiasm for things Germanic had been a widespread movement that found expression not only in academic disciplines but also in popular forms. The radical anti-Christian turn in Germanic ideology, like its development into a Germanic faith, had already been relatively widespread in völkisch circles before 1914. Above all in the turbulent years after the defeat of the First World War the mythology of the Germanic hero was revived as a political force, plumped up with racial doctrines and set up as an ideal in contrast to the 'levelling-down' practised by the western democracies.[69] As we have seen, Himmler too was part of this world; his Germanic awakening had taken place in 1923–4 when he read the novels of Werner Jansen.

Presumably in 1937 Himmler set down on paper the following thoughts:

We live in an era of the ultimate conflict with Christianity. It is part of the mission of the SS to give the German people in the next half-century the non-Christian ideological foundations on which to lead and shape their lives. This task does not consist solely in overcoming an ideological opponent but must be accompanied at every step by a positive impetus: in this case that means the reconstruction of the Germanic heritage in the widest and most comprehensive sense.[70]

On the basis of this premise Himmler developed a 'work plan'. A research group made up of subject specialists from among the SS was to begin a collection of source material on the 'Germanic heritage' in some five volumes, and as a second step investigate the 'so-called Christian Middle Ages in order to trace the various streams of Germanic heritage'. The results were to serve first and foremost the ideological 'direction' of the SS.

Himmler's research organization Ahnenerbe (Ancestral Heritage) was in fact to embark on such studies in the years to come, if not in the concentrated form in which Himmler had imagined in 1937.[71]

What he imagined the social order and the experience of the Teutons actually to have been, and why this lost world should represent an ideal, is, it must be said, hard to discover. His pronouncements on the Teutons of the Dark Ages are decidedly sparse.[72] It was only in his 'Schutzstaffel' speech of 1935 that he went into this topic in greater detail. In it he praised Germanic law as exemplary, in particular the principle, embedded in its belief in an all-embracing divine order, that nature and animals are worthy of protection; in addition, he praised the highly developed craftsmanship of the Teutons and their alleged ability to develop a plough that was far superior to anything comparable; their reverence for their ancestors, manifested in graves made of giant stones; their bravery and strength; their knowledge of astronomy; and finally their runes, the 'mother of all written languages'.

As Himmler regarded their conversion to Christianity as the Teutons' decisive original sin, preventing Germanic virtues from unfolding to their full extent in the medieval empire,[73] the 'missionary to the heathen', St Boniface, was the particular object of the SS leader's anger. He refused to forgive him for the felling in 723 of the Donar oak, revered by the Teutons as holy, and even 1,214 years later in 1937 he still was indignant at how 'anyone could be such a swine as to chop down that tree'.[74] But in Himmler's view the Christianization of the Teutons was above all the fault of 'Charles the Frank', that is, Charlemagne, whom he repeatedly accused in public speeches of slaughtering the Saxons;[75] his son, Louis the Pious, was for Himmler simply 'infected with Jewishness'.[76]

Himmler's negative appraisal of Charlemagne made no impression on Hitler, however, who in his speech to the party conference in 1935 emphasized that in the process of forming the empire of the early Middle Ages Christianity had been effective in creating communities, and declared Charlemagne the historic unifier of the Reich, a judgement he backed up with comments in his private circle.[77] Thereupon Himmler reversed his opinion: in the SS Guidance Booklets there appeared an article by H. W. Scheidt, head of the indoctrination office of Alfred Rosenberg (usually regarded as Himmler's main ideological competitor), in which the latter declared that the 'true reason for the conflicts with the Saxons and the other methods of subjugation employed by Charlemagne was his thoroughly Germanic will to power and his recognition that the centralized political power he enjoyed needed urgently to be extended'.[78] Himmler himself was strikingly slow to comment. Only in 1944 did he concede that Charlemagne was the 'subject of much controversy, much revered and in the final analysis—in spite of all the things we [...] don't like about him and which we must nevertheless understand as part of the power struggle involved in forming an empire—a great man, because he founded the Reich'.[79]

On the other hand, he took a quite different view of the German King Henry I: reverence for him was probably the most powerful expression of Himmler's efforts to reveal anti-Christian roots in the Middle Ages. In 1936, for the thousandth anniversary of the king's birth, Himmler visited his burial-place in Quedlinburg cathedral in order to inaugurate a new tradition. The annual 'King Henry celebrations' were to become a fixture of the SS commemorative calendar. Himmler's speech, published the same year, on the anniversary of the king's death[80] was designed to reveal parallels between Henry and Hitler. As was clear from the speech, Henry came to power at the same age as Hitler and, it was suggested, had to overcome similar problems: 'When, in 919, at the age of 43, Henry Duke of Saxony, a member of the Liudolfing family of soil-based aristocracy, became the German king, he came into the most dreadful inheritance. He became king of a German empire that hardly existed even in name. The whole of the eastern part of Germany had [...] been lost to the Slavs.'

Himmler listed a whole series of virtues in Henry that he considered exemplary. At his election in 919 he refused to be anointed by the church, and thus testified to the fact that, astutely acknowledging the prevailing circumstances, he was unwilling to tolerate the church's intervention in political matters in Germany under his rule. Himmler continued: 'He reintroduced the old and yet ever new Germanic principle of the loyalty of the duke to his liegeman, in sharpest contrast to the Carolingian methods of ruling based on church and Christianity.' In addition, according to Himmler, Henry was an advocate of 'open discussion among men'. Above all, 'he never forgot for a moment that the strength of the German nation lies in the purity of its blood and the ancient Germanic traditional rootedness in one's own soil'. He was owed heartfelt thanks 'for never making the mistake that Germans and also European statesmen have made for centuries up to the present day: that of seeing his goal as lying outside the living-space [*Lebensraum*]—today we would say geopolitical space—of his nation'.

Unfortunately, Himmler was forced to concede, the celebrations had one blemish: 'The earthly remains of the great German leader no longer rest in their burial-place. We do not know where they are.'[81] This 'source of shame for the whole German nation', as Himmler called it elsewhere,[82] gave him no rest. He instituted a thorough search for Henry's bones, which met with the desired success the following year. As *Das Schwarze Korps* promptly reported on the occasion of the King Henry celebrations, 'scientific evidence has established that the remains discovered during excavations in the crypt of Quedlinburg cathedral are in fact those of Henry I'.[83] 'Himmler has dug up the bones of Henry I', as Propaganda Minister Goebbels noted laconically in his diary.[84]

In the years that followed Himmler appeared annually in Quedlinburg to commemorate the dead king in a solemn ceremony in the crypt of the cathedral, the interior of which was festooned with a huge cloth bearing the SS runes.[85] During the war the commemoration went ahead without Himmler, however, and apparently in his absence the accustomed solemnity was somewhat lacking. At any rate, in 1944 Himmler's adjutant complained that after the most recent commemoration far too much alcohol had been consumed.[86]

If Himmler celebrated Henry I as the actual founder of the Reich and as one whose attitude to Christianity was distant, the rule of the Hohenstaufens in the High Middle Ages was for him an era in which 'the Reich at its height attained and radiated a power that outshone the rest of the world'. Emperor Frederick II and his contemporary Henry the Lion held pride of place on his roll-call of German heroes.[87]

Another model he drew from the Middle Ages was the order of Teutonic Knights. In 1939 the SS took over the headquarters of the order in Vienna, which had been requisitioned. Himmler exploited the occasion to expatiate on history. The order had, he said, been founded

very early [. . .] in the so-called [*sic*] Holy Land, when, led astray by the Christian church, the powerful forces of Germanic expansion bled to death in the far, far east. This order of knights then made the bold move to East Prussia and there became the order of Teutonic Knights. It founded the state, the order's own state of East Prussia, in accordance with its strict, soldierly code and Christian outlook. [. . .] It is my firm intention to appropriate from it all that was good about this order: bravery, extraordinary loyalty to a revered idea, sound organization, riding out into far countries, riding out to the east.[88]

In recent German history, however, Himmler found relatively few points of contact for his Germanic view of history. In the second half of the war he referred variously to Prussia and Prussian virtues and to the Prussian king Frederick II, the Prussian reforms, and Bismarck's founding of the Kaiserreich,[89] but that was as far as it went. His historical borrowings were thus basically concerned with appropriating the supposed Germanic heritage from the Dark Ages. The establishment of a cult of the Teutons within the SS was, as already indicated, entirely in accord with Himmler's youthful passion for Germanic heroes and virtues. Yet the veneration of the Teutons as practised by the SS cannot be explained merely as the influence of an individual quirk of the Reichsführer-SS. Rather, Himmler's intention was to secure for the SS a lasting role at the ideological heart of National Socialism as preserver of the Germanic heritage and its interpretation. In a system so profoundly rooted in ideology as National Socialism such a position held out the promise of considerably enhanced prestige and power.

The fact that the zeal with which many National Socialists emphasized the Germanic heritage in the first years of the Third Reich had since the mid-1930s been losing impetus did not discourage the Reichsführer-SS. Even the fact that in his public statements Hitler used only non-specific set phrases in comments on the Germanic past, and in private indicated clearly that he was not particularly interested in the Germanic heritage and considered any intensive engagement with this topic, of the kind Himmler went in for, as slightly bizarre,[90] did not reduce the latter's commitment. For, by contrast with Hitler, Himmler's concern with this matter was not primarily linked to effective mass propaganda, but rather he saw in it the way to underpin an identity specific to the SS.

He therefore went to considerable lengths not only to conjure up the existence of a Germanic empire and the continuation of Germanic features in the German people, but also to support these with scientific proof. He was not, however, alone in seeking to do this. The official head of NS ideology, the 'Führer's commisioner in charge of all intellectual and ideological training and education in the NSDAP', Alfred Rosenberg, had since 1933 been pursuing the plan of centralizing all prehistory in a 'Reich Institute for Pre-History and Early History'[91]—for Himmler, an additional spur to speed up research into the Germanic heritage through his own academic organization.

The Ahnenerbe (Ancestral Heritage)

Himmler's encounter with Hermann Wirth in October 1934 clearly provided the first impetus for the founding of this society. He met the private scholar and researcher into prehistory, who was universally rejected by the scholarly community in his subject, at a private soirée, also attended by Darré.[92] Commissioned by Himmler and Darré, in the spring of 1935 Wirth began work; first of all he prepared two exhibitions, the purpose of which was to present Germanic customs from a Nazi perspective.[93]

On 1 July 1935 Himmler founded the society for the study of intellectual prehistory, German Ancestral Heritage (Deutsches Ahnenerbe), which was set up entirely with Wirth's activities in mind.[94] Wirth became president of the society and Wolfram Sievers, Wirth's former private secretary, was appointed general secretary.[95] At first the Ahnenerbe was part of the work of the Race and Settlement Main Office and thus very much under Darré's influence.[96]

Soon, however, Himmler began to fear that the development of the institute could be adversely affected by the fact that Wirth was not regarded as a serious academic.[97] In addition, Wirth used the funds at his disposal in a very headstrong and lavish manner.[98] For these reasons, in the course of 1936 Himmler engineered a parting of the ways with Wirth, who, while retaining the honorary presidency and without in the process breaking with Himmler personally, was finally dismissed from the service of the Ahnenerbe in 1938.[99] The Indo-Germanic expert and Munich university professor Walter Wüst, who since the autumn of 1936 had been in charge of a newly created Ahnenerbe department for lexicology, became Wirth's successor.[100] (Wüst demonstrated his particular gratitude by, among other things, presenting Himmler, on the latter's thirty-seventh birthday, with a replica, made by the Allach factory, of a 'beautifully shaped, Lower Saxon bossed urn'—according to Wüst, a greeting 'across more than one-and-a-half millennia and full of profound meanings'.[101])

Before 1939 Himmler removed the Ahnenerbe in stages from the influence of the Race and Settlement Main Office and finally transformed this academic organization into an office of the SS, attached to his Personal Staff.[102] At the beginning of 1939 he introduced a new set of rules in which he made himself president, while Wüst, who was de facto director of the organization, became 'curator' and Sievers remained administrative head.[103]

From the start the main task of the Ahnenerbe was to support the SS's ideological indoctrination programmes with publications on Germanic prehistory and in the field of genealogy. Thus, Himmler demanded from members of the SS not only certificates of descent but in addition wanted SS leaders to display coats of arms. To this end he commissioned research into the 'clan emblems' and 'family crests' of their forebears and those of other prominent Nazis.[104]

The Ahnenerbe expanded rapidly. From 1936 onwards branches emerged all over the Reich. In the main they were working in isolation and were charged with the most diverse tasks. In 1939 the Ahnenerbe finally had around two-dozen research institutions at its disposal, mostly in the fields of prehistory, linguistics, and folklore but to a lesser extent also in other humanities disciplines, as well as, and increasingly, in the field of the natural sciences.[105] For example, in addition to Wüst's department of lexicology, in 1936 the Ahnenerbe had incorporated the Centre for Germanic Studies in Detmold (which immediately assumed responsibility for the Externsteine*). In 1937 the centres for Indogermanic–Finnish cultural relations[106] and for family and clan emblems were added,[107] as was the Centre for Folk Tales and Sagas a little later. In 1938 the Ahnenerbe set up a department of ethnic research and folklore in Frankfurt am Main[108] and a department of classical philology and archaeology.[109]

In 1938 Himmler decreed that all SS archaeological excavations should be concentrated in the new Ahnenerbe Centre for Excavations. Several such excavations already existed: alongside projects, such as the ultimately 'successful' search for the remains of Henry I, that were controversial in the academic world there were serious ones such as the excavation, which from 1937 enjoyed Himmler's personal patronage, of the early medieval trading settlement of Haithabu (Hedeby) near Schleswig, led by the famous archaeologist Hubert Jankuhn. In addition, the SS supported prehistoric excavations at the fortification of Erdenburg near Bensberg, at Altchristburg in East Prussia, and on the Hohenmichele, a prehistoric burial-site near Sigmaringen.[110] Further departments and research centres grew up: for Indogermanic religious history, for the Near East, for Germanic buildings, and for

---

* *Translators' note*: A natural rock formation in the Teutoburg Forest (discussed later in this chapter).

medieval and modern history.[111] Finally, there was the research centre headed by the Tibet scholar Ernst Schäfer for Central Asia and expeditions, which was refounded in 1943 as the Sven Hedin Institute.[112]

Himmler's interest in scientific research was originally aimed entirely at finding proof of the Cosmic Ice Theory (or World Ice Theory), which will be treated in detail later. To this end he had already founded a centre for meteorology, later for geophysics, under the directorship of the meteorologist Hans Robert Scultetus in Berlin in 1937. The research centre for astronomy at the Grünwald observatory near Munich was established for the same purpose.[113] In the following years Himmler extended almost at will the scientific and/or pseudo-scientific research activities of the Ahnenerbe. Amongst other things, he created a department of dowsing; a centre for geology and mineralogy, among the activities of which was prospecting for gold in Upper Bavarian rivers; a research centre for botany; and a department for the study of karst and caves.[114] In addition, a department of animal geography and animal history were planned, as well as one devoted to the investigation of the so-called occult sciences.[115]

The Ahnenerbe even developed an active line in journalism. From 1936 it had been contributing to the popular science journal *Germania*, described in its subtitle as 'a Germanic-lore monthly to promote things essentially German', and gradually brought it under its control. Himmler always followed the publications with great interest. In addition, the Ahnenerbe had since the end of 1936 been financing the strongly anticlerical journal *Nordland*, an 'organ of ideological struggle', and was joint editor of a number of specialist academic journals. Apart from these, a series called 'Deutsches Ahnenerbe' had existed since 1935. The year 1939 saw the start of elaborate conferences.[116]

The Ahnenerbe was, however, much more than a learned society. Staff of the Ahnenerbe acted as 'inquisitor, censor, and confiscator', in particular in the wake of a robust acquisitions policy.[117] Wüst himself made the self-critical observation in 1938 that the Ahnenerbe seized 'important objects and institutions' without going on to take appropriate care of them.[118] As in the case of many other SS projects, on more than one occasion the Gestapo gave the Ahnenerbe's activities the muscle they needed: for example, in 1938 the Ahnenerbe took over from the Munich Gestapo the valuable library confiscated from the author Lion Feuchtwanger, and the same year it used the Gestapo to seize part of the wealth of the Salzburg University Club and the whole of its library.[119]

The Ahnenerbe also attempted to gain a foothold in the universities by offering holders of chairs a headship of department or conferring on them a high rank in the SS. An SS presence in the universities not only held out the promise of influencing teaching and research, and thus of gaining prestige, but was designed to facilitate recruitment into the SS from the student body.[120] On several occasions Himmler intervened successfully in chair appointments,[121] especially as his influence in the Reich Education Ministry was growing. In April 1937 Heinrich Harmjanz, a member of the SS since 1930, took over the department for the humanities, and the chemist Rudolf Mentzel, in the SS since 1932, had been responsible since May 1939 for the science department; both were well disposed towards the Ahnenerbe. The Ahnenerbe returned the favour in autumn 1938 by setting up a department of ethnic research and folklore in Frankfurt am Main for Harmjanz, where he held a professorship alongside his position in the ministry. In spite of such initiatives, however, Himmler was never to succeed in developing a university and science policy.[122]

This lack of coherence characterizes the Ahnenerbe as a whole. A 'policy of unplanned expansion, dependent on random factors',[123] and the proliferation—not to say dissipation—of its activities led to the Ahnenerbe assembling in its ranks not only acknowledged experts in their fields, but also laypeople from outside the academic world, as well as outright charlatans. Consistent scholarly standards were never established.

The war was to do nothing to change this. The focus of research shifted now to projects 'important to the war effort'. As part of the resettlement projects organized by the SS the Ahnenerbe, for example, transferred cultural objects from the South Tyrol and the Baltic States, and in the occupied territories went in for cultural plunder on a grand scale.[124] Under the banner 'The Humanities' War Effort', numerous Ahnenerbe specialists were working on projects relevant to ideological conflicts with the enemy.[125] At the same time the Ahnenerbe got involved in animal- and plant-breeding (for example, in breeding a horse that would withstand the winter of the steppes for the militarized peasants in the east); in developments in armaments, some of a fantastical kind; but also—as part of the work of the Institute of Applied Military Research—in human experiments with frequently fatal results.[126]

In summary one can say that, with regard to the original purpose of the Ahnenerbe—research into prehistory and early history—substantial results were achieved. However, without a consistent research strategy to provide a framework for individual achievements, and the means of exploiting them ideologically to benefit the SS, these successes simply vanished. The fact that such a strategy never emerged is due to a whole series of factors; in essence, however, what did emerge was that science and scholarship were not capable of providing proof of Himmler's notion of a lost, culturally pre-eminent Greater Germanic Reich.[127]

'Under wraps'

Reverence for the Teutons, a fundamentally anti-Christian standpoint, and the eternal opposition of 'Germanic' and 'Asiatic' forces describe only some facets of Himmler's vision of the world, namely those the Reichsführer supported in public, if at times only in an attenuated form. Himmler linked these elements with a series of fantastical theories or myths that in the inter-war period were very widespread to form a much more comprehensive vision, though one he, for the most part, kept to himself.

The Reichsführer was, for example, an enthusiastic supporter of the Austrian engineer Hanns Hörbiger's Cosmic Ice Theory, mentioned above. Though unanimously rejected by contemporary science, this theory was extremely popular in the inter-war years. It assumed that what happens in the cosmos is determined by the antagonism between suns and ice planets, and that this can both explain global catastrophes in the recent history of the earth and also provide the key to myths, for example, the myth of the lost city of Atlantis.[128]

Unimpressed by the unequivocally negative reaction of scientists, in July 1936 Himmler not only committed leading supporters of the Cosmic Ice Theory in Bad Pyrmont to extending this theory under his patronage,[129] but attempted in particular, as part of the activities of the Ahnenerbe, to prove that it was correct. Two Ahnenerbe institutions, the Centre for Meteorology headed by the meteorologist Hans Robert Scultetus and the Research Centre for Astronomy at the Grünwald observatory, had been set up specifically for this purpose. Himmler even thought about putting Werner Heisenberg (whom he considered 'decent', in spite of the fact that he had just been heavily criticized in *Das Schwarze Korps*) in touch with 'our Cosmic Ice Theory people'.[130]

Himmler repeatedly approached the Ahnenerbe personally to have elements of the Cosmic Ice Theory checked. In December 1940, for example, his adjutant Brandt enquired 'whether the sun's being obscured by fog in some places might lead to the mutation of genetic material'—a question raised by the Reichsführer-SS. The Ahnenerbe specialist responsible for the Cosmic Ice Theory, the senior civil servant Scultetus, was, however, forced to deny there was such an effect.[131] In September 1941 Brandt sent, on Himmler's behalf, an essay entitled 'Butterflies Fly from South Africa to Iceland' to the administrative head Sievers, and asked for comments on it from the perspective of the Cosmic Ice Theory.[132] A few months later Himmler asked Sievers to pursue indications that frozen horses or mammoths had been found in Siberia, one of 'the few tangible proofs of a catastrophe to affect the earth however many thousands of years ago that would correspond to the earth catastrophe of the last moon-capture and its consequences, as stated in the Cosmic Ice Theory'.[133]

Himmler was outraged by a negative response to the Cosmic Ice Theory sent to him by a civil servant in the Reich Education Ministry; yet his letter betrays a certain defensiveness, for the Reichsführer clearly felt compelled to make use of Hitler's authority: 'I am willing to defend freedom of research in all its forms, and therefore freedom of research into the Cosmic Ice Theory. I even intend to give the warmest support to free research and in this I am in the best of company, as even the Führer and Chancellor of the German Reich Adolf Hitler has for many years been a convinced supporter of this theory, though it is frowned upon by the journeymen of science.'[134]

Even so, as early as 1938 he gave the Ahnenerbe the instruction to keep the Cosmic Ice Theory 'strictly under wraps', in other words, 'in no way to make it public' and to subject it 'to critical scrutiny from the point of view of very precise and limited fields of work'.[135] The Berlin meteorological office promptly changed its name to Centre for Geophysics.

The effects of cosmic events on the earth and on human life aroused Himmler's particular interest—in the mid-1920s he had already shown himself to be open-minded about astrology.[136] At the beginning of 1945 he set up an investigation into what knowledge was available concerning the 'influence of the weather on human beings': 'How far is there a connection with cosmic events. Is there an astrological way of calculating the weather?' It was his intention after the war, according to Himmler, to give the astrologer Wilhelm Wulff, who in the second half of the war wrote astrological reports for him, and his Cosmic Ice Theory specialist Scultetus the joint task of answering this question.[137] In addition, the Reichsführer-SS was convinced 'that the Teutons had possessed a remarkable, religiously based knowledge of the universe that even today has not been super-seded'.[138] After the end of the war he planned to set up an observatory at every SS location in order, as his adjutant explained in a letter, 'to give the broadest range of people the opportunity of taking an interest in astronomy and by this means to discover a partial substitute for the Christianity we plan to transcend'.[139]

Himmler was also attracted by the myth of Tibet—the idea, that was widespread in a variety of versions, that in the mountains of Tibet an advanced civilization had once existed, possibly the product of an original, sophisticated race that had sought refuge there from a global catastrophe. In Himmler's view it was clear that the civilization in question must have been connected to the legend of 'Atlantis', and that the stranded ruling class of Atlantis had spread out from there to Europe and East Asia. The conviction that Tibet was the 'cradle of humanity' accounts for Himmler's speculations about the common roots of European (in particular Germanic), Asian, and other elites.[140]

In connection with this the Reichsführer showed particular interest in the Japanese samurai, whom he took to be distant relations. On 1 November 1935 Himmler expounded to Hitler his view 'that the SS should become the German samurai', and the Führer agreed.[141] In 1937 he wrote a short foreword to Heinz Corazza's book *The Samurai: Honourable and Loyal Imperial Knights*, an extended version of a series of articles published in *Das Schwarze Korps*.[142] In the foreword Himmler explained to his readers that the history of the samurai demonstrated clearly 'that in distant times this people in the Far East had the same code of honour as our fathers had long ago in a past all too soon destroyed', and 'that it is frequently minorities of the highest calibre who give a nation eternal life in earthly terms'. He wisely did not go into his Tibet theory, however.

Behind the scenes, nevertheless, Himmler pressed strongly for the discovery of proof of the central role of Tibet as the land of origin of Germanic and Asiatic elites. In 1935 the young zoologist Ernst Schäfer, who had already taken part in two expeditions to eastern Tibet, came to his notice. Himmler made Schäfer a member of the SS,[143] and when the latter was preparing for a further expedition to Tibet these preparations were closely linked to the work of the Ahnenerbe. The cooperation collapsed, but Himmler nevertheless acted as patron to the expedition, which finally went ahead in 1939, paid for the participants' hurried flight home in view of the strained international situation in August 1939, and on their return made a point of welcoming them personally at the airport. One of the team was Bruno Beger, an employee of the Race and Settlement Main Office, who was conducting anthropological research primarily aimed at proving that the inhabitants had 'Aryan racial elements'.[144]

Himmler had given Schäfer a special mission: along with thirty SS troops and a considerable arsenal of weapons he was to be smuggled into Tibet through the Soviet Union, in order to stir up unrest among the population against British forces stationed there.[145] Although this mission came to nothing, the Reichsführer-SS had an Ahnenerbe 'Research Centre for Inner Asia and Expeditions' set up for Schäfer, which focused first of all on evaluating the materials from the expedition.[146] Nevertheless, Himmler kept Schäfer on a short leash. At the end of 1939 he obstructed Schäfer's plan for public showings of a film about the expedition,[147] and in March 1940 made it clear 'that nothing will appear in the newspapers about you, your work, your film, or about the expedition in general'.[148] In 1943 he went a step further and tried to forbid the publication of Schäfer's book *Secret Tibet*, as 'the first part is written in such a German manner, so objective by comparison with the English', while on the other hand the indigenous states and nations are presented 'in a very amiable but also mocking manner. This might do us immense damage among the coloured nations.' And in his typically opinionated manner he added: 'The reservations I had about the public showing of the film were justified after all.'[149] In fact, the real motive behind Himmler's efforts, unsuccessful though they were, to suppress publication was most likely embarrassment about exposing in public his search for proof of his eccentric vision of the world.

This vision was not, it must be said, restricted to Tibet. In 1938–9 Himmler also worked on plans to send an expedition to Bolivia, Peru, and Chile. The private scholar Edmund Kiss was to lead the expedition.[150] Himmler regarded him as particularly suitable because he had come to prominence by putting forward a theory which explained the mountains in the north of South America by means of the Cosmic Ice Theory.[151] The outbreak of war put an end to this plan, however.

Himmler also preferred to keep from public gaze the fascination he had had since his student days for the occult. The significance he in fact attached to it is, however, suggested by his relationship with his closest adviser in this field, Karl Maria Wiligut, who from October 1934 was first of all director of the archive section of the Race and Settlement Main Office, and then from January 1936 in charge there of special commissions.[152]

Ill. 14. One of Himmler's pet projects was research into and preservation of the 'ancestral heritage' of distant Germanic prehistory. He took part on a number of occasions in inspections of sites and archaeological excavations in order to make detailed observations. Here he is shown with Wiligut in a quarry in the Palatinate thought to contain runes.

Wiligut, whose name in the SS was 'Weisthor', was a retired colonel in the Austrian Imperial Army and already 66 years old when Himmler engaged him. We know little about his earlier life, and what we do know is not particularly reliable: one of the most important publications about 'Himmler's Rasputin' originates from the very circles in which Wiligut was admired.[153] According to it, Wiligut had frequented völkisch and esoteric circles in Vienna before the First World War and had been involved in journalism along the same lines. In 1903 his book *Seyfried's Runes* appeared.[154] He did not come to prominence as a figure within völkisch occultism until after the First World War, however. Wiligut claimed to be the 'bearer of the tradition' of an ancient Gothic clan, the Asa, and furthermore to be the bearer of a secret German kingship. Thanks to the abilities he claimed to have as a medium he was, being childless and the last of his line, capable of making contact with his ancestors and calling up occult knowledge thousands of years old. Himmler is said to have tried everything to boost the ageing Wiligut-Weisthor's ability to work, with the help of injections and drugs, and to salvage as much as possible of his store of occult knowledge; according to his biographer Mund, although this treatment certainly did bring about a reactivation of Wiligut's energies, they manifested themselves above all in over-indulgence in nicotine and alcohol.

Weisthor prepared pieces for Himmler on prehistory and early history and on religious questions, and sent him poems he had written himself.[155] Among other things the former colonel suggested that Himmler introduce an ancient Germanic religion in Germany.[156] Above all, however, he supplied him with what he claimed to be orally transmitted occult knowledge from the 'Asa-Uana clan': for example, the 'nine commandments of God', which he 'had set down in written form' for the first time 'since 1200', as the 'records on this subject were publicly burned by Louis "the Pious" '. The ninth commandment was: 'God is beginning without end—the universe. He is perfection in nothingness and yet everything in three times threefold knowledge of all things. He closes the circle [. . .] from consciousness to the unconscious so that this may become conscious again.'[157]

In summer 1936 Himmler read Wiligut's *Description of Human Development*, which he claimed originated from the 'occult transmission of our Asa-Uana clan Uilligotis':

Mankind, as the highest expression of intelligence and reason in creation on earth at any given time, falls into seven epochs, of which four are complete; the fifth is humanity in the present, and the sixth and seventh are the ages still to come. Each of these four epochs of development now completed was, according to oral occult teaching, brought about by an enormous earth catastrophe that ended with the union of our earth with one of these stars that gravitated towards us. [. . .] The fragments of humanity remaining on earth assimilated in this process with the intelligent beings who had come 'from heaven' (the stars) to 'Earth' and were being shaped in a similar way. Thus they formed the new humanity in each particular case, which represented new racial types, as of course such 'first' human beings were always to be found at different points of the earth, as it was assuming its new shape.[158]

In other words, clear evidence for the Cosmic Ice Theory!

Wiligut enjoyed several promotions, and in 1936, as an expression of his special esteem, Himmler bestowed on him the rank of SS-Brigadeführer.[159] At the beginning of 1939, however, Himmler broke with Weisthor. One reason was that Hitler had made a public statement opposing occultism, and another was the discovery that Himmler's adviser on the occult had spent three years in a Salzburg institution for the mentally ill and in 1925 had been legally incapacitated.[160]

Himmler did not, however, give up the relationship entirely. Significantly, the Reichsführer kept Wiligut's death's-head ring, which he had had to give back when he left the SS, in his own strongroom.[161] And he still called on Wiligut for advice, for example in the summer of 1940, when he was having an emblem designed for the graves of fallen SS men. Wiligut agreed with Himmler's suggestion that in place of the 'Christian cross the cross with bars of equal length can be used to accord with our ancient German religion', as it signifies 'God as spirit, God as strength, and God as matter in eternal change'; the Reichsführer gave orders for this to be carried out.[162] Finally, Himmler's office diary for November 1941 indicates a lunch with 'Colonel Wiligut' in Berlin.[163]

The following general picture emerges from all of this. Central to Himmler's vision of the world was the restoration of a de-Christianized, Germanic environment, which with the help of the myths of Atlantis and Tibet was to be linked to long-lost examples of sophisticated cultures, and via the Cosmic Ice Theory/astrology/astronomy to the history of the cosmos. Just as Himmler supposed that, with the help of his adviser Weisthor, he could penetrate directly to the world of the Germanic ancestors, so he believed he could be 'reincarnated' in his own bloodline—his vision therefore most certainly reached into eternity. Through the mixture of history, historical myth, Teutonic cult, astrology and astronomy, theories of how the earth came to be and how reincarnation is possible, a real substitute religion was created, possibly interwoven with notions of a primitive Germanic religion.

This construct admittedly suffered from the fact that, to put it mildly, it was not yet coherent. Himmler was aware of this, and for that reason spent a significant amount of his time—and this during the war—collecting 'evidence' to support his ideas. Tellingly, his view of the world can be reconstructed only from original sources, for he clearly never expounded it as a coherent whole.

It was not, however, only the incoherence and the protests from the academic world he anticipated that prevented Himmler from propounding his theory of the world to the public. His realization that the great majority of his fellow men would be unable—as yet—to recognize the intellectual consistency of his vision, and in particular that he would meet with vigorous opposition from Hitler should he, as one of the most important leaders of the NSDAP and Chief of the German Police, cause a stir by founding a substitute religion, made him cautious.

What was taught inside the SS and police under the heading of ideological indoctrination reflected, therefore, only in part Himmler's much more far-reaching beliefs: topics such as the Cosmic Ice Theory, Tibet myth, and Atlantis were excluded from the start, and overly aggressive attacks on Christianity also had to be avoided. It is therefore no surprise that Himmler did not design the ideological aspect of indoctrination (about which more will be said later) as a complete system of thought based on written texts. Rather, he tried to emphasize the communication of concrete role-models and heroic stories. Indoctrination was geared to affect the disposition rather than the intellect. Precisely because of its imprecise and mythical nature, the ideology he espoused could be turned into 'indoctrination' to only a limited degree, and other ways of getting it across had to be found: he considered gifts with symbolic meanings, ceremonies, and special 'holy' places to be particularly suitable for this.

By means of 'the things that are conferred, ceremonies, all the inner life that has been reawakened here', the SS had, in Himmler's opinion in 1938,

perhaps done something more important [. . .] for Germany than the SS can do by means, let's say, of exemplary organization or a regiment that can march faultlessly or fine sporting successes. I believe that these inner things connected with the heart, with honour, and with a mind filled with the most real and deep vision of the world are truly in the last analysis the things that give us strength, strength for today, and that will give us strength for every conflict and every hour of destiny that will confront Germany, and perhaps us personally, in the next thirty, fifty, 100 years.[164]

Symbols, festivals, rituals

By 'the things that are conferred' Himmler was referring to a series of gifts, heavy with symbolism, that he used to distribute within the SS.

At Christmas, which Himmler intended to change into the festival of the winter solstice, or Yuletide, he gave so-called Yule lights. These candle-holders, which were about 20 centimetres tall and had on them images that were supposed to commemorate the Germanic past, held two candles. Their significance and function Himmler explained as follows: 'The small light at the bottom of the candle-holder is to burn as a symbol of the last hour of the year that is ending: the big light is to burst into flame in the first moment the new year begins. There is a deep wisdom in the old custom. May each SS man see the small flame of the old year burn out with a pure and upright heart and be able to ignite the light of the new year with an exalted will.'[165]

The Reichsführer wished the family of every married SS man to have a Yule light. 'The wife in particular, when she loses the myth of the church, will want to have something else to fill her mind and the mind and heart of her child', Himmler told the Gruppenführer in November 1936. He would, therefore, this year again give away a larger number of Yule lights.[166] In 1937 it was 8,000[167] and in 1939 it was already over 52,000.[168]

In 1939 Himmler hit on the idea of having an additional 'solstice light' made, but he did not like the design. As, in the meantime, war had broken out he set the matter aside.[169] During the war newborn babies of SS families received 'life lights'.[170] Himmler continued this custom until the spring of 1945, though the recipients were informed that in the circumstances the gift could not be sent until after the war.[171]

All SS men with a membership number less that 2,000, as well as all SS leaders after they had been members for several years, received the death's-head ring.[172] Himmler committed this circle of SS leaders 'to wear the ring permanently on the ring finger of the left hand [...] The conferral of the ring is the external sign of inner worth, gained through struggle and duty, and of a community, tried and tested through the years, of loyalty to the Führer and to his vision.'

Those distinguished by receiving the death's-head ring were sent a lengthy letter by Himmler making them aware of the significance of the ring and how it should be treated. According to this, the death's-head ring was a

sign of our loyalty to the Führer, of our unchanging obedience towards our superiors, and of our unshakeable solidarity and comradeship. The death's head admonishes us to be ready at any time to commit our individual life for the life of the whole community. The runes on the opposite side of the death's head are the sacred symbols of our past, with which we are reconnected through the ideology of National Socialism [...] The ring is garlanded with leaves from the oak, the ancient German tree.

He goes on to say that the ring 'cannot be purchased', must never be allowed 'to fall into the hands of outsiders', and will revert to the Reichsführer-SS after 'you leave the SS or this world'. There was even an instruction that the making of 'illustrations and copies' was an offence, 'and you are to prevent this'.[173]

Lastly, Himmler presented selected SS leaders with swords of honour: 'I confer on you the sword of the SS. Never draw it without need! Never sheath it without honour! Preserve your own honour as unconditionally as you are committed to respecting the honour of others and to acting chivalrously to defend the defenceless!' By contrast with the ring, the sword was allowed 'to remain in your clan, if you have carried it for a lifetime without blame'. If not, the Reichsführer demanded it back.[174]

In 1936 Himmler announced the introduction of a brooch that every SS man should present to his wife on her becoming a mother, and which could be worn only by SS wives who were mothers.[175] The model for this piece of jewellery was a 'brooch decorated with runes arranged in the shape of the hagal rune', which Himmler had given to his wife.[176] When a third child and any subsequent children were born to SS wives they received from Himmler a letter of congratulation as well as a life light and Vitaborn juices.[177] From the fourth child onwards Himmler gave a birth light, on which were the words: 'You are only a link in the eternal chain of the clan.'[178]

In the course of time Himmler also developed diverse ceremonies, from birth and marriage ceremonies to burial rites. His stipulations for these were very detailed. A set of instructions dating from 1937, from the Race and Settlement Main Office's indoctrination section, for the 'ceremony of marriage of members of the party and its component organizations' makes clear how such a ceremony was envisaged. At its heart is the abolition of the division introduced by Christianity between the public ceremony of marriage and the private celebration; the intention was to return to what was allegedly the Germanic form of marriage ceremony.

The ceremony was introduced by music, though the document was obliged to confirm, with regret, that 'wedding music appropriate to our times is not yet available'. Then, to open the proceedings, sayings should be read out, preferably 'quotations from the Führer's speeches and book', followed by Nietzsche quotations from 'Child and Marriage' (*Thus Spake Zarathustra*) and an address by an SS leader. After a musical interlude the registrar concluded the marriage formally, whereupon the bride and groom were to light a candle 'as a sign of the commencement of a new Germanic blood-line'. Salt and bread were given to them and the couple committed—

by handshake—'to a shared life and shared work for the nation'. If the bridegroom was an SS man, the SS leader had the task of explaining to the young woman the fact that she would be received into the SS and of handing over the SS clan book or a certificate. The ceremony closed with everyone singing the 'SS anthem of loyalty'.[179]

When he conducted the ceremony himself Himmler was accustomed to give the couple a pair of silver goblets, and he recommended this practice to the SS commanders. For the exchange of rings, he introduced the following line: 'I wish not only, as of old, that your love should be without beginning or end, but I wish that your clan may be without beginning or end.'[180]

Christian baptism was to be replaced by a 'name consecration'. A set of instructions still in existence shows how such a ceremony was to be structured.[181] It was to be held in special 'consecration rooms', in which there was to be an altar draped with a flag bearing the swastika, on which, in place of the holiest Christian symbol, there was to be a picture of Hitler. Behind the altar three SS men had to stand holding an SS standard, while the walls were to be decorated with a black flag bearing the SS runes. The 'consecrator' took the place of the priest and the 'loyal guardian' that of the godparent.

The child had to be laid before the altar. Then texts from *Mein Kampf* were spoken or sung in chorus. The 'consecrator' delivered the following articles of faith on behalf of all present: 'We believe in the God of the universe / And in the mission of our German blood / that grows eternally young from the German soil. / We believe in the nation, the bearer of this blood / And in the Führer, whom God has given us.' If Himmler was 'guardian' at birth ceremonies he gave as a present a small silver cup and a spoon. A lovely old custom, as he said, recommending it to the Gruppen-führer in 1936, was that of giving the child 'the large blue sash denoting new life and made of blue silk'.[182]

When, in 1937, Karl Wolff's third child received the name Thorismann, Himmler presided over the ceremony, which was carried out by his prehistory adviser Weisthor. Weisthor wrapped the child in the blue 'sash of life', then gave the Wolffs the cup, the spoon, and a ring; the child should not wear it until, 'as a youth you have proved yourself worthy of the SS and your clan'.[183]

The celebration of the solstices was Himmler's particular hobby-horse, and above all the summer solstice of 21 June: he wished to give this day back its 'ancient meaning'. What he meant by this he explained rather ponderously to the SS Gruppenführer in November 1936—as always, when awkward subjects were being dealt with, 'quite openly', but 'without this being something that should immediately be released for publication for the masses or, as I should perhaps better say, the rank and file of our SS leaders and men'.

'You see,' Himmler began his train of thought, 'our men often complain and say, "Where for heaven's sake are we supposed to meet decent women, decent girls we can marry!"' In order to respond to this emergency he intended to make the summer solstice again a festival 'of Maytime, a festival of life, a festival of marriage'. For in ancient times 'the time between the spring festival and the summer solstice was the time for young people to compete with each other. It was then customary that the young people danced and leapt around the summer-solstice fire. Marriages were made.'

On this pattern, the 'SS men's sporting competitions, which we shall put on every year,' were 'always to take place between Easter and the summer solstice'. Himmler's ideas went far beyond the sporting aspect, however: 'I can imagine my initiative being adopted by the BDM (Bund Deutscher Mädel) and the Women's League, with competitions arranged for girls at the same time as the SS establishes competitions for men [. . .] If this process of selection were supported by a racially based selection of the participants in the female competitions it is my view that in the course of the years the summer solstice will be brought back to its true, ancient, and necessary significance.'[184]

As he let the Ahnenerbe know in a circular in September 1938, Himmler was assuming that in certain Germanic tribes it was usually only at the summer solstice that 'children were procreated and thus sexual intercourse took place'.[185] The summer solstice as a festival of copulation was symbolized, as Himmler said in 1936 at the Leadership School for German Doctors at Alt-Rehse in Mecklenburg, by 'the ancient custom that the finest boy leaps through the fire with the finest girl (both having been chosen through physical contests)'.[186]

Himmler naturally insisted on taking part every year in the summer solstice ceremonies.[187] In 1935 they were in the Sachsenhain at Verden, in 1936 on the Brocken mountain. In 1937 he was at Ludendorff's funeral on that day, but in 1938 he again celebrated the summer solstice, this time at Wolfsberg in Austria, and in 1939 on the Baltic near Kolberg (Kołobrzeg).

Himmler constantly intervened in what was to happen at the ceremonies. In 1936 he called on the Standarten to rehearse a 'torch dance for fifty-one dancers' created specially for this occasion, and to perform it at as many ceremonies as possible.[188] In 1938 he once again issued an order for the summer and winter solstice celebrations to be carried out in a uniform manner for the next three years,[189] and after the summer solstice he asked for reports on the celebrations from the whole of the Reich. He may well have been extremely enthusiastic about the results, for the various SS units had proved to be particularly imaginative in this year: while one Standarte could report the 'demonstration of a gymnastic dance by the BDM in dresses with colourful bodices, which led into a general folk-dance around the fire', in SS Abschnitt XVII 'ribbon dances' and 'bridal waltzes' had been practised. The Oberabschnitt Danube reported graphically that, 'after the anthem of loyalty and the national anthems members of the Hitler Youth hurled hoops of fire into the valley and young couples formed to jump together through the slowly subsiding fire'.[190]

If the summer solstice celebrations as conceived by Himmler formed the finale to the annual trials of physical strength within the SS,[191] at every winter solstice 'intellectual contests in the SS' were to take place, as Himmler informed the Gruppenführer in 1937. To this end, in 1937, he explained, genealogical tables as well as family histories and pieces on the significance of reverence for ancestors were to be produced.[192] Apropos of how to conduct the winter solstice, Himmler explained in 1936 to the Gruppenführer:

The winter solstice is not only the end of the year, Yuletide, after which come the twelve holy days, when the new year begins, but rather it was above all the festival when ancestors and the past were remembered, and when the individual realized that without his ancestors and his worship of them he is nothing, a small atom that can be swept aside at any time. Yet integrated into the infinite chain of their family in true modesty, ancestors and grandsons are everything.[193]

Accordingly, at the Yule celebrations gradually twelve candles were to be lit, and at each one a saying connected with the light was to be recited, which was followed by a general response: 'May their light shine.' The sayings revolved around the thought that the life of an individual was absorbed into the ancestral line.[194] In November 1937 Himmler issued the order that, following the winter solstice, SS men and their wives or fiancées in SS units had to celebrate Yuletide together. On this occasion the newly married SS members were to be given the Yule lights donated by the Reichsführer-SS.[195] In November of the following year Himmler asked the young SS scholars who belonged to 'team houses' to 'encourage young writers to compose German songs for Yuletide that could be sung at the celebrations of the party and its organizations in place of Christian hymns'.[196]

Himmler even turned his mind to the subject of funerals. In 1936, as he explained to his Gruppenführer, he had assigned the task of 'producing designs for tasteful coffins'. Wreaths of artificial flowers were not to be used under any circumstances. 'I suggest that throughout the winter the departments of the SS should give wreaths only of conifers—spruce, pine, or Scotch fir. That is simple and, if the wreaths are properly made, the nicest and best thing. In summer use oak and beech leaves and twigs for wreaths and add some nice flowers.'

Once again, what was important to him was 'that gradually a style should emerge. For everything we do must gradually conform to our innermost being. How we live, what sort of furniture, morals, and customs we have, all of this must be an expression of our inner selves. We must achieve this, and indeed in these first years of the SS we must lay the foundation stone.' Himmler emphasized, nevertheless, that he had no objection to Christian burials, if the relatives wanted them, referring to the death of his father which had occurred only a few days previously. The religious ceremony had, however, to be kept strictly separate from the SS ceremony.[197]

In 1942 the SS Main Office issued a publication, *Suggestions on How to Conduct a Funeral*. Himmler wrote the preface: 'For us death has no terrors. [...] The individual dies, but even during his lifetime in his children his nation develops beyond him.' An SS funeral was to consist of the funeral service, the funeral procession, and the solemn burial. To supplement the ceremony, quotations from the Führer, aphorisms, and literary sources were recommended. The funeral of Heydrich on 9 June 1942 was considered the paradigm for a truly successful occasion of this kind (see Ill. 13).

The responsibility for conducting these diverse ceremonies could not, however, in the Reichsführer's view be placed in the hands of those in charge of SS indoctrination; that would lead to the creation of a new 'priesthood' within the SS. 'We do not want that in the SS.' It was, he said, the task of commanding officers to officiate at the ceremonies.[198] When, in April 1940, he caught an SS leader planning to conduct an SS marriage ceremony that was outside his sphere of responsibility as a commander, Himmler threatened him thus: 'If I should catch you or another

SS leader again acting as a speaker or organizer of a clan ceremony [...] I shall strip you or the person concerned of his rank and lock you up for several years for attempting to re-found the priesthood.'[199]

In November 1936 Himmler requested the SS-Gruppenführer not to conduct birth or marriage ceremonies on SS premises or in public, but rather within the family.[200] Any report in the press was to be avoided.[201] The private nature of these ceremonies, as Himmler explained to the Gruppenführer, should prevent any 'priest' from turning up and objecting that a 'heathen marriage' or 'something like a church ritual' was being carried out. He wished to avoid, he said, 'taking a step out of time, one for which people are not ready and that would not yet be understood and so would make a ridiculous impression'.[202] There were good reasons for Himmler to be nervous about making the SS cult, which he had expressly designed, all too public, as will become clear through other examples. He feared not only ridicule from the public, but in particular Hitler's negative attitude with regard to any too pronounced revival of the Germanic heritage: 'Rosenberg, Himmler, and Darré have to stop this nonsense with cults', he had said in 1935, according to Goebbels's diary.[203]

As far as the normal SS social gatherings were concerned, Himmler was tireless in trying to prevent them from degenerating into all-too-vulgar events, 'bleak evenings of drinking', as he himself called them; instead, it was his wish to incorporate them into his plan of education. In 1941 he produced an eight-point sheet of guidelines for a—to his mind—successful 'comradeship evening'.[204]

First of all, we read, one thing is crucial: 'In all circumstances such social evenings must be properly planned.' And: a 'responsible leader' must supervise the 'organization of the programme' and 'have a firm hold on the evening's events'. He must, for example, ensure that before the evening starts the men have eaten properly so that they are not 'obliged to drink on an empty stomach'. Furthermore, on attending such an evening Himmler had noticed that 'people had forgotten the self-evident custom that no one may smoke until the highest-ranking officer gives permission'. He had, he wrote, gained the impression that 'a number of men and officers had succumbed so heavily to a smoking addiction that they could not last a quarter of an hour without smoking'. In addition, officers on these occasions had not 'to huddle together in a group and create their own clique, but had rather to sit among their men, which is why they are called "comradeship evenings"'. Himmler warned his readers: 'To have any value, the first part of any such evening has to serve to celebrate the education of officers and men. Regimental music or music played by a few of the men, "hearty songs" [...] a very few (one or two) well-delivered poems, a speech by the commander or someone of high rank—these are the things that have to make up the programme of a comradeship evening.' Even a good atmosphere came down, in Himmler's view, to organization.

Locations

In Himmler's opinion the rituals and festivals he had designed required a suitably dignified space, and he took pains to create locations that symbolized the continuity of 'Germanic' culture to a high degree. The Reichsführer-SS made it his aim that 'as far as possible each Standarte [regiment] shall have a cultural focus for German greatness and the German past, and that it should be put in order again and restored to a state worthy of a nation of culture'.[205]

The most important of these 'cultural foci' were to be situated in northwest Germany, the place of origin of the house of Saxony so esteemed by Himmler. The burial-place of Henry I in Quedlinburg on the eastern border of the Harz mountains was one of these SS 'holy places', but it was by no means the first.

As early as 1933 Himmler had set out to find a suitable building for the planned SS 'Reich leadership school'. In November he had viewed the Wewelsburg near Paderborn, a three-cornered castle built in the seventeenth century, the owner of which, the district of Büren, no longer wished to maintain it. Himmler took the view that the Wewelsburg was exactly right for his purpose.[206] After alterations, the castle was transferred to Himmler in a solemn ceremony on 22 September 1934 by the district administrator of Büren. Manfred von Knobelsdorff became the first captain of the castle (this designation was introduced in 1935). Up to that point he had been the SS chief indoctrination officer and he was Darré's brother-in-law.[207]

In 1935 Himmler moved responsibility for the project from the Race and Settlement Main Office to his Personal Staff;[208] its official designation was now Wewelsburg SS School.[209] In the meantime, however, the institution's emphasis had shifted: now its function was research on National Socialist ideology.[210] In fact, the impression created is of 'uncoordinated pseudo-scientific research undertaken for a specific purpose and determined by the individual ideas of whoever was working there at the time', the main emphasis lying on the task of creating a genealogical chart of the Himmler family.[211] When, from 1936 onwards, the Ahnenerbe took over by degrees the SS research projects that were ideologically relevant, vague plans were made that increasingly envisaged the castle as a site for ceremonial and prestigious occasions.[212]

Between May 1935 and November 1937 Himmler visited the Wewelsburg many times, and on some occasions for several days. In May 1938 a meeting of all the most senior officers of the SS took place there. Alongside Sepp Dietrich, Eicke, and Wolff were Daluege, the head of the Main Office, Werner Lorenz, August Heissmeyer, Heydrich, Walter Schmitt, and Pohl.[213] In November 1938 Himmler announced that he intended in future to hold a conference of Gruppenführer every spring at the Wewelsburg,[214] and to use the occasion to swear in the new Gruppenführer.[215] The first such gathering was planned for March 1939, but the occupation of Czechoslovakia meant that it did not take place.[216]

While staying there in January 1939 Himmler made various decisions. He was not prepared to open this 'treasure' to the 'hyenas of the press', and therefore publications about the Wewelsburg were as far as possible to be suppressed. He planned a planetarium for the castle, and in addition— clearly under the influence of the romanticism surrounding castles—he intended to establish a hoard of gold and silver 'for a rainy day'.[217] For his own room he wanted a 'long, narrow Gobelin tapestry [. . .] depicting a maidenly young woman, a future mother'.[218]

The death's-head rings that reverted to the Reichsführer-SS after the death of their wearers were to be stored in a special cabinet.[219] The family coats of arms of deceased Gruppenführer were to be hung in the castle so that, as he explained to the Gruppenführer in 1939, 'those who come after us must always take counsel together before our plaques, and must always stand upright in our presence so that they will do things as we did them'.[220] Those Gruppenführer with no coat of arms—in other words, the majority—were called upon by the Personal Staff to have one designed, a move that occasioned extensive correspondence.[221]

Comprehensive structural changes were made to the Wewelsburg, and the Reichsführer-SS had it equipped with numerous objects from the applied arts. The Gruppenführers hall, which was to be decorated with, amongst other things, coats of arms, was largely completed, and also a crypt in the castle tower, although neither was ever used. Nor did ceremonies, celebrations, or cult rituals take place at the castle, and only once, in June 1941, did the Gruppenführer actually hold their conference at the Wewelsburg.

Up to the end of the war a special Wewelsburg construction management team was drawing up plans for a grandiose extension of the site, which Himmler approved at each stage. Yet neither these nor any other remaining documents throw light on what function the Wewelsburg was supposed to assume in the life of the SS. The numerous contradictory and erratic instructions that Himmler gave out over the course of time for the extension of the castle indicate that he himself was not clear what this project was actually about.[222]

About 20 kilometres north-east of the Wewelsburg, near Detmold, were the Externsteine, a further 'cultural focus' of the SS. The Externsteine were a striking group of rocks that, according to a view prevalent in völkisch circles, represented a Germanic sanctuary. There was particular speculation that it was in fact Irminsul, the legendary chief sanctuary of the Saxons destroyed by Charlemagne.

Himmler was firmly convinced that the Externsteine played a significant role as a site of Germanic worship, and with the help of the Ahnenerbe he wished to provide scientific proof of this theory. What is more, he set about, by means of a foundation specially created for this purpose, developing the Externsteine into a neo-Germanic sanctuary. In 1934 and 1935 he ordered excavations of the Externsteine, which like all archaeological efforts before it produced no evidence of a 'Germanic' past history to the stones.[223]

Himmler did not, however, loosen his grip. In April 1937 he issued a detailed assignment: a medieval relief on one of the stones showing the descent from the Cross was to be investigated to see if what was there was not a 'Christian reworking of a Germanic depiction'.[224] A few months later, in November 1937, he voiced concrete speculations about why the rocks were blackened by fire. One explanation, he said, was, 'as SS-Brigadeführer Weisthor and I have long supposed, fire, which in some degree served astronomical purposes and whose function it was to indicate phases of the sun, months, and perhaps also days'.[225] Himmler did not, however, want to subject such speculations to expert scientific debate. Similarly, in November 1937 he instructed the Ahnenerbe to check any publication about the Externsteine in advance; the aim was to obstruct any 'that might in any way provoke a debate about the Externsteine'.[226]

After a further visit to the stones he wrote, on 20 April 1940, to Pohl that 'a lot of things' had to 'happen' on the site. Once again Himmler had very precise ideas about the development of the publicly accessible site: 'At both entry gates, halls or houses must be erected in the style of the farmhouses of Lippe [. . .] At the Externsteine themselves the ascents to rocks 1, 2, and 3 must be altered.' Various demolitions and changes had to be undertaken, and after that

the foundation's entire site must be put in our care. We shall also take on responsibility for the forest and protect the bird life as far as possible. I am declaring the site a reserve in perpetuity, where the only game that may be shot are boar, as I believe these could at best be a nuisance to visitors. Feral cats and dogs may still be shot. All other animals shall be able to run free here. We intend [. . .] to ensure that the forest again becomes as it once was and that animals can survive in it [. . .], not by artificial feeding but rather through the planting of trees and shrubs, including wild fruit bushes. [. . .] At the same time we must arrange for one of the South Tyrol hoteliers to come to Horn and build a decent hotel there. [. . .] We must keep a constant eye on all details such as noticeboards, signs, and waste-bins to make sure they are tasteful and placed so that they are easily spotted. [. . .] All in all, the public must be educated to behave as if in a truly sacred place.[227]

It was not only the adversities of war that made the development of the site difficult and caused Himmler to postpone his plans until peacetime.[228] In February 1942 Hitler told him, explicitly and unambiguously at an evening party, that the Externsteine had 'certainly never been a ritual site'.[229]

The so-called 'Saxons' grove' (Sachsenhain) near Verden was created by Himmler to commemorate the execution of allegedly 4,500 Saxons by Charlemagne in 782. The building-work began in the winter of 1934–5. In memory of the Saxons 4,500 boulders were set up; a village of Lower Saxon half-timbered houses that had been pulled down elsewhere completed the site.[230]

At the summer solstice of 1935 Himmler and Rosenberg conducted the official inauguration of the site. In his speech the Reichsführer-SS recalled 'the ancient law of German religion [. . .] that ascendancy is followed by downfall and downfall then followed by new life, as long as the will and the strength of blood live on in an earthly being'.[231] The invocation of 'German religion' referred to the fact that the Sachsenhain was intended as a monumental accusation in stone of the cruelty of Christian methods of conversion—a reproach that was, as it happens, untenable, for Himmler's repeated assertion that the Saxons had been killed as a result of the emperor's policy of conversion was completely without foundation.[232]

There is evidence that Himmler revisited the site in the summer of 1938 and gave various instructions for its design.[233] After Hitler, however, had 'rehabilitated' Charlemagne in his speech to the party conference in 1935, there was no more question of making the Sachsenhain a central ritual site for the SS. Up to the end of the war, however, it served the SS as a location for indoctrination and meetings.

As the history of all three sites graphically illustrates, Himmler's attempt to celebrate SS ideology by means of holy places, special rituals, and gifts with symbolic significance did not get beyond the preliminary stages: the manifestations of the 'cult' remained in the end as undefined as their content. From Himmler's perspective the reason was, no doubt, clear: it was not that he was on the wrong track, but rather that National Socialist Germany was simply not yet ready for his substitute religion.

II

Himmler's Leadership Style

Himmler added to the ideology and rituals peculiar to the SS an unmistakable leadership style, aimed at aligning the SS with him as an individual and with his goals. He saw himself primarily as the educator of his men: he not only personally established the principles on which members of the SS were selected, trained, disciplined, and made to conform to a model of family life governed by the SS ethos, but also monitored pedantically whether they were being observed.

As part of this process, his whole apparatus of control was designed exclusively around himself, and the management structure was decidedly unclear. By distributing the executive authority for his various areas of responsibility (police, SD, concentration camps, General SS, Waffen-SS, and others) over several SS Main Offices, Himmler ensured that the SS did not fragment into diverse, autonomous power-blocs. He had no deputy, nor was there a body composed of the top SS leaders that met regularly. Gruppenführer meetings were effectively no more than roll-calls. Himmler therefore could—and was obliged to—intervene repeatedly and make decisions over matters large and small. The creation of the Higher SS and Police Leaders (*Höhere SS und Polizeiführer* = HSSPF) allowed him at the same time to direct control over regional offices. Despite his pedantry, Himmler was not first and foremost a bureaucrat. He did not wish to create an administrative apparatus that controlled his sphere of power according to fixed rules. Bureaucratic institutions, as he was aware, tend to compel even their own leadership to act within the rules, to limit their room for manoeuvre and to make their actions predictable. By contrast, Himmler's style of leadership was highly unpredictable.

This type of leadership reflected his mistrust of others and his need to be in control. Himmler attempted to guide the extensive apparatus over which he had authority through voluminous instructions, in part concerned with absurdly minor matters, through countless decisions on individual cases, or through direct interventions; as a precaution he reserved final judgement in numerous cases for himself. He instructed and advised, criticized and commanded. No detail was too insignificant for him.

If Himmler was in his office, he worked long hours. As a rule he arrived at 10 a.m. and, apart from short breaks for lunch and supper, rarely left before 1 or 2 in the morning.[1] He preferred, however, to size up situations in their own location and then to make a point of reaching decisions on the spot rather than from his desk at headquarters. He recommended this procedure to his men also; for example, on 16 September 1942 to the SS and Police Leaders he had assembled at his headquarters at Hegewald: 'It is really no accident that I make decisions on most problems when I am on the spot. I don't decide them in Berlin but go to Lublin, Lemberg [Lvov], Reval [Talinn], and so on and eight, ten, twelve big decisions are made that evening. You should do this too!'[2]

Throughout his career Himmler was constantly on the move: as a Gau assistant in the mid-1920s he roared through Lower Bavaria on his motorbike; as deputy Reich propaganda chief he travelled the length and breadth of the Reich with the aid of the Reich railways; and as Reichsführer-SS he travelled through the whole of Europe during the war by special train, by plane, und by jeep. He particularly enjoyed inspection tours of newly conquered territories where the smoke of battle had hardly dispersed, in the company of a small entourage. In such cases he liked to get behind the wheel himself.

Significantly, among the photos he sent during the war to Gmund on Lake Tegern, to give his daughter Gudrun an idea of her father's daily work, there are none that show him at a desk in a fixed location. Instead there are numerous shots of him in animated conversation, on journeys and inspections, or making speeches.[3] That is exactly how the Reichsführer-SS wanted to be seen: as communicative, ubiquitous, as a leader who took care of everything, had everything under his control, and shared the privations of his men.

This 'soldierly' image was something he was to cultivate throughout his life; the corresponding habitus was essential to his leadership style. In order to lend credibility to this self-stylization he had no qualms about slight enhancements to his biography. Thus, for example, at the summer solstice of 1936 he spoke out about drunkenness in the SS, though, adopting the pose of the old soldier, he made certain allowances for this vice: 'Those of us who have been to war and come from that generation [...] have learned to booze and to fight as front-line soldiers. I tell you, if you are in battle and don't know if you'll survive the next few hours, you're hungry and haven't eaten for days, then it's easy to get used to smoking and boozing.'[4] Speaking to Wehrmacht generals in May 1944: 'in 1917 I became an ensign and as a young ensign I experienced the Revolution.'[5] Similarly, he failed to correct biographical details released to the press that stated that he had been a soldier at the front.[6] In fact he did not join the army until January 1918 and, as we know, because of this late call-up he had never seen active service and spent the Revolution at his parents' home on leave.

Himmler hoped to conceal his awkwardness and lack of confidence with others behind military 'objectivity' and 'sobriety', and to transform them into positive virtues conditioned by his profession. This was true in his private life as well as in the professional sphere. 'Do not take it amiss', he wrote to a publisher in 1933, 'if I ask you not to publish a biography of me at the moment. [...] when you get to know me you will understand that for the time being I have an absolute aversion to being photographed or interviewed, and to biographies and intrusive questions.'[7] And when, in 1942, his friend the Nazi writer Hanns Johst advised him against sending an actress a crate of fruit-juice as a token of his admiration—his motives might be misinterpreted—Himmler thanked him, saying that in the world of the theatre such things were 'understood and judged quite differently from how we down-to-earth soldiers intend them'.[8]

In personal matters Himmler set great store by being seen as very correct. Thus, he insisted that he be billed for the cigars he smoked in the Berlin SS mess[9] and refused to accept invitations from business-people trying to make a splash.[10] Nor was he willing to charge the SS bureaucracy for the cost of private journeys.[11] But another feature of Himmler's pernickety way of dealing with personal expenditure was that he claimed the generous tips he gave out on his travels as expenses.[12]

In his dealings with his staff, with visitors, or—when travelling—with his hosts he took pains to observe the formalities, and behaved in a friendly and genial, easygoing, good-natured, and polite manner. As far as food, drink, and personal comfort were concerned, his demands were modest. 'As a human being,' according to a typical statement by his bodyguard Josef Kiermaier, 'the Reichsführer-SS was naturally frank, friendly, and polite to everyone,' though only 'as long as he was sure that friendliness was not inappropriate'.[13] Then his demeanour could easily change, and Himmler

became, as Otto Wagener, one of the leading party functionaries of the
'time of struggle' remembered, 'ironic, sarcastic, cynical'.[14] According to
Albert Speer's description, he was 'correct in a friendly, slightly forced way',
but 'never warm'.[15] This rather artificial correctness and excessively schematic participation in the lives of others was also demonstrated by the way
that Himmler maintained his extensive present-giving with the aid of an
elaborate set of records: a specially created card-index system made it
possible at any time to establish who had received what presents from the
Reichsführer-SS and when.[16]

Recruitment and career of SS members

At first the fundamental requirement for acceptance into the SS was to be at
least 1.70 metres tall—at 174.5 centimetres (measured by himself and, as he
noted, 'in stockinged feet'), Himmler, incidentally, fulfilled this criterion.[17]
From 1933 onwards candidates for membership (and not only SS members
wishing to marry and their future wives) were also checked for their
'hereditary health' and 'Aryan descent'. Gradually even the old SS men
had to submit retrospectively to this procedure. A genealogy stretching back
at least to 1750 was required, in which there was to be no evidence of 'non-
Aryan' ancestors. Himmler would have liked to put the relevant date for all
SS applicants back to 1650, as he declared in 1936 at the celebration of the
summer solstice on the Brocken mountain, but it seems that because of the
expense this ruling was applied only to SS leaders.[18] If a non-Aryan forebear
was found in anyone's family tree the person concerned was excluded from
the SS on principle.[19]

   The actual 'racial examination', which always included a medical examination, involved an assessment of the applicant's overall appearance, according to the criteria of 'physical build' and 'racial evaluation', and both were
graded under the combined heading of 'appearance'. Negative 'racial'
characteristics could be compensated for by means of 'overall appearance'
and 'mental attitude'.[20] An intelligence test and sports test rounded off the
general evaluation of the candidate.[21] In cases where, although the 'certified
proof of descent' was fully in order, the 'overall appearance' nevertheless
aroused 'strong suspicion of traces of alien blood', Himmler decreed that a
special 'racial-biological examination' be carried out.[22]

Himmler intervened repeatedly in the recruitment process. In 1938, for example, he ruled that a 'considerably more lenient standard' was to be used when judging eye defects. Problem cases, such as where an otherwise 'eligible candidate' had lost an eye in an accident, were to be referred to him personally.[23] In the case of the Security Service also, Himmler took the view in May 1935 that, as far as the physical examination was concerned, 'full eligibility for SS membership' was not necessary. If, however, a 'racial examination gives rise to doubt or suggests ineligibility, every individual case is to be referred to me for a decision'. This ruling was designed above all with Gestapo members in mind, who, when admitted to the SS, were assigned to the SD.[24]

In 1937 Himmler asserted in a speech to Wehrmacht officers that only 10 to 15 per cent of candidates were accepted into the SS.[25] In actual fact the SS was much less choosy: in the SS–Oberabschnitt Elbe, for example, in the years 1935 and 1936 the available figures on applicants rejected on 'racial', physical, or age grounds show that 75 to 80 per cent of candidates were accepted.[26]

Nevertheless, candidates for membership continued to be examined thoroughly even after the outbreak of war; indeed, Himmler refined the process in December 1939 by ordering the introduction of a special 'race chart'.[27] It provided those conducting examinations with those 'characteristics that occur primarily when blood from another race is present', for example, 'jet-black hair' or a 'hooked' nose (by that was meant the 'Near-Eastern' or distinctly 'Jewish' nose). By particular request of the Reichsführer-SS, the 'Greek nose' ('no or only a slight indentation at the root of the nose') was included in order to avoid mix-ups. When the head of the SS Race Office, Bruno Kurt Schultz, wanted, in view of wartime conditions, to limit the 'proof of ancestry' to six generations and to make a decision about any 'compromised' SS members by means of a racial and character assessment, Himmler was outraged. Schultz, he declared, was unsuitable to be head of the Race Office.[28]

Early in 1935, at an SS leaders' conference for Oberabschnitt Silesia, Himmler set out his view of the career of the normal SS member: 'In future a member of the SS will first of all be selected according to the most rigorous principles, which will get more rigorous from year to year. At 18 he will join us as a cadet. For eighteen months he will train with us as a cadet. He will be on duty for long periods, four times a week and on two or three Sundays a month. Above all, during this time and while he is still young and can develop and be educated he will be ideologically trained.' At 19 he would have a further six months' labour service and then he was to serve for a year 'in a state organization'. When national service was introduced two months after this speech it naturally replaced the latter service.

Thereafter, Himmler continued, the young man would return to the SS in order to train for a further fifteen months as a cadet, before he was officially 'recognized as an SS man'. From this point up to his twenty-fifth birthday he would belong to the active General SS. 'In these years the following service is required: twice a week and two to three Sundays a month.' After that he was to be transferred to Reserve I, then, aged 35 to 40, to Reserve II, and at 45 to the division of permanent members. 'It is impossible to leave the SS on the grounds of age.'[29] Anyone who had placed himself under the authority of the Reichsführer-SS was to remain under it until death.

SS virtues

'I have reserved for myself matters to do with our conduct and all ethical questions and shall deal with them myself', Himmler declared in November 1938 to the head of the Indoctrination Office, when the latter reported to him; that is to say, 'questions of the relationship of the individual to the clan, family, the nation, and the state'.[30] In order to make these 'ethical questions' clear once and for all, Himmler in numerous speeches to SS members worked his way through a positive 'catalogue of SS virtues'. Central to it were the concepts of loyalty, obedience, and comradeship, and he frequently emphasized bravery, honesty, hard work, and fulfilment of duty. But he demanded repeatedly, and above all, one thing from his SS men—decency![31]

Let us examine more closely the virtues Himmler proclaimed.

For Himmler loyalty meant voluntary and total submission to a leader. Loyalty was a question of race and could be genuinely shown only by people of 'Germanic blood'. In the final analysis loyalty could not be rationally based, but rather it was an emotional tie, a 'matter of the heart', as Himmler put it.[32] It was a fundamental attitude that produced a reliable, extremely stable basis for the relationship between subordinate and leader.[33]

The SS was naturally loyal above all to Adolf Hitler. 'The political creed of the SS is Adolf Hitler', wrote the writer Hanns Johst, a friend of Himmler and at that time an SS-Oberführer, in *SS Guidance Booklets* in 1937: 'This order's concept of honour is pledged to this man firmly and irrevocably through the magic power of loyalty. The order serves and this service guarantees the immortality of Adolf Hitler and his will.'[34] Or to quote Himmler himself: 'The Führer is always right, whether the subject is evening dress, bunkers, or the Reich motorways.'[35]

Loyalty was lauded in the 'SS anthem to loyalty'.[36] It was strengthened towards Hitler by the oath sworn by every SS member. 'I swear to you, Adolf Hitler, as Führer and Chancellor of the German Reich, that I will be loyal and brave. I pledge obedience unto death to you and to those you appoint to lead. So help me God.'[37] On being appointed by Himmler, the SS-Gruppenführer were committed by a further oath to adhere strictly to his specifications when accepting candidates, even if 'it means rejecting my own children or the children of my clan [. . .] I swear by Adolf Hitler and by the honour of my ancestors—so help me God.'[38]

There was a positively ritual quality to the way loyalty was maintained, for example in the letters that Himmler regularly exchanged with SS leaders. Congratulations he sent on promotions, birthdays, and births, letters of condolence on the deaths of close family members, greetings at New Year and 'Yuletide' were normally acknowledged by a personal letter of thanks, which frequently culminated in renewed vows of loyalty. Himmler's birthday was in turn the occasion for personally written letters from his close associates to the Reichsführer-SS.[39]

This correspondence reveals an almost limitless repertoire of formulae expressing loyalty. On Himmler's thirty-seventh birthday he was, for example, congratulated by Theodor Eicke, leader of the SS Death's Head regiments, as follows: 'I have only one aim, that of welding together the men entrusted to me into a fighting unit resolute to the death, in the spirit of the SS and in loyalty to our symbol. All our strength belongs to you and thus to the Führer. Devotion to duty and loyalty are and will remain the morning prayer of the SS Death's Head units.'[40]

Gruppenführer Wilhelm Rediess, who received the gift of a Yule light from Himmler in 1935, sent his thanks: 'In its light I renew, along with my family, the vow of loyalty I made to the Führer and to you. I wish you, Reichsführer, a long life for the sake of the nation and therefore for all our sakes until your actions and aims have become irrevocable laws shaping the life of the whole German nation. These are my wishes for the New Year, to which I add hearty greetings from my clan to yours.'[41]

During the war the vows of loyalty became even more intense. As Ruth Bettina Birn has already indicated, many SS leaders were no longer satisfied with assuring Himmler of their loyalty in general terms, but reinforced their vow with the promise of the utmost commitment to duty and service.[42] Now it really was a case of loyalty unto death. Thus, in October 1944 Obergruppenführer Benno Martin sent thanks for his promotion to this rank by 'announcing' to Himmler that 'I will carry out my duty to you and to the idea of the SS to my last breath. Reichsführer, you can be equally certain of the commitment of my leaders and of the SS men and police under my command.'[43]

Hermann Fegelein, the former head of the main SS Cavalry School in Munich and now commander of the 8th SS cavalry division, wrote Himmler a letter in October 1943 on the latter's birthday, in which he not only vowed loyalty but claimed he was doing so because he owed the Reichsführer his entire existence:

Just as previously when we played sports, now in wartime too we have ridden undaunted, even in the most difficult times, assured in our hearts of victory under your command and in obedience to your orders. The fallen comrades of your cavalry units are testimony to this; they died on the field of honour, fulfilling your saying: 'We have to do more than our duty: as knights without fear or reproach.' In the heaviest fighting, in all seasons, summer or winter, we have served undaunted, loyal and obedient, true to you, Reichsführer, and to our word, carrying out everything we promised in peacetime. [...] In my life you have been the great patron, a strict superior officer, and an unfailingly helpful comrade. Together with SS-Obergruppenführer Jüttner you have made me what I am today. I have often had to carry out orders of yours that were heavy with responsibility and sometimes looked as if they were suicide missions. But my men and I have come through them all, through the mentality of our teams and through our precise way of thinking as Prussians. By nature I have the impetus, but it is you who have taught me to be conscientious and aware of my responsibilities, and ready to carry out my duty to the letter, and I believe I can say today that I have always proved how sacred your orders were to me. Perhaps, Reichsführer, you could tell the Führer that we feel this in our hearts simply and in faith and with the instinct of the German soldier, whose ancestors fought just like us for 2,000 years for the good of the Reich and who, when necessary, also fell.[44]

Friedrich Jeckeln, the Higher SS and Police Leader Ostland (the Baltic States and Byelorussia) and Russia North, reported to Himmler in May 1944 that two of his children had died. His letter ends as follows: 'My wife is distraught. I can bear even heavy blows of fate and still be committed and have the strength to work.' Himmler answered: 'It is terrible when fate suddenly strikes. I know that you as a profoundly loyal National Socialist and SS man grieve for your two sons, one of whom died a hero's death and the other of whom died so tragically as a child. I know too, however, that you always remain the same, unbowed and committed.'[45] Six months later Jeckeln let Himmler know that his home had been completely destroyed in a bombing raid. 'My entire earthly possessions have gone up in smoke. My wife and my four small children are safe at her parents' farm [. . .] And now we've really got to act!'[46]

The idea of loyalty had been internalized by many SS leaders to such an extent that the mere suspicion that they might have lost the Reichsführer's confidence could become a nightmare. The Viennese police chief Josef Fitzthum, who came under suspicion of having been too liberal with the profits of the 'Aryanization' programme, wrote in September 1940 to Himmler: 'The sense that I may have lost the confidence you have placed in me up till now is unbearable. Your reassurance that I still have it means a thousand times more to me than any formal exoneration.'[47]

Obedience, the second pillar in Himmler's doctrine of virtue, was the practical consequence of loyalty. If loyalty was an emotional attachment, obedience had to be demonstrated in practice; loyalty was an 'attitude of mind', the internalized willingness to be obedient that found expression in achievement and in the fulfilment of one's duty.[48]

Disloyalty meant in effect treason, and in principle was unforgivable. If instances of disobedience did occur, however, Himmler's approach was distinctly flexible; for disobedience, he explained, was a weakness of the Teutons, who were by nature headstrong. In certain circumstances, therefore, a mild punishment or even a pardon was possible—as long as the foundation of the relationship, namely loyalty, was not compromised. Gottlob Berger, head of the SS Main Office, was aware of this flexibility when, in July 1942, he told Himmler with regard to a conversation with General Steiner, who was under suspicion of disobedience, that he had gained the impression that 'he was loyal to the core', whereupon Himmler assured Steiner in a letter: 'I trust you implicitly.'[49]

'Anyone who is disloyal', as Himmler said in his programmatic SS speech of 1933, 'excludes himself from our society. For loyalty is a matter of the heart, never of the intellect. The intellect may stumble [. . .] but the heart must always go on beating, and when it stops a human being dies, just as a nation dies, when it breaks its oath of loyalty.'[50]

If Himmler demanded of his men not only obedience but absolute loyalty and elevated loyalty to the supreme law of the SS, then this was certainly also the result of his own insecurity in his relations with others. Although he developed considerable diplomatic skill in the course of time in concealing this weakness, in essence he could sustain personal relationships in the long term only if he controlled the relationship or if, as in his relationship as a young man with Röhm or Strasser or as in the case of Hitler, he subordinated himself to the other person. On the other hand, close personal relationships with people he regarded as equals he found difficult, as becomes clear from his complicated or cool relations with other leading party members. His strong need to reinforce obedience (something that went without saying in the SS) with an emotional element (that of loyalty), to have this confirmed by the repetition to him of formulaic expressions of loyalty, and to invent regular rituals of loyalty was no doubt deeply bound up with this deficiency of character.

By comparison, his elucidations of another central term in the catalogue of virtue, 'comradeship', remained insipid. We can infer from one of his few comments on this subject that comradeship in the final analysis supported men's training in obedience.[51] 'I ask that you train each other in your Sturm. You must be vigilant that in your Sturm no one lacks decency!', Himmler proclaimed in December 1938 when speaking to an SS Standarte.[52] But how comradeship was to be developed emotionally, how it was to be lived in everyday life inside and outside the SS, and whether and how far it was to encompass personal affection, friendship, and mutual trust—these were matters on which Himmler was silent. We have already indicated that, in particular in 1936–7, Himmler had opposed tendencies to regard the SS as a male league and had vehemently attacked Blüher's theory that such leagues were based, in the final analysis, on homoerotic attachments. Yet Himmler had no alternative to offer beyond mere commitment to loyalty and obedience.

On the other hand, in almost every speech there is an appeal to the SS to carry out their tasks 'decently'. 'Decent' (anständig) was a word he frequently connected with terms such as 'pure' and 'chivalrous'; what was meant was generous, understanding behaviour, free from selfish motives. 'Decency' was omnipresent in Himmler's world. 'May each of us live through every good day as decently as every bad one', was his message to his men in the foreword to the 1937 SS calendar.[53] Decency was required above all, however, when Himmler was demanding 'relentlessness' and 'severity', in particular when executions were to be carried out: 'Soldiers have to do many things,' he said looking back on 30 June 1934, 'but they must always do them decently, cleanly, setting aside understandable Schadenfreude and personal advantage. [. . .] Only if these principles are observed have we the moral strength and resolve to do these things and thus to be the kind of instrument the Führer requires.'[54] Sadistic torture or reviling of victims was, in Himmler's view 'not decent' and therefore to be rejected.

During the war Himmler was to stand by the claim that the SS killed its enemies 'decently'. His best-known declaration on the subject of decency and mass murder was made to the SS-Gruppenführer in Posen in October 1943, and referred to the mass murder of the Jews: 'Most of you will know what it is like to see 100 corpses lying side by side or 500 or 1,000 of them. To have coped with this and—except for cases of human weakness—to have remained decent, that has made us hard.'[55]

Even in 1936, however, he had drawn a distinction, and not during a secret meeting of his Gruppenführer but in a public statement to the Prussian State Councillors. The principle of a 'decent fight' applied only to 'any opponent worthy of such treatment'; it was, on the other hand, 'madness' to apply 'this chivalrous attitude [. . .] to Jewry and to Bolshevism', or to the treatment of a 'Jesuit fighting to gain earthly power' or 'Jewish or Jewified Freemasonry'.[56]

In his Posen speech of 1943 he took the line that it was necessary

to be honest, decent, loyal, and comradely [. . .] to those of our own blood and to no one else. How the Russians or the Czechs fare is a matter of indifference to me. [. . .] Whether or not 10,000 Russian women collapse with exhaustion while digging an anti-tank ditch concerns me only insofar as the anti-tank ditch is being dug for Germany. We will never be brutal and callous unless it is necessary: that is obvious. We Germans, who alone on this earth have a decent attitude to animals, will of course adopt a decent attitude to these human animals, but it is a crime against our own blood to worry about them and to apply ideals to them so that our sons and grandsons have an even harder time with them. If anyone comes to me and says: 'I can't make the anti-tank ditch with women or children. It's inhuman because they'll die', then I am forced to say: 'You are murdering your own blood, for if the ditch is not made then German soldiers will die and these are the sons of German mothers. It is our blood.' That is what I would like to inculcate in the SS and have, I believe, inculcated as one of the most sacred laws of the future: our concern, our duty, is towards our nation and our blood; that is what we must be concerned about, must think about; for that we must work and fight, and for nothing else.[57]

'Decency' towards 'animals in human form' was, therefore, for Himmler not a moral imperative but purely a matter of expediency, because, as he explained in a speech in May 1944, the 'many little subhumans in our service' were 'attached to their master with doglike devotion [. . .] because he was decent to them'.[58]

Himmler's concept of decency can be read as a cipher for double standards; it stands for norms that were in themselves contradictory. On the one hand decency, even towards enemies, is declared to be virtuous, but on the other it is labelled as 'madness'. Decent treatment could be expedient, but there was always the danger of treating enemies too well and thus doing damage to one's own cause—and that was morally reprehensible. Accordingly, it was decent not to treat one's enemies decently.

This is the only way of explaining how the SS on the one hand laid claim to being honourable and chivalrous, and yet on the other found every possible way of degrading, torturing, and murdering human beings with the greatest cruelty. The aura of dread surrounding the SS was a component in their strategy of terror, and Himmler knew how to exploit this effect. 'I have no intention, at least not during the war, of dispelling the bad reputation we have, which is only advantageous for Germany, because it keeps enemies at a distance', we read, for example, in a speech Himmler made to senior naval officers in December 1943.[59]

The demands of decency posed major problems even for Himmler himself. However firmly and repeatedly he declared 'decency' to be his life's motto, it was impossible to disguise the fact that, just once in a while, he wanted to be allowed to be 'not decent' and 'not well-behaved', as he had confessed to his fiancée at the beginning of their relationship.[60] The context in which he confessed to this is important; he was referring to his stomach problems, caused, he believed, by precisely those constant efforts to be 'decent'. He knew, therefore, that his rigid self-control, his torturous system of rules and virtues, was causing psychosomatic disorders. His body bridled at the imposition of decency—it wanted instead 'not to be decent'.

Himmler's constant appeals to 'decency' can be read as the expression of his strenuous efforts to resist temptations 'not to be decent': to be cruel, to torment or revile his enemies, to benefit from their downfall or to take malicious pleasure in it—'understandable Schadenfreude', as he called it in 1936. The imposition of 'decency' seems essentially to be a way of combating those feelings, which were only too familiar to him.

As far as the 'decency' of his leadership corps was concerned, the Reichs-führer-SS manifestly had similar doubts. Significantly, he could not bring himself to decide in the summer of 1942 to issue an order against anony-mous letters in the SS. He told his administrative chief Pohl that he would be able to ban such things only 'when I am sure of again having peacetime commanders and chiefs to whom any reasonably decent SS man can and does confidently come when he is deeply troubled. At this point I know that this will not be true of the majority of the people in question.'[61]

Below the level of 'virtues' there was a series of Himmler orders regulating the conduct of SS members, most of which he produced on 9 November each year and which he regarded as the 'basic laws' of the SS; over the years they were collected numerous times in a constantly growing catalogue.[62]

Alongside the engagement and marriage orders of 31 December 1931, the 'honour law' of the SS of 9 November 1935 was the most important of these basic laws. It committed SS members to 'defend' their 'honour by the use of arms'. This could certainly be understood as promoting duelling (as a former member of duelling fraternity, Himmler had obtained Hitler's express approval for this regulation).[63] In practice, however, Himmler tended if possible to avoid such duels and instead to settle these conflicts by concilia-tion. To this end, he set up special 'arbitration courts' that decided whether in actual cases of someone's honour being slighted a duel was appropriate or not. This judgement had to be confirmed by the Reichsführer,[64] for 'duelling with swords should not be done as lightly as in the past, otherwise duelling will be turned into a completely devalued formality'.[65] If a duel was judged to be unavoidable it had also to be approved in advance by Hitler;[66] at the beginning of 1943 duels of this kind were forbidden on principle 'during wartime'.[67]

The regulation concerning the 'sacredness of property' of November 1936, according to which in future there were to be no more locks on lockers in SS troops' accommodation, was also a basic law, along with the 'duty to save' and the 'sacred task [. . .] of giving help of every kind to the wives and children of dead comrades'.[68] During the war the order 'Last Sons' was added: it laid down that members of the Schutzpolizei and the SS who were the 'only or last surviving son' in their family should be sent home from the front and told: 'It is your duty, through the procreation and birth of children of good blood, to ensure as quickly as possible that you are not the last son [. . .] so that you can be deployed again in the front line of battle.'[69]

There was little that escaped Himmler's attention. His men were supplied with a constant stream of rules of conduct and prohibitions. He felt obliged to take steps to curb cheating and other discreditable practices in sports; at SS sports events he demanded 'incorruptible honesty', 'chivalrous bearing', and 'strict adherence to the standards of good behaviour'.[70] He reminded his men of the need to observe the speed limit,[71] and forbade high-ranking SS leaders who held a pilot's licence to fly while on duty.[72] SS men were not allowed to address each other as 'Herr' but had to use their rank, and on Mother's Day they had to ensure they were at home.[73] Men should acknowledge each other 'not with a limply bent arm, but in a soldierly fashion, with arm and hand outstretched'.[74] And when shaking hands, remove gloves! Or, to use Himmler's words: 'When SS men greet each other with a handshake, even if this takes place between a man and his superior officer, they must shake hands and not gloves.'[75]

Indoctrination

According to Himmler, 'indoctrination' was of the greatest importance in ensuring the enforcement of SS virtues and for the loyalty and commitment of SS members. At first it was the responsibility of the Race and Settlement Main Office.[76] A suitable organization was built up in the course of 1934: every SS unit down to the Sturm had an individual head of indoctrination who was appointed by the Race and Settlement Main Office and who was to ensure that all SS men within his field of responsibility took part once a week in an indoctrination hour. This indoctrination organization was directed by the thirteen full-time race officers from the SS-Oberabschnitte, who since April 1937 had been called 'SS Race and Settlement leaders' (*RuS-Führer*). It also came within their remit to implement the marriage order and, from 1938, to carry out the racial examination of whole population groups, initiate resettlement measures, and more besides.[77] To brief the indoctrination leader, at first indoctrination letters were issued sporadically and then replaced in 1936 by the *SS Guidance Booklet* (*SS-Leitheft*), which appeared regularly with guidelines and information.[78] In 1937 the indoctrination organization of the SS took on the ideological training of the police.[79] In August 1938 Himmler withdrew responsibility for indoctrination from the Race and Settlement Main Office, with whose head he had quarrelled, and transferred it to the SS Main Office.[80] At this point the indoctrination office had thirty-one full-time staff members and 430 honorary indoctrination leaders.[81] At the beginning of 1939 Himmler transferred responsibility also for the so-called team houses (*Mannschaftshäuser*) from the Race and Settlement Main Office to his Personal Staff. The total of sixteen team houses accommodated SS members who were receiving special ideological training and being toughened up in martial sports. They were to form the core of an academic SS elite.[82]

According to the principle of their ideological training, SS men were not to 'know about' National Socialism; rather, they were to 'live' it. 'The indoctrination leader must fire the emotions of his SS men. He can do that only if he propounds our intentions on the basis of his own most profound inner experience', as one set of instructions put it. 'The indoctrination leader must be a man's man himself and a living example of every word he says.'[83]

It would seem more than doubtful whether this could be realized in practice: indoctrination was schematized and formalized to the extent that there was little scope for improvisation. 'Flights of ideological imagination are something I most decidedly will not tolerate', as Himmler informed his indoctrination leaders.[84] *Das Schwarze Korps* then also described the attitude of many SS comrades to indoctrination as follows: 'Of course, this or that person thinks, "We ought to go along, especially because our superior officer is also going to be there (promotion!). In any case," as these people console themselves in a typically philistine manner, "the cosy get-together afterwards is always really nice."'[85]

In February 1936 the head of the Race and Settlement Main Office ordered that the 'basic indoctrination' of SS members had to take place in a total of twenty-eight weeks, split into four blocks and spread over twenty-one months in all. In every indoctrination week two teaching units of forty minutes each were to be held and had to follow a particular pattern: reading and discussion of an extract from *Mein Kampf* and of a short essay on a particular topic, followed by the presentation of a practical example derived from the procedure for approving marriages, so that the SS men were given some direction when choosing the right wife.[86] The four blocks of basic indoctrination covered the following topics: blood and soil (eight weeks), Jewry, Freemasonry, Bolshevism (eight weeks), history of the German nation (eight weeks), the SS year and customs, honouring the dead (four weeks).

The matching teaching materials can be found in the first seven editions of the *SS Guidance Booklets*, which even after the 'basic indoctrination' was completed remained the most important training resource.[87] Booklet 9 was concerned, among other things, with the history of the SS, while other booklets concentrated on the SS's spring games,[88] topics from prehistory and early history, and German history.[89] In addition there are constant 'tips' on choosing the right partner[90] and—under the heading 'For the family'— hints on how to choose 'good' German first names, in order to prevent aberrations, which were clearly quite frequent.[91]

Himmler himself took control of the design of the *SS Guidance Booklets*. At the meeting to discuss Booklet 10 he imparted some general instructions to Joachim Caesar, the head of the Indoctrination Office: 'It is my wish that the material used in indoctrination is not always taken from *one* area of life. Every area of life should be touched on and indeed in such a way that the trainee looks forward to the next indoctrination session and to reading the booklet. Above all, the way things are presented is what counts. The articles are never to be longer than 5–6 pages.' In particular he recommended *The Loyalty Book* and *The Passion Book*, works by his favourite writer Werner Jansen, as models.[92]

In line with the example of Jansen's books, Himmler advocated above all heroic stories in the *SS Guidance Booklets*—sagas, as he put it.[93] 'We must get rid of the idea', he declared in a lecture some years later, 'that a "saga" is something untrue, something made up. Rather, Norway's or Denmark's sagas are the history of these nations, and the saga of our nation is the history of our nation from its earliest time. And the human heart, that of men and women in Germany, can respond to this form of saga, of story, with its sensitive voice, much, much more than scholarly, didactic writing can teach men or women.'[94] In 1937 the *SS Guidance Booklets* did in fact move more towards putting historical material across in the form of 'heroic sagas'.[95]

The SS's 'ideological training' therefore moved further and further away from its initial ambition of passing on to SS members a comprehensive 'vision of the world', and concentrated instead on the 'most imaginative' dissemination possible of heroic role-models. First and foremost, SS men were to 'believe' in the order's mission; above all, emotional attachment to the organization was promoted. Through membership of the SS they had taken their place in a phalanx of heroic figures who had fought an eternal battle against 'subhumanity' to protect their families and their 'blood'. In this struggle private decisions regarding marriage and children played a significant role. As we shall see, the Reichsführer-SS therefore devoted particular care and attention to these questions, beyond the scope of indoctrination in general.

12

Himmler as Educator

Himmler's educational ambitions were not confined to the behaviour of his subordinates while on duty. Rather, they embraced all aspects of his men's lives: their appearance, their economic circumstances, their relationship to alcohol, their health, and, as we shall see in the next chapter, marriage and family planning. The Reichsführer-SS reserved for himself the right to demonstrate in an exemplary fashion to members of the SS, down to those of the lowliest rank, his severity and omnipotence. This he did by means of targeted interventions in the most diverse areas of their lives. The most senior members of the SS leader corps in particular had to endure painstakingly precise surveillance of their entire existence.

In the second half of the 1930s and during the Second World War the SS leadership—in other words, those who had reached at least the rank of Gruppenführer—was drawn overwhelmingly from two groups: young First World War volunteers and the so-called 'war youth generation'. The young volunteers were those born in the 1890s (mostly after 1895) who had seen service in the First World War, most of them from the outbreak, and had predominantly served as young lieutenants and then been members of the Free Corps. Members of this cohort had helped decisively to build up the SS before 1933. The so-called 'war youth' generation (that is, those born after 1900 who, although they had been fully aware of the war, had been too young for active service—Himmler's cohort) began to fill leading posts from 1933 onwards. There were, of course, also older men among the leaders, yet on closer inspection it appears that the majority of these played no active role in the SS but rather had been rewarded by Himmler with a relatively high rank in the General SS as part of his strategy of cultivating contacts. The Gau leaders of the veterans' organization, the Reichskrieger-bund, for example, had, when their organization was taken into the SS, received the rank Gruppenführer, without as a result achieving any signifi-cant influence on the leadership of the SS. The situation with regard to police officers (some of them long-serving officers, others Nazi activists appointed after 1933) was different; Himmler conferred corresponding SS ranks on them in order to incorporate them into the 'state protection corps' he was aiming to form. As the police became increasingly important after Himmler's appointment as Chief of the German Police, but in particular after 1939, when the racial utopia he advocated was being implemented (for example, in the fight against asocials in the 1930s or the mass executions carried out by the order police in eastern Europe during the war), these latecomers joining the SS in a sideways move should be taken into account in any analysis of Himmler's tactic of attaining his goals with the help of a subtle personnel strategy.[1]

At this point, however, the two cohorts mentioned above (young war volunteers and the war youth generation), who put their stamp on the SS in the 1930s, are the focus of attention. I have already discussed the specific biographical characteristics of the young war volunteers in the SS leader-ship, whose period as First World War soldiers was frequently followed by a frustrating and unsuccessful civilian career and who thus saw the SS as their last chance. Those who attained leading positions in the SS before 1933 were presented in Chapter 6; after 1933 further war volunteers moved up into the top positions.

Herbert Gille, born in 1897, was one example. He was to become the commanding general of the 2nd SS Tank Corps. A former cadet and professional soldier, Gille had taken work after the First World War as an estate manager, until in 1929 he was 'cut back' without any prospect of further work in agriculture. Until 1931 he got by as a travelling salesman and then as an independent insurance salesman. In 1932 he gave up this work for a full-time post as chief of staff of the SS-Abschnitt IV.[2] In March 1933, immediately after the seizure of power, he was, however, relieved of his position, taken into custody for three months, and expelled from the SS; precise reasons for these measures were never given to him. Although rehabilitated in March 1934, he was, as his brother wrote to Himmler, 'financially ruined and psychologically very low'. In a personal interview with Himmler in April 1934 he regained his spirits a little,[3] and Himmler gave him an interim position as a Standartenführer. He clashed with his superiors, however, again lost his job, and was judged by his superior officer Jeckeln as 'unsuitable for a leading role in the higher echelons'.[4] Gille was given a third chance: he was moved to the political action squad (*Politische Bereitschaft*) in Ellwangen and this time he was successful in carving out a career in the armed SS (*Verfügungstruppe*).[5]

Georg Lörner, born in 1899 and later head of Amtsgruppe B in the SS Main Office for Economy and Administration, had taken part in the First World War. After completing a course at a business school, in 1923 he went into his brother's firm: 'Because of the adverse economic circumstances and various failures the firm was forced in February 1930 to declare itself bankrupt', he wrote in his curriculum vitae.[6]

Carl-Albrecht Oberg, born in 1897 and deployed in the war as a Higher SS and Police Leader, had been a war volunteer and Free Corps fighter who in 1921 assumed the role of go-between linking the Reichswehr and the Patriotic Associations in Schleswig-Holstein. 'In January 1926 I was again employed as a businessman, as my political post up to that time, being financed by private means, was not sustainable.' In the end he found work with a company importing bananas, but not for long. 'This firm was liquidated after about a year and a half, making me jobless. In November 1930 I bought my present cigar shop.' The following year he became a member of the NSDAP and in 1932 of the SS.[7]

Günther Pancke, in the Second World War a Higher SS and Police Leader in Denmark, was born in 1899 and fought in the First World War as an officer cadet. After the Revolution he was active in the Free Corps in the Baltic region, then spent the time between 1920 and 1926 in Argentina, where he worked on cattle ranches. On a visit to Germany in 1926 he found a job. 'In June 1930 I joined the party and in 1931 the SS. After a tear-gas attack in protest at a private showing of the film *All Quiet on the Western Front* put on by the Reichsbanner, I was dismissed without notice from my firm and put in prison for six weeks. The sentence was suspended and on 1 January 1932 I went as a teacher to the SS School at Kreiensen.' A full-time post in the SS followed, and Pancke's career rapidly took off.[8]

For Otto Hofmann also the seizure of power meant a unique opportunity to return to the military milieu. Born in 1896, he was a war volunteer and member of a flying unit. After his divorce in 1926 he had lost his post as general manager in his parents-in-law's wine wholesale business and then worked as a salesman for a wine merchant. In April 1933 he decided to take a full-time post in the SS, to which he had belonged for a number of years. In 1940, after numerous promotions, he became head of the Race and Settlement Main Office.[9]

Georg Ebrecht, originally an artist, was born in 1895 and volunteered as a soldier in 1914, ending the war as a lieutenant. Up to 1924 he was active above all in various military organizations; long travels abroad followed and eventually he settled in East Africa as a planter of sisal. In 1922 he had already separated from his first wife; his divorce in 1926 was followed four weeks later by marriage to a woman who was already living on his plantation in Africa. In 1931 he was economically finished: 'When, after the huge collapse of prices on the world market, the plantation I had painstakingly built up became uneconomic, I went back to Germany.' He joined the NSDAP, in which he was active as a speaker, without support from any occupational income. The seizure of power opened up to him a professional career as a party functionary, first as a district leader, then as a Gau Inspector. In 1935 he moved to the Race and Settlement Main Office, where in 1937 he became a section head.[10] In 1938 his second marriage ended in divorce, on the grounds of 'complete breakdown', the court commenting that because of his function in the Race and Settlement Main Office he took the fact that the marriage was childless particularly to heart.[11] Ebrecht married a third time and had two daughters.[12]

Hanns Albin Rauter, a Higher SS and Police Leader in the Netherlands in the Second World War, was born in 1895 and fought in the Austrian Army for the whole of the First World War. He was then head of the Styrian paramilitary Heimatschutz, but in 1933 was expatriated from Austria as a result of National Socialist activities. Without career or money, he joined the NSDAP and the SS.[13]

The SS leaders from the war youth generation had also frequently been active in Free Corps and military groups, the young ones often in radical right-wing paramilitary youth organizations. This cohort, Himmler's contemporaries, was not only preoccupied with the trauma of defeat and the failure of the putches, it also shared an attitude that veered between disappointment at having arrived too late and a defiant posture of 'We'll show the older generation'. We have already been introduced to a number of members of this group, who joined the NSDAP before 1933—for example, Heydrich, the discharged naval officer, and Fritz Weitzel, the junior fitter with a conviction for aiding an abortion.[14]

In general the members of the war youth generation had better prospects of successful careers than the cohort of young soldiers, who had lost decisive years through their military service. A number of later SS leaders from this group went to university, in particular to study law. In the late 1920s and early 1930s they had mostly completed the second state examination in law. But with the onset of the economic crisis, and in view of the surplus, widely bemoaned, of candidates for graduate professions, they had only the slimmest chance of a post in the civil service, and even if they did get one they had first to accept years of unpaid work as trainees. The prospects for establishing themselves as lawyers were also poor. Those who had studied other subjects were confronted with similar problems; Himmler's failed career in agriculture illustrates the difficult situation. A takeover of power by the Nazis offered the prospect of a suitable career in the state or in one of the party organizations, and this undoubtedly provided one of the powerful motives propelling this group towards the NSDAP from the end of the 1920s. For many people, even for those who were not university educated, there was no comparable alternative.

Born in 1903, Werner Best, who in 1939 became a departmental head in the Reich Security Main Office and organizer of the Einsatzgruppen in Poland, had, after his law degree, become a junior judge. In 1930 he joined the NSDAP in the Hesse-Darmstadt Gau and headed its legal section. When in 1931 the so-called 'Boxheim documents', papers providing evidence that Best had made concrete plans for a National Socialist coup, were passed on to the authorities, he was dismissed from state service. The Nazi takeover of power provided him with the means in March 1933 of gaining a position as state commissar for police in Hesse; he became involved, however, in internal power struggles in the party and in September 1933 was removed from his post. In this situation Himmler offered him the opportunity of taking over the SD-Oberabschnitt South-West.

The following can also be cited as examples of university graduates who saw in the SS comparatively good career prospects: Hermann Behrends, doctor of law and trainee lawyer from 1930 to 1933, was in the SS from February 1932 and in the SD from the end of 1933, where he took over the central department for ideological evaluation. In 1936 he moved to the Gestapo, became staff manager of the Coordination Centre for Ethnic Germans (*Volksdeutsche Mittelstelle* = VoMi), and in 1944 a Higher SS and Police Leader in Serbia.[15] Otto Ohlendorf, born in 1907, studied law and political science and worked at the Kiel Institute for World Economics. From 1936 he made a career for himself in the SD, where he began by being responsible for reporting on economic affairs and from 1939 headed the 'German Home Affairs' department. In 1941–2 he was in addition chief of Einsatzgruppe D and responsible for the murder of tens of thousands of

Jews; Himmler clearly wanted to test out Ohlendorf's 'severity', as the latter was considered an intellectual.[16]

Hermann Fegelein was born in 1906, and as commander of SS cavalry units participated decisively in 'combating partisans' and the 'cleansing campaigns' that were to cost thousands of civilians their lives. He had completed his grammar-school education in 1926, studied for two semesters, and then broken off his studies. He entered the Bavarian State Police, but left again in 1929. He worked at his father's riding school until, in 1933, he joined the SS.[17]

Fritz Katzmann was born in 1906, and in the Second World War, as an SS and Police Leader, was chiefly responsible for the systematic mass murder of hundreds of thousands of Jews in Galicia. After being trained as a carpenter he worked from 1923 to 1928 in various towns. 'From 1928 to 1933 without work. From July 1933 to November 1933 in charge of the works police at United Steel in Duisburg-Hamborn. December 1933 to January 1934 in Duisburg as district head of the German Labour Front.' In February 1934 he was taken on full-time as an SS Leader.[18]

Erwin Rösener, later Higher SS and Police Leader for the Alpine region, and born in 1902, attended a technical school up to the age of 13, became an apprentice electrician between 1917 and 1921, and then worked for various firms. He was actively engaged in the Nazi movement, moved in 1929 from the SA to the SS, and was therefore sacked by his employer. 'Now I was able to devote myself completely to the movement. I then had short-term employment but always had to leave because of my political activities.'[19]

Numerous members of both cohorts suffered considerably as a result of failing to gain a foothold in a career. Marital problems, alcoholism, debts, and long-term medical consequences took their toll on many. Of course, the SS leaders were not alone in having these difficulties: we are not dealing with a negative selection of damaged lives, but rather with life-stories representative and typical of the time. Large segments of the German population had similar experiences. And the biographies of a whole series of leading SS men from the same generation developed without any striking interruptions.

Himmler, it must be said, knew how to exploit for his own purposes the susceptibilities evident from the ruptures described in the biographies of many members of the SS leader corps. He was able to make these men dependent on him in sometimes subtle ways. After all, many of the weaknesses he encountered in his dealings with his men were most probably familiar to him from his own experience and from personal acquaintances and friends of his own age.

Vices and inadequacies

On 26 July 1939, a few weeks before the outbreak of the Second World War, SS-Obergruppenführer Friedrich Jeckeln, Higher SS and Police Leader based in Brunswick, received a letter from the Reichsführer-SS. Himmler had received information, he wrote to Jeckeln, that a few weeks previously the latter, 'while under the influence of alcohol', had roared through towns and villages in his car at a speed of 80 to 100 kilometres an hour, 'showing disregard for drivers and pedestrians'. Himmler demanded that Jeckeln answer three questions: '1. Did you drive on this particular stretch of road? 2. How much alcohol had you drunk on that day? 3. Were you in breach of the rules of the road?' Jeckeln knew where Himmler had got his information. On the evening of 23 June a Hamburg businessman and active member of the NS Motor Corps (NSKK) had given chase and, after catching up with Jeckeln at a level-crossing after a fairly long and very eventful pursuit, had challenged him about his inconsiderate and dangerous driving, obviously fuelled by alcohol. Jeckeln revealed himself to be an SS-Obergruppenführer and drove on, but the NSKK man had not let the matter rest there.

Jeckeln, who years before had admitted to Himmler that he had an alcohol problem, then sent his Reichsführer the following 'report': at lunchtime on the day in question he had met a number of notable people for an 'intimate lunch', the purpose of which was 'to maintain good social relations and comradeship'. He had left this occasion, which was to go on into the evening, shortly before eight and set off to his hunting lodge. With the exception of minor infringements he had, as he emphasized, observed the rules and above all had driven safely. Jeckeln attempted to allay suspicion that he had had too much to drink by listing all the drinks he had consumed that day: '4–5 glasses of Moselle wine', '3 or at most 4 glasses of schnapps', then possibly '3 glasses of beer on top'. Jeckeln's calculation that if he admitted to ten or twelve alcoholic drinks Himmler would not count these as excessive drinking seems to have worked; on the evidence of his personal file the evening's drive had no further consequences for him.[20]

During a comradeship evening in May 1936, following, of all things, an inspection of Dachau concentration camp, an 'argy-bargy'—as Kaul later described it, in order to play it down—occurred between Brigadeführer Kaul and Oberführer Unger. In the course of this the two opponents tipped wine and beer over each other's uniforms. Unger was not prepared in retrospect to take the 'idiocies' particularly seriously either, and excused the incident by referring to the good atmosphere that had prevailed at this cheerful evening's drinking: 'It was also already very late and the large amount of alcohol consumed had created a very good and jocular mood.'[21] Himmler decided not to go along with the suggestion of von dem Bach-Zelewski, the Oberabschnittsführer in charge, of initiating formal proceedings but rather gave his chief of staff the task of summoning the two SS leaders and giving them a dressing-down in Himmler's name.[22]

In February 1942 Karl-Heinz Bürger, who at this point was preparing himself for his future tasks as a Higher SS and Police Leader in the Ukraine, received a letter from Himmler. The Reichsführer reproached him with having, in his earlier post as 'desk officer responsible for ideological questions' and during his inspection of educational establishments, taken part in a 'massive drinking bout'. During this he had 'manifestly more or less lost the power of rational thought and all self-control', and fired his pistol. Bürger candidly admitted the facts, claiming the incident had happened during the celebrations to mark the opening of the official residence of his boss Heissmeyer in January 1941. 'The devil must have got into me when I fired two shots at the ceiling lights. At the time this frivolity caused me much unease and I could explain it only by the fact that the deep sense of dissatisfaction I had felt during my assignment to the administrative office of SS-Obergruppenführer Heissmeyer was finding violent release.' Himmler's reaction was extreme indignation: an 'ideological educator who himself so abandons education and proper conduct' had 'morally no right [. . .] to pass on ideology to other people'. Nevertheless, he did not intend, he wrote, to take disciplinary action—on the assumption that this was an 'exceptional case'. He impressed on Bürger the need in future 'to bring the ideology he preached [sic], his bearing and the conduct of his life—in particular with regard to alcohol—into line with each other'.[23]

The fact that such free use of firearms was not an isolated incident is shown by an instruction Himmler issued some months after the reproof to Bürger: 'I am repeatedly being informed that a member of the SS or the police has felt the need to use his firearm in a completely inappropriate and irresponsible manner. Usually this happens in the company of others and under the influence of alcohol and indeed particularly in the eastern territories.' Such 'firearms abuse', Himmler went on, was 'not only irresponsible' but also 'absolutely un-German', for 'a German uses his weapon in battle and leaves such gunfights to the Slavs'.[24]

Matthias Kleinheisterkamp, commander of a Waffen-SS division, was called to order by Himmler in the most blistering manner in the autumn of 1941 because of an excessive drinking binge in the division mess: 'As a captain or battalion commander you could afford the odd lapse. After I, in spite of serious doubts, had entrusted you with a division, you were under an obligation to face up to the fact that your time for getting drunk—should you wish to count that activity among the high points of your life—was well and truly over.' The 'repellent scenes of drunkenness' had, according to Himmler, revealed a 'character flaw you must make serious efforts to eradicate by the end of your period of service'. Kleinheisterkamp, Himmler went on, had escaped being relieved of his command only because Himmler would have had to divulge to the Wehrmacht the reason for this personnel decision—and for the sake of the prestige of the Waffen-SS he would not do this. Thus the only punishment Kleinhasterkamp could expect was a ban on alcohol: 'I require of you not to drink any alcohol in the next two years, after showing that at the age of 49 you are not yet capable of handling it.'[25]

Himmler had regarded an alcohol ban for some time as a tried-and-tested method of discipline: 'If anyone is unable to handle alcohol and treats it as would a small child, I take it away from him. Just as one takes away a pistol from a small child because he does not know how to use it properly', he declared in 1938.[26] Two years previously he had propounded the principle that in the case of alcohol-related offences the culprits were to be given the alternative: 'Either you show you can handle alcohol and follow our example, or a pistol will be sent to you so that you can put an end to things. So make up your mind; you have twenty-four hours to do so.'[27] Curt von Gottberg had received a three-year alcohol ban as early as 1936, after he lost a foot in an alcohol-related accident.[28] Otto Rahn, an SS-Untersturmführer whose main occupation was as a writer, was also obliged to accept a two-year alcohol ban.[29]

Significantly, however, Himmler grew more lenient with regard to alcohol bans during the war: when serving at the front, particularly in the east, he made it known, alcohol consumption was 'justified, naturally within the bounds of moderation, and occasionally even to be recommended on health grounds'. Thus 'alcohol bans already imposed and/or those still to be imposed' were 'to be set aside during service at the front'.[30] In the east the disinhibiting effect of alcohol was clearly welcome.

These examples show that, in the case of members of the SS leader corps guilty of alcohol-related excesses, although Himmler delivered moral condemnations he nevertheless shied away from disciplinary punishments and preferred to use 'educative' means.[31] This is the more curious because he generally took the view that alcohol-related misdemeanours were to be treated particularly strictly,[32] for he assumed that in the case of two-thirds of all people who had 'run aground, alcohol was the most deep-seated reason for this shipwreck'.[33]

Why, then, this leniency towards excessive drinkers in the SS? Had he realized that draconian punishments would not achieve anything? Or did he not really intend to get rid of alcohol-related offences at all? Had he recognized that binge drinking and intoxication were a fixed component of the SS subculture, and that this bad habit among his men gave him repeated opportunities to call individual SS leaders to account and to subject them to his educative methods?

In 1941 a further measure was introduced: the Reichsführer had a rehabilitation home set up at Buchenwald concentration camp for SS members with alcohol problems.[34] In this measure Himmler saw 'not punishment but health education in their own interests for those SS men and police referred there'; he wanted, he said, to 'create an exemplary compulsory recovery home, in which the inmates were to be weaned off alcohol abuse by means of unconditional withdrawal of alcohol, coupled with health measures such as sport, toughening up, and so forth, and educated into being healthy men, robust in body and mind, with cause to be grateful to the Reichsführer-SS for his intervention'. Another practical measure was the imposition of a smoking ban. He also ordered that 'food be as free as possible of meat' ('In particular oatmeal is always to be served in the morning with grated apple or Maggi seasoning or similar additions'), and advised that a sauna be constructed.[35] The decision about who should be sent there was, of course, his.[36]

Financial exigencies among his subordinates similarly required the Reichsführer's regular interventions. The fact that many members of the SS leader corps had significant debts made them, to his mind, susceptible to all kinds of temptations, as he confirmed in June 1937 in an order: 'Thus,' he said, the situation still arose 'in which industrial and commercial circles or personalities try to make SS leaders benevolent and well disposed towards them by means of unusual concessions, usually of a material kind.'[37]

There were numerous instances of SS leaders in financial difficulty turning to Himmler. He gave von dem Bach-Zelewski financial support several times, for example in 1938 by lending him 7,000 Reich marks to buy a farm; in total the payments recorded in the files amounted to at least 11,000 Reich marks.[38] SS-Brigadeführer Paul Moder informed Himmler in 1937 that he had taken an interest-free loan of 15,000 Reich marks from the Hamburg entrepreneur Hermann Reemtsma, as his wife was demanding a large sum before she would agree to a divorce.[39] SS-Gruppenführer Paul Hennicke, the chief of the Weimar police, was 'for the moment completely broke', as a friend of the Himmler family informed the Reichsführer in September 1939; the police chief's salary was at the time being impounded.[40] Obersturmbannführer Otto Hofmann, a wine merchant up to 1933 and then a full-time SS leader, asked Himmler in 1934 for financial help as he was suffering a 'dire emergency'; Himmler doubted this information when, a short time later, he got wind of the fact that Hofmann had allegedly taken part in a 'champagne binge'.[41]

SS-Oberführer Erwin Rösener informed the head of the Personnel Office that he was suffering 'acute financial embarrassment at the moment', for in the 'time of struggle' he had, 'like any other party comrade, been forced to take on heavy debts and to be supported by my parents and siblings. Now I have to make that up somehow to the aforementioned by supporting them.' Asked for his advice, Himmler decided that no additional payments should be made.[42] When Marianne Bürger, who was employed at the SS officer-training college in Brunswick and married to Obersturmbannführer Karl-Heinz Bürger, asked Himmler for a monthly supplement to her income—she was expecting her fourth child—Himmler not only refused this request but also gave Frau Bürger instructions personally about how she might manage on the available money.[43]

Obersturmbannführer Ludolf von Alvensleben, the son of an aristocratic landowner, was, by his own admission, financially 'at rock bottom' in 1928.[44] In 1934 he had managed to clear around a third of his enormous debts of 750,000 Reich marks. In the autumn of 1934 Himmler got wind of the fact that von Alvensleben had failed to respond to the demand of a creditor for 2,500 Reich marks. Himmler ordered that von Alvensleben 'be questioned at a minuted interview', and furthermore decreed: 'If Obersturmbannführer v. Alversleben is unable to give satisfactory explanations to show that he has treated the matter in the manner required of a National Socialist and SS leader, his continued membership of the SS is impossible. The private debts of an SS leader are a matter which his superiors must take the keenest interest in.'[45]

In July 1937 Himmler ordered von Alvensleben, who in the meantime was head of SS-Abschnitt X and had by his own account cleared his debts with only 12,000 Reich marks remaining, to appear in the Four Seasons Hotel in Munich, and accused him there in the presence of the Chief of his Personal Staff of enjoying free use of a car that had been offered to him at a very attractive price by the Mercedes works. Himmler forbade von Alvensleben to acquire the car on these exceptional terms.[46]

Before this meeting Himmler had already issued a regulation in which he described the case in detail, without mentioning von Alvensleben by name, and impressed on his men that he wanted 'my SS leaders to remain free and independent, including in financial matters'. He expressly demanded that 'every SS leader refuse strictly and proudly to accept favours of any kind, even if they are dressed up as having a professional purpose, such as the claim that the high-level work of the recipient in question will be made easier'.[47]

Whereas Himmler made a show of intervening here in order to prevent von Alvensleben from losing his independence to a company for the sake of a relatively small financial advantage, only a year later he appeared significantly more generous: in order finally to secure for von Alvensleben a life free of debt, Himmler approved a consultancy contract between the SS leader and the Salzgitter works that boosted von Alvensleben's monthly income by 1,000 Reich marks.[48]

Why did Himmler consent to the consultancy, when he refused the car purchase? It appears that in the case of the consultancy his consent in the matter was a means of showing, at least to outward appearances, that things were under his control; he heard about the car purchase, however, only when the deal was in train, and was forced to intervene because his authority was being called into question. For that is primarily what was at stake in this case, and possible corruption was a secondary issue.

Old debts from the 'time of struggle' were, however, by no means the only reason for financial difficulties. In a staff order of December 1936, for example, the head of the Race and Settlement Main Office stated that 'a considerable proportion of members of the Main Office are heavily in debt. The debts have arisen almost exclusively by the thoughtless acquisition of radios, cameras, motor vehicles, etc., on which only a down-payment has been made. Most of those in debt are unmarried and comparatively well paid according to the salary scale, but by their frivolous purchases are so indebted that on the first of the month they have only small change left out of their salary.' This, he continues, is leading to an 'escalating amount of borrowing' among comrades, in pubs and from businessmen, amounting to what is 'ultimately stealing from comrades in the case of weaker personalities. But those in debt are also a good subject for the attentions of the opposition's intelligence services.' The SS members working full-time at the Main Office were therefore asked to hand in a declaration of debt. Any frivolous incurring of debt would result in immediate dismissal.[49]

In 1936–7 Himmler initiated serious measures to combat debt: he saw to it that the SS took out a loan, first of a million, later of 2.5 million Reich marks, in order to pay off the debts of first the Main Office staff, then the entire leader corps, and finally the SS as a whole.[50] At the beginning of 1937 a questionnaire was used to establish the financial liabilities of the Main Office SS leaders, and in the spring of 1937 he set up a department for economic support: SS debt counsellors negotiated with creditors a partial settling of the debts; the SS men in question had to pay the sums owed to the SS and to undertake never again to incur debts and—and this was a particular concern of Himmler's—never again to enter into hire-purchase agreements.[51]

'A considerable number of old Nazis are still carrying liabilities and debts from the time of struggle and the years of economic misery', asserted Himmler at a Gruppenführer meeting in February 1937. 'In the long run I consider this untenable.' For the future he recommended the following 'way of life': an 'SS man buys nothing he cannot pay for'; he 'will never buy anything in instalments'; the 'SS man is the most honest human being that exists in Germany'.[52] In his November speech to the Gruppenführer in Munich he announced an additional ten-point 'Basic Law concerning compulsory saving', in which one requirement was to create a savings fund into which salaried SS men each had to pay 1 mark a month.[53]

Alcohol abuse and indebtedness were not the only aspects of the lives of his leader corps that Himmler disapproved of. He repeatedly criticized his men, for example, for excessive ambition or exaggerated vanity. Hermann Behrends, liaison officer at the Coordination Centre for Ethnic Germans, was in fact, in Himmler's estimation, 'personally a decent, able, and courageous man in his work', but Himmler was disturbed by his 'consuming and unhealthy ambition'. For he suspected that the person behind Kaltenbrunner's recommendation of Behrends as Kaltenbrunner's replacement as

Ill. 15. Although right-handed, Himmler practised shooting with his left hand as well and stipulated that the SS as a whole should do the same. His men were supposed to learn to make up for physical weaknesses and other inadequacies through self-discipline and willpower.

Higher SS and Police Leader Danube was in fact Behrends himself.[54] Himmler was highly displeased when SS leaders pressed for their own promotion, and put them firmly in their place.[55]

In June 1942 he reproached SS-Brigadeführer Walther Schröder, Higher SS and Police Leader in Riga, with being 'addicted to being constantly in the newspapers', and 'made it clear' to him that 'the next time he was mentioned in a newspaper article' he would be 'demoted':

It is not the task of the SS and Police Leader to put on a public show and make a name for himself in the rear area post of Riga, rather it is to work from morning till night to care for his troops, to train and lead his men, learn about the region and its people, and learn also about the minutiae of workplace procedures. Public display and newspaper propaganda are not necessary for this. What is required is that your superiors, not the public, are convinced of your effectiveness, for the public does not promote or demote you. Take this final warning to heart.[56]

There were also instances of his finding fault with the 'company kept' by senior SS leaders. Thus, in March 1943 SS-Gruppenführer Gerret Korsemann received a letter from his Reichsführer containing the reproach that Korsemann had been a guest at the home of a major who was held by the officer corps of the order police to be a man 'about whose worth and character opinion has often been divided'. He knew, however, that he could expect of Korsemann 'that in future in choosing your friends and close associates you apply the care and acuteness of judgement I must demand of a Gruppenführer for his intimate circle'.[57]

SS members who committed suicide were reprimanded by him even after death. According to Himmler, 85 per cent of suicides in the SS were 'committed for reasons that can never be acknowledged: fear of punishment, fear of being tested, after a reproof from a superior, after a quarrel with parents, after breaking off an engagement, jealousy, an unhappy love life, and so forth'. Such suicides were, he claimed, 'seen by us SS men as an escape, an evasion of the struggle, of life itself'. In such cases no notice was to be taken of the suicide and the SS was to keep away from the funeral.[58] Suicides were not to be buried with a formal ceremony but had to be 'put in the ground' (verscharrt).[59] Himmler explained the rising number of suicides in the SS at the end of the 1930s by claiming that the cohorts reaching adulthood in the Weimar Republic were 'hothouse plants'.[60]

Ailing SS officers

The Reichsführer showed himself similarly concerned about the health of the SS. He prescribed medical examinations, read the diagnoses, and gave his men tips on nutrition and lifestyle. Occasionally he decreed where men should go on holiday and for how long, and forbade them to read official files while there.[61] The constant pressure and ceaseless 'deployment' led to numerous members of the SS leader corps, although only in their late thirties or early forties, suffering considerable physical wear and tear, and above all psychological and psychosomatic problems, during the war years. In the medical reports the same keywords recur: fatigue, exhaustion, problems with 'nerves', depressive conditions.

For example, the report on Gruppenführer Waldemar Wappenhans from April 1944 read: 'He seems agitated and exhausted. Purely physically his heart and circulation are no worse than at the last examination. [. . .] But I was unhappy about his state as a whole. I think that from a medical point of view he urgently needs some mental rest to regain his equilibrium.'[62]

In the case of SS-Gruppenführer Karl Gutenberger, Himmler ordered a 'comprehensive medical examination' after hearing about his health problems. The SS-Reich Medical Officer Robert Grawitz recorded that at the examination the 38-year-old seemed 'a little absent-minded', and showed a 'slight degree of indifference, a kind of euphoria, a tendency to see everything on the same level'. 'Possibly what we are seeing is the beginning of a post-traumatic change'—which caused Grawitz to prescribe an examination by a consultant at the psychiatric clinic at the Charité hospital in Berlin.[63] On the basis of the results Himmler sent Gutenberger first of all for four weeks to the SS 'Höhenvilla' in Carlsbad (Karlovy Vary), a sanatorium in which similar cases were treated.

When Erwin Rösener, Higher SS and Police Leader for the Alps, was examined in May 1944, a specialist in internal and nervous illnesses came to the conclusion: 'this particularly strong and healthy 42-year-old man presents with a state of nervous exhaustion that on the one hand derives from excessively prolonged pressures without a break and that on the other was already apparent and made worse as a result of autonomic dysfunctions consequent on a malfunctioning thyroid. We therefore have here a state of exhaustion attributable to his having consumed his very considerable reserves of strength.'[64] In August 1944 a medical report recommended that Rösener be admitted to the Höhenvilla in Carlsbad.[65]

At the end of 1944 the doctors diagnosed Karl Gustav Sauberzweig, commander of the Croat SS Volunteer Mountain Division, as having a 'distinct state of excessive nervous excitability tending [. . .] towards psychosis': 'He tries to be on his own; he does not wish to see anyone else; the sound of gunfire or the sight of blood distress him; his powers of concentration are distinctly deficient and he fears having to take responsibility, etc., etc.'[66]

In 1942 Himmler was forced to pension off the head of his Personnel Main Office, Walter Schmitt, as he was suffering from urinary frequency, attributable, according to a medical report, 'to a general neurosis that perhaps was worsened by his professional work'.[67] In addition, Richard Hildebrandt, Higher SS and Police Leader for the Vistula and responsible for annexed Polish territory, complained in 1942 of 'dizziness' and 'tiredness'; the doctor who examined him could find no organic cause.[68]

In cases in which a specific medical diagnosis could not be reached the Munich specialist for internal medicine, Dr Karl Fahrenkamp, who took particular account of psychological causes, was frequently consulted.[69] Fahrenkamp's special position was also demonstrated by the fact that inside the Personal Staff a department F was set up for him that in turn supported an 'Estate for Experimental Nutrition' near Salzburg. In addition, before 1940 Fahrenkamp conducted experiments on plants at Dachau concentration camp, and in 1942 he set up a laboratory in the neighbouring training camp, in which, amongst other things, herbally based cosmetics and beauty products were produced; because these goods were produced within the SS the strict government controls on cultivation could be circumvented.[70] Himmler was one of the grateful recipients of these products—skin-care products, mouthwash, and suchlike[71]—and was also one of Fahrenkamp's patients.[72] In November 1941 Himmler assured Fahrenkamp 'that I am eternally grateful to you for treating my men, who are extremely difficult patients, with such skill and common sense'.[73] As Himmler attributed his own stomach problems to psychosomatic causes, Fahrenkamp's patient reports gave him access to highly interesting material that allowed him to compare the course of his own illness with that of his SS leaders.

The 45-year-old Waffen-SS General Felix Steiner, for example, seemed to Fahrenkamp to be 'a very closed and inaccessible man, who answers serious questions with a smile and a certain self-irony'. It was his view 'that in this case a very vigorous man with a rigid military bearing arrives already wearing a mask and that behind this mask is concealed a sort of depression that under no circumstances' is to be shown. [74]

In the case of Ulrich Greifelt, head of the Four-Year-Plan Office in the Personal Staff, Fahrenkamp's findings, set down on the eve of Greifelt's forty-second birthday, were as follows:

Damage to the sight of the left eye as a result of flying. In 1918 quit his career as an officer. Through extraordinary efforts made a new career as technical director of a large factory. Lost this post in 1932 through no fault of his own. Has always worked hard [. . .] Herr G. suffers greatly from inner agitation and sleeplessness. Is unable to fall asleep and wakes up again early. Becomes very tense about new tasks but does not know why. Psychologically, his enjoyment of life is severely impaired. [. . .] Herr G. is depressed by two changes of career, in particular because he was forced to leave a sphere of activity he found very satisfying.[75]

Werner Lorenz, head of the Coordination Centre for Ethnic Germans, struck Fahrenkamp as someone who, although organically healthy, was nevertheless a 'tired, exhausted man'. He suspected 'psychological causes [...] as factors in his present condition [...] SS-Obergruppenführer L. says that you, Herr Reichsführer, know about his personal family circumstances.' It was, he continued, 'obvious that this refined and very alert man, whom I did not feel has a very robust constitution, is experiencing the effects of a psychological depression in the form of lassitude and exhaustion.'[76]

Many SS leaders reacted to illness and pain with 'severity' towards themselves, such as Heinz Johst, for example, commander of the security police in the Baltic States, who announced to his Reichsführer in July 1944 that, as a result of the long-term effects of diphtheria, he was suffering from serious heart complaints and circulation problems: 'Because of the situation, I have tried up to now to tackle the condition through my own vigour. Increasingly bad attacks of dizziness and now disturbances to my vision mean I can no longer do this.'[77]

Wilhelm Rediess, Higher SS and Police Leader in Königsberg, complained in October 1939 to Fahrenkamp of serious headaches on the left side, and in general admitted to having a 'very tired and preoccupied mind.' The doctor stated that he found Rediess to be a 'healthy and strong man' and therefore concluded that the complaints must 'be caused by a general exhaustion'. Fahrenkamp continued that advising him was 'difficult because he is more brutal with himself than anyone can be without in the long run damaging his overall fitness. However obvious it is that even pain can be conquered by force of will, medical experience shows that this attitude has its limits and one day, despite every effort of the will, good health gives way to illness.' Prevention, he writes, should not be confused with 'being soft', as Rediess believed.[78]

Erich von dem Bach-Zelewski, as Higher SS and Police Leader for Russia Centre, responsible amongst other things for 'combating partisans' and for the mass murder of Jews, suffered a physical and mental breakdown in March 1942. The Reich Medical Officer Grawitz reported to Himmler:

At the moment I have some concern about his frame of mind: from fear of his haemorrhoid problems SS-Obergruppenführer v. d. Bach had already been going without food for many months, both quantitatively and qualitatively, during the eastern deployment; I have already reported repeatedly that the delayed and somewhat halting process of recovery was caused by the serious physical, nervous, and psychological exhaustion in which the patient arrived for treatment. Now that he is beginning to recover physically he is torturing himself with notions of inferiority ('exaggerated sensitivity to pain, lassitude, lack of will power') and with his anxiety about being fully fit for service very soon and able to put himself at your disposal again, Reichsführer.

Grawitz's assumption was that although Bach-Zelewski would quickly be fit again, he would nevertheless 'grapple for a considerable time with various manifestations of depression'.[79]

Von dem Bach-Zelewski, whom Daluege in 1933 judged to be 'loyal and honest, very impulsive, in many cases unrestrained', and suitable for promotion only if 'his impulsive nature is held in check in his work and by his own efforts',[80] was anxious above all not to admit to himself the seriousness of his illness and to appear to Himmler as unchanged and still healthy. In a letter to his Reichsführer he claimed to have been wrongly treated at first, and only after that to have suffered a physical and mental breakdown:

It is untrue that I entered the field hospital completely exhausted and battle-weary. As your old fighter, whose energy is returning more strongly each day, I will not accept such a distortion of the facts, despite assertions of this being made at my bedside all day long. [...] I after all submitted to the operation only because the doctors estimated that a full recovery would take four weeks and I wanted to be 100 per cent fit again for the major battles in the spring. Up to fourteen days after the operation I was in daily contact with Mogilew by radio and courier [...] Only when the cramps began, and my body and then my mind began to be poisoned because my intestines had been put out of action, was there anything like a breakdown. It was less the appalling physical pains that caused the collapse than my conviction of having had the wrong treatment and the threat of the disgrace of dying in a hospital bed at a time when every soldier has the right to a decent soldier's death. [...] Reichsführer, I will prove to you this year that your old warriors cannot be kept down even by such experiences.[81]

Himmler assured him immediately that he had 'never been in any doubt that you are still your old self'.[82] Seemingly somewhat restored, von dem Bach-Zelewski plunged again into the fray.

There was, however, to be no fundamental change to his maladies. Two years later a specialist characterized his condition as follows: 'Irregular bowel movements', 'Constipation and weak anal muscles', 'very sensitive rectal mucosa'. 'The Gruppenführer lacks the concentration required to strengthen the sphincter. Given that we are dealing with an already highly strung disposition such as the Gruppenführer's, I attribute this failure to the fact that in the field there is limited hygiene, such as bathing facilities and suchlike, and thus the abovementioned complaints are made worse.'[83]

Alongside Fahrenkamp, Himmler's old schoolfriend Karl Gebhardt, now professor of medicine and director of the Hohenlychen sanatorium in the Uckermark in Brandenburg, played a key role in Himmler's efforts to maintain the health of his men.[84] Himmler's mistress Hedwig Potthast was to give birth to their first child at Hohenlychen in 1942, and Karl Wolff, head of the Personal Staff, recovered there in 1943 from a break-down, Himmler giving Gebhardt a gift of a dinner service for twelve in gratitude.[85] The sanatorium was also open to prominent figures who were not members of the SS. Thus, Gebhardt performed a knee operation in June 1938 on Lieutenant-General Walter von Reichenau, who played a signifi-cant political role among the generals, and sent Himmler a detailed report of the operation when the work was done.[86] Gebhardt sent a stream of reports about the treatment of famous patients, including members of the higher echelons of the European nobility.[87] When he repaired the ruptured Achil-les tendon of Himmler's friend Darré in August 1938, he also let his old schoolfriend know about it.[88]

After the assassination attempt on Heydrich in 1942 Himmler sent Gebhardt to Prague. After even Gebhardt was unable to prevent Heydrich's death, Himmler thanked him 'for being such a brave comrade and good friend to our dear Heydrich in his last days and hours'.[89] When, in 1936, Himmler's father developed cancer Gebhardt had again been on hand with advice: he made discreet investigations into the history of the illness and advised against an operation. Himmler followed his counsel.[90]

Even in more trivial matters Himmler turned to Gebhardt for his opin-ion. In January 1938 he sent him an 'old remedy for tuberculosis that has been passed down several generations of a family I know': 'a pinch (1 gram) each of lungwort, liverwort, ribwort plantain, centaurium, coltsfoot, Ice-land moss, Irish moss, sweet flag, hibiscus, salad burnet, speedwell, rhubarb root, ground and mixed well into one old measure (c. a kilo) of honey. The honey must be warmed beforehand [. . .] If diarrhoea should set in, then stop taking for 2 days.' Gebhardt's answer was, however, a disappointment to Himmler: no remedial effect in the case of tuberculosis could be ex-pected, and in addition this tea mixture was already long familar from folk medicine.[91]

Himmler's intensive efforts to secure the physical well-being of his men stretched even to making suggestions about their diet. When, in 1942, Sturmbannführer Ernst Günther Schenk, Waffen-SS Nutrition Inspector, sent in a memorandum on the improvement of the troops' rations in the SS,

Himmler reacted with comments in a twenty-two-point list—a veritable explosion of ideas—which he passed on to Pohl: 'The attention of all units must be drawn most vigorously to the toasting of bread. In all circumstances, even in marshland, bread can be sliced, warmed, and toasted on an open fire as on a hunt, and in the form of rusks would be an easily digested diet for those with intestinal problems.' After the war, he continued, the SS would have to create its own sources of food, if only for use in the east and for specific types of food:

It is only the specific types of food that influence our species that we must provide for ourselves: fruit and in particular pomaceous fruit, nuts (limitless supplies, especially for the winter), mineral water from natural springs, fruit juices, oat flakes, and oil for cooking [. . .]. Exaggerated stockpiling inside the borders of the Reich, as practised by the church in the Middle Ages, must absolutely be avoided. It is, however, our task, by promoting hand-operated mills in some of our own bakeries and in manual bakeries in the areas where we live, to influence and determine the preparation of these foodstuffs.

All in all, he placed great emphasis on accustoming the SS man and his family 'to our natural food in national-political training centres, in barracks, officer-training colleges and team houses, and in Lebensborn homes', 'so that later the boy will never eat anything else'. 'Slowly, imperceptibly, and in a sensible manner', the 'consumption of meat' was to be 'restricted for future generations'. Himmler's wish was 'a steady growth into a better future after centuries of aberrations and false starts. Only when meat and sausages are replaced imperceptibly by equally tasty foods that satisfy the palate as well as the body can there be any hope of success. Moral sermons are of no use here. We know ourselves that only good, cheap mineral water and excellent fruit juices, as well as good cheap milk can displace alcohol.'

In peacetime he intended, furthermore, 'to design and order the provisioning of the entire SS and police and their families, first for five years and then for all time'. It might be possible also to consider setting up 'nutrition supervisors' in the SS units, though the possibility that some kind of soldiers' council or commissar might emerge from this institution, even if only in the distant future, was to be avoided.[92] Standard menus were, in addition, to be planned for the SS: 'These menus must contain hot meals, in the form of soup, jacket potatoes, and a cold side-dish, at least three times a week and five times in the winter. A good herbal tea must be provided every evening. [. . .] Boiled and salted potatoes are to be strictly avoided.'[93]

Himmler's solicitous strictness

Himmler carried on a lively correspondence with senior SS leaders, using it again and again to dispense praise, blame, advice, and criticism in professional and personal matters. To old comrades-in-arms the Reichsführer sent personally written letters of encouragement. Thus, in a letter of January 1943 he thanked Theodor Eicke, whose division was facing immediate further deployment on the eastern front, for the 'loyal wishes for this difficult new year [. . .] As far as you are concerned I have only one wish: stay well and uninjured, for the SS and I need you as a loyal, brave and resolute old soldier, so that if the going gets tough we can do everything the Führer and the Reich expect of us.' His concern turned out to be justified: a little more than five weeks later Eicke was dead. His plane was shot down during a reconnaissance flight.[94]

Himmler's former adjutant Ludolf von Alvensleben received an express letter from Himmler in November 1943, when he was promoted to SS-Gruppenführer and Lieutenant-General of the police. In it Himmler pronounced the 'firm expectation that in the Crimea you will be a pillar of faith, confidence, strong action, and will never yield. Take care that even the last SS soldier or member of the police always keeps calm and is there when vigorous action and fighting are required.' Himmler signed off using the formula: 'In sincere and long-standing solidarity, Faithfully yours.'[95] Other standard forms were: 'I shake your hand sincerely' or 'My greetings in sincerest friendship'.[96]

Himmler sent Waffen-SS Major-General and Brigadeführer Walter Krüger a personal letter when the latter was taking over command of a police division fighting on the eastern front. Its confidential nature was underlined by Himmler's request to 'leave it in Germany'. Himmler exhorted Krüger 'to supervise or set in motion a good many things that would usually be passed on simply as commands'. Krüger was to be guided always by the principle that war was 'the best teacher of war itself'. Himmler concluded with the request that Krüger 'be sustained by faith in our SS men, that means therefore by faith in the good blood we have here and faith in these inspiring hearts, capable of sacrifice. I require you to eliminate any trace of defeatism. Reports from Unterführer, leaders, company commanders, or commanders that their unit is not ready to attack are to be answered with a court martial ending in a death sentence. A squad is ready to attack until it has suffered 80 per cent losses, definitely not before then.'[97]

But Himmler was also not slow to lecture and criticize. Friedrich Karl von Eberstein, Himmler's Higher SS and Police Leader in Munich, was forced in October 1942 to put up with Himmler reminding him in clear terms of his duties. Himmler accused Eberstein of being too 'phlegmatic', for the latter had communicated a decision of Himmler's in a tricky personnel matter by letter to the treasurer of the NSDAP and not, as Himmler expected, personally and 'in a nice manner'. Himmler admonished him:

It is not the task of a Higher SS and Police Leader to rule from his desk. I can just as well put an official behind a desk. Similarly, I am not [. . .] satisfied with the work of the fire police and the police after the air raid on Munich. After air raids and bomb damage you must be on the move day and night until the last German lying under the rubble has been recovered. The recovery of people within 5 days is imperative. Imagine if your child had lain beneath the rubble. I must ask you to regard your work not as being a ministerial quill-and-desk job but rather, as in the time of struggle, as requiring you to be highly active and mobile, working alongside the people and the troops. That is what I want from my Higher SS and Police Leaders, who are of course my representatives.[98]

Emil Mazuw, the Higher SS and Police Leader for the Baltic Region, was also reproached in December 1944 for inadequate activity: 'If I had wanted to have the Higher SS and Police Leaders as offices for passing on complaints or as letter-writing centres I would have indicated this, and in place of an SS-Obergruppenführer and General I would have appointed an administrator and secretary. In future you will do your duty better. Apart from that you are a representative of the SS and not that of the local mayor or of the local party offices working against the SS. You are to take special note of this last point.'[99]

In August 1942 the SS Police Leader for Estonia, Hinrich Möller, was also accused of being phlegmatic and overweight. After a visit to Reval (Talinn), Himmler wrote to Möller that he expected him 'to be on duty 6 evenings a week out of 7 with the squad and the men [. . .] I regard it as unheard of that a man of 36 is so phlegmatic, fat, and complacent. It is in your interests to change this as quickly as possible.'[100]

When Erhard Kroeger, who was the leader from June to December 1942 of an Einsatzkommando in the Ukraine and after that in the SD Main Office, betrayed signs of being less than happy about being moved to the

Waffen-SS, Himmler wrote to him in no uncertain terms: 'This ability to obey without comment is a characteristic you have yet to acquire. Only then will you be a proper SS man and come up to what I have always wanted you to be. Be assured that at the proper time you will be placed where you can be fully effective. I wish you every success for the fight.'[101]

SS-Obergruppenführer Hermann Höfle, Higher SS and Police Leader and German commander-in-chief in Slovakia, received an irate letter from his Reichsführer on 14 January 1945. Himmler reproached Höfle with 'softness, dependence, and lack of self-reliance with regard to your colleagues and staff'. He went on:

I can only request you to be firm, to understand finally that you are the commander and your chief of staff as well as your Ia [1st General staff officer] are your colleagues. They are not there to be your brain. Remember the basic concept of obedience, according to which we were both brought up, even if people around you try to talk you round. If I had had any notion how much this command I entrusted to you and which you took up with such hesitation overstrains your psychological reserves I would never have moved you there, to spare you and me this distress. This is the last time I shall express the hope that things will change and that in 1945 you will avoid the errors of 1944 and no longer commit them.[102]

In March 1943 the head of the Race and Settlement Main Office, Otto Hofmann, was given to understand in unmistakable terms that, as a result of a series of events, Himmler considered that he was not performing adequately in his job. By contrast with others, Hofmann had apparently been spending too little time at his desk. Himmler concluded his letter with a serious, if not quite syntactically correct, admonition:

Gruppenführer Hofmann, to establish a Main Office on a sound footing requires ceaseless application, skill, and serious work that does not neglect even the smallest details, until these things have become second nature to your subordinates. It is my wish that you refrain from so much work-related travel and from being constantly out of the office in order to make appearances as a great commander and general. All in all I am obliged to say that as the weeks go by I like your Main Office less and less.[103]

In April 1943 Hofmann was replaced as head of the Race and Settlement Main Office. Himmler recorded in a note that he had formed the impression that 'Hofmann lacks the calm and serenity required of one who has to remain in the background with the Race and Settlement Main Office during the war'. He assured Hofmann, however, 'that I have in no way, either personally or professionally, lost my confidence in him and he still retains it completely.'[104]

Yet even in his new position as Higher SS and Police Leader for the South-West Hofmann brought upon himself the wrath of his Reichsführer. He had taken decisions in an area that Himmler regarded as exclusively his own: ideological training. Himmler rebuked him 'for starting a competitor to the SS *Guidance Booklets* in the form of army postal service letters.' The

discovery of this fact merely confirmed to me how right it was to relieve you of the responsibilities of head of the Race and Settlement Main Office. I have made a clear decision to remove the Indoctrination Office from the SS Race and Settlement Main Office. I consider it incompatible with the obedience expected of an SS man to circumvent an instruction, not its letter but, and this is even more serious, its spirit. Although you have no more influence in this matter I have felt obliged, in order to set you on the right path, to declare to you my clear and unambiguous opinion for the benefit of your future professional life.[105]

Hofmann tried to expunge this serious reproach by declaring his loyalty:

The accusation of disobedience that you have levelled at me hits me exceptionally hard, as neither in this case nor at any time have I intended to circumvent one of your instructions. I have always regarded you as the epitome of the man who, after the Führer, claims my reverence as well as my loyalty and obedience. This is my true attitude and so I would request you, Reichsführer, not to burden me with this serious reproach.[106]

Yet Himmler did not withdraw the accusation but rather, a year later, added a further, much more serious one to it, namely, that of cowardice. In a devastating letter in November 1944 he claimed that the SS and Security Police agencies 'seem to have fled in panic and in a cowardly manner' from Alsace (for which Hofmann, as Higher SS and Police Leader for the South-West, was responsible). And he added: 'To give you clear direction in this matter I wish to apprise you that I had a Security Police chief in Paris shot for similar things.'[107]

Himmler's criticism of Gerret Korsemann was similarly devastating. He relieved the Gruppenführer and police general in July 1943 of his post as deputy Higher SS and Police Leader for Russia Centre because he considered the accusation levelled at Korsemann of having been in too much of a hurry to retreat from the Caucasus as justified. Himmler summoned Korsemann and 'urgently' brought home to him the need 'to cleanse himself by the most committed effort from the charge attaching to him of lack of courage'. To this end, Himmler would, he said, move him to the SS division Leibstandarte, where as soon as possible he was to take over a company 'going into action'.[108] Himmler gave express instructions to the commander of the division that Korsemann, in the rank of a Waffen-SS Hauptsturmführer, was to be 'deployed on the front line. I forbid you to deploy him in a rearguard position [...] I have given Korsemann the opportunity to see action with the tank division "Leibstandarte Adolf Hitler" so that he can clear himself through this action of the accusation of lack of courage and weakness of nerve.'[109]

The Waffen-SS generals were also admonished and told off; remarkably, such letters nevertheless often end in a conciliatory manner, in spite of frequently vehement reproaches. In November 1942 Himmler wrote a positively exemplary warning letter to Theodor Eicke. Now leader of the SS Death's Head division, Eicke had once again sent an SS leader assigned to him back to Berlin, in this case Kleinheisterkamp, as the latter 'was ill and at the end of his tether'. 'Dear Eicke,' was Himmler's riposte, 'I cannot resist the impression that if anyone is ill and at the end of his tether it is you and not Kleinheisterkamp.' Himmler reproached Eicke with two instances of 'impossible behaviour': first of all that he had 'blatantly gone against my order', and secondly that, 'at the most difficult time', he

had taken away from the 3rd Death's Head regiment an able, experienced commander, respected by his men, simply because you do not get on with him [...] You cannot justify to your men what you did here. You have placed your headstrong ego in what are surely private differences of opinion above the well-being of your division. You may be in no doubt that by this you will not gain the affection of your men or an increase in the respect shown you.

After this accusation Himmler changed his tone. His next words are solicitous:

The only explanation I can find, as I am really not willing to accept that you are consciously annoying and disappointing me in this way, is that you are not yet recovered and your nerves are not at all as they should be. In my view you came out too soon and the pain your foot gives you naturally has an effect on your decisions. That is not right, however, and must change. Either one is in good health and takes all decisions calmly and in a fit state or one is not in a healthy state and is ill (by no fault of one's own, of course). In that case one must not occupy this position and make life difficult for others by one's bilious mood.

I now expect from you an impartial report, not based on Herr Eicke's idiosyncrasies, but a clear statement from my old comrade Eicke about how his health is. If it is not good—as I unfortunately assume—then come back here for four weeks and get properly better. If on the other hand you believe you are fit, then you cannot afford any further episode of this kind under any circumstances.

Himmler's closing words were: 'I have never doubted your personal loyalty for a single moment. What I want to eradicate is your irrational self-will and your irrational waywardness. [...] I am sorry this letter was necessary. Yours, Heinrich Himmler.'[110]

In July 1938 he reprimanded Sepp Dietrich, the leader of the Leibstandarte, in a similarly fatherly and gentle manner for having wilfully exceeded his authority. In response the Wehrmacht High Command had sent in a complaint. 'Dear Sepp,' Himmler admonished him, 'you know what we are facing in the weeks ahead and how much unnecessary bother all these arbitrary actions on the part of your subordinates cause me and, in the final analysis, cause you also; so please put a final stop to them.'[111]

When, in 1943, he got wind of the fact that in the Ministry for the Eastern Territories a comment of Dietrich's was being spread about to the effect that 'even' [sic] Dietrich 'no longer believes that we can defeat the Russians', he first of all made it clear in a letter to Dietrich that 'an opinion of yours concerning the combat strength of the Russians' must have been 'misunderstood', before telling him to 'contact Rosenberg' or write 'a short note to him along these lines'. Himmler added: 'I know your view of the war in Russia very well. We are well aware that it is not easy. At the same time, however, we are certain that we can and will defeat the Russians, and indeed in the foreseeable future. Sincere greetings and Heil Hitler, Your good old friend Heinrich Himmler.'[112]

In July 1943 Himmler asked the head of the SS Main Office, Berger, to have a talk with one of his most important Waffen-SS generals, Felix Steiner. Himmler had been annoyed by his exchange of telegrams with Finnish volunteers. 'I want to spare Berger', Himmler wrote, 'being spoken to by me personally. I think I am well known for having shown the greatest generosity towards the vanity sported by soldiers and in particular by the typical general.'

Himmler had been struck by the fact that, in his telegram, Steiner had used the formulation 'in the ranks of my troops'. 'In this instance Steiner should really have given pride of place to the Führer and, as befits an SS man and Obergruppenführer, he should have remained in the background.' Apart from that, Himmler went on to complain, 'I have no recollection of a greeting "Hail to you" being used in the SS. Since I have been a National Socialist SS man the greeting has been "Heil Hitler".' Furthermore, wrote Himmler to Berger, it was his wish that in future Steiner be addressed by his SS rank and not as general. In addition, he was to be so good as to desist from 'the backbiting tone that quite a few men in the 'Viking' division still feel free to use towards me as Reichsführer-SS in their conversations in the mess, etc.'.[113]

Only a month later Himmler wrote to Steiner directly, because the deployment of an SS-Oberscharführer on the staff of the 'Viking' division that he had ordered had been arbitrarily changed. Admittedly, he avoided putting the blame on Steiner himself, but rather expressed 'the expectation that you will find the guilty man on your staff and will, by means of an exemplary punishment, lend my orders the weight I must require [. . .]. I must also say here candidly that even in the messes of the Viking division it should be unheard of for SS leaders to discuss the actions of the Reichsführer in a tone of criticism that goes beyond the proper limits of mess discussions.' Since his warning the month before, therefore, there had clearly been no change. Himmler insisted that 'the last trace of this spirit in the leadership of the Germanic corps be extirpated completely and that orders from the Reichsführer-SS be carried out blindly, unconditionally, and without hesitation'.[114] After Steiner had assured him of his loyalty, Himmler let him know that as far as he was concerned the matter was closed. 'I have absolute confidence in you.'[115]

In a letter of March 1943 Himmler levelled serious accusations at Paul Hausser, the commanding general of the 2nd SS Tank Corps, but in the end went no further than a reprimand. On his own initiative Hausser had approached the supreme army command of the Wehrmacht to which his tank corps was subordinated and requested replacement personnel from among members of the Wehrmacht (in this case a Luftwaffe division assigned to an army formation). Himmler was critical:

You cannot expect me, as Reichsführer-SS and founder of the SS, with my own hand to reduce to rubble the foundation on which the successes of your tank corps were ultimately built, namely racial and human selection and education. The moment I make a move to integrate a division of the army or air force, lock, stock, and barrel, into my old divisions, we might as well give up. I doubt very much, dear Hausser, for all that I acknowledge your merits, if you can take that upon yourself. Even in the exigencies of war neither you nor your chief of staff can resort to actions that tie my hands as Reichsführer-SS.[116]

'Punishments should be few but just and severe'

If lectures and reprimands were not sufficient, Himmler took active steps to educate his men. Disciplinary transfers to the 'front line', alcohol bans, and treatment for addiction have already been discussed; SS leaders who, in Himmler's view, spent too much time hunting could in a similar fashion receive a 'hunting ban' from the Reichsführer.[117] Smoking bans were also issued.[118]

Himmler developed idiosyncratic methods of dealing with disputes among SS leaders. 'My procedure when two are in conflict', he told Obergruppenführer Arthur Phleps in May 1944, 'is always on principle to transfer both [...] Similarly, even if there has been no conflict, I never appoint the man who has hitherto been his subordinate as successor to his superior officer; for otherwise the door is opened wide to intrigue.'[119] In a concrete case, as he told the Gruppenführer in 1938, he had 'sent word to two Oberführer who were in an unresolved dispute with each other [...] that I would make my office, with a bottle of water and two glasses, available to them from eight in the morning to eight at night. I would assume that by evening they would have had a chance to discuss every last issue. In future I will do the same in every individual case.'[120]

This procedure had potential to be extended: in 1942 the SS *Guidance Booklets* contained a report, headed 'A Chance to Talk Things Through... The Reichsführer's Order Concerning Comradeship', about an order of Himmler's to make two SS leaders who had fallen out live together for six weeks in one room. The SS *Guidance Booklets* commented that this example showed that 'the Reichsführer-SS gives precise consideration to every disciplinary case, looks into the motives, and takes measures accordingly—and that he most certainly tries out "amusing" punishments if he is convinced that his aims will be achieved.'[121]

'Amusing' punishments were a true speciality of Himmler's, and a tendency to sadism is undeniably present in them. In October 1942 the Reichsführer issued an order to all Waffen-SS and police leaders, reminding them of their duty to pay detailed attention to their men's diet. 'Leaders who fail to obey this command shall experience personally what a negative effect poor nourishment has on the performance and morale of the troops, and shall learn at the same time how to do better. I shall therefore consign these leaders to the House of Poor Nourishment I have set up. They shall stay there long enough to gain first-hand experience of how bad it is for the men to be forced to eat poor food provided by their commanders.'

Himmler had personally planned in detail the 'House of Poor Nourishment', which was to be situated next to the SS catering school in Oranienburg. Inmates were to spend up to four weeks there, and were not allowed to leave the building. 'Three-quarters of the time those taking part in the disciplinary course at the House of Poor Nourishment will receive poor and insufficient food, while for the remaining quarter they will be given an exemplary diet for troops.' The 'poor nourishment' was to be produced on the following principles: 'No variety. Overcooked. Tinned food with no fresh vegetables. Badly prepared.' If he encountered 'particularly bad menus', Himmler went on, 'I reserve the right to serve the commander in question this menu for the duration of the punishment'.[122]

In August 1944 Rudolf Brandt informed Standartenführer Guntram Pflaum, whom Himmler had put in charge of pest control, about a new idea Himmler had had. After the war Himmler intended to set up a 'Fly and Gnat Room'. 'All SS leaders and police who are either uninterested in the nuisance created by flies and gnats or even dismiss it with a superior smile will find they will be taken into care there for some considerable time, during which they will have the opportunity to study the question of flies and gnats from a theoretical angle as well as to enjoy the attentions of the hundreds and thousands of flies and gnats in the room itself.' Even now, Brandt continued his exposition of Himmler's reflections, thought should be given to 'collecting the appropriate literature for both rooms. The culprits to be accommodated there were to study this literature in depth and to write long and detailed essays on it, for example "Flies as carriers of disease", "Why do we need insect screens?", and so on.' 'Fly and Gnat Rooms' were, according to Himmler's concept, to form part of a 'House of Correction', for which he occasionally set down further detailed instructions.[123]

Up to 1939 the SS punished its members exclusively according to formal disciplinary procedures, on the basis of the 'Disciplinary and Appeals Regulations', by means of reprimands or, in serious cases, exclusion or 'expulsion' of those concerned.[124] However, from 1937 onwards there is clear evidence that Himmler had been working towards creating a separate jurisdiction for SS and police, comparable to the military courts.[125] In October 1939 he received Hitler's approval for this, and from then on the

SS had its own courts, which could dispense a whole catalogue of punishments provided for in the military and civil codes, including capital punishment. As we shall see, Himmler was to make this penal system his special province.[126]

Willing executioners: three case studies

Himmler's idiosyncratic approach to discipline produced extraordinary successes precisely in the case of SS leaders whose career histories were seriously flawed. In his hands they became willing instruments of his policies. The cases presented here of Oskar Dirlewanger, Curt von Gottberg, and Odilo Globocnik, though extreme, are nevertheless perfect examples of Himmler's methods.

Born in 1895 and a commando during the First World War, Oskar Dirlewanger was by the end of it 'a mentally unstable, violent fanatic and alcoholic, who had the habit of erupting into violence under the influence of drugs'.[127] The fact that he had succeeded, even after the ceasefire, in fighting his way back from the front in Romania to Germany with his men became for him the defining experience. Henceforth he adopted an unrestrained mode of life, characterized by contempt for the laws and rules of civil society. A student from 1919, he fought in a number of Free Corps units. Yet again, whatever troops he was leading became known for their excessive violence. Disciplined in 1921 by the college of commerce in Mannheim for 'anti-Semitic incitement', and with several convictions for possession of firearms, he gained his doctorate in politics the same year. He had an unstable career, in the course of which he lost a number of posts on the grounds of embezzlement, though no charges were brought. Meanwhile he was active in radical right-wing organizations, and in 1922 had become a member of the NSDAP. Promoted to deputy director of the labour exchange in Heilbronn after the Nazi takeover of power, in 1934 he was sentenced to two years' imprisonment for indecent behaviour committed against a 14-year-old girl in his official car. When, after his release, he pressed for his case to be reopened, the Gestapo took him into protective custody for several months on the grounds of his 'disturbing the peace by malicious complaints'. After this he volunteered for service with the Condor legion in Spain, but his conviction again got him into serious difficulties there. Back in Germany he approached Himmler for 'permission in the event of mobilization to march with the SS'. Dirlewanger declared that he had actually been convicted 'as the result of personal and political motives': 'I admit that I have done wrong but I have never committed a crime.'[128]

Himmler hesitated in responding to Dirlewanger's request, as he wanted to await the outcome of the procedure for reopening the case.[129] But in Gottlob Berger Dirlewanger had found a strong ally whose influence was probably responsible for securing his final acquittal.[130] And now Himmler gave this man who was on his beam-ends a second chance: he took Dirlewanger into the SS, though in the meantime he had joined the Wehrmacht, and gave him the task of forming a special unit made up of convicted poachers. These men, later known as Sonderkommando Dirlewanger, were particularly known for their extraordinary brutality in combating partisans. First they were deployed in the General Government (German-occupied Polish territories not annexed by Germany)[131] and then in Byelorussia; and in 1944 they took part in the suppression of the Warsaw uprising, after which they were used to combat the Slovakian uprising.

Dirlewanger's leadership of the Sonderkommando was characterized by continued alcohol abuse, looting, sadistic atrocities, rape, and murder—and his mentor Berger tolerated this behaviour, as did Himmler, who so urgently needed men such as the Sonderkommando Dirlewanger in his fight against 'subhumanity'. It was important to the Reichsführer, however, that the detachments within the Sonderkommando did not belong to the Waffen-SS, but merely served it.[132] It was not until 1945 that Dirlewanger succeeded in incorporating his unit, which accepted criminals of every hue and so was growing unstoppably, into the Waffen-SS as the 36th Grenadier Division.

Curt von Gottberg, born in 1896, was discharged in 1919 as a lieutenant after five years' military service. At first he joined the Ehrhardt brigade, and with it took part in the failed Hitler putsch of 1923.[133] He tried various lines of work; in 1932, having meanwhile become a property developer in East Prussia, he was involved in a financial scandal leading to a one-year ban on holding office in the NSDAP. In spite of this, in October 1933 Himmler entrusted to him the leadership of the political action squad in Ellwangen, in other words, of an armed SS unit.[134] Himmler was, however, to relieve him of this task because he 'behaved like a common freebooter'.[135]

Like so many SS leaders, von Gottberg had a massive alcohol problem. At the beginning of 1936 he lost a foot in a serious car accident for which he was to blame.[136] Though he insisted that he had drunk no more than two glasses of beer and a corn schnapps,[137] he was forced, after Himmler's intervention, to make a declaration on his word of honour (to Jeckeln, of all people, the leader of the Oberabschnitt responsible for him) 'that for three years beginning from today I shall desist from the consumption of alcohol in any form'.[138]

A vigorous man, von Gottberg restored his mobility to an astonishing extent with the help of an artificial leg. On 1 July 1937 he took on a new job as head of the Settlement Office within the Race and Settlement Main Office. In 1938, however, while out riding he suffered a serious heart attack, apparently the result of damage to the heart muscle that had occurred while he was ill. Von Gottberg ignored the warning signals. The supposed heart attack was not diagnosed until February 1939, when, on Himmler's instructions, von Gottberg was forced to report to Dr Fahrenkamp for a through examination. The report Fahrenkamp wrote for Himmler depicts an old warrior distinctly the worse for wear. In addition to the battered heart and amputated foot, the doctor noted old war wounds (bullet lodged in the stomach, bullet wound to the thigh, stab wound in the right upper arm). At the age of 27 von Gottberg had also accidentally lost two fingers while working a threshing machine.

Fahrenkamp summed up the result of his diagnosis as follows: 'Up to now he has made extraordinary demands on his body and has expended much energy disregarding accidents, war injuries, and illnesses.' Von Gottberg was, he reported, almost 'a textbook example of what even a seriously impaired body can do if the mind is strong'. Now he was in a psychological state in which medical help of the normally recognized kind would be of no use. 'Medical treatment in the usual sense is not appropriate for this patient. There are people a doctor cannot help. [. . .] As far as his state of mind in general is concerned, so many unresolved issues have accumulated that mental relief is more important than treatment of the body. For this patient a frank discussion with his boss would provide psychological relief.' 'Medical considerations', therefore prompted him, Fahrenkamp, to refer this request to Himmler.

Whether Himmler granted this 'psychological relief' in the following months cannot be established from the files. At the end of 1939 von Gottberg suffered another heavy blow: only six months after Himmler had appointed him acting head of the Land Office in Prague, thereby placing responsibility for settlement policy in the Protectorate in his hands, Günther Pancke, head of the Race and Settlement Main Office, ordered him to report sick immediately and to give up all his posts.[139] Pancke's explanation for this was that von Gottberg had claimed that Walter Darré, Agriculture Minister and, up to 1938, head of the Race and Settlement Main Office, was 'of Jewish extraction'; in addition, 'while in a fairly drunken state' he had made megalomaniacal statements in front of quite a large number of people', treated his colleagues 'in a humiliating fashion', and had deliberately misinformed him, Pancke. Pancke threatened KZ detention if von Gottberg continued spreading rumours. In fact the reasons for von Gottberg's demotion were more complicated: he had been involved in a dubious financial affair and was possibly also the victim of an intrigue initiated by Darré.[140]

Himmler gave instructions that, until the accusations were finally cleared up, von Gottberg was to be deployed as steward of an estate in the east and 'strictly to avoid any political involvement'.[141] Four months later he felt compelled to call von Gottberg, who was still in the Protectorate, to order after his two sons had caused a roof to catch fire: 'I do not believe that the unfortunate action of your two unsupervised children has increased respect for Germany or for the SS in the Protectorate. Six- to eight-year-olds should not be allowed to play with matches.'[142]

But in July 1940 Himmler rehabilitated von Gottberg and moved him to the SS Main Office, where, in October, the latter took over the recruitment department. At the close of the investigation the charges against him were declared to be unfounded and it was Pancke who received a sharp reprimand from Himmler.[143] In November 1942 von Gottberg became SS and Police Leader in White Ruthenia and, as we shall see, made rapid career progress in the war against the partisans as head of the 'Gottberg combat group'.

Von Gottberg is an almost perfect example of an SS leader whose dependence on Himmler was virtually total and existential. A physical wreck, alcohol-dependent, and burdened with a variety of transgressions and accusations, he developed an immensely strong need to prove himself and achieve psychological release, which only Himmler could provide. And Himmler bent von Gottberg to his will, through criticism and demotion, by overlooking misdemeanours and, on a number of occasions, by giving him the chance to redeem himself.

When, in November 1939, a retired lieutenant-colonel named Michner complained to the Führer that the former Gauleiter of Vienna, Odilo

Globocnik, had, without warning, broken off his engagement to Michner's daughter, Friedrich Rainer, the Gauleiter of Salzburg, rushed to the defence of his old comrade-in-arms. Rainer appealed for leniency to be shown towards Globocnik on the grounds of the latter's varied career in the service of the party and the movement. He claimed it was necessary to bear in mind that

from the start of the struggle in the Ostmark this man has been continuously in the most prominent and dangerous position, [...] endured over a year's detention with a number of interruptions during the time of struggle, for whole periods was absolutely penniless and survived only through handouts from good comrades, endured illnesses as a result of overexertion, and then after the liberation of the Ostmark he plunged without a break into preparations for the referendum and re-establishment of the party; then, again without a break, he took over the extremely difficult Gau of Vienna; then, when threatened with dismissal, he fought desperately for his achievements to be acknowledged and to defend his personal honour, while also weighed down by the constant anguish of a private concern, with the Michner family insisting ever more urgently on the engagement and on his keeping his word.[144]

In fact Globocnik had been removed from office as Gauleiter of Vienna in January 1939 because of his self-willed style of leadership; on top of that, during this time a financial audit by the punctilious Reich Treasurer of the NSDAP, Franz Xaver Schwarz, prompted by a number of murky financial deals, was hanging over him. This audit was not concluded until the spring of 1941, with Schwarz levelling massive criticism at Globocnik for his actions at the time in question.[145] If Himmler had not shielded Globocnik, Schwarz would hardly have been so obliging. Himmler, who in spite of this affair had appointed Globocnik SS and Police Leader in Lublin in November 1939, wrote to Schwarz that Globocnik would have to admit 'quite candidly' that 'in this financial matter I have behaved foolishly and in the revolutionary period I behaved thoughtlessly'. Though his behaviour was not 'excusable', 'I am convinced that Globocnik has in no instance behaved in a way that was not decent'.[146]

Meanwhile, Globocnik was highly active in the district of Lublin.[147] The Lublin auxiliary unit (*Selbstschutz*) subordinate to him, the leadership of which was assumed in spring 1940 by the former West Prussian Selbstschutz leader Ludolf von Alvensleben, committed such acts of cruelty in the course of the so-called AB Action, the systematic murder of members of the Polish elites, that even the Governor-General Hans Frank spoke of the 'band of murderers of the SS and Police Leader for Lublin'.[148]

In April 1941—the Viennese audit had just been completed—Globocnik approached Himmler about a personal matter: he had a new girlfriend, he joyfully told his Reichsführer (his engagement from the Vienna period had in the meantime finally been broken off), and in July he asked Himmler for permission to get engaged. Himmler reminded him gently of the prescribed marriage application procedure and said he 'confidently' hoped he would soon be able to give permission.[149] In August 1941 Himmler helped Globocnik by forwarding him the sum of 8,000 Reich marks so that the latter could settle the 'Michner matter'—clearly he had incurred debts with his former prospective father-in-law. Globocnik thanked Himmler for the non-repayable 'assistance', and assured him: 'I shall do all I can to deserve your support, Reichsführer.'[150]

And Globocnik was to keep his word. In the following months he became the driving force in the 'Final Solution' in the General Government. Since the end of 1939 he had already set up camps on a large scale for Jewish forced labour in Lublin. The major raids he organized to seize Jewish workers led, however, to considerable economic problems and brought him into conflict with the civil administration.[151]

In October 1941 he appears on his own initiative to have obtained Himmler's permission to build an extermination camp in the Lublin district to murder the Jewish civilian population that could not be deployed as forced labour. As a result of these preparations he was charged by Himmler with implementing Aktion Reinhardt, the systematic murder of the Jews in the General Government. In July 1941 Himmler also appointed Globocnik to set up the SS and police bases in the new eastern territories. We shall return to look in detail at all these measures taken by Globocnik; our focus here is the personality of this mass murderer and his personal relationship with Himmler.[152]

In August 1942, at the height of Aktion Reinhardt, Globocnik once more turned to Himmler concerning a private matter: an anonymous denunciation had been made about his fiancée. In view of the concerns that Himmler had already expressed about his engagement, Globocnik now asked him whether he should break it off. Himmler, who had received a negative report about the behaviour of Globocnik's fiancée in a pub, said he should, and Globocnik duly obeyed.[153]

It is clear from an appraisal of Globocnik from May 1943 that his superiors recognized that his hyperactivism was problematic, but tolerated it in the interests of 'the cause':

A full-blooded character with a typical mixture of positive and negative sides. Careless about externals, fanatically committed to the task in hand, engaged in it up to the hilt without concern for his health or public acknowledgment. One of the best and most vigorous pioneers in the General Government, responsible, courageous, a man of action. His daredevilry often causes him to overstep the boundaries, but not from personal ambition but for the sake of the cause. His achievements definitely speak in his favour.

However, there was a note of warning: 'It is important for SS-Gruf. Globocnik to get married soon in order to counteract the restless, pioneering life he is leading, and which is getting him down, with the calming influence of a wife and a home. This would undoubtedly help SS-Gruf. Globocnik to conserve his energies in order to prepare him for the major tasks which he is undoubtedly capable of carrying out.'[154]

In the summer of 1943 Himmler decided to recall Globocnik from Lublin because of his repeated clashes with the civilian administration.[155] In August 1944 Globocnik, who in the meantime had become Higher SS and Police Leader in the Adriatic coastal region, where he was not only ruthlessly pursuing partisans but also energetically organizing Jewish deportations, once again approached the Reichsführer-SS concerning an affair of the heart. He believed, so he informed Himmler, he had 'found the girl whom you, Reichsführer, would give me permission to marry'. Himmler agreed in principle to become Globocnik's best man. When the marriage, which was arranged by Globocnik's crony Friedrich Rainer, took place in August 1944, Himmler was unable to attend because of a prior engagement but sent the Globocniks a gift of a twelve-piece 'dinner and tea service'.[156]

It will have become apparent that Globocnik was entirely dependent on Himmler and showed him a positively doglike devotion. This total subordination manifested itself not only in the fact that he permitted the Reichsführer-SS to make decisions concerning his private life, but above all in his attempt to prove to Himmler that he was more or less permanently ready for action. Yet his exceptional commitment, impulsive and ruthless style of leadership, as well as his consequent inability to carry on a private life that conformed to SS requirements inevitably kept getting him into difficulties, and only one person was able to get him out of them: Reichsführer Himmler.

13

The SS Family

The SS is a National Socialist order of soldiers of Nordic race and a community of their clans bound together by oath. [...] Fiancées and wives, as well as their husbands, also belong, according to our laws, to this community, this order. [...] Let us be very clear about this: it would make no sense to collect together good blood from the whole of Germany and establish it here with a serious purpose, while at the same time allowing it through marriage to flow into families at will. Rather, what we want for Germany is a ruling class destined to last for centuries and the product of repeated selection, a new aristocracy continuously renewed from the best of the sons and daughters of our nation, a nobility that never ages, stretching back into distant epochs in its traditions, where these are valuable, and representing eternal youth for our nation.[1]

This exposition by Himmler, dating from 1937, makes it plain that, from the point of view of its Reichsführer, the SS had moved a long way from the idea of a purely male league. Instead, it was the 'clan' and its 'nurture' that were becoming ever more prominent.

Himmler had presented these ideas to Hitler as early as 1 November 1935 and noted his 'complete agreement and approval'. Himmler had gone into the details of his plans: 'half or $\frac{2}{3}$ of all new admissions should be sons of SS families, in order to sift out imperfect material, and at least $\frac{1}{3}$ must come from non-SS families, so that good blood of those outside the SS and destined to lead others should not be left untapped in the nation.' He had made sure he got precise confirmation from Hitler of every word of the progammatic formulation that the SS was 'an order of soldiers of Nordic race and a community of their clans bound together by oath'—a typical procedure of Himmler's to back up his decisions that makes clear how much he had built his own position and that of the SS on absolute loyalty to the 'Führer'.[2]

The SS, as Himmler stated on another occasion, was 'nation, tribe, clan, community', an 'order of knights that no one who, by virtue of his blood, has been accepted into can ever leave; he belongs to it body and soul as long as his earthly life shall last'.[3] Wives of SS men, Himmler explained in 1943 at a conference of naval commanders, 'also belong to this SS order, both during their husbands' lifetime and after their husbands' death. Wives and widows of SS men will never be excluded. After one year they become members of the SS and after ten years their children also become members, and they enjoy all the protection and care that we offer our clan.'[4]

It goes without saying that the SS remained first and foremost a male organization.[5] Nevertheless, the distinction Himmler drew between the SS and the typical purely male league (his warning of 1937 against a too pronounced 'masculinization of the Nazi movement', which would undoubtedly lead to homosexuality, should be borne in mind) resulted in the wives of SS members participating, at least peripherally, in the SS world: they were not only congratulated and sent a gift on the birth of their third child by the Reichsführer himself, but were also exposed to his solicitude and surveillance in a wide variety of ways.[6]

Approval of marriages

As leader of the 'clan order' of the Schutzstaffel, Himmler set great store by the 'correct' choice of a wife, by which was meant someone who satisfied his 'racial' criteria. This notion can be traced back to a very early stage in his plans. He had already established the basis for turning it into reality by issuing the Engagement and Marriage Order of 31 December 1931.

In 1934–5 the process for gaining approval for marriages was formalized. SS members who wished to marry had to produce family trees for themselves and their fiancées stretching back to 1800 and complete a questionnaire and a handwritten curriculum vitae, which they submitted at first to the Race Office and from 1935 onwards to the Clan Office of the Race and Settlement Main Office. In addition, they had to provide statements from two sponsors, full-length photographs showing 'the applicant and his future bride standing side by side', as well as pictures of the families of both partners. Both had to be examined by an SS doctor, who then completed a questionnaire on their hereditary health and on the results of the medical.[7]

The process was protracted and expensive. The very time the procedure took made it almost impossible for engagements to be dependent on obtaining approval. Even though Himmler took exception to it, in many

cases applications were received from SS men who had already got engaged.[8] If in the course of the approval process the bride-to-be turned out
not to conform to SS requirements—if, in other words, she was racially
'unsuitable', had a hereditary illness, or was infertile—and if the applicant
refused to terminate the relationship, he was obliged to leave the SS. In
doubtful cases 'leave to marry' was granted on the couple's 'own responsibility', which meant that the family was excluded from the 'SS clan community', which was to be catalogued in a special 'SS clan book'. This
differential treatment of SS members with a view to creating a 'new
aristocracy' had, however, a fundamental shortcoming: Himmler could
never bring himself to set down in detail how the clan book was to be
established.[9] In the end the remodelling of the male order into a 'clan
community' remained purely rhetorical, for no systematic biological 'selection' took place.

Significantly, the Marriage Order came to be repeatedly disregarded, so
that Himmler was continually obliged, on threat of punishment, to remind
his men that it was still in force.[10] In March 1936 he complained of many
instances of SS members 'applying to get engaged and married only when
the bride-to-be was eight or nine months pregnant'.[11] Approvals were in
general granted in a relatively relaxed way. In April 1935 the Reichsführer
had already told his office heads that the 'criteria for approving brides-to-be
of SS men cannot yet be very strict, as we have as yet hardly made any
progress towards instructing people about what we want and what we don't
want'. At any rate, long-standing relationships, where there might already
be children, were to be respected.[12]

In July 1935 Himmler extended the existing racial criteria by adding the
provision that all full-time SS leaders, sub-leaders, and team members under
25 could marry only if they were able to show evidence of being in a
position to support their future family (SS pay on its own did not enable
them to do so).[13] If a young SS man had already fathered a child, Himmler
allowed the marriage if his relatives undertook to allow the bride-to-be 'to
stay in their home and to provide for her'.[14] In August 1935 he demanded
that prospective wives should have taken a course in motherhood.[15] In the
autumn he instructed that all SS members submitting applications for
marriages to be approved must as a first step have obtained the permission
of their superior officer.[16] In 1937 he required that fiancées of SS men
should obtain the Reich Sport Badge.[17]

On principle Himmler had the final word on particular requests: all marriage applications from SS leaders, all refusals, and all requests to marry women who were not German nationals had to be referred to him.[18] During the war he ruled that he wanted to see all applications involving marriage to ethnic Germans who had formerly had Polish nationality,[19] to those belonging to 'Germanic' nations,[20] and to women of 'alien ethnic background'.[21]

This was the theory. In practice the Clan Office was simply incapable of meeting the heavy demands of this procedure. The Race and Settlement Main Office complained repeatedly about considerable 'backlogs' in processing requests. As early as 1936 Himmler was forced by lack of staff in the Clan Office to suspend until further notice the requirement for SS applicants to produce their family tree and to disregard marriage requests.[22] In May 1937 20,000 marriage applications were already awaiting processing.[23]

Himmler had no alternative but to relax the strict rules in the case of long-standing SS members, who if necessary had to obtain permission to marry after the event.[24] In June 1937 he gave the instruction that future infringements of the Marriage Order were not to be punished.[25] At that point at least 308 SS members had been excluded in the first six months of 1937 alone for this very reason.[26] At the end of 1940 he deferred the decision on how to punish infringements of the Marriage Order until the end of the war. In line with this instruction, during the following years no steps were taken against SS men for ignoring the order.[27] Himmler even went as far as to allow former SS members who had been excluded for this reason to be received back into the SS in certain circumstances.[28]

Regardless of the fact that the approval process could not be implemented in the rigorous manner desired, Himmler repeatedly intervened in an attempt to perfect it. On 18 May 1937 he issued the following directive: 'My wish is that SS members will found racially superior and healthy German families. For that reason the highest standards must be demanded of prospective wives with regard to appearance, health, and hereditary soundness.' The required gynaecological examination was to take the following form:

Be thorough but treat women sensitively! The ability to bear children should be assessed with reference to general appearance, the external measurement of the pelvis, and above all a tactfully conducted but nevertheless searching medical history (previous gynaecological illnesses or haemorrhages, discharges, menstruation, inflammations, abortions, etc.). There is reason to conduct an internal examination—which in some

circumstances need only be carried out rectally—only if the medical history or findings are equivocal. If the external pelvic measurements give rise to doubts, the internal
measurement can, if necessary, be carried out gently and precisely by means of
an X-ray.[29]

In August 1937, in a perplexing instruction, he encouraged full-time SS
leaders to marry young: 'I require full-time SS leaders to marry early.' He
went on, however, in the next sentence to say that on principle people in
this group would not be allowed to marry before the age of 25. Aspiration
and reality—in this case the relatively modest financial circumstances of SS
members—diverged dramatically.[30] In April 1938 Himmler came up with a
further suggestion: he asked the Race and Settlement Main Office to
consider 'if the medical questionnaire for prospective wives of SS men
could not have the questions added: Does the person in question have
prominent cheekbones? Has she a Mongolian eyelid crease?'[31]

Ill 16. As the supreme guardian of the 'clan order' of the SS Himmler made
efforts to incorporate wives into the 'SS family'. There was no strict separation
of private and professional life for Himmler or for his men. On this SS wedding
photo Himmler is seen on the right next to the bride. On the left is the head of
the Race and Settlement Main Office, Walther Darré, and behind him the Chief
of Himmler's Personal Staff, Karl Wolff.

During the war the procedure for approving marriages was further simplified. On 1 September 1939 Himmler ordered that, in the event of mobilization, it should be shortened in such a way that approval could be sent out from the Race and Settlement Main Office 'within a few hours'.[32] In January 1940 he directed that the documents normally required on submission of the request could also be sent in after the war and the 'marriage provisionally approved'.[33]

'At the start of the war,' he confided later to the Higher SS and Police Chief for the Elbe, Obergruppenführer Udo von Woyrsch, in March 1943,

I had to confront the huge question: should I give very strong backing to the men's willingness to marry and make it possible, without being in a position in wartime, where training for battle claims most of one's attention, to give the men adequate instruction about racial laws, life experience, and all the things necessary to make a successful union of two biologically well-matched people? Or should I stick to very strict selection by refusing a certain number of requests to marry? If I had done the latter I would have put an enormous brake on the willingness to marry precisely of young soldiers at the front. I therefore decided to limit the formalities, give a powerful boost to marriage, and to accept the mistakes that are made by individual SS men in wartime to a much greater extent than in peacetime.

The most important thing, Himmler continued, 'that I can and will achieve is to ensure as far as possible that every SS man who dies in the war has a child'. If the number of children became 'larger in total, I will accept what from a breeding point of view might be called poor results, which always do occur in the wider population'. Precisely because it was wartime, he said, he worked on the principle: 'Better to have a child of any kind than no child at all.'[34]

A few months later he reiterated this position when the head of the Marriage Office, SS-Brigadeführer Otto Heider, suggested that, in view of the large number of marriage applications that did not meet the strict racial demands of the SS, an attempt should be made 'to influence SS men's choice of partner and by this means to achieve an element of "breeding"'. Himmler replied that Heider should be in no doubt that he 'was fully aware of these matters'. It would be 'one of our most important peacetime tasks to instruct and direct all young SS men so that they choose a biologically appropriate future wife and mother of their children. [...] But during the war this was impossible.' The Reichsführer considered it more important, the reply said, 'for SS men simply to reproduce than for the Reichsführer to forbid them to marry hastily and thereby prevent children from being born'.[35]

In 1941 the Clan Office stated that since 1931, when the Marriage Order was issued, a total of more than 40,000 'provisional decisions' had been made, of which the office had been able subsequently to finalize only about 1 per cent because of the volume of work.[36] This situation never fundamentally changed: in fact, in the first six months of 1942 there were an additional 5,590 'provisionally' processed applications. In January 1942 the Clan Office made 522 decisions: eighteen approvals, nine rejections, forty-three cases of 'leave given on the applicant's own responsibility'; 452 decisions were merely 'provisional'.[37] Meanwhile, in the autumn of 1941 Himmler's assiduity was shown by his requirement that the medical questionnaire include the 'shape of the legs' under the three headings of 'straight, bow legs, knock knees', and subheadings 'slim, medium, and fat'.[38]

Himmler examines and decides

Whenever Himmler dealt personally with requests to marry he did not confine himself simply to rejecting or approving the application. Rather, he used the opportunity to intervene in a sustained and detailed way in the personal affairs of his men and their partners. His reactions and comments are revealing about his attitude to the opposite sex, his position regarding sexuality—and, last but not least, about the state of his own marriage.

In August 1940 Himmler was sent the marriage request of an SS man who wished to marry a Czech woman, who had been designated 'of good race' by the race inspectors. Himmler viewed the matter as a question of principle, in other words, from a racist perspective. As he wrote to the Higher SS and Police Leader von dem Bach-Zelewski, from a 'purely national point of view such a marriage should of course be rejected', but on the other hand, 'from a racial perspective the SS man' had made 'absolutely the right choice, for it would be good to remove this woman of good race from the Czech nation and incorporate her as a mother of Nordic blood into the German nation'. To achieve this, the couple should move to Reich territory and not return for the foreseeable future to the bride's home town.[39] He would make a final decision on the case at the end of the war.[40]

When approving requests to marry women from 'alien' or slightly dubious 'ethnic German' backgrounds, Himmler frequently stipulated that the couple should move away from territories that were occupied, annexed, or had a politically problematic ethnic mix to the so-called Old Reich territory.[41] His conditions could be much more stringent, however. Rottenführer G., a member of the guard unit at Dachau KZ, asked for permission in 1942 to marry Lucie B., the mother of his three children. Both were natives of the Warthegau. Himmler withheld permission for the foreseeable future, as the woman 'is not in a position to bring up G.'s children as Germans. G. has only himself to blame for this refusal, as he failed to teach B., whose father is German and mother is Polish, to master the German language and use it all the time.'

Himmler, however, held out hope for the marriage, if Frau B. and her children submitted to a programme of Germanization, which Himmler set down in detail: the children were to be transferred immediately by the Race and Settlement Main Office to a 'good German children's home', where the 'purely German and other aspects of their upbringing' were to be monitored. 'An SS leader from the Race and Settlement Main Office near the children's home is to be given personal responsibility for checking on and visiting the children. He should take a kind interest in them, as would an uncle with his nephews and nieces. The mother, Frau B., if she really wants to marry the father of her children, is to be sent for a year to a mothers' school run by the NS Women's Organization (*Frauenschaft*).' She would not be allowed to marry G., Himmler continued, until she had been given a positive assessment there: 'My decision should be communicated to G. by his commanding officer personally in a long, very positive, and kind conversation.'[42]

By contrast, Obersturmführer Adalbert K., a member of the Death's Head division, was transferred 'to the east immediately' in 1943 on Himmler's orders for having submitted a request to marry 'a girl who was admittedly good-looking' but who came from a strongly nationalist Czech family.[43] In this case Himmler decided clearly in favour of the 'national point of view'. Even in the case of Hauptsturmführer Dieter Wisliceny, who had played a decisive role in organizing the deportations of the Slovakian, Greek, and Hungarian Jews, the Reichsführer took the view that, given that the prospective bride regarded herself as an 'ethnic Hungarian', though 'of good race', the most important factor was whether she had the right 'attitude to Germany'.[44]

Himmler was indignant when couples wishing to marry did not submit their applications until the bride was about to give birth. Such behaviour,

Himmler informed an applicant in February 1943, was 'reckless and un-chivalrous (*unritterlich*)', and he requested him, he said, 'to make up for his past recklessness by conducting his marriage in a decent and chivalrous manner'.[45] An Oberscharführer who had made a girl pregnant while aware that her hereditary health was compromised and had then submitted a request to marry was dismissed by Himmler from the SS.[46]

Where the bride lacked 'reproductive capability', Himmler invariably intervened in both word and deed. Thus, Frau F. received the following communication in July 1941 from the Personal Staff of the Reichsführer-SS: 'As the results of examinations so far indicate that in your case we must anticipate a lack of reproductive capability, before making a final decision the Reichsführer-SS has ordered that you be sent to Prof. Dr. Clauberg for hormone treatment.' The SS was to bear the costs.[47] When the treatment proved successful, Himmler approved the marriage.[48]

On numerous occasions Himmler's guiding principle was: first children, then marriage. 'Fate itself' should decide, as he put it.[49] He seems to have enjoyed insisting on this principle when the potential father came from the so-called more exclusive social circles. One example is the case of SS-man Adrian Count A., a member of the propaganda squad—in Himmler's view, 'rather an odd character and his fiancée seems even odder'. Himmler came to the decision: 'At his age, for the SS to approve a marriage makes sense only if the wife has a reasonable prospect of having children. In the case of this woman that seems extremely doubtful.' Accordingly there was 'only one possibility, namely that the Count should take steps before the mar-riage. If they are successful, I shall be more than willing to approve the marriage. This method, tried and tested in countless German peasant villages, might bring success even in such an elevated family as the Count's.'[50]

Himmler made a similar judgement in 1942 in the case of Franz Alfred Six, head of an office in the Reich Security Main Office. He requested that Six should be informed in Himmler's name 'that he could give him leave to marry only when it is clear that his fiancée is expecting a child. The Reichsführer-SS wishes this personal discussion to be conducted in a very kind manner and for it to be made clear to SS-Hauptsturmführer Six that his fiancée, as he is aware, had syphilis in 1928 and a marriage without children would be pointless for him.'[51]

If Himmler considered that an applicant had chosen a very inappropriate bride, that man was liable to face serious repercussions. On 27 September

1942 he asked the chief of the SS Leadership Main Office, Hans Jüttner, to summon SS-Hauptscharführer Konrad H. and tell him 'that as far as his choice of bride, Fräulein Emma B.—this painted Czech girl—is concerned, I think he has taken leave of his senses. By making this choice H. has shown that he was clearly responsible for his two divorces, one as the guilty party and the other as jointly guilty. But he has also shown that he has not the remotest understanding of the principles of the SS.' In addition, Himmler called on Jüttner to see to it 'that in order to cool his passion Herr H. is moved to the healthy air of the front'.[52]

On 17 June 1943 Himmler wrote to Ernst Kaltenbrunner, asking him to inform SS-Sturmbannführer Wilhelm B., an official of the Alsace Gestapo, that Himmler was refusing his request to marry (the 38-year-old wished to marry Frau Z., who was considerably older). The applicant was, in addition, to be informed of the following:

I am abiding by my refusal, as I consider your marriage as a 38-year-old German man to a 50-year-old woman to be as irresponsible as your saying you refuse to marry again because you have suffered a disappointment. [. . .] You have not yet served at the front and therefore, like everyone who is given that opportunity, you must see to it that the sacrifice of many hundreds of thousands of lives at the front was not in vain and that the gaps they left in the nation are filled in future by children.

Immediately after this communication B. was to be 'transferred to the territory where the most difficult anti-partisan fighting was going on and to stay there for two years until he grows up or until his injuries land him in hospital'.[53]

Himmler could also show kindness. In individual cases, for example if petitioned by the bride-to-be, he could actually be persuaded to review his previous marriage prohibition.[54] In another case Himmler discovered that the fiancée of an SS-Sturmführer had been unfaithful. He imposed a year's 'self-examination' on her, during which a child was to be conceived; after that, he said, he would be prepared to approve the marriage.[55]

Himmler's counsels or requirements, as has been indicated, often affected the most private areas of a marriage. He sent a message to one bride-to-be that, although leave to marry would be granted, she was to be subjected to an examination by the SS doctor, Brustmann, because of her 'excess weight', as this might be 'attributable to a malfunctioning of the ductless glands'.[56] An Untersturmführer whose marriage he approved was nevertheless informed:

'In the view of the Reichsführer-SS, B.'s bride, who seems to be a painted doll, is not suitable for an SS man.'[57] Obersturmführer Werner K. was in turn told that 'his fiancée should not paint herself in that way. It is not the done thing in the SS.'[58] Gunner Richard A., on the other hand, was to 'suggest to his fiancée that she would [...] look more beautiful if she lowered her eyebrows'.[59]

On this evidence, women's use of cosmetics was a difficult subject. Himmler was not prepared to approve the marriage of SS man B. until the bride was pregnant, as in spite of a four-year engagement B. had not managed to wean her off 'make-up and dressing up'.[60] Rottenführer Z., however, was advised 'to father no more children after the child his fiancée is expecting at the moment. I believe this solution to be the best as otherwise both run the risk of marrying healthy partners and then, despite this, not having healthy children because of their own impairment.'[61] Himmler gave two people who wished to marry, but who were both confirmed as having a serious hereditary 'impairment', the advice to marry but to 'have themselves sterilized at the same time'.[62]

Even in the case of racial examinations Himmler reserved the right to adjust the results. In the case of a girl who, when examined, was designated as an 'uneven cross-breed', with western and eastern Baltic racial elements, mixed with some Dinaric ones, Himmler noted on reading through the documents: 'This girl is 1.68 metres tall, which in a woman absolutely indicates Nordic blood. The skin is pinkish-white, which is not strong evidence of western Baltic, eastern Baltic, or Dinaric racial origin. The head is of medium width and oval and there are no prominent cheekbones. The occiput is moderate and the colour of the eyes greenish.'[63]

On another occasion he reached the verdict that 'Frl. X.'s facial features are typically Slav', and recommended the examiner, one Oberführer Berndt,

to take a course in racial theory. I assume that his medical appraisal of 16. 2. 43 stems from ignorance and not from exaggerated solicitude based on a misunderstanding of the nature of comradeship. To identify in Frl. X. the predominance of Dinaric racial characteristics with an element of Baltic is more than strange. The main comment to be made here is that Herr SS-Oberführer Berndt will perhaps learn in his first remedial lesson in racial theory that only an eastern Baltic race is known in the terminology of that science.[64]

In February 1940 he made the following criticism:

Frl. L.'s medical questionnaire seems to me very peculiar and determined by an absolutely provincial point of view. She was examined on 18. 12. 1939 by an SS doctor, Dr M.. I find it incomprehensible how a woman aged 30, 1.74 metres tall, weighing 64 kilos, with pinkish-white skin, grey eyes, light blond straight hair, and categorized as Nordic on the basis of the predominant racial component, should make a very mediocre impression on the doctor. This so-called SS doctor in my view examined Fräulein L. not as a doctor but as a philistine from Insterburg.

Himmler in fact suspected that the woman, who wished to marry an SS doctor who was still married, was the victim of small-town tittle-tattle. Casting the net of suspicion more widely, he continued: 'If the same young woman had come to him anonymously he would probably have had a better impression. As it was, no doubt every gossip-monger in East Prussia knew what was going on.' He reserved the right to dismiss the doctor for incompetence.

Himmler exploited this incident to expound the principles underlying marriage and the admissibility of 'decent' separations: 'I know precisely how the Führer regards this matter. [. . .] When a couple separates it makes no sense to prevent another couple from forming and having children. In these matters too I would ask you when making judgements to attempt to reach a more profound understanding of the laws made by the Führer and under his leadership, such as the new divorce law, and not to stick rigidly to ways of thought that are in the final analysis profoundly Christian.' And he added: 'People should behave in a manner that is decent and chivalrous, and if they no longer get along together my view is that they should separate in a decent and chivalrous manner. I don't need to labour that point.'[65]

Himmler therefore turned down requests from SS men to marry considerably older women, if there was no prospect of children. In such cases he typically asked the applicant's superior officer 'to inform him in a kind and comradely manner that he considers his marriage to Fräulein X. to be unsound from an ethnic point of view'.[66] The refusal could, however, be delivered in a less 'friendly' form: 'After R. [. . .] was dissuaded from marrying a woman of 43, he is now attempting to marry a woman of 42½. Although I can see he has improved by six months, I consider this tendency to be positively aberrant. Saying he is too old to have more children shows that R. is as yet unaware of the attitude and views an SS man must have with regard to these matters in life.'[67]

If a child had already been born or the woman was pregnant he took a softer line:

It is of course correct that marriages in which the man is so much younger than the wife are biologically undesirable, as they can lead to the wife quickly ceasing to have children—at an age when the husband can still father children—and as a result there is a considerable risk of divorce. During the war, where soldiers on short leaves have less time than they have in peacetime to choose a partner, my view is that marriage to a woman who is carrying his child must be permitted and all doubts put aside.[68]

He was not prepared to give Oberscharführer Willy M. leave to marry a woman eleven years older until she confirmed 'conclusively' that she was pregnant. In this instance Himmler also ordered the applicant to come to Berchtesgaden so that he could communicate the decision to him in person and reprimand him 'most severely' for the 'immature and arrogant behaviour' he had displayed during the application process.[69] To be in a better position to gauge the likelihood of a pregnancy in such cases, he turned in August 1942 to the director of Lebensborn (Spring of Life) with the request that he should 'establish in an appropriate manner when the women giving birth at Lebensborn started menstruating and up to what age they might have children'.[70]

In 1942, 'in spite of serious misgivings', Himmler gave a 17-year-old Unterscharführer leave to marry a woman fourteen years older than him (she was expecting his child), though not without adding a piece of personal advice for the applicant:

You and your fiancée must nevertheless be in no doubt that in ten years at most this marriage will undergo a severe test, as, purely biologically and in accordance with nature's laws, the trajectories of men's and women's lives diverge at this point. Embark on this marriage if you are convinced that your future wife has the human qualities that in some form or other fate will demand of her. If difficulties arise, you and your wife have my permission to approach me for a solution, should I be spared till then.[71]

In another case on which he also reached a decision in 1942, Himmler had already refused the request of a Hauptscharführer to marry on the grounds that the woman was too old. Then, however, he changed his mind after receiving a personal letter from the woman. Himmler replied that he was gratified by the 'very decent attitude' that emerged from the letter, and particularly by the woman's willingness to 'release [the Hauptsturmführer] immediately and without hesitation if he should ever be obliged to demand this in order to preserve the nation'. Then his tone became more personal:

I can put myself in your position very easily. I simply ask you, in view of the great love that binds you to this man, to be clear in your own mind even today that for you a time may come when fate, in accordance with the laws of nature, tears apart the threads it has woven round the two of you, or when you, showing kindness and understanding, will be forced to be very generous. Delightful as the idea is of including children not your own in your family, in the majority of cases, and in spite of all the love and care your husband may show towards them, they will not be able to replace the child of his own blood he might have fathered.[72]

The timing of this letter was probably no accident. Himmler, who of course was himself married to a woman considerably older than himself, knew the problems he describes from personal experience. At any rate, in 1942 he became the father of a child born out of wedlock.[73]

Yet what purpose was served by this minute examination of individual cases, the imposition of these conditions with their far-reaching consequences, if the process was, as we have seen, for the most part a farce and Himmler was unwilling to treat the whole matter so rigorously that it turned into a massive impediment to marriage for his men? On the one hand, the examples set out here indicate that Himmler quite clearly took a strongly voyeuristic interest in these procedures, as is evidenced in particular by his obsessive demand for details, and not least by his obvious curiosity with regard to female anatomy. Evidently he derived pleasure from intervening in other people's most intimate concerns and controlling and organizing them in a confident manner—as he had done in his youth. One is reminded in this connection of the love-letters he wrote for a friend, or of the 'Paula affair' of 1923, when he tried to engineer the breaking-off of his brother's engagement. Yet again, the manner in which he fulfilled his duties as Reichsführer-SS was closely linked to his personal inclinations: for on the other hand, the process for approving marriages gave Himmler a further opportunity to discipline and educate his men. In the clan order of the SS getting married was not a private matter—and, as we shall see, nor was being married.

Himmler intervenes

When examining requests to marry, Himmler, for example, directed particular attention to any available divorce judgements. If his men had behaved in an 'unchivalrous' manner when the previous marriage was dissolved, he was implacable. He disapproved of the fact that Obersturm-führer C., who wished to remarry, had petitioned for divorce from his first wife, naming her as the sole guilty party, even though the marriage had clearly broken down. But that was not all: 'I consider it unchivalrous and outrageous for an SS man to demand marital relations of his wife shortly before she is due to give birth.' In addition, C.'s 'appearance is peculiar from a racial point of view (I merely draw attention to the shape of the mouth)'. Himmler ruled that C. should be 'dismissed from the Waffen-SS and the General SS after the war', but for the time being—and that meant 'imme-diately'—he was to be 'transferred to a Waffen-SS anti-aircraft division at the front'.[74]

In the case of Oberscharführer H., a member of the Waffen-SS, Himmler immersed himself in two divorce judgements issued against H., from which it was clear 'that he mistreated and abused his wife'. H. should 'be in no doubt', Himmler threatened, 'that I shall intervene if he mistreats and abuses his third wife'. Such behaviour would not lead to divorce but rather to 'years of disciplining and instruction' by the Reichsführer, 'to rid him of his violent temper and inculcate the self-control and kindness towards others required if people are to live in communities'.[75] In autumn 1939 Himmler dismissed Günther Tamaschke, the commandant of the female concentra-tion camp of Lichtenburg, for neglecting his wife.[76]

In November 1937 he declared to the Gruppenführer that 'another thing' he would 'not tolerate' was 'when any leader—I noticed a Standartenführer or Oberführer recently who fell into that category—is henpecked. I have often made myself clear on this matter: leaders who are incapable of leading a unit of two, in this case himself and his wife, are incapable of greater things.' Himmler called on the Gruppenführer to take such people in hand.[77]

Occasionally he did this personally. Brigadeführer Hermann Behrends was urged to 'take the lead' in his marriage,[78] and Günther Pancke, his Higher SS and Police Leader in Denmark, had also to submit to a lecture on how his wife, who lived in Brunswick, was leading an overly extravagant life. 'In addition, I would ask you to instruct your wife to the effect that she should not go round proclaiming her opinion loud and clear in all kinds of places about this or that political event in the Gau or about the Gauleiter. I also consider it unnecessary for you as a dutiful husband to come charging down from Denmark by car after every air raid on Brunswick, in order to report to her. You have no idea how much people are talking about this!'[79]

Pancke was deeply distressed by what, in his view, were unjust reproaches and responded with a self-assured and angry letter: 'From her youth my wife has been a National Socialist and at the age of 35 and as the mother of 4 children she has the maturity and experience of life not to need today to be instructed and directed by me.'[80]

Pancke's anger was not surprising, for Himmler had on occasions expressed criticism of the behaviour of wives that in essence was aimed at the SS leaders themselves, who were, it was implied, incapable of instructing and directing their wives as he saw fit: 'I disagree with several things about the way the wives of SS leaders appear in public,' Himmler declared to the Gruppenführer in 1936, for example, 'I am opposed to SS wives wearing make-up and going about with painted faces.' Make-up, he claimed, was

merely the inferior tendency of those of lesser races [...]. And our foolish German women, precisely those of superior race, think they have to copy this stupid fashion. In my opinion, anyone who piles on make-up—and I'm never petty about this—anyone who gets herself up like a half-caste is completely forgetting that she is denying her own good blood. [...] I at any rate intend, if I encounter extreme examples in company, to speak to the women about it.

He was also 'opposed to SS women smoking in public'. In Berlin, 'this swamp and mass grave of our nation,' he had in addition noticed that 'the 16- and 17-year old daughters of party comrades, even sometimes of SS members, were already appearing prominently by invitation at large state festivities [...] If we do not wish to bring up a generation of good-for-nothings, I would like urgently to request that SS leaders, those in high positions in particular, bring up their children in a simple and austere fashion [...] The same goes for the sons.'[81]

Himmler's intervention in the married life of his men could take on drastic proportions. This was true in the case of Erwin Rösener, the Higher SS and Police Leader for the Alps: he approached Wolff in April 1942 with the request that he inform Himmler cautiously that Rösener's second marriage had also broken down as the result of his being the prospective father of an illegitimate child. He was, he said, ashamed of appearing before the Reichsführer and saying to him, 'Reichsführer, here I am for the second time, causing you this unhappiness'.[82] After the divorce, and when Rösener had remarried, Himmler consistently exploited Rösener's weakness and started to keep his marriage under regular surveillance. He admonished him to go to Berlin at least every four weeks, 'in order to maintain married life', and made it abundantly plain that he would 'not tolerate a third shipwreck'.[83]

Herbert Becker, a 56-year-old SS-Gruppenführer and police lieutenant-general, was called upon by Himmler in 1943 to respond to the question of whether his wife was involved in a lesbian relationship; private correspondence to which Himmler had access aroused this suspicion. In a three-page letter Becker challenged this accusation vigorously and assured Himmler that, as a result of a full and frank discussion with his wife, they had both decided not to abandon the marriage, as previously planned, but 'to find a way back to a married life based on National Socialist principles'. Himmler was relieved. He wrote to Becker that he regretted having done his wife an injustice, and expressed the hope 'that your marriage [. . .] may yet acquire true and lasting meaning and content through the birth of children'. He also immediately suggested a gynaecologist who might be helpful if there were complications.[84]

Illegitimate births

In 1936 and 1937 Himmler, with striking frequency, concerned himself with different aspects of sexuality, on which he made a variety of comments and statements. We have already seen that at the Gruppenführer meeting of February 1937 he had warned very insistently about the dangers of homosexuality that could result from any too pronounced 'masculinization' of the National Socialist movement. At that time, as a means of protecting the particular 'at-risk' group (16- and 17-year-old boys), he had recommended relaxed and innocent social contact with girls (dance lessons!), at the same time rejecting the notion that this would promote premature sexual relations among adolescents.

In the months that followed he appears to have given further intensive thought to these problems. What was to happen with these young people when they were a few years older? In June 1937 Himmler had the opportunity to present the fruits of his deliberations and researches to a particularly well-qualified panel, the Expert Advisory Panel on Population and Racial Policy. 'We have attempted to use police resources,' Himmler explained,

bringing in our own departments as well, in order to discover what is really happening. At what age do young German men and girls begin to be sexually active? [. . .] We are almost all from middle-class backgrounds and want to look out into the world beyond our protected bourgeois upbringing. I am forced to say: it is completely different from what all of us have been told and from how we perhaps would like it to be. By the age of 22—I am using figures that are absolutely indisputable—the majority of men have been with a woman. Any officer, any soldier, can confirm this.

At this point Himmler permitted himself a small digression that makes clear how much he had abandoned his earlier self-stylization as a celibate—or rather, how concerned he still was to distance himself from this ideal he had held in his youth: 'The fact still remains, however, that soldiers who have had, and are still having, a lot of experience with girls are often precisely the ones who are good soldiers. In the movement, during the time of struggle, we too found that the very prim and proper ones were not always the best fighters.'

This was not his main topic, however: 'I merely want to state that sexual activity begins in the case of men—and the social context is of course an important factor here—between the ages of 18 and 21 and in the case of girls at 25.' What was to be done? The ideal solution in Himmler's view was certainly to marry early. He was, he admitted, in no doubt that most young men and women were not yet financially in a position to found a family, which was the reason why he had forbidden his own full-time SS men to marry early. Another, realistic solution had to be found: pre-marital sexual relations and illegitimate births had to become acceptable. (It goes without saying that the word 'contraception' does not occur anywhere in Himmler's statements on this subject.)

He expounded the problem to the Expert Advisory Panel as follows: 'I have come to the following conclusion: all the moral views we've had up till now that say, "All right, but not before marriage", are not going to get us anywhere.' As the SS's highest authority for approving marriages, Himmler after all had relevant experience to draw on: 'My SS men's requests to marry land on my desk and every day I look at twenty because I want to keep in touch with what is being done in practice. [. . .] I have reserved the right to deal with any refusal of a marriage in the whole of the SS so that during the first decades, while a certain way of doing things is still getting established, the criteria set are not too stringent.' Among the family trees in the applications there were few without some illegitimate children, he said, and so this matter should be 'treated to some extent with Germanic generosity'. He summed up the conclusion he had drawn from all this as follows: 'I shall vigorously resist any legal or strong moral restriction on relationships between men and young women. In this I am certainly not alone, but am acting with the Führer's approval, for I have had repeated conversations with him about this subject.' And now he came full circle: 'For anyone we restrict too severely will end up on the other side, in the homosexual camp.'[85]

Over a year before this, in April 1936, Himmler had made use of a stay in Gmund to put down on paper his thoughts about the problem of illegitimate births in relation to the SS.[86] There is an evident difference between this memorandum, intended for internal purposes, and his remarks to the Expert Advisory Panel: in the case of the SS he wanted not only to accept illegitimate births but to promote them, as an integral part of a population strategy. Beyond that, the paper clarifies the extent to which, for reasons based on population policy, he condemned the hostile attitude of the churches to sexuality. For the SS was to assume the role of an avant-garde as far as population policy was concerned, by absolutely rejecting the church's teaching on sexual morality. The time was not yet right, however, to go public with such ideas. He was to decide to take this step only after the beginning of the war.

'Certainly not later than a hundred years from now,' Himmler stated in the memorandum in question, 'and perhaps much sooner, we shall be happy about every additional human being in Germany, and the time might come when we are heartily thankful for every battalion we can send to our eastern border to fight against Bolshevism.' 'Welcoming illegitimate children', however, should never be allowed to 'do damage to the institution of marriage'. He intended to set a requirement within the SS, he said, for 'young men of 25 and at most 28 who have a paid position to marry, and once they are married, to have children'. It could not, however, be expected that young men and women should live 'lives of sexual abstinence' up to this point.

However commendably motivated, no allegedly moral laws instituted by Christianity provide a solution for this. They merely have one purpose for Christianity, namely, to make it indispensable as an institution with the power to forgive the sins of others. [. . .] In the SS I intend once and for all to part company with this dishonesty and in doing so I hope to set the whole of the German nation an example. My ideas are moving between the two poles of marriage on the one hand and the sure knowledge on the other that in most cases men and young women follow nature's imperative.

By this means he was hoping, he continued, to obtain '200–300 children per year from every battalion of the Verfügungstruppe'. 'I not only resolve to do all I can to raise our SS men's illegitimate, in most cases highly talented, children of good race and make them soldiers and officers or, alternatively, superior wives for our nation, but I shall expend an equal amount of effort on giving the girls in question [. . .] an honoured place beside the married mothers.' In the case of SS families who had the 'misfortune' not to be able to produce sufficient children of their own, it should become 'an accepted custom to take in illegitimate or orphaned children of good blood and bring them up'. Indeed, they should receive 'the number of children that should be the norm for an SS family', namely 'between four and six'.

Meanwhile, however, Himmler had also made a practical start towards ensuring 'racially high-quality' offspring from extramarital relationships: in September 1936 he announced in a circular to all SS leaders the founding of the Lebensborn association, which had in fact taken place in December 1935.[87]

By contrast with the formulation chosen for its statutes,[88] supporting 'racially and eugenically high-quality families with many children' played only a subordinate role in the association's activities.[89] What it was actually doing above all was looking after single mothers, to whom Lebensborn, with its special maternity homes, offered the chance of giving birth far away from their normal environment and keeping it secret. If desired, the baby became the association's ward.[90] In addition to single mothers, the homes were also available to married women, in particular to wives of SS men.

In every case the basic precondition for acceptance into the homes was an examination of both the mother and the father by an SS doctor, using the same racial criteria that prospective wives of SS men had to satisfy. The SS doctors were committed to confidentiality beyond the normal medical demands 'by a particular obligation imposed by the Reichsführer-SS'. In cases where 'special circumstances' applied, Himmler reserved the right to keep the birth and the father's identity completely secret.[91]

Though to the outside world the Lebensborn was an association, it was firmly integrated into the SS organization, reporting to the Race and Settlement Main Office. In 1937 its administration was part of the remit of the SS administrative head, Pohl. On 1 January 1938 the Lebensborn was taken out of the Race and Settlement Main Office and subordinated to the Personal Staff. The association's council was reorganized, and Himmler put himself at its head.[92] The organization was financed by compulsory levies on SS members. Those who were childless had to pay the most, while anyone with four or more children, whether legitimate or illegitimate, no longer had to contribute.

The Lebensborn opened its first maternity home in August 1936 in Steinhöring in Upper Bavaria. Six more were opened up to the outbreak of war. Head of the medical team for the whole of the Lebensborn was Himmler's former family doctor in Munich, Gregor Ebner, like him a member of the Apollo duelling fraternity and a friend on first-name terms with the Reichsführer.[93] The existence of the Lebensborn homes gave rise to all sorts of rumours about their purpose. The Lübeck woman who sent in a request to the SS for information about the nearest SS 'copulation home (*Begattungsheim*)'[94] was not an isolated case, and to this day in fact the Lebensborn is associated with the notion of a 'breeding institution'.

Himmler now also gave his attention to gaining support within the SS for extramarital procreation, naturally in a moderate form: he attempted to convey to his men that they did not have to marry the first person who came along: 'The sort of girl you meet at dances and parties is not the sort you marry,' he explained to the Gruppenführer in November 1936, two months after he had announced the founding of Lebensborn:

We must teach our men to recognize that they don't have to marry the first girl they meet out dancing. I see from the requests to marry that our men often marry having no idea what marriage is. Reading the requests I often wonder: my God, does an SS man have to marry this woman of all people, this walking mishap with a bent and sometimes ghastly frame. A little eastern European Jew or a little Mongol can marry her; that's all a girl like that is good for. In by far the most cases the men in question are radiant and handsome.

Before getting married SS men should 'have a good look at the sisters, brothers, and parents' of the bride. If the chosen one is the 'only acceptable one, while the other family members are dreadful', it is an exercise in 'practical racial awareness' to recognize that the bride's family has 'blood that is undesirable' for the SS man. He was not prepared to accept the excuse that a man might already have become involved in an established relationship before discovering that 'her brother or uncle was in a lunatic asylum': 'No, gentlemen, the man must be so good as to ask beforehand.'

For an unmarried man it was, Himmler said, 'no disgrace to have a girlfriend. He must, however, be clear in his own mind from the outset:

I shall not marry you because I cannot justify doing so. How he makes the girl accept that is his business; everyone has to be the judge in matters of his own conscience. But SS men must never behave in a way that is not decent but must rather be open and say: I'm sorry, I can't marry you as there have been too many serious illnesses in your family.' SS men were to be urged, 'in many individual conversations', to take these ideas on board.[95] For the rest, he was hopeful, as he confided to the Gruppenführer in 1937, that 'in the course of a thoroughly reasonable, open, and extremely tactful discussion with the young man or girl their sense of duty and their awareness of the immense responsibility they bear can be boosted to the point where they can both be educated to accept a life without sex up to the age of 18, 19, 20'.[96]

In 1936 and 1937, whenever Himmler's topic was sexual politics his ideas always revolved around the same considerations: the threat to young people of homosexuality; the toleration of sexual relations between unmarried young people; acceptance of illegitimacy; early marriage. It is obvious that Himmler had entered a phase in which he was settling accounts with his earlier attitude to the subjects of sexuality and masculinity. In the early 1920s the model before his eyes was that of the celibate, heroic warrior, the figure of the 'lonely freebooter'. He had already given up this image of himself in 1927–8, when he met his wife and set about founding a family. Now, some ten years later, this blueprint for life was gradually turning out to be flawed. If his prescriptions in matters of sexual politics from the 1936–7 period are read as reflections on his own development, then he clearly reproached himself with not having gained sexual experience earlier and not having married a woman of his own age earlier and founded a family with her. It was obvious to him which institution had caused him these difficulties: the Catholic Church.

The fact that Himmler gave voice to views on matters of sexual politics in 1936–7 in a manner that can be read as a critical commentary on his own previous life, and the fact that he showed himself so liberal with regard to extramarital sex and illegitimate births, most certainly had roots in his private experience. In autumn 1937 the Himmlers spent a relatively harmonious holiday together in Italy, and yet a precise reading of the entries in Margarete's diary, something she began to keep during this holiday, reveals deep dissatisfaction. After the seizure of power the Himmlers were certainly in a position to cultivate a lifestyle in keeping with their membership of the country's political elite: first of all they moved from Waldtrudering to a flat in the exclusive Möhlstrasse in Munich, which they moved out of again in 1934 to live near Lake Tegern, where in 1936 Himmler bought a village house (Lindenfycht) from the renowned singer Alois Burgstaller, extending it in 1937.[97] In addition, Himmler immediately rented a lakeside house,[98] as well as a hunting lodge in the mountains nearby.[99] In Berlin too he had comfortable accommodation, at first in a flat in Tiergartenstrasse 6a and from November 1934 in Hagenstrasse 22,[100] before he finally moved into a spacious house befitting the position he had in the meantime attained, Dohnenstieg 10 in the exclusive suburb of Dahlem. It had fourteen rooms,[101] and as his official residence was provided for him free of charge.[102]

The financial worries of the first years of marriage were therefore over, and Margarete's diary entries certainly convey her pride in Himmler's professional successes. At the same time, it is impossible to overlook her complaints that he is almost permanently away from home,[103] her doubts about whether his commitment to his work is really being adequately rewarded and whether it is all worth it.[104] On their tenth anniversary she wrote: 'In spite of the happiness marriage brings, I have had to do without many things in my marriage for H. is almost never there and his life is all work.'[105]

After attaining considerable social status as Himmler's wife, her lack of social confidence grew into a contempt for others, with undertones of aggression. She seems above all to have taken out her frustration on her domestic staff: there was constant annoyance in the Himmler household because the servants were 'insolent and lazy'.[106] In one diary entry, occasioned by just such an episode, she vented her resentment and fury: 'Why are these people not put under lock and key and made to work until they die. Sometimes I wonder if I live with human beings or not.'[107] In March 1939 two further employees left, and she complained: 'The notion of duty and service doesn't exist any more.'[108]

She had additional troubles on account of her foster-child Gerhard, whom the Himmlers had taken in. The son of a dead SS man, he was a year older than their daughter Gudrun. The complaints pile up in Margarete's diary: the boy is a 'criminal type', has stolen money, and 'is an appalling liar', she writes.[109] His natural mother was not prepared to have her wayward son back under these circumstances either, thereby displaying an attitude that, as Margarete confided to her diary, did nothing to 'unsettle' her 'opinion about human beings'.[110] In March 1939 Gerhard passed the entrance examination for a National Socialist educational establishment—these schools, designed to train up the future National Socialist elite, had in the meantime also become part of Himmler's empire—but in October he was forced to leave again.[111] In the light of these entries the Himmlers' domestic situation at the end of the 1930s can hardly be described as harmonious.

Early in 1936 a young woman named Hedwig Potthast took up a post as Himmler's private secretary. The two gradually became close, and at the end of 1938, it is believed, confessed to each other that they had fallen in love; they could not have started a relationship earlier than 1940, however. There is little point in speculating whether Himmler's rather barren domestic situation prompted his relationship with Hedwig Potthast, or whether his growing interest in the young woman created the backdrop against which Margarete's frustration must be viewed. As is usual in human relationships, both aspects most probably reinforced each other. Nevertheless, Himmler's statements of June 1937 to the Expert Advisory Panel on Population Policy reveal clearly the explosive potential he saw in his growing private conflict: in his view, he explained, it was 'absolutely clear, that the German nation is in absolute disarray on sexual matters, that as a nation we have the greatest possible tensions in this area, and we must face up to the fact that, if a nation is not living in accord with its most fundamental natural laws, then that is dynamite for the whole nation'.[112]

Divorce, adultery, remarriage

If SS members wanted to get divorced, Himmler in principle had no reservations. The Reichsführer declared openly to the Gruppenführer in 1937 that if the couple had grown apart he had 'complete sympathy' with their wish to divorce. At the same time, he set a condition: 'I require the guiding principle of the SS leadership corps to be that whatever fate decrees must happen in this area of life should be carried through in a way that is ordered, decent, and extremely generous on the part of the individual concerned.'[113]

Generosity was something Himmler himself inclined to: if in the course of disciplinary or criminal proceedings 'marital lapses' came to light, it was Himmler's policy for the wife not to be informed, 'in the interests of upholding the marriage'.[114] The requirement to be 'decent' and 'chivalrous' was not infringed, therefore, as long as the marital lapse did not come out into the open. In 1944 Himmler even approached the Reich Minister of Justice in an individual case to remove the legal ruling according to which adultery was to be regarded as an 'impediment to marriage'.[115] If proceedings were initiated in SS or police courts on the grounds of adultery, Himmler reserved for himself the decision on how they should be handled. In such cases he wished to be comprehensively briefed; amongst other things, photographs of all those involved (in particular, of any children) had to be included.[116]

The privilege of a 'second marriage' was something Himmler by no means took advantage of only for himself. His study of Germanic prehistory had convinced him of the existence of the 'second or Friedel-Ehe,* which the free Teuton of good race could enter into',[117] and he also permitted his men to enter into such an arrangement, on condition that they intended to have children. Thus, in 1944 Himmler allowed a married Obersturmbannführer, who on account of his wife's 'nervous condition' was unwilling to leave her, to cohabit with another woman. That was, however, with the proviso that the new relationship produced children.[118] On a visit to the acting Gauleiter of Westphalia-South, Obergruppenführer Schlessmann, Himmler advised him that in view of his marital problems he should look for 'a loving woman', who 'would be prepared to give children to the German nation with me [Schlessmann]'. Some time after this conversation Schlessmann 'reported' to Himmler that he had now found 'this loving woman', who was his secretary and was now three months pregnant with his child. No stranger to this type of relationship himself, Himmler was very pleased, granted the second wife accommodation, and promised 'complete secrecy'.[119]

Marriage orders and number of children

In spite of all these efforts the number of marriages among SS members was, in Himmler's view, still too low, and the lack of children produced when the war was causing many losses became a problem that threatened the future viability of the SS. In June 1942 he explained to the leadership corps

---

* *Translators' note*: Quasi-marriage or 'lover' marriage between a man and a woman of lower status.

of the SS-Division 'Das Reich' 'that the number of children does not replace even half of those who have fallen [. . .] A terrible loss, much more terrible than the death of the men themselves.'[120] Specific challenges had to be issued.[121] In December 1944 Himmler requested the commandant on Obersalzberg, Obersturmführer Frank, to 'enquire' of the unmarried leaders and Unterführer under his command 'what they had done so far to put an end to their unmarried state or what they were intending to do in the foreseeable future'.[122] In 1943 Himmler had his 'acute displeasure' conveyed to one Hauptsturmführer Schwarz for 'still being unmarried at the age of 44'; if this were still the case by the end of the war, he would be dismissed from the SS.[123]

If all cajoling and admonitions produced no results, in particularly extreme cases Himmler ordered his men to marry. Hauptsturmführer Arnold, for example, received such a letter from his Reichsführer in June 1943:

Dear Arnold!
    As far as I am aware, you are your parents' only son. In my opinion you are under an obligation to marry and ensure that the Arnold clan does not die out.
    I expect an answer to this letter.[124]

To make doubly sure, Himmler sent a letter the same day to Arnold senior, suggesting it would be good if the latter 'were to influence him in the same direction'.[125]

Fritz Bauer, a sports teacher at the SS sanatorium in Hohenlychen, reported as early as October 1936 that he had carried out just such an order from his Reichsführer: 'With regard to your order to marry by 30 January 1937, I am pleased to report that I intend to obey the order on 12 December 1936.'[126] Himmler was delighted, and donated 500 Reich marks for the wedding.[127]

The case of SS-Hauptsturmführer Feierlein was somewhat more complicated. At first he received an unequivocal instruction from Himmler: marry by 20 April 1938—the Führer's birthday! When the date passed, nothing had happened and Wolff sent him a reminder, Feierlein attempted to wriggle out of it by saying he had not understood Himmler's instruction to be an order. The Chief of the Personal Staff did not, however, accept this 'lazy excuse', and passed on to him a formal order from the Reichsführer that Feierlein 'had until 31. 12. 38 to report the execution of your order to marry'.[128] When, however, a short time later a suspicion arose that Feierlein might be involved in a corruption scandal in Vienna, Wolff informed him that the order had been suspended and he was forbidden 'to get engaged or married without receiving further communications'.[129] In May the following year Feierlein asked for his marriage prohibition to be suspended, as in the meantime he had met 'a girl'; his wish was granted, and in June he 'gave notice' of his impending marriage.[130]

In 1936 Himmler prescribed four as being the 'smallest number of children to be expected of a good and healthy marriage'.[131] On occasion he spoke, in reference to Hitler, of four sons.[132] Himmler personally attended to the creation of the right circumstances in which his men could use their leave to father children: wives of SS men were to be given the opportunity to holiday near the places where their husbands were deployed, in order to boost the birth rate, as he decreed in an order of October 1942.[133] To one childless wife of an SS man Himmler provided the services of a healer.[134] On the other hand, if the wife's family tree revealed a 'non-Aryan', he demanded that already married SS men should have no more children.[135]

The results of Himmler's efforts to produce more marriages and children among the SS were extremely meagre, in fact positively pitiful. According to the SS Statistical Yearbook for 1938, a mere 39.7 per cent of the SS were married. Taking into account that only some 2.5 per cent of the under-25s were married, this means that among older SS men only 57.3 per cent were married.[136] The number of children per married SS man was a mere 1.1. Apart from this, only very few SS men had responded to Himmler's call to bring children into the world outside wedlock: a total of 741 unmarried SS men had, according to the figures, produced in all 811 illegitimate children up to this point.[137] For the war period there are no equivalent statistics, and yet Himmler's constant lament about the lack of children produced by his men, and his attempts to encourage them to father a new generation, even if partly illegitimate, show clearly that the fertility of SS members had basically not altered at all. But SS members disappointed Himmler's expectations with regard to marriage and children not only in terms of quantity but also of quality: the procedure for approving marriage requests broke down, as we have seen, because it was impracticable, while the Reichsführer's notions of breeding never got off the ground. The 'clan order' was above all a construct of Himmler's imagination.

Even in his private life he indulged this illusion of a 'clan order'. Anyone, relative or friend, who was close to him was gradually integrated into the 'order'. His parents may have observed the beginnings of his political career with a sceptical eye, but by the early 1930s at the latest they looked upon their son's career with pride. His father collected newspaper cuttings, mostly from the *Völkischer Beobachter*, containing mentions of his son,[138] and in 1932 he even worked his way through a copy of the second volume of *Mein Kampf* that Heinrich had given him. His final comment on it was that Hitler was a man who engaged his interest and whom he viewed with true admiration.[139] In 1933 both parents became members of the NSDAP.[140]

Even in the years that saw Himmler advance to the position of chief of a terror apparatus surrounded by an aura of horror, no shadow seems to have fallen on the relationship. Although in the period that followed Himmler senior repeatedly approached his son in the name of petitioners who were frequently suffering from his persecution, the two also carried on an avid correspondence during these years about their family history.[141] When Gebhard Himmler died in 1936 Heinrich organized a grand funeral, at-tended by an official SS delegation, which in many respects resembled a state funeral.[142]

Himmler's younger brother Ernst, who had completed his university course in electrical engineering in 1928, got a job in 1933 with Heinrich's help with the Berlin radio and at the same time joined the SS. He had already become a member of the NSDAP in 1931. In the Reich broadcast-ing organization Ernst quickly rose to become deputy technical director and then, in 1942, director.[143] In 1937 Himmler approved a loan for his brother, who in the meantime had established a family, from an SS fund and thus enabled him to buy a house that had formally belong to a trades union.[144] Ernst, in turn, supplied Heinrich on various occasions with internal information from the world of broadcasting and from other areas his professional activities gave him knowledge of, not scrupling even to make a denunciation.[145]

The oldest of the Himmler brothers, Gebhard, who since 1925 had been teaching at a college of further education, also advanced his career during the Third Reich. In 1933 he became leader of the Bavarian Further Educa-tion Association, and the same year joined the NSDAP. He insisted, however, on his membership dating from May 1932, the date when his wife joined, because as a civil servant he had at that point not been permitted to become a member. In June 1934 he joined the SS and in 1935 he became head of a college of engineering in Munich.[146] In 1939 he entered the Reich Education Ministry as a desk officer and in 1944 became head of the department responsible for further education throughout the

Reich.[147] Within the SS he rose to the rank of Standartenführer, though Ernst made it only as far as Sturmbannführer. In their careers it is clear that both brothers succeeded in getting to the top of their respective professions. Both took trouble to keep in close touch with Heinrich: in 1944 Ernst and Gebhard, as his 'technical brothers', offered to give Himmler the benefit of a comprehensive account of their views on the future development of military technology.[148]

The fact that Himmler arranged for his schoolfriends Falk Zipperer and Karl Gebhardt to work for him professionally, the one as a legal historian, the other as director of a clinic, has already been mentioned. He maintained his friendship also with Alois Rehrl, ten years his senior, on whose estate he had done his agricultural work placement in 1921–2. It goes without saying that Rehrl, like Zipperer and Gebhardt, joined the SS.[149]

It was probably at the end of the 1920s that Himmler met a man with whom he established a particularly close friendship: the völkisch writer Hanns Johst, already mentioned, who was a National Socialist and, as chair of the Reich Writers Chamber, a powerful Nazi state functionary in the field of literature.[150] From 1934 onwards Johst addressed Himmler in letters as 'my friend Heini Himmler',[151] and although he was ten years older, called Himmler his 'big brother'.[152] They paid each other frequent visits (Johst lived on Lake Starnberg, not far from Himmler's home on Lake Tegern), played badminton, bathed, and fished in their leisure time, travelled together, and went on tours of inspection.[153] In 1935 Himmler accepted Johst into the SS, giving him the relatively high rank of Oberführer; Johst was repeatedly promoted in the years following, finally becoming a Gruppenführer on 30 January 1942.[154]

The extensive correspondence between the two was marked on Johst's side by an exuberant and at times emotive and high-flown style, in which he expressed his unbounded admiration for Himmler's life's work and his leadership style; indeed, he positively idolized him. After recovering from an appendectomy in 1940, he wrote to his friend that he was 'happy to be an SS man and that on top of that life has given me our friendship, Heini Himmler, which makes this dubious existence of ours worth living'.[155] In 1943 he praised Himmler's rhetorical gifts in the most exalted terms: the Reichsführer was a 'typically masculine speaker'. 'What you say lives and works on the level of insight, [. . .] enriches us with your vision [. . .] even more: it makes us resemble you and transforms us from being mere listeners to being followers.'[156] Johst gave Himmler poems and books with a personal dedication,[157] and published various contributions, for example to the *SS Guidance Booklets* and to *Das schwarze Korps*, in which he praised the SS and its leader in the most elevated poetic language.[158]

Himmler responded to Johst's effusions in his more reserved manner, but he did repeatedly make efforts to show appropriate appreciation of the outpourings of emotion that he inspired. Himmler also revered Johst, as the writer possessed abilities he himself lacked. In March 1942 Himmler assured Johst how important their correspondence was to him: 'You may be confident that your letters are always precious to me. They are like emissaries from a world I greatly love but which, because fate has chosen to put me where I am, remains closed to me for most of my time and most of my life. I am all the more delighted to receive regular salutations from the intellectual world of our blood, which you embody as one of Germany's finest.'[159] Though each wrote in his own typical manner, the friends exchanged what can almost be called love-letters.

Another, and very close, relationship of Himmler's is noteworthy. From 1939 onwards the Reichsführer was a patient of the celebrity masseur Felix Kersten, a Baltic German who after the First World War had acquired Finnish nationality. Through intensive massages Kersten was capable of relieving Himmler's physical pains, at least for a time. Under the hands of the masseur, who, two years older than Himmler and with a massive frame, exuded an atmosphere of calm, Himmler relaxed generally, and Kersten took advantage of the treatments to build up a relationship of trust with the Reichsführer.[160] Whether Himmler really allowed him access to his more intimate thoughts, as Kersten asserted in his memoirs, or whether Kersten made up these conversations after the war must remain in doubt; at any rate, Kersten was to take on an important role, particularly in the final phase of the war, in setting up foreign contacts for Himmler.

It is evident that the more Himmler established his position as Reichsführer-SS and extended his power, the more the boundaries between his own family and personal life and his official function became blurred. While on the one hand he made his brothers, his closest friends, and even his favourite writer SS leaders, on the other he treated SS members in many respects like members of an extended family. Adopting the pose of a strict and solicitous father, he educated, commended, punished, admonished, and pardoned his men. The rigid notions he held, and prescribed for his men, about marriage partners, sexual morality, and family planning reflected strongly his experiences as an individual, including the shortcomings he saw in his own marriage. A certain voyeuristic tendency was also involved in his interventions in the private lives of others.

His ideas on the virtues and values of the SS, which he was constantly relaying formulaically to his men, reflected his efforts to replace the emotional void he sensed in his relationships with others with a dense network of rules of conduct. And if he constantly admonished his men to be 'decent', it is not difficult to see behind this his own exertions to keep under control the emerging desire to be allowed for once not to be 'decent'. His ambivalent attitude to this matter expressed itself in particular through his repeated and explicit bans on treating enemies 'decently'.

Himmler had succeeded in establishing his personal predilections, foibles, phobias, and hostilities securely within the SS. He tried as hard as he could to develop an SS cult out of his passion for the Teutons, and in large measure he drew on the Ahnenerbe to bolster his quasi-religious speculations about God and the cosmos. Amalgamated with the police to form a state protection corps, his SS persecuted a range of 'subhumans' that, in his view, were setting about a final conflict with the 'Aryan race'. These were made up of a collection of enemies, all of whom had some kind of close connection with his own life history: communists, Freemasons, politically engaged and morally censorious Christians, Jews, and homosexuals.

As a consequence, Himmler carried over his personal beliefs to an astonishing extent into the organization he headed; leading the SS was not for him simply a political office, it was part of who he was. The task he had set himself in life was to create a strong internal organization for the SS, to extend it and to guarantee its future through his Germanic utopia. By working tenaciously to fulfil the tasks Hitler had entrusted to him, and by linking them adroitly, Himmler built up a unique position of power, which he shaped in line with his own idiosyncratic ideas.

PART IV

At War: Ambition and Disappointment

14

War Preparations and Expansion

'Sometimes', Himmler remarked at a meeting of SS-Gruppenführer in February 1937,

National Socialists dream that one day we shall conquer the world. I'm all in favour of that, even if we're not talking about it at the moment. But I'm convinced that we must do it in stages. At the moment we wouldn't have the numbers to populate even another province, a zone, or a country half the size of Germany. It ought to be obvious that we can't simply take over a population, that if we have to take over a province that is not ethnically German, then it will have to be cleared out down to the last grandmother and the last child and without mercy—I hope there's no doubt about that. I hope there's also no doubt about the fact that we shall then need a population and a population of high racial quality in order to be able to settle it there and breed from it, so that we can begin to surround Germany with a hundred million Germanic peasants. This will then enable us to set out once more on the path to world domination, which was our position in the past, and really to organize the earth according to basic Aryan principles so that it's in better shape than it is now.[1]

Thus, the fantasy of this fine Aryan world, which Himmler was outlining here, was a long-term objective to be achieved 'in stages'. The addition of the 100 million settlers required—Himmler had already mentioned the same number in a speech in 1931[2]—had to be largely secured by an expansive population policy, an effort that would take several generations. In 1938 Himmler prepared the SS leadership for a 'conflict', a 'fateful hour' that would 'confront Germany in the next 30, 50, 100 years and with which we ourselves might be faced'.[3]

At the same time, Himmler assumed that a life-and-death struggle would occur in the course of the next ten years, as he explained to the Gruppen-führer in November 1938:

We must be clear about the fact that during the next ten years we shall be faced with extraordinary and critical conflicts. It won't be simply a struggle among nations; that's merely a smokescreen put up by our opponents. It will be an ideological struggle waged by all the Jews, Freemasons, Marxists and church people in the world. These forces—and I am assuming that the Jews are in the driving seat as the embodiment of everything that is negative—are aware that if Germany and Italy are not destroyed, then they themselves will be destroyed. That is a simple conclusion. The Jews cannot survive in Germany. It's only a matter of years—we shall be increasingly driving them out with unparalleled ruthlessness [. . .]

Be in no doubt that if we succumb in this decisive struggle they wouldn't even allow a few Germans to survive in a reservation; everyone would be starved and slaughtered. Everybody will be affected, whether they are enthusiastic supporters of the Third Reich or not; it will be enough that they speak German and have a German mother.[4]

Only a few months later, in February 1939, Himmler had changed the timing he envisaged for the outbreak of a great war, a world war: now it could be expected to occur not within the next decade but in the foresee-able future, if not immediately, and as a direct result of the Jewish policy initiated by the November 1938 pogrom. Himmler's notes for a speech given to Oberabschnitt Rhine in Wiesbaden read as follows: 'Radical solution of the Jewish problem is prompting Jewry to fight us, if necessary by unleashing a world war.'[5] There is a clear link here with Hitler's well-known 'prophecy' in his speech to the Reichstag on 30 January 1939, in which he stated that a 'world war' unleashed by 'international finance Jewry' would result in the 'annihilation of the Jewish race in Europe'.[6]

Himmler probably used the term 'greater Germanic empire' for the first time in the presence of SS leaders when referring to his fantasy of a future Germanic Reich in his 1938 speech to the Gruppenführer at the annual commemoration of the 9 November 1923 putsch: 'Germany's aim for the future is either the greater Germanic empire or it is nothing. I believe that if we in the SS do our duty then the Führer will be able to achieve this greater Germanic Reich, the greatest empire that has ever been achieved by human beings and that the earth has ever seen. So, bearing this in mind, now go off and do your duty and get to work.'[7]

Himmler does not appear, however, to have believed that this empire could be created during the lifetime of Adolf Hitler; when referring to 'the Führer' he must have meant a successor. That becomes clear if one draws on another text from this period. In 1939, before the start of the war, Himmler once again spoke of a ring of settlements surrounding Germany composed of 80–100 million 'Germanic peasants'. But this was intended merely as the starting point for considerably more gigantic plans, 'so that starting from that basis Germany can create the great Germanic empire that we are dreaming of and that the Führer is aiming for'.[8]

The vision of the settlement of 100 million peasants with the subsequent establishment of a great empire, mentioned here once again, evidently referred to the distant future and was not envisaged as the outcome of the world war, which Himmler was expecting to break out at any moment. For, in 1938, the Third Reich did not possess the 80–100 million 'Germanic peasants' and would not do so even in thirty or fifty years' time. At the end of 1938 and beginning of 1939, world war and the creation of an empire appear to have been distinct ideas in Himmler's mind. At this point he evidently regarded the military conflict that was expected as, in the first instance, a struggle for the existence of National Socialist Germany that would then provide the basis for the later empire.

The takeover of ethnic policy

Although this empire was still a distant prospect, during 1936–7, Himmler had begun to launch a number of initiatives to prepare for its creation. Opportunities were provided by ethnic policy, that is to say, relations between the Reich and ethnic German minorities mainly in eastern and south-eastern Europe, by his contacts with Hitler's foreign policy advisers, as well as through international police links; furthermore, he tried to gain influence within the diplomatic service.

Himmler had already gained experience in the field of ethnic policy after the SD had begun to take an interest in the Sudeten Germans in 1934. Himmler's intelligence agency ran the so-called Sudeten German Control Centre, which Hitler's deputy, Hess, had set up in December 1933 with the help of a Gestapo functionary from Dresden in order to identify any Czech spies among Sudeten German refugees.[9] During the following years the SD also became involved in Czechoslovakia itself; above all it focused on the internal affairs of the Sudeten Germans with the aim of using the Sudeten-land as its base for the surveillance and pursuit of German émigrés in Czechoslovakia. For example, the murder of the engineer Rudolf Formis, near Prague in January 1935—Formis was a former colleague of the Nazi dissident Otto Strasser—was carried out by an SD commando. The SD also supported the 'Aufbruch' circle, a group opposing Konrad Henlein's Sudeten German Heimatfront.[10] The German consul in the Bohemian town of Reichenberg, Walter von Lierau, had been a member of the SS since 1932 and was registered as a member of the SD Office.[11]

From the end of 1937 onwards Himmler intervened personally to direct the regime's ethnic policy. The situation was confused because in some cases Nazi ethnic politicians found themselves in irreconcilable disagreement with those with more traditional views on ethnic politics.[12] This requires a brief explanation.

Since 1933 the Nazi regime had made considerable efforts to take over so-called ethnic work; that is to say, to look after the affairs of and acquire influence over the roughly 10 million members of German minorities in the rest of Europe. At the time of the Nazis' takeover of power there were a number of organizations and institutions, the majority of which were conservative and nationalist in outlook, that were actively involved in developing relations with the ethnic German minorities, including in particular: the Verein—from 1933, Volksbund—für das Deutschtum im Ausland (Association—since 1933, the National League—for Germans Abroad); the Deutsche Schutzbund (German Protection League); the Deutsche Ostmarkenverein (German Association for the Eastern Marches); the Bund Deutscher Osten (BDO) (League of the German East); and the Deutsche Auslands-Institut (German Foreign Institute) in Stuttgart. However, a number of Nazi politicians claimed a leading role in ethnic policy or at least the right to have a say. That was true of the head of the Nazi Party's Auslandsorganisation (Foreign Organization), Ernst Wilhelm Bohle, who tried to extend his responsibility for dealing with Germans abroad to include ethnic Germans with a foreign nationality;[13] it was also true of Hitler's ambitious special representative for foreign affairs, Joachim von Ribbentrop, as well as of Alfred Rosenberg, who was head of the Nazi Party's foreign policy department.

A few months after the takeover of power Hitler assigned to his deputy, Rudolf Hess, wide-ranging powers in the sphere of ethnic policy.[14] Hess's task was a difficult one. A ruthless coordination of the existing, not genuinely

Nazi, ethnic organizations appeared inopportune, since the Nazi leadership had no interest in alienating the large numbers of conservative ethnic activists and thereby possibly creating a movement opposed to the Nazi regime among German minorities abroad. Moreover, in view of the extent of the new regime's diplomatic isolation, it wanted to avoid creating the impression that it intended to use the Germans abroad as a means of causing disruption or even as a fifth column.

In the autumn of 1935, however, Hess decided to reorganize ethnic policy and set up an office under the direction of Otto von Kursell, a painter and art teacher who had been an active supporter of the Nazis since the early 1920s and had been appointed to the Reich Ministry of Education in October 1934. Its function was to coordinate ethnic policy. Formally the 'Kursell Office', which was soon renamed the Volksdeutsche Mittelstelle or VoMi (Coordination Centre for Ethnic Germans), was subordinated to Hess's representative for foreign affairs, Joachim von Ribbentrop, in order to provide him with a vehicle for his ambitions in the sphere of ethnic policy.[15]

In 1936 Kursell, who had the rank of an SS-Obersturmbannführer, had a disagreement with Himmler. When Kursell learned that the SS was favouring a Sudeten German group, which was in opposition to Henlein's Sudeten German Party, which Kursell supported, he persuaded Göring to issue an edict which made the issuing of foreign currency in matters involving ethnic politics subject to his, Kursell's, approval. In this way he hoped to be able to control Himmler's activities in the Sudetenland. Irritated by Kursell's high-handedness, Himmler now evidently sought an excuse to get rid of Kursell and to intervene in ethnic policy directly himself. He accused Kursell, in his role as head of the Baltic Brotherhood, an association of Baltic Germans living in the Reich, of engaging in activities hostile to the state and involving Freemasonry.[16] And at the beginning of 1937 Kursell was in fact replaced as head of VoMi by Himmler's man, SS-Obergruppenführer Werner Lorenz.

Lorenz, who had been a member of the SS since 1930, had been substantially involved in establishing the SS in Danzig (Gdansk), had taken over SS-Oberabschnitt North in Königsberg in 1931, and Oberabschnitt Hamburg in 1934, in the latter case as the 'permanent representative of SS-Obergruppenführer Ambassador von Ribbentrop'.[17] Although inexperienced in ethnic politics, he was chosen because he had excellent social contacts, a self-confident bearing, and a friendly manner. His close contacts with Ribbentrop, who was regarded as 'the coming man' in the regime's foreign policy, were also in his favour, for VoMi was still answerable to Hess via Ribbentrop.[18] Hermann Behrends, who had been involved in the SD, became Lorenz's deputy, and in his new capacity continued to act as Heydrich's agent.[19] Behrends, who became the real strong-man in VoMi, recruited a number of SS leaders into it, among them Walter Ellermeier, who was to become Lorenz's adjutant.

Under its new leadership VoMi, which according to Lorenz was 'the supreme agency dealing with all matters concerning ethnic Germans',[20] soon succeeded in subjecting the various organizations involved in this sphere to stricter control.[21] Thus, in 1937 Behrends took over control of the Bund Deutscher Osten from Theodor Oberländer and thereby became largely responsible for 'borderland activities'.[22] Evidently Himmler had already been planning, in connection with the dismissal of Kursell, to get rid of Hans Steinacher, the conservative chairman of the most important ethnic German organization, the Volksbund für das Deutschtum im Ausland (VDA), as well and to replace him with a 'very senior SS leader'.[23] In fact, on 19 October 1937 Hess suspended Steinacher from his post as head of the VDA after Lorenz had informed him that Steinacher was not sticking to various agreements made with VoMi.[24]

As far as cooperation with the ethnic German organizations abroad was concerned, although the new VoMi leadership favoured Nazi organizations,[25] it refrained from subordinating them formally to itself. The organizations remained de facto independent, which, among other things, reflected foreign policy considerations.[26]

On 2 July 1938 Hitler made VoMi responsible for 'overseeing the work of all state and party agencies involved in ethnic and borderland issues (German minorities abroad and alien minorities at home) and for the efficient deployment of all the resources at their disposal'. VoMi, which was not a state organization, was thereby given the right to issue directives to Reich ministries. This represented an important invasion of the Reich's responsibility for foreign affairs.[27] On 3 February 1938 the VDA was 'coordinated' and turned into a 'cover organization' of VoMi, as the Führer's Deputy put it in his directive. All the other ethnic organizations, with the exception of the Bund Deutscher Osten, which was responsible for borderland issues, were to be incorporated into the VDA, whereas in future all party organizations were to be banned from getting involved in any 'ethnic activity'.[28]

Lorenz and Behrends also managed to put an end to, or at least mitigate, conflicts among the leaderships of the German organizations abroad.[29] In general they restricted themselves to working with those ethnic German organizations that supported the Third Reich, and in most cases they ensured that these groups dominated the political work of the ethnic German minorities. In Romania VoMi succeeded in getting the Deutsche Volkspartei (German People's Party), which was opposed to the Deutsche Volksgemeinschaft (German National Community), to join its competitor.[30] In Yugoslavia VoMi recognized the Schwäbisch-Deutscher Kulturbund (Swabian-German Cultural League) as the official representative of the ethnic Germans after imposing a change of leadership.[31] In Hungary it favoured the Volksbund der Deutschen in Ungarn (National League of Germans in Hungary), which was founded in November 1938.[32]

In the Sudetenland from 1937 onwards VoMi regarded Konrad Henlein's Sudeten German Party as the official representative of the Sudeten Germans,[33] particularly after Henlein had radically altered his position in November 1937. Instead of demanding more autonomy for the Sudeten Germans within Czechoslovakia, Henlein now demanded their absorption into the Reich.[34] In doing so he was adopting the line of his deputy, Karl Hermann Frank, who had close links to Himmler.[35] In 1938 VoMi, in partnership with Henlein, introduced a 'strict system of command' into the organization of the Sudeten Germans.[36]

In May 1938 VoMi tried to establish an organization to include all the ethnic Germans in Poland but failed as a result of the diversity of the various associations.[37] After the Munich Agreement of November 1938 the Germans managed to gain official recognition for the ethnic Germans in Slovakia, established a German Party sympathetic to Nazism, and secured the appointment of the leader of the German ethnic group as a state secretary.[38]

Thus, up until the outbreak of war Himmler's influence on ethnic activities remained indirect and informal. It sprang from the authority he exercised over the leading VoMi functionaries and their effective control over the ethnic German organizations. VoMi was not yet an integral part of the SS empire but only an extended arm of it.

The fact that Himmler was anxious to enlarge the activities of the SS to include ethnic matters was clearly linked to the leadership role which he envisaged the SS playing in the revival of the 'Germanic race' and the impending expansion of the Reich. If the German Reich was to be determined in future by ethnicity and race, then it was necessary to secure the adhesion of ethnic German minorities to Nazi Germany. Himmler's plan to surround the Reich with a ring of 100 million Germanic peasants is clearly relevant here. Furthermore, by involving the SS in ethnic policy it would be possible to extend the range of the concept of a comprehensive 'state protection corps', with the SS acting in diplomatic crises as the defender of ethnic Germans, for example through encouraging the formation of ethnic German 'self-defence leagues'. Indeed, this actually occurred during the Sudeten crisis and in the Free City of Danzig during the preparations for war.[39]

Himmler's good personal relations with Ribbentrop, to whom Hitler had given various special diplomatic assignments, and who since 1935 had had a 'Bureau' at his disposal for this purpose, provided the Reichsführer-SS with further opportunities for acquiring diplomatic influence.[40] Himmler considered that it was his achievement to have drawn Ribbentrop into politics during the negotiations preceding the formation of the Hitler government at the turn of the year 1932–3.[41] As early as May 1933 he had appointed Ribbentrop SS-Standartenführer, and he kept promoting him, for the last time on 20 April 1940 to Obergruppenführer.[42] From 1937 onwards the Ribbentrop Office and the SD Main Office cooperated closely,[43] and the Himmler and Ribbentrop families were good friends. For example, on 2 February 1938, two days before Ribbentrop's appointment as Foreign Minister, the Ribbentrops stayed the night with the Himmlers,[44] and, during a stay in a clinic in February 1939, Margarete Himmler noted with gratitude that her friend had telephoned.[45]

When, in June 1933, his former adjutant, Josias, Hereditary Prince of Waldeck and Pyrmont, was appointed to the Foreign Ministry's personnel department, for Himmler this represented the first step towards the SS's infiltration of the diplomatic service. In June 1934 the Hereditary Prince left the service, but in the meantime he had ensured that of the ten attachés who had been appointed to the personnel department since he had joined five were members of the SS.[46] After the Hereditary Prince's dismissal the official in the NSDAP's liaison staff responsible for foreign affairs, SS-Standartenfuhrer Herbert Scholz, was appointed to the Foreign Ministry. Scholz, who was soon transferred to the German embassy in Washington as an attaché, saw his role during his future career as being to act as a representative of the SS. In February 1939, after meeting him, Himmler asked Scholz to propose 'suitable people in the diplomatic service based in the United States' for membership of the SS. In January 1940 he recommended two people in the embassy.[47]

Up until February 1938 there is evidence of 50 out of a total of 500 senior officials in the diplomatic service being members of the SS. Around half of these diplomats, who were very often attachés at German embassies, joined the SS between September 1936 and February 1938, evidently following increased efforts at recruitment by the SS.[48] Foreign Minister Konstantin von Neurath was appointed an SS-Gruppenführer in September 1937.[49] On 13 September the head of the Foreign Organization of the NSDAP and state secretary in the Foreign Ministry, Wilhelm Bohle, was admitted to the SS by Himmler at the party rally. Bohle recruited numerous functionaries of the Foreign Organization (i.e. Nazi sympathizers among ethnic Germans abroad) into the foreign service, most of whom were in the SS. After he left the Ministry in 1941 Bohle ensured that the Foreign Organization would continue to provide intelligence for the SD, and gave Himmler information concerning foreign service personnel.[50]

Thus, with the appointment of Himmler's friend Ribbentrop to the post of Foreign Minister on 4 February 1938, initially it looked as if Himmler had secured a significant increase in influence over German foreign policy. Ribbentrop not only brought with him twenty members of his office, who were simultaneously members of the SS,[51] but suggested that the new state secretary, Ernst von Weizsäcker, and Ernst Woermann, who had been appointed head of the political department, should also be admitted to the SS. On 30 April 1938 Himmler acceded to this request.[52] In March 1938 he placed another intimate in the Foreign Ministry in the shape of Wilhelm Keppler, who was appointed a state secretary and the Foreign Ministry's special representative for Austria. The two men had got to know each other at the beginning of 1933 when they were arranging the meeting between Hitler and Papen in Ribbentrop's house, and since then Keppler and Himmler had used the intimate 'du' form of address with each other. Keppler, who had initiated the donor organization 'The Friends of the Reichsführer-SS', had also been a member of the SS since March 1933.[53] In November 1939 Himmler strengthened the bonds between the two still further when, in his capacity as Reich Commissar for the Consolidation of the Ethnic German Nation, he gave Keppler the job of dealing with all matters concerning the property of the refugee Baltic Germans.[54]

Emil Schumburg, the head of the Foreign Ministry's department dealing with Germany (Referat Deutschland) and a member of the SS since October

1936,[55] increasingly took on the role of a 'liaison officer'[56] for Himmler. However, soon this close cooperation with the SS appears to have aroused Ribbentrop's suspicion. According to a report by the Gestapo chief Heinrich Müller, Schumberg's 'frank, invariably helpful and positive cooperation with us' had led 'the new leadership of the FM' 'to marginalize Dr Schumburg'.[57] It did not, in fact, come to that;[58] however, as Müller's reference to 'the new leadership of the FM' suggests, Ribbentrop's appointment as Foreign Minister did not actually increase Himmler's opportunity to influence foreign policy in any way. On the contrary, Ribbentrop, who always reacted very sensitively to anyone encroaching on his responsibilities, resisted Himmler's attempts at infiltration and their personal relationship began to cool quite markedly.

Himmler, however, still retained the right to appoint police attachés to German embassies, who could then act as the extended arm of the Gestapo and SS abroad. Thus, he installed one of these special representatives in Spain. In May 1936, in other words, shortly before the outbreak of the Spanish Civil War, criminal commissar Paul Winzer, a member of the SS since 1933, was assigned to the German embassy in Madrid at the express wish of the Chief of the German Police in order to investigate Spanish communism and anarchism. In November 1936, again at Himmler's express wish, he became an official liaison officer to the Spanish political police and finally acted as a police attaché at the embassy.[59] During the following years he expanded his office quite considerably; by the end he had twenty staff, of whom some were deployed in the Spanish protectorate of Morocco to act as the ears of the SD in North Africa.[60]

By the outbreak of war Himmler had appointed police attachés to the German embassies in Rome, Tokyo, and Belgrade.[61] When, after the outbreak of war, Hitler ordered that all personnel employed at German diplomatic missions should be subordinate to the Reich Foreign Minister,[62] Himmler worked out a deal with Ribbentrop to the effect that his representatives at the various missions were permitted to have their own separate line of communication to the Reich Security Main Office (RSHA).[63]

In August 1940 the head of the SD Foreign Department, Heinz Johst, made an agreement with the desk officer in the Foreign Ministry responsible for liaising with the SS, Rudolf Likus, that the SD was permitted to run its own intelligence service, so long as reports with any diplomatic significance were sent to the Foreign Ministry's department dealing with Germany. Moreover, the SD was entitled to act abroad on its own responsibility.[64]

Himmler also attempted to acquire influence over German foreign policy by utilizing links to foreign police forces. Fascist Italy was the most obvious partner. On 30 March 1936 a German–Italian police conference was held in Berlin. Led by Himmler, the German delegation consisted of Heydrich, Werner Best, Gestapo chief Heinrich Müller, as well as other representatives of the police and the Foreign Ministry. The Italian delegation included the police chief Arturo Bocchini and other high-ranking police officers. The main topic of the conference was cooperation in the fight against communism. In October a German delegation led by Himmler reciprocated with a visit to Rome, where Himmler was received by Mussolini.[65] Further bilateral police conferences with communism as their target took place during the following months with Finland, Bulgaria, and probably with Hungary, and contacts along the same lines were established with Poland and Yugoslavia.[66]

Between 30 August and 3 September 1937 Himmler hosted an international police congress attended by representatives from Belgium, Brazil, Bulgaria, Finland, Greece, Hungary, Italy, Japan, the Netherlands, Poland, Portugal, Switzerland, Uruguay, and Yugoslavia. According to a Foreign Ministry statement, he discussed with them how 'the fight against Communism could be boosted', and above all how 'Germany could take the lead [. . .] in this vital campaign in which they were all involved'.[67] Himmler considered the topic of the conference to be so sensitive that he ordered that no information about the conference should be released.[68] The Italian delegation was once again led by Police Minister Bocchini, and he invited Himmler to make an official visit to Italy in October 1937.[69]

Himmler and Bocchini got on so well that after the end of his official visit the Italian police chief invited his German colleague to stay on for a private holiday in Italy lasting several weeks. Beforehand Himmler had to take part in the obligatory ceremonies in Munich to commemorate the 9 November putsch, but a few days later he and his wife departed on the only big foreign holiday the couple ever had. This was reason enough for Margarete to begin a diary, which she enthusiastically kept during the journey, though unfortunately only occasionally adding further entries.[70]

'We arrived in Rome at midday on 14.11.37', she noted. We learn that the couple had travelled in a saloon carriage and were received by Bocchini personally. During the days that followed they visited the sights: the Colosseum, Castel Gandolfo, the Castel Sant'Angelo, the Capitol and the Vatican, the Roman forum, where Himmler impressed his wife with his 'knowledge of history'. And then Margarete noted a small victory: 'Thanks to the kindness of the police we were able to go for a drive in the Vatican park in our car with the SS pennant.'[71]

On 17 November they went on to Naples. Unfortunately, Himmler had 'a stomach upset'. Neverthless, the following day they visited Herculaneum and Pompeii, where—and that was naturally particularly interesting—'mosaic floors with a swastika' had been excavated. Margarete Himmler noted her impressions of the country and its people without any inhibitions. 'In Italy they take cooking very seriously. Apparently there are no drunkards here; they are used to drinking wine.' 'One comes across children everywhere; what a blessed country it is.'[72]

On 19 November she continued her tour of Naples in the company of Eugen Dollmann. Dollmann, a historian who had been living in Italy since 1928, had come into contact with leading Nazis, including Himmler, through his acquaintanceship with the Hitler Youth leader Baldur von Schirach. He acted as Himmler's interpreter during his trips to Italy. In fact Dollmann had a special place among Himmler's representatives abroad. Attached to the German embassy, he was not answerable to the police liaison officer, Herbert Kappler. In future his reports would keep Himmler up to date with developments in Italy.[73]

In the meantime, Himmler had spent a very disagreeable day—according to Margarete, he had 'driven up Vesuvius, where it rained and was very windy'. In the afternoon they went on to Cosenza in Calabria, a trip of 350 kilometres involving several breakdowns, arriving after midnight. On the following day the Himmlers visited the fortress that dated back to the Hohenstaufens and then went on to Taormina in Sicily. And here they began a fortnight's holiday, reading, playing bridge, and bathing. Himmler played a lot of tennis. They also made trips, for example to Syracuse, where they visited the 'catacombs with a Franciscan guide. He was a sly one who didn't answer any of H's questions.' At the beginning of December they went on to Palermo, where Himmler, always on the lookout for 'Germanic' remains, bought some antiquities.

On 4 December the Himmlers flew to Libya and, on the following day, visited the archaeological sites in Leptis Magna, a city which, Margarete noted, 'the Romans had built with infinite greatness, richness, and nobility'. 'I keep thinking,' she asked herself, 'why are these people now so poor? Perhaps because there are no longer any slaves.' In view of the pomp with which his host, the governor Italo Balbo, celebrated their visit, Himmler's tourist garb was somewhat inappropriate. For he was wearing a 'ridiculous young person's hiking-type knickerbocker suit', as Dollmann disapprovingly noted.[74]

On 6 December the Himmlers visited a Tuareg camp and on the following evening they were invited to dine with the Balbos. Beforehand the Himmlers had visited a mosque and the Jewish quarter. Margarete described her impressions: 'Awfully dirty and the smell! The Arabs are much cleaner.'

On 9 December the Himmlers flew to Naples, on the following day visited Paestum and the National Museum, and on the eleventh were taken to Rome by car. That evening, after dining with the German ambassador to the Vatican, von Bergen, Himmler once again felt 'very bad. Immediately said it was the lobster.' But the following day he had recovered enough to be able to accept an invitation from Bocchini, and on the thirteenth they returned to Berlin by train.[75]

On 10 December, while still in Naples, Himmler had summarized some of his impressions of the trip in a letter to Walther Wüst, the head of the Ahnenerbe, and had drafted a substantial research project. He wrote that, while visiting Italian museums and archaeological sites, he had kept coming across 'evidence of Germanic remains': references to runes in a Latin inscription in the Roman forum, the swastikas in Pompeii and Herculaneum, and other things. Wüst was therefore instructed 'to create a department in the Ahnenerbe with the task of studying Italy and Greece in the light of their Indo-Germanic-Aryan associations'. Himmler fully recognized that this was naturally a 'very big' task. But he expressed himself confident that 'we shall thereby achieve our main goal of coming closer to proving that the Aryan and Nordic people have spread outwards from the centre of Germany and the Baltic basin to almost all parts of the earth, and that now at least we are coming closer to providing evidence for the intellectual dominance of the world by the Aryan Teutons'.[76]

Their trip, with its little difficulties, had shown that the Himmlers had not yet quite achieved this high aspiration in their private lives.

The Blomberg–Fritsch crisis

At the end of 1937 Hitler made an important change in the policy of the Third Reich: he embarked on a policy that was openly expansionist. On 5

November 1937, in an address to the Reich Minister of War, Werner von Blomberg, the Reich Foreign Minister, Konstantin von Neurath, and the commanders-in-chief of the army, navy, and Luftwaffe, he justified the need for military expansion in order to acquire for Germany the 'living-space' that was necessary to secure its future as a great power.[77]

Hitler then went into the details of when and how, and suggested two possible scenarios. In the first place, he told his audience that he was determined to conduct a major war at the latest by 1943 to 1945 in order to solve 'Germany's space problem'. Their opponents would be France and Great Britain. Secondly, he elucidated possible situations in which Germany might be able to act before these dates. If, for domestic or diplomatic reasons, France should prove incapable of intervening then he wanted to use the opportunity to attack and annex Austria and Czechoslovakia.

The concerns and the criticism expressed by the military chiefs and Neurath about his military plans following his talk helped to convince Hitler that the transition to a more aggressive foreign policy would be possible only if he replaced the conservatives, who were filling leading positions within the state apparatus, with more biddable followers.

By chance, a few months later the Reich War Minister's involvement in a marriage scandal provided the opportunity for a major reshuffle along the lines Hitler was seeking. In January 1938 Blomberg married a much youn-ger woman, who, it was revealed shortly after the wedding, had several convictions for 'immoral behaviour' and was registered with the police as a prostitute. The affair—an affair of state, since Hitler and Göring had acted as witnesses at the wedding—led to Blomberg's retirement.[78] At the end of January 1938 Göring, who regarded himself as the obvious successor to Blomberg and had personally informed Hitler of the marriage scandal, unexpectedly presented Hitler with material that compromised his most important rival for the post, the Commander-in-Chief of the army, Werner von Fritsch. Himmler's Gestapo had provided him with the material and Göring gave Hitler a file which appeared to show that Fritsch was homo-sexual.

Hitler immediately seized on the accusation, arranging a confrontation in the Reich Chancellery between von Fritsch and the sole witness, a man who had previous convictions for blackmailing his sexual partners. The witness claimed to recognize Fritsch as a previous customer, an accusation that Fritsch strenuously denied. The Gestapo was assigned to investigate the matter further. It was a scandal that, during the following days, threatened to plunge the regime into a crisis. On 4 February, however, Hitler took control of the situation by dismissing both von Blomberg and von Fritsch, by taking over the supreme command of the Wehrmacht himself without replacing the War Minister, and by appointing Walther von Brauchitsch as the new Commander-in-Chief of the army. At a stroke the whole structure of the military leadership had been transformed.

The reconstruction of the leadership of the Wehrmacht was followed by extensive changes in personnel. During the first days of February twelve generals were removed and fifty-one other posts in the military hierarchy had new incumbents. The Foreign Ministry was also affected: Foreign Minister von Neurath was promoted 'upstairs' to chair the Secret Cabinet Council (which never met), and was replaced as Foreign Minister by Hitler's slippery 'special ambassador', Joachim von Ribbentrop, who appointed Ernst von Weizsäcker, the head of the Political Department (in the Foreign Ministry), to be his state secretary. The ambassadors in Rome, Tokyo, London, and Vienna were replaced. Finally, Hjalmar Schacht was replaced as Reich Economics Minister by Walter Funk, a former business journalist and hitherto a state secretary in the Propaganda Ministry.[79]

In the meantime the Gestapo was investigating Fritsch, who had to appear before the Reich Military Court in March. In fact the court had begun its own investigation into the affair and—by contrast with the Gestapo investigation—evidence had also been sought that might exonerate Fritsch; and indeed, such evidence had been found. The main hearing, which was conducted by Göring personally, ended with a sensation: the prosecution witness was forced to confess that he had confused General von Fritsch with a retired cavalry officer named Frisch. Fritsch was pronounced innocent and officially rehabilitated.[80]

Fritsch considered Himmler primarily responsible for his fall. He made serious accusations against the 'main villain': 'Your whole attitude in this affair shows [...] that you were determined in a biased manner to portray me as the guilty one.' Fritsch even contemplated challenging Himmler to a duel.[81] In fact Himmler had been convinced of Fritsch's guilt from the start, and he ensured that the investigation would be carried out one-sidedly. It is possible—and we shall come back to this—that he thought that he would boost his career by exposing the scandal. However, he certainly did not, as Fritsch assumed, intentionally fabricate and initiate the affair. In the light of the homophobic horror scenarios that Himmler painted in 1936–7, he may well have actually believed that the plague of homosexuality had already infected the highest ranks of the Wehrmacht. Goebbels noted at the height of the crisis, at the beginning of January, that the fact that the Gestapo could not come up with the required results made Himmler 'very depressed. Fritsch has still not confessed.'[82]

Himmler's depression may well have increased when it became clear that the accusations against Fritsch made by him were completely groundless. Goebbels noted of a meeting with Hitler in March: 'The trial of von Fritsch is going very badly. The whole thing seems to be based on a case of mistaken identity. Very bad news, particularly for Himmler. He is too quick to act and also too prejudiced. The Führer is very annoyed.'[83]

Hitler's annoyance hit Himmler hard, and the blow was deserved. The Reichsführer-SS and Chief of the German Police had completely failed in a highly embarrassing affair of state. As late as August, at the time of von Fritsch's final rehabilitation, Goebbels noted: 'Terrible defeat for Himmler.'[84] Himmler's position in the Fritsch affair was made particularly awkward because he was simultaneously facing the accusation that the uncompromising pursuer of homosexuals was all the time tolerating one in a key position within the SS. For, in February 1938, he was compelled to suspend Gruppenführer Kurt Wittje, until 1935 head of the SS Main Office, because of rumours of his alleged homosexuality. Himmler instructed the 'Reichsführer-SS's Great Court of Arbitration' to conduct an investigation, which, however, produced no concrete evidence to support the allegations. Himmler, though, was not satisfied. He produced a seven-page response to the court's report, subjecting it to a detailed and devastating critique, then conducted his own meticulous examination of the Wittje case and ordered his dismissal from the SS on the grounds that his homosexuality had been 'definitely' proved. He then sent the whole file back to the court with the comment that they should consider the affair as a 'classic example' of how such cases should be dealt with in the future. He could not resist teaching the court a lesson, and did so in great detail.[85]

It is clear from Himmler's statement that the case was particularly awkward because Hitler had already informed him in 1934 that he had been told by the War Minister, Blomberg, that Wittje, a former officer, had been dismissed from the Reichswehr on the grounds of suspected homosexuality. Himmler must have considered this information particularly alarming because the elimination of the SA leadership in 1934 had been justified primarily on the grounds of Röhm's and his followers' homosexuality. Had the rumour been confirmed, the SS's opponents would have been able to claim that the SS leadership was also involved in the homosexual conspiracy allegedly led by Röhm.

Himmler's detailed statement on the Wittje case from 1938 is thus also a piece of self-justification, comprehensive proof that, at that time, he himself had carefully examined the accusations but had been *forced* to consider them baseless. As far as Himmler was concerned, the case was particularly tricky because, after the removal of Fritsch with the aid of a fictitious scandal, now he himself was in danger of being confronted with the accusation that he had tolerated a homosexual and former officer in the ranks of the SS. He was thus concerned to prevent any suspicion of this arising.

Himmler told the court that the detailed examination of the affair that was carried out at that time had not given rise to any suspicion on which one could act. According to Wittje's personal file, the only evidence was that on two occasions during his Reichswehr service, when drunk, he had, as Himmler indignantly noted, 'put his arms round, hugged, and kissed a subordinate'. As a result Wiitje had been requested by his superiors to hand in his resignation. At the time, Himmler noted in 1938, he had come to the conclusion that Wittje's behaviour was the result of his excessive alcohol consumption. He had thus warned him to avoid 'getting drunk', a warning that unfortunately Wittje had not heeded. In May 1935 Himmler had relieved Wittje of his post as head of the Main Office at his own request, 'on health grounds', but had let him keep his rank of Grup-penführer. In 1937 there had been a further complaint from Wittje's former driver, which in Himmler's view was quite clear: 'Hugging, kissing, touch-ing.' However, the driver had withdrawn his accusation.

In fact there was more evidence against Wittje. He had gone on holiday with a young SS man. As far as Himmler was concerned, the case was clear. 'In my eyes it is completely abnormal for a man of 43 to offer to use the familiar "du" form with a young chap of 25 after only a few weeks and then to go on holiday not with his wife and children, who were going to East Prussia, but with this young man to Kreuth and Salzburg and then, despite the fact that Wittje has recently been in financial trouble, to pay for his trip.' The trip with this young man, instead of with his family, was 'outrageous and could be attributable only to abnormality'. Wittje and his companion were therefore to be dismissed from the SS, even if there is 'a danger that I'm being unjust to someone', since 'I would prefer to be too strict in this area rather than allow the plague of homosexuality to enter the SS'.[86]

In November 1938 Himmler returned to the case at a meeting of Grup-penführer, and justified Wittje's dismissal, since 'there must be a reasonable question as to whether he has not seriously incriminated himself under §175 [of the Penal Code]'.[87] However, Himmler did not continue to hold this affair against Wittje. In 1942 he helped him to find another career.[88]

The Blomberg–Fritsch affair, or rather the Blomberg–Fritsch–Wittje affair, is reflected in Margarete Himmler's diaries: 'H has a lot of worries and even more work', she wrote on 26 January, not without compassion for the focus of Himmler's hard work: 'I feel really sorry for poor old Blomberg.' On 30 January she noted: 'Day after day H hasn't been getting back from work before midnight. I don't know how he can put up with it.' And on 4 February she noted: 'Big news. The Führer has taken over the Wehrmacht himself. Ribbentrop has become Foreign Minister. Many changes. H is very tense. Has had to work on it night and day and yet hasn't been promoted himself.' Thus, presumably Himmler had thought he had a chance of being promoted to minister, possibly to Minister of Police.[89]

A month later, on 5 March, she reflected on her husband's permanent overwork and his position in the Third Reich: 'We spent almost 8 days in Gmund and two in Munich. Here on Tuesday we got back to lots of excitement. I lie in bed till midnight waiting for Heini. H is so tired and exhausted from all the annoyance and I always think he gets so little credit. I sometimes rack my brains thinking why things are as they are. Are his enemies really so powerful? But H is cheerful and brave and I try to be cheerful too.'

The Anschluss with Austria

'Austria is now part of the German Reich. H was the first to arrive in Vienna.' Margarete Himmler noted this with satisfaction in her diary on 13 March 1938. For her this marked the end of a period in which the political tension had had a direct impact on the atmosphere in Himmler's family. 'We could never escape the tension. Every day brought something new. H, who naturally knew what was going on, was in a good mood, indeed really cheerful. But for me, who could only watch the comings and goings and had to pack his military uniform, it was all too stressful.'[90]

In January 1938 the German police had begun extensive preparations for the mobilization of around 20,000 policemen, allegedly for a big parade. In fact the police were preparing for the invasion of Austria, in which eventually, on 12 March, motorized police units from all over the Reich participated side by side with Wehrmacht units.[91]

The excuse for Hitler to undertake the so-called Anschluss, which had been planned for months and was carried out by force, was provided by the sudden announcement by the Austrian Chancellor Kurt von Schuschnigg, on 9 March, of his intention to carry out a plebiscite only a few days later on the maintenance of Austrian independence. His aim was thereby to demonstrate Austria's determination to retain its independence in the face of increasing German pressure. Hitler was not prepared to wait for this plebiscite, and indeed insisted that it should not take place. He succeeded in forcing Schuschnigg's resignation and his replacement as Chancellor by the leader of the Austrian Nazis, Arthur Seyss-Inquart. Seyss-Inquart then requested German troops to be sent in, as he had been instructed to do by the German government.[92]

In fact Himmler had flown to Vienna in the early morning of 12 March, before German units at the head of an armed commando occupied the city. The journal Die Deutsche Polizei (The German Police) informed its readers that the Reichsführer-SS 'landed unexpectedly this morning around 5 o'clock at Aspern airport near Vienna before any German units had crossed the border. Accompanied by, amongst others, SS-Gruppenführer Heydrich, he took the initial measures necessary to maintain law and order and thus was the first representative of the National Socialist Reich to step onto Austrian soil.'[93] The paper spoke of a 'bold coup by Reichsführer-SS Heinrich Himmler', by which 'this revolution, one of the most epoch-making in the history of the world [. . .] was carried out without a single shot being fired and without any blood being spilt'. However, the article did not have the resonance it sought. Goebbels had the paper confiscated, since in the article concerned 'virtually all the secrets of 10–13 March were betrayed'.[94] This was something of a disgrace for the Chief of Police and Secret Police.

But to return to Himmler's appearance in Vienna on 12 March: here he hoped that, by issuing tough-sounding orders, he would be able to wipe out the memory of the defeat that his SS had suffered in 1934 after the attack on the Viennese Federal Chancellery. One of his announcements, for example, read: 'in Vienna 800 Austrian SS men are protecting the Seyss-Inquart government in the Federal Chancellery from armed Reds.'[95]

Himmler, accompanied by Seyss-Inquart, then moved on from Vienna to Linz, where he arrived around midday in order to greet Hitler, who had arrived in his homeland.[96] On 14 March Himmler had not been able to resist marching into Vienna with Sepp Dietrich, 'at the head of the Leib-standarte', as *Die Deutsche Polizei* reported. The next day he travelled west to meet Hitler, who was on his way from Linz to Vienna. He met him halfway there, at St Pölten; from there he accompanied him to Vienna, where, on the same day, the big demonstration took place in the Heldenplatz at which Hitler announced the 'entry of my homeland into the German Reich', to the applause of a huge crowd.

On 18 March Himmler ordered the establishment of a Gestapo head-quarters in Vienna modelled on the organization he had created in the 'Reich', as well as the establishment of Gestapo district headquarters in the provincial capitals of the Austrian provinces.[97] On 14 March he had already appointed the Gestapo chief Hermann Müller to be Inspector of the Security Police in Austria. He remained in this post until the summer of 1938. His successor was Walter Stahlecker.[98]

On 21 March Himmler appointed two new special staffs who had responsibility for supervising the establishment of the order and security police and liaising with the central agencies in Berlin.[99] At the beginning of April 1938 he toured the Austrian provincial capitals in order to inspect their police departments,[100] and between 23 and 25 May he once again visited Vienna. In general Himmler succeeded in integrating the police of the Austrian 'corporate state' into the German system without generating too much friction. One of their most pressing tasks was to organize a wave of arrests of political opponents, in particular communists and socialists.[101]

As in the two previous years, and in the midst of this reorganization of the Austrian police, between 2 and 10 May the Reichsführer undertook an official visit to Italy.[102] As before, he was accompanied by his wife Margarete, and again the visit was not without its hiccups. Margarete's refusal to follow court protocol and curtsey when being received by the Queen of Italy—we should not have to do that!—caused offence. The 'whole court', she wrote in her diary, was 'peeved'. And, all in all: 'there was a lack of order and there were some funny situations. What a way to be treated. Such courts have funny customs. They don't regard anyone who isn't a courtier as a human being.'[103]

Ill 17. Himmler and his SS were to play a central role in the annexation of foreign territories by the German Reich. The picture shows Himmler and the chief of the order police, Kurt Daluege, at the ceremony where the Austrian police swore an oath of loyalty to Hitler on 15 March 1938.

Operations in the Sudetenland

A substantial number of motorized police units participated in the occupation of the Sudetenland in October 1938, as well as two Einsatzgruppen of the security police. The latter had originally been established with the aim of operating throughout the country in the event of a German attack on Czechoslovakia.[104] However, when this had to be postponed as a result of the Munich Agreement of 30 September, which granted the Sudeten German territory to Germany, the two Einsatzgruppen entered the Sudetenland. They confiscated Czech police documents and, by the end of the year, had carried out a large number of arrests, possibly affecting as many as 10,000 Czechs and Germans.[105] Armed SS units—the whole of the SS Verfügungstruppe as well as four Death's Head battalions—also marched into the Sudetenland, representing the SS's first military action.[106] By the end of September other Death's Head units had arrived to reinforce the

Sudeten German Free Corps formed from refugees entering Czech territory and occupying a small amount of border territory.[107]

On 1 October this Free Corps, which had been trained by the SA and supplied with arms by the Wehrmacht, was subordinated to the SS. However, the SS proved incapable of taking on the provisioning of food and other necessities, which had hitherto been supplied by the SA and paid for by the Wehrmacht. According to the Wehrmacht High Command's liaison officer with the Free Corps, this provoked 'discontent among the leaders of the Free Corps, threatening to jeopardize the internal structure of the corps which it had taken considerable effort to establish. The fear, which was justified, was that the SA leaders who had proved themselves in action and in establishing [the corps] would be replaced by ones from the SS.' There were signs that the force was liable to disintegrate. Moreover, the SS began to try to recruit members of the Free Corps, which created 'bitterness' among SA leaders. 'In order to win over the leadership of the Free Corps the deputy leader of the Sudeten Germans and his chief of staff were offered high-ranking positions in the SS. However, they rejected them.'[108] 'It was shocking to experience how two components of the state (leaders of the SA and SS) were involved in a more or less latent opposition to one another, whose effects were having a negative impact on the leadership and the unity of the force', concluded the lieutenant-colonel concerned.[109] Clearly, five years after the Röhm affair relations between the SS and the SA were anything but harmonious.

The SS's engagement in the Sudetenland had, however, increased Himmler's military ambitions. On 8 November, after the conclusion of the occupation, Himmler reported to his Gruppenführer in Munich that during the Sudeten crisis he had mobilized 5,000 SS men between the ages of 45 and 50, of whom the SS had kept on 3,500 in the force. As a result of this mobilization it had been possible to remove active Death's Head units from the concentration camps and establish six new battalions. In addition, he had mobilized 11,000 men to act as police reinforcements.[110]

Pogrom

The Nazi regime's move to an overt policy of expansion went hand in hand with increased persecution of the Jews. This became particularly apparent after the Anschluss with Austria in March 1938, when Nazi activists satisfied their pent-up desire to indulge in anti-Jewish acts, particularly in Vienna, where there was a large number of attacks on Jews as well as arbitrary and illegal expropriation of property.[111]

The fact that, after the annexation of Austria, the SD, which was really a party organization, succeeded in acquiring executive powers in the sphere of Jewish policy proved decisive for the development of SS Jewish policy. Adolf Eichmann, who had been sent to Vienna as the SD's Jewish expert, managed to persuade the Reich Commissar in Austria, Josef Bürckel, to establish a 'Central Agency for Jewish Emigration' on 20 August 1938, and to assign to the SD responsibility for running this organization. With the aid of this agency Eichmann introduced a system by which Jews who were compelled to emigrate were rapidly processed through all the various bureaucratic procedures. The whole process was financed by the property which the Viennese Jews were forced to hand over as they passed through it.[112]

After the Anschluss the Nazis increased the persecution of the Jews. A new wave of anti-Jewish laws was issued, which among other things prepared for the 'aryanization' of what property the Jews still possessed. In the course of the 'asocial' action of June 1938, as has already been indicated, the Kripo also arrested a large number of Jews and placed them in preventive detention.[113]

What then, at this stage, did Himmler intend to do with the Jews who were resident in Germany?

As has already been pointed out, prior to 1938 Himmler made relatively few comments, either public or private, on the 'Jewish question'. The reason for this was not because he was not anti-Semitic, but presumably simply because, unlike in the case of other issues such as the fight against 'asocials' and homosexuals or the church question, in Himmler's view Jewish persecution required little engagement on his part. There was a consensus among the most important actors in Jewish policy—Hitler, the Four Year Plan organization under Göring, as well as the Reich Interior Ministry under Frick—to radicalize the persecution in stages, in order thereby to exclude German Jews completely from the economy and society and try to persuade them to emigrate. Within the context of this policy Heydrich's security police and the SD performed their role so effectively that Himmler was rarely obliged to intervene himself.

In the spring of 1938 Himmler took a decision in an individual case concerning the request of a female German Jew living abroad to enter

Germany, the justification for which helps to reveal his long-term objective for dealing with the Jews. The Reichsführer responded to the request by saying that the person concerned could enter the country, so long as she 'commits herself to staying in Germany because Germany [is not prepared] to give up its most valuable pawn, the Jews'. This decision was in complete contradiction to the forced-emigration policy which the SD in particular was pursuing after the Anschluss, and thus caused considerable consternation in its Jewish department. In response, the department asked Himmler whether his decision meant that 'all rich Jews', as well as 'all well-known Jews or those suitable to act as pawns', should be excluded from the emigration programme. Himmler initialled the document without commenting further, and in July announced that the matter was closed.[114] The idea of keeping wealthy Jews as hostages reflected Himmler's extreme utilitarian mentality, and was to preoccupy him again and again in the coming years.

Between May and July 1938 there were renewed attacks on Jews by party activists in various parts of the Reich. In Berlin, in particular, Goebbels attempted to create a real pogrom atmosphere. However, the Sudeten crisis persuaded the Nazi leadership to stop anti-Jewish attacks for the time being in order to demonstrate Nazi Germany's peaceful intentions. At the beginning of October, though, the moment the crisis was ended by the Munich Agreement, the attacks began again with full force. Among other things, at least a dozen synagogues were damaged during these weeks. There were increasing signs that the party's rank and file were moving in the direction of a full-scale pogrom.

On 28 October, in the midst of this charged anti-Semitic atmosphere, Himmler ordered the expulsion of Polish Jews resident in the Reich within three days, in order to pre-empt the Polish government's move to deprive them of their nationality.[115] During the next few days, in the first major deportation, 18,000 people were arrested and driven over the German–Polish border in inhuman conditions.[116]

On 7 November 17-year-old Herschel Grynspan assassinated Ernst vom Rath, the legation secretary in the German embassy in Paris, in revenge for the deportation of his parents, who came from Poland. This provided the Nazi regime with a welcome excuse to satisfy the militant anti-Semitic sections of the party's rank and file by launching the pogrom for which they were pressing. Already on 7 November, the day of the assassination, the Nazi press began issuing threats to the Jews living in Germany, and, in accordance with the instructions of the Propaganda Ministry, announced that Grynspan's deed, an attack by 'world Jewry', would have unforeseeable consequences for the situation of the Jews in Germany.[117] On 7 and 8 November, in Hesse in particular, party activists attacked synagogues and Jewish shops.[118]

In this situation, on 8 November Himmler made his annual speech to the SS-Gruppenführer, who had assembled in Munich to take part in the ceremonies commemorating the putsch of 1923 on the following day. In his speech Himmler referred to the 'Jewish question'. 'During the next ten years,' he announced, 'we shall undoubtedly face extraordinary and critical conflicts', for it was a question of surviving the 'ideological struggle' with 'all the Jews, Freemasons, Marxists, and churches in the world'. He did not omit to add that 'I consider the Jews as the driving [force], as the essence of everything that is negative [...] the Jews cannot remain in Germany—it's only a matter of years—we shall increasingly drive them out with unparalleled and ruthless brutality'.[119] However, Himmler made no reference to the actual situation, and the formulation that they would drive the Jews out in the course 'of years' does not suggest that at this point he was working on the assumption that there was about to be a dramatic new development in the persecution of the Jews.

The following day, 9 November, vom Rath died of his wounds. The news, which was not unexpected, arrived in Munich in the afternoon. His death was officially announced that evening during the usual commemoration ceremony for the 'old fighters' in the Munich town hall. Hitler left the event, while Goebbels roused the party leaders who were present with a fiery tirade and in this way initiated the pogrom. The chronology of these events, however, indicates that before the meeting took place Goebbels had already agreed with Hitler on how to proceed.[120]

Himmler was also present in the town hall.[121] It is not clear what he did after Goebbels's speech or whether he issued any orders to the SS. In any case, throughout the Reich members of the SS, who had come together that evening for the commemoration, took part in the attacks. It is impossible to establish whether special orders would have had to be issued centrally by the Reichsführer-SS or whether the SS simply joined in the local attacks.[122]

Later that evening Himmler went to Hitler's Munich flat and was present when, shortly before half past eleven, reports came in about the extent of the destruction.[123] Presumably he then gave instructions to the Gestapo chief Müller, based in Berlin, who then informed his officials shortly before midnight that soon 'action would be taken against the Jews, in particular against synagogues'; no one should interfere. Looting and major acts of violence should, however, be prevented. And, more important: the concentration camps should prepare to receive 20,000–30,000 prisoners.[124]

At midnight Himmler joined Hitler for the oath-taking ceremony for SS candidates on Odeonsplatz and then returned to his hotel, the Vierjahreszeiten, where he met Heydrich. Put in the picture by Himmler, Heydrich then sent a telex to the offices of the security police and SD in which he announced that 'demonstrations against the Jews are to be expected throughout the Reich', which the police should not hinder. Instead, the police should restrict themselves to preventing the burning of synagogues where there was a threat to neighbouring buildings, as well as to stopping looting and attacks on non-Jewish businesses.[125]

Müller's order and Heydrich's telex, sent about one-and-a-half hours later, show that the police reacted relatively late to these events and were evidently surprised by the extent of the violence. Throughout the Reich Nazi activists—members of the SA and SS, members of the party and other Nazi organizations—had begun to destroy synagogues, Jewish institutions, and businesses; to smash the furniture in Jewish houses; to drag Jews from their homes by force, to humiliate, mistreat, and in many cases to murder them. The official death-toll was later put at ninety-one, which is probably too low. There were numerous suicides, and of the 25,000–30,000 Jewish men who were arrested during the night and taken to concentration camps many did not survive their imprisonment or died later as a result.[126]

During the following weeks further steps in so-called 'Jewish policy' were discussed at a number of conferences attended by high-ranking officials.[127] At the meeting held on 12 November 1938 Heydrich raised the question of Jewish emigration, and among other things mentioned the experience of the SD with the 'Jewish Emigration Office' in Vienna. He proposed the establishment of a similar agency to cover the whole of the Reich. Göring accepted the idea. Furthermore, Heydrich proposed an 'emigration programme for the Jews in the rest of the Reich', covering a time-span of 'at least 8–10 years'.[128] The fact that his proposal for an organized expulsion of the Jews met with general approval at this meeting was the decisive precondition for Heydrich's future leadership role in Jewish policy. The idea of a programme for the comprehensive expulsion of the Jews developed by the 'Jewish department' of the SD during the previous years, which had thoroughly assessed its domestic, diplomatic, and economic implications, now became the official policy of the regime.

On 24 January 1939 Göring ordered the establishment of a 'Central Office for Jewish Emigration' along the lines of the emigration agency created by Eichmann in Vienna, and put Heydrich in charge of it. In parallel with this, Göring began the amalgamation of all the various Jewish organizations and associations to form an integrated compulsory organization in the shape of the Reich Association of the Jews in Germany (Reichsvereinigung der Juden in Deutschland), under the supervision of the Reich Interior Ministry.[129] It replaced the Representative Council of the Jews in Germany (Reichsvertretung der Juden in Deutschland) created in 1933. On 4 July 1939, under the 10th Decree for the Implementation of the Reich Citizenship Law, all Jews living in Germany and all Jewish organizations were obliged to become members of this body.[130]

The pogrom was followed by a wave of anti-Semitic legislation. Jews were largely excluded from further economic activity, their businesses were compulsorily 'aryanized', their insurance claims arising out of the damage caused by the pogrom were nullified. Instead, they were obliged to pay an 'atonement contribution' amounting to 1 billion Reich marks.[131]

Himmler too issued a number of decrees during these weeks. Thus, on 10 November he banned Jews from possessing firearms, a measure which the Reich Minister of the Interior confirmed the following day by issuing an official decree to that effect.[132] On 2 December, on the basis of a general police decree issued the day before,[133] he ordered a curfew for all Jews to coincide with the 'National Solidarity Day'. Since Jews 'had no part to play in the solidarity of the German people', they were not permitted to leave their place of residence between the hours of 12.00 and 8 p.m.[134] On 3 December 1938 Himmler signed a decree which banned Jews from possessing motor vehicles, with immediate effect. Their driving licences and permits were declared invalid and had to be handed in.[135]

This continuing and increasingly threatening harassment had its effect. The negotiations with the International Committee for Political Refugees, which Schacht began on Hitler's instructions at the end of 1938 in order to realize Heydrich's proposal for a large-scale 'emigration programme', in the end collapsed.[136] However, the panic produced by the November pogrom and the loosening of the restrictions on immigration in several countries led to increasing numbers of Jews leaving Germany.[137]

The occupation of Prague

At the beginning of April 1939 Himmler's daughter Gudrun received a letter from Karl Wolff, her father's adjutant: 'Dear Püppi,' he began, 'I'm writing this letter in order to give you and, in particular your children and grandchildren, a valuable document.' According to Wolff, on 15 March he had personally witnessed the Führer's entry into the old imperial castle of Prague, the Hradschin. He described it as follows: 'The Führer went into a barely furnished room, turned to your father, and embraced him, delighted that it had been granted to him to win Bohemia and Moravia for Germany. The Führer then said: "Himmler, isn't it wonderful that we are standing here, here we are and we shall never leave". Later on the Führer once again said to your father: "I don't want to praise myself, but I really have to say: it was very elegantly done".' 'I hope, dear Püppi,' Wolff concluded his letter, 'that I will have made you very happy with my story.'[138]

There was a good reason why Hitler turned to Himmler in his euphoria, for the SS and police had in fact played a leading role in the largely smooth occupation of the Czech part of Czechoslovakia on 15 March 1939, just as they had in the invasion of Austria and the Sudetenland. In addition to two regiments of order police,[139] Himmler had assigned two Einsatzgruppen of security police to the occupying force, who immediately began seizing documents and—as part of 'Operation Iron Bars'—arrested large numbers of communists and German émigrés—by the beginning of May around 6,000 people. It took until 1 September before the status of the security police in the 'Protectorate of Bohemia and Moravia' had been legally defined. In the meantime the security police could impose an arbitrary regime unrestrained by legal limits.

In fact legalization changed little, because effectively it simply legalized the arbitrary regime already established by Himmler and Heydrich. The decree laid down that not only the Czech authorities but also the German administration were obliged to follow the orders of the Gestapo, and that 'the Reichsführer-SS, in agreement with the Reich Protector, [. . .] can [implement] [. . .] the administrative measures necessary for the maintenance of law and order outside the normal limits'. The Reich Protector, the former Foreign Minister von Neurath, was, however, de facto excluded from security matters, because the Deputy Reich Protector, Karl Hermann

Frank, who had been appointed Higher SS and Police Leader, was subordinate to Himmler as far as his practical responsibilities were concerned. Moreover, the security police were authorized to give instructions to the regional authorities in the Protectorate on 'matters concerning the state police', and it was Himmler who appointed the commander of the security police. In fact, the first appointee to this post, Otto Rasch, was replaced after only a few weeks by Stahlecker. The order police operated with the same degree of autonomy.[140]

The revival of settlement policy

Up until 1938 Himmler showed very little interest in the settlement activities of his Race and Settlement Main Office. It is true that, on 3 September 1935, he issued an order to the effect that the Race and Settlement Main Office (RuSHA) was responsible for all matters concerning the settlement of SS members. This applied to the choice of settlers for both the project 'Re-establishment of the German Peasantry' and the 'homestead settlement' programme, in other words urban settlement,[141] and in 1938 the head of the Race and Settlement Main Office had extended this order to the police.[142] In fact, however, the SS's settlement activities were initially on a modest scale. Thus, in 1938, for example, only fifty-five peasants had been settled on a total area of less than 5,000 hectares as part of the 'New Peasant Settlement' programme, while 102 SS houses were planned in the SS-Oberabschnitt West as part of the homestead programme.[143]

This minimal amount of activity, and the limited personal interest shown by the Reichsführer-SS in the settlement issue, can be attributed to the fact that, by appointing Reich Minister of Agriculture Darré as head of the Race and Settlement Main Office at the beginning of the 1930s, Himmler had intended to ensure that he would be made responsible for 'eastern settlement'. Although at the time it looked as though this would become important only in the distant future, his aim was to ensure that, through the alliance with Darré, the SS would have a strong position in a key sphere of the Nazi fantasy empire.

Although Darré had emphasized, in a speech in January 1936, that the future of German peasant settlement lay in eastern Europe up to the Urals,[144] his RuSHA had not made any significant preparations for this future project. In 1937, however, Hermann Reischle, the head of the staff office of the Reich Food Estate, for which Darré was also responsible, had given instructions to start secretly planning the settlement of Czechoslovakia. Reischle insisted that he was not prepared to put up with the 'absurd situation' that in Nazi Germany 'nobody was thinking [how] in practice' the central demand of Nazism for 'new space' could be realized. The strict secrecy of these drafts prevented Reischle, who was also head of the Race Office of the Race and Settlement Main Office, from involving the SS in these plans. Indeed, it may well be the case that, in his function as head of the Race Office, he wished as far as possible to prevent the SS from developing their own settlement plans and so providing unwelcome competition.[145]

SS settlement activity only really got going in 1938, utilizing settlement land in the annexed Sudeten territory and in Austria. In June 1938 the German Settlement Society (Deutsche Ansiedlungsgesellschaft = DAG), which was controlled by the RuSHA,[146] was given the task of buying land in Austria for a Wehrmacht training area and resettling the residents in 'aryanized' property. This was followed by three more such contracts for military training areas. In all it involved a total of 35,000 hectares.[147] The fact that DAG ran 'a precise, punctual and smooth operation' led to it being given further, similar tasks.[148]

The RuSHA was even more heavily involved in the Sudetenland. In October Günter Pancke, who had replaced Darré as head of the RuSHA in the late summer of 1938, wrote to his boss Himmler that 'the opportunity provided by the Sudetenland' should be exploited for far-reaching changes in the 'whole settlement field'. The Sudetenland should be intensively utilized as a test-bed for settlement in order to secure SS responsibility for settlement issues for the whole of the Reich or, as Pancke put it, so that, 'by being able to refer to real achievements, the SS can work towards gaining the post of Reich Settlement Commissar in the old Reich as well'. Thus, his appointment as Reich Commissar for the Consolidation of the German Ethnic Nation (Reichskommissar für die Festigung deutschen Volkstums), which represented the decisive step in increasing Himmler's responsibility for settlement, was already being prepared the previous year. In July 1939, with specific reference to an order from the Reichsführer-SS, the Race and Settlement Main Office requested from the SD 'documents, statistics, as well as maps dealing with the agricultural and geopolitical conditions in Czechoslovakia, Lithuania, Latvia, Estonia, and Romania'. The fact that, at the same time, a request was made for documents concerning the 'work of

Catholic Action in the above countries' indicates who was envisaged as providing the land for future settlement.[149]

The real change in SS settlement policy, however, came in spring 1939, when Hitler gave Himmler the task of organizing the resettlement of the German minority in South Tyrol. It was only then that settlement policy acquired the dimensions of a full-scale 'ethnic population policy', and it was only then that Himmler not only came to focus on it but saw it as a chance to shift the emphasis in the expansion of the SS empire from the concept of the 'state protection corps' to 'Lebensraum policy'.

Such a reorientation of policy would have been impossible with Darré. The SS's settlement policy needed to acquire a more racial and military emphasis than Darré's peasant form of settlement policy. In the SS the future settlers were seen in the first instance as 'military peasants' (*Wehrbauern*).[150] Thus, Himmler considered the removal of Darré, whom he had long regarded as a political partner and personal friend, as unavoidable

Himmler parts company with Darré

Darré's personal records show that by 1937 at the latest he had come to mistrust Himmler. On 17 April 1937, on the occasion of a visit to Himmler, Darré had noted that the Reichsführer-SS had behaved in a 'very warm and friendly way' towards him, but 'had been remarkably pessimistic about the damage to my public position and my relationship with the Führer'. Himmler was referring to Darré's unfortunate appearance at the Reich Peasant Rally in 1936, which had seriously damaged his prestige within the Nazi leadership. In the view of leading Nazis, Darré's long-winded speech, which focused on ideology, had failed to articulate agricultural policy. The whole event had served only to document the Reich Peasant Leader's political isolation.[151] Now, wrote Darré, on this visit he had 'refrained from commenting' and 'simply calmly listened to what he had to say, since my friendship with Himmler means a lot to me'.[152]

On 8 December 1937 he had a 'serious talk' about the SS with his state secretary, Herbert Backe:

I don't believe for a moment that the RFSS could have anything against me, but his entourage or some of them must have a very strong influence over him so that he's beginning to do things and he's not aware of their repercussions [. . .] What should one do? Wait! [...] I can't give up my post as head of the Race and Settlement Main Office [...] dangerous gaps in the flank of the Nazi struggle in support of the peasantry [...] Is the SS developing into a feudal praetorian guard? [...] People are pulling the wool over Himmler's eyes with the slogan 'good blood' that has to be saved and yet behind the scenes all the key positions are being filled by SS donors.[153]

Two weeks later Darré noted: 'Conversation with Backe: plan to turn the SS into a samurai order and at the same time to amalgamate it with the police (Plan RFSS). That won't do. Cui bono?' And, at the beginning of 1938: 'Very worried about the way the SS is going [...] Wolff is creating an alternative regime with opponents of the SS.' Two weeks later he noted: 'Worried about the future of the SS. Would it be better for me to give up the Race and Settlement Main Office since the SS is developing into a capitalist praetorian guard under a Jesuitical high command?'[154]

In February 1938 he did in fact offer his resignation as head of the Race and Settlement Main Office. Himmler had strongly criticized Joachim Caesar, the head of the indoctrination department in the Race and Settlement Main Office, accusing him of excessive 'intellectualism', and evidently wanted to dismiss him over Darré's head. According to Darré, he was the third head of the indoctrination department whom Himmler had rejected, and therefore the Reichsführer was obviously dissatisfied with the way in which 'my [Darré's] ideas of blood and soil, of breeding and race are being imparted to and anchored in the SS'. His dismissal as head of the Race and Settlement Main Office was therefore unavoidable.[155] Although this resignation statement was phrased in such a way that it gave Himmler the opportunity of rejecting it, in fact he accepted Darré's resignation without further discussion.[156] A draft of this letter has survived that is even more direct. 'I owe it to the Führer', Darré had written, 'to vacate my office, since it no longer provides the guarantee that my place in history will be clear.' In the last sentence he had also described his decision as 'irrevocable', whereas in the letter that was actually sent he wrote that he 'could not see an alternative course of action'.[157]

Darré's resignation was announced to the public as resulting from the burdens imposed by his other duties. According to a note of Darré's, 'at the moment nothing could be worse' than having 'this solution exploited by somebody to drive a wedge between the SS and the peasantry'.[158] After Himmler had secured Hitler's approval for Darré's dismissal he initially sent him on leave, because, as he wrote to him, he had been 'unable to issue final instructions and make a new appointment' as a result of his preoccupation with other urgent political matters.[159] At that time he had on his desk a proposal from Pohl to abolish the Race and Settlement Main Office, in order to be rid of its 'chronic financial difficulties [. . .] once and for all'.[160] In the end Himmler could not bring himself to do this, but, as Pohl had proposed, transferred the indoctrination office, hitherto subordinate to the RuSHA, to the SS Main Office, thereby considerably restricting Darré's former sphere of operations.

A successor to Darré, namely Pancke, was not appointed until 11 September 1938, after Darré had pressed for his dismissal to be made official on the grounds that the existing hiatus was creating problems. Two of his closest colleagues, the chief of staff of the RuSHA, Georg Ebrecht, and the head of the Race Office, Reichsle, left with him.[161] However, Darré asked Himmler to appoint him as a 'close personal adviser without any particular function', since, during the next few years, Himmler would not be able to realize the 'concept of the SS as an order' that both of them were trying to achieve because the task of 'state protection' would have priority. Thus, Darré continued to hope that he would be able to realize his far-reaching ideological dreams over the medium term with the aid of Himmler and the SS. Significantly, Himmler did not respond to his request.[162]

This rejection may well have confirmed Darré in the opinion that he noted down when he was informed by Himmler's adjutant of the Reichsführer's acceptance of his resignation as head of the Race and Settlement Main Office: 'Himmler has never understood the fundamental importance of my ideas.' At the time he added that he wanted 'to try to retain his friendship'.[163] And indeed, Darré and Himmler were subsequently anxious publicly to demonstrate that their personal relationship remained intact.[164] Nevertheless, they continued to drift apart, and by 1939–40 Darré's initial mistrust had turned into enmity.

South Tyrol and the Protectorate

Now, without Darré, SS settlement policy could be geared to the concept of living-space. The prelude to this was Himmler's assignment to resettle the ethnic Germans from South Tyrol.[165] Immediately after the occupation of Prague, either at the end of March or the beginning of April, Hitler gave Himmler and the Gauleiter and Governor of Tyrol, Franz Hofer, oral instructions to prepare to deprive 30,000 ethnic Germans living in South Tyrol of their German citizenship.[166] The background to this was the attempt to defuse German–Italian relations through a clear demarcation of their respective spheres of interest. For the invasion of Prague represented a clear breach of the Munich Agreement, for which Mussolini had been largely responsible, and contradicted the statement made by the Germans to the Italian government that German expansion would stop at the German 'ethnic frontier'. Hitler now aimed to allay the suspicion of his most important potential ally through a generous policy regarding South Tyrol. Hitler's demonstrative step in the South Tyrol question was the essential precondition for the Pact of Steel of 22 May 1939, which was intended to consolidate the German–Italian alliance.

It was understandable that Hofer, the Gauleiter of Tyrol, should have been assigned this task, but why was Himmler brought in? There were several reasons. First, he could point to the experience gained by the Race and Settlement Main Office through the resettlement programmes involved in the establishment of military training areas in Austria and the Sudetenland. But much more important were his police responsibilities, which promised to ensure that the 'de-settlement' of the South Tyroleans would take place in an orderly manner, and that any objections from those affected would be immediately suppressed. In addition, there was his excellent relationship with the most senior officials of the Italian police, as well as, above all, the role that he had taken on in the past as the coordinator and most senior authority in the field of ethnic policy.

Right from the start, Himmler interpreted the task of resettling 30,000 South Tyroleans as the first stage in the complete clearing of South Tyrol of German-speakers.[167] On 30 May 1939 he stated in a memorandum that, 'the Führer's fixing of the border between German and Italy' was to be 'permanent'. It was thereby 'clearly and irrevocably established that South Tyrol has been abandoned as ethnic German territory and is of no more interest to us'. This did not, however, mean that 'Germany has given up the 200,000 South Tyroleans who want to be German'. The problem could be solved only in the context of 'what may be a historically uniquely generous process': Germany would 'create somewhere in the territory under its control, for example in the east, a space for 200,000 people', a specially designated area from which all the existing population would be removed. Such an area could, for example, be established in North Moravia, which would also have the advantage that 'Moravia would acquire an additional

200,000 national elements [*sic*], who are of good racial stock and very self-consciously and militantly German'.

That, however, was the 'strategic final goal'. Until then they should aim for a 'solution in stages', for example through resettlement from the South Tyrol to the German Reich, above all to North Tyrol. They had already requested the Coordination Centre for Ethnic Germans to produce a 'central registry' of all these immigrants, in order to be able later on to have the possibility of transferring the South Tyrolean immigrants to the designated settlement area. The resettlement programme would have to be closely coordinated with the Italian agencies, preferably in cooperation with their responsible police authorities.[168]

On 23 June a meeting between German and Italian officials, chaired by Himmler, took place in Berlin; the Italian delegation was led by the ambassador, Bernardo Attolico. Himmler noted that the meeting had resulted in an agreement to begin the 'return' of those people who were citizens of the German Reich (that included numerous Austrians who had changed their citizenship as a result of the Anschluss). A central 'Office for Emigration and Returnees' was to be established in Bozen (Bolzano), with four branch offices in other parts of South Tyrol, in order to organize this population-transfer of several thousand people within the space of a few weeks, but also to prepare the other South Tyroleans for their future emigration. After the conclusion of this first operation 'those Tyroleans who were not bound to the soil' were to move to Reich territory and, in particular, to North Tyrol; the peasant population would follow later.

Moreover, according to Himmler, the Italians had agreed to help ensure that the real-estate of the South Tyroleans was not sold off at knock-down prices. The Italian state would therefore introduce a special commission into the sales process. Himmler, on the other hand, had made a commitment to the Italians to stop the small amount of motor traffic on the frontier between North and South Tyrol, in order to avoid damaging 'popular morale'. He also had requested the Italians to ask the Vatican, with which 'I have only inadequate contacts', for support so that the Catholic clergy in both parts of Tyrol could 'prevent the whipping up of chauvinistic nationalism and the demand for Anschluss with Germany'. According to Wolff's minutes, Himmler was 'irritated' by Attolico's question as to where the Germans intended settling the Italians: 'What's it got to do with the Italians where we resettle the South Tyroleans?'[169]

At the beginning of August 1939 Himmler received 'a number of South Tyrolean men', representatives of the minority, 'in order to explain to them quite frankly the Führer's intentions and the purpose of the whole resettlement programme', and to request them, 'despite the great sadness they must feel at the loss of their homeland, to obey the order to leave and to show the utmost discipline in carrying it out'.[170]

Despite a few problems, in fact the German–Italian negotiations over the implementation of the resettlement programme, initiated by the Berlin meeting of June 1939, reached a conclusion acceptable to both sides in October 1939.[171] Those people with German citizenship living in South Tyrol were expected to resettle within three months. The South Tyroleans of Italian nationality who opted for Germany would leave by the end of 1942. Those who did not would remain in their homeland and become Italians; in other words, speak Italian and adopt Italian culture.[172] The so-called option procedure by which the South Tyroleans had to opt for Germany or Italy was, as envisaged, basically completed by the end of 1939. This did not, however, resolve the issue of where the South Tyroleans were to settle; indeed, it was to preoccupy Himmler for years.

In the spring of 1939 Himmler's attention was initially focused on the Protectorate. On 18 April 1939 an 'Einsatzgruppe Land Office', composed of representatives of the State Police Office, the SD, and the RuSHA, had taken over the department in the Czech Ministry of Agriculture responsible for keeping the records of landholdings, the so-called 'Land Office'. It had been established after the end of the First World War in connection with the programme of land reform in the Republic of Czechoslovakia.[173]

On 17 May Curt von Gottberg, head of the Settlement Office in the RuSHA, was appointed head of the Land Office by the Reich Protector. By the time of his dismissal in December 1939 he had confiscated a total of 256,000 hectares of land for the SS and its settlement associations, and had secured for the Land Office, through transfer to an intermediate foundation, a total of 145,000 hectares of state forest. Property was expropriated from Jews, as well as from the Catholic Church and the state.[174] The aim was to settle Germans and expel 'non-Germanized' Czechs to the Reich, where they would be used as labour. Responding to a query from Himmler, in July 1939, only two months after his appointment, Curt von Gottberg could announce that they were ready to settle 12,000 South Tyroleans.[175]

In his role as Reich Minister of Agriculture and Reich Peasant Leader, Darré was primarily interested in 'peasant policy', and he now protested in vain at the appointment of a representative of the SS as head of the Land Office and at the resultant gearing of future settlement in the Protectorate to the requirements of population policy. The working-group, which Reischle, the head of Darré's staff office, had already set up in 1938 to prepare for the settlement of Bohemia and Moravia, had long been aware of the fact that control over the Land Office would be the decisive administrative prerequisite for the transfer of agricultural property in the Protectorate, and had, therefore, also sought to secure it.[176] However, the SS had beaten Darré's people to it, for they had the impression that Darré and his agrarian experts considered the settlement issue too much in terms of 'food policy'.[177]

During the following months Darré, supported by the Reich Protector's office, kept complaining about Gottberg's policy and, as Pancke reported to Himmler, trying to 'torpedo' it.[178] A particular problem was the fact that the acting headship of the Land Office lacked clear administrative authority, as 'hitherto its legal position [has been based] exclusively on the policing role assigned to the Reichsführer-SS'.[179]

Gottberg aimed at 'promoting' his Czech Land Office to be 'the Reich Protector's supreme settlement authority'.[180] By trying to take over the DAG (German Settlement Society), founded by Darré, through an association of which he was the chairman, Gottberg sharpened the conflict with Darré, who in response tried to have it transferred to the state.[181] Darré may well not have been entirely innocent in Gottberg's involvement in a dubious financial affair in connection with the purchase of the DAG. As a result, the latter was first relieved of his post as head of the Settlement Office in November 1939 and then, in December, also of the headship of the Land Office.[182] The views on settlement policy of Gottberg's successor, Theodor Gross, who came from the Reich Protector's office, were much closer to those of the Ministry of Agriculture than to those of the SS.[183]

Thus Himmler's move to take over settlement policy failed initially, above all as a result of the opposition of Darré. After the latter had been kicked out, Himmler had envisaged a comprehensive settlement policy based on effective cooperation between the individual parts of his organization. His contacts and responsibilities as Reichsführer-SS and Chief of the German Police had appeared to make him predestined to become commissar for the resettlement of the South Tyroleans, and his control of the police in the Protectorate, which was not constrained by any legal restrictions, enabled him to take over the Land Office. Nevertheless, his attempt had failed. Himmler appears to have learnt one thing above all from this experience: if he was to achieve his goal of completely controlling settlement policy, he would have to deploy his police powers far more brutally than he had done in Prague.

The role that Himmler's SS played in the annexation of Austria and the Sudetenland and in the occupation of the Czech parts of Czechoslovakia, his involvement in the resettlement of the South Tyroleans for the purpose of strengthening the German–Italian alliance, as well as the extensive confiscation of land by the SS in the Protectorate—all of these developments show that, during 1938–9, Himmler was placing the SS more and more at the service of a policy of expansion, preparation for war, and the permanent occupation of conquered territory.

When, in March 1939, the Polish government, strengthened by an Anglo-French guarantee, declined to accede to Germany's demands for the integration of Danzig into the Reich and for concessions over the Polish Corridor, Hitler decided to resolve the issue by going to war with Poland. The following months saw careful preparations for the military conflict: through various forms of provocation of Poland, through the strengthening of the alliance with Italy, and finally through the Nazi–Soviet Pact, which sealed the fate of the Polish state, Hitler believed that he could exclude the possibility of the western powers entering the war in the event of renewed German aggression, despite the fact that they had indicated they would do so. At any rate, he did not imagine that the military action against Poland would immediately lead to the major European war that he had envisaged since 1937, and which, since the beginning of 1939, Himmler had reckoned would occur at any moment.

Himmler was prepared for war: he controlled armed units with 40,000 men; the police was ready to deploy a substantial number of its personnel for military purposes and to fill the gaps with reservists; his concentration camps had a large capacity for containing actual and potential opponents of the regime.

Five days before the start of the war mobilization was in full swing, and affected a wide range of people. Among others, Professor Werner Jansen, author of the Teutonic novels that Himmler liked so much and a member of the SS since 1935, reported to his Reichsführer for duty. A physician and professor at Berlin University, he requested Himmler, 'with warm greetings, to let me participate in the great struggle as your historian'.[184] Himmler responded positively, assigning Jansen to the staff of the division which had been formed in the meantime from the Death's Head units, where in fact he remained during the next few months.[185] For Himmler, things had come full circle: the man who had been a major inspiration for the development of his Teutonic fantasy became his chronicler at the very moment when the SS set out to realize this fantasy. Jansen, however, did not succeed in writing this epic. He died in December 1943 following a long illness, two days after Himmler had appointed him SS-Standartenführer.[186]

15

War and Settlement in Poland

The start of the Second World War represented an extraordinary opportunity for Himmler. During the previous years, under the slogan 'State Protection Corps', he had endeavoured to integrate his various functions to make them as coherent and unified as possible. In this way, under the pretext of pursuing a policy of general prevention, an ever-expanding and oppressive police apparatus had been created, which was intended to be merged with the SS 'order', supplemented, in particular, by armed units, by responsibilities in the field of ethnic population policy, and—from 1938 onwards—by various settlement and resettlement activities. Now he could begin expanding and reorganizing his various power centres, and directing the various individual parts of his empire to undertake complementary tasks, thereby producing synergies.

The military engagement of the various armed SS units at last offered him the opportunity of realizing his long-held idea of a large, unified, and autonomous military force, the Waffen-SS. Its 'blood sacrifice' in war must increase the aura of the SS as an elite organization and underpin its role as the 'State Protection Corps'. Moreover, in the context of the war he could move against all 'enemies of the state', at home but also in the territories to be conquered, with the utmost brutality and in this way expand his power base. Above all, the war offered the option of greatly expanding the SS's settlement policy in conquered territory, thereby providing the foundations for that 'ring' of 80,000–100,000 peasants that he had envisaged as protecting the frontiers of the Reich. With the outbreak of war this vision, that he had originally envisaged as a task for future generations, appeared to Himmler to be increasingly relevant to his own 'settlement' activities: the future of the Greater Germanic Reich lay in the present, and to a large extent in his own hands.

In July 1939, at the ceremony which took place annually in Quedlinburg to commemorate the German emperor, Henry I (the Fowler), Himmler had the idea of commissioning the Ahnenerbe to investigate 'how quickly major achievements have been carried out in German history'. He was particularly interested in discovering whether his idol, Henry, could be used as a measure of comparison for the political achievements of Adolf Hitler. Nine days after the outbreak of war he had the first results of the Ahnenerbe investigation, which, however, did not begin to provide an answer to his question.[1] However, Himmler, who when in doubt invariably preferred his own ideas to those of the experts, did not allow this to prevent him from viewing the war as the fulfilment of a historic mission.

The SS at war

The Gestapo and SD were substantially involved in the preparations for war.[2] A Central Office II P (Poland) had already been set up in the SD Main Office in May 1939, in order to handle centrally the affairs of 'ethnic Germans in Poland' and to create a register of those persons against whom they would want to proceed in the event of war. From July 1939 onwards the Gestapo and SD took concrete measures for the event of war by once more forming Einsatzgruppen.[3]

The SD was assigned the important role of staging a number of frontier violations directly before the planned attack, which would be blamed on the Poles and used to justify the outbreak of war.[4] Heydrich directed the highly secret operation himself, and Himmler made a short visit in the middle of August to inspect the sections of the frontier that had been selected.[5] After careful preparation, on 31 August, the night before the invasion, SD commandos attacked the Gleiwitz radio station, a customs post, and a forestry house on the German–Polish border, in order to fake Polish provocations. Statements in German and Polish were broadcast by the Gleiwitz station. They left behind a number of KZ prisoners who had been dressed in Polish uniforms and then killed. This was to provide the justification for the German 'retaliation'.[6]

Another, much smaller commando, composed of members of the Death's Head units, played a key role in the early hours of the war. The SS men had been smuggled into the Free City of Danzig in order to strengthen the 'home guard' (*Heimwehr*), a force composed of Danzig SS members which, after secret preparations, the Nazi-controlled Danzig Senate had officially established on 18 August 1939 as the 'SS-Danzig Home Guard'. On the morning of 1 September 1939 the Home Guard participated among other things in the attack by German troops on the Westerplatte, the Polish fortress in Danzig. It also had the task of capturing the post-office. However, armed post-office officials, who were Polish army reservists, had barricaded themselves in the building, which was not finally taken until the evening.[7]

Himmler, who liked to see himself as a soldier, could at last now 'go to the front'. But he did this in a rather comfortable manner, appropriate to his high rank. At the beginning of September he left Berlin with his mobile headquarters in the special train 'Heinrich' (which he had to share with Ribbentrop and the head of the Reich Chancellery, Hans-Heinrich Lammers). During the next few weeks he tried to keep as close to Hitler's headquarters as possible, which at this point was also in a train, and which changed its location several times in the course of the war.[8]

Publicly, and particularly vis-à-vis the Wehrmacht, Himmler had always justified the establishment of armed SS units in terms of the SS's role in maintaining internal security. In fact, however, since 1934 he had been systematically constructing a military force, training a large number of potential officers in the officer-training colleges and militarizing the Death's Head concentration camp guard units.[9] Now, in the war against Poland, he could at last strengthen the various armed units, create more of them, and thereby establish a unified SS military force. His aim was to create an autonomous SS army corps, as he had already explained to the Gruppenführer in November 1938. This would, he said, underpin the 'moral' position of the SS as an organ of repression:

If I may describe the overall task of the SS as being, together with the police [...] to guarantee Germany's internal security, then this task can be performed only if a section of the SS, of this leadership corps, serves and sheds blood at the front. If we did not make a blood sacrifice and if we did not fight at the front we would have lost the moral right to shoot those at home who avoid serving and are cowards. That is the role of the Verfügungstruppe [military SS], which has the most glorious duty of being able to serve at the front.[10]

In August 1939 Hitler had ordered the integration of the units of the Verfügungstruppe (VT) into the field army, as had been envisaged in the event of mobilization. The 'Leibstandarte', the regiments 'Germania' and 'Deutschland', as well as other units, were distributed among various armies and participated in the war against Poland.[11] With the end of hostilities came the next step: the VT *division*, which had long been planned, was created out of the units of the Verfügungstruppe; it was later to be called 'Das Reich'.[12] Right at the beginning of the war Himmler made Theodor Eicke commander of the Death's Head Standarten. The KZ guards now went into action as military formations; their role in the concentration camps was taken over by the so-called police reinforcements. Three Death's Head Standarten operated in the rear areas of the 10th and 8th Armies and carried out 'cleansing and security measures', in reality using the most vicious methods to terrorize the civilian population, and murdering countless people. Eicke carried out the operations using Hitler's special train as his base.[13]

As early as September 1939 Himmler received permission from Hitler to form the Death's Head Standarten into a division. When the three Standarten left Poland in October for Dachau, where the division was formed, they were replaced by new Death's Head units that had been established since 1938.[14] In the same month Himmler ordered the creation of a police division from members of the order police and Wehrmacht units.[15]

Thus, shortly after the outbreak of war Himmler controlled an SS armed force comprising three divisions as well as the 'Leibstandarte'. In the course of 1940 the force acquired the collective name Waffen-SS.[16] The name signified the existence of a force independent of the Werhrmacht, and suggests that the various SS units were regarded as being of equal value to it.

'Shoot them on the spot'

The war against Poland was fought by the Nazi leadership to some extent as a war of racial extermination. Here too Himmler played a central role from the start.[17]

On 22 August Hitler had spelled out unmistakably to the generals how he wanted this war to be fought, as is clear from a record of his speech in note form taken at the time: 'The destruction of Poland has priority. The aim is to eliminate active forces, not to reach a definite line [. . .] Close your hearts to pity. Act brutally. 80 mill. people must obtain what is their right.

Their existence must be made secure. The stronger man is always right. The greatest harshness.'[18]

On 3 September Himmler gave an order that 'armed Polish insurgents, who are caught in the act', were to be 'shot on the spot'. In the event of insurgents emerging, senior officials in the local administration should be taken hostage. His permission should be sought if large numbers of insurgents were captured or if it was intended to shoot hostages. Four days later Himmler issued an order by telephone that the shootings should be carried out by the police and not the army.[19]

On 7 September Heydrich announced, at a meeting of departmental heads, that 'the leading elements in Polish society should as far as possible be rendered harmless',[20] and on 14 October he demanded in front of the same group that the 'liquidation of leading Poles' that was already under way should be concluded by 1 November.[21] In accordance with these instructions, special police and SS units, as well as Wehrmacht units, murdered tens of thousands of Polish citizens during the hostilities and in the first months of the occupation. The pretext for this was provided by claims of Polish atrocities, according to which more than 50,000 people were alleged to have lost their lives. In fact the total number of all ethnic Germans who died in various ways during the war amounted to between 4,500 and 5,000, among them about a hundred victims of the 'Bromberg Bloody Sunday', which was portrayed by Nazi propaganda as a Polish atrocity with thousands of deaths.[22]

The planned mass murder of particular groups of Poles, which was disguised as 'retaliation', was to a significant extent controlled and carried out by the Einsatzgruppen of the security police, which had once again been established as in the previous annexations. There were seven Einsatzgruppen in all, comprising around 2,700 men, of which five were assigned to the high commands of the five armies deployed in Poland.[23] Officially they were supposed to combat all those 'elements hostile to the Reich and anti-German in enemy territory behind the front line', as was stated in the agreement reached with the Army High Command in July. However, a minute by Heydrich from July 1940 indicates that they had received further instructions that 'were extremely radical (for example, an order to liquidate numerous members of the Polish elites running into thousands)'. In practice this meant legitimizing the murder of members of the intelligentsia, the clergy, the aristocracy, and the Jewish community.[24] The Reich Security Main Office had been preparing relevant search lists since May 1939.[25]

It is not clear who issued the instructions referred to by Heydrich, or when they were issued. Leading members of the Einsatzgruppen stated after the war that a meeting had already taken place in August, at which Himmler and Heydrich had made it clear that it was to be left up to their own initiative how they eliminated the Polish intelligentsia,[26] a procedure that was to be typical of the way in which orders were issued within the SS throughout the war.

The Einsatzgruppen received support above all from the Volksdeutscher Selbstschutz (Ethnic German Self-Defence Force). Himmler had given orders for the creation of this force shortly after the start of the war.[27] The matter was taken in hand by Gottlob Berger, the head of the SS Recruitment Office responsible for recruiting members of the armed SS. The Selbstschutz recruited the greater part of the German minority who were 'fit for action' (amounting to a total of 100,000 men within a few weeks) was heavily dependent on the SS for its organization, and in September was integrated into the order police.[28]

During the actual hostilities the Einsatzgruppen and the Selbstschutz, but also the order police, the Waffen-SS, and elements of the Wehrmacht, shot thousands of Polish civilians,[29] among them hundreds of Polish Jews, who in a number of cases were locked in their synagogues and burned alive.[30] These murders represented the culmination of the unrestrained violence to which the Jews had been subjected since the start of the war.[31] After September 1939 the Einsatzgruppen and the Wehrmacht drove tens of thousands of Jews by force over the demarcation line into the Soviet-occupied zone.[32]

On occasion Himmler intervened directly in the actions of the Einsatzgruppen. Thus, on 3 September, responding to the news of alleged disturbances in the industrial district of eastern Upper Silesia, he ordered SS-Obergruppenführer Udo von Woyrsch to establish an Einsatzgruppe z. b.V. ('for special assignments') and made him responsible for 'radically crushing the Polish uprising that is flaring up [...] with all available means'.[33] After it had become clear that there was no significant uprising in the 'area of operations', Himmler extended von Woyrsch's mission. He appointed him 'Special Police Commander' in the area of the 14th Army and ordered him to 'disarm and crush the Polish bandits. Executions.' Himmler was offering von Woyrsch, whom he had had to dismiss as leader of Oberabschnitt East for being involved in unauthorized murders associated with 30 June 1934, a chance to 'prove himself' by taking radical action in Poland. What was required was murderous initiative, and in fact Einsatzgruppe z.b.V. was to carry out numerous pogroms against Jews in its path through Poland.[34] On 11 September, prompted by Hitler, Himmler gave Einsatzgruppe IV the order 'to arrest 500 hostages to be drawn mainly from the Polish intelligentsia in Bromberg and additionally from communists and, in the event of the slightest sign of insurrection or attempts at resistance, to act ruthlessly by shooting the hostages'.[35]

After the end of the German–Polish war this terror was systematized. From the end of October onwards the Einsatzgruppen and the Selbstschutz, directed by the Reich Security Main Office, carried out the so-called 'Intelligentsia Operation',[36] which was in fact a campaign of murder directed above all at teachers, university graduates, former officers and officials, clergy, landowners, leading members of Polish nationalist organizations, and above all Jews.[37]

As mentioned already, during the first four months of the German occupation tens of thousands of people were murdered in this way. The new Reich Gau of Danzig–West Prussia was a particular focus of the operation.[38] Here, in addition to members of the Polish elites and Jews, asylum patients, 'asocials', prostitutes, women who allegedly had sexual diseases, as well as Gypsies were shot; here it became clear to what extent subordinate bodies, acting on their own initiative, could carry out a 'cleansing' of the conquered territories on the basis of 'racial hygiene'.[39]

From mid-September onwards the leader of the Selbstschutz in Danzig–West Prussia who was responsible for these murders was Ludolf von Alvensleben, previously Himmler's adjutant.[40] The 'reward' that Himmler thought up for this mass murder represented not only an expression of his gratitude to and recognition of von Alvensleben, but also had a pedagogic purpose. On 20 March 1940 Himmler informed Heydrich that he had assigned to von Alvensleben, of whose precarious financial position he had been well aware since the 1930s,[41] two estates in the territory that had been annexed which until 1918 had belonged to his family. However, this was only a provisional measure and by no means represented a transfer of property; he did not intend to give von Alvensleben preferential treatment. Rumours to that effect that had been circulating among ethnic Germans in the Gau, and had presumably prompted Heydrich to contact Himmler, were without foundation. Rather, he, Himmler, had agreed to Alvensleben's taking over the running of the estates 'in order to provide SS-Oberführer von Alvensleben, who, as leader of the Selbstschutz had played a significant part in the executions but of whom it was said by some ethnic Germans that he was not really bothered and would soon be leaving, with the opportunity to return as a citizen and inhabitant and thereby to be a good and courageous example to the ethnic Germans'.[42]

Himmler's henchmen also set about systematically murdering Polish patients in mental hospitals, at least 7,700 people in total.[43] This action has clear parallels with the so-called 'euthanasia' programme in the Reich. There the Chancellery of the Führer of the NSDAP, operating under the code title T4, was responsible; in Poland it was the SS. Those who took part in the shooting of patients between the end of September and December 1939 in the new Reich Gau of Danzig–West Prussia included members of the 'Wachsturmbann Eimann', a unit composed of SS men from Danzig, the Ethnic German Self Defence force, as well as members of Einsatzkommandos. In November patients from the Owinska (Teskau) asylum in the new Reich Gau of Wartheland were murdered.[44] From the end of November onwards patients from two asylums were deported to Posen, where the Gestapo had a base in Fort VII, part of a nineteenth-century fortress. Here a new murder technique was applied, whose effects Himmler was able to observe for himself when he paid a visit on 12 December 1939. The victims were poisoned with carbon monoxide gas in a hermetically sealed room—the first mass murder carried out by the Nazis with poison gas.[45] At the beginning of 1940 this facility was replaced by gas vans.[46]

Mental patients, however, were shot by Himmler's commandos in the Reich as well, in neighbouring Pomerania. In September–October 1939 Gauleiter Franz Schwede had evidently offered to place the Stralsund sanatorium at Himmler's disposal. In November and December 1939 between 1,200 and 1,400 psychiatric patients were 'transferred' from the Pomeranian asylums to West Prussia and executed there by the Wachsturmbann Eimann. At the beginning of 1940 patients began to be deported to the Kosten asylum in the Warthegau, which had just been 'cleared', where they were murdered in gas vans.[47] The asylums in the annexed territories in Poland and in Gau Pomerania, which had been 'cleared' in such a murderous manner, were then occupied by SS units, used as accommodation by the Wehrmacht or as prisons, as well as for accommodating ethnic German being resettled from the Baltic States who were in need of care.[48]

The murder of mental patients in the occupied territories continued until the middle of 1941. The Sonderkommando Lange, named after its commander, criminal commissar and SS-Untersturmführer Herbert Lange,

Ill. 18. During the war with Poland Himmler kept in close proximity to Hitler to demonstrate clearly the key role that his SS was playing in this Nazi ideological war of annihilation. The photo shows Hitler's Luftwaffe adjutant Nikolaus von Below (standing on the left), and his army adjutant Gerhard Engel (standing next to him), to the left of Hitler Martin Bormann, and to the right of Hitler his Wehrmacht adjutant, Rudolph Schmundt.

which was responsible, killed thousands of people with the aid of gas vans, above all in May and June 1940 as well as in June and July 1941.[49] In the autumn of 1941 Lange's commando began to murder the Jewish population of the Warthegau. At the end of 1941 it established a gas-van base in Chelmno in order to carry out these murders on a larger scale.[50] In the process Lange's unit became an important organizational link between the systematic murder of the handicapped and of the Jews. In the winter of 1939–40, however, Himmler and his henchmen were not yet contemplating the mass killing of Jews with poison gas. At this point the 'final solution' they were seeking involved ghettoization and expulsion, and, although in 1939–40 the SS had already killed thousands of Jews in Poland, there was no question yet of the systematic murder of the Jewish population in special extermination camps.[51]

During the war with Poland members of the Wehrmacht had not only taken part in the murder of civilians in the occupied territories, but—much more seriously—at the beginning of the war the Wehrmacht leadership had agreed to a 'division of labour' with the SS and police. When, on 12 September 1939, Admiral Canaris, the head of military intelligence, spoke to the chief of the Wehrmacht High Command, General Keitel, about the plans for wide-ranging executions in Poland, the latter referred him to a decision of Hitler's. The Führer had made it clear that 'if the Wehrmacht didn't want to have anything to do with it, it must accept that the SS and the Gestapo would act alongside it'.[52] On 21 September the Commander-in-Chief of the army, von Brauchitsch, informed army commanders that Hitler had assigned the Einsatzgruppen in Poland certain 'tasks of an ethnic-political nature' that lay outside the army's area of responsibility.[53] The Wehrmacht had thereby made a significant contribution towards creating the preconditions for the war in Poland to acquire the features of an ideologically driven extermination campaign. However, it left the vast majority of the mass murders to Himmler's henchmen.[54]

It was only after the end of this war that the military, but also the civil, administration opposed the uncontrolled behaviour of the Einsatzgruppen and the Selbstschutz.[55] There had been repeated confrontations between their leaders and Wehrmacht officers. In the middle of November the army commander in the newly created military district of Danzig, Lieutenant-General Fedor von Bock, complained to the Gauleiter and Reich Governor Albert Forster that, despite a promise made to him in the middle of October,[56] murders were continuing to be carried out by the Selbstschutz.[57] Although on 8 October Himmler had ordered the dissolution of the Selbstschutz by the end of the month, in some occupied districts this process lasted until the spring of 1940.[58] The commander of the military district in the Warthegau, General Walter Petzel, also contacted the Commander-in-Chief of the Reserve Army and informed him of the arbitrary shootings, looting, and acts of violence being carried out by the SS special formations.[59] In February 1940 the military commander in the southern section of the frontier, General Wilhelm Ulex, used the word 'bestiality' to describe the atrocities.[60] In November 1939 and January 1940 the military commander in the east of Poland, Johannes Blaskowitz, complained to the Commander-in-Chief of the army about the murders of Jewish and non-Jewish Poles.[61]

The behaviour of the SS in Poland caused so much concern among the officer corps that, as we shall see, at the beginning of 1940 Himmler felt compelled to respond to the issue of SS terror.

Reich Commissar for the Consolidation of the Ethnic German Nation

Himmler instructed the Race and Settlement Main Office (RuSHA) to send three special Einsatzkommandos to western Poland, the so-called RuS-Advisers, small groups of eight or nine SS members, who worked in close cooperation with the Einsatzgruppen of the security police.[62] In September 1939 they advanced with the German troops and began registering all Polish and Jewish agricultural land as well as confiscating farms that appeared valuable. The names of the owners were passed on to the security police, 'so that the owners of the farms can be arrested'. Thus, already during the war the SS was making practical preparations for the policy of Germanization and, as the head of one of the adviser commandos put it, in order 'to secure the necessary land for the impending appointment of the Reichs-führer-SS as Reich Commissar for the Settlement of the East'.[63] This evidently happened in a great hurry in order to pre-empt any measures by the Reich Ministry of Agriculture, which considered itself responsible for settlement policy and was regarded with suspicion by the RuSHA.[64] As has already been shown, the Ministry under Darré had succeeded in frustrating the ambitions of the SS's settlement experts in the Protectorate and was preparing, at the latest from August 1939 onwards, to take over settlement matters in occupied Poland.[65]

At the beginning of October 1939 the Reich Ministry of Agriculture discovered that, in pursuit of their settlement activities in the conquered territories, the SS were referring to a 'Führer edict'. During the following days this edict acquired concrete form, despite the bitter opposition of Darré and his great disappointment, which he was to express in letters to Lammers and Himmler. But Darré was engaged in a fruitless struggle. For, on 7 October, on Himmler's thirty-ninth birthday Hitler made Himmler 'very happy', as Margarete noted in her diary: 'The Führer has made him Settlement Commissar for the whole of Germany. The crowning acknowl-edgment of his work. He works day and night.'[66] With the Decree for the

Consolidation of the Ethnic German Nation, Hitler gave Himmler responsibility for the two tasks of 'admitting into its territory and arranging the
settlement within the Reich of [. . .] those Germans who were hitherto
obliged to live abroad', as well as 'arranging the settlement of the ethnic
groups [within the area under Germany's control] so as to improve the lines
of demarcation between them'. In practice this involved 'repatriating' Reich
and ethnic Germans, 'eliminating the harmful influence of those alien
sections of the population which constitute a threat to the Reich and the
German national community' (for which purpose, it stated below, Himmler
could 'assign specific areas of settlement to the population groups in question'), as well as 'forming new German settlements through the resettlement
of populations'. In order to carry out these tasks the Reichsführer-SS was to
make use of 'the existing authorities and institutions'.[67]

However, Himmler, who in future called himself 'Reich Commissar for
the Consolidation of the Ethnic German Nation', was successfully thwarted
by Lammers in his attempts to turn the Reich Commissariat into a 'supreme
Reich authority'.[68] A few days before Hitler was supposed to assign
Himmler the new task, Lammers had received a concerned letter from
Darré who, 'in the interests of our great settlement project', expressed
'the urgent wish' that 'this task, to which I am particularly committed,
should not be restricted by any special commissions assigned to some other
agency'. After all, 'everybody in Germany' knows 'that the precondition
for the organization of this task being located in the SS was my seven years
of devoted work as head of the Race and Settlement Main Office. Without
my work the SS would not be remotely in a position to raise the whole
issue.' Darré explicitly opposed Himmler's idea of 'military peasants'. He
argued that the historical examples of Austria and Russia showed that this
model was suitable only for weakly defended borders or territories that lay
outside one's own borders that needed to be protected. But the new border
with Russia would be defended by the Wehrmacht.[69]

On 5 October Himmler received a letter from Darré, in which he was
still addressed as 'Dear Heini!' Darré's exclusion from the eastern settlement
programme was, he wrote, 'one of the greatest disappointments of my life'.
Furthermore, he complained that Himmler had failed 'to inform me of what
had already been going on for two weeks in relation to the re-creation of
the German peasantry in Poland'. 'In order to have it documented', Darré
concluded with the following statement: 'This past summer I have been
carefully observing the goings on in this matter and those involving von

Gottberg, as well as the most recent events concerning the re-creation of the German peasantry in Poland. I have been aware of them and I have made a careful note of them.'[70]

Darré met Lammers and Himmler on 7 October, and from their conversation concluded that Himmler had agreed that he, Darré, should perform the 'executive functions' in the settlement programme.[71] When, a few weeks later, it became clear that Himmler had no intention of letting Darré participate in settlement policy in Poland, the latter turned to Göring, complaining he was bitter about the fact that, 'on the question of settlement the Reichsführer is throwing me on the scrapheap like a squeezed lemon after he has sucked out from my brain and my talents what seemed useful to him and his SS'.[72] But this intervention by the Agriculture Minister could not alter the fact that, shortly after the beginning of the war, Himmler had succeeded in taking substantial control of settlement policy in the newly conquered territories and outmanoeuvering Darré in the process.

16

A New Racial Order

As Reichsführer-SS, Chief of the German Police, and Settlement Commissar Himmler now had all the instruments in his hands necessary for subjecting the conquered territories to a radical 'ethnic reordering'. To begin with he started to construct an organizational setup in the conquered territories along the same lines as the one in the Reich.

In October 1939 Friedrich Wilhelm Krüger was appointed Higher SS and Police Leader (HSSPF) East and thereby as Himmler's representative in the General Government.* There was a change to the usual organizational arrangements, in that Himmler sought to improve the coordination of his various responsibilities by appointing SS and Police Leaders in the four districts of the General Government. Himmler saw them as 'advisers of the government district chiefs', who would be obliged to follow the latter's instructions 'as long as they are not countermanded by orders from the HSSPF or his representatives'.[1] Krüger, who was 'directly' subordinate to the Governor-General, Hans Frank (which, according to his and Himmler's interpretation, meant that he was not subject to any bureaucratic control by Frank's office[2]), soon acquired a special position for his office within the administration of the General Government. In September 1941, as his relationship with the Governor-General reached a critical point, Himmler reserved the right to subject instructions which Governor-General Frank gave to Krüger on police matters to prior examination before they were implemented. Frank naturally rejected this.[3]

In November 1939 Himmler appointed Bruno Streckenbach commander of the security police in the General Government. The former inspector of the security police in Hamburg had commanded an Einsatzgruppe during

* *Translators' note*: German-occupied Poland excluding the territories annexed to Germany.

the war with Poland. Streckenbach, to whom the commanders of the security police in the four districts of the General Government were subordinated, commanded about 2,000 members of the Gestapo and Kripo. Alongside them there was an equivalent organization of the order police.[4] As far as the Polish territories annexed to Germany were concerned, SS-Gruppenführer Wilhelm Koppe was appointed HSSPF for the new Warthegau, and SS-Gruppenführer Richard Hildebrandt HSSPF for the new Gau of Danzig–West Prussia, while the territories annexed to Upper Silesia and East Prussia were assigned to Erich von dem Bach-Zelewski, based in Breslau, and Wilhelm Rediess, based in Königsberg, respectively.

The Higher SS and Police Leaders were to play a key role in population policy in the east. Himmler not only made them responsible for transporting the people who were to be 'outsettled' and of settling the ethnic Germans, but above all placed the whole executive responsibility for population policy in their hands. In East Prussia, Silesia, and the Warthegau he appointed them 'permanent representatives' of the Reich Governors whom he had appointed as his 'representatives' in the sphere of population policy. In Gau Danzig–West Prussia and in the General Government the HSSPF were even to act as Himmler's representatives in his role of 'consolidating the ethnic German nation', as he did not have sufficient trust in either Reich Governor Forster or Governor-General Frank.[5] The reality of these, in some cases, complicated arrangements was that, as in the Reich, Himmler had created in Poland a network of responsibilities, lying outside the orbit of the civil administration, which he essentially controlled.

From the beginning his police apparatus in Poland pursued a policy of brutal suppression. Blissfully ignorant of the country—it was, for example forbidden to learn Polish—a negative selection of police officials set about crushing any Polish insubordination through a policy of exceptionally tough punishments, mass arrests, and summary executions. In the spring of 1940 this strategy reached its initial unhappy high point when the security police killed around 3,500 members of the Polish intelligentsia and political functionaries, as well as around 3,000 people who were described as criminals.[6] Against this background any attempt to penetrate the Polish underground, let alone try to play off the various factions of the Polish underground movement against each other, was hardly possible.[7] Within a very short time the Germans had succeeded in alienating the very people who, in view of their anti-Russian and anti-Soviet attitudes, might have been won over in the summer of 1941.

In February 1940, with the aid of a 'Decree for the Combating of Acts of Violence in the Annexed Eastern Territories', Himmler undertook a first attempt at introducing a massive increase in penalties for the Polish and Jewish populations and in certain cases the 'immediate passing and carrying out' of sentences through police courts martial. In other words, the arbitrary violence of the previous months was to be retrospectively legitimated. Although this initiative was opposed by Lammers and Göring, the Reich Ministry of Justice adopted the increases in penalties proposed by Himmler in one of its decrees. In response Himmler agreed to put an end to the police courts.[8]

However, his restraint did not last long. Since Himmler did not wish to dispense with a judicial responsibility for the police in the annexed eastern territories, in December 1941, with significant support from Bormann, he compelled the Reich Justice Ministry to issue a penal code for Poles in the annexed territories. This was a special penal code for Poles and Jews, which, although implemented by the judiciary, was so draconian that it applied the death penalty even for minor cases of insubordination. The Reich Minister of Justice could not prevent Himmler from using the negotiations preceding this decree to reintroduce SS and police courts martial, albeit restricted to certain situations.[9]

The start of Jewish persecution in Poland

Given this background, it is hardly surprising that, right from the start, and based on Himmler's wide-ranging powers, the new gentlemen of the black order aimed to target the approximately 1.7 million Jews who had come under German rule as a result of the war. Himmler and the SS leadership had already developed far-reaching plans for what to do with them.[10]

Heydrich reported to the meeting of departmental heads of the security police on 14 September that Himmler was currently putting to Hitler proposals for dealing with the 'Jewish problem in Poland', which, because of their major diplomatic implications, could be decided only by the Führer himself.[11] A week later, on 21 September, Heydrich informed the departmental heads that Hitler had approved Himmler's plans for 'deporting the Jews into the foreign Gau', for 'driving them over the line of demarcation'.* It is clear from a telex to the commanders of the Einsatzgruppen

---

* *Translators' note*: The line of demarcation with the Soviet-occupied zone.

from the same day exactly what was envisaged in practice.[12] The Polish Jews were initially to be 'concentrated' in large cities and then deported to an area near the eastern border of occupied Poland, where a 'Jewish state under German administration' was envisaged, as Heydrich explained to Brauchitsch the following day.[13] In addition, Heydrich mentioned in his telex a—top-secret—'final goal' of the anti-Jewish measures. This presumably referred to the comprehensive programme that Heydrich had explained to his departmental heads on 21 September in bullet-point form: the deportation of the Jews from the 'Greater German Reich' into the 'Jewish reservation' and their possible 'expulsion' into the part of eastern Poland occupied by the Soviet Union.

The Soviets and the Germans reached agreement on 28 September about the demarcation line between their respective occupation zones. The territory between the Vistula and the Bug, the later General Government district of Lublin, had been assigned to the Germans, and the future 'reservation' was planned for this area, with its role expanded. The 'Nature-conservation area' or 'Reich ghetto', as Heydrich called it, was intended to absorb those Poles from the territories annexed to Germany who were regarded as 'undesirable' in addition to the Jews.[14]

On 29 September Hitler informed Alfred Rosenberg that he wanted to divide the newly conquered Polish territory into three parts. The area between the Vistula and the Bug was to be separated from the west by an 'eastern wall', and the Jews from the whole of the Reich, as well as 'all elements who are in any way unreliable', were to be settled there. A broad strip on the old German–Polish border was to be Germanized and colonized, and between these two territories there was to be a 'form of state' for the Poles.[15] In fact, during the coming weeks the Nazi leadership treated the idea of a 'Jewish reservation' as anything other than 'top secret'.[16]

At the beginning of October 1939 the Reich Security Main Office (RSHA) began to make concrete plans for the deportation of the Jews living in the Reich to the 'reservation'. As early as 6 October, the day before the signing of the Decree for the Consolidation of the Ethnic German Nation, Adolf Eichmann, the head of the Central Agency for Jewish Emigration in Prague, was ordered by Gestapo chief Heinrich Müller to prepare for the deportation of 70,000–80,000 Jews from the government district of Kattowitz (Katowice)—in other words, from annexed Polish territory that was now part of Silesia. According to Müller, the Jews from neighbouring Mährisch-Ostrau (Ostrava) in the Protectorate could also be deported.[17]

Eichmann, however, was already engaged in a more far-reaching task. Hitler, he told the Silesian Gauleiter, has, 'to start with, ordered the transfer of 300,000 Jews from the Old Reich [pre-1938 Germany] and the Ostmark [Austria]'. He, Eichmann, had to report to Himmler on the first deportations and, on the basis of this report, Hitler would then make a final decision.[18] In view of the wider perspective opened up by this, Eichmann extended the preparations for deportation to include the Jews of Vienna and requested a list of all the Jews who had been registered in the Reich.[19] The deportations planned by Eichmann were also intended to include Gypsies.[20]

In mid-October Eichmann and Walter Stahlecker, the commander of the security police and SD in the Protectorate, decided on Nisko on the river San as the railway station to which the Jews should be sent and as the location for a 'transit camp'. This camp, which lay directly on the border of the district of Lublin, was intended to be a staging post through which the Jews would arrive in the 'Jewish reservation'.[21] A conscious decision was taken not to go through with the original plan to house the deportees in barracks.[22]

Between 20 and 28 October 4,700 people from Vienna, Kattowitz, and Mährisch-Ostrau were in fact deported to Nisko, where their guards simply forced them to disperse into the autumnal countryside.[23] However, on the day of the very first transport the RSHA banned further transports.[24] An important reason for the ban will have been the fact that, in the meantime, Himmler, as Settlement Commissar, was developing much more far-reaching resettlement plans which the Nisko action would have interfered with. For Himmler was not primarily concerned with the rapid deportation of the Jews from the Reich, but rather with his plan to deport undesirable Poles and Jews from the annexed eastern territories so that they could make room for the settlement of ethnic Germans. However, despite Himmler's new priority and despite the halt to the Nisko action, the RSHA remained basically committed to the deportation of Jews from the Reich to the district of Lublin.[25]

Germanization in the annexed territories

With his intervention in the Germanization policy in the east Himmler had in fact achieved a coup, as is clear from Darré's horrified response. Up to this point Himmler had strongly supported the rapid deportation of the Jews from the whole of the Reich. However, as we have seen, in his role as Settlement Commissar he had called a halt to these measures after a few weeks. The 'Jewish question' was now to be 'solved' within the much wider framework of the ethnic 'reordering' of Poland.

In his new sphere of activity, as the historian Isabel Heinemann puts it, Himmler relatively quickly achieved a 'strategic division of labour' with the Haupttreuhandstelle Ost (Main Trustee Office East).[26] This body, which had been established by Göring in October 1939, had the task of registering, confiscating, and administering commercial property in those parts of Poland that were to be annexed. Göring respected Himmler's responsibility for the confiscation of agricultural property. Moreover, in the course of the planning for South Tyrol, an agency for immigration and resettlement had been established under Ulrich Greifelt, and this now developed into the headquarters for carrying out the task of 'consolidating the ethnic German nation'. From June 1941 onwards it had the title Staff Headquarters of the RKF (Reichskommisar für die Festigung deutschen Volkstums).[27]

Hardly had he been appointed when Himmler leapt into action. As early as 11 October he signed 'provisional planning guidelines':

One Gau will be settled with Swabians, another with Franconians, and a third with Westphalians, Lower Saxons, Schleswig-Holsteiners, and so on. A village with around twenty-five farms will have a hard core of ten to twelve farms from a particular clan. These will be joined by ten to twelve ethnic German ones so that, with the aid of the Germans from the Old Reich, the ethnic Germans can once more be integrated into German life. Two or three SS military peasants will be settled in each village who can fill the posts of local peasant leader, parish councillor, and suchlike.[28]

On the same day he informed the heads of the main departments, Lorenz, Heydrich, and Pancke as well as Greifelt and the Reich Governors, Artur Greiser and Wilhelm Forster, of his views:

I envisage the [ethnic German] population of Riga forming the clan basis for the cities of Gotenhafen [Gdynia] and Posen [Poznań]. The urban population of Dorpat [Tartu] and Reval [Talinn] can be deployed in the same way. The selection of the population will be carried out by the chief of the security police in agreement with SS Obergruppenführer Lorenz. In order to settle Germans in those cities it will be essential to expel the Poles and clear their dwellings. Members of the Polish intelligentsia should be the first to be expelled.[29]

On 24 October Himmler visited Arthur Greiser, recently appointed Reich Governor in Posen. In the evening he spoke about settlement plans in the club of the civil administration. To begin with, he tried to elucidate the historical dimension of settlement:

As early as 3,000 years ago and during the following period Teutons lived in the eastern provinces in which we now find ourselves. Despite the poor transport conditions of those days and the other primitive conditions that existed, it was possible to settle Germans. These ancient German settlements have more or less survived racially to the present day in closed communities and as islands, even if in some cases they no longer speak the language. What was possible then must be even more feasible today.

Himmler explained the 'concept of the military peasant', for whose creation concrete preparations had already been made: 'It involves, among other things, the compulsory saving that I introduced into the SS. An SS man, who in due course saves 2,000 to 3,000 Reich marks, has thereby laid the foundation for a settlement. The brickworks and stone quarries that I have established were begun with the aim of providing the basis for future peasant settlements.' With his penchant for going into detail, Himmler explained to his audience how he envisaged the life of the future settlers:

The settlements that I envisage should not be built of clay, with walls one course of stone thick, but rather we should build houses as in the old days, two or three stone courses thick and with good foundations. We don't need to buy the land for settlement; settlement land already exists [...]. Polish workers must provide the cheap labour for settlement and for ploughing the fields. [...] The Germans will always provide the leadership for everything; the Poles will do the dirty work.

Great emphasis was to be put on cleanliness: 'I envisage that in every settler's house there will be a room in the cellar where one can do the washing, where there will be a bath and a shower for the peasant when he comes home sweaty from the fields.' There was always to be enough space for 'healthy families with several children'. The houses were to be built

according to plans and drawings that we shall produce. All the kitsch and urban rubbish that there is such a lot of in this area must be got rid of and our settlers should live in a healthy, peasant milieu. The peasant houses should be neither luxurious nor primitive. [...] In fifty to eighty years' time 20 million German settlers should be living in this vast settlement area in the east, of whom 10 million will be peasants with eight to ten children. The perpetuum mobile will then stand still. If there is no more land to be distributed then, as is always the case throughout history, new land will have to be got with the sword.[30]

Himmler announced an initial comprehensive plan for the 'resettlement of Poles and Jews' on 30 October 1939. The following population groups were to be expelled to the General Government: 'all Jews' from the annexed territories, 'all Congress Poles' (in other words, all Poles who came from the parts of Poland that had belonged to Russia between 1815 and 1916) from the province of Danzig–West Prussia, as well as 'a number, still to be determined, of particularly hostile Poles from the provinces of Posen, East Prussia, and eastern Upper Silesia'.[31]

On 8 November Streckenbach, the commander of the security police in the General Government, who had been assigned the 'central planning of settlement and evacuation in the east', informed the Higher SS and Police Leaders who were responsible for carrying out the deportations that, by the end of February 1940, 'all Jews and Congress Poles from the annexed territories' should be 'evacuated', and the Polish population that remained should be divided into 'Poles, 'ethnic Germans', as well as 'Poles who are still regarded as desirable'. In all, it was now planned 'initially, by the end of February 1940, to evacuate around 1,000,000 Jews and Poles [. . .] from the Old Reich and the newly occupied eastern territories',[32] of whom around 700,000 would come from the annexed territories.[33]

The RSHA produced a 'long-range plan': first, to deport all Jews and politically undesirable Poles to the General Government; then the 'racial assessment' and expulsion of the mass of the Polish population. A 'short-range plan' envisaged, to begin with, the deportation of 80,000 Poles and Jews from the Warthegau in order to resettle the Baltic Germans. They had been provisionally accommodated in camps following their repatriation after the occupation of the Baltic States by the Soviet Union.[34] These totals were actually exceeded, with the deportation of more than 87,000 people— 'politically compromised Poles, Jews, Polish intelligentsia, criminals, and asocials'[35]—from the Warthegau to the General Government between 1 and 17 December.[36]

On 21 December Heydrich announced that he had appointed Eichmann to be his special adviser 'to coordinate all security police matters involved in the implementation of the clearing of the eastern territory'.[37] During the first months of 1940 Eichmann had to ensure that, in the process of implementing a second short-range plan, 600,000 Jews would be deported into the General Government,[38] an action that kept being postponed,[39] while those responsible cited very different figures for those to be deported.[40] Finally, on 23 January 1940 the head of the Settlement Commissariat's main planning department produced a general plan for the settlement of the eastern territories that had been annexed, according to which, over the long term, 3.4 million Poles were to be deported. The deportation of the roughly 3.4 million Jews living in this area already formed part of the plan.[41]

However, on 30 January 1940 Heydrich came up with a new idea. Now, between 800,000 and a million Poles were to be provisionally sent from the annexed Polish territories for 'labour deployment' in the Reich. Only 40,000 Jews and Poles were to be deported to the General Government from the 'eastern Gaus' to make room for the resettlement of the Baltic Germans, and only around 120,000 Poles were to be sent there to make room for the resettlement of the Volhynian Germans. Subsequently, all the Jews—not only those from the annexed Polish territories but also those from the whole of the Reich—as well as 30,000 Gypsies were to be deported to the General Government.[42]

In fact, only part of this far-reaching scheme was achieved. By the beginning of 1941 almost 308,000 Poles and Jews from the annexed eastern territories had been deported to the General Government.[43] After that the General Government was, to a large extent, no longer treated as a 'reception area'. Initially used as an assembly area for the invasion of the Soviet Union, it was then declared to be a potential region for German settlement.[44] By the end of 1942 another 57,000 'racially undesirable' people had been resettled from the annexed eastern territories. After that we have no more statistics, but there cannot have been substantial population movements.[45] In addition, there were hundreds of thousands of Jewish inhabitants of the annexed territories who were not deported, but 'concentrated' in ghettos during 1940–1 and who, from the end of 1941 onwards, were to be murdered in the extermination camps.

Himmler assigned the 'racial assessment' of the people who were to be resettled, both Germans and Poles, to the Race and Settlement Main Office, which, because of its role in the examination of SS members and their wives, had accumulated years of experience in the sphere of 'racial selection', and, as a result of these new tasks, acquired considerable importance.[46]

★

The compulsory resettlement of hundreds of thousands of people required the creation of an elaborate organization. A 'Central Office for Immigration' (Einwandererzentralstelle = EWZ) was established in the middle of October 1939 on Heydrich's orders, and from January 1940 onwards it was based in Łódź, with a number of branch offices. With the help of the RuSHA experts assigned to it, it undertook a 'racial assessment' of the ethnic Germans and decided where they were to be 'settled'.[47] It had a counterpart in the shape of the Central Office for Resettlement (Umwandererzentralstelle = UWZ) in Posen, also with several branch offices,[48] which was responsible for the expulsion of Poles and Jews from the annexed Polish territories. The three Race and Settlement adviser units, which the RuSHA had sent to Poland at the start of the war, now formed SS Land Offices, which were run from the Central Land Office in Berlin. By the end of 1942 they had confiscated a total of 686,054 farms with 6,043,901 hectares of land, which amounted to 91.7 per cent of farms.[49] Moreover, in March 1940 so-called SS settlement staffs were created to organize the expulsion of the indigenous population and the settlement of ethnic Germans in the various localities.[50] These staffs were filled with former Selbstschutz leaders,[51] who had experience in exercising terror. Terror and resettlement policy were inextricably linked.

On 13 December 1939, on a visit to the transit camps in the Łódź district (on the previous day he had witnessed how people were gassed in a gas chamber), Himmler declared that the racial assessments were designed to prevent 'mongrel types from emerging in the territories that are to be newly settled. I want to create a blond province.'[52] On the same day he took advantage of an inspection of the EWZ in Łódź to comment on the racial classification of 'returnees', and ordered the head of the Race and Settlement Main Office to work out binding guidelines for this procedure. The results of the examination and assessment process were, according to Himmler, 'of decisive importance for the fate of the individual and of the German east'. The work should be carried out 'not bureaucratically but with generosity of spirit'. A careful distinction should be made in judging personal appearance between 'physical and racial characteristics. The racial appearance of all members of the family should be assessed.'[53]

In response Pancke worked out guidelines for the 'selection of people who are to be earmarked for the newly won eastern territories', according to which there were four categories who came into consideration for this project: ethnic German returnees, indigenous ethnic Germans, Reich applicants for settlement, as well as people whom the Reich Food Estate had already registered as applicants to become peasants.[54] The head of the Clans Office (Sippenamt), Hofmann, had already issued 'Instructions for Assessing the Suitability of Returnees', which followed the SS's principles for selection and divided people into four categories.[55]

Originally it was envisaged that only those who were classified in categories I and II would be settled in the east; anyone who was in category III was to be deported to the Old Reich and anyone in category IV would be deported to the country from where they came. However, on the occasion of a visit to Łódź in January 1940, Himmler gave instructions that people in category III were also to be settled in the east.[56] As a result, the criteria for membership of this group were made stricter.[57]

During this visit Himmler also ordered that 'those returnees placed in category IV are to be transferred to the Old Reich without exception [...] The returnees in categories I and II are to be settled in the new eastern Gaus without exception.' He himself determined the size of farms to be allocated to the farmers in groups I to III.[58]

Any 'returnees' who were defined as 'ethnically alien' (for whom the special category IVf had been created) were to be sent to the General Government. In January Himmler ordered that each such 'evacuation' of 'dubious ethnic Germans' was to be submitted to him for approval.[59] Those affected were obliged to await his decision in camps, 'probably in Franconia'.[60] Himmler also reserved for himself the decision on 'applications for citizenship from those in categories I and II with professional occupations'.[61]

As always when a project particularly interested him, Himmler concerned himself with the smallest details. When a form which had been sent to him for final evaluation had, in his view, not been filled in correctly, the RuSHA representative at the Central Office for Immigration in Łódź was instructed to remind his assessors that Himmler paid particular attention to 'the information concerning body size, hair colour, colour of eyes, the mongol wrinkle, the epicanthus, slit eyes'.[62]

Himmler's habit of reserving certain decisions for himself or of personally intervening in individual cases once again illustrates the arbitrary nature of the racial assessments that took place. They were not made on the basis of objective criteria but were basically determined by the value-judgement of the individual assessor, for whom the 'overall impression' not only of the individual subject but of the whole family being assessed was decisive.

From November 1939 to March 1940, to start with around 62,000 ethnic Germans from Latvia and Estonia were 'transited'. During the winter they were followed by those being resettled from the eastern Polish territories occupied by the Soviet Union, 128,000 in all, followed by around 30,000 ethnic Germans from the General Government (the area round Chelm and Lublin), and 137,000 ethnic Germans from the Romanian territories annexed by the Soviet Union in the summer of 1940 (Bessarabia and North Bukovina), to whom were added, at the request of the Romanian government, a further 70,000 ethnic Germans from Romania. At the beginning of 1941 they were followed by 48,000 Lithuanian Germans, as well as 12,000 ethnic Germans who were subsequently being resettled from Estonia and Latvia. By the end of 1940 Himmler's racial assessors had dealt with half-a-million, by the end of 1944 more than a million ethnic German 'returnees'.[63]

However, the results of the assessment of the returnees by SS assessors turned out to be far poorer than anticipated, given the high expectations that had been placed on the racial standards of the ethnic Germans who were being resettled. The assessment of the 'racial value' of the Estonian and Latvian Germans was all in all a positive one: of 55,600 people over 6 years of age, somewhere between 60.1 and 74.4 per cent were placed in the categories I and II and were thereby considered 'suitable for settlement'.[64] But of the ethnic Germans from Volhynia and Galicia, more than 45,500 people in all, only 44 per cent met the criteria for placement in groups I and II.[65]

The following comment by a racial assessor can be read as a declaration of bankruptcy for a population policy based on racial ideology:

In racial terms the average is a more or less balanced mixture of the Falian race with various elements of the main European races, of which the East Baltic race represents a high proportion. If strict criteria had been applied then the proportion of families in category IV would have been considerably larger. It was only as a result of repeated and urgent requests by the senior officials that many families on the borderline were categorized as III.[66]

The SS assessors also assigned the majority of ethnic Germans from Bessarabia, Bukovina, and Dobrudscha to group III.[67] But this figure may also have been the result of subsequent adjustment, for at a meeting there was mention of a figure of between 40 and 60 per cent being in group IV.[68]

What is more, although the 'racial assessment' of the ethnic Germans produced such disappointing results, there were not enough farms available for the ethnic Germans who had been selected as being 'of good racial quality', despite the ruthless expulsion of the indigenous population. By the end of 1940 the settlement staffs had allocated farms in the Warthegau to more or less all the 5,000 Baltic Germans with farming backgrounds (the majority of ethnic Germans from this region lived in urban centres) and also to more than half the Volhynian, Galician, and Narev Germans from eastern Poland and also to those from Chelm and Lublin, in other words, the vast majority of the agrarian population from these territories. However, the more members of the indigenous population they expelled, the more the planners ran the risk that these measures would affect people who might in fact have been categorized as 'capable of being Germanized' (and indeed, after the opening up of the General Government to German settlement in the summer of 1941, the search began for such 'Germanizable' people among those who had been 'de-settled' in 1939 and 1940).

At the beginning of 1941, however, it became clear that the Poles could no longer be expelled from the annexed territories to the General Government in such large numbers, because of the pressures on space created by the mobilization of the Wehrmacht for the Russian campaign, a situation that was to persist after the outbreak of war with the Soviet Union. This meant that there was now hardly any chance of accommodating the next wave of resettlement of over 200,000 ethnic Germans from Bukovina, Bessarabia, and Dobrudscha in farms in the annexed territories. By April 1941 there were already 275,000 settlers stuck in VoMi reception camps, 228,000 of them in the Old Reich, representing more than half the people who had hitherto been resettled.[69]

In March 1942 Himmler's population experts reckoned that, of the total of 510,000 people who were being resettled, only barely 287,000 had been 'settled' in the annexed eastern territories and 93,000 in the Old Reich (most of them housed in provisional accommodation). That meant there were still 131,000 people in the camps.[70]

In view of this situation the SS leadership had the idea of employing young ethnic German girls as housemaids in the Old Reich, especially in large families or working for people connected with the SS leadership. Frau Himmler herself received household staff from Volhynia. In the summer 1940 Karl Brandt reported to Koppe that the Reichsführer's wife—who, as we have seen, generally placed heavy demands on her servants—appeared to be 'satisfied with the girls', but required 'another girl because one of the girls wants to marry soon'.[71] Moreover, according to Brandt, 'the Reichsführer-SS

[...] requires a second girl, who must be sent as soon as possible for a well-known family'. But that was not the end of it: 'Furthermore, SS-Gruppenführer Wolff requests a cook and a housemaid for SS-Sturmbannführer Sachs in Schweinfurt.' It is clear from the same letter that the Cosmic Ice Theory researcher in the Ahnenerbe, Scultetus, also wanted to be provided with servants. Wilhelm Koppe was able to meet all five requests.[72] And the numbers of those who were interested in acquiring servants grew: in May 1941 Himmler asked Greifelt 'to supply 12 ethnic German girls for the SS sanatorium Hohenlychen and three more girls who are to be employed by members of the Reichsführer's family'.[73]

All the measures for settling ethnic Germans described hitherto have referred to the annexed eastern territories, the enlarged 'living-space' of the Nazi Reich. By contrast, at that time the General Government was envisaged in the minds of the planners as simply an area in which to dump people who were 'inferior'. In summer 1940 Himmler included the General Government for the first time in his plans for Germanization in another way, and in the form of an experiment strictly limited to the SS. He assigned to Globocnik the task of establishing what the latter termed a model 'military settlement'. Himmler decided that this type of settlement should be given the name 'SS and police base' (SS- und Polizeistützpunkt), and on 2 November ordered Globocnik to establish six such bases. In March 1941 the latter had transformed six former rural estates into bases. They were administered by SS members, and when necessary could be occupied by police units.[74] At this point it was not planned to turn them into core areas for substantial settlement projects.

The Ethnic German List [*Volksliste*] and re-Germanization

Apart from racial assessment of ethnic German returnees, 'racial assessment' of the indigenous population of the annexed Polish territories also formed part of the duties of the SS. On 25 May 1940 Himmler gave Hitler a memorandum with the title 'A Few Thoughts on the Treatment of the Ethnically Alien Population in the East'. Himmler's basic idea was that 'in the east we must endeavour to recognize and foster as many individual groups as possible', in other words, 'to divide them up into as many segments and splinter groups as possible'. For 'only by dissolving this ethnic mishmash of 15 million people in the General Government and 8 million in the eastern provinces will we be able to carry out the racial screening process that must form the basis on which we can fish out the racially valuable people from this mishmash, bring them to Germany and assimilate them there'.

Within four or five years, 'for example, the term "Kaschubian" will be unknown because there will no longer be a Kaschubian people'. 'I hope to see the term "Jew", Himmler continued, 'completely eliminated through the possibility of a large-scale emigration of all Jews to Africa or to some colony'; and that it will be possible, 'over a slightly longer period [...] to ensure the disappearance of the ethnic categories of Ukrainians, Gorales, and Lemkes from our territory'. The same should also apply, 'making allowances for the larger area involved, to the Poles'.

A key to solving this problem was the 'question of schools'. The non-German population in the east should have only elementary schools with four classes and no schools at a higher level. The elementary schools should simply teach : 'Basic counting up to 500 at the most, how to write one's name, and that it is God's commandment to be obedient to the Germans and to be honest, hardworking, and well-behaved. I consider it unnecessary to teach reading.' Parents who wanted to give their children a better education would have to apply to the Higher SS and Police Leader, whose decision would be primarily determined by racial considerations:

If we recognize such a child as being of our blood then the parents will be informed that the child will be placed in a school in Germany and will remain in Germany indefinitely. However cruel and tragic each individual case may be, if one rejects the Bolshevik method of physically exterminating a people on the grounds that it is fundamentally un-German and impossible, then this method is the kindest and the best one.

Himmler sketched the future as follows:

After these measures have been systematically implemented over the next decade, the population of the General Government will inevitably consist of an inferior remnant, which will include all the people who have been deported to the eastern provinces as well as from those parts of the German Reich which contain the same racial and human type (for example, the parts containing the Sorbs and Wends). This population will be available as a leaderless labouring class [...] it will get more to eat and have more from life than under Polish rule and, while lacking culture itself, under the strict, consistent, and fair leadership of the German people will be called upon to participate in their eternal cultural achievements and monuments. Indeed, in view of the amount of hard labour required to produce them, it may even be indispensable.[75]

Himmler noted that Hitler had endorsed the memorandum in principle, and had agreed that it should be given to a small group of top functionaries for them to read as a guideline authorized by him, but that it should not be handed out generally.[76]

Himmler had already developed two Germanization programmes. Since, according to the memorandum, the General Government was to be re-served for 'inferiors', these applied only to the annexed territories. In the first place, there was the 're-Germanization' of those Poles who, because of their 'positive' racial characteristics, were to be excluded from the mass of people who were to be deported to the General Government. Secondly, there was the tracking down of 'people of German origin' in the annexed Polish territories through the procedure of racial screening, which acquired the title 'Ethnic German List' (*Volksliste*).

Re-Germanization had the dual function of, 'on the one hand, utilizing racially valuable families for the German programme of labour mobilization and, on the other hand, removing from the Polish nation those Nordic families from which, experience has shown, the Polish leadership is pre-dominantly drawn'.[77] In order to carry out this task, Himmler, in his role as Settlement Commissar, had already established a special office of the Race and Settlement Main Office in the Łódź branch of the Central Office for Resettlement [UWZ] in March 1940.[78]

Since the summer of 1940 a total of around 30,000–35,000 Poles had been re-Germanized.[79] This figure was far below Hitler's and Himmler's guide-lines. They had originally envisaged up to a million Poles 'capable of being re-Germanized', a figure that matched calculations produced by the NSDAP's Office for Racial Policy.[80] In October 1940 Himmler reduced the target to around 100,000, and justified this by the need for careful 'racial selection'.[81] In May 1941 he explained his position once again to the Higher SS and Police Leaders based in Poland:

People can't be Germanized by the party taking them in hand and politically indoctrinating them, for the German administration and the German military have been trying this kind of thing in West Prussia and Posen for over a hundred years in a different form, with the result that during the period of German rule people served as Germans and were German citizens and during the period of

Polish rule they served as Poles and were Poles. This old method has historically been proved to be the wrong one.

Germanization of the eastern provinces can be done only on the basis of racial theory and that is by screening the population of these provinces. The racially valuable people, who in terms of their bloodline can be absorbed into our national body without causing damage (in some cases even with positive results), must be transferred to the old Reich as individual families. The other group, who on racial grounds cannot be absorbed, will remain in the country for as long as we need its labour for the development of the provinces and will then, in the course of the next 5–10 years, without exception or mercy be got rid of to the General Government, which is the place for people for whom on racial grounds Germany has no use.[82]

Ill. 19. Between the autumn of 1939 and the spring of 1941 Himmler regarded settlement policy in Poland as his most important task. He not only pushed these plans forward to a megalomaniacal extent but involved himself in every detail from the installation of showers in settlement houses to the criteria for racial examinations. Here he is explaining an exhibit at the exhibition 'Construction and Planning in the East' to the head of the Chancellery of the Führer of the NSDAP, Philipp Bouhler, Reich Armaments Minister, Fritz Todt, Hitler's Deputy, Rudolf Hess, and Heydrich.

In view of the slow results, in the middle of 1940 Himmler ordered the Race and Settlement Main Office to look for re-Germanizable families also among the Polish agricultural workers who had come to the Reich after the outbreak of war and whom Himmler had been obliged to let in 'un-screened' because of the shortage of time.[83] The aim was to select several thousand who would be able to live in Germany over the long term.[84]

As far as the introduction of the Ethnic German List was concerned, Reich Governor Arthur Greiser had already begun the process in 1939 by introducing a list in the Warthegau, for which, however, the decisive criteria were political and cultural, a line that was clearly contrary to the racial policy of the SS.[85] On 12 September 1940 Himmler issued his own guidelines for an ethnic German list in the annexed Polish territories based on the principle that any 'attempt at a general Germanization of the eastern provinces that is not based on racial principles will, in the end, lead to failure and to the loss of the eastern provinces'.

Once again Himmler envisaged four categories: groups I and II would include those who were clearly categorized as Germans; these people would be given German citizenship. Group III was intended for those who, 'over the years, had established links with the Poles' but nevertheless had the 'racial potential' to become 'full members of the German national commu-nity'. This group would receive German citizenship, but without the privilege of being a 'Reich citizen'. However, this had little practical importance since the status of Reich Citizen, which had been introduced by the Reich Citizenship Law of 1935, was never precisely defined and in practice never materialized. Ethnic Germans who had 'thrown in their lot with the Poles politically' belonged to group IV and received German citizenship only on a provisional basis. Members of groups III and IV were obliged to move to the Old Reich.[86]

As usual, Himmler had very detailed ideas as to how the process of 'racial assessment' should proceed: '1. The most important principle is that the racial assessment should be disguised as a medical examination [. . .] 2. The rooms used must be such that, at the end of the assessment, the person who is to be assessed returns to the dressing-room. 3. A shower facility for the purpose of personal hygiene is an essential precondition for the assessment procedure.' Himmler also laid down that assistant assessors should be em-ployed, that coloured boards should be used, that cheekbones, eyelids, and body hair should be examined, as well as other details of the physical examination, and, in addition, required that there should be a 'proper drill' for the whole procedure in order that the 'thorough assessment' of up to 400 people a day could be managed.[87] As usual, he made the final decision on any complaints.[88]

The main problem with the Ethnic German List was deciding on who belonged in groups III and IV, who was German and who was Polish. The Race and Settlement Main Office pursued the policy of subjecting these 2 million or so people to individual assessment, a task which in 1942 was to be handled by eleven offices of the Ethnic German List in the annexed Polish territories. It is unclear, however, how many people were actually assessed.[89] For Himmler was to come up against considerable opposition to his plan for individual racial assessments from the Reich Governors in the Warthegau, Danzig–West Prussia, and Upper Silesia, who preferred a simpler procedure.[90] In any case, during the war it proved impossible to carry out major resettlement programmes on the basis of the Ethnic German List.

Thus, all three Germanization programmes that Himmler had initiated in the autumn of 1939 in his role as Settlement Commissar had come to a halt in 1940–1, and had more or less failed. The settlement of ethnic Germans from the Baltic States in the annexed territories had only partially succeeded; re-Germanization achieved far poorer results than originally envisaged. The process of registration for the Ethnic German List does not appear to have been successfully concluded. The main obstacle to the realization of these programmes was the fact that the expulsions to the General Government could not be carried out to the extent required. The various population movements got in each other's way to such a degree that even the 'evacuation' of the Jewish population from the Reich that had originally been envisaged and confidently announced could not be carried out directly after the defeat of Poland, as had been planned.

'Jewish emigration'

Three months after the deportations associated with the Nisko project had been halted in November 1939 because of the priority being given to the settlement of ethnic Germans, the Reich Security Main Office organized a further, limited expulsion. On 12 and 13 February 1940 over 1,100 Jews from the district of Stettin, comprising almost the whole of the city's Jewish community, were deported to the Lublin region, and on 12 March around 160 people were deported from Schneidemühl to Glovnev near Posen.[91]

On 19 February Himmler justified these transports to the Gauleiters by the need to find room for the Baltic Germans. According to Himmler, he was explaining this so that his audience did not have any 'false hopes' as to subsequent deportations from their Gaus.[92] During the coming year, however, he intended, 'provided the war goes on for the whole year', to tackle 'Jewish emigration' 'to the extent that the numbers permit', in other words, to the extent that the conditions in the General Government allowed. Evidently this compulsory resettlement was to be distinguished from the 'normal emigration from the Old Reich, the Ostmark, and the Sudetengau'. This would 'continue [...] despite the war'. 'We then still want to emigrate [sic] 6,000–7,000 Jews per month to Palestine, South America, and North America.' However, working along these lines it was possible to expel at most 80,000 people annually. Thus the deportations into the General Government had to be restarted in accordance with the following priorities:

First, I must try to get the Jews out of the eastern provinces, Posen and West Prussia, eastern Upper Silesia, and southern East Prussia, from the four provinces. That's the first thing to do. Then comes the Old Reich and then the Protectorate. Here too I want at some point to get the 150,000 Jews in the Protectorate out. The Gypsies are another problem. If I can, I want to get them out this year as well. There are around 30,000 in the Reich as a whole, but they do a lot of racial damage.[93]

Himmler had good reason to warn against 'false hopes', for expansive deportation plans to the General Government were increasingly coming up against the opposition of the Governor-General, Hans Frank. At a top-level meeting on 12 February Frank had opposed the 'continuation of the resettlement programme as practised hitherto' and had received a promise from Himmler and Göring that in future he would be consulted more about the evacuations.[94] After a further conversation with Hitler, on 29 February, Frank reckoned that 'at least 400,000–600,000 more Jews' would be arriving, and on 4 March he informed the district and city chiefs in the Lublin area that their district continued to be envisaged as 'a sort of Jewish reservation'.[95] Thus, a few days later the German authorities postponed the planned creation of a ghetto in Warsaw; in view of the fact that the

General Government was going to act as a dumping ground, there no longer seemed any point in going ahead with it.[96]

On 24 March Göring made all deportations into the General Government subject to his and Frank's express approval.[97] This meant that de facto the transports had been halted. The project for a Jewish reservation in Lublin was permanently abandoned and the preparations for a ghetto in Warsaw were restarted.[98] Himmler's announcement to the Gauleiters had been far too rash.

Ethnic policy in the former Czechoslovakia reviewed

In the autumn of 1940 the population of the Protectorate of Bohemia and Moravia was also subjected to a 'racial stocktaking'.[99] The initiative came from the Higher SS and Police Leader in Prague, Karl Hermann Frank, and received a positive response from Hitler. The investigation was the responsibility of the Race and Settlement Main Office, which, in October 1940, was ordered by Himmler 'as soon as possible to draft a questionnaire for Czech school doctors', which superficially was intended to assess schoolchildren's health, but in fact was designed 'to clarify what are for us important questions' concerning the 'racial' make-up of Czech youth. Himmler then laid down the criteria for the racial test: 'exact height, age, weight, eye colour divided into three categories: 1. blue, blue-green—2. brown, dark brown—3. black, and finally the skin colour, which is to be divided into 1. Blond, dark blond—2. Brown, dark brown and black.'[100]

Himmler sent Frank the questionnaire that had been drafted by the RuSHA in accordance with his guidelines and, in addition, recommended that 'profile and full-face photographs' should be made of every child. In this way, according to Himmler, for the first time they would have 'in practice a racial stocktaking of the Czech people'.[101] In order to carry out this ambitious task, at the beginning of 1941 the RuSHA established a well-staffed branch office in Prague.[102]

In the meantime, a member of the RuSHA, Walter König-Beyer, had composed a memorandum on the racial-political conditions of the Bohemian–Moravian region which concluded that, after a thorough racial and political assessment of the indigenous population, around 55 per cent should be resettled to the General Government.[103] However, at this point Himmler's assignment as Settlement Commissar did not yet apply to the Protectorate, so that initially no concrete steps could be taken to implement such a project. It was only when Heydrich was appointed deputy Reich Protector in October 1941 that plans for the Germanization of the Protectorate received a decisive impetus.

At this point Slovakia also became a target of the SS and its ambitious population policy. Independent Slovakia, which had been created in March 1939, had a German minority of about 130,000 people. The leadership of this group, which had Nazi views, sought affiliation with the Reich, which, in view of the areas of ethnic German settlement, would have implied the annexation of large parts of Slovakia. This was opposed to the official policy of the Nazi regime, which was much more in favour of a Slovakian state dependent on Germany than of bringing these ethnic Germans 'home to the Reich'.[104]

In May 1940 Franz Karmasin, the leader of the ethnic German group, appealed to the RuSHA to join him on a visit to the ethnic Germans who were living dispersed in the Beskydy mountains in order to 'assess and examine their racial value'. Günther Pancke, the head of the RuSHA, duly undertook a study trip to the area, informing the Reichsführer of its results: 'The whole of Slovakia is a huge graveyard for ethnic Germans.' On the basis of this observation Pancke developed a plan that, far from aiming to strengthen the ethnic German group, instead envisaged a fusing of the Slovakian population with 'the ethnic Germans'. In Pancke's view, after the removal of Jews and Gypsies, as well as the 'exclusion' of the population of Hungarian origin, amounting to around 500,000 people, it would be possible to win back this territory completely for German ethnicity, particularly if, in addition, some 100,000 ethnic German families were settled there.[105] In March 1940 the SS not only began clandestinely to examine the ethnic Germans in Slovakia but at the same time set about forming an elite from the Slovakian Hlinka guards, which might act as the core of the fusion policy advocated by Pancke.

The resettlement of the South Tyroleans

Apart from these plans for large-scale settlement and population movements, Himmler was still confronted with the problem of sorting out the task Hitler had given him prior to his appointment as Reich Commissar for the Consolidation of the Ethnic German Nation, namely, the resettlement of the South Tyroleans.

A few days after the outbreak of the Second World War Himmler informed his 'highly valued friend', the Italian Minister of Police Bocchini, that he would stick to his original promise to oblige all Reich Germans to leave South Tyrol within three months (the first stage in the resettlement), 'despite the changed conditions and tension inevitably created by the war'. Naturally, the South Tyroleans who decided to emigrate 'should not be permitted to look down on' those people who decided to remain in Italy, 'thereby indicating that they wanted to become Italians both as regards their outward behaviour and as far as their innermost feelings are concerned'.[106]

After further negotiations Himmler interrupted the intensive planning for the population movements in Poland and, between 11 and 13 October, met Bocchini in Tremezzo on Lake Como in order to deal with the problems that had arisen in the meantime. He used the occasion to advocate a radical shortening and acceleration of the planned operation. Originally the South Tyroleans with Italian nationality had been given a deadline of 30 June 1940 within which to decide whether they wanted to become German or remain Italian. This was now reduced to 31 December 1939, with a corresponding simplification of the bureaucratic procedure.[107]

On the return journey from Tremezzo Himmler took some fundamental decisions relating to the resettlement of the South Tyroleans. He noted, in a piece that was intended for publication, that they should be 'placed en bloc in a new settlement area', for example in the lower reaches of the Netze (Notec) river or in an area on 'the northern slopes of the Beskyda', in other words, in the mountain range in southern Poland that bordered on Slovakia. In accordance with an order from Hitler, the resettlement was to be carried out in a 'generous manner'. 'Rural and urban communities will be re-established under their old names.' Himmler had already thought of a name for the settlement, which was not meant cynically: East Tyrol.[108]

On 21 October 1939, after further negotiations, the first agreement concerning the resettlement was reached,[109] and five days later, on 26 October, the emigration guidelines were issued. However, this prompted a propaganda campaign by the Italians against the resettlement that was tolerated by the prefect in Bolzano. Moreover, the Italian authorities kept arresting South Tyroleans sympathetic to the Nazis who were supporting the emigration.[110] On 14 November Himmler intervened, with a pointedly friendly letter to Bocchini in which he nevertheless complained strongly about the propaganda campaign, the arrests, and about the fact that the Italians had not kept to certain parts of the agreement concerning the right to opt for German or Italian nationality[111] On 15 November Wolff and the under-state secretary in the Italian Interior Ministry, Buffarini Guidi, came to an agreement in Rome which, in particular, ensured the release of those who had been arrested.[112] The option process, which had been completed by the end of 1939, resulted in a large majority opting to emigrate.[113]

Of the 200,000 people who had opted for Germany or were German citizens, 56,000 had left their homeland by the end of 1940. However, during the last months of 1940 the numbers of resettlers were declining significantly. By the middle of 1942 only a further 20,000 people had left South Tyrol, and then the whole project came to a halt. The vast majority had emigrated to Austria, around 21,000 to other parts of the Reich.[114]

While the majority of South Tyroleans were housed in makeshift resettlement camps, Greifelt's RKF office stuck to the plan for a settlement of the South Tyroleans en bloc. Himmler's original idea of resettling the South Tyroleans in the Beskyda was dropped fairly quickly, in view of the negative response of those affected.[115] After the victory over France in June 1940, Greifelt put forward a new plan. On 10 July he produced a memorandum which envisaged the resettlement of the South Tyroleans in Burgundy. A week later Himmler made a surprise revelation of this idea, which had allegedly already been approved in principle by Hitler, to a delegation of those who had opted for Germany. The delegation went on a tour of inspection to the proposed settlement area, and on 23 July was received by Himmler for a final meeting. Although work continued on the project during the following years, the annexation of French territory and the expulsion of the indigenous population in order to 'free up' the settlement area would have damaged German–French relations to an extent that made it inconceivable during the war.[116]

After the occupation of Yugoslavia in the spring of 1941 a new settlement area was discussed and then rejected, namely Lower Styria, which had been annexed by Germany. Finally, in mid-1942 the most outlandish plan of all was mooted: to settle the South Tyroleans in the Crimea, a scheme proposed to Himmler in May 1942 by the former Gauleiter of Vienna, Alfred Frauenfeld, who had been designated as the future Commissar-General of the Crimea. Himmler discussed this project with Hitler and both men liked the idea. It was agreed, however, that its implementation would have to be postponed until after the war. Himmler told Frauenfeld that 'we shall simply find another national group or another population' for Burgundy.[117]

The strategy developed by Himmler in October 1939 had involved committing himself to carrying out a rapid resettlement of a whole population to a particular area without an area actually being available. Conceived in the euphoria of Germany's victory and inspired by the expansion of his resettlement task in his new role as Settlement Commissar, it proved to be a disaster with catastrophic consequences. However, the abortive resettlement of the South Tyroleans was not the only fiasco produced by Settlement Commissar Himmler.

The Reichsführer on the defensive

At the beginning of 1940 Himmler was faced with massive criticism from the leadership of the Wehrmacht. At its heart were orders relating in various ways to Himmler's radical policy of ethnic reordering but also affecting the status of the Wehrmacht, namely the mass murders committed by the SS in Poland, which in the view of the officer corps threatened to damage the honour of the Wehrmacht, and also Himmler's so-called 'Procreation Order' of October 1939.

As has been shown above,[118] from 1939 onwards there was an increasing number of complaints from Wehrmacht commanders about atrocities carried out by the SS in Poland. In particular, in November 1939 and January 1940 the Military Commander East, Colonel-General Johannes von Blaskowitz, complained to the Commander-in-Chief of the army, Walther von Brauchitsch, in two memoranda.[119]

After a meeting between Blaskowitz and von Brauchitsch in January the latter had two meetings with Himmler, on 24 January and 2 February, at which, among other things, he raised these complaints, though without trying to press Himmler too hard. During the second meeting Himmler was conciliatory, admitted 'mistakes', and emphasized that he was concerned to maintain good relations with the army.[120] Brauchitsch was satisfied with this. Indeed, on 13 March he invited Himmler to give a speech to the senior commanders in Koblenz. Himmler used the opportunity to play down the reports of atrocities by the SS and, in addition, to indicate that he was doing nothing without Hitler's knowledge. Thus, his radical population policy was covered by the authority of 'the Führer'.[121] In the end, the outrage within the officer corps at the crimes of the Waffen-SS in Poland fizzled out without having made any impact, apart from the fact that in future the military was much more reserved in its response to proposals from the SS leadership to integrate SS command structures or agencies into the military command structures.

At von Brauchitsch's meeting with Himmler on 2 February, Himmler's 'Children's Decree', as the Commander-in-Chief politely described it, was also the subject of discussion. This was the order of 28 October, which within the Wehrmacht was known as the 'Procreation Order' (*Zeugungsbe-fehl*), and which may well have caused more agitation than the crimes committed by the SS in Poland.[122]

On issuing this order Himmler had provided the following justification: 'Every war is a bloodletting of the best blood. Many a military victory won by a nation has been at the same time a crushing defeat for its vitality and its blood.' However, the 'inevitable death of its best men, however sad, is not the worst thing' about it; it is rather 'the non-existence of the children who have not been produced by the living during the war and by the dead after the war [. . .] He who knows that his clan, that all that he and his ancestors have wanted and sought to achieve, will be continued through his children can die in peace. The best gift to the widow of a fallen soldier is always the child of the man she loved.' And then Himmler came to the point: 'Beyond the limits of bourgeois laws and conventions, which are perhaps necessary in other circumstances, it can, even outside marriage, be a noble task, under-taken not frivolously but from deep moral seriousness, for German women and girls of good blood to become mothers of the children of soldiers going to war of whom fate alone knows whether they will return or die for Germany.'

Thus Himmler had decided publicly to propagate the views on illegiti-mate births that he had pursued above all during 1936–7. Although he had addressed his order to procreate children 'outside marriage' to 'the whole of the police and SS', in fact he spoke generally about 'soldiers going to the front', and so it was also intended to be a general appeal to go beyond 'the bounds of bourgeois laws and habits'.

Apart from that, Himmler recalled in his order—referring once again not only to the police and SS—the

sacred duty to become mothers and fathers. Let us never forget that the victory gained by our swords and the blood shed by our soldiers would be pointless unless it were followed by the victory involved in the birth of children and the settlement of our new land. During the last war many a soldier decided out of a sense of responsibility to have no more children during the war so that his wife would not be left in need and distress after his death. You SS men need not have such concerns and anxieties.[123]

In January 1940, however, Himmler felt it necessary to elucidate the Procreation Order through a further order. His October order, which—how could it be otherwise!—'was conceived with decency and construed in a decent sense and deals candidly with problems that can be anticipated in the future', had 'led to misconceptions and misunderstandings on the part of some people'. As far as this involved the question of illegitimate children, Himmler commented briefly and succinctly: 'this is not a matter for discussion.' However, the order had also been interpreted to mean that SS men were being encouraged 'to approach the wives of soldiers serving at the front', and Himmler emphatically denied this.[124] On 30 January he issued a specific ban on members of the police and SS having sexual intercourse with the wives of front-line soldiers. Himmler made it clear in the order that breaches would be treated as disobeying a military order and punished accordingly.[125]

After the two meetings with von Brauchitsch in January and February 1940 Himmler also dealt with the murders in Poland and the controversial Procreation Order in a speech to the Gauleiters and other high-ranking party functionaries. Unlike the appearance before the senior commanders of the Wehrmacht arranged with von Brauchitsch, here Himmler was basically performing in front of his home crowd, and so did not have to adopt a remorseful pose.

As far as the Procreation Order was concerned, Himmler noted that, 'with a very few exceptions', he 'had been clearly and correctly understood' by the party, but outside the party he had 'largely' met with 'criticism and opposition'. Himmler explained that he had issued the order because the father of an SS man who had been killed had asked him whether his son had left behind an illegitimate child. This enquiry had made him realize that, 'in our hypocritical age, for we are still socially hypocritical, it is necessary for a chap to be dead and buried before his parents can be happy and suddenly understand the age-old truth that it is important for a family to go on and for its blood not to be lost'. In response he had 'drafted this order and given it to the Führer, not—and I would ask you to appreciate this—because I wanted to tell the world that the Führer had approved it, but only in order to find out: does the Führer agree with it or does he not? If he agrees with it then the order will be issued. If there's a negative response we shall have to deal with it ourselves and not refer to the Führer.'

After having covered his back by citing the highest authority, he then gave them a lecture that was simultaneously grammatically confused and condescending:

Gentlemen theoreticians, you fail to see that this increase in the number of males born in the war years will bring nature back into balance by itself, but that this equilibrium will not be produced in the cohorts of women now aged between 35 and 40, but in fact will be produced by war widows, though not all of them in the legal sense of the word, but rather by women whose husbands or future husbands have fallen and are not there, women who are still of child-bearing age. I reckon that these amount to 100,000, it may be 2, 3, 4 or 500,000, indeed it may well be half-a-million who have a problem in that their husband is dead.

In addition, 'there is a huge silent burden which unfortunately continues to weigh on our nation' in the shape of homosexuality, a 'lethal illness for a nation'. While Himmler naturally assumed that the fight he had been waging for years—he had previously estimated there were 2 million homosexuals— had made a significant impact, 'I think we must still reckon there are half-a-million' of them.

This problem, 'that there are women here and no men for these women', cannot 'simply be solved with moralizing words'. 'I am opposed and I think we are all opposed to this continuing social hypocrisy, to the fact that flirting or, if you like, friendship, or a relationship are socially acceptable but an illegitimate child is not socially acceptable and so the mother isn't either.' The attitude he was putting forward did not, he claimed, undermine marriage; on the contrary, 'marriages which produce many children form the core of the nation'. Himmler devoted seventeen pages of his speech to the controversial order, before moving on to his second topic. The point was to ensure that 'in the provinces which now belong to Germany [...] the problem of the existence of a Polish minority is dealt with and elimi- nated during our time'. And, in order to clarify matters, he emphasized: 'I don't want to be misunderstood: the Polish nationality and the Polish people must both be dissolved.'

After commenting on the supposed percentage of Germanic blood in the Slavs, he came to the point with a combination of half-hearted assertions of his innocence and relatively subtle counter-attacks:

Then there's the question of alleged atrocities. It is of course quite possible that in the east a train gets frozen in and not only during evacuations and that the people freeze to death. That's possible. Unfortunately that's happened to Germans as well. You simply can't do anything about it if you're travelling from Łódź to Warsaw and the train gets stuck for hours on end. Then you can't blame the railways or anybody. That's the fault of the climate there. It's regrettable for the Germans, it's regrettable for the Poles, and, if you like, it's regrettable for the Jews as well, if anyone feels like being sorry for them. But it's not intended and it can't be helped. I think it's wrong to make a big song and dance about it.

Himmler continued:

Also, the fact that a lot had to be done on foot. Well, good God, I can't help it. I couldn't help the fact that the Germans had to go on route marches either. So my first concern is going to be for the Germans. If I can change things for them I will certainly do so. And then, if I have the time and opportunity, I will happily change things for the Poles and Jews as well. But that has the lowest priority. And I think it's wrong for people to get excited here in Berlin and to tell a lot of stories about atrocities. I don't deny at all—in fact, I'm well aware of it—that here and there in the east excesses have occurred, shootings when people were drunk, cases where people may well have deserved to be shot but shouldn't have been shot by someone who was drunk, where looting has occurred throughout the east sometimes in a manner that I must say I didn't believe possible. Done by every conceivable agency and by every conceivable person in every conceivable uniform. [. . .] When a case like that occurs, then one must calmly note it:—for example, if I've been informed by a few Gauleiters that police sergeant so-and-so has sent some parcels home, I'm very grateful for that. We shall note it and then deal with the man.[126]

In September 1940 Himmler referred once again to the murders in Poland, this time in a speech to the commanders of the 'Leibstandarte' and this time without attempting to describe the crimes as an accident. On the contrary: internally, he openly admitted the murders when he reminded people that in Poland, in temperatures of minus 40 degrees, 'we had to cart off tens of thousands, hundreds of thousands of people. We had to be tough enough—you're going to listen to this and then immediately forget it again—to shoot thousands of leading Poles. We had to be tough enough to cope with bringing in tens of thousands of Germans this winter in −40° because otherwise we would later come to regret not having done it.'[127]

A change in Himmler's private life

If Himmler had simultaneously to defend his public support for illegitimate births and the mass murders in Poland, this was not by chance. In both cases, albeit in very different spheres, his ethnic policy had come up against what were still widely accepted ethical boundaries and he had determined to ignore them.

This was also true, as has already been indicated, of his private life. The Reichsführer-SS took his own 'Procreation Order' to heart and planned to have children outside his marriage. While he was not among those who risked their lives at the front, his self-image as a soldier made it appear to him as his duty to procreate during the war, even if in doing so he was forced to break with convention.

At the beginning of 1936 Hedwig Potthast had become Himmler's private secretary,[128] responsible, among other things, for the distribution of the Reichsführer's gifts as well as for his role as godfather.[129] She was 23 years old at the time and the daughter of a Cologne businessman. After training as a secretary qualified in foreign languages she had got a job in Koblenz, but in 1934 transferred to the Gestapa in Berlin. At some point Himmler and Hedwig Potthast became intimate. At Christmas 1938, as she told her sister three years later, they had confessed to each other that they were hopelessly in love. During the next two years they had thought carefully about whether there was any 'decent' way by which they could be together—Himmler did not want a divorce, out of consideration for his wife—until in the end they decided to have children within a sort of second marriage.[130]

Thus, Himmler probably decided to have children with Hedwig Potthast in 1940, the year in which he publicly supported illegitimate births. The letter also reveals that Himmler wanted to inform his wife of his extramarital relationship only after children had been born. On 15 February 1942 Hedwig's and Himmler's son, Helge, was born in Hohenlychen, the sanatorium headed by Himmler's schoolfriend Gebhardt.[131]

According to Hedwig Potthast's own statement, she gave up her job as Himmler's secretary at the beginning of 1941. To begin with, Himmler sent her to live in Brückenthin in Mecklenburg, very near to a manor house, the home of Oswald Pohl and his second wife, Eleonore, who was a friend of hers.[132] In 1942 she moved to Berchtesgaden, where she gave birth to a second child by Himmler on 20 July 1944, who was given the name Nanette–Dorothea.[133]

Unfortunately, we know hardly anything about the relationship between Hedwig Potthast and Heinrich Himmler. In view of Himmler's full diary the couple cannot have seen much of each other, and they cannot possibly have lived together. Presumably he did not reveal the secrets of his work, his plans, and projects to her any more than he did to his wife, Margarete. One cannot assume that because she had been his private secretary he let her in on official secrets.

On the outbreak of war Margarete had looked for a task in which she could engage. As a trained nurse she began work in a Red Cross hospital,[134] but soon experienced friction and problems with the doctors.[135] At the beginning of December 1939 the Red Cross appointed her supervisor of its

Ill. 20. After his relationship with his wife deteriorated Himmler tried to develop a close and loving relationship with his daughter Gudrun. He kept in close touch with Gudrun and during the war kept her regularly informed about his daily life. From time to time she was allowed to accompany him on official trips (here together with the chief of Himmler's personal staff, Karl Wolff).

hospitals in Military District III, Berlin–Brandenburg, which were mainly involved in treating transports of wounded soldiers;[136] 'my train stations', as she proudly called them.[137]

This responsible task also involved trips to the occupied territories, where, as usual, she commented on the land and its people. For example, in March 1940 she noted on a journey to Poland: 'Then I was in Posen, Łódź, and Warsaw. This Jewish rabble, Polacks, most of them don't look like human beings and the dirt is indescribable. It's an incredible job trying to create order there.'[138] 'These Polish types', she wrote in the same month, 'don't die so easily from infectious diseases, are emune [sic]. Almost incomprehensible.'[139] In April 1941, on a visit to inspect Red Cross establishments in Alsace, she proved how sharp her racial antennae were: 'Very poor population. Sloping foreheads.'[140]

Margarete found out about Heinrich's new liaison at the latest by February 1941. She felt humiliated and bitter.[141] When an acquaintance divorced her husband because he had made another woman pregnant, she commented in her diary: 'Men think of doing that only when they're rich and successful. If not, their not-so-young wives have to feed them, help them, or stick it out with them. What times we live in!'[142] However, Heinrich Himmler regularly visited Gmund, where Margarete was now living with their daughter Gudrun, in order to make sure everything was all right. His meetings with Margarate must have been tense. Margarete, at any rate, did not look forward to them: 'Now Heini's coming, there'll be a lot of trouble. One can't look forward to anything. I will and must put up with it all for the sake of my child.'[143] He too was more concerned about his daughter during these visits. He telephoned Gudrun, whom he still called Püppi, every second or third day;[144] both of them sent letters to each other more or less every week,[145] and he sent her photos which documented his life in his headquarters or on trips and which he provided with appropriate captions.[146] They had a close and loving relationship, and after 1945 Gudrun Himmler tried as hard as possible to keep these memories alive, refusing to distance herself from her father.[147]

17

Repression in the Reich

The Reich Security Main Office (Reichssicherheitshauptamt = RSHA), established shortly after the outbreak of war, provided Himmler with a central organization with which to subject Germany and the occupied territories to a regime of repression and terror during the coming years. The initial impetus for the creation of the Reich Security Main Office came from Heydrich. From the beginning of 1939 Heydrich had been aiming to complete the unification of the security police and SD within a new organizational structure, and in particular to establish a distinct career path for its members and to transfer the whole organization onto the books of the Reich budget.[1]

In February 1939 Heydrich instructed his colleague Walter Schellenberg to produce a plan for a reorganization of the security police and the SD. Schellenberg followed the principle that the security police should become the state protection corps by 'being absorbed into the SS', 'and not the other way round'.[2] This was a pointed reference to the views of Werner Best, the administrative chief of the Gestapo, whose aim was nothing less than to turn the leadership of the SD into civil servants.[3]

At the core of this dispute was the question of who would have control over this organization designed for political repression and created through a merger between the security police and the SD—lawyers or 'political fighters'—and during the following months this produced a major clash. In view of Himmler's well-known hostility to lawyers Best's position had little prospect of succeeding, and in 1940, partly as a consequence of this conflict, Best left Heydrich's sphere of operations. However, Heydrich and Schellenberg failed in their attempt to create a structure that would preserve the autonomy of the SD and secure the leadership of the SD/SS vis-à-vis the security police, at least in the form in which they envisaged it.[4]

While this basic issue was being fought over, the headquarters of this unified organization of repression began to take shape. In July 1939 Heydrich announced the creation of a Reich Security Main Office, which he based on a plan drawn up by Schellenberg, who was also responsible for the title; and on 27 September 1939 Himmler officially established it by issuing an edict.[5]

The outbreak of war, however, prevented the realization of Heydrich's and Schellenberg's far-reaching ambitions. In the final analysis, what emerged was an organizational torso; lawyers and SD leaders were employed side by side and the SD continued to be financed by the Reich Treasurer of the NSDAP. Himmler, however, did not give up the idea of a 'state protection corps', and in 1941–2 attempted to realize his aim with the aid of a 'Führer Edict concerning the SS and Police', but without success.[6]

The Reich Security Main Office was initially divided into six—from March 1941, seven—Offices or *Ämter*. Apart from the Administration Office that initially had one and then two departments, the Reich Security Main Office was composed of the Gestapo (Office IV), the criminal police (V), SD Home Affairs (III), the SD's foreign intelligence service (VI), as well as the Office for Research into and the Combating of Opponents (to begin with Office II, then Office VII). There were major changes in March 1941, not only as a result of the division of the Administration Office but above all because of the transfer of responsibilities from Office II (VII) to other Offices.

During the first years of the war the five operational Offices of the RSHA were organized as follows: Office IV, the old Secret State Police Office (Gestapa), which continued to be under the direction of Heinrich Müller, contained five departments—A: political opponents; B: religious confessions, Jews, Freemasons, émigrés, pacifists; C: protective custody; D: occupied territories; and E: counter-intelligence.[7] The reorganization of the RSHA in March 1941 had a major impact on Office IV. A new department for Churches and Jews was created. This was above all the result of the fact that the churches' department in the Research Office (VII) had been disbanded and its work was now to be continued by the Gestapo. In the course of this reorganization Eichmann's section 'Emigration and Evacuation' was now transferred from department IV D4 to the newly formed department IV B4 (Jewish affairs/evacuation affairs).[8]

Office V, under Arthur Nebe (which was identical with the Reich Criminal Police Office), initially consisted of six departments, which were consolidated into four in March 1941: crime policy and prevention; operations; police records and tracing; and the Institute of Criminal Technology. The establishment of an Institute of Criminal Biology in December 1941 underlined the great importance that the Kripo continued to assign to prevention based on 'the biology of heredity'. Finally, in 1943 an Institute of Criminal Medicine was established, based in Vienna.[9]

Office III (SD Home Affairs), under Otto Ohlendorf, which essentially emerged from Central Department II1 (Assessment of the Various Spheres of National Life) of the SD Main Office, consisted of four departments responsible for issues of ethnicity, legal and constitutional matters, culture, and the economy. The SD Home Affairs Office produced the 'Reports from the Reich', the detailed monthly reports on the population's 'mood and bearing', and had the task of watching out for developments in the individual 'spheres of life'—such as culture, the economy or 'ethnic matters' (*Volkstum*)—that ran counter to Nazi aims and reporting them to the appropriate authorities.[10]

Office VI (SD Foreign Affairs), the successor to Office III of the SD Main Office, was the largest Office in the RSHA, with a total of eight departments and thirty-eight sections,[11] and was headed by Heinz Jost. Born in 1904, he was a lawyer by profession, had been a party member since 1927, and was a senior official in the SD.[12] Nevertheless, the foreign department of the SD achieved only modest successes during the first two years of the war. It succeeded in building networks of agents in the important neutral countries, namely Switzerland, Sweden, Spain, and Portugal, as well as in Italy, Germany's ally, and it worked closely with the secret services of the south-east European countries. However, it failed to achieve significant espionage successes against Great Britain, the United States, or the Soviet Union.[13]

Office VII (Research into and the Combating of Opponents) was initially composed of the departments: Basic Research, Ideological Opponents, Domestic Issues, and Foreign Issues. In March 1941 the work of Office VII, whose head, Franz Alfred Six, was simultaneously pursuing his academic ambitions,[14] was reduced to 'scholarly' research on opponents, while various sections involved in combating opponents using intelligence methods were transferred to the Gestapo. Others which were involved in the *active investigation* of opponents were assigned to the Home Affairs and Foreign Intelligence Offices.[15]

Although its research contribution—in other words, the Office's *raison d'être*—was in the final analysis minimal, the officials tasked with dealing with the various issues were very industrious. In the academic sphere they exercised considerable influence on the assessment of qualifications and on appointments, and in the occupied territories they pursued a systematic policy of plunder, 'acquiring' libraries, archives, and collections on a large scale.[16]

The development of the Reich Security Main Office was characterized by a certain amount of fragmentation of responsibilities, which meant that the pre-war years had seen the work of the Gestapo and the Kripo increasingly overlapping. From now on the Gestapo concentrated on the actual pursuit of political opponents, which during the war was extended above all to cover the increasing number of foreigners living in Germany. In view of the imminent outbreak of war, Heydrich had already considerably restricted the tasks of the Gestapo through an edict of 31 August 1939. Its engagement in matters involving the religious confessions, Jews, Freemasons, émigrés, reactionaries, and party affairs was substantially restricted, while the majority of those cases involving homosexuality and abortion were transferred to the Kripo.[17] 'Preventive' measures using terror directed at 'asocials' and criminals were also now largely the responsibility of the criminal police. These instructions were modified during the course of the war.[18]

The SD, which in the pre-war period had often acted as an auxiliary agency of the Gestapo, now tended to withdraw from an executive role.

The Gestapo

A few weeks after the outbreak of war, and with the police reorganization still going on, Himmler was confronted with his first challenge. At 9.20 on the evening of 9 November 1939 a bomb exploded in the Bürgerbräukeller in Munich, killing eight people and injuring numerous others. The explosion occurred only thirteen minutes after Hitler had left the building, considerably earlier than his programme had envisaged. If he had not altered his plans he would undoubtedly have fallen victim to the explosion, which occurred next to the rostrum and had been detonated with the aid of a timing device. By chance the assassin was arrested on the same evening. Georg Elser, a joiner, who had prepared and carried out the assassination attempt on his own, was caught by German frontier guards while trying to flee to Switzerland, and, after the attack became known, was brought to Munich.

Himmler and the Gestapo officials investigating the affair initially did not believe Elser's claim that he had carried out the attack without any outside help. Instead, they believed that it had been an attack by the British Secret Service. Himmler had already officially committed himself to this account of the events, and the propaganda covering it was designed accordingly.[19] Since, on the very same day, an SD commando had kidnapped two British agents, Captain Sigismund Payne Best and Major Richard Stevens, in the Dutch town of Venlo near the German border, Hitler and Himmler immediately speculated that they had disrupted a secret operation of the British Secret Service aimed at removing the dictator and destabilizing the Nazi regime.[20]

As a result, an attempt was made to force Elser to reveal information about the 'men behind the scenes'. According to a post-war report by two Gestapo officials, Himmler even interrogated Elser personally in order to explore the background; in the process he kicked him brutally several times, abused him, and had him tortured by a Gestapo official in a side room. This is, in fact, the only example in his whole career of Himmler personally using physical force.[21] However, during the night of 13–14 November Elser undermined Himmler's assumptions and deductions by explaining in detail how he had planned and carried out the act on his own.[22]

As a result, Himmler was faced with the threat of being accused of incompetence in relation to the assassination, on the grounds both of having led the investigations in the wrong direction and, as the supreme chief of police in the Reich, of being responsible for the inadequate security arrangements at the Bürgerbräukeller that had enabled Elser painstakingly to assemble his bomb.

On 8 September 1939 the Reich Ministry of Justice issued a brief and terse press release: 'The Reichsführer-SS and Chief of the German Police has announced that Johann Heinen, of Dessau, was shot on 7.9.1939 for refusing to cooperate in implementing safety measures required for national defence. He also had a criminal record for theft.' The announcement mentioned two further cases: another person with a previous conviction who was shot for 'arson and sabotage' and a Jehovah's Witness shot for 'conscientious objection'.

The Reich Justice Minister, Franz Gürtner, was concerned about the legal grounds for these 'executions without a trial'. It was not until a few weeks later that he learned that Hitler himself had ordered the three shootings and, in the meantime, had ordered the execution of two bank-robbers, as the courts 'had not shown themselves equal to the special wartime conditions'. By January 1940 Hitler had instructed Himmler to arrange the immediate execution of a total of eighteen criminals, including a confidence-trickster who had pretended to be a successful U-boat officer, a rapist, a handbag thief who had taken advantage of the blackout, an arsonist, and sex offenders who had abused children. In some cases sentences had already been passed on these offenders, in others no trial had yet taken place.[23]

There was, in fact, no legal basis for these executions; the Gestapo had nevertheless already developed a standard procedure for them. On 3 September Heydrich had informed the Gestapo branches of the 'Basic Principles for Maintaining Internal Security During the War', which stated, among other things:

Any attempt to undermine the unity of the German people and its determination to fight must be ruthlessly suppressed. In particular, any person who expresses doubts about the victory of the German nation or questions the justification for the war is to be arrested [...] The Chief of the Security Police must then be informed without delay and a decision requested on the further treatment of the arrested persons, since the ruthless liquidation of such elements may be ordered at a high level [...].[24]

Himmler's organization was thus entitled to execute anyone arousing such a suspicion, even in the case of relatively minor offences. The term used to describe this police licence to kill was 'special treatment' (*Sonderbehandlung*). It was carried out in concentration camps, police prisons, or in work re-education camps, and later on in the war also in public, for example in businesses or in public places.[25] All cases which regional Gestapo offices deemed suitable for 'special treatment' had to be referred to Himmler. It is clear that the Reichsführer made the decision himself, which was final, just as he did in doubtful cases involving the approval of marriage, applications for re-Germanization, and the punishment of his men for indulging in banned sexual relations.[26]

Within the territory of the Reich itself 'special treatment' was directed above all against an 'opposition' group that the Nazi policy of conquest had itself created: foreigners living in Germany. By the end of 1939 the party and state agencies were already engaged in intensive discussions about how the large numbers of Polish POWs and workers who had been brought into the Reich should be treated, and above all how they should be kept separate from the German population. It was clear that people from a subjugated country who were potentially hostile to Nazi Germany posed a threat. Propaganda hostile to the regime, the undermining of work discipline, espionage, but also ordinary criminality could all be anticipated. The assumed 'racial inferiority' of the Poles increased the problem in the eyes of the regime, and Himmler made it his task not only to develop the surveillance of foreigners into a new focus for the work of the Gestapo, but to do so in particular in racial terms.

A few days after the outbreak of war Himmler asked Hitler how they should proceed if Polish POWs made friends with, or even had sexual relations with, German women and girls. Hitler replied, as Himmler noted in a minute, 'every POW who has relations with a German girl or a German woman should be shot', and the German woman should be publicly denounced by 'having her hair shorn and being sent to a concentration camp'.[27] On 8 January Heydrich informed the Gestapo offices that the POWs concerned would be transferred by the Wehrmacht's POW department to the Gestapo.[28] (In December, at Himmler's request, Best had already ordered all Poles who left their place of work without permission to be imprisoned in a concentration camp).[29]

On 29 February 1940 Himmler expressed his views on the treatment of Polish agricultural workers, who were being brought into the Reich in ever-increasing numbers, to a group of senior party functionaries. It was impossible to 'screen' a million Poles within a few weeks and to allow only 'racially valuable and decent people' into the Reich. Instead, the Poles were being 'brought in en bloc and treated as Poles en bloc'. They would be given a badge, and as a matter of principle 'they would not be allowed to form relationships with Germans [. . .] If a Pole has sex [. . .] with a German woman the man will be hanged and it will be done in front of his camp. Then the others won't do it.' Moreover, Himmler reassured his audience that they were making sure 'that there are a sufficient number of Polish women and girls coming over as well so that there can be no question of there being any need'. The German women who had forbidden relations with Poles, Himmler added, would be 'mercilessly taken to court' and, if there was insufficient evidence to secure a conviction, 'sent to a concentration camp'. There was 'no point', the Reichsführer concluded, in 'theorizing' about this. It would be 'better if we didn't have them—we all know that—but we need them'.[30]

Barely two weeks later, on 8 March 1940, the question of how Polish civilian workers living in the Reich were to be treated was finally and comprehensively dealt with by the so-called 'Polish decrees', a collection of ten documents in total.[31] In this connection Himmler informed Gestapo offices through a telex from the Reich Security Main Office that they should be responsible for punishing insubordinate behaviour by Poles—habitually negligent work, strikes, leaving the workplace without permission, acts of sabotage, and so on—on their own initiative through consignment to a work re-education camp or a concentration camp, and, in particularly serious cases, through 'special treatment'—in other words, execution. In the case of sexual intercourse between Polish workers and Germans, the Pole should be shot without waiting for the sentence of a court; the German partner, whether male or female, should be sent to a concentration camp.[32] If the case did go to court and there was no guilty verdict, imprisonment in a concentration camp should nevertheless be imposed. In a decree of May 1940, reflecting Hitler's instruction of September 1939, Himmler added that, 'if the local women and girls wish publicly to denounce the woman concerned or to cut off her hair before she is transferred to a concentration camp the police should not intervene to prevent it.'[33]

In July the application of the March decrees was extended to cover POWs who had been released.[34] Large numbers of executions of Polish POWs for having sexual relations with German women began after the victory over France in June 1940. However, after July 1941 Himmler ordered the RSHA to examine every single case, in order to establish through 'a racial assessment' whether the Polish man concerned was capable of being 'Germanized'. If this was the case he was sent to a KZ for a relatively short time. If the racial assessment was negative he was executed.[35] The press reported the incidents with the standard formula: 'hanged [. . .] on the orders of the Reichsführer-SS and Chief of the German Police for illicit sexual relations.'[36]

It would, however, be a mistake to imagine that at the start of the war the Gestapo had begun to pursue all actual or potential 'enemies' of the regime with the same degree of harshness. The number of cases brought against left-wingers and critical or opposition members of religious denominations appears even to have reduced.[37] The historian Eric Johnson has shown that, as in the pre-war period, more than 40 per cent of the preliminary investigations were directed against 'ordinary Germans',[38] who in wartime too were treated relatively mildly and got away with a warning or a fine.[39]

By contrast, the surveillance and persecution of the Jews was drastically increased after the outbreak of war. This also had organizational repercussions. Department IV D4, established in the RSHA at the beginning of 1940 under Eichmann, and shortly afterwards renamed IV B4 (Jewish affairs, evacuation affairs), focused on the 'Jewish question'.[40] Among other things, the section controlled the Reich Association of Jews, created in July 1939, to which all the Jewish communities that still existed and all remaining Jewish associations, organizations, foundations, and so on were subordinated.[41]

During the first months after the outbreak of war the exclusion of Jews from German society was completed.[42] Joseph Walk's collection of anti-Jewish legislation reveals that between the November pogrom of 1938 and the outbreak of war 229, and between 1 September 1939 and the start of the deportations in October 1941 exactly 253 anti-Jewish measures were enacted, often by Himmler or the security police. On 10 September 1939 Himmler issued an unpublished edict imposing a 8 p.m. curfew for Jews.[43] On 12 September 1939 the security police limited the Jews to certain shops,[44] and on 23 September the Gestapa ordered the 'immediate' confiscation of all radios in the possession of Jews throughout the Reich.[45] Further measures imposed by other authorities included the removal of telephones,[46] discriminatory treatment in relation to air-raid precautions,[47] as well as discrimination in the allocation of rationed goods, which was ensured by marking Jews' ration-books with a J.[48] Moreover, the whole of the Jewish population capable of work was obliged to perform compulsory labour,[49] and more and more Jews had to vacate their flats and move into specified 'Jew houses' (*Judenhäuser*).[50] From May 1941 onwards Gestapo offices began to set up special 'Jew camps' (*Judenlager*), particularly near large cities.[51]

The SD reported that, in the first quarter of 1940, 10,312 Jews had emigrated from Germany.[52] On 24 April 1940 the Reich Security Main Office instructed Gestapo offices that they must 'continue to press ahead with Jewish emigration from the Reich, and to an even greater extent during the war'.[53]

The Kripo

During the war the criminal police (Kripo) had to cede a large part of its personnel to agencies in the occupied territories as well as to Einsatzkommandos, the Gestapo, and to the Wehrmacht's Secret Field Police. The gaps were inadequately filled by the reactivation of pensioned officers as well as through the appointment of outsiders.[54]

At the same time, the Kripo acquired numerous new responsibilities. It was expected to impose greater control and discipline on young people, who were subject to a variety of bans to prevent them from going astray;[55] it also had to pursue the so-called war-economy offences, in other words, breaches of the numerous rationing regulations such as slaughtering animals without a permit, participating in the black market, or distributing forged ration books.[56] During the later war years it also had to exercise control over the millions of foreigners living in Germany, as well as deal with some of the consequences of Allied bombing.

The criminal police responded to these new demands above all in two ways: on the one hand, they no longer pursued so-called petty offences, which among other things resulted in the statistics for certain offences such as fraud showing a decline.[57] On the other hand, they gradually extended the 'preventive combating of crime' until it became a policy of systematic mass murder as the conditions in concentration camps were made considerably harsher.

To begin with, the Kripo imposed preventive police detention on more and more sections of the population. After the outbreak of war all those 'unworthy of military service' (that is to say, those who were excluded from military service because of significant previous convictions), women who were suspected of working as prostitutes, as well as so-called criminal psychopaths were consigned to concentration camps.[58] On 18 October Himmler ordered that 'work-shy' people with previous convictions who were arrested during police raids should no longer be reported to labour exchanges but immediately transferred to concentration camps.[59] During the first weeks following the outbreak of war Himmler also had numerous members of the socialist labour movement sent to concentration camps, as well as 2,000 people of Polish origin.[60] Moreover, the Kripo rearrested those Jews who had been taken into protective custody in November 1938 and had then been released in return for their promise to emigrate, but who had remained in the country.[61] Furthermore, the Reich Criminal Police Office ordered that all people who, on account of 'mental instability', were suspected of spreading discontent among the population should be taken into preventive police custody.[62] In addition, the persecution of clergy was increased. Numerous new legal regulations which were issued immediately after the outbreak of war, for example, the ban on listening to foreign broadcasts, the Decree against National Pests, or the War Economy Decree, provided the justification for imposing preventive custody.[63]

As far as crime-prevention was concerned, between the summer of 1940 and the autumn of 1941—that is, during the phase of Blitzkrieg victories— the Kripo appears to have already been preparing for the post-war period. The preventive measures were now extended to the annexed territories (the Protectorate, western Poland, Alsace and Lorraine) and within the Reich were increasingly geared to the priorities of population policy. Homosexuals, sex offenders, and people who cohabited in order to avoid the regulations of the Marriage Health Law all suffered ever-increasing persecution.[64] Above all, as previously indicated, conditions for those imprisoned in concentration camps became much harsher.

Concentration camps (KZ) and the establishment of the SS's business empire

Himmler was determined to respond to the increase in the number of prisoners during the war by expanding the KZ system and to prevent any camps being established outside the system he had created. During the winter of 1939–40 he had to intervene with several Higher SS and Police Leaders on these grounds. In December 1939 he reprimanded Richard Hildebrandt, the HSSPF responsible for the new Gau of Danzig–West Prussia, for establishing his own camp in Stutthof. Hildebrandt was intending to retain the Wachsturmbann Eimann, a formation created from the Danzig SS, after the end of the war as an autonomous unit, among other things to act as guards for 'his KZ'. Himmler complained that by setting up such an autonomous force Hildebrandt was helping to bring about 'the end of the SS as a unified organization'. He told him, in no uncertain terms: 'concentration camps can be established only with my permission.'[65]

Himmler had a copy of this letter sent to the leaders of the Oberabschnitte, though he did not mention Hildebrandt by name. Furthermore, he instructed the acting Inspector of Concentration Camps, August Heissmeyer, to find out whether there were any other HSSPF camps in the Reich. The camps were then inspected by the Concentration Camps Inspectorate (IKL), and none of them was considered worth retaining. Even Stutthof remained a detention camp with purely regional responsibilities. The Wachsturmbann Eimann was disbanded.[66]

When Himmler learnt in January 1940 that the HSSPF in Breslau, von dem Bach-Zelewski, was intending to establish a regional detention camp in a former artillery barracks near the town of Auschwitz, 'along the lines of a state concentration camp',[67] he seized the property, using his powers as Settlement Commissar. In fact, in February 1940[68] Richard Glücks, who had taken over the IKL from Eicke in November 1939, proposed establishing a concentration camp there under its auspices. Himmler agreed and, at the beginning of May 1940, Hauptsturmführer Rudolf Höss, hitherto Schutzhaftlagerführer in Sachsenhausen concentration camp, was appointed its commandant. Initially the majority of prisoners incarcerated there were Polish civilians.[69]

At the beginning of 1941 the IG Farben chemicals concern expressed an interest in constructing a large plant for the manufacture of Buna (synthetic rubber) in Auschwitz. Its favourable geographical location and the prospect of prisoners providing cheap labour were positive factors influencing the decision.[70] Himmler devoted a great deal of attention to the IG Farben project, and gave his personal assurance that there would be a sufficient number of prisoners to carry out the building work. He first visited the KZ on 1 March 1941 and took decisions concerning both the design of the camp and cooperation with IG Farben.[71] The construction of the camp accelerated plans for the 'Germanization' of the town; Jews and Poles were expelled. Himmler wanted Auschwitz to become a German 'model town', a model for the settlement of the east.[72]

Around January 1940 Himmler transformed the previous branch camp of Neuengamme near Hamburg into an autonomous concentration camp. The number of prisoners was doubled and plans were made for the large-scale production of clinker-brick.[73] Gross-Rosen in Lower Silesia, which initially had been established as a satellite camp of Sachsenhausen and was

intended for the quarrying of granite, was raised to the status of an autonomous concentration camp in May 1941. Himmler and Glücks had already
visited the camp in the autumn of 1940.[74] Natzweiler in Alsace also became
an autonomous concentration camp in May 1941. In August 1940, like
Neuengamme, it too had been established as a satellite camp of Sachsenhausen. This camp was also primarily designed for the quarrying of stone.[75]

Thus, by spring 1941 four new concentration camps had been established
in addition to the six existing ones: Auschwitz, Neuengamme, Gross-Rosen,
and Natzweiler. Moreover, KZ Niedernhagen (the camp was intended for
prisoners working on the Wewelsburg), as well as KZ Hinzert (a former
police camp for disciplining workers on the Western Wall fortifications
project), were subordinated to the IKL.[76]

After the outbreak of war conditions in all the concentration camps were
made more harsh: food supplies were reduced and mistreatment increased;

Ill. 21. Himmler and his entourage during a visit to KZ Mauthausen. Himmler
had already announced to Wehrmacht officers in 1937 that, in the event of war, the
SS saw it as its task to secure 'Germany at home' as a fourth 'theatre of war'
alongside those on the land, water, and in the air. And after the outbreak of the
Second World War Himmler did indeed focus on this task with extreme brutality.
He reserved decisions in cases of 'special treatment', in other words the summary
murder of people who were opponents of the regime or guilty of serious offences,
to himself.

the barracks were seriously overcrowded. As a result, after the outbreak of war the death-rate increased sharply.[77] Soon, however, German inmates came to represent only a minority among the numerous prisoners whom the Gestapo had arrested in the occupied territories, particularly in the east.[78] The number of KZ prisoners quadrupled from around 21,000 in August 1939 to around 70,000 in spring 1942.[79]

In January 1941 Heydrich ordered a 'division of the concentration camps into distinct levels reflecting the personality of the prisoners and the degree of threat they pose to the state'. Accordingly, the prisoners were divided into three categories, for each of which particular concentration camps were responsible: 'the less incriminated prisoners in protective custody who are definitely capable of rehabilitation' were sent to Dachau, Sachsenhausen, and Auschwitz; those more seriously incriminated but nevertheless capable of being rehabilitated were assigned to 'Level II', namely Buchenwald, Flossenbürg, Neuengamme, as well as to Auschwitz II, which was still to be built; the 'seriously incriminated' prisoners who were 'unlikely to be capable of rehabilitation' were to be sent to Mauthausen, which at this stage was the only KZ in 'Level III'. And it was, in fact, there that the most dreadful conditions and the highest death-rate were to be found.[80]

As we have seen, the exploitation of prisoners' labour played a major role in the establishment of the four new concentration camps, as indeed had been the case with the Mauthausen and Flossenbürg camps established in 1938. It was to be utilized both for the SS's own building-materials business as well as—as in the case of Auschwitz—for building projects. Thus, in addition to the German Earth and Stone Works (Deutsche Erd- und Steinwerke), founded in 1938 and responsible for stone-quarrying by KZ prisoners, a further 199 holding companies were established for KZ businesses.

The Deutsche Ausrüstungswerke GmbH (German Equipment Works Ltd.), founded in May 1939, gradually took over the workshops in the camps in order, in the first instance, to provide equipment for armed units of the SS and for concentration camps. In 1940–1 the number of objects produced was reduced; the main focus was now on furniture for the KZ and SS forces, but also for ethnic Germans who were being resettled. At the end of 1941 the Deutsche Ausrüstungswerke had plants in Dachau, Sachsenhausen, Buchenwald, Auschwitz, Lublin, and Lemberg (Lvov), and a total of 4,800 workers, overwhelmingly KZ prisoners and Jewish forced labourers.[81] Similarly, the Gesellschaft für Textil und Lederverwertung

(Textiles and Leather Processing Company) acted as an umbrella company for all the plants providing the SS with clothing with the aid of KZ workshops.[82]

With the establishment in January 1939 of the German Research Institute for Food and Nutrition (Deutsche Versuchsanstalt für Ernährung und Verpflegung = DVA), which initially focused above all on research into and the planting of medicinal herbs, Himmler had succeeded in realizing a project particularly close to his heart. The institute was primarily dependent on the extensive herb gardens in KZ Dachau, but during the following years in addition bought a total of sixteen experimental farms. In October 1940 Himmler directed the research institute to focus on experiments that had been suggested by people working on the ground or which had not yet been carried out by academic scientists or had even been rejected by them. It was particularly important to develop careful processing methods; their effectiveness should be assessed in collaboration with the SS physicians.[83]

Himmler utilized the SS farms in particular in order to carry out experiments involving biological-dynamic methods of cultivation.* Although this agrarian theory inspired by anthroposophy, like all other 'secret knowledge', had been officially banned after Hess's flight to Scotland— the Führer's Deputy was portrayed as being a victim of such circles— Himmler pressed on with these experiments, although the term now used was 'natural methods of agriculture' (naturgemäße Landbauweise). Himmler gave detailed instructions[84] for the experiments which demonstrated his hostility to artificial fertilizers. After all, as he pointed out to his administrative chief Pohl, having worked as a laboratory assistant in the Schleissheim fertilizer factory he knew what he was talking about.[85]

Himmler was aware of the fact that, as with many of his other projects, it would be sensible not to make a big song and dance about his controversial experiments. For example, he expressly rejected the idea of getting Bormann to inform Hitler about their progress. The people involved should 'work quietly and in some cases not talk so much about the natural methods of agriculture. Nobody [would] bother us if we quietly, decently, and successfully got on with tilling the land.' The office in charge of the project should be moved out of Berlin and transferred to one of the farms, ideally in the east.[86] In fact it came to be based in the Wertingen state farm near Himmler's Hegewald headquarters in the Ukraine. The person in charge,

---

* *Translators' note*: This refers to a method of cultivation advocated by Rudolf Steiner.

Obersturmführer Grund, was given a special new task by Himmler,[87] namely, 'analysing the performance of the biological–dynamic method in the Russian territories'. Himmler's weakness for unconventional projects had once again acquired gigantic dimensions.[88]

However, the expansion of the SS's business operations involved not only enterprises that were mainly based in the concentration camps. In April 1939 the SS established the Sudetenquell GmbH (Sudeten Spring Ltd.) near Marienbad, which a short time later began producing its own drink with the enticing name 'Green Sour Spring Water' (*Grüner Sauerbrunn*). This enterprise was rooted in Himmler's ambition to get the 'SS men used to quenching their thirst with non-alcoholic drinks instead of their excessive consumption of beer, wine etc.'; good-value mineral water was to be offered as an alternative.[89]

During the following years the SS, by buying up firms, tried to acquire a monopoly of mineral-water production in order to break the cartel that was assumed to operate in this market. By 1944 75 per cent of German mineral-water production was in the hands of the SS; Himmler's efforts, initially focused solely on reforming SS members, had acquired their own momentum.[90] The same intention was behind the purchase of fruit-juice factories, in which, among other things Himmler's prized 'Vitaborn' (Life Spring) juices were produced. Himmler used to give them as presents, and they represented a particular token of his esteem.[91]

Another development, however, was to prove more significant for the future of the SS business empire. In November 1939 Himmler succeeded in persuading the Haupttreuhandstelle Ost (Main Trustee Office East), which under Göring's auspices was administering the property confiscated from Poles and Jews in the annexed eastern territories, to seize all the brickworks in the area under their control for the benefit of his settlement commissariat. The aim was to place their production at the disposal of ethnic German settlers. In January 1941 the Ostdeutsche Baustoffwerke (East German Building Materials Works) was established, which in the course of the year restarted 300 brickworks, most of which were small-scale operations; in addition, there were the works producing building materials in the General Government. In his capacity as Settlement Commissar, Himmler also took over building-materials works in annexed Lower Styria as well as in the district of Bialystok, in other words, the area in eastern Poland that, after its conquest in the summer of 1941, had acquired a special administrative status.[92]

Thus, most of the SS enterprises served either the needs of the SS itself or, often, Himmler's political-ideological aims (as can be shown with the manufacture of mineral water, medicinal herbs, and building materials for German settlers), or they sprang from the need to control the employment of KZ prisoners in order to keep them out of the hands of the authorities responsible for labour deployment. As a result, almost all the businesses operated at a loss.

In 1940 this was to change. Since 1939 all SS businesses had been subordinated to Oswald Pohl, the administrative head of the SS, and from spring 1940 onwards he had been managing them with the aid of his new Administration and Business Main Office (Hauptamt Verwaltung und Wirtschaft). In July 1940 Pohl instigated the establishment of Deutsche Wirtschaftsbetriebe GmbH (German Businesses Ltd.), which was intended to unify all SS enterprises.[93] To begin with, Pohl was the sole general manager. In July 1942 a second manager was appointed, although Pohl retained complete control.[94] During 1940–1, under the management installed by Pohl, SS business policy underwent a significant change. From now on economic factors were taken much more into consideration—the watchwords were the maximizing of profit, business expansion, and the market.[95]

The SS and police acquire their own judicial system

Himmler's plans for the SS and police to establish their own judicial system along the lines of the military can be traced back to 1937. However, he was able to achieve his objective only in October 1939. All armed SS units, the full-time members of the HSSPF staffs, as well as all police units who were deployed in the war were subjected to the new judicial system.[96] Regulations equivalent to those of the military code were now applied to the SS, including the death penalty and penal servitude, with the SS and police courts responsible for all offences, not only those against the military code.[97] The SS disciplinary code—in other words, the possibility of demoting or expelling SS members—remained unaffected by the new jurisdiction.

It was not by chance that the SS and police judicial system was introduced immediately after the war with Poland. It is obvious that Himmler wished to have the responsibility for investigating and, where he felt it appropriate, punishing the assaults and crimes committed by members of the SS and police during the war.[98] Himmler also banned the press from reporting the proceedings of the SS and police courts.[99] However, other motives for creating this special judicial system were decisive. In view of the general intensification of repression in the autumn of 1939, the Reichsführer did not want any complaints that offences by members of the SS and police were being treated too laxly. At the same time, having achieved his own judicial system, he considered it very important to ensure that it fully embodied the principles of virtue, decency, and discipline that he had been preaching for years.

During the Second World War he gradually expanded the responsibility of the SS judicial system to include the whole of the police, the General SS (including those serving in the Wehrmacht), all foreigners fighting in SS units and the 'ethnic alien' protection forces, as well as auxiliary organizations attached to the police such as the Technical Emergency Unit, the Air Defence Police, and the Fire Service (including the voluntary fire brigades).[100] In a number of occupied territories, for example in the Protectorate, the Netherlands, and to the greatest extent in Norway, it became an instrument of occupation policy, since it was applied even to offences committed by inhabitants of these countries.[101]

With a decree of 4 April 1943 the Wehrmacht handed over the prosecution of civilian offenders in the occupied territories entirely to the SS and police courts if the offence was largely directed against the SS or police.[102] When Himmler took over the Reserve Army in July 1944, thereby acquiring responsibility for the POWs of the Wehrmacht, this group too became subject to the SS and police jurisdiction.[103]

Himmler played a central role in shaping this judicial system.[104] He not only provided the Court Main Office, to which the SS and police judiciary was subordinate, with regular instructions, he also appointed an 'SS Judge on the Staff of the Reichsführer-SS and Chief of the German Police' in the shape of Horst Bender, to whom he gradually transferred the powers that he himself possessed as 'Supreme Judge' (*Gerichtsherr*) of the SS and police.[105] Himmler provided himself with the power to suspend sentences,[106] and in a number of cases reserved to himself the right to confirm sentences, as, for example, with offences against the ban on sexual relations with the wives of front-line soldiers and prosecutions of adultery,[107] as well as all sentences of SS leaders and police officers.[108]

The right of confirming sentences also extended to offences committed by members of the SS and police against his ban on sexual relations with 'women from an ethnically alien population' in the occupied eastern territories. In such cases he generally called for the papers prior to the initiation of a preliminary investigation in order to decide, on the basis of photos and a report on the general racial impression made by the woman, whether such an offence had in fact been committed, as significantly the term 'alien' (*andersartig*) was never properly defined.[109] SS judges deployed in the east decided at a conference held in May 1943 that Himmler's ban on sexual relations with indigenous women must be 'urgently' amended, since, as one of the judges put it, probably 'at least 50 per cent of all members of the SS and police' were breaching this ban. As he had discovered from one unit, the view taken by the force was that 'relationships and sex were permitted as long as there were no consequences'.[110]

In June 1942 Himmler had already relaxed the ban on 'sexual relations with women and girls from a population of an alien race'[111] which he had issued in April 1939, for members of the SS and police based in the General Government: 'I recognize the difficulties facing the men of the SS in the General Government from a sexual point of view. I do not, therefore, object to sex in brothels or with prostitutes subject to medical and police supervision, as neither procreation nor close personal relations are likely to occur as a result.'[112] Himmler's 1939 ban kept causing problems right up until the end of the war, problems in which, typically, Himmler took a personal interest. Thus, in January 1945, for example, he decided 'that GV [sex] with racially inferior Croatian women [is] merely undesirable'.[113]

Himmler's right to confirm sentences was extended by a Führer decree of 1941 laying down that, 'in the event of there being serious doubts about the correctness of a verdict', the Reichsführer would have the right on his own initiative to suspend verdicts that had already been reached under due process and to insist on a retrial.[114] He wished to be informed of all cases which involved breaches of 'ideological obedience' (and for that to be done right at the start of proceedings), as well as of 'all sentences of SS and police courts' that involved the death penalty, penal servitude for life, or penal servitude of over ten years.[115] Moreover, prosecutors, and eventually SS judges as well, received an enormous number of individual directives from their Reichsführer.[116]

The measures that Himmler instituted to govern the SS judicial system were thus not only comprehensive but involved an elaborate system of multiple stages of supervision and reveal a positively manic need to exercise control. Everything was designed to enable him to make the final decision.

Himmler gave this caricature of a legal system its ultimate expression when, following the death of the head of the SS Court Main Office, Paul Scharfe, who was not in fact a lawyer, Himmler issued the 'Basic Directive No. 1 for the SS Judicial System', which stated quite baldly: 'I hereby decree that the head of the SS Court shall never be a lawyer.'[117] It would, however, be too simple to interpret Himmler's excessive need to exercise control merely as megalomania finding release in arbitrary actions. For, seen in the light of his pedagogic mentality, with its ideological bent, his control mechanisms were altogether rational: Himmler was endeavouring to create a special SS penal code, designed to put into practice ideas for the ideological indoctrination of his men and the inculcation of SS norms of living. A particular instrument used to achieve this was the juridical trick of judging breaches of internal SS prohibitions as military disobedience, in other words, as a serious offence under the military penal code.[118]

Himmler, therefore, ensured that the SS and police judicial system punished sexual contacts with 'alien races' to an extent far beyond the provisions of the Blood Protection Law of 1935, prosecuted sex with the wives of front-line soldiers with conspicuous harshness, and took extremely tough action against offences linked to alcohol, homosexuality, and property crime, in other words, all those offences which he, as Reichsführer-SS, had already tried to eliminate through educational and disciplinary methods before the introduction of the SS judicial system.

Himmler advocated the uncompromising punishment of members of the SS and police as a matter of principle. The nation should know, he wrote to Daluege in 1942, 'that a disloyal policeman or police officer will be punished. This will not damage our reputation but will rather strengthen and increase it.'[119] Similarly, in 1943 he emphasized to the Gruppenführer that, as 'Reichsführer-SS, as Chief of the German Police and now as Reich Minister of the Interior, [he did not have] the moral right to prosecute any national comrade and we could not summon up the strength to do it if we did not brutally insist on impeccable conduct in our own ranks'.[120]

When he considered it necessary he imposed punishment without a formal sentence. Thus, in one case he postponed the sentencing of an SS-Obersturmführer found guilty of the mistreatment of a subordinate involving grievous bodily harm resulting in death, and ordered that the person concerned 'should be provided with a pistol and given the opportunity of executing judgment on himself', which he then did.[121] Subsequently, as often happened in such cases, he showed consideration by ordering that the dependants should be looked after as if the person involved had fallen in battle. 'That is the point of providing the pistol.'[122]

Himmler also kept issuing penal guidelines. For example, in January 1945, when members of the 256 Volksgrenadierdivision (a Wehrmacht unit set up and led by the SS) had participated in looting, he ordered that, in the case of looting in Reich territory, 'as a deterrent a death sentence should be imposed in a suitable case and should be carried out in the presence of members of the units of the division concerned'.[123] And after a lecture by the SS Judge on the Staff of the Reichsführer-SS concerning the 'prosecution of those who have shot Jews without authorization', Himmler decided that the decisive point was the 'motives' of those involved in such incidents: 'In the case of political motives there should be no prosecution unless required for the maintenance of public order [...] In the case of selfish, sadistic, or sexual motives they should be prosecuted and, where appropriate, for murder or manslaughter.'[124] Thus, even in the face of unparalleled mass murder Himmler did not want to abandon the right to claim that his SS murdered 'decently'.

18

Shifting Borders:
The Year 1940

Himmler was unable to exploit the conquests of 1940—the occupation of Norway, Denmark, France, the Netherlands, Belgium, and Luxembourg—in the same way that he had done with the campaign against Poland; he was prevented from acquiring a comparable position of power in the territories that had been newly occupied. Similarly, he was largely unsuccessful at realizing the foreign-policy ambitions that he developed during this period. Nevertheless, he had a significant impact on the German occupation of northern and western Europe. By pursuing a decidedly racist policy in France involving 'ethnic political' measures, with his comprehensive plans for deporting the Jews, as well as his attempts to recruit ethnic Germans and 'Teutons' for his Waffen-SS, Himmler ensured that German rule differed significantly from conventional occupation policies.

Ever since the Anschluss with Austria Himmler had been able to acquire experience of the annexation of occupied or conquered territories. While the position of the police in Austria had been regulated along the lines of the situation prevailing in the Reich, Himmler's police organization in the Protectorate had been granted the greatest possible autonomy vis-à-vis the Reich Protector, von Neurath.[1] In the satellite state of Slovakia, which had been created after the occupation of the 'remainder of Czechoslovakia', Himmler aimed to establish a Gestapo branch which could control the Slovakian secret police, the USB (Ustredna statna bezpecnost), and treat the allied state de facto as German territory. To achieve this, between June 1939 and August 1940 he sent three police commissions one after the other to Pressburg (Bratislava). However, apart from causing tension with the German Foreign Ministry, nothing much came of this.[2] In July 1941 the 'Office of the Reich Security Main Office in Pressburg' was finally closed.[3]

The only official who remained was a police attaché attached to the German embassy.[4]

The behaviour of Himmler's organization and his forces in Poland had prompted the Wehrmacht to object to the integration of security police and SD Einsatzkommandos into the army as part of the planning for future military campaigns. Heydrich commented on this in a document, noting that in many cases 'among senior army commanders' there was 'a fundamentally different attitude towards basic issues involving the combating of enemies of the state' compared with that of the SS. The directives for the deployment of the police in Poland had been 'extremely radical' ('for example, the order to liquidate numerous members of the Polish elites, amounting to thousands'). Since the Wehrmacht could not be let in on this, the actions of the police and SS had appeared to outsiders arbitrary, brutal, and unauthorized. The Selbstschutz, which 'in some cases had carried out impossible and uncontrollable acts of revenge',[5] had added to the problem. Thus, at the end of March Heydrich was obliged to inform his office chiefs that the planned participation of Einsatzkommandos in the invasion of Belgium and Holland had been cancelled.[6]

On 9 April 1940 the Wehrmacht mounted a surprise landing in Norway in order to pre-empt a feared intervention by Britain. While the German troops, engaged in fierce fighting with Norwegian and British forces, were still endeavouring to bring the country under their control, the structure of the future German occupation began to take shape under the Essen Gauleiter Josef Terboven, whom Hitler had appointed Reich Commissar on 24 April.

Himmler had tried to acquire influence in Norway right from the start,[7] and, despite opposition from the Wehrmacht, on 20 April 1940, at a meeting with Hitler attended by Terboven, Göring, and Bormann, he succeeded in securing the appointment of a Higher SS and Police Leader and the deployment of an Einsatzgruppe. Improvising, Heydrich produced a unit of which the core was formed by eighty Gestapo and SD officials who had originally been intended for 'a special deployment in the West', which had been kept secret from the Wehrmacht.[8] SS-Obergruppenführer Fritz Weitzel was appointed HSSPF in Norway. However, while staying in Düsseldorf during June he was killed in an air raid and was replaced by the Königsberg HSSPF, Wilhelm Rediess. In fact, both Weitzel and Rediess allowed themselves to be controlled by Terboven to a large extent, even though they were not officially subordinate to him.[9] The same was true of

Heinrich Fehlis,[10] hitherto head of the security police/SD group in Oslo. In the autumn of 1940 Fehlis replaced SS-Oberführer Stahlecker, previously commander of the security police in the Protectorate, as the commander of the around 200-strong Einsatzgruppe of the security police and SD which had arrived in Norway at the end of April. Thus Terboven had some success in blocking Himmler's attempt to intervene in the occupation administration through his own men. In Heydrich's opinion, the deployment of security police and SD in Norway occurred in any case 'to some extent [...] too late' for them still to be able to combat 'the enemies of the state' there effectively.[11]

In the case of the occupation of Denmark, which occurred simultaneously with that of Norway, Himmler had no success at all. German plans for the occupation envisaged the stationing of troops; however, interventions in the work of the Danish government and administration were only to occur for military purposes. Thus, no proper occupation administration was established; instead, the German envoy in Copenhagen, who had the additional title 'Reich Plenipotentiary', communicated the wishes of the Reich government to the Danish government and deployed a small staff to observe whether or not they were carried out.[12]

On 10 May German troops invaded Belgium, Luxembourg, the Netherlands, and France. The Dutch armed forces had already capitulated on 15 May. Two days later Himmler embarked on a trip to the newly conquered territory in order to visit his Waffen-SS units and get to know the country and its people. He was accompanied by, among others, Wolff, his adjutant Joachim Peiper, his old schoolfriend and personal physician Gebhardt (probably because of the latter's personal connection with the Belgian royal family), as well as the latter's colleague, the physician Ludwig Stumpfegger.

Himmler recorded his impressions in a diary, in which the trip is also documented by a series of photographs: 'This part of Holland and Maastricht itself make a distinctly friendly and clean impression. The population was by no means hostile but greeted our soldiers. If we asked for information it was given to us freely and correctly.' On the evening of the first day they stayed at the Hotel Warson in Hasselt. The commander of the Standarte 'Der Führer' and his deputy, who were based nearby, joined the party. There was a victorious mood: 'We had a very nice meal in the evening, drank some wine, and the two of them talked about their experience of the fighting'.

Next day the group left for Eindhoven and Tilberg to visit the headquarters of the 18th Army. That night they stayed in the Hotel La Suisse. Himmler was very content: 'The food was good and incredibly plentiful. All the Dutch cities made an excellent impression; the population is friendly and its racial quality is high. It was really nice seeing the men, women, and children. They are a great gain for Germany.' Thus, for Himmler it was clear that the Netherlands were going to be annexed.

On the following day the group went on an excursion—Himmler, as he noted, was at the wheel—in the direction of Rosendaal, where they met up with the SS-Standarte 'Germania'. On 19 May, after a flying visit to Antwerp, which involved a roundabout route because bridges had been blown, on the way to Brussels they went through a small town:

When we came through Runst, a Flemish town with lots of brickworks, we were met by members of the town militia who were obviously hanging around waiting for the first German troops to arrive. They took us to meet the mayor and the town council, who surrendered the town of Runst to us. At the same time they wanted us to provide them with water, gas, and electricity. At the end Gruppenführer Wolff told these good people that I was the head of the Gestapo.

Next they visited the town of Leuven (Louvain), which was badly damaged. Himmler tried to convey his impressions: 'Apart from a few soldiers there was hardly anybody in the town, which looked very odd.'[13] Finally they got to Brussels, and on the following day went sightseeing. After a meeting with the commander of the Leibstandarte the group returned to the Felsennest Headquarters, where on 22 May Himmler gave Hitler a first-hand account of his impressions.[14]

Before starting out on his trip Himmler had already proposed to Hitler that Arthur Seyss-Inquart, at the time Deputy Governor of the General Government, should become the new Reich Commissar for the Netherlands.[15] Seyss-Inquart was an old acquaintance of Himmler's and, following his usual practice, in October 1938 the latter had awarded him the rank of SS-Gruppenführer, backdated to 12 March, the date of the Anschluss.[16]

On 18 May Seyss-Inquart was indeed appointed Reich Commissar in the Netherlands; from Himmler's point of view this provided the prospect of his being able to appoint a HSSPF in the Netherlands. He chose Hans Albin Rauter, chief of staff of the SS-Oberabschnitt South-East in Breslau, whom Seyss-Inquart integrated into the occupation administration in the role of

Commissar-General for Security. This meant that Rauter was subordinate both to the head of the civil administration and to the Reichsführer-SS and Chief of the German Police. In the event of a conflict between the two, in practice his loyalty to Himmler had clear priority.[17]

Heydrich, however, was once again dissatisfied with the situation: here too the appointment of a HSSPF had occurred 'almost too late', as 'naturally, because of a lack of practical experience and expertise, the work carried out under the direction of military intelligence had been relatively ineffective at capturing émigrés as well as documents and archives relevant to the police, compared with what would have been possible if the Gestapo, with all the records and information at its disposal, had been able to act immediately'.[18]

Ill. 22. During the war, in particular, Himmler's leadership style was marked by a high degree of mobility. He was continually on the move through occupied Europe inspecting his units and offices and giving his people detailed instructions on the spot. In this way the Reichsführer-SS conveyed the impression that he was personally involved in all matters concerning his extensive area of responsibilities and ready to share the wartime stresses and strains with his men.

At the end of May Hans Nockermann, who had already arrived in Amsterdam immediately after the Dutch capitulation as leader of an SD commando, was appointed commander of the security police and SD in the Netherlands.[19] However, Nockermann did not stay long. After the Dutch population had publicly and demonstratively expressed their sympathies for the royal family on 29 June, Himmler replaced him with Wilhelm Harster, who had briefly held the same post in Prague in 1939. Harster immediately began to transform the Einsatzkommandos of the Dutch Einsatzgruppe into units with permanent bases in the country.[20]

The long-term aim of the German authorities was to integrate the Netherlands into the German Reich as part of a 'Germanic Reich'. In the short and medium term, however, the independence of the Netherlands was to be maintained, not least in view of the continuing existence of the Dutch administration in their colonies. Moreover, in the shape of the Nationaal-Socialistisch Bewegung (NSB) under Anton Mussert the occupiers found a not-insignificant partner (the NSB had, after all, won 8 per cent of the vote in the elections of 1935), which was ideologically close to them, but which was not prepared to give up political independence in favour of an alleged 'Germanic' blood relationship.[21]

On 2 June Himmler arrived in The Hague to discuss with the radical Dutch Nazi Meinoud Rost van Tonningen, the internal party rival of Mussert, the establishment of a Dutch SS, which he had just ordered the week before.[22] The two had known each other since 1937, and Himmler hoped that with the support of Rost van Tonningen he would be able to realize his planned 'Germanic' policy in the Netherlands. Hitler declared that this appointment met with his 'strong approval'. However, it made a conflict between the Reichsführer and Mussert inevitable.[23]

At the beginning of 1941 Seyss-Inquart received a letter from Himmler in which he outlined once again the principles of this policy: as Reich Commissar, Seyss-Inquart had the 'historically important task of returning, with a firm but nevertheless very gentle hand, 9 million Germanic-Low German people, who for centuries have been alienated from the Germans, and of integrating them once more into the German-Low German community [...] Of course we both clearly understand that this task of creating a community of 110 million will be the basis for a really large Germanic Reich.'[24]

On 25 May, only a few days after his first trip to the Netherlands, Himmler proposed to Hitler the appointment of a Reich Commissar in

Belgium, which was about to capitulate. However, this time Hitler ignored Himmler's wishes and instead appointed a military administration, which was also responsible for Luxembourg and for two French *départements*.[25] On 15 June Himmler made another attempt, but again without success. Daluege, who in the meantime had arrived in Brussels to install a commander of the order police, had to return to Germany.[26]

Heydrich too was initially able to base only a small group in Brussels. Max Thomas, acting as the representative of the Chief of the Security Police and SD for Belgium and France, opened an office which, at the beginning of July, was reinforced by a small SD commando. This had been requested by Eggert Reeder, SS-Oberführer and district president in Düsseldorf, who in the meantime had been appointed head of the military administration.[27] The Office of the Representative of the Security Police and SD responsible for the Area under the Control of the Military Commander for Belgium and Northern France that emerged from this development took its orders from the Reich Security Main Office,[28] so that in the end Himmler and Heydrich were in fact able to exercise influence on the military administration of Belgium.

However, the SS was not content with this development; as far as they were concerned, the initial weeks of the occupation that were so decisive for security and intelligence operations had passed without being made use of. An HSSPF was only finally appointed in 1944. In France the situation was no different, which explains why, referring to both countries, Himmler noted in July 1940 'that the army high command [...] is engaged in operations that are clearly of a political police character [...] completely excluding the Reich bodies that are the leading experts in combating enemies of the state and crime in general'.[29]

In fact the military administration in France in 1940 was not prepared to grant the Reich Security Main Office a significant role.[30] The SS's position was not exactly helped by Werner Best, who had left the RSHA as a result of the dispute with Heydrich, being given the post of administrative chief in the office of the military commander in France. Although Best pursued a strictly racist policy, he relied in the first instance on his own organization.[31] After the armistice of 22 June a small security police/SD commando (Heydrich referred to ten or fifteen men[32]) under the command of Helmut Knochen began to operate in Paris, in order, according to its commission, to monitor 'Jews, communists, émigrés, lodges, and churches'.[33] However, the commando was bound by the directives of the military administration and had no executive functions. It was only in January 1941 that Knochen

acquired the right in cases of emergency to carry out arrests and expropria-
tions without the permission of the military authorities.[34]

On 25 July 1940 Thomas and Knochen met the *chef du cabinet* of the
French Interior Minister, Adrien Marquet, who requested them both to put
him in contact with 'someone close to the Führer' so that the minister could
pass on his 'views and requests' to the German leadership, bypassing the
military administration. Himmler was only too glad to take on this role.
A few days later Heydrich proudly informed Ribbentrop of the existence of
an 'informal link' to the French government that 'had been established
and was being run by the Reichsführer-SS's security service'. They were
pleased to be placing it at the disposal of the Foreign Ministry in order to be
able 'to deal with particular problems in accordance with its wishes'. Apart
from enabling him to make this patronizing dig at the Foreign Minister,
Heydrich welcomed the agreement because he was now in a position
'illegally to place security police and SD informants in all the *départements*'.[35]

Although the military restricted the influence of the security police and
SD following the occupation of France, it is clear from this example that in
the occupied territories they benefited from their terrifying reputation.
As a result they were able to establish important contacts, with whose
help they could build up their organization behind the backs of the military.
However, the atrocities committed by the SS in Poland, and the affront to
the moral code of the officer corps represented by the 'Procreation Order',
evidently had negative repercussions for the Reichsführer's claims to power.
If one considers the role of the SS in connection with the invasions of 1940,
Himmler was successful only in the Netherlands and to a limited extent in
Norway; in those countries which were subordinated to a military admin-
istration its few representatives had to fight to win their positions.

Himmler also encountered difficulties in France in his role as Reich Commissar
for the Consolidation of the Ethnic German Nation (RKF). Nazi ethnic experts
worked on the assumption that in France, including Alsace and Lorraine, there
were around 1.6 million ethnic Germans, who could be returned to the
German ethnic identity—'won back', as the contemporary idiom put it.[36]
Thus, in June 1940 the Reich Security Main Office was already beginning to
make preparations for the racial screening of these people in occupied France.[37]

Alsace and Lorraine were not formally annexed. Instead, Gauleiters
Robert Wagner (Baden) and Josef Bürckel (Saar-Palatinate) took over the
civil administration in Alsace and Lorraine respectively, and thereby

incorporated these French territories into the administrative structure of the Reich. Their main task, according to Hitler's instructions, was to create the conditions for the 'Germanization' of these territories by carrying out various political measures relating to population issues.[38]

Around 100,000 people were expelled or driven into the unoccupied zone in France in order to make room for German settlers from the Reich.[39] However, in carrying out these resettlements Gauleiter Bürckel, whom Himmler had appointed RKF representative for Lorraine, pursued his own strategies. With Hitler's support, Bürckel did not place the main emphasis on racial criteria, but instead gave particular importance to language, political reliability, and economic factors. This was contrary to the policy of Settlement Commissar Himmler, whose colleagues deployed in Lorraine wished to 'screen' the population according to racial characteristics. In September 1940, following his usual practice, Himmler had established a Land Office (Bodenamt) in Metz in order to take over agricultural properties that had 'become vacant'. It was headed by Friedrich Brehm, who had gathered appropriate experience as boss of the land office in Kattowitz (Katowice). Moreover, in October 1940 Bruno Kurt Schulz, a leading racial expert from the RuSHA, took over its branch office in Metz. However, all these appointments came too late to exercise a significant influence on the Gauleiter's expulsions and to be able to organize them according to racial criteria.[40] By the end of 1940 Bürckel had already expelled over 80,000 people from Lorraine.

By the end of 1940 Gauleiter Wagner had deported or driven around 100,000 people from Alsace into the unoccupied zone, including 22,000 Alsatian Jews.[41] Although Bruno Schultz, the RuSHA's representative in Metz, had already initiated 'racial assessments' of the Alsatian population in 1940, it was only during the course of 1941 that Himmler, in his capacity as Settlement Commissar, succeeded in imposing his will on the further resettlement programme in Alsace. In June 1941 he appointed Carl Hinrichs head of the Strasburg Land Office, thereby creating the material preconditions for measures to be taken along the lines he wanted.

Volunteers for the Waffen-SS

It is clear from a letter to Lammers, dated March 1939, that during the prewar period Himmler had already been aiming 'to win over [. . .] men of

Nordic blood for the active regiments of the SS [. . .] from all Germanic-type nations with the exception of the Anglo-Saxons'. He had already raised this topic 'a long time ago with the Führer and received his approval'.[42] On 8 November 1938 he had told the Gruppenführer of his aim that, 'at the latest within two years the Standarte "Germania" would contain only non-German Teutons'.[43] After the defeat of France the time had come to implement this project on a large scale.

On 15 August 1940 Himmler ordered the creation of an SS Leadership Main Office (SS-Führungshauptamt) to operate 'as a headquarters for the military leadership of the Waffen-SS and for the pre- and post-military leadership and training of the General SS'. Himmler initially reserved the right to head this new main office himself. The new arrangement worked at the expense of the SS Main Office (Hauptamt), which, however, still continued to be responsible for the recruitment and indoctrination of the Waffen-SS, as well as for the Business and Administration Main Office, the Personnel Main Office, and the SS Court Main Office. These offices in turn continued to be responsible for their particular areas insofar as they affected the Waffen-SS. As a result, rivalries and conflicts among the Main Offices were unavoidable.[44]

On 7 August, a week before the introduction of this new arrangement, Gottlob Berger, the head of the recruitment office in the Main Office, who was responsible for the recruitment of the Waffen-SS, approached Himmler to request a considerable expansion of his existing role. On 15 August Himmler responded to Berger's ambitions by promoting him to be de facto head of the SS Main Office; the dismissal of August Heissmeyer, the relatively weak acting head of the Main Office, was now merely a matter of time.[45] In a letter dated 15 August, Berger informed Himmler that the number of recruits which the Waffen-SS could rely on securing during the coming years would in all probability be insufficient to cover the increasing demands being made on the force.[46] Berger, however, had devised a solution to this problem: 'The Wehrmacht will not object to the further expansion of the Waffen-SS provided it can succeed in securing some of its recruits from those German and Teuton ethnic groups which are not drawn upon by the Wehrmacht. I consider this to be a particular issue that the Reichsführer still has to resolve.' Berger, who had already asked Himmler on 15 May 1940, the day of the Dutch capitulation, whether he could have permission to try to recruit for the Waffen-SS from 'the Dutch and later the Flemings',[47] was now looking further afield to Denmark and Norway as well as to the German ethnic minorities in Romania, Yugoslavia, and Hungary. As the organizer of the 'ethnic German self-defence force' in Poland, he already had relevant experience in this sphere. His ambitions, however, were not limited to Europe: 'As far as ethnic Germans throughout the world are concerned, we still have around 5 ½ mill. in North America and Canada[,] 1.2 mill.(of pure blood) in South America[,] 77,000 in Australia.'

As far as Himmler was concerned, Berger was pushing at an open door. The Reichsführer had already begun to recruit 'Germanic' volunteers on 20 April 1940, when he secured a Führer order for the establishment of an SS-Standarte 'Nordland', which consisted half of Germans and half of Danes and Norwegians.[48] After Vidkun Quisling, the leader of the Norwegian Nazis, appealed for recruits in January 1941, 300 Norwegians volunteered during the weeks that followed. On 28 January 1941 Himmler travelled to Norway in order personally to attend the swearing-in of the members of this first 'Germanic' SS unit.[49] 'After the passage of many generations', he told the men on this occasion

you are the first Norwegian men who have determined to take up the fight and to do so on your own initiative, not having been compelled to do it by a government dependent on England. For the first time you are standing lined up in the midst of your comrades, men of the Hird [the paramilitary organization of the Norwegian Nazis] and SS men from the Reich [...] We are admitting you as comrades, as brothers into our ranks, into the ranks of a formation that has always thought in Germanic terms and is Germanic in spirit.[50]

Himmler used his stay to have a look at the country and its people. On 2 February he visited a 'country farm near Trondheim typical of the central Norwegian landscape',[51] and made a speech to a German police battalion. In the evening he took part in a German–Norwegian 'comradeship evening'. On the fourth he went to Narvik, and stayed in northern Norway until the middle of the month.[52] In May 1941 he once again went to Norway in order to establish a Norwegian SS division. At a solemn ceremony he appointed Jonas Lie, the Norwegian state councillor responsible for the police, to be leader of the country's SS, and swore in the first 150 Norwegian SS men.[53]

SS recruitment in Denmark began in July 1940 and was carried out by the DNSAP, the Danish Nazis. On 1 September the Waffen-SS recruitment office opened a branch in Copenhagen.[54] However, following opposition from the Foreign Ministry, which had been bypassed, it had to be closed down again for the time being.[55]

On 25 May 1940 Himmler had ordered the creation of an SS-Standarte 'Westland' for Dutch and Flemish volunteers. The two new Standarten, 'Westland' and 'Nordland', together with the Regiment 'Germania' which was composed of Germans, were intended to form the Waffen-SS division 'Viking'.[56] In the autumn of 1940 Himmler created a Dutch as well as a Flemish General SS, thereby rounding off his establishment in the two countries.[57]

In February 1941 Berger received permission from Himmler to recruit Finns. At the start of the war with the Soviet Union 400 Finns were already serving in the 'Viking' Division.[58]

At the beginning of April 1941 Hitler also gave permission for the establishment of an SS-Standarte 'North West' for volunteers from the Netherlands and Flanders, who did not need to meet the 'racial' criteria for membership of the SS and were not to be admitted into it.[59] A few months later, after the outbreak of the war against the Soviet Union, these first steps towards recruiting volunteers who did not count as 'Teutons' were to lead to the creation of 'legions' in the Waffen-SS. Despite the relaxation of the selection criteria, however, Himmler's first recruitment programme in northern and western Europe was not particularly successful. Up until June 1941, apart from the Finns, the SS had recruited only 2,000 west European volunteers.[60]

The ethnic German minorities in eastern and south-eastern Europe proved more productive. They were to provide a reservoir not only for the Waffen-SS but also for armed self-defence units operating under the aegis of the SS. Shortly after the start of the Second World War the Waffen-SS had already begun recruiting among the ethnic Germans from Yugoslavia who were working in the Reich. The Waffen-SS's recruitment office had also begun to take steps to register the ethnic Germans in Yugoslavia itself, even though Göring had forbidden it.[61] On Himmler's instructions, Berger recruited 200 ethnic Germans from Yugoslavia and, after the country was occupied in April 1941, increased these efforts considerably. The other ethnic German minorities in the Balkans now also became a target for SS recruiters.

First moves in this direction were made as early as 1940. In August 1940 the German Reich forced through Hungarian claims to territory at the expense of Romania in the so-called Second Vienna Award, thereby

documenting its dominant position in the Balkans. This had direct repercussions not only for the aspirations to independence of the ethnic German
groups in both countries but also for Himmler's and Berger's recruitment
measures.

In the summer of 1939 the Waffen-SS had already recruited a group of
sixty to eighty ethnic German grammar-school boys from Romania and
brought them to Germany. There these young men joined the Waffen-SS
and received basic military training.[62] In the spring of 1940 a further
thousand young men, who allegedly were needed in the Reich as agricultural labour, were given a preliminary medical then taken over the border to
Vienna and there given their final medical examination; 700 of them joined
the Waffen-SS.[63] This recruitment drive, which became known as the
'1,000-man action', represented the start of the systematic recruitment of
ethnic Germans from Romania for the Waffen-SS, which reached its high
point in 1943.

The Second Vienna Award and the consequent ceding of territory
brought about the abdication of the King of Romania. The pro-German
Marshall Ion Antonescu formed a new government and, on 9 November
1940, Nazi sympathizers within the German minority exploited the political
upheaval to found the NSDAP of the Ethnic German Group in Romania,
Berger's son-in-law, Andreas Schmidt, taking over the leadership.[64]

Despite this close connection between Schmidt and Berger, the party's
foundation had taken place without the prior approval of Himmler, who in
the meantime had become the central figure in ethnic German politics. In
fact, Himmler regarded the founding of this party, which called itself
National Socialist and displayed the swastika flag, as 'entirely detrimental
to us'; the other Balkan states would consider it a threat to their independence and it would cause unnecessary annoyance to Russia. Thus, the party
should display 'the swastika as little as possible'.[65] 'As always happens in
ethnic German questions,' Himmler complained to Berger, he 'was told
about it only when the damage had been done': 'If something goes well
then it's always the others who are responsible, but if something doesn't go
off as planned then it's the Reichsführer's fault.'[66]

In connection with the Vienna Award the Germans imposed a minority
agreement on the Hungarian government, according to which the already
Nazi-inclined National League of Germans in Hungary was declared to be
the sole legitimate representative of the ethnic Germans in Hungary and
membership of the ethnic group was linked to a commitment to Nazi

ideology.[67] However, Franz Basch, the leader of the ethnic group, rejected an initial move by Berger to recruit 500 ethnic Germans from Hungary for the Waffen-SS. Nevertheless, Hungarian Germans who had fled to the Reich or were declared to be 'itinerant workers' did join the Waffen-SS.[68]

In the autumn of 1940 Sturmbannführer Viktor Nageler, whom the SS had sent to Slovakia in the summer of 1940 as an adviser to the Hlinka Guard, began to assess volunteers for the Guard in accordance with 'racial' principles. Between November 1940 and January 1941 the Danube SS recruitment office carried out an assessment, disguised as a medical examination, of a total of 4,694 men. More than half of the candidates proved to be 'suitable'; 40 per cent were even 'eligible for the SS'. In January 1941 Himmler approved further assessments but did not want to do anything 'for the time being'.[69]

The SS had also created a paramilitary organization within the German ethnic group in Slovakia, which called itself the 'Voluntary Protection Squad', and, in addition, a clandestine SS unit with the title 'Einsatztruppe', which, in accordance with Himmler's instructions, was expanded to form an 'ET Sturmbann' and served as a source of recruitment for the Waffen-SS.[70] At the end of 1940, however, Berger informed Himmler that Franz Karmasin, the leader of the ethnic group, was causing 'the men all sorts of difficulties' because he considered the SS was exerting too much influence on the formation of the Hlinka Guard. For, in the meantime, Sturmbannführer Nageler, who had been assigned to the Hlinka Guard as an adviser, had started to create an elite unit from the members of the Guard, the so-called Wehrmannschaften (defence teams), who were envisaged as in the future helping the SS to integrate Slovakia into a greater Germanic empire. By creating such an elite, Nageler intended nothing less than to select racially 'valuable' Slovaks in order to amalgamate them with the 'Germanic' population. This was a project with which Himmler sympathized and which he was to return to in the following year.[71] However, the implementation of such ideas would have damaged in the long term the privileged position the German ethic group was claiming for itself in Slovakia, and this was the reason for Karmasin's opposition.

By contrast, and in direct opposition to Nageler's scheme, Berger advocated creating out of the ET Sturmbann a Standarte of the General SS in Slovakia. However, Himmler considered such ideas 'premature'.[72] At this point Himmler was concerned above all to avoid anything that might damage German–Slovak relations; the accusations being made against him in connection with the failed legionnaires' putsch in Romania, to which we shall return in the next section, made this appear advisable.[73] Nevertheless, despite Karmasin's obstruction and Himmler's cautious approach, by the end of 1941 the Waffen-SS had managed, through individual commitment, to recruit 600 ethnic Germans from Slovakia.[74]

During 1940 the SS also began trying to recruit from the ethnic Germans in Alsace, though with only moderate success. At the beginning of 1941 there were only around 200 volunteers. At short notice Himmler expected those responsible to produce an immediate increase to 500 recruits: 'Germanic tribes who do not have a single son participating in the current great freedom struggle for the reordering of Europe will lose all self-respect and will be unable to retrieve it for decades.'[75]

Himmler has a go at foreign policy

On 23 October 1940 Hitler met the Spanish dictator, Franco, at the railway station in Hendaye in order to discuss the modalities of Spain joining the Axis alliance, without, however, achieving a really significant result. A few days before this meeting Himmler had travelled to Spain and, among other things, had met Franco. Evidently the presence of the Reichsführer was intended to reinforce the final discussions concerning security for the meeting of the two dictators in Hendaye.[76] Moreover, Himmler will have used his visit to discuss the relatively intense German–Spanish police relations. The official reports, however, gave the impression of it being primarily a tourist visit.

On 20 October, after stops in San Sebastian and Burgos, Himmler arrived by train in Madrid. According to the *Völkischer Beobachter*: 'The streets leading to the North Station were packed with people and Falangists in uniform together with units of the newly formed Spanish police lined the route to the Ritz Hotel. Flags were flying throughout Madrid in celebration. The Reichsführer-SS was warmly greeted by the population on his drive through the streets.'[77] On the same day Himmler was received by Franco, and in the afternoon he attended a bullfight where, according to the *Völkischer Beobachter*, his arrival was greeted 'with loud applause'.[78]

On the following day Himmler went to Toledo in order to look at the historic fortifications, the Alcázar, which in the meantime had become a pilgrimage site for Spanish nationalists. In 1936, at the beginning of the Civil

War, for two months Franco supporters had withstood a siege by superior Republican forces.[79] The day after he visited the archaeological museum in Madrid, studied intently a map of the barbarian invasions, and asked the director of the museum to provide him with a copy of some of the exhibits.[80]

That evening Himmler spoke at a meeting of the Madrid branch of the German NSDAP, in which he gave the audience some of his impressions of his recent trip. He was quoted by the *Völkischer Beobachter* as saying: 'One can still see in the Germanic physiognomies of the northern Spanish traces of the German blood that over the centuries has been lost to the Reich. However, since the year 1933 this tragic development has ceased.' Himmler then turned 'to the great settlement project in the German east', and 'gave graphic details of the huge trek involved in the resettlement programme'. In the east, according to Himmler, 'not only [...] were settlements being constructed but the landscape is being given a new appearance'. Himmler noted with approval that in Spain they had begun the necessary reforestation of the barren Karst areas and the plains, and continued—now evidently mounting one of his hobby-horses: 'We too must create windbreaks in the German east by planting dense forests. This would block the Asiatic wind coming from the Steppes.'[81] On 23 October he flew to Barcelona, from where on the following day he set out for home.[82]

During the coming years official state visits by Himmler such as the one to Spain were to be relatively infrequent. This was not simply because the number of states with which the Third Reich still maintained diplomatic relations continually declined, but above all because Foreign Minister von Ribbentrop regarded all diplomatic activities undertaken by Himmler with great suspicion and endeavoured to restrict them. The reason for this change in attitude was the SD's unsuccessful initiatives in Romania at the beginning of 1941.

In January 1941 the SD intelligence network in Romania had supported an unsuccessful putsch by the Iron Guard, the paramilitary organization of the Romanian fascists, against the dictator Antonescu, a close ally of Nazi Germany, and subsequently helped the leader of the putsch, Horia Sima, to escape to Germany. This dilettante action not only discredited the SD in the eyes of the Nazi leadership but also weakened Himmler's position vis-à-vis the Foreign Ministry. Hitler explicitly disapproved of the SD's independent initiative and instructed Himmler to keep Jost's SD foreign department on a tight leash.[83] On 21 February Himmler met Jost and the people responsible for the security police's and SD's activities in Romania for a discussion of these events.[84] Himmler always rejected accusations that he himself had supported Sima's putsch. In fact, when, during the planning stage of the so-called legionnaires' putsch, he had been asked for support he had sent Sima a letter in Hitler's name admonishing him to work collegially with Antonescu. However, he could not dispute the reproach that his agents in Romania had at the very least acted without authorization.[85]

From now on Himmler showed a demonstrative lack of interest in Romanian domestic politics. A few years later, at a meeting with Antonescu in March 1944, he claimed that 'after the unfortunate legionnaires' putsch I [kept] my people out of Romania'. Antonescu, at least, was not convinced by this retreat: he made it unmistakably clear to Himmler at this meeting that the SD was encouraging opposition to him in Bucharest. Himmler replied with disarming naivety that, 'all in all', he could not 'believe that', as the police attaché had only 'two or three assistants'.[86]

As a direct consequence of the 'unfortunate legionnaires' putsch', in April 1941 Ribbentrop wanted to cancel the agreement he had reached with Himmler at the start of the war about police attachés. The agreement had, in particular, granted the SD the right of reporting independently to the RSHA.[87] Ribbentrop now demanded from all members of German foreign missions a declaration, on their word of honour, that they were not working for the SD or for military intelligence.[88] The closing down of the 'Office of the Reich Security Main Office in Pressburg' in July 1941, which had already begun intelligence operations in Slovakia comparable to those in the Reich, must be seen in this context. Evidently the Foreign Ministry feared that, as in Romania, independent initiatives by the SD could jeopardize relations with a Reich ally.[89]

Ribbentrop's response put an end to his friendship with Himmler. 'It seems to be all over between Ribbentrop and Heini,' Margarete Himmler wrote in her diary on 8 May 1941. 'Herr v. R is too full of himself.'[90] The cooling of personal relations most probably contributed to the slow progress of negotiations between the SS and Foreign Ministry concerning the future position of police attachés at German foreign missions that produced an agreement only after several months; as Heydrich noted, 'a peace agreement that was so important for the Reichsführer in human terms'.[91] In the agreement of August 1941 Himmler and Ribbentrop concurred on the following points: the representatives of the SS and police working abroad should refrain from all diplomatic activities; if, in the course of their intelligence work, they came across material relevant to foreign policy this should be handed over to the Foreign Ministry. Himmler's agents would in future be led by police attachés, who were responsible to the heads of mission and would be required to report to them.[92]

At this time so-called police liaison officers were attached to the German diplomatic missions in Sofia, Shanghai, Rome, Tokyo, Lisbon, Pressburg (Bratislava), Madrid, Paris, Belgrade, and Bucharest. Representatives of the SD's foreign department were located in Addis Ababa, Sofia, Shanghai, Reval (Tallin), Athens, Teheran, Tokyo, Belgrade, Bucharest, Leningrad, Bern, Pressburg, Ankara, and Budapest.[93] Furthermore, the August agreement included the sending of further police attachés to German foreign missions. As a result, at the beginning of 1942 Ribbentrop sent Himmler's representatives to Helsinki, Stockholm, and Bern. However, he was not prepared to go beyond the agreement that had been reached and therefore declined to accept the appointment of SS leaders to the consulates in Izmir and Trapezunt (Trabzon), Casablanca, and Marseilles.[94]

After the crisis of 1941 Ribbentrop claimed the right to approve Himmler's foreign trips. To support his stance he could refer to a circular of August 1941 from Hans-Heinrich Lammers, head of the Reich Chancellery, that established the requirement for all leading figures to secure permission for trips abroad.[95] When Himmler wanted to make a flying visit to Belgrade in October 1942 to inspect the 'Prince Eugene' division, Ribbentrop instructed that 'the Reichsführer-SS's trip to Belgrade should be treated just like any other foreign trip'.[96] However, Himmler visited Belgrade even without permission,[97] and the Foreign Ministry decided that it was advisable to take no further action.[98] When, in spring 1943, Himmler planned a visit to Mussolini, Ribbentrop once again intervened in the preparations for the visit, and it did not in fact take place.[99]

Ribbentrop also attempted to subject the visits that Himmler received from abroad to a confirmation procedure which, however, the latter always succeeded in smoothly avoiding. Thus, Ribbentrop complained to Himmler in 1944 that 'the Hungarian Interior Minister Vajna's trip to Germany should have been submitted to the Führer for approval via the Foreign Ministry'; in future he should please ensure that this happened.[100] Himmler replied that in principle this was true, but Vajna was a 'special case' which '[I] have of course cleared with the Führer'.[101]

The extension of Jewish persecution

In the spring of 1940 the Nazi government was once more engaged in planning a 'final solution' of the 'Jewish question'. Now, after victory in the west, the French colony of Madagascar appeared to be the answer.[102] This was by no means an original idea. Ever since the end of the nineteenth century the notion that one could settle European Jews in large numbers in Madagascar had been very popular in anti-Semitic circles in various European countries.[103]

Himmler provided an important impetus, presenting Hitler, on 25 May 1940, with a memorandum 'Concerning the Treatment of the Alien Population in the East' in which he expressed the intention of seeing 'the term "Jew" [...] completely eliminated through the massive emigration of all Jews to Africa or to some colony'. However, when discussing the plan to steal children 'of good racial quality' from Poland he distanced himself from the 'physical extermination of a people'; that would be 'fundamentally un-German and impossible'. Hitler approved the memorandum in principle,[104] and during the summer made a number of positive comments about the Madagascar project,[105] which was now being developed both by the Foreign Ministry and by the Reich Security Main Office.

Franz Rademacher, the head of the 'Jewish Affairs' desk in the Foreign Ministry, presented a plan on 3 July. A few days earlier Heydrich had requested to be allowed to participate in the planned 'territorial solution', which would affect the 3.25 million people concerned.[106] Rademacher's motto, 'all Jews out of Europe', makes clear how the 'territorial solution' had come to be envisaged in the meantime. Rademacher proposed that France should give Germany Madagascar as a mandate 'for the solution of the Jewish question': 'The part of the island that is not required for military purposes will be placed under the administrative control of a German police governor, who will be subordinate to the Reichsführer-SS. Apart from that the Jews will be allowed to govern themselves in this territory.' This would ensure that the Jews would be 'hostages in German hands for the future good behaviour of their racial comrades in America'. Thus, the Madagascar project was envisaged as hostage-taking (as indeed had been the case with the plan for a 'Jewish reservation' in Poland).

A memo of Rademacher's dated 2 July ('Plan for Solving the Jewish Question') contained more details of this project:

From the German point of view the Madagascar solution represents the creation of a large ghetto. The security police are the only people who have the necessary experience in this area; they have the means of preventing escapes from the island. Moreover, they have the experience to enable them to impose the appropriate punishments that will be necessary in view of the hostile acts committed against Germany by Jews in America.[107]

During the following weeks the Reich Security Main Office produced its own version of the Madagascar Plan, which was issued as a booklet on 15 August. It referred to the creation of a 'police state' in Madagascar for the 4 million Jews under German rule. A time-scale of four years was envisaged for their transportation by ship.[108]

Furthermore, in August Viktor Brack, the official within the Chancellery of the Führer of the NSDAP responsible for organizing the 'Euthanasia' programme, put forward a proposal 'to use the transport organization that he has developed during wartime for the Führer's "special assignment" for transporting the Jews later on to Madagascar', a suggestion that was explicitly approved by Rademacher.[109] The fact that Philipp Bouhler, the head of the Chancellery of the Führer of the NSDAP, was being considered as governor of a future colony in East Africa[110] also demonstrates how sinister the whole Madagascar project was. The idea that over a period of years millions of Jews would be deported to Madagascar, where a large number of them would presumably succumb relatively quickly to the inhospitable conditions—leaving aside the 'punishments' to be inflicted by the security police—clearly demonstrates that, in the final analysis, this project envisaged their physical extermination even if, in the event of 'good behaviour' by the United States, this might have been subject to revision. Thus, the plans, in which the Reich Security Main Office was heavily involved, were developing step by step in the direction of the 'extermination' that Himmler had himself rejected in May.

However fantastic the Madagascar project may sound, the Reich Security Main Office took it seriously. The Madagascar plan provided a substitute for the plans for a 'Jewish reservation' that they had not been able to realize in Poland and in which they now included the west European Jews. They most likely assumed that if Madagascar failed to work out then in good time they would find some other territory. What is remarkable about

Rademacher's August memo, at any rate, is the fact that he now estimated the number of Jews to be sent to Madagascar as 6.5 million, an indication that the Jews from south-east Europe as well as those from the French colonies in North Africa were to be included in the deportation plans.

The Madagascar plan had a direct impact on German Jewish policy in Poland. As Governor-General Frank informed his colleagues a few days later,[111] on 8 July Hitler had assured him that in the light of the Madagascar project there would be no further deportations into their territory. On 9 July Himmler announced to the Reich Security Main Office that there would be no more deportations into Frank's territory, thereby finally closing down the project for a 'Jewish reservation' in the General Government.[112]

Right from the start it had been Frank's civil administration that had been responsible for the measures directed against the Polish Jews—their registration and public identification through a badge and their exclusion from the economy. Moreover, it had gradually introduced ghettoization.[113] In addition, in June 1940 the civil administration took over responsibility for Jewish forced labour from the SS. This was, above all, the result of the high-handed and brutal forced-labour policy pursued by Odilo Globocnik, the SS and Police Leader in the Lublin district, which had caused serious problems and by the summer of 1940 was considered to have failed. However, the new distribution of responsibilities did not prevent Globocnik from maintaining forced-labour camps in order to pursue his pet project: the creation of the 'Moat', a dilettante plan for a defensive line along the border with the Soviet-occupied zone. Globocnik's unstoppable activity in the field of Jewish forced labour was also primarily responsible for the fact that the Lublin district developed into the centre for slave labour within the General Government. It was here that Jews from other districts tended to be deployed on major projects and housed in special camps under primitive and completely inadequate conditions.[114]

Between autumn 1940 and January 1941 the German leadership finally gave up the Madagascar plan, after they had been forced to accept that there would not be a separate peace with Britain. Within the context of the planning for 'Barbarossa'[115] (the invasion of the Soviet Union), a new 'post-Madagascar project was being developed.[116]

On 22 October, in a speech to party comrades during his stay in Madrid, Himmler had once again stated that 'all Jews from the Greater German Reich' would be placed in a 'closed ghetto' in the General Government.[117]

However, in view of Frank's opposition to deportations into his territory, and against the background of the start of German planning for the war against the Soviet Union, it was obvious that this objective would have to be revised.

A memo of Eichmann's, dated 4 December, in which he produced figures for a speech by Himmler, provides an indication of how the Reich Security Main Office was envisaging the future 'final solution of the Jewish question' at this time.[118] Eichmann distinguished between two phases: 'the initial solution of the Jewish question through emigration' and the future 'final solution of the Jewish question', by which he meant 'the resettlement of the Jews away from the economic sphere of the German people to a territory which is still to be designated'. According to Eichmann, this project would 'involve around 5.8 million people', whereas the Reich Security Main Office had used a figure of 4 million. Thus, in the meantime, the territories of Germany's allies and satellites in south-east Europe as well as the French colonies in North Africa were now also being included.

In a speech to the Reich leaders and Gauleiters on 10 December 1940, on the subject of 'Settlement', Himmler described the 'emigration' of the Jews from the General Government as a vital future task in order 'to make more room for Poles'. Himmler had thereby clarified the link between the settlement of ethnic Germans in the annexed Polish territories, the further expulsion of indigenous Poles to the General Government, and the need to deport the Jews from the General Government in order to make way for this new wave of immigration. The Reichsführer-SS did not, however, say what the destination of this 'Jewish emigration' was to be.[119]

At the end of 1940 and beginning of 1941 Hitler gave Heydrich the task of working out a 'project for a final solution' to be implemented after the war, which he presented to the 'Führer' in January 1941. Hitler had given his instructions to Heydrich via both Himmler and Göring; thus the Hitler–Göring–Heydrich chain of command in Jewish policy that had existed since 1936 was still intact, alongside that of Hitler–Himmler–Heydrich. We do not have the text of Heydrich's plan, but the content can be reconstructed from various documents.[120]

The draft envisaged the deportation of all Jews from Europe. The destination of the transports was to be the General Government, but that would serve only as an intermediate stopping place.[121] The (top-secret) final destination of the deportations was to be the Soviet territories that were to be occupied. When Heydrich went to see Göring in March 1941 in order to discuss the matter and his responsibilities, Göring pointed out the need for a clarification of Rosenberg's position. This was because he had been designated as the future Reich Minister for the Occupied Eastern Territories.[122]

It is not absolutely clear, however, what those involved actually meant at this point by a 'final solution' within the Soviet Union that was going to be occupied, and presumably it was not yet clear to them either. At the beginning of 1941 Himmler, at any rate, temporarily considered the idea of a mass sterilization of Jews. He asked Viktor Brack to work out a plan for it. However, after he received the plan in March 1941 he appears not to have pursued this idea any further.[123] It seems that Himmler and the other decision-makers preferred to postpone dealing with the issue of what was to happen to those who had been deported until after the anticipated victory over the Soviet Union.

PART V

The Greater Germanic Reich: Living-Space and Ethnic Murder

19

An Ideological War
of Annihilation

The Nazi leadership had been preparing for a renewed extension of the war since the beginning of 1941: late in July 1940 Hitler had decided to invade the Soviet Union in the spring of 1941. Again this war was planned as a Blitzkrieg, in other words, the expectation was that the Soviet Union would collapse like a house of cards under the blows delivered by the Wehrmacht and would by autumn be completely defeated. What was new about this war, however, was that from the start it was conceived as an ideological and racist war of annihilation. The Soviet Union was not simply to be defeated; the intention was to eliminate its ruling class, decimate the nations living on its territory by the violent destruction of millions of people, and to exploit the survivors as slave labour for the construction of the new German 'living-space' (Lebensraum).[1]

Himmler assumed that he would play a key role in the conquest, control, and reshaping of this gigantic territory. He planned to deploy four divisions and a series of further fighting units, mostly at the most forward part of the front: his police organization would employ his methods of terror to dominate the conquered territory, and he himself as Settlement Commissar would organize the necessary expulsions and resettlements of the indigenous population, in order to make way for 'Germanic' settlers. The vision of a forcible seizure of land to colonize in the east that he had outlined as the SS's future task suddenly seemed to come within reach. On 10 June 1941 he put to the head of the Reich Chancellery, Hans Heinrich Lammers, his suggestion that he, Himmler, should be given responsibility for maintaining control in all occupied eastern European territories in police 'and political' security matters, so that, as Settlement Commissar, he could 'see to the pacification and stabilization of the political situation'.[2] This claim to power put him in direct competition with Alfred Rosenberg, whom Hitler had already appointed on 20 April to be 'responsible for the central coordination of questions concerning eastern Europe', though with the qualification that Himmler would in future 'occupy a special position' alongside him in the east. The negotiations that Himmler then conducted with Rosenberg about their future responsibilities in the east turned out to be tough: 'To work with Rosenberg, let alone under him, is definitely the most difficult thing there is in the NSDAP', as Himmler wrote to Bormann.[3]

Now 40 years old, Himmler hoped that his new tasks would boost his career, which in the previous few years had stagnated, and result in his being admitted to the innermost circle of Nazi leaders. After the great political successes of 1933 and 1936, since 1938 he had had to accept several painful defeats: his misdirected investigations into von Fritsch had seriously threatened the relationship between Hitler and the Wehrmacht, had played a significant role in provoking a state crisis, and brought down Hitler's displeasure on him. He had found himself increasingly forced to keep his various 'Germanic' and occult activities 'under wraps', as he was in no doubt that Hitler regarded these ventures with suspicion. His radical pro-posals regarding the role of the church could not be put into practice. The atrocities carried out by the SS in Poland and his order to procreate had provoked massive criticism from the Wehrmacht, with the result that he had to give way publicly and accept being marginalized during the police 'processing' of the conquered north and west European states. In Romania his SD had supported the Iron Guard's failed putsch and as a result had destabilized German–Romanian relations; for that reason Ribbentrop, the Foreign Minister, curtailed Himmler's foreign-policy ambitions wherever possible. Even Himmler's various resettlement programmes had ground to a halt. And although Waffen-SS units had been deployed in the very van-guard of Blitzkrieg operations from the autumn of 1939 onwards, since the end of 1939 he had been able to establish only one additional division, 'Viking'; the concentration of these units into an independent SS army corps that he had planned as early as 1938 had not come about. Instead, his units had always been distributed over the whole of the front, with the result that he was unable to establish a link between their military effectiveness and strategically decisive operations.

Now that there was a prospect of conquering vast territories in the east Himmler hoped to be able to turn the situation again to his advantage.

Preparations

As a result of the predominantly negative experiences Himmler had had in cooperating with the Wehrmacht during the military campaigns of 1940, he attempted early on to reach agreement with the military about the deployment of security police and SD in the attack on Russia.

Heydrich had been negotiating with the army Quartermaster-General on this question since February 1941.[4] On 13 March Keitel, chief of the Wehrmacht High Command, issued guidelines stating that 'special responsibilities in the zone of army operations' would be given to the Reichsführer-SS 'at the Führer's request [. . .] in preparation for the political administration'. These special responsibilities, as the guidelines ominously put it, 'result from the impending final struggle between two opposing political systems'.[5] What was meant by these special responsibilities was made abundantly clear by Hitler to his generals during March, in a number of statements. He stated unequivocally that the coming war was a 'battle between two ideologies'[6] that could be won only if the 'Jewish-Bolshevik intelligentsia'[7] were annihilated.

Keitel's guidelines of 13 March also indicated, however, that in fulfilling their 'special responsibilities' the units of the Reichsführer-SS would no longer be subordinate to the Wehrmacht, as they had been in the war against Poland, but were rather to act independently. By this means the leadership of the Wehrmacht believed it could distance itself from the renewed and extended mass murders which, if Poland had been anything to go by, were in the offing.

Against the background of these provisions Heydrich, in close consultation with Himmler,[8] agreed a draft arrangement with the Quartermaster-General at the end of March.[9] In the 'Regulations for the Deployment of the Security Police and the SD in Conjunction with the Army' we read that 'the carrying out of particular tasks by the security police outside the scope of the army units' made it 'necessary to deploy special security police (SD) units in the field of operations'. Their duties were, however, only vaguely defined: where they were near the army front line they were to 'secure' documentation and people; in the rear area they had responsibility, amongst other things, for 'identifying and combating activities hostile to the state and the Reich'. The special units (*Sonderkommandos*) had to execute their duties 'on their own responsibility', but were to be subordinate to the armies or to the commanders of the rear areas 'with regard to marches, provisions, and quartering'.[10] What was actually meant by the formulation 'on their own responsibility' was that the anticipated mass liquidation of communist officials in the area of army operations was to be carried out by the Sonderkommandos, but that they could rely on the army's logistical support in carrying this out.

The negotiations had just been concluded when unforeseen events occurred: on 27 March the Yugoslav government, which was friendly towards Germany, was toppled in a military putsch, and the Nazi regime had to reckon with the country entering the war on the side of the British. Hasty preparations were therefore made to attack Yugoslavia and also Greece (which at the time was already at war with Italy). On 6 April the Nazi attack began; Yugoslavia capitulated on 17 April and mainland Greece was occupied by the end of the month.[11]

An extremely simple solution was found to the question of what role Himmler's security police and SD were supposed to play in this improvised war: Heydrich's draft agreement with the Quartermaster-General provided the basis for action, though with a small but very significant change. When the people whom Himmler's henchmen were to 'secure' were listed, not only 'émigrés, saboteurs, and terrorists' were included but specifically 'communists and Jews' also. This revealed that the war in the Balkans was to be waged as an ideological war, just as was planned for the war against the Soviet Union. In accordance with the agreement two security police and SD Einsatzgruppen took part in the fighting, one in Yugoslavia and one in Greece—from the perspective of the SS leadership a significant improvement over the affront they had been forced to endure the previous year when France, Belgium, and the Netherlands were occupied.[12]

One day before Yugoslavia's surrender, on 16 April, Himmler, who had set up his headquarters during hostilities in Bruck an der Mur, had a meeting in a hotel in Graz with Heydrich, Wolff, Daluege, the chief of his Leadership Main Office Hans Jüttner, and the army Quartermaster-General Eduard Wagner. On the basis of the draft of 26 March, they came to a final agreement about the 'Regulations for the Deployment of the Security Police and the SD in Conjunction with the Army' for the imminent war against the Soviet Union. Although 'communists and Jews' were not expressly mentioned in the final version, the events that led up to the agreement demonstrate that the participants were in no doubt as to who was meant as the prime target of the 'war of two ideologies'.[13]

At the beginning of May Himmler interrupted his war preparations and made a flying visit to Greece, which had recently been occupied, just as he had taken a look at the newly conquered western territories the previous year. On 6 May he flew to Athens, arriving the following day after a stopover in Budapest. There he visited the Peloponnese and Corinth, and finally German troops in Larissa. From Athens he flew on to Belgrade, where he inspected an ethnic German village.[14]

Back in Germany on 11 May, he was confronted with an alarming situation: the previous day Rudolf Hess, Hitler's Deputy, had flown on his own initiative to Scotland in a Messerschmitt and parachuted down in order put a peace proposal to the British government.[15] Leaving Gmund, where he had wanted to relax for a few days, Himmler had a meeting on 11 May in Munich with Göring to discuss the situation then travelled with him to Obersalzberg, where talks continued into the night. Himmler's Gestapo was to take responsibility in the days that followed for arresting and interrogating important close friends of Hess. Two days later there was a hurried meeting of Reich and Gau leaders on the Obersalzberg, which Himmler most probably also attended.[16]

Hitler dealt relatively quickly with the crisis occasioned by Hess. The Führer's former Deputy was declared insane, and was succeeded in the role (but without the title) by Martin Bormann, who had up to that time been the Deputy's deputy. Bormann, who was now head of the Party Chancellery, was friendly with Himmler. They both belonged to the radical wing of the party and this expressed itself, for example, in the strong anticlericalism that was fundamental to both of them. Bormann's appointment therefore increased Himmler's chances of finding Hitler disposed to listen to his ideas, and in fact Himmler's position grew more secure in the course of the ensuing months.

One result of Hess's flight was a Gestapo campaign in June against astrologers, clairvoyants, dowsers, spiritualists, and representatives of other occult teachings, which Hess in part espoused; this was a means of providing evidence to show the outside world that Hess had quite simply been the victim of mumbo-jumbo. The campaign was not without its dangers for Himmler, as it threatened circles he felt connected to, for example the adherents of anthroposophical agriculture or of the Cosmic Ice Theory. For

Himmler this experience was sufficient reason to keep such occult interests even more firmly 'under wraps'.[17]

On 18 May he returned to Berlin, where he had a meeting with, among others, Victor Brack from the Führer's Chancellery, one of those mainly responsible for the 'Euthanasia' programme. Some weeks earlier Brack had sent him a report about the possible mass sterilization of Jews, which they very likely discussed.[18] A few days after this meeting Professor Carl Clauberg, whose advice Himmler usually sought concerning gynaecological matters, suggested a further process for carrying out mass sterilization. Presumably these plans were connected with the projected deportations of European Jews to the Soviet territories that were to be conquered: any possibility of the deportees procreating was to be excluded.

On 21 May Himmler issued an order in which he outlined the main features of the deployment of SS and police units in the future occupied territories, about which agreement had been reached with the Wehrmacht in mid-April: in the east, as in the Reich itself, the Higher SS and Police Leaders (HSSPF) would play a central role. The relevant HSSPF was to be put in charge of 'SS and police troops and security police for special deployment' (not only the Einsatzgruppen, who had been the subject of negotiations with the army, but also units that had not been mentioned in the agreement and to which Himmler was giving an even greater degree of independence in this order), so that he could 'implement tasks I [Himmler] shall give directly to him'. Comprising these units were, on the one hand, troops belonging to the order police, who were to 'fulfil their tasks according to my directives', and on the other, units of the Waffen-SS, who were responsible for similar tasks as well as 'special tasks I shall give them'.[19]

What Himmler was alluding to obliquely rather than directly was the fact that in the months to come these particular SS and police units were to carry out mass murder on a devastating scale among the civilian population of the occupied Soviet territories, and especially its Jewish members, and in so doing open the floodgates for the annihilation of the European Jews. How did Himmler prepare the members of these units for this? Let us take a closer look at the individual units and what we know about the instructions given to them.

From the spring of 1941 onwards four Einsatzgruppen, in total about 3,000 strong, were set up in the security police's NCO training school at Pretzsch near Leipzig.[20] They were made up of members of the SD, Gestapo, criminal police and order police, Waffen-SS, and ancillary staff, in part from the SS and police administrative apparatus.[21] It is striking that a particular type was dominant in the leadership, namely the 'specialist'; he had already had an academic education, often in law, a practical training within the police administration, and was a skilled bureaucrat, while at the same time being a man of radical action and conviction and strongly committed to Nazi ideology.[22] Of the seventeen members of the leadership cadre of Einsatzgruppe A, all without exception long-standing employees in the SS and police apparatus, there were, for example, eleven lawyers, nine of whom had doctorates; thirteen had joined the NSDAP or one of its affiliated organizations before 1933.[23]

At first the order police[24] went into the war against the Soviet Union with twenty-three battalions (in total 11,640 men and 420 officers), consisting of long-serving career policemen, who made up the bulk of the leadership corps and NCO corps in the remaining units also, as well as of older police reservists[25] without any service record and also of younger volunteers.[26] All these units were led by more senior police officers, many of whom had gained experience back in the civil war and border conflicts of the post-war period, while a significant number of more junior officers had been trained in the SS officer-training colleges.[27]

In addition to the security and order police Himmler, by concentrating the SS Death's Head units into a 'Commando Staff (Kommandostab) RFSS', equipped himself with a reserve force ready for deployment on his 'special tasks'.[28] As early as 7 April 1941 he had created his own task force, which on 6 May was renamed Commando Staff RFSS.[29] On 1 May he formed two motorized SS brigades from SS Death's Head regiments and simultaneously two SS cavalry regiments in Cracow and Warsaw were merged and later became the SS Cavalry Brigade.[30] A number of these Death's Head units had already carried out numerous acts of violence in Poland.[31] In July 1941 Himmler had a total of more than around 19,000 Commando Staff troops at his disposal.[32] In this way he enabled himself to intervene directly to combat racial and political enemies in the occupied eastern territories and to set clear priorities in this process.

In the weeks before the Russian campaign, 'Operation Barbarossa', these forces were initiated into their tasks. The relevant orders that Hitler had issued to the Wehrmacht in themselves spoke volumes about the coming war. In May he ordered that criminal acts perpetrated by members of the Wehrmacht against the civilian population in the east were as a rule no longer to be prosecuted by the military courts, and thus were to go unpunished. Crimes committed by enemy civilians were also not to be punished by the military courts, but rather in such cases the perpetrators were to be 'finished off', 'put down' on the spot; 'collective violent measures' against communities were permitted.[33] In the 'Guidelines on the Treatment of Political Commissars' signed on 6 June by Keitel, the head of the Wehrmacht High Command, it was stated that Soviet commissars, as 'the initiators of barbaric Asiatic methods of fighting', were to be 'finished off' by the fighting force.[34] In the 'Guidelines on the Conduct of Troops in Russia' of 19 May, which were disseminated down to company level, 'Bolshevism' was characterized as being the 'mortal enemy of the National Socialist German nation', and for this reason 'ruthless and vigorous measures against Bolshevik agitators, partisans, saboteurs, and Jews' were required, as well as 'the eradication of all active and passive resistance'.[35]

Himmler and Heydrich, however, went considerably further than these instructions. The Reichsführer insisted on personally putting the most senior SS leaders in the right frame of mind for the extermination they were going to carry out. To that end he summoned them specially to the Wewelsburg from 11 to 15 June.[36] He had invited about a dozen people, among them his close colleagues Wolff and Brandt; his two police chiefs Daluege and Heydrich; the HSSPFs earmarked for the territories to be conquered, namely Prützmann, von dem Bach-Zelewski, and Jeckeln; Pohl, the head of the SS Main Office; and his friend, the writer, President of the Reich Chamber of Literature, and SS-Brigadeführer Hanns Johst. In 1939 and 1940 Johst had accompanied Himmler on journeys to Poland, published a small volume about the first journey,[37] and thereafter had requested from Himmler the privilege of accompanying him in future on important assignments so that he could act as Himmler's semi-official biographer.[38] Thus he was promoted to the role of 'Bard to the SS',[39] and so was indispensable for capturing the atmosphere of these historic days at the Wewelsburg.

At this meeting, Himmler, according to a post-war testimony of von dem Bach-Zelewski, put at 30 million the number of human beings by which the Soviet Union was to be 'decimated', in other words, a figure corresponding to the scale of population growth since 1914 in the territories to be conquered.[40] This statement characterizes the climate prevailing in the highest echelons of the SS in these days and weeks immediately before the invasion: they had a clear sense of embarking on a campaign of racial annihilation of incalculable proportions.

Heydrich then went on to apprise the leaders of the Einsatzkommandos along the same lines, both at a meeting in the Prince Charles Palace in Berlin, which presumably took place on 17 June, and also in Pretzsch on the Elbe, when the Einsatzkommandos were officially given their marching orders shortly before the outbreak of the war.[41] After this Heydrich wrote a summary of his instructions: on the one hand, in a letter of 29 June to the leaders of the Einsatzgruppen, in which he alluded only to the 'efforts at self-cleansing' that the commandos were supposed to set in motion;[42] and on the other, in a communication to the HSSPFs of 2 July, in which he informed them about the 'most important instructions I have given to the security police and SD Einsatzgruppen and Einsatzkommandos'.[43]

In the 2 July letter he stated clearly: 'All of these are to be executed', and there followed a list—'Comintern officials (and professional communist politicians) [,] the senior, middle-ranking and radically inclined lower-ranking officials of the party, the Central Committee, the regional and district committees [,] people's commissars [,] Jews in party and state posts [,] other radical elements (saboteurs, propagandists, snipers, assassins, agitators, etc.).'

The 'all' at the beginning and the 'etc.' at the end of the list, as well as the fact that in this instruction Heydrich also emphasized that the 'attempts of anti-communist and also anti-Jewish circles at self-cleansing in the territories to be occupied [. . .] were not to be impeded'—on the contrary, they were to be promoted, 'though invisibly'[44]—reveal that the scope of those to be executed was set very wide. The formulation 'all [. . .] Jews in party and state posts' was similarly only code for the instruction to kill an extremely vaguely defined Jewish elite, consisting first and foremost of men. It was largely left to the commandos' own initiative to determine the details of who was to be counted as part of this elite.

After the June conference at the Wewelsburg Himmler went to Berlin, where he had numerous meetings. He met, amongst others, Hermann Fegelein, who reported to him that the two SS cavalry regiments were ready for deployment; Jüttner, the head of the SS Leadership Main Office; and Gauleiter Alfred Meyer, Rosenberg's most important colleague in the setting up of the Ministry for the East. He also visited Hitler several times in the Reich Chancellery.[45] At this time of high excitement he was regularly restored to fitness between appointments by his masseur Felix Kersten.[46]

On 18 June, at around midday, however, he interrupted his Berlin duties and flew to Bavaria in order to spend the following day with his wife and daughter in his home in Gmund. Before the start of the great struggle he

Ill. 23. The Himmlers on 19 June 1941, two days before the outbreak of the war with the Soviet Union.

wanted once more, even if only briefly, to relax: private photographs have survived showing the Himmlers on this beautiful summer day in the wonderful mountain scenery around Lake Tegern—picking flowers.

By lunchtime on 20 June Himmler was back in the Reich Chancellery and had a meeting in the afternoon with Jeckeln. The next day he met Daluege and had lunch again with Hitler and others. The following morning the attack on the Soviet Union began. Himmler had a considerable fighting force among the invading armies: as well as the Einsatzgruppen, the order-police squads, and the troops of the Command Staff, his three Waffen-SS divisions, the police division (incorporated in 1942 into the Waffen-SS), and the 'Leibstandarte' division all took part in the invasion.

Phase 1: Executions of Jewish men

On 25 June Himmler took his special train 'Heinrich' to Hitler's headquarters near Rastenburg in East Prussia. On 30 June he set off through occupied

Lithuanian territory; Heydrich accompanied his Reichsführer on this train journey, first to Grodno and then to Augustowo. In Grodno Himmler and Heydrich found that, although the town had been occupied the week before, not a single member of the security police or the SD was there, which provoked Himmler to reprimand the commando leader and admonish him in future to demonstrate 'the greatest flexibility in tactical troop deployment'.[47]

In Augustowo they came across a commando of the Gestapo base at Tilsit that had already made a start on 'punishment campaigns' in the wake of the advancing Wehrmacht. Himmler and Heydrich approved of these 'comprehensively', as the Tilsit Gestapo reported to the Reich Security Main Office.[48] Three days later the Tilsit commando shot over 300 people, mainly Jewish civilians.[49] The next day, already back in his headquarters in East Prussia, Himmler met Göring, and on 3 July he had a meeting with the chief of his Command Staff, Kurt Knoblauch, and with Jüttner, head of the Leadership Main Office. Two days later, on Saturday, he inspected the troops of the 1st SS Cavalry Regiment.[50]

On 8 July he returned to the newly occupied territories, this time accompanied by the chief of the order police, Daluege. The same day he arrived in Bialystok,[51] where at a meeting of SS and police officers—at least according to what von dem Bach-Zelewski, who was also present, said after the war—he made statements to the effect that, 'as a matter of principle any Jew' was 'to be regarded as a partisan'.[52] The way in which this order was passed down through the levels of the hierarchy in the days that followed can be reconstructed: on 9 July, speaking to members of the police regiment Centre, Daluege issued a call for 'Bolshevism finally to be eradicated',[53] and on 11 July the commander of the police regiment Centre in Bialystok passed on the order of the HSSPF for special assignments (z.b.V.) attached to the commanding officer of the rear army area Centre, that all Jewish men between the ages of 17 and 45 'caught' looting were to be executed.[54] This gave carte blanche for mass murder: in the middle of July two battalions of the regiment were responsible for a massacre that claimed the lives of about 3,000 Jewish men.[55]

On the way back from Bialystok Himmler, now accompanied by Heydrich, once more stopped off in Grodnow. Both were supplied with evidence to satisfy them that the murder commandos had made up for the passivity for which they had been criticized on 30 June. 'In the first days in Grodnow and Lida initially only 96 Jews were liquidated,' a report from

Einsatzgruppe B read. 'I gave the order that operations here were to be considerably stepped up. [...] The necessary liquidations will be guaranteed under all circumstances.'[56] Himmler's tours of inspection and personal interventions on the spot in the first weeks of the war therefore did much to initiate and intensify the mass murder of Jewish civilians.

As Christian Gerlach has shown, in his indispensable study of German occupation policy in Byelorussia, senior-ranking SS men were demonstrably present at almost all sizeable 'operations' (*Aktionen*) in the first weeks of the war against the Soviet Union: if neither Himmler, Heydrich nor Daluege was there, their place was frequently taken where the murders were committed by the responsible officer for the region, von dem Bach-Zelewski, Nebe, or the chief of the police regiment Centre, Max Montua. Himmler's inspection tours were therefore an integral part of a system of leadership in which the senior leaders ensured that the overall policy was adhered to through checks and constant intervention on the ground.

Almost all the security police and SD Einsatzkommandos, and also a whole series of police battalions, had begun in June to shoot Jewish men of military age en masse, hundreds or thousands at a time. These executions were carried out on a variety of pretexts: 'reprisals', punishing 'looters', combating 'partisans'. The diverse units followed a set pattern, even if individual murder operations showed variations: some units set the upper age-limit of the male victims higher than others; in some places the entire male population in a particular age-group was murdered, in other places it was 'only' some, and here again to varying extents. The leaders of the units therefore quite clearly had a certain amount of room for manoeuvre. When the order was passed down it had, of course, been clear that initiative and individual judgement were required.

And mass murders committed by the units were not the whole story. In numerous places they succeeded, as Heydrich had ordered, in provoking 'efforts at self-cleansing', in other words, pogroms carried out by the local population. In the territories occupied by the Soviets between 1939 and 1941, above all in Lithuania, Latvia, and the western Ukraine, there is evidence for pogroms in a total of at least sixty places, and estimates suggest there were at least 12,000 victims, possibly 24,000.[57]

On 13 July in Stettin (Szczecin) Himmler inspected 200 members of the Waffen-SS who had been transferred to the Finnish front to reinforce the SS combat group North, which had not only suffered heavy losses in the first days of the war but had been unsuccessful in an attack on and in the ensuing counter-attack from the Red Army. The unit was showing widespread signs of disintegrating. Himmler admonished the men and then spoke to the twenty-five commanders as a separate group. They were, he explained, engaged in a struggle with a 'nation of 180 million, a hotch-potch of races and peoples whose very names are unpronounceable and who are physically built in such a way that they can be shot en masse without mercy', 'animals', in other words. 'This nation has been united by Jews in a religion, a world-view, called Bolshevism [...].'[58]

'Police and political security matters'?

On 16 July, around three weeks after the beginning of the war to which Himmler attached such high hopes, Hitler in his headquarters made the essential decisions concerning the structure of future occupation policy in the east. Present were Göring, Keitel, Rosenberg, and Bormann—not Himmler, and the outcome of that meeting was to be a disappointment to him as well. Hitler ruled[59] that at the end of hostilities the administration of the occupied territories should pass to civilian agencies: to Reich commissariats under the newly appointed Reich Minister for the Occupied Eastern Territories, Alfred Rosenberg.[60] Rosenberg was, admittedly, instructed to observe the jurisdictions of other central agencies—and that meant in particular Himmler's responsibilities, which were defined by Hitler as 'providing security in the newly occupied territories through the police'. To this end Himmler was allowed to appoint Higher SS and Police Leaders and SS and Police Leaders.[61]

Himmler's ambitions, however, as we have seen, extended far beyond this. On 10 June he had asked Lammers for control over 'police *and political* security matters', and thereby provoked Rosenberg's objection.[62] Two days after the outbreak of the war he had gone further and given Konrad Meyer, his head of planning, three weeks in which to incorporate Soviet territories into the planning already in train for German settlement policy in the east ('General Plan East').[63] On 11 July Himmler gave the Coordination Centre for Ethnic Germans the responsibility for producing a survey of 'ethnic Germans' in the occupied Soviet Union, an activity that was to proceed in close consultation with the Einsatzgruppen.[64] On 15 July Meyer's outline plan was on his desk. The fact that the following day Hitler denied him the central role he craved in the political reorganization of the east was a bitter personal defeat. At the same time, this day marks the commencement of a decisive change in Himmler's policy, a change that can be explained by his practice of not allowing setbacks to divert him from doggedly pursuing the goals he had set himself.

First of all, it is striking that he stubbornly persisted in acting as if the responsibilities he had been given as Reich Settlement Commissar in October 1939 for the 'consolidation of the ethnic German nation' also applied in the occupied Soviet territories, a claim vigorously contested by both Rosenberg and Göring.[65] In concrete terms, Himmler made use of his police jurisdiction to initiate settlement measures in the occupied eastern territories, thus proving once again his ability when necessary to make very effective combined use of the individual parts of his empire.

Three days after his setback he travelled to Lublin, where he gave Globocnik a series of orders that underlined the significance of the Lublin district as the future hub of the 'ethno-political' reordering of the east. In the town of Lublin, according to Himmler, a large complex of camps was to be set up, and in the area around Zamosc preparations were to be made for the settlement of ethnic Germans. In addition, he instructed Globocnik to create a network of police and SS posts in the newly occupied territories stretching out from Lublin.[66]

Himmler's stubborn attempts to exploit his police responsibilities as the basis for a 'new ethnic order' in the east were not, however, restricted to settlement measures. And this brings us to the real change he effected from the middle of July 1941. The task of 'consolidating the ethnic German nation' that Hitler had given him in October 1939 included not only the 'creation through resettlement of new German settlement areas', but also the 'elimination of the damaging influence of [. . .] alien elements in the population'. In Poland Himmler had attempted to put this latter aspect into practice by beginning mass deportations of Poles and Jews from the annexed territories. Yet this huge resettlement programme, designed to create space for ethnic Germans, had in essence failed: the planned numbers were far from being attained, the expulsions had led to considerable chaos in the General Government, and the majority of ethnic Germans were still stuck in resettlement camps.

The conclusion Himmler drew from these experiences was that 'ethnic cleansing' in the east should be tackled right away and not, as originally assumed, after the war. As a first step to 'neutralize' the 'alien elements in the population' whole regions were now to be made 'free of Jews' through mass executions and the ghettoization of those who could still be exploited as slave labour.

At the back of this was a gigantic programme of expulsion, resettlement, and extermination, to which some 30 million people in the east (this was the extent of the operation planned at the outbreak of the war, according to von dem Bach-Zelewski) were to fall victim. Yet such a programme of annihilation directed at the indigenous population as a whole was a complete pipe-dream in the summer of 1941. It was possible neither simply to shoot 30 million people nor to cut them off from any food supplies and let them starve. From the perspective of the conquerors, however, these reservations did not apply to the Jews, a much smaller population group: it was claimed they could be clearly distinguished 'racially' from the rest of the population, and as allegedly strong supporters of the communist regime they were said to be the most dangerous enemy of the Nazi leadership and so must be dealt with first. Himmler had, in any case, set in motion a systematic policy of discrimination and terror against the Jews, who were concentrated over-whelmingly in the towns, as part of his police duties. He needed only to extend and step up these measures to turn 'providing security through the police' into a policy of ethnic extermination. The Jews' homes and posses-sions were a very welcome source of booty into the bargain, as they provided valuable resources that could be used to make further resettlement measures considerably easier. By 'neutralizing' the Jews while the war was still in progress, Himmler calculated, he stood out as the man with the necessary brutality and the requisite means at his disposal to turn the regime's overblown notions of a new ethnic order for the entire 'eastern area' into reality.

In addition, the fact that in August 1941 Himmler began to connect his utopian ideas of a new order in the east with the 'neutralization', the systematic murder, of the Soviet Jews was in harmony with the general policy of the Nazi regime towards the Jews in this critical period. For in August 1941 Hitler was attuning the regime to the idea of fighting the war in future under the banner of a 'war against the Jews'. As relations with the United States, which sooner or later would enter the war, deteriorated, the propaganda machine intensified its anti-Semitic rabble-rousing: now the Germans were no longer fighting only 'Jewish Bolshevism'—this old Nazi propaganda slogan had been promptly and extensively reactivated at the time of the invasion of the Soviet Union—but also a comprehensive 'Jewish world conspiracy', held together, allegedly, by an incipient coalition of communism and capitalism. From the end of August onwards the propaganda machine had been spreading appropriate catchphrases on a huge scale. In this context the regime also stepped up its persecution of German Jews. In September they not only had to suffer new types of discrimination, but in the wake of a decision from Hitler of 18 August[67] they were obliged to wear badges identifying them as Jews and thus, according to propaganda, be made visible as 'the enemy within'. In August the assumption among the Nazi leadership was still that the German Jews would be deported to the east only a few months later, after the generally anticipated victory over the Soviet Union.[68]

Against this background Himmler could rest assured that any initiative to radicalize anti-Jewish policy would be favourably received by his 'Führer'. The extension of the mass executions in the Soviet Union was not a case of Himmler acting independently, but rather an anticipation of what Hitler had in any case planned for the period after the war: the physical extermination of the Jews, whatever form that might take. And so Himmler made no bones about his radicalization of Jewish policy in the east. The reports from the Einsatzgruppen were being read daily by a large number of people at the Berlin headquarters, and conveyed a vivid impression of Himmler's anti-Jewish extermination policy. They were also shown to Hitler. According to a radio telegram from the Gestapo chief Müller to the Einsatzgruppen: 'Regular reports on the work of the Einsatzgruppen in the east are to be sent to the Führer.'[69]

Phase II: Women and children

With Hitler's instruction of 16 July and the decision in principle it indicated about the structure of the civil administration, the moment had come for Himmler, in spite of his clear setback, to deploy the three SS brigades of his Commando Staff for their actual purpose—for those 'special tasks I shall give them', as he had announced in his order of 21 May.[70]

Himmler probably discussed the planned deployment of the SS cavalry units[71] with von dem Bach-Zelewski as early as 8 July, when he visited Bialystok. With the orders of 19 and 22 July—in other words, immediately after Hitler had given him control of 'providing security in the newly occupied eastern territories through the police' and had significantly enhanced the status of the HSSPFs—Himmler placed the two cavalry regiments, which were to be concentrated into one cavalry brigade at the beginning of August, under von dem Bach-Zelewski's command and the 1st Infantry Brigade under the command of the HSSPF Russia South, Jeckeln.[72] On 21 July Himmler had a meeting with the commanding officer of the rear area of army South, Karl von Roques, presumably in order to discuss the activities of Jeckeln's 1st Infantry Brigade within von Roques's sphere of responsibility.[73]

Himmler personally planned the first deployment of the SS cavalry, which was to be in the Pripet marshes. He travelled there via Kaunas and Riga. On 29 July he flew to Kaunas, looked round the city, and spoke with Hinrich Lohse, the new Reich Commissar for the Ostland (the Baltic States and Byelorussia). On 31 July he continued his journey to Riga, where amongst other things he inspected the central prison and its new inmates. The following day he met Lohse again and also the HSSPF Hans Adolf Prützmann.[74] Immediately after Himmler's visit the latter's men extended the mass murders of Jews in Lithuania and Latvia. From 5 August Einsatz-kommando 3, as the detailed report of its leader, Karl Jäger, shows, began with the help of Lithuanians to shoot men, women, and children indiscriminately.[75] Einsatzkommando 2, stationed in Latvia, also began in August to shoot women and children; in September 18,000 people had been murdered.[76] Einsatzkommando 'Tilsit' likewise began, at the end of July or beginning of August, to shoot women and children in considerable numbers.[77]

On the afternoon of 31 July Himmler flew from Riga to Baranowicze, where he gave the final order for the creation of the Cavalry Brigade led by Hermann Fegelein from the two regiments. He then discussed with von dem Bach-Zelewski the SS cavalrymen's continuing 'pacification' campaign.[78] For this deployment Himmler had already issued the brigade with special 'Guidelines for Cavalry Units Combing Marshlands': 'As, nationally speaking, the population is hostile, racially and humanly inferior, or even, as is often the case in marsh areas, composed of criminals who have settled there, all those who are under suspicion of helping the partisans are to be shot, women and children are to be deported, livestock and food are to be confiscated. The villages are to be burnt to the ground.'[79]

On his visit to Baranowicze on 31 July Himmler radicalized this order, as can be inferred from a radio message of 1 August from the 2nd Cavalry Regiment: 'Express command of the RFSS. All Jews must be shot. Jewish women to be herded into the marshes.'[80] The equivalent order delivered by the commander of the cavalry battalion of the 1st Cavalry Regiment on 1 August was equally brutal : 'No Jewish male to remain alive, no remnant of any family in the villages.'[81]

If the wording of these orders is a guide, Himmler had obviously instructed that all Jewish men were to be shot and also that the women were to be subjected to violence, though not explicitly that the latter should be murdered. The same pattern is followed repeatedly: the gradual inclusion of new groups of victims of the shootings was not the response to a single and absolutely unequivocal order from Himmler, but rather there was a longer process in which the unit leaders were progressively accustomed to their own atrocities, indeed positively educated into being mass murderers.

Future developments show also that Himmler's order was understood in very different ways. The 1st Cavalry Regiment had been murdering thousands of Jewish men, women, and children indiscriminately since 3 August in Chomsk, Motol, Telechany, Swieta Wola, Hancewicze, and other places.[82] On 11 August the cavalry detachment of the regiment reported 6,504 victims; in fact the number was most probably closer to 11,000.[83] By contrast, the cavalry battalion of the 2nd SS Cavalry Regiment shot almost exclusively Jewish men: according to information given by the regiment, between 5 and 11 August a total of 6,526, in fact presumably around 14,000.[84] Apart from this the regiment reported: 'Herding woman and children into the marshes was not as successful as it should have been, for the marshes were not so deep that people sank into them.'[85] Was that an attempt deliberately to misinterpret Himmler's command?

In the weeks to come the Cavalry Brigade continued its 'cleansing operation' almost continuously and murdered thousands of Jews, and from the beginning of September onwards even the members of the 2nd Regiment began shooting women and children.[86] In fact, in August the Cavalry Brigade had most probably already murdered more than 25,000 Jews.[87] This then triggered the spread of the mass murders to the whole Jewish population in the rear area of the Army Group Centre, in which von dem Bach-Zelewski as HSSPF had control.

In the meantime Himmler had long since returned from the occupied eastern territories: on 3 August he had flown to Berlin and on 5 August had set off for his headquarters in Rastenburg, where a series of meetings took place in the following days.[88] From Rastenburg Himmler observed above all the development of the mass murders committed against the Soviet civilian population in the area of HSSPF Russia South, Jeckeln, whom he had put in command of the 1st SS Infantry Brigade for this purpose. Jeckeln and his brigade were supposed to play the same central role on the southern section of the front assumed by von dem Bach-Zelewski with the help of the Cavalry Brigade further north. The 1st Infantry Brigade began as early as the end of July also to shoot Jewish women, doing so as part of a 'cleansing operation' that took place between 27 and 30 July in the Zwiahel area.[89] The brigade reported that as a result of this 'operation' it had executed 800 people, 'Jews and Jewesses aged 16 to 60'.[90] After this mass murder brigade units carried out further 'operations', in the course of which they murdered an estimated 7,000 Jewish men, women, and children.[91] Himmler was not satisfied. He ordered Jeckeln to his headquarters on 12 August and appeared 'indignant' about the latter's activity, which still left something to be desired,[92] whereupon Jeckeln increased the number of murders.[93]

At the end of August the series of mass murders organized by Jeckeln reached its peak. In a hitherto unprecedented massacre, 23,600 people,[94] the vast majority Jews who had been deported across the border by the Hungarian authorities in July–August as 'troublesome foreigners',[95] were murdered within three days in Kamenets-Podolsk. Massacres followed in Berdychiv[96] and Shitomir;[97] Jeckeln also played a leading role in the massacre of the Kiev Jews at Babi Yar, in which 33,771 Jews were reportedly executed at the end of September.[98] This wave of mass murders gave the decisive impetus that led to commandos under Jeckeln's jurisdiction (Einsatzgruppe C and several police battalions that had in part already participated in Jeckeln's 'operations') also beginning a blanket extermination of the Jewish population in the summer.[99]

By the beginning of October 1941 Einsatzkommando 6 belonging to Einsatzgruppe C was the only one that had not yet executed any Jewish women. That was to change after Himmler paid a visit to the unit on 3 October in Krivoy Rog, whereupon members of Einsatzkommando 6 shot the Jewish women there also, the city being reported on 20 October as being 'free of Jews'.[100]

On 14 October Himmler set off again for Baranowicze, this time with a large entourage. Flying with him were, amongst others, Wolff, Prützmann, and also the Reich theatre designer Benno von Arent, who had the rank of SS-Oberführer, the 'Führer's cameraman', Lieutenant Walter Frentz (who was received into the SS during this journey), and a further SS photo reporter. The reason why they were there was to become clear in the days that followed. On arriving in Baranowicze, where von dem

Bach-Zelewski apprised Himmler of the results to date of the 'cleansing operation', the party of notables proceeded the same day to Minsk and took up residence in the Lenin House.[101]

The next morning an execution was on Himmler's itinerary—'partisans and Jews', as his work diary noted. The mass shooting took place outside Minsk: squads of eight to ten order or security policemen, members of Einsatzkommando 8, took turns to shoot the victims, who included women. There are strong indications that Frentz filmed the execution; an entry for 19 November in Himmler's diary reads: 'Dined on the train. Newsreel and film of Minsk.'[102]

Watching the execution, Himmler seems to have assumed the pose of a neutral and businesslike observer. A lieutenant of the criminal police in charge of one of the execution squads gave the following testimony after the war: 'After the first salvo Himmler came right up to me and looked personally into the ditch, remarking that there was still someone alive. He said to me, "Lieutenant, shoot that one!"' The man obeyed. 'Himmler stood beside me while I did it [...] For Himmler and his entourage the whole thing was simply a spectacle.'[103]

Afterwards Himmler made a speech to the members of the firing-squads, in which he said that although the shootings were a heavy burden for the marksmen they were nevertheless necessary in 'the war of ideologies'. On this occasion, according to the testimony of Otto Bradfisch, the leader of Einsatzkommando 8, Himmler stated that the Führer had issued a command concerning the shooting of all Jews that must be obeyed at all costs.[104] There is nothing to corroborate this statement. If it is indeed accurate then it took several weeks more for the new order to reach all the murder squads, a fact that makes it unlikely that Himmler, above and beyond his comment to Bradfisch at Minsk, was already announcing openly that all Jews were to be murdered, as was asserted in post-war testimonies.[105]

Before lunch at the Lenin House the party visited a prisoner-of-war camp, and in the afternoon, after a drive through the ghetto, Novinki hospital, a psychiatric institution north-west of Minsk. Five weeks later a German police commando murdered 120 patients by gassing them. Everything points to Himmler, still under the immediate impression of the execution, having given instructions for this murder when he inspected the institution on 15 August, apparently as part of the search for a less bloody method of murder.[106]

The next day, culture, or properly speaking cultural looting, was on Himmler's itinerary. On the occasion of a visit to a Minsk museum he gave Arent the task of sifting the city's art collections for possible exhibits to be sent back to Germany. On the morning of 16 August Himmler flew back to Rastenburg. That evening he met the former administrative head of Lebensborn, Standartenführer Guntrum Pflaum, whom he had given authority on 11 July 'to receive ethnic German children of good and unmixed blood' in the Volga German republic. Himmler now extended this task 'to the entire occupied territories of the European Soviet Union.'[107] In August the Main Office of the Reich Commissariat for the Consolidation of the Ethnic German Nation set up a branch office in Riga which was to take care of unresolved questions relating to the property of ethnic Germans.[108] In July Himmler had already had the Sonderkommando R (Russia) set up under Brigadeführer Horst Hoffmeyer to seek out ethnic Germans still living in the Soviet Union.[109]

Himmler was therefore continuing his efforts to extend his sphere of influence as Settlement Commissar to the occupied Soviet territories. His order, discussed above, to Globocnik to pursue an independent settlement policy in the east, and his attempt to make Lublin the base for it, were projects that also belong in this context. For Himmler regarded the mass murders of Jews, to which he devoted so much attention during these weeks, as an integral part of a much more broadly based policy of ethnic reordering.

On 17 August Himmler had lunch with Hitler. In the weeks following he remained almost without a break in his own headquarters in East Prussia, where he had numerous meetings with Hitler and also had discussions with Ribbentrop, Lammers, Göring, Heydrich, Daluege, and others.[110] By the beginning of September he had finally got his way over a decisive matter: Hitler declared that the scope of the responsibilities of the Reich Settlement Commissar should now include the occupied eastern territories.[111] Yet the Reichsführer-SS was still not satisfied: on 18 September Heydrich sent a draft decree to Lammers which provided for more powers to be given to the SS and police, as well as to Himmler in his capacity as Settlement Commissar both in the General Government and the Protectorate as well as in the territories controlled by the heads of the civil administration (in other words, in Lorraine, Alsace, Luxembourg, Carinthia–Carniola, Lower Styria, the occupied Netherlands, and Norway). The SS and police were now to be responsible for 'control of security' in 'internal political' matters, and no longer only for 'police' matters in these occupied territories. In addition, Himmler wanted authority over the Minister for the East, Rosenberg. Lammers was to indicate to Himmler several weeks later, however, that such formal extension of his competency was not possible for the time being.[112]

At a meeting on 4 October 1941 representatives of the Ministry for the East, led by Gauleiter Meyer, attempted to gain acceptance for the view that the responsibilities Hitler had just confirmed as being Himmler's related only to the 'implementation' of settlement policy, while planning fell properly to the Ministry for the East. Heydrich rejected this interpretation, however, and instead suggested that the central offices and the institutions subordinated to them on various levels in the occupied eastern territories should coordinate their activities better.[113]

On the same day that Heydrich sent Lammers his extensive demands, Himmler himself set about enlarging his role as Settlement Commissar by issuing instructions on the spot. On 18 September he embarked on further 'travels in the Ostland', accompanied by Heydrich, Wolff, and others: he flew to Riga, went on the following day to Mitau (Jelgava) and Reval (Tallinn), then to Dorpat and Pleskau (Pskov), returning to Rastenburg on 21 September. He used this opportunity to issue various instructions about the deportation of Russians from Estonia, and gave his HSSPF in Riga, Prützmann, the task of examining whether those children whose parents had been deported by the Soviets in 1940–1 were 'capable of Germanization'.[114]

On 24 September Himmler took part in a discussion at the Führer's headquarters at which Hitler appointed Heydrich Deputy Reich Protector in Prague, and thereby created the precondition for a more radical policy towards the Jews in the weeks to follow.[115] On 30 September he set off on yet another tour of inspection, this time to the Ukraine. On 2 October, only two days after the Babi Yar massacre, he met Jeckeln in Kiev and then spent three days in Krivoy Rog. There he visited Einsatzkommando 6, which, as described above, began immediately afterwards also to shoot Jewish women.[116]

At the request of the Wehrmacht, Himmler decided on 4 October—he was still in Krivoy Rog—that Sonderkommando Lange, which since 1940 had been murdering Jews by means of gassing vehicles, should be brought by plane to Novgorod in order to kill the patients in three psychiatric hospitals there, because the accommodation was urgently needed for troops.[117] On the

Ill. 24. Himmler used his visits to the newly conquered territories to enquire into a whole range of matters. As usual he was interested in anything and everything. This photo from the year 1941 shows him, together with Karl Wolff, inspecting a captured Soviet tank.

same day Himmler paid a visit to Nicolajev, where Einsatzgruppe D was based, and apparently also to Cherson, as a note indicates.[118]

At the end of September—in other words, a few days before his visit— Einsatzgruppe D had murdered the inhabitants of the ghetto in Nikolajev, about 5,000 men, women, and children.[119] Now Himmler addressed the members of Einsatzgruppe D, calling the shootings a difficult task but a necessary one.[120] Presumably only a few days later Sonderkommando 11a executed virtually all the Jewish inhabitants of Cherson.[121] With these mass murders Einsatzgruppe D finally began murdering all Jewish members of the civilian population in their territory, and it is evident that Himmler's visit brought about this radicalization.

On 5 October he was back again at the Führer's headquarters in Rastenburg, meeting Hitler in the evening and entertaining him with his recent impressions of the journey: he reported to his 'Führer' that the inhabitants of Kiev had made an unfavourable impression on him and a good '80–90% of them' could be 'dispensed with'.[122]

On 7 October, his forty-first birthday, Himmler held court: Daluege, Heydrich, Wolff, Jüttner, Grawitz, Knoblauch, and many others put on a reception to congratulate him. In the evening he gave a dinner attended by many of the above and also by Ribbentrop and Lammers.[123] On 13 October he discussed the 'Jewish question' with Globocnik in the latter's district of Lublin (we shall return to this), on 14 October he had a lengthy interview with Heydrich,[124] and on 23 October he visited the slave-labour camp in Mogilev. It was at this time that plans were made to extend this camp significantly; only a few days before, on 18 October, the deportation of Jews from Reich territory had begun, and on 8 November the first of these transports was due to reach Minsk, which lay about 150 kilometres west of Mogilev. In mid-November the construction of a large crematorium for the camp in Mogilev was commissioned, just as at the other destinations of deported German Jews, in Chelmno and Riga, preparations were made to build mass extermination complexes (which we shall also return to in more detail). On the day of Himmler's visit to the Mogilev camp 279 people were executed there. Four days previously the ghetto had been liquidated; most of the inhabitants had been shot.[125] On 24 October Himmler made a lightning visit from Mogilev to Smolensk and met the senior commander of the Army Group Centre, von Bock. During their meeting the shootings of Jews in the army group's area were discussed, according to the testimony of von dem Bach-Zelewski, who was also present.[126]

On 25 October Himmler returned to his headquarters, where he had a meeting with Globocnik.[127] That evening Himmler and Heydrich were with Hitler. Records of Hitler's monologues give us an indication of the topics discussed. After recalling his 'prophecy' of 30 January 1939, the dictator stated: 'This race of criminals has the two million dead of the World War on its conscience, and now it has hundreds of thousands more. Let nobody say to me: We can't send them into the swamps! Who's worrying about our people? It's good if the fear that we are exterminating the Jews goes before us.'[128]

Around three weeks later, on 15 November 1941, Himmler had a meeting with Rosenberg in Prague to discuss cooperation in 'police and settlement matters'; the encounter was made necessary by Rosenberg's complaint of 14 October. The upshot of this discussion was an agreement signed by both men on 19 November establishing that the HSSPFs and the SSPFs should answer 'personally and directly' to the Reich and general commissars. The territorial commissars had 'authority in specialist matters' over them.[129] The question of whether the 'treatment of the Jewish problem' was a 'police matter' or had to be resolved in 'the context of overall policy' (a clear indication that Himmler's radical action had strained his authority as police chief to the point that Rosenberg was justified in perceiving a threat to his own political leadership in the east) was to be solved by means of 'dual accountability': The person responsible for 'Jewish questions' on the HSSPF's staff would have the same responsibility in the Reich commissar's office.[130] On 16 November, the following day, both came to report to Hitler that they had reached agreement over the most important bones of contention. In reality they had done little more than use set phrases to express a compromise that in the following months Himmler would increasingly interpret to his own advantage.[131]

The truly astounding amount of travelling Himmler did in these weeks and months reveals that, after being passed over during discussions of occupation policy, he did everything he could from the end of July to the end of September/beginning of October to step up the mass executions of Jews in the Soviet Union (which his murder units had already begun under the pretext of their duties as 'security police'), to the point of turning them into a comprehensive genocide: in all the territories where his Einsatzgruppen were operating the decisive impetus to move to the systematic murder of the Jewish civilian population came in every case from him personally. 'I decided', he was to explain on 6 October 1943 to the SS-Gruppenführer, 'in this case also to find a clear solution. I did not see myself as justified in eradicating the men—by that I mean in killing them or having them killed—only to let their children grow up to avenge them by killing our sons and grandsons.'[132] And on 24 May he expressed himself in almost exactly the same terms in Sonthofen to the Wehrmacht generals: 'I did not consider myself justified—as far as Jewish women and children were concerned—in allowing children to grow up to be the avengers who would kill our fathers and our grandchildren. I would have seen that as cowardly. As a result the issue was solved uncompromisingly.'[133] The formulations Himmler chose in these addresses indicate that he really did take the decision to murder the women and children on his own initiative— secure in his confidence that such actions reflected the intentions of the highest authority, those of Hitler himself.

His strategy of using a campaign of bloody ethnic cleansing to extend what at first were responsibilities solely for police matters into the task of enforcing a comprehensive 'ethnic policy' in the newly occupied territories was in the end successful. This method was not new: in the Protectorate and in occupied Poland he had already made use of the brute force of the security police to advance his ambitions in the field of 'settlement policy'. Himmler's technique of meshing his very diverse spheres of responsibility in the most varied policy areas had proved effective yet again, though with fateful consequences.

20

From Mass Murder to the 'Final Solution'

From the autumn of 1941 onwards the Nazi regime began gradually to extend the mass murder of the Jews to the whole of Europe. The so-called territorial plans for 'solving the Jewish question' had already envisaged deporting the European Jews to Madagascar, an area which lacked adequate facilities for survival, and so to destroy them there. From the beginning of 1941 the leadership was determined to achieve this aim within the territory of the Soviet Union that was scheduled for conquest, in other words, in the area where, since summer 1941, Himmler's commandos had been engaged in a campaign of mass murder of the local Jewish population. It was inevitable that the Jews who were being deported to 'the east' from autumn 1941 onwards would be caught up in this murderous policy, and this evidently created a situation in which the objectives as far as the 'final solution' was concerned became even more radical. Now it was no longer simply a question of letting the Jews who had been deported die out over the medium or long term, but rather of 'eliminating' them completely through mass murder and doing so during the course of the war.

The widespread view that this process resulted from a single order from Hitler does not do justice to its complexity. There was in fact a consensus within the leadership of the regime, and also among numerous senior functionaries in the occupied territories, that the 'Jewish question' should be 'solved' in a murderous fashion. But the realization of this aim occurred through the interplay of guidelines from above and initiatives from below that was characteristic of the regime.

Three elements can be determined that were essential for setting in motion the process of systematic mass murder: the preparation and actual commencement of deportations 'to the east'; the expansion of the murder campaigns beyond the occupied Soviet territory to embrace particular regions of east and south-east Europe; and finally the planning and construction of sites for mass extermination in occupied Poland. During the first months of 1942, out of these elements Himmler and Heydrich fashioned step by step a programme that envisaged the extermination of the majority of European Jews before the end of the year.[1] Himmler played a key role in this process: continually referring back to Hitler, he issued orders in the latter's name, made suggestions, encouraged initiatives.

In August 1941 Hitler was still insisting that they could start deporting Jews to the occupied eastern territories only after Germany had defeated the Soviet Union.[2] However, from the beginning of September he was evidently considering revising this decision. He left the soundings to Himmler. On 2 September, following lunch with Hitler, the Reichsführer-SS discussed the topic 'Jewish question—deportations from the Reich' with Friedrich-Wilhelm Krüger, the Higher SS and Police Leader (HSSPF) in the General Government. However, when he became aware that the General Government could not be used for that purpose, on 4 September he approached Wilhelm Koppe, HSSPF in the Warthegau. Koppe wrote to him on 10 September suggesting they could put '60,000 Jews in the Litzmannstadt [Łódź] ghetto'.[3]

Other people were also raising the issue. On 14 September the Minister for the East, Alfred Rosenberg, proposed to Hitler that they should immediately begin the deportation of the central European Jews that had long been planned, because the previous day the Soviet government had begun to deport the Volga Germans.[4] Two days later Otto Abetz, the German ambassador in Paris, passed on a proposal from his 'Jewish expert' that the Jews from the whole of Europe should be deported to the eastern territories. Himmler responded positively: Jewish prisoners in camps could be deported to the east as long as transport was available.[5] On the same day he discussed the topic 'Jewish question. Settlement of the east' with Ulrich Greifelt, the head of his Staff Main Office for the Consolidation of the Ethnic German Nation, as well as with Konrad Meyer, his chief planning officer for the eastern settlement programme. Moreover, on this same day Abetz met Hitler, who expressed his opinion in the most brutal manner on how his future eastern empire should be organized.[6]

On 17 September Hitler discussed Rosenberg's proposal with Ribbentrop, and on the eighteenth Himmler informed Arthur Greiser, the Reich Governor of the Wartheland, of Hitler's express wish that as soon as possible the Old Reich and the Protectorate should be cleared and freed of Jews from west to east. I am therefore anxious, as a first step, to transport the Jews from the Old Reich and the Protectorate to the eastern territories that the Reich acquired two years ago and to do it if possible this year in order to be able to get rid of them further east next spring. For the winter I intend to put around 60,000 Jews from the Old Reich and the Protectorate in the Litzmannstadt ghetto, which I gather has room to spare.[7]

The reasons for Hitler's decision not to make the deportation of the Jews living in the areas Germany controlled dependent on the ending of the war were complex. The fate of the Volga Germans was only a pretext. In August 1941, as has already been mentioned, Hitler decided in future to fight the war under the slogan of 'a war against the Jews'. In view of the fact that it was looking increasingly likely that America would enter the war, he believed he had found a formula that would explain the impending coalition between communism and capitalism: the 'Jewish world conspiracy' covered both opponents. As a result, from his point of view the European Jews were to be seen as members of the enemy camp, and their deportation was the logical consequence. On 21 September Wilhelm Koeppen[8], the Ministry of the East's liaison official in Hitler's headquarters, noted that 'in the event of America's entry into the war' Hitler was considering 'retaliatory measures against the German Jews because of the way the Volga Germans had been treated'. That the deportations were intended to be understood as a threat to the United States is underlined by the fact that they took place in full view of the public, were commented on in the presence of foreign correspondents in Germany,[9] and received considerable attention in the international press.[10] Since Hitler was completely convinced of the existence of a Jewish world conspiracy, he relied on awareness of the deportations influencing American foreign policy in his favour.

There was also a domestic-policy motive for the deportations. By being carried out in public and placed in context by propaganda, they could be used to denounce and punish the Jews as 'the people who were pulling the strings behind the air raids',[11] while the household goods of the deportees could be donated to the non-Jewish victims of air raids and to other people who were in need who could also be assigned 'Jewish housing'.[12] The calculation behind it was that the numerous beneficiaries of the deportations would thereby make themselves complicit in the Jewish policy. However, there are various indications that the deportation of the central European

Jews was intended right from the beginning to be the first step on the way to a programme involving the deportation of all European Jews.[13]

The background to this was provided by the reaction of the occupiers to the growing resistance in the territory under their control. The German attack on the Soviet Union resulted in the mobilization of resistance to the hated occupation throughout German-occupied Europe. In particular, the communist underground movement gradually overcame the paralysis that had been caused by the Hitler–Stalin pact of August 1939. In the summer and even more in the autumn of 1941 the Germans experienced an increasing number of acts of sabotage and assassinations. As a result they increased their repressive measures.

Thus, the military commander in Serbia had already begun shooting hostages in large numbers in July as a 'reprisal' for acts of resistance.[14] In France such executions took place for the first time on 6 September, and then, on Hitler's instructions, increasingly in October; in Belgium on the 15 and 26 September; and in Norway, after strikes in Oslo, also in the middle of September.[15]

In Norway Reich Commissar Terboven imposed a civil state of emergency on the district of greater Oslo on 10 September 1941. On the same day he asked Himmler whether SS and police jurisdiction could not be extended to the whole of the Norwegian population, in order to prevent 'German justice in the form represented by the Ministry of Justice from taking root here'. Himmler agreed by return of post and, only five days later, transferred judicial responsibility for the Norwegian population to HSSPF Friedrich Rediess. By 17 September, when the new arrangement came into effect, Terboven had achieved his goal.[16]

After the attack on the Soviet Union the commander of the security police and SD in the Netherlands, Wilhelm Harster, ordered mass arrests of communists.[17] On 16 September the OKW issued an order that in general the execution of fifty to 100 communists was to be considered 'appropriate' in reprisal for the assassination of one German soldier.[18]

Heydrich, who had become deputy Reich Protector of Bohemia and Moravia at the end of September, imposed a civil state of emergency immediately following his appointment and introduced courts martial; 404 men and women were shot during the period of the state of emergency.[19]

The resistance movement in Greece carried out a number of assassinations at the end of August and in September.[20] In response, at a meeting with Hitler at the beginning of November, Himmler proposed punishing the large Jewish community in Saloniki and deporting it.[21] In his presentation Himmler made the following points: first, he spoke generally about 'moving people of alien race (Jews)', mentioned the cities of Riga, Reval (Talinn), and Minsk as 'main centres', and finally referred to Saloniki, where he saw a particular 'threat because of the links between Jews and Levantines'. His presentation clearly shows that at this point he already conceived the deportations in terms of a Europe-wide project. Hitler approved Himmler's presentation and assigned him the task of removing the 'Jewish element' from Saloniki. In fact, the deportations of the Jews from Saloniki did not take place until 1943.[22]

Himmler was not alone in wanting to focus reprisals on the Jews. Since the autumn of 1941 the military occupation authorities in Serbia and France had been taking the initiative to concentrate their reprisals on the Jewish minority. In October 1941 the Wehrmacht in Serbia began systematically shooting Jewish men, whom they had targeted for internment since August, as 'a reprisal' for assassinations. By the beginning of November 8,000 Jews had already fallen victim to these murders; their dependants were interned during the winter and murdered in gas trucks the following spring.[23]

The military authorities in France had been arresting thousands of mainly foreign Jews since spring 1941. In December 1941 they no longer responded to assassinations with the shooting of hostages but began to threaten to deport a number of communists and Jews 'to the east'. At first, however, the threat could not be implemented because of the transport situation. The first transport of a thousand hostages to Auschwitz left France only in March 1942.[24]

From the point of view of the Nazi leadership, the intensification and expansion of repressive measures against the Jews was only logical. As they worked on the assumption that communism and the Jews were substantially identical, they imagined that it was the Jewish minorities who were mainly behind the resistance activity even outside eastern Europe. Thus, the fact that the Nazi leadership was so determined to initiate the deportation of the Jews in the late summer of 1941 was no doubt due in part to the spectre of a Jewish–communist resistance movement.

To start with, however, it proved extremely difficult to carry out the deportations. At the beginning of October the plan to place 60,000 Jews in the Łódź ghetto met with strong opposition, not only from Georg Thomas, the head of the Wehrmacht Armaments' Office,[25] but also from the district governor, Friedrich Uebelhoer, putting him in bad odour with

Himmler as a result.[26] According to Uebelhoer, the Łódź ghetto was not a 'decimation ghetto' into which one could pack more and more people, but a 'work ghetto'.[27] The Reich Governor's office eventually worked out a deal with Eichmann reducing the original figure of 60,000 to 25,000 Jews and Gypsies. Himmler had evidently offered Greiser a deal: 'in return' he could murder no fewer than 100,000 indigenous Jews.[28] At the beginning of October the Reich Security Main Office also gave orders that the Riga and Minsk ghettos would have to take 50,000 people between them.[29]

On 6 October Hitler announced to his luncheon guests that all Jews had to be 'removed' from the Protectorate and the Jews from Vienna and Berlin should 'disappear' simultaneously with the 'Protectorate Jews'.[30] Four days later, on 10 October, Heydrich announced the deportation of the first 5,000 Jews from Prague.[31] They could be 'put in [...] the camps with the communist prisoners' in the eastern territories.[32] On the same occasion Heydrich stated that Hitler wanted 'the Jews to be removed from German territory, if possible by the end of the year'.

From the spring of 1941 the government of the General Government was also aiming to have 'their' Jews deported in the course of the year to the Soviet territory that was going to be conquered. However, in mid-October Rosenberg made it clear to Frank that for the time being there was no chance of that happening. As a result the government of the General Government began to contemplate 'solving' the 'Jewish question' in its own territory.[33] That same month Governor-General Frank held a series of meetings in the capitals of the various districts, at which Jewish policy was discussed in distinctly radical terms. It was decided that in future the death penalty would be imposed on people who left ghettos. This inaugurated a manhunt directed at all Jews who were outside the ghettos.[34]

On 1 August 1941 Galicia was incorporated into the General Government. During the weeks prior to its being absorbed the so-called Einsatz-kommando z.b.V ('for special assignments') had launched a campaign of terror in the district, targeted in particular at Jewish men, especially those in prominent positions. After the incorporation of Galicia into the General Government this commando, which in the meantime had been designated as the headquarters of the commander of the security police in Galicia, did not let up in its campaign of terror.[35] From the beginning of October the security police in Galicia applied their murderous policy to all Jews without distinction, as the other Einsatzkommandos were doing at the same time in the Soviet districts. Terrible massacres were taking place week after week.[36]

Thus the practice of systematic mass murder had already reached the General Government at the same time as Rosenberg was giving his negative response to Frank.

In the same period concrete preparations were being made for the systematic murder of Jews in the district of Lublin bordering on Galicia, in other words, the district that in 1939 had been envisaged as forming the 'Jewish reservation' (and in spring 1942 was actually to serve as the reception area for the Jews deported from the Reich). A central role was played by the local SS and police leader Odilo Globocnik, to whom three months earlier Himmler had assigned vital tasks in the future ethnic reorganization of the east. On 13 October Globocnik met his Reichsführer[37] in order to discuss a proposal made two weeks before to restrict the 'influence of the Jews', who must be 'targeted' for the sake of political security'.[38] It can definitely be assumed that Globocnik proposed the construction of a primitive extermination camp and that Himmler gave him permission.[39]

This meeting marked a turning-point. Two or three weeks later, at the beginning of November—in the meantime the 'Jewish question' had been discussed at several government meetings in the General Government—work began on the construction of Belzec extermination camp.[40] The fact that its capacity was initially restricted and that no further extermination camps were built in the General Government before spring 1942 indicates that in autumn 1941 Globocnik had not yet received the order to prepare for the extermination of all the Jews in the General Government. His commission concerned the district of Lublin and possibly also that of Galicia.[41]

On 20 October 1941, a week after his conversation with Globocnik, Himmler, together with Ribbentrop, met a high-level Slovakian delegation at the Führer's headquarters consisting of the President, Josef Tiso, Prime Minister and Foreign Minister Vojtech Tuka, as well as Interior Minister Alexander Mach. Himmler used the occasion to offer the Slovakian leadership the possibility of deporting 'their' Jews to a specially designated territory in the General Government. His proposal received a unanimously positive response.[42] There are indications that, as a result of this meeting, the construction of a second extermination camp was initiated in the district of Lublin–Sobibor.[43]

It was probably during his visit to Minsk in mid-August or shortly thereafter that Himmler issued his instructions to find a method of killing that exposed his men to less stress than the massacres.[44] A few days after Himmler had witnessed a mass shooting there, von dem Bach-Zelewski tried—probably in vain—to get Herbert Lange, the chief of the SS Son-derkommando that for some time had been murdering patients in the Warthegau in gas vans, to give a demonstration in Minsk.[45] Arthur Nebe, the commander of Einsatzgruppe B, who was probably present during Himmler's visit, also initiated experiments. Following attempts to kill mental patients through the use of explosives,[46] patients from asylums in Mogilev and Novinki near Minsk (which Himmler had visited on 15 August) were killed in hermetically sealed rooms through car-exhaust fumes introduced from outside.[47] Finally, the decision was made in favour of using gas vans. Before the end of the year all four Einsatzgruppen were using this method.[48]

From November 1941 onwards gas vans were also deployed in the Warthegau, where from mid-October to 9 November[49] 20,000 Jews ar-rived from the Reich as well as 5,000 Gypsies from the Burgenland, in a total of twenty-five transports. The gas vans were used for murdering indigenous Jews as had been agreed, 'in return' for the deportations. There is evidence for the use of gas vans in Chelmno from 8 December, where in the meantime a base for gas vans had been established.[50] This was the first extermination camp to begin its fearful work, and from January 1942 inhabitants of the Łódź ghetto were being killed in Chelmno.[51]

Alongside the development of gas vans, in the autumn of 1941 gas chambers were being installed in occupied eastern Europe. On 25 October Erhard Weitzel, the desk officer for racial questions in the Ministry of the Eastern Territories, informed Reich Commissar Hinrich Lohse of the con-struction of such a gas chamber: Oberdienstleiter Brack of the Chancellery of the Führer of the NSDAP, the organizer of the 'Euthanasia' programme, would soon be coming to Riga in order to make the necessary prepara-tions.[52] However, the announcement was premature: the murders in Riga were carried out in gas vans, not gas chambers.[53]

In the General Government, as we have seen, the construction of Belzec extermination camp had begun at the start of November and a second extermination camp (Sobibor) may have been prepared at the end of 1941.[54] Brack played a role here. He met Himmler on 14 December and agreed to send his specialists to the General Government to help establish and run the extermination camps. By the summer of 1942 Brack had assigned a total of ninety-two specialists in murder.[55]

Gas was also the murder method that came to be used in Auschwitz concentration camp, which had been considerably enlarged since the start of the war with the Soviet Union. Experiments were carried out with the poison gas Zyklon B, which was already used in the camp for the purposes of disinfection.[56] The first of these occurred at the beginning of September, when 600 Soviet POWs and 250 sick prisoners were killed with Zyklon B in a cellar of Block 11. Later, in the middle of September, 900 Soviet POWs were murdered in the same way in the morgue of the crematorium.[57] By the end of the year it can be assumed that a number of small groups of prisoners—in all likelihood exhausted Jewish forced labourers from Upper Silesia—had fallen victim to the Zyklon B experiments in Auschwitz.[58]

In November 1941 the SS ordered the construction of a large crematorium in Mogilev (around 150 kilometres east of Minsk), which suggests that a large extermination camp was going to be located there. During the early months of 1942, however, the SS decided to expand their extermination facilities in Poland instead. The ovens that were originally planned for Mogilev were sent to Auschwitz in 1942.[59]

This evidence can be summarized as follows: while experiments with Zyklon B were going on in Auschwitz, in the autumn of 1941 the SS began building installations for murdering people with gas near those ghettos that were the destinations for the initial wave of deportations from the Reich—in Riga, near Łódź (Chelmno), in Belzec, probably also in Mogilev, in other words, in the Minsk area. In those regions that were of central importance for the future transfers of population being planned within the context of the racial 'New Order', at the very least the indigenous Jewish population that was 'incapable of work' was to be exterminated. In addition, it was still the intention to deport the remaining Jews to the occupied Soviet territory, a 'final solution' plan which was also based on the physical extermination of the European Jews.

The deportations to Minsk began on 8 November. The day before, on 7 November, the German security police had murdered around 12,000 inhabitants of the Minsk ghetto with the help of indigenous auxiliaries. Eight transports with around 8,000 people arrived in Minsk before the deportations were interrupted at the end of November as a result of the poor transport situation. In view of the approaching winter Himmler had to abandon his original intention of deporting the central European Jews 'to the east'[60] before the end of the year; the plans now ran into the coming spring.[61]

When the deportations to Riga began on 19 November the construction of the KZ that was intended for the German Jews had not even begun.[62]

The first five transports intended for Riga, with around 5,000 people from the Reich, were therefore diverted to Kaunas, where all the deportees were shot by members of Einsatzkommando 3 in Fort IX of the historic fortress.[63] Meanwhile more mass murders were taking place in the Riga ghetto. Between 29 November and 1 December the local HSSPF had around 4,000 Latvian Jews and, on 8 and 9 December, probably more than 20,000 inhabitants of the ghetto shot.[64] While in Soviet custody, Jeckeln stated that he had received the order to liquidate the ghetto from Himmler himself.[65]

Moreover, during the first massacre a thousand Jews who had just been deported from Berlin were shot immediately on their arrival in the early morning of 30 November. However, after this mass murder Himmler called a halt to the murder of Jews from Reich territory for the following months; he had also attempted to prevent the shooting of the Berlin Jews. There is a relevant entry in Himmler's office diary for 30 November which states: 'Jewish transport from Berlin: do not liquidate.'[66] The phone-call, however, came too late; the massacre had already occurred.[67]   Himmler then threatened Jeckeln, in a wireless telegram dated 1 December, that he would 'punish' 'independent actions and contraventions' of 'the guidelines that I have issued or the Reich Security Main Office has given out in my name' concerning how 'the Jews resettled to the Ostland area' are to 'be treated'. At the same time, he summoned Jeckeln and discussed the 'Jewish question' with him on 4 December.[68] The choice of words indicates that Jeckeln had not contravened an express order of Himmler's, but rather had not correctly understood the policy contained in Himmler's 'guidelines' (which we do not know). In contrast to those living in the target areas, the Jews deported from the Reich in the autumn of 1941 were not (yet) to be killed en masse.

It is not surprising that Jeckeln had 'misunderstood' Himmler. In the autumn of 1941 more and more leading Nazis could be heard talking openly about the coming 'annihilation' or 'extermination' of the Jews. At dinner on 25 October Hitler once again recalled his 'prophecy' of 30 January 1939, and told his guests among other things that it was 'a good thing if people are scared by talk that we are exterminating the Jews'.[69] The weekly journal *Das Reich* published a leader article by Goebbels in its issue of 16 November 1941 in which he too recalled Hitler's prophecy of 30 January 1939, and commented: 'We are experiencing the realization of this prophecy and the Jews are meeting a fate that, though hard, is more than merited.' 'World Jewry', according to Goebbels, was now undergoing 'a gradual process of annihilation'. Two days later Rosenberg spoke at a press conference of the impending 'biological elimination of the whole of European Jewry'.[70] It was probably not a coincidence that this statement of Rosenberg's was preceded by a discussion with Himmler on 15 November lasting several hours, which, among other things, was concerned with Jewish policy.[71] Evidently it was the leadership's intention to extend the 'solution of the Jewish question' beyond the murders that had hitherto been limited to specific areas in order to pursue a still more radical 'final solution', even if they were not yet clear about the 'how', the 'where', and the 'when' of a programme of 'annihilation' that was being demanded with increasing stridency. The mood within the top leadership circles can only be described as murderous.

This matched the situation in the occupied territories. It was not a coincidence that a variety of functionaries on the 'periphery' seized the initiative to embark on or advocate mass murders of Jews more or less simultaneously. The deportations were directed to ghettos that were already completely full up, to camps which did not yet exist (Riga, Mogilev), or to key regions that were envisaged as settlement areas for ethnic Germans. In this way 'impossible situations' were being brought about quite systematically.

During these months Himmler behaved as he had in July–August when it came to the inclusion of women and children in the mass murder. The initiative for the intensification of Jewish policy—in this case, the start of the deportations—once again came from Hitler, but Himmler, like other leading functionaries, intuited such a decision, felt his way forward, and acted in advance of it and took on an active role as soon as the time was ripe. The first suggestion that gas might be used as a method of murder appears to have come from him; he took advice from the experts who had acquired relevant experience in the context of the 'Euthanasia' programme; he made suggestions, adopted proposals such as that from Globocnik to establish an extermination camp in Belzec, gave the initiators enough space to develop their ideas, but intervened if his subordinates went too far. Thus the murder process was typically set in motion by the tension between, on the one hand, orders that had been framed in general terms and were intended to be understood intuitively, and on the other, individual initiatives on the part of those who were responsible at the local level. At the same time, the leadership—and that meant very largely Himmler himself—could intervene as required in order to speed up or slow down the process.

On the evening of 7 December Himmler dined at Hitler's headquarters. Afterwards they discussed the most recent world political events, as is clear from Himmler's office diary: 'Japan's declaration of war on America and England.' As a result of Japan's attack on Pearl Harbor, which immediately preceded its declaration of war, the Second World War had finally become a 'world war'.

As an ally of Japan, Hitler was determined to declare war on the United States. From his point of view this was a relatively risk-free undertaking, as America's armed forces would be tied down in the Pacific for years, while in the meantime he could bring his European war to a successful conclusion and in any case could attack American transports to Europe by sea at will. On 12 December, at a special session of the Reichstag, Hitler officially declared war as an ally of Japan, a decision that was enthusiastically received by the Nazi members of parliament, among whom was Reichstag deputy Himmler.[72]

On the following day Himmler took part in a meeting of the Gauleiters and Reich leaders which was held in Hitler's private rooms in the Reich Chancellery. Hitler made some observations about the critical situation on the eastern front, as well as about the situation created by the declaration of war on the United States. As Goebbels noted, he referred once more to his 'prophecy' of 30 January 1939: 'As far as the Jewish question is concerned, the Führer is determined to sort things out. He prophesied to the Jews that if they once more brought about a world war they would bring about their own annihilation. That wasn't just words. The world war has happened; the annihilation of the Jews must be the necessary consequence. We must treat this question without any sentimentality.' To feel any compassion was inappropriate. 'Those responsible for this bloody conflict [...] will have to pay with their lives' for the German losses.[73]

However radical these statements were, they did not differ in tone from the earlier threats of annihilation that Hitler, Rosenberg, and Goebbels had been making during the previous months. Thus they represent neither a change of policy nor a 'fundamental decision' in Jewish policy.[74] They were simply a further demand to extend and speed up the mass murder of the Jews that had been in progress for months. When Himmler had a lengthy meeting with Hitler on 18 December his notepad contained numerous points for discussion, which in the first instance referred to the organization, equipment, deployment, and appointments of the armed SS, but also issues concerning the order police. However, he had noted the 'Jewish question' as the first point, and wrote next to it, evidently as a result of this meeting: 'to be exterminated as partisans.' In fact, since the summer Jews were being murdered en masse in connection with the combating of partisans or, to put it more accurately, under this pretext. It appears that Himmler simply wanted this practice (or this use of words) once again to be confirmed by the highest authority in the regime.[75]

21

The Murder
of the European Jews

Himmler spent Christmas 1941 on the eastern front. On 23 December he set off from Rastenburg for Poltava in the Ukraine to meet Walter von Reichenau, the commander of Army Group South. On the following day he flew to Mariupol, where he visited Colonel-General Ewald von Kleist, the commander of the 1st Panzer Army. From there he continued his journey to Taganrog on Lake Asov to spend Christmas Eve with wounded members of the 'Leibstandarte'. The next day he travelled to the divisional HQ of the 'Leibstandarte' in Nikolajevka to meet the divisional commander, Sepp Dietrich; on 26 December he inspected the front-line positions of the 'Viking' division and met the divisional commander, Felix Steiner. On the following day he flew back to Poltava, stayed there overnight, and next day attended a briefing at the HQ of Army Group South.

On 3 January 1942, six days after his return to headquarters, he embarked on another trip to the front, this time to the northern sector of the eastern front, where he visited the other two Waffen-SS divisions that were in action, the Death's Head and the police division. He returned on 6 January, and during the following days concentrated on dealing with matters that had arisen as a result of his trips to the front: promotions, the setting up of hospitals for the Waffen-SS in the east, improvements to the combating of lice infestation, 'warm things' for the police deployed in the east. He even had time to watch the film *Request Concert*. On 14 and 15 January the heads of the SS Main Offices met under his chairmanship to discuss a redistribution of responsibilities. On 17 January Himmler took part in a hunting party which the East Prussian Gauleiter Erich Koch had organized in Leissienen, and on the eighteenth as well as the twentieth he had lunch with Hitler.[1]

On 21 January his routine was broken by a phone-call from Heydrich concerned, among other things, as he noted, with the 'Jewish question. Meeting in Berlin'. The head of the Reich Security Main Office informed him about the results of a conference that had taken place the day before at the SS's guest-house on the Wannsee. Referring to his assignment from Göring 'to make all the preparations necessary [. . .] for an overall solution to the Jewish question in Europe', Heydrich had invited all the important agencies involved—SS and police, Party and Reich Chancelleries, the Ministry of the Eastern Territories, the government of the General Government, the Reich Justice, Interior, and Foreign Ministries, Göring's Four-Year Plan agency—to a 'general discussion', 'in the interests of achieving a common viewpoint'. Originally scheduled for 9 December 1941, the conference was postponed at short notice because of America's entry into the war, as some of those invited would have been unable to attend.[2]

The participants focused above all on the question of whether or not the 'half-castes' (*Mischlinge*) and those living in 'mixed marriages' should be included in the 'final solution'. Discussion of this issue took up most of the conference, without resolving it.[3] Before Heydrich opened the discussion he gave a general overview of the state of Jewish persecution throughout Europe. We do not have a verbatim account of his statement; we have only the minutes prepared by Eichmann at Heydrich's request, subsequently revised in accordance with instructions from the Gestapo chief Müller, and then sent to the participants.[4]

The central passage in Heydrich's address ran as follows: 'As previously authorized by the Führer, emigration has now been replaced by the evacuation of the Jews to the east as a further solution.' These 'actions' (in other words, the deportations that had already started) were merely 'provisional options'; they would, however, provide 'the practical experience', which, 'in view of the impending final solution (*Endlösung*) of the Jewish question', was of vital importance. The 'final solution' would involve a total of 11 million Jews; a statistical appendix attached to the minutes broke the numbers down according to countries, including not only Jews from neutral states but even those living in Great Britain. It was clear from this that the 'final solution' that was being sought could be fully achieved only after victory had been won.

According to Heydrich, 'during the course of the final solution the Jews are to be suitably assigned to labour in the east under appropriate direction. Jews capable of work will be brought to these territories and will be put to work building roads in large labour columns with the sexes separated. In the course of this work a large proportion will undoubtedly disappear through natural diminution.' 'The remaining remnant, which will undoubtedly constitute the segment most capable of resistance, will have to be appropriately dealt with', to prevent it from becoming a 'germ cell of a Jewish reconstruction'. Heydrich left open the question of the fate awaiting those Jews who were not 'capable of work', in particular the women and children, though it is clear from the context that these people would have to be killed in order to avoid creating a 'germ cell of a Jewish reconstruction'.

The Jews were to be initially brought to 'transit ghettos', 'from there to be transported further east'. Jews over 65 years of age, according to Heydrich, would be accommodated in a 'ghetto for the aged' in order to avoid 'frequent interventions',[5] and presumably also to give added plausibility to the alleged 'labour deployment in the east'.

Thus, at this point in time, as at the beginning of 1941, the Reich Security Main Office assumed that the 'Jewish question' would be solved in the occupied eastern territories; it would be solved only after the end of the war and through a combination of forced labour and mass murder.[6] However, the Wannsee conference also conceived of the possibility of murdering the Jews in the General Government and in the occupied Soviet territories at that time and irrespective of the overall plan. In mid-December 1941, on his return from the conference of Reich leaders and Gauleiters on 12 December, Governor-General Frank had told his colleagues that, as far as dealing with the Jewish question was concerned, he had been tersely advised: 'Liquidate them yourselves.'[7] While at the time Frank had been asking himself how that could be done,[8] his state secretary, Josef Bühler, now suggested to the conference that they should 'begin solving this question in the General Government', 'because here the transport problem would not play a significant role and issues of labour deployment would not get in the way of this action being carried out'; in any case, the majority of Jews there were 'incapable of work'. 'In conclusion,' according to the minutes, 'the various possible solutions were discussed, Gauleiter Dr Meyer and state secretary Dr Bühler both advocating carrying out certain preparatory measures connected with the final solution themselves at once, although the population must not be alarmed in the process.'[9] By 'preparatory measures' they can have been referring only to the establishment of extermination camps along the lines of Belzec, which was already in the process of being built.

Thus Bühler had put forward an alternative solution that rendered the deportation programme to the east just proposed by Heydrich largely superfluous. During the following months Himmler and the Reich Security Main Office were to adopt this proposal and develop it further. As a result, the main focus of the European 'final solution' shifted from the occupied eastern territories to occupied Poland.

Extermination through work

The fact that the mass murder that was in progress during the spring and early summer of 1942 expanded into a comprehensive programme of extermination had much to do with the development of labour deployment within the SS empire. It was the concept of 'extermination through work' that led to the systematic distinction being made between 'those capable of work' and 'those incapable of work', and, as a result, to the organization of forced-labour camps and extermination centres on a vast scale, with the aid of which the European Jews were to be eliminated.

In the summer of 1941 Himmler had already begun contemplating how best to exploit the labour of the concentration camp inmates—initially for the SS's major building projects in eastern Europe.[10] However, when in September the Wehrmacht agreed to assign him a large number of Soviet POWs he no longer pursued these ideas, and instead ordered the expansion of Auschwitz-Birkenau and Lublin-Majdanek concentration camps to operate as forced-labour camps for POWs.[11] In fact, these plans came to nothing; the majority of the Soviet soldiers, who were already exhausted at the time they were taken prisoner, did not survive the catastrophic conditions in the Wehrmacht POW camps during the autumn and winter of 1941. By the end of 1941 Himmler had received only 30,000 prisoners from the Wehrmacht, and after that he did not receive any more.[12]

However, the SS's need for prisoners was continually growing. For a long time it had been trying to reach deals with armaments concerns for the labour deployment of KZ inmates.[13] In January 1941, as already mentioned, IG Farben had decided to set up a Buna plant near Auschwitz for the industrial production of synthetic rubber. It is clear that access to the Auschwitz prisoners played an important part in this decision. Himmler had approved the deployment of prisoners for this purpose in his order of 26 February, in which he had ordered the 'evacuation' of the Jewish

population of the town of Auschwitz. The building work began in April
and cost the lives of around 25,000 prisoners. In fact the plant never
produced significant amounts of Buna.[14]

The SS also deployed thousands of prisoners for a project proposed by
Ferdinand Porsche, the managing director of the Volkswagen Company.
Porsche persuaded Himmler to use prisoners to build a light-metals foundry
in the VW plant. In return he promised to provide the Waffen-SS with
modern amphibious jeeps. Hitler, who was brought in on the affair, signed
an order on 11 January 1942 in which he assigned to Himmler the task of
'constructing, equipping, and operating' the foundry, expressly stating that
it should be done with the aid of KZ inmates. The use of the word
'operating' implied for the SS the expectation that at last they were going
beyond simply supplying labour and were now actually becoming involved
in armaments production.[15]

Ill. 25. In July 1942 Himmler visited Auschwitz-Monowitz and presumably also
met representatives of IG Farben. Among the inmates employed in the Buna
works was the Jewish resistance fighter Primo Levi, who later recorded his
experiences in the book *Is This a Man?*

Far more workers, however, were required for the SS's so-called building programme for peacetime (*Friedensbauprogramm*), which involved in particular plans for the reorganization of the occupied eastern territories. In December 1941 Pohl had submitted to Himmler the first construction programme, which had a budget of 13 billion Reich marks and had been drafted by Hans Kammler, the head of the SS Main Office Budgets and Building.[16] When it finally became clear, at the beginning of 1942, that he could no longer count on receiving Soviet prisoners, Himmler revived his plans of the previous summer to deploy KZ inmates as forced labour for his own building projects. But for this to happen the camps had to be filled up first. On 26 January 1942 he informed the Inspector of Concentration Camps, Richard Glücks, that 'in view of the fact that we cannot anticipate receiving Russian prisoners in the immediate future, I shall consign a large number of Jews and Jewesses who will be emigrated [*sic*] from Germany to the camps. In the course of the next four weeks, therefore, you must prepare to receive 100,000 male and up to 50,000 female Jews in the concentration camps. During the coming weeks the concentration camps will be expected to carry out major economic tasks.'[17] In fact, during the following months tens of thousands of Jews were deported to the district of Lublin, where those who were designated 'capable of work' were forced to work in Majdanek and other camps. In Auschwitz Jews from Slovakia were deployed as forced labour.[18]

Himmler not only filled his camps with new prisoners, however, but also concentrated on exploiting more effectively those who were already there. On 19 January, the day before the Wannsee conference, he ordered the amalgamation of Pohl's Main Offices—Budgets and Building and Administration and Business—with the Administration Office in the SS Leadership Main Office, that was also controlled by Pohl, to form the SS's Business and Administration Main Office (Wirtschafts- und Verwaltungshauptamt = WVHA). In March 1942 he also incorporated the Concentration Camp Inspectorate into the new Main Office, which, on the one hand, emphasized the economic importance of the camps, but was also intended to provide a barrier to any future encroachment on the part of Fritz Sauckel. For Sauckel's appointment as General Plenipotentiary for Labour Mobilization threatened to generate disagreements over who was in charge of the concentration camp inmates.[19]

Meanwhile, Kammler revised his draft of the peacetime building programme. Himmler had been dissatisfied with the first draft and specifically demanded that Kammler should be more ambitious. The latter responded by proposing to spend the incredible-sounding sum of 20 to 30 billion Reich marks—among other things, for building extensive settlements in 'the east'— involving the deployment of 175,000 forced labourers: 'Prisoners, POWs, Jews, etc.'[20] At the end of March 1942 Himmler gave his views on Kamm- ler's plans. Among other things, he criticized his assumption that a prisoner's productivity would be only half that of a German worker. Himmler in- structed Pohl that the 'biggest reserve of labour power was contained' in the prospect of increasing the productivity of the individual prisoner. 'By being given responsibility for the Concentration Camp Inspectorate, the head of the Business and Administration Main Office has been provided with the opportunity of achieving that.'[21] The message was clear: with the aid of terror to get the maximum productivity out of the prisoners with the minimum expenditure. The prisoners, who in a short time would be worked to death, were to be replaced by new slave labour.[22]

Oswald Pohl, the head of the WVHA, hurried to prove to Himmler that he had understood what was expected of him. In a report of 30 April he emphasized that 'keeping prisoners on the grounds of security, re- education, or prevention was no longer the priority'; the 'main emphasis' had 'shifted towards economics'.[23] In an order from the same day Pohl made KZ commandants 'responsible for labour deployment. In order to achieve maximum performance this deployment must be exhausting in the truest sense of the word.'[24]

Thus, as part of the preparations for the 'final solution' that were already under way, Himmler geared his organization to combine mass murder and mass production in the form of 'extermination through labour'. This move not only enabled him to expand the concentration camp system but also to demonstrate its compatibility with the conditions created by the war. Himmler hoped above all to counter the accusation that was being increas- ingly levelled, given the deteriorating war situation, that the SS was point- lessly eliminating labour that was urgently needed. The new plan explained the extermination of people who were 'incapable of work' as a 'practical' necessity.

This maxim had already been applied in the occupied Soviet territories from the late summer of 1941 onwards. The Einsatzgruppen allowed only those Jews to live who were 'capable of work'. They then died in the camps, debilitated from forced labour and as a result of the catastrophic living conditions. In the forced-labour camps in Upper Silesia under the direction of the Breslau police chief Albrecht Schmelt, from November 1941 onwards selections were being carried out among the Jewish forced labourers, initially sporadically but soon systematically. Those no longer capable of work were deported to Auschwitz and murdered.[25]

In the autumn of 1941 the SS had initiated a huge forced-labour project in the district of Galicia in the General Government, in which, apart from Ukrainians and Soviet POWs, large numbers of Jews were deployed. This was the road linking Lemberg (Lvov) and the Donets basin, the so-called Transit Road IV, and can be described as a pilot project for the new policy.[26] In the camps set up for the forced labourers living conditions were terrible and a brutal regime was enforced. There were continual selections of those incapable of work, particularly among the Jewish forced workers, who were then murdered. Here the scenario which Heydrich had outlined at the Wannsee conference of Jewish labour columns 'building roads' had long been reality.

The turning-points in spring 1942

At the Wannsee conference of 20 January 1942, apart from the old plan of deporting the European Jews to the occupied Soviet territories and killing them there through forced labour and 'special treatment', another variation of systematic mass murder had been discussed: the killing of the Jews living in the General Government *in situ* with the means that were available, in other words, in gas chambers such as had already been built in Belzec and Auschwitz.

Initially Himmler aimed, with the aid of Globocnik, to continue in the spring of 1942 the mass murders in the districts of Lublin and Galicia for which preparations had been made or which had already begun in the autumn of 1941. Belzec extermination camp, which he had ordered to be built the previous October, was completed in March 1942; it was to become the prototype for the extermination camps in the General Government. On 13 March Himmler travelled to Cracow, had discussions with HSSPF Krüger, and on the following day went on to Lublin to meet Globocnik, the key figure in Jewish policy in the General Government.[27]

Immediately after his visit, between 16 March and 20 April, the ghetto in the city of Lublin, the district capital, was almost completely cleared.[28] In the course of this bloody 'action', which took place in two stages, numerous people were shot in the ghetto itself; a few thousand were kept in Lublin as workers, and around 30,000 were deported to Belzec where they were murdered. On 24 March deportations from the rural parts of the district of Lublin began, from which Globocnik and his people selected some 14,000 Jews for Belzec. Then the camp was temporarily closed so that it could be extended.[29]

There is a variety of evidence to show that at this time Globocnik had instructions from Himmler to murder all the Jews from the district who were 'incapable of work'. Thus, on 27 March Goebbels made a note in his diary concerning the Lublin Jews that '60% of them will have to be liquidated while only 40% can be deployed for work'.[30] In the neighbouring district of Galicia, between mid-March and the beginning of April 1942 Globocnik's staff also deported around 15,000 inhabitants of the Lemberg ghetto who were deemed 'incapable of work' to Belzec. Thousands of people from the smaller ghettos in the district were forced to follow the same path, while further thousands were murdered *in situ*.[31] Thus Globocnik's orders did not apply only to Lublin.

The deportation of Jews from the Reich and Slovakia to the district of Lublin, which had already been designated as a 'Jewish reservation' in September 1939, began simultaneously with the clearing of the Lublin ghetto. By the beginning of March 1942 Eichmann had concocted a programme according to which 55,000 Jews would be deported from the Reich, a number which presumably had been reached by June. At the same time he had announced that, as had been agreed at the Wannsee conference, the intention was to deport most of the remaining elderly Jews to Theresienstadt by the autumn.[32] The deportation trains destined for the district of Lublin[33] usually stopped in the capital, Lublin, where the men judged 'capable of work' were separated out and sent on to the Majdanek camp. The other people were put in the ghetto that had just been cleared where, as a result of the miserable conditions, the majority did not survive the coming weeks and months.

In February 1942 Himmler repeated the offer that he had made to the Slovak leadership in October of the previous year.[34] He sent a request to the Slovak government via the Foreign Ministry for it to send 20,000 workers to the Reich for deployment 'in the east', to which the Skovaks agreed. Between 26 March and 7 April four transports with a total of 4,500 young men arrived in Majdanek and four transports with a total of 4,500 young women arrived in Auschwitz, who were all deployed as forced labour.[35]

On 30 March, in addition to the transports from Slovakia, the first transport of Jewish hostages from France arrived in Auschwitz . They had been deported 'to the east' in 'retaliation' for attacks by the French resistance movement. While the preparations for this transport were being made, Heydrich announced the deportation to Auschwitz of a further 5,000 Jewish hostages from France during the coming months.

Apart from that, transports from the forced-labour camps of the 'Schmelt Organization' in Upper Silesia were continually arriving in Auschwitz. Anyone who worked for it and was considered no longer fit to work was killed. For this purpose, during the spring and summer of 1942—following the experiments with Zyklon B on non-Jewish prisoners the previous autumn—the camp authorities constructed gas chambers in two farmhouses that lay on the edge of the Auschwitz-Birkenau camp. The process of transforming it into a proper extermination camp with four more gas chambers and crematoria had not even begun yet. On 20 March 1942 the first of these converted farmhouses, the so-called Red House or Bunker I, was used for the first time for murdering Jews from the Schmelt camps who were 'incapable of work'. During the following weeks and months it was above all Jews from Upper Silesia who were being gassed here.[36]

In the meantime Himmler had once again used the Foreign Ministry to get the Slovak government to agree to deliver up all its Jews (a further 70,000 people) to Germany.[37] On 10 April Heydrich visited Bratislava in order to explain the deportation programme.[38] Already on the following day a transport with entire Jewish families left Slovakia. By 20 June seven more transports had arrived in Auschwitz, where the deportees were deployed as forced labour; during the same period a further thirty-four transports arrived in the district of Lublin.[39] Here—like the people who were being deported from Germany at the same time—they were incarcerated in ghettos whose original inhabitants had been transported to the Belzec and Sobibor extermination camps shortly beforehand.[40]

Thus, in April 1942 three major deportation programmes were in operation: the Jews from Lublin and Galicia were being deported to Belzec; those from the Reich and Slovakia were being sent to Lublin and Auschwitz; and the deportations to Auschwitz from France had begun. At this point Himmler and Heydrich intervened once more: in April they made decisive preparations for the expansion of what had hitherto been a programme of mass murder of Jews 'incapable of work' limited to a particular region to one that would encompass all European Jews. Himmler's office diary for this period contains references to a remarkable series of meetings: within a period of eight days, between the end of April and the beginning of May, Himmler met Heydrich a total of seven times in three different places (Berlin, Munich, and Prague). On either side of these unusually intensive exchanges there occurred two lengthy meetings between Himmler and Hitler, which took place on 23 April and 3 May in the Führer's headquarters.[41] Even if we know nothing about the content of these meetings, the chronology of the events that followed, which will be outlined below, indicates that it was during these days that Hitler, Himmler, and Heydrich established the essential parameters for a Europe-wide extermination programme that was to be put into effect from May–June 1942 onwards.

But why at this point in time? The essential precondition for the stepping-up of the policy of murder appears to have been the fact that in the spring of 1942 Himmler was able to bring Jewish policy in the General Government under his control, and so could authorize Globocnik to go beyond his function as HSSPF in the district of Lublin and to organize mass murder throughout the General Government, in other words, in an area inhabited by approximately 1.7 million Jews. In no other area under German control was there anything like that number of Jews.

By the beginning of March Governor-General Frank had already had to cede important responsibilities for the police to Himmler. This was prompted by Frank's involvement in a serious corruption scandal. When he was subjected to 'personal and comradely' interrogation by Himmler, Bormann, and Lammers on 5 March, his response was not especially convincing. Subsequently, Himmler criticized his 'very theatrical behaviour'. Having been put on the spot in this way, Frank had to make considerable political concessions: HSSPF Krüger was made state secretary for 'all matters concerning the police and the consolidation of the ethnic German nation', and in this role was answerable to Himmler. Furthermore, Globocnik was to be appointed governor of the district of Lublin. In fact this never happened, because evidently Frank's agreement to it was enough to enhance Globocnik's position vis-à-vis the civil administration.[42]

The agreements of the beginning of March concerning Krüger came into effect in May and June. On 7 May Krüger was appointed state secretary for security matters, and he became Himmler's representative within the General Government in his role as settlement commissar. Moreover, Himmler was authorized to give him direct instructions concerning security and ethnic matters.[43] Finally, under a supplementary decree of 3 June regulating

Ill. 26. On 13 March 1942 Himmler, accompanied by HSSPF Krüger, inspected a police unit in Cracow. On the following day he travelled on to Lublin where he met Globocnik, who two days later initiated the first 'ghetto action'.

his new position as state secretary, Krüger was expressly given the responsi-bility for all 'Jewish affairs'.[44] At the same time, in May or June a start was made on the construction of the largest extermination camp in the General Government, Treblinka.[45]

In the light of these impending developments, at the end of April and beginning of May Himmler and Heydrich decided to include large areas of occupied Poland in the mass murder of the Jews. Given his central role in Jewish policy and the fact that he was kept closely informed during these weeks, we have good reason for assuming that Hitler was in agreement. From 5 May onwards the rural districts of Lublin were systematically 'cleared' of Jews irrespective of whether or how many Jews were arriving from other countries. By 10 June more than 55,000 people had been deported to Sobibor, the second extermination camp in the General Government, which had been completed in the meantime.[46] In the middle of May Upper Silesia was caught up in the murder programme. By August 1942 20,000 people from Sosnowitz, Bendzin, and other places had been deported straight to Auschwitz and murdered there, and around 18,000 people had been sent to the forced-labour camps of the Schmelt organization.[47] At the end of May deportations from the district of Cracow to Belzec began.[48]

These dramatic developments in occupied Poland were bound to have an impact on Jewish policy as a whole. While the programme of murder in the General Government was stepped up, the deportations of Jews from the Reich and Slovakia to this region were increased beyond the totals agreed in March. Moreover, the deportees were no longer incarcerated in ghettos; the majority were murdered when the transports arrived at their destinations in the east. Thus Himmler had evidently revoked his ban on the murder of German Jews from the Reich issued at the end of November 1941.

To summarize, the following major changes in policy towards the German Jews occurred during May and June 1942: in May a fourth wave of deportations from the Reich began. By September 1942 around 16,000 people had been deported to Minsk,[49] where they were no longer put in the ghetto, as had occurred in the winter of 1941, but forced to leave the trains at a stop near the estate of Maly Trostinez. Here, from 11 May 1942 onwards, almost everybody arriving on the transports was either shot or murdered in gas vans.[50] The vast majority of those Jews who had been deported from the Reich to Łódź in autumn 1941 and who had survived the catastrophic conditions—more than 10,000 people—were now deported to Chelmno between 4 and 13 May and murdered there.[51] From mid-June onwards the last transports of the third wave of deportations from the Reich were generally sent to Sobibor extermination camp, where the majority were gassed.[52] Moreover, in the middle of May, for the first time people who had been deported from Theresienstadt to the General Government were murdered in Sobibor.[53] From June 1942 onwards the same thing happened with people who were in deportation trains coming from the Reich; there is reliable evidence for this occurring in the middle of the month.[54] Moreover, from the beginning to the middle of June the members of a total of ten transports from Slovakia, who had been designated as 'incapable of work' at the selection in Lublin—in other words, mainly women and children—were no longer accommodated in a ghetto but deported straight to the Sobibor extermination camp and murdered there.[55]

In the spring of 1942 Himmler also made great efforts to reduce the number of Jews who were 'deployed in work' and therefore for the time being still protected. The fact that he issued an order to this effect is revealed in a letter that the Gestapo chief Müller wrote to the commander of the security police in Riga, Karl Jäger, on 18 May. Müller wrote that, in accordance with a 'general order from the Reichsführer and Chief of the German Police', 'Jews and Jewesses aged 16 to 32 who are capable of work are to be excluded from special measures until further notice. These Jews are to be put to work en bloc. KZ or labour camp.'[56] The letter makes it clear that the 'special measures'—in other words, the murder of the prisoners— was now the rule, 'deployment for work', which was ultimately designed to be equally lethal, the exception.[57]

At the same time, the pressure on the Jews still working in the Reich increased still further. The Reich Security Main Office interpreted the special regulations for the Jews who were 'deployed in work vital for the war effort' with increasing strictness,[58] and on 28 May Hitler promised Goebbels that he would request Speer 'to ensure that Jews employed in the German armaments industry are replaced by foreign workers as soon as possible'.[59] It was only a lack of transport that prevented this order from being implemented in the summer, and in the autumn Hitler once again urged that it should be carried out.

At the same time as these events were occurring the Einsatzgruppen resumed on a large scale the mass murder of Soviet Jews that had begun the previous summer. This applied in particular to Byelorussia, where

Heydrich, on a visit to Minsk in April,[60] evidently provided the impetus for it, as he did for the Reichskommissariat Ukraine.[61]

However, while the Jewish persecution, which had followed the turning-points that took place during the last days of April and the first days of May, was still escalating an event occurred that within weeks led to a further radicalization of the whole extermination process and to Himmler showing his determination to murder the vast majority of European Jews in the course of 1942: the assassination of Reinhard Heydrich, Himmler's most important aide in the organization of the Holocaust.

The Assassination of Heydrich

On 27 May 1942 two Czech agents, who had been trained by the British Secret Service and dropped by parachute in the Protectorate, carried out an assassination attempt on the deputy Reich Protector, Heydrich, seriously injuring him, though at first it appeared that the injuries were not life-threatening.[62]

On the same day as the assassination attempt Hitler ordered that anyone who had assisted the assassins should be 'shot together with his whole family'. Furthermore, 10,000 Czechs who were suspect or politically incriminated should be arrested or, if they were already in custody, 'shot in the concentration camps'.[63] On the same evening Himmler pressed for 'the whole of the opposition intelligentsia to be arrested'. That same night 'the hundred most important' opposition figures should be executed.[64] A state of emergency was declared for Prague, and a few hours later this was extended to cover the whole of the Protectorate.

Daluege had already arrived in Prague on the afternoon of 27 May, and that evening he received instructions to take over the work of the Reich Protector which hitherto had been being carried out by Heydrich for von Neurath. Substantial units of the order police entered the Protectorate the following day and carried out raids lasting for days. However, on 28 May Hitler revoked his order to shoot 10,000 Czechs after Karl Hermann Frank, HSSPF in the Protectorate, advised him against it.[65]

Although seriously injured, Heydrich appeared to be recovering until, after a few days, septicaemia set in and he died on 4 June. On 31 May Himmler said his farewells to the dying man and then, on 4 June, immediately after his death, once again visited Prague in order to see the deceased for the last time and to meet his widow. On 7 June he attended the funeral there.[66]

On 9 June Hitler received the Czech government of the Protectorate in the presence of Frank, Himmler, Bormann, and others. After receiving its declaration deploring the assassination, Hitler gave an address which culminated in the threat 'to resettle a few million Czechs [. . .] if necessary during the war',[67] a plan that was as impossible to carry out as the mass shooting of Czechs that had already been dismissed. Instead of that, it was decided to focus Germany's revenge on a particular place, but to do so with extreme brutality.[68]

Immediately after the meeting with Hitler, Frank ordered the commander of the security police in Prague 'to shoot [. . .] all the male inhabitants' of the village of Liditz (Lidice) and to 'transfer all the women [. . .] to a concentration camp'. The children should be 'collected and, in the case of those who are fit to be Germanized, should be given to SS families in the Reich'; the village itself should be 'burnt down and razed to the ground'. The fact that Frank issued this order expressly 'on the basis of a meeting with the Führer' indicates that this idea of carrying out an act of revenge came from the senior SS functionaries who were closeted with Hitler at this juncture. It is not clear why the village of Lidice near Kladno was selected. No particular link with the assassins could be proved. Nevertheless, as Frank had ordered, 199 men were shot, the women were deported to Ravensbrück concentration camp, and after a few of the ninety-eight children had been selected as 'racially valuable' the rest were murdered in Chelmno extermination camp.[69]

A further 'act of retaliation' was aimed directly at the Prague Jews: on 10 June 1942 thousands of them were deported to Majdanek and held here and in surrounding camps.[70] Nevertheless, at this time the Nazi leadership must have had the idea of exacting even harsher retaliation on 'the Jews' for Heydrich's death. The decision-making process can no longer be reconstructed in detail. However, the numerous meetings between Hitler and Himmler at the end of May and beginning of June suggest that the intensification of Jewish persecution that was to occur was worked out in close agreement between the two men.[71]

The fact that the head of the security apparatus and absolute ruler of the Protectorate should have been the victim of an assassination came as a serious shock to the Nazi leadership. There was a mood for revenge. On 9 June Heydrich received a pompous state funeral (see Ill. 13). The service took place in the new Reich Chancellery, in the presence of Hitler and the entire leadership of the Third Reich; Himmler gave the funeral oration. Reflecting the measures taken in the Protectorate, the Reichsführer emphasized the motif of revenge: 'We have the sacred duty to atone for his death, to carry forward his work, and now, even more than before, mercilessly to annihilate the enemies of our people without showing any weakness.'[72]

With Heydrich, Himmler had lost his most important colleague, the man who during the 1930s had built up the security police apparatus, who after the outbreak of war had established the Einsatzgruppen, who in past months had been largely responsible for organizing the mass murders in the Soviet Union, and who had prepared and initiated the deportations from various European countries. Himmler had always been sure of Heydrich's loyalty, even if, with Hitler's assignment to Heydrich of preparations for the 'final solution', a second chain of command had been created alongside Himmler's general responsibility for combating all 'enemies of the Reich'. These competing chains of command do not, however, appear to have led to serious rivalry between Himmler and Heydrich. On the contrary, Himmler considered that in the first instance and above all it was his own power that had been adversely affected by his colleague's murder.

Heydrich was buried in the Invaliden cemetery. In the evening Himmler made another speech to the leaders of the SS-Oberabschnitte and the heads of the SS-Offices. Apart from the admonition not to neglect their own security—'for we want to kill the enemy, the enemy mustn't kill us'—Himmler spoke about the future tasks of the SS: the further 'amalgamation with the police', the 'bringing in and amalgamation of the Germanic peoples with us', as well as 'settlement and ethnic migration in Europe'. 'We shall certainly have concluded the ethnic migration of the Jews within a year,' he continued, 'then no one will be migrating any more. For now things have finally got to be sorted out.'[73]

From the weird perspective of Himmler and the Nazi leadership the assassination of Heydrich had to be avenged with a further radicalization of Jewish persecution; they were in a 'war against the Jews', and felt massively challenged by the assassination and especially by *this* enemy. The SS leadership—Himmler took over the RSHA himself—immediately began to press for the further stepping-up of mass murder that had begun in May. The planners in the RSHA and on Globocnik's staff benefited from the fact that, because of the summer offensive, a transport ban was imposed between 19 June and 7 July. During this period they could revise the existing deportation plans. Under the title 'Operation Reinhardt' (in honour of the dead Heydrich), Globocnik's responsibility was now extended to cover the murder of all Jews in the General Government.[74]

After the assassination: Himmler launches the Europe-wide extermination programme

After the death of Heydrich the deportations from the Reich continued with undiminished intensity. When the transport ban was imposed in the east those Jews who had hitherto been exempted from the 'transports to the east' became the focus of the planners: the elderly and infirm, decorated war veterans and their dependants, as well as other 'privileged' groups. Between June and October 1942 around 45,000 people were deported to Theresienstadt, which now served as a 'ghetto for the elderly'.[75]

In view of the transport ban, Himmler had the idea of deporting more Jews from western Europe 'for labour deployment'. Following his orders, on 11 June 1942 the SS Jewish experts in the various countries arranged to transport '15,000 Jews from the Netherlands, 10,000 from Belgium, and 100,000 from France'. They also obeyed Himmler's instruction that '10% of Jews incapable of work' could 'be included'.[76] According to Himmler's order of May 1942, this meant that these people would be subjected to 'special measures', in other words, would be murdered in the gas chambers of Auschwitz immediately on arrival.

On 23 June, when informed that the total planned for France could not be achieved for organizational reasons, Himmler responded indignantly: the tempo envisaged hitherto (of three transports of 1,000 people each per week) would have to be 'significantly increased [...] with the aim of completely freeing France of Jews as soon as possible'.[77] This order must be seen as part of the acceleration of the extermination of the Jews throughout Europe that had been initiated in May and June. The appointment of Carl-Albrecht Oberg, hitherto SS and Police Leader in the Polish district of Radom, as HSSPF in France from 1 June will have convinced Himmler that the organizational preconditions for such a comprehensive deportation of the Jews were now in place.[78] In fact, following Himmler's order, the tempo of deportations from France was significantly increased. Whereas in March and June, prior to his intervention, only five transports had been achieved, between July and November 1942 a total of fifty-three transports, most of them containing 1,000 people, left France bound for Auschwitz.[79] And on 21 July, for the first time, 'Jews incapable of work', whom Himmler had insisted be deported, were separated from the other deportees immediately on arrival and murdered in the gas chambers.[80]

The first 'selection' had, however, already occurred in Auschwitz some weeks earlier. From the beginning of July 1942 onwards transports from Slovakia no longer went to the district of Lublin but to Auschwitz, where on 4 July 'those incapable of work' were for the first time murdered immediately on arrival. There is evidence that by 21 October deportees from eight transports from Slovakia had been murdered in this way.[81] After the lifting of the transport ban most of the transports from the Reich were sent to Minsk, and in the following months also to Riga, Treblinka, and Auschwitz. Most of the deportees were now killed immediately after the trains had arrived.[82]

After the lifting of the transport ban in July deportations from occupied Poland also began again in large numbers. The aim of making the General Government 'free of Jews' in the near future corresponded to the Germanization policy that was being simultaneously initiated. On 12 June Himmler had already ordered the 'Germanization' of large areas in the east, including the General Government, to be speeded up and completed within twenty years. At the beginning of July HSSPF Krüger advocated approving the settlement of Germans in the General Government.[83]

Deportations from the district of Cracow to Belzec began again in the second week of July, after the period of the transport ban had been used considerably to enlarge the capacity of the gas chambers.[84] On 9 July Himmler discussed with Krüger and Globocnik the latter's proposals of 3 July. Although these have not survived, we know that they were particularly concerned with Jewish policy in the district of Lublin.[85]

On 11, 12, and 18 July Himmler had frequent meetings with Hitler. Afterwards he pressed for increased transport capacity. Karl Wolff, the head of his private office, telephoned the state secretary in the Reich Transport Ministry, who assured him that from 22 July there would be 'every day a train with 5,000 Jews from Warsaw to Treblinka, as well as a train from Przemysl (Lublin district) to Belzec twice weekly'.[86] While we can only assume that Himmler discussed the details of the mass murder of the Polish Jews with Hitler, we can be certain that, as far as the occupied Soviet territories were concerned, Himmler had received explicit instructions from Hitler to make these 'free of Jews'.[87]

On 17 and 18 July Himmler visited Auschwitz and used the opportunity to witness a demonstration of how people were murdered in a gas chamber.[88] On the evening of 17 July, at a social occasion put on by the Gauleiter of Upper Silesia, contrary to his normal habits he drank several glasses of wine and gave the appearance of being relaxed and content. His behaviour and comments led one of those present to assume that the Nazi leadership had now decided to murder the European Jews—a piece of information that was passed on to Switzerland and from there was telegraphed to the west via the representative of the Jewish World Congress, Gerhart Riegner.[89]

Himmler travelled on from Auschwitz to visit Globocnik in Lublin, where, on the following day, he ordered Krüger to ensure that the 'resettlement of the whole Jewish population of the General Government has been carried out and completed by 31 December 1942'. After this date Jews would no longer be permitted to reside in the General Government, apart from in four large camps.[90] Three days later the dissolution of the Warsaw ghetto began, which was to take place in stages. The majority of the inhabitants were deported to the Treblinka extermination camp, which had just been built and was located only 50 kilometres from Warsaw.[91] By 12 September over 250,000 people had been deported, a rough average of 5,000 per day.

At the same time Himmler's organization took over the whole system of Jewish forced labour, in other words, the area of operation that represented the only barrier to the complete annihilation of the Jewish population. In the hands of the SS forced labour, in the sense of 'extermination through labour', now became an integral part of the murder programme in the General Government.[92]

In May and June 1942 it had looked as if Jewish workers would still be deployed in large numbers in the General Government, that is to say, that the extermination policy in the General Government was still targeted primarily at the Jewish population that was 'incapable of work'. However, hardly had HSSPF Krüger taken over responsibility for all 'Jewish affairs' at the beginning of June when the policy changed radically. His July order to the effect that only Jews aged between 16 and 32 were permitted to be employed proved decisive. This restriction, which is reminiscent of Himmler's directive of May 1942 (which referred to people aged between 16 and 32), represented a death sentence for all those outside this age cohort.[93] On 14 August Krüger went a step further and ordered the dissolution of all

Jewish forced-labour camps. Also, on 5 September, Field-Marshal Keitel ordered the Wehrmacht to replace all Jewish workers in the General Government with Poles.[94] All Jews in the General Government were now exposed to the strategy that Himmler had been pressing for since the beginning of 1942, of combining forced labour and mass murder to form a comprehensive extermination programme.

As this chapter has shown, in the summer of 1942 Himmler's anti-Jewish policy had culminated in the inclusion of a whole series of European countries in the policy of systematic mass murder. However, in the second half of the year he was to press for the murder-rate in those countries that had already been included in the Holocaust to be stepped up still further and, in addition, to extend the deportation programme to more countries.

The following chapters will show that for Himmler the launching of the Holocaust in Europe was only the first step on the path to a much more comprehensive vision of a new order. For it is clear from an assessment of his ceaseless activities during these months that the final decision to murder the European Jews was just the first of a number of fundamental turning-points that Himmler was to engineer during the coming months, and which had the object of securing the central role in the establishment of the Nazi empire for his SS and an unique historical position for himself.

To this end, the Reichsführer sought to combine what, at first glance, seem completely different topics to form a political programme, geared to the racial domination and reordering of Europe. Thus, in the next two chapters we shall examine more closely two fields in which Himmler also took important decisions in the summer of 1942: settlement policy and the recruitment of non-German citizens for his Waffen-SS. However, in order to explain the importance of these turning-points in the summer of 1942, it is necessary first to look at the chronology both before and after this period. Only then will we turn our attention to the second half of 1942.

The events of 1942 strikingly demonstrate that Himmler was a man who knew how to combine ambitious ideological notions with a sure instinct for power. And this is apparent in the way he systematically exploited the functions he had acquired as Reichsführer-SS. What begins to become evident in 1942 is a fantasy world displaying the most extreme degree of brutality, inhumanity, and absolute ruthlessness in power politics, a fantasy world that has Himmler's characteristic stamp upon it and which he believed he could turn into reality in a very short space of time.

22

Settlement Policy and Racial Selection

Precisely at the point when he was setting about drawing the whole of Europe into the Holocaust, in May and June 1942 Himmler took decisive steps to standardize the diverse SS settlement plans and extend them to the whole territory of the future Reich. The systematic murder of the Jews was only the beginning (as the coincidence of these decisions makes clear) of his project to subject the whole of Europe to a radical racial 'reordering'.

Himmler had a mental picture of the European map separated into a number of zones, distinguished by the 'racial calibre' of their inhabitants and the latter's future role in a Greater Germanic Reich. By comparison, national boundaries were of secondary importance for him. In the top rank according to his estimation were the countries whose inhabitants he classed as 'Teutons' (*Germanen*): these were places where 'Germanic' volunteers could be recruited into the Waffen-SS and where later potential settlers for the east could be found. In a Greater Germanic Reich these countries would stand side-by-side with the German Empire as equal partners. In practice, however, he could treat only Norway and the Netherlands, which were administered by civil commissars, fully as Germanic territories, and thus he intervened in the internal politics of those countries. The fascist movements he supported and their leaders, Quisling and Mussert, met with little success, however. In Belgium conditions were more difficult: only the Flemish could really count as Teutons, whereas by origin the Walloons could not. Yet a process of mental revision seems to have occurred in him, for he reacted very positively to attempts by the Walloons to present themselves to him as 'romanized Teutons', and he supported research projects designed to prove this theory. The fact that the Belgian territories were subject to military rule was, however, an obstacle for it was less open to his influence. He also in fact regarded Denmark as 'Germanic', but in this case the restrained German occupation policy prevented him from taking any significant action. Sweden was undoubtedly 'Germanic', but neutral, and so in the case of this potential 'brother country' he also had to exercise severe restraint. All in all, therefore, his attempts at Germanic integration remained pipe-dreams; the only degree of success he achieved was in recruiting volunteers and bringing national police forces into line with the German pattern (as discussed elsewhere in this volume).

The second zone on Himmler's map of Europe consisted of those areas the Reich had already annexed or was going to annex, where the inhabitants would have to be sorted on the basis of racial criteria: the Protectorate belonged to this zone, also the occupied Polish and Soviet territories, as well as Alsace and Lorraine (which were under the authority of German Gauleiters as chiefs of the civil administration and thus already half integrated into the Reich) and the Yugoslav territories annexed in 1941.

The third zone was made up of those eastern and southern European states allied to the Third Reich in which there were significant ethnic German minorities. Acting on Hitler's instructions, Himmler assumed the leadership of these ethnic Germans and represented their 'interests' (as he himself defined them) with regard to the governments of these countries. The countries in question were Slovakia, Croatia, Hungary, and Romania; Serbia, which was under military rule, was a special case. Even here his main concern was in the final analysis the recruitment of 'volunteers' from the ethnic German population; though he did not state it openly, at bottom he became more and more convinced that these populations should be dispersed and those belonging to them used to further his settlement projects in eastern Europe.

The remaining European territories that were not to become part of the racially based empire that was to be created interested him by comparison far less: thus France was significant to him above all because he was responsible for the security of the occupying forces. Italy was German's most important ally, and its autonomy had to be respected at all costs, which is why he gave complete support to Hitler's policy of strengthening this alliance by abandoning the claims of the ethnic Germans to South Tyrol. Finland was regarded as a loyal ally, to whose population he accorded high status because of its particular racial ancestry, even if they were not 'Teutons'.

The settlement policy that will be discussed in this chapter therefore related exclusively to the territories designated here as the second zone, namely, territories that the German Reich had annexed or intended to annex.

In an earlier chapter we have traced the early stages of Himmler's racist, 'selection'-based settlement policy and seen that his efforts were concentrated at first on Poland and then extended to the Protectorate as well as Alsace and Lorraine.

After the Balkan war Himmler also included Yugoslav territory in his endeavours—more precisely, the territories that under the names of Lower Styria and Upper Carniola had been annexed by the Reich. In his capacity as Settlement Commissar Himmler subjected the Slovenian population to a racial 'selection' and had almost 40,000 people—members of the intelligentsia and immigrants from other parts of Yugoslavia—relocated to Serbia and Croatia. In June 1941 he ordered that all racially 'suitable' persons from Lower Styria and southern Carinthia be 'included in the measures to deploy persons capable of re-Germanization from the eastern territories and General Government'.[1] As a first step, however, these people were to be taken to west and central Germany. In November 1941 and January 1942, after a preliminary selection, a total of more than 33,000 people were transferred to VoMi camps in the Reich, where in spring 1942 a more thorough racial examination was conducted. In this process 15,000 people were identified as being 'capable of re-Germanization', in other words, suitable for settlement in the east. Most, however, remained in the VoMi camps until the end of the war.[2] The German ethnic minority from Gotschee, an area near Ljublyana now part of the Italian zone of occupation, was in turn forcibly resettled in the now-vacant areas of Lower Styria and southern Carinthia.[3]

The outbreak of the war against the Soviet Union compelled Himmler to revise his entire settlement planning.[4] Two days after the Germans launched their attack, on 24 June, he gave his head of planning, Konrad Meyer, in the Main Office of the Settlement Commissariat the task of adapting the planning to the new circumstances.[5] Meyer was ready in July with a first version of the revised 'General Plan East'. It was now envisaged that the General Government and the territories being annexed to the east of it would be Germanized, though only two days later this project turned out already to be outdated, because Hitler, at a meeting about the future of the east, sketched out more extensive plans for annexation.

Meanwhile the Reich Security Main Office was working on its own general plan for the east. It was presented in 1941 and assumed that, in addition to the annexed Polish territories and the General Government, the Bialystok district, the Baltic States, the western Ukraine, and Byelorussia would also be settled by Germans. The precondition for this was the expulsion of 31 million inhabitants of these territories.[6]

On 28 May 1942 the Reich Settlement Commissariat Main Office produced a new version of its General Plan East. The suggestion was now that so-called 'settlement marches' be set up in the Baltic area, the Ukraine, and the Leningrad region, as well as thirty-six settlement bases, which would function also as SS and police bases. In the meantime there was no more talk of extensive relocation of indigenous populations, and instead discussion focused on 'decimating' the urban population above all by means of starvation and forced labour.[7]

Himmler read the plan, which he considered 'very good on the whole', and charged Meyer with enlarging it into a European 'Comprehensive Settlement Plan' incorporating the older projects for the annexed eastern territories but also including Alsace and Lorraine, Upper Carniola and Southern Styria, and Bohemia and Moravia. In addition Himmler ordered the complete 'Germanization' of Estonia and Latvia. The period envisaged for this settlement process was, he instructed, to be reduced from between twenty-five and thirty years to twenty years.[8]

From documents Meyer presented at the end of 1942 it is apparent that the plans now aimed to 'transfer' within thirty years a 'pool of settlers', amounting to more than 10 million people from the Reich, more than a million from the 'Germanic' countries, and 200,000 more from overseas, to the territories to be settled. A process of 'complete Germanization' was envisaged; further details about the fate of the native, non-German population were, in the author's view, clearly superfluous.[9] Himmler responded by instructing Meyer to include Lithuania, White Ruthenia (Byelorussia), the Crimea, and Taurien in the comprehensive plan also.[10] Work to refine these plans continued until some time in mid-1943.

The efforts put into a comprehensive settlement plan can therefore be described as Himmler's attempt to harmonize settlement planning as a whole throughout his various offices.[11] The period in which he made these fundamental decisions, in May and June 1942, coincided, as must be emphasized once again, with the phase in which he was also laying the foundations for the whole of Europe to be included in the Holocaust and even accelerated this process under the impact of Heydrich's assassination.

In a speech on 16 September 1942 to the SS and police leaders from the Russia South area Himmler set out how he saw the settlement of the eastern territories. In the next twenty years the annexed Polish territories, the General Government, the Baltic States, White Ruthenia, Ingria (the area around Leningrad), and the Crimea were to be settled by 'Teutons'. In the remaining occupied Soviet territories bases would be established on the main transport routes so that 'settlement enclaves' would arise—first of all 'from the Don to the Volga', but later 'as far as the Urals'. 'This Germanic east reaching to the Urals must', according to Himmler's vision, 'be a seedbed for Germanic blood, so that in 400–500 years [. . .] instead of 120 millions there will be 500–600 million Teutons.' The indigenous population would be sifted according to those of 'inferior' race and those 'of good race'.[12] What lay at the heart of the settlement of the east he had summed up succinctly in the summer of 1942 as the maxim of the 'ethno-political monthly' *Deutsche Arbeit* ('German Work') in the words: 'Our task does not consist in Germanizing the east in the traditional sense, that means by teaching the German language and German laws to the people who live there, but rather to ensure that only people of actual German and Germanic blood live there.'[13]

By the end of 1942 Himmler had made considerable progress with his resettlement strategy: according to the report he sent to Hitler dated 20 January 1943, a total of 629,000 ethnic Germans had been resettled. Of those, 429,000 had come from territories previously under Soviet rule, 77,000 from Romania, 34,000 from Yugoslavia, and 79,000 from the South Tyrol. Of these 629,000 ethnic Germans, 445,000 had been 'settled', 332,000 of them in the annexed Polish territories, 13,500 in Carniola and Lower Styria, 6,600 in the Protectorate, 5,000 in Alsace and Lorraine, 17,000 in Lithuania (as part of a special scheme for returning Germans), and in addition 70,000 (apart from the South Tyroleans) in the 'Old Reich', including annexed Austria. In many cases, however, the settlers ended up not in neat farmhouses on their own bit of land, as Himmler's planners had pictured them, but rather in resettlement camps or in mostly cramped accommodation in towns.

To create space for these people 365,000 Poles from the annexed Polish territories had been expelled into the General Government, 17,000 Slovenians had been deported to Serbia, and 37,000 as forced labour to Germany.

In addition, 100,000 people from Alsace, Lorraine, and Luxembourg had been deported to unoccupied France, Germany, or to the occupied eastern territories. Himmler's assumption was that he could also resettle a further 400,000 ethnic Germans, consisting of 143,000 South Tyroleans and 250,000 from the occupied eastern territories.[14]

After this general survey we shall look in greater detail in the following sections at the most important resettlement projects. These also include Himmler's vigorous efforts to identify 'good blood' among the non-German population in the occupied territories and to make a start at least in conducting a racial selection among the foreign slave labourers in the Reich.

The Protectorate

In the Protectorate Heydrich had been pressing on with plans for Germanization from the autumn of 1941 onwards. A start was actually made in compiling the 'racial inventory' of the population that the Race and Settlement Main Office had been preparing since the previous autumn. It was disguised as an X-ray screening connected with the introduction of the German identity card in the Protectorate. The head of the RuSHA, Bruno Kurt Schultz, took on responsibility for the academic supervision of the operation as a whole, and to this end was appointed to a chair in racial biology specially created for him at Prague University. It is impossible to establish now how many people were examined in detail; certainly the racial examiners were occupied with 'establishing the racial composition' of the Protectorate until late 1942.[15]

Even the Prague Land Office was reactivated on Heydrich's orders as an instrument of racial policy: the director up to that point, Theodor Gross, a dietitian, was replaced by a member of the SD, as had happened before in 1939;[16] Heydrich, significantly, reproached Gross with not having implemented the policy of expropriation consistently enough. Now the Land Office applied itself with renewed zeal to the preliminary steps towards requisitioning large tracts of land for German settlers.

By means of racial testing and settlement planning the intention was to have all the necessary documentation ready so that Germanization could begin immediately after the war. In November 1941 Heydrich received the cover for his back that he needed for these preparations: on Himmler's urging, Hitler included the Protectorate in the former's responsibilities as

Settlement Commissar and Himmler immediately entrusted Heydrich with carrying out these tasks.[17]

After Heydrich's death Himmler accelerated what was already in progress. In the confidential address he delivered at Heydrich's memorial service in Berlin he announced that Bohemia and Moravia also should have an 'entirely German' population within twenty years. A few days later he directed that Bohemia and Moravia, as well as Alsace, Lorraine, Upper Carniola, and Southern Styria were to be integrated into the general settlement plan. The corresponding detailed work carried out by the Reich Settlement Commissariat Main Office anticipated that about 50 per cent of the Czech population would be 'Germanized' and the other half expelled. In addition to the 236,000 Germans already living in the Protectorate, the intention was to bring 1.4 million German settlers into the country.[18]

What was to happen to the Czechs who were destined to be 'expelled'? Heydrich had already made a clear statement on the matter: in February 1942, two weeks after the Wannsee conference, he had declared in a speech to representatives of the administration of the German occupation that in the process of the envisaged deportation of 11 million European Jews to 'open up further the Arctic region' the Czechs could be used 'as supervisors and foremen, etc. as a positive indication of their pro-German orientation'. The 'final solution to the Jewish question', which at this point was still confined to the deportation of the Jews to the eastern territories, was therefore, as this comment makes clear, embedded in the gigantomania of the SS's population-policy plans.[19]

But it all remained a fantasy: no concrete measures to resettle the Czechs were taken during the war. In the General Government, in the Soviet Union, and in France, on the other hand, Himmler did set settlement pilot projects in train in order to lend weight to his claim after the war to a leading role in the reordering of 'living-space'. The key decisions for all these projects were taken, surprisingly, within a relatively short space of time, in July and August 1942.

The General Government

At the end of 1939 Hitler and Himmler had already declared the General Government to be territory to which 'inferior' beings from the new eastern provinces incorporated into the Reich, but also some from the Old Reich, were to be 'consigned', and by the end of 1942 365,000 Poles had in fact been deported to this territory, as has already been mentioned, while from the end of 1940 to the spring of 1941 the SS resettled around 30,000 ethnic Germans and 'alien nationals of good race' in the opposite direction, from the General Government to the Warthegau and the Old Reich: the General Government as dumping ground could simply not be a suitable home for people of German descent.[20] Thus Himmler's fundamental decision, dating from the summer of 1941, in future to 'Germanize' the General Government also marks a radical change of direction.

Significantly, the SSPF for the Lublin district, Odilo Globocnik, who was simultaneously organizing the mass murder of Jews, became the central figure in the settlement policy of the General Government. During his visit in July 1941 to Lublin Himmler not only made Globocnik his 'appointee in charge of setting up the SS and police bases in the new eastern region', but also empowered him to extend the district operation 'Search for German Blood' to the whole of the General Government and to establish a 'large-scale settlement area' near Zamosc,[21] so that from there the whole Lublin district could be Germanized.

In the autumn of 1941 Globocnik, who for months had maintained his own planning office to look after his special responsibilities for 'population policy',[22] introduced a series of measures and prepared his men for what was to come. 'Enemy nations' must 'move slowly towards their own destruction', and 'in this territory a bulwark' must 'be created against the Slav nations through the settlement of German farmers and farmers of German descent',[23] he proclaimed in November 1941 at a leaders' conference in Lublin.

The same month several thousand people were forcibly expelled from various villages in the Lublin district by SS-Sonderkommando Dirlewanger, which was notorious for its brutality, so that the ethnic Germans of the district could be concentrated there.[24] Simultaneously, a specialist adviser from the RuSHA specifically attached to Globocnik began a 'general review' of the Polish population and their property.[25] In addition, from the autumn onwards Globocnik had been extending the system of SS and police bases, on which he had been working since 1940. Each base was to comprise several estates as well as the administrative offices of various branches of the SS and police, and thereby fulfil a dual function: as a centre for the combating of partisans and as an outpost for Germanization thanks to exemplary agricultural production and training on the farms.

In March 1942, in parallel with the equivalent measures in the annexed eastern territories, the procedure of the Ethnic German List (*Volksliste*; see Chapter 16 above) was applied also to those of German descent in the General Government.[26] At roughly the same time five new commissions of the Central Office for Immigration began, in the wake of the 'search for German blood,' to register ethnic Germans throughout the General Government and also to investigate the 'proportion of German blood' in those people who between 1939 and 1941 had been expelled on account of their 'inferiority' from the annexed eastern territories into the General Government. The operation went on until the autumn of 1943.[27]

From 18 to 20 July Himmler was again staying in the Lublin district in order to find out about the progress of the Germanization process there. Immediately beforehand he had convinced himself in Auschwitz that the mass murder of the European Jews was in operation. In Lublin he now made further decisions concerning the Germanization of the district, in particular with regard to the settling of ethnic Germans in the Lublin and Zamosc areas. On 19 July, along with Krüger and Globocnik, he made a through inspection of the area identified for it and spent an afternoon with the ethnic German settlers. He showed particular interest in the process of racial examination: at his request, individual families from a variety of categories were presented to the Reichsführer.[28] Himmler also used the opportunity to be brought up to date by Krüger and Globocnik about the progress of 'Aktion Reinhardt', the murder of the Jews in the General Government. The order, mentioned above, to Krüger to ensure that the 'resettlement of the whole Jewish population of the General Government is accomplished by 31 December 1942' dates from this day.[29]

The Zamosc settlement project got under way in November 1942, Himmler having given detailed instructions for it. At this point the Jewish inhabitants in the area had already been murdered; now 50,000 Poles were to be expelled in order to make room for around 2,500 families of settlers, in total about 10,000 people. The Poles, who were driven from their homes with violence by Globocnik's men, were channelled into a camp in which employees from a branch office of the Central Office for Resettlement sorted them into the familiar four 'racial groups': those assigned to the first two groups, a small minority, were deported to the Reich to be 're-Germanized', but the vast majority were deployed in the Reich or on the spot as forced labour. In this way the native Polish farmers were made to work for the German settlers. Anyone classified as 'inferior' was sent to Auschwitz; those unfit for work were consigned to so-called pension villages (*Rentendörfer*), in other words, death colonies. Progress as a whole was, however, slow. By the end of 1943 the racial examiners had dealt with only a third of the 50,000 people they were to cover. This changed when a series of 'anti-partisan' operations was initiated in the war zone: treatment of the Polish population became more brutal, the examination procedure was radically simplified and accelerated, and within a few weeks the target of 50,000 deportees had almost been achieved.[30]

The Soviet Union

Although the order that Himmler gave to Globocnik on 17 July 1941 to construct a network of SS and police bases in the newly occupied territories led to the creation of an extensive administration (the Office of the Representative Responsible for Setting up the SS and Police Bases in the New Eastern Region), because of a lack of resources there were no practical results. Globocnik therefore confined himself again to establishing bases in the General Government.[31] Himmler's attempt to use his police powers to introduce settlement measures in the occupied eastern territories thus had failed, but it had also become superfluous. He had, after all, managed to convince Hitler in September 1941 that the occupied Soviet territories should be placed under his control in his capacity as Settlement Commissar.

Apart from that, Himmler had found yet another foothold in ethnic policy by which to secure his position in the Soviet Union: the 'protection' of ethnic Germans. He had already used the same method in Poland and Yugoslavia. The Sonderkommando R (Russia) he had set up in July 1941 under Brigadeführer Horst Hoffmeyer established an armed defence unit in the ethnic German territories, opened German schools, and appointed liaison officers. The investigations pursued by the Sonderkommando into 'Black Sea Germans' indicate that at the end of 1941 there was still an assumption in the SS that these people, like the ethnic German 'settlers' from the Soviet Union before them, were to be brought 'home to the Reich'. In 1942, however, a change began in settlement policy: now ethnic Germans were to be gathered into settlement centres and act as pioneers within the project of Germanization.[32] As in the General Government, in the autumn of 1942 three race and settlement leaders were installed as part of the HSSPF group in the conquered Soviet territories. Their task was to ensure the preservation of 'valuable blood' and to help in the preparations for future settlement. They concentrated, for example, on gaining control of the collective farms.[33]

In August 1942 Himmler called his leading staff in the area of ethnic policy to a meeting in his headquarters in the Ukraine. Meyer, Greifelt, Lorenz, Berger, Prützmann, HSSPF for Russia South, and Stuckart, state secretary in the Reich Ministry of the Interior, were present.[34] In the Ukraine, 45,000 ethnic Germans in 'around 486 villages' had at first been looked after by the VoMi, but were now, as was generally acknowledged, being neglected since the transfer of responsibility to the civil administration. Here, 'life as a völkisch community [. . .] was now dead'. In order to change this unsatisfactory situation Himmler announced that he was going to involve the HSSPF in looking after the German minority by setting up 'ethnic German control centres'. In addition, he instructed that these people should be 'settled together'; in the first instance 10,000 were to be based in and around Shitomir.

'In accordance with the Führer's order,' Himmler continued, in his initiation of his audience into Hitler's plans for the occupied eastern territories, 'in the next twenty years parts of the Ukraine will be populated entirely by Germans.' Settlements in any of the territories were to be established first and foremost on the main traffic routes—at intersections there should be towns of 15,000 to 20,000 inhabitants surrounded by 'a rural population which is entirely German'. Settlements in the other territories were to be established as follows: first of all the Reich Commissariat Ostland, 'in view of the Estonians' capacity for Germanization', while on the other hand 'it is imperative that the Latgalians be expelled' from Latvia and 'there is no possibility of Germanizing the Lithuanians, as they are intellectually slow and have an extraordinary amount of Slavic blood'; secondly, so-called Ingria, the territory around Leningrad; thirdly, White Ruthenia, which would be comparatively easy, as the local population had 'no intelligentsia or political ambition'; and finally, fourthly, the Crimea.

Only the projects relating to the Ukraine (including the Crimea) were set in motion. But as a preliminary the number of ethnic Germans living there had to be established. Reich commissar Lohse, whom Himmler put in charge of 'Germanization' on 9 September, therefore gave instructions for the Ethnic German List to be introduced in September 1942.[35] The population in question was split into three groups: first Germans, secondly Germans in mixed marriages and their families (insofar as they professed themselves to be German and their families made a 'good impression'), thirdly people of German descent and their families who no longer felt themselves to be German, and in addition orphaned children of German blood. Those who, although they felt they were German culturally, were judged to be 'racially alien' and were not married to a German were not entered in the Ethnic German List. Thus Himmler's racist policy had triumphed completely in this territory: being German was a matter of 'blood' and not of attitude.[36]

In November 1942, after a stay in the Crimea, Himmler gave the SSPF Crimea, SS-Sturmbannführer Heinze, the task of preparing for the settlement of the peninsula (including the neighbouring territory of Taurien between the Dnieper estuary and the Azov Sea). Thereupon Heinze set up an ethnic German control centre, the so-called Crimean Commando, which derived from Commando R and comprised around 10,000 ethnic Germans, and made preparations for the territory to be settled later.[37] The plan temporarily floated to settle the South Tyroleans in the Crimea had had to be shelved in 1942. Instead, in 1943 the Crimean Commando hit on the idea of moving the Palestine Germans there who had been interned by the British. But in the meantime the Wehrmacht was in retreat, and when, from autumn 1943, the Crimea was being abandoned the settlers were also evacuated, for the time being to the Warthegau.

The second settlement project was in fact realized: the settling of a total of 30,000 ethnic Germans (for a time the assumption was there would be 43,000) in the General Commissariat of Shitomir, in three areas around Himmler's headquarters in Hegewald.[38] Between the middle of October and the middle of November 1942 a specially created Sonderkommando of the Reich Settlement Commissariat, the Henschel unit, expelled a total of almost 15,000 Ukrainians from the settlement areas of Hegewald and Försterstadt and moved 10,000 ethnic German settlers there. Himmler showed great interest in this: on 20 October he made a 'journey to the ethnic German villages' from his headquarters, accompanied by a group of SS leaders, among them his writer friend Hanns Johst, the 'SS bard', and Himmler's former employer from Fridolfing, Alois Rehl, who in the meantime had become an Obersturmführer and was visiting for a few days. Both Johst and Rehrl also accompanied Himmler to the Crimea to inspect ethnic German settlements.[39]

Ill. 27. During his visit to the Crimea at the end of October 1942 Himmler, who had studied agriculture, found the time to inspect the local cotton plantation.

In 1943, however, German resettlement policy in the General Commissariat of Shitomir had to go on the defensive: the special Henschel unit's main task was now to withdraw ethnic Germans from territories threatened by partisans and from dispersed settlements. The plan was in fact to accommodate them in two further settlement areas around Shitomir, but even that turned out to be impossible, one reason being that any further large-scale expulsion of Ukrainians seemed inopportune in view of the tense overall situation. Thus, in the end 30,000 ethnic Germans were squashed into the settlements at Hegewald and Försterstadt and a few thousand were taken to the third settlement area of Kalinowka. The 'settlement' programme was a failure: apart from small garden plots, it had not been possible as a rule to give the settlers any land of their own. Instead they were put to work on large farms; many were living in camps. At the end of 1943 the settlements were abandoned and the ethnic Germans were brought in 'treks' by horse and cart to the Warthegau.[40]

France

In the summer of 1942 Alsace and Lorraine also claimed more of Himmler's attention. In this case the Reich's resettlement supremo was concerned above all to 'remove' those who were considered undesirable on racial grounds in a future greater Germanic Reich. The Gauleiters Robert Wagner and Josef Bürckel, who were established as heads of the civil administration in Alsace and Lorraine, simply wished to consign these people to the occupied eastern territories—regardless of the fact that Himmler had introduced pilot schemes here that were based on careful racial 'selection'. In his view only truly 'Germanic elements' could be considered for settlement, and not those 'inferior beings' whom Bürckel and Wagner wanted to get rid of. It was, however, to be no easy job for Himmler to get his way in the face of opposition from these Reich governors.

In 1940 he had come off second-best against Bürckel in Lorraine when the latter, as already described, had more than 80,000 people deported to France and, in spite of great difficulties, settled Reich Germans and ethnic Germans. In the autumn of 1941, however, the situation changed. For in September Bürckel (who was the official representative of the Reich Commissar for the Consolidation of the Ethnic German Nation in Lorraine) appointed HSSPF Theodor Berkelmann as his representative for settlement matters in Lorraine, and thereby effectively handed his responsibility for ethnic issues back to Himmler. In doing so he was acknowledging that his settlement policy—he had had recourse, above all, to people from his home Gau of Saar-Palatinate—had largely been a failure.[41]

Berkelmann now set about organizing a comprehensive racial examination of the Lorraine population on the same lines as the Ethnic German List: in October 1941 the racial 'suitability test' was introduced.[42] His aim of implementing a carefully prepared settlement policy on a racial basis was, however, in conflict with Bürckel's plan to resettle 40,000 Lorrainers in the Ukraine—a request Hitler himself granted Bürckel in August 1942.[43] Greifelt, the head of the Main Staff Office in the Settlement Commissariat, was extremely vexed by 'the need to carry out such an immediate mass evacuation' as a result of Bürckel's initiative, for it necessarily jeopardized ethnic policy in Lorraine and in the Ukraine. But Himmler's response was:

'Nothing can be done about these things. The Führer has made his decision.'[44]

Himmler agreed with Bürckel that Lorrainers who were 'racially worthless and asocial' should emigrate to France, as should the female relatives of Lorrainers living in France, if they 'are past childbearing age or are racially worthless'. The same applied to male relatives if they were no longer fit for military service. The opportunity generously granted to Lorrainers who were not opting for German nationality of going to France did, however, have a catch, as is clear from the agreement: 'Those Lorrainers opting for emigration to France will be noted down at the receiving offices until this Saturday. They will then be immediately transferred to concentration camps as communist elements.'[45]

The plan to resettle 40,000 Lorrainers in the Ukraine, like many a grand 'population project', never came to fruition, as a result of wartime developments, with the result that Himmler's men did get their way: in February 1943 10,000 Lorrainers, handpicked on the basis of racial tests, were resettled, mostly in the Old Reich. In May 8,000 of them were still in VoMi camps.[46]

In Alsace Robert Wagner, the Gauleiter, had by the end of 1940 deported about 100,000 people to unoccupied France. In the second half of 1941 Himmler gradually brought his influence to bear on resettlement policy. The precondition for this was the setting up of a Land Office in Strasbourg.[47] On 19 March Wagner informed Himmler that he had recently received Hitler's permission for a 'final cleansing' in Alsace. The timing, he said, was still open, but it was to involve 'the removal of anybody unusable or racially inferior'; Hitler would determine, 'according to the political situation', whether 'such elements' should be 'consigned to France or settled in distant parts of the east'.[48]

Three months later Himmler returned to this matter in a letter to Wagner. In principle he was, of course, in agreement with Wagner that Alsace must 'be cleansed of unreliable elements of any kind'. Under no circumstances, however, could these be 'consigned to the east', as the east was being kept in view 'by us as an area for Germanic settlement by good racial elements' and so was not a 'penal colony'. Wagner might also consider that if 'some elements' were deported to France there was a danger of, 'by this means putting people of German blood at the disposal of the French and thus promoting the rebuilding of the French nation'.[49]

As Himmler saw it, dealing with 'undesirable elements' was therefore essentially a racial problem: among the Reich's political enemies there could be valuable 'Germanic blood' that in France and in the occupied eastern territories might cause damage in the long term. Wagner adopted Himmler's standpoint on this and proposed a solution that promised not only to free his territory from 'undesirables' but also to avoid the loss they feared of 'valuable blood': 'racially valuable' persons were to be 'resettled' in the Old Reich, while the 'racially inferior' were to be 'resettled' in France.

This principle was accepted on 7 August 1942 by the representatives of various SS offices responsible for ethnic policy who met in Berlin in order, on the basis of Wagner's detailed proposals, to issue 'Guidelines for the Treatment of Resettled Alsatians'. Wagner had drawn up a list of those 'inferior people' whom he intended to get rid of by means of a 'second resettlement operation' (the first had taken place in October 1940): 'Negroes and coloured people of mixed race, Gypsies and their descendants, Jews from half-Jews upwards, those in Jewish mixed marriages', and in addition, 'those of alien races and their descendants', the 'patois population',[50] 'asocials', and 'the incurably mentally ill'.[51]

Two days later, on 9 August, in the Fuhrer's headquarters Himmler met first of all Hitler, then Wagner and Bürckel, Gustav Simon, head of the civil administration in Luxembourg, the state secretary in the Reich Ministry of the Interior, Stuckart, as well as Ribbentrop and Keitel, to discuss the principles of ethnic policy in the west.[52] Bürckel reported later that on this occasion Hitler had made the decision in principle that 'asocials', 'criminals', 'all inferior elements', and 'anyone who does not belong to us by blood' should be sent to France, while 'anyone who belongs by blood to the German nation and must not be handed over to France [. . .]—is to be resettled in the Reich without regard to political or other attitudes, insofar as these elements in the population cannot be sustained in Alsace'.[53] Though warning that at the time there was no scope for larger-scale operations, Hitler had allowed the possibility of smaller ones (in 'individual and special cases').

By persuading Wagner, Himmler had therefore succeeded in making Hitler revise his original position that 'inferior people' should simply be sent off 'to the east'. Now a racial examination was to be the first stage and the deportations diverted to France. This was by no means merely a question of geography, but rather Himmler had managed to pin his 'Führer' down to Himmler's own principles: the crucial factor in official membership of the

German nation was not now political loyalty, language, or cultural tradition but race (scrutinized on an individual basis by SS experts). A German-speaking inhabitant of Alsace who felt himself to be 'German' and was loyal to the Third Reich could be deported to France as being 'of inferior race', while an opponent of German policy who defined himself as French and spoke French could, if the racial examination was positive, be moved to the Reich on the grounds that he was 'capable of being re-Germanized'. It was precisely this group that stubbornly resisted the imposition of 'Germanness' who attracted the particular attention of the racial examiners, for the latter detected behind this obstinacy the possibility of the influence of Nordic blood.[54]

With regard to France, Himmler pursued many far-reaching plans. On 12 April 1942 he came out with the view, during a meal with Hitler, that 'once a year there should be a trawl through the Germanic population of France for good blood. There should be an attempt to move the children of this section of the population while very young to German boarding schools and direct them away from their accidental French nationality towards their Germanic blood and to the fact that they belong to the great German nation.'[55]

A start had been made some considerable time before on establishing the number of ethnic Germans and those of German descent in France.[56] An 'advisory centre for returning ethnic Germans' established at the headquarters of the military command in Paris in 1940 had already registered 74,000 ethnic Germans in France by May 1941.[57] In June 1941 Heydrich therefore created a branch office of the EWZ (Central Office for Immigration, based in Łódź) in Paris that was not only to register the ethnic Germans but also to examine their racial characteristics. Lambert von Malsen-Ponickau, who was at the same time head of the EWZ in Łódź, was put in charge of the office, for which Himmler laid down special guidelines. By the end of 1944 almost 20,000 people in France had been registered and settled in Alsace, Lorraine, the Old Reich, and in the annexed Polish territories.[58] These results fell far short of the SS's expectations: 'The racial profile of the returning ethnic Germans processed in February can only be described as moderate', we read for example in 1942 in the summary produced by the branch office in Paris in its report for that month.[59]

In northern France, on the other hand, the racial examiners encountered a sizeable group of around 15,000 people, originally from Poland, who had lived for a considerable time in Germany, mostly in the Ruhr, and had emigrated to France after the First World War, where they called themselves ethnic Germans. In 1943 they were the object of a 'special emigration operation', and 5,000 of them were registered in the Ethnic German List. In March 1943 Himmler consented to their being given German nationality. The decisive factor in this decision was not, however, that these people regarded themselves as Germans, but that, even though their ancestors originated from Poland, they had proved by their stubborn attitude as migrants that they represented a racial selection and therefore had 'Germanic' roots.[60]

Marriage ban and 'Germanization' in the Reich

Himmler's Germanization policy in no way stopped at his plans for resettlement. As a result of the war against the Soviet Union he rather became increasingly convinced that in the 'inferior' population of the Soviet Union there must nevertheless still be genetic remnants of extinct Germanic peoples, which by, as it were, a back-cross with living 'Germanic' people could again be made fruitful. The immense number of people needed for the new order envisaged for the east led to a certain generosity in defining what was to be understood by 'Germanic'.

Himmler, therefore, from time to time contemplated including all the eastern workers brought into the Reich in the process of re-Germanization.[61] The fact that forced labourers from the east could not be examined as part of their whole family—something that, as Himmler repeatedly stressed, was crucial for the 'overall impression'—did, however, run counter to this. The process of re-Germanization for eastern workers was therefore applied only in particular individual cases, and in September 1944 halted altogether.[62] It was above all those Soviet agricultural workers earmarked for 'individual deployment' on German farms who, as part of a 'rough-and-ready selection process', were tested for their 'capacity for re-Germanization'. Underlying this was concern about the biological 'threat' to the female rural population.[63]

By contrast, racial testing of female domestic staff from eastern Europe developed differently. In October 1941 Himmler had already ordered that girls from Poland, the Ukraine, and the former Baltic States who, after careful racial examination, were judged to be 'capable of re-Germanization' should be brought to the Reich as housemaids,[64] in order to relieve German housewives of work and thus promote in them a greater desire to have children. If these girls, as Himmler expressed his thoughts in July 1941,

have, depending on their age, worked impeccably for 3–5 years as housemaids, cooks, or nannies in a family with three or more children or where there is one child and the mother is expecting a second, they will be given German nationality and also be entitled to marry a German. Furthermore, such girls should be given the prospect of their family also being judged by the girls' behaviour and attitude and then later having the opportunity of coming to Germany and being Germanized.[65]

Yet only 3–5 per cent of these eastern European girls, for whom members of the elite eagerly placed orders at the Race and Settlement Main Office, satisfied the racial criteria.[66] As their 'capacity for re-Germanization' had been overestimated, in 1942 another method was tried: the search for suitable workers was extended to the occupied Soviet territories, particularly to the Ukraine and Byelorussia, and the racial criteria were relaxed. Now the aim was not primarily to identify those capable of being re-Germanized but to conduct a 'preliminary selection', in other words, to exclude particularly 'primitive' people. Girls belonging to Racial Group III did still seem to be acceptable, though not for subsequent citizenship. As many as 50,000 girls may have been brought to the Reich with this proviso.[67] The supposed biological risks associated with these girls being employed in German households were therefore considered much less serious than those to which lonely farmers' wives saw themselves exposed by Soviet agricultural workers.

Even though sexual intercourse between Germans and 'ethnic aliens' had been ruled as strictly forbidden, Himmler did not apply without exception the rigorous punishment originally envisaged for such cases. Instead, he instructed that a differentiated procedure be adopted, based on the findings of the 'racial' examination of the 'ethnic alien' involved and designed to ensure that no 'valuable blood' was lost. From 1941 onwards he no longer had slave workers caught in 'cases of sexual intercourse' summarily executed, but rather first subjected to a racial examination; if this had a positive outcome they were sent to a concentration camp.[68] German women who had become pregnant by civilian workers or prisoners of war were also subjected to a racial test, on the outcome of which depended whether the Race and Settlement Main Office would require the pregnancy to be terminated.[69]

From December 1942 onwards pregnant workers from the east were also required to undergo a racial examination. If a child 'of good race' could be expected the mother was allowed to carry the child to term but not to keep it. Rather, it was handed over after birth to a German foster-family. If the child was 'racially undesirable' considerable pressure was often put on the mother to agree to a termination, and sometimes even force was used. If such 'undesirable' children were nevertheless born they were put in 'care facilities for foreign children', where most died of systematic neglect—without doubt several tens of thousands of infants in all.[70]

The dangers to 'racial policy' created by mass deportations from eastern Europe to Germany and the numerous provisions for individual cases that were made either to contain these risks or to filter out 'good blood' seem to have prompted Himmler to introduce a radical reversal of racial policy in the spring of 1942. In March that year he decreed, in his capacity as Settlement Commissar, that the term 'related' (artverwandt), which up to that point had been used consistently in Nazi racial terminology to refer to the non-German European nations, was to be replaced by a set of new prescribed terms. The term 'related', it was claimed, was based on the 'presupposition [. . .] that the racial structure of all European nations is so closely related to that of the German nation that if interbreeding occurs there is no danger that the German nation's blood will be racially contaminated'. This, it was claimed, is not at all the case, however: even in the European context, 'racial intermingling' was a threat, particularly in the case of contact with 'Slavdom'.

The corresponding directive states that at a meeting in the Party Chancellery of the party branch offices involved it had therefore been decided, 'with immediate effect' (until a comprehensive law protecting German blood was passed after the end of the war), to divide the term 'related' into, first, 'German blood and blood of related (= Germanic) races' (to which members of 'non-Germanic' nations who were 'capable of re-Germanization' also belonged, in other words those who exhibited 'Nordic-Faelish (nordische-fälische) racial elements'), and secondly, 'related blood but not from related races', by which was meant all non-Germanic European nations (Slavs, Latins, Celts, Balts).[71]

The introduction of this terminology heralded Himmler's policy of permitting Germans in future to have sexual relations only with other Germans or 'Teutons'. Although at first intercourse was banned only with Slavs, the directive made a basic distinction undoubtedly intended to prepare the way for a future ban on sexual relations between Germans and those of Latin, Baltic, or Celtic origin.

Seizure of children

The SS not only took children 'of good race' from female slave workers sent to Germany, but also forcibly removed tens of thousands of them from the occupied and annexed territories. The historian Isabel Heinemann, who has done pioneering work on the activity of the Race and Settlement Main Office, concludes that as a result at least 50,000 children in eastern and south-eastern Europe were forcibly removed from their families.[72]

In 1942 the staff headquarters of the Reich Settlement Commissar took the initiative in this matter, calling on the responsible authorities in the Warthegau to search for children of German extraction in Polish orphanages and then to check all children placed in foster-families.[73] The children were first sent for observation to a central children's home and then handed over to the Lebensborn organization, which placed the older ones in 'German boarding schools' and offered the younger ones to SS families for adoption. The remaining annexed Polish territories, the General Government, and the occupied Soviet territories were gradually also drawn into this initiative.

As early as 18 June 1941 Himmler had spoken to Arthur Greiser, the Reich Governor in the Warthegau, about this matter: 'I consider it right that young children of particularly good race from Polish families should be collected together and brought up by us in smallish special crèches and children's homes. The removal of the children should be justified on the grounds of health risks. Children who fail to do well must be returned to their parents.'[74] Rudolf Creutz, the chief of staff at staff headquarters, expressed reservations about this proposal, however, insofar as it applied to 'Polish children of good race whose parents were still alive'; 'serious problems' could arise from such an operation.[75] It does, in fact, seem that Himmler's idea of forcibly separating children from intact families was not systematically implemented, but it certainly did occur in a number of cases, though the number cannot be precisely quantified.[76]

As far as the Soviet Union was concerned, as early as July 1941 Himmler had charged Guntram Pflaum, the administrative head of the Lebensborn, with taking care of ethnic German children 'of good race'. Pflaum set up a children's home in Bobruisk for children 'of good race', who were offered for adoption in Germany.[77] These were by no means all from ethnic German backgrounds, but also included 'racially valuable' children from Byelorussian families, and the home was not confined to orphans. In the Ukraine children 'without parents' were also gathered in camps and subjected to 'racial selection'.[78] During a journey through the Reichskommissariat Ostland in autumn 1941 Himmler had in addition given instructions to gather information on the children of people deported by the Soviets, establish whether they were 'capable of Germanization', and if so to move them to the Reich.[79]

On Himmler's orders, 'those of German origin' in the General Government who were unwilling to be entered in the Ethnic German List were punished by being put in concentration camps and having their children removed.[80] In addition, at least 4,500 Polish children from the Zamosc district, whose parents had been 'resettled'—in other words, turned into slave labour or sent to Majdanek—were transported to the Reich.[81]

Himmler regarded the whole matter as extremely simple. 'It is our task', he emphasized to the SS and Police Leaders from Russia-South on 16 September 1942, 'to remove everybody of good race from here.'[82] And on 4 October 1943, at the conference of Gruppenführer at Posen (Poznań), he spoke openly in favour of the forcible removal of children: 'Whatever we find in the way of good blood from our race we will take, if necessary by stealing children and raising them ourselves.'[83]

This also applied to the children of resistance fighters and partisans who had been killed or imprisoned (or those suspected of such activities).[84] The best-known case is the barbaric action taken at Lidice. As part of the 'retribution' for the assassination of Heydrich eighty-eight children, whose fathers were shot and whose mothers were put in a concentration camp, were first taken to a camp belonging to the Central Office for Resettlement in Łódź , where seven were identified as being 'capable of Germanization' and the remaining eighty-one deported to the Chelmno extermination camp and murdered.[85]

Shortly after, on 25 June 1942, Himmler issued 'Guidelines for Action Against Partisans and Other Bandits in Upper Carniola and Lower Styria'. They clearly stated that, 'in principle men in any culpable family, in many cases even those of the entire clan, are to be executed, the women from these families are to be arrested and sent to a concentration camp, the children to be removed from their homeland and collected together in

Ill. 28. On his Minsk trip in August 1942 Himmler is shown demonstrating to
his two companions, Josef Kiermaler, the head of his personal security service
(first from left), and Karl Wolff (second from left), the racial examination of a local
boy. The photo was taken by the 'Führer's photographer', Walter Frenz, who
was accompanying the group.

the part of the Gau belonging to the Old Reich. I shall expect additional reports on the number and racial value of these children.'[86] On 6 January 1943 he ordered that in 'operations against the bandits' men and women suspected of such activity were in future to be deported to the camps in Lublin and Auschwitz and their children to an 'internment camp for children and adolescents'. The 'racial and political inspection' that was to take place there can be interpreted as an indication that those racially 'valuable' children who did not understand their situation and so were not potential avengers of their parents were also considered for 'Germanization'.[87]

A further group of 'Germanic children' that Himmler refused to relinquish were those children fathered by German soldiers in the occupied countries.[88] He was particularly concerned about 'Germanic' countries. Assessors from the Race and Settlement Office took on responsibility for the racial examination of children born in the Netherlands and Norway, and from 1942–3 the Lebensborn organization was involved in their care. In Norway alone Lebensborn maintained six maternity homes, in which an estimated 6,000 such children of the occupation were born.

Even the children of German soldiers and Russian women became an object of Himmler's desire, above all because it was assumed that there was a colossal number of such births; even if the mothers were in principle considered to be 'racially inferior ethnic aliens', there was a chance that the superior racial genetic make-up of the father would produce passable results.[89] Hitler had brought his attention to the problem, the Reichsführer-SS explained in his address to the SS and Police Leaders from Russia-South in September 1942, 'that in Russia probably a good 1 to 1½ million children had been fathered by German soldiers'. He conceded that it was possibly slightly fewer, 'but it will certainly be several hundred thousands or almost a million'. These children were, he said, 'an unheard-of boost, both in quantity and in racial quality, to the Russian nation, which at this point has lost a great deal of blood'. For that reason Hitler had let him know 'that we, the SS, must first of all establish where all these children are, so that they can be inspected. The children who are of good race and healthy will be taken away from their mothers and taken to Germany, or if the mothers are of good race and healthy we shall take them too.'

The 'children of poor race', on the other hand, were to be left behind. 'My view is that even that is damaging to us. For even a child produced by a German father and a Russian mother of poor race gives something positive to the Russians; for we cannot tell what may suddenly emerge from his blood in the third, fourth, fifth, sixth, and even later generations, if it combines again with similar blood.' According to another record of the speech, he already had a solution to hand for this problem: He spoke of the 'eradication' of the undesirable progeny.[90]

Hitler and Himmler may, however, have greatly overestimated the virility of German soldiers stationed in the east. Realistic estimates suggest that no more than 10,000–11,000 children were fathered by German soldiers with local women.[91] In this case too the Race and Settlement Main Office played its part in conducting racial examinations; the children were handed over to the National Socialist Welfare organization (NSV). In all the German occupied territories probably more than 10,000 children of German soldiers were taken into NSV institutions.[92]

Racial examination: methodical arbitrariness

As the previous sections of this chapter have shown, in 1941–2 Himmler began to define racial criteria in a highly flexible manner. And it emerged that the flexibility he prescribed was highly compatible with the examination process. For the vast majority of people examined by the racial assessors were diagnosed as being a 'mixture' of European 'principal races' as defined by racial theory: the subjects were therefore people showing 'traces of blood' of a variety of races—'Nordic', 'Faelish', 'Mediterranean' (*westisch*), 'Dinaric', 'Alpine' (*ostisch*), or 'East Baltic'. The racial criteria were met either if the 'Nordic' element could be clearly recognized or if the other components were 'well balanced' (in other words, even if there were no 'Nordic' elements at all). An applicant was given a clear negative appraisal if, in the view of the assessor, 'Slavic', Negroid', 'oriental' ('Jewish'), or other 'alien' influences were demonstrable (or were 'presumed'), or if the traces of European elements 'resulted in an 'unbalanced' appearance—in other words, one in which the features were too 'Dinaric', 'Alpine' or 'East Baltic'.[93]

This overview by itself reveals the arbitrariness of the whole procedure and the absurdity of the so-called racial doctrine underlying it. If the overwhelming majority of those tested were classed as 'of mixed race' (*Mischling*), then the German population could neither be defined unequivocally on the basis of 'racial' criteria nor could it be clearly distinguished in racial composition from neighbouring nations. The evident differences in appearance among those tested were, however, not simply accepted as variants but rather the attempt was made to relate them back to specific 'ideal types', which in their pure form—the 'Nordic' type, the 'Dinaric' type, and so on—existed only in the imagination of race theorists. For racial theory was based on the proposition that the origins of human beings in the twentieth century could be traced back to prehistoric, pure 'primal races' (Urrassen)—an assumption that was essentially a historical myth with no anthropological foundation.

The arbitrariness of the racial examinations is not only reflected in these results but characterized the process as a whole: the decisive element in the assessment was, in the end, the 'overall picture' presented by the candidate, the immediate impression gained by the assessor at the examination. Family context (the preference was for examining the whole family), geographical origin, religious affiliation, nationality, and possible membership of the Nazi Party were noted and formed part of this 'overall picture'. Yet even the purely biological criteria were subject to interpretation. If, for example, the shape of the head ('short') and the amount of body hair ('abundant') indicated negative racial characteristics, the criterion 'erect bearing' could fully compensate for these inadequacies. In the final analysis, where there were so many criteria, it was virtually always possible in assessing a candidate presenting a 'mixed' racial appearance to give weight to one or several as clear 'proof' of a 'positive' (or 'negative') overall picture.

A sober appraisal would put Himmler himself in the racially average band, or to some extent even below it: his face was round rather than oval, his nose more broad than slim, his normal bearing more 'sagging' than 'erect', and his chin—and for the racial assessors this was a particularly negative feature—fell clearly into the 'receding' category.

23

The 'Iron Law of Ethnicity': Recruitment into the Waffen-SS

During this summer of 1942 that was proving so promising for Himmler—he had, after all, succeeded in including the whole of Europe in the systematic mass murder of the Jews, while at the same time advancing his settlement plans—the Reichsführer-SS made progress in another area as well: the expansion of his Waffen-SS. He succeeded in massively extending its basis of recruitment both inside and outside Germany.

In May 1942 Himmler had managed to persuade Hitler to establish an SS army corps under Colonel-General of the Waffen-SS Paul Hausser, composed of the 'Leibstandarte', 'Das Reich', and 'Death's Head' divisions, which were withdrawn from the front in order to fill the gaps left by their losses and to re-equip them as Panzer grenadier divisions. By the end of the year the army corps had been renamed the SS Panzer Corps.[1] This meant that Himmler had brought together his most effective divisions under a unified command, and right up to the end of the war SS divisions were used as a 'fire brigade', always being deployed where critical situations developed on any of the fronts. In this way, through deployments involving very heavy losses, the Waffen-SS was able to build up its reputation as a superior elite force.

Finally, in August 1942, Himmler succeeded in persuading Wilhelm Keitel, the chief of the Wehrmacht High Command, to triple the quota of recruits for the Waffen-SS from the 1924 age cohort. This measure provided the SS with new divisions. In September 1942 Hitler ordered that the SS Cavalry Brigade should be expanded to form the SS Cavalry Division 'Florian Geyer'.[2] In December he ordered the creation of two new German SS divisions from which, in 1943, a new SS army corps was to emerge.

However, as has already been described, in 1940 the Waffen-SS had already begun to try to recruit outside Germany, in the so-called Germanic countries and among ethnic German minorities in south-eastern Europe. The Reich's intervention in the Balkans and the attack on the Soviet Union, which in propaganda terms was fought as a crusade of civilized Europe against 'Bolshevism', changed the context in which recruitment took place. It was now necessary to spread the net widely in the search for allies in the war against Bolshevism. As Himmler regarded the recruitment measures among ethnic German minorities in south-east Europe and in the occupied countries in northern and western Europe as anticipating the future Greater Germanic Reich and the new order which this new power would impose on Europe after the end of the war, the recruitment policy of the Waffen-SS forms part of the same project as Himmler's other racial and foreign-policy ambitions. It is clear from the numerous relevant entries in his office diary just how seriously he took issues involving the recruitment, establishment, and equipment of the Waffen-SS. These matters also figured prominently in his 'leader's lectures'.[3]

National legions

Apart from the two sources of recruitment already referred to that the Waffen-SS had utilized outside Germany—ethnic Germans and 'Germanic volunteers'—in 1941 Himmler focused on another small group: volunteers from occupied or allied countries who were to be organized in national 'legions'. Hitler agreed to this project on 29 July 1941.[4]

Following negotiations with the Wehrmacht, it was agreed that the Waffen-SS would recruit legions from Norwegians, the Dutch, Swedes, Danes, and Flemings and retain the Finnish volunteer battalion that had already been set up at the start of 1941, while the Wehrmacht would form Croatian, Spanish, and French units. Although the majority of the Waffen-SS legionnaires came from 'Germanic' countries, they were carefully differentiated from the true 'Germanic' volunteers from these countries. They were not considered members of the SS, and so were not subject to the SS's racial criteria for selection or to the Marriage Order; they were foreign legionnaires in the service of Germany. These legions were intended to signify, in an explicitly nationalist manner, the participation of the countries concerned in the common 'crusade' against Bolshevism, while the idea of the 'Germanic' volunteers implied an integrative purpose.

There were, however, considerable teething troubles involved in setting up the legions; the Swedish one did not even get going.[5] In Denmark, where recruitment was in the hands of the Danish Nazis, the SS began to establish a so-called Free Corps 'Denmark' in July 1941, and by the end of the month was able to send 600 volunteers to Germany for training.[6] In July 1941 Dutchmen and Flemings were withdrawn from the Standarte 'North-West' established in April to form the core units for the 'Flanders' and 'The Netherlands' legions[7], and at the end of July the SS Leadership Office ordered the creation of the 'Norway' legion.[8] However, by the time the men had finished their training at the end of 1941 none of the legions had achieved regimental strength[9]—by then they had been able to recruit a total of only 5,816 men.[10]

In the directives that Himmler issued for the new force he emphasized that the legionnaires were not members of the SS; thus, they did not wear SS runes on their uniform, but instead badges symbolizing their 'member-ship of their nation'. They had to swear an oath of loyalty to Hitler, and received the same wages and family support as all other members of the Waffen-SS.[11]

The first military engagement of the Flemish and Netherlands legions, which occurred in January 1942 and was designed to block a Soviet counter-attack in the Leningrad area, proved extremely costly. The Nor-wegian legion also took part in military operations in the Leningrad area in February 1942; the Danish legion had been fighting on the eastern front since 1941 as part of the 'Death's Head' division.[12] The military engagement of the Finnish legion was considerably delayed. In January 1942 Aaltonen, the chief of the Finnish state police, told a colleague of Berger's in no uncertain terms that the volunteers were so discontented, above all with the arrogance of the German officers and their rough treatment, that 'Finnish volunteers [...] going into action for the first time would shoot their German SS officers'.[13] It was only after a number of serious abuses had been dealt with that the Finnish authorities permitted the battalion to leave for the front. From January 1942 onwards it fought for several months as part of the 'Viking' division.[14]

The complaints made by the Finns—discriminatory treatment, failure to keep the promises with which they had been recruited, failure to take account of the military experience and ranks that they had acquired in their own army—were also made by the members of other nations. Berger warned Himmler in February 1942 that 'the recruitment of volunteers from the Germanic and ethnic German areas is becoming more and more difficult and will cease altogether if fundamental changes are not made'.[15]

In response, on 6 March 1942 Himmler transferred to Berger responsibility for the 'recruitment of the Waffen-SS legions, police units, and guard battalions', the 'military supervision of all the Germanic volunteers', and the 'establishment, leadership, and training of the Germanic SS in the individual countries',[16] and introduced a series of concrete measures to meet the legionnaires' complaints. The men whose period of enlistment had come to an end were in fact discharged; foreigners were also now allowed to be trained as officers at the SS officer-training college at Bad Tölz; and from now on German personnel who were transferred to the legions had to go through an orientation course. Himmler also reserved the right to appoint officers to the foreign units of the Waffen-SS himself.[17]

Since little changed as far as the poor treatment of foreigners was concerned, and the war soon began to take a turn for the worse, during 1942 the number of volunteers decreased. The legions' losses could no longer be covered, so that they could no longer be deployed in their existing form.[18] As a result, the legions had a poor reputation with the leadership of the regime. In April 1942, during one of his table talks, Hitler was already expressing scepticism about 'all the foreign legions on the eastern front': as the legionnaire was not 'inspired by ethnic membership of the Germanic Reich he must consider himself a traitor to his nation'.[19]

In view of the lack of new recruits, at the end of 1942 the decision was taken to reorganize the legions; as part of this reorganization the term 'legionnaire' was replaced by 'SS volunteer'. German members of the SS and 'Germanic volunteers' were now deployed to reinforce the Danish, Dutch, and Norwegian legions, and the legions were transformed into the 'Denmark', 'Netherlands', and 'Norway' regiments. This provided the basis for the future SS Volunteer Panzer Grenadier division 'Nordland' ('Northland').[20] The complicated name clearly indicates the difference between it and the proper Waffen-SS divisions, which were composed only of Reich Germans and 'Teutons'.

A year later the 'Netherlands' regiment was removed from the 'Nordland' division. The new autonomous brigade finally became the 23rd SS Volunteer Panzer Grenadier 'Netherlands' Division. A new Flemish legion was established with the name 'Langemarck' and later transformed into the

27th SS Volunteer Grenadier Division. The Wehrmacht transferred its French and Wallonian volunteer units to the SS, which deployed each of them as a division within the Waffen-SS, even though their numbers were below those normally required for a Waffen-SS division.[21]

The Finnish government, however, recalled its battalion in May 1943 following the wrangles referred to above.[22] Himmler issued an emotional order of the day to the departing Finns: 'During these recent most difficult and testing times we have been linked by a fraternal bond, which can never be broken by any outward separation.'[23]

Germanic volunteers

The recruitment of 'Germanic' volunteers was much more successful. Although, like the German SS members, these volunteers had to undergo racial screening[24] and submit to the obligations of the Engagement and Marriage Order,[25] according to a (possibly too generous) estimate, during the Second World War the Waffen-SS was able to recruit over 100,000 men from northern and western Europe. However, about half of these joined during the last year of the war, in other words, in circumstances under which the 'volunteers' had few alternatives. According to this calculation there were 50,000 Dutch, 40,000 Belgians (with equal numbers from Flanders and Wallonia), and 6,000 each from Denmark and Norway, as well as a further 1,200 volunteers from other countries, above all Switzerland, Sweden, and Luxembourg, and about 1,000 Finns.[26]

On 12 August 1942 Hitler declared that the Reichsführer-SS was responsible for 'dealing with all the ethnic German groups in Denmark, Norway, Belgium, and the Netherlands [. . .] on behalf of the NSDAP, its formations, and affiliated organizations'.[27] Six months later he extended this monopoly of responsibility to the civilian administrations in the occupied territories, so that they were now obliged to consult Himmler if they wished to contact the 'ethnic German' elements in the various countries concerned.[28] As a result, Himmler had not only strengthened his position vis-à-vis the recruitment of 'Germanic' volunteers in north-west Europe, but above all had had his 'Greater Germanic' policy confirmed. Ever since the occupation of these countries in 1940 he had been endeavouring to establish relations with indigenous fascist movements so that they could help him not only to recruit for his Waffen-SS but also provide the political basis for a future amalgamation with the Reich as part of the 'Greater Germanic' concept. However, by the time Hitler sanctioned this policy in August 1942 it had already basically failed.

In Denmark the SS had initially worked with the Danish Nazis, and in particular used their organization to recruit volunteers. However, through this cooperation the Danmarks Nationalsocialistiske Arbejderparti (DNSAP) had discredited itself in the eyes of the majority of its fellow countrymen. When elections were due in 1943 the DNSAP was to gain representation in parliament only through massive electoral support from the German minority. As a result the SS had to seek a new partner. In 1943 it broke with the DNSAP, and instead the SS established a quasi-militia, the Schalburg Corps, named after the leader of the 'Denmark' Free Corps, Christian Frederik von Schalburg, who had been killed in Russia. Fritz Clausen, the head of the DNSAP and formerly Himmler's most important partner in Denmark, volunteered for front-line duty and eventually, following his increasing abuse of alcohol, was confined to a mental hospital by Himmler.[29]

In Norway Himmler had relied on Vidkun Quisling and his party, Nasjonal Samling. Quisling, however, who had been appointed Prime Minister by the occupation authorities in February 1942, was completely isolated among his own population. His attempts to extract commitments concerning the future of his country from the German leadership were stalled.[30]

In the Netherlands Himmler's attempts to recruit volunteers met with resistance from Anton Mussert, the very man whom the occupation authorities regarded as their main ally in the country. The 'Leider' of the fascist Nationaal-Socialistische movement, the only party that had been permitted to exist in the Netherlands since the summer of 1941, was pursuing his own policy. He hoped to achieve a 'Greater Netherlands' through amalgamation with Germanic Flanders. Right from the start he regarded SS attempts at recruitment as an affront to Dutch sovereignty. Although Himmler succeeded in neutralizing Mussert's resistance to Waffen-SS recruitment and in forcing through the establishment of a 'Germanic' General SS in the Netherlands, in doing so he had aroused Mussert's mistrust. He feared that the 'Greater German Reich' propagated by Himmler would simply result in the annexation of the Netherlands. Although Himmler was often provoked by Mussert,[31] he could not avoid supporting him in public for the simple reason that there was no alternative.[32] The person who was originally his closest ally, Rost van Tonningen, leader of the radical wing of the Dutch Nazis, had been rejected as a volunteer by the SS-Standarte 'Westland' because he could not prove his Aryan identity and thus was not a feasible candidate for such a function.[33] Rost van Tonningen had been born in Indonesia, a fact that was used by his opponents to cast doubt on his racial 'purity'. Instead, in April 1941 he took over as head of the Dutch national bank and became state secretary in the Finance Ministry. From then on he focused his attention on currency matters.[34]

Himmler's interest in Belgium was initially concentrated on Flanders, which after the war he intended to incorporate into the Reich as 'Reich Gau Flanders'. The head of the SS Main Office, Gottlob Berger, who regarded himself as an expert on Flanders and devoted a considerable amount of effort to the Germanization of this area, initially attempted to infiltrate the fascist Vlaamisch Nationaal Verbond (VNV) and persuade it to adopt a Greater Germanic policy, an attempt which, however, failed. It supported a policy of seeking a Greater Flanders through the incorporation of the Netherlands. In 1941 Berger, therefore, turned to the Deutssch-Vlamisch Arbeitsgemeinschaft (DeVlag) (German-Flemish Working Group) in order, with Himmler's full support, to build it up as a counterweight to the VNV. The result was that the Flemish forces who were prepared to collaborate were now working against each other.[35]

Himmler's attempts to create a basis for his 'Greater Germanic' fantasies through cooperation with fascist mass movements in north European countries had led nowhere. The fact that he utilized these organizations for the attempt to recruit for the Waffen-SS damaged their reputation in the eyes of the indigenous population, which saw them not as the avant-garde of a better political future but as collaborators and traitors. And from the point of view of the fascist movements those volunteers recruited by the SS now left a gap as political activists in the countries concerned.

Given this limited progress, and at the same time the Waffen-SS's urgent need for recruits, Himmler began to consider whether the concept of 'Germanic volunteers' could not be extended. For example, in the French-speaking Wallonian part of Belgium, which Nazi racial experts generally regarded as 'Roman', there was the fascist Rexist movement under the leadership of Léon Degrelle. Since the beginning of 1943 he had been deputy commander of the SS Storm Brigade 'Wallonia', a unit of Belgian volunteers that had been transferred by the Wehrmacht to the Waffen-SS. Himmler supported Degrelle, if only for the simple reason that he was able to recruit more volunteers for the SS in Wallonia than was possible in the 'Germanic' Flemish part of Belgium.[36] Moreover, Himmler approved of the way in which Degrelle was prepared to adapt his original policy of a 'Greater Belgium' to the SS's vague 'Germanic' ideas. For Degrelle utilized the transfer of his men to the Waffen-SS to proclaim, in a major speech, that the Walloons were members of the 'Germanic race'.[37] Hitler was delighted (and evidently surprised) by this move, and noted in January 1943 that it was 'extremely interesting that the Walloons were now suddenly deciding to be Teutons'.[38]

Himmler, at any rate, was thinking along the same lines. In 1943 he initiated racial-biological investigations in Wallonia which, according to a report by Professor Frank Petri, appeared to confirm that 'the whole of the north and west of France reaching right into the Paris basin contains a very significant proportion of Germanic-north German bloodlines'. Petri, who was a medievalist and leading 'researcher of the west', held the rank of senior councillor for military administration and acted as the expert for 'ethnic German and ethnic Flemish affairs' on the staff of the military administration. He provided Himmler with the intellectual backing for his attempt to claim that Wallonia should belong to the future Greater Germanic Reich.[39] Himmler's Flanders expert, Gottlob Berger, could already see a 'Reich Gau Wallonia', in other words, another Germanic province, beginning to emerge.[40]

In July 1944 Himmler explained his views on the Wallonia question to Hitler in the following terms:

We must take care in our dealings with the movement for Wallonian renewal. Its leader, Léon Degrelle, is an extremely clever but very adaptable politician, who has at last persuaded the Rexist movement to take on board the idea of a Greater Germanic Reich but who is capable of suddenly reverting to the notion of a Greater Burgundian Reich of the Walloons. Degrelle's idea that the Walloons are romanized Teutons is a view that we could very well adopt ourselves.[41]

However, given the way the war was developing such plans soon proved irrelevant: a few weeks later Himmler's romanized Teutons were already outside his control.

At the same time, on occasion Himmler contemplated assimilating young Slovaks through service in the SS. In October 1941 he adopted a project which Nageler, his adviser with the Hlinka Guard, had been pursuing for some time.[42] During a meeting with the Slovak President Tiso, and his

Interior Minister Mach, Himmler proposed recruiting volunteers for the Waffen-SS from the Hlinka Guard. According to Himmler, Mach responded 'enthusiastically'. This was the same visit during which he proposed to his Slovak guests that 'their' Jews should be deported to the General Government, a further example of how seamlessly the 'positive' and 'negative' sides of Himmler's racial policy meshed together: integration on the one hand, exclusion and mass murder on the other. After the meeting Himmler immediately issued detailed instructions for the recruitment of Slovaks. They should be 'subject racially to the strictest Germanic criteria'. One should 'never be able to distinguish a Slovak volunteer in the Waffen-SS from a German or a Germanic volunteer when in uniform'.[43] The idea was that, through such a process of racial selection, an elite could be created in Slovakia that could be merged with the majority population of a future Greater Germanic Reich.

On 1 September 1942 Himmler appointed Nageler his special representative for the recruitment of volunteers in Slovakia. In fact, from January 1943 onwards, with the support of the Slovak government, several thousand men were to be 'recruited' for the Waffen-SS, sometimes under considerable pressure, although these came mostly from among the German minority. Himmler's idea of 'Germanizing' a Slovak elite through service in the SS was dropped.[44]

Ethnic Germans

Under the changed circumstances of the war Himmler now benefited from the fact that in 1936–7 he had acquired the primary responsibility for ethnic German policy and during the following years, with the help of VoMi, had managed to bring the individual ethnic German communities increasingly under his control. As early as April 1941 the Waffen-SS began recruiting among the German minorities in western Banat (which, as part of Serbia, was under German military administration); in the new state of Croatia, which was dependent on Germany; as well as in Blatschka, which had been transferred from Yugoslavia to Hungary.[45] This was rapidly extended to other countries: Hungary, Romania, and Slovakia where Himmler's recruiters were already active. Since Himmler regarded the German ethnic groups in the first instance not as citizens of their respective countries but as Germans, who were living in those countries purely as a result of historical accident, his methods could easily be transferred from one ethnic group to the next, as will become clear in what follows. He had little interest in the fact that his recruitment of people who, in terms of international law, were foreigners would have serious repercussions for bilateral relations; conflicts with the Foreign Ministry were thus inevitable.

While stationed in Yugoslavia in April 1941 the 'Das Reich' division received the order to go ahead and recruit ethnic German volunteers into its ranks. The divisional commander, Paul Hausser, began systematically to carry out medical examinations in ethnic German villages of the Banat and to train the recruits. Ethnic German soldiers of the Yugoslav army who had been captured by the Germans were released if they agreed to join the Waffen-SS. As a result, in one way or another around 1,000 men became members of the Waffen-SS during the spring of 1941.[46]

From April 1941 on an SS recruitment agency was operating among ethnic Germans in Croatia.[47] However, this provoked protests from the Foreign Ministry, which wanted to follow a different path. On 16 September 1941 the German envoy, Siegfried Kasche, made an agreement with the War Minister, Slavko Kvaternik, about the recruitment of ethnic Germans. According to this, 10 per cent of ethnic German recruits were to be reserved for the Wehrmacht (Berger, however, claimed them for the Waffen-SS), but the bulk of the ethnic Germans were to serve in special ethnic German units of the Croatian army.[48]

Himmler, however, was unimpressed by this. In the late summer of 1941 he established a 'German Force' along the lines of the General SS as a security militia as well as a task formation for combating partisans, both of which were formally attached to the Croatian militia, the Ustasha.[49]

In November 1941, responding to a request from Hess issued in February, Himmler established an Office for Ethnic Questions within the NSDAP, which was to 'deal with all ethnic issues involving the NSDAP' with representatives from all four of the main offices that in the meantime had acquired responsibilities for ethnic issues: VoMi, the RuSHA, the RSHA, and the Staff Main Office of the RKF.[50] The precise definition of his party responsibilities for 'settlement issues', which involved difficult questions of competence, particularly in relation to the Soviet Union, proved problematic, and Himmler was unable to realize his aim of now being able to act as 'the representative of the NSDAP for the consolidation of the ethnic German nation'.[51] Nevertheless, by establishing the office he was clearly expressing his claim to be the main point of contact within the

NSDAP for all ethnic German matters. In March 1942 the office was even raised to the status of a Main Office for Ethnic Questions within the NSDAP's headquarters.[52]

Hardly had the office been created when, in November 1941, Himmler met the leaders of the ethnic German groups in Croatia, Slovakia, and Serbia. On this occasion Sepp Janko, who represented the Germans in Banat in Serbia, offered to establish an ethnic German home guard in regimental strength for the purpose of relieving the Wehrmacht units based in Banat. In view of the relevant experience he had gained there, Branimir Altgayer, the leader of the Germans in Croatia, was to provide assistance with the training.[53] A few weeks later Hitler approved this plan.[54] Moreover, in January 1942 Himmler appointed August von Meyszner as the first HSSPF in Serbia.[55] Meyszner not only acquired command over all the police in Serbia,[56] but was also given the task of recruiting ethnic Germans for the Waffen-SS.[57] In February Himmler ordered von Meyszner to call upon the German ethnic group in Banat to join a self-defence force attached to the Waffen-SS.[58] However, de facto the recruitment of volunteers turned into compulsory recruitment by agencies of the ethnic group. Those members of the German minority of military age were also recruited for a new division of the Waffen-SS, which finally received the name 'Prince Eugene'.[59] In this way, by April 1942 some 10,000–15,000 men had been recruited from the Banat, who did not in fact have to meet the SS's 'racial' criteria. They counted as 'SS volunteers', not as 'SS members'.[60] In addition, also at the beginning of February 1942, the 'Banat Staff Guard' was set up, an ethnic German auxiliary police force, which was formally subordinate to the Serbian Interior Ministry but in fact answered to the German commander of the order police in Belgrade.[61]

Thus, within a very short period Himmler had managed to mobilize large sections of the German minority in south-east Europe for his military ambitions. That may have been responsible for the fact that, from spring 1942, he floated the idea that in principle ethnic Germans were subject to military conscription just like the Germans in the Reich. However, Berger vetoed that idea in June. He warned that the introduction of military conscription was 'not possible' under international law, but in any case it was 'not at all necessary', for 'those who do not volunteer will simply have their houses smashed up'.[62] As a result, in July Himmler modified his position accordingly: he now declared that the ethnic German groups throughout south-east Europe must be clear that, although they might not be subject to it in legal terms, they were subject to military conscription by the 'iron law of their ethnicity', and indeed 'from the age of 17 to 50'.[63]

From September 1942 onwards all ethnic German males aged between 17 and 60 in Banat who were not already on active military service were in fact required to perform service in the 'German Force', a militia similar to the SS, which, like the one in Croatia, performed security duties. Himmler's order to establish the German Force corresponded to an order (to which we shall return) that he had issued the previous month for the mobilization of the Germans in the General Government and occupied Polish territories.[64] All these instructions were designed to achieve a single goal: the total mobilization of all ethnic Germans under the command of the SS.

On 17 October 1942 Himmler visited the 'Prince Eugene' division in Kraljevo on his way back from a visit to Italy. On the following day ethnic Germans in the Balkans celebrated the birthday of the person whose name their division bore.[65] Recruitment for the division was carried out throughout the Balkans. In the autumn of 1941 the Waffen-SS had already recruited so many ethnic German men in Croatia that the quota of 10 per cent settled on in the agreement of 16 September 1941 was soon exceeded. However— and this point was emphasized by Martin Luther, head of the German department in the Foreign Ministry—this recruitment was jeopardizing the existence of the ethnic German task formation, which had been created to combat the continually increasing partisan movement. Thus, in October 1941 the SS Main Office agreed to cease recruitment.[66] However, when it became apparent that the ethnic Germans who, according to the agreement of 16 September, were supposed to serve with special units of the Croatian army were in fact receiving their training from Wehrmacht units, Himmler made a strong complaint to the Wehrmacht and finally succeeded in ensuring that in future the recruitment and training of ethnic Germans throughout south-east Europe would be in the hands of the SS.[67]

In June 1942 Himmler permitted recruitment to begin again. All 17–30-year-old ethnic Germans from Croatia were to be inspected for admission to the 'Eugene' division. In consequence, around 20,000 members of the ethnic German minority who lived in the Bosnian territories which belonged to Croatia, and which had been made insecure as a result of the activities of Yugoslav partisans, had to be resettled because they had been rendered virtually defenceless as a result of the recruitment of their young men. Moreover, putting an end to such 'scattered settlements' and their replacement by 'concentrated settlement' in closed areas reflected the policy that Himmler was simultaneously pursuing in Poland and the Soviet Union in his role as Settlement Commissar. The Foreign Ministry temporarily stopped or slowed down the recruitment,[68] but then gave way after massive pressure from Berger.[69]

Voluntary recruitment was in reality a farce, as is clear from the principle enunciated by Himmler in July that ethnic Germans were subject to the 'iron law of ethnicity'. In fact, all members of the relevant age cohorts were inspected by commissions organized by Obersturmführer Nageler, and the organizations of the ethnic group concerned also applied pressure.[70] By the end of November 28,000 men had been inspected and over 6,500 conscripted.[71] In December 1941 Hitler ordered the transfer of the 'Eugene' division to Croatia in order to fill it with the new recruits. During the first months of 1943 the ethnic German troops of the Croatian Wehrmacht and the task formations were integrated into the division.[72] Meanwhile, in December 1942, however, new complications had arisen: the Croatian government wanted to withdraw Croatian citizenship from those ethnic Germans who had joined the SS. But the Germans finally managed to persuade it to agree to postpone dealing with the matter until the end of the war.[73]

In September 1942, while recruitment was going on, the Reich and Croatian governments made an agreement that, as Himmler had planned, more than 18,000 ethnic Germans were to be resettled. The majority of them ended up in a camp near Łódź; the others were housed in camps scattered throughout the Reich.[74] Himmler, however, wanted more: the removal of all Germans living in Croatia. His proposal can be explained partly in terms of his irritation at the difficulties that had arisen in relation to recruitment in Croatia. But he justified his proposal with the argument that this would be a way of demonstrating to their Italian allies (with whom they shared the occupation of Croatia) that the Reich was not pursuing any long-term interests of its own in the country. Himmler's real motive, however, was probably his overarching Lebensraum project. For in the meantime Himmler had abandoned the idea of using the German minority to exercise influence in Croatia and instead planned to move them to settlement areas in eastern Europe for which there were not yet nearly enough potential settlers. At this point he also proposed the 'resettlement' of the ethnic Germans living in Transnistria, which indicates that his plans for ethnic Germans covered the whole of south-east Europe.

Since the autumn of 1941 Nageler's men had been at work in Blatschka, which had previously been Serbian but which had been annexed by Hungary, with their operations disguised as a racial-biological research project. By October 1941 they had recruited 2,000 Germans for the Waffen-SS. By the summer of 1941 hundreds of young men from the old Hungarian territory had already been sent to the Reich for 'sports training'.[75]

On 18 November Himmler announced to Franz Basch, the leader of the ethnic German group in Hungary, that the Waffen-SS was now aiming to recruit to a far greater extent than before from the Hungarian German men who were living in the core part of Hungary.[76] He showed little concern for the political and legal problems created by such a course of action, given that it involved people who had lived there a long time and had Hungarian citizenship. For him these people were merely pawns in his scheme to create a Greater Germanic Reich. The statement that he made in December to the effect that it would be possible to secure around 60,000 ethnic German volunteers from Hungary, Romania, and Slovakia[77] is further proof that he regarded the very different conditions prevailing in these various countries as of secondary significance.

The Hungarian government agreed to the recruitment of 20,000 ethnic Germans. The recruitment programme lasted from 24 February to 3 April 1942, and was once again led by Nageler. A total of 25,000 men reported for inspection, 18,000 of whom were graded as fit for combat.[78] In June 1942, under pressure from Himmler, Ribbentrop arranged another recruitment programme with the Hungarian government for 1943.[79] (An agreement similar to that with Hungary was intended to be made with Romania in 1943.)[80] However, from an 'ethnic-political' point of view the Hungarian programme had a flaw: the Hungarians had insisted that, on joining the Waffen-SS, the ethnic Germans would lose their Hungarian citizenship.[81] This meant that the potential of the German minority for exercising influence was much reduced. Himmler was not only prepared to accept this, he even appears to have been willing to go a step further. Basch reported after the war that Himmler had confided to him that he was planning to resettle the Hungarian Germans in the Warthegau.[82]

Thus, what originally began as the recruitment of volunteers for self-defence units had led to the de facto military conscription of the ethnic Germans; in the course of this development the SS had not only acquired complete control of the national groups concerned but had even been able to recruit members of their leadership. However, the recruitment programmes normally had the effect of weakening the national group concerned to the extent that the abandonment of the country in which they had lived for centuries came under discussion and in some cases was actually carried out.

This approach was opposed by the Foreign Ministry. Martin Luther, the head of its German department, had already objected to the resettlement of the German minority in Croatia, complaining in September 1942 that this step would 'immediately weaken the sense of ethnic solidarity' of the other 2.5–3 million ethnic Germans in the south east.[83] Luther, who had joined the Foreign Ministry in a sideways move from the party and was one of the main figures responsible for the nazification of the ministry, was nevertheless sceptical about SS policy. At the beginning of 1943 Helmut Triska, who was responsible for ethnic policy in the Foreign Ministry, and like Luther had originally come from the party and therefore was basically in favour of the 'revolutionary' drive of Nazi ethnic policy, strongly criticized Himmler's approach in a paper with the title 'On Radical Measures Taken by the Reich Leadership of the SS Concerning the Policy Towards Ethnic German Groups Abroad'.

In particular Triska complained that, in recruiting 20,000 ethnic Germans from Hungary, Himmler had accepted the loss of their Hungarian citizenship and as a result the group had suffered the permanent loss of its most active members. In Croatia too 'the physical threat to the German settlements was considerably increased. The German settlements in Bosnia had to be removed and resettled during the war.' In Serbia, 'the conscription that was originally going to be carried out by the leaders of the national groups [...] was carried out directly by the division itself and this was done rigorously, ignoring any political considerations'. As far as Romania was concerned, despite 'all assurances to the contrary by the Reich leadership of the SS, [...] numerous ethnic Germans from Romania were illegally conscripted into the ranks of the Waffen-SS, which led to resistance from the Romanian government' and made 'Reich policy appear suspect'.

In conclusion, according to Triska, the fact was that

the Reich leadership of the SS [...] has pursued policies towards ethnic German groups which have made it virtually impossible to plan future work involving these ethnic groups. [...] The measures taken have created such political confusion, not only among the foreign governments but also among the agencies of the Reich leadership of the SS, that nobody has any idea whether the ethnic groups in the various countries concerned are to be prepared for future resettlement, consolidation, or political and economic expansion.

The Reich leadership had 'either taken, initiated, or advocated measures that have promoted expansion, measures that have consolidated the status quo, and measures that have involved removal, in other words resettlement'. 'These measures reveal no clear political line.'[84]

There could hardly be a more apposite description of the chaos that Himmler's policies had created among the ethnic German minorities in south-east Europe (but not only there).[85] For the ruthless policy of recruitment had drained the ethnic German minorities, threatening their very existence, while the Reichsführer's plans for a new ethnic order remained too nebulous to offer these people an alternative life in another area.

24

A Europe-wide Reign of Terror

In the second half of 1942 a whole series of developments coincided within Himmler's empire. As has been shown in the two previous chapters, settlement policy and the increased recruitment of citizens of other countries for the SS were being vigorously pursued, as was the deportation and murder of the European Jews. However, for various reasons a number of obstacles were emerging. In this chapter we shall see how these measures of Himmler's corresponded with those in other spheres in which he was active during the decisive summer months of 1942. Himmler was successful in securing the responsibility for 'combating partisans', in order above all to be in a position to drive forward the annihilation of the Jews in eastern Europe. Combating resistance in the occupied territories generally went hand in hand with an increase in Jewish persecution. He was also to make a serious attempt to establish an SS armaments concern. When that failed he turned to hiring out KZ prisoners as forced labour to industry. In order to increase their number, among other things he had the 'asocials' transferred from prison to concentration camp. By taking over the responsibility for punishing slave labourers from eastern Europe he was able to consign them to concentration camps for the slightest offence and thereby to increase his reservoir of labour. These measures, which were motivated partly by racial, partly by security, and partly by economic priorities, were also driven by the Reichsführer-SS's concern to hold together and combine the various parts of his empire as it expanded in all directions, in order not only to increase his power but above all to be able to realize the political objectives of his grand project to establish a new order on the European continent under the leadership of the SS.

On 28 July, only a few days after the final launching of the European Holocaust, Himmler embarked on a journey to Finland.[1] Despite a programme packed with meetings, he was intending to make time for a bit of relaxation. After a stopover in Reval he landed in Helsinki on the morning of 9 July, where he was officially welcomed by the President, Risto Ryti, and in the evening attended a dinner given by the Prime Minister, Johan Wilhelm Rangell. On the following day he was given a tour of the city and in the afternoon flew to Mikelli, the headquarters of the Finnish Commander-in-Chief, Marshall Carl Gustav Emil Mannerheim, whom he met in the evening. During the following days he had meetings with Colonel-General Eduard Dietl in Rovaniemi and with the commander of the SS Division 'North', Matthias Kleinheisterkamp, in Kananeinen, and inspected Waffen-SS units. On 2 August Himmler travelled for two days of relaxation on the island of Petays, which had been recommended to him by his masseur, Felix Kersten, for the 'magnetic healing' properties of its sunbathing. On 2 August he met Prime Minister Rangell on Petays and, according to the latter's post-war testimony, raised the question of Finland's attitude to its indigenous Jews. Rangell claims to have evaded the issue by remarking that that there was no 'Jewish question' in Finland, which had around 2,000 assimilated Jews.[2] In fact the small Jewish minority was not affected by the Jewish policy of its mighty German ally. After a bit of sightseeing in Helsinki on 5 August Himmler flew back to his headquarters the following day.

In parallel with Himmler's initiative in Finland, during July and August 1942 the RSHA tried to get other allies to hand over their Jews. When viewed together, these various actions clearly indicate that the RSHA was now determined to try to deport Jews from as many European states as possible in the course of 1942.

In July the police attaché at the embassy in Zagreb was instructed to initiate 'the resettlement' of the Croatian Jews to 'Germany's eastern territories'. The Ustasha regime had already created the preconditions for this: from the spring of 1941 onwards it had introduced anti-Semitic legislation modelled on Germany's and interned more than half of the 30,000 Jews living in Croatia in camps, in which the majority were murdered or died as a result of the appalling conditions.[3] In August the Germans organized four deportation trains to Auschwitz, where nearly 5,000 Jews were murdered.

Since the summer of 1941 Romania had been actively involved in the German policy of exterminating the Jews in the newly conquered eastern territories. In the territories of Bessarabia and the Bukovina, which had just been reconquered from the Soviet Union, the Romanians murdered around 50,000 Jews; the Jewish inhabitants of this area who survived, around 150,000 people, were deported to the territory occupied by Romania between the Dniester and the Bug rivers. At least 65,000 of these people died of hunger and in epidemics or were shot.[4]

In July 1942 the Reich demanded control over the Jews in the core Romanian territory. The adviser on 'Jewish questions' at the German embassy in Bucharest, SS-Hauptsturmführer Gustav Richter, made an agreement with the Romanian government that the around 320,000 Jews affected, who since 1938 had been subjected to increasingly tough anti-Semitic legislation, should be deported from 10 September 1942 onwards. The German ambassador in Bucharest, Manfred von Killinger, informed the Foreign Ministry that the destination of the transports was to be the district of Lublin, where 'those capable of working would be deployed in labour columns while the remainder would be subjected to special treatment'.[5]

In Hungary the situation was different. Although anti-Semitic legislation had been passed, in the view of the Germans it was not sufficiently effective, as it hardly went beyond the Nuremberg laws.[6] When, in July 1942, the Hungarian military attaché in Berlin submitted his government's proposal that all Jews living in Hungary 'illegally' should be resettled to Transnistria,[7] Himmler decided to postpone the deportation of Jewish refugees requested by Hungary until the Hungarians had agreed to include their indigenous Jews in the proposed measures.[8]

As far as Bulgaria was concerned, in the summer of 1942 the RSHA considered that its Jewish legislation was also inadequate to initiate deportation.[9] Moreover, they were making no progress in the case of Greece either. Attempts by the RSHA and the Foreign Ministry during the second half of 1942 to persuade their Italian allies to adopt a tougher anti-Semitic policy in their two occupation zones in Greece—namely, to introduce the marking of Jews with a badge—came to nothing.[10]

During July and August the RSHA also increased the tempo of deportations in the occupied western territories. Following Himmler's order of June to deport all French Jews, ten initial transports with a total of around 10,000 people were sent to Auschwitz between 19 July and 7 August. Those being deported, stateless Jews who had often lost their citizenship only as a result of German Jewish policy, were arrested in a major raid that took place in Paris on 16 and 17 July.[11] As had been agreed with the Vichy government in July, from August onwards they also began deporting Jews from the unoccupied zone. Moreover, between 14 and 26 August over 2,000 Jewish children were sent to Auschwitz in six transports, despite the fact that most of them were French citizens. Both the French Prime Minister, Pierre Laval, and the RSHA had given their express approval for this action.[12]

The deportations from the Netherlands began in the middle of July: around 38,000 people had been sent to Auschwitz by the end of the year.[13] From 4 August 1942 trains from Belgium travelled in the same direction.[14] By the end of 1942 almost 17,000 people, all of them foreign or stateless Jews, had fallen victim to these measures.[15]

Meanwhile, at the end of July HSSPF Fritz Katzmann had once again begun the mass murder of Jews in the General Government, in accordance with Himmler's order to make the territory 'free of Jews' by the end of the year. In the major 'August action', which took place between 10 and 25 August, he had more than 40,000 Jews arrested in the district capital of Lemberg (Lviv) alone, around half of the city's population of Jews, and then deported in goods trains to Belzec, where they were murdered.[16]

This mass murder was in full swing on 17 August when Himmler arrived in Lemberg for a meeting that was attended by, among others, Governor Otto Wächter, Katzmann, and Globocnik. On this day alone Katzmann had had 3,051 people arrested, who were then deported to Belzec.[17] On the following day Himmler, as usual, wanted to see for himself; to begin with he inspected various SS offices and then a number of camps for Jewish forced labour working on the Transit Road IV. In the evening he flew back to Berlin.[18] Three days later he once again met Globocnik, this time in Lublin, and travelled with him to the area round Zamosc to see what progress had been made towards its 'Germanization'.[19]

Between 31 August and 3 September Himmler had to deal with a completely different issue: air-raid damage. He undertook a journey lasting several days to cities in north and west Germany which had been hit particularly badly by the increasing Allied air raids, gained a clear picture of the extent of the damage, and then issued instructions for its clearing-up. In the process he demonstrated once again how flexible he was in linking his various responsibilities. Teams of KZ prisoners, who had originally been intended for building-projects in the east, were now utilized for the clearance of air-raid damage in the west and KZ workshops were used to provide door- and window-frames.[20]

A few weeks later Himmler had to face the fact that his plan to make the whole of the General Government 'free of Jews' by the end of the year could not be achieved. At the armaments conference held between 20 and

23 September 1942 Hitler agreed with the proposal of the head of labour mobilization, Fritz Sauckel, that in view of the dramatic shortage of labour Jewish skilled workers in the General Government should continue to be employed.[21] Himmler, who evidently discussed the consequences of this decision with Hitler on 22 September,[22] reacted quickly. Since his attempt from the beginning of the year to integrate forced labour into the extermination programme had resulted in his now having to slow down mass murder in favour of slave labour, he would now have to increase the number of KZ prisoners who could be forced to work. He would do this through mass arrests of non-Jews (which will be discussed below), as well as by confining ghetto inhabitants in concentration or forced labour camps. On 9 October 1942 he ordered that 'so-called armaments workers' in textile and other plants in Warsaw and Lublin should be gathered together in concentration camps. Those Jews who were employed in 'real armaments plants' should be removed in stages so that there would be only 'a few big Jewish concentration camp plants' left, preferably in the east of the General Government. 'However, even there, according to the Führer, the Jews should disappear one day.'[23] Police regulations issued in October and November 1942 confined 'Jewish residential districts' to restricted areas.[24] For all those Polish Jews who were not engaged in armaments production these regulations represented certain death. At the end of 1942, according to official German data, only 298,000 of the 2.3 million Jews who had been originally living in the General Government were still alive.[25]

Himmler also intervened directly in the extermination process in the Soviet Union, to which the basic instructions for the systematic murder of European Jews issued in May and June 1942 had particularly applied. In doing so he made use of the fact that in July 1942 Hitler had given him responsibility for 'combating bandits'.

In May 1942 the Einsatzgruppen had resumed their murderous activity systematically and on a large scale in the General Commissariat of White Ruthenia. At the end of July Commissar-General Wilhelm Kube reported that 'during the past 10 weeks around 55,000 Jews [have] been liquidated'.[26] In the Reich Commissariat Ukraine, where a new wave of murders had also begun in May, the scale of murder was stepped up in July, a development exactly matching that in the General Government, where Himmler had ordered the annihilation of the Jewish population by the end of the year, and which was also directly linked to the responsibility for 'combating bandits'. This involved, as we shall see, not simply the elimination of actual partisans but all 'suspect elements', and by definition these included the Jewish population. A letter from Himmler to Berger dated 28 July 1942 provides documentary evidence that this responsibility was the equivalent of an order from Hitler for the systematic murder of the Soviet population in the occupied Soviet territories: with a hint of self-pity, he declared: 'The occupied eastern territories will become free of Jews. The Führer has placed the implementation of this very burdensome order on my shoulders. Nobody can relieve me of this responsibility.'[27]

At the end of August 1942 there was a further escalation in the Ukraine: the aim was now the complete annihilation of the Jewish population. It is worth remembering in this context the settlement plans Himmler was pursuing at the same time for the Ukraine, where he had based his headquarters throughout the summer months. These involved 'the settlement together' of 10,000 ethnic Germans in and around Shitomir and the idea that parts of the Ukraine would be completely 'German' within a period of only twenty years. Against this background it is not surprising that the occupying authorities concentrated on systematically murdering, district by district, all the Jews living there, in particular in the General Commissariats of Volhynia-Podolia and Shitomir, centres of Jewish life in the Ukraine.[28] It is true that the settlement of ethnic Germans occurred directly at the expense of the Ukrainians (and not of the Jews). However, the indirect link between the future of the ethnic Germans and the 'Jewish question' within the context of a 'new ethnic order' is obvious.

The SD office in Pinsk began to dissolve the city ghetto at the end of October. This was prompted by a written order from Himmler of 27 October 1942:

According to my information, the ghetto in Pinsk can be regarded as the headquarters for all the bandit activity in the Pripet marshes. I therefore recommend that, despite any economic concerns you may have, you immediately dissolve and liquidate the ghetto in Pinsk. If possible 1,000 male workers are to be secured and transferred to the Wehrmacht for the construction of the wooden huts. The work of these 1,000 workers must, however, be carried out only in a closed camp under the strictest guard. If this guard cannot be provided then these 1,000 workers should also be annihilated.[29]

The instruction was immediately carried out. Between 29 October and 1 November at least 16,200 people were murdered, in a massacre lasting four days.[30]

Ill. 29. This is how Himmler liked to see himself: constantly on the move in order to take decisions on the spot, drive things forward, and personally intervene to sort things out. The photo comes from a collection of private photos that Himmler sent his daughter Gudrun, in order to keep in touch with her.

At the end of 1942 there were only a few thousand Jewish skilled workers still left in the Ukraine.[31] The HSSPF for South Russia, Hans Prützmann, reported to Himmler on 26 December 1942 that in the course of 'combating the bandits' in the area for which he was responsible, which included the Ukraine and Bialystok, between 1 September and 1 December 1942 a total of 363,211 Jews had been 'executed'. On 29 December Himmler passed on the report to Hitler, who took note of it.[32]

From September onwards, however, there were increasing signs that the deportations, which since the summer of 1942 had come to involve the whole of Europe, would by no means proceed smoothly. The problems were not confined to the General Government. In a number of places there were even intentional delays and resistance.

At the armaments conference from 20 to 22 September 1942 referred to above Hitler had spoken of the 'importance of removing the Jews from the

armaments plants'.[33] A few days later he emphasized to Goebbels his determination, 'under all circumstances to get the Jews out of Berlin'; Jewish
workers were to be replaced by foreigners.[34] At that point, however, it was
simply not possible. It was only the increased recruitment of foreigners and
POWs for armaments production from the beginning of 1943 onwards, and
the general toughening of domestic policy after Stalingrad, that provided the
preconditions for a new wave of deportations from the Reich. Nevertheless,
Himmler did all he possibly could to realize Hitler's aim of making the Reich
'free of Jews'. In September he made an agreement with the Reich Minister
of Justice, Otto Georg Thierack, that he would take over all 'asocial elements' who were in prison, including all Jews, Gypsies, Russians, and Poles,
for 'extermination through labour'.[35] On 29 September he inspected Sachsenhausen concentration camp, and on the same day instructed Glücks, the
Inspector of Concentration Camps, 'to make all concentration camps based
in the Reich free of Jews and [...] to transfer all Jews to Auschwitz
concentration camp and the POW camp in Lublin', an instruction which,
on 5 October, the RSHA passed on to the relevant offices and which was
substantially carried out during the following months.[36]

In France, after the transports in July and August the deportation
programme came to a halt. As a large number of children were held in the
camps, the attempt to continue the deportations aroused public opposition
from the Catholic Church and the population was vehemently hostile. Thus,
at the beginning of September the Vichy government informed the Germans
that further arrests and deportations could no longer be carried out in the
unoccupied zone.[37]

Thus, in view of the threat to the domestic reputation of Prime Minister
Laval, in September HSSPF Carl Oberg persuaded Himmler, as a kind of
gesture of good-will towards the French, not to deport any more French
citizens from the occupied zone for the time being.[38] This was a remarkable
change of policy, given the fact that as recently as June the Reichsführer had
demanded the complete deportation of all Jews from France by the end of
the year. Now the occupation authorities increasingly concentrated on
arresting foreign Jews in the occupied zone, who were deported to the
east during November in four more transports. After that there was a stop to
the deportations; by then 42,000 people had been deported from France.[39]

In Norway a wave of arrests began on the 25 October after the RSHA had
been pushing for the deportation of the small Jewish minority. In November the first of a total of 770 Jews were deported—930 had fled to Sweden.[40]

The Foreign Ministry and the RSHA also had little success with their allies in the autumn of 1942. Despite several initiatives it became clear that, apart from Croatia, all the allies who during 1942 had been included in the German deportation plans had by the autumn frustrated their intentions. In Slovakia the deportations had come to a complete halt by October 1942;[41] Romania was evidently stalling the procedure that had been agreed in July.[42] In January 1943 Himmler finally realized that there was no point in pushing the Romanian government to deliver up its Jews; he therefore suggested that the 'Jewish adviser' at the German embassy in Bucharest should be withdrawn.[43] Bulgaria[44] and Hungary[45] also showed a lack of commitment in October 1942.

At the end of November Himmler had still believed that the deportations from Hungary could soon be set in train. For this purpose he offered Ribbentrop the services of an experienced expert, for example Dieter Wisliceny, to act as the 'desk officer for Jewish questions' at the German embassy in Budapest. As a 'first instalment' 100,000 Jews could be deported from the territories annexed from Slovakia and Romania.[46] However, in December he had to accept that the Hungarians had no interest in deporting their indigenous Jews.[47]

In October 1942 under-state secretary Luther's attempts, made via the German missions in Rome and Zagreb, to clarify the Italians' attitude towards the deportation of Croatian Jews from their occupation zone met with no more success.[48] Even Himmler could not make a difference. At a meeting with Mussolini during a visit to Italy in October 1942 the two men discussed the 'Jewish question'. On this occasion Himmler gave Mussolini an insight, partly realistic and partly glossed over, into its violent 'solution'. However, before he could get round to discussing Italian Jewish policy, Mussolini ended the interview with a 'friendly enquiry about the programme for my stay in Rome and my next travel programme'.[49] By this time the Jews living in Croatia had already been interned by the Italian occupation authorities. This had removed them from German clutches.[50]

The combating of partisans and repression in the occupied territories

In view of the increasing threat posed by Soviet partisans, in July 1942 Hitler decided that in future the police should be responsible in the first instance for combating them.[51] This decision was made at precisely the moment when Himmler was involving the whole of Europe in the extermination programme, and it underlines once more the close link between the Holocaust and 'combating partisans'. The maxim that Jews were 'to be exterminated as partisans' had been in force ever since the invasion of the Soviet Union; as already mentioned, Hitler had specifically confirmed it to Himmler on 18 December 1941 and, by transferring to him this responsibility, provided him with further room for manoeuvre vis-à-vis the programme of mass murder.

However, that was not the only point. Himmler had already proved how brutally he could act against 'bandits' even when the murder of Jews was not the main priority. On 25 June 1942 he had ordered that 'bandit activity' in Upper Carniola and Lower Styria—in other words in the territory annexed from Yugoslavia—should be 'totally' crushed in a 'four-week-long campaign' under the direction of the HSSPF for the Alpine region, Erwin Rösener. 'Every last German man in this territory but also from outside this area from the old Gaus of Kärnten and Styria, who is capable of bearing arms and aged between 17 and 55, is to be mobilized for this campaign [...] The campaign is to be purposeful, tough, and ruthless.'

Himmler spelled out what this involved in detailed 'guidelines'.

The campaign must neutralize all elements of the population who have willingly supported the partisans by providing manpower, food supplies, weaponry, and shelter. The men of a guilty family, in many cases even the clan, are to be executed as a matter of principle; the women of these families are to be arrested and sent to a concentration camp and the children are to be removed from their home and to be collected together in the Old Reich part of the Gau. I shall expect separate reports about the number and racial quality of these children. The possessions of the guilty families are to be confiscated.

'The campaign', according to Himmler, 'will require from the leaders and men the utmost in the performance of their duty and in discretion as well as in physical performance and exertion in the difficult mountain terrain I expect leaders and men of the SS and police to fulfil the expectations that have been placed in them.'[52] In fact the coming months saw a large number of executions, arrests, and compulsory adoptions in this occupied territory.[53]

On 28 July 1942 Himmler made an official announcement that the 'Reichsführer-SS and Chief of the German Police' had now, 'in agreement with the OKW', become 'the supreme agency for combating the so-called partisans'. 'I am personally assuming [command of this] struggle against bandits, *francs-tireurs*, and criminals.'[54] A few days later he ordered that the term 'partisan' should not be used in future, and that instead the term to be used should be 'bandits' (*Banden*).[55] On 18 October Hitler confirmed Himmler's general responsibility for 'combating bandits', and stated specifically that Himmler should be 'solely responsible' in the Reich Commissariats, whereas in the districts under military administration the Wehrmacht should be in charge.[56]

Already on 9 July the Reichsführer-SS had summoned high-ranking SS functionaries to Berlin to a meeting about the future combating of partisan activity. As usual Himmler was not slow to put forward proposals: for example, the population of the occupied Soviet territories should be forced to cut down trees and bushes on either side of the roads and railways to a depth of 400 to 500 metres in order to deprive the partisans of cover. For a variety of reasons the Reich Ministry for the Eastern Territories failed to implement this.[57]

He had more success with another suggestion. On 17 August Himmler, with the Führer's approval, imposed on those Germans living in the General Government and occupied Soviet territories who were not serving in the Wehrmacht, police, or SS the 'duty of honour' 'to increase the combat strength of the SS/police by placing themselves at its disposal in their free time, and particularly during emergencies', by serving in 'alarm units'. Himmler admitted that this would mean that in future they would lose their weekends because of having to carry out exercises, but he was convinced that those affected 'would be happy, even if they were not liable for military service,[58] to be able to serve the Fatherland in some capacity by bearing arms'.[59] It is clear that this provided the local SS and police agencies with a powerful weapon for putting pressure on members of the civilian administration or employees of German firms; the total mobilization of all Germans in the occupied east strengthened the power of the SS and police.

On 7 August Himmler issued detailed orders for two major campaigns against partisans in the General Commissariat of White Ruthenia and the district of Bialystok.[60] The operations 'Marsh Fever' and 'Wisent' took place during August–September and September–October 1942. However 'Marsh Fever', which was commanded by the HSSPF for Russia-North, Jeckeln, proved to be something of a failure as far as combating partisans was concerned. In order to make the result appear more impressive, in addition to 389 'bandits' who had allegedly been shot in combat and 1,274 bandits who had been 'found guilty', Jeckeln had more than 8,000 Jews shot out of hand, among them almost the whole population of the Baranowicze ghetto. Although this mass murder fitted in with Himmler's aim of pushing on with the murder of Jews under the cover of 'combating bandits', at the same time he wanted to see more dead 'bandits'. As a result, the responsibility for 'combating bandits' in White Ruthenia was transferred to the HSSPF for Russia-Centre, von dem Bach-Zelewski, who was considered more effective.[61]

Ernst von dem Bach-Zelewski was to become Himmler's most important commander in the field of 'combating bandits'. However, at this point, as HSSPF for Russia-Centre, the dynamic Bach was responsible only for territory under military administration. But, according to the Führer directive of 18 August, the Wehrmacht was responsible for 'combating bandits' in this area. Bach, therefore, requested Himmler to appoint him 'Inspector for the Combating of Bandits in the Whole of the Eastern Territories'.[62]

On 22 September Himmler discussed this proposal with Hitler in the context of a conversation lasting several hours which, apart from the threat from partisans, covered the settlement of ethnic Germans in the eastern territories and 'Jewish emigration',[63] a further indication of the extent to which these three topics were linked in Himmler's conception of the reordering of living-space in the east. Hitler agreed, and on 24 October Himmler appointed his HSSPF Russia-Centre not only as 'The Reichsführer-SS's Plenipotentiary for Combating Bandits' but also signed a total of five edicts regulating this new office.[64]

Above all, Himmler subordinated to him the General Commissariat White Ruthenia, which was under civilian administration, for the duration of the planned 'pacification campaign'. This was followed in November by the appointment of Curt von Gottberg as the new SS and Police Leader in White Ruthenia. Thus, Gottberg, who had been in the political wilderness since 1939 as a result of the Prague 'Land Office affair',[65] was being given the chance to rehabilitate himself in the eyes of his Reichsführer by particularly ruthless action. By transferring the Sonderkommando Dirlewanger, which was largely composed of criminals,[66] to Byelorussia Himmler was placing at von dem Bach-Zelewski's and Gottberg's disposal a particularly brutal force for carrying out the planned 'pacification campaign'.[67] Thus Himmler had appointed a handpicked trio for 'combating bandits' in this area: three former losers who wanted to earn the respect of their superior. Between November 1942 and the beginning of May 1943 alone the SS, police, and Wehrmacht killed over 40,000 people in White Ruthenia in the course of eighteen major campaigns.[68]

On 30 October 1942 Himmler ordered that during all the campaigns against partisans in the occupied Soviet territories 'every member of the population who can be spared and is capable of work should be taken prisoner and sent to work in Germany'.[69] In this he was following a directive from Göring, about which he was evidently not happy. As late as February he was refusing to transfer the men who had been taken prisoner during the anti-partisan campaigns to the Plenipotentiary for Labour Mobilization, Fritz Sauckel; the people locked up in concentration camps were 'suspect bandits', and should not be released as 'free workers'.[70] However, in view of the acute labour shortage in the German war economy, from the summer of 1943 onwards he had to give way.

By being given the responsibility for combating bandits, Himmler had acquired the authority he needed to suppress all opposition in the occupied eastern territories. In the 'east', as a matter of principle, the security police and SD did not confine themselves to responding to acts of resistance that had already occurred but rather proceeded prophylactically: at the latest from 1942 onwards they were instructed to kill all communists in the occupied Soviet territories, even if there was no evidence that they had committed any actual acts of resistance. This practice became routine.[71] Moreover, in the Polish territories which had been temporarily under Soviet occupation from 1939 to 1941 the 'eastern types' and 'Soviet people' who had come to this area during this period were often murdered or put in forced labour camps simply because of the suspicion that they might be loyal to the Soviet state. Those functionaries who had been evacuated eastwards by the Soviets were particularly affected by these measures. Furthermore, all those who were assumed to be of 'asiatic' descent were suspect. They were considered per se to be agents of the Soviet regime and were killed arbitrarily and without pity.[72]

Himmler's policy in the eastern territories was basically quite simple: by acting with extreme brutality he aimed to reorganize the 'living-space' that had been conquered. He rejected concessions or favours to the indigenous population. Thus, he not only objected in April 1942 to Rosenberg's proposal for a 'new agrarian order' offering the rural population the prospect of having private property (a scheme which failed anyway);[73] he also vehemently opposed any attempt to promise the Russians a 'nation state'.[74] The pamphlet *The Subhuman* issued by Himmler's SS Main Office clearly illustrates—with photographs to demonstrate the inferiority of the Soviet peoples—their view of 'eastern people': 'a frightful creature [...] just an approximation to a proper human being [...] but intellectually and spiritually inferior to any animal.'[75]

The 'new agrarian order' was not the only bone of contention between Rosenberg and Himmler. Responsible in the meantime for the liberally interpreted 'police measures for guaranteeing the security' of the occupied eastern territories, the 'consolidation of the ethnic German nation', and the combating of bandits—a responsibility that he was to extend to the whole of the Soviet Union in 1943—Himmler could envisage neutralizing Rosenberg. His correspondence with the Minister for the East concerning disputes over responsibility fill several files, but the extensive memoranda Rosenberg composed in the course of these disputes merely document his inexorable retreat.[76]

In April 1942 Himmler even went so far as openly to express his total contempt for Rosenberg in a letter to Alfred Meyer, of all people, who was the state secretary in the Ministry for the East and Rosenberg's deputy. After expressing a hypocritical regret at his frankness, he went on to write that, of course, Rosenberg was 'not a soldier and none of us expects him to be or to become one. We party comrades value and honour him for making his name as the Reich leader of the NSDAP responsible for ideology. But, even if he is Minister for the East, Party comrade Rosenberg must leave soldierly matters to the people who are responsible for them and who have to answer for them.'[77] As far as Himmler was concerned, Rosenberg was nothing but a wimp. At the beginning of 1943, since Heydrich, his original contact-man with Rosenberg, was no longer available, he agreed with the Minister for the East that in future the head of the SS-Main Office, Berger, would fulfil this role in the rank of a state secretary.[78]

Although not directly affected by Himmler's responsibility for combating bandits, during 1942 the occupied countries of central, western, and northern Europe were also exposed to repression at the hands of the SS and security police.

In Norway the SS and police court intervened in the political persecution of the population for the first time from the middle of 1942 onwards; that is to say, it dealt with cases in which the investigations were carried out and the charges were brought by the security police. By the middle of 1944 a total of 127 death sentences had been passed in such trials.[79] Moreover, in response to acts of sabotage, in October 1942 the German occupation authorities declared martial law in the district of Trondheim. Thirty-four people were summarily executed. At the same time the security police ordered the arrest of all male Jews in this district, a measure that two weeks later was extended to every Jew in the country and led finally to the deportation of the Norwegian Jews. Once more, as in France and in the Protectorate, an 'act of reprisal' in a German-occupied country had concluded with violent anti-Jewish measures.[80]

Belgium was under military administration, and the Wehrmacht's Secret Field Police, which was responsible in the first instance for the suppression of resistance, repeatedly shot hostages. Here the representative of the Chief of the Security Police and SD attached to the head of the military administration—Belgium was the only country in which Himmler did not succeed in appointing a HSSPF until 1944—pursued an independent policy of repression. From June 1941 until August 1942 he succeeded in getting the RSHA to issue 600 orders for protective custody and deporting those involved to concentration camps in the Reich.[81]

In France Himmler succeeded in appointing a HSSPF in March 1942, in other words, at the same time as the first transports of Jewish hostages to Auschwitz.[82] Carl Oberg, who was appointed to the post on 1 June 1942, secured the right to issue directives to the French police and, through the transformation of the stations of the Secret Field Police, which were distributed throughout the country, into stations of the security police and SD, acquired an executive apparatus operating throughout the country. Helmut Knochen, who had been in charge of the Sipo commando in Paris since 1940, became the commander of the security police.[83] In July 1942 Oberg used his strong position to secure an agreement with the French police chief René Bosquet for close cooperation between the German and French police, which in turn was granted greater freedom of action in the occupied zone.[84]

During the course of the summer Oberg and Knochen not only drove forward the anti-Jewish policy in the occupied and unoccupied zones but ordered further mass executions of hostages on 11 August and 21 September. However, as attacks by the resistance in September and October increased Oberg came to the same conclusion that the military administration had reached the previous year, namely, that from the point of view of the occupation authorities 'reprisal' executions were counter-productive (at the same time he successfully persuaded Himmler to take account of the

doubts of the Vichy government about the wisdom of deporting French
Jews). Oberg now prepared other types of 'atonement', which from 1943
onwards took the form above all of the deportation of Jews and opponents
to German concentration camps.[85]

The excessive revenge taken by the security police in the Protectorate
after Heydrich's death in June 1942 has already been referred to. After this
wave of terror the HSSPF tried to calm the general situation. The most
important priority of the occupation authorities was to exploit the country
economically, and that required quiet on the political front. Although
arrests were made and death sentences passed for resistance activities, the
reprisals were far less severe than the terror that reigned in Poland or
Yugoslavia.[86]

As is evident from the examples of France and the Protectorate, Himmler's top functionaries in the occupied territories were by no means always
in favour of a policy of boundless terror. That was not only a reflection of
security police considerations but a result of the fact that another factor was
becoming increasingly important: the growing need for forced labour in the
concentration camps. In view of this it seemed more advisable to deport
resisters to concentration camps rather than shoot them.

The failure of the SS armaments concern

Until the beginning of 1942 the SS, in the shape of the official responsible
for economic matters, Oswald Pohl, had largely been responding to requests
from industry without developing a strategy for building up its own armaments capacity.[87] That changed during the winter crisis of 1941–2, when
the switch from 'Blitzkrieg' to a more substantial mobilization of all the
resources required for fighting what looked like turning into a total war was
becoming evident. As a contribution to solving the emerging shortage of
labour, Himmler ordered the employment of Jewish workers en masse and,
as has already been shown, with the establishment of the Business and
Administration Main Office created the preconditions for the 'economization' of the concentration camp system.

On 16 March Richard Glücks, who was in charge of the Concentration
Camp Inspectorate, met representatives of the Armaments Ministry in order
to discuss various possibilities of deploying prisoners. Glücks explained that
the SS did not wish to have any influence on the decisions about what was

to be produced, but, in accordance with a 'decree of the Reichsführer-SS [. . .] the actual production process itself [had to] take place within the camps'.[88] Walter Schieber, the departmental head within Speer's Armaments Ministry, then set about establishing such projects. For example, it was arranged that the Wilhelm Gustloff Works in Weimar would produce rifles in KZ Buchenwald, and a number of other projects were under discussion.[89]

In July 1942 Himmler seized the initiative. After a meeting with Schieber he produced for Pohl a list of various armaments projects (for example, apart from rifles, the production of pistols and anti-aircraft guns) to be carried out in four camps. Himmler was particularly interested in an Opel factory near Auschwitz which the SS was to construct and operate. He hoped that this would accelerate the SS's motorization.[90] It was not by chance that an SS armaments concern was being created at this juncture. For in this same month of July Himmler introduced de facto military conscription for ethnic Germans in south-east Europe, which he envisaged leading to a further expansion of the Waffen-SS. These recruits had to be armed and equipped.

In fact, however, all these initiatives more or less came to nothing. It was possible to begin producing rifles in Buchenwald only in the spring of 1943, and even then production was slow to get going. In August 1944 the production facilities were destroyed in an air raid. The plan to produce hand-guns in Neuengamme had to be aborted, and the same happened to most of the other projects. It was only in Auschwitz that fuses for shells were produced—instead of the planned anti-aircraft guns.[91]

Factory production never got going in the concentration camps because high-calibre machine tools were difficult to acquire, because productivity in the KZ plants was comparatively low as a result of the terrible living and working conditions,[92] but above all because Himmler had overlooked the fact that the precondition for his plans—a cooperative relationship with industry[93]—could not exist so long as the SS controlled production. For industry was determined to keep control of the manufacturing processes that had been transferred to the concentration camps.

On 15 September 1942 Speer and Pohl reached agreement on the need to deploy more KZ prisoners for armaments production. Pohl informed Himmler of the details, addressing the decisive point quite openly: 'we must no longer narrow-mindedly insist on all the manufacturing processes being transferred to our camps. So long as we were engaged only in piddling things, as you Herr Reichsführer quite rightly described our previous operations in view of their limited scope, we could demand that this should happen.' But in the case of armaments plants with 5,000 or more prisoners this was no longer feasible; as Speer pointed out, these had to be situated 'on green-field sites'. According to the agreement with Speer, Pohl went on, the SS should take over vacant or understaffed plants, fill them '100% with our prisoners', and run them as SS armaments plants, but outside the camps. In this way Speer wanted to 'accommodate 50,000 Jews capable of work in closed plants that already existed'. Pohl wanted these prisoners 'withdrawn from the eastern emigration'.[94]

By doing this Pohl had ignored Himmler's instruction that production should be moved to the camps. But in any case, the agreement was unrealistic since the KZ prisoners who were being thrown together and who were not adequately trained would not have been in a position to take over complete production processes at short notice. Moreover, the SS did not have the requisite experience to prepare and organize the production processes.

In the armaments conference, which ran from 20 to 22 September, Speer then alerted Hitler to the fact that it would be inadvisable to move the manufacturing facilities to the KZs and that Himmler's demand that the SS should have a 'decisive influence on these businesses' was inappropriate. The more sensible solution would be to introduce a second shift of KZ prisoners in certain plants. Hitler agreed with Speer and, as compensation for the prisoners that he was placing at the disposal of industry, promised Himmler that between 3 and 5 per cent of production would be allocated to the Waffen-SS.[95] That represented the end of the SS armaments concern. In future the SS restricted its role to hiring out prisoners, and for this purpose established satellite camps all over the Reich linked to the relevant plants.

In September 1942 Speer aborted one more ambitious armaments project that Himmler had been pursuing since the end of 1941. As already mentioned, according to a Führer order of January 1942 the Reichsführer had been promised 'the establishment, equipping, and running' of a light metal foundry in the VW works. From spring onwards hundreds of prisoners had been employed there: a special KZ ('workers' village') had been built near the plant. In the middle of September 1942 Speer banned the construction of the building on the grounds that the economic relevance of the project to armaments production was dubious. This meant that Himmler's attempt to engage in armaments production through this show project had also failed.[96]

Terror at home

When, in the autumn of 1941, it began to become clear that the war was not going to end soon the criminal police (Kripo) acquired new tasks. On the previous assumption that the war would soon be over, from the summer of 1940 onwards it had concentrated on the regime's aims in the sphere of population policy. But now the effects of the air war, wartime economic offences, and the increased surveillance of young people and foreigners created new priorities for the criminal police, operating under the terms of a completely new interpretation of 'preventive policing'.

The air war confronted the Kripo with a variety of problems: bomb victims had to be identified and looters brought to book. Above all, in the second half of the war property offences, facilitated by the black-out measures and the damage to or destruction of buildings, rose enormously in the cities that had been attacked. Moreover, many people's normal inhibitions were removed by the immediate threat under which they were living and by the destruction of their usual way of life. Youth gangs emerged in the rubble of the bombed cities and the black market flourished. Cases of homicide and robberies also increased.[97]

The so-called delinquency of young people was of particular concern to the Reichsführer. On 26 January 1942 he sent Heydrich a report by the Reich Youth Leadership which described the leisure activities of the so-called 'Swing Youth' (*Swing-Jugend*)in Hamburg: young people from main-ly middle-class backgrounds, who played banned 'swing music' at parties and elsewhere, expressed their opposition to the Hitler Youth and other institutions of the Nazi state. Himmler was livid:

All of the leaders, and that means both male and female leaders and those teachers who are hostile to us and support the Swing Youth, are to be sent to a concentra-tion camp. There the young people must first receive a beating and then be made to perform the toughest possible exercises and forced to do hard work. I consider that a work camp or a youth camp is inappropriate for these blokes and these useless girls. The girls must be forced to do weaving and in summer to work on the land. These young people must be confined to a concentration camp for a lengthy period of two or three years. It must be made clear that they will never be allowed to study. Enquiries must be made to see how far their parents have supported them; if they have supported them then they too should be sent to a concentration camp and their property should be confiscated. Only if we act brutally will we be able to get on top of this anglophyle [*sic*] trend at a time when Germany is fighting for its existence and prevent it from spreading.[98]

From 1942 onwards the regime was concerned that increasing criminality and evidence of social delinquency might damage Germany's image as an orderly state and have a negative impact on the mood of the home front. In Hitler's view, it was the 'mob' who were primarily responsible for starting the revolution of 1918. In his draconian opinion, in the event of a revolt breaking out, 'within two days all criminals should be killed'.[99] The transition to the systematic extermination of criminals and 'asocials' in the second half of 1942 was a logical consequence of this attitude. It was largely carried out by the Reichsführer-SS.

This new murderous form of 'criminal prevention' was also aimed at the east European forced workers in the Reich, who in the meantime numbered millions. In September 1941 Himmler had objected in vain to the decision to bring civilian workers into the Reich in addition to Polish workers and Soviet POWs. The amount of resources that were involved in pursuing escaped POWs or foreign workers who were returning to their home countries of their own accord was considerable. In the first six months of 1943 over 300,000 people were arrested as a result of this search activity.[100]

Himmler's veto was, however, ignored,[101] and so, on 20 February 1942, Heydrich issued the so-called Eastern Workers' Decrees, which regulated the treatment and guarding of civilian Soviet workers. The Gestapo was now made solely responsible for combating criminality, sexual relations with Germans, and other offences, and it was to impose very harsh sentences on offenders. Consignment to a concentration camp or 'special treatment' were the two options. According to these regulations, offences by Soviet forced workers were to be dealt with by the judicial system only when a death sentence could be anticipated.[102]

On 18 September 1942 the Reich Minister of Justice, Otto Thierack, and his state secretary, Curt Ferdinand Rothenberger, met Himmler in his Ukrainian headquarters to deal with a number of agreements involving the judicial authorities. The results of this meeting were far-reaching. In the first place, in future 'inadequate' judicial verdicts were to be subject to 'correction' by 'police special treatment', with Himmler and Thierack reaching agreement on individual cases. If they failed to agree then Hitler's opinion was to be sought via Bormann.

Secondly, they agreed on the 'handing over of asocial elements from the prison system to the Reichsführer-SS for extermination through work'. This was to affect, without exception: 'those in preventive detention, Jews, Gypsies, Russians and Ukrainians, Poles serving a sentence of over three years, Czechs, and Germans serving a sentence of over eight years with the approval of the Reich Minister of Justice.' It is not surprising that, as already mentioned, the 'handing over' of these prisoners was agreed at the very same moment when the decision was made increasingly to employ KZ prisoners in armaments production. Moreover, Himmler and Thierack were in agreement that in future 'Jews, Poles, Gypsies, Russians, and Ukrainians [should no longer be tried] by the normal judicial process'; instead, in future such cases would be 'dealt with by the Reichsführer-SS'.

In addition, during the meeting Himmler proposed that 'many more special institutions should be established in the prison system in accordance with the principle that those who were incapable of rehabilitation should be confined together, while those who were capable of rehabilitation should be confined together according to their particular offence (e.g. fraudsters, thieves, violent criminals)'. While the Justice Minister considered the proposal to be 'correct' in principle, he objected to Himmler's more far-reaching demand that the prosecution service should be integrated into the police apparatus. He agreed to look into Himmler's further demand that criminal records should in future be kept by the police.[103]

On the basis of this agreement, from the autumn of 1942 onwards commissions of assessors composed of officials from the Justice Ministry visited prisons to select which prisoners should be sent to a concentration camp—by mid-1943 a total of 17,307 judicial prisoners. By 1 April 1943 5,935 of them were already dead. The selections continued.[104]

Furthermore, in summer 1942 the regulations for political surveillance were made more strict. Anyone considered 'unworthy of serving in the armed services' was in danger of being taken into preventive detention if he committed the most minor offence.[105] Moreover, in December 1942 the Reich Criminal Police Office issued orders that those 'criminals and asocials who cannot be arrested' were to be sent to the camps, where they 'should be appropriately detained', a formulation which must be seen as an indication that this group of people should be murdered.[106] It has been estimated that in the middle of 1943 there were far more than 20,000 prisoners in preventive detention in concentration camps. By the end of 1943 a total of between 63,000 and 82,000 had been in preventive custody, of whom between 26,000 and 34,000 are estimated to have died.[107] Himmler himself remarked, in a speech on 14 October 1943, that at that time there were 40,000 political prisoners as well as 70,000 'asocials', 'career criminals', and 'preventive detainees'.[108]

However, the agreement between Thierack and Himmler of September 1942 was not restricted to the substantial emptying of German prisons and the 'relief' of the judiciary from the trouble of prosecuting east European forced workers. It also helped Himmler to achieve a goal that he had been pursuing for two years: police control of the prosecution of Poles in the annexed eastern territories. The Reich governors were strongly opposed, because they feared that this would worsen an already tense situation, and Thierack finally revoked his approval. However, typically, the RSHA ignored this and instructed the Stapo offices to 'deal with' such cases themselves, although, in view of the Reich governors' opposition,[109] to do so with some discretion.

Himmler and the Greater Germanic Reich: a reconstruction

As has been shown in detail in the preceding chapters, between April and September 1942 Himmler took a number of far-reaching decisions covering a whole range of areas; some of these had very serious consequences.

First, at the end of April and beginning of May the Reichsführer-SS made the final arrangements for the inclusion of the whole of Europe in the murder of the European Jews. At the end of May and beginning of June, after Heydrich's assassination, he decided to extend and speed up this programme of mass murder to the extent that the 'final solution' would essentially be achieved by the end of the year. During the following months he was exceptionally preoccupied with pursuing this goal. Moreover, the extension of the deportation programme to the whole of Europe from the middle of March 1942 also strengthened the position of the apparatus of repression that he had built up in the occupied countries concerned and of his 'advisers' in the allied states.

Secondly, in July 1942 Hitler assigned to Himmler responsibility for 'combating bandits' in the occupied eastern territories. The fact that at the end of the year Himmler reported to him that, as the result of this assignment, over 363,000 Jews had been shot in the area of Russia–South alone (well over 90 per cent of all the victims of his 'combating bandits') clearly indicates how he understood this task.

Thirdly, in June 1942 Himmler ordered his chief planner, Konrad Meyer, to broaden the settlement plans in order to develop an 'overall settlement plan' for the whole of Europe, which would cover Poland, large parts of the occupied Soviet Union, Alsace and Lorraine, Upper Carniola and South Styria, as well as the Protectorate of Bohemia and Moravia. At the same time, he ordered that the period during which settlement was envisaged as taking place should be reduced by five–ten years to a period of twenty years. In June he announced the Germanization of the Protectorate; in July he laid down parameters for the settlement of the district of Lublin; in August he was taking decisions concerning settlement policy in the Ukraine and at the same time was intensively involved in the ethnic 'cleansing' of Alsace and Lorraine.

Fourthly, in the summer of 1942 Himmler was able significantly to broaden the basis of recruitment for the Waffen-SS. In July 1942 he declared that, 'on the grounds of the iron law of ethnicity', ethnic Germans throughout eastern Europe were liable to military conscription, and therewith initiated a systematic policy of recruiting the ethnic Germans of south-east Europe. In August 1942 Hitler assigned to Himmler sole responsibility for 'relations with all Germanic ethnic groups in Denmark, Norway, Belgium, and the Netherlands [. . .] involving the NSDAP', which strengthened his position for the recruitment of 'Germanic volunteers'. Also in August 1942 Himmler mobilized all Germans in the General Government and the Soviet Union who were capable of bearing arms into 'alarm units' subordinate to him; and he created special militias for those ethnic Germans who were not recruited into the SS. During August he was also able to expand recruitment into the Waffen-SS within Germany itself.

Fifthly, in July 1942 Himmler made another attempt to establish an SS armaments concern in order to free the Waffen-SS from dependence on Wehrmacht allocations. However, when these attempts failed in September 1942, and when the SS's major construction projects, for which it wanted to utilize most of the KZ prisoners, were postponed, he moved to hiring out KZ prisoners to industry. He immediately concentrated on increasing the number of prisoners; they were to double during the following six months.

Sixthly, on 18 September 1942 he made an agreement with Justice Minister Thierack for 'asocial elements' among judicial prisoners (in particular those from 'racially inferior' population groups) to be transferred to concentration camps. His aim of subjecting these people to a regime of 'extermination through work' was in accordance with both his strategy of racial extermination and his merciless utilitarian policy of exploitation.

Seventhly, by simultaneously removing from Thierack the responsibility for the prosecution of Poles, Russians, and Ukrainians in Reich territory he had created the opportunity of filling his camps. For now, if civilian forced workers made themselves in the least suspect they were liable to be sent to a concentration camp. The same is true of the regulations he issued in October, that in future persons suspected of being partisans were on principle to be punished with KZ incarceration, and that ghetto inhabitants in Poland who were required for armaments projects should also be confined to concentration camps or forced labour camps.

It is clear from these turning-points that, believing the victory of the Third Reich was in sight, Himmler was pushing forward certain developments and was combining them in such a way that, taken together, they represented an attempt to create a qualitatively new regime and one in which the SS would have the key role. It should once more be emphasized that in the case of the majority of these decisions there is evidence of prior consultation with Hitler, and in the other cases we can assume that he was acting in the spirit of his 'Führer', a procedure that had characterized Himmler's political style since his earliest days in the NSDAP. In order to describe the new regime that he envisaged Himmler fell back on the term 'Greater Germanic Reich' that he had already used at the end of the 1930s. But now, in 1942, his image of this regime had acquired far clearer contours.

The Greater Germanic Reich was not to be simply a Greater German Reich enlarged by annexed territory, but a qualitatively new supranational regime under totalitarian rule that was systematically constructed on the basis of a racial hierarchy. A ruling elite composed of members of the Germanic nations would in future dominate the European continent and assign to other nations their respective places according to their racial quality: as allies of the new empire, as nations under its 'protection', or—the role envisaged for the Slav nations—as work-slaves who would not have the right of an independent national existence.

In the meantime, however, Himmler had ensured that without the SS this empire would be inconceivable:

- The SS had constructed a Europe-wide apparatus of repression, which not only brutally suppressed all opposition tendencies and any resistance but, in addition and above all, systematically and massively murdered all *potential* opponents and 'racial inferiors' on the basis of alleged biological criteria, a policy that in the first instance was directed at the Jews but also targeted, above all, east European Gypsies and sections of the Slav population. Basically it represented a version of the policy of racial 'general prevention' that Himmler had developed for the Reich during the late 1930s but which in a radicalized version was now being extended to the whole of Europe. The victims of this policy were now no longer being placed in preventive detention but murdered. But this bloody task, the difficulty of which he often complained about in tones bordering on self-pity, was, as far as he was concerned, an unavoidable aspect of a more far-reaching project to transform Europe and secure the future of the 'Teutons' (*Germanen*).

- The SS worked on an overall plan to Germanize large areas of central and eastern Europe, and had either begun or already carried out a number of resettlement projects. It controlled the ethnic German groups in south-east Europe and was responsible in the first instance for relations with the 'Germanic forces' in north-west Europe. This provided it with important sources of future settlers.

- By opening the Waffen-SS to ethnic Germans, 'Germanic volunteers', and non-Germanic legionnaires from European countries, Himmler had created a model for the new regime within the SS itself, in which the individual was already being graded in accordance with his racial 'value'.

- With the massive amount of forced labour carried out by KZ prisoners, and the idea of 'extermination through work', the SS was providing proof that it was in a position not only usefully to employ an army of slave workers, but also to utilize this deployment as an effective instrument of repression and for the liquidation of all political and racial undesirables.

- The SS had successfully enforced its claim that it alone possessed the necessary expertise authoritatively to define the new racial hierarchy and, using the 'proven' instrument of racial assessment, to determine on what level of this racial hierarchy each individual was placed. The SS was not concerned about the fact that racial assessments were largely arbitrary, as the criteria with which they were operating in fact represented racial fantasies. For it had both the power to force through this policy of racial segregation and the 'world-view' to legitimize these measures.

Furthermore, the turning-points between spring and autumn 1942 indicate that Himmler's view of how this new regime should be constructed had shifted dramatically. While at the end of the 1930s he had assumed that the Reich would be able to achieve the status of a world power only in the course of several generations, now his view of the period involved had been reduced as if in a time lapse. The huge Reich was already in the process of being created, and he must act now in order to secure a decisive role for himself and his SS. The motive of speeding up developments that were already in progress was decisive here, for in view of the Wehrmacht's impending victory a window appeared to be opening which would permit the realization of ideas that had previously appeared utopian. The 'final solution' of the European 'Jewish question' had to be implemented *now* and not after the end of the war. Further settlement projects in eastern Europe had to begin *at once* and not in the distant future. The extermination of the 'asocials' had to happen *immediately*. Himmler wanted to initiate a dynamic which, within a few months, would have subjected the area controlled by Germany to a process of quasi-revolutionary change.

It is important to bear in mind the exceptional amount of power that Himmler had concentrated in the SS leadership in the months between spring and autumn 1942. Despite the reverses and delays referred to, he had installed an unbridled system of terror and mass murder throughout Europe; using the instrument of 'extermination through work', he ruled over an army of slave workers; he had begun the resettlement of millions of people, selected according to racial criteria, and was in the process of setting up a second army alongside the Wehrmacht, whose composition ignored national boundaries and whose structure prefigured the future Greater Germanic Reich.

In September 1942 Himmler could assume that he had successfully laid the foundations of the Greater Germanic Reich of which he dreamt. However, this situation lasted only a few weeks. For, with the landing of the Allies in North Africa in November 1942 the fortunes of the war began to change, and as a result the prospects of further decisive steps in the direction of a Greater Germanic Reich rapidly disappeared. In particular, large-scale settlement projects were even less viable than they had been before and, in view of the war situation, it was inadvisable to differentiate too obviously between the 'Germanic brother nations' and other Europeans.

Himmler, however, was not frustrated by this development, nor did it mean a decline in his power. His original idea might not succeed, but nevertheless, as far as he was concerned, he was still a winner. For in many areas the dynamic of the development that he had unleashed or driven forward could not be stopped. The mass murder in the camps, the slave labour, as well as the 'combating of bandits' and merciless repression in the occupied territories were, not least thanks to his own efforts, so firmly integrated into the Nazi conception of war that they continued undiminished, all the more so as the situation deteriorated.

Thus Himmler soon found a new role. Now he projected an image of himself as the man who, through the use of exceptional terror, was guaranteeing the internal security of the Reich and of the territories occupied by Germany. In the two-and-a-half years remaining to him as Reichsführer-SS he accumulated a monopoly of power for this purpose that he had never previously achieved. The more the Third Reich headed towards its downfall, the more powerful became the Reichsführer-SS.

PART VI

Downfall in Stages

25

A Turn in the War—A New Opportunity?

With the landing of Allied troops in North Africa in November 1942 the military initiative was passing more and more to the Allies. From now onwards the southern flank of Axis-dominated Europe was increasingly exposed and, on 11 November 1942, Germany and Italy decided to occupy the unoccupied zone in the south of France. As a result Himmler acquired a new task: the elimination of all 'enemies' of the Reich who, under the protection of the Vichy regime, had hitherto been able to evade persecution.

He envisaged that a crushing blow against this army of 'enemies' who were allegedly concentrated in the south of France would mark the start of a generally harsher policy of repression. This would now have to take precedence over the vision of a Greater German Reich that had so preoccupied him during the previous months. Now that the threat to the Reich from outside was growing Himmler felt it incumbent upon him to secure the 'internal theatre of war',[1] and that meant the merciless elimination, using all available means, of all enemies within the area controlled by Germany. This would be carried out by crushing political resistance in the occupied territories, by including countries in the campaign of Jewish persecution that had not hitherto been involved, along with a renewed escalation in the murder programme, as well as by extending the 'campaign against bandits' to the whole of eastern Europe. Moreover, during the coming months Himmler was able substantially to increase his power. He considerably enlarged the Waffen-SS by recruiting 'ethnic alien' volunteers; he was appointed Reich Minister of the Interior, thereby acquiring control over the Reich's internal administration; he significantly increased the slave army in the concentration camps; and, when he took over responsibility for the missile programme, it looked as if he was going to get his hands on a substantial part of the armaments industry. However, his impact as head of the Waffen-SS, Interior Minister, and organizer of armaments production turned out in fact to be modest. The more the Third Reich came under military pressure during the coming years, the more Himmler's role became reduced to that of head of a merciless terror machine.

This development began at the end of 1942, when he tried to bring the south of France, which had just been occupied by German troops, under his control. On 14 November, four days after the occupation, he instructed the commander of the security police in France, Helmut Knochen, to send him 'daily reports of arrests of politically dangerous elements and leading figures in the previous regime. Every effort must be made to catch these dangerous opponents.'[2]

As always when he wished to enlarge his sphere of responsibilities or to give it a new focus, he appealed directly to Hitler. On 10 December, in the course of a long interview, he explained the situation in the south of France to his Führer, and why as radical a policy as possible was required to deal with it. It was minuted that Himmler had been informed that

there are currently at least 1.5 million deadly enemies of the Axis living and moving around freely in the previously unoccupied part of France, namely 600,000–700,000 Jews, 500,000–600,000 anti-Fascist Italians, 300,000–400,000 red Spaniards, around 20,000 Anglo-Saxons, 80,000 Poles, Greeks, etc. They represent a not inconsiderable threat to the supplies and security of the German–Italian Mediterranean army. In addition, there are hostile French amounting to a number many times larger than that and consisting primarily of communists, Gaullists, and church people.[3]

Hitler was impressed with this account of the situation. He instructed Himmler, as the latter carefully noted, to 'get rid of' the 600,000 to 700,000 Jews in France, including North Africa. The 'red Spaniards' were to be 'made to work', the Gaullists, English, and Americans were to be arrested, and the Italians in the unoccupied area were to be deployed as forced labour and their leaders locked up in concentration camps.[4]

A few days later Himmler once again approached Hitler. He wanted the whole of the French police force to be centrally organized under Bousquet, the police secretary-general of the Vichy government. Moreover, what was needed in order to 'strengthen its effectiveness' was for 'every brave and manly French policeman to have the absolute backing of his superior' (which was equivalent to giving them carte blanche for arbitrary behaviour), for 'officers to have financial security', for Himmler's own police apparatus 'to have the right to use all the facilities of the French police in the way of records and for search operations', the creation of a special police unit for combating the 'political enemies of Europe', and the deportation to Germany of 'all those others guilty of destroying the unity of Europe such as Blum, Gamelin, Daladier'.[5]

During the following days Himmler developed the idea of making an example of the south of France, which had just been occupied. In order to leave no doubt about the new radical policy, he wanted to carry out a 'major operation' and one that would involve the French police. He calculated that this would enable him to make it complicit in his policy of persecuting what were, after all, 1.5 million 'deadly enemies' and binding it closer to the occupation authorities. Marseilles was selected as the location of the operation. In Himmler's mind this Mediterranean port was a labyrinthine 'nest of criminals' that simply needed exterminating.

A punishment operation in Marseilles

In the middle of December 1942 a police regiment specially established for this purpose arrived in Marseilles and, from this point onwards, Himmler became personally involved in the 'measures' to eliminate 'the criminals' in the city, referring to a commission from Hitler to the SS.[6] On 3 January several bombs went off in Marseilles; the communist resistance had carried out a number of attacks on the occupation authorities. The following day Himmler ordered his most senior representative in the country, HSSPF Oberg, to launch an energetic and concerted operation to be carried out by the order and security police: 'I demand the toughest and most radical action. Naturally, you are also responsible for the part of France that has hitherto remained unoccupied. However, the image of the French government and its definite independence must be preserved.'[7]

On the same day, however, the Wehrmacht—as Himmler presumed, after consultation with Oberg—had already declared a state of emergency in Marseilles, so that it would be responsible for any retaliatory measures. Himmler was annoyed, and reminded Oberg on 5 January that 'the Führer has definitely given us the responsibility for Marseilles'.[8] The 'Marseilles affair', he insisted to Oberg in a telex sent on the same day, is 'a purely police

matter dealing with sabotage by a subhuman insurgency going on there'.
Oberg should kindly leave his Paris office and get down to Marseilles. He
also sent Daluege, the chief of the order police, and Major-General of Police
Walter Schimana, using this opportunity to inform Oberg of Schimana's
appointment as chief of the order police in France.[9]

On the following day Oberg received another telex from his Reichsführer, once again reproaching him for having ceded the impending operation in Marseilles, contrary to the Führer order:

The moment something happens in Marseilles, without consulting me, you, Herr
Oberg, change the Führer order, run after the Wehrmacht, and ensure that a
divisional commander takes command in Marseilles. I must say I didn't expect
such bureaucratic-type behaviour from you. Any other SS man, above all, any
other Higher SS and Police Leader, would have been glad for the SS to be able to
tackle such a difficult task on its own and would have taken care of it himself and
would have felt able to leave his comfortable office in Paris.

Moreover, Oberg had also contravened another Führer order: four tanks,
which on Hitler's instructions had been sent to reinforce the order police in
France, could not be put into operation there, allegedly on account of a lack
of suitable personnel.

You have had the honour of becoming a Higher SS and Police Leader and so you
should also have been prepared to take on the burden, just as I have, of seeing to
everything personally, from whether the prostitutes in a small French town are
subject to inspections to prevent our troops from catching diseases, to whether
there are men available to drive tanks that have been placed at your disposal. But
this cannot be done simply through meetings or at soirées.

'Disobeying any more Führer orders or changing them in a bureaucratic
manner' would lead to his dismissal.[10] A few days later he ordered Oberg to
deploy the French police 'to clear out this French nest of criminals'. After
all, they could expect losses and he wanted to avoid them being German
ones.[11]

On 18 January he urged Oberg to 'arrest the great mass of criminals in
Marseilles and put them in concentration camps'—he gave a figure of
'around 100,000'! Moreover, Himmler demanded 'the extensive dynamit-
ing of the crime district. I do not want German lives to be put at risk in the
underground alleys and cellars.' The 'lower part of Marseilles' should be
blown up in such a way that 'those living there are killed simply by the
effects of the blast'. The French police should not only be obliged to

participate but should also understand that 'they ought to be deeply grateful to us for doing it'.[12]

Hitherto there had not been a comparable police action in the occupied western territories. Had Himmler got his way, German occupation policy would have been reduced to that of a brutal regime of terror, which would undoubtedly have had serious consequences for the relationship between occupiers and the indigenous population in the rest of the western territories. Oberg appears to have been only too conscious of the fact. Despite Himmler's increasingly urgent requests and threats, he pursued his own policy. In his negotiations with the French police during the following days he managed to evade Himmler's draconian instructions,[13] and reached agreement with his interlocutors on the following course of action: on 22/3 January 1943 the French police carried out raids in Marseilles and, instead of the figure of 100,000 that had been requested, arrested 6,000 people; the 20,000 inhabitants of the harbour quarter were driven from their homes and had to undergo an inspection. The German security police delivered up 2,200 people, most of them Jews, to the police prison camp at Compiègne near Paris, and 782 Marseilles Jews were deported to Sobibor. Part of the harbour quarter was then in fact blown up. Surprisingly, Himmler expressed himself satisfied with Oberg's minimalist version of his massive cleansing plans. Evidently the German and French security authorities had found a compromise through which Himmler's strategy of extermination could be modified.

Himmler, however, stuck rigidly to one feature of the Marseilles cleansing operation: he was determined to send 1,500 French prisoners to build a railway in the Narvik district in Norway, and put the RSHA under pressure with a stream of telexes so that his 'firm' promise to Hitler could be kept.[14]

The reasons why Himmler was only partially successful in enforcing his extremely brutal policy in Marseilles, and why his orders were evaded by Oberg, even though the latter was already a target of Himmler's disapproval, may have had nothing to do with events in the south of France. For, at the beginning of 1943, it cannot have been a secret within the security apparatus that, immediately after he had managed to persuade Hitler to agree to his hard line over Marseilles, Himmler had fallen into bad odour with his 'Führer'; for a time the authority of the Reichsführer appeared seriously damaged.

For, on 16 December 1942, the former leader of the Romanian Iron Guard, Horia Sima, who with 260 followers had escaped to Germany after his unsuccessful coup of January 1941, had fled German internment to Rome, despite having given his word of honour that he would stay. This flight was extremely embarrassing for Himmler. He had never been able completely to free himself from the suspicion that he had personally approved the 1941 coup, which had been supported by members of the SD. And now it appeared as if, by tolerating the flight, he had once again tried to sabotage the German policy vis-à-vis Romania of supporting the Antonescu regime. What made it worse was the fact that he had not immediately reported the flight to Hitler, so that the latter did not hear of it until days later. A serious crisis developed in relations with Romania when, on 26 December, Marshall Antonescu demanded Sima's extradition. Hitler was extremely annoyed about Himmler's behaviour with regard to Sima and demanded that the latter keep him continually informed about the progress of the hunt for him. Finally, after considerable efforts, Sima was arrested in Rome and brought back to Germany. Hitler revoked his original order to execute him, and instead he and his followers were put in concentration camps.[15]

Resistance throughout Europe

Oberg not only survived the Marseilles affair but continued to oppose Himmler's radical policy, despite repeated admonitions from the Reichsführer. Oberg controlled over 200 security police throughout France, in other words, a relatively widely spaced network, whose members, mostly unqualified and not able to speak French, were basically unable to cope with the increasing activities of the resistance.[16] Thus, contrary to Himmler's wishes, Oberg considered it inadvisable to attempt to become the overlord of the French police, but preferred rather to adopt a policy of cooperation. He delayed the transfer of French politicians and American journalists from French internment to German concentration camps long enough until, in April 1943, after a conversation with the French police chief Bouquet, Himmler reluctantly came to agree with him.[17]

At the end of 1943, however, Himmler put an end to the cooperation of Oberg and Bousquet. He ordered Oberg to request Prime Minister Laval to dismiss Bouquet (the previous month Oberg had vigorously opposed such a step)[18] and to appoint Joseph Darnand, chief of the French militia, the Vichy regime's special force, as his successor. This appointment was clearly intended to bring about the amalgamation of the militia and the police along German lines. Moreover, Darnand was an Obersturmführer in the French Waffen-SS.[19]

In February 1944 a quarrel broke out between Berger, the head of the Main Office, and Oberg. 'On the express orders of the Reichsführer SS', Berger wanted to establish an Einsatzkommando of the Waffen-SS for France and to amalgamate the French right-wing paramilitary leagues in order to provide a counterweight to the Free French army in the event of an Allied landing. Berger concluded his missive with an argument that was hard to refute: 'German mothers won't be weeping for foreigners who get killed. And I'm saying that on the anniversary of my son's death.'[20] Oberg, who was primarily concerned to prevent anything that threatened to disturb French domestic politics, opposed this policy and did so with a very ingenious argument. 'In accordance with the Führer's directives, while on the surface we should be following a policy of cooperation,' nevertheless we should 'never [lose] sight of the fact that our aim is to destroy France once and for all.' The 'creation of such a unified, French national organization, or something similar, with the aid of the SS would, however, provide the basis for a truly national reconstruction of France, in other words be contrary to the Führer's directives'. And the 'creation of such a unified organization' would remove 'the possibility, when the time comes, of playing off the various political forces in France, including Darnand's militia, against one another'.[21]

Himmler informed Berger that he must drop his plans for the time being, but he wanted to discuss the matter thoroughly with him.[22] In fact, the right-wing leagues in France were not amalgamated into a unified militia, nor did Berger achieve his aim of establishing a recruiting office for the Waffen-SS in France. Once again Oberg had succeeded in imposing his relatively careful approach and in using delaying tactics to block Himmler's radical policy.[23]

Himmler's brutal orders for the suppression of all opposition provoked resistance from his own people in the other occupied territories as well. The regional German police authorities, most of which were dependent on the cooperation of local forces, frequently modified Himmler's draconian orders. It became apparent that the Higher SS and Police Leaders and commanders of the security police did not simply represent Himmler in the occupied territories, but increasingly the reverse—namely, the interests of the area for which they were responsible, as they understood them, vis-à-vis Himmler. In fact he himself must, in the meantime, have reached the conclusion that the indiscriminate shooting of hostages, which had been the norm in 1941, was not necessarily conducive to keeping the resistance at bay. Thus, despite his verbal advocacy of shootings, in practice he tended to support mass arrests and deportations to German concentration camps, particularly as he had an increasing need for slave labour. His policy of repression was, therefore, clearly contradictory: his brutal announcements and extreme orders cannot disguise the fact that he lacked a strategy to cope with the complex demands of the European resistance movements. Thus his approach varied from country to country, as will become clear from the following examples.

In the Protectorate, as already mentioned, the retaliatory excesses of June 1942 were followed by a certain degree of calm. In 1943, however, Himmler demanded a tougher policy. On 3 July, against the background of increasing Czech hostility to the Germans, he ordered the acting Reich Protector, Daluege, 'immediately to take into protective custody and send to a concentration camp all those officials and employees of the Czech authorities who have shown a lack of commitment to their service or work', and also, as a 'preventative and deterrent measure', 'immediately to take 500 Czechs into protective custody and transfer them to a concentration camp'.[24] In fact this no longer meant Auschwitz, because two months before he had instructed the Gestapo not to send any more Czechs there as the President of the Protectorate, Emil Hácha, had expressed concern about the 'high death-rate' in the camp.[25] In September 1943 Himmler authorized his HSSPF Karl Frank, 'for the purpose of restoring order as quickly as possible [. . .] to have Czech troublemakers and saboteurs hanged on the spot'. According to his own statements, Frank ensured that around 100 death sentences were passed each month, but these were announced only locally in order to play down the importance of the resistance movement.[26]

In Denmark too Himmler followed a comparatively cautious policy during the first half of 1943. He received first-hand information about the country from Werner Best, who had been appointed Reich Plenipotentiary in November 1942 and with whom his relationship had improved somewhat since the latter had left the RSHA in 1940. The former administrative chief of the Gestapo was answerable to the Foreign Ministry, but also supplied Himmler with his regular assessments of the situation.[27] In return Himmler initially supported Best's political line of continuing the low-key and cooperative policy as practised hitherto. The Reich Plenipotentiary limited himself to submitting 'recommendations' to the Danish government, which was substantially independent. Even the relatively small Jewish minority in the country and refugees from other countries were left in peace.[28] In July 1943 Himmler informed Best that he had told Hitler that, 'from a purely security and sabotage point of view', Denmark was 'at the moment the best country'.[29]

Only a few weeks later, however, Himmler was to judge the situation very differently. During the summer of 1943 more and more acts of sabotage, strikes, and disturbances took place, and at the end of August Hitler responded by imposing a military state of emergency. And in this critical phase of German occupation policy the Danish Jews were also no longer going to be protected. Despite the state of emergency the acts of resistance increased. Finally, in December 1943 Himmler appointed a Higher SS and Police Leader in Denmark in the shape of Günther Pancke, a clear denigration of Reich Plenipotentiary Best and a critique of his low-key policy towards the Danes, since he was thereby deprived of his control over the German police in the country. Himmler had good reason to tell Best, in a personal letter in October, 'not to be sad' about the appointment of his rival.[30] The Reich Plenipotentiary responded by altering his policy: at the end of 1943 he subordinated Danish civilians to SS and police jurisdiction by creating a 'Police Field Court', and in January 1944 had this measure sanctioned by Hitler. During the following period this court repeatedly sentenced members of the resistance movement to death.[31]

In the occupied Netherlands the Higher SS and Police Leader, Hanns Rauter, had long been taking a hard line with the local resistance movement. In February 1943 he proposed to his Reichsführer responding to an act of sabotage that had just taken place by arresting 5,000 students ('sons of plutocrats') who belonged to the 'reactionary camp', returning all former NCOs of the Dutch armed forces to prisoner-of-war camp, and shooting fifty hostages. Himmler agreed, but advised: 'I would not shoot the hostages if we are going simultaneously to arrest the five thousand.'[32] After a further attack a few days later, however, he wanted the number of 'sons of plutocrats' increased. Moreover, in 'most cases' the fathers ought to be arrested at the same time. Civil servants who could be shown to have given false information 'also belonged in the KZ, but they should be put in the quarry'. And 'there mustn't be any climb-downs. The emigration of the Jews must be kept going.'[33]

When, on the following day, a member of Mussert's militia was murdered, Himmler informed Rauter that the previous day Hitler had reiterated that 'there must be absolutely no concessions; the toughest possible action must be taken'. Not only must the 5,000 'sons of plutocrats' and their fathers be arrested, but, in addition to the NCOs, the 'prominent pro-English reserve officers' should also be interned.[34]

A few weeks later a doctors' strike broke out, and once again Himmler told Rauter: 'I'm in favour of taking really tough action.' Three or four hundred strike leaders should be arrested and deported straight away to concentration camps in the Reich.[35] At the beginning of May there was another strike, and this time almost a million Dutch people took part. Rauter broke it in the most brutal fashion, among other things by carrying out a hundred summary executions. His Reichsführer was full of praise for Rauter's 'vigorous action'.[36]

In September 1943 Rauter suggested establishing police courts martial. Himmler approved, and added that offenders' families should also be punished by 'confiscating their property, furniture and other effects, in fact everything'.[37] At the same time Rauter worked out how one could deal with the resistance without becoming obviously involved in the role of the occupying power. As 'retribution' for an attack they should not be content with 'locking up 100 well-known agitators' from the province concerned in a concentration camp; rather, they could use 'suitable men from the 'Germanic SS' 'to carry out a reprisal under the leadership of our people and finish off three of the leading agitators'.[38] Once again Himmler approved the plan, and Rauter lost no time in carrying it out. The very same month the Germanic SS went into action, and a total of fifty-five people fell victim to the so-called 'Operation Silver Pine'.[39]

This represented the birth of a new concept of 'counter-terror' for combating the European resistance movements. In retaliation for attacks by the resistance, prominent persons who were known to be opponents of the Nazis were, where possible, ambushed and murdered, with the identities and motives of those involved remaining a mystery. The aim was to leave it uncertain as to whether the attacks were carried out by the occupation authorities themselves or on their instructions, or whether indigenous right-wing forces acting on their own initiative were responsible. The counter-terror was thus used in the first instance in the 'Germanic countries' in which the Nazi regime claimed that, because of 'blood ties', there was a broad basis for collaboration with the Reich; and in fact in a number of cases indigenous 'comrades' supported the SS's counter-terror.

On 30 December 1943 Hitler summoned Best, Pancke, and the commander of Wehrmacht troops in Denmark and ordered them to engage in counter-terror. The whole operation was organized by Alfred Naujocks, who had been responsible for the attack on the Gleiwitz radio station in 1939. At the beginning of 1944 he brought a commando to Denmark, which the SS sabotage expert, Otto Skorzeny, had placed at his disposal. Danish Nazis who had joined the Schalburg corps, a unit not unlike the SS, participated in the preparation of the attacks. During the following weeks numerous individuals engaged in Danish public life were murdered in the street or in their own homes, and public buildings were blown up.[40]

In the summer of 1944 the counter-terror was extended to Norway and Belgium. In Oslo, during the course of 'Operation Flower Picking', a commando of the German security police murdered around two-dozen people who were suspected of supporting the resistance movement.[41] In Brussels the 'Jungklaus Office', which had supposedly been established to recruit volunteers for the Waffen-SS, but in fact was the control centre for all the activities of the SS and SD in Belgium, became involved in the preparations. The attacks, to which Himmler gave his express approval on 4 June 1944 and for which he issued detailed guidelines, were carried out with the aid of Belgian fascists and were largely directed at well-known figures who had been prominent opponents of collaboration.[42]

In occupied eastern Europe, however, where in Himmler's view they were dealing with 'subhumans', the methods of repression were far more brutal. In the spring of 1942 he had already effectively emasculated Hans Frank through the appointment of Krüger as state secretary for security and omnipotent RKF representative, and with the aid of Bormann and Lammers he continued to put Frank under pressure, among other things by carrying out major police and resettlement operations in order to demonstrate Frank's incompetence and that of his administration. Hitler was not, however, prepared to dismiss Frank, who had in fact become disillusioned, for fear of a loss of German prestige in the General Government. Meanwhile, Himmler was hoping that an increase in terror would strengthen the SS's position in this region.

In November 1942, following reports about a Polish uprising that was alleged to be about to take place, Himmler ordered that a large number of Poles suspected of subversion should be sent to concentration camps.[43] The uprising did not take place, and yet in January 1943 Himmler raised the matter again. Now, however, he associated the 'bandit activities' with unemployment in the General Government. As with the 1938 'asocial operation' in the Reich, his main concern was to increase the numbers held in concentration camps through a programme of massive arrests: 'I therefore order that from now onwards all proletarian types whether male or female should be sent to the KL [concentration camps] in Lublin, Auschwitz, or in the Reich. The numbers arrested must be sufficiently large to decrease significantly those people who are not in employment in the GG and thus achieve a distinct alleviation of the threat from bandits.'[44]

As a result, between 15 and 22 January Himmler's men arrested around 20,000 people indiscriminately; the 'action' affected above all people who were not unemployed, producing considerable unrest among the population and thereby increasing the potential threat of resistance. The civilian population, who had not been warned in advance, objected strongly, and Krüger not only had to admit that mistakes had been made but eventually felt obliged to reassure the civilian administration that such actions would not be carried out in future.[45] Himmler did not allow himself to be affected by this. 'We must not be put off such actions by unavoidable mistakes, since all in all the removal of asocial, criminal types will in the final analysis alleviate the situation.'[46] Apparently among the 'mistakes' was the fact that, in the course of the mass arrests, Himmler had wanted to 'transfer' to concentration camps the 20,000 Polish officers who were still held as prisoners of war. In the event, the Foreign Minister, Ribbentrop, intervened to prevent this.[47]

On 19 June 1943 Himmler was able to persuade Hitler to extend his range of responsibilities for 'combating bandits', and to convince him for this purpose to 'return' to him a number of SS and police units that had been transferred to the front. As in the previous September, in order to achieve this he utilized a meeting in which the 'partisan problem' and the 'Jewish question' formed the subject of discussion. Himmler's commission to expand the 'combating of bandits' was evidently linked to Hitler's order to him 'to carry out ruthlessly [...] the evacuation of the Jews [...] in the course of the next three to four months'.[48]

Two days later Himmler appointed von dem Bach-Zelewski commander of the units involved in combating bandits. At the same time he declared the territories of Upper Carinthia and Lower Styria, the General Government, the district of Bialystock, the regions of Russia-Centre and Russia-South/ Reich Commissariat Ukraine, as well as Croatia to be 'bandit combat areas'.[49] He was now in a position to engage in unrestricted terror over large parts of south-east and eastern Europe. In April 1944 upper and central Italy were added to the 'bandit combat areas'.[50]

In the case of the General Government its classification as 'a bandit combat area' meant that among other things the powers of the security police courts martial were extended. Now, on principle, Poles who were guilty of the slightest offence 'against the work of German reconstruction' could be shot on the spot without any formal legal process.[51] Between October 1943 and July 1944 (in other words, before the Warsaw uprising) the occupation authorities murdered 8,000 people in Warsaw alone.

The extent of the terror, disguised as 'combating bandits', that was exercised in the occupied Soviet territories and the very varied motives that lay behind it may be illustrated by the following example. In the course of 1943 the Nazi leadership developed the notion that the threat posed by the partisans in occupied Soviet territories could be effectively combated by the creation of 'dead zones', an idea that was also affected by economic considerations. Initial experiments were undertaken.[52]

On 10 July 1943 Himmler announced in an order that Hitler had decided 'that the territories of the northern Ukraine and Russia-Centre plagued by bandit activity' were to be 'cleared of all their population'. The whole of the male population capable of work was to be 'transferred' to Sauckel, 'on the basis of POW conditions'. The women would be assigned to Sauckel 'for work in the Reich'. 'Part of the female population and all children without parents will be placed in our reception camps.' The territories that had been emptied in this way were to be managed by the Higher SS and Police Leaders, with some areas being planted with Kok-Sagys, a rubber-type plant in which Himmler was particularly interested, and others 'exploited for agriculture'. 'The children's camps are to be established on the borders of these territories so that the children can be used as labour for Kok-Sagys cultivation and for agriculture.'[53]

Anyone who remained in the 'dead zones' after the civilian population had been deported or murdered, their property plundered, and their houses destroyed, would then automatically be considered 'a bandit suspect' and shot on sight. In the General Commissariat of White Ruthenia in August 1943 the 'dead zones'—contiguous territories—already made up 16 per cent of the arable land; in July 1944 in the area under military administration in eastern Byelorussia as much as 75 per cent![54]

Thus the order benefited security through the depopulation of territories 'suspected of harbouring bandits', and the economy by providing forced labour; the establishment of camps for the 'bandit children' corresponded to Himmler's racial principles; and with the production of Kok-Sagys he hoped to be able to deliver a raw material important for the war economy. (The day before, Himmler had had himself appointed by Göring as 'Special Representative for Plant Rubber' in order to be able to embark on large-scale Kok-Sagys production.)

Himmler had already issued the order to transfer people from 'territories plagued by bandits' to the Reich as labour in October 1942, but the operation had not got under way. His order of 10 June was, however, actually put into effect. In September 1943, in his role as commander of the units involved in combating bandits, von dem Bach-Zalewski gave the requisite instructions and ensured that they were carried out during the coming months.[55] In the process the motives for and methods of combating partisans had changed radically by comparison with those of the previous year. Whereas in 1942 'combating bandits' was primarily motivated by the aim of murdering the Jews as 'bandit suspects', now, since the murder of the Jews in eastern Europe had been largely achieved, it was primarily a matter of securing labour. This developed into a key motive for the combating of partisans.[56]

By contrast, an alternative strategy, continually discussed within the German leadership, of trying to gain allies among the indigenous population by promising them some form of political autonomy or other privileges invariably met with strong resistance from Himmler. 'We must never', he noted in a minute from November 1942, 'promise the Russians a national state. Otherwise we may be making commitments [. . .] which one day we shall have to keep.'[57] In his notorious Posen speech to the SS-Gruppen-führer of 4 October 1943 he adopted a similar tone, when he firmly rejected the idea that was current in the Wehrmacht that they could work with the Russian general Andrei Andreyevitsch Vlasov, who was a German POW, to recruit Russian auxiliaries to fight Stalin. The motto: 'We can't defeat the Russians; that can be done only by the Russians themselves', would lead to defeatism.[58] A year later, however, having in the meantime become commander of the Reserve Army and personally responsible for providing Wehrmacht replacements, Himmler was to reconsider his position. Yet, in Posen he reiterated to his leadership corps: 'I don't care in the least what happens to the Russians or the Czechs [. . .] Whether other nations are

Ill. 30. On 16 September 1944 Himmler, now commander
of the Reserve Army, came to an agreement with General
Vlasov on the deployment of Russian troops alongside the
Wehrmacht. The photograph taken afterwards showing the
men shaking hands was purely for show, as in private
Himmler had never concealed his contempt for the general.

prosperous or die of hunger only interests me in so far as we have slaves for
our culture; otherwise it doesn't interest me.'[59]

From the autumn of 1942 onwards, in the light of the change in the war
situation, Himmler had also been intensifying the repressive policy in the
Reich. In the first place this affected the millions of foreigners who were
living there, as already described in the previous chapter.

In December 1942 Himmler decided to transfer the leadership of the
RSHA, which he had taken on himself after Heydrich's assassination, to
Ernst Kaltenbrunner. Kaltenbrunner, who had been HSSPF Danube in
Vienna since 1938, had little experience of police command but had the
reputation of knowing something about secret intelligence matters, and was
regarded as absolutely loyal to Himmler. In view of the military and political
changes that were likely to happen, the Reichsführer valued these qualities
particularly highly. Moreover, he approved of Kaltenbrunner's robust

behaviour when dealing with other institutions of the Nazi state.[60] The official appointment occurred on 30 January 1943.

One of the challenges facing the new head of the RSHA came from the Reich Ministry of Justice. In November 1942 Thierack had withdrawn from the agreement he had made in September that in future Poles and eastern workers would be subject to punishment by the Gestapo. He had responded to objections from the Reich governors in the eastern territories.[61] However, after negotiations lasting several months Kaltenbrunner managed to force the ministry once more to give up this responsibility. On 30 June 1943 the RSHA informed the Stapo offices that, as a matter of principle, the punishment of Polish and Soviet Russian forced workers was 'to be carried out' by the Gestapo using 'Gestapo methods' or 'special treatment'. The RSHA laid down in this edict that cases involving Soviet and Polish forced workers should be handed over to the judiciary only if a sentence by a court was considered necessary 'for political reasons of morale', and if assurances had been given by the court that a death sentence could be anticipated.[62] The RSHA had already ensured in March 1943 that it could arrest Poles who had been released from prison after serving a sentence of more than six months and order that they should be consigned to a concentration camp.[63]

Escaped POWs, the crews of aircraft that had been shot down, or Allied paratroopers who had been caught also faced harsh treatment. In the summer of 1943 Himmler issued an edict which could be interpreted as a licence for lynch justice. It was 'not the task of the police to interfere with conflicts between German national comrades and British and American terroristic airmen who have bailed out'.[64] On 4 March Gestapo chief Müller decreed that, following their capture, escaped POWs (except for Britons and Americans) were to be transferred to the security police and SD, who should send them to Mauthausen, where they were to be shot. The internal code-name for this procedure was 'Operation Bullet'.[65]

Persecution of the Jews intensifies

With the Anglo-American landings in Morocco and Algeria in November 1942 the Jews throughout Europe also came under further pressure. Initially that applied particularly to the Jewish minorities in the Mediterranean. As a counterstroke to the Allied landings in North Africa German troops occupied Tunisia and brought around 85,000 Tunisian Jews under their control.

A specially formed Einsatzgruppe Tunisia introduced a regime of forced labour, and around twenty Jewish men were deported to the extermination camps. The total victory of the Allies in North Africa in May 1943 prevented a catastrophe.[66]

The anti-Jewish measures had much more far-reaching consequences in the south of Europe, which the Germans feared might come to form the rear area for a new southern front of 'Fortress Europe'. We have already seen from the example of Marseilles that, after the occupation of southern France by German and Italian troops on 11 November 1942, Himmler was determined to clear this area of Jews as well.[67] In January and February Jews were arrested in large numbers in both northern and southern France, and in February the deportations were restarted. However, since on the one hand the Italian authorities were not prepared to support anti-Jewish measures in their occupation zone of south-east France and offered sanctuary to Jewish refugees, and on the other, the deportation of Jews with French citizenship threatened to disrupt the policy of collaboration, in March the security police developed a new strategy: they demanded that the French government strip those Jews who had acquired French citizenship of their nationality. The deportations were postponed for the time being, on the assumption that this would be approved.[68]

Italy's attitude became a serious problem,[69] as Himmler frequently explained to Ribbentrop. Their ally's policy provided 'the excuse for many circles in France and throughout Europe to stall over the Jewish question because they can point out that not even our Axis partner is prepared to cooperate over the Jewish question'.[70] In February, therefore, he 'urgently' requested the Foreign Minister to approach the Italians and 'urge them no longer to sabotage [. . .] the Reich Security Main Office's Jewish measures. Our attempts to persuade the governments of Croatia, Romania, Bulgaria, and Slovakia to deport the Jews in these countries are also facing serious difficulties because of the Italian government's attitude.'[71]

Nevertheless the RSHA increased the pressure on Bulgaria as well as on Greece. In February a special commando arrived in Saloniki to organize the deportation of the local Jewish community, which Himmler had already announced in November 1941. Between mid-March and mid-August 1943 a total of 45,000 Jews were deported from Saloniki and the adjacent Macedonian communities to Auschwitz, where almost all of them were murdered.[72] The Bulgarian Jewish commissar, Alexander Belev, and the German Jewish adviser in Sofia, Dannecker, signed an agreement on 22

February that envisaged the deportation of 20,000 Jews by May 1943.[73] In fact in March 1943 the over 3,000 Jews living in Thrace and the over 7,000 living in Macedonia—both territories had been occupied by Bulgaria—were arrested by the Bulgarians and deported to the General Government, where the majority were murdered in Treblinka.[74] The deportation of the Jews from Old Bulgaria was thwarted by increasing opposition from within the country itself.[75]

At the beginning of 1943 the Nazi leadership had resumed on a large scale its extermination and deportation programme in the General Government. The 'labour deployment' in the Reich had been reorganized so that Jewish workers could now be dispensed with. For this reason, in February the SS removed the remaining German Jews still employed in armaments production in the Reich from their factories ('Operation Factory') and deported them to the east.[76]

In January 1943, while on a visit to Warsaw, Himmler ordered the dissolution of the Warsaw ghetto. Of the 40,000 Jews still living there 8,000 were to be 'deported in the next few days'. The 16,000 people who at that time were still working in various plants were to be deported 'to a KL, preferably Lublin', and those plants that were actually involved in armaments production, but only these, should be 'concentrated in some place in the General Government'.[77] The others were to be closed. The transfer of production to Lublin at short notice proved impossible, however. On 15 February, therefore, Himmler ordered Pohl to establish a concentration camp within the ghetto itself for those ghetto inhabitants whom armaments plants claimed to need as workers.[78] However, the deportation of those not required as workers ordered by Himmler began a few days after his visit. From 18 January onwards the transports from Warsaw to Treblinka were under way. Between 5,000 and 6,000 people arrived there during the following days.[79]

Then something completely unexpected happened. When, on 19 April, the occupation authorities set out finally to clear the Warsaw ghetto they were confronted by several hundred armed resisters. It took troops under the command of SS-Brigadeführer Jürgen Stroop, who were heavily armed and far superior in numbers, four weeks to subdue the insurrection. On 16 May 1943 they managed to destroy the last pocket of resistance of the desperate Jewish fighters.[80]

The courage and stamina of the Jewish defenders surprised—indeed, shocked—the Nazi leadership. It was now that the decision was taken to conclude the 'final solution'—and not only in the General Government—as soon as possible and no longer to take into consideration the possible utility of Jewish labour. In May, before the end of the ghetto uprising, Himmler used the occasion of a presentation by Ulrich Greifelt, the head of his Main Office for Ethnic Issues, to insist that it was a 'priority in the General Government [...] to remove the 300,000–400,000 Jews still living there'.[81] Friedrich-Wilhelm Krüger, the HSSPF responsible for the General Government, explained on 31 May that he had 'only recently received the order to carry out the dejewification in a very short period of time'. According to Krüger, Himmler also wanted to put an end to the employment of Jews in the armaments industry and in forced labour camps.[82]

Under the impact of the Warsaw ghetto uprising, from April 1943 onwards the SS accelerated the bloody liquidation of those ghettos that still existed as well as the small forced labour camps, a campaign that had begun in March. In May 1943 SSPF Katzmann ordered the dissolution of all ghettos in the district of Galicia.[83] Between May and the end of June 1943 around 80,000 people fell victim to this mass murder, which was carried out with extreme brutality. At the end of June 1943 Katzmann reported to the HSSPF-East, Krüger, that 'with effect from 23 June 1943 all Jewish quarters have been dissolved' and, as a result, 'apart from those Jews in the camps under the control of the SS and Police Leader, the district is now free of Jews'.[84]

In June 1943 only a few tens of thousands of Jews were still living in the General Government, mainly in forced labour camps, which were largely controlled by the SS. Nevertheless, on 19 June Himmler ordered that 'the evacuation of the Jews must be carried out ruthlessly and must be got through despite the unrest that will occur during the next three to four months as a result'. Resistance in the area did increase—this provides part of the context for the declaration that the whole of the General Government was now a 'bandit combat area', by which Hitler increased Himmler's freedom of action there.[85]

In order to pre-empt potential resistance from employers, who might insist on continuing to employ their Jewish workers, Himmler now pursued a policy of transforming the remaining ghettos and camps into concentration camps. This ensured that the inmates were now at last totally subject to the SS and prevented any attempt by other agencies to gain access to them. Himmler endeavoured to ensure that only those Jews could remain alive for the time being who, on the basis of the strictest criteria, really were essential to war production.

The Warsaw ghetto, which had already been declared a concentration camp in February 1943, was finally dissolved in June 1943. Moreover, Himmler ordered the removal of all traces of its existence.[86] In July 1943 he also ordered that Sobibor extermination camp should be transformed into a concentration camp and that the prisoners should sort captured ammunition.[87] Those Jews in the General Government who had survived June were concentrated in forced labour camps, most of which operated as satellite camps of Majdanek.[88] In January 1944 the work camp Plaszow (near Cracow) as well as those in Lemberg, Lublin, and Radom were declared to be concentration camps.[89]

With his order of 21 May 1943 that all Jews from Reich territory, including the Protectorate, were to be deported 'to the east' or to There-sienstadt, Himmler closed the last bolt-hole for those Polish Jews who had hitherto been able to stay alive in Polish territories directly administered by the Reich, namely eastern Upper Silesia, the Warthegau, and the district of Bialystock.[90] Between 22 and 24 June 1943 the SS deported 5,000 Jews from Sosnowitz and Bendzin to Auschwitz, and in the first half of August the last ghettos in Upper Silesia were cleared.[91] Himmler encountered difficulties, however, with the transformation of the Łódź ghetto into a concentration camp, for Arthur Greiser, the Reich Governor of the Warthegau, blocked the order which would have deprived him of 'his ghetto'.[92] The dispute lasted from June 1943 until February 1944, when Himmler and Greiser agreed to permit the ghetto to remain as a 'Gau-ghetto'. However, only as many Jews were permitted to live there as had to be 'definitely retained in the interests of the armaments economy'.[93] On the other hand, Himmler's order of August 1943 that the more than 100 Jewish forced labour camps in the Warthegau should be liquidated had been carried out by October.[94] The Bialystock ghetto was also finally dissolved between 16 and 23 August, after Globocnik had reported to Himmler on 21 June that the workshops there were being transferred to Lublin. More than 25,000 people were deported to Treblinka or to Majdanek, where they were to be deployed as forced labour.[95]

However, it was not only the occupation authorities for whom the Warsaw ghetto uprising had acted as a wake-up call. Jewish resistance to the extermination policy now flared up in other places as well. The SS were faced with an armed resistance group when clearing the Bialystock ghetto,[96] and the same thing happened in August in the Glubokoje ghetto near Vilnius.[97] Moreover, in August there was an organized mass break-out from Treblinka, and on 14 October the inmates of Sobibor revolted, killing eleven SS men.[98] And this was happening against the background of the inexorable advance of the Soviet army. The Sobibor uprising probably gave Himmler the final impetus to order Krüger to liquidate the last important camps in the Lublin district. At the beginning of November the prisoners in the Lublin camps were shot in a massacre lasting two days, code-named 'Harvest Festival'. The same thing was occurring simultaneously in other camps in the General Government. There were around 42,000 victims in the Lublin district alone.[99]

After the Warsaw ghetto uprising Himmler acted in the same way in the occupied Soviet territories, namely in the Reich Commissariat Ostland, where a significant number of Jews still remained. On 21 June 1943, after meeting with leading SS functionaries, he ordered that 'all Jews living in ghettos in Ostland territory are to be placed in concentration camps'. At the same time he banned 'Jews from leaving concentration camps for work', and reiterated an order that he had already issued in April to build a concentration camp near Riga.[100] Those 'members of the Jewish ghetto not required' were to be 'evacuated to the east', in other words, to be murdered.[101] This guaranteed Himmler total control over the Jewish forced workers in Reich Commissariat Ostland. One should recall in this context the commission to conclude the 'final solution' that he had been given by Hitler two days previously. Confining surviving Jews in concentration camps; continually selecting Jewish forced workers in the concentration camps for extermination; reducing the work opportunities for Jews outside the camps, for example with the Wehrmacht; and hunting for Jews in hiding under the cover of 'combating partisans' with the aid of von dem Bach-Zelewski, who, as already mentioned, on this very 21 June had been appointed head of the units for combating bandits—these were the methods with which Himmler hoped to carry out as quickly as possible Hitler's commission in the General Government and in Reich Commissariat Ostland.[102]

In this way his extermination policy continued its merciless course in the Reich Commissariat. The two last large ghettos in the Baltic states apart from Riga, Kaunas[103] and Vilnius,[104] were liquidated in September 1943, their inhabitants deported to Estonian and Latvian work camps or murdered. Some of the inhabitants of the Kaunas ghetto, however, were retained by the SS and the ghetto was transformed into a concentration camp. Also in September, and linked to these measures, the KZ Valvara in

Estonia was established as a transit camp.[105] The last three ghettos in the General District of White Ruthenia were destroyed between August and October 1943.[106]

The Warsaw ghetto uprising had an impact in other European countries dominated by Germany. In May 1943 another two transports left Croatia for Auschwitz, with around 2,000 people.[107] In Slovakia the Germans pressed in June for deportations to be restarted, but their request fell on deaf ears.[108] In May the RSHA ordered the number of those to be deported from the Netherlands to be suddenly increased. Between 18 May and 20 July almost 18,000 people were deported to Sobibor in eight transports. In Belgium the Gestapo office in Brussels informed Mecheln camp on 29 June that, following an order from Himmler, 'now the Jews with Belgian nationality are to be immediately included in the deportation programme'.[109] On 20 September 1943 the first deportation train left the country with only Belgian Jews on board. Five more were to follow by the end of the year. Almost 6,000 people were deported to Auschwitz.[110]

In June 1943 Himmler returned to the plan that he had been following since the beginning of the year, of persuading the French government to deprive French immigrant Jews of their French citizenship and thereby make them free for deportation. Himmler pressed Oberg, his HSSPF in France, for the immediate publication of the deprivation-of-citizenship law, which Laval had already signed.[111] In the Reichsführer's view the deportations ought to be finished by 15 July 1943.

Once again, however, Himmler's order could not be carried out. This time it was Laval, not Oberg, who was responsible. On 25 July, the day of Mussolini's fall, the Prime Minister decided to cancel the publication.[112] Laval managed to put off Oberg and Knochen for several weeks[113] before finally declaring, on 24 August, that he would not sign the law.[114] In response the security police began acting independently, seeking out Jews and deporting them. Also, when they acquired the opportunity to get their hands on Jews who had fled to the Italian zone of occupation in south-east France this was to have an impact on Jewish persecution throughout France.

Gypsy policy

At the end of 1942, as part of the programme of racial selection and systematic mass murder that applied throughout the area controlled by

Germany, Himmler and the SS began also significantly to increase the persecution of the so-called Gypsies.

After the outbreak of war Gypsies in the Reich had been kept in camps 'pending their ultimate deportation', as stated in the relevant RSHA directive.[115] In the autumn of 1939 the idea had been that, as part of the Nisko plan, the Reich German Gypsies would be deported to the General Government along with the German Jews.[116] In fact that happened only in May 1940; under a specific order of Himmler's, 2,500 Gypsies were deported from Reich territory to the General Government.[117] However, after a certain amount of to-ing and fro-ing about the progress of the deportations, in the summer of 1940 Himmler announced that the 'evacuation of Gypsies and Gypsy half-castes from Reich territory' was to be postponed 'until the Jewish question [has] been generally solved'.[118] In November 1940 the Reich Criminal Police Office held out the prospect that the 'the Gypsy question' in Reich territory 'would be finally settled' after the war.[119]

This remained the situation until 1942. During this period evidently neither Himmler nor the RSHA had concrete ideas about the future fate of those who had been deported. They were left to themselves; the majority—there are no exact figures—died as a result of the miserable conditions in the General Government. A minority survived or returned to the Reich during the war, where some of them were able to hide until the end.[120]

In November 1941 the halt to the deportations decreed in 1940 was lifted for a particular group of Gypsies: 5,000 Gypsies from the Burgenland were transported to the Łódź ghetto in the course of the deportation of Jews from the Reich. Himmler endeavoured to set aside concerns of the district governor responsible, Friedrich Uebelhoer, that the Gypsies might engage in arson by advising Uebelhoer to shoot ten Gypsies for every fire in the ghetto. 'In this way,' Himmler advised, 'you will get the best possible fire brigade for the ghetto; it will be the keenest there has ever been.'[121] In January 1942 all those Gypsies who had not succumbed to living conditions in the ghetto were killed by gas vans in Chelmno.

On 20 April Himmler telephoned Heydrich with the order: 'Gypsies not to be exterminated', as is clear from his notes on telephone conversations.[122] It is unclear whether this order of Himmler's applied to the Gypsies who were still living in the Reich, to those who had been deported to the General Government, or whether it was a general directive applying to all Gypsies. It appears, however, that with this directive the Reichsführer-SS was initiating a more differentiated Gypsy policy. For in the summer of 1942

Himmler began to distinguish between settled and nomadic Gypsies. He ordered that 'police measures should not be taken' on principle against indigenous Gypsies in the General Government, provided they were settled;[123] they were not, therefore—as had been the norm in occupied Poland since 1939—to be murdered. During 1942 the security police applied the same policy as in the General Government to the occupied Soviet territories, where in many places Gypsies had been shot by the Einsatzgruppen irrespective of their way of life,. Finally, in autumn 1943 Himmler ordered nomadic Gypsies in Soviet territories to be sent to concentration camps, and in spring 1944 Gypsies from Lithuania and Byelorussia were in fact deported to Auschwitz.[124]

From 1942 onwards Himmler also pursued a differentiated policy towards the Gypsies living in the Reich, though in a very different form. He imposed on the SS and police apparatus his view that in future they should distinguish between the 'pure-race' Sinti and Lalleri (including 'half-castes' capable of being integrated into these groups) as well as the Roma on the one hand, and the remaining 'half-castes' on the other. After the end of the war the Gypsies 'of pure race' should be placed in a 'reservation' and continue the way of life 'peculiar to their kind' there in isolation. The other Gypsies should be deported to camps.[125]

In order to provide a scholarly basis for this differentiation, in September 1942 Himmler assigned to the Ahnenerbe the task of researching the future of the Gypsy language and customs.[126] In October 1942 the RSHA issued a directive on his instructions, according to which 'pure-race Gypsies' would 'in future [enjoy] a certain freedom of movement', that is to say, 'to wander in a certain area' and to live according to their 'traditions and customs' and to follow 'an occupation peculiar to their kind'.[127] At the beginning of November 1942 there is more evidence of Himmler's personal interest in the plan to 'reorganize the treatment of the Gypsies in the Reich'.[128]

Thus, as far as Germany was concerned, Himmler ensured that the persecution of Gypsies was focused primarily on Gypsy half-castes, who had become settled and, therefore, in his view had departed from the way of life 'peculiar to their kind'; in Poland and the Soviet Union, on the other hand, it was precisely the nomadic Gypsies who were persecuted.

On 10 December 1942, therefore, Himmler ordered that 'Gypsy half-castes, Roma Gypsies, and members of Balkan Gypsy clans not of German blood' living in the Reich be sent to concentration camps.[129] 'Socially adjusted' Gypsies were not to be deported, although the criteria for this classification remained unclear.[130] Beforehand he had managed to meet the concerns expressed by Hitler and the Party Chancellery[131]—Himmler's idea of a racially differentiated treatment of the various Gypsy groups in the Reich was directly opposed to the attitude of the state and party leadership, who regarded all Gypsies as 'inferior' and wanted them all murdered. With his decision of December 1942 to deport Gypsies the Reichsführer-SS demonstrated his implacable determination to implement the negative aspect of his policy towards the Gypsy population. By contrast, the positive measures to maintain 'pure-race' Gypsies were postponed until the end of the war.

If one bears in mind that since December 1942 the regime had been simultaneously preparing the last great wave of Jewish deportations from the Reich, and that, in autumn 1942, Himmler had agreed with Thierack to deport 'asocials' to concentration camps,[132] one can appreciate the broader context within which he took his decision to deport the Gypsies in December 1942: the Reichsführer was relentlessly pursuing the 'cleansing' of the area that was one day to be the core territory of the Greater Germanic Reich.

On 15 January 1943 a meeting took place in the RSHA at which representatives of the Reich Criminal Police Office, the SD, the RuSHA, as well as members of the Research Centre for Racial Hygiene and Population Biology were present.[133] The meeting was designed to establish the precise criteria for the differentiation of the two groups of Gypsies, as well as to deal with the question of what was to be done with those who were not to be deported. The 'solution' reached was to sterilize the great majority of the 'half-castes'. A telex from the Reich Criminal Police Office dated 29 January 1943[134] instructed the Kripo offices to register those 'socially adjusted Gypsy half-castes' who were not to be deported.[135]

Between February and July 1944 some 20,000 Gypsies living in the Reich—around three-quarters of the people who belonged to this minority—were transported to Auschwitz, where they were compelled to live in a special 'Gypsy camp'.[136] Together with those people who had been deported from territories occupied by Germany, the total number of Gypsies transported there amounted to around 23,000.[137]

From April 1944 onwards Gypsies 'capable of work' were transferred from Birkenau to concentration camps in the Reich, a total of barely 1,600 people. Of the other Gypsies deported to Birkenau, around 6,000 were still alive in spring 1944. In August the camp authorities took the decision—presumably in light of the deportation of the Hungarian Jews to

Auschwitz—to liquidate the 'Gypsy camp'. In all, around 5,600 Gypsies were murdered with gas in Auschwitz.[138] There is no evidence of a direct order from Himmler for this; however, in view of the detailed instructions for dealing with the Gypsy question that Himmler had given hitherto, it can be assumed that this decision was treated as 'a matter for the boss' and at the very least would not have been taken without his approval.

In the occupied Soviet territories at least 10,000 people and possibly many more were victims of the Gypsy persecution,[139] in Poland around 8,000.[140] In Serbia the Wehrmacht and police murdered around 1,000 Gypsies.[141] In Slovakia measures to arrest Gypsies were only seriously adopted after the German intervention in the summer of 1944: SS-Einsatzgruppe H may also have murdered up to 1,000 Gypsies.[142] At the end of 1944, under the rule of the Arrow Cross, numerous Roma were deported from Hungary to forced labour in concentration camps in Germany.[143]

In the Netherlands, Belgium, and France, by contrast, the persecution consisted of control measures, bans on settlement, and the confinement of Gypsies and other members of the 'travelling population' to particular sites. Here a differentiated Gypsy policy was not pursued and the number of victims remained in the hundreds.[144]

All in all, as is clear from this overview, the SS murdered tens of thousands of Gypsies, but not with the same determination and systematic approach as was the case with the Jews. Himmler's notion of a differentiated treatment of the Gypsies in the future Greater Germanic Reich affected specific Gypsy groups with its brutal arbitrariness, depending on whether the Reichsführer, operating in his fantasy world, considered them either particularly racially valuable or particularly dangerous.

More men for the Waffen-SS

In 1942 Himmler had extended the recruitment basis of the Waffen-SS both within and outside Germany; from the end of the year onwards he endeavoured to establish new divisions from German SS members. In February 1943 Hitler agreed to his setting up a division formed from members of the Hitler Youth (which later acquired the title 'Hitler Youth Division'), and in October two more SS-Panzergrenadier divisions—'Götz von Berlichingen' and 'Reichsführer-SS'—composed of members of the Reich

Labour Service. In the same month the divisions 'Leibstandarte', 'Das Reich', 'Death's Head', 'Viking', and 'Hohenstaufen', which were already substantially mechanized, were renamed SS-Panzer divisions.[145]

By recruiting from the Hitler Youth age cohorts and from Reich Labour service camps, which in some cases involved exerting considerable pressure—Himmler himself spoke of our 'involuntary volunteers'[146]—the SS had finally given up the voluntary principle in Germany as well. Members of the General SS were in any case drafted into the Waffen-SS en masse, and the recruitment of non-members of the SS, which had increased from 1942 onwards, now became the norm.[147] The main focus of recruitment, however, continued to be abroad. It is clear from a register from the end of 1943 that at this point 54,000 ethnic Germans from Romania, 22,000 from Hungary, more than 5,000 from Slovakia, 21,000 from the Banat and Serbia, more than 18,000 from Croatia, and 1,292 from North Schleswig were serving with the Waffen-SS, the vast majority of them on account of the 'duty of military service' introduced by Himmler for ethnic Germans.[148]

On 12 May 1943 the German and Romanian governments signed an agreement that regulated the recruitment of ethnic Germans for the Waffen-SS and ensured that volunteers retained their Romanian citizenship.[149] On the basis of this agreement, in the second half of 1943 an increasing number of ethnic Germans from the Romanian part of the Banat and from Siebenbürgen were transferred to the 'Prince Eugene' division.[150] In fact the recruitment had already begun weeks before the agreement had been signed, and some of the 'volunteers' had been forced into military service.[151] As early as 30 July 1943 Berger reported that 41,560 men had been recruited. Himmler responded by sending him 'hearty thanks': 'As with so many of your other actions and achievements you have done an enormous amount for our German fatherland and the Führer.'[152]

During his trip to Germany in June 1942 the Hungarian Prime Minister, Miklós Kállay, had promised Ribbentrop a further 10,000 ethnic Germans for the Waffen-SS.[153] In May 1943 an agreement concerning recruitment was worked out with the Hungarian government.[154] However, Franz Basch, the leader of the ethnic German group, was 'gloomy' about its success: the volunteers would lose their Hungarian citizenship; he advocated compulsory enlistment.[155] This is in fact what happened, and in August of 22,000 'volunteers' 18,000 were enlisted as fit.[156]

The occupation of Hungary on 12 March 1944 opened up quite new perspectives, from Himmler's point of view. The Reichsführer-SS planned to establish a cavalry and two grenadier divisions each from ethnic Germans of Hungarian nationality and 'Hungarian citizens of mainly German origins', in other words, a total of six divisions. Evidently in this way he wanted to create another SS army out of thin air.[157] The agreement for such an SS recruitment programme was signed on 14 April 1944.[158] Moreover, Himmler forced the Hungarian government to transfer ethnic Germans serving in the Hungarian army to the Waffen-SS. He had already made the same agreement with the Slovakian government at the beginning of 1944. In this way the SS secured an additional 50,000 ethnic German soldiers from both countries, although too few to create separate divisions for each of them.[159]

Of the approximately 25,000 ethnic Germans from Croatia liable for military service around 17,000 were serving in the Waffen-SS after the existing militias, task forces, and Croatian-German territorials had been integrated into the 'Prince Eugene' division.[160] A mass mutiny which occurred in the summer of 1943 sheds some light on conditions in the division. As a result, 173 members of the division, all of them ethnic Germans from Croatia, were arrested and sent to Dachau concentration camp. On 17 October Himmler wrote to the divisional commander, Arthur Phleps, in exceptionally moderate terms; evidently he was well aware of conditions in the division, in which many were serving by no means voluntarily. According to Himmler, what was decisive about the case was the fact that the ethnic Germans were being continually insulted by their superiors. In particular, the 'nice Balkan habit' had spread of 'cursing the mother of the person concerned'. Himmler ordered drastic counter-measures. He instructed that 'in every such case in which NCOs or men curse a comrade's mother, they are to be shot on the spot'. In particularly serious cases the person should be hanged. He had nevertheless, so he informed Phleps, 'consigned' the 173 ethnic Germans to a camp so that they could be trained 'to be good volunteers of the Waffen-SS' and improve their knowledge of German.[161]

Apart from the recruitment of ethnic Germans and 'Germanic' volunteers, from 1942 onwards Himmler began increasingly to recruit men who, in Nazi jargon, were termed 'ethnic aliens'. As early as 1940 he had formed 'legions' in north-west Europe—with limited success, as we have seen— whose members did not have to meet the high 'racial' standards of the SS, and during the following years he engaged in massive recruitment in Wallonia and France. But if he was permitting men of 'Roman' or other non-Germanic origins to serve in the SS volunteer divisions then surely this practice could be expanded?

He embarked on one of the most audacious plans in this sphere in February 1943, after he had received Hitler's approval for establishing a division of Bosnian Muslims along the lines of the Bosnian-Herzogovinan regiments of the Austrian empire.[162] He met with opposition from the Croatian authorities, however. Furious, he told his representative in Croatia, Konstantin Kammerhofer, 'to intervene using all your weight'.[163] In the end the latter had the recruits conscripted on the basis of the general duty of military service. The men received their training in France and Silesia. Like their predecessors in the Austrian empire, the soldiers of the 13th SS Volunteer Mountain Division (Croatia) wore a red fez (in their combat uniforms it was grey) with a tassel and a badge which combined an eagle, the SS skull, and a swastika. Instead of the SS runes, on their right collar they wore a model of a 'Handschar', or scimitar. With reference to that, in May 1944 the division was renamed 'Handschar'.

Himmler was quite prepared to respect the culture and way of life of his Islamic volunteers, and, as always when he was interested in something, got involved in details. He enquired of the Grand Mufti what Islamic food regulations should be adhered to as far as supplying the division was concerned, and then announced in August 1943 that he would grant to all 'Islamic members of the SS and police [. . .] as an absolute special privilege [. . .] that, in accordance with their religious laws, they should never be served pork or sausage containing pork and should never be given alcohol to drink'. He should be informed of all contraventions of this order. And, 'I also forbid any joking about these matters such as typically occurs among comrades or any "pulling the legs" of the Muslim volunteers'.[164] He also concerned himself with practical questions: the new fezes of the division did not meet with his approval. He told Pohl that their colour had to be changed and they had to be slightly trimmed.[165]

Himmler was not only prepared to allow the Grand Mufti to appoint several imams for his Bosnian division, he even aimed to allow members of the division to pursue Islamic studies; indeed, he went so far as to envisage establishing an 'Islamic institute somewhere in Germany in which the Mufti can train imams so that he can have a corps of priests who are personally loyal to him and at the same time have been appropriately politically trained'.[166] For after all, Islam and Nazism were linked by their common hostility to 'the Jews'.

Ill. 31. The mountain infantry company of the 'Handschar' division on the parade ground.

'Why should anything come between Muslims in Europe and in the whole world and us Germans?' he asked the 13th SS Mountain Division in a speech in January 1944:

We have the same aims. There can be no more solid a basis for living together than common aims and common ideals. For 200 years Germany has not had the slightest cause for friction with Islam [...] Now we Germans and you in this division, you Muslims, share a common feeling of gratitude that God—you call him Allah, but it's the same—has sent our tormented European nations the Führer, the Führer who will rid first Europe and then the whole world of the Jews, these enemies of our Reich, who robbed us of victory in 1918 so that the sacrifice of two million dead was in vain. They are also your enemies, for the Jew has been your enemy from time immemorial.[167]

Reading this speech, one might conclude that Himmler's expression of respect for the world religion of Islam was genuine. In fact, however, his emphasis on common ideals was nothing more than cynical hypocrisy. Two weeks later Himmler reiterated to the Reich propaganda offices why he valued the Croatian volunteers so highly: 'I must say I have nothing against Islam; for it preaches to its members in this division and promises them paradise if they have fought and died. A practical and agreeable religion for soldiers!'[168]

In battle, however, the division disappointed his expectations. Deployed against partisans in their homeland at the end of 1943, the force proved relatively ineffective and, what is more, increasingly rebellious. At the end of 1944 Himmler ended the experiment.[169] Two other Muslim units—the 21st SS Mountain Division 'Skanderbeg' composed of Albanians and a Croatian division named 'Kama'—were also short-lived. Both had been established only in 1944. 'Skanderbeg' was dissolved in autumn 1944 and 'Kama' appears never to have been ready for combat.[170] As a result, Himmler's original plan of establishing two army corps of Bosnian and Albanian troops in the Balkans and, by the end of 1944, of combining them with the 'Prince Eugene Division' to form an autonomous SS army had failed.[171]

In May 1942 Himmler had still been hesitating with regard to Baltic units. At the end of August 1942, however, he approved the establishment of an Estonian legion and shortly afterwards the Wehrmacht transferred a number of Estonian battalions to the Waffen-SS for this purpose.[172] In January 1943 Himmler personally inspected a group of fifty-four Estonian legionaries who were attending a Waffen-SS training course for NCOs, and received a 'good impression' of their 'racial quality'. He therefore considered it worthwhile to encourage German-language lessons and ideological indoctrination for the soldiers.[173]

Himmler never formally recognized the Estonians as Teutons, for that would have brought him into conflict with German occupation policy in that country. In his view, however, they were so similar to Teutons that there would be no danger in racially mixing with them. 'The Estonians', so he informed the heads of his Main and Leadership Offices, 'really belong to the few ethnic groups with whom, after having excluded a very few elements, we could mix without incurring any damage to ourselves.'[174] As we have seen, he had reached similar conclusions about the Slovaks and the Walloons.

At the end of 1942, on Berger's advice, Himmler secured Hitler's approval for a Latvian Waffen-SS legion.[175] In April 1943 6,500 Estonians and Latvians had been recruited.[176] The Estonian and Latvian legions were strengthened by the addition of German SS and transformed into the Estonian and Latvian Volunteer Brigades. Shortly afterwards they were expanded into divisions.[177] For this purpose Himmler introduced compulsory military service into the Reich Commissariat Ostland: Estonians and Latvians—Himmler considered Lithuanians unreliable—could now be conscripted into the Waffen-SS.[178] A third Baltic SS division was created out of the police battalions of the auxiliary police, which Himmler had established in 1941.[179]

From April 1943 onwards he allowed Ukrainians from the old Austro-Hungarian territory to be recruited for a Galician division. Out of 100,000 applicants 30,000 were accepted.[180] Himmler visited the division, which was given the title 14th SS-Waffengrenadier division after it had completed its training. In a speech to its commanders he dealt, among other things, with criticism that had emerged within its ranks. The tough drill was not harassment, and Galicians too had the possibility of being promoted. To prevent 'unrest', he forbade the men to engage in 'politics' and, apart from that, preached his list of virtues in a slightly altered form. Apart from obedience, comradeship, and loyalty, he considered it particularly important to explain to the Ukrainians the importance of 'order'.[181] The division did not last long. It was deployed against the Red Army and in July 1943 almost completely wiped out.[182]

The establishment of other 'ethnic alien' volunteer units during 1944 met with an equal lack of success. Apart from two Russian, two Hungarian, one mixed German and Hungarian, and two Cossack divisions, there were several smaller units such as the 'SS–East Turkish Armed Unit', the 'Caucasian Armed Unit', as well as Serbian, Romanian, and Bulgarian units, and the SS tried to reorganize the Indian legion that had been taken over from the Wehrmacht and had been recruited in POW camps. A British legion, also to be composed from POWs, could not be formed in 1943 because of lack of interest.

If these units were ever deployed—in several cases this did not happen—their military performance was far inferior to that of the average German units.[183] Hitler himself was very critical of the whole programme. In view of the occupation of their homelands the members of these units naturally lacked motivation and were unreliable, as he commented in 1945, shortly before the end of the war. Given the serious shortage of armaments, deploying these units was 'a luxury', 'stupid', 'nonsense'.[184]

For Himmler, however, their immediate military usefulness was not necessarily the main point. Right from the start of the recruitment programme Himmler had made a sharp distinction between full Waffen-SS divisions, whose members had to satisfy the same 'racial' criteria as all other members of the SS, and volunteer units composed of foreigners who did not have to satisfy these criteria. In his view, the big increase in the Waffen-SS must not be allowed to lead to a dilution of the racial criteria for acceptance into the SS.[185] Himmler made it clear, for example, that one should not speak of a Ukrainian SS man, but only of 'Ukrainians serving in armed units of the SS'. The 'term SS man, which means so much to us and which we regard so highly,' should not be used for 'the numerous members of alien ethnic groups which we are now organizing under the command of the SS'.[186]

Himmler insisted that only men in groups I and II of the four-level racial scheme of the RuSHA should be allowed to become members of the SS. Men in group III could 'join the volunteer units of the Waffen-SS' or the order police, 'which are under the command of the RFSS'.[187] The same applied to Reich German SS volunteers who were not considered racially suitable for the SS.[188]

In spring 1943 Himmler ordered the establishment of a further SS corps, the so-called Germanic Panzer corps, which was intended to comprise the 'Viking' division and a new unit formed out of the existing volunteer corps, the 'Northland' division.[189] Himmler explained his ultimate aim in establishing such a corps, composed of members of various nations, in a note of February 1944: the Germanic corps was intended to form the cadre for recruitment and training in the event of 'having to introduce legal conscription in the Germanic countries later, which will undoubtedly be necessary'.[190] In September 1943 Himmler asserted that Hitler had approved this view in principle, and was of the opinion that the formation of the Wehrmacht in Germanic countries should take place under the control of the SS'.[191]

If one takes into account Himmler's successful compulsory recruitment of ethnic Germans living outside Germany and bears in mind the fact that, from 1943 onwards, he concentrated on recruiting 'ethnic alien' units to serve within the framework of the SS, it becomes clear how he envisaged the armed forces of a future Germanic empire. Alongside the Wehrmacht there would be a Waffen-SS whose elite troops would comprise Reich Germans, ethnic Germans, Dutch, Flemings, Danes, Norwegians, and, if necessary, troops from other countries classified as 'Germanic'. Around this core would be grouped units whose 'ethnic alien' members would not be seen as being SS-worthy, but (and this is clear from the recruitment attempts during the last phase of the regime) could come from almost every European nation (with the exception of Poland), a kind of gigantic foreign legion, whose members would serve in separate 'national' units.

In his speech to the Gau and Reich leaders in Posen on 3 August 1944 Himmler mentioned his aim of forming thirty SS 'European divisions' in the post-war period. Effectively this represented the future peacetime strength of a European SS, which could then be expanded in the event of war. Together with its purely German troops, the Waffen-SS would have reached a sufficient size to make it a second autonomous land-based military force alongside the Army.[192] (Himmler's ambitions seem to have gone beyond the creation of a land-based army. In 1944 he reached agreement with the Navy to establish a 'Germanic Naval Reserve Section', which was based in Sennheim in Alsace—in other words, a safe distance from the sea—and was being prepared for deployment with the Navy.)[193]

Viewing Himmler's efforts at recruitment during the last years of the war from this perspective, it is clear that what at first sight appears to be a hectic and desperate cobbling together of the last and least militarily effective reserves represented from Himmler's point of view a logical and integral part of his Greater Germanic vision.

Himmler as Reich Minister of the Interior

On 10 August 1943 Hitler appointed Himmler Reich Minister of the Interior.[194] At this point he was of the opinion, as he informed Goebbels, that the Reichsführer was 'a quite exceptional figure in our regime'.[195] The previous incumbent, Dr Wilhelm Frick, who had held the post since 1933, was fobbed off with the purely representative office of Reich Protector in Bohemia and Moravia.[196]

Hitler did not expect that in his new role Himmler would carry out structural changes to the state machine or fundamentally alter the relationship between party and state. Rather, his appointment was intended to strengthen further his reputation as the man primarily responsible for the 'security' of the Third Reich and to round off his area of responsibilities. 'Himmler is undoubtedly the right man to control domestic policy', Goebbels noted in his diary. 'At any rate, he will guarantee our internal security under all circumstances.'[197]

Nevertheless, Himmler's assumption of his office on 26 August was followed by a number of changes within the ministry. Himmler reorganized it into two areas of activity: he placed the departments for the constitution and administration, civil defence, personnel, and local government in the section 'Internal Administration' under state secretary Wilhelm Stuckart, and assigned the other section, health administration, to state secretary Dr Leonardo Conti.[198]

He transferred the tasks of the ministry's department IV, to which were subordinated the existing institutes for Ethnic Research, and Research into Foreign Countries and Peoples, to the SD's foreign department in the RSHA. In this way Himmler had not only taken a step towards ensuring that these institutions could be utilized for foreign espionage; in addition he had brought such important institutions as the Ethnic German Working Groups, the German Foreign Institute, and the Wannsee Institute, which was responsible for research on Russia, under his control, thereby acquiring Nazi research capabilities in the fields of ethnicity and foreign countries that he could utilize for his long-range plan for 'living-space'.[199]

Himmler, who visited the Interior Ministry only two or three times during the period of his incumbency, controlled it from his field headquarters, where his long-term assistant Rudolf Brandt acted as head of the ministerial office. In fact, the Interior Ministry under Himmler as minister operated to a large extent independently under state secretary Stuckart.[200] Himmler kept his distance from the Ministry, not only on account of his numerous other tasks but also because of his distrust of the state bureaucracy and his general dislike of lawyers and officials. As Interior Minister he continually inveighed against bureaucratic formalism and schematic approaches. For example, in order to break through the anonymity of administrative documents he often demanded that the official dealing with the issue should sign the correspondence personally.[201] He supported the idea that county administrators (*Landräte*) should hold their posts for a maximum of ten years only, which resulted in a lengthy dispute with Bormann.[202] He considered it necessary to make frequent ostentatious statements that in future he would be relentless in rooting out corruption in the administration,[203] and he signed an edict restricting the employment of close relatives in the same government body, which, given the actual situation in small local authorities, was singularly naive.[204]

Himmler admonished his officials to treat citizens in a way 'that is worthy of a German Teuton person'. In the event of such admonitions having no effect, in a speech to the mayors of large cities he advised them: 'you should try treating these gentlemen officials in the same offensive way as they treat the nation.' Himmler had found a new task: 'We shall jolly well teach these people, and anyone who doesn't get the message will one day get the boot.'[205]

The new minister placed a particular emphasis on 'strengthening self-administration'* as he put it.[206] The reason why he was particularly concerned with rearranging the responsibilities of mayors and county administrators was that, as part of the wartime rationalization of the administration, from 1943 onwards attempts had been made to delegate administrative tasks to the lowest level. The Party Chancellery had been a particular advocate of this because, by transferring responsibilities to a new middle-tier authority between the Reich and county levels (an enhanced Gau) as well as by strengthening the municipalities vis-à-vis the directly state-controlled counties, it was aiming to increase the authority of the party at the expense of the state bureaucracy. Gauleiters were to be given more independence from ministerial bureaucracy and Nazi mayors from county administrators.

---

* *Translators' note*: Self-administration (*Selbstverwaltung*) is the technical term referring to the rights and partial autonomy of local government vis-à-vis the state supervisory authorities.

While Frick had always opposed this policy of Bormann's, Himmler was more sympathetic to such ideas. When in the coming months he advocated 'strengthening self-administration' his main ulterior motive was, in close alliance with Bormann, to weaken the state administration in favour of the party. They had both discussed the future policy of the Interior Ministry a few days before Himmler's appointment.[207]

Himmler's inimitable personal contribution to this attempt at a structural shift in power was the way in which he tried—with references to the 'Germanic tradition of cooperation', to Henry I as a founder of cities, or to the historic role of 'German mayors as supporters of the tradition of the Reich'—to provide these administrative changes with an ideological gloss.[208] But in the final analysis little came of it.[209]

It is true that Himmler was able to achieve limited successes at regional level with his attempts at meeting the wishes of the party through administrative restructuring. For example, he secured Führer edicts to divide up the Prussian provinces of Saxony and Hesse-Nassau into a total of four new provinces, as well as for the reorganization of the Lower Weser area, thereby serving the needs of the Gauleiters affected by these changes.[210] However, he rejected Bormann's attempt to close district governors' offices (*Regierungspräsidien*), thereby strengthening Lammers's and Stuckart's position, which was vital for maintaining the authority of the state vis-à-vis the ambitions of the Gauleiters.[211] These examples show the extent to which Himmler became involved in the details of the power struggle between party and state without being in a position to develop a uniform political line and get it implemented.

This inability became evident to all those involved at a series of big meetings at which Himmler tried to give the office heads the impression that, with his appointment as Reich Minister of the Interior, a fresh wind was blowing though its dusty offices. Whether at the 'Assembly' of the government of the General Government in Cracow on 18 November 1943,[212] or at the conference of all the district governors on 10–11 January 1944 in Breslau,[213] or at the meeting of mayors of large cities (Oberbürgermeister) and Landeshauptmänner* on 12 and 13 February in Posen[214]— at all of them the pressing problems with which the administration saw itself

---

* *Translators' note*: The Landeshauptmänner were the highest-ranking Prussian officials, who had traditionally been elected by the provincial assemblies and were responsible for matters that were 'self-administered' by the provinces.

confronted during the war (shortage of personnel, the consequences of the air war, and so on) came under discussion. But Himmler invariably limited himself to generalities; he had no solutions to offer.[215]

Despite his limited success, however, through his promotion to Reich Interior Minister Himmler joined the leadership group of Goebbels, Bormann, and Speer, which was pressing for German society to be forced to adjust to the requirements of 'total war'. Goebbels, in particular, repeatedly noted the 'absolute agreement of our views'[216] and praised Himmler's policy.[217] However, he did not want Himmler to take over any more responsibilities: 'Himmler has already got too much to do and cannot do most of it by himself', as he observed in his diary.[218]

Goebbels also carefully noted that Bormann, who since his appointment as head of the Party Chancellery had been considered one of Himmler's closest allies, now began increasingly to distance himself from him: 'Bormann has become a bit sceptical about Himmler because he is taking on too many things. It's not good if someone in the NS leadership gets too big; the others must then make sure that he is brought back into line.'[219] Power-political rivalry and common interests balanced one another among this group. There also seem to have been tensions between Speer and Himmler. In May 1944, at any rate, Goebbels advised Speer to resolve his differences with Himmler and Bormann, for both 'belong to our most active circle'.[220]

In his role as Reich Minister of the Interior Himmler found himself faced with a fundamental conflict of interest: For political-ideological reasons he supported the policy, developed above all by Bormann, of replacing state administration by Nazi 'leadership' (*Menschenführung*). As Interior Minister in time of war, however, he had to be concerned to maintain traditional administrative structures. And if he actually tried to introduce changes to the administrative structure of the state he would be accused of being hungry for power. Himmler 'solved' this complicated situation by leaving things unsettled.

The SS and armaments

As we have already seen, Himmler's attempt to establish his own armaments concern failed in September 1942 as a result of the SS's lack of the relevant skills, and of opposition from industry and from Speer. The majority of the armaments projects that Himmler had wanted to carry out in the concentration camps never materialized, or not nearly to the extent that had been envisaged;[221] most SS plants, whether based inside or outside concentration camps, did not transfer their production to armaments.[222] The only plants to engage in full-scale armaments production were the German Earth and Stone Works Company and the furniture factories based in the Protectorate.[223] When Himmler claimed, in a speech to the Gruppenführer in October 1943: 'We have armaments plants in the concentration camps', this was, to put it mildly, somewhat exaggerated.[224]

Himmler, however, did not give up. But he now concentrated above all on exotic projects. In autumn 1943 he promised Hitler 'to meet the Waffen-SS and police oil requirements by processing oil shale ourselves', and for this purpose in May 1944 founded the German Oil Shale Co. Ltd. (Deutsche Schlieferöl GmbH). Ten oil-shale plants employing only concentration camp inmates were established in Württemberg. This was followed in September 1944 by the establishment of the German Peat Processing Co. Ltd. (Deutsche Torfverwertung GmbH) to collect peat to produce motor-vehicle fuel.[225]

Moreover, the Reichsführer could not stop thinking about the cultivation of Kok-Sagys. From the beginning of 1942 onwards he had been hoping that this rubber-containing plant, which was cultivated in eastern Europe, could make a major contribution to the provision of rubber for the German war economy.[226] When, during an interview with Hitler in February 1943, Himmler pointed out the benefits that wide-scale cultivation of this plant would bring, the Führer immediately made him responsible for achieving these production goals. In response to Himmler's objection that he was only marginally concerned with this question, Hitler replied, as the baffled Reichsführer noted at the time, that 'he was not interested in organizational matters and he was giving me responsibility for it!'[227] Himmler immediately formed the organizations involved into a Kok-Sagys working group,[228] organized a Kok-Sagys conference,[229] and after Göring had appointed him on 9 July 'my special representative for all matters involving rubber plants',[230] created an 'administrative office' to run the show.[231] An experimental farm was also established in Auschwitz.[232]

Although it quickly became clear that the plant could cover only a tiny amount of Germany's overall requirements for rubber (a maximum of 1.7 per cent),[233] Himmler made great efforts to secure an extensive area for its cultivation. We have already referred in this chapter to the attempts made to utilize areas in northern Ukraine and Russia-Centre 'plagued by bandits' for this purpose.[234] Himmler reckoned initially on using a total of 30,000 hectares in the annexed eastern territories for its cultivation, in the General Government,[235] in the Ukraine, in Reich Commissariat Ostland, as well as in France. In September 1943 Romania also became a target for the Kok-Sagys planners as a potential area of cultivation.[236] After the occupation of Hungary the SS sought another 10,000 hectares there to compensate for the recent loss of territory in the east.[237] Himmler advised that they should focus in particular on former Jewish landed property.[238] The more the occupied territories had to be given up, the more the cultivation of Kok-Sagys had to be concentrated in Reich territory, where in 1944 a total of 16,700 hectares were provided, with 18,500 envisaged for 1945—land that was urgently needed for planting with foodstuffs.[239]

The practical results of the cultivation were catastrophically bad. At the end of 1943 the person responsible for reporting from the west of Ukraine noted 'a complete failure', since '95% of the acreage' had 'not produced anything'.[240] In the Reich as well, in 1944 almost everywhere it was reported that the harvest had failed.[241] In March 1944 the head of the raw-materials and planning office in the Armaments Ministry, Hans Kehrl, advised Himmler in future to give up cultivating Kok-Sagys completely.[242] Himmler replied sharply, and reminded Kehrl of his duty of obedience: 'I myself am not prepared to break with this tradition of obedience, which I have regarded as sacred ever since I joined the move-ment, in the interests of some sort of capitalist speculations.' He considered Kehrl's objections to be a 'typically narrow-minded big-capitalist attitude, which obviously regards plant-sourced rubber as undesirable competition for the IG Farben invention of Buna'.[243] But who was it, Himmler continued, who had enabled IG Farben to construct a big Buna works in Auschwitz? He, the Reichsführer! Himmler did not mention the total lack of success of the Kok-Sagys enterprise; the whole thing had become purely a matter of prestige. The plantations of the 'Special Representative for all Matters concerning Plant-sourced Rubber' had not produced any signifi-cant yields by the end of the war.

As the SS failed to establish its own armaments concern, from autumn 1942 onwards the Business and Administration Main Office shifted its focus towards hiring out prisoners to armaments factories. The employment of prisoners by the Oranienburg Heinkel works became a trial project in which, in the end, almost 7,000 prisoners, who were accommodated in a camp located directly next to the works, were employed. Numerous industrial concerns followed this example.[244]

By September 1942, through his agreement with Thierack concerning the 'handing over of asocial elements from the penal system to the Reichs-führer-SS for liquidation through work', Himmler had attempted to fill his camps in order to satisfy the growing demand for prisoners as workers. His order of 31 December to consign 35,000 additional prisoners to the concentration camps must be seen in the same context.[245] As a result of this policy the number of prisoners in the camps doubled between September 1942 and April 1943, from 110,000 to 203,000.[246] It was, however, only from autumn 1943 onwards that the really massive deployment of prisoners occurred, as the number of forced workers recruited by Sauckel began gradually to fall. Now the system of satellite camps, situated directly next to industrial plants, began rapidly to expand.

Moreover, in summer 1943 it looked as if the SS would succeed after all in moving beyond the hiring-out of prisoners and a modest amount of production to becoming involved in a promising major armaments project, namely, in the development and production of the so-called A4, the first ballistic missile.

Militarily, the A4 with its conventional warhead of 1,000 kilograms of explosives, was of relatively little value; the much cheaper and technically less advanced Luftwaffe competitor, the flying bomb, Fi 103, could carry almost the same amount of explosives. However, from a technical point of view neither the Fi 103 nor the A4 represented a reply to the Allied bomber fleets, which in a single attack could drop thousands of tons of explosives with increasing accuracy on their planned targets. It was presumably Himmler's penchant for exotic, utopian-type projects that made him so enthusiastic about the Army's idea for a rocket. Moreover, he was probably also tempted by the thought that, with the help of prisoner labour, he would at last be able to get hold of a major armaments project.

Himmler's interest was aroused after Hitler had given his basic approval to the A4 rocket programme in November 1942. On 11 December he attended a rocket trial launch at the Peenemünde testing ground; he was not put off by the fact that the trial ended with the rocket exploding four seconds after take-off. On the contrary, he supported the head of the project's attempt to gain an audience with Hitler, though without success.[247] In March 1943 he had the military commander at Peenemünde dismissed. There were doubts about his reliability because of his alleged links to the Catholic Church, and vague accusations were made, which later turned out to be without foundation. Himmler installed a successor who could be relied upon to toe the line.[248] This example shows how he was prepared to use his police powers ruthlessly when bent on gaining an advantage. On 28 June Himmler was received at Peenemünde by Wernher von Braun wearing the uniform of an SS-Hauptsturmführer. The visit went off satisfactorily: Himmler appointed von Braun Sturmbannführer and backdated the promotion to the day of his visit.[249]

In the meantime the A4 special committee of the Peenemünde test facilities responsible for rocket production had decided to request KZ inmates from the SS for the envisaged manufacture of the rockets, and this was approved in June.[250] However, when a British air raid on Peenemünde in August 1943 caused some damage, Himmler suggested to Hitler that rocket production should be placed entirely in his hands. The A4 rocket was to be produced underground with the aid of KZ prisoners— the SS had already agreed to a request from the A4 Armaments special committee—and the development programme could be carried out at a testing ground of the Waffen-SS in Poland. Hitler approved this proposal and Himmler assigned the responsibility to Hans Kammler, the head of Department C (Buildings) in the Business and Administration Main Office. A cave system near Nordhausen in Thuringia was selected as the production site, the so-called Mittelwerk, where in autumn 1943 an autonomous concentration camp was established named Mittelbau.[251] On 20 August Speer and his deputy Karl-Otto Saur met the recently appointed Interior Minister, Himmler, to discuss the details. The following day Himmler summed up the main result of the meeting in a note to Speer: 'I, as Reichsführer-SS, [..] am taking over responsibility for the production of the A4 equipment.'[252]

This statement was, however, a little premature, for while Hitler had ordered that Himmler should support Speer with this work, he by no means wished to give him responsibility for the production process.[253] Himmler, however, did not allow himself to be put off: in March 1944 von Braun and two of his leading colleagues were arrested and imprisoned for several weeks. They were accused of making comments in which, among other things, they had criticized the conduct of the war and emphasized the importance of civil space exploration.[254] Braun's army superior managed, however, to get the technical director freed, albeit only on a temporary basis. According to von Braun, Himmler's aim in doing this was to gain control of the development work on the rocket, though he was to prove unsuccessful.[255] In spring 1944, however, Himmler's man Kammler became heavily involved in the transfer of German aircraft production underground; Mittelwerk became the model for this. On 4 March 1944 Göring appointed Kammler his 'Representative for Special Building Work', whereupon, supported by the SS and with the aid of KZ prisoners, he set about transferring aircraft production underground in mines, tunnels, and so forth. This meant that the SS had in fact at last managed to get a foothold in Luftwaffe armaments production, but at a time when German planes could no longer compete with those of the Allies.[256]

The collapse of Italy and its consequences

On 4 October 1943 the SS-Gruppenführer gathered in Posen for one of their regular meetings. Himmler gave a speech lasting several hours covering the political and military situation. In the process he came to talk about a subject that he usually refrained from discussing in his speeches:

Today I am going to refer quite frankly to a very grave chapter. We can mention it now among ourselves quite openly and yet we shall never talk about it in public. I'm referring to the evacuation of the Jews, the extermination of the Jewish people. Most of you will know what it is like to see 100 corpses lying side by side or 500 or 1,000 of them. To have coped with this and—except for cases of human weakness—to have remained decent, that has made us tough. This is an unwritten—never to be written—and yet glorious page in our history. For we know how difficult we would have made it for ourselves if, on top of the bombing raids, the burdens and the deprivations of the war, we still had Jews today in every town as secret saboteurs, as agitators and troublemakers.[257]

Two days later the Gau and Reich leaders, the party elite, came to Posen. Once again Himmler referred to the issue, 'which for me has become the most difficult question I've had to face in my life, the Jewish question'. Once again, to justify the genocide he emphasized 'that we would not have been able to withstand the burdens of the fourth and would not withstand the fifth and sixth years of war that are perhaps still to come, if we had still had this corrupting plague in our national body'. Later on in his speech he dealt specifically with the murder of women and children:

For I did not consider myself justified in exterminating the men—in other words, killing them or having them killed—and then allowing their children to grow up to wreak vengeance on our children and grandchildren. The difficult decision had to be taken to make these people disappear from the face of the earth. For the organization that had to carry out this duty it was the most difficult that we have ever had to undertake.[258]

Himmler's aim in making these two speeches was clearly, by being 'frank', to confirm officially the widespread rumours and bits of information that were going around about the true scope of the Jewish policy; in this way his audience were to be turned into accomplices, complicit in the unparalleled crime. To make quite sure, he had a list prepared specially of those Gruppenführer who were not present at his speech on 4 October 1943.[259]

The fact that Himmler made this confession in October 1943 was not a matter of chance. For at this point, in the aftermath of Italy's breaking her alliance with Germany and the consequent German occupation of Italy and of Italian-occupied territory, Himmler initiated a further escalation of his Europe-wide extermination policy. On 1 October, only a few days before his speech, he had tried to get hold of the Danish Jews; but the majority of his potential victims had already fled to Sweden.

Himmler became involved in the aftermath of Italy's breaking of the Axis alliance in various ways. On 19 July he had prophesied to Bormann and Ribbentrop that Mussolini was about to fall, which then actually happened on 25 July.[260] He had acquired his information from a German archaeologist working in Italy, and not, as he claimed, from 'intelligence sources'—in other words, the SD's foreign department. His Waffen-SS took part in the occupation of Italy in September in the shape of the 'Leibstandarte' division. Originally, Hitler had ordered the deployment of the whole SS Panzer corps with three divisions, but the situation on the eastern front made that inadvisable.[261] The SD not only organized the kidnapping of Mussolini from his imprisonment in the mountain hotel on the Gran Sasso, but a small commando under the leadership of Otto Skorzeny, who was in charge of Group S (Sabotage) in the SD's foreign department, actually took part in the action to free the Duce, which was carried out by German paratroopers.[262]

German troops had hardly arrived in the country before Himmler had organized an SS and police apparatus along the lines of those in the other occupied territories. In the 'Führer's Instruction Concerning the Appointment of a Plenipotentiary of the Greater German Reich in Italy and the

Organization of Occupied Italian Territory', provision was made for the appointment of a 'special police adviser to the Italian national government'.[263] The post was filled by Karl Wolff, previous head of Himmler's personal staff, who simultaneously acted as HSSPF for Italy, later even as the 'Highest SS and Police Leader'.[264] Wolff established a network of SSPF in his area of responsibility. Mussolini, who was now head of a Fascist government based in northern Italy, became merely a puppet of the Nazi regime. As his 'special police adviser' Wolff supervised the contacts between the Italian authorities and the German SS and police and controlled the establishment, armament, and deployment of Fascist combat units. From July 1944 onwards, as General Plenipotentiary, he was also responsible for combating partisans behind the front line.[265]

After the occupation of Italy Himmler also pursued the idea of getting his SS to 'collect' members of the Fascist militia and party for later 'formations'.[266] In October 1943 he wanted to begin by integrating two divisions into the Waffen-SS.[267] But the project made little progress: at the end of 1944 only 5,000 men were ready for action in an Italian Waffen-SS division instead of the 20,000 originally planned.[268]

It was not only in Italy itself and the area hitherto occupied by Italy that Jews became caught up in the extermination programme; the same thing happened in other countries where Jews had managed to survive up until then.

In the first place the RSHA was determined ruthlessly to deport the around 33,000 Jews from those parts of Italy that were now controlled by Germany.[269] In October Dannecker arrived in Rome at the head of a small Einsatzkommando.[270] After a raid on 16 October he had more than a thousand Jews deported from the Italian capital to Auschwitz; by the end of the year, after further raids in other cities, the SS had managed to deport nearly 1,400 people to Auschwitz. The RSHA, however, considered that this way of proceeding had produced 'no significant results', for in the meantime the vast majority of Jews living in Italy had managed to hide.[271]

Therefore, at the beginning of December representatives of the Foreign Ministry and the RSHA agreed to involve the Italian authorities in the persecution and thereby make them complicit.[272] Since the Fascists could in any case hold their own against a widespread resistance movement only with the help of a terror regime, domestic political considerations no longer played a part in German plans. At the beginning of 1944 Dannecker's mobile commando was replaced by a special Jewish department attached to the commander of the security police in Italy, which dealt with the deportation of the Jews who had already been interned by the Italians. During 1943–4 a total of 6,400 Jews were deported from Italy; the total of those killed was 5,596, which meant that every sixth Jew who had been living in Italy in 1943 was murdered.[273]

Operating with a section of the 'Einsatzkommando Reinhard', Odilo Globocnik, who came from Trieste and was one of those mainly responsible for the extermination of the Polish Jews, wreaked havoc from September 1943 onwards among the Jews in the 'Adriatic Coast zone of operations', the area round Trieste that had been incorporated into the territory of the Greater German Reich. Himmler had appointed him HSSPF, and Globocnik ensured that between December 1943 and February 1945 twenty-two transports with more than 1,100 Jews left Trieste in the direction of Auschwitz. Over 90 per cent of those deported were murdered.[274]

In the former Italian occupation zones in Greece, Albania, and in the Dodecanese (the group of islands in the eastern Aegean which had belonged to Italy since 1912) around 16,000 Jews fell into the hands of the Germans.[275] Between March and April 1944 the new occupiers deported a total of 5,000 people from the Greek mainland alone.[276] Between May and August 1944 around 3,800 members of the Jewish communities in the Greek islands, mainly from Crete, Rhodes, and Corfu, were deported.[277]

In Croatia, which up until September had also been under Italian occupation, the majority of Jews, who in the meantime had been interned on the island of Rab, managed to escape into the area controlled by the people's liberation army. The Gestapo caught a few hundred people and deported them in the second half of March to Auschwitz.[278]

On 8 September 1943 the Germans also moved into the zone previously occupied by the Italians in southern France. Eichmann's colleague Alois Brunner, who had already organized the deportation of Jews from Vienna, Berlin, and Saloniki, arrived hot-foot with his Sonderkommando.[279] Without French support, however, he was unable to deport more than a fraction of the Jewish refugees, 1,800 people in all, to Drancy.[280] In the eyes of the Germans the existence of the Italian occupation zone had hindered Jewish persecution in the whole of France.[281] Now that it was gone, measures could be drastically radicalized throughout French territory. From now on all Jews living in France were to be deported to the east, irrespective of their citizenship.

In August 1943 the Gestapo had already begun to arrest more and more Jews in France.[282] From December 1943 on it was being supported by the French police in the provinces, since in the meantime the head of the Vichy militia, Joseph Darnand, had replaced René Bousquet as general secretary of police, not least owing to pressure from Himmler.[283] However, it was only after the reshuffle in the Vichy government had been concluded in March 1944[284] that the Germans could at last ignore French concerns about the deportations. The new government was, in any case, so disliked by the population that the country could now be controlled only by a terror regime.

On 14 April 1944 Brunner and Knochen, the commander of the security police in France, ordered that all Jews should be arrested, irrespective of their citizenship. In the four months until the fall of Vichy in August 1944 more than 6,000 people were deported.[285] In all, the occupying authorities had deported a total of almost 76,000 Jews from France to the extermination camps and killed a further 4,000 in other ways. Himmler's SS men had murdered every fourth Jew living in the country, including around 24,000 French citizens.[286]

In October 1943, as previously mentioned, the RSHA also wanted to deport the small Jewish minority in Denmark. The Reich plenipotentiary appointed in November 1942, Werner Best, former administrative chief of the Gestapo, had prompted the 'action' in order to bring about a fundamental change in German occupation policy, which had hitherto been relatively restrained. However, fearing failure as he lacked sufficient police, he allowed the date of the planned deportation to leak out, and so the great majority of the around 7,000 Jews living in Denmark were able to escape.[287]

The Hungarian Jews were less fortunate. During 1943 the Nazi regime put more and more pressure on the Hungarian government to persuade them to deport the Jews living in Hungary.[288] As it became increasingly clear that the Kallay government was not prepared to hand over the Jews to the Germans,[289] the Nazi authorities decided to 'solve' the 'Jewish question' without Kallay.

At the beginning of 1944 German–Hungarian relations increasingly deteriorated. It was clear that Hungary too wanted to leave the alliance with Germany. In March 1944, therefore, German troops occupied the country. Prime Minister Kallay was replaced by the man who had hitherto been head of the Hungarian mission in Berlin, Döme Sztójay. Hitler appointed SS-Brigadeführer Edmund Veesenmayer to be the new envoy and plenipotentiary of the Greater German Reich in Hungary, and Himmler established an SS organization there. This created the political and technical preconditions for the deportations.[290]

Under the pretext of labour deployment from now on the SS organized the comprehensive deportation and extermination of the Hungarian Jews. Prompted by Veesenmayer, as early as April the Sztójay government was offering the Reich 50,000 Jews for armaments projects, with the promise of another 50,000 to follow.[291]

The system of concentration and deportation developed over the years by Himmler's persecution machine was instituted and operated to perfection with the active support of the Hungarian authorities. During March and April the Germans had the Hungarian government introduce a comprehensive set of anti-Jewish legislation.[292] A Jewish council was established, initially for the capital and then for the whole country, in accordance with instructions from the RSHA Sonderkommando which had been sent to Budapest and was led by Eichmann in person.[293] The country was divided into zones, and later it took only a matter of days to clear the Jews from each zone; they were then sent to Auschwitz zone by zone.[294]

The first trains began rolling at the end of April. At the beginning of May the tempo of the deportations was speeded up considerably. From 14 May onwards as a rule four transports left the country every day, each carrying 3,000 Jews. By the beginning of July a total of 437,000 people had been deported from the five zones. When, at the beginning of July, the deportations from the last zone, Budapest, were scheduled to begin[295] Sztójaj informed Veesenmayer that, in response to world-wide protests,[296] the Reich Governor, Horthy, had ordered a halt to the deportations.[297] To begin with, Himmler was powerless in the face of this decision: if he had demanded the immediate resumption of the deportations he would have risked Germany losing another ally. The opportunity to continue the deportations was only to occur under changed domestic political circumstances.

Against the background of the continuing deportations from Hungary, and in the course of a programme of 'ideological-political indoctrination' lasting several months, Himmler now frequently referred openly to the murder of the European Jews in front of Wehrmacht generals and declared his belief in the need for the genocide. By means of a whole series of speeches the Reichsführer wanted to make it clear to senior officers, among whom rumours and bits of information about the Holocaust had been circulating for years, that, in the event of a military defeat, they would not be able to pretend they were unaware of the fact that the murder of the European Jews was one of the regime's war aims.

'The Jewish question has in general been solved in Germany and in the countries occupied by Germany', Himmler declared to Army officers on 5 May. 'It was solved uncompromisingly, as was appropriate in view of the struggle in which we are engaged for the life of our nation, for the survival of our blood [...] You may appreciate how difficult it was for me to carry out this military order that I was given, that I have followed and carried out for the sake of obedience and with complete conviction.' Once again Himmler referred to the murder of women and children:

In this conflict with Asia we must get used to condemning to the past the rules and customs of past European wars which we have grown fond of and which are more natural for us. In my view, despite all our heartfelt sympathy, as Germans we must not permit hate-filled avengers to grow up, with the result that our children and grandchildren will then be obliged to confront them because we, the fathers and grandfathers, were too weak and too cowardly and left it to them to deal with.[298]

A few weeks later, on 24 May 1944 he informed the generals:

The Jewish question was [...] solved ruthlessly in accordance with orders and a rational assessment of the situation. I believe, gentlemen, that you know me well enough to know that I am not a bloodthirsty person or a man who enjoys or takes pleasure in having to do something harsh. On the other hand, I have sufficiently strong nerves and a sufficiently strong sense of duty—I think I can claim that for myself—that if I consider something to be necessary then I will carry it out uncompromisingly. I did not consider myself justified—I'm referring here to the Jewish women and children—in allowing avengers to grow up in the shape of the children who will then murder our fathers and grandchildren. I would have considered that a cowardly thing to do. As a result the question was solved uncompromisingly.[299]

'It was the most fearful task and the most fearful commission that could be assigned to any organization: the commission to solve the Jewish question', he emphasized on 21 June in another speech. 'I would like once again to say a few frank words about it in this company: It's good that we were tough enough to exterminate the Jews in our area.'[300] He could not have expressed it more bluntly. He had now made sure that the Army knew about it.

26

Collapse

The failed attempt on Hitler's life on 20 July 1944 made it possible for Himmler to accumulate an unprecedented range of powers. He was to succeed for a final time in redefining his and the SS's role within the Nazi state, namely, as the guarantor of internal security and embodiment of executive power in its entirety.[1]

Again Hitler enabled him to do this by authorizing individual actions in the weeks and months following 20 July. Himmler's reputation had clearly not been damaged by his failure either to expose the extensive preparations for the coup or to prevent the attempt on his Führer's life. Obviously the (overwhelmingly conservative) opponents of the regime and resistance groups had not managed to keep the Gestapo completely in the dark about their various deliberations and activities, and some members of these circles had already been arrested in the months running up to the assassination attempt.[2] But in July 1944 Himmler's henchmen were not remotely close to uncovering the actual coup.[3]

On 21 July he therefore spoke to his officers in terms that were as grandiose as they were vague about what was known before the assassination attempt: 'As an old Nazi [. . .]—and let's be open and German about this with each other—I have always been expecting something to come from these circles. And as Reichsführer-SS, with all the information sources at my disposal and with my instinct for political developments, I was in a position to anticipate for a very long time some initiative from reactionary elements on the political spectrum. I knew it would come some time or other.'[4]

On 3 August 1944 he was similarly vague when addressing the party's Reich leaders and Gauleiters: 'We had been [. . .] on the trail, shall we say, of all these reactionary conspiracies for a long time.' In this connection he

named, among others, Johannes Popitz, Franz Halder, and Erich Fellgiebel
as suspects even before 20 July; while making the most derogatory remarks
about those conspirators who had meanwhile been exposed, he avoided any
comment about the extent to which he had been aware of concrete preparations for the coup.[5]

After 20 July Himmler became very active in order to compensate in
retrospect for his own failure. During the night of 20–1 July Otto Skorzeny,
celebrated in propaganda as the man who freed Mussolini, advanced on the
Bendler block with an SS company in order to occupy the building where
the headquarters of the Reserve Army (Ersatzheer) and of the conspirators
were located and begin questioning the officers who were already there or
who had been ordered to report there.[6]

On 21 July the 20 July Special Commission was created in Office IV, the
Gestapo headquarters, of the Reich Security Main Office, and was composed of up to about 400 staff organized into eleven groups. In the following
days 600–700 arrests were made and the commission succeeded in establishing relatively quickly the detailed sequence of events of the attempted coup:
Kaltenbrunner, head of the RHSA, gave Himmler a daily report on the
progress of the investigation. Nevertheless, the Gestapo remained ignorant
of the actual extent of the conspiracy.[7]

On 30 July Himmler discussed with Hitler how to proceed against the
perpetrators. Himmler noted: '1. Judicial process. 2. Stauffenberg family. 3.
Members of the Seydlitz family.'[8] In addition to the planned conviction of
the conspirators and their accomplices by the People's Court, these headings
indicate that 'clan custody' (*Sippenhaft*) was to be applied to the family of the
attempted assassin, Claus Schenk von Stauffenberg, and to that of General
Walther von Seydlitz, chair of the 'League of German Officers' founded by
German prisoners of war in the Soviet Union.[9]

Above and beyond the Stauffenberg and Seydlitz families, the Gestapo
took more than 140 family members into custody in July and August.[10] On
25 October Kaltenbrunner let Bormann know that Himmler had refused 'to
establish specific guidelines regarding clan custody. The whole of Count
Stauffenberg's family must be taken into custody. Otherwise every case
must be examined individually.'[11] On 21 November Müller gave instructions on how to proceed with clan custody: thereafter Himmler intended to
decide personally whether this form of internment was to be imposed.[12]
The regime was to make use of clan custody up to the end of the war. In

April 1945 200 people in this category were still interned in Dachau concentration camp, to which they had eventually been moved.

In addition, Himmler exploited the attempted coup to justify a new wave of mass arrests. He obtained Hitler's permission to do so on 14 August 1944, as he noted in his calendar: 'Arrests of S.P.D. and K.P.D. bigwigs.' At the same time he recorded: 'Thälmann is to be executed.' Four days later the former head of the KPD, who had been in a concentration camp since 1933, was in fact murdered.[13]

The arrest of the 'bigwigs' extended to all former KPD and SPD members of the Reichstag and regional assemblies and town councillors throughout the Reich. In this 'Operation Thunderstorm', as Müller, the Gestapo chief, made clear in instructions to the regional offices, it was 'irrelevant [...] whether there is any evidence against them at this point'. Even 'former SPD party and union secretaries' were to be included in the operation, which was to be carried out in the early hours of 22 August. The day before, Müller, again on Himmler's orders, gave instructions for former elected representatives belonging to the Catholic Centre Party also to be arrested, among them the former mayor of Cologne, Konrad Adenauer. Far in excess of 5,000 people were targeted, the majority of whom were, however, released after two to four weeks. The whole operation was evidently designed to intimidate overwhelmingly any actual or potential opponents.[14]

The Gestapo did, however, see to it that opponents of the regime in their custody, either prominent ones or those the Gestapo considered the most dangerous, did not survive the war. In April 1945 an official in military intelligence, Hans von Dohnanyi, former head of military intelligence Wilhelm Canaris, his deputy Hans Oster, the military judge Karl Sack, the theologian Dietrich Bonhoeffer, and Georg Elser, who had attempted to assassinate Hitler, were murdered in concentration camps.[15]

Himmler assumes command of the Reserve Army

The campaign of retribution against the 20 July plotters and all other opponents was, however, only one of the consequences of the failed coup. On the very day of the assassination attempt Hitler appointed Himmler chief of the Reserve Army in succession to Colonel-General Friedrich Fromm, Stauffenberg's immediate superior, who had been aware of the conspiracy. Thus Himmler acquired one of the most important posts within the army: the range of his responsibilities covered, among other things, military equipment, law-enforcement throughout the army, prisoners of war, reserve personnel, and training, in other words, all army training establishments. In fact, in the summer of 1944 the Reserve Army consisted of almost 2 million men. Although this appointment was made as an immediate response to the coup attempt and was intended to humiliate and punish the military, from whose ranks the conspirators came, it was not a complete surprise. For on 15 July, five days before the coup, Himmler had decisively invaded Fromm's sphere of influence, something that, incidentally, may well have contributed to Fromm's final realization that a coup was unavoidable if the army were not to be at the mercy of the SS in the short or long term.

On 15 July Hitler had transferred to Himmler the responsibility in future for 'training, National Socialist indoctrination, disciplinary penal codes, and courts martial' in the case of fifteen planned new army divisions—a significant encroachment by the Reichsführer-SS on the army and one that gave rise to the expectation that in future Himmler would be put entirely in charge of the creation of new Waffen-SS units. For Himmler, this extension of his powers and the prospects arising from it were of decisive strategic importance, for they provided the means of overcoming the shortage of personnel that threatened the SS in 1944; for the recruitment quota conceded to it by the army was no longer adequate to cover the SS members required to replace German Waffen-SS casualties. And a further aspect is important: there was a subtle connection between this task of Himmler's to establish new army divisions and 'train' them as National Socialists and his addresses to the generals in May and June, in which he had openly admitted the murder of the Jews. By this means the army was being told in no uncertain terms that it was now an instrument of the political and ideological objectives of the regime, and shared responsibility for the criminal consequences of the latter's policies.

On the afternoon of 15 July Himmler spoke with Fromm, who only a few hours beforehand had been curtly informed by Hitler in the Führer headquarters of the new arrangement. In this interview Fromm, who had been steamrollered by events, subordinated the new divisions to Himmler 'with regard to their deployment', allowed him to have a say about who should fill the officer posts, and agreed to the subordination of the planned divisions (which after 20 July were to be given the martial name of National

Grenadier Divisions) to three SS general commandos yet to be formed, which could be established only with massive support from the army.[16]

The boundaries between army and Waffen-SS had therefore already been almost completely obliterated when on 20 July Himmler gained control of a substantial part of the army in the form of the Reserve Army. Having been appointed Reich Minister of the Interior the previous year, he prepared to unite in his own person this monopoly of power spanning the whole Reich territory—a reinvention of the old idea of a state protection corps, though one now operating under the conditions of war and of positively gigantic proportions.

If his appointment is viewed in the context of a series of other important shifts of responsibility it also becomes apparent that the failed assassination provided an opportunity for a group of Nazi political leaders who for some time had been demanding 'total war' to get their way. These men had agreed amongst themselves and attempted to pressure Hitler in this direction. As has already been mentioned, Himmler must be counted as one of this group, along with Goebbels, Bormann, and Speer. On 25 July Hitler gave Goebbels authority and far-reaching powers to move to total war,[17] and empowered Bormann to execute all necessary measures to 'bring about a total war effort' within the party and its structures. Bormann was to exploit this responsibility, among other things, to extend Himmler's monopoly of power. According to a decree from the Führer of 20 September 1944, in the event of enemy forces penetrating into Reich territory executive power in the field of operations was removed from the military commanders and transferred to the so-called Reich defence commissars (the Gauleiters). It was then Himmler's task to 'coordinate throughout the Reich' the measures to be taken in the field of operations by the Reich defence commissars.[18] The 'gang of four', namely, Goebbels, Bormann, Himmler, and Speer, therefore had the Nazi apparatus of power de facto in their hands to a considerable extent, while at the same time being careful neither to question Hitler's leadership nor to take any steps openly against the official number two in the state, Göring. They operated only within a sphere of activity determined by Hitler and made no serious attempt to exceed these boundaries. None of the four, for example, took any initiative to convince the others that the war could be ended only without Hitler; in each case their link to the 'Führer', both personal and as part of the political power structure, was too strong. Thus the powerful foursome moved towards inevitable and total defeat.

In the night of 20–1 July Himmler, in his new capacity as commander of the Reserve Army, gave his first instructions. He reversed the orders that had been issued the previous day in Fromm's name and began to fill the top posts in his new sphere of operations with reliable SS leaders. On 21 July he appointed Hans Jüttner, director of the SS Leadership Main Office, as his deputy and Chief of Staff.[19]

How Himmler saw his responsibility was something he revealed a few days after his appointment, when he wrote to Fegelein, his liaison officer in Hitler's headquarters, that 'everyone who opened his mouth' would have to 'be shot ruthlessly' by 'detection commandos [. . .] composed of the most brutal commanders'.[20] He gave his first address to officers from the army armaments office and the General Army Office on 21 July. The coup had occasioned 'deep grief for us soldiers', he announced, even though he could by no means be sure about the grief of those present. As an antidote to the spirit of revolt he advocated a return to the 'genuine, ancient military virtues', and to illustrate his point invoked the familiar catalogue he had been making the SS commit to for years. To the virtues of loyalty, obedience, comradeship, hard work, and truthfulness he added another, however: faith. 'All your training, selection, and skill', he impressed on the officers, 'has been in vain if it is not founded on unshakeable faith in the German prerogative and German victory. I base this faith on the merits of our Germanic faith and of our race. I am convinced that we are of greater worth than the others.'[21]

In the following days there were more speeches to officers of army divisions that were similarly constructed round the catalogue of virtues, 'decency' of course being one of them. No attentive listener could fail to notice, however, that the 'faith' that Himmler conjured up in these speeches was only supposed to conceal the fact that he could not come up with anything to counter the increasingly hopeless situation of the Third Reich.[22]

Yet on 3 August 1944, to the party's Reich leaders and Gauleiters, Himmler presented a completely different face. There was no more talk of communal 'grief'. Instead, Himmler was settling scores with the military leaders, 'this clique'. Every undesirable development, crisis, and defeat suffered by the German army since the end of the First World War was, he claimed, the result of a conspiracy of reactionary and incompetent General Staff officers: from 1941 onwards 'these staffers' were increasingly to blame 'for the spread of defeatism from the top to the bottom of the army'.[23]

At the beginning of August Hitler authorized Himmler, 'for the purpose of reducing staff to examine and simplify the entire organizational and administrative basis of the army, the Waffen-SS, the police, and the OT [Organisation Todt, the Wehrmacht's construction group]'. By so doing he was giving Himmler leave to intervene in the organization of the Army as a whole.[24] Himmler delegated this task to Pohl, the Head of the Business and Administrative Main Office, though Pohl discovered that a special appointee in the shape of General Heinz Ziegler had only a few months previously been given the job by Hitler of standardizing the Wehrmacht's organization. Pohl was therefore in favour of discretion, but Himmler let him know that that he was 'not interested' in whether 'General Ziegler is still there or not'.[25] Two months later he expressly forbade Pohl 'to make even the slightest concession' to the Wehrmacht High Command.[26]

Soon this new task was beginning to have consequences: in November 1944 Himmler had the recruitment offices for army officer candidates merged with those of the Waffen-SS and incorporated into the SS administration. The Waffen-SS was given a quota of 17.3 per cent of those potential recruits called for examination in 1944, and the Wehrmacht High Command finally conceded the right to the SS Main Office to reserve 20 per cent of those army volunteers born in 1927 and 1928. In addition, it became accepted practice to use Wehrmacht soldiers to fill up SS units.[27] Gottlob Berger, Head of the SS Main Office, wanted to go further and take control of the entire process of deployment both in the military and in the civil realm, but time ran out for that.[28]

Prisoners of war were also Himmler's responsibility as commander of the Reserve Army, though he delegated this area to Berger.[29] Now that Soviet POWs fell within his field of responsibility the Reichsführer-SS was once more confronted with an initiative that he had hitherto rejected vehemently, namely, the recruitment of Soviet POWs as a separate auxiliary force of the Wehrmacht. In his speech in Posen on 6 October the previous year he had called General Vlasov, the main advocate of this idea among the Russians, the 'Russian swine'.[30] In July 1944 he nevertheless decided to cooperate with Vlasov as a result of mediation on the part of Gunter d'Alquen, the editor-in-chief of *Das Schwarze Korps* and commander of the SS-Standarte for war reporting. That same month, after his first contact with Vlasov, Berger set up a 'Russian operations centre', the head of which acted as Himmler's liaison officer with Vlasov.[31]

On 16 September Himmler received the Russian general personally for talks.[32] At the very beginning of the interview Vlasov raised the matter of Himmler's theory of subhumans; the latter was evasive and immediately declared himself willing to have the brochure entitled *The Subhuman* that he had had circulated withdrawn (and indeed, Himmler did shortly after issue an internal instruction for all propaganda against subhumans to be stopped). Himmler and Vlasov agreed to establish a 'Committee for the Liberation of the Russian Nations', and Himmler made Erhard Kroeger, former leader of the ethnic German population in Latvia, who had been in command of an Einsatzkommando in 1941, political appointee responsible for the Vlasov initiative and put Gunter d'Alquen in charge of psychological warfare. He then had himself photographed with Vlasov (see Ill. 30).

Vlasov, whose activities were supported by Ribbentrop and Goebbels, was given the opportunity on 14 November 1944, in a 'Prague Manifesto', of issuing a call to liberate his homeland.[33] Meanwhile Himmler cannily had Vlasov's troops established under the umbrella of the Wehrmacht, by contrast with the Galician or Ukrainian SS volunteer units; he had not revised his position so radically that he was willing to integrate them into his Waffen-SS. In April 1945 Vlasov, who on 28 January 1945 was officially appointed supreme commander of the Russian forces, would have more than 45,000 men at his disposal. As far as the course of the war was concerned that was no longer of any significance.[34]

The fact that Himmler was now in control of the Wehrmacht penal system[35] was indicated rapidly by a brutalization of military justice. According to the new commander of the Reserve Army, 'the penal system will without exception be placed directly in the service of the war'.[36] The Wehrmacht's judiciary took this information on board: between January and May 1945 alone something like 4,000 death sentences were passed. Drumhead courts martial handed out 6,000–7,000.[37]

In the following months Himmler also saw to it that Wehrmacht armaments were merged on the level of personnel and organization with the SS. Thus the A4 rocket project seemed finally to have fallen into his hands. On 6 August 1944 he gave Kammler, the Head of department C in the Business and Administration Main Office, complete authority to ensure the 'most rapid' deployment of the A4.[38] Kammler did as he was told,[39] and on 6 September the first raid on London using the A4 (or V2, as it was also called) took place. In all more than 3,000 V2s were to be launched, more than half of which landed on the British capital.[40]

Himmler claimed to be convinced that the V rockets would bring about a turn in the war. At the end of July he had declared in a speech to the officer corps of a new grenadier division: 'I know that we still have crises and shortages to get through. We should not forget, however that V1 and the V2, V3, and V4 to come are not a bluff [. . .].' He had, he said, news from London according to which the constant bombardment of the city in the previous weeks with V1s (the 'doodlebug' flying-bombs developed by the Luftwaffe) had already led to 120,000 deaths, which 'absolutely matches the numbers of V1s we have sent over and for which I have precise figures. For we know more or less what effect they have and thus we can work out ourselves the numbers of dead.'[41] It remains Himmler's secret how he could claim to know the damage done by a weapon whose impact on southern England could not be verified by the German side. At any rate, the figures he gave were almost fifty times larger than the actual number of victims.[42]

The drive with which Himmler in his new capacity attempted to expand his power in all directions did, however, meet with resistance. When, on 23 August, Goebbels suggested to Hitler that, as part of the measures to promote total war, Himmler should be put in charge of all the district headquarters of the Wehrmacht, Hitler's reaction was negative: 'But the Führer fears that Himmler is so overloaded with work that it will get too much for him and the same tragedy will befall him as befell Göring. He too had so many offices that he lost track of them.' Himmler's work would have to be 'concentrated'. As Goebbels explained further, Himmler had 'tried once more to take charge of the entire A4 programme, which the Führer had categorically rejected. To do this Himmler would have had to build up a new apparatus without being in a position to dismantle the existing apparatus. So nothing is going to change here.'[43]

In the end, in January 1945 Himmler was forced to give up not only the A4 programme but also armaments as a whole, having been put in charge of them in the meantime as commander of the Reserve Army. Thus the miracle weapon, the capabilities of which had been completely overestimated, had been placed once and for all beyond his grasp.[44]

Terror and mass murder to the end

The nearer the Third Reich came to its downfall, the more Himmler stepped up the use of terror in the occupied territories. On 30 July 1944

Hitler issued a secret order henceforth suspending completely any court-martial proceedings against the indigenous populations of the occupied territories. Instead, 'terrorists and saboteurs' caught in the act were to be 'crushed on the spot',[45] while those caught later were to be handed over to the security police and SD. Himmler's henchmen were now instructed to take independent action against resistance groups, in other words, to pronounce 'administrative death sentences'. Thus, for example, in occupied Norway at least sixty-eight people were shot without any legal process on the orders of the Oslo security police and SD.[46]

Similarly, in August 1944 the commander of the security police in the Netherlands, Eberhard Schöngarth, had several hundred political prisoners in Vught concentration camp shot without trial.[47] After an assassination attempt on HSSPF Rauter in March 1945, which, though severely injured, he survived, Schöngarth ordered the shooting of a further 250 people.[48]

In Denmark too the military courts were suspended and security police and SD boosted their anti-terror activities. In August alone eleven prisoners were shot 'while escaping'.[49] In September 1944 Himmler ordered that the entire Danish police force be arrested, claiming they were supporting the resistance and should therefore be deported en masse to Buchenwald. Thereupon more than 2,000 Danish police were taken into custody in an operation led by HSSPF Pancke and sent to Buchenwald concentration camp.[50]

The extensive destruction of Warsaw that followed the suppression of the Polish uprising in August and September 1944 also seems to have been Himmler's work. At any rate, in a speech to commanding officers of the military districts and commanders in charge of training he boasted that he had given the order to 'raze Warsaw to the ground'. 'Every block of buildings must be burnt down and dynamited', he claimed to have said in his orders.[51]

Above all, however, this terror campaign was directed at Jewish minorities who had hitherto managed to escape deportation. In the summer of 1942 the Slovak government had increasingly dragged its feet with regard to the deportation of Slovakian Jews. As a result Himmler took care that, after the start of the uprising there and the country's occupation by German troops in August 1944, this persecution was again advanced with violent measures. He appointed his head of the SS Main Office, Gottlob Berger, who up to that point had shone as a desk-bound perpetrator, as commander of German troops in Slovakia, named Hermann Höfle, who had played a key role in 'Aktion Reinhardt', as HSSPF, and put in place a commanding officer for the security police, even though the country was not formally occupied but in fact still had the status of an ally. The latter had his own Einsatzgruppe at his disposal, and it embarked on a campaign of persecution of the Jewish community in Slovakia. In the face of opposition from the Slovak government the SS got its way and deportations were resumed. Between September 1944 and March 1945 eleven transports deported 8,000 people to Auschwitz, more than 2,700 to Sachsenhausen, and more than 1,600 to Theresienstadt.[52]

As we have already seen, in July 1944 the Hungarian government had ordered a stop to deportations. After Eichmann, acting on his own initiative, had had more than 2,700 Jews sent to Auschwitz in the second half of July,[53] the Hungarian government finally gave way to strong German pressure and agreed at the beginning of August to their resumption.[54] Shortly after, however, under the influence of Romania's defection from the Axis on 23 August, Horthy again withdrew this agreement,[55] and on 29 August expressly instructed the newly formed Hungarian government under Prime Minister Géza Lakatos to put a stop to the persecution of the Jews.

Surprisingly, however, Himmler himself had already issued an order on 24 August to cease further deportations from Hungary.[56] Sonderkommando Eichmann left the country in September.[57] At first sight, and in view of stubborn attempts by the Germans in the previous months to set the deportations in motion, Himmler's decision seems incomprehensible.[58] If, however, it is assumed that from the perspective of the Nazi regime the deportations represented an important means of pressurizing their Hungarian allies, as accomplices in an unprecedented crime, into binding themselves for good or ill to the Reich, then Himmler's change of course becomes comprehensible. If in these circumstances he had insisted upon a resumption of the deportations, there was the threat of a severe political crisis, the end of the Horthy regime, and thus possibly the loss of the Hungarians as allies. And the Germans had as yet no political alternative to offer.

In the middle of October the situation changed. In the wake of secret negotiations with the Soviet Union Horthy had announced that Hungary would withdraw from the war, and the Arrow Cross Party under Ferenc Szálasi mounted a successful putsch with German support.[59] Again the SS tried to resume the deportations, to implicate their new Hungarian partner too in mass murder and so bind it irrevocably to the Greater Germanic Reich.

Nevertheless, the original intention to deport the Jews of Budapest to Auschwitz was now out of the question. The transport situation was poor, and in addition the gas chambers in Auschwitz had already been dismantled; all traces of the annihilation process were supposed to be obliterated promptly and completely before any possible advance by the Red Army into Upper Silesia.[60] Eichmann, who had returned to Budapest directly after the putsch, now reiterated the demand of April 1944 that 50,000 Jewish workers be supplied to the Reich so that they could be used in the underground production of armaments.[61] From the end of October onwards those affected were marched towards the Hungarian border.[62] As a result of the high death-toll from these marches (deaths which were not concealed behind camp fences but took place in full public view) Szálasi put a stop to them on 21 November. Those Jews remaining in Budapest were confined to the ghetto. Most of them managed to survive until the capital fell to the Red Army in February 1945.[63]

From the middle of 1944 onwards Himmler had been making various attempts to offer the Allies Jews who were in his power in exchange for foreign currencies or materials important for the war, presumably with the primary purpose of putting out feelers to probe the possibility of separate peace negotiations with the western powers. We cannot be absolutely certain whether he or Hitler would actually have been prepared to release a large number of Jewish prisoners in exchange for some suitable trade-off, or whether such negotiations were simply an excuse to establish contact with the western Allies. Presumably from the outset Himmler's negotiating position was set to move in a number of possible directions: if the western Allies were prepared to enter into such negotiations one could attempt first of all to bypass such 'humanitarian' issues and sound out the political possibilities of ending the war. Secondly, these contacts could be exploited to sow mistrust between the western Allies and the Soviet Union. Thirdly, the United States and Great Britain could be 'exposed' as the puppets of Jewish interests and the negotiations broken off.

Himmler's idea of using the Jews as hostages with which to blackmail the western powers was not new: he had recommended this strategy before the so-called 'Kristallnacht' ('Night of Broken Glass'), and the mass arrests of Jews during this November 1938 pogrom—accompanied by simultaneous international negotiations to improve the opportunities for emigration—fitted into this scenario. Holding Jews hostage in order to prevent the

Americans from entering the war seems to have figured both in the Madagascar plans of 1940 and in the commencement of the deportation of German Jews in the autumn of 1941, and since 1942 the SS leadership had repeatedly allowed individual prominent Jews to emigrate to a neutral country in exchange for large amounts of foreign currency.[64] Himmler had obtained Hitler's express permission to do this in December 1942, and in this connection had ordered that about 10,000 Jews should be held back in a special camp as 'valuable hostages'.[65] The 'holding camp' of Bergen-Belsen was established in spring 1943 with this in mind.[66] And again in 1942, Dieter Wisliceny, Himmler's adviser on Jewish matters in Slovakia, accepted a large sum in dollars from Jews, though it is not clear whether the halt called to deportations from Slovakia was actually related to this payment or whether the SS had in any case notified the end of deportations from Slovakia because German policy towards the Jews was meeting with increasingly strong resistance from the Slovak government.[67]

Whatever the case, when Wisliceny came to Budapest as part of the Sonderkommando Eichmann, representatives of the Zionist Support and Rescue Committee (Vaada) in Budapest contacted him in order to negotiate the emigration of a large number of Hungarian Jews in exchange for foreign currency or goods. The SS's desire for 10,000 lorries soon emerged as the key element in the talks. The Jewish side paid several large sums in dollars in advance. Two emissaries from Vaada travelled to Istanbul to obtain assurances from the Allies to support the envisaged agreement with Eichmann. Should Himmler have had hopes of making indirect contact with the Allies via Jewish representatives, these were quickly dashed. The British had the two Vaada representatives arrested.[68]

Finally, two concrete agreements were reached in Budapest between the SS and Vaada. First of all, at the end of June 15,000 Hungarian Jews were deported as forced labour to Austria instead of to Auschwitz, so that, according to Eichmann's assurances, they could be held in readiness for further exchange negotiations. But this was not a concession of any kind on the part of SS, for its intention was in any case to deploy Hungarian Jews as forced labour in the Vienna area. In the second place, agreement was reached to move 1,684 Hungarian Jews, also at the end of June, by special transport to the holding camp of Bergen-Belsen. From there they emigrated in two groups in August and December to Switzerland. The material quid pro quo was negotiated by Kurt Becher, director of the equipment staff at the HSSPF office in Hungary, first with Vaada representatives and then, from August 1944, also with the representative of the American Jewish Joint Distribution Committee in Switzerland, Saly Mayer. Up to January 1945 there were further talks on Swiss soil between representatives of the SS and Jewish organizations about feasible exchange deals: Jews for goods or money or—according to Himmler's instructions to Becher at the end of 1944—for Romanian ethnic Germans who in the meantime had been cut off behind the German–Soviet front. When, at the end of November, a representative of the American War Refugee Board took part in one of these Zurich meetings it was the first time that Becher had had contact with an American government office. Yet if this raised in Himmler the hope of being able to advance to possible peace explorations, he was again disappointed, for in this respect the talks were completely fruitless.[69]

In parallel with this, in October 1944 in Vienna and in January 1945 in Wildbad in the Black Forest Himmler himself was conducting negotiations with Jean-Marie Musy, the former President of the Swiss Confederation, over the release of Jews. As a result, 1,200 people were allowed to travel from Theresienstadt to Switzerland.[70] Himmler was to refer to these exchange projects in the final phase of the war when making a last attempt to establish contact with the Allies.

Thus Himmler was fully prepared to give up fairly small groups of Jewish prisoners if thereby he could achieve concrete returns and had the chance of establishing politically useful connections with the enemy. He also seems to have been willing to pursue serious negotiations for the release of larger groups of Jews if that would prolong the life of the Third Reich. Himmler was too strongly focused on utilitarian considerations to support the maxim of dragging as many 'enemies' as possible down to destruction with him. Instead, human lives were ruthlessly used as bargaining-chips. If exchanging them promised to bring advantages, he was as ready to take such a step as he was to commit mass murder. Having acted in close consultation with Hitler on the question of the exchange of Jewish prisoners at the end of 1942, what is not clear is up to what point in time and with what particulars Himmler kept Hitler informed about these negotiations. Although Himmler asserted that Hitler had found out about the release of the 1,684 and 1,200 Jews only after the event and had been highly indignant, this may have been a trick to show himself in a better light to his negotiating partners.[71]

Himmler's idea of holding talks with the Allies about the exchange of Jewish prisoners rested, however, on the assumption that he would retain control over the prisoners up to the last possible moment. For this reason (and because the working prisoners were, from the perspective of the SS, valuable capital, who furthermore were not to be left to the enemy as witnesses to the horrors of the concentration camps) Himmler decreed that the concentration camps were to be vacated and 'evacuated'.

As early as 17 June 1944 Himmler had transferred the command of the concentration camps to the Higher SS and Police Leaders in the event of so-called 'Situation A' arising (defined at first as an uprising (Aufstand) on the part of the prisoners and then principally as the approach (Annäherung) of enemy troops).[72] The process of clearing and evacuation was to result in renewed selection of the prisoners: as a rule, the guards murdered weak and ill prisoners before the evacuation; in a number of concentration camps German prisoners were released. The prisoners were normally made to march on foot, mainly in winter weather and in catastrophic conditions. Anyone who got left behind was killed by the accompanying guards, and in many cases with local assistance. Concentration camps located further inside the Reich were the destination of these death marches from the main camps. The process of collecting a large number of prisoners in a decreasing number of camps resulted frequently in an almost complete breakdown in provisioning. Living conditions that were in any case disastrous became even more wretched.[73]

First of all the former ghettos and camps for Jewish forced workers in the Baltic States, which on Himmler's instructions had been redesignated as concentration camps, had been cleared since the summer of 1944. Prisoners from the Kaiserwald camp complex close to Riga, from the Kowno concentration camp, and from Vaivara were deported by the SS mainly to Stutthof but also to Auschwitz.[74] From September 1944 onwards a large number of prisoners were killed in two improvised gas chambers with Zyklon B.[75] At the end of the year the first rail transports of prisoners left the main Stutthof camp and in January eleven columns were formed, each with a thousand prisoners, who were supposed to march on foot to Lauenburg (Lębork), 140 kilometres away. Only about one-third of the prisoners reached the city.[76]

From the summer of 1944 onwards Auschwitz was also being gradually cleared. At that time the camp still held some 130,000 prisoners, half of whom were now being moved to other concentration camps.[77] The evacuation of the remaining 67,000 prisoners began in the middle of January 1945: the prisoners were marched westwards in columns; guards shot around a quarter of them during the march. Part of the marching columns reached Gross-Rosen concentration camp in Lower Silesia, which became a transit camp for the camps and prisons in the east that had been cleared.[78] Finally, 44,000 prisoners from the Rosen concentration-camp complex were taken in rail transports to camps situated further westwards.

Even if one of the motives behind Himmler's evacuation of the camps was to retain as long as he could a large number of prisoners as potential objects of exchange, treatment continued to be harsh. The fact that the evacuation resulted in the death or murder of many prisoners was clearly not contrary to his intentions. The supposed humanitarian pose that Himmler adopted in conducting negotiations towards the end of the war for the release of Jews must be viewed against the background of this brutal and cynical evacuation process.

A military commander at last

At the beginning of September Hitler gave his commander of the Reserve Army the task of preventing troop units from retreating from those occupied territories the Germans still held but which were outside the actual theatre of operations, and of setting up combat units in the rear area.[79] In a speech on 21 September to the commanders of the military districts and those in charge of training, Himmler reported proudly how in the previous weeks he had criss-crossed the areas under threat ('down the whole of the western front from Trier to Mühlhausen (Mulhouse), Colmar, Metz'), spoken with 'thousands of soldiers', and wherever he considered necessary had intervened, taking to task the negligent commander of a troop transport and personally demoting the incompetent commanding officer in Trier. 'Brutal action against signs of indiscipline in the rear area' was what he recommended to the officers present.[80] The fact that in his entire military career Himmler himself had never made it beyond precisely this rear area (and never would do) did not seem to trouble him.

In Hitler's eyes, however, Himmler's stance as a merciless enforcer and fanatical driver of men clearly qualified him for further military responsibilities. In September he entrusted to him the task of creating a home guard (*Volkssturm*). The idea for a militia that would take on security responsibilities as the need arose was something Himmler had been considering for years. Back in January 1942 he had created the rural guard (*Landwacht*), and in December this was extended to be a rural and urban guard. In line with an agreement reached between Himmler and Bormann, members of the SA, SS, and Nazi Party who had had not been called up for military service were the preferred source of recruits. This force was deployed, for example, to supervise forced workers or recapture escaped prisoners.[81]

Since June 1944 the Nazi leadership had been contemplating some kind of home guard in the event of a direct threat to Reich territory by enemy forces.[82] In the middle of September Bormann, Himmler, and Keitel agreed that a home defence force (*Volkswehr*) should be set up. On 26 September Hitler signed the 'Decree Concerning the Formation of the German "Volkssturm"'—that sounded distinctly more martial and historically significant. The decree stated that all men capable of bearing arms between the ages of 16 and 60 would be called up to the Volkssturm; 'establishment and leadership' would be the responsibility of the Gauleiters, while Himmler, in his capacity as commander of the Reserve Army, would be responsible for 'military organization, training, equipment, and supplies for the German Volkssturm'. Even 'combat operations', Hitler's decree read, were, 'in line with my instructions', placed under Himmler's control.[83]

Himmler had already announced the creation of a home guard to commanders of the military districts and commanders in charge of training on 21 September,[84] and the official notification came on 18 October in Königsberg at a roll-call of the Volkssturm there. For his speech, which was broadcast on the radio, Himmler had chosen a heavily symbolic date. This day, 18 October, he reminded his listeners, was the 131st anniversary of the Battle of the Nations at Leipzig, an ideal opportunity to make reference to the Volkssturm of 1813 and its role in the Wars of Liberation. Himmler tried to bolster the people's courage: back then an improvised militia had succeeded, in a military situation judged to be hopeless, in making an important contribution to the victory over Napoleon. A similar role was to be reserved for the present Volkssturm: 'Our enemies must be taught to understand that every kilometre they advance into our country will cost them rivers of their own blood. Every building in the town, every village, every farm, every forest will be defended by men, young and old, and—if necessary—by girls and women too.'[85] On 12 November, in all Gaus, at least as far as the conditions of war permitted, the Volkssturm guard was ceremoniously sworn in.[86]

Himmler appointed Berger as Chief of Staff of the Volkssturm, and the latter gathered a suitable team. A dynamic character, Berger soon exceeded his powers, which in fact were entirely confined to the military side of the Volkssturm's creation, and this led Bormann to complain to Himmler.

Although Himmler admonished Berger to 'stick to his proper task', in the end the two of them had their way over Bormann.[87]

On 16 October Berger issued training instructions for the Volkssturm, which required 'ideological activation' in particular, as well as weapons training and field exercises.[88] In theory 6 million men were potentially available, more than were in the regular army.[89] The military quality of this final call to arms was, however, more than inadequate: for their 'service' in the Volkssturm (exercises in the evenings and at weekends) people wore worn-out civilian clothing or uniforms belonging to any and every military and non-military organization. An armband was the sign identifying the wearer as a combatant as defined by international laws of war.[90] The Volkssturm had few weapons at its disposal, and its firearms, collected from all sorts of places, were mostly of doubtful value. Military training as a rule was limited to a superficial orientation.[91]

It was believed in all earnestness that such serious inadequacies in a fighting force consisting primarily of adolescent boys and old men could be compensated for by guerrilla tactics, by means of which—supported by tricks and guile—every copse and every farm was to be fought for. Borrowing an idea from the Chief of the General Staff, Heinz Guderian, Berger recommended to the men of the Volkssturm the novels of Karl May★ as 'training literature'.[92]

In fact the Volkssturm was used above all for basic tasks such as evacuating towns and villages before enemy troops arrived.[93] From October, however, battalions were deployed at the front in East Prussia,[94] and from November on the western front near Metz. But the results were so negative that in February Hitler ordered that Volkssturm units should in future be used only to protect the rear areas. Nevertheless, in the following months Volkssturm units were to be repeatedly sent to the front, above all in the east.[95]

Even if the military value of this last effort remained slight, the fact that the structure of the Volkssturm, down to its local groups, mirrored that of the party organization[96] showed what Himmler's and Bormann's first priority was with regard to it, namely, that all men capable of bearing arms should be recorded and disciplined by the party (Volkssturm soldiers were subject to the jurisdiction of the SS and police courts). The primary motive for the creation of the Volkssturm was therefore, in all probability, the Nazi leadership's fear that the war could be brought to a premature end by means

★ See *translators' note*, p. 80.

of a rebellion on the home front. Nazi leaders at the highest level in the final phase of the war were driven by this anxiety, and the memory of 1918, which was constantly adduced in this connection, reveals to what extent members of the Nazi elite had fallen victim to the myth of the stab in the back, which they themselves had conjured up often enough.

In his radio address of 18 October Himmler alluded to a further organization that he had brought into being along with the Volkssturm: 'Even in the territory they believe they have conquered,' he warned the Allies, 'the German will to resist will constantly spring to life again, and, like werewolves, death-defying volunteers will damage and destroy the enemy from the rear.'[97] On 19 September Himmler had already appointed Obergruppenführer Hans Prützmann, former HSSPF for Russia-South, as 'General Inspector for Special Intelligence', and authorized him to create small undercover units that would carry out acts of sabotage behind enemy lines on German territory under threat of occupation. These partisans were to be trained in the camps of the guerrilla combat troops, special anti-partisan units led by Otto Skorzeny. They were placed under the HSSPF. Preparations for guerrilla fighting on German soil were given the name 'Werewolf'.

This was an allusion to the title of a book (*Der Wehrwolf*) by Hermann Löns,* much read in its day and one disseminated by the regime, a heroizing portrayal of a secret resistance group of peasants from the Lüneburg Heath at the time of the Thirty Years War who defend their homes against marauding freebooters. The spelling 'Werwolf', which Himmler himself used, was at the same time a reminder of the creature of folklore, a human being who under cover of night transforms into an animal.

The fact that the werewolf units were originally conceived for fighting in border areas temporarily occupied by the enemy was responsible for the relatively late preparations for an armed underground in Gaus located in the German interior. Only a few more far-reaching plans to continue the fight even after a surrender were developed, as such considerations were forbidden on principle in view of the Nazi rhetoric of ultimate victory.

In spite of these significant obstacles, the creation of the werewolf units was by no means without effects and consequences. For the idea current today that they all simply broke up after the Allies swept over them is not entirely accurate. Although the attempt to build up a guerrilla movement in

---

* *Translators' note*: (1866–1914), a writer on rural and patriotic themes, often located in the Lüneburg Heath area.

occupied Germany was unsuccessful (the decisive prerequisite—namely, support from the population, which was in fact sick of war—was lacking), new research indicates that werewolves and other fanatics from the civilian population who continued the fight against the Allies on their own initiative even after the occupation did in fact carry out thousands of attacks, and hundreds of allied soldiers and German 'collaborators' fell victim to them.[98]

The most spectacular werewolf operation was the murder on 25 March 1945 of Franz Oppenhoff, who had been appointed Oberbürgermeister of Aachen by the Allies on 31 October 1944. The Aachen district court, which carefully reconstructed this case in 1949, discovered that the murder was carried out on the personal orders of Himmler, passed on by Prützmann in November 1944 to the responsible HSSPF. The HSSPF's attempt to ignore them was in vain. Himmler issued numerous reminders in letters and by telephone, and the murder was eventually carried out by a commando group that had been smuggled through the front line.[99]

When, in the autumn of 1944, after Allied troops had occupied almost the whole of France, the western frontier of the Reich came under threat, Himmler was given a further military task: in November Hitler appointed him Commander-in-Chief of the Upper Rhine, with the powers of an army group commander, his job being first and foremost to construct a sort of defensive front out of the assorted units of the Reserve Army, Volkssturm, border patrols, and police.

In the first week in January units of the army group Upper Rhine reinforced the offensive of army group C, located north of it in Alsace (Operation North Wind), which was designed to exploit the retreat of American troops from the Saar front following the Ardennes offensive. Army group Upper Rhine mounted as part of this operation three fairly large assaults without achieving any strategic advantage.[100] In the war diary of the Wehrmacht High Command there is no trace of any contribution made to the fighting by the Commander-in-Chief Upper Rhine.

During this period Himmler set up his headquarters in a special train at Triberg station in the Black Forest. The main advantage of this remote location was that the mobile headquarters could be moved into the security of railway tunnels in the event of air raids.[101] On 21 January 1945 Himmler and his train went to Schneidemühl,[102] where he took up a new post: Hitler had appointed him Commander-in-Chief of the army group Vistula. As Goebbels noted in his diary, this decision was 'mainly due to the fact that the troop formations retreating from the advancing Soviets have become fairly disordered and a firm hand is required to turn them back into solid fighting units'.[103] This task was 'absolutely safe' in Himmler's hands.[104]

As he confided to Goebbels, Hitler appeared at this time 'extremely pleased with Himmler's work'. The propaganda minister thereupon suggested that Hitler appoint Himmler 'as soon as possible Commander-in-Chief of the army', in other words, transfer to him the function Hitler himself had assumed since 1941. Hitler was not yet willing, however, 'to take this far-reaching measure until Himmler has proved his ability by handling successfully several large operations'.[105] This was precisely what Himmler was to attempt on the Vistula.

With regard to Himmler's work as commander of the army group Vistula, we have the record of his most important military colleague in this function, the memoirs of Colonel Eismann, who in the middle of January 1945 was made 1st General Staff Officer of the group.[106] Hans-Georg Eismann first met Himmler in January 1945 in Schneidemühl, where the train of the Reichsführer-SS was parked. He recalled: 'Himmler received me seated at the desk of his elegant saloon wagon, listened to my report, and then moved to a larger table in the middle of the room on which a map of operations from the Wehrmacht High Command was lying. He questioned me briefly about my previous experience and then proceeded to deliver a kind of lecture about the current situation with reference to the map.'

The army group Vistula was tasked with closing a 120-kilometre gap that had been opened in the front between the army groups Centre and North, in order, as Eismann wrote, 'to form a viable defensive front at least along the general line of Central Silesia to the lower Vistula'. The section of the front that had to be defended quickly lengthened to 450 kilometres, however.

On his induction by Himmler, Eismann recorded: 'The essence of the somewhat unclear explanations was, however: With the army group Vistula I shall stop the Russians in their tracks, then beat them and force them to retreat. That was a tall order [. . .] It was difficult to avoid the reaction that this was a blind man discoursing on colour.' When Eismann posed the question of 'what reinforcements would be available and at what time', he received 'from my commanding officer a rather loud and ungracious lecture on my having the typical attitude of the General Staff', which 'reached its climax in the assertion that General Staff officers only ever had concerns and were scholars with only academic learning who could not improvise. Their mindset was defeatist and so on. He, Himmler, would put a stop to such concerns and get to grips with things with single-minded energy. That was the only way to get on top of difficult situations.' Of course, these comments, as Himmler assured him when he asked, had not been directed at Eismann personally.

Eismann also produced a very detailed description of his new boss:

To look at, medium height, a slightly elongated upper body, slightly bow-legged, a little plump rather than slender. He wore the familiar simple grey uniform. His head viewed face-on resembled a fairly pointed triangle. Particularly striking was his profile with its receding chin. Very lively eyes, usually somewhat screwed up, which in conjunction with his cheekbones gave his face a slightly Mongolian appearance. Narrow lips, though not cruel-looking. Altogether this large face had nothing daemonic or cruel or in any way significant. It was the face of the man in the street. His hands were striking, at least for anyone who attaches any importance to what hands tell us. They were not at all elegant. Rather clumsy, not large hands with long fingers and broad fingertips, but rather soft like women's hands when he shook hands with you. Apart from that my impression of Himmler was of an animated man with varied interests, perhaps a little over-active and with very strong views.

The staff that Eismann found in place was completely inadequate, and essentially had neither equipment nor communications at its disposal. In the special train there was only a telephone. There were no communication links to the two subordinate armies.

How did Heinrich Himmler, Commander-in-Chief of the army group Vistula, assess the situation described above? The answer is: not at all. He was simply unable to reach an operational assessment of the situation as a whole. He stared, mesmerized, at the vast gap he had to close. [. . .] The words 'method of attack' and 'strike at the flank' were ones he used constantly but it did not occur to him that the Russians were on the point of capturing the flank of his own desperate second army. Yet one glance at the map he had constantly in front of him made this plain. For him there seemed to be nothing but 'attack'.

In July 1944, in an address to officers, the Reichsführer-SS had summarized his military maxims in the following insight: 'The time for intelligent operational methods is past. In the east the enemy is on our borders. The only type of operation available here is to advance or stand still.'[107]

Himmler concentrated on holding the strongholds of Thorn, Posen, and Schneidemühl. On 30 January 1945 he put forward the commandant of

Schneidemühl, 'as an example of a staunch and undaunted commander and fortress commandant', for a military honour, because the latter had 'personally shot with his own weapon' a number of his retreating soldiers and had ordered a sign to be hung round their necks with 'This is what happens to all cowards' on it.[108] The same day he gave orders for SS-Standartenführer Karl von Salisch, the former police chief of nearby Bromberg, to be shot for 'cowardice', as well as dismissing the former district governor and the city's mayor and having them drafted into a 'probation battalion'.[109] But in the final analysis such drastic measures were the helpless expression of a rigid defensive stance, which was catastrophic for the operational leadership of the army group, and which, according to Eismann's observations, was the result of Himmler's fear of Hitler: 'The dreaded Reichsführer-SS was completely at the mercy of his own fear of Hitler. It made him unable even to present any kind of reading of the military situation to Hitler with forcefulness, let alone to gain acceptance for it. This fundamentally subaltern attitude did much damage and cost a great deal of unnecessary bloodshed.' Eismann was forced to state that Himmler not only 'lacked any previous knowledge and experience for such a difficult and purely military task', but he also complained that the latter as commander of the Reserve Army was incapable of 'obtaining suitable reinforcements of men and materials promptly for his own army group'.

On a visit to Berlin at the beginning of March Himmler met Goebbels, who was surprised at how 'disproportionately optimistic' Himmler was about the situation.[110] Himmler's colleague Eismann had a completely different impression: 'The more unfavourable and difficult the situation became for army group Vistula, the more Himmler realized that there were no laurels he could gather there. He now also doubtless recognized that he was not up to the responsibilities of military leadership and became aware that his enemies in the Führer's headquarters were making the most of this.'[111] Shortly after Hitler visited army group Centre in March Himmler suffered an angina attack. From then on, Eismann recalls, the lectures on the situation took place, if at all, at his sickbed; finally Himmler went to Hohenlychen, to the sanatorium of his schoolfriend Gebhardt, until on 21 March Hitler relieved him of his duties as Commander-in-Chief of army group Vistula.

As military commander of the Volkssturm, commanding officer of the Reserve Army, and last but not least, as Chief of the German Police Himmler still had scope for finding a role in the defence of the Reich. In the final weeks of the war he issued a series of martial decrees designed to ensure steadfastness and create terror. On 28 March 1945, for example, he ordered: 'The displaying of white flags, the removal of anti-tank obstacles, the failure to report for Volkssturm duties, and similar behaviour are to be dealt with with the greatest severity [. . .] All males in a building where a white flag is displayed are to be shot. There must be no delay in implementing these measures.' On the 15 April the order was: 'No German city will be declared an open city. Every village and town will be defended and held by every means possible. Any German man who fails to uphold this fundamental national duty will forfeit his honour and his life.'[112]

In the final months of the war the Gestapo murdered thousands of people. At the latest in February 1945, the lower level regional offices of the Reich Security Main Office were given permission to make their own decisions about the 'special treatment' of prisoners, and Gestapo offices made considerable use of this freedom. At the end of March Himmler issued a command that anyone bearing arms had the right to shoot looters on the spot: in many places, after air raids in particular, the Gestapo therefore killed suspects. In addition, in the last weeks of the war the Gestapo dismantled a large number of their prisons. Those prisoners who had been destined for 'special treatment' or who were not freed by the Allies were shot as part of mass executions. The main victims of all these measures were foreign workers.[113]

Putting out feelers for peace

After the Allies made a successful landing in June 1944, followed in the succeeding weeks by heavy German military defeats, Hitler attempted to break up the Allied coalition by preparing a counter-offensive in the west and by circulating rumours about a separate peace. It is quite clear that he intended to cause confusion by creating the spectre of a separate peace and thus to set about preparing the ground for an actual separate peace treaty. Among Hitler's closest associates these ideas were treated seriously.

When, for example, the Japanese ambassador Hiroshi Oshima apprised Hitler in September 1944 of his government's proposal to approach the Soviet Union with the aim of initiating peace negotiations with Germany, Goebbels encouraged Hitler in a detailed memorandum to make a similar approach to Stalin.[114] In the same month Foreign Minister Ribbentrop sought permission from Hitler to make contact on the broadest basis with the enemy powers, and Hitler had false information spread via Spain about a Soviet offer to make a separate peace in order to lay the bait for the western powers.[115] It is in this context that notes Himmler made in preparation for a discussion with Hitler on 12 September should be viewed. There we read the significant words: 'England or Russia' and 'Russia–Japan'.[116]

A few years ago a short note by Churchill was discovered in the Public Record Office in London that may possibly be connected with these soundings. This note, dated 31 August, reveals that the Secret Service had passed to Churchill a series of documents, including a 'Special Message from Himmler'. It is impossible now to reconstruct the content of this message, as Churchill had made the handwritten comment (which was an extremely unusual occurrence) on the document: 'Himmler telegram left and destroyed by me.'[117] How such a telegram could have been conveyed emerges from a letter from the Spanish Foreign Minister Ramón Serrano Súñer, who at the beginning of 1944 had offered Himmler his good services should the latter wish to make contact with Churchill. Himmler had the letter forwarded to the German Foreign Ministry.[118] Whether he availed himself of this or a similar offer in order to make an approach to Churchill or whether the 'Himmler telegram' refers to something completely different is impossible to establish.[119] Everything, however, points to the fact that he would never have ventured such a step without the agreement of his 'Führer'.

Only after Himmler had been in a position (as commander of the Reserve Army, Commander-in-Chief of the Upper Rhine, Commander of the army group Vistula, and as military head of the Volkssturm) to acquire an impression of the true hopelessness of the military situation did he make a series of attempts, albeit hesitatingly and indecisively to the last, to come to a political agreement to end the war. The fact that Hitler, even in the final stages of the war, was not prepared to initiate serious moves to end it by political means did, however, prove an obstacle to the realization of such ideas of Himmler's. Hitler was realistic enough to recognize that, with the prospect of imminent victory, the Allies would no longer be interested in such proposals, and he was as unwilling to resign as he was to surrender.

The Goebbels diaries indicate that from January 1945 onwards the propaganda minister was in virtually continuous discussions with Hitler about the possibility of making peace, but that in view of the constantly deteriorating military situation Hitler saw such an initiative as bound to fail. Instead, he at first pinned his hopes on a split in the enemy coalition.[120] The (therefore purely theoretical) discussions between Goebbels and Hitler during these months about the prospects for peace thus focused as a rule on the western powers.

At the beginning of March, however, Goebbels was confronted with the news that Hitler considered a separate peace to be a possibility, if at all, only in the east: 'The Führer is convinced that if any of the hostile powers were to enter into talks with us, the Soviet Union would certainly be the first.' On the other hand, 'the war against England' was to be continued 'with the greatest vigour and ruthlessness'. Ribbentrop's efforts 'to put out feelers towards the western countries' were, therefore, 'completely hopeless at the moment'.[121]

Two days after his discussions with Hitler, on 7 March, Goebbels had a two-hour meeting with Himmler at the sanatorium at Hohenlychen. Himmler, who had 'suffered a bad angina attack', looked 'slightly battered' to Goebbels. In the main the two were in complete agreement about 'the situation in general': 'He speaks of Göring and Ribbentrop in the most critical terms, describing them as the two sources of error in our general conduct of the war, and he is absolutely right.' As Goebbels noted, Himmler was 'very worried' about the situation at the front, but even more so about food supplies. 'The morale of the troops is without doubt affected. Himmler admits this on the basis of the experience of the army group Vistula.' But in addition and above all, 'neither in the military nor in the civilian sector do we have strong leadership at the centre, because everything has to be put to the Führer himself and yet that is feasible in only a very few cases. Göring and Ribbentrop are obstacles at every turn to a successful conduct of the war.'

What, therefore, should be done? It was, after all, impossible 'to force Hitler to break with the two of them'. This comment suggests that at this meeting there may have been talk of using more forceful methods of making Hitler adopt another political course, yet both were wary of taking this idea further. According to Goebbels,

Himmler sums up the situation correctly in what he says. His reason tells him that we have little hope of winning the war by military means, but his instinct tells him that in the long run a political route will open up so that we can still turn the war in our favour. Himmler sees this possibility more in the west than in the east. He believes that England will come to its senses, though I am somewhat doubtful about that. Himmler's analysis shows he is focused completely on the west and expects nothing from the east.

Goebbels took a different view, as is shown by his diary comments on Himmler's statements: 'I believe we would achieve more in the east and that Stalin is more realistic than the English–American maniacs.' What, according to his own notes, he did not tell Himmler, was that the latter's judgement that it was in the west that a political solution was to be sought was diametrically opposed to Hitler's. By keeping this fact from him he advisedly allowed Himmler and his western option to slide into a political blind alley. He left the Reichsführer in a reasonably cheerful mood: 'In the atmosphere surrounding Himmler there is something very nice, modest, and absolutely National Socialist, and this has an extraordinarily beneficial effect. One can only be thankful that, at least as far as Himmler is concerned, the old National Socialist spirit still prevails.'[122]

A few days later Goebbels was obliged to comment that Hitler was harbouring considerable resentment against the Reichsführer. 'The Führer is placing a large part of the blame directly on Himmler. He says he was continually ordering Himmler to move our troops to Pomerania, and that as a result of repeated indications from the Department of Foreign Armies he made the mistake of believing in the push towards Berlin and making corresponding dispositions.' Even when he, Hitler, gave clear orders, they were 'constantly undermined by secret sabotage. In this regard he levels the most severe reproaches at Himmler [...] Clearly Himmler fell victim to the General Staff the moment he took over as army group commander. The Führer accuses him of rank disobedience and intends on the next occasion to give him a piece of his mind and impress on him that if such a thing should occur again the result would be an irreparable rupture between them.' Goebbels added: 'I regarded entrusting Himmler with the command of an army group as a mistake in the first place. In the present situation that is not what he should be doing, particularly not if it might lead to a rupture with the Führer.'

And this breach evidently went far deeper still. Hitler confided to Goebbels that if, as Goebbels had suggested, he had transferred the supreme command of the army to Himmler 'the catastrophe would have been even worse than it is anyway'—an altogether damning verdict for Himmler.[123] In the days that followed Hitler was to send Goebbels the minutes of his military briefings so the latter could see for himself that his 'Führer' had in fact warned of a Soviet push towards Pomerania in the face of contradiction from his military advisers.[124]

Hitler informed Goebbels two days later that Himmler bore 'the historic guilt for the fact that [...] Pomerania and a large part of its population had fallen into Soviet hands'.[125] Goebbels, however, was intelligent enough to recognize that this failure was rooted in the system: unfortunately, he wrote, Hitler had 'neglected to convert his opinion, which was based more on intuition than on knowledge, into clear orders. As a result everyone has done what he wanted, including Himmler.' Goebbels was clear-sighted about the issue: 'Rather than making long speeches to his military colleagues, the Führer would do better to give them brief orders but then to ensure with ruthless rigour that these orders are obeyed. The many routs we have suffered at the front are the result of poor leadership methods and wrong information.'[126]

On 15 March, the following day, Hitler informed his propaganda minister that Himmler had been to see him and that he had given him 'an extraordinarily vigorous dressing down'.[127] At the same time, or a few days later, Hitler also let Goebbels know that he intended to remove Himmler from the command of the army group Vistula. Goebbels commented on Himmler's unsuccessful excursion into the higher echelons of the military command as follows: 'Unfortunately, he was tempted to chase after military laurels, but he has been a complete failure. He's bound to destroy his good political reputation by this.'[128]

In spite of this dishonourable discharge, Himmler, after his sudden recovery, insisted, as Colonel Eismann records, 'on celebrating in grand style the transfer of command to his successor', though inevitably his 'theatrical swansong, which was not clouded by any kind of specialist knowledge, made a strange and indeed positively repellent impression in the midst of such an extremely grave situation'.[129]

At the end of March another serious occurrence caused a further deterioration in the relationship between Hitler and Himmler. Hitler accused, of all people, the 'Leibstandarte'—the original core unit of the armed SS, which during the whole of the war had been deployed repeatedly in critical military situations and suffered heavy losses, and whose leader, Sepp Dietrich, was celebrated by the Nazi media as a war hero—of failure on the Hungarian front, and compelled Himmler to issue the so-called 'armband order': members of the unit were made to remove the strip with the words 'Leibstandarte Adolf Hitler' from their uniforms—an extraordinary humiliation for the SS and its Reichsführer.[130]

When, in March 1945, Himmler was giving more intense thought to the possibility of taking soundings towards ending the war by political means, he was doing so, therefore, in a situation in which he had failed as an army commander and had been seriously discredited in Hitler's eyes. In the weeks previously he had pursued his old idea of using Jewish prisoners as hostages, and it appears that his escalating conflict with Hitler strengthened his resolve to develop this project into a political mission. As the Third Reich was conducting a war against the Jews, the key to ending the war logically lay in the latter's hands.

In mid-March Himmler's personal physician Felix Kersten, who had moved to Sweden and had offered his services to the Swedish Foreign Minister as an intermediary, came to Germany, where he still had an estate. Himmler told him that the concentration camps would not be blown up as the Allies advanced; further killings there were forbidden and the prisoners were instead to be handed over to the Allies.[131] He was to reaffirm this several times in the following days,[132] and a short time later Himmler did in fact issue the order to camp commandants not to kill any more Jewish prisoners and to take all measures to reduce mortality among them. The order was delivered to the commandants by Pohl personally.[133]

Back in Stockholm Kersten informed his link-man to the World Jewish Congress, Hillel Storch, that Himmler had in addition declared his willingness to release 10,000 Jewish prisoners to Sweden or Switzerland.[134] As early as February Himmler had been in direct contact concerning the release of prisoners with the Vice-President of the Swedish Red Cross, Count Folke Bernadotte, who acted on behalf of the Swedish government. Himmler met Bernadotte for the first time on 19 February, when the latter was in Germany, and again at the beginning of March.[135]

Agreement was reached that Scandinavian concentration-camp inmates should first be assembled at Neuengamme, and finally Bernadotte, who was continually including new groups of prisoners in his demands, gained consent for them to be brought by Swedish Red Cross medical teams via Denmark to Sweden. Himmler's assent, given to Kersten, to the release of 10,000 prisoners was an important step forward in this negotiation process. In fact far more than the 8,000 Swedish prisoners—actually more than 20,000 people—were to be rescued.[136]

Bernadotte was, however, surprised at the manners and behaviour of his opposite number, as he noted after their discussion in February: 'He appeared strikingly, indeed astoundingly, obliging, showed his sense of humour, even a touch of gallows humour, a number of times and liked to make a joke to lighten the tone a little.'[137] It is quite obvious that Himmler was still versatile and in the process of changing roles again in the very last phase of the Third Reich, by presenting himself as a poised and conciliatory negotiating partner who was at pains to bring things to a sensible conclusion.

After visiting Himmler in mid-March, Kersten also brought to Sweden a letter to himself from the Reichsführer. It is one of the most surprising documents that Himmler wrote in his entire time as Reichsführer-SS. In the letter Himmler first gave Kersten official notification of the release of the 2,700 Jewish men, women, and children to Switzerland, and added: 'This is to all intents and purposes the continuation of the course my colleagues and I had been pursuing consistently for many years until the war and the unreason unleashed by it in the world made it impossible to carry through.' From 1936 to 1940, he goes on, 'in conjunction with Jewish-American organizations', he had worked intensively towards a solution through emigration, with 'very beneficial' results. 'The journey of the two trains to Switzerland', the Reichsführer-SS continues, 'is, in spite of all difficulties, the deliberate resumption of this beneficial process.'

Himmler then felt obliged to refer to the situation at the Bergen–Belsen camp. He wrote that on hearing the rumour that 'a typhus epidemic of catastrophic proportions had broken out', he immediately sent a team led by his chief medical officer of health to the camp. 'Cases of this type of epidemic typhus' were 'very often found in camps containing people from the east, but should be regarded as under control through the use of the best modern clinical treatments'. Finally, he said he was sure that 'if demagoguery and superficialities are excluded and all differences set aside, wisdom and reason, along with humane sentiments and the willingness to help, will inevitably, notwithstanding the bloodiest wounds, come to the fore among all parties'. He concluded the letter 'with all good wishes'.[138]

The effrontery of this letter is breathtaking: did Himmler really believe that by posing as a detached, humanitarian intermediary he could construct a negotiating position with the western Allies? After all, by this point the concentration camps of Majdanek and Auschwitz had long since been liberated, and for months detailed reports about mass murder in gas chambers had been circulating in the international press. Confronted with his own downfall, had Himmler drifted into a world of illusions?

From a biographical perspective another explanation for his behaviour can be found: for him it was simply important to preserve the outward forms until the very end, and he did this by adding to the various roles he had assumed during the Nazi dictatorship a further one, that of the honest broker. If the chance arose to establish contact with the western Allies via Bernadotte or other intermediaries, to extend the human trafficking, and possibly also to begin negotiating about a separate peace, then the other side would not be dealing with an ice-cold, calculating Reichsführer-SS who presided over life and death, but rather (and Himmler's letter to Kersten was designed to pave the way for this) his negotiating partners would have to accept him in the role of a man of honour guided by the best intentions.

On the Allied side, it must be said, there was a different view. When the Swedish representative of the World Jewish Congress suggested involving the British embassy in the transfer of prisoners to Sweden, the British Foreign Secretary Eden wrote to Churchill that he was unwilling to have anything to do with the business, and for one reason only: Himmler was behind it. Churchill wrote 'good' on the report, and noted clearly in the margin: 'No link with Himmler.'[139]

On 2 April Bernadotte had a further meeting with Himmler. After his return to Stockholm the Count informed the British ambassador, Victor Mallet, about their discussions.[140] According to Bernadotte's report, Himmler now, in contrast to the previous meeting, gave the impression of a man who knew all was lost. When Bernadotte suggested that the best course of action was now to surrender, Himmler responded that Hitler opposed any such move and he felt bound by his oath.

Himmler knew, Bernadotte said, that he was No. 1 on the Allied list of war criminals; he had complained that outside Germany he would be regarded as brutal. In fact he loathed brutality. When, thereupon, Bernadotte reproached him with a concrete instance of a massacre by the Gestapo, Himmler at first denied it but at a further meeting the following day conceded that, on the basis of enquiries he had made in the meantime, this regrettable incident had in fact taken place. After this conversation Himmler sent a message to Bernadotte via his secret-service chief Walter Schellenberg to say that, in the event of Hitler's radically revising his position, he hoped that Bernadotte would go to Allied headquarters and attempt to mediate. Was this an attempt to introduce the possibility of a coup? Bernadotte took pains to get to the bottom of it, and a few days later had the message sent that he would be prepared to make an attempt at mediation if Himmler assumed power in Germany and dissolved the NSDAP.[141]

Himmler remained indecisive, however, even as the days passed. He could neither bring himself to declare himself Hitler's successor and then offer the Allies the Reich's capitulation—a step even the serving Finance Minister, Ludwig Count Schwerin von Krosigk, advised him to take on 19 April—nor was he prepared to brace himself for a partial military capitulation in northern Germany.[142]

On 19 April a further emissary travelled from Sweden to Germany. To Kersten, Himmler had declared himself willing to speak directly to a representative of the World Jewish Congress. Hillel Storch asked Norbert Masur, a Jew of German descent who had emigrated to Sweden, to take on this mission. The two-and-a-half-hour discussion took place during the night of 20–1 April at Kersten's property near Berlin and lasted until five in the morning. In addition to Masur and Himmler, who had just arrived from Hitler's last birthday celebration, Schellenberg, Brandt (Himmler's private secretary), and Kersten were also there.

In this discussion too Himmler played the role of the man of honour. In lengthy explanations to his Jewish guest he tried to defend, or else to gloss over, the regime's policy towards the Jews. The first plan had been the emigration of the Jews, but after the outbreak of war the regime had been confronted with hostile masses of eastern Jews who had to be brought under control. The war against the Soviet Union had been forced on Germany, he claimed; in view of the dreadful conditions in the east many Jews had died, but many Germans had suffered in the war as well. The concentration camps had been severe but just. Yes, there had been abuses, but he had punished those who were to blame. As a result of epidemics the death-rate had been high, and that was why they had been forced to build large crematoria.

Himmler gave figures for the number of Jews still alive in the individual concentration camps, and claimed that 150,000 had been left behind in Auschwitz and 450,000 in Budapest. This greatly exaggerated total for the number of survivors was clearly a brazen lie. He then complained that although he had handed over the camps of Bergen-Belsen and Buchenwald, atrocity stories were being circulated as propaganda about the alleged horrific conditions in the camps and he was being blamed personally. Nobody had been dragged through the mud by the press in the last few years as much as he.

At this time reports and pictures of the Bergen-Belsen camp, which had been handed over to the British army on 15 April, were in fact circulating in the world's press: between January 1945 and the liberation 35,000 prisoners had died in the camp, which was piled high with unburied corpses, and a further 14,000 died in the first two months after the liberation.[143] Buchenwald had been liberated on 11 April; in the preceding days the SS had transferred more than half of the prisoners elsewhere. There was no hand-over of the camp.

Masur repeatedly objected to Himmler's blatantly false presentation of events, but was nevertheless determined to listen to the essential points in the latter's sermon in order not to put his mission in jeopardy. Overall, according to his estimation, Himmler gave the impression of being intelligent, educated, and historically aware. For the most part, Masur recorded, Himmler had spoken calmly even when the discussion had become controversial. His tense inner state had, all the same, been evident. Another thing struck Masur: Himmler's need to keep talking, which was almost unstoppable.

Finally, Himmler declared to Masur that he was ready to hand over a thousand Jewish women from Ravensbrück to the Red Cross, and additionally a series of smaller groups of prisoners of various nationalities. By then the discussion had touched on every possible political question, and Himmler had exploited the opportunity to give a wide-ranging defence of the regime. It was possible to infer from this account that he considered Germany's defeat to be inevitable. The country would not, however, surrender, he said. He himself had no fear of death. The best of the German nation, as he had told Kersten on parting, would perish with the Nazi leadership, and what happened to the rest was of no importance.[144]

Bernadotte was to meet Himmler on two more occasions: first of all early on 21 April, immediately after Himmler's talks with Masur, in Hohenlychen, where Bernadotte achieved further concessions with regard to the release of prisoners,[145] and finally after Himmler had called for him once again—in the meantime the Reichsführer had been forced to leave Hohenlychen for the north-west because of the approach of Soviet troops, and had established himself with a fairly large entourage in the police barracks in Lübeck.[146]

In the night of 23–4 April the two men met in the Swedish consulate in Lübeck. Himmler declared to him, according to Bernadotte's account of the conversation,[147] that Hitler had turned away from life and would be dead in a few days. He, Himmler, now felt entitled to act even without Hitler's consent. Now he asked Bernadotte straight out to convey to the Swedish government his wish to arrange a meeting with Eisenhower, so that the German western front could surrender. The eastern front would be held as long as possible. Although Bernadotte immediately explained that he considered such an initiative to be unrealistic, he declared himself willing to communicate Himmler's request on condition that Denmark and Norway were included in the offer of surrender. Himmler agreed. Beyond that, Himmler told Bernadotte, if his offer were refused he would take over command of a battalion on the eastern front and die in battle.[148]

In the days that followed Himmler waited anxiously for a response. On 28 April, at the Wehrmacht High Command, he chanced to meet Grand Admiral Karl Dönitz, supreme commander of the navy, and asked if the latter would be ready to assume a 'role in the state' in the event of Hitler no longer being in Berlin and a successor having taken over his office. In making his offer Himmler had already made it plain whom he regarded as Hitler's successor.[149]

Bernadotte confidentially informed the British and American ambassadors in Stockholm about his meeting with Himmler. In addition, Himmler had given Bernadotte a letter to the Swedish Foreign Minister, Christian Günther. As expected, the western powers turned down the offer of a partial surrender, and exposed Himmler—who had expressed to Schellenberg[150] his fears of that very thing happening—to all the world by publishing his offer at the end of April in the world's press.

Charles de Gaulle, President of the provisional French government, tells in his memoirs of a final attempt by Himmler to get his head out of the noose: via 'unofficial channels', he had received a memorandum from Himmler with an offer of an alliance. France was to join with a defeated Germany to prevent a situation where it was treated by the Anglo-Saxon powers as a satellite state. De Gaulle, for whom this train of thought 'unquestionably contained a grain of truth', could not bring himself to respond to the friendly proposal—for, as he succinctly put it, Himmler had 'nothing to offer'.[151]

Meanwhile, on 29 April Hitler in his Berlin bunker had also learned of Himmler's initiative from the international press. He flew into a rage. In his Political Testament, written the same day—the day before his suicide—he expelled 'the former Reichsführer-SS and Reich Minister of the Interior Heinrich Himmler' from the party and from all offices of state. To complete the picture, it is worth mentioning that Himmler's successors were the Breslau Gauleiter Karl Hanke, as Reichsführer-SS, and the Gauleiter and Bavarian Prime Minister Paul Giesler, as Reich Minister of the Interior. Hitler used his testament to heap further blame on Himmler; Göring, who a few days before had also been removed from all his offices for flouting Hitler's authority, was similarly criticized. As Hitler wrote, 'through secret negotiations with the enemy, which they held without my knowledge and against my will, and through their attempt in defiance of the law to seize power in the state,' both had 'done untold damage to the country and to the whole nation, quite apart from their treachery towards me personally'.[152]

The accusation of being a faithless traitor to his leader and his country was sure to be an extraordinarily heavy blow to Himmler, the more so because he no doubt considered it unjust. He had delayed his initiative to the very last moment, until the day, 22 April, that he heard from Führer headquarters about Hitler's last briefing, at which the 'Führer' declared that he was no longer in a position to give orders and thereby had effectively abdicated. Himmler had good reason to assume that, after Hitler had excluded himself, he had the right, in the name of the Reich leadership, to initiate a move to end the war by political means, as it was impossible to tell whether Hitler, who seemed to have lapsed into passivity, had settled on the succession. Yet Himmler did not realize that behind Hitler's withdrawal of 22 April was his calculation that, while keeping a door open for last-minute negotiations, he could nevertheless hold onto the possibility to the last of distancing himself once more from the peace soundings, should they fail, and of thus not tarnishing his historical reputation with the disgrace of surrender.[153]

As the last chapter of the history of the concentration camps shows, Himmler failed to keep his agreement given to Kersten in March to hand over the camps to the approaching Allied troops. Although Bergen–Belsen had been handed over, this was only because the outbreak of a typhus epidemic prevented any further 'evacuations'.[154] Meanwhile Dora-Mittel-bau and Buchenwald were cleared at the beginning of April on his express orders. Of the total of 48,000 inmates at Buchenwald the SS removed some 28,000; by the end of the war at least a third of them had died.

In the middle of April the group of officers in the SS Business and Administrative Main Office responsible for the concentration camps had a final meeting at which, in line with a directive from Himmler, it is very likely that the evacuation of the last camps not yet liberated by the Allies was discussed. The camps in question were Sachsenhausen, Dachau,

Neuengamme, Flossenbürg, and Ravensbrück. There is proof that Himmler instructed Dachau and Flossenbürg directly that no living prisoners were to fall into enemy hands. In the days that followed the SS leadership also refused requests by the Red Cross for the last camps to be handed over.

The fact that Himmler broke his word is probably attributable on the one hand to fear that his consent would be taken by Hitler, who disapproved strongly of his trade with concentration-camp prisoners, as a breach of confidence. On the other, the world should not be deceived by Himmler's appearance in the guise of a humanitarian intermediary: he was prepared to save human lives only if he received tangible returns from the opposing side. He still viewed prisoners as human capital, and intended to exploit them to the end as bargaining-tools—hence his determination to keep them with him at every stage of his retreat.

In view of the emerging division of the as yet unoccupied parts of the Reich, the last death marches went in two separate directions. Prisoners from Flossenbürg and Dachau marched southwards, while those from Ravensbrück, Sachsenhausen, and Neuengamme marched north. These evacuation marches collapsed into chaos, and frequently a large proportion of the prisoners were shot by the guards. At the end of April more than 3,000 prisoners were transported in indescribable conditions by ship from Stutthof near Danzig to Neustadt on the Bay of Lübeck, where those who had survived the rigours of the voyage were killed on the beach by guards and marines. American troops liberated Flossenbürg on 23 April, Dachau on 29 April, and Mauthausen on 5 May.[155] Of the more than 714,000 prisoners still in the concentration-camp system at the beginning of 1945, estimates suggest that between 240,000 and 360,000 fell victim to the evacuations.[156]

On the run

Himmler's crowded diary in the last months of the Third Reich did not allow for any more visits to his family in Gmund or to his mistress Hedwig Potthast and their children in Berchtesgaden. Letters and telephone-calls acted as a substitute. Both women were unswervingly loyal to him to the end; no evidence has survived that suggests they came to have any doubts about their relationship with this mass-murderer or about their life at his side.

On 16 January Margarete Himmler received a visit from her brother-in-law Gebhard, Heinrich's elder brother. Her diary entry makes one suspect that Gebhard—who since 1933 had enjoyed rapid success in his brother's slipstream in his career in vocational training—had, in view of the imminent destruction of the Third Reich, brought up the fatal role his brother had played in it and the fact that the Himmler family were actually staunch Catholics. If his intention had been to cause Margarete to reflect in some manner, then this attempt was a total failure. 'He then wanted to have a talk with me on my own. I sensed something unpleasant was coming. But that it would become so awful, hearing him say such mean things about other people, and that he would talk about his parents and Heini, raising his eyes to heaven in that Catholic way! I'll never understand it.'[157] Two weeks later she wrote of Heinrich: 'How wonderful that he has been called to great tasks and is equal to them. The whole of Germany is looking to him.'[158] On 21 February she noted that she intended to stay in Gmund, as that was what Heinrich wanted.[159]

Margarete remained in contact with Himmler into April. Then she left Gmund as American troops were advancing. Mother and daughter fled towards the south and fetched up in a British internment camp in Italy. A British Secret Service officer who questioned both of them thought that no interrogation was necessary, as his impression was that Margarete's life had remained relatively unaffected by her husband's professional activities. He also attested that Himmler's wife had retained a 'small-town mentality'.[160]

Hedwig Potthast saw Himmler for the last time in March in Hohenlychen, returning from there to her house in Berchtesgaden. After that both spoke daily on the telephone, with the last conversation on 19 April. 'Even though I am still telling myself that the new year will be hard, perhaps burdensome,' she had written almost cheerfully to him in her last New Year letter, 'I am almost curious to see what it will bring. Above all I wish you strength for the task you have been entrusted with by the Führer and the fatherland.' A few of her letters from January 1945 are preserved, basically describing her daily life in Berchtesgaden: she reported on their children's progress, and we learn that she kept up neighbourly contact with the Bormanns and that Frau Fegelein, Eva Braun's sister, paid her visits. She also enjoyed the winter scenery in Berchtesgaden. 'Why is it that you can't ski?, she asks in the last existing letter, dated 12 January 1945.[161] Indeed: Why had Himmler never learnt to ski?!

Cut off from his family and his second family, and still in the Lübeck police barracks, Himmler tried, after the failure of his attempt to make contact with Eisenhower, to defend himself against the charge of being a faithless traitor. In a radio message of 30 April to Kaltenbrunner, who had set up his headquarters in southern Germany, he distanced himself from Allied reports about his talks with Bernadotte, and about an announcement of the Führer's death, which he had allegedly written. The fight, as he stressed, must be continued under all circumstances.[162]

That same day he was paid an unexpected visit by Grand Admiral Dönitz, who had just received a radio message from Bormann from the Führer's bunker in Berlin informing him of Himmler's treachery and calling on him unequivocally to take 'swift and implacable' measures against all traitors. Dönitz confronted Himmler with the accusations that he had sought contact with the Allies behind Hitler's back, which Himmler denied. Dönitz, who—by contrast with Himmler—had no instruments of power at his command, noted this declaration of innocence and returned to his headquarters in Plön. There news arrived, still on the same day, that meanwhile the succession as laid down in Hitler's will 'had come into force'. In this manner Dönitz heard the news of Hitler's death and that he was to succeed him.[163]

Dönitz thereupon asked Himmler to come and see him; he arrived during the night accompanied by six armed SS men. Dönitz informed him about the dispositions for the succession. Visibly shaken, Himmler immediately offered himself as 'second-in-command', an offer that Dönitz refused with thanks, pointing to the non-political nature of the government he was to head.[164]

Himmler reappeared several times unbidden in Dönitz's headquarters, until on 6 May the latter officially dismissed him as Reich Minister of the Interior (Hitler's dismissal of Himmler in his testament had, in the view of those concerned, never become legally effective). The dismissal had been preceded by negotiations with Himmler, who was still trying to gain some form of official recognition from the new government in his capacity as Reichsführer-SS. After his dismissal it was made clear to Himmler that he was to keep his distance from the seat of government, whatever it did.[165] Walter Lüdde-Neurath, the Grand Admiral's adjutant, and Count Schwerin von Krosigk, Dönitz's Foreign Minister, both agree in their memoirs that at this time Himmler made a decidedly optimistic, cheerful impression and spoke of how he and his SS would take on an important role in the emerging post-war order, while claiming that if that were not to come off he could manage to go into hiding.[166] To conclude from this that Himmler harboured illusions even up to May 1945 about his future fate would be going too far. Others who observed him more closely during these days gained the opposite impression. To Bernadotte, Himmler appeared in April to be exhausted and under great strain—'he was manifestly having a serious battle to maintain the external appearance of calm'[167]—and Schellenberg similarly describes Himmler as in an extremely agitated state that he was unable to control.[168]

Throughout his life Himmler had been at pains to govern and conceal his emotions and responses, to present himself to others as even-tempered and very positive, and, whenever circumstances permitted, to be as amiable as possible to those with whom he had dealings. As he saw it, his office, his position with regard to his subordinates and vis-à-vis his negotiating partners required such a demeanour. For that reason nothing definitive can be said about his actual state of mind in those days. The reports of Schellenberg and Bernadotte indicate that he was fighting against the threat of psychological breakdown, concerned to maintain his vaunted self-discipline and self-control.

To the end he made ever more hectic attempts to find some kind of solution to avert his inevitable downfall. As he may have told himself, he still had considerable instruments of power at his disposal: several Waffen-SS divisions remained under his command, and in the territory not yet occupied by the Allies he was in charge of the organization of the Reserve Army, had command of the police, the Volkssturm, his network of agents, and finally of the terror organization Werewolf, which was to be active behind enemy lines. In addition, he was holding hundreds of thousands of prisoners in the camps as bartering-counters.

At the beginning of May, when all attempts had failed, he stood empty-handed. He had not managed to make really effective preparations for flight or for a life under cover of a false identity. To whom could the head of the SS and police apparatus turn with a request like that, without appearing to his staff as a boss whose calls for endurance and whose displays of optimism had simply been empty rhetoric?

Thus, his only recourse was to a forged paybook that gave his identity as Sergeant Heinrich Hitzinger, the name he chose hinting at his inner reservations about actually denying his identity. As far as disguising his appearance was concerned, though he had got himself some civilian clothing and an eyepatch he had not even changed his spectacles. To the end he was recognizable as who he was: Heinrich Himmler.

In practical terms he was equipped for suicide. Like all Nazi leaders he possessed lethal poison. Yet beyond that he had evidently made no preparations at all regarding the circumstantial aspects of a possible suicide. He had neither chosen a place of significance (for example, some north German Germanic sanctum) nor does he appear to have drawn up a declaration in the event of his death, or, as far as one can tell, written a farewell letter. To die in a last battle, as he had proclaimed he would, was not something he wanted to do either, and he lacked the decisiveness to hand himself over officially as a prisoner as, for example, Göring had done. To present himself candidly to the Allies, take responsibility for his deeds and misdeeds, and defend his SS men—even had he possessed the courage to take this path, he had blocked it off through his own contradictory behaviour in the previous weeks and months. He could calculate that in any war-crimes trial not only his crimes would come out but also his attempts to use lies, deception, and shady deals involving human lives to avert at the last moment the downfall threatening him and save his own skin. How, for instance, could he explain the letter that he had given Kersten in March, in which he had pretended to be working for a humanitarian solution to the 'Jewish question'?

All that remained for him in this situation was to go on the run in a more or less aimless way. On 11 May, now superficially disguised as Sergeant Heinrich Hitzinger, he left the Flensburg area together with his private secretary Rudolf Brandt, his adjutant Werner Grothmann, and a further adjutant by the name of Heinz Macher, Heinrich Müller, the chief of the Gestapo, and the chief of his personal security service, Josef Kiermaier. The group of six men went first to Friedrichskoog in the district of Dithmarschen, about 100 kilometres to the south.

In Friedrichskoog the weather was bad. Not until 15 or 16 May could the six men cross the Elbe estuary, which was several kilometres wide, in a fishing-boat and continue their journey to Neuhaus in Lower Saxony; according to Grothmann, the intention was to get to the Harz mountains, where Himmler would hide out for a time and then make his way to the Alps. After Neuhaus they travelled on foot to the Meinstedt area. There Brandt, Müller, and Kiermaier split off from the group in order to have their identification papers stamped by the British commandant of the town, but never returned. Müller was the only member of the group who actually succeeded in disappearing without trace.

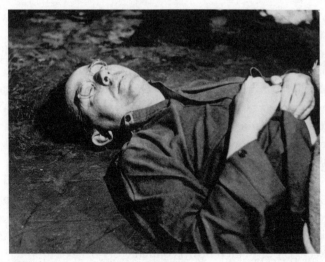

Ill. 32 Himmler's corpse

Himmler, Grothmann, and Macher continued their march, but on 21 May they landed at a checkpoint near Bremerförde, which had been set up by Soviet POWs released from captivity. On this and the following two days Himmler was sent to several camps, one after the other, until—exhausted but outwardly calm, and without visible emotion—he stood before his British interrogators, who had in the meantime ascertained his identity. The fact that from his perspective only suicide was now an option will have become clear to him during these hours. He could determine only its timing now, and this he wanted to delay. When, however, it became evident that in the course of an alleged medical examination an attempt would be made to remove the poison capsule concealed in his mouth, the moment had arrived: by biting on the capsule he could remain in control to the last.[169]

Conclusion

What role did Reichsführer-SS Heinrich Himmler play in the history of National Socialism? How can his contribution to the 'German catastrophe' be assessed?

These are the central questions that I have pursued in this biography. If in a number of the preceding chapters I have focused quite intensively on the development of Himmler's personality, then this was not because I was assuming it would be possible to attribute the Reichsführer's later misdeeds solely to a defective personality development—for example, to his having suffered childhood trauma or having been socialized in an environment where violence was accepted. Psychoanalytical interpretations have not been the focus of this historical biography. If, however, it is possible to strip away the outer layers to reveal some kind of core personality, then a sensible interconnection between biography and structural history can help us to a better understanding of his political actions. The picture that emerges can be summed up as follows.

Nothing in Himmler's childhood and youth, spent in a sheltered, conservative Catholic home typical of the educated bourgeoisie of Wilhelmine Germany, would suggest that someone with clearly abnormal characteristics was growing up there. There are no indications at all of any particular problems with his upbringing, of any marked tendency to be cruel, or any noticeable aggressiveness; and it would certainly also be mistaken to see Himmler's later development as decisively determined by a father–son conflict rooted in an unusually authoritarian upbringing, even granted that the Himmler household was indeed very strict and his father monitored Heinrich down to the detail of how he structured his diary—a tendency to overstep personal boundaries that Himmler was to demonstrate later in life in different circumstances with regard to his SS men. With the exception of minor skirmishes, however, he does not seem to have reached the point of rebelling against his father; nor is there any evidence of serious political differences between father and son.

If a key to Himmler's personality is sought in his childhood and adolescence, it is his obvious weaknesses that are striking, and above all the counter-measures he took to overcome them. Physically weak and often unwell, Heinrich was emotionally inhibited and backward in his social development: he suffered from an attachment disorder that made it difficult for him to build up strong and lasting relationships. Throughout his life Himmler was to struggle with these difficulties, which determined his behaviour towards others. Yet he learned to compensate for these deficiencies or to disguise them, on the one hand by means of the strong tendency towards self-control and self-discipline rooted in his upbringing, and on the other by positively drilling himself in the forms and practices of social intercourse.

For Himmler, who was born in 1900, as for many of his generation, the First World War with its far-reaching consequences represented a rupture with the past. Himmler became part of the so-called war youth generation, which, although united by the experience of the war, itself suffered from a complex caused by having been too young to take an active part in it. Though trained as an ensign in 1918, Himmler had no opportunity to serve in the military.

The fact that he had not had the chance to prove himself in combat was responsible in significant measure for his continuing to model himself as a young man on the concept of the ideal soldier, even after he left the army; he regarded himself henceforth primarily as an officer who had been prevented from exercising his vocation. This attitude explains his decision to study agriculture, which was typical of disbanded officers who, seeing themselves as warriors in waiting, were passing the time until the next great conflict by acquiring the skills to earn a living but above all by engaging in a huge range of paramilitary activities.

This soldierly world, which can be summed up in the words: sobriety, distance, severity, objectivity, but also order and regulations, particularly appealed to Himmler with his lack of self-confidence. He was constantly indulging in self-stylizations as a soldierly man, although they remained confined to the realms of the imagination. Though a member of various paramilitary organizations, he took no part in any fighting in the immediate post-war period. The fact that there was little place for women in this male world made it even more attractive to him, as someone with evident difficulties in relating to women. Himmler was determined, as a soldierly man, not to give in to erotic temptations, and when he was in the grip of them he tried to suppress them with images of violence and war or to act them out through his penchant for voyeurism. He compensated for his lack of experience by interfering in the private lives of others, a tendency that can also be observed when he was Reichsführer-SS. It was only much later that he discerned 'homosexual dangers' in this way of life, with its protective cocoon of male solidarity and its self-imposed celibacy, and this was a disturbing insight that strengthened his latent homophobia.

In the years immediately following the First World War Himmler lived in a fantasy world shaped by the paramilitary subculture of the German post-war period; he came into contact with the reality of the Weimar Republic only in 1922, when as a result of the inflation he was unable to embark on a second programme of study and was forced to take up a post as an assistant in a factory that produced fertilizers. In the meantime he had been awarded a diploma in agricultural studies. It was precisely at this point that his politicization and commitment to the radical Right began. Himmler had originally regarded himself as a supporter of the German Nationalist Party, but the general radicalization of politics in Bavaria in 1922–3, and the fact that right-wing conservatives and right-wing radicals merged from time to time, smoothed the way for him to join the Nazis. In doing so he may well have been impressed more by the strong presence of the Nazi movement in the paramilitary world than by the political party as such. His model in this period was above all Ernst Röhm, not Adolf Hitler. It was not until 1923–4 that he gradually developed a coherent völkisch vision, involving also a rejection of the Catholic faith. To the essential elements of this ideology— anti-Semitism, extreme nationalism, racism, and a rejection of modernity— he added occult beliefs and Germanophile enthusiasms; from these elements arose an ideology that was a mixture of political utopia, romantic dream-world, and substitute religion.

The failure of the putsch of 9 November 1923, the subsequent banning of the Nazi Party, and the general economic and political normalization left Himmler, who had now given up his job, on the brink of personal and political bankruptcy. And yet this young man from a comfortably off family decided to remain loyal to the political far Right and harness his professional future to it. His highly developed powers of endurance, coupled with an indulgence in political illusions, his self-image as a soldier, and the fact that he could see no professional alternative are all likely factors in his decision to commit himself to what at that point was hardly a promising cause. In addition we see a character trait emerging that was to manifest itself repeatedly in Himmler's political life: failure led him neither to give up nor to turn back, but rather to redouble his efforts in pursuing the goal he had set himself, even if he was to learn to do this in a very flexible manner that corresponded to the power relations at the time. It was precisely these features of his personality that made him persevere with the NSDAP in the coming lean years and made him appear suitable for a 'soldierly' role within the party's paramilitary activities. After a few years as a rural agitator and then as a low-ranking official in the Munich Party Office, and still under the wing of his mentor Gregor Strasser, in 1927 he became deputy Reichsführer of the protection squads, who acted as bodyguards to party members. From the perspective of the party leadership it made sense to place the organization of speaking engagements by prominent party members (for which Himmler, as deputy Reich propaganda chief, was responsible) and their protection in the same hands. Although up to this point he had frequently failed to make a good impression, it was in this position that he finally showed what he could do, and at the beginning of 1929 the leadership of the still fairly insignificant SS fell into his lap.

Himmler now set about building up the SS, which at the point when he took it over comprised only a few hundred members, into the National Socialist movement's second paramilitary organization. He was helped in this by the long-standing conflict between the party leadership and the SA, which erupted twice, in the summer of 1930 and the spring of 1931, into revolts, above all on the part of the Berlin SA. On both occasions Himmler placed the SS at the party's disposal as a reliable means of protection. Though the SS remained subordinate to the SA leadership under Röhm, his old mentor, Himmler was nevertheless successful in making the SS stand out as clearly distinct from the SA. His SS was more disciplined, did not provoke the party, and, by contrast with the ruffians in the SA, saw itself as an elite, a feature that manifested itself not least in what purported to be racial criteria for acceptance and permission to marry. Himmler regarded the SS as the racial vanguard for future 'Blood and Soil' policies, a claim he strengthened through his alliance with Richard Walther Darré, the party's agrarian expert and settlement ideologue. In contrast to the ideal of rough, unfettered masculinity propagated by the SA, Himmler advanced the deliberately 'soldierly' image of the SS man, who should, if possible, be head of a clan (*Sippe*) with many children. Himmler's own new orientation is reflected in this: in 1927 the man who had been a 'lonely freebooter' entered into a relationship with Margatete Boden, seven years his senior, and married her in 1928. In 1929 their only child was born.

As this survey of Himmler's development in his 'formative years' reveals, the familiar clichés about his personality do indeed accurately reflect specific characteristics visible in the Reichsführer. His contemporaries frequently thought him impassive, cold, and pedantic. Constantly striving to keep his emotions at a distance and his lack of self-confidence under control, Himmler conducted his relations with others in a manner that was organized down to the smallest detail, and thus made the impression of being insipid and impersonal. He attempted to compensate for the emotional void he felt by taking refuge in utopian dreams and quasi-religious speculations, which in turn were regarded by his contemporaries either as 'romantic' or simply as crackpot. Himmler never got too carried away with such daydreams, however; rather, as his first years as Reichsführer-SS showed, he was able to combine ideological flights of fancy with power politics in a an effective manner and to exploit the political power-struggles in the NSDAP for his own purposes, an indication of the extreme utilitarian outlook he had adopted in general. Anything useful to him was permissable. The fact that he did not shy away from violence in the process may not be surprising in the light of his biography. From the outbreak of the First World War Himmler believed himself to be in a military conflict. After experiencing the war for three-and-a-half years from the everyday standpoint of the home front, he had joined the Bavarian army at the beginning of 1918 at the age of 17 and from that time on had moved permanently in circles dominated by the military and by violence. He regarded the turbulent post-war years merely as a continuation of the war and as a chance now to triumph over the enemy within. After the failed putsch he survived by sheltering in the paramilitary environment fostered by right-wing radicalism. As Reichsführer-SS he then regarded himself as a commander in a civil war in which the use of any kind of violence, including political assassination, was permitted.

Himmler assumed the leadership of the SS at a time when Nazism was on the point of rapidly becoming a mass movement, and he was inevitably drawn into the maelstrom of its galloping expansion: in the space of about four years his SS grew to 50,000 members. To make sense of Himmler's development from this time it is therefore necessary to trace it with close reference to the history of Nazism as a whole, a history that can be described as the rapid succession of dynamic processes: the conquest, extension, and assertion of power, expansion, racial war of annihilation, and finally progressive self-destruction. Himmler the politician was inextricably bound up in this welter of historical developments; a purely biographical explanation of his political activity would therefore be totally inadequate. We are dealing here with complex political events that cannot be reduced to the psychology of the individual actors.

If, however, Himmler's career is reconstructed in detail, it becomes evident to what extent he imprinted his personality on his various offices. One example of this is his idiosyncratic style of leadership, which encompassed the private lives of his men and their families. Himmler saw his role as that of the educator of his SS, as a father-figure. The 'compliance' that had bound him to his parents was something he now demanded of his SS leaders; he could act out his voyeuristic and manipulative tendencies by snooping into their private affairs. At the same time he was at pains to extend his 'soldierly' self-image to the SS as a whole. Members of the SS were not to bond as mates but to submit to an iron discipline and employ the same reserved and sober social forms behind which Himmler concealed his own lack of social ease.

And if he expressly made the claim that in everything it did his SS was guided by particular moral principles, and in formulaic fashion repeatedly held up an obligatory SS 'catalogue of virtues', then there is an unmistakable link to features that define his personality. At the beginning of their relationship he had confided to his fiancée that he wished he could for once be allowed not to be 'decent' (*anständig*) and to remove the straitjacket of rules, maxims of conduct, and self-control. The SS was to supply him with plentiful opportunities for doing just that. In order to paper over the contradiction between high moral claims and obscure temptations, however, the façade of virtue and constant concern for 'decency' had to be maintained to outward appearances at all costs; this double standard was a feature of Himmler the man as well as of his SS.

Himmler's attempts, by means of a special SS cult, to guarantee the cohesion of the 'order' and to strengthen its elite character as keeper of the Holy Grail of Nazism similarly reveal his personal weaknesses. Himmler himself needed symbols and insignia, myths and shrines, festivals and rituals, both to orientate himself as well as to give sensuous expression to his fantasy world and to be able to share it with others, even if imperfectly. The peculiar primness and artificiality of this cult, in which Himmler was constantly playing the role of master of ceremonies, provided an unconscious illustration of his inhibited personality.

Gradually the personality and the office became one. Private life and career became increasingly interlinked: his brothers and friends joined the SS, while Himmler treated SS members like members of his own family. Unbidden, he made their family life, their health, their private debts, and their alcohol consumption his business. And when he was considering breaking free of his now-unsatisfying marriage and forming a new attachment, he recommended 'second marriages' to his men and the fathering of illegitimate children.

Above all, his position in the Nazi state seemed to open up to him the opportunity of transforming dreams and ambitions that had long enthused him in private into political reality on a grand scale: liberation from the chains of the Christian religion and the rejection of restricting moral obligations; the re-evaluation of procreation and marriage from the point of view of racial breeding and selection; a career as an officer and army commander; the creation of an ideology that would be an adequate substitute for religion; finally, the restoration of a lost Germanic world, and in particular the radical extirpation of the hated 'subhumans' as the prerequisite for the realization of this utopia.

In this way, and over time, he created a position of power geared completely to himself personally and defined by his specific predilections and peculiarities. Himmler was the complete opposite of a faceless functionary or bureaucrat, interchangeable with any other. The position he built up over the years can instead be described as an extreme example of the almost total personalization of political power. This phenomenon can be explained only by means of the specific power structures in Nazism and their dynamic: leadership by a charismatic Führer, the absence in this system of law and regulations, the permanent pressure to adapt power structures to altered political goals—these resulted in a situation where large parts of the apparatus of power were indeed linked directly to the 'Führer' by means of tasks and responsibilities that had been designed with specific people in mind, but these confidants of Hitler had extraordinary freedom of action in the discharge of these responsibilities.

In Himmler's case, a series of relatively distinct phases in his political career can be discerned, in each of which the Reichsführer set out a specific vision of the SS. In so doing he was reacting to the processes of change affecting the regime and was contributing also to those changes: he was, however, unable to direct or control them entirely.

In 1933 he at first had to content himself with the post of Chief of the Political Police in Bavaria. By exploiting, among other things, the mounting conflict between the party and state leadership on the one hand and the SA on the other, and recommending himself to the former as a reliable ally, he was able within a relatively short time to propel himself upwards to the post of Chief of the Political Police in the other German states and finally in the entire Reich. The successful liquidation of the SA leadership—his erstwhile mentors Röhm and Strasser fell victim to it—was to strengthen considerably the position of his SS and remove any doubts about his loyalty to Hitler. From this position he developed a comprehensive programme for the leadership of the police as a whole, which after Hitler had appointed him Chief of the German Police in 1936 he intended to amalgamate with the SS to form a 'state protection corps'.

When, at the end of the 1930s, the Third Reich moved to expand, he redefined his goals: Alongside settlement and 'racial selection' of the population in the territories 'to be Germanized', he expanded the Waffen-SS, deployed it as part of the policy of repression in the occupied territories, and introduced a policy of systematic, racially based mass murder. In the period 1938–40, however, he not only gained a string of new responsibilities but had to accept several painful defeats and setbacks. Among them were his failure in the Fritsch crisis and the criticism from the Wehrmacht he was forced to suffer on account of SS atrocities in Poland and of his so-called 'procreation order'; in the newly conquered countries of northern and western Europe he was not able to be as effective everywhere as he had imagined, and in occupied Poland his massive resettlement programme had ground to a halt.

With the invasion of the Soviet Union he hoped he would be able to leave this period of stagnation behind. In the summer of 1941 it was unequivocally Himmler who seized the initiative to extend the executions already being carried out by his Einsatzgruppen and other murder squads of 'suspect' Jews in the Soviet Union to a blanket genocide of the Jewish minority in the occupied eastern territories. In doing so he was convinced that he was acting in harmony with Hitler's long-term plans. This initiative was Himmler's response to a further defeat: his marginalization with regard to occupation policy in the east, which he had heard about in mid-July. By now employing the police powers he enjoyed for the purpose of geno-cide—and this was his calculation—he secured for himself and his SS the much more wide-ranging task of subjecting the conquered territories to a gigantic programme of deportation, resettlement, and extermination. From his perspective the murder of the Jews was only the first step towards a much more extensive 'new order' based on racist criteria.

In the autumn and winter of 1941 Himmler played a key role in the intensification of the persecution of the Jews, that is, in the preparation of the first waves of deportations and the inclusion of additional territories in eastern Europe in the extermination programme. Behind this too were considerations that went far beyond the 'elimination' of the Jews: at the height of the Nazi politics of conquest he replaced the notion of a 'Germanic' Reich with the vision of a 'Greater Germanic' Empire.

In the spring of 1942 it seemed to him that the moment had arrived when he could finally achieve a breakthrough for this aim: he saw an opportunity of extending the Holocaust to more and more groups of Jewish victims. First the whole of occupied Poland was caught up in the whirlwind of mass extermination, followed by—and the assassination of Heydrich clearly played an important part in this—the rest of the European countries. By September 1942, immediately after these fundamental decisions taken mainly between April and June 1942, he set the course of a development that, seen in its totality, amounted to nothing less than the creation of a new order on the European continent under SS leadership. This was made possible by his linking together a number of diverse tasks: he took over responsibility for 'combating bandits' in the occupied territories, had a complete settlement plan drawn up for the territory under German domination, constantly expanded the Waffen-SS's recruitment opportunities, concerned himself with the integration of the 'Germanic countries' into the new Reich, planned to build up his own arms business, tackled the systematic removal of 'asocial' elements, and, under the banner of 'extermination through labour', ensured the expansion of the concentration-camp system.

From Himmler's perspective the sequence of brilliant military victories won by the Wehrmacht from 1939 onwards was like a time-lapse, making the span of several generations that he had hitherto estimated as being necessary to establish a Greater Germanic Reich drastically shrink: in 1942 there seemed to him a window allowing him and his SS to turn ideas that had up to then been regarded as utopian into reality. What looked from his standpoint like a huge acceleration of historical processes and the entirely justified expectation of turning utopian dreams into reality in a very short time seems to me an absolutely decisive factor in explaining his actions in implementing the 'Final Solution' and organizing gigantomaniacal 'plans for a new order'. Up to this point he had, in his own estimation, been ultimately successful with almost everything he had tackled. Nothing and nobody seemed capable of stopping him.

Yet very shortly after this, at the end of 1942, came the turn in the war, and Himmler was forced to put his extensive plans on hold. If one examines more closely the diverse projects to which he had given powerful impetus, most in any case ran aground fairly swiftly: his projects for new settlements were inadequately carried out or ended in a fiasco; his plan to build bridge-heads in the 'Germanic countries' by forming alliances with local leaders and agencies willing to collaborate was largely unsuccessful; his own arms business never materialized; the 'combating of bandits' turned out to be a hopeless endeavour; the large-scale recruitment of ethnic Germans into the Waffen-SS weakened the position of German minorities in south-eastern Europe, and the recruitment of volunteers from 'alien nations' to the Waffen-SS had mainly negative results.

Now he concentrated fully on what had always represented the core of his power: the exercise of violence and terror, with the help of which he now intended to guarantee the 'security' of the territory still dominated by Nazi Germany. By taking on further offices, in particular that of Reich Minister of the Interior and commander of the Reserve Army, towards the end of the war he to all intents and purposes united in his own person all the instruments of violence belonging to the Nazi state.

Nevertheless, he was unable to stop resistance movements in the occupied territories, nor is there evidence to suggest that he had developed even the beginnings of a coherent idea of how to do so. The situation in Germany itself was, however, different: up to the military capitulation in May 1945 he was largely successful in what he had set himself in 1937 as his chief task in the event of a new war, namely, to cover the regime's back in the 'internal theatre of war' inside Germany. The fact that the Third Reich did not collapse from within but only under the force of the Allied armies—a prolongation of its existence that cost millions of lives—really was to a considerable extent the work of Heinrich Himmler.

In the final phase of the war Himmler tried for the very last time to redefine his role in the Third Reich: as an honest broker, who, acting from allegedly humanitarian motives, was opening up the way for peace. He made efforts to establish contacts with the western Allies via neutral states, offering in the process the possibility of exchanging concentration-camp prisoners and even seeking to contact Jewish organizations—an absurd course of action that possibly underlines his tendency to indulge political illusions as much as his striving to adjust to whatever circumstances he found himself in. When these efforts failed and Hitler repudiated him in the final days of the war he took refuge in hectic activity, without finding anything with which to counter his inner or outer collapse.

What is remarkable in all this is above all Himmler's ability, in the course of the Nazi dictatorship, on the one hand to create all-embracing plans for the power complex he controlled, and on the other to allocate to the individual component organizations of his empire tasks connected with the realization of these plans that, from the regime's perspective, not only made sense ideologically and in terms of power politics, but also gave the impression of forming a coherent whole. Although he was extremely careful in each individual case to obtain Hitler's confirmation of any new powers, he was nevertheless the one who was able to combine these separate powers tactically into a system. In this way he made successive additions to his areas of responsibility, until finally, at the end of the war, he was probably the most powerful Nazi politician after Hitler.

And yet Himmler's career cannot be interpreted one-sidedly in terms of a continuous and persistent process of realizing existing ideological tenets. Although a particular theme—the refrain of the eternal struggle of 'Germanic' heroes against 'Asiatic' subhumans—runs through his mind and actions, this way of seeing the world was so general and vague that he could adapt it to fit any political situation. This ability to combine ideology flexibly with power politics was his real strength.

It should finally be emphasized that Nazi policy took its particular explosiveness and dynamic to a considerable extent from the manner in which Heinrich Himmler brought together the police, the camp system, racial selection, settlement policy, combating of partisans, forced-labour programmes, and the mobilization of 'Teutons' and 'ethnic Germans'. From this an SS and police complex arose, the internal coherence and full scope of which can be understood only if the person who united all these powers is taken into account. If Himmler had been replaced in the 1930s by someone else, this specific and highly dangerous network of different powers would not have come into being. If, on the other hand, these responsibilities had been distributed among several Nazi politicians as separate domains, Nazi policy could not have led to its dreadful consequences in quite the same way.

If we consider Himmler's empire and the plans and utopian fantasies he developed in their entirety, it is also evident that he had amassed a potential for destruction that far exceeded the catastrophes that Nazism itself actually caused: for the systematic murder of the European Jews, with which above all the name Himmler is connected today, was not in his eyes the ultimate goal of his policies but rather the precondition for much more extensive plans for a bloody 'new ordering' of the European continent.

Endnotes

PROLOGUE

1. Himmler and his companions were apprehended by two freed Soviet POWs who were deployed to reinforce a British patrol; see 'Die letzten Tage von Heinrich Himmler. Neue Dokumente aus dem Archiv des Föderalen Sicherheitsdienstes', presented and with an introduction by Boris Chavkin and A. M. Kalganov, in *Forum für osteuropäische Ideen- und Zeitgeschichte*, 4 (2000), 251–84.

2. On Himmler's time in Camp 31 see the report Selvester wrote in 1963 at the request of the Himmler biographers Roger Manvell und Heinrich Fraenkel, who subsequently used it in their biography (*Himmler: Kleinbürger und Massenmörder* (Herrsching, 1981), 227 ff.). Before passing the report on to Manvell and Fraenkel, Selvester sent it for approval to the Public Relations Department of the War Office. The paragraph on the plan to drug Himmler (PRO, WO 32/19603) was crossed out. Written almost twenty years after the event, the report contains a number of inaccuracies, particularly with regard to the chronological sequence of events, as is clear from a comparison with the report written on 23 May 1945 by Smith, the chief interrogating officer, and the 2nd British Army communication concerning the events dated 24 May 1945. All these documents are in PRO, WO 208/4431.

3. PRO, WO 208/4431, War Diary, Second Army Defence Company, 23 May 1945.

4. Ibid. War Diary, 26 May 1945. On the location of the grave see further correspondence in this file.

CHAPTER I

1. Letters in the *Süddeutsche Zeitung* of 9/10 August 1980.

2. Ibid.

3. BAK, NL 1126/26, Family tree of the Kiene family created by Gebhard Himmler, September 1921. Agathe Kiene lived from 1833 till 1916. On the family history of the Himmlers see Bradley F. Smith, *Heinrich Himmler 1900–1926. Sein Weg in den deutschen Faschismus* (Munich, 1979), 23 ff.

4. In the *Amtliches Verzeichnis des Personals der Lehrer, Beamten und Studierenden an der Königlich-Bayerischen Ludwigs-Maximilians-Universität zu München* he is registered as a student from the winter semester 1884/5 to the summer semester 1890; it is also registered that he interrupted his studies from winter semester 1898/9 until summer semester 1890.

5. Himmler's great niece, Katrin Himmler, discovered the information about the stay in Russia through oral family history; see Katrin Himmler, *Die Brüder Himmler. Eine deutsche Familiengeschichte* (Frankfurt a. M., 2005), 35.

6. I was informed that there is no record of Himmler's role as tutor to Prince Heinrich in the Private Archive of the Wittelsbach dynasty (BHStA, Abteilung III).

7. According to the *Blätter für das Gymnasial-Schulwesen* 33 (May/June 1897), 528. The *Festschrift zur Vierhundert-Jahr-Feier des Wilhelms-Gymnasiums, 1559–1959* (Munich, 1959), 57, shows that Himmler was employed as a grammar-school teacher there during the years 1894–1902. According to Himmler, *Brüder Himmler*, 37, he was employed at the Ludwigsgymnasium from 1890 and from 1893 as a private tutor.

8. BAK, NL 1126/26, Family tree of the Heyder family created by Gerhard Himmler, 1931. Anna Maria Heyder was born on 19 January 1866. Her father, Franz Alois Heyder, born on 2 July 1810 in Abensberg (Lower Bavaria), died on 17 April 1872. His ancestors, who can be traced back to the sixteenth century, were foresters. In 1839 Alois Heyder had married a widow who was eighteen years older than him before, in 1862, he married Anna Hofritter, the mother of Himmler's mother, who was fourteen years younger than him. Cf. Smith, *Himmler*, 29.

9. Himmler, *Brüder Himmler*, 38, mentions 300,000 Goldmarks, which for those days represented considerable wealth. However, the Himmlers' lifestyle does not suggest that they possessed significant income from property in addition to the income he earned as a civil servant.

10. BAK, NL 1126/1, Gebhard Himmler to Prinz Heinrich, 21 June 1900 (a thank-you letter for his agreeing to become godfather), 8 October 1900 (announcement of the birth) and 19 October 1900 (re the christening); cf. Smith, *Himmler*, 38 f.

11. Smith, *Himmler*, 30 f.

12. As in a farewell letter that he wrote to his wife before embarking on a journey to Greece in 1912 (Himmler, *Brüder Himmler*, 48). The fact that the family regularly attended mass is clear from Heinrich's diary. Apart from Heinrich's holiday diaries for 1910 and 1911 (Lenggries), 1912 (Lindau), und 1913 (Brixlegg) in Nachlass Himmler, BAK, NL 1126/6, the Himmler diaries that have survived are in the Hoover Institution, Stanford University, also as microfilm in Nachlass Himmler (BAK, NL 1126). In future they will be referred to in the notes as TB.

13. Himmler, *Brüder Himmler*, 46 ff., demonstrates this in exemplary fashion from family history by means of the farewell letters that Himmler's father wrote prophylactically to Gerhard and Ernst.
14. Smith, *Himmler*, 46 f.; TB, 18 September 1915.
15. BAK, NL 1126/1, Gebhard Himmler, 'Notes on the schooling of our dear children' (*Schulnotizen*); see Smith, *Himmler*, 43.
16. Himmler, *Brüder Himmler*, 46 ff.
17. At first they lived in the bride's flat on the first floor of Sternstrasse 13 (*Adressbuch für München 1898*). Agathe Himmler, an employee of the District Office (*Bezirksamt*), was also registered as living at this address. In 1900 and 1901 the family lived on the second floor of Hildegardstrasse 6, from the 1 April 1901 on the third floor of Liebigstrasse 5, k (*Adressbuch für München 1900 und 1901*). Cf. Smith, *Himmler*, 39.
18. Smith, *Himmler*, 50.
19. The correspondence is contained in BAK, NL 1126/1. Katrin Himmler describes the visits in *Brüder Himmler*, 39, based on the manuscript of the memoirs of her great-uncle, Gerhard Himmler, which are in the possession of the family.
20. On the cultural changes during the period of the Prince Regent and on the decline of Munich as an artistic centre see above all David Clay Large, *Hitlers München. Aufstieg und Fall der Hauptstadt der Bewegung* (Munich, 1998), as well as the collection of essays edited by Friedrich Prinz and Marita Krauss, *München—Musenstadt mit Hinterhöfen. Die Prinzregentenzeit 1886–1912* (Munich, 1988), in particular Roger Engelmann, 'Öffentlichkeit und Zensur. Literatur und Theater als Provokation', 267–76. For a general account of this period see Karl Möckl, *Die Prinzregentenzeit. Gesellschaft und Politik während der Ära des Prinzregenten Luitpold in Bayern* (Munich and Vienna, 1972).
21. *Blätter für das Gymnasial-Schulwesen*, 38, 9/10 (September–October 1902), 665.
22. BAK, NL 1126/1, correspondence between Gebhard Himmler and the family doctor, Quernstedt (15 July 1903), as well as with Prince Heinrich (the prince's enquiry about Heinrich's state of health, 25 June 1903, and Himmler's replies of 30 August and 20 December 1903); Smith, *Himmler*, 40 ff.
23. *Blätter für das Gymnasial-Schulwesen*, 40, 9/10 (September–October 1904), 684; *Adressbuch für München 1905*; see Smith, *Himmler*, 42.
24. Smith, *Himmler*, 42 f.; BAK, NL 1126/1, School reports. Himmler's father mentions here five different occasions when Gebhard was ill during this year, which led to 147 days off school.
25. See in particular the reflections on this in Himmler, *Brüder Himmler*, 66 f., BAK, NL 1126/1, Schulnotizen.
26. BAK, NL 1126/1, Schulnotizen.
27. Smith, *Himmler*, 44 f.
28. See the holiday diaries for 1910 und 1911 (Lenggries), 1912 (Lindau), and 1913 (Brixlegg) in Nachlass Himmler, BAK, NL 1126/6.
29. TB, 1911, Landaufenthalt in Lenggries; cf. Smith, *Himmler*, 44 ff.

30. Smith, *Himmler*, 51.

31. BAK, NL 1126/1, Schulnotizen.

32. George W. F. Hallgarten, 'Mein Mitschüler Heinrich Himmler', in *Germanica Judaica*, 1/2 (1960–1), 4–7.

33. Smith, *Himmler*, 52; Himmler, *Brüder Himmler*, 49.

34. BAB, NS 19/3667. On Zipperer see Smith, *Himmler*, 53 f.

35. Falk Zipperer, 'Eschwege. Eine siedlungs- und verfassungsgeschichtliche Untersuchung', in *Festgabe für Heinrich Himmler* (Darmstadt, 1941), 215–92. Zipperer's dissertation, which appeared in a series of the SS academic organization, Ahnenerbe, was concerned with the customs of Upper Bavaria: *Das Haberfeldtreiben. Seine Geschichte und seine Bedeutung* (Weimar, 1938); see also BAB, BDC, SS-O Zipperer.

36. BAB, NS 19/3535.

37. Alfons Beckenbauer, 'Eine Landshuter Jugendfreundschaft und ihre Verwicklung in die NS-Politik. Der Arzt Dr. Karl Gebhardt und der Reichsführer-SS Heinrich Himmler', in *Verhandlungen des Historischen Vereins für Niederbayern*, 100 (1974), 5–22.

38. Smith, *Himmler*, 48.

39. Alfons Beckenbauer, 'Musterschüler und Massenmörder. Heinrich Himmlers Landshuter Jugendjahre', in *Verhandlungen des Historischen Vereins für Niederbayern*, 95 (1969), 93–106.

40. TB, 28 July 1915.

41. TB, 4 September 1915.

42. TB, 16 February 1915.

43. TB, 29 July 1915.

44. On the war youth generation see in particular: Ulrich Herbert, *Best. Biographische Studien über Radikalismus, Weltanschauung und Vernunft, 1903–1989* (Bonn, 1996), 42 ff. Herbert believes that this generation was concerned above all to transfer an idealized version of the 'front-line soldier' to the domestic political situation. Herbert refers in particular to the book by Günther Gündel that was particularly influential at the time: *Sendung der Jungen Generation. Versuch einer umfassenden revolutionären Sinndeutung der Krise* (Munich, 1932). The other work referred to by him in this context, by Helmut Lethen, *Verhaltenslehren der Kälte. Lebensversuche zwischen den Kriegen* (Frankfurt a. M., 1994), focuses on authors of the 'Neue Sachlichkeit' and so is not relevant for the early history of right-wing radicalism in the Weimar Republic. Michael Wildt, *Generation des Unbedingten. Das Führungskorps des Reichssicherheitshauptamtes* (Hamburg, 2003), has provided supporting evidence for the picture sketched by Herbert by showing that, with a 60 per cent membership, the upper ranks of the Reich Security Main Office (*Reichssicherheitshauptamt* = RSHA) were dominated by the war youth generation. On the war youth generation see also Barbara Stambolis, *Der Mythos der jungen Generation. Ein Beitrag zur politischen Kultur der Weimarer Republik* (Bochum, 1982).

45. On war games see TB, 1 September 1914, 1 and 18 February1915.
46. KAM, OP 54540, report of the head of the Landshut Jugendwehr, 26 June 1917.
47. TB, 25 September 1915. On the Jugendwehr see Smith, *Himmler*, 61.
48. TB, 16 February and 31 July 1915.
49. TB, 27 September 1914.
50. BAK, NL 1126/3, Membership card; date of entry was 6 February 1917.
51. Smith, *Himmler*, 69.
52. Ibid. 68 f. and 72; Himmler, *Brüder Himmler*, 57.
53. Smith, *Himmler*, 72.
54. KAM, OP 54540, certificate of the district liaison officer for youth military training, 25 June 1917.
55. Hofverwaltung, Frau Prinzessin Witwe Arnulf, Hofmarschall Pflaum, 4 and 11 June 1917; Smith, *Himmler*, 72 ff.
56. BAK, NL 1126/1, questionnaire 1. Btl. 1. Inf.-Regiment, completed by Gebhard Himmler on 23 June 1917.
57. KAM, OP 54540, school report of 15 July 1917. Himmler was rated 'very good' in the subjects Religious Studies and History, 'good' in German, Latin, French, Maths, and Gymnastics, and 'satisfactory' in Physics.
58. BAK, NL 1126/1, Magistrat Landshut to Gebhard Himmler, 6 October 1917, as well as KAM, OP 54540, Certificate of the Magistrate of 24 December 1917. On this episode see also Smith, *Himmler*, 74 f.
59. KAM, OP 54540, letter from Hofmarschall Pflaum to the commander of the 11th Bavarian Infantry Regiment, 17 August 1917.
60. Ibid. Archiv des fr. Bay. III. A.K., letter to Major Ritter v. Braun re promotion to lieutenant, 18 March 1921; Smith, *Himmler*, 82 f.
61. BAK, NL 1126/11, letter of 4 January 1918.
62. Ibid. correspondence with his parents (January); Smith, *Himmler*, 76 ff.
63. Details in BAK, NL 1126/11.
64. Ibid. 29 January 1918.
65. Ibid. correspondence with his parents (February); Smith, *Himmler*, 79.
66. Himmler, *Brüder Himmler*, 60 f.
67. BAK, NL 1126/11, 23 March 918.
68. Ibid. 7 May 1918, also 6, 15, and 22 May 1918.
69. Smith, *Himmler*, 82 f.
70. BAK, NL 1126/11, 20 June and 17 September 1918.
71. Thus, for example, in his letter of 5 August 1918, in which he wrote that he had reported sick and the doctor had prescribed rest.
72. BAK, NL 1126/11, 23 June and 29 August 1918.
73. Ibid. 29 August 1918.
74. Ibid. 4 August 1918.
75. KAM, OP 54540, assessment of 14 September 1918. In this assessment Himmler's performance was rated good to very good, and he was considered suitable for a commission at a later date.

76. BAK, NL 1126/11, 13 August 1918.
77. Smith, *Himmler*, 85.
78. BAK, NL 1126/11.
79. Ibid. 23 October 1918; Smith, *Himmler*, 85.
80. Smith, *Himmler*, 86f. Details are to be found in his letters to his parents of 30 November as well of 6, 10, 11, and 17 December 1918 (BAK, NL 1126/11).
81. BAK, NL 1126/11, 6 December 1918.
82. Ibid. 23 June and 29 August 1918. Cf. Smith, *Himmler*, 87 f.
83. BAK, NL 1126/11, 6 December 1918.
84. KAM OP 54540, Archive des fr. Bay. III. A.K., letter to Major Ritter v. Braun re promotion to lieutenant, 18 March 1921; Smith, *Himmler*, 88.

CHAPTER 2

1. BAK, NL 1126/13, Teacher notebook of Gebhard Himmler's: War Special Class A, Gymnasium Landshut. Class teacher Himmler, Konrektor; cf. Smith, *Himmler*, 89.
2. Poems by the two friends can be found in BAK, NL 1126/19; Smith, *Himmler*, 90 f.
3. On the revolution in Munich see Allan Mitchell, *Revolution in Bayern 1918/ 1919. Die Eisner-Regierung und die Räterepublik* (Munich, 1967); Karl Bosl (ed.), *Bayern im Umbruch. Die Revolution von 1918, ihre Voraussetzungen, ihr Verlauf und ihre Folgen* (Munich and Vienna, 1969); Heinrich Hillmayr, *Roter und Weißer Terror in Bayern nach 1918. Ursachen, Erscheinungsformen und Folgen der Gewalttätigkeiten im Verlauf der revolutionären Ereignisse nach dem Ende des Ersten Weltkrieges* (Munich, 1974); Hans Fenske, *Konservatismus und Rechtsradikalismus in Bayern nach 1918* (Bad Homburg v. d. H., 1969), 40 ff.; Heinrich August Winkler, *Von der Revolution zur Stabilisierung. Arbeiter und Arbeiterbewegung in der Weimarer Republik 1918 bis 1924*, 2nd edn (Berlin and Bonn, 1985), 184 ff.
4. 4 BAK, NL 1126/18, Reports of the Regensburg secretariat of the BVP, 23 and 30 December 1918 and 9 January 1919; cf. Smith, *Himmler*, 93.
5. According to his great-niece Katrin (though she does not provide any further evidence) he took part in the attack on Munich and in the fighting in the centre of the city as a member of the Landshut Free Corps (*Brüder Himmler*, 71). However, this is highly improbable. It would be the only example of Himmler having been involved in combat in his entire life, so one can assume that he would have referred to this event in later years. After all, throughout his life 'Miles Heinrich' tried to portray himself as a 'soldier', which is why he constantly referred to his period of military service. The fact that he never mentioned the fighting in Munich is an important indication that he did not take part in it. His army file in the Kriegsarchiv München, which was kept open until 1921, also fails to refer to any such action. His 1921 request for an abridgement to his university course—a special dispensation for those who had fought in the war—does not refer to it either.

6. This is based on a short note in Himmler's handwriting signed by his company commander on 13 July 1919 (it was concerned with permission to receive food), see BAK, NL 1126/1. See also Himmler, *Brüder Himmler*, 71.

7. Beckenbauer, 'Musterschüler', esp. 97 f.

8. BAK, NL 1126/12, letter of 10 August 1919 (I), also the letters to his parents of 1, 3, 10 (II), 15, and 24 August 1919. On his period of training see Smith, *Himmler*, 97 ff. His special work diary will in future be referred to as ATB.

9. ATB, 10 August 1919.

10. ATB, 2–23 September 1919. Three letters to his mother, who initially remained in Landshut, have survived: 11, 15, and 20 September 1919.

11. ATB, 25 September 1919. On this see also the letters from Quenstedt to Gebhard Himmler of 24 September and 18 October 1919 (BAK, NL 1126/1). The doctor attributed the enlargement of the heart to the excessive physical demands of his military service. On his illness see Smith, *Himmler*, 99 ff.

12. BAK, NL 1126/8, Leseliste [Reading list] no. 1—28, NL 1126/9 contains a transcription that was used for this book, which in future is referred to as Leseliste. See in detail Smith, *Himmler*, 102 ff.

13. Leseliste no. 10: 'A, to begin with nauseatingly insipid but in the end stimulating, novel, too naturalistic.'

14. On the history of forgery see Nick Groom, *The Forger's Shadow: How Forgery Changed the Course of Literature* (London, 2002).

15. Leseliste no. 23, Friedrich Wichtl, *Weltfreimaurerei, Weltrevolution, Weltrepublik. Eine Untersuchung über Ursprung und Endziele des Weltkrieges* (Munich, 1919). The book appeared in 1928 already in its 11th edition. On Wichtl's book see Helmut Neuberger, *Freimaurerei und Nationalsozialismus. Die Verfolgung der deutschen Freimaurerei durch völkische Bewegung und Nationalsozialismus*, vol. 2: *Das Ende der deutschen Freimaurerei* (Hamburg, 1980), 40 ff.

16. Leseliste no. 19.

17. TB, 16 October 1919. On Himmler's period in Munich during the years 1919–20 see Smith, *Himmler*, 107 ff.

18. TB, 18 October 1919; BAK, NL 1126/1, matriculation certificate from the same day.

19. TB, 12 December 1919, about his examination by Dr Quenstedt.

20. Smith, *Himmler*, 107.

21. In the 1920 *Adressbuch für München* there is the entry: Anna Loritz, widow of a chamber singer, boarding house, Jägerstr. 8 I; Smith, *Himmler*, 107 f.

22. TB, 22 November 1919; on visits to von Lossow see also TB, 23 October and 26 December 1919.

23. TB, 16 December 1919 and 11 January 1920.

24. On his visits see among others TB, 22 November, 15 and 26 December 1919, and 12, 16, and 24 January 1920.

25. TB, 21 February 1920.

26. TB, 19 November 1919 (joining). On life in the fraternity see among other references TB, 20 November, 2, 4, 11, 13, and 17 December 1919, and 10 and 27 January 1920. On Apollo see Smith, *Himmler*, 114 f.
27. TB, 27 January 1920.
28. On his religious activity see among other references TB, 12 and 19 October, 16 and 28 November, 2, 8, and 26 December 1919, and 1, 10, 11, and 18 January 1920. On his attitude to religion at this period see Smith, *Himmler*, 119 ff.
29. TB, 9 November 1919.
30. TB, 24 December 1919.
31. BAK, NL 1126/3, admitted on 10 November 1919.
32. Ibid. receipt of the 14th Alarm Company, 16 May 1920.
33. TB, 4, 7, and 8 November 1919. On his military activities see in addition TB, 14 November and 1 December 1919.
34. TB, 11 December 1919.
35. TB, 4 November 1919.
36. TB, 1 December 1919.
37. TB, 16 January 1920.
38. TB, 17 October 1920. The names mentioned are undecipherable.
39. BAK, NL 1126/12, 18 January 1920. Ibid. letters of 20 and 24 March 1920.
40. Ibid. letters of 20 and 24 March 1920.
41. On joining the Einwohnerwehr on 16 May 1920 he received from the Alarm Company '1 rifle with 50 bullets, 1 helmet, 2 bullet holders, 1 satchel' (receipt) as well as an Einwohnerwehr booklet. He was a member of the machine-gun detachment of the 5th District in the Einwohnerwehr; see Programme of 5 August 1920 for the month of August (shooting practice and training evenings in the gym hall). All documents are in BAK, 1126/1.
42. Ibid. membership card of the Schützengesellschaft Freiweg.
43. BAK, NL 1126/1.
44. TB, 17 November 1919.
45. TB, 11 November 1919.
46. TB, 31 December 1919.
47. On Himmler's early anti-Semitism see also Smith, *Himmler*, 125 f.
48. The issue of how far Jewish students ought to be allowed to take part in the social life of their fellow students was intensively discussed in the aftermath of World War I. Thus the question of whether Jews should be allowed to become members of the Deutsche Studentenschaft was one of the main subjects for discussion at its founding meeting in Würzburg in 1919, until finally an ambiguous formula for membership was worked out. The majority of the Burschenschaften (fraternities) agreed a resolution at the fraternities conference in 1920 that banned the membership of Jews and those in 'mixed marriages'. The Verband der Vereine Deutscher Studenten (League of German Student Associations) resolved in 1920 that Jews should no longer be eligible to be given 'satisfaction' (i.e. allowed to take part in duels). See Helma Brunck, *Die Deutsche Burschenschaft in der*

Weimarer Republik und im Nationalsozialismus (Munich, 1999), esp. 184 ff.; Heike Ströle-Bühle, *Studentischer Antisemitismus in der Weimarer Republik. Eine Analyse der burschenschaftlichen Blätter 1918 bis 1933* (Frankfurt a. M. etc., 1991), esp. 84 ff.; and Marc Zirlewagen, *Der Kyffhäuser-Verband der Vereine Deutscher Studenten in der Weimarer Republik* (Cologne, 1999), 65 ff. Also Michael H. Kater, *Studentenschaft und Rechtsradikalismus in Deutschland 1918–1933. Eine sozialgeschichtliche Studie zur Bildungskrise in der Weimarer Republik* (Hamburg, 1975), esp. 146 ff. On the continuation of anti-Semitic traditions among students from Imperial Germany see Norbert Kampe, *Studenten und 'Judenfrage' im Deutschen Kaiserreich. Die Entstehung einer antisemitischen Trägerschicht des Antisemitismus* (Göttingen, 1988).

49. TB, 15 December 1919.
50. TB, 26 December 1919.
51. TB, 12 November 1919.
52. TB, 4–9 January 1920.
53. TB, 3 January 1920, refers to the 'street ballad, which Lu and I are doing for the benefit of Vienna children, and which we want to sing for the party at Loritz's'. On 13 January he wrote about the origin of the piece. In BAK, NL 1126/1 there is a programme note, 'For the children of Vienna'.
54. TB, 25, 28, 30 November, 9, 14, and 30 December 1919, and 13, 20, 23 January 1920.
55. See e.g. TB, 25 January 1920; previously there are entries concerning rehearsals of the piece, for example on 14 January 1920.
56. TB, 15, 16, 17, 19, and 20 October, 1 and 9 November 1919. Thereafter Himmler's visits to the Hagers decreased. On Himmler's earlier relationship with Luisa Hager see Smith, *Himmler*, 67 f. During his stay in the Ingolstadt hospital he noted of Ottilie Wildermuth's book *Aus dem Frauenleben*, 'Very suitable for Luisa' (Leseliste, no. 18).
57. TB, 20 October 1919.
58. TB, 1 November 1919; the same formulation occurs on 2 November 1919.
59. TB, 9 November 1919.
60. TB, 28 October 1919.
61. TB, 30 October 1919.
62. TB, 2 November 1919.
63. TB, 5 and 15 November 1919.
64. TB, 17 October and 20 December 1919.
65. TB, 19 October and 13 November 1919.
66. TB, 24 November, 1, 8, and 19 December 1919.
67. TB, 17, 23, and 29 November 1919.
68. TB, 3 November 1919.
69. TB, 4 November 1919.
70. TB, 8 November 1919, also 9 November 1919.
71. TB, 7 November 1919.
72. TB, 13 November 1919.

73. TB, 11 November 1919. On his plans to emigrate see Smith, *Himmler*, 127.
74. In the diary there are numerous entries about his learning Russian, e.g. on the 17, 18, 26, and 27 November, 1, 9, 19, 22, 23, 25, and 29 December 1919, as well as on the 3 and 13 January 1920.
75. TB, 14 November 1919.
76. TB, 12, 17, 20–6 November 1919.
77. TB, 16 November 1919.
78. TB, 26 and 27 November 1919.
79. TB, 28 November 1919.
80. TB, 30 November 1919.
81. TB,1 and 2, and 7, 8, 11, and 13 December 1919.
82. TB, 8 December 1919.
83. TB, 10 December 1919.
84. TB, 31 December 1919.
85. TB, 11 January 1920.
86. TB, 12 January 1920: 'Afterwards continued a very unsatisfactory conversation with Gebhard. A sorting out.'
87. TB, 14 January 1920.
88. TB, 28 January 1920; on the development of his sexuality see also Smith, *Himmler*, 117 ff.
89. TB, 24 November 1919.
90. TB, 18 December 1919.
91. Leseliste no. 43, *Der Priester und der Messnerknabe und andere apokryphe Erzählungen* (Hanover, 1919). The book was erroneously attributed to Oscar Wilde.
92. TB, 30 January 1920.
93. TB, 6 December 1919.
94. TB, 7 December 1919, similarly on 21 December 1919.
95. TB, 31 December 1919: 'In the evening I read and discussed politics with father'; 4–9 January 1920: 'On 7.1. and 8.1. dear Daddy was there until 1 p.m.'; 20 January 1920: 'Very nice letter from Daddy.' But see also on 24 November 1919: 'In the morning I got a letter from father that one felt like sticking up on the wall. We were both flabbergasted. Gebhard was annoyed. I wasn't.' His personal crisis in spring 1921 is also revealed by two letters from Ludwig Zahler to him in which the latter gave him advice and tried to cheer him up; BAK, NL 1126/18, 14 and 19 April 1921; see also Smith, *Himmler*, 110.
96. For a classic study see John Bowlby, *Attachment and Loss*, 3 vols. (London, 1969–80). See also Gottfried Spangler und Peter Zimmermann (eds), *Die Bindungstheorie. Grundlagen, Forschung und Anwendung* (Stuttgart, 1995).
97. See Ulrich Herbert, *Best. Biographische Studien über Radikalismus, Weltanschauung und Vernunft 1903–1989* (Bonn, 1996), 142 ff.
98. Leseliste no. 36, Albert Ludwig Daiber, *Elf Jahre Freimaurer!* (Stuttgart, 1905), 26–30 October 1919: 'A book that says nothing particularly new about Freemasonry and portrays it as terribly harmless. I'm dubious about the author's position.'

99. Leseliste no. 44, read 23/4 March 1920. According to his list of reading, Himmler had evidently not read Flex's main work, *Der Wanderer zwischen beiden Welten* (Munich, 1917), which was probably the most widely read book by middle-class young people during the post-war years, in which Flex tried to create a link between the youth movement and the 'front-line experience'.

100. Leseliste no. 32, read November 1919.

101. Ibid. no. 39, read 23 January–1 February 1920.

102. Ibid. no. 45, *Tagebuch einer Verlorenen: von einer Toten*, ed. Margarete Böhme (Berlin, 1905), read March 1920, in Munich and Ingolstadt.

103. Ibid. no. 32, read February 1920.

104. Ibid. no. 47, read 8–17 April 1920.

105. Ibid. no. 51, read 1–10 August 1920.

106. Ibid. no. 50, read 5–7 May 1920. The book's overarching theme was 'work and don't despair'.

107. Hans Wegener, *Wir jungen Männer* (Düsseldorf and Leipzig, 1906), 62.

108. Ibid. 75 f.

109. Leseliste no. 50.

110. BAK, NL 1126/12, 15 September 1920.

111. BAK, NL 1126/3, membership card of the Touring Club; on the journey to Fridolfing that turned out to be rather hair-raising on account of the bad weather see BAK, NL 1126/12, letter to his parents of 9 September 1920; Smith, *Himmler*, 130.

112. BAK, NL 1126/12, 19 and 26 September, 10 October, and 18 November 1920 as well as 2 June 1921. On his stay in Fridolfing in general see also Smith, *Himmler*, 130 ff.

113. BAB, NS 19/3535. In autumn 1942 Hauptsturmführer Rehrl—he joined the SS in 1936—spent several days at Himmler's headquarters and accompanied him on a trip to the Crimea; in 1943/4 the Reichsführer-SS allocated him KZ prisoners and Jehovah's Witnesses, as forced workers for his farm, and, as late as Christmas 1944, he sent a present to Rehrl's daughter, see 'Der Dienstkalender Heinrich Himmlers 1941/42', im *Auftrag der Forschungsstelle für Zeitgeschichte in Hamburg*, ed. and introduced Peter Witte *et al.* (Hamburg, 1999), 20, 22, and 24–7 October, and 1 November 1942; Friedbert Mühldorfer, 'Fridolfing', in Wolfgang Benz and Barbara Distel (eds), *Der Ort des Terrors. Geschichte der nationalsozialistischen Konzentrationslager*, vol. 2: *Frühe Lager, Dachau, Emslandlager* (Munich, 2005), 327; BAB, BDC, SS-O Rehrl.

114. BAK, NL 1126/12, 11 November and 14 December 1920, and 6 and 26 February, 7 March, and 22 May 1921.

115. Documents concerning the memberships in BAK, NL 1126/3.

116. BAK, NL 1126/12, 10 October 1920 (choral society), 14 May 1921 (peasant marriage), 2 June 1921 (gymnastics society), 2 June 1921 (Corpus Christi procession).

117. BAK, NL 1126/1, programme for the district Einwohnerwehr shooting match of 3–5 December 1920 in Titmoning, Shooting results for 'Himmler from Fridolfing'.
118. BAK, NL 1126/12, 4 October and 28 November 1920, and 2 June 1921.
119. Ibid. 19 September and 4 October 1920, and 18 January 1921.
120. Ibid. 10 October 1921, and 20, 29 March and 24 June 1921.
121. Ibid. balance sheet from 2 April to 10 July 1921.
122. Ibid. 14 May 1921.
123. This was his assessment of *Pillars of Society and Brand* (Leseliste nos. 60 and 65).
124. Leseliste no. 63, read 5–15 October.
125. Ibid. no. 60, read 3 September 1920.
126. Ibid. no. 65, read 20 October–3 November 1920. He gave up on Ibsen's *The Pretenders* (no. 79, read 2–12 February 1921).
127. Ibid. no. 62, read 26–30 September 1920, and no. 72, read 14/15 December 1920.
128. Ibid. no. 53, *Kampf und Tod Karls XII.* (Munich, 1917), read 16 August 1920.
129. Ibid. no. 90, read 23–6 May 1921.
130. Ibid. no. 67, read 1–12 December 1920.
131. Ibid. no. 92, read 20 June–5 July 1921.
132. Ibid. no. 75, Heinrich Schierbaum, *Reden der Nationalversammlung zu Frankfurt a.Main* (Leipzig, 1914).
133. Ibid. no. 58, Christian Meyer, *Zur Erhebung Deutschlands 1813 bis 1814* (Munich, 1915), read 24–30 August 1920.
134. Ibid. no. 57, Julius Haupt, *Die deutsche Insel. Ein Gedenkbuch kriegsgefangener Offiziere* (Munich, 1920), read 25–8 August 1920.
135. Ibid. no. 77, *Wider Kaiser und Reich* (Munich, 1909), read 15–23 January 1921.
136. Ibid. no. 78, *Bankrott. Historischer Roman* (Munich, 1908), read 9–11 February 1921.
137. Ibid. no. 70, *Der Teufel in der Schule. Volkserzählung* (Munich, 1908), read 20–1 December 1920, and no. 71, *Die Sünde wider den Heiligen Geist* (Munich, 1908), read 22–3 December 1920.
138. The change of location can be gathered from his correspondence with his parents (BAK, NL 1126/12); in NL 1126/1 there is a copy of the reference given him by the agricultural machinery factory, Vereinigte Fabriken; cf. also Smith, *Himmler*, 148.

CHAPTER 3

1. BAK, NL 1126/3, the address is clear from the various documents in the same file (among other things the membership card of the veterans' association of the Munich Technical University (Technische Hochschule)); Smith, *Himmler*, 149.
2. Ibid. 149 f.

3. TB, e.g. 12, 15, and 20 January, 13 February, 3 March, 30 May, 20 and 27 June 1922.
4. BAK, NL 1126/12, e.g. 21 November and 9 December 1921, and 20 January, 3 and 13 February, and 3 March 1922.
5. TB, 16 January 1922.
6. BAK, NL 1126/12, e.g. 2 November 1921 and 1 February 1922.
7. Ibid. 2 November 1921, and 20 January, 21 February 1922.
8. TB, e.g. 1, 6, and 20 November 1921, and 22 January, 5, 12 February, 26 March, 28 May, 15 and 29 June 1922.
9. TB, among others 1, 2, 4, 5, 18, 27, and 30 November 1921, and 12, 14 January and 26 March 1922; such examples are also mentioned in letters to his parents, e.g. in BAK, NL 1126/12, 2 November 1921 and 20 January 1922.
10. TB, 9 November 1921.
11. TB, 17, 18, and 21 November and 6 December 1921, and 13, 14, and 30 January, 28 February, 16 and 17 June 1922; Smith, *Himmler*, 151 f.
12. TB, among others 26 November 1921, and 11, 16, 18, 22, and 23 February, 1 and 28 June, and 4 July 1922. On his involvement in the relationship during his second stay in Munich see also Smith, *Himmler*, 152.
13. TB, 15 and 22 January, 11 and 26 February 1922.
14. TB, 19 and 26 November 1921, and 20 February and 17 June 1922.
15. Thus on a trip to a meeting of the fraternity in Nuremberg he stayed with a fellow member and accepted medical assistance from another (TB, 21 June 1922).
16. TB, 11 November 1921.
17. TB, 2 February 1922.
18. TB, 24 February 1922.
19. TB, 4 July 1922.
20. In 1922 he was registered as a member of the war veterans' organization of the Munich Technical University, of the German Touring Club, as well as of the German Agricultural Society (BAK, NL 1126/3); he took part in a meeting of the Alpine Club on 30 January 1922 (TB), he was admitted into the Officers' Association on 10 February 1922 (ibid.). On his membership of associations see also Smith, *Himmler*, 151.
21. 21 TB, 11, 15, 16, 17, 18, 24, and 28 November, 2 and 7 December 1921, and 30 January, 13 and 18 February, and 29 May 1922. On the dances see TB, 8, 9, and 11 November 1921, and 31 January, 5, 17, 18, 27, and 28 February 1922; Smith, *Himmler*, 151 f.
22. TB, 14 February and 6 June 1922.
23. Thus on 1 July 1922, 'chatted the time away' with Alphons. On further lengthy conversations with friends and acquaintances see TB, 4 and 9 November 1921, and 22 February, 4 and 25 March 1922; Smith, *Himmler*, 150 f.
24. TB, 11 and 17 February 1922. There are similar descriptions in the entries for 26 January, 10 and 27 February 1922.

25. TB, 18 February 1922.
26. TB, 21 June 1922.
27. TB, 15 and 17 January, 14 and 28 February 1922.
28. TB, 5 February 1922.
29. TB, 1 March 1922.
30. TB, 28 June, also 30 June and 1 July 1922.
31. TB, 6 March 1922.
32. TB, 1 July 1922.
33. TB, 22 January 1922.
34. TB, 6 June 1922.
35. TB, 19 February 1922.
36. TB, 25 February 1922.
37. TB, 7 November 1922.
38. TB, 26 May 1922.
39. TB, 27 May 1922.
40. TB, 4 March 1922.
41. Leseliste, no. 115.
42. Klaus Theweleit, *Männerphantasien* (Munich and Zurich, 2000) (1st edn, 2 vols., Frankfurt a. M, 1977–8), 59.
43. Ibid. 131.
44. TB, 15 January 1922.
45. TB, 19 November 1921. There are also general references to emigration plans in the entry for 14 January 1922.
46. TB, 22 November 1922.
47. TB, 23 November 1922.
48. TB, 25 January 1922.
49. TB, 27 March 1922.
50. TB, 1 December 1921.
51. TB, 26 January 1922.
52. TB, 4 February 1922.
53. TB, 21 February 1922. Similar self-criticism can be found in the entries for 13 and 18 November, as well as for 4 December 1921; see also Smith, *Himmler*, 158.
54. TB, 27 February 1922.
55. TB, 18 November 1921.
56. TB, 27 November 1921.
57. TB, 5 February 1922.
58. TB, 17 February 1922.
59. TB, 27 May 1922.
60. TB, 4 and 18 February 1922 concerning stomach problems. On 2 March 1922 he writes: 'Had to drink a whole glass of beer in one go. Hugo, the new Senior, did not know that I had been given permission not to drink beer.' On the following day he noted: 'terrible stomach ache.'

61. TB, 28 January 1922.
62. TB, 8 June 1922.
63. Ibid.
64. TB, 24 November 1921.
65. TB, 7 December 1921. On the quarrel with Käthe see also the entries for 10 November and 7 December 1921, as well as for 16, 17, and 18 January and 22 February 1922.
66. TB, 5 March 1922.
67. TB, 30 June 1922.
68. TB, 7 June 1922.
69. TB, 8 and 25 June, and 5 July 1922.
70. TB, 6 June 1922. Meister was quoting here from Emmanuel Geibel's 'Fahnen-treu', written in 1850; see Smith, *Himmler*, 167.
71. TB, 21 February 1922.
72. TB, 18 January 1922.
73. TB, 21 February 1922.
74. TB, 23 February 1922.
75. BAK, NL 1126/1, letter to the examination board of the Department of Agriculture of the Munich Technical University and the board's positive reply dated 3 June 1921. See also NL 1126/12, letters to his parents concerning exams that he was taking during his practical training in Munich (e.g. 6 February and 7 March 1921).
76. TB, 13 June 1922.
77. TB, 23 March 1922, as well as the following days. There are no diary entries for the period between 28 March and 26 May 1922.
78. TB, 30 May, 8, 14, and 30 June, as well as 2 July 1922.
79. TB, 15 June 1922: 'Father: Afterwards 10 o'clock in the Augustinerkeller. Talked politics. About women, love, life, particularly nowadays, about esoteric knowledge, about patriotic activities, talked to Gebhard and Paula etc. till 12 o'clock, enjoyed ourselves very much. Home again.'
80. TB, 4 Feb, 1922. Hugo Stinnes (1870–1924), who was not in fact a Jew, was one of the most influential businessmen during the post-war period.
81. TB, 4 March 1922. On the anti-Semitic entries in the diary see also Smith, *Himmler*, 165.
82. Leseliste no. 106, read 25 December 1921–5 January 1922. 'A book that really makes one scared and that, by providing evidence, once again clearly shows what one suspects is going on but is always forgetting about. A marvellous collection of material.'
83. Ibid. no. 107, read 11 February 1922.
84. TB, 22 June 1922.
85. TB, 3 July 1922.
86. TB, 12 January 1922.
87. TB, 9 June 1922.

88. On the conflict between Bavaria and the Reich see Ernst Rudolf Huber, *Deutsche Verfassungsgeschichteseit 1789*, vol. 7: *Ausbau, Schutz und Untergang der Weimarer Republik* (Stuttgart, etc., 1984), 249 ff.
89. *Münchner Neueste Nachrichten*, 16 June 1922.
90. TB, 24 June 1922.
91. TB, 26 June 1922.
92. TB, 28 June 1922.
93. TB, 2 July 1922.
94. TB, 4 June 1922.
95. TB, 5 July 1922. Himmler had allowed himself to be recruited for an anti-Republican initiative, which, however, was unsuccessful in getting its proposal put to a referendum. There is a copy of the statutes of the League in Staatsarchiv Freiburg, A 40/1, no. 174.
96. TB, 5 July 1922.
97. TB, 19 June 1921.
98. TB, 9 June 1922; see Smith, *Himmler*, 163.
99. TB, 2 July 1922.
100. TB, 13 November 1921.
101. Gebhard completed his diploma in Mechanical Engineering in July 1923, Ernst completed his diploma in Electrical Engineering in 1928; see Himmler, *Brüder Himmler*, 95 and 131.
102. TB, 9 June 1922. He was already complaining about the high lecture fees and the high prices of textbooks on 4 November 1921.
103. *Zahlen zur Geldentwertung in Deutschland 1914 bis 1923*, bearb. im Statistischen Reichsamt (Berlin, 1925), 5. On the effects of hyperinflation on Munich see Martin H. Geyer, *Verkehrte Welt. Revolution, Inflation und Moderne, München 1914–1924* (Göttingen, 1998), 319 ff.
104. This is shown by a comparison of the cost-of-living indices and the salaries of senior Reich officials (the incomes of senior Bavarian officials were similar):

February 1920	January 1921	January 1922	April 1922	July 1922	October 1922	January 1923
Cost of living compared with 1913 (= 1):						
8	11	20	34	54	221	1120
Salaries compared with 1913 (= 1):						
2	4	8	10	20	80	373

105. See Smith, *Himmler*, 162.
106. BAK, NL 1126/1, copy of the diploma.
107. BAK, NL 1126/17, letter from Prof. Hudezeck, 15 August 1922; see Smith, *Himmler*, 222.

108. BAK, NL 1126/1, copy of the reference from Stickstoff-Land-GmbH Schleissheim, 30 August 1923.

109. On the 1923 crisis and the prehistory of the Hitler putsch see Gerald D. Feldman, *The Great Disorder: Politics, Economics, and Society in the German Inflation, 1914–1924* (New York and Oxford, 1993), 631 ff.; Fenske, *Konservativismus*, 188 ff.; Heinrich August Winkler, *Weimar 1918–1933. Die Geschichte der ersten deutschen Demokratie* (Munich, 1993), 186 ff.

110. On the course of the Hitler putsch see Hanns Hubert Hofmann, *Der Hitlerputsch. Krisenjahre deutscher Geschichte, 1920–1924* (Munich, 1961); Harold J. Gordon, *Hitlerputsch 1923. Machtkampf in Bayern 1923–1924* (Frankfurt a. M., 1971); John Dornberg, *Hitlers Marsch zur Feldherrnhalle. München, 8. und 9. November 1923* (Munich, 1983).

111. StA München, Pol. Dir. München 6712, interrogations of Seydel und Lembert.

CHAPTER 4

1. In his diary entry for 14 February 1924 Himmler expressed his frustration and disappointment at his unsuccessful attempts to find work. It is clear from a letter from an acquaintance, Maria Rauschmayer, dated 13 June 1924 (BAK, NL 1126/17), that, prompted by Himmler's mother, she had been trying to ask around about a job in agriculture for him.

2. TB, 11, 13, 14, and 15 February 1924; evidently he was awaiting mail which was supposed to be left in the Schützen or 'Fasching' pharmacy. (According to Karl Wolff, his fellow fraternity member, Fasching, worked in the Schützen pharmacy: StA München, 34865/9, interrogation of 16 February 1962.) On 11 February Himmler referred to arrests of putschists in his diary; on 15 February he noted more details about the role of one of those arrested.

3. TB, 15 February 1924.

4. In 1924 Gebhard Himmler was registered as living at Marsplatz 8 (II Floor), see *Adressbuch für München 1924*.

5. BAB, BDC, Research Ordner 199, NSDAP headquarters to Himmler, 12 August 1925, with enclosure: National Socialist local branches in Lower Bavaria.

6. On his work on the article for the *Langquaider Zeitung* see TB 11, 12, and 17 February 1924; on its publication in the *Rottenburger Anzeiger* see TB, 23 February 1924.

7. TB, 24 February 1924.

8. TB, 25 February 1924.

9. TB, 24 February 1924.

10. Lothar Gruchmann and Reinhard Weber, with the assistance of Otto Gritschneder (eds), *Der Hitler-Prozess 1924. Wortlaut der Hauptverhandlung vor dem*

Volksgericht München I, 4 vols. (Munich,1997–9), here vol. 2 (Munich, 1998), 642. This shows that the defence offered to call Himmler as a witness to the aggressive behaviour of a Reichswehr officer who, on 9 November, was placed with his troops opposite to the Reichskriegsflagge in front of the War Ministry.

11. BAK, NL 1126/7, letters from Hajim (?) Mazhar, 24 November 1923, 16 April 1924, and 15 March 1925; reference in TB, 14 February 1924.

12. TB, 11, 14, and 15 February 1924.

13. TB, 12 February 1924.

14. BAK, NL 1126/17, Robert Kistler to Himmler, 17 June 1924.

15. Ibid. letter of 5 November 1924.

16. TB, 7 November 1921 and 31 May 1922. On the 'Paula affair' see also Smith, *Himmler*, 198ff.

17. TB, 12 November 1921 He had read the book in December 1920 and commented on it as follows: 'A book that presents the ideal of a woman as pure feeling and shows us woman simply as a goddess, as she often appears as a goddess to a true man. It is a hymn of praise to woman and to a feeling that is beautiful and idealized.—If only it could come true in the world we live in and if only the goddess woman did not have so many flaws' (Leseliste no. 72).

18. This is suggested by Paula Stölze's comment in her letter to Gebhard of 4 March 1924 that at the time she had considered Heinrich's letter to be 'not quite right' (BAK, NL 1126/13).

19. Ibid. Himmler to Paula Stölzle, italics in the original. It was a draft of 18 April 1923, which was sent in that or similar form as is clear from Paula's response, in particular her unwillingness to be 'lectured to' by Heinrich.

20. Ibid. 1 July 1923.

21. Ibid.

22. Ibid. 11 February 1924.

23. The break-up is clear from various letters in BAK, NL 1126/19: Gebhard Himmler's letter to the parents of his fiancée, 27 February 1924, as well as to Paula, 28 February 1924; Paula's reply as well as that of her father, Max Stölzle, both dated 4 March 1924. Gebhard then replied on 10 March 1924.

24. BAK, NL 1126/13, 4 March 1924.

25. Ibid. letter from the private detective, Max Blüml, dated 14 March 1924, to Himmler, who had given him the job on 9 March 1924.

26. Ibid. letter to Rössner, 12 March 1924, reply of 18 March 1924.

27. TB, 18–22 February 1924. A reference to a further stay with these friends is contained in the Leseliste no. 202 (28 February–5 March 1924).

28. BAK, NL 1126/17, 23 May 1924.

29. Maria Rauschmayer, born on 29 May 1901 in Dillingen, began her study of German at Munich University in winter semester 1919. She submitted a dissertation on the Reformation in 1924, but did not complete the degree (information from the Munich University archive).

30. TB, 2 June 1922.

31. BAK, NL 1126/17, Maria Rauschmayer to Himmler, 13 June 1924, received on 17 June 1924, see also the letter from Maria Rauschmayer of 18 November 1923.

32. Ibid. 2 August 1924.

33. Leseliste no. 175, Friedrich Zur Bonsen, *Das zweite Gesicht* (Cologne, 1916), read 29 November–4 December 1923: 'Intellectually serious and lucid study.'

34. Geyer, *Verkehrte Welt*, 309 ff., points out that during the hyperinflation medical and religious cranks were popular and that 'alternative' doctrines like Theosophy, Occultism, Spiritualism, and Anthroposophy had a big impact. See also Ulrich Linse, *Barfüßige Propheten. Erlöser der Zwanziger Jahre* (Berlin, 1983).

35. Leseliste no. 246, Heinrich Jürgens, *Pendelpraxis und Pendelmagie* (Pfullingen, 1925), read 25 August 1925.

36. BAK, NL 1126/17; however, he was turned down because the astrologer did not have enough facts (letter from Studienrat C. Heilmaier to Himmler, 19 September 1925).

37. Leseliste no. 148, Max Eyth, *Der Kampf um die Cheopspyramide*, 8th edn (Heidelberg, 1921), read 19–23 February 1923.

38. Ibid. no. 148, Karl Du Prel, *Der Spiritismus*, new edn (Leipzig, 1922), read January and February 1923: 'A serious little work with a philosophical basis which has really made me believe in Spiritualism and has really introduced me to it for the first time.'

39. Ibid. no. 86, Matthias Fidler, *Die Toten leben! Wirkliche Tatsachen über das persönliche Fortleben nach dem Tode* (Leipzig, 1909), read 30 April and 2 May 1921.

40. Ibid. no. 111, read December 1923.

41. Ibid. no. 191, read 9 February 1924.

42. Ibid. no. 167, Christian Heinrich Gilardone, *Eppes Kittisch!! Noch ä Beitraagk zu Israels Verkehr und Geist* (Speyer, 1843), read 8–14 October 1923.

43. Ibid. no. 171, Theodor Fritsch, *Handbuch der Judenfrage*, 29th edn (Leipzig, 1923), read 25 September–21 November 1923.

44. Ibid. no. 176, Theodor Fritsch, *Der falsche Gott. Beweismaterial gegen Jahwe* (Leipzig,1920), read 1–5 December 1924.

45. Ibid. no. 200, Erich Kühn, *Rasse? Ein Roman* (Munich, 1921), read 27 February 1924: 'Naturally deals with the Aryan and Jewish racial problem. The seduction and incarceration of this German girl is handled particularly well'. Ibid. no. 201, Edward Stilgebauer, *Die Lügner des Lebens. Das Liebesnest* (Berlin, 1908), read 20–9 February 1924: 'Jewish blood and Jewish sensuality depicted fairly well. The novel deals with inferior people with only a few exceptions.'

46. Ibid. no. 216, *Eine unbewusste Blutschande. Der Untergang Deutschlands. Naturgesetze über die Rassenlehre* (Grossenhain i. S., 1921), read 17 September 1924: 'A marvellous book. It's a pioneering work. Particularly the last part on how it's possible to improve the race again. It's on a terrifically high moral level.'

47. Ibid. no. 223, read 22–4 October 1924.
48. Ibid. no. 173, Heinrich Böhmer, *Die Jesuiten*, 4th completely revised edition (Leipzig and Berlin, 1921), read 5–24 November 1923.
49. Ibid. no. 193, Carl Felix von Schlichtergroll, *Der Sadist im Priesterrock* (Leipzig, 1904), read 19 February 1924: 'History of the seduction of women and girls in a sadistic manner in Paris. Moral constraint and hypnosis.'
50. Ibid. no. 207, Alfred Miller, *Ultramontanes Schuldbuch. Eine deutsche Abrechnung mit dem Zentrum und seinen Hintermännern* (Breslau, 1922), read 19 May 1924.
51. Ibid. no. 229, K. v.Widdumhoff, *Die entdeckten schwarzen Henker des deutschen Volkes* (Weissenburg i. B., 1924), read October 1924–20 January 1925.
52. Ibid. no. 189, Adolf-Viktor von Körber, *Adolf Hitler: sein Leben und seine Reden* (Munich, 1923), read 16 January 1924. Ibid. no. 208, Dietrich Eckart, *Der Bolschewismus von Moses bis Lenin. Zwiegespräch zwischen Adolf Hitler und mir* (Munich, 1924), read 19 May 1924. 'A down-to-earth and witty conversation between Hitler and Eckhardt, which reveals both of their personalities so accurately and so well. It provides a perspective through all epochs and opens one's eyes to many things that one hasn't been aware of. I wish that everyone would read this book.'
53. Ibid. no. 162, Björnstjerne Björnson, *Mary* (Berlin, 1910), read 15–19 September 1923: 'Mary is a purely Nordic, Germanic woman.'
54. Ibid. no. 165, Werner Jansen, *Das Buch Treue. Nibelungenroman* (Hamburg, 1916), read 28 September–3 October 1923.
55. Ibid. no. 179, read 1 October 1923–5 January 1924.
56. Ibid. no. 217, Werner Jansen, *Das Buch Leidenschaft. Amelungenroman* (Braunschweig, 1920), read 18–20 September 1924. The book was based on the 'Amelungenlied', a literary reconstruction produced in the nineteenth century.
57. Ibid. no. 218, read 24 September 1924.
58. Ibid. no. 220, Werner Jansen, *Gudrun: Das Buch Liebe* (Brunswick. 1920), read 4–21 October 1924.
59. Ibid. no. 202, Hans Günther, *Ritter, Tod und Teufel* (Munich, 1921), read 28 February–5 March 1924 as well as July–November 1924. In a letter of August 1924 (BAK, NL 1126/17), which was concerned among other things with the essence of 'völkisch' and which refers to conversations with Himmler, his friend Maria Rauschmayer mentioned both *Das Buch Treue* and Günther's work.
60. According to a post-Second World War report written by Gregor Strasser's brother Otto, which is not very reliable, Himmler had already met Gregor during 1923. He claims that Himmler was visiting Gregor when the police arrested him in Landshut directly after the putsch. Otto Strasser also maintains that during the previous months Himmler had assisted Gregor with the organization of his own paramilitary unit based in Landshut, acting as his 'adjutant'. This statement is not supported by any other evidence and appears

improbable in view of Himmler's involvement with the Reichskriegsflagge (Otto Strasser, *Hitler und ich* (Konstanz, 1948), 47 and 66 f.).

61. On Gregor Strasser see above all Udo Kissenkoetter, *Gregor Straßer und die NSDAP* (Stuttgart, 1978) and Peter D. Stachura, *Gregor Strasser and the Rise of Nazism* (London, 1983). Strasser outlined his views on 'National Socialism' in his book *Kampf um Deutschland. Reden und Aufsätze eines Nationalsozialisten* (Munich, 1932).

62. It is clear from Himmler's Leseliste that he was based in Landshut from July 1924.

63. BAK, NL 1126/17, letter to Robert Kistler, Milan, 22 August 1924.

64. *Kurier von Niederbayern*, 9 December 1924.

65. In October 1924 the Völkische Bloc had joined the NS-Freiheitsbewegung, which had brought together the Deutschvölkischen and the Nazis.

66. BAB, BDC, Research Ordner 199, letter of 8 July 1925.

67. Ibid. 4 August 1925.

68. See the further correspondence between Himmler and headquarters between September 1925 and February 1926 (ibid.).

69. Ibid. letter of 17 February 1926. He finished the year 1925 with a considerable deficit in his payments to party headquarters. See the letter from headquarters to Himmler of 19 January 1926.

70. Ibid. Himmler to Maurer, editor of the *Völkischer Beobachter*, 9 July 1925.

71. BAB, BDC, Research Ordner 199, 12 August 1925, Headquarters to Himmler.

72. Ibid. Himmler to Headquarters, 29 September 1925, and reply, 26 October 1925.

73. Ibid. Report for the period 15 October 1925–1 May 1926.

74. *Kurier von Niederbayern*, 28 August 1924, concerning a speech on 25 August in Aidenbach; ibid. 4 June 1925, concerning a speech in Viechtach; ibid. 21 September 1924 about a forthcoming speech in Fürstenzell on 24 September; on 3 April the paper reported on a speech in Malgersdorf on 26 March 1926.

75. On 9 March he spoke in the Dingolfing local branch and on 26 March in Malgersdorf on this topic (ibid. 18 March and 3 April 1926).

76. 'History and Locarno', Landshut local branch, speech on 19 November 1925 (ibid. 22–3 November 1925).

77. He spoke about the 'Dubious Machinations of the Jews' on 30 May 1924 in Viechtach (ibid. 4 June 1924) und he expanded on the topic 'Jewry and Bolshevism' on 13 June 1925 in Zwiesel (ibid. 21 June 1925). He had spoken about 'The Threats from the Jews' on 30 April 1926 in Malgersdorf (ibid. 11 May 1926).

78. Leseliste no. 235, Franz Haiser, *Freimaurer und Gegenmaurer im Kampfe um die Weltherrschaft* (Munich, 1924), read January–18 March 1925: 'We need such books. They strengthen one's belief in what one instinctively feels and yet, because one has been corrupted, doesn't dare believe [...].' In future years Himmler was to recommend this book and Wichtl's piece of anti-Freemasonry

propaganda, which he had read in 1919, as essential reading for an understanding of this problem (BAB, NS 18/5022, letter to Lindner, 27 August 1927).

79. *Kurier von Niederbayern*, 17–18 May 1925. He made similar statements on 15 May 1925 in Vilsbiburg (ibid. 20 May 1925). For speeches relevant to this topic see also 24 June 1925 in Deggendorf (ibid. announcement of 21 June 1925); 4 June in Straubing: 'The Freemasons' Lodge as a Tool of the Jews' (ibid. 3 June 1925).

80. He made similar speeches on 19 March 1926 in Irlbach and on 20 March 1926 in Strasskirchen (ibid. announcement of 17 March 1926).

81. 'The Agricultural Situation', in *Nationalsozialistische Briefe*, 1 April 1926.

82. 'Wake Up, Peasants!' of 20 July 1926.

83. *Kurier von Niederbayern*, 17 September 1925.

84. Ibid. 22–3 November 1925.

85. Ibid. 12 November 1925, announcement of a speech in Rotthalmünster: 'What Does National Socialism Want?'; ibid. 3 April 1926, about a speech on 26 March 1926 in Malgersdorf: 'National or International Socialism'; ibid. 18 March 1926, about a meeting in Dingolfing on 9 March 1926; on 27 March 1926 he spoke in Plattling on the same topic (ibid. 27 March 1926), and in Landshut he took the same line on 25 March 1926 (ibid. 31 March 1926).

86. Ibid. 3 December 1924.

87. Ibid. 18 March 1926.

88. Ibid. 3 April 1926. Himmler also spoke in September 1925 in Thuringia (see ibid. 7 October 1925) and between 10 January and 15 February 1926 undertook a speaking tour through north Germany (ibid. 18 February 1926.)

89. Leseliste no. 276, read La[ndshut], Mu [nich] and [on] journeys, 1925–19 February 1927.

90. Richard Breitman, 'Mein Kampf and the Himmler Family: Two Generations React to Hitler's Ideas', *Holocaust and Genocide Studies*, 13 (1999), 90–7.

91. On this see StA München, Pol. Dir. München 10081, Minute of the Munich police, Abt. VIa, of 13 January 1926; Report of Himmler's interrogation of 12 January 1926.

92. Elke Fröhlich *et al.* (eds.), *Die Tagebücher von Joseph Goebbels*, 2 Parts, 9 and 15 volumes (Munich, 1993–2006), 13 April 1926.

CHAPTER 5

1. Wolfgang Horn, *Der Marsch zur Machtergreifung. Die NSDAP bis 1933* (Düsseldorf, 1972), 243; Peter Hüttenberger, *Die Gauleiter. Studie zum Wandel des Machtgefüges in der NSDAP* (Stuttgart, 1969), 26 ff.; Dietrich Orlow, *The History of the Nazi Party*, vol. 1: *1919–1933* (Newton Abbot, 1971), 76 ff.

2. *Völkischer Beobachter*, 17 September 1926.

3. BAB, BDC, Research Ordner 199, 30 January 1927. On the party headquarters in this period see Horn, *Marsch*, 278 ff.; Albrecht Tyrell, *Führer befiehl... Selbstzeugnisse aus der 'Kampfzeit' der NSDAP. Dokumentation und Analyse* (Düsseldorf, 1969), 355 ff.

4. Hans-Walter Schmuhl, 'Philipp Bouhler—Ein Vorreiter des Massenmordes', in Ronald Smelser, Enrico Syring, and Rainer Zitelmann (eds), *Die Braune Elite II. 21 weitere biographische Skizzen* (Darmstadt, 1993), 39–50.

5. See Mathias Rösch, *Die Münchner NSDAP 1925–1933. Eine Untersuchung zur inneren Struktur der NSDAP in der Weimarer Republik* (Munich, 2002), 512, who does not attribute much importance to the later Oberbürgermeister of Munich during this period.

6. Peter Longerich, *Geschichte der SA* (Munich, 2003), 53 f.

7. On Hitler's political style during this period see Tyrell, *Führer befiel*, 146; Ian Kershaw, *Hitler*, vol. 1: *1889–1936* (Stuttgart, 1998), 359 ff.

8. Gerhard Paul, *Aufstand der Bilder. Die NS-Propaganda vor 1933* (Bonn, 1990), 64, and Kissenkoetter, *Straßer*, 33.

9. Paul, *Aufstand*, 65.

10. Ibid. 65 f.; a copy of the pamphlet is in the printed materials collection in the Institut für Zeitgeschichte (IfZ) in Munich.

11. On Himmler's planning of the 'Hitler meetings' see above all the file BAB, NS 18/5002, correspondence with the individual local branches, in particular Himmler's circulars dated 31 March 1928. Himmler had already sent questionnaires to local branches on 10 January 1928 in order to find out when, as a result of 'the largest hall having already been booked or because of festivities', a Hitler meeting could not take place (ibid.).

12. Reichspropagandaleitung (ed.), *Propaganda* (Munich, 1928), 36 ff.

13. BAK, NL 1126, appointments calendar for 1927.

14. BAB, NS 19/1789, 'National or International Socialism'.

15. StA München, Pol. Dir. München 18001, police report concerning the membership meeting of the Neuhausen section on 6 October 1926, 'Capitalism and Productive Labour'. The report is dated 14 October 1926.

16. Ibid. report on the public meeting of the Regensburg NSDAP local branch, 11 April 1927. The meeting took place on 9 April 1927.

17. BAB, NS 18/5007, letter from Fritz Schusnus to the Reich Party headquarters, 27 October 1926. Election results from the *Statistische Jahrbücher des Deutschen Reiches*.

18. BAB, NS 18/5007, 2 December 1926.

19. Ibid. Himmler's figures.

20. Ibid. Himmler to the Gau headquarters, 21 April 1927.

21. Ibid. Party headquarters to Himmler, 28 April 1927.

22. Ibid. Heinz Schulz to Himmler, 1 May 1927.

23. Ibid. Himmler to the Gau headquarters, 2 May 1927.

24. Ibid. 18 May 1927.

25. On the meetings and the election result see Beate Behrens, *Mit Hitler zur Macht. Aufstieg des Nationalsozialismus in Mecklenburg und Lübeck 1922–1933* (Rostock, 1998), 76 f.; on the election in general see ibid. 74 ff.

26. Circular from Himmler dated 24 December 1928, printed in Tyrell, *Führer befiel*, 255 ff. (quotes BAB, formerly Slg. Schumacher 373).

27. Paul, *Aufstand*, 68.

28. Tyrell, *Führer befiel*, 225; Paul, *Aufstand*, 66 f.

29. On the shift of Nazi propaganda to rural areas after the Reichstag election of 1928 see Johnpeter Horst Grill, 'The Nazi Party's Rural Propaganda before 1928', *Central European History*, 15 (1982), 149–85; Peter D.Stachura, 'Der kritische Wendepunkt? Die NSDAP und die Reichstagswahlen vom 20.Mai 1928', *Vierteljahrshefte für Zeitgeschichte*, 26 (1978), 66–99; Tyrell, *Führer befiehl*, 225 ff.

30. BAB, NS 18/5008, Himmler to G. Feder, 21 April 1928, and in NS 18/5011, to A. Göpfert, 2 August 1930.

31. BAB, NS 18/5001, Himmler to the Hof local branch.

32. BAB, NS 18/5005, Himmler to the *Westdeutscher Beobachter*, 6 November 1928.

33. BAB, NS 18/5007, 20 April 1927.

34. Ibid. 19 April 1927.

35. BAB, NS 18/5005, Himmler to Robert Scherl, band leader, 10 August 1928.

36. BAB, NS 18/5022, Himmler to Hans Lustig, Stettin, 27 July 1927.

37. BAB, NS 18/5006, Himmler to Herr H. Götz, Kronach, 10 May 1928. Similarly NS 18/5013b, Himmler to Karl Schick, Rossbach (Pfalz), 30 July 1930.

38. BAB, NS 18/5004, various letters.

39. BAB, NS 18/5006, letter to Coburg district headquarters (*Bezirksleitung*), 16 March 1928.

40. BAB, NS 18/5001, Propaganda department to Aschaffenburg local branch, 2 February 1927.

41. BAB, NS 18/5005, 24 October 1928.

42. Ibid. 27 October 1928.

43. Ibid. 31 October 1928.

44. Ibid. Himmler to the *Westdeutscher Beobachter*, 6 November 1928.

45. Tyrell, *Führer befiehl*, 146.

46. Himmler expressed his views on the origins of the agricultural crisis in an undated article and demanded as a response 'an ethnic (*völkisch*) peasant policy', which he used as the title of the piece (BAB, NS 19/1789). According to Himmler, in eastern Germany 'there are now huge amounts of land belonging to large estates that are on sale', which ought to be settled with peasants and

agricultural workers. At the same time, according to Himmler, this [was] 'the only effective defence against the intrusion of masses of Slavs from the east'.

47. Michael H. Kater, 'Die Artamanen. Völkische Jugend in der Weimarer Republik', *Historische Zeitschrift*, 213 (1971), 577–683; Peter Schmitz, *Die Artamanen. Landarbeit und Siedlung bündischer Jugend in Deutschland 1924–1935* (Bad Neustadt a. d. Saale, 1985).

48. Kater, 'Artamanen', 614.

49. Ibid. 623.

50. Ibid.

51. This is clear from documents in the archive of the German youth movement (see n. 57 below).

52. BAB, NS 18/5011, Himmler to Geheimrat von Konopath, 26 June 1930.

53. BAB, NS 18/5005, letter of 16 May 1929. Himmler recommends to his party comrade from Duisburg, Karl Muefeld, the principles of the Artam league, 'which has implemented in an exemplary manner the aims you have expressed in so far as it is possible to carry them out at the moment. I can only recommend that you should join the ranks of the Artam league and work for the realization of these goals.'

54. BAB, NS 18/5014, Himmler to the Pomeranian Gau headquarters, 21 August 1929, Re: request for the expulsion of five named party comrades.

55. BAB, NS 18/5004, Himmler to Rudolf Hager, Vienna, 21 June 1928.

56. BAB, NS 18/5011, Himmler to Maria Giessing, Bad Reichenhall, 16 July 1930.

57. Archiv der Deutschen Jugendbewegung, A 2-82/82, note by Alwiss Rosenberg of 23 May 1969, and A 2-82/10, Alwiss Rosenberg: 'Streit in der Artamanenbewegung' (MS).

58. Kater, 'Artamanen', 623.

59. The newspaper first appeared as a supplement to the *Berliner Arbeiterzeitung*. There is evidence for its existence until July 1929. Himmler was still using notepaper with the Bundschuh heading in 1931 (BAK, NL 1126/14, note of 16 February 1931).

60. BAK, NL 1126/6.

61. BAK, NL 1126/14, 29 September and 16 October 1927.

62. See the note in the catalogue of BAK, NL 1126. According to that the Himmler letters are in private hands. The archivist in the Federal Archive (*Bundesarchiv*), Josef Henke, was able on the basis of a microfilm to convince himself of their authenticity.

63. BAK, NL 1126/14.

64. Ibid. 21 November 1927.

65. Ibid.

66. Ibid. 22 November 1927.

67. Ibid. 2, 4, and 12 November 1927.

68. Ibid. 22 November 1927. She had already asked in her letter of 21 November what was the reason for his 'disappointment'.

69. Ibid. 26 November 1927.
70. Ibid.
71. Ibid. and 13 December 1927.
72. Ibid. 20, 21, and 22 December 1927.
73. Ibid. 22 and 24 December 1927.
74. Ibid. 24 December 1927.
75. Ibid. 20 December 1927.
76. Ibid. 24 December 1927. After she had got to know him a bit better she wrote on 11 March 1928: 'You know, sweetheart, I'm astonished by your submissiveness. All I can say to you is: "as you make your bed so you must lie on it".'
77. Ibid. 4 January 1928; 5 January 1928: 'Why are you so afraid of Berlin?'
78. Ibid. 21December 1927. On 24 December 1927 she enquired: 'What did the doctor say?' There are further mentions of stomach problems from 9 to 12 April 1928.
79. Ibid. 4 January 1928. The topic of 'decent' and 'not decent' comes up repeatedly in her early letters: 'And on the struggle about not being decent and not being good. I didn't want you suddenly to want to be like that and I wanted to help you' (31 December 1927). 'Yesterday evening I read your old letters, my dear fathead who wants to be decent' (4 January 1928).
80. Ibid. 24 December 1927.
81. Ibid. 27 December 1927.
82. Ibid. 29 December 1927 (two letters).
83. Ibid. 22 December 1927.
84. Ibid.
85. Ibid. 30 December 1927.
86. Ibid. 2 January 1928.
87. Ibid. 31 December 1927.
88. Ibid. 2 January 1928 (two letters).
89. Ibid. letter arrived in Munich on 2 January 1928.
90. Ibid. 31 December 1927.
91. Ibid. 5 May 1928.
92. Ibid. 6, 7, and 24 January 1928.
93. Ibid. 6 and 7 February 1928. There is an entry in the office diary for 8 February referring to his stay in Berlin, BAK, NL 1126/6.
94. On his travel preparations see BAK, NL 1126/14, 11 February, 21 April, und 13 May 1928.
95. Ibid. 31 December 1927 and 4 January 1928.
96. Ibid. 2 March 1928.
97. Ibid. 11 February 1928.
98. Ibid. 6 March 1928.
99. Ibid.

100. Ibid. 3 March 1928. 'You know, sweetheart, from your letter I once again get the feeling that you've told your parents something and don't want to tell me what they've replied for fear of offending me.'

101. Ibid. 21 April 1928; and 3 and 18 May 1928.

102. Ibid. 10 May 1928.

103. In her letter of 10 February 1928 (ibid.) she is already talking of leaving the clinic and sharing her life with Himmler. It is clear from the letter of 20 February 1928 (ibid.) that at this point she is determined to sell her shares in the clinic.

104. Ibid. 26 April 1928.

105. Ibid. 21 May 1928.

106. Ibid. 12 and 20 April 1928.

107. Ibid. 13, 20, 23, 25, and 27 June 1928.

108. Ibid. 24 und 27 June 1928.

109. StA München, Amtsgerichte 21849, 141, 19 September 1928.

110. BAK, NL 1126/14, 17 June 1928.

111. Ibid. 21 June 1928. See also 19 May and 15 and 18 June 1928.

112. StA München, Pol. Dir. München 18001, driving-test certificate. According to this Himmler had had driving lessons between 16 March and 22 June 1928.

113. BAK, NL 1126/14, wedding announcement of 3 July 1928.

114. Ibid. 21 January and 18 June 1929.

115. Ibid. 20 March 1929.

116. Ibid. 5 May 1929.

117. Ibid. 6 May 1929.

118. Ibid. 24 September 1929: 'Your parents do understand that the child will be baptized as a Protestant, don't they?'

119. Ibid. 22 September 1929.

120. Ibid. 13 October 1929.

121. Robert Lewis Koehl, *The Black Corps: The Structure and Power Struggles of the Nazi SS* (Madison, Wisc., 1983), 86.

122. On the early years of the SS see Heinz Höhne, *Der Orden unter dem Totenkopf. Die Geschichte der SS* (Gütersloh, 1967), 23 ff., and Koehl, *Black Corps*, 18 ff.

123. BAB, NS 19/1934, Guidelines for the Establishment of Protection Squads, sent out by the supreme command of the SS on 21 September 1925. On SS uniforms see also Andrew Mollo, *Uniforms of the SS*, vol. 1: *Allgemeine SS 1923–1945* (London, 1969).

124. BAB, NS 19/1934, Guideline no. 1, 21 September 1925.

125. Ibid. undated. Copy in the *Völkischer Beobachter* of 6 August 1926; Höhne, *Orden*, 28.

126. Longerich, *Geschichte der SA*, 45 ff.

127. BAB, NS 19/1934, Ernst Wagner to Hitler, 20 May 1926.

128. Ibid. Circular no. 1, 14 April 1926.

129. Koehl, *Black Corps*, 25 f.

130. Ibid. 26; Höhne, *Orden,* 29.

131. Koehl, *Black Corps,* 26 f.

132. BAB, NS 19/1934, 13 September 1927.

133. Ibid. and order no. 2 of 4 November 1927 (in the same file).

134. BAB, NS 19/1934, order of 20 January 1929. On the history of the SS in the years 1929–30 see in particular Koehl, *Black Corps,* 32 ff.

135. The figure of 280 men often quoted in the literature from the official party history written by Gunter d'Alquen (*Die SS. Geschichte, Aufgabe und Organisation der Schutzstaffeln der NSDAP* (Berlin, 1939), 8) is unreliable. D'Alquen's booklet is simply an expanded version of a Himmler speech from January 1937 and is not based on his own research. On Himmler's figures see BAB, NS 19/4013, 5 May 1944 (260), NS 19/4011, 16 December 1943, speech at a conference of Naval commanders (290), NS 19/4014, speech of 21 June 1944 in Sonthofen to Wehrmacht generals (300). In Heinrich Hoffmann, *Das Braune Heer. 100 Bilddokumente: Leben, Kampf und Sieg der SA und SS* (Berlin, 1932), 45, there is a caption under a Himmler portrait which states: 'He began his work with 300 or 400 men.'

136. *SS-Leitheft* 7/1b (1941/42), 'Im Dienst des Führers...Vom Kampf der SS. Ein geschichtlicher Rückblick', 10–14.

137. BAB, NS 19/1934.

138. A 'fundamental order' issued by the SA leadership on 12 April 1929 ('Grusa VIII') regulated in particular the formation of SS units and details of SS service (ibid.).

139. BAB, NS 19/1934.

140. Ibid. SS-Order Party Rally 1929, 26 July 1929.

141. *Völkischer Beobachter,* 4–5 August 1929, Standarten dedication ceremony and Announcement no. 29 of the Supreme SA Leader; *Völkischer Beobachter,* 6 August 1929, 'The swastika as the banner of freedom to come. The great march-past in the presence of the Führer.'

142. *Tagebücher Goebbels,* 5 July 1929.

143. Ibid. 1 August 1929.

144. Ibid. 20 November 1930.

145. Ibid. 22 November 1929.

146. Ibid. 13 January und 20 March 1930.

147. Ibid. 23 March 1930.

148. Paul, *Aufstand,* 70; Kissenkoetter, *Straßer,* 55 f.

149. *Tagebücher Goebbels,* 28 April 1930.

150. Ibid. 2 May 1930.

151. Ibid. 12 May 1930.

152. Ibid. 24 May 1930.

153. Himmler had third place on the list of candidates for the district of Upper Bavaria, which in fact ensured that he gained a seat in the Reichstag; had the party done badly in this district he would have got into parliament through

the Reich list, where he had a secure place at no. 15 (*Völkischer Beobachter*, 28 and 31 August 1930).

154. Details are contained in the file BAB, NS 18/5014. On his handing over of the post see also Kissenkoetter, *Straßer*, 59.

155. BAB, NS 19/1722, NSDAP Reichstag group to Himmler, 20 February 1931. 'We wish to point out', the reprimand stated, 'that the way the group's mail is being handled is by no means conducive to its efficient functioning.'

156. BAB, NS 19/1721, Schwenningen local branch to Himmler, 21 September 1932; Himmler's reply of 1 October 1932. The false statement is in Heinrich Himmler, *Der Reichstag 1930. Das sterbende System und der Nationalsozialismus* (Munich, 1931), 57.

CHAPTER 6

1. Longerich, *Geschichte der SA*, 103 f.; these events are documented in particular in StA München, Pol. Dir. München 6808, Report of the Landeskriminalamt Berlin of 16 September 1930; see also *Tagebücher Goebbels*, 30 August and 1 September 1930.

2. StA München, Pol. Dir. München 6810, Police report on a meeting of 14 October 1930; Eberhart Schön, *Die Entstehung des Nationalsozialismus in Hessen* (Meisenheim a. Glan, 1972), 129 f.; see also Longerich, *Geschichte der SA*, 102 and 105.

3. BAB, NS 19/2817, Himmler's report from memory of the resignation of the supreme SA-Führer Pfeffer von Salomon in 1930, written on 4 June 1941.

4. This is the version contained in the introduction to 'Die Pflichten des SS-Mannes und SS-Führers', BAB, NS 19/3973, as well as in the article 'Entstehung und Geschichte der SS', in *SS-Leitheft*, 2/9 (1936), 11–13.

5. BAB, NS 19/1934, SS order no. 20, 1 December 1930.

6. BAB, formerly Slg. Schuhmacher 403, SA order from Hitler dated 3 September 1930.

7. On the conflict between Hitler and Röhm during the early history of the SA see Longerich, *Geschichte der SA*, 15 ff., 33 ff., and 45 ff.

8. The memorandum, which appears to have been written by August Schneid-huber, one of the highest-ranking SA leaders, summarized the criticism of the party leadership that was widespread within the SA (StA München, Pol. Dir. München 6822, notes for a speech at an meeting of SA leaders, 30 November 1930). On the meeting with Hitler and Röhm's appointment see Longerich, *Geschichte der SA*, 108 f.

9. BAB, NS 19/1934.

10. BAB, BDC, Research Ordner 238 I (also NARA, T 580 R 36), Röhm to Himmler, 28 March 1930: 'I would like to thank you very warmly for your

letter of 29 January 1930, which more than any other I have received made me want to return soon to Germany.'

11. Ibid. (also NARA, T 580R 36), Himmler to Röhm, 4 November 1929.

12. Ibid. (also NARA, T 580 R 36), Röhm to Himmler, 28 March 1930. Röhm's letters of 7 September 1929 und 27 August 1930 have also survived (ibid.).

13. Longerich, *Geschichte der SA*, 147.

14. BAB, NS 19/1934.

15. Koehl, *Black Corps*, 41.

16. BAB,NS 19/1934. The order dealt with various other details.

17. Ibid. staff order no. 9 of 12 February 1931 and provisional instruction for the reinforcement, training and deployment etc. of the SS motorized units, 21 March 1931.

18. BAB, NS 19/1934, 12 May 1931.

19. StA München, Pol. Dir. München 6822, report of the General Inspector to the Chief of Staff, 17 December 1931.

20. On the numerous conflicts between the SA and the SS see Longerich, *Geschichte der SA*, 149 ff.; Michael H. Kater, 'Zum gegenseitigen Verhältnis von SA und SS in der Sozialgeschichte des Nationalsozialismus von 1925 bis 1939', *Vierteljahrsschrift für Sozial- und Wirtschaftsgeschichte*, 62/3 (1975), 339–79.

21. BAB, NS 19/1934, Oberführer Süd, Oberführer order no. 8, guidelines for the training of the SS in Abschnitt South, 1 April 1931.

22. Longerich, *Geschichte der SA*, 110 f.; see also in particular *Tagebücher Goebbels*, 1–10 April 1931.

23. BAB, NS 19/1934. The meeting took place on 13 and 14 June 1931.

24. 'Wir sind das Heer vom Hakenkreuz', 'O Deutschland hoch in Ehren', 'Noch ist die Freiheit nicht verloren', 'Wenn alle untreu werden', 'Heil mein Lieb, der Morgen graut', 'Brüder in Zechen und Gruben', 'Ich hatt' einen Kameraden', and 'Drei Lilien' were cited.

25. BAB, NS 19/1934, Provisional Service Regulations for the Work of the SS, June 1931.

26. Ibid. SS order C, no. 28, of 9 June 1931.

27. Ibid. SS order A, no. 35 of 13 July 1931.

28. Ibid. SS order A, no 1 of 24 January 1932.

29. Ibid. SS order A, no. 30 of 8 June 1931.

30. Shlomo Aronson, *Reinhard Heydrich und die Frühgeschichte von SA und SD* (Stuttgart, 1971), 34 ff.

31. Ibid. 37 f.; Wildt, *Generation*, 241.

32. Aronson, *Heydrich*, 54 ff., on the creation of the SD.

33. Ibid. 60 f.

34. Longerich, *Geschichte der SA*, 111.

35. BAB, formerly Slg. Schumacher 415, figures on the strength of the SA and SS, 18 May 1931; BAB, NS 19/1934, Himmler to Supreme SA leader, 2 October 1931.

36. Ibid. Report of the Landeskriminalpolizeiamt Berlin of 1 November 1931.

37. Doc. PS-1992 (A), Lecture by Himmler on the nature and role of the SS to a Wehrmacht course on national politics, 15–23 January 1937, in *International Military Tribunal: Der Prozess gegen die Hauptkriegsverbrecher vor dem Internationalen Militärgerichtshof, 14. Oktober 1945 bis 1. Oktober 1946*, 42 vols. (Nuremberg, 1947–9), here vol. 29, 206 ff.

38. BAB, NS 19/1934, SS order A, no. 65, of 31 December 1931.

39. BAB, NS 19/4013, speech of 5 May 1944. The same line was taken in an article published by the head of the Race Office, Schultz, in the journal *Volk und Rasse*, 17 (1942), in January 1942 to mark the tenth anniversary of the Engagement and Marriage Order: 'This order provoked a huge amount of malicious distortion and vicious sarcasm but the SS was unshakeable in standing its ground . . .' (1 f.).

40. This account of subcultural aspects of the SA derives above all from a large amount of literature that was published by the SA or those close to it immediately after the seizure of power. For details see Longerich, *Geschichte der SA*, 115.

41. BAB, NS 19/1934, SS order A, no. 67, 31 December 1931.

42. This is based on the rules of procedure of 12 May 1931 (ibid.).

43. On Darré see Anna Bramwell, *Blood and Soil: Richard Walther Darré and Hitler's 'Green Party'* (Bourne End, 1985); Horst Gies, *R. Walther Darré und die nationalsozialistische Bauernpolitik in den Jahren 1930 bis 1933* (Frankfurt a. M., 1966); BAB, BDC, SS-O Darré.

44. Isabel Heinemann, *'Rasse, Siedlung, deutsches Blut'. Das Rasse- und Siedlungshauptamt der SS und die rassenpolitische Neuordnung Europas* (Göttingen, 2003), 55 ff.

45. BAB, NS 19/1074.

46. BAB, BDC, SS-O Wolff; Jochen von Lang, *Der Adjutant. Karl Wolff, der Mann zwischen Hitler und Himmler* (Munich, 1985), 12 ff.

47. BAB, BDC, SS-O Heissmeyer, undated cv.

48. BAB, BDC, SS-O Wege, particularly the cv of 12 May 1932.

49. BAB, BDC, SS-O Hildebrandt, particularly the cv of 15 April 1936.

50. BAB, BDC, SS-O Krüger, cv.

51. Richard Breitman, 'Friedrich Jeckeln, Spezialist für die "Endlösung im Osten" ', in Ronald Smelser und Enrico Syring (eds), *Die SS. Elite unter dem Totenkopf. 30 Lebensläufe* (Paderborn etc., 2000), 267–75; BAB, BDC, SS-O Jeckeln, in particular Jeckeln to Himmler, 28 February 1932.

52. BAB, BDC, SS-O Lorenz, in particular the cv, 31 March 1937.

53. BAB, BDC SS-O Wittje, especially the undated cv.

54. BAB, BDC, SS-O Zech; Zech, born in 1892, had served in the Reichswehr until 1920 as a captain. See *Reichstags-Handbuch, IX, Wahlperiode 1933* (Berlin, 1934).

55. BAB, BDC, SS-O Moder, in particular the undated cv.

56. BAB, BDC, SS-O Schmauser, in particular the undated cv.

57. TB, 6 July 1922.

58. Anke Schmeling, *Josias Erbprinz zu Waldeck und Pyrmont. Der politische Weg eines hohen SS-Führers* (Kassel, 1993).

59. BAB, BDC, SS-O Woyrsch.

60. BAB, BDC, SS-O Eberstein.

61. Charles Messenger, *Hitler's Gladiator: The Life and Times of Oberstgruppenführer and Panzergeneral-Oberst d. Waffen-SS Sepp Dietrich* (London etc., 1988); Christopher Clark, 'Josef "Sepp" Dietrich. Landsknecht im Dienste Hitlers', in Smelser and Syring (eds), *Die SS. Elite*, 119–33; BAB, BDC, SS-O Dietrich.

62. BAB, BDC, SS-O Daluege; Caron Cradle, 'My Honor is Loyalty: The Biography of General Kurt Daluege', unpublished diss., Princeton 1979, particularly 74 ff. concerning his switch to the SS.

63. BAB, BDC, SS-O Rodenbücher, in particular the cv of 13 October 1933.

64. BAB, BDC, SS-O Weitzel, in particular the undated cv.

65. Ibid. Gerichts- und Rechtsamt, re: Standartenführer Hirt, 12 October 1937.

66. Ibid. Himmler to Hartmann, 30 October 1931.

67. BAB, BDC, SS-O Rediess, undated cv; appointment documents of 1 January 1931, 4 and 12 July 1932 (in July 1932 Rediess took over Abschnitt XII, though only for a week).

68. BAB, NS 19/1934, SS order D, no. 68, 31 December 1931.

69. Ibid. SS order D, no. 1, 14 January 1932, list of SS Air units. Himmler dealt with further details in SS order D, no. 3, of 18 March 1932.

70. Koehl, *Black Corps*, 53, who adopts the figures in the *Statistisches Jahrbuch der Schutzstaffel der NSDAP 1937* (Berlin, 1938), 4. For comparison: in June 1932 the SA had 397,000 members (Longerich, *Geschichte der SA*, 159).

71. Jan Erik Schulte, *Zwangsarbeit und Vernichtung. Das Wirtschaftsimperium der SS. Oswald Pohl und das SS-Wirtschafts-Verwaltungshauptamt 1933–1945* (Paderborn, etc., 2001), 24.

72. Schulte, *Zwangsarbeit*, 22 ff., on the beginnings of the SS administration.

73. BAB, NS 19/1934, SS order D, no. 69.

74. Mollo, *Uniforms*, 8. On Himmler's first appearance in the new uniform see the statement by Wolff (StA München, Staatsanwaltschaften 34865, vol. 9, 23 January 1962).

75. StA München, Staatsanwaltschaften 34865, vol. 9, 23 January 1962.

76. BAB 19/1074, note of 6 January 1939.

77. StA München, Staatsanwaltschaften 34865, vol. 9, 23 January 1962.

78. Ernst Hanfstaengl, *Zwischen Weißem und Braunem Haus. Memoiren eines politischen Außenseiters* (Munich, 1970), 98.

79. Albert Krebs, *Tendenzen und Gestalten der NSDAP. Erinnerungen an die Frühzeit der Partei* (Stuttgart, 1959), 209.

80. On this see Gerhard Schulz, *Von Brüning zu Hitler. Der Wandel des politischen Systems in Deutschland 1930–1933* (Berlin and New York, 1992), 819 ff.; Winkler, *Weimar*, 444 ff.

81. Richard Bessel, *Political Violence and the Rise of Nazism: The Storm Troopers in Eastern Germany 1925–1934* (New Haven and London, 1984), 87 ff.

82. BAB, BDC, SS-O Wappenhans, 13 April 1938.

83. See Schulz, *Brüning*, 961 ff.; Winkler, *Weimar*, 510 f.

84. Between June 1932 and the beginning of 1933 the SS only grew from around 41,000 members to around 50,000: Koehl, *Black Corps*, 53 and 79.

85. BAB, NS 19/1934, Abschnitt IV, Braunschweig: Mood of the SS, 23 September 1932.

86. Ibid. Gruppe East, 21 September 1932.

87. Ibid. Gruppe South, 21 September 1932.

88. Ibid. Gruppe South-East, 22 September 1932.

89. Ibid. Gruppe West, 21 September 1932.

90. Ibid. Abschnitt VII, Danzig, 23 September 1932.

91. Longerich, *Geschichte der SA*, 159 ff.

92. BAB, formerly Slg. Schuhmacher 407, 17 December 1932.

93. BAK, NL 1126/2, letter from Himmler, 4 April 1933.

94. Henry Turner, *Hitlers Weg zur Macht. Der Januar 1933* (Munich, 1997), 97 f.; Joachim von Ribbentrop, *Zwischen London und Moskau. Erinnerungen und letzte Aufzeichnungen,* aus dem Nachlass, ed. Annelies von Ribbentrop (Leoni a. Starnb. See, 1953), 37 f.

CHAPTER 7

1. On terror during the period of the seizure of power see in particular Klaus Drobisch and Günther Wieland, *System der NS-Konzentrationslager 1933–1939* (Berlin, 1993), 11 ff.; Johannes Tuchel, *Konzentrationslager. Organisationsgeschichte und Funktion der 'Inspektion der Konzentrationslager' 1934–1938* (Boppard a. Rh., 1991), 35 ff.; George C. Browder, *Foundations of the Nazi Police State: The Formation of Sipo and SD* (Lexington, Ky., 1990), 50 ff.

2. Drobisch und Wieland, *System*, 27 ff., emphasize that the essential feature of protective custody was precisely the absence of legal certainty.

3. Tuchel provides an overview of the various types of concentration camp during the years 1933–4 in *Konzentrationslager*, 38 ff.

4. On the 'seizure of power' in Bavaria and the construction of the terror apparatus there see Jochen Klenner, *Verhältnis von Partei und Staat 1933–1945, dargestellt am Beispiel Bayerns* (Munich, 1974), 44 ff.; Ortwin Domröse, *Der NS-Staat in Bayern von der Machtergreifung bis zum Röhm-Putsch* (Munich, 1974), 80 ff.; Martin Faatz, *Vom Staatsschutz zum Gestapo-Terror. Politische Polizei in Bayern in der Endphase der Weimarer Republik und der Anfangsphase der nationalsozialistischen Diktatur* (Würzburg, 1995), 381 ff. (See in particular 398 ff. on the expansion of the office of the police chief); Tuchel, *Konzentrationslager*, 121 ff.; Aronson, *Heydrich*, 94 ff.

5. Aronson, *Heydrich*, 100 f.

6. *Münchner Neueste Nachrichten*, 13 March 1933; see also *Völkischer Beobachter* of the same day.

7. BHStA, StK 5255, radio message from Wagner, 15 March 1933; see Klenner, *Verhältnis*, 859.

8. BHStA, StK 6288, Wagner edict, 27 March 1933; see Klenner, *Verhältnis*, 82 f.; Faatz, *Staatsschutz*, 417 ff.

9. BHStA, StK 6288, Wagner edict, 27 March 1933; see Klenner, *Verhältnis*, 82 f.; Faatz, *Staatsschutz*, 417 ff. 9 Wagner order, 1 April 1933, in *Bayerische Staatszeitung und Bayerischer Staatsanzeiger*, 21 (1933), 4 April 1933; also published in Aronson, *Heydrich*, 323; see Klenner, *Verhältnis*, 59.

10. Aronson, *Heydrich*, 99 f.

11. BHStA, StK 6288, Wagner edict, 10 April 1933.

12. Domröse, *NS-Staat*, 185 ff., on the special commissars.

13. BAB, R 2/28350, chronicle of the whole SS camp complex in Dachau quoted from Tuchel, *Konzentrationslager*, 124. On the establishment and early history of the Dachau camp see Barbara Distel and Ruth Jakusch, *Konzentrationslager Dachau 1933–1945* (Brussels, [1978]); Stanislav Zámecník, *Das war Dachau* (Luxembourg, 2002); also id., 'Dachau-Stammlager', in Wolfgang Benz and Barbara Distel (eds), *Der Ort des Terrors. Geschichte der nationalsozialistischen Konzentrationslager*, vol. 2: *Frühe Lager, Dachau, Emslandlager* (Munich, 2005), 233–74; id., 'Das frühe Konzentrationslager Dachau', in Wolfgang Benz and Barbara Distel (eds), *Terror ohne System. Die ersten Konzentrationslager im Nationalsozialismus 1933–1935* (Berlin, 2001), 13–39; Günther Kimmel, 'Das Konzentrationslager Dachau. Eine Studie zu den nationalsozialistischen Gewaltverbrechen', in Martin Broszat und Elke Fröhlich (eds), *Bayern in der NS-Zeit*, vol. 2: *Herrschaft und Gesellschaft im Konflikt. Part A* (Munich, 1979), 349–413; Lothar Gruchmann, 'Die bayerische Justiz im politischen Machtkampf 1933/34. Ihr Scheitern bei der Strafverfolgung von Mordfällen in Dachau', in Martin Broszat and Elke Fröhlich (eds), *Bayern in der NS-Zeit*, vol. 2: *Herrschaft und Gesellschaft im Konflikt. Part A* (Munich, 1979), 415–28; Hans-Günter Richardi, *Schule der Gewalt. Die Anfänge des Konzentrationslagers Dachau 1933–1934. Ein dokumentarischer Bericht* (Munich, 1983).

14. *Völkischer Beobachter*, 21 March 1933; See Tuchel, *Konzentrationslager*, 124.

15. Archiv Gedenkstätte Dachau, 16.103, quoted in Tuchel, *Konzentrationslager*, 125.

16. Tuchel, *Konzentrationslager*, 125 f.; Richardi, *Schule*, 55 ff. and 88 ff. The SS finally took over the camp on 30 May 1933.

17. IfZ, Nuremberg documents, PS-1216; see Tuchel, *Konzentrationslager*, 126.

18. Sybille Steinbacher, *Dachau—die Stadt und das Konzentrationslager in der NS-Zeit. Die Untersuchung einer Nachbarschaft* (Frankfurt a. M. etc., 1993).

19. On the investigations of the Munich public prosecutor see Gruchmann, 'Justiz', 416 ff. Prosecutor Wintersberger's report of 2 June 1933 is published

as doc. D-926, in *IMT*, vol. 36, pp. 55 ff. On the meeting with Epp on 2 June see Gruchmann, 'Justiz', 420 f.

20. On Eicke see Tuchel, *Konzentrationslager,* 128 ff., and Aronson, *Heydrich,* 105 ff.

21. BAB, BDC, SS-O Eicke, Eicke to Himmler, 29 March 1933.

22. Ibid. Eicke report of 20 March 1933 on the events in Ludwigshafen; Himmler order of 3 April 1933.

23. Ibid. Eicke to Himmler, 29 March and 13 April 1933; Report of Heyde, 22 April 1933.

24. Ibid. letter to Eicke on Himmler's behalf, 20 May 1933; Himmler to Heyde, 2 June 1933.

25. BAB, BDC, SS-O Koegel, Eicke to the head of the Bavarian auxiliary political police [Hilfspolizei], 27 November 1933; see Bernd Wegner, *Hitlers Politische Soldaten. Die Waffen-SS 1933–1945: Leitbild, Struktur und Funktion einer natio-nalsozialistischen Elite,* 5th edn. (Paderborn, 1997), 179.

26. On the Dachau model see Tuchel, *Konzentrationslager,* 141 ff.; Richardi, *Schule,* 119 ff.

27. Partly reproduced in doc. PS-778, in *IMT,* vol. 26, pp. 291 ff.

28. BAB, R 22/1167, Service Regulations for Sentries and Prison Guards, see Tuchel, *Konzentrationslager,* 144 f.

29. Details in Richardi, *Schule,* 183 ff.

30. Ibid. 189 ff. and 209 f. At the cabinet meeting on 26 July 1933 Interior Minister Wagner announced that he had directed Himmler 'to provide him with daily reports on important events and on significant measures that were being planned' (BHStA, MA 99 526).

31. Richardi, *Schule,* 179 ff.

32. Published in Distel und Jakusch, *Dachau,* 80; see also Tuchel, *Konzentrationsla-ger,* 142 f.

33. The acting Minister of Justice had already advocated restricting the use of protective custody at the cabinet meeting on 7 April 1933; on 16 May the ministers criticized the unauthorized measures taken by the Bavarian political police chief against Jewish institutions in Munich. It was minuted that 'actions of the political police chief had repeatedly caused great concern' (BHStA, MA 99 525). On 26 July the Reich Governor complained about the measures taken by the political police against the Nuremberg Jews; Prime Minister Siebert suggested that Himmler should be assigned an 'experienced administrative lawyer'. In the cabinet meeting on 27 February 1934 the Justice Minister declared that the practice of the political police in carrying out arrests was 'intolerable', and won support for his suggestion that decisions on the applica-tion of protective custody should in future be made by the Interior Minister (MA 99 526). But Himmler's work was not seriously affected by these repeated criticisms from the government.

34. Dok. D-926, in *IMT,* vol. 36, pp. 47 f. In a letter to Justice Minister Frank of 29 November 1933 Wagner refers to Himmler's commission of 18 November

1933, according to which the investigations of deaths in Dachau were to be abandoned 'for political reasons of state'. See Gruchmann, 'Justiz, 423 ff.

35. BHStA, MA 99 525, meeting of 6 December 1933.

36. Doc. D-926, in *IMT*, vol. 36, pp. 54 f., minute of Stepp, 6 December 1933.

37. This is the accurate characterization in Tuchel's *Konzentrationslager*, 149.

38. In Bavaria by 13 April 5,400 people had already been taken into protective custody, more than half of them communists. See Hartmut Mehringer, 'Die KPD in Bayern 1919–1945. Vorgeschichte,Verfolgung und Widerstand', in Hartmut Mehringer, Anton Grossmann, and Klaus Schoenhoven (eds), *Bayern in der NS-Zeit*, vol. 5: *Die Parteien KPD, SPD, BVP in Verfolgungund Widerstand* (Munich, 1983), 1–286, here 73 ff. In June 1933 over 1,000 Social Democrats were incarcerated in a further wave of arrests, see Hartmut Mehringer, 'Die bayerische Sozialdemokratie bis zum Ende des NS-Regimes. Vorgeschichte, Verfolgung und Widerstand', ibid. 287–432, here 338 ff.

39. Tuchel, *Konzentrationslager*, 153 f.

40. Ibid. 53 ff.

41. On the takeover of the political police see the overview in Hans Buchheim, 'Die SS—Das Herrschaftsinstrument', in id. *et al.*, *Anatomie des SS-Staates*, 7th edn. (Munich, 1999), 13–212, 39 ff., and the detailed account in Browder, *Foundations*, 98 ff.

42. Wegner, *Politische Soldaten*, 81 ff.; James J. Weingartner, *Hitler's Guard: The Story of the Leibstandarte SS Adolf Hitler, 1933–1945* (Carbondale, Ill., etc., 1974), 1 ff.

43. Even after Himmler had appointed Dietrich leader of the SS-Oberabschnitt East, Dietrich continued to emphasize the special position of the Leibstandarte. In April 1934, however, he agreed to the subordination of the Leibstandarte to the Oberabschnitt East; see Wegner, *Politische Soldaten*, 83, and Weingartner, *Guard*, 8 f.

44. On the takeover of the political police in Hamburg see Browder, *Foundations*, 100 ff.; Michael Wildt, 'Der Hamburger Gestapochef Bruno Streckenbach. Eine nationalsozialistische Karriere', in Frank Bajohr and Joachim Szodrzynski (eds), *Hamburg in der NS-Zeit. Ergebnisse neuerer Forschungen* (Hamburg, 1995), 93–123;Henning Timpke (ed.), *Dokumente zur Gleichschaltung des Landes Hamburg 1933* (Frankfurt a. M. ,1964); Ludwig Eiber, 'Unter Führung des NSDAP Gauleiters. Die Hamburger Staatspolizei (1933–1937)', in Gerhard Paul and Klaus-Michael Mallmann (eds), *Die Gestapo. Mythos und Realität* (Darmstadt, 1995), 101–17; BAB, BDC, SS-O Kaufmann.

45. *Dokumente zur Gleichschaltung*, 169 ff.

46. Ibid. 31.

47. BAB, BDC, SS-O Hans Nieland, SS-OA Nord, 21 March 1934, to RFSS. This appointment only occurred orally but was made formal on 30 April 1934 (Head of the SS Office to OA Nord, 7 April 1934). Nieland had joined the SS officially on 1 November 1933. See *Dokumente zur Gleichschaltung*, 177.

48. *Dokumente zur Gleichschaltung*, 177 f.

49. BAB, BDC, SS-O Streckenbach; Wildt, 'Streckenbach', 101; *Dokumente zur Gleichschaltung*, 176.

50. BAB, BDC, SS-O Kaufmann, Himmler to Kaufmann, 15 November 1933.

51. BAB, BDC, SS-O Georg Friedrich Ahrens, cv of 25 June 1942 and letter from Himmler dated 14 August 1934.

52. BAB, BDC, SS-O Streckenbach.

53. *Dokumente zur Gleichschaltung*, 176.

54. Ibid. 231 ff.

55. BAB, BDC, SS-O Hildebrandt and SS-O Ludwig Oldach (SS date of entry: 26 September 1933); Browder, *Foundations*, 104 f.; *Völkischer Beobachter*, 13 December 1933: 'Himmler becomes leader of the political police in Mecklenburg.'

56. On Himmler's appointment in Württemberg see Browder, *Foundations*, 106 ff.; Paul Sauer, *Württemberg in der Zeit des Nationalsozialismus* (Ulm, 1975), 58 ff. On Stahlecker see Jürgen Schuhladen-Krämer, 'Die Exekutoren des Terrors. Herrmann Mattheiss, Walther Stahlecker, Friedrich Mussgay, Leiter der Geheimen Staatspolizeistelle Stuttgart', in Michael Kissener and Joachim Scholtyseck (eds), *Die Führer der Provinz. NS-Biographien aus Baden und Württemberg* (Konstanz, 1997), 405–43, esp. 416 ff.

57. BAB, R 18/5642, minute by Pfundtner on a conversation with Murr, 31 May 1934. Murr told Pfundtner: the 'Führer is particularly keen on these units, which are similar to the Wecke unit, and, according to Herr Himmler, wants them to be introduced in all the states'.

58. BAB, NS 19/1724, Himmler to Murr, 4 December 1933: 'I would like to inform you that if you officially appoint me police chief in Württemberg I will be very happy to accept.' In a letter to Murr of 15 December 1933 Himmler referred to 'Würrtemberg as the first state with which I have been cooperating in the very important sphere of the political police for months'.

59. Herbert, *Best*, 138.

60. BAB, BDC, SS-O Murr.

61. Browder, *Foundations*, 108; see also Herbert, *Best*, 137 f.

62. Michael Stolle, *Die Geheime Staatspolizei in Baden. Personal, Organisation, Wirkung und Nachwirken einer regionalen Verfolgungsbehörde im Dritten Reich* (Konstanz, 2001), 85 ff.

63. Browder, *Foundations*, 106 f.; Inge Marssolek and René Ott, *Bremen im Dritten Reich. Anpassung—Widerstand—Verfolgung* (Bremen, 1986), 121 ff. and 176 ff.; BAB, BDC, SS-O Laue and Schulz. According to his cv of 7 June 1935, from 1930 onwards the latter was in the Intelligence department, which de facto was the political police. From November 1933 he was acting head of the Secret State Police in Bremen. On Schulz see in particular Wildt, *Generation der Unbedingten* (Hamburg, 2003), 561 ff. See also BAB, NS 19/1718, telegram from Himmler's Adjutant's office to the Bürgermeister of Bremen, 18 December 1933, according to which Himmler was happy to become political police chief in Bremen.

64. Browder, *Foundations*, 106.

65. Buchheim, 'SS', 39; Browder, *Foundations*, 110. Prime Minister Alfred Freyberg joined the SS in November 1933 and from spring 1934 was registered as a
leader in the SD Office. Reich Governor Loeper (who was also responsible for
Brunswick) was given the rank of SS-Gruppenführer shortly after Himmler's
appointment: BAB, BDC, SS-O Friedrich Wilhelm Loeper, Himmler's telegram of congratulation on his appointment dated 12 February 1934; SS-O
Alfred Freyberg.
66. Browder, *Foundations*, 111.
67. Buchheim, 'SS', 42; Browder, *Foundations*, 111.
68. On Saxony see Aronson, *Heydrich*, 160 f. In Dresden the SD had a valuable
contact in the shape of Herbert Mehlhorn, from 1 September 1933 deputy
president of the Saxon Secret State Police. Mehlhorn was a member of the
SD. On Himmler's appointment in Saxony see also Browder, *Foundations*, 111 f.
69. BAB, NS 19/1724, 17 December 1933; BAB, BDC, SS-O Loeper, Himmler's
letter of congratulation dated 12 February 1934. On the context see Gerhard
Wysocki, *Die Geheime Staatspolizei im Land Braunschweig. Polizeirecht und Polizeipraxis im Nationalsozialismus* (Frankfurt a. M. and New York, 1997), esp. 58 f.
70. BAB, BDC, SS-O Klagges.
71. Aronson, *Heydrich*, 166; on this conflict see also Browder, *Foundations*, 94 ff.
72. In June 1933 Klagges brought Jeckeln back to Brunswick from SS headquarters
in Munich, where he had been sent in 1932 because of his involvement in
bomb attacks. Jeckeln had cooperated with Klagges in the conflict with the SD:
see Wysocki, *Geheime Staatspolizei*, 63; BAB, BDC, SS-O Jeckeln, letters of
appointment dated 6 February 1933 and 9 August 1933.
73. Browder, *Foundations*, 109 f.
74. Ibid. 115.
75. For a summary of the reasons for Himmler's success see ibid. 114 f.
76. On Braunschweig, Hessen, and Saxony see ibid. 111 ff.; on Baden see Stolle,
Geheime Staatspolizei, 87; Eiber, 'Führung', 109 ff., points out that Gauleiter
Kaufmann's control of the political police in Hamburg was such that he was
able to delay the systematic persecution of the Social Democrats—in view of
the strong position of SPD supporters within the administration—until autumn 1934.
77. This arrangement lasted until the Bavarian political police was finally
incorporated into the Gestapo in 1937. See Ludwig Eiber, 'Polizei, Justiz
und Verfolgung in München 1933 bis 1945', in Richard Bauer *et al.* (eds),
*München—'Hauptstadt der Bewegung'. Bayerns Metropole und der Nationalsozialis-
mus* (Munich, 2002; 1st edn. 1993), 235–43.
78. The assertion that Himmler was seeking to create a unified German police
force right from the start (Aronson, *Heydrich*, 134; Herbert, *Best*, 137 f.; put in a
rather more general way by Browder, *Foundations*, 98 f.) is supported only by
the retrospective statements by Best and Eberstein. Significantly, there is no
contemporary evidence for it.

79. On the police in Prussia in 1933 see Browder, *Foundations*, 50 ff.; Tuchel, *Konzentrationslager*, 47 ff. On Daluege's role see Aronson, *Heydrich*, 75 ff., and Cradle, 'Honor', 92 ff.

80. For details on Daluege's alienation from Himmler see Aronson, *Heydrich*, 80.

81. On the formation of the Prussian Gestapo see ibid. 82 ff.; Browder, *Foundations*, 55 ff.; Christoph Graf, *Politische Polizei zwischen Demokratie und Diktatur. Die Entwicklung der preußischen Politischen Polizei vom Staatsschutzorgan der Weimarer Republik zum Geheimen Staatspolizeiamt des Dritten Reiches* (Berlin, 1983), 108 ff.; Tuchel, *Konzentrationslager*, 53 ff. The Law Concerning the Creation of a Secret State Police Office of 26 April 1933 is crucially important, see *PrGS* 1933, 122 f.

82. Browder, *Foundations*, 58 f., provides a number of examples: the head of the Gestapo office in Breslau, Emanuel Schaefer, was an SD member as was his subordinate, Günther Patschowski, whom Schäfer had recruited (see also ibid. 115; BAB, BDC, SS-O Emanuel Schäfer, Assessment by SD-Führer Oberabschnitt South-East dated 12 July 1937); the heads of the Gestapo offices in Frankfurt an der Oder and Aachen, Hans Moebus and Hans Nockermann, joined the SS in summer 1933 (BAB, BDC, SS-O Hans Nockermann, Entry into the SS in summer 1933), the file reveals that he was assigned to the SD from 1 August 1935).

83. Aronson, *Heydrich*, 68, refers to file no. 464 of the former Sammlung Schumacher in the Bundesarchiv (BAB), which has been dissolved and can no longer be reconstructed.

84. This refers to the figures in the original plan (Tuchel, *Konzentrationslager*, 46).

85. Edict of 21 April 33, quoted in Aronson, *Heydrich*, 79, BAB, formerly Slg. Schumacher 464.

86. Edict of 7 June 1933, quoted in Aronson, *Heydrich*, 71, BAB, formerly Slg. Schumacher 464.

87. Letter of 25 June 1933, quoted in Aronson, *Heydrich*, 87 f., BAB, formerly Slg. Schumacher 462; for details see Graf, *Politische Polizei*, 179 ff.

88. GStA, Rep 90 P 1, H. 1, Volk to Göring, 24 March 1934, here also Göring's minute of approval.

89. Browder, *Foundations*, 87; GStA, Rep 90 P 2, H.2, Gestapa organizational chart, 22 January 1934: Department V, Sohst, liason officer to the SA, SS, to the RFSS, and to the Schutzpolizei.

90. For example Guenther Patschowski, hitherto Himmler's contact in the Silesian Gestapo, whom he appointed head of the new Department IV, Treason and Counter-espionage, in the Gestapa, an office that worked closely with the Reichswehr. Patschowski brought his own staff with him (Browder, *Foundations*, 115 f.; Aronson, *Heydrich*, 156 ff.; for the source see the account by an insider publishing in 1945 under a pseudonym, 'Heinrich Orb', *Nationalsozialismus: 13 Jahre Machtrausch*, 2nd edn. (Olten, 1945), 127 f. and 146).

91. Browder, *Foundations*, 86 f. and 119; Aronson, *Heydrich*, 175; Graf, *Politische Polizei*, 187.

92. BAB, BDC, SS-O Daluege, Reichsführung-SS, Führungsstab, to Daluege, 2 October 1933, and Daluege's reply of 3 October 1933 (also in Aronson, *Heydrich*, Dokument 12, 320), in which he clearly expressed his disappointment about this.

93. See above pp. 156 f. and Browder, *Foundations*, 98 f.

94. Browder, *Foundations*, 91 ff. On the SD in 1933 see above all Aronson, *Heydrich*, 139 ff.

95. BAB, BDC, SS-O Heydrich, order of 22 July 1933 with retrospective effect to 19 July 1933; Browder, *Foundations*, 96.

96. Browder, *Foundations*, 96.

97. IfZ, Party Chancellery Order of 13 November 1933.

98. Browder, *Foundations*, 97; Aronson, *Heydrich*, 140; BAB, BDC, SS-O Heydrich.

99. George C. Browder, *Hitler's Enforcers: The Gestapo and the SS Security Service in the Nazi Revolution* (New York, etc., 1996), 116 f.

100. Aronson, *Heydrich*, 164.

101. IfZ, Partei-Kanzlei, Order of 9 June 1934; this arrangement came into effect on 15 July 1934.

102. Tuchel, *Konzentrationslager*, 78 ff.

103. Browder, *Foundations*, 88. See also BAB, R 19/423, Complaint from Hinkler who had now been appointed police president in Altona–Wandsbek, 22 December 1933. Daluege wrote to Röhm in this connection (ibid., 23 February 1934) to say that Göring had requested documents from Halle concerning Hinkler's previous career as a teacher and said 'that in view of the report on Hinkler provided by two professors from the University of Halle and given that we are old Nazi fighters we must all be considered mad'.

104. Browder, *Foundations*, 87 ff.; Diels's promotion occurred on 9 November 1933.

105. See ibid. 76 ff.; Graf, *Politische Polizei*, 139 ff.

106. BAB, R 18/5642; significantly a Reich Interior Ministry 'Memorandum Concerning the Creation of a Secret Reich Police Force and of a Secret Reich Police Office' was presented to Frick on 19 December 1933.

107. Law Concerning the Secret State Police of 30 November 1933, in *PrGS* 1933, 413; Browder, *Foundations*, 89 f.

108. Decree Concerning the Implementation of the Law Concerning the Secret State Police of 8 March 1934, in *PrGS* 1934, 143; Browder, *Foundations*, 123 f.

109. Browder, *Foundations*, 121 ff. According to Orb, *Nationalsozialismus*, 85 ff., Behrends knew Heydrich from his period as a naval officer and was devoted to him.

110. Browder, *Foundations*, 123; on 9 January 1934 Frick had already requested the states to reduce the use of protective custody, and in January Göring had also

issued similar instructions for Prussia (BAB R 58/264, letter of 9 January 1934; see Aronson, *Heydrich*, 183). Göring issued a further order about this in March (BAB, R 58/264, 11 March 1934).

111. BHStA, Reichsstatthalter Epp 148, Meeting with the Reich Governors, 22 March 1934.

112. Browder, *Foundations*, 123; Gruchmann, 'Justiz', 550; BAB, R 43 II/398, Reich Governor to Prime Minister, 20 March 1934, Wagner's comment, 13 April 1934.

113. BAB, R 58/264, edict of 12 April 1934; see Aronson, *Heydrich*, 184.

114. GStA, Rep 90 P 2, H. 1, 28. April 1934, Göring to Himmler, and Himmler's reply, 1 May 1934. As part of this compromise Frick also had to accept that Himmler became chief of the political police in the states of Lippe and Schaumburg Lippe, the last two titles that were missing from Himmler's collection of political police-chief titles (Browder, *Foundations*, 125 f.; NLA, StA Bückeburg, L4/10193/1–2).

115. Graf, *Politische Polizei*, 208 ff.

116. BAB, NS 19/4006, Speech to Oberabschnitt North-West, 5 March 1939; similarly in a speech to Oberabschnitt Rhine, 26 February 1939, and in a speech to police officers in Wiesbaden on 27 February 1934 (ibid.). On the SS's expansion after the seizure of power see Koehl, *Black Corps*, 91 f.

117. Doc. PS-1992 (A), speech to a Wehrmacht course on national politics from 15 to 23 January 1937, in *IMT*, vol. 29, pp. 206 ff.

118. Schulte, *Zwangsarbeit*, 77.

119. BAB, NS 19/4042, 6 February 1934.

120. Ibid. Himmler order of 9 February 1934 concerning the reorganization of the Reich leadership of the SS.

121. On Pohl and his switch to the SS see Schulte, *Zwangsarbeit*, 32 ff.

122. BAB, BDC, SS-O Pohl, letter to Himmler, 24 May 1933.

123. BAB, BDC, SS-O Pohl.

124. Reinhard Rürup (ed.), *Topographie des Terrors. Gestapo, SS und Reichssicherheitshauptamt auf dem 'Prinz-Albrecht-Gelände'. Eine Dokumentation* (Berlin, 1987), 11 ff.

125. Longerich, *Geschichte der SA*, 206 f.; Wolfgang Sauer, 'Die Mobilmachung der Gewalt', in Karl Dietrich Bracher *et al.*, *Die nationalsozialistische Machtergreifung. Studien zur Geschichte des totalitären Herrschaftssystems in Deutschland 1933/34* (Cologne and Opladen, 1960), 685–972, 897 ff.; Heinz Höhne, *Mordsache Röhm. Hitlers Durchbruch zur Alleinherrschaft 1933–1934* (Reinbek b. Hamburg, 1984).

126. On the history of the SA after the seizure of power see Longerich, *Geschichte der SA*, 179 ff.

127. Ibid. 204.

128. Sauer, 'Mobilmachung', 948 on Diels (based on his memoirs *Lucifer ante Portas*, 378 ff.) and 948 for Fritsch.

129. Höhne, *Mordsache Röhm*, 224 ff.

130. Klaus-Jürgen Müller, *Das Heer und Hitler* (Stuttgart, 1968), 106 f.

131. Sauer, 'Mobilmachung', 951.

132. Höhne, *Mordsache Röhm*, 226 f.

133. Ibid. 224 ff.; Herbert, *Best*, 141 f. Best was assigned SD-Oberabschnitt South (Bavaria) and kept his existing function, Oberabschnitt South-West (Baden und Württemberg).

134. BAB, NS 23/1, 16 May 1934.

135. Höhne, *Mordsache Röhm*, 228 f.

136. Vom Woyrsch, the then head of SS-Oberabschnitt South-East, was ordered by Himmler to come to Berlin on 25 June; the head of SS-Abschnitts XXI (Görlitz), Hildebrand, was also present at this interview. Himmler informed the two SS-Führer that an SA revolt was expected and that Silesia was the main centre of the trouble. See IfZ, GM 07.06, Statement by Udo vom Woyrsch, 12 July 1949; charge issued by the public prosecutor at the Osnabrück state court, 21 April 1956; Judgment, 2 August 1957; also Sauer, 'Mobilmachung', 955. The date of 28 June 1934 as contained in Herbert, *Best*, is only based on Best's statements.

137. Sauer, 'Mobilmachung', 956.

138. Röhm was shot by the commandant of KZ Dachau, Eicke, and his deputy. Gregor Strasser was murdered by an SS man in a cell in the Gestapo prison in Berlin; see Höhne, *Mordsache Röhm*, 294 ff.

139. Herbert, *Best*, 156.

140. *Völkischer Beobachter*, 26 July 1934.

141. See the summary in Herbert, *Best*, 146.

142. Browder, *Foundations*, 148 ff.

143. GStA, Rep 90 P 1, H. 1, Göring to Frick, 5 July 1934. On the same day Göring informed all Oberpräsidenten and Regierungspräsidenten in a radio message that this edict did not apply to the Prussian Gestapo (ibid.); see. Aronson, *Heydrich*, 217 f.

144. GStA, Rep 90P 1,H. 1, 4 July 1934.

145. Ibid. also in BAB, R 58/239.

146. Ibid. letter from Frick dated 7 July 1934, published in Günter Plum, 'Staatspolizei und innere Verwaltung 1934–1936', *Vierteljahrshefte für Zeitgeschichte*, 13 (1965), 191–224, doc. no. 2. In his reply of 9 July 1934 (GStA, Rep 90 P 1, H. 1) Göring welcomed the new arrangement without referring to the basic question raised by Frick of the position of the 'special political police'. There are more toughly worded drafts in this file; the final version is published in Plum, 'Staatspolizei', doc. no. 3. See Aronson, *Heydrich*, 219.

147. GStA, Rep 90 P 1, H. 1, Frick to Göring, 13 July 1934; Frick to the Ober- and Regierungspräsidenten, 16 July 1934, published in Plum, 'Staatspolizei', doc. no. 4; see Aronson, *Heydrich*, 219 f.

148. On the Vienna July putsch see Gerhard Jagschitz, *Der Putsch. Die Nationalso-zialisten 1934 in Österreich* (Graz, etc., 1976). For a summary see Sven Felix Kellerhoff, 'Schüsse am Ballhausplatz. Der Putsch gegen Österreichs Kanzler Dollfuß 1934', in Alexander Demandt (ed.), *Das Attentat in der Geschichte* (Cologne, etc., 1996), 345–60.

149. Jagschitz, *Putsch*, 74 ff.

150. *Tagebücher Goebbels*, 24 June 1934.

151. Jagschitz, *Putsch*, 81 f.

152. On the course of the putsch see ibid. 99 ff.

153. On the Dollfuss myth see ibid. 190 ff.

154. On the crushing of the putsch see ibid. 130 ff.

155. Ibid. 145.

156. Ibid. 179 ff.

157. Ibid. 82 ff.

158. Ibid. 184.

159. A copy of the report is in BAB, NS 19/3633 and 3634 and published as *Die Erhebung der österreichischen Nationalsozialisten im Juli 1934. Akten der Histor-ischen Kommission des Reichsführers SS* (Vienna, etc., 1965).

160. *Erhebung*, 69.

CHAPTER 8

1. On the diplomatic and domestic background to Himmler's appointment as Chief of the German Police see Browder, *Foundations*, 166 f.

2. BAB, BDC, Research Ordner 425; see Koehl, *Black Corps*, 109 ff.

3. Published in Paul Hausser, *Soldaten wie andere auch. Der Weg der Waffen-SS* (Osnabrück, 1967), 232 ff. The edict also stated that up to 25,000 men could be recruited to bolster the political police.

4. Details in Wegner, *Politische Soldaten*, 94 f.

5. Ibid. 89.

6. Ibid. 90.

7. Ibid. 91; Klaus-Jürgen Müller, *General Ludwig Beck. Studien u. Dokumente zur politisch-militärischen Vorstellungswelt und Tätigkeit des Generalstabschefs des deutschen Heeres 1933–1938* (Boppard a. Rh., 1980), 68; remarks by the RFSS to the head of the Truppenamt on 10 October 1934, ibid. doc. no. 14a, 372 ff.

8. Müller, *Beck*, 68 ff.

9. Wegner, *Politische Soldaten*, 92 f.

10. BAB, NS 15/35.

11. BAB, NS 31/70, RFSS order of 14 January 1935.

12. Schulte, *Zwangsarbeit*, 62 ff. On the development of the Administration Office within the SS Main Office see ibid. 45 ff.

13. Tuchel, *Konzentrationslager*, 159 ff.; Karin Orth, *Das System der nationalsozialis-tischen Konzentrationslager. Eine politische Organisationsgeschichte* (Hamburg, 1999), 31 ff.; on the camp see Stefanie Endlich, 'Die Lichtenburg 1933–1939. Haftort politischer Prominenz und Frauen-KZ', in Wolfgang Benz and Bar-bara Distel (eds), *Herrschaft und Gewalt. Frühe Konzentrationslager 1933–1939* (Berlin, 2002), 11–64.

14. Tuchel, *Konzentrationslager*, 184 ff.

15. Ibid. 187 ff.; Dirk Lüerssen, '"Moorsoldaten" in Esterwegen, Bürgermoor, Neusustrum. Die frühen Konzentrationslager im Emsland 1933 bis 1936', in Wolfgang Benz and Barbara Distel (eds), *Herrschaft und Gewalt. Frühe Konzen-trationslager 1933–1939* (Berlin, 2002), 157–210, here 182 ff.

16. Tuchel, *Konzentrationslager*, 192 ff.; Carina Baganz, *Erziehung zur 'Volksge-meinschaft'. Die frühen Konzentrationslager in Sachsen 1933–34/37* (Berlin, 2005), 251 ff.

17. Kurt Schilde, 'Vom Tempelhofer Feld-Gefängnis zum Schutzhaftlager: Das "Columbia-Haus" in Berlin', in Wolfgang Benz and Barbara Distel (eds), *Herrschaft und Gewalt. Frühe Konzentrationslager 1933–1939* (Berlin, 2002), 65–81; Udo Wohlfeld, 'Im Hotel "Zum Großherzog". Das Konzentrationslager Bad Sulza 1933–1937', in Wolfgang Benz and Barbara Distel (eds), *Instrumentarium der Macht. Frühe Konzentrationslager 1933–1937* (Berlin, 2003), 263–75.

18. BAB, NS 19/1447, and GStA, Rep 90 P 13, H. 1, Himmler to the Prussian Finance Minister (referring to the conversation), quoted in Tuchel, *Konzen-trationslager*, 309 f., who comments extensively on the document.

19. BAB, NS 19/4002, speech by Himmler to officials and employees of the Secret State Police Office on 11 October 1934.

20. BAB, NS 19/4003, speech by the RFSS to the Prussian State Councillors, 5 March 1936: 'I believe that few people are more aware of just how inadequate the organization of the Secret State Police Office was during the years 1933/34 and still was at the beginning of 1935 than the Prime Minister and I.'

21. Tuchel, *Konzentrationslager*, 160.

22. GStA, Rep 90 P 1, H. 1, letter from Göring dated 15 October 1934, Procedural instructions for the Secret State Police, also in BAB, R 58/239; see Aronson, *Heydrich*, 222 f.

23. GStA, Rep 90P 1, H. 2, 20 November 1934; see Aronson, *Heydrich*, 239.

24. GStA, Rep 90P 1, H. 2, circular order from Göring, 20 November 1934, also in BAB, R 58/239; see Aronson, *Heydrich*, 223.

25. Browder, *Enforcers*, 124 ff.

26. Aronson, *Heydrich*, 202 ff.

27. Browder, *Enforcers*, 127 and 132 ff.

28. On the Foreign Department at this time see Thorsten J. Querg, *Spionage und Terror. Das Amt VI des Reichssicherheitshauptamtes 1939–1945*, Phil. Diss. Berlin 1997 [Microfiche], 157 ff. According to Browder, *Enforcers*, 176, Department

III had only 41 staff in 1937. On the early activities of the SD abroad see Höhne, *Orden*, 210 ff. and 259 ff.

29. Browder, *Foundations*, 175.

30. Browder, *Enforcers*, 92.

31. Quoted in Aronson, *Heydrich*, 196 (from the dissolved Slg. Schumacher [BAB]).

32. BAB, R 58/243, Police Institute Charlottenburg, Organization of the Secret State Police. The service instruction is undated but was issued before Himmler's appointment as Chief of the German Police.

33. IfZ, Partei-Kanzlei, circular 24/36 of the Führer's deputy, 14 February 1936, which repeats the order of the head of the Security Main Office of 8 December 1935.

34. Browder, *Foundations*, 179, quotes a summary which is in the BAM in Freiburg under file no. Z 518z.

35. On the whole subject of the relations between military intelligence (the Abwehr) and the Gestapo during the first years of the regime see Browder, *Foundations*, 172 ff.

36. BAB, R 58/242, minutes of the meeting dated 17 January 1935; see also Browder, *Foundations*, 180 ff.

37. Browder, *Foundations*, 180 f.

38. Ibid. 181; GStA, Rep 90 I, H. 2, Blomberg to Pr. Finance Minister and to the Reich and Pr. Interior Minister 22 January 1935, Minutes of the meeting dated 17 January 1935 enclosed; BAB, R 43 II/391, Blomberg's letter of 1 July 1935.

39. Browder, *Foundations*, 183; Herbert, *Best*, 184; the agreement was made on 21 December 1936.

40. BAB, NS 19/3576; Martin Broszat, 'Nationalsozialistische Konzentrationslager 1933–1945', in Hans Buchheim et al., *Anatomie des SS-Staates*, 7th edn. (Munich, 1999), 321–445, here 352; Tuchel, *Konzentrationslager*, 108; Browder, *Foundations*, 188.

41. Browder, *Foundations*, 192 f.

42. *RVBl* 1935, 577 f.; see Browder, *Foundations*, 194.

43. BAB, NS 19/1447; Tuchel, *Konzentrationslager*, 108 f.

44. GStA, Rep. 90 P 104, also doc. PS-3751, in *IMT*, vol. 33, pp. 56 ff.; see Aronson, *Heydrich*, 235.

45. BAB, R 22/1462; Göring sent Himmler's draft out on 3 May 1935.

46. GStA, Rep 90 P 2, H. 3, meeting of 27 June 1935; see also BAB, R 22/1462, Gürtner's minute of 27 June 1935; see Gruchmann, 'Justiz', 553 f.

47. On the persecution of the KPD in this period, Horst Duhnke, *Die KPD von 1933 bis 1945* (Cologne, 1972), 189 ff.; Klaus Mammach, *Widerstand 1933–1939. Geschichte der deutschen antifaschistischen Widerstandsbewegung im Inland und in der Emigration* (Cologne, 1984), 84 ff. and 162 ff.; Allan Merson, *Kommunistischer Widerstand in Nazideutschland* (Bonn, 1999), 82 ff.

48. GStA, Rep 90 P 104; discussed by Browder, *Foundations*, 189 f., and Aronson, *Heydrich*, 238 ff.

49. Duhnke, *KPD*, 190 f.; Merson, *Widerstand*, 157.

50. Duhnke, *KPD*, 199 f.

51. Detlev J. K. Peukert, *Die KPD im Widerstand. Verfolgung und Untergrundarbeit an Rhein und Ruhr 1933–1945* (Wuppertal, 1980), 144.

52. Mammach, *Widerstand*, 51.

53. Ibid.

54. Ibid. 53.

55. Mehringer, 'KPD in Bayern', 85 ff.

56. Ibid. 135.

57. BAB, R 58/2271, Deputy Chief and Inspector of the Gestapo, 12 July 1935; Johannes Tuchel, 'Gestapa und Reichssicherheitshauptamt. Die Berliner Zentralinstitutionen der Gestapo', in Gerhard Paul und Klaus-Michael Mallmann (eds), *Die Gestapo. Mythos und Realität* (Darmstadt, 1995), 84–100, here 91 f.

58. BAB, R 58/389, note for Heydrich, 18 September 1935; see also Tuchel, *Konzentrationslager*, 312.

59. Duhnke, *KPD*, 201. According to a survey initiated by the KPD party leadership, at the end of 1935, of 422 leading functionaries (members of the Central Committee, the district headquarters, and the mass organizations) 119 had been arrested and 24 killed; 125 had emigrated and around 10 per cent had left the party as a result of the persecution (Mammach, *Widerstand*, 57).

60. Browder, *Foundations*, 197 has provided various examples. Thus the political police in the two small Lippe states were subordinated to the Prussian Gestapo in March and April 1935 to act as branches of it; in order to enhance the authority of the Gestapo leadership, already in May 1934 the Gestapo had begun to promote individual local branch offices to regional branches with authority over neighbouring Stapo local branches. Internally they were repeatedly instructed to avoid committing arbitrary acts against prisoners, and in September 1935 Best ordered that in future press statements about 'measures taken by the state police' should be made more convincing (BAB, R 58/243, 20 September 1935).

61. Browder, *Foundations*, 196 f.; on Best's appointment see Herbert, *Best*, 147 f.

62. However, he had been unable to achieve his original intention of promoting the Gestapa to be a ministry. The regulation that the chief of the Gestapo should himself decide what action was required to combat all 'activities threatening the state' was somewhat modified by the formula, 'in agreement with the Minister of the Interior'. While the law envisaged closer links between the district offices of the Stapo and the district governors (Regierungspräsidenten) (*PrGS 1936*, 21 f.), this aim was undermined by various decrees implementing the law signed by Göring which, in particular, qualified the requirement contained in the law for the Stapo offices to report to the provincial governors (Oberpräsidenten) and receive instructions from them

(BAB, R 58/241, Position of the Oberpräsidenten vis-à-vis the Organs of the Gestapo, 10 February 1936, and 2 April 1936 re: the Ending of the Situation Reports of the Regierungspräsidenten, published as doc. no. 8 in Plum, 'Staatspolizei'). The complaint of the Oberpräsident of the province of East Prussia to the Prussian Prime Minister dated 28 March 1936 clearly shows how the offices of the state police in East Prussia managed to remove themselves from the authority of the internal state administration (GStA, Rep 90 P 3). On this question see Gruchmann, 'Justiz', 559, and Browder, *Foundations*, 214 ff. See also Göring's instructions of 29 February 1936 (BAB, R 58/243): 'The Regierungspräsidenten shall inform the Gestapa about the political situation and about political events through bi-monthly situation reports and reports of events. The Gestapa shall determine the details of what these reports are to cover [. . .] The district offices of the Gestapo shall inform the Geastapa and the responsible Oberpräsidenten and Regierungspräsidenten about the political situation and political events. The Gestapa shall determine the details of what these reports are to cover.'

63. *Das Schwarze Korps*, 8, 15, 22, and 29 May 1935.
64. See above all the following articles: 'Die Gestapo' (the style of the article suggests that Werner Best was the author), *Völkischer Beobachter*, 23 January 1936; Reinhard Heydrich, 'Die Bekämpfung der Staatsfeinde', *Deutsches Recht*, 1936, 121–3 (April 1936); Werner Best, 'Die Geheime Staatspolizei', *Deutsches Recht*, 1936, 125–8 (April 1936); id., 'Der Reichsführer SS and Chef der Deutschen Polizei', *Deutsches Recht*, 1936, 257–8 (July 1936); Himmler's speech of 5 March 1936 (BAB, NS 19/4003) is also available as a booklet: *Rede des Reichsführers-SS vor den Preußischen Staatsräten. 5. März 1936 im Haus der Flieger* (1936).
65. *Völkischer Beobachter*, 23 January 1936: 'The state must not be content with investigating crimes of high treason and treason that have already taken place and punishing the offenders. It is much more important to pre-empt such crimes and thereby to destroy the roots of these threats to the state.'
66. In his articles in the *Deutsches Recht* Best opposed any attempt at subjecting the political police to 'legal norms' (April 1936); they required no 'specific legitimation by law' in order to be able to carry out their duties (July 1936).
67. The term 'State protection corps' (Staatsschutzkorps) is used in an article in the *Völkischer Beobachter* of 23 January 1936; it refers to the Gestapo. In his series of articles in *Das Schwarze Korps* of May 1935 Heydrich had already referred to the SS, insofar as it was serving in the state police, as the 'domestic political protection corps of the National Socialist state' (29 May 1935).
68. The Gestapo article in the *Völkischer Beobachter* of 21 January 1936 states that the Gestapo knows that it 'must directly hurt a large number of people'.
69. Published as a booklet: Heinrich Himmler, *Die Schutzstaffel als antibolschewistische Kampforganisation* (Munich, 1936).
70. BAB, NS 19/4003.

71. See above p. 183.

72. In his letter to the Reich Finance Minister of 21 September 1935 Frick demanded the reintegration of the political police into the general police and the transfer of the police from the states to the Reich (BAB, NS 19/3581, also in R 18/5627; see also Tuchel, *Konzentrationslager*, 313). In November 1935 Frick sent the head of the Reich Chancellery, Hans Heinrich Lammers, a memorandum composed by Daluege which was intended to prove the need to transfer the police to the Reich (BAB, R 43 II/391). It is unclear whether at this point Frick was fully informed about the shift in power relations in Himmler's favour that had already occurred. See also doc. PS-775, in *IMT*, vol. 26, pp. 289 ff., undated memo by Daluege in which he presented the alternatives of locating responsibility for all questions involving the political police either with the Reich Interior Minister or with the Gestapa, which in this case would become a Reich ministry.

73. BAB, NS 19/1447, 18 October 1935; see also Herbert, *Best*, 169.

74. The mention of Frick's 'Gestapa edict' must refer to his letter of 21 September 1935 (see n. 72); see also Tuchel, *Konzentrationslager*, 313.

75. BAB NS 19/3582, note by Himmler 18 October 1935. The minute states: 'There were lengthy discussions about the question of the leadership academies, internal unrest and the Verfügungstruppe, about the question of the asocial elements and how to secure them in special re-education camps, as well about tougher action against the communists. The Führer approved the leadership schools in principle and, within the framework of the consolidation of the whole of the police force, they are to become the responsibility of the Reichsführer-SS either in the role of a state secretary in the Interior Ministry or directly under the Führer.' See Wegner, *Politische Soldaten*, 109. The mention of 'approval for the leadership academies', which had in fact already been founded, must refer to their financing being taken over by the state.

76. Browder, *Foundations*, 207; Peter Hoffmann, *Die Sicherheit des Diktators. Hitlers Leibwachen, Schutzmaßnahmen, Residenzen, Hauptquartiere* (Munich, etc., 1975), 51 ff.; BAB, R 18/5627, note by Pfundtner for Frick, 21 October 1935, and R 43 II/102, Lammers to Himmler, 22 October 1935; NS 19/2196, Himmler's minute after his interview with Hitler, 18 October 1935: 'After Lammers had been immediately summoned the security commando was subordinated to the Reichsführer-SS.'

77. BAB, NS 19/1269, two letters to the Reich Minister of Justice, 6 November 1935; see also Tuchel, *Konzentrationslager*, 315 f.

78. BAB, R 22/1467, Himmler's agreement in principle of 6 January 1936, and R 22/5032, Gürtner to Frick, 27 March 1936, concerning the arrangement agreed in the meantime with Himmler. For further details see Gruchmann, 'Justiz', 571 ff.

79. Edict Concerning the Appointment of a Chief of the German Police in the Reich Ministry of the Interior, *RGBl* 1933 I, 487 f.

80. BAB, R 43 II/391, contains a copy of Himmler's order of 26 June 1936, appointing Daluege and Heydrich as heads of the new main offices. There is also a copy of a Himmler order for the allocation of duties within the sphere of the Chief of the German Police in which he determined the respective responsibilities of the order and security police.

81. *RMBliV* 1936, Sp. 1339.

82. Thus, for example, in a letter dated 10 December 1937 the Baden Gauleiter, Wagner, complained about the fact that 'the Reich Governor who carries the political responsibility has no influence on the political police' (Stolle, *Geheime Staatspolizei*, 95, quoting Generallandesarchiv Karlsruhe, 233/27892).

CHAPTER 9

1. BAB, R 19/379. In the report in the *Völkischer Beobachter* about Himmler's induction as Chief of the German Police the anti-Semitic statements in Himmler's speech were excluded, probably in view of the caution being exercised in Jewish persecution in the Olympic year of 1936.

2. Best, 'Reichsführer SS', referred here to the 'potency of the State protection corps', in that it 'now links the German police with the ideological commitment of the SS'.

3. Hans Frank *et al.*, *Grundfragen der deutschen Polizei. Bericht über die konstituierende Sitzung des Ausschusses für Polizeirecht der Akademie für Deutsches Recht am 11. Oktober 1936* (Hamburg, 1936), Himmler's contribution, 11–16.

4. Günter Neliba, *Wilhelm Frick. Der Legalist des Unrechtsstaates. Eine politische Biographie* (Paderborn, etc., 1992).

5. 'Aufgaben und Aufbau der Polizei des Dritten Reiches', in Hans Pfundtner (ed.), *Dr. Wilhelm Frick und sein Ministerium. Aus Anlaß des 60. Geburtstages des Reichs und preußischen Ministers des Innern Dr. Wilhelm Frick am 12. März 1937* (Munich, 1937), 125–30, quotations 128–30.

6. Reinhard Heydrich, 'Aufgaben und Aufbau der Sicherheitspolizei im Dritten Reich', ibid. 149–53, quotation 150. The volume also contained a contribution from Kurt Daluege: 'Die Ordnungspolizei und ihre Entstehung im Dritten Reich', 133 –45.

7. Himmler, *Schutzstaffel*, 29.

8. BAB NS 19/4004.

9. Ibid.

10. On the German Police Day see Robert Gellately, *Hingeschaut und weggesehen. Hitler und sein Volk* (Munich, 2002), 67 ff.

11. On the Gestapo myth see Robert Gellately, 'Allwissend und allgegenwärtig? Entstehung, Funktion und Wandel des Gestapo-Mythos', in Gerhard Paul and Klaus-Michael Mallmann (eds), *Die Gestapo. Mythos und Realität* (Darmstadt, 1995), 47–70. Gellately has shown here and in his book *Hingeschaut*, with

numerous examples, that there was extensive reporting of the Gestapo and of the existence of concentration camps. As examples of such articles, in some cases by leading figures in the police apparatus, that often pointed the way ahead see Dr B. (Best), 'Rechtsstellung des Reichsführers-SS und Chefs der Deutschen Polizei', *Völkischer Beobachter*, 4 June 1937; Best, 'Die präventive Aufgabe der Geheimen Staatspolizei', *Frankfurter Zeitung*, 3 March 1938; Heydrich, 'Die deutsche Sicherheitspolizei. Zum Tag der Deutschen Polizei', *Völkischer Beobachter*, 28 January 1939, elucidates the concept of police preventive action; the article 'Die SS-Totenkopfverbände', *Völkischer Beobachter*, 26 January 1939, contains comments about the function of the KZ.

12. BAB, NS 19/4004, Tag der Deutschen Polizei, 16 January 1937. Heydrich made similar comments in the *Völkischer Beobachter* of 15 January 1937 ('Zum Tag der Deutschen Polizei'), where he wrote the police need people to 'offer to help' in order 'to secure the existence and the strength of the nation against all threats and all attacks'.

13. BAB, NS 19/4003, speech at the celebration of the summer solstice on the Brocken, 22 May 1936.

14. On the history of the Gestapo see Holger Berschel, *Bürokratie und Terror. Das Judenreferat der Gestapo Düsseldorf 1933–1945* (Essen, 2001); Browder, *Enforcers*; id. *Foundations*; Wolfgang Dierker, *Himmlers Glaubenskrieger. Der Sicherheitsdienst der SS und seine Religionspolitik 1933–1941* (Paderborn, etc., 2002); Robert Gellately, *Die Gestapo und die deutsche Gesellschaft. Die Durchsetzung der Rassenpolitik 1933–1945* (Paderborn, etc., 1993); id., *Hingeschaut*; Eric A. Johnson, *Der nationalsozialistische Terror. Gestapo, Juden und gewöhnliche Deutsche* (Berlin, 2001); Paul and Mallmann (eds), *Gestapo*; Reinhard Mann, *Protest und Kontrolle im Dritten Reich. Nationalsozialistische Herrschaft im Alltag einer rheinischen Großstadt* (Frankfurt a. M., etc., 1987); Stolle, *Geheime Staatspolizei*; Wildt, *Generation* (on the Gestapo in this period see 214–62).

15. Mann, *Protest*, 292. Other police authorities, administrative agencies, businesses, or Nazi organizations were responsible for initiating 33 per cent of the investigations, 13 per cent were the result of interrogations. There was, however, a selective procedure according to which some categories of case (e.g. investigations of Jews) were not represented and others (e.g. investigations of communists) are under-represented.

16. Johnson, *Terror*, 392 ff.

17. Burkhard Jellonnek, 'Staatspolizeiliche Fahndungs- und Ermittlungsmethoden gegen Homosexuelle. Regionale Differenzen und Gemeinsamkeiten', in Gerhard Paul and Klaus-Michael Mallmann (eds), *Die Gestapo. Mythos und Realität* (Darmstadt, 1995), 343–56, here 350, notes a figure of 87.5 per cent for denunciations in cases of malicious statements (*Heimtücke*) for the Saarbrücken Gestapo office; according to Johnson, *Terror*, denunciations of Christians, Jehovah's Witnesses, homosexuals, and those subject to political persecution were relatively infrequent (pp. 251, 269, 312 ff., and 393). Robert Gellately

notes in his study of the Würzburg Gestapo that 54 per cent of all cases of 'racial disgrace' (sexual relations of 'Aryans' with Jews) and 59 per cent of all cases which involved too close contact with Jews derived from denunciations by the population; 24 per cent and 7 per cent respectively derived from interrogations, 7 and 14 per cent respectively derived from information from other organizations (*Gestapo*, 162). For a distribution pattern of denunciations for the individual categories see Stolle, *Geheime Staatspolizei*, 252 ff.

18. Johnson, *Terror*, 392 ff.
19. Elisabeth Kohlhaas, 'Die Mitarbeiter der regionalen Staatspolizeistellen. Quantitative und qualitative Befunde zur Personalausstattung der Gestapo', in Gerhard Paul and Klaus-Michael Mallmann (eds), *Die Gestapo. Mythos und Realität* (Darmstadt, 1995), 219–35, 221 ff. There are figures for January 1934 and June 1935 in GStA, Rep 90 P 13, H. 2, and Rep 90 P 14, H. 1; BAB, R 58/610, contains the results of a questionnaire 'Personnel complement of the Stapo offices and Stapo regional offices on 31 March 1937'.
20. Kohlhaas, 'Mitarbeiter', 227; Browder, *Foundations*, 56, on those who came in from outside.
21. BAB, R 58/610, figures for 31 March 1937. The actual strength is given, the number of posts planned for is usually somewhat higher. Stapo offices, which also had to watch over sections of the frontier, were invariably better staffed; thus the Köstlin office had 86 officers, although the district had a population of only about 700,000. See Kohlhaas, 'Mitarbeiter', 226 f.
22. Walter Otto Weyrauch, *Gestapo V-Leute. Tatsachen und Theorie des Geheimdienstes. Untersuchungen zur Geheimen Staatspolizei während der nationalsozialistischen Herrschaft* (Frankfurt a. M., 1989). According to Weyrauch the Frankfurt Stapo had a list of 1,200 informal agents (p. 11); see also Kaus-Michael Mallmann, 'Die V-Leute der Gestapo. Umrisse einer kollektiven Biographie', in Gerhard Paul and Klaus-Michael Mallmann (eds), *Die Gestapo. Mythos und Realität* (Darmstadt, 1995), 268–87.
23. Circular edict of the RFSSuChdDtPol, 15 February 1938, in *RMBliV* 1938, cols. 285 ff.
24. On the SD after 1926 see Browder, *Enforcers*, 210 ff.; Wildt, *Generation*, 378 ff.; and Michael Wildt (ed.), *Die Judenpolitik des SD 1935 bis 1938. Eine Dokumentation* (Munich, 1995).
25. Wildt (ed.), *Die Judenpolitik*, 27.
26. BAB, R 58/239.
27. Aronson, *Heydrich*, 212 f. Reinhard Höhn, head of Central Department II 1, became a professor of law at Berlin University in 1935 and had to leave the SD in 1937 (Wildt, *Generation*, 378 f.); Franz Six, head of Department II (Inland) in the SD Main Office, who was an expert on the press, became a lecturer in Königsberg in 1937 and a full professor and Dean of the Faculty of Foreign Studies at Berlin University in 1940 (Lutz Hachmeister, *Der Gegnerforscher. Die Karriere des SS-Führers Franz Alfred Six* (Munich, 1998)); before joining the SD

Otto Ohlendorf had worked at the Kiel Institute for the World Economy (Hanno Sowade, 'Otto Ohlendorf—Nonkonformist, SS-Führer und Wirtschaftsfunktionär', in Ronald Smelser and Rainer Zitelmann (eds), *Die braune Elite. 22 biographische Skizzen* (Darmstadt, 1989), 188–200); the German-ist Hans Rössner, who was an employee in the SD Culture Group, appears to have been considered for a chair at Strasbourg in 1941 (Wildt, *Generation*, 386 ff.); his predecessor, Wilhelm Spengler, also a Germanist, established the 'Literature Office' (Schrifttumsstelle) at the German Book Centre (Deutsche Bücherei) in Leipzig, which systematically scrutinized the output of German publishers (ibid. 174 ff.). The physician Gustav Scheel, who had a dual career in the SD und the NS Student League (he became Reich Student Leader in 1936), played an important role in recruiting young academics for the SD (ibid. 172 ff.); according to his own testimony, Walter Schellenberg, who later became head of the SD Foreign Department, was put in contact with the SD by his university tutor (George C. Browder, 'Schellenberg—Eine Geheim-dienst-Phantasie', in Ronald Smelser and Enrico Syring (eds), *Die SS. Elite unter dem Totenkopf. 30 Lebensläufe* (Paderborn, etc., 2000), 418–30).

28. Mann, *Protest*, 180.
29. Johnson, *Terror*, 305 ff.
30. Duhnke, *KPD*, 194; Stolle, *Geheime Staatspolizei*, 222 f.; Johnson, *Terror*, 191 ff., discovered that around 70 per cent of the Krefeld Gestapo files for 1933 and 1934 dealt with communists; after the beginning of 1935 the number declined.
31. Gestapa, 'Lagebericht für 1937', published in Margot Pikarski und Elke Warn-ing (eds), *Gestapo-Berichte über den antifaschistischen Widerstandskampf der KPD 1933–1939*, vol. 1: *Anfang 1933 bis August 1939* (Berlin, 1989), doc. no. 16; Duhnke, *KPD*, 201.
32. BAB, NS 19/4004, speech at the Gruppenführer meeting in Munich in the officers' quarters of the SS-Standarte Deutschland, 8 November 1937. In a similar way in his speech to Wehrmacht officers in January 1937 he defended the policy he had pursued in Bavaria of not letting communist functionaries go free: doc. PS-1992 (A), in *IMT*, vol. 29, pp. 206 ff., here 217.
33. Thus in his address to Gestapo officials and employees on 11 October 1934 he placed the blame for the 'corruption' of the SA leadership on the Jews, the Freemasons, and Ultramontanism (BAB, NS 19/4002); on 5 March 1935 he told Prussian state councillors that, apart from the Jews and Bolshevism, the Gestapo was focusing its efforts on 'jewified world Freemasonry' (ibid.); in January 1937 he announced at a course on national politics run by the Wehrmacht that he considered that 'Bolshevism led by Jews and Freemasons' to be the main enemy (doc. PS-1992 [A], in *IMT*, vol. 29, pp. 206 ff., quotation 229), and he explained to SS-Gruppenführer on 8 November 1938 that they were dealing with a 'war being fought by all the Jews, Freemasons, Marxists, and Churches in the world' against Nazi Germany (NS 19/4005, published in

Heinrich Himmler, *Geheimreden 1933–1945*, ed. Bradley F. Smith and Agnes F. Peterson (Munich, 1974), 25 ff., quotation 37).

34. *Das Schwarze Korps*, 15 May 1935; on this series see also above pp. 196 ff.
35. Neuberger, *Freimaurerei*, ii. 16 ff.
36. Ibid. 101 f.
37. Ibid. 119 f.
38. Ibid. 23 f.
39. BAB, NS 19/1720, RFSS to a Frau Käthe Oswald, 25 August 1932.
40. Neuberger, *Freimaurerei*, ii. 45 f. and 108.
41. Wildt (ed.), *Judenpolitik*, 27.
42. BAB, R 58/239; on this order of Heydrich's concerning the demarcation of the responsibilities of the SD and the Gestapo see p. 188 above.
43. In January 1935 he told SS leaders in Breslau, that they were involved in a 'struggle with those who have been the oldest opponents of our nation for thousands of years, with Jews, Freemasons and Jesuits' (BAB, NS 19/40029, 19 January 1935, meeting of leaders of SS-Oberabschnitt South-East in Breslau, published in Himmler, *Geheimreden*, 57). In January 1937 he talked to Wehrmacht officers about 'our natural opponents, international Bolshevism led by Jews and Freemasons' (doc. PS-1992 [A], in *IMT*, vol. 29, pp. 206 ff., quotation 229), and he told Napola heads in July 1938, that they had ranged against them the whole of capital, all the Jews, all Freemasons, all the democrats and philistines, all the Bolshevists in the world, all the Jesuits in the world, and last but not least all the nations who regret that they did not kill the lot of us in 1918' (BAB, NS 19/4005, speech in the Ahrenshoop tent camp, 3 July 1938, published in Himmler, *Geheimreden*, 57 f.).
44. From summer 1933 onwards the Gestapo offices reported on Jewish organizations; in the summer of 1934 they received instructions to report on all areas of public life in which Jews and non-Jews cooperated (Berschel, *Bürokratie*, 171).
45. Ibid. 275 ff.; BAB, R 58/269, edicts of 28 January und 6 March 1935.
46. BAB, R 58/276, 10 February 1935 (published in Joseph Walk (ed.), *Das Sonderrecht für die Juden im NS-Staat. Eine Sammlung der gesetzlichen Maßnahmen und Richtlinien. Inhalt und Bedeutung*, 2nd edn. (Heidelberg, 1996), i, 514).
47. Ibid. i. 516, 12 February 1935.
48. Circular edict of 27 July 1936 re: regulations for the implementation of the Law concerning Public Houses in *RMBliV* 1936, col. 1067; Uwe Dietrich Adam, *Judenpolitik im Dritten Reich* (Düsseldorf, 1972), 155.
49. Uwe Dietrich Adam, *Judenpolitik im Dritten Reich*, 156 and 169 ff. It was only in January 1938 that the law concerning the alteration of surnames and first names was issued. The decree to implement it contained a list of first names that Jews were no longer allowed to use.
50. BAB, R 58/23a, 7 July 1936.

51. OA Moscow, 501-1-18, Gestapa Berlin, II 1 B 2, published in Otto Dov Kulka and Eberhard Jäckel (eds), *Die Juden in den geheimen NS-Stimmungsberichten 1933–1945* (Düsseldorf, 2004), doc. no. 447.

52. On 17 August 1935 the Gestapa, ordered the Stapo offices to start keeping a list of members of Jewish organizations; but during the coming months those Jews who were not members of organizations were also registered. A national register was started in Gestapo headquarters. Further measures to register German Jews were the identity-card decree of 23 July 1938 and the national census of May 1939, in which a statement of racial identity was required (details in Adam, *Judenpolitik*, 182 ff.).

53. Wildt (ed.), *Judenpolitik*, 38.

54. Ibid. 34.

55. See below p. 217 f.

56. BAB, NS 19/4005, speech in Alt-Rehse (1938). On Himmler's hatred of Christianity see Josef Ackermann, *Heinrich Himmler als Ideologe* (Göttingen, etc., 1970), 88 ff.

57. BAB, NS 19/3666, published in Himmler, *Geheimreden*, 50 f.

58. BAB, NS 19/4009, 9 June 1942, published in Himmler, *Geheimreden*, 145 ff., quotation 159 f.

59. BAB, NS 19/4009.

60. BAB, NS 19/4042, 10 January 1934.

61. IfZ, PS-2204, 15 October 1934 and 25 March 1935.

62. BAB, NS 19/3901, 20 September 1935, with reference to the earlier order of 15 October 1934. 'German Christians' were a group within the Protestant Church sympathetic to the Nazis [trs.].

63. Friedrich Zipfel, *Kirchenkampf in Deutschland 1933–1945. Religionsverfolgung und Selbstbehauptung der Kirchen in der nationalsozialistischen Zeit* (Berlin, 1965), 108, quotes the order of 18 November 1937 in the BDC.

64. IfZ, PS-2204, 15 September 1934.

65. Ibid. minute concerning an interview with Hitler on 23 October 1935. As is clear from the minute of 1 November 1935 (ibid.), eight days later Himmler presented him with an order concerning matters involving the religious confessions, which Hitler approved.

66. BAB, NS 19/3901, 24 July 1937.

67. June 1937; published in Jürgen Matthäus *et al.*, *Ausbildungsziel Judenmord? 'Weltanschauliche Erziehung' von SS, Polizei und Waffen-SS im Rahmen der 'Endlösung'* (Frankfurt a. M., 2003), doc. no. 7.

68. BAB, NS 2/53, Himmler to Pastor Friedrich in Halberstadt, 11 March 1937.

69. BAB, NS 19/3481, Himmler to Hans Schulze, 14 August 1941.

70. *Statistisches Jahrbuch der Schutzstaffel der NSDAP 1938* (Berlin, 1939), 99. According to this, on the set date of 31 December 1937 54.2 per cent of SS men were Protestant and 23.7 per cent Catholic. 0.2 per cent were categorized as 'others'.

71. BAB, BDC, SS-O Weitzel to Himmler, 30 April 1936, and reply of 2 July 1936.
72. BAB, NS 19/4004, 18 February 1937.
73. BAB, NS 2/53, Himmler to Pastor Friedrich in Halberstadt, 11 March 1937.
74. Speech to the officers of a Grenadier division at the Bitche training camp on 26 July 1944, published in Himmler, *Geheimreden*, 215 ff., quotation 217. See also the RFSS's speech at the meeting of the NSDAP's foreign organization in Stuttgart (BAB, NS 19/4005, 2 September 1938): '1. I will not put up with anyone in the SS who does not believe in God. 2. I will not tolerate anyone's feelings being hurt on account of their religious convictions.'
75. BAB, NS 19/4003, speech at Gruppenführer meeting in Dachau, 8 November 1936.
76. BAB, NS 10/4007, speech to party comrades after November 1940.
77. On Hartl see Dierker, *Glaubenskrieger*, 96 ff.
78. Petra Madeleine Rapp, *Die Devisenprozesse gegen katholische Ordensangehörige und Geistliche im Dritten Reich. Eine Untersuchung zum Konflikt deutscher Orden und Klöster in wirtschaftlicher Notlage, totalitärer Machtausübung des nationalsozialistischen Regimes und im Kirchenkampf 1935/1936* (Bonn, 1981); on the participation of the SD in the preparation of the trials see Dierker, *Glaubenskrieger*, 173 ff.
79. Hans Günter Hockerts, *Die Sittlichkeitsprozesse gegen katholische Ordensangehörige und Priester 1936/1937. Eine Studie zur nationalsozialistischen Herrschaftstechnik und zum Kirchenkampf* (Mainz, 1971), 4 ff.
80. Ibid. 12 ff.
81. Dierker, *Glaubenskrieger*, 178 ff.
82. Hockerts, *Sittlichkeitsprozesse*, 63 ff.
83. Dierker, *Glaubenskrieger*, 183 ff.
84. Oron J. Hale, *Presse in der Zwangsjacke, 1933–1945* (Düsseldorf, 1965), 148 ff.; Dierker, *Glaubenskrieger*, 189 ff.
85. Dierker, *Glaubenskrieger*, 85 ff.
86. On the role of the Gestapo in church politics focusing on the Protestant Churches during the years 1935–7, see Dierker, *Glaubenskrieger*, 192 ff.
87. Ibid. 198 f.
88. Ibid. 408 f.
89. On Himmler's and the SS's role in church politics during the years 1937–8 see ibid. 407 ff.
90. *Tagebücher Goebbels*, 15 February 1937. The conversation took place during a railway journey.
91. Dierker, *Glaubenskrieger*, 335 ff., and 241 f.
92. BAB, NS 19/688.
93. Dierker, *Glaubenskrieger*, 336 ff.
94. BADH, ZB I/668, RFSS's adjutant's office to the Security Police Main Office, 30 April 1937.

95. Dierker, *Glaubenskrieger*, 346.

96. BADH, ZB I/1686, minute of a meeting on 5 November 1937.

97. Dierker, *Glaubenskrieger*, 341 ff.

98. On the persecution of the Jehovah's Witnesses see Detlef Garbe, *Zwischen Widerstand und Martyrium. Die Zeugen Jehovas im 'Dritten Reich'* (Munich, 1993).

99. Ibid. 149 ff.

100. Ibid. 96 ff.

101. Ibid. 159 ff.

102. Ibid. 215 ff.

103. Ibid. 234.

104. Ibid. 239 ff.; on the persecution in Baden see also Stolle, *Geheime Staatspolizei*, 226 ff.

105. Garbe, *Widerstand*, 247 ff.

106. See the edited volume *Himmlers Hexenkartothek. Das Interesse des Nationalsozialismus an der Hexenverfolgung*, ed. Sönke Lorenz *et al.*, 2nd edn. (Bielefeld, 2000), and in particular the contribution by Jörg Rudolph, '"Geheime Reichskommando-Sache!" Hexenjäger im Schwarzen Orden. Der H-Sonderauftrag des Reichsführers-SS, 1935–1944', 47–97.

107. Ibid. 56.

108. Himmler, *Schutzstaffel*, 5.

109. For more details see Rudolph, 'Geheime Reichskommando-Sache!', 52.

110. Ibid. 84.

111. Blank reported on it after the war; see *Nordwestdeutsche Hefte*, 3/1 (1948), 3–6.

112. BAB, NS 19/2963, Kaltenbrunner to Himmler, 18 June 1943, and Brandt to Chief of the Security Police, 26 June 1943.

113. BAB, NS 19/4013, speech to the Wehrmacht generals on 5 May 1944 in Sonthofen; similarly in his Sonthofen speech of 21 June 1944 (BAB, NS 19/4014).

114. *RMBliV* 1936, cols. 1152 ff., regulations implementing the circular edict on the reorganization of the state criminal police of 20 September 1936, 16 July 1937; Patrick Wagner, *Volksgemeinschaft ohne Verbrecher. Konzeptionen und Praxis der Kriminalpolizei in der Zeit der Weimarer Republik und des Nationalsozialismus* (Hamburg, 1996), 234 ff.

115. Wagner, *Volksgemeinschaft*, 237.

116. Ibid. 238.

117. Ibid. 239 ff.

118. BAB, R 58/242, edict of Frick on the appointment of inspectors of the security police, 20 September 1936; enclosed are 'official instructions for the inspectors of the security police'. There is also an overview dated 24 September 1938 of the appointments of inspectors of the security police that had been made by 15 September 1938. Edict and instructions are also in *RMBliV* 1936, cols. 1243 f. See also Wagner, *Volksgemeinschaft*, 246 f.; Friedrich Wilhelm,

Die Polizei im NS-Staat. Die Geschichte ihrer Organisation im Überblick (Paderborn, etc., 1997), 79 ff.

119. On the Kripo as part of the security police see Wagner, *Volksgemeinschaft*, 243 ff. Both Kripo and Gestapo continued to investigate cases of racial disgrace after Heydrich had ordered that, as a matter of principle, the bulk of these investigations should be handed over to the Kripo (Walk (ed.), *Sonderrecht*, ii. 141, edict of 27 March 1936; Berschel, *Bürokratie*, 212 ff.).

120. Doc. PS-1992 (A), lecture to a Wehrmacht course on national politics from 15 to 23 January 1937, published in *IMT*, vol. 29, pp. 206 ff., quotation 220.

121. Printed in the booklet *Vorbeugende Verbrechensbekämpfung*, published by the Reich Criminal Police Office (IfZ, Dc 17.02); see also Wagner, *Volksgemeinschaft*, 254 f., and the detailed account in Karl-Leo Terhorst, *Polizeiliche planmäßige Überwachung und polizeiliche Vorbeugungshaft im Dritten Reich. Ein Beitrag zur Rechtsgeschichte vorbeugender Verbrechensbekämpfung* (Heidelberg, 1985), 115 ff.

122. Wagner, *Volksgemeinschaft*, 256 ff.

123. See in detail ibid. 254 ff.

124. Ibid. 265 ff.

125. IfZ, Dc 17.02, collection of edicts concerning the preventive combating of crime; Wagner, *Volksgemeinschaft*, 259. On this whole issue see Terhorst, *Überwachung*.

126. The directives for implementation dated 4 April 1938 (in IfZ, Dc 17.02, collection of edicts concerning the preventive combating of crime) contain a detailed list of the groups who should form the main target of the preventive combating of crime: 'Beggars, tramps (Gypsies), prostitutes, alcoholics, persons with infectious diseases, particularly sexual diseases, who try to evade the measures taken by the health authorities', as well as 'the work-shy and those who refuse work'. See also Wolfgang Ayass, '"Ein Gebot der nationalen Arbeitsdisziplin": Die Aktion "Arbeitsscheu Reich" 1938', in *Feinderklärung und Prävention. Kriminalbiologie, Zigeunerforschung und Asozialenpolitik* (Berlin, 1988), 43–74, here 53 f.

127. Ayass, '"Gebot"', 45 ff.

128. OA Moscow, 500-1-261; published in 'Das Schicksal der Juden im Saarland 1920–1945', ed. Hans-Walter Herrmann, in *Dokumentation zur Geschichte der jüdischen Bevölkerung in Rheinland-Pfalz und im Saarland von 1800–1945*, published by the Landesarchivverwaltung Rheinland-Pfalz and the Landesarchiv Saarbrücken (Koblenz, 1974), 257–491, here 447 ff.; see Ayass, '"Gebot"', 54 f.

129. Ayass, '"Gebot"', 67 ff.

130. Decree to Secure the Labour Requirements for Tasks of Particular Political Importance (*RGBl* 1938 I, 652) as well as the decree to implement it of 20 June 1938, both published in Timothy W. Mason (ed.), *Arbeiterklasse und Volksgemeinschaft. Dokumente und Materialien zur deutschen Arbeiterpolitik*

1936–1939 (Opladen, 1975), 669 ff. Up to the beginning of the war 800,000 workers were conscripted, particularly for the construction of the West Wall (ibid. 667).

131. On the press reporting see Peter Longerich, *'Davon haben wir nichts gewusst!' Die Deutschen und die Judenverfolgung 1933–1945* (Munich, 2006), 112 ff.

132. Wagner, *Volksgemeinschaft*, 292 ff.

133. According to official figures, the number of murders and cases of manslaughter declined by 46.2 per cent between 1932 and 1938, the number of cases of grievous bodily harm by 58.3 per cent, of serious cases of theft by 58.7 per cent, of blackmail by 39.6 per cent, of arson by 45.2 per cent, and of counterfeiting currency by 88.2 per cent (*Deutsche Justiz*, 101 [1939], 1476). For an interpretation of the statistics see Wagner, *Volksgemeinschaft*, 214 ff. and 297 f.

134. Michael Zimmermann, *Rassenutopie und Genozid. Die nationalsozialistische 'Lösung der Zigeunerfrage'* (Hamburg, 1996), 114 ff.

135. Ibid. 81 ff.; see also Guenter Lewy, *The Nazi Persecution of the Gypsies* (Oxford and New York, 2000), 15 ff.

136. Zimmermann, *Rassenutopie*, 86 ff.

137. Ibid. 106 ff.

138. Ibid. 125 ff.; see also Lewy, *Nazi Persecution*, 43 ff.

139. IfZ, Dc 17.02, circular edict of the RFSS, 8 December 1938; instructions on implementation from the Reich Criminal Police Office of 1 March 1939.

140. Ibid. 5 June 1939; Zimmermann, *Rassenutopie*, 101 ff.

141. BAB, NS 19/4004, 16 January 1937. For Himmler's attitude towards homosexuality see Burkhard Jellonnek, *Homosexuelle unter dem Hakenkreuz. Die Verfolgung von Homosexuellen im Dritten Reich* (Paderborn, 1990). Apart from this important study see also: Geoffrey Giles, 'The Institutionalization of Homosexual Panic in the Third Reich', in Robert Gellately and Nathan Stoltzfus (eds), *Social Outsiders in Nazi Germany* (Princeton, etc., 2001), 233–55; Günter Grau (ed.), *Homosexualität in der NS-Zeit. Dokumente einer Diskriminierung und Verfolgung*, 2nd rev. edn. (Frankfurt a. M., 2004); Richard Plant, *Rosa Winkel. Der Krieg der Nazis gegen die Homosexuellen* (Frankfurt a. M., etc., 1991); Peter von Rönn, 'Politische und psychiatrische Homosexualitätskonstruktion im NS-Staat', Part I: 'Die politische Genese des Homosexuellen als Staatsfeind', Part II: 'Die soziale Genese der Homosexualität als defizitäre Heterosexualität', both in *Zeitschrift für Sexualforschung*, 11 (1998), 99–129 and 220–60; Hans-Georg Stümke, *Homosexuelle in Deutschland. Eine politische Geschichte* (Munich, 1989).

142. Report of the president of the Higher State Court (Oberlandesgerichtspräsident) in Frankfurt, 2 September 1937, who repeats information from the Frankfurt police chief of 26 April 1937 (BAB, R 3001/1460); StA Marburg, LRA Eschwege Nr. 1718, Kassel criminal police department, guidelines for combating homosexuality and abortion of 11 May 1937, refers to the same comment. See Jellonnek, *Homosexuelle*, 122.

143. BADH, ZM 1668, Akte 13.

144. 'As a German, as a National Socialist, I wish to make the following point quite soberly: People dispute about how many homosexuals there are and how many abortions take place: I don't want to give any figures here' (*Grundfragen der deutschen Polizei*, 14).

145. BAB, NS 19/4004; excerpts also in Himmler, *Geheimreden*, 93 ff.

146. BADH, ZM 1668, Akte 13.

147. BAB, NS 19/4005, speech by the RFSS at a meeting of the NSDAP's Foreign organization in Stuttgart, 2 September 1938.

148. BAB, NS 19/4004; excerpts also in Himmler, *Geheimreden*, 93 ff.

149. BADH, ZM 1668, Akte 13.

150. BAB, NS 19/4005, speech by the RFSS at a meeting of the NSDAP's Foreign organization in Stuttgart, 2 September 1938.

151. BADH, ZM 1668, Akte 13. The figure of 400,000 is based on ten annual cohorts each with 40,000 capable of being recruited.

152. BAB, NS 19/4004; excerpts also in Himmler, *Geheimreden*, pp. 93 ff.

153. *Statistisches Jahrbuch 1937*, Secret (page stuck in) Reasons for the Exclusions and Expulsions mentions 23 exclusions and 29 expulsions on the basis of paragraph 175.

154. See below pp. 368 ff.

155. Jellonnek, *Homosexuelle*, 95 ff.

156. Ibid. 110 ff.

157. Edict of 10 October 1936, published in Grau (ed.), *Homosexualität*, doc. no. 27.

158. Jellonnek, *Homosexuelle*, 122 ff.; Wagner, *Volksgemeinschaft*, 249 ff.

159. IfZ, Annual report of Office V of the RSHA, 1940, 61; Jellonnek, *Homosexuelle*, 129 ff.

160. On the statistics see Jellonnek, *Homosexuelle*, 122.

161. 'Das sind Staatsfeinde', *Das Schwarze Korps*, 4 March 1937. See also: 'Homosexualität und Kunst' (11 March 1937), 'Achtung der Entarteten' (1 April 1937), and 'Was sage ich meinem Kinde?' (15 April 1937), in which Himmler's demand for a positive attitude towards the question of sexual relations between young people was addressed.

162. StA Marburg, LRA Eschwege Nr. 1718, Kassel criminal police, guidelines for combating homosexuality and abortion, 11 May 1937.

163. BAB, R 22/865, Statement by Himmler of 2 March 1937; see also Jellonnek, *Homosexuelle*, 116.

164. Edict of 29 October 1937, in IfZ, Dc 17.02, collection of edicts concerning the preventive combating of criminality.

165. Jellonnek, *Homosexuelle*, 156. Himmler took the view that this principle should never affect the position if one offered a preventive prisoner the possibility of release in the event of his agreement; since preventive detention did not carry a fixed term this 'offer' implied a threat of possible life imprisonment.

166. IfZ, Annual report of Office V of the RSHA, 1940, decree of 12 July 1940.
167. BAB, NS 19/4007, 29 February 1940, published in Himmler, *Geheimreden*, 115 ff., quotation 120 f.
168. BAB, R 58/261.
169. BAB, NS 19/2376, Edict of 7 March 1942; Jellonnek, *Homosexuelle*, 30.
170. Jellonnek, *Homosexuelle*, 34 ff.; NS 19/1916, statistics of the SS Court Main Office for the first quarter of 1943 contain 22 sentences, none of which is a death sentence. Geoffrey Giles, 'The Denial of Homosexuality: Same-Sex Incidents in Himmler's SS and Police', *Journal of the History of Sexuality* (2002), 256–90, examined four cases contained in the SS and police judicial records in which sentences were imposed for such offences. Himmler confirmed two of the sentences (one of them a death sentence) and in the other two cases ordered 'front-line duty' instead of the sentences of imprisonment that had been imposed.
171. *Das Schwarze Korps*, 25 May 1939.
172. BAB, NS 19/688, correspondence about orders in 1937 and 1940. Himmler's response to Rahn can be adduced above all from Brandt's letter to Naumann (Propaganda Ministry) dated 2 November 1943 as well as from Brandt's letter of 9 May 1944. On Rahn's activities and his role in the SS see Hans-Jürgen Lange, *Otto Rahn. Leben und Werk* (Engerda, 1995), and id., *Otto Rahn und die Suche nach dem Gral. Biografie und Quellen* (Engerda, 1999). Lange, *Leben und Werk*, 54 ff. documents the correspondence between Himmler and Rahn for the years 1936–9, which can be found among other things in Rahn's SS-O-Akte in the BDC.
173. Referred to in the letter from the head of OKW, Amtsgruppe Inland, 16 March 1944 (BAB, NS 19/688).
174. BAB, R 43 II/391, Himmler's decrees of 26 June 1936 concerning the distribution of responsibilities within the sphere of the German police and concerning the appointment of a chief of the order police and a chief of the security police; see also Wilhelm, *Polizei*, 83 f.
175. Wilhelm, *Polizei*, 84 f.
176. Circular edict of the RFSS, 15 August 1936, Provisional Regulations Concerning the Replacement of Constables in the Schutzpolizei, in *RMBliV* 1936, col. 1180c.
177. The facts concerning personnel numbers and the duties of the order police have been gleaned from two addresses given by Daluege, one to SS leaders on 23 January 1939 and the other at a conference of Prussian district and provincial governors (Regierungs- and Oberpräsidenten) on 23 June 1939 (BAB, R 19/381). On the history of the order police see also Martin Hölzl, 'Grüner Rock und Weiße Weste. Adolf von Bomhard und die Legende von der sauberen Ordnungspolizei', *Zeitschrift für Geschichtswissenschaft*, 50 (2002), 22–43; Heiner Lichtenstein, *Himmlers grüne Helfer. Die Schutz- und Ordnungspolizei im 'Dritten Reich'* (Cologne, 1990); Hans-Joachim Neufeld, Jürgen

Huck, and Georg Tessin, *Zur Geschichte der Ordnungspolizei 1936–1945* (Koblenz, 1957).

178. Wilhelm, *Polizei*, 113 ff.

179. Ibid. 110 ff.; on the strength of the fire brigades see Daluege's statements of 23 January 1939 (BAB, NS 19/381).

180. Orth, *System*, 35 ff.; Tuchel, *Konzentrationslager*, 326 ff.

181. Hermann Kaienburg, *Der Militär- und Wirtschaftskomplex der SS im KZ-Standort Sachsenhausen-Oranienburg. Schnittpunkt von KZ-System, Waffen-SS und Judenmord* (Berlin, 2006), 19.

182. Himmler to the Justice Minister, 8 February 1937, quoted in Falk Pingel, *Häftlinge unter SS-Herrschaft. Widerstand, Selbstbehauptung und Vernichtung im Konzentrationslager* (Hamburg, 1978), 63. On KZ Sachsenhausen see Hermann Kaienburg, 'Sachsenhausen-Stammlager', in Wolfgang Benz und Barbara Distel (eds), *Der Ort des Terrors. Geschichte der nationalsozialistischen Konzentrationslager*, vol. 3: *Sachsenhausen, Buchenwald* (Munich, 2006), 17–72; Gerhard Finn, *Sachsenhausen 1936–1950: Geschichte eines Lagers* (Berlin, 1988); Kaienburg, *Sachsenhausen-Oranienburg*; Günter Morsch (ed.), *Mord und Massenmord im Konzentrationslager Sachsenhausen 1936–1945* (Berlin, 2005).

183. On the history of the camp see Harry Stein, 'Buchenwald–Stammlager', in Wolfgang Benz and Barbara Distel (eds), *Der Ort des Terrors. Geschichte der nationalsozialistischen Konzentrationslager*, vol. 3: *Sachsenhausen, Buchenwald* (Munich, 2006), 301–56; id., *Konzentrationslager Buchenwald 1937–1945. Begleitband zur ständigen historischen Ausstellung*, published by the Gedenkstätte Buchenwald (Göttingen, 1999); Jens Schley, *Nachbar Buchenwald. Die Stadt Weimar und ihr Konzentrationslager 1937–1945* (Cologne, etc., 1999). Himmler's visit on 22 May 1937 is clear from his office diary (Michael Wildt, 'Himmlers Terminkalender aus dem Jahr 1937', *Vierteljahrshefte für Zeitgeschichte*, 52 (2004), 671–91, here 686).

184. Zámečník, 'Dachau-Stammlager', 245 ff.

185. Jörg Skriebeleit, 'Flossenbürg-Stammlager', in Wolfgang Benz and Barbara Distel (eds), *Der Ort des Terrors. Geschichte der nationalsozialistischen Konzentrationslager*, vol. 4: *Flossenbürg, Mauthausen, Ravensbrück* (Munich, 2006), 17–66.

186. On the history of the camp see Florian Freund and Bertrand Perz, 'Mauthausen-Stammlager', in Wolfgang Benz and Barbara Distel (eds), *Der Ort des Terrors. Geschichte der nationalsozialistischen Konzentrationslager*, vol. 4: *Flossenbürg, Mauthausen, Ravensbrück* (Munich, 2006), 293–346; Hans Maršálek, *Die Geschichte des Konzentrationslagers Mauthausen. Dokumentation*, 3rd edn. (Vienna, 1995).

187. Hermann Kaienburg, *Das Konzentrationslager Neuengamme 1938–1945*, published by the KZ-Gedenkstätte Neuengamme (Berlin, 1997).

188. On KZ Ravensbrück see Annette Leo, 'Ravensbrück-Stammlager', in Wolfgang Benz and Barbara Distel (eds), *Der Ort des Terrors. Geschichte der*

nationalsozialistischen Konzentrationslager, vol. 4: *Flossenbürg, Mauthausen, Ravensbrück* (Munich, 2006), 473–520; Bernhard Strebel, *Das KZ Ravensbrück. Geschichte eines Lagerkomplexes* (Paderborn, etc., 2003).

189. Doc. PS-1992 (A), lecture to a Wehrmacht course on national politics, 15–23 January 1937, published in *IMT*, vol. 29, pp. 206 ff., quotation 222.

190. Orth, *System*, 32 and 38 f.

191. Ibid. 40 ff.

192. Doc. PS-1992 (A), published in *IMT*, vol. 29, pp. 206 ff., quotation 217.

193. BAB, NS 19/4004, speech at a Gruppenführer meeting in Munich in the leaders' quarters of the SS-Standarte Deutschland, 8 November 1937.

194. Hermann Kaienburg, *'Vernichtung durch Arbeit'. Der Fall Neuengamme. Die Wirtschaftsbestrebungen der SS und ihre Auswirkungen auf die Existenzbedingungen der KZ-Gefangenen* (Bonn, 1990), 72.

195. Schulte, *Zwangsarbeit*, 103 ff.

196. On the date when the agreement was made see ibid. 112. It is no longer possible to discover who took the initiative, Speer or Himmler (details ibid. n. 86).

197. Ibid. 114 ff.; on these businesses see also Hermann Kaienburg, *Die Wirtschaft der SS* (Berlin, 2003), 454 ff., and Michael Thad Allen, *The Business of Genocide: The SS, Slave Labor, and the Concentration Camps* (Chapel Hill, NC, 2002), 58 ff.

198. There are overviews of prisoner conditions in Drobisch and Wieland, *System*, 106 ff. and 205 ff., and in Orth, *System*, 54 ff.

199. BAB, NS 19/1542, letter to Gürtner, 16 May 1938.

200. Ibid. 31 May 1939. On the hanging of Emil Bargatzky on 4 June 1938 see Stein, 'Buchenwald-Stammlager', 336.

201. Doc. PS-1992 (A), lecture to a Wehrmacht course on national politics, 15–23 January 1937, published in *IMT*, vol. 29, pp. 206 ff.

202. BAB, NS 19/4006, 29 January 1939.

203. Kaienburg, 'Sachsenhausen-Stammlager', 48.

204. Doc. PS-1992 (A), lecture to a Wehrmacht course on national politics, 15–23 January 1937, published in *IMT*, vol. 29, pp. 206 ff., quotation 221. For references to Himmler's visits to concentration camps see BAK, NL 1126/7, diary entry for 15 February 1935 (KZ Lichtenburg). According to Drobisch and Wieland, Himmler also visited Lichtenburg at the end of May 1938, *System*, 303. According to Wildt, 'Terminkalender', Himmler was in Sachsenhausen on 30 September 1937.

205. Walter Janka, *Spuren eines Lebens* (Berlin, 1991), 60 ff. BAK, NL 1126/7, diary entry of 16 February 1935: Sachsenburg. On this visit see Baganz, *Erziehung*, 278.

206. Blank, 'Hakenkreuz', 3. Blank dates the visit to 10 October 1942. On the dating see BAB, NS 19/3959.

207. Account by retired Landtag deputy Ludwig Soswinski, published in Doku-mentationsarchiv des österreichischen Widerstandes, '*Anschluß*' *1938. Eine Dokumentation*, ed. Heinz Arnberger *et al.* (Vienna, 1988), 539 f.

208. Reinhard Vogelsang, *Der Freundeskreis Heinrich Himmler* (Göttingen, etc., 1972), 88 f.; Drobisch and Wieland, *System*, 303 f.; NS 19/1396, note for Himmler concerning the planned visit by journalists, 1 March 1938.

209. Wegner, *Politische Soldaten*, 112.

210. Ibid. 97.

211. Ibid. 103.

212. Orth, *System*, 62 f.

213. BAB, NS 19/1652, Führer edict of 17 August 1938 concerning the armed units of the SS; words added: draft of 3 June 1938 with alterations made by Himmler on 10 June 1938; Wegner, *Politische Soldaten*, 112 ff.

214. Doc. PS-1992 (A), lecture to a Wehrmacht course on national politics, 15–23. January 1937, published in *IMT*, vol. 29, pp. 206 ff., quotation 231.

215. Ibid. 228.

216. Himmler, *Geheimreden*, 25 ff., quotation 31.

217. Wegner, *Politische Soldaten*, 104.

218. BAB, NS 19/4005, Speech to a Gruppenführer meeting in Munich, 8 November 1938.

219. Wegner, *Politische Soldaten*, 120 ff. The author shows in detail how this restriction could be got round.

220. Ibid. 124 f.; Charles W. Sydnor, *Soldaten des Todes. Die 3. SS Division 'Totenkopf' 1933–1945* (Paderborn, etc., 2002), 30 f.

221. BAB, NS 19/4005, speech to a Gruppenführer meeting in Munich, 8 November 1938.

222. The post of Higher SS and Police Leader was created by a decree of the Reich Interior Minister's of 13 November 1937 (BAB, NS 19/2850, here also further orders affecting the HSSPF). Ruth Bettina Birn has researched them thoroughly in *Die Höheren SS- und Polizeiführer. Himmlers Vertreter im Reich und in den besetzten Gebieten* (Düsseldorf, 1986).

223. Speech of 8 November 1938, in Himmler, *Geheimreden*, 25 ff., quotation 26.

224. On the creation of the HSSPF see Birn, *Die Höheren SS- und Polizeiführer*, 10 ff.

225. Wilhelm, *Polizei*, 93 ff. This was the purpose of the following edicts of the RFSSuChdDtPol: 18 January 1938, in *RMBliV* 1938, cols. 157 ff.; 24 March 1938, in *RMBliV* 1938, col. 537 (after the Anschluss with Austria); 4 March 1938, in *RMBliV* 1938, cols. 390 f.; 23 June 1938, in *RMBliV* 1938, cols. 1089 ff. (for the security police); 12 November 1940, in *RMBliV* 1940, col. 2167 (further concessions on admission to the SS for members of the order police).

226. Buchheim, 'SS', 102.

227. Edict of the RFSSuChdDtPol of 10 May 1937, announcement of a Führer decision of 16 January 1937, in *RMBliV* 1937, col. 758.

228. Werner Best, *Die deutsche Polizei* (Darmstadt, 1940), 96.
229. Buchheim, 'SS', 111 f.
230. See below pp. 353 ff.
231. See below p. 312.
232. *RMBliV* 1938, col. 2132a, Order of the RFSSuChdDtPol, 12 December 1938.
233. See below pp. 485 ff.
234. BAB, NS 19/4004, 16 January 1937.

CHAPTER 10

1. *Statistisches Jahrbuch 1937*, 15; *Statistisches Jahrbuch 1938*, 16.
2. *Statistisches Jahrbuch 1938*, 107.
3. BAB, NS 19/4003, speech at the Gruppenführer meeting in Dachau, 8 November 1936.
4. BAB, NS 19/4005, speech at the Gruppenführer meeting in Munich, 8 November 1938.
5. BAB, NS 19/4007, speech to the officer corps of the Leibstandarte on the evening of the Metz conference, 7 September 1940, published as doc. PS-1918, in *IMT*, vol. 29, pp. 98 ff., quotation 107.
6. Mayerhofer, 'Der Sippenorden', *SS-Leitheft*, 9/2 (1943), 14–17. On the SS as an order see Ackermann, *Himmler*, 97 ff.
7. BAB, NS 19/4003, speech of 8 November 1936. On 18 February 1937 he declared to the Gruppenführer that his intention was, 'perhaps in a decade to bring together SS und police in one body' (NS 19/4004). On 8 November 1937, in his speech to the Gruppenführer on the occasion of the second year of his 'Ten-Year Plan', he expressed the hope 'that in ten years we shall be an order and not only an order of men but an order of clan communities' (NS 19/4004, final passage, also published in Himmler, *Geheimreden*, 61).
8. Buchheim, 'SS', 201 ff.; *Dienstkalender*, 33 ff. (esp. the Personal Staff).
9. BAB, NS 19/3901, SS order of 9 November 1936.
10. Elisabeth Kinder, 'Der Persönliche Stab Reichsführer-SS. Geschichte, Aufgaben und Überlieferung', in Heinz Boberach and Hans Booms (eds), *Aus der Arbeit des Bundesarchivs. Beiträge zum Archivwesen, zur Quellenkunde und Zeitgeschichte* (Boppard a. Rh., 1977), 379–97, 383.
11. Kinder, 'Der Persönliche Stab', 381.
12. BAB, NS 19/3901, Order concerning the reorganization of the system of command within the whole of the SS. The intention was to guarantee uniform command arrangements in the regions by subordinating the SD-Oberabschnitte and the Race and Settlement Office to the Oberabschnittsführer in each case.
13. BAB, NS 2/3 Order from the chief of the RuSHA 19/35, 10 April 1935; cf. Heinemann, *Rasse*, 69 f.

14. Heinemann, *Rasse*, 99; BAB, NS 2/86, order of the RFSS of 1 August 1938.
15. Buchheim, 'SS', 202 f. On the administration of the SS in this period see Schulte, *Zwangsarbeit*, 62 ff.
16. Aronson, *Heydrich*, 202 ff.
17. For a detailed account see Schulte, *Zwangsarbeit*, 247 ff.
18. Buchheim, 'SS', 205.
19. Schulte, *Zwangsarbeit*, 76 ff.; further details can be found in BAB, NS 3/465 and 468, SS budget plans for 1935 and 1938. In 1935 the General SS received more than a million Reich marks in the form of membership dues and extraordinary payments by non-party comrades in the SS; in 1938 840,000 Reich marks were expected. Payments by sponsoring members amounted to 5,544,000 Reich marks in 1935, 4,800,000 in 1936 and 1937, and then 3,960,000 in 1938.
20. Vogelsang, *Freundeskreis*, 22 ff.
21. BAB, BDC, SS-O Keppler.
22. Vogelsang, *Freundeskreis*, 52 ff.
23. On the meetings see ibid. 78 ff.
24. Ibid. 136.
25. Ibid. 88 f., also Wildt, 'Terminkalender', 681.
26. Vogelsang, *Freundeskreis*, 92 ff.; draft speech for 12 Dezember 1943 (IfZ, NO 5637).
27. A list is printed in the appendix to Vogelsang, *Freundeskreis*, 139 ff., taken from IfZ, NI 9971. In Himmler's appointments calendar for 8/9 February 1937 there is the first known list with 38 names, to which Wildt ('Terminkalender', 679) alludes.
28. Vogelsang, *Freundeskreis*, 108 ff.
29. Ibid. 101 ff.
30. BAB, R 2/12 1172a; see Schulte, *Zwangsarbeit*, 98 ff., and Kaienburg, *Wirtschaft*, 123 ff. and 137 ff.
31. For the most detailed account of these enterprises see Kaienburg, *Wirtschaft*, 159 ff. and 185 ff. On the early SS businesses see also Allen, *Business*, 31 ff.; Enno Georg, *Die wirtschaftlichen Unternehmungen der SS* (Stuttgart, 1963), 12; and Schulte, *Zwangsarbeit*, 93 f.
32. These were Franz Nagy, the sculptor Theodor Kärner, and Bruno Galke, who was the man responsible in the Personal Staff for, among other things, the SS businesses. Albert Knoll, 'Die Porzellanmanufaktur München-Allach. Das Lieblingskind von Heinrich Himmler', in *KZ-Außenlager. Geschichte und Erinnerung*, Dachauer Hefte 15 (Dachau, 1999), 116–33; Gabriele Huber, *Die Porzellan-Manufaktur Allach-München GmbH. Eine 'Wirtschaftsunternehmung' der SS zum Schutz der 'deutschen Seele'* (Marburg, 1992), 12 ff.
33. Huber, *Porzellan-Manufaktur*, 46.
34. Ibid. 27, in 1940.
35. Knoll, 'Porzellanmanufaktur', 120.

36. Himmler to Pohl, 26 September 1939, published in Heinrich Himmler, *Reichsführer!... Briefe an und von Himmler*, ed. and intr. by Helmut Heiber (Stuttgart, 1968), no. 52.
37. Huber, *Porzellan-Manufaktur*, 44 ff.
38. Ibid. 51 ff.
39. On the course in national politics see doc. PS-1992 (A), in *IMT*, vol. 29, pp. 206 ff. It took place from 15 to 23 January 1937. For the speech to the Gruppenführer see BAB, NS 19/4005, 8 November 1938, published in Himmler, *Geheimreden*, 25 ff.
40. *Schutzstaffel*, 3. In his speech of January 1937 he said that the coming decades would mean a 'battle to the point of annihilation of those subhuman enemies I have mentioned throughout the world against Germany as the core nation of the Nordic race, against Germany as the core nation of the Germanic nation, against Germany as the bearer of culture for humanity. They will mean the to be or not to be of white men, of which we are the leading nation' (*IMT*, vol. 29, pp. 206 ff., quotation 234).
41. In his speech at the Reich Peasants' Rally of 1935 Himmler had asserted that 'our common and eternal enemy, the Jew' was responsible for the violent Christianization of the Saxons, the Spanish Inquisition, the witch hunts, and the outbreak of the Thirty Years War (*Schutzstaffel*, 5).
42. BAB, NS 19/4012, speech to the conference of Reich chief propaganda officials, 26 January 1944.
43. BAB, NS 19/4009, speech in the Haus der Flieger, 9 June 1942, published in Himmler, *Geheimreden*, 145 ff., here 147. On the battle between Asia and Europe see also NS 19/4009, speech at the SS officers' training college (Junkerschule) at Bad Tölz, 23 November 1942, and NS 19/4014, speech to representatives of the German judiciary in Kochem, 25 May 1944; ibid. speech in Sonthofen, 21 June 1944.
44. 'This struggle is a conflict [...] of two leader classes or leadership classes, on the one hand the leadership of the subhumans: Jews, commissars and politruks, who are convinced to their core of their ideology, fanatical supporters of this doctrine of destruction, for this idea of an Asian empire, and in reality prepared to use ultimate and brutal means for the sake of this conviction. [...] This is a battle of ideologies, as was the battle with the Huns at the time of the migrations, as was the battle throughout the Middle Ages with Islam, where not only religion was at stake but also a battle of the races.' BAB, NS 19/4014, speech to the Oberabschnittsführer and chief officers in the Haus der Flieger, 9 June 1942, published in Himmler, *Geheimreden*, 145 ff., quotation 150. For the term 'politruk', see below Ch. 12, n. 92.
45. BAB, NS 19/4014, speech in Sonthofen, 21 June 1944.
46. Ibid. speech in Sonthofen, 24 May 1944. In his Vienna speech of 1939 he had already spoken of the 'unfortunate doctrine of an Asianized Christianity' (BAB, NS 19/3666, published in Himmler, *Geheimreden*, 51). On 16 Septem-

ber 1942, in a speech made in his headquarters at Hegewald, he imputed to the church typically 'oriental' concepts (NS 19/4009).

47. BAB, NS 19/4005, speech at the Gruppenführer meeting in Munich, 8 November 1938, published in Himmler, *Geheimreden*, 25 ff., here 9. In the same speech, however, Himmler also spoke of the future 'Germanic' Reich (ibid. 38 f.). The topos of the 'Greater Germanic state' can be found in a speech he made at the end of 1940 (NS 19/4007, undated). 'Greater Germania' was then invoked above all in his speech in Posen on 24 October 1943 (NS 19/4011), as well as in Sonthofen on 24 May 1944 (NS 19/4014). Cf. Frank-Lothar Kroll, *Utopie als Ideologie. Geschichtsdenken und politisches Handeln im Dritten Reich* (Paderborn, 1998), 217 ff.

48. BAB, NS 19/4012, speech on the occasion of the conference of Reich chief propaganda officials, 26 January 1944.

49. BAB, NS 19/4009.

50. BAB, NS 19/4007, speech to the Gauleiters, 29 February 1940, also published in Himmler,*Geheimreden*, 116 ff., quotation 125.

51. BAB, NS 19/4013, speech in Sonthofen, 5 May 1944: 'Out of countless millions of possibilities, two who share in the inheritance of the blood came together in some kind of embrace which reunited the few drops of Aryan blood so copiously lost in this territory of Russia–Eastern Europe–Asia, as much of this genetic material, which alone is capable of organizing and giving organized leadership, as is needed to produce a dangerous Attila or Genghis Khan or Stalin or Lenin from a brutal Asian unrestrained by any moral feeling. Woe to the European, Germanic, Aryan human beings every time that over there such a one has emerged, capable of organizing and leading armies and powerful forces made up of this mass of subhumanity.'

52. As in his speech in Posen on 4 October 1943 (BAB, NS 19/4010), also published as doc. PS-1919 in *IMT*, vol. 29, pp. 110 ff., esp. pp. 145 f.; also his speech in Posen of 6 October 1943 (ibid.), published in Himmler, *Geheimreden*, 162 ff., esp. 169.

53. For this reason I consider Kroll's attempt (*Utopie*, 209 ff.) to interpret this vision of the world as a more or less coherent whole and largely independent of its timing as not entirely convincing, as this necessarily involves disregarding changes over time and smoothing over blatant contradictions. Kroll's correct observation that, for example, Himmler's ideology of a Greater Germanic Reich contains 'a considerable measure of pragmatic political calculation' (p. 219) should have led, in my opinion, to a deconstruction of these texts, whereas Kroll's analysis is directed towards reconstructing a vision of the world that probably never existed in such a clear and abstract form as this.

54. See above, pp. 218 ff.

55. See above, p. 220.

56. BAB, NS 19/4011, 16 December 1943. On Waralda see also the speech of 26 July 1944, published in Himmler, *Geheimreden*, 215 ff., 217.

57. NARA, T 580/150/229, RFSS to Wüst, 28 May 1940.
58. BAB, NS 19/3670 (undated).
59. BAB, NS 19/4013, 26 November 1944.
60. Himmler to Pohl and Müller, quoted from the report 'Tätigkeit der Zeugen Jehovas in der Neuzeit: Deutschland', *Jahrbuch der Zeugen Jehovas* (1974), 66–253, here 196 f.
61. On 6 January 1943 Himmler ordered that Jehovah's Witnesses under arrest should be made to work in SS households (Garbe, *Widerstand*, 451). He offered 'Bible students' to, among others, his old friend Rehrl and also to a farmer in Valepp, where he owned an alpine hut; see Mühldorfer, 'Fridolfing'; Johannes Wrobel, 'Valepp/Schliersee (Bauer Marx)', in Wolfgang Benz and Barbara Distel (eds), *Der Ort des Terrors. Geschichte der nationalsozialistischen Konzentrationslager*, vol. 2: *Frühe Lager, Dachau, Emslandlager* (Munich, 2005), 522 f. From March 1944 to April 1945 Himmler had a work detail of twenty prisoners carry out construction work on air-raid shelters on his property in Gmund. Margarete Himmler observed the progress of the work and complained about the prisoners' poor performance; one of them died while at work. See Hans-Günter Richardi, 'Der gerade Weg. Der Dachauer Häftling Karl Wagner', in *Dachauer Hefte* 7, 52–101, esp. 52 ff. Wagner worked there from March to April 1944.
62. BAB, NS 19/3947, 21 July 1944, published in Ackermann, *Himmler*, 305 f.
63. BAB, NS 19/4003, speech at the Gruppenführer meeting in Dachau, 8 November 1936. On ancestor worship cf. Ackermann, *Himmler*, 64 ff.
64. BAB, NS 19/4003, speech at the Gruppenführer meeting in Dachau, 8 November 1936.
65. BAB, NS 19/4004, speech at the Gruppenführer meeting in Bad Tölz, 18 February 1937. On this matter see also Ackermann, *Himmler*, 68 ff.
66. BAB, NS 19/2241, 25 February 1937.
67. Karl August Eckhardt, *Irdische Unsterblichkeit. Germanischer Glaube an die Wiederverkörperung in der Sippe* (Weimar, 1937). Himmler had at first reversed his original agreement to have a special edition of the book printed for the SS, upon which Eckhardt, deeply offended, withdrew his suggestion to found an institute; Eckhardt to Wolff, 9 December 1937. Himmler and Eckhardt discussed the matter, however, after which the plans for the institute were realized (see also the correspondence in the same file).
68. On Himmler's view of history as 'eternal recurrence' see Kroll, *Utopie*, 245 ff.
69. See Klaus von See, *Deutsche Germanenideologie. Vom Humanismus bis zur Gegenwart* (Frankfurt a. M., 1970); Rainer Kipper, *Der Germanenmythos im Deutschen Kaiserreich. Formen und Funktionen historischer Selbstthematisierung* (Göttingen, 2002); Joachim Heinzle, *Die Nibelungen. Lied und Sage* (Darmstadt, 2005).
70. Published in Ackermann, *Himmler*, doc. no. 8, 253 ff. (undated).

71. See Michael H. Kater, *Das 'Ahnenerbe' der SS 1935–1945. Ein Beitrag zur Kulturpolitik des Dritten Reiches*, 4th extended edn. (Munich, 2006), 95 f. and 108 f.
72. As Kroll notes (*Utopie*, 236 f.).
73. On Himmler's re-Germanization of the early Middle Ages see in particular ibid. 237 ff.
74. BAB, NS 19/4004, speech in Bad Tölz, 18 February 1937.
75. BAB, NS 19/4003, speech by Himmler in Quedlinburg cathedral, 2 July 1936; Himmler, *Schutzstaffel*, 5.
76. Himmler, *Schutzstaffel*, 12.
77. Hitler did not, however, name Charlemagne but rather praised 'those great German emperors [...] who with a merciless sword and disregarding the fates of the individual tribes strove to bring more German people together' (*Parteitag der Freiheit. Reden des Führers und ausgewählte Kongressreden am Reichsparteitag der NSDAP 1935* (Munich, 1935), 123, closing address). On Hitler's vigorous rejection of criticism of Charlemagne see *Tagebücher Goebbels*, 15 November 1936.
78. H. W. Scheidt, 'Die Christianisierung Germaniens im Lichte nationalsozialistischer Geschichtsbetrachtung', *SS-Leitheft*, 3/5 (1937), 58–62, quotation 60.
79. BAB, NS 19/4014, speech to Wehrmacht officers in Sonthofen, 24 May 1944. Similar comments are to be found in his speech at a conference of Oberbürgermeister and senior local government officials that took place on 12 and 13 February 1944 in Posen: Charlemagne was, he said, the first 'great uniter of the Reich' (BAB, NS 19/4012). See also the ideological training materials issued by the Reichsführer-SS: In the booklet entitled *Rassenpolitik* ('Racial Policy') issued by the SS Main Office (Berlin, 1943) there is on p. 42 the still somewhat ambivalent statement: 'And however much we reject Charlemagne's methods of compulsion in individual cases, we must acknowledge that he made the Europe of his day into a powerful unit.' *Erzählte Geschichte*, Part 3 (Berlin, no date), the textbook for German lessons intended for SS members of German ethnic groups and Germanic units, did not make heavy weather of it, celebrating Charlemagne as 'the uniter of Europe' (29 ff.).
80. Heinrich Himmler, *Rede des Reichsführers-SS im Dom zu Quedlinburg am 2. Juli 1936* (Magdeburg, 1936).
81. In the *SS-Leithefte* of 1937, on the occasion of the memorial celebrations for Henry, the comparison of Henry and Hitler was once again explicitly made. See H. Löffler, 'Der Gründer des Ersten deutschen Reiches', *SS-Leitheft*, 3/4 (1937), 52–5: 'He erected his Reich on the same foundation on which a thousand years later Adolf Hitler also erected his Third Reich: on a free peasantry rooted in the soil and on an army ready for service' (p. 55). In view of this persistent interpretation of the medieval emperor, the assertion that Himmler had regarded himself as a reincarnation of the emperor seems misplaced.

82. The journal *Germanien*, which was edited by the Ahnenerbe, produced a special number on Henry I in 1936, for which Himmler wrote a preface.
83. *Das Schwarze Korps* of 1 July 1937.
84. *Tagebücher Goebbels*, 3 July 1937.
85. Documents on the celebrations, which were accorded a great deal of space in the newspapers, can be found in BAB, NS 19/3901 and NS 19/3666.
86. BAB, NS 19/397, cost-sheet for King Henry celebrations of 1942, 1943, and 1944; note by Brandt from 19 August 1944, who considered it more than questionable whether 'the dignity of the King Henry celebrations and more particularly living conditions in the fifth year of war are compatible with the expenditure of 300 Reich marks on alcohol for a group of 21 people'.
87. See e.g. his speech of 24 May 1944 (BAB, NS 19/4014). In the ideological training materials issued by the Reichsführer-SS and the SS Main Office the opportunity was taken to give particular prominence to Frederick II and Henry the Lion: see booklet *Rassenpolitik*, 51, and also *Erzählte Geschichte*, Part 3, pp. 48 f.
88. BAB, NS 19/3666, printed in Himmler, *Geheimreden*, 50 f. In the *SS-Leithefte* of 1937 Hermann Löffler, who worked in the Race and Settlement Main Office, praised the order for its 'policy of re-Germanization' and 'extension of living-space in the east'; see 'Der Deutsche Ritterorden', *SS-Leitheft*, 3/6 (1937), 67–78, quotation 67.
89. BAB, NS 19/4014, speech in Sonthofen, 24 May 1944; NS 19/4015, speech in Grafenwöhr, 25 July 1944, and speech made at the army training grounds at Bitch, 26 July 1944. See also the ideological training materials produced by the Reichsführer-SS: the booklet entitled *Rassenpolitik* conveys a positive image of Bismarck (91 ff.), as does the textbook for German lessons *Erzählte Geschichte*, Part 3, pp. 74 ff., which, without going into the difference between ideas of a smaller and greater German unification, states plainly on p. 79 that 'Adolf Hitler is completing Bismarck's work'. Prussia is praised in the article 'Preußentum und Weltanschauung', in *SS-Leitheft*, 10/3 (1944), 25–7. On Himmler's view of Prussia see Kroll, *Utopie*, 242 ff.
90. See e.g. Hitler's comments, made in Himmler's presence in February 1942, on the primitiveness of the Teutons (Adolf Hitler, *Monologe im Führer-Hauptquartier 1941–1944. Die Aufzeichnungen Heinrich Heims*, ed. Werner Jochmann (Bindlach, 1988), 263 f.). On his rejection of 'cultic nonsense' as practised by Himmler, see below, p. 293.
91. Kater, *'Ahnenerbe'*, 22 ff. This study, a doctoral dissertation of 1966 first published in 1974, has now appeared in its 4th edition and remains essential reading on the SS scientific organization. Additional information can be found in Heather Pringle's *The Master Plan: Himmler's Scholars and the Holocaust* (New York, 2006).
92. Kater, *'Ahnenerbe'*, 26; on Wirth see ibid. 11 ff., also Ingo Wiwjorra, 'Herman Wirth—Ein gescheiterter Ideologe zwischen "Ahnenerbe" und Atlantis', in

Barbara Danckwortt *et al.* (eds), *Historische Rassismusforschung. Ideologen, Täter, Opfer* (Hamburg and Berlin, 1995), 95–112.

93. Kater, *'Ahnenerbe'*, 26 f.
94. According to its ordinances (NARA, T 580/207/733) its purpose was to research 'intellectual prehistory', as Wirth usually described his own programme of research.
95. On Sievers see Kater, *'Ahnenerbe'*, 28 ff.
96. Ibid. 37 ff.
97. Ibid. 41 ff.
98. Ibid. 60.
99. Ibid. 58 ff. See also NARA, T 580/128/47, correspondence between Himmler/Ahnenerbe and Wirth. This reveals that at least until 1942 Wirth received funds from the Ahnenerbe.
100. NARA, T 580/207/733, ordinances of 11 March 1937; cf. Kater, *'Ahnenerbe'*, 58.
101. NARA, T 580/128/47, Wüst to Himmler, congratulations on 7 October 1937.
102. Kater, *'Ahnenerbe'*, 40 f., 64 ff., and 91.
103. NARA, T 580/207/733, ordinances of 1 January 1939; cf. Kater, *'Ahnenerbe'*, 92.
104. Ibid. 53 ff. and 70 ff.
105. The Ahnenerbe Memorandum of 1939, an expensively produced work that was distributed to prominent members of the SS, names 34, but not all existed; cf. Kater, *'Ahnenerbe'*, 112.
106. Ibid. 45 f.
107. Ibid. 76 ff.
108. Ibid. 75 f.
109. Ibid. 95. This was the immediate consequence of Himmler's journey to Italy in 1937 (see below pp. 397 ff.). The department was later named Research Centre for Classical Studies.
110. On the excavations see Kater, *'Ahnenerbe'*, 80 ff. The popular science journal *Germanien* gave its readers regular updates on the SS's archaeological projects.
111. Kater, *'Ahnenerbe'*, 95 ff.
112. Ibid. 211 ff.
113. Ibid. 86 f.
114. Ibid. 87 and 127 f., and 265 f.
115. For a survey see ibid. 87 f.
116. In the early summer a first 'annual conference' was held in Kiel and designed as an exhibition particularly highlighting folklore and prehistory; see ibid. 104 ff. and 113 ff.
117. As Kater comments, ibid. 121.
118. NARA, T 580/128/47, Wüst to Sievers, 9 January 1938; cf. Kater, *'Ahnenerbe'*, 122.

119. Ibid. 122.

120. Ibid. 130 ff.

121. Ibid. 137.

122. Ibid. 273 ff.

123. Ibid. 88.

124. Ibid. 147 ff.

125. Ibid. 170 ff.

126. Ibid. 216, 218 ff., and 227 ff.

127. On this see Kater's summing up, ibid. 353 ff.

128. Brigitte Nagel, *Die Welteislehre. Ihre Geschichte und ihre Rolle im 'Dritten Reich'* (Stuttgart, 1991); Kater, *'Ahnenerbe'*, 51.

129. NARA, T 580/194/165, 19 July 1936; Nagel, *Welteislehre*, 72 f.

130. Facsimile of the letter of 21 June 1938 to Heydrich, in Samuel A. Goudsmit, *Alsos: The Failure in German Science* (London, 1947), 116; Nagel, *Welteislehre*, 74.

131. NARA, T 580/150/229, Brandt (Personal Staff RFSS), to the Ahnenerbe, 5 December1940, and the answer from Scultetus, 15 May 1941.

132. Ibid. Brandt to Sievers, 10 September 1941.

133. BAB, NS 19/3042, 26 June 1942. The Cosmic Ice Theory was based on the assumption that in the course of its history the earth had 'captured' several planets, which later collapsed.

134. BAB, NS 19/1705, published as Appendix 28 in Nagel, *Welteislehre*; on this incident see ibid. 84 ff.

135. BAB, NS 21/327, Sievers to Brandt, 7 August 1942, published as Appendix 38 in Nagel, *Welteislehre*.

136. See above p. 77.

137. BAB, NS 19/212, Field HQ to Schellenberg, 23 February 1945. After the war Wulff wrote an account of his activities: *Tierkreis und Hakenkreuz. Als Astrologe an Himmlers Hof* (Gütersloh, 1968).

138. Himmler, *Schutzstaffel*, 11 f.

139. BAB, NS 19/3165, Adjutant of the RFSS, 17 January 1943, to Rifleman Albrecht in the SS hospital in Hohenlychen. Himmler told the latter, when he enquired, to study astronomy. When the SS man contacted him again the adjutant replied by sending him additional information about Himmler's observatory plans.

140. On the background to these 'theories' see *Mythos Tibet. Wahrnehmungen, Projektionen, Phantasien*, ed. Art and Exhibition Gallery of the Federal Republic of Germany in association with Thierry Dodin and Heinz Räther (Cologne, 1997); Nicholas Goodrick-Clarke, *Die okkulten Wurzeln des Nationalsozialismus,* 2nd edn. (Graz and Stuttgart, 2000). See NARA, T 580/186/366, Himmler to Wüst, Director of the Ahnenerbe, 25 October 1937, with approving comments on the latter's statement on the book by Sigurd Wettenhovi-Aspa, *Fenno-Ägyptischer Kulturursprung der Alten Welt.*

Kommentare zu den vorhistorischen Völkerwanderungen (Helsinki, 1942). In the letter Himmler makes the assumption that Finns and Egyptians, and also Chinese and Japanese, were once nations colonized by an 'elite from Atlantis'.

141. IfZ, PS-2204, note on file about a discussion with Hitler on 1 November 1935.

142. Heinz Corazza, *Die Samurai. Ritter des Reiches in Ehre und Treue* (Berlin and Munich, 1937); cf. Ackermann, *Himmler*, 68.

143. BAB, BDC, SS-O Schäfer. Schäfer was born in 1910. He had written two books about the expedition begun in 1934 that collapsed in the highlands of central Tibet, making it necessary for him to turn back in difficult circumstances: *Unbekanntes Tibet. Durch die Wildnisse Osttibets zum Dach der Erde* (Berlin, 1937), and *Dach der Erde. Durch das Wunderland Hochtibet. Tibetexpedition 1934/36* (Berlin, 1938). In the foreword to *Unbekanntes Tibet* he acknowledged Himmler's support. On this whole subject see Reinhard Greve, 'Tibetforschung im SS-Ahnenerbe', in Thomas Hauschild (ed.), *Lebenslust und Fremdenfurcht. Ethnologie im Dritten Reich* (Frankfurt a. M., 1995), 168–99.

144. Peter Mierau offers the most detailed account in *Nationalsozialistische Expeditionspolitik. Deutsche Asien-Expeditionen 1933–1945* (Munich, 2006), 311 ff.; see also Greve, 'Tibetforschung', 171 ff., Christopher Hale, *Himmler's Crusade: The True Story of the 1938 Nazi Expedition into Tibet* (London, 2003), and Kater, '*Ahnenerbe*', 211 f.

145. BAB, NS 19/2709, Himmler to Schäfer, 7 September 1939. In this letter Schäfer had to put up with severe criticism from the Reichsführer, because he had spoken to Admiral Canaris about his mission and thus was putting its secrecy at risk; Schäfer to Himmler, 3 November 1939, on the state of preparations (ibid.). The enterprise failed not least because of the financial cost, put by Schäfer at 2–3 million Reich marks (letter to Wolff, 6 April 1940, ibid.). On the mission see Greve, 'Tibetforschung', 177, Kater, '*Ahnenerbe*', 212, also Mierau, *Expeditionspolitik*, 365 ff.

146. Greve, 'Tibetforschung', 177 ff., and Mierau, *Expeditionspolitik*, 394 ff.

147. BAB, NS 19/2244, Brandt to Tobis-Filmkunst, 24 November 1939.

148. Ibid. Himmler to Schäfer, March 1940, no day.

149. BAB, BDC, SS-O Schäfer, Himmler to Schäfer, 24 February 1943. The book in fact appeared in 1943 with the subtitle *Erster Bericht der deutschen Tibet-Expedition Ernst Schäfer 1938/39*.

150. See BAB, NS 19/500, Otto to Brandt, Gmund, 5 August 1939, on the secondment of a Luftwaffe major for the South America expedition. In a letter Sievers wrote on 9 August 1939 to Himmler as President of the Ahnenerbe he reminded him that in discussions with Kiss he had voiced the intention of informing the governments of Bolivia, Peru, and Chile about the Ahnenerbe expedition arranged for 1940 (ibid.).

151. Edmund Kiss, *Das Sonnentor von Tihuanaku und Hörbigers Welteislehre* (Leipzig, 1937).

152. BAB, BDC, SS-O Weisthor.

153. The account in question was *Der Rasputin Himmlers. Die Wiligut Saga* (Vienna, 1982) by Rudolf J. Mund and published by the Volkstum-Verlag. It is based above all on letters, notes, and oral material from Wiligut's adherents and admirers, of whom the author was one. Goodrick-Clarke, *Wurzeln*, took some important material from it. Hans-Jürgen Lange is more critical: *Weisthor. Karl Maria Wiligut. Himmlers Rasputin und seine Erben* (Engerda, 1998).

154. Karl Maria Wiligut, *Seyfried's Runen (Rabensteinsage)* (Vienna, 1903), reprinted in Winfried Katholing, *Die Sage von Ritter Seyfried und der Rebenstein bei Znaim* (Aschaffenburg, 2003), 73–115.

155. Amongst the papers Wiligut sent Himmler were the article 'Gotos Raunen—Runenwissen!', which had appeared in the journal *Hagal* in 1934, with a personal dedication from Wiligut, a mythological poem in seven stanzas, a 'mythological idyll', a number of letters, and an Irminic prayer from 1934. The documents are published in Lange, *Weisthor*. In addition Wiligut prepared for Himmler a detailed commentary on a book dedicated to Himmler's father, *Erklärung der Gebräuche bei der Ausstellung der Heiligen Sakramente in der rechtgläubigen Kirche* (W. Michailowskij, St Petersburg, 1870), NS 19/3944.

156. BAB, NS 19/3670 (undated).

157. BAB, NS 19/3671, 'For my Reichsführer-SS Heinrich Himmler from a loyal German!' Initialled on 1 May 1934 by Himmler.

158. Ibid. initialled on 17 June 1936 by Himmler.

159. BAB, BDC, SS-O Weisthor, promotion w.e.f. 9 November 1936.

160. Ibid. Wolff to Pancke, 5 February 1939; according to this Weisthor had 'left the SS w.e.f. 1. 1. 39 at his own request for reasons of age and of the fragile state of his health'.

161. Ibid. Chief of the Personal Staff, Wolff, to Schmitt, 22 August 1939.

162. BAB, NS 19/1573, correspondence between Brandt und Wiligut, who was in Salzdetfurt being treated for rheumatism, from 18 August to 11 September 1940.

163. *Dienstkalender*, 28 November 1941, lunch with Colonel Wiligut, Frau Ruppmann, Frau Baltrusch.

164. Speech in 1938 in Himmler, *Geheimreden*, 79.

165. 'Zur Erkenntnis deutschen Wesens. Julzeit—heilige Zeit', *Germanien*, 8 (1936), 369–72, 371; cf. Huber, *Porzellan-Manukfaktur*, 133 ff.

166. BAB, NS 19/4003, speech at the Gruppenführer meeting in Dachau, 8 November 1936.

167. BAB, NS 19/4004, speech at the Gruppenführer meeting in Munich in the leaders' quarters of the SS-Standarte Deutschland, 8 November 1937.

168. Knoll, 'Porzellanmanufaktur', 122 f. Huber, *Porzellan-Manufaktur*, 24, even mentions 60,000.

169. BAB, NS 19/457, Himmler to Diebitsch, 9 June 1939, and also Personal Staff (Brandt) to the Personal Staff Munich, 5 April 1940 (ibid.); cf. Huber, *Porzellan-Manufaktur*, 136 f.

170. Huber, *Porzellan-Manufaktur*, 136. There was also a life light embellished with a 'children's frieze' and known as a 'children's frieze light'.

171. Various letters in BAB, NS 19/3034 and in 3666.

172. BAB, NS 19/3901, Order for the Conferral of the Death's Head Ring, 10 April 1934. All SS leaders from Sturmführer upwards received the ring if they had either joined the organization before 1933 and had belonged to it for at least two years or had joined after 30 January 1933 and had been members for three years, and also all SS leaders who through belonging to the Reichswehr and police had not been able to join before 30 January 1933 received it after they had been members for two years. For a detailed account of the ring see Klaus D. Patzwall, *Der SS-Totenkopfring. Seine illustrierte Geschichte 1933– 1945*, 4th. rev. edn. (Norderstedt, 2002), 58 f.

173. See e.g. BAB, BDC, SS-O Daluege, Himmler to Daluege, 24 December 1933.

174. Ibid. Himmler to Daluege, 15 September 1933.

175. BAB, NS 19/4003, speech to the Gruppenführer meeting in Dachau, 8 November 1936.

176. Ibid. For a time this was nothing more than an announcement: see BAB, NS 19/3081, Personal Staff to Frau Gahr, 8 June 1939, and further correspondence on the design that was finally put forward.

177. Examples in BAB, NS 19/3034 and 3666; cf. Gudrun Schwarz, *Eine Frau an seiner Seite. Ehefrauen in der 'SS-Sippengemeinschaft'* (Hamburg, 1997), 64.

178. Ackermann, *Himmler*, 66.

179. BAB, NS 19/1148, referred to RFSS with a letter of 17 April 1937; published with a commentary in Schwarz, *Frau*, 53 ff.

180. BAB, NS 19/4003, speech at the Gruppenführer meeting in Dachau, 8 November 1936. See also speech at the wedding ceremony of SS-Sturmbannführer Deutsch, 2 April 1936 (ibid.).

181. Instructions for the Organization of Name Consecrations, formerly Slg. Schumacher (BAB), discussed in detailed in Ackermann, *Himmler*, 84 ff.

182. BAB, NS 19/4003, speech at the Gruppenführer meeting in Dachau, 8 November 1936.

183. A facsimile of the official record of the ceremony is published in Lang, *Adjutant*, 43 f.

184. BAB, NS 19/4003, speech at the Gruppenführer meeting in Dachau, 8 November 1936.

185. NARA, T 580/143/167, circular 5/38, 30 September 1938.

186. BAB, NS 19/4005, speech in Alt-Rehse.

187. BAB, NS 19/3667, list of summer-solstice celebrations in which the RFSS has taken part.

188. BAB, NS 2/6, Wolff to RuSHA, 26 October 1936.
189. BAB, NS 2/54, 28 February 1938.
190. BAB, NS 19/530, summary report of the SS Main Office dated 25 October 1938, enclosing the reports from senior SS leaders sent in at the request of the Personal Staff.
191. 'Frühjahrswettkampf der SS', *SS-Leitheft*, 3/1 (1937), 45–7, also 'Sonnen-wendkämpfe der SS', *SS-Leitheft*, 3/3 (1937), 62–4 (for the second quotation).
192. BAB, NS 19/4004, speech to the Gruppenführer meeting in München in the officers' quarters of the SS-Standarte Deutschland, 8 November 1937.
193. BAB, NS 19/4003, speech to the Gruppenführer meeting in Dachau, 8 November 1936.
194. BAB, NS 19/2240, correspondence of the Personal Staff concerning the 'light sayings' for the celebrations in 1936 and 1937.
195. Ibid. 16 November 1937; cf. Ackermann, *Himmler*, 65, and Schwarz, *Frau*, 63.
196. BAB, NS 19/1312, Brandt to Ellersiek, 8 November 1938.
197. BAB, NS 19/4003, speech at the Gruppenführer meeting in Dachau, 8 November 1936. Italics in the original.
198. Ibid. Gruppenführer meeting 8 November 1936; similarly BAB, NS19/4004, Gruppenführer meeting in Bad Tölz, 18 February 1937.
199. BAB, NS 2/231, 16 April 1940.
200. BAB, NS 19/4003, Gruppenführer meeting in Dachau, 8 November 1936.
201. Schwarz, *Frau*, 57, with reference to a letter from the head of the SS Main Office of October 1935.
202. BAB, NS 19/4003, Gruppenführer meeting in Dachau, 8 November 1936.
203. *Tagebücher Goebbels*, 21 August 1935.
204. BAB, NS 2/56, RFSS's Guidelines for Comradeship Evenings, 22 February 1941.
205. Doc. PS-1992 (A), in *IMT*, vol. 29, pp. 206 ff.
206. Karl Hüser, *Wewelsburg 1933–1945. Kult- und Terrorstätte der SS. Eine Doku-mentation* (Paderborn, 1982), 11 ff.
207. Ibid. 26 ff.
208. Ibid. 23 ff.
209. BAB, NS 19/3901, order of 6 November 1935.
210. Hüser, *Wewelsburg*, 24.
211. Ibid. 32 f.
212. Ibid. 61 ff.
213. NS 19/3667, RFSS's guest list at the Wewelsburg between 1935 and 1938. On the dates of 12/13 May, 25/26 May, and 1 July 1935 see BAK, NL 1126/7, appointments diary for 1935; for 4 to 6 February and 7 to 9 May 1937 see the diary for 1937 (Wildt, 'Terminkalender', 689).
214. Speech of 8 November 1938, in Himmler, *Geheimreden*, 25 ff., here 26.
215. Hüser, *Wewelsburg*, 43 f.
216. Ibid. 65.
217. BAB, NS 19/1446, on his visit to the castle from 15 to 18 January 1939.

218. BAB, NS 19/1446; this instruction is undated (also published in Ackermann, *Himmler*, doc. no. 21).
219. Speech from 1938, quoted in Himmler, *Geheimreden*, 79. BAB, NS 19/3901, Himmler's instruction regarding the transfer of death's-head rings belonging to fallen SS men to the Personnel Main Office, 6 December 1939.
220. BAB, NS 19/4004, speech in Bad Tölz, 18 Februar 1937. Cf. Ackermann, *Himmler*, 105.
221. This can be found in the personal files of numerous SS leaders (BAB, BDC, SS-O).
222. Hüser, *Wewelsburg*, 50 ff.
223. Uta Halle, *'Die Externsteine sind bis auf weiteres germanisch!' Prähistorische Archäologie im Dritten Reich* (Bielefeld, 2002), 180 ff.
224. BAB, NS 19/1631, Wolff to Galke, who was the person in the Personal Staff with responsibility for the Externsteine, 27 April 1937.
225. Ibid. Himmler to Galke, 5 November 1937.
226. Ibid. Himmler to Galke, 4 November 1937.
227. Ibid. 20 April 1940.
228. This is clear from his letter of 20 April 1940.
229. Hitler, *Monologe*, 4 February 1942.
230. Justus H. Ulbricht, '"Heil Dir, Wittekinds Stamm". Verden, der "Sachsenhain" und die Geschichte völkischer Religiosität in Deutschland', *Heimatkalender für den Landkreis Verden* (1995), 69–123, and also (1996), 224–67, esp. 245 ff.
231. *Verdener Anzeigenblatt*, 22 June 1935, quoted in Ulbricht, '"Heil Dir"', 258.
232. Ibid. 97 f.
233. BAB, NS 19/3666, Personal Staff to Diebitsch re dispositions made by Himmler on his visit on 18 June 1938.

CHAPTER 11

1. PRO, WO 208/4474, Himmler dossier, testimony from Josef Kiermaier, who was responsible for Himmler's personal security, 5 August 1945. See in addition the testimony given by Himmler's adjutant Rudolf Brandt at the Nuremberg Doctors' Trial, published in *Der Nürnberger Ärzteprozess 1946/47. Wortprotokolle, Anklage- und Verteidigungsmaterial, Quellen zum Umfeld*, commissioned by the Foundation for Twentieth-Century Social History, ed. Klaus Dörner *et al.*, final editing by Karsten Linne (Munich, 1999), 4933 ff. Himmler's *Dienstkalender* (office diary), which exists for the years 1941 and 1942, shows that he seldom began work before 10 and most often still had appointments late into the evening. Colonel Eismann of the General Staff, Himmler's closest military colleague in his capacity as commander of the army group Vistula, claims in his memoirs that in general Himmler began work around 10.30 (BAM, N 265/127, notes of Colonel Eismann).

2. BAB, NS 19/4009, speech at the SS and Police Leaders' Conference in the HQ at Hegewald, 16 September 1942.

3. This album is one of four photograph albums belonging to the Himmler family that were given in 2004 to the archive of the US Holocaust Museum.

4. BAB, NS 19/4003, speech at the summer solstice on the Brocken, 22 May 1936.

5. BAB, NS 19/4013, speech on 5 May 1944 in Sonthofen.

6. OA Moscow, Himmler file. In 1934 he edited a piece of writing about him that contained false information about his school-leaving exams (Abitur) and his service in the 'field'.

7. BAB, NS 19/1718, letter of 30 October 1933 to Ferdinand Bruger as a response to the latter's request of 13 August 1933.

8. BAB, BDC, SS-O Johst, Johst to Himmler, 30 April 1942, and Himmler's reply, 14 May 1942; see Rolf Düsterberg, *Hanns Johst: 'Der Barde der SS'. Karrieren eines deutschen Dichters* (Paderborn, 2004), 290.

9. BAB, NS 19/3666, note on file for SS Oberführer von Alvensleben, 5 December 1938.

10. OA Moscow, Himmler file, correspondence with photographic business, 17 and 27 June 1938.

11. Ibid. Wolff to RFSS cash fund, 2 June 1937.

12. BADH, ZM 766 A 19, travel expenses of RFSS from 1939 and 1940.

13. PRO,WO 208/4474, Himmler dossier, testimony of Josef Kiermaier, 5 August 1945; see also a similar statement by Himmler's adjutant Rudolf Brandt in the Nuremberg Doctors' Trial, published in *Nürnberger Ärzteprozess*, 4978; on his modest requirements see also the recollections of Colonel I. G. Eismann (BAM, N 265/127).

14. Otto Wagener, *Hitler aus nächster Nähe. Aufzeichnungen eines Vertrauten 1929–1932* (Frankfurt a. M., 1978), 76 ff.

15. Albert Speer, *Erinnerungen* (Berlin, 1969), 382.

16. Evidence of the extensive administration of Himmler's present-giving can be found in files BAB, NS 19/116, 424, 569, 1076, 3535, 3972, and 4044. The personal files of the SS leaders (BDC) also contain summaries of gifts received.

17. BAK, NL 1126/7, diary for 1935, entry for 28 December 1935.

18. BAB, NS 19/4003, 22 May 1936. Himmler stuck to this wish, as he told Hildebrandt, the head of the Race and Settlement Main Office, on 17 December 1943 (NS 19/1047).

19. Himmler issued a decision personally in cases of doubt. When in April 1940 Untersturmführer Küchlin was to be dismissed from the SS as it turned out that one of his ancestors, born in 1643, had been of the 'Mosaic' faith, Himmler, after a personal interview with Küchlin, instructed that a new investigation be conducted and let the Untersturmführer stay in the SS until final clarification. His declared reason can only be described as bizarre: he did not, he said, believe that the ancestor had really been a Jew, as the man's daughter had married the

landlord of an inn called 'The Wild Man'; he, however, knew that owners of inns with this name had been 'very race-conscious and inwardly unchristian men and members of German [. . .] heathen secret societies and they would certainly not have permitted anyone to marry a Jew' (BAB, NS 19/453).

20. The 'mental attitude of a free member of the master race', as Himmler explained in a speech to members of the Hitler Youth on 22 May 1936, was in cases of doubt more important than external characteristics (Himmler, *Geheimreden*, 61 f.).

21. On the examination see in particular BAB, NS 2/53, Himmler's order concerning proof of Aryan descent and genetic health, 13 July 1934. In 1936 Himmler ruled that applicants who had submitted their applications in the previous two years should be admitted to the SS before the completion of the examination of their descent (NS 2/166, Himmler's order of 1 October 1936). See also instructions on this matter of 20 April 1935 (NS 2/280) and 26 May 1939 (NS 2/152). Further relevant dispositions are found in files NS 2/166 and NS 31/279; see also Heinemann, *'Rasse'*, 59 ff.

22. BAB, NS 2/152, letter from head of RuSHA, 2 August 1939.

23. Ibid. letter from RuSHA, 22 March 1938.

24. BAB, NS 2/166, order of 20 May 1935, reproduced in letter of 3 June 1936.

25. Doc. PS-1992 (A), lecture by Himmler on the nature and purpose of the SS as part of a Wehrmacht course on national politics, 15 to 23 January 1937, in *IMT*, vol. 29, pp. 206 ff., here 210.

26. Heinemann, *'Rasse'*, 61.

27. BAB, NS 2/152, RuSHA circular, 22 December 1939.

28. BAB, NS 19/1047, Hildebrandt to Himmler, 1 December 1943, and Himmler's reply, 17 December 1943, published in Himmler, *Reichsführer!*, no. 288a.

29. BAB, NS 19/4002, speech at the leaders' conference of SS-Oberabschnitt South-East in Breslau, 19 January 1935; see also Ackermann, *Himmler*, 106 ff. Himmler also described the 'path' of the SS man in similar terms in other speeches: NS 19/4005, speech at the camp at Ahrenshoop to Napola senior staff, teachers, and pupils, 3 July 1938; doc. PS-1992 (A), lecture by Himmler on the nature and purpose of the SS as part of a Wehrmacht course on national politics, 15 to 23 January 1937, in *IMT*, vol. 29, pp. 206 ff.

30. BAB, NS 2/86, note by Caesar, reporting to Reichsführer-SS, 21 November 1938.

31. Such catalogues of virtue can be found, for example, in the following speeches: BAB, NS 19/4005, speech in Znaim, 11 December 1938; NS 19/4009, The Hague, 17 May 1942; NS 19/4013, speech to the 13th SS Alpine division, 11 January 1944; *Berliner Tageblatt* of 15 June 1937, report on the speech on the occasion of the consecration of the memorial for Gauleiter Loeper, Leopoldshalle in Stassfurt, 13 June 1937.

32. Himmler, *Schutzstaffel*, 23 (speech of 12 November 1935 in Goslar).

33. This is Birn's convincing explanation, in *Die Höheren SS- und Polizeiführer*, 365 ff. On loyalty see also Ackermann, *Himmler*, 149 ff.

34. *SS-Leitheft*, 11 (January 1937), 29 f.

35. BAB, NS 19/4005, speech at the Gruppenführer meeting in Munich, 8 November 1938, published in Himmler, *Geheimreden*, 25 ff., here 43.

36. Ackermann, *Himmler*, 150.

37. Ibid.

38. NS 19/3902, order of 9 November 1936; cf. Ackermann, *Himmler*, 119 f.

39. Birn, *Die Höheren SS- und Polizeiführer*, 367 ff.

40. BAB, BDC, SS-O Eicke, 6 October 1937. For further declarations of loyalty (in addition to those examples cited in the text and in Birn, *Die Höheren SS- und Polizeiführer*, 363 ff.) see, among others, BDC, SS-O Gerhard Klopfer, 12 December 1942, on his promotion; SS-O Albin Rauter, 20 June 1943 (promotion); SS-O Friedrich Wilhelm Krüger, 7 October 1938 (birthday); SS-O Heissmeyer, letter of thanks for Yule light, 6 January 1936; SS-O Alfred Wünnenberg, New Year letter, 15 December 1942.

41. BAB, BDC, SS-O Rediess, 22 December 1935, also published in Birn, *Die Höheren SS- und Polizeiführer*, 370.

42. Birn, *Die Höheren SS- und Polizeiführer*, 376 f.

43. BAB, BDC, SS-O Martin, 3 August 1944.

44. BAB, BDC, SS-O Fegelein, 5 October 1943.

45. BAB, BDC, SS-O Jeckeln, 18 May and 1 June 1944.

46. Ibid. 7 November 1944; quoted by Birn, *Die Höheren SS- und Polizeiführer*, 394.

47. BAB, BDC, SS-O Fitzthum, 4 September 1940.

48. Birn, *Die Höheren SS- und Polizeiführer*, 375 f.; Hans Buchheim, 'Befehl und Gehorsam', in id. *et al.*, *Anatomie des SS-Staates*, 7th edn. (Munich, 1999), 213–320, 235; Ackermann, *Himmler*, 152 ff.

49. BAB, NS 19/1667, Berger to Himmler, 28 July 1943; BDC, SS-O Steiner, letter from Himmler of 25 August 1942. Birn, in *Die Höheren SS- und Polizeiführer*, 381, emphasizes in particular the examples of Woyrsch und von Alvensleben, who in spite of inadequate performance were able to maintain their relationship of loyalty with the Reichsführer. Also instructive in this respect is the example of Eicke (see above p. 152).

50. Himmler, *Schutzstaffel*, 23.

51. Birn, *Die Höheren SS- und Polizeiführer*, 379.

52. BAB, NS 19/4005, speech in Znaim, 11 December 1938.

53. BAB, NS 2/50. On Himmler's concept of 'decency' see Ackermann, *Himmler*, 153 ff.

54. BAB, NS 19/4002, speech at the leaders' conference of SS-Oberabschnitt South-East in Breslau, 19 January 1935.

55. BAB, NS 19/4010, 4 October 1943, published as doc. PS-1919 in *IMT*, vol. 29, pp. 110 ff., quotation 145.

56. BAB, NS 19/4003, also published as Himmler, *Rede des Reichsführers-SS vor den Preußischen Staatsräten.*

57. BAB, NS 19/4010, 4 October 1943, published as doc. PS-1919 in *IMT*, vol. 29, pp. 110 ff., quotation 123.

58. BAB, NS 19/4013, speech in Salzburg, 14 May 1944.

59. BAB, NS 19/4011, speech at the conference of Naval commanders, 16 December 1943.

60. See above p. 105.

61. BAB, NS 2/59, Brandt to all heads of Main Offices, 28 July 1942 (quoted from a letter from Himmler to Pohl of the same date).

62. BAB, NS 19/3973, compilation of December 1940, published in Ackermann, *Himmler*, 262 ff. The booklet *Rassenpolitik*, edited in 1943 by the SS Main Office, gives as 'basic laws of the SS' the order to marry, the law of honour, dispositions for the Lebensborn, basic law concerning the care of widows and orphans, and the SS order to last surviving sons (pp. 57 ff.). The list of 'Grundgesetze' as of 30 October 1942 (Erlass-Sammlung, BAK, NSD 41/39, 232 ff., published in Bianca Vieregge, *Die Gerichtsbarkeit einer 'Elite'. National-sozialistische Rechtsprechung am Beispiel der SS- und Polizeigerichtsbarkeit* (Baden-Baden and Berlin, 2002), 256 ff.) gives in addition the order concerning 'ethnic self-respect' of 19 April 1939, which forbade SS men and police to associate, and in particular to have sexual relations, with members of 'populations of other races', and also the instruction 'Tactful attitude towards those of other faiths' of 15 September 1934. The definitive list of basic laws, according to the head of the SS Main Office for the SS Court in April 1940, had been postponed by Himmler to the end of the war (BAB, NS 7/3, announcement of 1 April 1940).

63. IfZ, PS-2204, note for the file by Himmler on his discussion with Hitler on 1 November 1935.

64. See *Schied- und Ehrengerichtsordnung der SS*, Miesbach (*c.*1935). The arbitration courts decided cases that did not fall within the scope of disciplinary proceedings.

65. BAB, BDC, SS-O Kaul. In view of the conflict between Brigadeführer Kaul and Oberführer Unger, the responsible Oberabschnittsführer von dem Bach-Zelewski had suggested a duel (von dem Bach-Zelewski, 12 May 1936, to Heissmeyer; Himmler's decision of 31 May 1936).

66. BAB, NS 19/4004, speech at the Gruppenführer meeting in Munich in the leaders' quarters of the SS-Standarte Deutschland, 8 November 1937.

67. BAB, NS 7/218, order from Himmler of 5 January 1943 re the preservation of honour in war. Himmler is quoting here from a Führer order for the Wehrmacht, which was also appropriate for the SS.

68. BAB, NS 19/4004, speech to the Gruppenführer meeting in Munich in the leaders' quarters of the SS-Standarte Deutschland, 8 November 1937.

69. BAB, NS 19/3901, 15 August 1942.

70. Ibid. 11 November 1935.
71. BAB, NS 19/3903, 3 February 1940.
72. BAB, BDC, SS-O Heydrich, note in the file, 2 May 1937. The ban was directed at Heydrich and Weitzel.
73. BAB, NS 19/3901, 1 July 1936 and 4 May 1939.
74. Ibid. 31 May 1939.
75. Ibid. order of 13 June 1940.
76. On ideological training in the SS see Heinemann, 'Rasse', 62 ff., and also the volume of essays edited by Jürgen Matthäus et al., Ausbildungsziel Judenmord? 'Weltanschauliche Erziehun' von SS, Polizei und Waffen-SS im Rahmen der 'Endlösung' (Frankfurt a. M., 2003) and in particular Jürgen Matthäus's own essay 'Die "Judenfrage" als Schulungsthema von SS und Polizei. "Inneres Erlebnis" und Handlungslegitimation', 35–86.
77. Heinemann, 'Rasse', 116 ff.
78. Ibid. 94 ff. The first number appeared at the end of 1935 but was then withdrawn.
79. Ibid. 96 ff.
80. BAB, NS 31/234, order of 1 September 1931; on the other hand, Heinemann, 'Rasse', 99 ff., sees this order not as a step towards reducing the power of RuSHA but rather as motivated by financial difficulties.
81. Listed in BAB, NS 2/64; Heinemann, 'Rasse', 100.
82. BAB, NS 19/580, Himmler's order concerning the establishing of Mannschaftshäuser (team houses), 12 February 1939. In the file there is also a list of existing Mannschaftshäuser and of those to be set up in the near future, as on 22 June 1939; cf. Heinemann, 'Rasse', 92 f.
83. BAB, NS 2/277, directive from the head of the RuSHA, 16 October 1934, published in Matthäus et al., Ausbildungsziel Judenmord?, doc. no. 1.
84. BAB, NS 2/277, Himmler's instruction on ideological training in the SS, 28 June 1937, published in Matthäus et al., Ausbildungsziel Judenmord?, doc. no. 7.
85. 'Schulung hat nichts mit Schule zu tun', Das Schwarze Korps of 17 February 1938.
86. BAB, NS 2/277, instruction from the head of RuSHA on the implementation of ideological training, 17 February 1936, published in Matthäus et al., Ausbildungsziel Judenmord?, doc. no. 3. It was not possible to keep to the original schedule; the time allowed for basic training had to be extended by another five months; see Matthäus, '"Judenfrage"', 46.
87. Booklets 1 and 2 were concerned with blood and soil and with the peasantry, booklet 3 with the Jews, booklet 4 with freemasonry and bolshevism, booklets 5 and 6 contain material on German history, booklet 7 deals with traditions.
88. 'Frühjahrswettkampf der SS', SS-Leitheft, 3/1 (1937), 45–7; 'Sonnenwendkämpfe der SS', SS-Leitheft, 3/2 (1937), 62–4.
89. Vol. 3 (1937), booklets 2 and 4–6 as well as in numerous other articles.

90. 'Das Sonntagsmädel. Eine Geschichte zur richtigen Frauenwahl', *SS-Leitheft*, 7/4b (1941), 7–9, and also 'Gegensätze ziehen einander an . . . oder: gleich und gleich gesellt sich gern. Eine Unterhaltung über die rechte Frauenwahl', *SS-Leitheft*, 7/12a (1941), 23–4.

91. *SS-Leitheft* 6/6b (1940), supplement: Feier und Freizeit, containing 'Für die Familie'; 'Geburt und Namensgebung', *SS-Leitheft*, 2/12 (1936), 53–6.

92. 'Held oder Tor?', *SS-Leitheft*, 2/12 (1936), 9–12; 'Canossa', *SS-Leitheft*, 3/4 (1937), 40–6; 'Heinrich der Löwe', *SS-Leitheft*, 3/6 (1937), 9–19.

93. BAB, NS 2/86, note by Caesar, reporting to Reichsführer-SS, 21 February 1938. On further instructions see also Himmler's undated training instruction (cited according to the former Slg. Schumacher/238 I (BAB)).

94. BAB, NS 19/4011, speech to the conference of naval commanders, 16 December 1943. In it Himmler expressly referred to the *Leithefte*. Similarly NS 19/4012, speech at the conference of Reich chief propaganda officers, 28 January 1944, and also NS 19/4014, speech to Wehrmacht generals, 21 June 1944.

95. From booklet 4 onwards of volume 3 (1937) the *SS-Leithefte* each contained several such stories under the rubric 'From German History': in this booklet, for example, J. v. Leers, 'Stellinga', 13–18, and by the same author, 'König Heinrich I', 26–30; K. Pastenaci, 'Der Wiking Leif entdeckt Amerika!', 19–25. Though the format changed, this practice was continued in subsequent years.

CHAPTER 12

1. For this study all SS-Gruppenführer (and those holding higher ranks) were taken into consideration who had acquired their title between the middle of 1937 and 1944 (SS length-of-service lists of 1937, 1943, and 1944 in IfZ).

2. BAB, BDC, SS-O Gille, curriculum vitae and letter from his brother Kurt Gille to Himmler, 7 May 1934.

3. Ibid. Herbert Gille to Himmler, 6 May 1934; Kurt Gille to Himmler, 7 May 1934 (also on Herbert's arrest).

4. Ibid. assessment, 24 May 1934.

5. Ibid. assessment, 1 October 1940.

6. BAB, BDC, SS-O Lörner, c.v.

7. BAB, BDC, SS-O Oberg, c.v., 12 March 1933.

8. BAB, BDC, SS-O Pancke, c.v., 19 November 1935.

9. BAB, BDC, SS-O Hofmann, c.v.

10. BAB, BDC, SS-O Ebrecht, c.v., 9 March 1935; Birn, *Die Höheren SS- und Polizeiführer*, 333.

11. BAB, BDC, SS-O Ebrecht, verdict of 28 November 1938.

12. Ibid. birth announcement of his daughter Hela, 23 February 1940; on 14 July 1941 Ebrecht thanked Hildebrandt for his congratulations on the birth of his daughter Antje.

13. BAB, BDC, SSO Rauter, c.v., 15 February 1935.

14. See above pp. 134 ff.

15. BAB, BDC, SS-O Behrends, *inter alia* c.v., 16 February 1932.

16. BAB, BDC, SS-O Ohlendorf; Sowade, 'Otto Ohlendorf'.

17. BAB, BDC, SS-O Fegelein, c.v.

18. BAB, BDC, SS-O Katzmann, c.v.

19. BAB, BDC, SS-O Rösener, c.v., 4 March 1937.

20. BAB, BDC, SS-O Jeckeln, Himmler to Jeckeln, 26 July 1939; Jeckeln's reply of 28 July 1939; report of NSKK-Oberscharführer Heinz W. Hussmann of 26 June 1939.

21. BAB, BDC, SS-O Kaul, Kaul to Schmitt, the head of Personnel, 22 May 1936; Ungerto the Personnel Office, 22 May 1936. The incident took place on 8 May 1936.

22. Ibid. von dem Bach-Zelewski to Heissmeyer, 12 May 1936; Himmler to von demBach-Zelewski, 31 May 1936. In the view of von dem Bach-Zeleweski a duel would have been the appropriate way to resolve the conflict, but Himmler also rejected that.

23. BAB, BDC, SS-O Bürger, Bürger to Himmler, 16 February 1942, and Himmler's reply of 1 March 1942.

24. BAB, NS 19/3939, RFSS instruction, 24 October 1942.

25. BAB, BDC, SS-O Kleinheisterkamp, Himmler's letter of 9 October 1942.

26. BAB, NS 19/4005, speech of 11 December 1938.

27. BAB, NS 19/4003, speech to the Hitler Youth on 22 May 1936, published in Himmler, *Geheimreden*, 89.

28. BAB, BDC, SS-O Gottberg, von Gottberg's declaration of acceptance, 12 August1936.

29. BAB, BDC, SS-O Rahn, letter of 28 August 1937.

30. BAB, NS 7/245, communication of SS judge on RFSS staff to the Main Office of the SS Court, 18 August 1942.

31. In the case also of Harald Turner, the deputy head of the Race and Settlement Main Office, Himmler took a relatively gentle line when the former was involved in an alcohol-related lapse, sending Turner to the front. He emphasized that he had decided not to impose the punishment normally laid down, namely dismissal from the SS (BAB, BDC, SS-O-Turner, Himmler to Herff and Hildebrandt, 13 January 1945.).

32. BAB, NS 7/245. On 22 January 1942 Himmler issued the instruction that in the case of offences committed by members of the SS and police alcohol abuse should not be taken as a reason to commute the punishment but rather as 'one to make the punishment much more severe'.

33. Doc. PS-1992 (A), lecture by Himmler on the nature and purpose of the SS as part of a Wehrmacht course on national politics, 15 to 23 January 1937, published in *IMT*, vol. 29, pp. 206 ff.

34. BAB, NS 7/245, SS judge on RFSS staff to the Main Office of the SS Court, 21 July 1941, about Himmler's idea of imposing a 'rehabilitation stay' in such cases. Glücks, who was working out the details, suggested KZ Buchenwald in a letter to the RFSS of 23 July 1942; SS judge to Glücks, 18 August 1941, passes on Himmler's agreement. A letter of 18 November 1941 from the Main Office of the SS Court to the Personal Staff reveals that the process of admitting the first four candidates was already under way.

35. BAB, NS 7/24, SS judge to Glücks, 18 August 1942, on Himmler's ideas and instructions for the rehabilitation, which the Personal Staff sent to Glücks on 24 October 1941. Finally the Main Office of the SS Court made a summary of the stipulations in a directive about the arrangements for rehabilitation stays of 28 March 1942.

36. BAB, NS 7/245, SS judge to Main Office of the SS Court, 5 January 1942.

37. BAB, NS 2/2, order of RFSS of 25 June 1937.

38. BAB, BDC, SS-O Bach-Zelewski, correspondence from the years 1935 to 1938.

39. BAB, BDC, SS-O Moder, 15 October 1937.

40. BAB, BDC, SS-O Hennicke, Ludwig Guldener to RFSS, 9 September 1938.

41. BAB, BDC, SS-O Otto Hofmann, note for the file, head of department III, 28 August 1934.

42. BAB, BDC, SS-O Rösener, Rösener to Schmitt, 14 October 1938; Schmitt's reply, 12 November 1938.

43. BAB, BDC, SS-O Bürger, 16 January 1940; Bürger's reply, 28 February 1940, in which she basically apologizes for her request.

44. BAB, BDC, SS-O Alvensleben, letter from von Alvensleben of 11 December 1934.

45. Ibid. Himmler's response, 25 October 1934.

46. Ibid. note in the file about the meeting dated 26 July 1937.

47. BAB, NS 2/3, RFSS directive of 25 June 1937.

48. BAB, BDC, SS-O Alvensleben, von Alvensleben to managing director Rudolf Stahl, August 1938, in which he confirms that he will act as the latter's 'personal adviser' and mentions Himmler's approval. Draft agreement with Stahl sent to Wolff, 26 August 1938; Himmler's approval via a letter from Wolff to von Alvensleben, 24 November 1938.

49. BAB, NS 2/5, staff order 22/36, 10 December 1936.

50. BAB, BDC, SS-O Backe, Himmler to Herbert Backe, 30 June 1938; also to be found here are the details of the first loan of 1 million Reich marks.

51. BAB, NS 19/4004, Gruppenführer meeting in Bad Tölz, 18 February 1937.

52. Himmler explained the procedure to the Gruppenführer on 18 February 1937 (ibid.). In an order of 3 May 1937 Himmler forbade SS men to take on debt

obligations: 'In particular I forbid so-called hire purchase agreements.' The order of 30 September 1937 dealt with further details and confirmed that hire purchase was forbidden on principle (BAB, NS 2/176).

53. BAB, NS 19/4004, speech at the Gruppenführer meeting in Munich in the leaders' quarters of the SS-Standarte Deutschland, 8 November 1937.

54. BAB, NS 19/2651, Himmler to Werner Lorenz, Behrend's superior, 16 December 1942, published in Himmler, *Reichsführer!*, no. 180.

55. BAB, BDC, SS-O Rudolf Jung, Himmler to Hans Krebs, 19 January 1943.

56. BAB, NS 19/3221, letter of 24 June 1942.

57. BAB, BDC, SS-O Korsemann, Himmler to Korsemann, 12 March 1943.

58. BAB, NS 19/3901, instruction from Himmler, 19 March 1939.

59. BAB, NS 19/4005, speech at the Gruppenführer meeting in Munich, 8 November 1938, published in Himmler, *Geheimreden*, 25 ff., 44 f.

60. Ibid.

61. BAB, BDC, SS-O Fritz Weitzel, letter from Himmler of 24 Januar 1939: 'Dear Fritz, I strongly wish and command that first of all in the interests of your health you and your wife spend your leave in southern Italy and not in northern Italy (Tyrol), and secondly that this leave should last for three weeks without interruption. I forbid you to leave for Germany or to have files sent to you during this time, with the exception of one batch of items for reading and information only. A holiday has a purpose only if it takes one away completely from everyday things and other worries and so leads to proper relaxation and thus recovery. I need precisely the senior leaders for a long time yet and we cannot afford to wear them out within a few years from overwork.' See also SS-O Ebrecht, communication of 17 August 1938 concerning a period of leave imposed by Himmler.

62. Abschrift in BAB, BDC, SS-O Rösener, medical report, 28 April 1944.

63. BAB, BDC, SS-O Gutenberger, medical report, 13 March 1944. Also here see Herff to Gutenberger, 28 February 1944, und Herff to Himmler, 16 and 25 March 1944.

64. BAB, BDC, SS-O Rösener, medical report Braitmaier, 29 May 1944.

65. In the same file.

66. BAB, BDC, SS-O Sauberzweig, Prof. Koch, medical report for Gebhardt, 29 November 1944, cites a further report from his colleague Crinis, a neurologist at the Charité hospital in Berlin; Gebhardt to Herff, 12 March 1945.

67. BAB, BDC, SS-O Schmitt, medical certificate, 9 July 1942.

68. BAB, BDC, SS-O Hildebrandt, medical certificate, 3 February 1942.

69. The strong emphasis that Fahrenkamp placed on psychosomatic factors is evident in his book *Kreislauffürsorge und Gesundheitsführung* (Stuttgart, 1941).

70. BAB, NS 19/1630, list of members of the Personal Staff as around May 1943; NS 19/3666, correspondence of the Personal Staff with Fahrenkamp. See in addition NS 3/1136, construction of the cosmetics factory in Dachau, esp. correspondence with medical officer Dr. med. Karl Fahrenkamp (Personal

Staff Reichsführer-SS, department F). On Fahrenkamp's activities at Dachau see Kaienburg, *Wirtschaft*, 785, 817, and 830 ff.

71. BAB, NS 19/3666.

72. *Dienstkalender*, 3 January 1941 und 25 February 1942. Fahrenkamp advised him on 29 July 1940 to get a carbonic-acid bath as a way of helping his low blood pressure (OA Moscow, Akte Himmler).

73. BAB, BDC, SS-O Berger, 28 November 1941. On 12 November he had had a meal with Fahrenkamp (*Dienstkalender*).

74. BAB, BDC, SS-O Fahrenkamp, 1 March 1942.

75. BAB, BDC, SS-O Greifelt, medical report Fahrenkamp, 7 December 1938.

76. BAB, BDC, SS-O Fahrenkamp, 13 May 1944.

77. BAB, BDC, SS-O Jost, 22 November 1943.

78. BAB, BDC, SS-O Rediess, report from Fahrenkamp to Himmler, 2 October 1939.

79. BAB, BDC, SS-O Bach-Zelewski, report of Reich Medical Officer, 9 March 1942.

80. Ibid. 14 June 1933.

81. Ibid. letter to Himmler, 31 March 1942.

82. Ibid. Himmler to Bach, 6 April 1942.

83. Ibid. report from Ruppert (specialist), 22 March 1944.

84. Beckenbauer, 'Landshuter Jugendfreundschaft', sheds little light on the relationship between Himmler and Gebhardt.

85. BAB, NS 19/1292, Brandt, date illegible.

86. Ibid. Gebhardt to Himmler, 5 and 11 July 1938.

87. For example, Gebhardt reported a conversation he had had in Brussels with the Queen of Belgium while visiting a patient there and four weeks later on a conversation with the Queen Mother (ibid. reports from Gebhardt of 14 June and 14 July 1939).

88. BAB,BDC, SS-O Darré, report of 22 August 1936.

89. BAB, NS 19/1292, Himmler to Gebhardt, 9 October 1942.

90. BAK, NL 1126/13, Gebhardt to Himmler, 22 September 1936.

91. BAB, NS 19/1292, Himmler to Gebhardt, sent on 14 January 1938, Gebhardt to Himmler, 23 January 1938.

92. What is meant is a 'Politruk', the usual term for a political commissar in the Soviet army.

93. BAB, NS 2/59, Himmler to Pohl, 12 August 1942; published in Himmler, *Reichsführer!*, no. 136.

94. BAB, BDC, SS-O Eicke, 19 January 1943. See also a letter from Himmler to Eicke of 16 April 1942 that is similar in tone.

95. BAB, BDC, SS-O Alvensleben, 1 November 1943.

96. BAB, BDC, SS-O Jüttner, letter of condolence from Himmler, 8 Dezember 1943: 'I press your hand in sympathy.' Further examples in Birn, *Die Höheren SS- und Polizeiführer*, 371.

97. BAB, BDC, SS–O Krüger, 8 August 1941.

98. BAB, BDC, SS–O Eberstein, Himmler to Eberstein, 7 October 1942.

99. BAB, NS 19/382, 30 December 1944.

100. BAB, NS 19/3904, Himmler to Möller, 24 August 1942.

101. BAB, BDC, SS–O Kroeger, 12 April 1943.

102. BAB, BDC, SS–O Höfle.

103. BAB, BDC, SS–O Hofmann.

104. Ibid. memorandum on the meeting with Hofmann, 13 March 1943. Himmler also passed on to Hildebrandt his personal esteem for the latter's predecessor, Hofmann: 'Hofmann's departure is not in the slightest dishonourable' (SS–O Hildebrandt, letter of 15 May 1943).

105. BAB, BDC, SS–O Hofmann, 29 September 1943.

106. Ibid. 2 October 1943. Nine years previously Hofmann had tried using a very similar formula to avoid a punishment imposed on him. 'I am determined that my work will be guided only by National Socialist ideology. Because I believe that this way of thinking is so firmly rooted in me that I never consciously do anything wrong, and because I cannot reproach myself with having done anything wrong unconsciously, I would ask you, Reichsführer, to exempt me from this punishment' (ibid. [1934], cited in Birn, *Die Höheren SS- und Polizeiführer*, 373).

107. BAB, BDC, SS–O Hofmann, 29 November 1944.

108. BAB, BDC, SS–O Korsemann, Himmler to the head of the Personnel Main Office, 5 July 1943.

109. Ibid. Himmler to commander of the SS Panzer division 'Leibstandarte', January 1944 (no day given).

110. BAB, BDC, SS–O Eicke, 28 November 1942.

111. BAB, BDC, SS–O Dietrich, 23 July 1938.

112. Ibid. 30 August 1943.

113. BAB, NS 19/1667, 15 July 1943. Berger reported on 28 July 1943: 'Steiner's loyalty to the Reichsführer-SS is strong and inviolable.' Steiner's 'informal manner' accounted for much.

114. BAB, BDC, SS–O Steiner, 12 August 1943.

115. Ibid. Himmler to Steiner, 25 August 1943.

116. BAB, BDC, SS–O Hausser, letter of March 1943.

117. BAB, BDC, SS–O Krüger, RFSS to HSSPF East, Krüger, 25 April 1942. The ban was aimed at the director of the Land Office in the Warthegau, Standartenführer Hammer.

118. For an example of a smoking ban imposed on the grounds of protecting health see Himmler to SS-Sturmbannführer Adalbert Graf Kottulinsky, 16 September 1938, published in Himmler, *Reichsführer!*, no. 40.

119. BAB, NS 19/2601, Himmler to Phleps, 10 May 1944.

120. Speech of 8 November 1938, published in Himmler, *Geheimreden*, 25 ff., here 46.

121. *SS-Leitheft*, 7/10a (1941–2), 19. The ruling was occasioned by a case that the head of Office I of the RSHA, Streckenbach, described in a circular (BAB, R 58/261, 28 February 1942). According to this, Himmler had 'become aware that two older, married members of the uniformed police are living in the same building as enemies for trivial reasons, completely disregarding the obligation to be comradely. On one occasion a conflict concerning the keeping of hens resulted in their trading serious insults and blows. The Reichsführer-SS and Chief of the German Police placed a room at the disposal of these two policemen for six weeks to function as a communal living-room, thus giving them the opportunity to discuss their differences at length and to ponder together the concept of comradeship and the duties of Germans in wartime.'

122. BAB, NS 2/275, 5 October 1942.

123. BAB, NS 19/1415, note dated 22 July 1944. See also note by Brandt, 2 June 1944 (ibid.), that the Höhenvilla in Karlsbad should be the model: 'Guests to be thrown out in the morning at a fixed time on the grounds that all the rooms are being thoroughly cleaned. They are then too uncomfortable for anyone to stay in and so everyone disappears of his own accord.'

124. *Disziplinar- und Beschwerdeordnung* (Munich, 1933); Vieregge, *Gerichtsbarkeit*, 10 ff.

125. Vieregge, *Gerichtsbarkeit*, 13 f.

126. See below pp. 485 ff.

127. According to Knut Stang, 'Dr. Oskar Dirlewanger—Protagonist der Terrorkriegführung', in Klaus-Michael Mallmann and Gerhard Paul (eds), *Karrieren der Gewalt. Nationalsozialistische Täterbiographien* (Darmstadt, 2004), 66–75, quotation 67, on the basis of a characterization in a post-war testimony. Essential information on his career can be drawn in particular from the assessment by the SD-Oberabschnitt South-West of 14 May 1938 and also from the letter from the Chancellery of the Führer of the NSDAP to RFSS of 17 May 1940. Details of the indecent behaviour are contained in the judgement of the district court of Württemberg of 26 February 1936 (all in BAB, BDC, SS-O Dirlewanger).

128. Ibid. Dirlewanger to RFSS, 4 July 1939.

129. Ibid. reply from the Personal Staff, 16 August 1939.

130. The acquittal emerges from a report by the Stuttgart *NS- Kurier* of 25 May 1940. Berger had supported his admission to the SS (BAB, BDC, SS-O Dirlewanger, letter to Himmler of 4 June 1940); Berger had then also secured Dirlewanger's release from custody (ibid. Dirlewanger to RFSS, 4 July 1939).

131. It was SSPF Globocnik, of all people, who in a letter to Himmler of 5 August 1941 gave Dirlewanger an excellent testimonial for this period: 'During deployment on the construction of the forward trenches at Belcez and when in charge of the Jewish camp of Dzikow Dirlewanger was an excellent leader' (BAB, BDC, SS-O Dirlewanger). On Sonderkommando Dirlewanger see French L. MacLean, *The Cruel Hunters: SS-Sonder-Kommado Dirlewanger, Hitler's Most Notorious Anti-Partisan Unit* (Atglen, 1998); Hellmuth

Auerbach, 'Die Einheit Dirlewanger', *Vierteljahrshefte für Zeitgeschichte*, 10 (1962), 250–63; Hans-Peter Klausch, *Antifaschisten in SS-Uniform. Schicksal und Widerstand der deutschen politischen KZ-Häftlinge, Zuchthaus- und Wehrmachtstrafgefangenen in der SS-Sonderformation Dirlewanger* (Bremen, 1993).

132. BAB, NS 19/3978, Himmler to RuSHA re petition from Emil K., 5. September 1944. Himmler here draws attention to the fact that K. does not need permission to marry as, like most other members of the unit, he was not an SS man.

133. On him see Peter Klein, 'Curt von Gottberg—Siedlungsfunktionär und Massenmörder', in Klaus-Michael Mallmann and Gerhard Paul (eds), *Karrieren der Gewalt. Nationalsozialistische Täterbiographien* (Darmstadt, 2004), 95–103; Kaienburg, *Wirtschaft*, 259 ff.; BAB, BDC, SS-O Gottberg.

134. Ibid.

135. This was Darré's evaluation in a letter to Himmler, 18 August 1939 (ibid.).

136. Ibid. Gottberg's report on the accident, which had taken place on 5 January 1936, to Gruppenführer Schmitt.

137. Ibid.

138. Ibid. Jeckeln to SS Main Office, 19 August 1936, on the declaration made by Gottberg on 12 August.

139. Ibid. note on the file by Pancke, 13 November 1939.

140. On von Gottberg's activities and demotion see Heinemann, *'Rasse'*, 133 ff., Kaienburg, *Wirtschaft*, 313 ff. See also below pp. 414 ff.

141. BAB, BDC, SS-O Gottberg, Wolff to Pancke, 11 January 1940.

142. Ibid. Himmler to von Gottberg, 30 May 1940.

143. Ibid. RFSS to Pancke, no date, and Himmler to Gottberg, 6 April 1942.

144. BAB, NS 19/1140, letter from Michner of 8 November 1939; statement from Rainer, 24 November 1939.

145. BAB, BDC, SS-O Globocnik, Schwarz to Globocnik, 18 March 1941; ahead of this there had been an extensive correspondence in this matter: Schwarz to Himmler, 10 January 1941; Himmler to Schwarz, 20 February 1941; Globocnik to Schwarz, 3 March 1941, and also to Wolff, 4 March 1941 (all ibid.).

146. Ibid. Himmler to Schwarz, 20 February 1941.

147. Siegfried J. Pucher, '. . . *in der Bewegung führend tätig.' Odilo Globocnik— Kämpfer für den 'Anschluß', Vollstrecker des Holocaust* (Klagenfurt, 1997), 70 ff.

148. Christian Jansen und Arno Weckbecker, *Der 'Volksdeutsche Selbstschutz' in Polen 1939/40* (Munich, 1992), 77 f. The Selbstschutz was perforce dissolved in the summer of 1940; Globocnik, however, created a successor organization in the shape of the 'Sonderdienst' (ibid. 194 f.).

149. BAB, BDC, SS-O Globocnik, correspondence, 5 and 14 July 1941.

150. Ibid. Personal Staff to Globocnik, 16 July 1941, and letter of thanks to Himmler, 28 August 1941.

151. Pucher, *'Bewegung'*, 77 ff.; Bogdan Musial, *Deutsche Zivilverwaltung und Judenverfolgung im Generalgouvernement. Eine Fallstudie zum Distrikt Lublin 1939–1944* (Wiesbaden, 1999), 110 ff.

152. See below pp. 572 and 528.
153. BAB, BDC, SS-O Globocnik, letter of 30 August 1942 and Himmler's reply of 11 September 1942. In April 1942 a letter was already in Himmler's hands in which an SS Sturmbannführer complained that in Zakopane Globocnik's fiancée had flirted extravagantly and without embarrassment in front of everyone in a public house, annoying and repelling in the process all the other people there, whose attention she had meanwhile attracted, by her appearance and carry-on' (ibid. letter of 10 April 1942).
154. Ibid. assessment on the occasion of SS-Gruppenführer Herff's official tour of the General Government.
155. Ibid. Himmler to Krüger, 5 July 1943. At first Himmler planned to make Globocnik deputy HSSPF Russia-Centre. Shortly after, however, the District Governor Wendler asked Himmler to see to Globocnik's transfer 'as soon as possible' as it was impossible to work with him (letter to Himmler, 27 July 1943; Himmler's reply, 4 August 1943).
156. Ibid. letter of 1 August 1944; Himmler's reply, 6 August 1944; letter from the Personal Staff (Brandt) to Globocnik, 18 September 1944; Brandt to Rainer, 28 September 1944. On Globocnik's engagement in 1942 and marriage in 1944 see Pucher, 'Bewegung', 145 f.

CHAPTER 13

1. BAB, NS 19/4004, speech to the Gruppenführer meeting in Munich in the officers' quarters of the SS-Standarte Deutschland, 8 November 1937. On the SS as a clan community see in particular Schwarz, *Frau*, 17 ff.
2. IfZ, PS-2204, Himmler's note in the file concerning his discussion with Hitler on 1 November 1935.
3. BAB, NS 19/4002, speech at the leaders' conference of the SS-Oberabschnitt South-East in Breslau, 19 January 1935.
4. BAB, NS 19/4011, 16 December 1943.
5. 'Im Dienst des Führers...Vom Kampf der SS. Ein geschichtlicher Rückblick', *SS–Leitheft*, 7/1b (1941), 10–14, here 13: 'Thus although it can be still be said that the SS is a National Socialist order of men, it can never be said that it is meant to be an order for men alone.'
6. Schwarz, *Frau*, 64.
7. BAB, NS 2/166, leaflet on the submission of documents supporting petitions to get engaged or married, 27 April 1937. On the procedure for approving marriages see Heinemann, 'Rasse', 50 ff., also Schwarz, *Frau*, 24 ff. The most important orders from Himmler on procedures for the approval of marriages are in NS 2/232 (4 June 1934), 2/280 (20 April 1935 and 19 March 1936), and also 2/53 (11 March 1936).

8. BAB, NS 19/3483, Himmler to Kaltenbrunner re the application to marry from Wilhelm B., an administrator for criminal cases, 17 June 1943.

9. BAB, NS 2/183, suggestion by Hofmann, the head of the Clan Office to be presented to the RFSS, April 1939: 'Before suggestions can be made to the Reichsführer-SS on the form, content, and organization of the book, the Reichsführer-SS would really need to determine himself how he envisages the clan book and what he aims to do with it.'

10. BAB, NS 19/577, order of 6 June 1935; cf. Schwarz, *Frau*, 31.

11. BAB, NS 2/85, 19 March 1936.

12. BAB, NS 2/53, 20 April 1935.

13. BAB, NS 2/280, 6 July 1935; Schwarz, *Frau*, 32 f.

14. BAB NS 2/175, Himmler to Darré, 30 April 1936.

15. Schwarz, *Frau*, 34 f.

16. Ibid. 33 f.

17. BAB, NS 2/280, RFSS, 27 April 1937; detailed provisions for exemption followed on 25 May 1937 (ibid.).

18. BAB, NS 19/577, order of 31 March 1939; NS 2/176, order of 25 February 1937 concerning decisions on marriages to foreign women.

19. BAB, NS 2/288, RFSS to RuSHA, 4 March 1940.

20. BAB, NS 2/231, Himmler to Hofmann, 12 November 1942.

21. Ibid. letter from the head of the RuSHA, 5 February 1943.

22. BAB, NS 2/85, Chief of Staff of the RuSHA to Himmler, 18. June 1936: the processing of proofs of descent and marriage requests had to be suspended 'with immediate effect' through lack of staff. See also the note on the file by the head of the Clan Office on a discussion with Himmler on 12 August 1936.

23. BAB, NS 2/53, Chief of Staff of RuSHA to the Personal Staff, 13 May 1937. See also NS 2/85, for a similar complaint, 26 February 1937.

24. BAB, NS 2/280, RFSS to RuSHA, 21 April 1937, concerning the easing of the procedure in the case of SS men who were already party comrades before 1933. In March 1939 Himmler decided that in the case of all SS men who were married before 1936 but were not at that time members of the SS there was no requirement for permission to marry to be obtained after the event (ibid. 22 March 1939).

25. BAB, NS 2/175, letter from SS Court, 23 June 1937.

26. *Statistisches Jahrbuch der Schutzstaffel der NSDAP 1937* (sheet subsequently pasted in and classified as secret). According to this one of the 308 suffered the more severe form of exclusion, namely 'expulsion'.

27. BAB, NS 2/239, an unsent letter from Turner, head of RuSHA, to Himmler of 28 March 1944, refers to Himmler's order of 1 November 1940.

28. BAB, NS 47/33, order of 11 January 1940.

29. BAB, NS 2/179. The head of the Race and Settlement Office could not make up his mind when issuing the corresponding guidance leaflet to reproduce precisely the instructions Himmler had given for gynaecological examinations.

Under the heading 'Examination' he put merely: 'Thorough! Proceed sensitively in the case of women. Internal examination to be carried out only if necessary' (ibid.).

30. BAB, NS 2/280, RFSS, 30 August 1937.
31. BAB, NS 2/52, RFSS to RuSHA, 21 April 1938.
32. BAB, NS 2/55. On the procedure for approving marriage during the war see Schwarz, *Frau*, 38 ff.
33. BAB, NS, 19/3479, 26 January 1940.
34. BAB, NS 2/231, 22 March 1943.
35. Letter from Heider of 3 June 1943; reply from Personal Staff (Brandt), 16 June 1943, published in Ackermann, *Himmler*, 266 f.
36. BAB, NS 19/3479, head of RuSHA, comments on the August report from the Clan Office signed by Himmler.
37. BAB, NS 19/3482, statistics of the Marriage Office in the RuSHA, January to June 1942.
38. BAB, NS 19/3479, Personal Staff (Brandt) to Hofmann, 20 November 1941.
39. BAB, NS 19/3480, Himmler to von dem Bach-Zelewski, 7 August 1940.
40. Ibid. Personal Staff (Brandt) to the bridegroom, 27 January 1941.
41. For example: BAB, NS 19/3483, Personal Staff to the RuSHA, 5 March 1943, concerning Hauptsturmführer B., who wished to marry an ethnic German. He was to be transferred from Warsaw and deployed 'either in the Old Reich, in the occupied Russian territories or in one of the Germanic countries, Denmark, Norway, or the Netherlands', but under no circumstances 'in the General Government, in the Danzig–West Prussia Gau or in the Warthegau'. NS 19/3482, RFSS to the chief of the Order Police, 24 December 1941, concerning the marriage application of Oberwachtmeister S., who was evidently stationed in France. Himmler wished S. to be transferred immediately to Germany and the woman to move also so that she would be removed 'from French influence'.
42. BAB, NS 19/3483, RFSS to Hofmann, 30 November 1942. Further correspondence shows that these instructions by Himmler could not be put into effect; in the end he gave permission for the marriage even without these obligations (ibid. Brandt to Hofmann, 19 April 1943).
43. Ibid. Himmler to the chief of the order police, 24 June 1943.
44. BAB, NS 19/3978, letter to RuSHA, 24 October 1944.
45. BAB, NS 2/275, letter to SS Hauptscharführer Heinrich, 15 February 1943.
46. BAB, NS 19/3878, Himmler to Wolff re request from Hermann W., 23 March 1944.
47. BAB, NS 19/3481, letter from Personal Staff to Betty F., 26 July 1941.
48. Ibid. Brandt to the RuSHA, 10 October 1941. In the same file there is a case in which Himmler also instructed that Clauberg conduct an examination: marriage application M., letter from the Reich Medical Officer to the Personal Staff, 24 August 1941.

49. BAB, NS 19/3483, Himmler to Genzken re the application by Hauptsturm-führer Dr Kurt R. The same formulation can be found in Himmler's letter to Stormtrooper Willi W., 30 November 1944 (NS 19/3478).

50. BAB, NS 19/3482, Himmler to d'Alquen, 27 May 1942. Himmler had turned down the request once already on the grounds of the bride's infertility.

51. BAB, NS 19/3481, letter from the Personal Staff (Brandt) to Hofmann, 4 September 1942.

52. BAB, NS 19/3483, letter to Jüttner, 27 September 1942.

53. Ibid. Himmler to Kaltenbrunner, 17 June 1943. The transfer did not take place, however: Kaltenbrunner let Himmler know that B. had seen reason and promised 'to look for a young and healthy marriage partner as soon as possible' (ibid. 7 July 1943). Himmler agreed to the suggestion of leaving B. in (ibid. Brandt to Kaltenbrunner, 15 July 1943).

54. Ibid. Himmler to Gertrud S., 30 January 1943, and also the note on the file from the Personal Staff of 6 November 1943 about a similar case. In the case of Stormtrooper Hans B. in 1944 he revised the negative decision he had at first made (BAB, NS 19/3478).

55. BAB, NS 19/3219. These details emerge from the letter of 4 December 1942 from the fiancé, Sturmführer Lex, to the head of the Leadership Office.

56. BAB, NS 19/3480, Clan Office to Brunhilde F., 27 May 1941.

57. Ibid. Personal Staff (Brandt) to Jüttner, 24 May 1941.

58. BAB, NS 19/3483, letter to Jüttner, 2 October 1943.

59. BAB, NS 19/3478, letter of 1 December 1944 to the Marriage Office.

60. Ibid. Personal Staff to the RuSHA, 6 August 1944.

61. BAB, NS 19/3482, Himmler to Hofmann, 3 December 1942. See NS 2/59, communication from Hofmann to RFSS, 15 December 1942: after this disclo-sure Z. decided not to go ahead with the marriage.

62. BAB, NS 19/3478, Himmler to RuSHA re request of H. M., 5 October 1944.

63. BAB, NS 19/3483, Himmler to Hofmann re Frau K., 25 January 1943. A further example of Himmler's correcting 'ethnological' assessments can be found in his letter of 29 December 1944, in which, by contrast with the position adopted by RuSHA, he categorized a woman from Latvia as 'a woman originally of German descent capable of Germanization' (NS 19/3478, re request of Unterscharführer W.).

64. BAB, NS 19/3483, letter from Himmler re application of Hauptsturmführer Dr R., 26 February 1943.

65. BAB, NS 19/3481, letter to HSSPF Rediess re the case of R., 6 February 1940. The Reich medical officer charged with carrying out the examination, how-ever, retrospectively defended the result reached by the doctor (ibid. report of 12 February 1940).

66. BAB, NS 19/3482, Brandt to RuSHA, 20 November 1942, application by Hauptscharführer Sch. On similar cases see NS 19/3978, Himmler to SS Leadership Office re the petition of Unterscharführer Fritz D., 10 March

1944 (after Himmler had concluded that the woman was 'infertile' he turned down the application, ibid. 20 July 1944); NS 19/3482, Personal Staff (Brandt), to Streckenbach re the request from J., 28 November 1942; NS 19/3483, Himmler to Eicke re Rottenführer S., 30 November 1942, und Personal Staff to Berger re request of SS man S., 9 March 1943 (this case was later settled positively in consideration of the petitioner's two existing children).

67. Ibid. Himmler to Berger, 9 October 1942.
68. Ibid. RFSS to RuSHA re the request of Stormtrooper Erwin M., 20 February 1943.
69. Ibid. letter of 22 June 1942 to RuSHA.
70. BAB, NS 19/3684, Personal Staff (Brandt) to Ebner, with a copy to Grawitz, 4 August 1942. According to Brandt's information the enquiry was occasioned by the case of a woman who at the age of 49 or 50 had had her third child; she had not begun menstruating until she was 19.
71. BAB, NS 19/3482, Himmler to Unterscharführer S., 11 April 1942. In a similar case, where he had given consent, in spite of a sixteen-year age-gap, in view of the woman's pregnancy, he prepared the future wife for the fact that, in the face of the inevitable failure of her marriage, she would have to find a 'huge amount of wisdom, goodness, and generosity' (NS 19/3978, letter of 27 August 1944 to RuSHA re the request of Unterscharführer H).
72. BAB, NS 19/3482, Himmler to Frau R., 14 September 1942.
73. On 15 February 1942 Hedwig Potthast gave birth to their son (*Dienstkalender*).
74. BAB, NS 19/3483, Himmler to the head of the Personnel Office and head of the Race and Settlement Main Office, 9 December 1942. See also ibid. Personal Staff (Brandt) to Herff, 20 August 1943: 'The Reichsführer-SS asks you to communicate to Untersturmführer F. his most severe displeasure at his unchivalrous behaviour unworthy of an SS man in the matter of his divorce in that without warrant he petitioned to have his wife declared solely at fault.'
75. Ibid. letter of 12 January 1943 to the SS Leadership Office.
76. Schwarz, *Frau*, 68.
77. BAB, NS 19/4004, speech at the Gruppenführer meeting in Munich in the officers' quarters of the SS-Standarte Deutschland, 8 November 1937.
78. Himmler to Werner Lorenz, 16 December 1942, published in Himmler, *Reichsführer!*, no. 180. The admonition was given in case, as Himmler supposed, Frau Behrends was the 'driving force behind the unhealthy ambition' of her husband.
79. BAB, NS 19/3142, 16 May 1944, published in Himmler, *Reichsführer!*, no. 314.
80. Ibid. Pancke's reply of 6 June 1944.
81. BAB, NS 19/4003, speech at the Gruppenführer meeting in Dachau, 8 November 1936. See also BDC, SS-O Lorenz, Himmler to Kaltenbrunner, 19 June 1943, in which he tried to get to the bottom of rumours that the daughters of Obergruppenführer Lorenz behaved 'with little decorum in the Red Cross'; the younger daughter in particular had been transferred several times 'because everywhere she got too involved with the soldiers [. . .] I must gain a clear and unequivocal view of this matter'.

82. BAB, BDC, SS–O Rösener, Rösener to Wolff, 22 April 1942.

83. Ibid. Rösener to Himmler, 22 Juli 1943, responding to Himmler's letter of 17 July 1943.

84. BAB, BDC, SS–O Becker, letter from Becker of 13 February 1943 and Himmler's reply of 20 February 1943.

85. BADH, ZM 1668, file 13, comments of the RFSS on the occasion of the deliberations of the Expert Advisory Panel on Population and Racial Policy on 15 June 1937.

86. BADH, ZM 1645 Akte 7, statement on the problem of 'illegitimate children', 28 April 1936. On Himmler's attitude see also Ackermann, *Himmler*, 130 ff.

87. BAB, NS 19/3973, principles of the Lebensborn organization, 13 September 1936.

88. IfZ, Dc 012.017, statutes of the Lebensborn Association, 10 February 1938, published as a booklet without date or place of publication (1938).

89. Georg Lilienthal, *Der 'Lebensborn e.V'. Ein Instrument nationalsozialistischer Rassenpolitik* (Stuttgart and New York, 1985), 40.

90. Ibid. 41 ff.

91. IfZ, Dc 012.015, leaflet on admission to a Lebensborn Association home.

92. Lilienthal, *'Lebensborn'*, 47 ff.

93. Ibid. 45 ff.

94. BAB, NS 19/204, Lisamaria K., Lübeck, to Sturmbannführer of the Leipzig SS, copy sent via HSSPF Elbe to the Personal Staff, 20 July 1944.

95. BAB, NS 19/4003, speech at the Gruppenführer meeting in Dachau, 8 November 1936.

96. BAB, NS 19/4004, Gruppenführer meeting in Bad Tölz, 18 February 1937.

97. OA Moscow, Himmler file, mortgage declaration from the Bayerische Hypotheken- und Wechselbank of 15 November 1938; Galke to the accounts department of the Brown House, 16 June 1937. Further correspondence related to the purchase in the same file.

98. BAB, NS 19/440, arrangements for payment of rent (1938).

99. USHMM, Acc. 1999.A.0092, Margarete Himmler's diary, 13 June and 4 August 1939, on the completion of the Valepp hunting lodge.

100. OA Moscow, Himmler file, Wolff to the mayor for Tiergarten district, 5 November 1934, and Wolff to the landlord, the Mitteldeutsche Stahlwerke, 17 August 1937.

101. Ibid. letter from the Märkische Elektricitätswerk AG to the office of the RFSS, 9 July 1937.

102. Ibid. Bormann to Himmler, 10 July 1937.

103. USHMM, Acc. 1999.A.0092, diary of Margarete Himmler, for example 30 March and 26 June 1938 and also 29 March 1939.

104. Ibid. 5 February, 5 March and 2 April 1938.

105. Ibid. 3 July 1938.

106. Ibid. 1 April 1938. For further complaints about servants see 2 April, 16 August, and 31 December 1938, 13 August and 14 November 1939.
107. Ibid. 2 April 1938.
108. Ibid. 29 March 1939.
109. Ibid. 2 April 1938; in addition, 15 April and 31 December 1938.
110. Ibid. 8 April 1939. 'Yesterday I spoke to Gerhard's mother. She was very sad but naturally does not want him back. She won't even have him for Easter. And she still wants to go on drawing money for him too.'
111. Ibid. 15 March and 16 October 1939.
112. BADH, ZM 1668, file 13, comments of the RFSS on the occasion of the deliberations of the Expert Advisory Panel on Population and Racial Policy on 15 June 1937.
113. BAB, NS 19/4004, 18 February 1937, cited in Himmler, *Geheimreden*, 84.
114. BAB, NS 7/220, SS judge on the staff of RFSS to main department, SS Court, 24 November 1941.
115. BAB, NS 19/3978, Personal Staff (Brandt) to Dr Kümmerlein, judge in the Higher Regional Court (Oberlandesgericht), 29 March 1944.
116. BAB, NS 2/175, note on the file from the Clan Office, 25 August 1941.
117. Himmler to Wüst and Sievers, 17 August 1944, published in Himmler, *Reichsführer!*, no. 344. The 'Friedelehe', a term that has continued to provoke controversy, is a construct of the historian Herbert Meyer (*Friedelehe und Mutterrecht* (Weimar, 1927)). See also Schwarz, *Frau*, 89 ff., and also the comments that Himmler is claimed to have made on this matter to his masseur (Felix Kersten, *Totenkopf und Treue. Heinrich Himmler ohne Uniform. Aus den Tagebuchblättern des finnischen Medizinalrats Felix Kersten* (Hamburg. 1952), 223 ff.).
118. Obersturmbannführer Weigel to Himmler, 26 June 1944, and also Personal Staff (Brandt) to Hildebrandt, 2 October 1944, both published in Himmler, *Reichsführer!*, no. 326a and b.
119. Schlessmann to Himmler, 30 January 1945, and also Himmler's reply of 12 February 1945, both published ibid. nos. 380a and b.
120. BAB, NS 19/4006, speech to the leadrship corps of the SS Division 'Das Reich', 19 June 1942.
121. On these exhortations from Himmler cf. Ackermann, *Himmler*, 126 ff.
122. Letter of 6 December 1944, published in Himmler, *Reichsführer!*, no. 366.
123. Himmler to Brandt, 22 October 1943, published ibid. no. 277.
124. BAB, NS 19/2970, RFSS, 21 June 1943, published in Himmler, *Reichsführer!*, no. 215.
125. Ibid.
126. BAB, NS 19/3127, letter of 28 October 1936.
127. BAB, NS 19/3127.
128. BAB, NS 19/1275, Wolff to Feierlein, 14 July 1938; Feierlein's reply, 16 August 1938; Letter from Wolff, 29 August 1938.
129. Ibid. Wolff to Feierlein, 10 October 1938.

130. Ibid. Feierlein to Wolff, 7 May and 22 June 1939.
131. BAB, NS 19/3973, principles of the Lebensborn, 13 September 1936.
132. A doctor who in 1938 had been dismissed from the SS on account of a miscarriage he had induced in a nurse he had made pregnant was, according to Himmler's instruction, to be readmitted only if he declared himself in agreement with the 'Führer's clearly expressed view' that if possible a family should include four sons (Personal Staff (Brandt) to Personnel Main Office, 9 March 1943, published in Himmler, *Reichsführer!*, no. 217).
133. BAB, NS 19/3594, scheduled leave in accordance with the order of the RFSS of 2 October 1942.
134. BAB, NS 19/2651, Himmler to Frau E., 15 April 1942.
135. Himmler to Darré, 29 March 1938, and head of the Personnel Main Office, 13 September 1939, re the Mayr/Engler-Füsslin family, both published in Himmler, *Reichsführer!*, no. 27 and no. 50; cf. Schwarz, *Frau*, 49 f.
136. *Statistisches Jahrbuch der Schutzstaffel der NSDAP 1938*, 87 ff.
137. Ibid. 90.
138. BAK, NL 1126/34, 'From the political life of our dear son Heinrich.'
139. Breitman, 'Mein Kampf'.
140. Himmler, *Brüder Himmler*, 140.
141. Correspondence in BAK, NL 1126/13; Himmler, *Brüder Himmler*, 143 f.
142. *Brüder Himmler*, 165; see also *Völkischer Beobachter* (Munich edition) of 2 November 1936.
143. Himmler, *Brüder Himmler*, 131 ff., 144 f., 153 ff., 166 ff., and 192 ff.
144. BAB, NS 19/2651, 22 October 1937, Personal Staff to Obersturmführer Ernst Himmler re approval of a loan application.
145. Ibid. Ernst Himmler to Heinrich Himmler, 25 May 1944, in which he advises him to remove Major Schmidt, a Jew, as deputy manager of the Lorenz firm; see also NS 19/1541, report on Belgium, 1941. See Himmler, *Brüder Himmler*, 209 ff.
146. Himmler, *Brüder Himmler*, 117 f. and 156 ff.; BAB, BDC, SS-O Gerhard Himmler.
147. Himmler, *Brüder Himmler*, 174 ff.
148. BAB, NS 19/2651, Ernst Himmler to Heinrich Himmler, 25 May 1944.
149. See the relevant SS-O files in BAB, BDC.
150. Düsterberg, *Johst*, 287.
151. Correspondence in BAB, BDC, SS-O Johst; see Düsterberg, *Johst*, 289.
152. BAB, BDC, SS-O Johst, letter of 29 March 1938.
153. Düsterberg, *Johst*, 294.
154. BAB, BDC, SS-O Johst.
155. Ibid. 9 December 1940.
156. Ibid. letter of 3 April 1944. The letter refers to Himmler's speech in Posen on 'Freedom Day', 24 October 1943 (BAB, NS 19/4011); see Düsterberg, *Johst*, 318.

157. BAB, BDC, SS-O Johst, poem on Himmler's birthday, 1937; letter of thanks from Himmler, 15 April 1937; for further examples see Düsterberg, *Johst*, 289.

158. 'Der Neue Orden', *SS-Leitheft*, 2/11 (1936–7), 29 f.; 'Zum einjährigen Bestehen des Schwarzen Korps', in *Das Schwarze Korps*, 12 March 1936; see Düsterberg, *Johst*, 294 f.

159. BAB, BDC, SS-O Johst, 31 March 1943; see Düsterberg, *Johst*, 301.

160. See Kersten's memoirs, *Totenkopf*, and also the commentary on sources and literature in the appendix.

CHAPTER 14

1. BAB, NS 19/4004, Gruppenführer meeting in Bad Tölz, 18 February 1937.

2. See above pp. 122 ff.

3. Himmler, *Geheimreden*, 79. There are no further details on dates.

4. BAB, NS 19/4005, speech to the Gruppenführer meeting in Munich, 8 November 1938, published in Himmler, *Geheimreden*, 25 ff., quotation p. 37 f.

5. BAB, NS 19/4006, 26 February 1939.

6. Adolf Hitler, *Reden und Proklamationen 1932–1945. Kommentiert von einem deutschen Zeitgenossen*, 2 vols., ed. Max Domarus (Neustadt a. d. Aisch, 1963), ii. 1057.

7. BAB, NS 19/4005, speech to the Gruppenführer meeting in Munich, 8 November 1938, published in Himmler, *Geheimreden*, 25 ff., here 49.

8. BAB, NS 19/3666, published in: Himmler, *Geheimreden*, 51. There is no date given, but the speech must have been given between January 1939 and the beginning of the war.

9. Ronald Smelser, *Das Sudetenproblem und das Dritte Reich (1933–1938). Von der Volkstumspolitik zur nationalsozialistischen Außenpolitik* (Munich, etc., 1980), 151 f.

10. Ibid. 156 ff.

11. BAB, BDC, SS-O Lierau, in particular the letter of 6 December 1938 to Kelz.

12. On Nazi ethnic policy in the second half of the 1930s see Hans-Adolf Jacobsen, *Nationalsozialistische Außenpolitik 1933–1938* (Frankfurt a. M. and Berlin, 1968); Valdis O. Lumans, *Himmler's Auxiliaries: The Volksdeutsche Mittelstelle and the German National Minorities of Europe, 1933–1945* (Chapel Hill and London, 1993); Tammo Luther, *Volkstumspolitik des Deutschen Reiches 1933–1938. Die Auslanddeutschen im Spannungsfeld zwischen Traditionalisten und Nationalsozialisten* (Stuttgart, 2004).

13. Jacobsen, *Nationalsozialistische Außenpolitik*, 90 ff.

14. Ibid. 175 f.

15. Ibid. 225 ff.

16. Ibid. 231 f.

17. BAB, BDC, SS-O Lorenz, Schmitt, SS head of personnel, to Lorenz, 10 January 1938.

18. Jacobsen, *Nationalsozialistische Außenpolitik*, 234.

19. BAB, BDC, SS-O Behrends; Aronson, *Heydrich*, 161 f.

20. Hans-Adolf Jacobsen (ed.), *Hans Steinacher: Bundesleiter des VDA 1933–1937. Erinnerungen und Dokumente* (Boppard a. Rh., 1970), doc. no. 109, meeting with SS Obergruppenführer Lorenz, 23 April 1937.

21. Jacobsen, *Nationalsozialistische Außenpolitik*, 234 ff.; Lumans, *Auxiliaries*, 62 ff.

22. Jacobsen, *Nationalsozialistische Außenpolitik*, 249.

23. This is what Karl Haushofer said he believed in a letter to Hess, 10 December 1936, printed in Jacobsen (ed.), *Steinacher*, doc. no. 109.

24. Luther, *Volkstumspolitik*, 157.

25. Ibid. 155.

26. Luther demonstrates this with the example of the conflicts between German associations in Poland in 1937 and in Romania, as well as with the reluctance of VoMi to intervene in Yugoslavia. Also VoMi gave up favouring the (Nazi) Amerikadeutscher Volksbund over other American organizations, which was criticized by the Foreign Department (*Volkstumspolitik*, 154 ff.).

27. PAA, Inland IIg 214; Luther, *Volkstumspolitik*, 164 f.

28. IfZ, Party Chancellery, Order 5/39g of 3 February 1939; Luther, *Volkstumspolitik*, 165.

29. Luther, *Volkstumspolitik*, 166.

30. Karl M. Reinerth, 'Zu den innenpolitischen Auseinandersetzungen unter den Deutschen in Rumänien zwischen den beiden Weltkriegen', in Walter König (ed.), *Siebenbürgen zwischen den beiden Weltkriegen* (Cologne, Weimar, and Vienna, 1994), 149–67, here 160 f.; on Romania see also Johann Böhm, *Die Deutschen in Rumänien und das Dritte Reich 1933–1940* (Frankfurt a. M., 1999), 197 ff.

31. Akiko Shimizu, *Die deutsche Okkupation des serbischen Banats 1941–1944 unter besonderer Berücksichtigung der deutschen Volksgruppe in Jugoslawien* (Münster, 2003), 59 ff.

32. Norbert Spannenberger, *Der Volksbund der Deutschen in Ungarn 1938 bis 1944 unter Horthy und Hitler*, 2nd rev. edn. (Munich, 2005), esp. 141 ff.

33. Smelser, *Sudetenproblem*, 175 ff.

34. Luther, *Volkstumspolitik*, 160.

35. Smelser, *Sudetenproblem*, 185.

36. Luther, *Volkstumspolitik*, 166.

37. Otto Heike, *Die deutsche Minderheit in Polen bis 1939. Ihr Leben und Wirken kulturell, gesellschaftlich, politisch. Eine historisch-dokumentarische Analyse* (Leverkusen, 1985), 214 ff.

38. Ernst Hochberger, 'Die Deutschen in der Slowakei', in id., Anton Scherer, and Friedrich Spiegel-Schmidt, *Die Deutschen zwischen Karpaten und Krain* (Munich, 1994), 12–78, here 38.

39. By contrast, at this stage the recruitment of potential spies and future volunteers for armed SS units appears to have been a secondary motive for Himmler's activities in the field of ethnic German policy; see Lumans, *Auxiliaries*, 38.

40. Jacobsen, *Nationalsozialistische Außenpolitik*, 252 ff.

41. BAB, NS 19/1446, notes on statements made by Himmler at lunch on 30 January 1939.

42. Hans-Jürgen Döscher, *SS und Auswärtiges Amt im Dritten Reich. Diplomatie im Schatten der 'Endlösung'* (Berlin, 1991), 149.

43. Ibid. 150.

44. USHMM, Acc. 1999.A.0092, 2 February 1938.

45. Ibid. 2 February 1939: 'Apart from Herr v. R., nobody has given me a ring.'

46. Döscher, *Auswärtiges Amt*, 140 f.

47. Ibid. 141 ff., quotation 143.

48. Ibid. 115.

49. BAB, BDC, SS-O Neurath, letter of appointment from Himmler of 18 September 1937; see Döscher, *Auswärtiges Amt*, 136 ff.

50. Ibid. 160 ff.

51. Ibid. 153.

52. Ibid. 185 f.

53. Ibid. 175 ff.

54. BAB, NS 19/809, without giving day.

55. BAB, BDC, SS-O Schumburg, certificate of service dated 13 May 1937. On Schumburg see in particular Döscher, *Auswärtiges Amt*, 119 ff.

56. Gestapo Chief Müller described him in an assessment of 1944 as 'a sort of liaison with the Reich Security Main Office' (BAB, BDC, SS-O Schumburg, 19 July 1944).

57. Ibid.

58. Ibid. assessment of 19 July 1944; see Döscher, *Auswärtiges Amt*, 131. The plan to move Schumburg to a foreign posting was prevented by the outbreak of war. In October 1939 Schumburg took over the special German desk, which is where the link with the SS was located. Schumburg regarded himself as in the first instance a representative of the SS within the Foreign Ministry, and thus it was understandable that, in his 1944 assessment of him, Müller should have considered that 'his sympathies lie more with us than with the Foreign Ministry'.

59. PAA, Inland IIg 101, Heydrich to Foreign Ministry, 4 May 1936; note from the Foreign Ministry, 4 May 1936; RFSS to the Foreign Ministry, 24 November 1936, and further correspondence; see Döscher, *Auswärtiges Amt*, 129 f.

60. BAB, R 58/860, list of Winzer's, 12 August 1942.

61. PAA, Inland IIg 61, Schumburg to the state secretary, 13 July 1939.

62. Decree of 3 September 1939, published in *'Führer-Erlasse' 1939–1945. Edition sämtlicher überlieferter, nicht im Reichsgesetzblatt abgedruckter, von Hitler während des Zweiten Weltkrieges schriftlich erteilter Direktiven aus den Bereichen Staat, Partei,*

Wirtschaft, Besatzungspolitik und Militärverwaltung, compiled and ed. Martin Moll (Stuttgart, 1997).

63. This agreement was contained in a Ribbentrop edict of 26 October 1939, which is referred to by Likus in a note dated 8 August 1940 about the SD abroad (PAA, Inland IIg 71).

64. BAB, R 58/243, agreement of 8 August 1940 (Annex A of the RFSS's circular edict of 23 May 1942).

65. *Völkischer Beobachter*, 22 and 23 October 1936.

66. On the police conferences see Jacobsen, *Nationalsozialistische Außenpolitik*, 462 f.

67. PAA, Inland IIg 71; BAB, NS 19/253, programme for the German–Italian conference: NS 19/256, Bülow-Schwandte (Foreign Ministry) to Himmler concerning the impending conference, 24 August 1937.

68. BAB, NS 19/2736, Personal staff (Brandt) to the RFSS's press office, 28 August 1937.

69. 'Unter Kameraden' (articles and photos on the visit), in *Das Schwarze Korps*, 28 October 1937.

70. USHMM, Acc. 1999.A.0092.

71. Ibid. 15 November 1937.

72. Ibid. 14, 17, and 19 November 1937.

73. On Dollmann see PAA, Inland IIg 82, Pusch notes for Luther, 3 and 9 March 1942, which refer to a 'close relationship of trust' between them. See also Dollmann's memoirs, *Dolmetscher der Diktatoren* (Bayreuth, 1963).

74. Dollmann, *Dolmetscher*, 82.

75. USHMM, Acc. 1999.A.0092, 9–13 December 1937.

76. NARA, T 580/207/725, RFSS to Wüst, 10 December 1937.

77. Doc. PS-386, in: *IMT*, vol. 25, pp. 402 ff., minutes by Colonel Hossbach dated 10 November 1937 of the meeting of 5 November 1937; see in particular Walter Bussmann, 'Zur Entstehung und Überlieferung der "Hoßbach-Niederschrift"', *Vierteljahrshefte für Zeitgeschichte*, 16 (1968), 373–84, and Bradley F. Smith, 'Die Überlieferung der Hoßbach-Niederschrift im Lichte neuer Quellen', *Vierteljahrshefte für Zeitgeschichte*, 38 (1990), 329–36. On the 'decisive year 1937' see Klaus Hildebrand, *Das vergangene Reich. Deutsche Außenpolitik von Bismarck bis Hitler 1871–1945* (Stuttgart, 1995), 632 ff.

78. On the Blomberg–Fritsch affair see Müller, *Heer*, 255 ff.; Karl-Heinz Janssen and Fritz Tobias, *Der Sturz der Generäle. Hitler und die Blomberg–Fritsch-Krise 1938* (Munich, 1994).

79. On this reshuffle see Tobias, *Sturz*, 48 ff. Janssen und Tobias convincingly demonstrate that, with his reshuffle of 1938, Hitler found a way out of a crisis which was unexpected and which had initially baffled him, indeed plunged him into despair; this is also shown by the Goebbels diaries for this period.

80. Walter Schellenberg, *The Schellenberg Memoirs*, ed. Louis Hagen (London, 1956), 31 f.

81. Horst Mühleisen, 'Die Fritsch-Krise im Frühjahr 1938. Neue Dokumente aus dem Nachlaß des Generalobersten', in *Militärgeschichtliche Mitteilungen*, 56/ 2 (1997), 471–508. This contains Fritsch's letter to Himmler (doc. 5), which was not sent, in which he spelled out his failures and challenged him to a duel. In particular, in the statements published here as documents 7 and 8, Fritsch accused Himmler of having intentionally initiated the affair.

82. *Tagebücher Goebbels*, 31 January 1938.

83. Ibid. 18 March 1938.

84. Ibid. 12 August 1938.

85. All documents in BAB, NS 19/3940: with a letter of 28 February 1938 Himmler had initially assigned the investigation to the Small Arbitration Court, but, after receiving a report, subsequently ordered proceedings to be started by the Great Arbitration Court. See also the report of the Great Arbitration Court of 23 May 1938 and RFSS to the Arbitrator of the Great Arbitration Court, 17 June 1938.

86. Ibid.

87. BAB, NS 19/4005, speech to the Gruppenführer meeting in Munich, 8 November 1938.

88. BAB, BDC, SS-O Wittje, Himmler to Daluege, 11 September 1942.

89. Janssen and Tobias, *Sturz,* discuss the possibility that Himmler wanted to become War Minister or to take over a new ministry in the military field. In any case, Hitler made it clear to the generals that he decisively rejected such an idea (128 ff.).

90. USHMM, Acc. 1999.A.0092.

91. Neufeld, Huck, and Tessin, *Ordnungspolizei*, 9 ff.

92. On the occupation and annexation of Austria see Dokumentationsarchiv (ed.), *'Anschluß' 1938. Protokoll des Symposiums in Wien am 14. und 15. März 1978* (Vienna, 1981); Gerhard Botz, *Die Eingliederung Österreichs in das Deutsche Reich. Planung und Verwirklichung des politisch-administrativen Anschlusses (1938–1940)*, 2nd rev. edn. (Vienna, 1976); Norbert Schausberger, *Der Griff nach Österreich. Der Anschluß* (Vienna and Munich, 1978).

93. Helmuth Koschorcke, '"Unternehmen Otto". Die deutsche Polizei in den historischen Tagen der Wiedererschaffung Großdeutschlands', in *Die Deutsche Polizei*, 7, of 1 April 1938.

94. *Tagebücher Goebbels*, 3 April 1938.

95. Himmler order of 12 March 1938, published in *Die faschistische Okkupationspolitik in Österreich und der Tschechoslowakei (1938–1945)*, documents selected and introduced by Helma Kaden (Berlin, 1988), doc. no. 3. He had already organized the deployment of the order and security police for the occupation of Austria on the day before his flight: BAB, R 19/401, Himmler order re: 'Special assignment Austria', 11 March 1938.

96. Statement by Peter Revertera, the former director of security for Upper Austria, April 1946, published in Dokumentationsarchiv (ed.), *'Anschluß' 1938*, 328.

97. *RMBliV*, 23 March 1938, 472 ff. Heydrich had already issued the relevant instructions internally on 15 March; see Franz Weisz, 'Personell vor allem ein "ständestaatlicher" Polizeikörper. Die Gestapo in Österreich', in Gerhard Paul and Klaus-Michael Mallmann (eds), *Die Gestapo. Mythos und Realität* (Darmstadt, 1995), 439–62.

98. Weisz, 'Personell', 439 f. and 445.

99. Ibid. 440.

100. BAB, NS 19/3951, office diary for 1938.

101. See e.g. *Widerstand und Verfolgung in Wien 1934–1945. Eine Dokumentation*, published by the Dokumentationsarchiv des österreichischen Widerstandes, ed. Wolfgang Neugebauer, 3 vols. (Vienna, 1975), vol. 2, doc. no. 1, contains the report of an émigré newspaper of 2 April 1938 from which it is clear that 120 socialists had already been arrested in Vienna; the report of the Vienna Gestapo on the communist and Marxist movement from the beginning of 1939 states that since the Anschluss 890 communist suspects had been arrested (doc. no. 20).

102. BAB, NS 19/3951, office diary for 1938.

103. USHMM, Acc. 1999.A.0092, 4 May 1938.

104. Neufeld, Huck, and Tessin, *Ordnungspolizei*, 11; doc. USSR-509, in *IMT*, vol. 39, pp. 536 ff.: note of June 1938 concerning the deployment off the SD in the case of 'SR'; Gestapo presentation for Best concerning the deployment of the SD in the 'SR' 29 June 1938; Security Main Office proposal for the deployment of the SD in the event of an occupation of the whole of Bohemia–Moravia–Silesia, 29 September 1938.

105. Oldrich Sládek, 'Standrecht und Standgericht. Die Gestapo in Böhmen und Mähren', in Gerhard Paul and Michael Mallmann (eds), *Die Gestapo im Zweiten Weltkrieg. 'Heimatfront' und besetztes Europa* (Darmstadt, 2000), 317–39, esp. 317–21; Jörg Osterloh, *Nationalsozialistische Judenverfolgung im Reichsgau Sudetenland 1938–1945* (Munich, 2006), 185 ff.

106. George H. Stein, *Geschichte der Waffen-SS* (Düsseldorf, 1967), 21; details of the military deployment are contained in the bundle of documents PS-388 in the IfZ.

107. Werner Röhr, 'Das Sudetendeutsche Freikorps—Diversionsinstrument der Hitler-Regierung bei der Zerschlagung der Tschechoslowakei', *Militärgeschichtliche Mitteilungen*, 52 (1993), 35–66.

108. Doc. EC-366, in *IMT*, vol. 36, pp. 356 ff., Report on his activities as OKW liaison officer with the Sudeten German Free Corps, quotation 360.

109. Ibid. 361.

110. BAB, NS 19/4005, speech at the Gruppenführer meeting in Munich, 8 November 1938, published in Himmler, *Geheimreden*, 25 ff.

111. Herbert Rosenkranz, *Verfolgung und Selbstbehauptung. Die Juden in Österreich 1938–194* (Vienna, 1978), 20 ff.

112. On the background and establishment of the Central Agency see Hans Safrian, *Die Eichmann-Männer* (Vienna and Zurich, 1993), 23 ff.; Rosenkranz, *Verfolgung*, 120 ff.

113. Peter Longerich, *Politik der Vernichtung. Eine Gesamtdarstellung der nationalsozialistischen Judenverfolgung* (Munich and Zurich, 1998), 177.

114. The matter is in OA Moscow, 500-1-549.

115. Walk (ed.), *Sonderrecht*, II 569.

116. Longerich, *Politik*, 195 ff.; Trude Maurer, 'Abschiebung und Attentat. Die Ausweisung der polnischen Juden und der Vorwand für die "Kristallnacht"', in Walter H. Pehle (ed.), *Der Judenpogrom 1938. Von der 'Reichskristallnacht' zum Völkermord* (Frankfurt a. M., 1988), 52–73.

117. On the press coverage see Longerich, *'Davon'*, 124 ff.

118. On the events in Kurhessen see Dieter Obst, *'Reichskristallnacht'. Ursachen und Verlauf des antisemitischen Pogroms vom November 1938* (Frankfurt a. M., etc., 1991), 67 ff.; Wolf-Arno Kropat, *Kristallnacht in Hessen. Der Judenpogrom vom November 1938. Eine Dokumentation* (Wiesbaden, 1988), 21 ff.

119. BAB, NS 19/4005, speech at the Gruppenführer meeting in Munich, 8 November 1938, published in Himmler, *Geheimreden*, 25 ff., quotation 37.

120. *Tagebücher Goebbels*, 10 November 1938. Vom Rath, who was attended by Hitler's personal doctor with strict instructions 'to act as consultant and report directly', died around 4 p.m. (*Völkischer Beobachter*, 9 November 1938); the fact that news of his death reached Munich in the course of the afternoon was confirmed both by the Reich Press Chief Otto Dietrich (*12 Jahre mit Hitler* (Munich, 1955), 56) and by the Gauleiter of Magdeburg-Anhalt (Rudolf Jordan, *Erlebt und Erlitten. Weg eines Gauleiters von München bis Moskau* (Leoni and Starnb. See , 1971), 180).

121. This is clear from the seating arrangements, which are in the file Bürgermeister und Rat Nr. 458/3 (Handakten Fiehler) in the Munich city archive.

122. Obst, *'Reichskristallnacht'*; Hans-Jürgen Döscher, *'Reichskristallnacht'. Die Novemberpogrome 1938* (Frankfurt a. M., etc., 1988).

123. Statement by Karl Wolff, IfZ, ZS 317 II, 22 March 1948. Wolff's statement is supported by that of his colleague Luitpold Schallermeier: IMT, vol. 42, pp. 510 ff., and vol. 21, p. 392; see also IfZ, ZS 526, interrogation of 23 June 1947.

124. Doc. PS-374, in *IMT*, vol. 25, pp. 377 f.

125. Doc. PS-3051, in *IMT*, vol. 31, pp. 516 ff.

126. On the mass arrests see Heiko Pollmeier, 'Inhaftierung und Lagererfahrung deutscher Juden im November 1938', *Jahrbuch für Antisemitismusforschung*, 8 (1999), 107–30; Harry Stein, 'Das Sonderlager im Konzentrationslager Buchenwald nach den Pogromen 1938', in Monica Kingreen (ed.), *Nach der*

Kristallnacht. Jüdisches Leben und antijüdische Politik in Frankfurt am Main 1938–1945 (Frankfurt a. M., 1999), 19–54.

127. This refers to the sessions chaired by Göring on 12 November (doc. PS-1816, in *IMT*, vol. 28, pp. 499 ff.) and 6 December (Götz Aly and Susanne Heim, 'Staatliche Ordnung und "organische Lösung". Die Rede Hermann Görings "über die Judenfrage" vom 6. Dezember 1938', *Jahrbuch für Antisemitismusforschung*, 2 (1993), 378–404) and the meeting chaired by Frick on 16 December, in *Bevölkerungsstruktur und Massenmord. Neue Dokumente zur deutschen Politik der Jahre 1938–1945*, compiled and with a commentary by Susanne Heim and Götz Aly (Berlin, 1991), doc. no. 1, 15–21.

128. Doc. PS-1816, in *IMT*, vol. 28, pp. 499 ff. On this meeting see the account in Walter Strauss, 'Das Reichsministerium des Inneren und die Judengesetzgebung. Die Aufzeichnungen von Dr. Bernhard Lösener: Als Rassereferent im Reichsministerium des Inneren', *Vierteljahrshefte für Zeitgeschichte*, 9 (1961), 262–313, here 286 ff.

129. BAB, R 58/276.

130. *RGBl* 1939 I, 1097. For details on the background see Wolf Gruner, 'Poverty and Persecution: The Reichsvereinigung, the Jewish Population, and Anti-Jewish Policy in the Nazi State, 1939–1945', *Yad Vashem Studies*, 27 (1999), 23–60, here 28 ff., and Esriel Hildesheimer, *Jüdische Selbstverwaltung unter dem NS-Regime. Der Existenzkampf der Reichsvertretung und Reichsvereinigung der Juden in Deutschland* (Tübingen, 1994), 79 ff.

131. Adam, *Judenpolitik*, 213 ff.; Longerich, *Politik*, 212 ff.

132. *Frankfurter Zeitung*, 11 November 1938, Order of the Reichsführer-SS and Chief of the German Police; Decree Concerning the Banning of the Possession of Weapons by Jews of 11 November 1938, in *RGBl* 1938 I, 1573.

133. Ibid. 1676 and 1704.

134. Walk (ed.), *Sonderrecht*, II 37, order of 29 November 1938.

135. Ibid. III 47.

136. Herbert A. Strauss, 'Jewish Emigration from Germany. Nazi Policies and Jewish Response', *Leo Baeck Institute Yearbook*, 25 (1980), 313–61 (I), and 26 (1981), 343–409.

137. On these negotiations see Ralph Weingarten, *Die Hilfeleistungen der westlichen Welt bei der Endlösung der deutschen Judenfrage. Das 'Intergovernmental Committee on Political Refugees' IGC 1938–1939* (Bern, Frankfurt a. M., and Las Vegas, 1981).

138. BAB, NS 19/3666.

139. Neufeld, Huck, and Tessin, *Ordnungspolizei*, 11.

140. Decree Concerning the Establishment of the Administration and of the German Security Police in the Protectorate, *RGBl* 1939 I, 1682f.; Sládek, 'Standrecht'; Helmut Krausnick, 'Die Einsatzgruppen vom Anschluß Österreichs bis zum Feldzug gegen die Sowjetunion. Entwicklung und Verhältnis zur Wehrmacht', in id. and Hans-Heinrich Wilhelm, *Die Truppe des Wel-*

tanschauungskrieges. Die Einsatzgruppen der Sicherheitspolizei und des SD 1938–1942 (Stuttgart, 1981), 13–278, here 25 f.; Detlef Brandes, *Die Tschechen unter deutschem Protektorat*, vol. 1: *Besatzungspolitik, Kollaboration und Widerstand im Protektorat Böhmen und Mähren bis Heydrichs Tod 1939–1942* (Munich, 1969), 37 f.

141. BAB, NS 2/86, RFSS, Head of the Main Office, signed Himmler, 3 September 1935.

142. Ibid. undated, signed Himmler.

143. Ibid. undated and unsigned note. On the beginnings of settlement policy see Heinemann, *'Rasse'*, 71 ff.; Kaienburg, *Wirtschaft*, 251 ff.

144. Andrea D'Onofrio, 'Rassenzucht und Lebensraum: Zwei Grundlagen im Blut- und Boden-Gedanken von Richard Walther Darré', *Zeitschrift für Geschichtswissenschaft 'Berlin'*, 49 (2001), 140–57, with the text for the speech at the conference of Gau agricultural advisers in Weimar on 23–4 January 1936—see in particular p. 55; for further examples of similar comments by Darré or members of his entourage see Heinemann, *'Rasse'*, 71.

145. BAB, BDC, SS-O Reischle, two undated speeches on the topic of settling 'new space', given around March 1939. In fact Reischle wanted to resettle around 700,000 Czechs from the agrarian districts of the Bohemian–Moravian region to the towns and to settle a similar number of Germans from the Reich in the same area in two stages.

146. On the DAG see Kaienburg, *Wirtschaft*, 288 ff.; BAB, NS 2/86, Gottberg (Settlement Office) to the board of the Dresdner Bank re: the (disguised) takeover of the DAG by the SS, 24 October 1938, and report of the DAG to the head of the Ministry of Agriculture in Vienna, 8 November 1938; NS 2/55, Darré to Himmler, 20 September 1939: 'The German Settlement Association, Berlin, is working closely with the SS Race and Settlement Main Office; it has been provisionally designated by me as the official settlement association for the whole of the Reich including the Eastern March and most of the Sudetenland.'

147. On the activities of the DAG in Austria see Heinemann, *'Rasse'*, 121 ff.; Kaienburg, *Wirtschaft*, 294 f.

148. BAB, NS 2/86, Gottberg to the head of RuSHA, 20 August 1938.

149. BAB, NS 2/54, Pancke to Himmler, 7 October 1938; NS 2/64 Pancke to the Personal Staff, 15 July 1938.

150. Kaienburg elucidates this difference of opinion between Darré and Himmler, see *Wirtschaft*, 265 ff.

151. Gustavo Corni and Horst Gies, *Brot—Butter—Kanonen. Die Ernährungswirtschaft in Deutschland unter der Diktatur Hitlers* (Berlin, 1997), 184 f. and 194.

152. BAK, NL 1094, I 65a, so-called Darré Diary, edited by Hanns Deetjen. It is clear from the preface that in 1969 Deetjen prepared excerpts from the original diary.

153. Ibid.

154. Ibid. 25 December 1937 and 3 January 1938.

155. BAK, NL 1094, I 10, Darré to Himmler, 8 February 1938.

156. However, Himmler dismissed Darré 'subject to the Führer's approval' (ibid. Himmler to Darré, 28 February, confirmation by Darré of 1 March 1938).

157. BAK, NL 1094, I 10.

158. Ibid. note concerning a phone-call from the Reich Peasant Leader from Berchtesgaden, 28 February 1938.

159. Himmler had already secured approval on 2 March 1938 (BAB, BDC, SS-O Darré, note of 5 March 1938). He informed Darré of this decision only on 26 April 1938 (ibid. letter of 26 April 1938).

160. Pohl was prompted to make this 'bold suggestion' when the Finance Minister rejected an increase in the subsidy paid to RuSHA (BAB, BDC, SS-O Pohl, 30 March 1938). On the reorganization of the Indoctrination department see Himmler's order of 1 August 1938 (NS 2/86).

161. On his resignation see Heinemann, 'Rasse', 112 f.; Uwe Mai, 'Rasse und Raum'. Agrarpolitik, Sozial- und Raumplanung im NS-Staat (Paderborn, etc., 2002), 114 ff.; Kaienburg, Wirtschaft, 268 ff.; Bramwell, Blood, 133. On Pancke's appointment see BAB, BDC, SS-O Pancke, overview of service record.

162. BAB, BDC, SS-O Darré, Darré to Himmler, 6 July 1938.

163. BAK, NL 1094, 65a, entries for 17 April and 8 and 25 December 1937, 9 and 13 January, and 28 February 1938.

164. See the private correspondence between the two in BAK, NL 1094, I 58, and Darré's letter to Himmler of 6 July 1938 (BAB, BDC, SS-O Darré).

165. On the South Tyrol question see Conrad F. Latour, Südtirol und die Achse Berlin–Rom 1938–1945 (Stuttgart, 1962); Leopold Steurer, Südtirol zwischen Rom und Berlin 1919–1939 (Vienna, etc., 1980); Karl Stuhlpfarrer, Umsiedlung Südtirol 1939–1940 (Vienna, etc., 1985).

166. Stuhlpfarrer, Umsiedlung, 53. It is clear from Likus's (SS liason officer with the Foreign Ministry) note of 4 April 1939 that Himmler had already received the commission at this point; this is also the source of the 30,000 figure (BAB, NS 19/2070).

167. Stuhlpfarrer, Umsiedlung, 54. In his letter to Himmler of 14 April 1939, however, Hofer still appears uncertain as to whether South Tyrol is to be finally given up for ever (BAB, NS 19/2070).

168. BAB, NS 19/2070, memorandum of 30 May 1939; Stuhlpfarrer, Umsiedlung, 63 ff.

169. BAB, NS 19/2070, Himmler's note on the meeting. Wolff produced more detailed minutes and Greifelt another version (ibid.). On the German side, Lorenz, Behrends, Bohle, state secretary von Weizsäcker, and other representatives of the Foreign Ministry took part. See Stuhlpfarrer, Umsiedlung, 68 ff.

170. BAB, NS 19/2070, memorandum concerning the German–Italian negotiations on the question of the resettlement of the South Tyroleans (with a detailed chronology), 9 December 1939.
171. Stuhlpfarrer, *Umsiedlung*, 86 ff.; on the agreements reached on 21 October 1939 see ibid. 148 ff.
172. On the results of the negotiations see ibid. 97 ff. The deadline of three months for the Reich Germans was to start from the date at which the resettlement agencies had been established.
173. Liaison office with RuSHA in Prague, 18 April 1939, concerning the takeover of the Land Office 'on political grounds' in accordance with the agreement between the head of the SS Race and Settlement Main Office and the head of the SS Security Main Office. Pancke had proposed the takeover of the Land Office in a letter to Heydrich of 31 March 1939; Pancke referred to the recent 'abrupt takeover and securing of the Lithuanian and Jewish farms in Memel'. Pancke justified the SS acquiring responsibility as follows: 'Since in my view the settlement problem, particularly outside the old frontiers of the Reich, is primarily a political one, in my view it can only be dealt with by a political organization, in other words the SS, and not by ministerial agencies, which hitherto have generally demonstrated their unsuitability for carrying out political tasks.' On the takeover of the Land Office and its work under Gottberg see Schulte, *Zwangsarbeit*, 168 ff., Heinemann, '*Rasse*', 131 ff., and Kaienburg, *Wirtschaft*, 313 ff.
174. Heinemann, '*Rasse*', 139.
175. BAB, NS 2/164, Gottberg to Himmler, 12 July 1939; see Heinemann, '*Rasse*', 144.
176. That is clear from the speeches Hermann Reischle gave in the spring (BAB, BDC, SS-O Reischle). Reischle wanted to settle around 150,000 German peasant families on the land and to drive around the same number of Czechs into the towns of the Protectorate. Half of all the independent peasant farms should be given to Germans.
177. For example Pancke to Himmler, 15 April 1939 (BAB, NS 2/138); see Heinemann, '*Rasse*', 132 f.
178. BAB, NS 2/139, 11 August 1939. See also NS 2/138, letter from Darré of 17 May 1939, in which he objects to the SS taking over responsibility for settlement. On the Darré–Gottberg conflict and his dismissal see Heinemann, '*Rasse*', 146 ff., and Kaienburg, *Wirtschaft*, 327 ff.
179. BAB, NS 2/139, Pancke, report on the inspection of the Prague Land Office, November 1939.
180. BAB, NS 2/139, Gottberg to Reich Minister of the Interior, 9 August 1939.
181. Darré complained to Himmler about it on 20 September 1939 (BAB, NS 2/55); on the German Settlement Association (Deutsche Ansiedlungsgesellschaft) see in detail Kaienburg, *Wirtschaft*, 288 ff.
182. Heinemann, '*Rasse*', 148.

183. Ibid. 150; Kaienburg, *Wirtschaft*, 332.
184. BAB,BDC, SS-O Jansen, letter of 27 August 1939.
185. Ibid. Personnel Main Office (Schmitt) to Eicke, 18 January 1940. It states that Jansen expressed a wish to Himmler 'to spend some time at the front attached to a high-level staff in order to gain impressions he can use later in his writings'. Jansen's service with the Death's Head division is documented in a note of 21 August 1940.
186. BAB, BDC, SS-O Jansen.

CHAPTER 15

1. NARA, T 580/150/225, Ahnenerbe to Himmler, 9 September 1939. Among other things the brief study compared 'the chain of fortifications against the Hungarians [. . .] with the building of our West Wall'.
2. See in particular Wildt, *Generation*, 419–580.
3. Ibid. 421 f.
4. Thus, in his Reichstag speech of 1 September 1939 Hitler declared: 'Last night, for the first time the Polish army opened fire on our territory. Now, since 5.45 we have been returning fire' (Hitler, *Reden und Proklamationen* [Domarus], ii.1312 ff., quotation 1315).
5. IfZ, ZS 573, interrogation of Emanuel Schaefer, the former head of the Stapo office, on 13 June 1952, by the Cologne public prosecutor.
6. Jürgen Runzheimer, 'Die Grenzzwischenfälle am Abend vor dem deutschen Angriffauf Polen', in Wolfgang Benz and Hermann Graml (eds), *Sommer 1939. Die Großmächte und der Europäische Krieg* (Stuttgart, 1979), 107–47; see also id., 'Der Überfall auf den Sender Gleiwitz im Jahre 1939', *Vierteljahrshefte für Zeitgeschichte*, 10 (1962), 408–26; Höhne, *Orden*, 240 ff.; doc. PS-2751, statement by Naujock, 19 November 1945, in *IMT*, vol. 31, pp. 90 ff.
7. Rolf Michaelis, *Die Geschichte der SS-Heimwehr Danzig 1939* (Rodgau, 1990); Dieter Schenk, *Die Post von Danzig. Geschichte eines deutschen Justizmords* (Reinbek bei Hamburg, 1995).
8. Schellenberg, *Memoirs*, 71 ff.
9. Wegner, *Politische Soldaten*, 302.
10. BAB, NS 19/4005, published in Himmler, *Geheimreden*, 25 ff., here 31; see Wegner, *Politische Soldaten*, 127.
11. Wegner, *Politische Soldaten*, 126; for further details see Otto Weidinger, *Division Das Reich. Der Weg der 2. SS-Panzer-Division 'Das Reich'. Die Geschichte der Stammdivision der Waffen-SS* (Osnabrück, 1967), vol. 1: *1934–1939*, 139 ff. and 274 ff.
12. Wegner, *Politische Soldaten*, 126; Weidinger, *Das Reich*, i. 320 ff.
13. Sydnor, *Soldaten*, 33 ff.
14. Wegner, *Politische Soldaten*, 124 f.; Sydnor, *Soldaten*, 37 ff.

15. Wegner, *Politische Soldaten*, 126 f.; Friedrich Husemann, *Die guten Glaubens waren. Geschichte der SS-Polizeidivision (4. SS-Polizei-Panzer-Grenadier-Division)*, vol. 1:*1939–1942* (Osnabrück, 1971), 17 f.

16. Wegner, *Politische Soldaten*, 127 f.

17. For literature on the war against Poland and on the first phase of occupation see Dieter Pohl, *Von der 'Judenpolitik' zum Judenmord. Der Distrikt Lublin des Generalgouvernements 1939–1944* (Frankfurt a. M., etc., 1993); Jansen und Weckbecker, *'Selbstschutz'*; Horst Rohde, 'Hitlers erster "Blitzkrieg" und seine Auswirkungen auf Nordosteuropa', in Klaus A. Maier *et al.*, *Die Errichtung der Hegemonie auf dem europäischen Kontinent* (Stuttgart, 1979), 79–156; Czesław Madajczyk, *Die Okkupationspolitik Nazideutschlands in Polen 1939–1945* (Cologne, 1988); Krausnick, 'Einsatzgruppen', 32 ff.

18. *Akten zur deutschen auswärtigen Politik 1938–1945. Aus dem Archiv des Auswärtigen Amtes*, Series D: *1937–1941*, vol. 7: *Die letzten Wochen vor Kriegsausbruch* (Baden-Baden, 1967), no. 193; Winfried Baumgart, 'Zur Ansprache Hitlers vor den Führern derWehrmacht am 22.8.1939: eine quellenkritische Untersuchung', *Vierteljahrshefte für Zeitgeschichte*, 16 (1968), 120–49.

19. Krausnick, 'Einsatzgruppen', 44; Alexander B. Rossino, *Hitler Strikes Poland: Blitzkrieg, Ideology, and Atrocity* (Lawrence, Kan., 2003), 66 and 259.

20. BAB, R 58/825, 8 September 1941.

21. Ibid. 16 October 1941.

22. Jansen and Weckbecker, *'Selbstschutz'*, 27 ff.; Włodzimierz Jastrzębski, *Der Bromberger Blutsonntag. Legende und Wirklichkeit* (Posen, 1990).

23. Krausnick, 'Einsatzgruppen', 33 ff. There is a detailed account of the leadership in Rossino, *Hitler*, 29 ff.

24. Helmut Krausnick, 'Hitler und die Morde in Polen. Ein Beitrag zum Konflikt zwischen Heer und SS um die Verwaltung der besetzten Gebiete', *Vierteljahrshefte für Zeitgeschichte*, 11/2 (1963), 196–209, here 207.

25. Dorothee Weitbrecht, 'Ermächtigung zur Vernichtung. Die Einsatzgruppen in Polen im Herbst 1939', in Klaus-Peter Mallmann and Bogdan Musial (eds), *Genesis des Genozids. Polen 1939–1941* (Darmstadt, 2004), 57–70, here 57; Dan Michman, 'Why Did Heydrich Write the "Schnellbrief"? A Remark on the Reason and on its Significance', *Yad Vashem Studies*, 32 (2004), 433–47, here 439 f.

26. Weitbrecht, 'Ermächtigung', 59 ff.

27. IfZ, NO 2285, Himmler to the heads of the civil administration with the Army High Commands, 26 September 1939. The decisive conference must have taken place between 3 and 7 September 1939 (Jansen and Weckbecker, *'Selbstschutz'*, 48, which is based on Berger's Nuremberg statement: IfZ, MB 30, 3838 ff.). On 7 October 1939 Himmler issued 'provisional guidelines for the organization of the "Self-Defence" in Poland', quoted in Jansen and Weckbecker, *'Selbstschutz'*, 52 f., on the basis of documents in the Zentrale Stelle Ludwigsburg.

28. On the figures see Jansen and Weckbecker, *'Selbstschutz'*, 35.
29. On the role of the Selbstschutz see, in particular, ibid. 111 ff. On the participation of the Wehrmacht in the murders see Joachim Böhler, *Auftakt zum Vernichtungskrieg. Die Wehrmacht in Polen 1939* (Frankfurt a. M., 2006), and id., '"Tragische Verstrickung" oder Auftakt zum Vernichtungskrieg? Die Wehrmacht in Polen 1939', in Klaus-Michael Mallmann and Bogdan Musial (eds), *Genesis des Genozids. Polen 1939–1941* (Darmstadt, 2004), 36–57. On the Einsatzgruppen see Rossino, *Hitler*, 88 ff., and id., 'Nazi Anti-Jewish Policy during the Polish Campaign: The Case of the Einsatzgruppe von Woyrsch', *German Studies Review*, 24/1 (2001), 35–53. The role of the order police and the Waffen-SS has been investigated by Klaus-Michael Mallmann and Martin Cüppers in the volume edited by Mallmann and Musial, *Genesis des Genozids*.
30. For examples see Rossino, *Hitler*, 90 f. and 99.
31. Ibid. 88 ff.
32. Christopher R. Browning, *Die Entfesselung der 'Endlösung'. Nationalsozialistische Judenpolitik 1939–1942* (Berlin, 2006), 56 f.; Böhler, '"Verstrickung"', 45 ff.; id., *Auftakt*, 216 ff.
33. IfZ, NOKW 1006. On von Woyrsch see his SS-O file in BAB, BDC.
34. Krausnick, 'Einsatzgruppen', 41, and Böhler, *Auftakt*, 210 ff.
35. Quoted from Krausnick, 'Einsatzgruppen', 57. The hostage-taking was in the end done not by the Einsatzgruppe but by the Wehrmacht.
36. Jansen und Weckbecker, *'Selbstschutz'*, 154 ff.
37. Ibid. 96 ff. and 154.
38. Ibid. 154 ff. and 212 ff. In autumn 1939 German units also shot people in the Warthegau who came from the same target groups as in Danzig–West Prussia, though in smaller numbers (ibid. 156 and 224 ff.). Units that were based in the Polish territories which bordered East Prussia, in eastern Upper Silesia, and in the central and eastern Polish territories also carried out murders (ibid. 156 f. and 228 f.).
39. Volker Riess, *Die Anfänge der Vernichtung 'lebensunwerten Lebens' in den Reichsgauen Danzig-Westpreußen und Wartheland 1939/40* (Frankfurt a. M., etc., 1995), 173 ff.
40. Jansen and Weckbecker, *'Selbstschutz'*, 49 ff. and 64 ff.
41. See above pp. 325 f.
42. BAB, BDC, SS-O Alvensleben, Himmler to Heydrich, 26 March 1940.
43. This is Riess's assessment in *Anfänge*, 355.
44. Ibid. 243 ff.
45. Ibid. 290 ff.
46. Ibid. 321 ff.; Mathias Beer, 'Die Entwicklung der Gaswagen beim Mord an den Juden', *Vierteljahrshefte für Zeitgeschichte*, 35/3 (1987), 403–17, here 404 ff.; Eugen Kogon, Hermann Langbein, and Adalbert Rückerl (eds), *Nationalsozialistische Massentötungen durch Giftgas. Eine Dokumentation* (Frankfurt a. M.,

1986), 62 ff.; Ernst Klee, *'Euthanasie' im NS-Staat. Die 'Vernichtung lebensunwerten Lebens'* (Frankfurt a. M., 1983), 105 ff.

47. Riess, *Anfänge*, 222 ff.; see esp. Heike Bernhardt, *Anstaltspsychiatrie und "Euthanasie" in Pommern 1933–1945. Die Krankenmorde an Kindern und Erwachsenen am Beispiel der Landesheilanstalt Ueckermünde* (Frankfurt a. M., 1994).

48. Riess, *Anfänge*, 104 ff., 131, 135 f., 168, 256, and 334.

49. Ibid. 188 and 288 f.

50. See above p. 324.

51. Richard Breitman considers a note by Himmler dated 5 December 1939 as 'the earliest evidence for the plan for a kind of death factory which used poison gas to kill and crematoria to dispose of the corpses'. The note, concerning a conversation with Oswald Pohl, reads: 'Crematorium—delousing installation' (BAB, NS 19/1449; Richard Breitman, *Der Architekt der 'Endlösung'. Himmler und die Vernichtung der europäischen Juden* (Paderborn, 1996), 130 f.). In fact, however, it was not until 1942 that installations were built in which killing with poison gas was combined with the burning of the corpses in crematoria. If Himmler had already had such a plan in December 1939, for which in fact there is no further evidence, then in that case he was not pursuing it very thoroughly.

52. Note by Lieut.-Col. Lahousen, printed in Helmuth Groscurth, *Tagebücher eines Abwehroffiziers 1938–1940. Mit weiteren Dokumenten zur Militäropposition gegen Hitler*, ed. Helmut Krausnick and Harold C. Deutsch with Hildegard von Kotze (Stuttgart, 1970), 357 ff.

53. Printed in Müller, *Heer*, Annex no. 45.

54. On this see ibid. 422 ff.

55. On resistance by and protests from the army see in detail Krausnick, 'Einsatzgruppen', 80 ff.

56. Meeting between the chief of the general staff of the Wehrmacht commander in the recently established military district of Danzig and von Alvensleben, the Selbstschutz commander responsible for the West Prussian district, on 13 October 1939, in Jansen and Weckbecker, *'Selbstschutz'*, 175.

57. Quoted in Groscurth, *Tagebücher*, 409 ff.

58. Jansen and Weckbecker, *'Selbstschutz'*, 146 and 193 ff.

59. Complaint from the military district commander in the Warthegau, General Petzel, to the Commander of the Reserve Army, dated 23 November 1939, doc. D-419, in *IMT*, vol. 35, p. 88.

60. IfZ, NO 3011, Commander-in Chief East, notes for the Commander-in-Chief East's interview with the Commander-in-Chief of the army, 15 February 1940. They contain a long list of assaults and record Ulex's statement of his views of 2 February 1940.

61. Müller, *Heer*, 437 ff.; Blaskowitz's notes for an interview with the Commander-in-Chief of the army 6 February 1940, printed in Ernst Klee, Willi Dressen,

and Volker Riess (eds), '*Schöne Zeiten*'. *Judenmord aus der Sicht der Täter und Gaffer* (Frankfurt a. M., 1988), 14 ff.

62. The responsibilities were defined in the RuSHA order of 2 September 1939 (BAB, NS 2/157). The following tasks were envisaged: securing the offices of the Western March Association (Westmarkverein) insofar as they had been involved in matters to do with land; closing down the money and credit institutes and the agricultural cooperatives; establishing contact with the leaders of the German ethnic groups in order to 'register: (a) Jewish property, (b) the state forests and estates [. . .], (c) church property, (d) large private estates, (e) agricultural land in the hands of banks'. See also BAB, BDC, SS-O Brehm, Brehm report of 7 October 1940: 'After the invasion of Poland the head of the Settlement Main Office in the Race and Settlement Main Office, SS Ober-führer von Gottberg, gave me, as commander of an Einsatzgruppe, the task of getting hold of all documents concerned with Poland's land reform and undertaking the preparatory work for the establishment of a land office.' The Einsatzgruppen of RuSHA officially began their work on 11 September 1939 (NS 2/55, Pancke to RFSS, 11 September 1939). For a thorough account of the discussions see Heinemann, '*Rasse*', 201 ff.

63. BAB, NS 2/61, draft of a report for the office of the RKF. Head of the RuS-Advice section B, Theodor Henschel. It stated further that the consultation 'had the task of preparing for the Germanization of ethnically alien landed property and asserting the interests of the SS in the property that became available [. . .] Those involved in the discussions were forbidden to intervene actively on their own initiative, which meant that they had to maintain close contact with the Einsatzgruppen of the security police [. . .] Property in Jewish hands and large Polish farms (over 25 ha in size) were reported to the security police so that the owners could be arrested and, after the farms had become vacant as a result of their owners' arrest, they were assigned to the head of the civilian administration to be looked after by his agricultural department.' See also NS 2/60, Advice A, Report no. 13, 21 October 1939, and Himmler to Pancke, 28 November 1939.

64. See the material in BAB, NS 2/55. The Settlement Office discovered that the Agriculture Ministry had drafted 56 tenants of landed estates in order to deploy them to farm estates in Posen formerly belonging to the Polish state. More-over, it was suspected that the Ministry was trying to resuscitate the 'old Prussian Settlement Commission founded in 1886' (minute of 11 September 1939 and Pancke to Himmler of the same date).

65. Details in Madajczyk, *Okkupationspolitik*, 391.

66. USHMM,Acc. 1999.A.0092, 16 October 1939.

67. Doc. PS-686, in *IMT*, vol. 26, pp. 255 f. On the background see Stuhlpfarrer, *Umsiedlung*, 247 ff. The edict was based on the draft of a Führer edict concerning the organization of the South Tyrolean resettlement programme,

which Lammers had sent to Himmler on 12 August 1939. Himmler made some alterations. See BAB, R 43 II /1412.

68. Stuhlpfarrer, *Umsiedlung*, 253. Material in BAB, R 43 II/1412.
69. IfZ, NG 1759, Darré to Lammers, 4 October 1939.
70. IfZ, NG 1759.
71. This is clear from the letter to Göring of 27 October 1939 (ibid.).
72. Ibid. 27 October 1939.

CHAPTER 16

1. BAB, R 58/241, edict of 1 November 1939. On the establishment of the police and its relationship with the administration see Gerhard Eisenblätter, 'Grundlinien der Politikdes Reichs gegenüber dem Generalgouvernement, 1939–1945', unpublished doctoral dissertation, Frankfurt University (1969), 131 ff.
2. In June 1940, for example, Himmler was able successfully to insist that Frank's state secretary, Bühler, was not Krüger's superior (ibid. 143).
3. Martin Broszat, *Nationalsozialistische Polenpolitik 1939–1945* (Stuttgart, 1961), 81.
4. For details on the order police in the General Government see Eisenblätter, 'Grundlinien', 136 f.
5. BAB, R 75/3b; published in *Faschismus, Ghetto, Massenmord. Dokumentation über Ausrottung und Widerstand der Juden in Polen während des 2.Weltkrieges*, published by the Jewish Historical Institute Warsaw, selected, edited, and introduced by Tatiana Berenstein, Artur Eisenbach, *et al.* (Frankfurt a. M., 1962), 42 f.; on the role of the HSSPF in this context see Birn, *Die Höheren SS- und Polizeiführer*, 158.
6. Madajczyk, *Okkupationspolitik*, 187.
7. Michael Foedrowitz, 'Auf der Suche nach einer besatzungspolitischen Konzeption. Der Befehlshaber der Sicherheitspolizei und des SD im Generalgouvernement', in Gerhard Paul and Klaus-Michael Mallmann (eds), *Die Gestapo im Zweiten Weltkrieg. 'Heimatfront' und besetztes Europa* (Darmstadt, 2000), 340–61, esp. 340 ff.
8. Decree Concerning the Introduction of German Penal Law of 6 June 1940, in *RGBl* 1940 I, 84. On this see also Broszat, *Polenpolitik*, 142 ff.
9. Decree Concerning Penal Measures against Poles and in the Incorporated Eastern Territories of 4 December 1941, in *RGBl* 1941 I, 759.
10. Christopher R. Browning, 'Die nationalsozialistische Umsiedlungspolitik und die Suche nach einer "Lösung der Judenfrage" 1939–1941', in id., *Der Weg zur 'Endlösung'. Entscheidungen und Täter* (Bonn, 1998), 13–36; and Pohl, *Lublin*, 22.
11. BAB, R 58/825, 15 September 1939.
12. *Faschismus, Ghetto, Massenmord*, 37 ff.; IfZ, PS-3363.

13. Minutes of the conversation between Heydrich and von Brauchitsch, printed in Groscurth, *Tagebücher*, 361 f.

14. BAB, R 58/825, Meeting of departmental heads of 29 September, minutes of 1 October 1939. Correspondingly, the exceptional regulation referred to in the express letter of 21 September that no preparations for deportations were to be carried out in the area of Einsatzgruppe I was cancelled (YV, 053/87, Eichmann minute of 29 September 1939).

15. Alfred Rosenberg, *Das politische Tagebuch Alfred Rosenbergs aus den Jahren 1934/ 1935 und 1939/1940*, ed. Hans-Günther Seraphim (Munich, 1964), 81.

16. See Longerich, *Politik*, 255. Hitler himself mentioned it on 26 September to the Swedish industrialist Dahlerus (Andreas Hillgruber (ed.), *Staatsmänner und Diplomaten bei Hitler. Vertrauliche Aufzeichnungen über Unterredungen mit Vertretern des Auslandes*, vol. 1: *1939–1941* (Frankfurt a. M., 1967), 29 f.) and on 1 October explained to the Italian Foreign Minister the idea of an 'ethnic reorganization' in the east (*ADAP*, Series D, vol. 7, no. 176, Minutes of 2 October 1939). The German press was also informed confidentially about these plans and there was soon speculation about such a 'reservation' in the international press. (Vertrauliche Information [Information from the Propaganda Ministry], 9 October 1941, published in Jürgen Hagemann, *Die Presselenkung im Dritten Reich* (Bonn, 1970), 145). On 6 October Hitler announced in his Reichstag speech, that 'after the collapse of the Polish state' the 'most important task' was 'a reorganization of the ethnic situation, that is to say a resettlement of the nations'. In the course of the creation of this new order 'the attempt' must be made 'to sort out and regulate the Jewish problem' (*Verhandlungen des Reichstages. Stenographische Berichte*, vol. 460 (Berlin 1939), 51 ff.).

17. YV, 053/87 (Gestapo files from Mährisch-Ostrau); on Eichmann's further activities in this period see in detail Longerich, *Politik*, 256 ff. For literature on the deportations in autumn 1939 see Miroslav Kárny, 'Nisko in der Geschichte der Endlösung', *Judaica Bohemiae*, 23 (1987), 69–84; Seev Goshen, 'Eichmann und die Nisko-Aktion im Oktober 1939. Eine Fallstudie zur NS-Judenpolitik in der letzten Etappe vor der "Endlösung"', *Vierteljahrshefte für Zeitgeschichte*, 29/1 (1981), 74–96; Jonny Moser, 'Nisko: The First Experiment in Deportation', *Simon Wiesenthal Center Annual*, 2/1 (1985), 1–30; Seev Goshen, 'Nisko. Ein Ausnahmefall unter den Judenlagern der SS', *Vierteljahrshefte für Zeitgeschichte*, 40/1 (1992), 95–106; Hans Günter Adler, *Der verwaltete Mensch. Studien zur Deportation der Juden aus Deutschland* (Tübingen, 1974), 125 ff.; Browning, 'Umsiedlungspolitik'; Safrian, *Eichmann-Männer*, 68 ff. There is further material in the volume of conference proceedings edited by Ludmila Nesládková, *The Case Nisko in the History of the Final Solution of the Jewish Problem in Commemoration of the 55th Anniversary of the First Deportation of Jews in Europe* (Ostrava, 1995).

18. YV, 053/87, note by Günther 11 October 1939. Eichmann also referred to this 'commission from the Führer' during his visit to Becker, the 'special

representative for Jewish questions', on Bürckel's staff; he mentioned that the Jews still living in Vienna would be expelled in '3 to 4 years at the latest' (Gerhard Botz, *Wohnungspolitik und Judendeportation in Wien 1938. Zur Funktion des Antisemitismus als Ersatz nationalsozialistischer Sozialpolitik* (Vienna and Salzburg, 1975), 105).

19. YV, 053/87, note of 6 October 1939.

20. Ibid. telegrams from SD Main Office to Stapo branch office in Mährisch-Ostrau, 13 October 1939, and reply from SD Danube, 16 October 1939.

21. The meeting in the Stapo branch office in Mährisch-Ostrau on 9 October was concerned with details involving the construction of the barracks (ibid. Dannecker minute, 11 October 1939).

22. Ibid. minute of the central office in Vienna, 17 October 1939. Gauleiter Bürckel, who had been informed by a member of his staff about the recent conversation with Eichmann, declared that he was 'more than happy [...] that the planned resettlement of Jews into barracks did not need to take place because the cost per head for building the barracks alone would come to 300 Reich marks'.

23. See Safrian, *Eichmann-Männer*, 77 ff. On the carrying out of the deportations see Goshen, 'Eichmann', 86; on Vienna see Rosenkranz, *Verfolgung*, 215 ff.; on the deportation from Mährisch-Ostrau see Kárny, 'Nisko', 96 ff., and Luká Přibyl, 'Das Schicksal des dritten Transports aus dem Protektorat nach Nisko', in *Theresienstädter Studien und Dokumente* (2000), 297–342.

24. YV, 053/87, note of the Gestapo branch office in Mährisch-Ostrau, 21 October 1939. In a letter to Bürckel of 9 November 1939 Himmler once more made it clear that he had 'banned the deportation of the Jews for the time being because of technical difficulties' (Botz, *Wohnungspolitik*, 196, and doc. PS-3398, in *IMT*, vol. 32, pp. 255 ff.).

25. Thus, at the end of October the RSHA informed SD-Oberabschnitt Vienna that it was quite conceivable that 'individual transports of Jews from Vienna' might be included (YV, 053/86, SD-Danube to Stapo branch office in Mährisch-Ostrau, 28 October 1939). On 1 November 1939 the HSSPF East, Krüger, also referred to existing plans for 'a particularly large concentration of Jews' (Werner Präg and Wolfgang Jacobmeyer (eds), *Das Diensttagebuch des deutschen Generalgouverneurs in Polen 1939–1945* (Stuttgart, 1975), 56).

26. Heinemann, *'Rasse'*, 214. On the demarcation of responsibilities and on cooperation see BAB, NS 2/139, letter from RKF, Himmler, 15 February 1940, and IfZ, PS-2207, containing order of the RFSS re: Cooperation of the RFSS's agencies with the Main Trustee Office East, 10 November 1939.

27. Heinemann, *'Rasse'*, 191; Stuhlpfarrer, *Umsiedlung*, 251.

28. BAB, NS 2/60.

29. Ibid. also 11 October 1939, note to the same distribution list re: Accommodating the Volhynian Germans. Further instructions issued on this day to the heads of the SS Main Offices are in the same file.

30. Ibid. note.
31. BAB, R 75/3b, published in *Faschismus, Ghetto, Massenmord*, 42 f.
32. Minutes in *Biuletyn Głównej Komisji Badania Zbrodni Niemieckich w Polsce*, 12, doc.no. 3. See also Krüger's report to a meeting of the district administrators (Landräte) of Cracow district on the same day (Präg and Jacobmeyer (eds), *Diensttagebuch*).
33. Circular of the HSSPF Warthegau, Koppe, 12 November 1939, printed in *Faschismus, Ghetto, Massenmord*, 43 ff.
34. Heydrich to the HSSPF Cracow, Breslau, Posen, and Danzig and telexes of 28 November 1939 re: details of the short-range plan, in *Biuletyn Głównej Komisji Badania Zbrodni Niemieckich w Polsce*, 12, Docs. 4 and 5. Although the long-range plan has not yet been discovered there exists an undated and unsigned draft, which presumably was composed by Department III of the RSHA (BAB, R 69/1146, ed. Karl Heinz Roth in *1999*, 11 (1997), 50–71).
35. BAB, R 75/3b, final report, Koppe, 26 January 1940, printed in *Faschismus, Ghetto, Massenmord*, 48.
36. BAB, R 75/3b, HSSPF Koppe to RSHA, Posen, 18 December 1939, published in *Biuletyn Głównej Komisji Badania Zbrodni Niemieckich w Polsce*, 12, doc. 8.
37. BAB, R 58/276, also printed in *Biuletyn Głównej Komisji Badania Zbrodni Niemieckich w Polsce*, 12, doc. 9; the letter referred to the official meeting of 19 December 1939.
38. Götz Aly, '*Endlösung*'. *Völkerverschiebung und der Mord an den europäischen Juden* (Frankfurt a. M., 1995), 73 f., quoting Archivum Głównej Komisji Badania Zbrodni przeciwko Narodowi Polskiemu Warschau, UWZ, P 197. On these plans see also Frank's comments of 19 January 1940 (Präg and Jacobmeyer (eds), *Diensttagebuch*).
39. Aly, '*Endlösung*', 77, 81 f., and 89.
40. Details in Longerich, *Politik*, 266 f.
41. BAB, R 113/10, printed in *Mitteilungen der Dokumentationsstelle zur NS-Sozialpolitik*, 1 (1985), 45 ff., with an introduction by Karl Heinz Roth and supplementary documents. The document has survived in another version as an annex to a message from the OKW of 8 March 1940 and is also dated February (Rolf-Dieter Müller, *Hitlers Ostkrieg und die deutsche Siedlungspolitik. Die Zusammenarbeit von Wehrmacht, Wirtschaft und SS* (Frankfurt a. M., 1991), 130 ff.). RuSHA specifically welcomed the memorandum of the Office for Racial Politics of the NSDAP concerning the 'Treatment of the Population in the Former Polish Territories', which went beyond the 'basic planning'—among other things, it proposed deporting all Jews and over 5 million Poles from the annexed territories and Germanizing the remaining population, estimated to be 1.3 million (R 49/75, Hecht/Wetzel-Memorandum, 25 November 1939); Heinemann, '*Rasse*', 192 f.

42. BAB, R 58/1032, Meeting of 30 January 1940 in the RSHA, published in *Faschismus, Ghetto, Massenmord*, 50 ff. On the modifications to the deportation plans see Browning, *Entfesselung*, 91 ff.

43. In addition to the 80,000 people who were expelled as part of the first short-range plan, the following population movements took place: between 10 February and 15 March 1940, as part of the so-called intermediate plan, 40,128 Jews and Poles were deported from the annexed territories to the General Government (ibid. 104 ff.). Between April 1940 and January 1941 the second short-range plan came into effect in a revised version with the deportation of 130,000 Poles and 3,500 Jews to the General Government. In the course of the 'Cholm Action' 30,275 ethnic Germans from the area round Cholm and Lublin were settled in the Warthegau and 28,265 Poles were deported from there to the General Government (Aly, *'Endlösung'*, 157). Furthermore, during the so-called Saybusch Action between September 1940 and January 1941 a total of 18,000 Poles were driven out of the eponymous district in Upper Silesia and their farms were taken over by settlers from Galicia (Sybille Steinbacher, *'Musterstadt' Auschwitz. Germanisierungspolitik und Judenmord in Ostoberschlesien* (Munich, 2000), 133 f.).

44. See below p. 581 f.

45. According to the report of the Main Department I of the RKF of 28 January 1941, by 16 January 1941 a total of 307,958 people had been 'evacuated' (BAB, R 49/3127, resettlement and evacuation in the incorporated territories during 1941, 28 January 1941). According to Himmler's interview with Hitler on 20 February 1943, 366,000 people had been deported by the end of 1942 (R 43 II/1411).

46. After a meeting with Himmler on 7 November 1939 department head Pancke noted: 'Hofmann should consider how one can assess the racial characteristics of large masses of the German and Polish populations of the eastern territories. The Reichsführer-SS wants to use the Clan Office [Sippenamt] in the RuS-Main Office to integrate the RuS-Main Office into his Reich Commissariat so that, as a result, the whole deployment of people in the eastern territories can be controlled and the right decisions can be taken. As a result of the integration of the Settlement Office and the Clan Office into the Reich Commissariat the RuS-Main Office will acquire an absolutely decisive influence on the settlement of the eastern territories' (BAB, NS 2/139). On 16 December 1939 Himmler assigned to Hofmann, the head of the Clan Office, the job of taking over the responsibilities of the head of the Race Office in addition to his own (BDC, SS-O Hofmann). See Heinemann, *'Rasse'*, 194 f.

47. Heinemann, *'Rasse'*, 195 ff. and 232 ff.

48. Ibid. 197 ff. and 251 ff. There is important material on the activities of the Litzmannstadt office in the final report of the head of the Litzmannstadt office concerning the resettlement in the Wartheland under the second short-range plan at the end of 1940 (BAB, R 75/6).

49. End-of-year final report of the Central Land Office for 1942 (BAB, R 49/195); see Heinemann, *'Rasse'*, 212 ff.

50. Heinemann, *'Rasse'*, 217 ff.

51. For examples see ibid. 209 f.

52. BAB, NS 2/60, report of the RuS-leader with the EWZ, Künzel, 20 December 1939, and Pancke report of 20 December 1939.

53. Ibid. Künzel report of 20 December 1939.

54. Ibid. 20 December 1939.

55. BAB, NS 2/88, 14 October 1939; Heinemann, *'Rasse'*, 234 f.

56. BAB, R 69/178, EWZ North-East to Chief of Sipo and SD, 17 January 1940; IfZ, NO 4326, Hofmann, 25 January 1940.

57. Heinemann, *'Rasse'*, 236.

58. BAB, R 69/178, EWZ North-East to Chief of Sipo and SD, 17 January 1940.

59. USHMM, RG 15.015 M/162, RKF, signed Creutz, to HSSPF Warthe, North-East and South-East, 18 January 1940.

60. BAB, NS 2/61, meeting in the EWZ North-East on 1 April 1940.

61. BAB, R 69/598, report on the conference of the RuS offices as part of the conference of the Immigration offices on 11/12 January 1941 in Dresden, paper given by the head of the Clan Office, Richard Kaaserer.

62. BAB, R 69/598, letter of 18 November 1940. *Epikanthus medialis* is the medical term for the so-called Mongol fold or crease, a crescent-shaped fold at the internal edge of the eye, which was popularly known as 'slit eyes' and is common among many East Asian peoples. Himmler evidently wanted to be sure that this feature would be noted.

63. Heinemann, *'Rasse'*, 242 ff. BAB, R 49/14, Reich Ethnic German Commissar, Resettlement in the East. Figures for 31 December 1942; here the total number of ethnic Germans resettled from the Baltic up to this point is given as 126,000.

64. BAB, NS 2/88, EWZ North-East, Posen branch, RuS-Office to the head of the Posen Immigration branch office, 26 March 1940, final report on the processing of the Baltic Germans; see Heinemann, *'Rasse'*, 244 ff.

65. BAB R 69/516 EWZ North-East, Posen branch, RuS Office to HSSPF Koppe re: racial assessment of the ethnic Germans from Vollhynia, Galicia, and the Narev district who have been processed by 18 February 1940, 20 February 1940.

66. BAB, R 69/501, EWZ, Roving Commission I, addition to the Vollhynian and Galician statistics, 20 August 1940.

67. BAB, R 69/178, summaries. Included here were a total of over 147,000 people who had been resettled from these districts.

68. BAB, R 69/598, report on the meeting of the RuS offices as part of the EWZ meeting of 11–12 January 1941 in Dresden.

69. There is an excellent overview in the introduction to the *Dienstkalender*, 81 f. See also BAB, R 49/26, RKF, report to Himmler re: Statistics on the resettlement situation on 15 April 1941, 5 May 1941.

70. Heinemann, 'Rasse', 247 f.

71. BAB, NS 19/150, the date is unreadable.

72. Ibid. Brandt to Koppe, 9 August 1940: 'The five girls you sent from Berlin have arrived safely.'

73. Ibid. Personal Staff to Greifelt, 30 May 1941.

74. Schulte, Zwangsarbeit, 246 ff.

75. Himmler's Memorandum on the Treatment of the Ethnic Aliens in the East (May 1941), ed. Helmut Krausnick, Vierteljahrshefte für Zeitgeschichte, 5 (1957), 194–8.

76. According to Himmler's handwritten minute (28 May 1940) on the memorandum (see n.75) Hitler had considered it 'very good and correct'; but he [Himmler] should 'keep it absolutely secret' and show it to Frank 'to tell him that the Führer considers it correct'.

77. USHMM, RG 15.015 M/259, order concerning the deployment of Poles capable of being Germanized, 3 July 1940; on the re-Germanization process see Heinemann, 'Rasse', 282 ff.

78. Heinemann, 'Rasse', 197 ff. and 251 ff.

79. Ibid. 283.

80. BAB, R 49/75, Hecht/Wetzel memoradum, 25 November 1939. They assumed a figure of 1.3 million Poles in the annexed territories capable of being Germanized.

81. The aim of Germanizing a million people is contained in Himmler's Edict on the Inspection and Selection of the Population of the Occupied Eastern Territories of 12 September 1940, quoted in Heinemann, 'Rasse', 282. A note from the Reich Economics Ministry of 1 November 1940 states: 'In response to a telephone inquiry the Reich Commissar for the Consolidation of the Ethnic German Nation stated that in accordance with a decision of the Führer, up to a million Poles can be Germanized in Germany. At the moment around 800–900 people are being Germanized. However, the Reich Commissar estimates that the increasing numbers of those being registered will initially lead to the Germanization of around 100,000 people. In view of the very strict medical and racial criteria being applied the figure of 1 million will probably not be achieved' (USHMM, RG 15.007 M/125).

82. USHMM, RG 15.015 M/251, Himmler to the HSSPF East, North-East, Vistula, Warthe, South-East, 20 May 1941. The letter referred to the 'indigenous West Prussians'. However, Himmler made it clear that his comments applied to all the annexed territories.

83. See his remarks in his speech of 29 February 1940 (BAB, NS 19/4007, and below p. 475).

84. Heinemann, 'Rasse', 479 f.; Himmler's signed order as RFK 42I of 23 July 1941 (USHMM,RG 15.007 M/125) was of decisive importance.

85. Heinemann, 'Rasse', 261 f.

86. BAB, NS 19/3979, edict of 12 September 1940 concerning the Inspection and Selection of the Population of the Occupied Eastern Territories. The content of this edict was incorporated into the Reich Interior Minister's Decree Concerning the Ethnic List and German Citizenship in the Incorporated Eastern Territories of 4 March 1941, *RGBl* 1941 I, 118 f.; see Heinemann, *'Rasse'*, 262 f.

87. BAB, NS 2/88, Chief of RuSHA, Hofmann, to the head of the Race Office, Schultz, concerning interviews with Himmler on 22 November 1941, 25 November 1941. The instruction referred both to the 'selection procedure' for the Ethnic German List as well as to the assessments in the Litzmannstadt branch office. It was to be applied first to the assessments in Upper Silesia. For the date of the interviews see *Dienstkalender*.

88. USHMM, RG 15.007 M/113, RFSS, Guidelines for the composition and procedure of the Supreme Assessment Court for Ethnicity Issues in the incorporated eastern territories.

89. In the spring of 1942 nearly 100,000 people in the Warthegau and in East Prussia were assessed for membership of Groups III and IV. A start was evidently made on assessing the estimated 1.9 million candidates in West Prussia and Upper Silesia (Heinemann, *'Rasse'*,268).

90. On Himmler's disagreement with Forster about the implementation of the Ethnic List procedure see Himmler's letter of 20 November 1941, in Dieter Schenk, *Hitlers Mann in Danzig. Albert Forster und die NS-Verbrechen in Danzig-Westpreußen* (Bonn, 2000), 207; also BAB, NS 2/231, Brandt to RSHA and RuSHA, 2 December 1943. On the conflict with Forster see Heinemann, *'Rasse'*, 269 ff. In the Warthegau Reichsstatthalter Greiser gave in after Himmler insisted in September 1941 on the principle of using strict racial criteria for selection (ibid. 274 f.). On the conflict with the Upper Silesian Gauleiter Bracht see ibid. 172 ff.

91. Adler, *Mensch*, 140 ff.

92. Speech to the Gauleiters, 29 February 1940, in Himmler, *Geheimreden*, 139.

93. Ibid. 138 f.

94. Doc. EC-305, in *IMT*, vol. 36, pp. 299 ff.

95. Präg and Jacobmeyer (eds), *Diensttagebuch*, 2 and 4 March 1940.

96. Report by Schön, the head of the resettlement department attached to the governor of the Warsaw district, 20 January 1941, in *Faschismus, Ghetto, Massenmord*, 108 ff.

97. Paul Sauer (ed.), *Dokumente über die Verfolgung der jüdischen Bürger in Baden-Württemberg durch das nationalsozialistische Regime*, vol. 2 (Stuttgart, 1966), no. 408.

98. Report by Schön, the head of the resettlement department attached to the governor of the Warsaw district, 20 January 1941, in *Faschismus, Ghetto, Massenmord*, 108 ff.

99. See Heinemann, *'Rasse'*, 151 ff.

100. *Die Deutschen in der Tschechoslowakei 1933–1947. Dokumentensammlung*, compiled by Václav Král (Prague, 1964), 424.
101. Hitler to Frank, 6 January 1941, printed ibid. 425.
102. Heinemann, *'Rasse'*, 155 f.
103. Ibid. 154 f.
104. Tatjana Tönsmeyer, *Das Dritte Reich und die Slowakei 1939–1945. Politischer Alltag zwischen Kooperation und Eigensinn* (Paderborn, etc., 2003), 312 f.
105. Pancke to Himmler, 15 May 1940 and 18 June 1940, published in *Die Deutschen in der Tschechoslowakei*, 405 ff.; cf. Tönsmeyer, *Reich*, 46 f., and especially Johann Kaiser, 'Die Politik des Dritten Reiches gegenüber der Slowakei 1939–1945. Ein Beitrag zur Erforschung der nationalsozialistischen Satellitenpolitik in Südosteuropa', unpublished dissertation, Bochum University (1970), 427 ff.
106. BAB, NS 19/2070, Himmler to Dollmann, 6 September 1939; Stuhlpfarrer, *Umsiedlung*, 140 f.
107. Stuhlpfarrer, *Umsiedlung*, 142 f.
108. Quoted ibid. 623.
109. Ibid. 148 ff.
110. Ibid. 177 ff.
111. BAB, NS 19/2070.
112. Stuhlpfarrer, *Umsiedlung*, 170 f.
113. Ibid. 205 ff., for discussion of the various available figures and 155 ff. for the process of opting.
114. Ibid. 541 ff.; Latour, *Südtirol*, 74 ff.
115. Stuhlpfarrer, *Umsiedlung*, 617 ff.
116. Ibid. 649 ff.; on Himmler's comments on 18 and 23 July see BAB, R 49/2156, Kukla's report and a minute on the trip to Burgundy.
117. IfZ, NO 2417, Himmler to Frauenfeld, 10 and 27 July 1942; Stuhlpfarrer, *Umsiedlung*, 701 ff.
118. See above p. 433 f.
119. Blaskowitz note for the interview with the Commander-in-Chief of the army, 6 February 1940, printed in *'Schöne Zeiten'*, 14 ff.
120. Müller, *Heer*, 445 f.; on the meeting of 2 February see Franz Halder, *Kriegstagebuch. Tägliche Aufzeichnungen des Chefs des Generalstabes des Heeres 1939–1942*, ed. Hans-Adolf Jacobsen together with Alfred Philippi, vol. 1: *Vom Polenfeldzug bis zum Ende der Westoffensive (14. 8. 1939–30. 6. 1940)* (Stuttgart, 1962), 183, 5 February 1940.
121. Müller, *Heer*, 448 ff.; Halder, *Kriegstagebuch*, vol. 1, 229, 13 March 1940.
122. See Müller, *Heer*, 459 ff., on the 'disgust and outrage', which the edict had aroused in the officer corps, and which among other things is shown in Groscurth's diary (14 December 1939 and 22 January 1940). Himmler's friend, Johst, felt prompted to mount a defence of the edict in his book, *Ruf des Reiches, Echo des Volkes. Eine Ostfahrt* (Munich, 1940).

123. BAB, NS 19/3901; Facsimile in Norbert Westenrieder, '*Deutsche Frauen und Mädchen!*' *Vom Alltagsleben 1933–1945* (Düsseldorf, 1984), 42.

124. BAB, NS 19/3901, 10 January 1940. On 19 June 1940 regulations for implementing the RFSS's order of 28 October 1939, which modified the original purpose of the order: 'The first duty is to care for all children of good blood whose fathers have been killed in the war and their mothers [. . .] The second duty is to care for all children of good blood who have been fathered by SS men during the war. The SS will take responsibility for their care and for the care of expectant mothers in all cases where there is need and hardship. [. . .] The third duty is to care for the families of members of the SS who have been called up into the Wehrmacht or the Waffen-SS' (NS 2/275).

125. BAB, NS 7/221, The SS judge attached to the RFSS in the SS Court Main Office, 24 March 1942 (refers to the order of 30 January 1940). In this letter the SS judge accepts in Himmler's name that in individual cases punishment may not be appropriate: 'However, it is obvious that in all those cases where the culprit has exploited the absence of the husband and has behaved irresponsibly, with a lack of decency, or even in a mean way towards the husband or wife the court must be merciless in imposing punishment.'

126. BAB, NS 19/4007, 29 February 1940, see also Himmler, *Geheimreden*, 116 ff., quotation 117 ff. Italics in the original.

127. BAB, NS 19/4007, speech to the commanders of the 'Leibstandarte' on the evening of Metz Day, 7 September 1940.

128. PRO, WO 208/4474, Hedwig Potthast, Reichsführer Himmler's Mistress, 24 May 1945. I used this report of the British Secret Service to reconstruct her most important biographical data. During the 1980s Hedwig Potthast spoke to the journalist Peter Ferdinand Koch about her relationship with Himmler (see his book *Himmlers graue Eminenz. Oswald Pohl und das Wirtschaftsverwaltungshauptamt der SS* (Hamburg, 1988)). On Himmler's relationship with Potthast see also Himmler, *Brüder Himmler*, 233 ff.

129. BAB, NS 19/3672.

130. BAK, NL 1126/37, Letter of November 1941.

131. *Dienstkalender.*

132. Koch, *Pohl*, 57 and 79.

133. Ibid. 186 f.

134. USHMM, Acc. 1999.A.0092, 4 September 1939; on Margarete's life during the war see Himmler, *Brüder Himmler*, 241 ff.

135. USHMM, Acc. 1999.A.0092, 11 September, 16 October, and 3 and 14 November 1939.

136. Ibid. 3 December 1939.

137. Ibid. 2 June 1940. Further entries during the years 1942–3, for example on 16 August 1943: 'My stations were in perfect order.'

138. Ibid. 7 March 1940.

139. Ibid. 23 March 1940.
140. Ibid. 6 April 1941.
141. Ibid. 4 February 1941: 'Heini's been in Norway for the past week and I haven't heard anything from him via the staff for two days. I don't dare to ask because I'm treated appallingly and no one protects me and everyone is aware of it, otherwise I couldn't understand their behaviour. And every young girl is after a man. If they only knew how bitter life is. Will I be able to protect my daughter from the worst?'
142. Ibid. 1 March 1942.
143. Ibid. 6 September 1943.
144. This is clear from the *Dienstkalender*.
145. BAK, NL 1126/16, Gudrun Himmler's letters.
146. An album into which Gudrun stuck the photos of her father is in the US Holocaust Museum in Washington: Himmler Family Collection. Himmler often put captions on the photos: 'To my dear Püppi from Pappi.'
147. Himmler, *Brüder Himmler*, 277 f.

CHAPTER 17

1. Wildt, *Generation*, 259 ff.
2. BAB, R 58/826, Reorganization of the Security Service of the Reichsführer-SS in order to align its organization and personnel with those of the security police, 24 February 1939. Schellenberg was putting forward ideas that he had already proposed in a paper that he had submitted in the summer of 1938 (R 58/827, minute of 5. July 1938).
3. Ibid. Basic Principles for the Training and Career Development of the Leaders (senior officials) of the German Security Police, 1 March 1939. Best also advocated his views publicly in an article, which appeared under the title 'Criticism and Aporia of the "lawyer"' in the journal *Deutsches Recht* (1939), 196–9, and was printed in an abridged version in the *Deutsche Allgemeine Zeitung* of 12 April 1939. On the dispute see Herbert, *Best*, 228 ff.
4. Both wanted to achieve this through the Reich government taking over the SD but without subjecting it to state administrative law. On this dispute see BAB, R 58/826, Schellenberg minute of 4 April 1939; R 58/137, meeting with Heydrich on 15 April 1939 re: reorganization of the Sipo and SD; R 58/137, Schellenberg minute of 25 April 1939 re: critique of Best's position, R 58/826, Heydrich circular of 5 July 1939.
5. Ibid. circular edict of 5 July 1939; R 58/240, merger of the central offices of the security police and SD, 27 September 1939.
6. Material in BAB, R 43 II/393a; cf. Wildt, *Generation*, 278.
7. Wildt, *Generation*, 335 ff.
8. Ibid. 352 ff.

9. Ibid. 301 ff.; Wagner, *Volksgemeinschaft*, 265 ff.
10. Wildt, *Generation*, 378 ff. The SD homeland reports dealing with the whole of the Reich, which were collected by the RSHA, have been published in *Meldungen aus dem Reich 1938–1945. Die geheimen Lageberichte des Sicherheitsdienstes der SS*, ed. and with an introduction by Heinz Boberach, 18 vols. (Herrsching, 1984–5).
11. Querg, *Spionage*, 165; Wildt, *Generation*, 391 ff.
12. BAB, BDC, SS-O Jost.
13. Querg, *Spionage*, 183 ff.
14. Hachmeister, *Gegnerforscher*.
15. BADH, ZR 920/56, circular edict of the Intelligence Service of 4 August 1941; cf. Dierker, *Glaubenskrieger*, 331 ff., and Wildt, *Generation*, 364 ff.
16. Wildt, *Generation*, 377. Apart from Hachmeister's study see also the article by Jürgen Matthäus, '"Weltanschauliche Forschung und Auswertung". Aus den Akten des Amtes VII im Reichssicherheitshauptamt', *Jahrbuch für Antisemitismusforschung*, 5 (1996), 287–330, and the edited volume *Himmlers Hexenkartothek*.
17. BAB, R 58/239.
18. Wagner, *Volksgemeinschaft*, 330 ff.
19. See the reports in the German daily newspapers, for example: *Deutsche Allgemeine Zeitung* of 10 November 1938 (morning edition), Headline: 'The world's view of the assassination attempt. RFSS announces: the culprits are believed to be foreign'; *Völkischer Beobachter* of 11 November 1938: 'England and the Jews are the brains behind the Munich crime.'
20. Judged as an example of a professional secret service in action the kidnapping was of dubious value since it meant that the chance of infiltrating the Secret Service network in the Netherlands was thrown away. On the Venlo Action see Schellenberg, *Memoirs*, 82 ff.; Höhne, *Orden*, 263 ff.; Querg, *Spionage*, 224 ff.; Wildt, *Generation*, 399 f.
21. IfZ, ZS 1939, Albrecht Böhme, 19 May 1949, here another undated statement by Böhme, in which he repeats his story; ZS 735, Franz Josef Huber, 19 June 1969.
22. Elser's statement to the Gestapo has been published in various places, most recently in *Das Protokoll. Die Autobiographie des Georg Elser* (Königsbronn, 2006). The most comprehensive account remains Anton Hoch and Lothar Gruchmann, *Georg Elser. Der Attentäter aus dem Volke. Der Anschlag auf Hitler im Münchner Bürgerbräu 1939* (Frankfurt a. M., 1980).
23. Note by Gürtner 20 September 1939 published in Martin Broszat, 'Zur Perversion der Strafjustiz im Dritten Reich', with a documentary appendix, *Vierteljahrshefte für Zeitgeschichte*, 6 (1958), 390–443, here 408 f.; Gürtner note on a meeting with Hitler, 14 October 1939, published ibid. 411; list of victims compiled by the Reich Justice Ministry, ibid. 411 ff.
24. BAB, R 8/243, excerpts published in Broszat, 'Konzentrationslager', 399.

25. For examples of executions in work re-education camps see Gerd Wysocki, 'Lizenz zum Töten. Die "Sonderbehandlungs"-Praxis der Stapo-Stelle Braunschweig', in Gerhard Paul and Michael Mallmann (eds), *Die Gestapo im Zweiten Weltkrieg.'Heimatfront' und besetztes Europa* (Darmstadt, 2000), 237–54, here 241 ff.; on businesses see ibid. 246 ff. Bernd-A. Rusinek, *Gesellschaft in der Katastrophe. Terror, Illegalität, Widerstand–Köln 1944/45* (Essen, 1989), 350 ff., describes a public execution in Cologne. For further examples of such murders portrayed as executions see Hans-Joachim Heuer, *Geheime Staatspolizei. Über das Töten und die Tendenzen der Entzivilisierung* (Berlin, 1995); see also Hellmuth Auerbach, 'Der Begriff "Sonderbehandlung" im Sprachgebrauch der SS', in *Gutachten des Instituts für Zeitgeschichte*, vol. 2 (Stuttgart, 1966), 182–9.

26. This is indicated by the guidelines which the head of Gestapo Department II announced at a meeting of desk officers on 26 September 1939 (published in Martin Hirsch *et al.* (eds), *Recht, Verwaltung und Justiz im Nationalsozialismus. Ausgewählte Schriften, Gesetze und Gerichtsentscheidungen von 1933 bis 1945* (Cologne, 1984). Also the choice of words in the 'Basic Principles' of 23 September 1939 ('on higher authority') shows that Himmler could decide unilaterally and did not need to get Hitler's approval in every individual case.

27. Himmler minute, 20 November 1939, quoted in Ulrich Herbert, *Fremdarbeiter. Politik und Praxis des 'Ausländer-Einsatzes'in der Kriegswirtschaft des Dritten Reiches* (Bonn, 1999), 91, based on files of the Berlin public prosecutor's office.

28. Edict of 8 January 1940, quoted ibid. 91 f., based on files of the Berlin public prosecutor's office.

29. *Documenta Occupationis*, vol. 10: *Praca przymusowa polaków pod panowaniem hitlerowskim: 1939–1945* ('Polish Forced Labour under the Hitler Regime') (Posen, 1976), doc. no. II 3, 28 December 1939.

30. BAB, NS 19/4007, published in Himmler, *Geheimreden*, 116 ff., relevant passage on 134.

31. Herbert, *Fremdarbeiter*, 86 ff.

32. *Documenta Occupationis*, vol. 10, doc. no. II 4, Himmler's Edict Concerning the Treatment of Polish Civilian Workers Deployed in the Reich, 8 March 1940.

33. BAB, R 58/272, 7 May 1940.

34. Herbert, *Fremdarbeiter*, 94.

35. *Documenta Occupationis*, vol. 10, doc. no. II 9, Reichsführer-SS Guidelines Concerning the Use of Special Treatment for Polish Forced Workers and Prisoners of War, 5 July 1941; see Herbert, *Fremdarbeiter*, 148; Heinemann, 'Rasse', 488 ff.

36. See Herbert, *Fremdarbeiter*, 149, who refers to a report in the Essen newspaper, *Rote Erde*.

37. Johnson, *Terror*, 324 ff.

38. See the figures ibid. 550 ff. and 387.

39. Ibid. 352 ff.

40. Wildt, *Generation*, 358 ff.
41. Ibid. 132 ff. and 153 ff.
42. See Adam, *Judenpolitik*, 258 ff., and Avraham Barkai, *Vom Boykott zur 'Entjudung'. Der wirtschaftliche Existenzkampf der Juden im Dritten Reich 1933–1943* (Frankfurt a. M., 1987), 183 ff.
43. Walk (ed.), *Sonderrecht*, IV 2; Adam, *Judenpolitik*, 259.
44. Walk (ed.), *Sonderrecht*, IV 10, edict of the chief of the security police, 12 September 1939.
45. RSHA edict of 21 September 1939, referred to in Adam, *Judenpolitik*, 260.
46. Walk (ed.), *Sonderrecht*, IV 115.
47. Statutes of the Reich Air Raid Defence League of 28 June 1940, in *RGBl* 1940 I, 992; Walk (ed.), *Sonderrecht*, IV 127; Adam, *Judenpolitik*, 258 f.
48. Adam, *Judenpolitik*, 260 f.; Konrad Kwiet, 'Nach dem Pogrom. Stufen der Ausgrenzung', in Wolfgang Benz (ed.), *Die Juden in Deutschland 1933–1945. Leben unter nationalsozialistischer Herrschaft* (Munich, 1989), 545–659, 605 ff.; Walk (ed.), *Sonderrecht*, IV 67, edict of the Reich Minister of Economics of 23 January 1940 re: The Provision of Textiles.
49. Wolf Gruner, *Der geschlossene Arbeitseinsatz deutscher Juden. Zur Zwangsarbeit als Element der Verfolgung 1938–1943* (Berlin, 1997), 107 ff.
50. Details in Longerich, *Politik*, 231. On the 'Jew houses' see Gruner, *Arbeitseinsatz*, 249 ff.
51. Gruner, *Arbeitseinsatz*, 250, has demonstrated the existence of 38 such camps.
52. OA Moscow, 500-1-597.
53. OA Moscow, 503-1-324.
54. Wagner, *Volksgemeinschaft*, 305 ff.
55. Ibid. 311.
56. Ibid. 311 f.
57. Ibid. 310 f. and 317 f.
58. Reich Criminal Police Office, 1 September 1939, and edicts of the Reich Minister of the Interior of 9 and 12 September 1939 (all published in the pamphlet: *Collection of Edicts Concerning the Preventive Combating of Crime*, IfZ, Dc 17.02).
59. Circular edict of 18 October 1939, published ibid.
60. Broszat, 'Konzentrationslager', 399; Orth, *System*, 96 f.; Czesław Pilichowski, *Es gibt keine Verjährung* (Warsaw, 1980), 127 (on people of Polish origin).
61. Circular edict of 7 September 1939, published in *Collection of Edicts Concerning Preventive Combating of Crime*, IfZ, Dc 17.02.
62. Circular edict of 12 September 1939, published ibid.
63. Wagner, *Volksgemeinschaft*, 332. According to official figures from the Reich Criminal Police Office on 31 December 1940 7,269 persons were in preventive police detention compared with 6,018 in the previous year and 3,231 at the end of 1938: *Jahrbuch Amt V (Reichskriminalpolizeiamt) des Reichssicherheitshauptamtes SS 1939/40* (Berlin, 1940), 5 and 44. On 1 January 1940 4,845 'professional

criminals, habitual criminals or people who posed a threat to the public' were in police preventive custody and by the end of 1940 the figure was 6,530; the number of 'asocials' who were in preventive custody sank from 7,713 to 6,824: *Jahrbuch Amt V*, 44 f. Wagner, *Volksgemeinschaft*, 333, points out, however, that elsewhere in the same publication very different figures for 'asocials' in preventive custody on 31 December 1939 are referred to (p. 5: 8,212).

64. RSHA decrees of 12 July 1940 (Homosexuals) and 25 October 1941 (IfZ, Dc 17.02, *Collection of Edicts Concerning the Preventive Combating of Crime*); Wagner, *Volksgemeinschaft*, 333 f.

65. BAB, NS 19/1919, Himmler to Hildebrandt, 16 December 1939, from which Hildebrandt's query can be inferred. On this matter see Orth, *System*, 69 ff.

66. The relevant documents are in NS 19/1919: Himmler to Heissmeyer, 16 December 1939; Glücks to Himmler with the same date; Heissmeyer report of 25 January 1940; Glücks's reports of 30 and 31 January 1940 and letter from Himmler of 30 April 1940.

67. BAB, NS 19/1919, Heissmeyer report of 25 January 1941.

68. Ibid. Report of 21 February 1941.

69. BAB, BDC, SS-O Höss; Orth, *System*, 76 ff.; Steinbacher, *'Musterstadt'*, 179 f.

70. Steinbacher, *'Musterstadt'*, 205 ff.; Peter Hayes, *Industry and Ideology: IG Farben in the Nazi Era* (Cambridge, 2001), 347 ff.; Bernd C. Wagner, *IG Auschwitz. Zwangsarbeit und Vernichtung von Häftlingen des Lagers Monowitz 1941–1945* (Munich, 2000), 37 ff.; Hans Deichmann and Peter Hayes, 'Standort Auschwitz. Eine Kontroverse über die Entscheidungsgründe für den Bau des I. G. Farben-Werks in Auschwitz', *1999*, 11/1 (1996), 73–101.

71. *Dienstkalender.*

72. Steinbacher, *'Musterstadt'*, 209 ff.; Himmler order of 26 February 1941, reproduced in IfZ, NI 11086, Krauch to Ambros, 4 March 1941.

73. Kaienburg, *'Vernichtung'*, 152 ff.

74. Orth, *System*, 82 ff.; Isabell Sprenger, *Groß-Rosen. Ein Konzentrationslager in Schlesien* (Cologne, etc., 1996), esp. 88 ff.

75. Orth, *System*, 85 ff.

76. On Hinzert and Niedernhagen see ibid. 88 ff.

77. Ibid. 109 ff.

78. Ibid. 102 ff.

79. Ibid. 98; Kaienburg, *Neuengamme*, 229.

80. IfZ, PS-1063, edict of 2 January 1941; see Orth, *System*, 86 f.

81. Schulte, *Zwangsarbeit*, 125 ff.

82. Ibid. 131 ff.; Allen, *Business*, 72 ff. and 100 f.

83. BAB, NS 3/1427, summary of Himmler's comments on 4 October 1940; see also Kaienburg, *Wirtschaft*, 800.

84. BAB, NS 19/2122, Himmler to Pohl, 24 June 1941; see on these experiments in detail Kaienburg, *Wirtschaft*, 80 ff.

85. BAB, NS 19/3122, Himmler to Pohl, 29 November 1941, published in Himmler, *Reichsführer!*, no. 80a.
86. BAB, NS 19/3122, Brandt to Vogel, 20 March 1942. In a letter to Konrad Meyer, who on his instructions was preparing the 'General Plan East', Himmler wrote that he naturally rejected anthroposophy, but that further experiments should be carried out in order to develop alternatives to artificial fertilizers which, in the long run, would very probably prove dangerous (NS 19/3211, 15 July 1941; see Kaienburg, *Wirtschaft*, 801).
87. BAB, NS 19/3211, Report of 29 October 1943 and further material re: Wertingen.
88. Kaienburg, *Wirtschaft*, 462 and 771 ff.; Schulte, *Zwangsarbeit*, 137 f.
89. Himmler circular of 15 September 1939, published in Himmler, *Reichsführer!*, no. 51; see also Schulte, *Zwangsarbeit*, 136 f.
90. Kaienburg, *Wirtschaft*, 474 ff.; Schulte, *Zwangsarbeit*, 182 ff. However, the attempt to take over the Apollinaris Spring, which involved 'enemy property' under compulsory administration, failed; the firm was ultimately leased by the German Business Plants (Deutsche Wirtshaftsbetriebe); see Josef Henke, 'Von den Grenzen der SS-Macht. Eine Fallstudie zur Tätigkeit des SS-Wirtschafts-Verwaltungshauptamtes', in Dieter Rebentisch and Karl Teppe (eds), *Verwaltung contra Menschenführung im Staat Hitlers. Studien zum politisch-administrativen System* (Göttingen, 1986), 255–77.
91. Schulte, *Zwangsarbeit*, 183.
92. Kaienburg, *Wirtschaft*, 466 ff.; Schulte, *Zwangsarbeit*, 144 f.
93. Allen, *Business*, 83; Kaienburg, *Wirtschaft*, 412 ff.; Schulte, *Zwangsarbeit*, 147 ff.
94. Allen, *Business*, 92 ff. and 107 ff.; Kaienburg, *Wirtschaft*, 416 ff.; Schulte, *Zwangsarbeit*, 193 ff.
95. Schulte, *Zwangsarbeit*, 193 ff. emphasizes this 'paradigm shift'.
96. Decree of 17 October 1939, in *RGBl* 1939 I, 2107 f., and the decrees implementing it of 1 November 1939 and 17 April 1940 (ibid. 2293 ff., and *RGBL* 1940 I, 659). BAB, NS 7/2, edict of the Reichsführer-SS und Chief of the German Police Concerning the Decree Concerning the Jurisdiction of Special Courts in Criminal Cases Involving Members of the SS and Members of the Police Units Deployed on Special Missions, 20 November 1939. See on this whole matter Vieregge, *Gerichtsbarkeit*, 6 ff.
97. Vieregge, *Gerichtsbarkeit*, 30.
98. Ibid. 13 ff.
99. Laid down in the edict of the SS Court Main Office of 29 December 1939; see Vieregge, *Gerichtsbarkeit*, 16.
100. Ibid. 18 ff.
101. On the inclusion of the indigenous inhabitants in the jurisdiction see ibid. 26 ff. In the Netherlands in individual cases the Reich Commissar could transfer the pursuit of criminal offences committed by the indigenous inhabitants to the SS and police courts. In Norway in September 1941 the Reich

Commissar even transferred the passing of judgement on all contraventions of his orders to the jurisdiction of the SS and police (Birn, *Die Höheren SS- und Polizeiführer*, 144; Robert Bohn, *Reichskommissariat Norwegen. 'Nationalsozialistische Neuordnung' und Kriegswirtschaft* (Munich, 2000), 91 ff.). In July 1942 in the Protectorate the SS and police courts took over the punishment of all direct attacks by non-Germans on the SS and police if the RFSS considered this necessary in the interests of the SS and police (decree of 15 July 1942 in *RGBl* 1942 I, 475; Birn, *Höhere SS- und Polizeiführer*, 140 ff.). On the activities of the SS and police courts in relation to civilians in Denmark from the beginning of 1944 onwards see Erich Thomsen, *Deutsche Besatzungspolitik in Dänemark 1940–1945* (Düsseldorf, 1971), 201 f.

102. Vieregge, *Gerichtsbarkeit*, 27.
103. Führer decree of 5 September 1944, published in *'Führer-Erlasse'*, no. 365; Vieregge, *Gerichtsbarkeit*, 27 f.
104. Vieregge, *Gerichtsbarkeit*, 202 ff.
105. Ibid. 216. The file BAB, NS 7/57, contains a collection of such powers granted to Bender.
106. Vieregge, *Gerichtsbarkeit*, 213 ff.; BAB, NS 7/2, Himmler edict of 20 November 1939.
107. Vieregge, *Gerichtsbarkeit*, 214 f.
108. BAB, NS 7/52, Bender to the SS Court Main Office, 18 September 1940; see Vieregge, *Gerichtsbarkeit*, 215.
109. BAB, NS 7/265, Himmler to Bender, 24 October 1941, and Bender to SS Court Main Office, 12 November 1941; NS 19/3872, Circular from the SS Court Main Office of 9 December 1941; see Vieregge, *Gerichtsbarkeit*, 108.
110. BAB, NS 7/13, Note of the Field Command Headquarters, 13 May 1943.
111. Published in Vieregge, *Gerichtsbarkeit*, Appendix 6 (based on ZStL, Dokumentation ČSSR, no. 396).
112. BAB, NS 19/3939, 30 June 1942.
113. BAB, NS 7/265, Sturmbannführer Korff to Bender, 21 January 1945.
114. Führer Edict Concerning the Exceptional Reopening of Cases in the SS and Police Courts of 24 July 1941 and Himmler's regulations to implement it of 25 November 1941, both in BAB, NS 7/303; Viereggge, *Gerichtsbarkeit*, 196 ff.
115. BAB, NS 7/344, SS judge attached to the RFSS, 6 May 1942.
116. Vieregge, *Gerichtsbarkeit*, 106.
117. BAB, NS 19/1913, 16 August 1942.
118. On military disobedience as a 'general clause' see Vieregge, *Gerichtsbarkeit*, 95 ff.
119. BAB, NS 19/9, 9 October 1942.
120. Speech at the Gruppenführer meeting, 4 October 1943, doc. PS-1919, in *IMT*, vol. 29, pp. 110 ff., quotation p. 144.
121. BAB, NS 7/1001, SS judge attached to the RFSS and Chief of the German Police, 22 June 1943.

122. Ibid. minute of an interview with the RFSS concerning the Buchhold case.
123. BAB, NS 7/250, Telex Personal Staff, 4 January 1945.
124. BAB, NS 7/247, SS judge attached to the RFSS to the SS Court Main Office, 26 October 1942.

CHAPTER 18

1. Brandes, *Tschechen*, 37 f.
2. On the police missions of Tanzmann, the Vogt police commission, and the police liaison officer Hahn and his team there is extensive material in PAA, Inland IIg 100 and Luther files; see Tönsmeyer, *Reich*, 114 ff.
3. This was the name used in the report of the German envoy to the Foreign Ministry, 4 September 1941 (PAA, Inland IIg 100). The office was closed on 3 July 1941: BAB, R 70 Slowakei 301, Hahn to RSHA. Cf. Tönsmeyer, *Reich*, 124 f., and Kaiser, 'Politik', 488 ff.
4. His appointment was, however, delayed for more than a year: PAA, Inland IIg 100, German embassy to the Foreign Ministry, 5 November 1941; see Tönsmeyer, *Reich*, 120.
5. Minute by Heydrich of 2 July 1940, published in Krausnick, 'Hitler', quotation p. 207.
6. BADH, ZR 277, minutes of the meeting with the head of Office I, 2 April 1940. On 28 March 1940 Heydrich had ordered the establishment of a commando for the Netherlands and Belgium respectively (ibid.).
7. On the occupation of Norway see Hans-Dietrich Loock, *Quisling, Rosenberg und Terboven. Zur Vorgeschichte und Geschichte der nationalsozialistischen Revolution in Norwegen* (Stuttgart, 1970), 277 ff., and Bohn, *Reichskommissariat*, 31 ff.; on the role of the security police see Wildt, *Generation*, 508 ff.
8. BADH, ZR 277, note, 20 April 1940. The eighty men were really intended to be deployed in four Einsatzkommandos with the three SS divisions and the 'Leibstandarte', which was to be kept 'strictly secret' from the Wehrmacht (ibid. minutes of the meeting with the head of Office I, 2 April 1940).
9. Loock, *Quisling*, 356 ff.; Bohn, *Reichskommissariat*, 70 ff.
10. Bohn, *Reichskommissariat*, 74 ff.
11. Heydrich note of 2 July 1940, published in Krausnick, 'Hitler', quotation p. 207.
12. Thomsen, *Besatzungspolitik*, 11 ff.
13. BAB, NS 19/1678.
14. Wilfried Wagner, *Belgien in der deutschen Politik während des Zweiten Weltkrieges* (Boppard a. Rh., 1974), 131 f.
15. BAB, BDC, SS-O Seyss-Inquart, letter from Himmler to him, 16 May 1940, published in *De SS en Nederland. Documenten uit SS-Archieven 1933–1945*, introduced and edited by N.K.C.A. in 't Veld, 2 vols. ('s Gravenhage, 1976);

see also Konrad Kwiet, *Reichskommissariat Niederlande. Versuch und Scheitern nationalsozialistischer Neuordnung* (Stuttgart, 1968), 48.

16. BAB, BDC, SS-O Seyss-Inquart, document of appointment. Both corresponded with each other regularly before Seyss-Inquart's appointment to the post of Reich Commissar (ibid.).

17. Kwiet, *Reichskommissariat*, 83 ff. The appointment to HSSPF followed on 23 May 1940.

18. Heydrich note of 2 July 1940, published in Krausnick, 'Hitler', 207 f.

19. On the appointment of Rauter and Nockermann and the simultaneous establishment of an SS-Oberabschnitt North-West in the Netherlands see Himmler to the SS Main Offices, 24 May 1940, in BAB, BDC, SS-O Seyss-Inquart, published in *SS en Nederland*, doc. no. 23.

20. Guus Meershoek, 'Machtentfaltung und Scheitern. Sicherheitspolizei und SD in den Niederlanden', in Gerhard Paul and Michael Mallmann (eds), *Die Gestapo im Zweiten Weltkrieg. 'Heimatfront' und besetztes Europa* (Darmstadt, 2000), 383–402, here 387 ff.; Wildt, *Generation*, 511 ff.

21. Kwiet, *Reichskommissariat*, 2 ff.

22. See note 19.

23. Kwiet, *Reichskommissariat*, 107; see also Himmler to Seyss-Inquart, 4 June 1940 (BAB, BDC, SS-O Seyss-Inquart).

24. Ibid. letter of 2 January 1941.

25. Wagner, *Belgien*, 132 ff. On German occupation policy in Belgium see also, in particular, Werner Warmbrunn, *The German Occupation of Belgium, 1940–1944* (New York, 1993), and Wolfram Weber, *Die innere Sicherheit im besetzten Belgien und Nordfrankreich 1940–44. Ein Beitrag zur Geschichte der Besatzungsverwaltungen* (Düsseldorf, 1978). On the role of the security police in the occupation of Belgium see Wildt, *Generation*, 522 ff.

26. Wagner, *Belgien*, 166.

27. BAB, BDC, SS-O Reeder.

28. Warmbrunn, *German Occupation*, 118 f.

29. Heydrich note of 2 July 1940, published in Krausnick, 'Hitler', 209.

30. See Bernd Kasten, '*Gute Franzosen*'. *Die französische Polizei und die deutsche Besatzungsmacht im besetzten Frankreich 1940–1944* (Sigmaringen, 1993), 22 f.; on the role of the security police and SD in the first phase of occupation policy see also Ahlrich Meyer, *Die deutsche Besatzung in Frankreich 1940–1944. Widerstandsbekämpfung und Judenverfolgung* (Darmstadt, 2000), 13 ff., and Wildt, *Generation*, 514 ff.

31. Herbert, *Best*, 251 ff.

32. Heydrich note of 2 July 1940, in Krausnick, 'Hitler', 208; BAB, R 58/241, message from Heydrich to the Stapo offices referring to fifteen men in Paris.

33. Commando staff guidelines for cooperation with the representative of the Chief of the Security Police and SD, quoted in Kasten, '*Franzosen*', 23.

34. Claudia Steur, *Theodor Dannecker. Ein Funktionär der 'Endlösung'* (Essen, 1997), 48.

35. PAA, Inland IIg 81, Heydrich to von Ribbentrop, 27 July 1940; the minutes of the meeting are in the appendix.

36. Information on the numbers of the ethnic German groups in Europe, 25 June 1940 (AP Lodz, L 3571), quoted in Heinemann, 'Rasse', 305.

37. Ibid. 306.

38. Führer edict concerning the provisional administration of Alsace and Lorraine, 2 August 1940 ('Führer-Erlasse', no. 44); second Führer edict concerning the provisional administration of Alsace and Lorraine, 18 October 1940 (ibid. no. 58). On German 'ethnic policy' in Alsace and Lorraine see Heinemann, 'Rasse', 306 ff., and Lothar Kettenacker, Nationalsozialistische Volkstumspolitik im Elsaß (Stuttgart, 1973).

39. After the first expulsions, which affected around 20,000 to 25,000 people, there were large waves of expulsions: of around 60,000 people between 11 and 21 November 1940 and around 10,000 people in February 1942. Thousands also went 'voluntarily'; see Heinemann, 'Rasse', 306 f., 310, and 318.

40. Bruno Brehm criticized the fact that among the families being deported there were undoubtedly people with German nationality, indeed even SS applicants (BAB, BDC, SS-O Brehm, Brehm to RKF planning chief Meyer, 3 November 1940). See also R 49/74, head of the EWZ, Office West, draft of guidelines for the treatment of the alien and ethnically alien population in Lorraine by the security police, 25 February 1941; it proposes a comprehensive 'racial selection'. See Heinemann, 'Rasse', 307 f. and 315 ff.

41. Ibid. 318 f.

42. BAB, NS 2/55, Himmler to Lammers, 21 March 1939. In this letter Himmler expressed his doubts about a draft law banning the marriage of Germans with foreigners. He also made it clear that he aimed to 'win women of Nordic blood for Germany'.

43. BAB, NS 19/4004, speech of 8 November 1938, published in Himmler, Geheimreden, 25 ff., quotation p. 38.

44. Wegner, Politische Soldaten, 265.

45. BAB, R 31/96, Himmler order of 15 August 1940. Himmler ordered that Berger should initially be Heissmeyer's permanent representative, but would be assigned other tasks.

46. IfZ, NO 1825, Berger to Himmler, 7 August 1940. Berger worked on the basis of a recruitment quota of 2 per cent of each annual cohort; this corresponded to the quota in the Reich.

47. IfZ, NO 5717.

48. On the establishment of this unit and other early 'Germanic units' see Stein, Geschichte, 128 f.

49. Dienstkalender.

50. Völkischer Beobachter, 2 February 1941. He gave an 'important address' before the oath-taking ceremony of the SS leaders in Oslo. (Völkischer Beobachter, 31 January 1941).

51. *Berliner Börsenzeitung*, 3 February 1940.

52. *Völkischer Beobachter*, 3 February and 4 April 1940.

53. *Dienstkalender*, 21–2 May 1941.

54. Thomsen, *Besatzungspolitik*, 94 f.

55. PAA, Inland IIg 7, undated note, arrival stamp 22 September 1940.

56. BAB, NS 33/213, Hausser circular, 13 September 1940; Barbara Materne, 'Die Germanische Leitstelle der SS 1940–1945. Entstehung, Aufgabenbereiche und Bedeutung in der Machtstruktur des Dritten Reiches', MA diss. Düsseldorf (2000), 29.

57. Wagner, *Belgien*, 248; Himmler circular, 24 May 1940, published in *SS en Nederland*, no. 23.

58. Stein, *Geschichte*, 134.

59. Ibid. 135. Jüttner order, 3 April 1941, published in *SS en Nederland*, no. 65.

60. Stein, *Geschichte*, 137.

61. BAB, NS 19/1711, Berger to Himmler, 10 and 16 September 1940. According to this there were two commissions 'over there' who were conducting assessments of the ethnic Germans which were disguised as 'an assessment of the health of the nation'. The letter of 16 September 1940 contains a reference to the fact that this was contrary to a 'special order of the Reich Marshall'. Himmler agreed to the measures. See Thomas Casagrande, *Die volksdeutsche SS Division 'Prinz Eugen'. Die Banater Schwaben und die nationalsozialistischen Kriegsverbrechen* (Frankfurt a. M. and New York, 2003), 142 f.

62. Johann Böhm, *Die Gleichschaltung der deutschen Volksgruppe in Rumänien und das "Dritte Reich" 1941–1944* (Frankfurt a. M., etc., 2003), 284 f.

63. Ibid. 286 ff.

64. Ibid. 48; it is a reworking of an older work by the author: *Das nationalsozialistische Deutschland und die deutsche Volksgruppe in Rumänien 1936–1944. Das Verhältnis der deutschen Volksgruppe zum Dritten Reich und zum rumänischen Staat sowie der interne Widerstreit zwischen den politischen Gruppen* (Frankfurt a. M., etc., 1985). In the meantime he has published a monograph on the period before 1940; see Böhm, *Die Deutschen*.

65. BAB, NS 19/3888, Himmler to Berger, 27 November 1940, who stated that he had been surprised by the founding of the party (ibid. letter of 2 December 1940).

66. Ibid. Berger to Himmler, 4 December 1940, concerning a conversation with Schmidt, with Himmler reporting on it.

67. Spannenberger, *Volksbund*, 233 ff.

68. Ibid. 309 f.

69. BAB, NS 19/383, Berger to Himmler, 27 January 1941, here a handwritten note by Himmler. See also the report of the recruitment office of 24 January 1941 (ibid.), and Tönsmeyer, *Reich*, 175 f.

70. Kaiser, 'Politik', 436 f.

71. As he told Himmler on 14 June 1941, with his creation of a cadre within the Hlinka Guard Nageler was aiming to ensure that 'in the event of a change in the form of government he would have a suitable leadership available' (BAB, NS 19/240). On Nageler's ideas and Himmler's sympathy for them see Kaiser, 'Politik', 441.

72. Karmasin proposed to Himmler on 27 February 1941 that the existing volunteer protection squad should be expanded. Himmler replied on 17 March 1941 (BAB, NS 19/1846).

73. Ibid. Berger to Himmler, 12 December 1940. On the background see Kaiser, 'Politik', 436.

74. Lumans, *Auxiliaries*, 219; see also Martin Broszat, 'Heranziehung von slowakischen Staatsbürgern deutscher Volkszugehörigkeit zum Dienst in der Waffen-SS', in *Gutachten des Instituts für Zeitgeschichte*, vol. 1 (Munich, 1958), 412–17.

75. BAB, NS 19/3517, Himmler to Kaul, 30 January 1941.

76. Bernd Rother, *Spanien und der Holocaust* (Tübingen, 2001), 115 f.

77. *Völkischer Beobachter*, 21 October 1940.

78. *Völkischer Beobachter*, 22 October 1940.

79. *Völkischer Beobachter*, 23 October 1940.

80. *Berliner Börsenzeitung*, 23 October 1940.

81. *Völkischer Beobachter*, 23 October 1940. According to another copy of this speech, Himmler dealt with the plans for and figures involved in the mass resettlements that he was carrying out in Poland; among other things, he mentioned that in future 'all the Jews from the whole of the greater German Reich' would be accommodated in a 'closed ghetto' in the General Government. (BAB, R 49/20, published in Müller, *Ostkrieg*, doc. no. 8).

82. *Völkischer Beobachter*, 24 October 1940; *Berliner Börsenzeitung*, 25 October 1940.

83. On the involvement of the SD in the Legionnaires' putsch see Armin Heinen, *Die Legion 'Erzengel Michael' in Rumänien. Soziale Bewegung und politische Organisation. Ein Beitrag zum Problem des internationalen Faschismus* (Munich, 1986), 445; Andreas Hillgruber, *Hitler, König Carol und Marschall Antonescu* (Mainz, 1954), 16 ff.; Höhne, *Orden*, 267 f.; Wildt, *Generation*, 398 ff.

84. *Dienstkalender*.

85. PAA, Inland IIg 61, von Ribbentrop note, 10 March 1941; Heydrich statement, 2 April 1941, above all as a response to the report by von Killinger, the German envoy in Bucharest, who had written on 26 February 1941 that 'the behaviour of some German circles' had contributed to 'the attempted putsch', and then had gone on to name a number of SD representatives in Romania as well as SS members of the embassy (*ADAP*, Series D, vol. 12, no. 94).

86. PAA, Inland IIg 6a, 24 March 1944.

87. See above p. 394.

88. BAB, NS 19/1788, Heydrich to von Weizsäcker, 20 June 1941; Wildt, *Generation*, 649.

89. This was the line taken in the report of the German envoy to the Foreign Ministry, 4 September 1941, in PAA, Inland IIg 100. The office was closed on 23 July 1941 (BAB, R 70 Slowakei 301, Hahn to RSHA). See also Tönsmeyer, *Reich*, 124 f., and Kaiser, 'Politik', 488 ff.

90. USHMM, Acc. 1999.A.0092.

91. BAB, NS 19/1633, Heydrich to Wolff, 5 August 1941. On the course of the negotiations see also PAA, Inland IIg 61, Heydrich to von Weizsäcker, 20 June 1941.

92. BAB, NS 19/1633, agreement of 8 August 1941; Wildt, *Generation*, 649. The agreement contained 'a secret annex', negotiated on 28 August 1941, according to which it was the task of the police attachés to ensure that the agents and representatives of the RFSS refrained from any activity relating to foreign policy. On the same day the Foreign Ministry and the RSHA agreed on a set of 'official instructions' for police attachés (NS 19/1788), which reiterated the subordination of the attachés to the chief of mission. The Foreign Ministry's copy is in PAA, Inland IIg 71. If there was no police attaché at an embassy then ad hoc arrangements should be made for 'another clandestine special representative of the police' to take over the supervision of the RFSS's representatives (ibid. minutes).

93. PAA, Inland IIg 70, list of 5 July 1941.

94. PAA, Inland IIg 71, Luther to the Foreign Ministry's head of personnel, Schröder, 27 February 1942.

95. PAA, Inland IIg 118, circular of 1 August 1941.

96. Ibid. Sonnleithner to Luther, 19 October 1942.

97. Ibid. note for Luther, 19 October 1942.

98. Ibid. Luther to Gaus, 6 November 1942.

99. See the correspondence of May and June 1943 (PAA, Inland IIg 61).

100. Ibid. RAM office note for Wagner, 14 December 1944. See also the instruction to Vortragender Legationsrat Wagner for transmission to the RFSS field headquarters, 31 December 1944.

101. Ibid. note from the head of Inland II.

102. For literature on the Madagascar project see Adler, *Mensch*, 69 ff.; Magnus Brechtken, *'Madagaskar für die Juden'. Antisemitische Idee und politische Praxis 1885–1945* (Munich, 1997) (including comprehensive bibliography of previous publications); Christopher R. Browning, 'The Decision Concerning the Final Solution', in id., *Fateful Months: Essays on the Emergence of the Final Solution* (New York and London, 1985), 8–38, esp. 35 ff.; Hans Jansen, *Der Madagaskar-Plan. Die beabsichtigte Deportation der europäischen Juden nach Madagaskar* (Munich, 1997), esp. 320 ff.; Leni Yahil, 'Madagascar, Phantom of a Solution for the Jewish Question', in Bela Vago and George L. Mosse (eds), *Jews and Non-Jews in Eastern Europe, 1918–1945* (New York, 1974), 315–34.

103. See in detail Brechtken, *'Madagaskar'*.

104. Published in *Vierteljahrshefte für Zeitgeschichte*, 5 (1957), 194–8 (with a short introduction by Krausnick). Himmler further proposed taking 'racially valuable' children away from their Polish parents; while this was 'cruel' and 'tragic', it was preferable to their 'extermination'. The minute of Hitler's response is dated 28 May 1940.

105. Hitler and von Ribbentrop explained their plans to Mussolini and Ciano on 17 and 18 June; on 20 June Hitler mentioned the Madagascar project to Admiral Raeder, the Commander-in-Chief of the navy; at the beginning of August he mentioned the plan of expelling all the Jews from Europe to the German ambassador to France, Abetz, and in the middle of August he commented on it to Goebbels; see Galeazzo Ciano, *Tagebücher 1939–1943* (Bern, 1947), 249; Paul Schmidt, *Statist auf diplomatischer Bühne 1923–1945. Erlebnisse des Chefdolmetschers im auswärtigen Amt mit den Staatsmännern Europas* (Bonn, 1949), 494 f.; Gerhard Wagner (ed.), *Lagevorträge des Oberbefehlshabers der Kriegsmarine vor Hitler 1939–1945* (Munich, 1972), 106 ff.; PAA, Inland IIg 177, Luther note, 15 August 1940, published in *ADAP*, Series D, vol. 10, doc. no. 345; *Tagebücher Goebbels*, 17 August 1940.

106. PAA, Inland IIg 177, The Jewish Question in the Peace Treaties, published in *ADAP*, Series D, vol. 10, 92 ff. See Heydrich's letter of 24 June 1940 in the same file.

107. PAA, Inland IIg 177.

108. Ibid.

109. Ibid. 30 August 1940. Brack is wrongly referred to here as 'Oberbereichsleiter Brake'; his actual title was Oberdienstleiter.

110. Brechtken, *'Madagaskar'*, 261 f. A statement by Bouhler's deputy, Brack, at the Nuremberg doctors' trial, which is not totally reliable, claims that Bouhler was to be governor of Madagascar (ibid. 261).

111. Präg and Jacobmeyer (eds), *Diensttagebuch*, 12 July 1940.

112. Note on the meeting in department IV D 4, 9 July 1940, published in *Biuletyn Głównej Komisji Badania Zbrodni Niemieckich w Polsce*, 12 (1960), doc. no. 38. On 12 June Heydrich and Frank agreed that the major resettlement programme planned in December 1939 would not take place, but the 'current Volhynian operation' and the 'Jewish evacuations planned to begin in August this year' (i.e. the deportation of the Jews from the annexed eastern territories) would go ahead; see Günther (RSHA) telex to Höppner (UWZ Posen), 1 July 1940, published ibid. doc. no. 37.

113. Musial, *Zivilverwaltung*, 115 ff.; Pohl, *Lublin*, 79 ff.

114. Musial, *Zivilverwaltung*, 164 ff.

115. In this context Hitler's Directive no. 18 of 12 November 1940 (securing France and the Iberian countries, with a paragraph on 'Russia') and no. 21 of 18 December 1940 (Operation Barbarossa) are decisive; published in Walther Hubatsch (ed.), *Hitlers Weisungen für die Kriegführung 1939–1945. Dokumente des Oberkommandos der Wehrmacht*, 2nd edn (Koblenz, 1983).

116. On the deportation plans following the collapse of the Madagascar project see Browning, *Entfesselung*, 160 ff.

117. BAB, R 49/20, published in Müller, *Ostkrieg*, no. 8.

118. BAB, NS 19/3979.

119. BAB, NS 19/4007, Himmler's notes for the speech.

120. Note of Theodor Dannecker, appointed as the Gestapo Jewish expert in Paris, to Eichmann, of 21 January, CDJC, V-59, published in Serge Klarsfeld, *Vichy–Auschwitz. Die Zusammenarbeit der deutschen und französischen Behörden bei der "Endlösung der Judenfrage" in Frankreich* (Nördlingen, 1989), 361 ff., who also mentions the involvement of Göring and Himmler. Statement by Eichmann in the Propaganda Ministry, 20 March 1941, published in Adler, *Mensch*, 152; for details see Longerich, *Politik*, 287 f.

121. After a conversation with Hitler on 16 March Frank announced to his colleagues that the General Government would soon be 'dejewified', see Präg and Jacobmeyer (eds), *Diensttagebuch*, 25 March 1941, 335.

122. OA Moscow, 500-3-795, Heydrich note, 26 March 1941; see Aly, *'Endlösung'*, 270.

123. IfZ, NO-203, Brack to Himmler, 28 March 1941. According to a statement by Brack of May 1947, Himmler had given him this assignment in January 1941 because he feared the mixing of Polish and west European Jews (*Trials of War Criminals before the Nuernberg Military Tribunals under Control Council Law No. 10*, vol. 1 (Nuremberg, 1949), 732). Himmler had met Brack on 13 January 1941 (*Dienstkalender*).

CHAPTER 19

1. On the attack on the Soviet Union see, amongst others, Andreas Hillgruber, *Hitlers Strategie. Politik und Kriegführung 1940–1941*, 2nd edn (Frankfurt a. M., 1982); Horst Boog et al., *Der Angriff auf die Sowjetunion*, updated edn. (Frankfurt a. M., 1991); Peter Jahn and Reinhard Rürup (eds), *Erobern und Vernichten. Der Krieg gegen die Sowjetunion 1941–1945. Essays* (Berlin, 1991); Bernd Wegner (ed.), *Zwei Wege nach Moskau. Vom Hitler–Stalin-Pakt bis zum 'Unternehmen Barbarossa'* (Munich and Zurich, 1991); Gerd R. Ueberschär and Wolfram Wette (eds), *Der deutsche Überfall auf die Sowjetunion. 'Unternehmen Barbarossa' 1941*, revised edn. (Frankfurt a. M., 1991).

2. As he wrote in a letter to Lammers of 10 June 1941 (BAB, R 6/21); on this see also Rosenberg's response of 14 June 1941 and the memorandum about the duties and powers of the Reich minister for the occupied eastern territories and of the Reich commissars and on the powers of the Reichsführer-SS, Chief of the German Police, and Reich Commissar for the Consolidation of the Ethnic German Nation, which Rosenberg sent to Lammers on 27 August 1943 (IfZ, NO 3726).

3. BAB, NS 19/3874, 25 May 1941. On Rosenberg's appointment see *'Führer-Erlasse'*, 168 f. On the conflict between Rosenberg and Himmler in the preparatory phase of the war see Ernst Piper, *Alfred Rosenberg. Hitlers Chefideologe* (Munich, 2005), 517 ff.

4. Christian Gerlach, *Kalkulierte Morde. Die deutsche Wirtschafts- und Vernichtungspolitik in Weißrußland 1941 bis 1944* (Hamburg, 1999), 81.

5. Guidelines for special territories for directive no. 21 (Barbarossa), published in Hans-Adolf Jacobsen, 'Kommissarbefehl und Massenexekutionen sowjetischer Kriegsgefangener', in Hans Buchheim *et al.*, *Anatomie des SS-Staates*, 7th edn (Munich, 1999), 449–544, doc. no. 1.

6. Address by Hitler on 30 March to senior generals, published in Halder, *Kriegstagebuch*, vol. 2: *Von der geplanten Landung in England bis zum Beginn des Ostfeldzuges (1.7.1940–21.6.1941)*, 335 ff., here 336 f.

7. Hitler's instructions to Jodl for the final version of the 'Guidelines for Special Territories for Directive no. 21 (Barbarossa)', 3 March 1941, in *Kriegstagebuch des Oberkommandos der Wehrmacht 1940–1945*, by Helmuth Greiner and Percy Ernst Schramm (editors-in-chief), vol. 1: *1. August 1940–31. Dezember 1941* (Frankfurt a. M., 1965), 341. In a speech to generals on 17 March Hitler also spoke of the annihilation of 'the intelligentsia deployed by Stalin'; see Halder, *Kriegstagebuch*, ii. 317 ff., quotation 320. In his speech of 30 March (see n. 6) he spoke of 'annihilating the Bolshevik commissars and the communist intelligentsia'.

8. *Dienstkalender*, 10 March 1941, discussion with Heydrich on the cooperation of SS and police with the army.

9. On 26 March Wagner was in a position to present a first draft order agreed with Heydrich (BAM,RW 4v/575; published in Jacobsen, 'Kommissarbefehl', doc. no. 2).

10. BAM, RH 22/155, published in Jacobsen, 'Kommissarbefehl', doc. no. 3.

11. On the Balkan war see Klaus Olshausen, *Zwischenspiel auf dem Balkan. Die deutsche Politik gegenüber Jugoslawien und Griechenland von März bis Juli 1941* (Stuttgart, 1973); Karl-Heinz Golla, *Der Fall Griechenlands 1941* (Hamburg, etc., 2007).

12. BAM, RH 31-I/v.23; cf. Roland G. Förster (ed.), *'Unternehmen Barbarossa'. Zum historischen Ort der deutsch-sowjetischen Beziehungen von 1933 bis Herbst 1941* (Munich, 1993), 507 f., and also Walter Manoscheck, *'Serbien ist judenfrei'. Militärische Besatzungspolitik und Judenvernichtung in Serbien 1941/42* (Munich, 1993), 41 f.

13. *Dienstkalender*. The negotiations are described in detail in Andrej Angrick, *Besatzungspolitik und Massenmord. Die Einsatzgruppe D in der südlichen Sowjetunion 1941–1943* (Hamburg, 2003), 41 ff.

14. *Dienstkalender*, 6 to 10 May 1941.

15. On the Hess affair see Rainer F. Schmidt, *Rudolf Heß—'Botengang eines Toren?' Der Flug nach Großbritannien vom 10. Mai 1941* (Düsseldorf, 1997), 185 ff.

16. There is no entry in the *Dienstkalender* but there is evidence for the fact that he was present on the Obersalzberg on the evening of the eleventh; he went back to work again in Berlin only on 18 May 1941. On the conference see *Tagebücher Goebbels*, 14 May 1941.

17. On 9 May 1941 he discussed with Heydrich the Gestapo measures demanded by Bormann against these circles (*Dienstkalender*). After the war Ellic Howe, an expert on the astrology scene, collected relevant information: *Urania's Children: The Strange World of Astrologers* (London, 1967), 192 ff.; see also Peter Longerich, *Hitlers Stellvertreter. Führung der Partei und Kontrolle des Staatsapparates durch den Stab Heß und die Partei-Kanzlei Bormann* (Munich, etc., 1992), 153 f.

18. IfZ, NO 204. The Personal Staff thanked Brack for this report on 12 May 1941 and informed him that Himmler wished to speak with him about it very soon.

19. IfZ, NOKW 2079, published in Jacobsen, 'Kommissarbefehl', 184 f.

20. On the setting up of the Einsatzgruppen see Angrick, *Besatzungspolitik*, 74 ff.; Krausnick, 'Einsatzgruppen', 19 ff.; Peter Klein (ed.), *Die Einsatzgruppen in der besetzten Sowjetunion 1941/42. Die Tätigkeits- und Lageberichte des Chefs der Sicherheitspolizei und des SD* (Berlin, 1997); Hans-Heinrich Wilhelm, 'Die Einsatzgruppe A der Sicherheitspolizei und des SD 1941/42—eine exemplarische Studie', in Helmut Krausnick and Hans-Heinrich Wilhelm, *Die Truppe des Weltanschauungskrieges. Die Einsatzgruppen der Sicherheitspolizei und des SD 1938–1942* (Stuttgart, 1981), 281–636; by the same authors, *Die Einsatzgruppe A der Sicherheitspolizei und des SD 1941/42* (Frankfurt a. M., etc., 1996), 11 ff. A fifth Einsatzgruppe was finally set up at the headquarters of Eberhard Schöngarth, the commander of the security police in Cracow, and set out at the beginning of July for the eastern Polish territories; from August it was referred to as 'Einsatzgruppe z.b.V.' (Krausnick, 'Einsatzgruppen', 180 f.).

21. In October 1941 the 990 members of Einsatzgruppe A were composed of the following: 35 SD men, 41 Kripo men, 89 Stapo officials, 133 order police, 340 Waffen-SS; the remaining personnel were heavy-duty vehicle drivers, emergency services staff (who as a rule had not previously been members of the SS or police), telecommunications staff, administrative staff, and 13 female employees (Doc. L-180, Stahlecker report of 15 October 1941, published in *IMT*, vol. 37, pp. 670 ff.).

22. In his biography *Best* Ulrich Herbert elucidated this type by means of an exemplary case.

23. Wilhelm, 'Einsatzgruppe A', 281 ff.

24. For literature on the order police see, for example, Andrej Angrick, '"Da hätte man schon ein Tagebuch führen müssen". Das Polizeibataillon 322 und die Judenmorde im Bereich der Heeresgruppe Mitte während des Sommers und Herbstes 1941. Mit einer Auseinandersetzung über die rechtlichen Konsequenzen', in Helge Grabitz (ed.), *Die Normalität des Verbrechens. Bilanz und Perspektiven der Forschung zu den nationalsozialistischen Gewaltverbrechen. Festschrift für Wolfgang Scheffler zum 65 Geburtstag* (Berlin, 1994), 325–84; Christopher

R. Browning, *Ganz normale Männer. Das Reserve-Polizeibataillon 101 und die 'Endlösung' in Polen* (Reinbek bei Hamburg, 1993); Daniel Jonah Goldhagen, *Hitlers willige Vollstrecker. Ganz gewöhnliche Deutsche und der Holocaust* (Berlin, 1996); Konrad Kwiet, 'Auftakt zum Holocaust. Ein Polizeibataillon im Osteinsatz', in Bundeszentrale für politische Bildung (ed.), *Der Nationalsozialismus* (Frankfurt a. M., 1993), 191–208; Jürgen Matthäus, 'What about the "Ordinary Men"? The German Order Police and the Holocaust in the Occupied Soviet Union', *Holocaust and Genocide Studies*, 10/2 (1996), 134–50; Klaus-Michael Mallmann, 'Vom Fußvolk der "Endlösung". Ordnungspolizei, Ostkrieg und Judenmord', *Tel Aviver Jahrbuch für Deutsche Geschichte*, 26 (1997), 355–91; Neufeld, Huck, and Tessin, *Ordnungspolizei*.

25. These were members of the 'Reinforced Police Protection', composed of those born between 1901 and 1909, the full complement of which at the beginning of the war was supposed to be 95,000 (BAB, R 19/382, address by Daluege, 16 January 1941). At the beginning of 1942, of the 117,525 reservists who had been called up only 7,325 were with the battalions (NS 19/335, Daluege's lecture at the meeting of 1 to 4 February 1942). The total strength of all the battalions ran to just 60 000 men (ibid. memorandum from the chief of the order police, 20 August 1940).

26. The volunteers of the so-called 'operation 26,000 men' were recruited from those born between 1918 and 1920 (police trainees), as well as from the years 1905 to 1912 (recruited as corporals) (BHStA, Reichsstatthalter Epp, decrees from the RFSS of 11 und 31 October 1939, decree from the Reich Minister of the Interior of 25 October 1939). Volunteers were deployed in a total of 31 battalions, in other words, only about half of those recruited from operation 26,000 men (cf. BAB, NS 19/395, memorandum from the chief of the order police, 20 August 1940).

27. Wegner, *Politische Soldaten*, 142 and 149 ff.

28. On this matter see Yehoshua Büchler, 'Kommandostab Reichsführer-SS: Himmler's Personal Murder Brigades in 1941', *Holocaust and Genocide Studies*, 1/1 (1986), 11–25, here 13 f., and also Martin Cüppers, *Wegbereiter der Shoah. Die Waffen-SS, der Kommandostab Reichsführer-SS und die Judenvernichtung 1939–1945* (Darmstadt, 2005), 64 ff.

29. BAB, NS 19/3508, SS Leadership Office, 24 April and 6 May 1941.

30. Ibid. order from Himmler, 17 June, effective on 21 June 1941.

31. These are described in detail in Cüppers, *Wegbereiter*, 33 ff.

32. BAM, M 806 (copies from the Military Archive in Prague), actual strength end of July 1941.

33. BAM, RH 22/155, published in Reinhard Rürup (ed.), *Der Krieg gegen die Sowjetunion 1941–1945. Eine Dokumentation* (Berlin, 1991), 45; on the details of how this arose see Förster, 'Unternehmen Barbarossa', 511; Ralf Ogorreck, *Die Einsatzgruppen und die 'Genesis der Endlösung'* (Berlin, 1996), 19 ff. The accompanying letter from the supreme commander of the army of 24 May 1941

(Disziplinar-Erlass, in Jacobsen, 'Kommissarbefehl', doc. no. 10) took the line of preventing the fighting troops from interpreting this Führer order in too extreme a manner.

34. BAM, RH 2/2082; published in Rürup (ed.), *Krieg*, 46. On the commissar order in general see Förster, *'Unternehmen Barbarossa'*, 520 ff.

35. BAM, RH 22/12. On the conditioning of the troops through propaganda see Förster, *'Unternehmen Barbarossa'*, 525 ff.

36. BAB, NS 19/3957, 11 to 15 June 1941, see *Dienstkalender*.

37. Johst, *Ruf.*

38. Note on the file concerning a conversation with Johst on 26 February 1940 (BAB, NS 19/1446); see Düsterberg, *Johst*, 305.

39. As Rudolf Brandt called him (BAB, NS 19/1945, 10 August 1942).

40. *IMT*, vol. 4, pp. 535 f. Von dem Bach-Zelewski dated the meeting in Nuremberg to the beginning of 1941.

41. This emerges unanimously from the statements of the members of the Einsatzkommandos present.

42. BAB, R 70 SU/32.

43. BAB, R 70 SU/31, published in Peter Longerich (ed.), *Die Ermordung der europäischen Juden. Eine umfassende Dokumentation des Holocaust 1941–1945* (Munich, 1989), 116 ff.

44. This was also how it was put in a letter of 29 June 1941.

45. *Dienstkalender*, 16 and 17 June 1941.

46. On 16, 17, 18, and then again on 23 June 1941 (ibid.).

47. Ibid.; BAB, R 70 SU/32, deployment order no. 1 of 1 July 1941.

48. OA Moscow, 500-1-758, 1 July 1941.

49. EM 19. For the period 23 June 1941 to 24 April 1942 the RSHA compiled reports from the Einsatzgruppen, numbered according to the sequence of days, under the title 'News of events in the USSR'. The originals can be found in R 58/214–21.

50. *Dienstkalender*.

51. BAB, R 20/79, KTB Pol.Btl. 322.

52. Hearing of 20 April 1966 (ZStL, 73/61, vol. 6, pp. 1510 ff).

53. BAB, R 20/79, KTB Pol.Btl. 322, 9 July 1941.

54. BAB, R 20/80, KTB Pol.Btl. 322 (annexes), order of 11 July 1941.

55. Angrick et al., 'Tagebuch', 334 ff.; judgment of the regional court of Bochum against members of the police battalion 316 that also participated in this massacre (LG Bochum, 6 June 1968, ZStL, II 202 AR-Z 168/59).

56. *Dienstkalender;* EM 21.

57. Andrzej Zbikowski, 'Local Anti-Jewish Pogroms in the Occupied Territories of Eastern Poland, June–July 1941', in Lucjan Dobroszycki und Jeffrey S. Gurock (eds), *The Holocaust in the Soviet Union: Studies and Sources on the Destruction of the Jews in the Nazi Occupied Territories of the USSR, 1941–1945* (Armonk, NY, and London, 1993), 173–9, names 35 places for eastern Galicia

alone. Aharon Weiss, 'The Holocaust and the Ukrainian Victims', in Michael Berenbaum (ed.), *A Mosaic of Victims: Non-Jews Persecuted and Murdered by the Nazis* (New York, 1990), 109–15, identifies 58 pogroms in the western Ukraine, including Volhynia. See also Bogdan Musial, *'Konterrevolutionäre Elemente sind zu erschießen'. Die Brutalisierung des deutschsowjetischen Krieges im Sommer 1941* (Berlin and Munich, 2000), 172, with numerous references to further pogroms.

58. BAB, NS 19/4008, speech to the reinforcements for the North unit, 13 July 1941.

59. Set down in the Führer decree on the administration of the newly occupied eastern territories of 17 July 1941 (Doc. L-221, in *IMT*, vol. 38, pp. 86 ff.).

60. BAB, R 43 II/683a. Rosenberg had been designated for this responsibility since Hitler gave him the task at the beginning of April of setting up an 'office' for 'eastern questions'. On Rosenberg's preparations for the war against the Soviet Union see Yitzhak Arad, 'Alfred Rosenberg and the "Final Solution" in the Occupied Soviet Territories', *Yad Vashem Studies*, 13 (1979), 263–86, at 265 ff.

61. Hitler's decisions were laid down in several decrees drawn up on 17 July 1941, among them in particular the decree mentioned in note 59 and also the decree, important in this present connection, concerning the provision of security by the police in the newly occupied eastern territories (IfZ, NG 1688, published in *'Führer-Erlasse'*, no. 99).

62. See note 2.

63. BAB, NS 19/1739.

64. IfZ, NO 4724, RFSS to Lorenz and Heydrich, 11 July 1941.

65. This was how Rosenberg—as confirmation of his own idea—remembered on 9 August something that Göring had said, according to which Himmler was 'tasked exclusively with providing security through the police in this territory' and 'the Reichsführer-SS's responsibilities in relation to the consolidation of the German nation' were 'unequivocally restricted to the German Reich and did not apply to the eastern territories' (BAB R 6/23, note from Rosenberg). See also Müller, *Ostkrieg*, 98.

66. BAB, BDC, SS-O Globocnik, note on the file from Himmler, 21 July 1941.

67. *Tagebücher Goebbels*, 19 August 1941.

68. For details see Longerich, *Davon*, 159 ff.

69. OA Moscow, 500-1-25, copy also in ZStL, Doc. UdSSR, Nr. 401 and published in Klein (ed.), *Einsatzgruppen*, 342. On the Einsatzgruppen reports and their distribution see Ronald Headland, *Messages of Murder: A Study of the Reports of the Einsatzgruppen of the Security Police and the Security Service, 1941–1943* (Rutherford, 1992), and Longerich's summary in *Der ungeschriebene Befehl. Hitler und der Weg zur 'Endlösung'* (Munich and Zurich, 2001), 112.

70. IfZ, NOKW 2079, published in Jacobsen, 'Kommissarbefehl', 184 f. See also YV, M 36/3 (copies from the Military Archive in Prague), minutes of the meeting in the office of the operations officer, which make clear that Himmler

wanted to deploy the Commando Staff troops selectively: 'The units subordinated to the Commando Staff will be deployed in the realm of political administration. Larger companies may be deployed in the rear area. Members of the Commando Staff and of the units subordinated to it have no role to play in the field of operations or in the rear area.'

71. *Dienstkalender*, Cüppers, *Wegbereiter*, 136.
72. KTB Kdostab RFSS, published in *Unsere Ehre heißt Treue. Kriegstagebuch des Kommandostabes Reichsführer-SS, Tätigkeitsberichte der 1. und 2. SS-Infanterie-Brigade, der 1. SS-Kavallerie-Brigade und von Sonderkommandos der SS* (Vienna, 1965), 219 and 30. The Cavalry Brigade was formed on 2 August 1941.
73. *Dienstkalender*, 21 July 1941.
74. Ibid. 29–31 July 1941.
75. OA Moscow, 500-1-25, Jäger's report.
76. EM 96; Wilhelm, *Einsatzgruppe A*, 113.
77. Judgment passed at Ulm, 29 August 1958, published in *Justiz und NS-Verbrechen. Sammlung deutscher Strafurteile wegen nationalsozialistischer Tötungsverbrechen 1945–1966*, vol. 15 (Amsterdam, 1976), no. 465.
78. KTB Kdostab RFSS, 31 July 1933, published in *Unsere Ehre*, 33; BAB, R 20/45b, diary of von dem Bach-Zelewski. See also *Dienstkalender*.
79. KTB Kdostab RFSS, 28 July 1941, published in *Unsere Ehre*, 220 ff.
80. BAM, RS 3-8/36; on the meeting with Himmler see also BAB, R 20/45b, diary of von dem Bach-Zelewski, 31 July 1941.
81. BAM, RS 4/441, Abt.-Befehl Nr. 2; Cüppers, *Wegbereiter*, 143.
82. Cüppers, *Wegbereiter*, 142 ff.
83. BAM, RS 4/441; Cüppers, *Wegbereiter*, 151.
84. Cüppers, *Wegbereiter*, 253 ff. The discrepancies in the figures presumably arose from initial misunderstandings when they were passed on.
85. USHMM, RG-48.004, Reel 2, Box 24, 2nd Cavalry Regiment, mounted detachment, Report of 12 August 1941 (copies from the Military Archive, Prague), published in *Unsere Ehre*, 227 ff.
86. Cüppers, *Wegbereiter*, 194 ff.
87. Ibid. 203. In its final report of 18 September 1941 for both phases of their 'cleansing operation' the brigade notified a total of 14,178 looters shot, 1,001 partisans shot, and 699 members of the Red Army (USHMM, RG 48.004, Reel 2, Box 24).
88. Amongst others with Daluege, Jeckeln, and Knoblauch (*Dienstkalender*, 8, 12, and 13 August 1941).
89. IfZ, NOKW 1165, report of HSSPF South to Army High Command, 1 August 1941, report on cleansing operation. On the 1st Brigade's murders in July and August see Cüppers, *Wegbereiter*, 165 ff., and also Bernd Boll, '"Aktionen nach Kriegausbruch". Wehrmacht und 1. SS-Infanteriebrigade 1941', *Zeitschrift für Geschichtswissenschaft*, 48/9 (2000), 775–88.

90. Report from 1st SS Brigade, 30 July 1941, for 27 to 30 July, in *Unsere Ehre*, 197 ff. See also BAB, NS 33/39, report from 1st SS Brigade, 30 July 1941, on the period 27 to 30 July, and in addition NS 33/22, report on the activities of the Commando Staff RFSS, 6 August 1941, on the period 28 July to 3 August 1941.

91. Report from 1st SS Brigade for the period 3 to 6 August, in *Unsere Ehre*, 108 f.; see also Shmuel Spector, *The Holocaust of Volhynian Jews, 1941–1944* (Jerusalem, 1990), 76 f., for further details, and also Cüppers, *Wegbereiter*, 174, whose estimates have been used here.

92. *Dienstkalender*, BAB, NS 33/320, adjutant to RFSS, 11 August 1941, also NS 33/312, Commando Staff, 12 August 1941. A comparison of the numbers of victims shows that the Cavalry Brigade had already shot a considerably larger number of Jews.

93. Report from 1st SS Brigade of 10 August 1941 for the period 6 to 10 August, in *Unsere Ehre*, 111 ff.; EM 59 of 21 August 1941; NS 33/22, report of Commando Staff of 10 September 1941 on activity 1 to 7 September. On further units see Cüppers, *Wegbereiter*, 203 ff.

94. EM 60; see also NS 33/22, Jeckeln's reports to the Commando Staff, 27 to 30 August 1941.

95. Randolph L. Braham, 'The Kamenets-Podolsk and Délvidék Massacres: Prelude to the Holocaust in Hungary', *Yad Vashem Studies*, 9 (1973), 133–56; Klaus-Michael Mallmann, 'Der qualitative Sprung im Vernichtungsprozess. Das Massaker von Kamenez-Podolsk Ende August 1941', *Jahrbuch für Antisemitismusforschung*, 10 (2001), 239–64.

96. EM 88; see also NS 33/22, telex from HSSPF South, 5 September 1941.

97. EM 106.

98. On the Babi Yar massacre see Krausnick, 'Einsatzgruppen', 189 f.; Hartmut Rüss, 'Wer war verantwortlich für das Massaker von Babij Jar?', *Militärgeschichtliche Mitteilungen*, 57/2 (1998), 483–508; Erhard Roy Wiehn (ed.), *Die Schoáh von Babij Jar. Das Massaker deutscher Sonderkommandos an der jüdischen Bevölkerung von Kiew 1941 fünfzig Jahre danach zum Gedenken* (Konstanz, 1991); Klaus Jochen Arnold, 'Die Eroberung und Behandlung der Stadt Kiew durch die Wehrmacht im September 1941. Zur Radikalisierung der Besatzungspolitik', *Militärgeschichtliche Mitteilungen*, 58/1 (1999), 23–63.

99. On Einsatzgruppe C see Dieter Pohl, 'Schauplatz Ukraine. Der Massenmord an den Juden im Militärverwaltungsgebiet und im Reichskommissariat 1941–1943', in *Ausbeutung, Vernichtung, Öffentlichkeit. Neue Studien zur nationalsozialistischen Lagerpolitik*, ed. Norbert Frei, Sybille Steinbacher, and Bernd C. Wagner for the Institut für Zeitgeschichte (Munich, 2000), 135–73; Pohl, 'Die Einsatzgruppe C 1941/42', in Peter Klein (ed.), *Die Einsatzgruppen in der besetzten Sowjetunion 1941/42. Die Tätigkeits- und Lageberichte des Chefs der Sicherheitspolizei und des SD* (Berlin, 1997), 71–87. On the individual units there is the following information: Einsatzkommando 5 shot all inhabitants of one place, including women and children, for the first time in the middle of

September and then continued this practice (EM 119 of 20 October 1940: Bogusslaw, Uman, Cybulow, and others). In the Shitomir area Kommando 4a had been shooting women in large numbers, and very soon after children as well, from the beginning of August (ZStL, judgment of the regional court at Darmstadt, 29 November 1968). Police battalion 45, which belonged to the police regiment South began shooting Jews indiscriminately at the end of July/beginning of August (ZStL, II 204 AR-Z 1251/65, indictment and judgment). The commander, Besser, stated he had been acting in accordance with an order from the commander of the police regiment South, who in issuing the command had in turn referred to a general command from Himmler to liquidate (ibid. indictment). It can be verified that police battalion 314, also part of police regiment South, had been shooting women and children since 22 July (ZStL, 204 AR-Z 1251/65 D, note at the end of the file by the Bavarian State Criminal Police, 19 December 1977. In addition BAB, NS 33/22, telex from HSSPF South, 21, 24, und 27 August with reports of shootings carried out by battalion 314).

100. *Dienstkalender.*
101. Ibid.; on this journey see also in particular Gerlach, *Morde*, 571 ff.
102. Klaus Hesse, '"... Gefangenenlager, Exekution,... Irrenanstalt...". Walter Frentz' Reise nach Minsk im Gefolge Heinrich Himmlers im August 1941', in Hans Georg Hiller von Gaertringen (ed.), *Das Auge des Dritten Reiches. Hitlers Kameramann und Fotograf Walter Frentz* (Munich and Berlin, 2006), 176–94.
103. Paul D., testimony of 8 January 1963, ZStl 208 AR-Z 203/59, red file, Z-Prot. II, vol. 3, Quoted after Riess, *Anfänge*, 275 f. Riess rightly rejects all assertions as unproven that Himmler felt ill at this shooting and that this personal experience was responsible for the introduction of gassing vehicles in the east.
104. ZStL, 201 AR-Z 76/59, 8 October 1971, vol. 11, pp. 7605 ff.
105. Gerlach, *Morde*, 572 f. According to Gerlach the relevant testimony of von dem Bach-Zelewski provides no evidence that Himmler alluded to the murder of all Jews in his speech.
106. *Dienstkalender,* 15 August 1941.
107. Ibid.; BAB, BDC, SS-O Pflaum, letter to Himmler of 11 July 1941 and Pflaum's note of 25 August 1941.
108. BAB, R 6/23, Himmler to Rosenberg, 19 August 1941, also Rosenberg to Lammers, 23 August 1941.
109. Heinemann, *'Rasse'*, 420 f.
110. *Dienstkalender.*
111. OA Moscow, 1323-1-53, and BAB, R 43 II/684a, Lammers to Rosenberg re Himmler's spheres of responsibility, 6 September 1941.
112. In a discussion on 22 October Himmler and Lammers agreed for the time being not to approach Hitler concerning this matter, though in Lammers's view that would be necessary if the matter were to be pursued (BAB, R 43 II/

396, Heydrich to Lammers, 18 September 1941, and also Lammers's note of 23 October 1941, published in *Deutsche Politik im 'Protektorat Böhmen und Mähren' unter Reinhard Heydrich 1941–1942. Eine Dokumentation*, ed. Miroslav Kárny', Jaroslava Milotová, und Margita Kárná (Berlin, 1997), 82 ff. and 132; see also *Dienstkalender*, 22 October 1941. On 14 and 15 October Rosenberg complained again about SS and police attempts to extend their powers in the Soviet territories (BAB, R 43 II/684a, Lammers's notes of 23 and 28 October 1941). The consequence was the discussion between Himmler and Rosenberg of 15 November 1941, about which Himmler informed Lammers on 25 November 1941 (see below p. 538).

113. BAB, NS 19/1734.

114. BAB, R 6/9, note from HSSPF Ostland, 17 February 1942.

115. *Dienstkalender.*

116. Ibid.

117. Ibid.; PRO, HW 16/32, Himmler to HSSPF Koppe, Posen.

118. *Dienstkalender* and also BAB, NS 19/3957, itinerary on which Cherson is noted.

119. ZStL, 213AR 1898/66, indictment of 8 March 1966. See also IfZ,NOKW 3233, report on the activity of Sonderkommando 11a in Nikolajev, 18–31 August 1941; cf. Angrick, *Besatzungspolitik*, 241 ff.

120. *Dienstkalender*, 4. October 1941; what Himmler said emerges from a post-war testimony of the former head of Einsatzkommando 11a, Paul Zapp, who reports on it.

121. StAnw München, 118 Ks 268, indictment of 8 March 1966; BAM, RH 20-11/488, report on the activity of Sonderkommando 11a in Cherson, 22 August to 10 September 1941. See Angrick, *Besatzungspolitik*, 251 ff.

122. BAB, R 6/34a, published in Werner Koeppen, *Herbst 1941 im 'Führerhauptquartier'. Berichte Werner Koeppens an seinen Minister Alfred Rosenberg*, ed. and with a commentary by Martin Vogt (Koblenz, 2002), 59.

123. *Dienstkalender.*

124. Ibid.

125. Ibid.; Christian Gerlach, 'Failure of Plans for an SS Extermination Camp in Mogilev, Belorussia', *Holocaust and Genocide Studies*, 11/1 (1997), 60–78.

126. *Dienstkalender.*

127. Ibid.

128. Hitler, *Monologe*, 25 October 1941.

129. BAB, R 6/9, joint instruction from Himmler und Rosenberg, 19 November 1941.

130. BAB, R 43 II/684a.

131. BAB, NS 19/3885, note on the file from Himmler, 15 November 1941; R 6/9, note from Rosenberg, 19 November 1941. On the meeting with Hitler, attended also by Bouhler, see *Dienstkalender*. See also Piper, *Rosenberg*, 587. Three days previously Himmler had also, though unsuccessfully, tried to get

himself acknowledged by the party as having sole responsibility for the 'consolidation of the German nation'. He was, however, obliged to make do with an 'Office for National Identity (*Volkstum*)' (*Dienstkalender*, 13 November 1941).

132. BAB, NS 19/4010, published in Himmler, *Geheimreden*, 162 ff., quotation 169.
133. BAB, NS 19/4014, published in Himmler, *Geheimreden*, 203.

CHAPTER 20

1. The hypothesis that as early as the summer of 1941 the regime had taken a fundamental decision systematically to murder all European Jews and had drawn up relevant plans is no longer tenable, however (details can be found in Longerich, *Politik*, 421 ff.) Thus Richard Breitman's thesis that at the end of August, a few weeks after Heydrich's 'authorization' by Göring, Himmler had approved a completed 'plan' by Heydrich for the murder of the European Jews by gassing rests on an error: the entry in the diary kept by Himmler's private secretaries for 26 August 1941, on which Breitman's argument is based, in fact refers to the approval of a 'travel plan' by Heydrich, who intended to fly to Norway (Breitman, *Architekt*, 262 and 272; *Dienstkalender*, 26 August 1941). In addition, the testimony of the Auschwitz commandant Rudolf Höss that some time in 'summer 1941' he had been summoned to Himmler and told in confidence that Hitler had 'ordered the final solution to the Jewish question' and that he, Himmler, had identified Auschwitz for this, cannot be quite accurate, as the 'existing annihilation locations in the east', of which, according to Höss's recollection, Himmler spoke, at this point did not yet exist. If this interview took place at all a date of 1942 appears more plausible, the more so because in his post-war testimonies Höss frequently confused these two years (Rudolf Höss, *Kommandant in Auschwitz. Autobiographische Aufzeichnungen*, with an introduction and commentary by Martin Broszat (Stuttgart, 1958), 157 ff.; see also his corroborating statement of 14 April 1946 in *IMT*, vol. 11, pp. 438–66).
2. Longerich, *Politik*, 427.
3. Wolf Gruner draws attention to this: 'Von der Kollektivausweisung zur Deportation der Juden aus Deutschland (1938–1945). Neue Perspektiven und Dokumente', *Beiträge zur Geschichte des Nationalsozialismus*, 20 (2004), 21–62, at 48. On the sources see the details in the *Dienstkalender*, 2 and 4 September 1941. The editors point to the fact that Koppe's letter of 10 September is not preserved but that what it refers to can be reconstructed from the record of correspondence kept by the Personal Staff.
4. Otto Bräutigam, 'Aus dem Kriegstagebuch des Diplomaten Otto Bräutigam', with an introduction and commentary by H. D.Heilmann, *Beiträge zur nationalsozialistischen Gesundheits und Sozialpolitik*, 4 (1989), 123–87, 14 September

1941. Bräutigam was Rosenberg's liaison with the Wehrmacht High Command.

5. *Dienstkalender*. The author of this suggestion, Carltheo Zeitschel, had already formulated it in August (CDJC, V-821.8.41, published in Klarsfeld, *Vichy*, 367). Zeitschel informed Dannecker, the Gestapo officer for Jewish matters in Paris, about the meeting of Himmler and Abetz on 8 October (CDJC, V-16; published in Serge Klarsfeld, *Die Endlösung der Judenfrage in Frankreich* (Paris 1977), 25).

6. *Dienstkalender; ADAP*, Series D, vol. 13, 2, no. 327, 16 September 1941.

7. BAB, NS 19/2655, published in Longerich, *Ermordung*, 157.

8. BAB, R 6/34, Koeppen-Aufzeichnungen, 21 September 1941, published in Koeppen, *Herbst 1941*, 34 f. Koeppen had this information from the diplomat Gustav Adolf Steengracht, who belonged to Ribbentrop's Personal Staff. It is possible that at this point Steengracht was not yet aware of Hitler's decision to deport the Jews.

9. Goebbels gave the instruction that if correspondents asked questions they should be told that the Jews were being sent to the east 'to work' (NS 18 alt/622, minutes of the propaganda conference, 23 October 1941). On the details see Longerich, *Davon*, 182 f.

10. See for example the *Neue Zürcher Zeitung* of 20 October 1941, which published a UPI report on 18 October about the deportations from the Rhineland and Berlin. The *New York Times* had already carried a report on 18 October 1941 with further details about the situation of the Berlin Jews. On 22 October the *Neue Zürcher Zeitung*, on the basis of a UPI report of 20 October, wrote that the deportations were continuing and that a total of 20,000 people were affected.

11. Longerich, *Politik*, 427 ff.

12. Longerich, *Davon*, 199 f.

13. On 4 October Heydrich spoke of the 'plan to resettle all Jews outside Europe', referring on 6 October to a statement 'from the highest level' that 'Jewry' had 'to disappear from Europe once and for all' (BAB, NS 19/1734, at a meeting with representatives from the Ministry for the East and also CDJC, I 28, published in Klarsfeld, *Vichy*, 369 f., letter to the army Quartermaster-General). See also Longerich, *Befehl*, 188 ff.

14. Manoschek, *'Serbien'*, 43 ff.

15. Ahlrich Meyer, '"... daß französische Verhältnisse anders sind als polnische". Die Bekämpfung des Widerstands durch die deutsche Militärverwaltung in Frankreich 1941', in Guus Meershoek *et al.*, *Repression und Kriegsverbrechen. Die Bekämpfung von Widerstands- und Partisanenbewegungen gegen die deutsche Besatzung in West und Südosteuropa* (Berlin and Göttingen, 1997), 43–91; Weber, *Sicherheit*, 59 ff.; *Die Okkupationspolitik des deutschen Faschismus in Dänemark und Norwegen (1940–1945)*, documents selected and with an introduction by Fritz Petrick (Berlin and Heidelberg, 1992), 33.

16. Bohn, *Reichskommissariat*, 92 f. and 95 f., based on documents in the Norwegian state archive.

17. Meershoek, 'Machtentfaltung', 391.

18. Communist uprising in the occupied territories, 16 September 1941, published in *Kriegstagebuch des Oberkommandos der Wehrmacht*, vol. 1, doc. no. 101. On 28 September Keitel modified the order: now hostages from nationalist and democratic-bourgeois circles could be shot (doc. PS-1590, in *IMT*, vol. 27, pp. 373 f.).

19. Brandes, *Tschechen*, i. 207 ff.

20. Peter Klein, 'Die Rolle der Vernichtungslager Kulmhof (Chełmno), Belzec (Bełżec) und Auschwitz-Birkenau in den frühen Deportationsvorbereitungen', in Dittmar Dahlmann (ed.), *Lager, Zwangsarbeit, Vertreibung und Deportation. Dimensionen der Massenverbrechen in der Sowjetunion und in Deutschland 1933 bis 1945* (Essen, 1999),459–81, on 473.

21. A record of this meeting was made by Hitler's army adjutant Gerhard Engel: IfZ, ED 53/1, the so-called Engel Diary, which are in fact handwritten notes by Engel from the post-war period, presumably based on contemporary notes, 2 November 1941; in Gerhard Engel, *Heeresadjutant bei Hitler 1938–1943. Aufzeichnungen des Majors Engel*, ed. and with a commentary by Hildegard von Kotze (Stuttgart, 1975), 111, wrongly dated (2 October 1941) and at two points wrongly transcribed. Because of the incorrect transcription Engel's report has up to now been rejected in all the research literature, as Himmler was demonstrably not in the headquarters on 2 October. An entry in the *Dienstkalender* for 2 November does, however, confirm a meeting between Himmler and Hitler on 2 November 1941. Heydrich, Jodl, and Keitel were also present.

22. See below p. 663.

23. Manoschek, *'Serbien'*, 55 ff.

24. Ulrich Herbert, 'Die deutsche Militärverwaltung in Paris und die Deportation derfranzösischen Juden', in Christian Jansen (ed.), *Von der Aufgabe der Freiheit. Politische Verantwortung und bürgerliche Gesellschaft im 19. und 20. Jahrhundert. Festschrift für Hans Mommsen zum 5. November 1995* (Berlin, 1995), 427–50, at 437 ff.

25. BAB, NS 19/2655 11 October 1941, and also Himmler's reply of 22 October 1941.

26. Ibid. Uebelhoer to Himmler, 4 and 9 October 1941, Heydrich to Himmler,8 October 1941, Himmler to Uebelhoer and Greiser, 10 and 11 October 1941; further material on the matter can be found in the same file.

27. Ibid. 4 October 1941.

28. This emerges from a letter from Greiser to Himmler of 1 May 1942, in which he informed him that the 'special treatment operation approved by you in consultation with the Chief of the Reich Security Main Office, SS Obergruppenführer Heydrich, for around 100,000 Jews in my Gau' could be 'completed

in the next 2 to 3 months' (*Faschismus, Ghetto, Massenmord*, 278). Evidence that there was a target of 100,000 Jews, 'incapable of work' and thus to be murdered, can also be found in another document of January 1942: see YVA, 051/13b, communications interception report by the Research Office of 16 January 1942. See also Klein, 'Rolle', 474.

29. BAB, 19/2655, Heydrich to Himmler, 8 October 1941.

30. BAB, R 6/34 a, reports by Werner Koeppen, Rosenberg's permanent deputy at Hitler's HQ, published in *Herbst 1941*. According to Hitler, the Jews were not to be deported first to the General Government but sent 'on to the east right away'; he admitted that through lack of transport this was not possible at that time.

31. YVA, M 58/23 (copy from the State Central Archive, Prague, 114-2-56), published in *Deutsche Politik im 'Protektorat'*, doc. no. 29.

32. By this Heydrich may well have meant camps for civilian prisoners such as existed, for example, in Minsk and Mogilew (cf. Gerlach, 'Failure', 62).

33. Präg und Jacobmeyer (eds), *Diensttagebuch*, 14 October 1941.

34. At the meeting in Lublin on 17 October the Third Ordinance Concerning Residence Restrictions in the General Government was discussed, in which the death penalty was introduced for anyone leaving the ghetto (ibid. esp. 427 f. The ordinance was backdated to 15 October, see *Faschismus, Ghetto, Massenmord*, 128 f.). At the government meeting on 20 October in Cracow the Distict Governor Otto Wächter explained that, 'in the end a radical solution to the Jewish question is unavoidable, and that at that point no allowances—for example for interests linked to particular craftsmen—could be made (IfZ, MA 120, shortened version in Präg und Jacobmeyer (ed.), *Diensttagebuch*, 436). At the 21 October meeting in Lemberg Eberhard Westerkamp, head of the Main Department for Administration of the Interior in the government of the General Government, demanded that the 'isolation of the Jews from the rest of the population' should be carried out 'quickly and as thoroughly as possible'. Westerkamp also referred to the fact, however, that a 'decree from the government forbids the creation of new ghettos, as it is hoped that in the near future the Jews will be deported from the General Government', even though a few days before this Rosenberg had described this 'hope' as illusory (MA 120, shortened version in Präg und Jacobmeyer (ed.), *Diensttagebuch*, 436). See also statements made by Jost Walbaum, the head of the Health Main Office in the government of the General Government, at a conference of doctors that took place in Bad Krynica between 13 and 16 October: 'There are only two paths: either we condemn the Jews to starve to death in the ghetto or we shoot them' (ZStL, Poland 98, conference report).

35. Dieter Pohl, *Nationalsozialistische Judenverfolgung in Ostgalizien 1941–1944. Organisation und Durchführung eines staatlichen Massenverbrechen* (Vienna, 1996), 140 ff. An 'intelligentsia operation' typical of this phase took place in Stanislau on 3 August, when 600 men were shot (IfZ, Gm 08.08, 5 Ks 4/65, judgment of the

regional court of Münster, 31 May 1968). On these first murders see also Thomas Sandkühler, 'Endlösung' in Galizien. Der Judenmord in Ostpolen und die Rettungsinitiativen von Berthold Beitz 1941–1944 (Bonn, 1996), 148 ff.

36. For details see Pohl, Ostgalizien, 138 ff.

37. Dienstkalender.

38. BAB, BDC, SS-O Globocnik, letter to Himmler of 1 October 1941. See also Pohl, Lublin, 101.

39. This view is also taken by the editors of the Dienstkalender, 233, note 35. The fact that a decisive 'breakthrough' was achieved is made clear by a letter that a colleague of Globocnik, Hauptsturmführer Hellmuth Müller, sent on 15 October 1941 to Hofmann, the head of RuSHA, which reflects the state of affairs before the decisive meeting between Himmler and Globocnik two days previously (Globocnik went first to Berlin on 14 October, see Dienstkalender). Müller stated that Globocnik regarded 'the political circumstances in the GG in principle as a transitional phase'; he saw 'the gradual cleansing of the whole GG and Poland from Jews as necessary for the purpose of providing security etc. in the eastern territories', and was 'full of extensive and good plans in connection with this, the implementation of which was hampered merely by the limits to his authority in these matters imposed by his present post'. After Globocnik's journey to the Reich, however, this was to change fundamentally (BAB, BDC, SS-O Globocnik).

40. ZStL, 208 AR-Z 252/59, vol. 6, p. 1179, testimony of Stanislaw Kozak on the beginning of building work (1 November), published in Nationalsozialistische Massentötungen, 152 f.; Michael Tregenza, 'Belzec Death Camp', Wiener Library Bulletin, 30 (1977), 8–25, confirms this date.

41. Pohl, Lublin, 101 and 105 f.

42. Dienstkalender, 20 October 1941. The editors quote from a declaration from Mach of 26 March 1942 before the Slovakian State Council from which one can infer the German offer.

43. Klein, 'Rolle', 478, has already pointed this out. There are indications, though they are uncorroborated, that the building of Sobibor was already being prepared at the end of 1941 (ZStL, doc. 643, 71-4-442, testimony of the Polish railway worker Piwonski from 1975); cf. Jules Schelvis, Vernichtungslager Sobibór (Berlin, 1998), 37; Browning, Entfesselung, 525. Whether the building-works described were actually planned as an extermination camp cannot be established beyond doubt.

44. These instructions were reconstructed on the basis of witness testimony, see Beer, 'Entwicklung', 407; regional court in Munich, judgment against Karl Wolff, 30 September1964, published in Justiz und NS-Verbrechen, vol. 20, no. 580, here pp. 434 ff.; Dienstkalender, 15 August 1941.

45. Gerlach, Morde, 648; PRO, HW 16/32, 16 and 18 August 1941.

46. Beer, 'Entwicklung', 408; 'Die Ermordung psychisch kranker Menschen in der Sowjetunion. Dokumentation', compiled and translated by Angelika

Ebbinghaus and Gerd Preissler, *Beiträge zur nationalsozialistischen Gesundheits- und Sozialpolitik*, 1 (1985), 75–107, on 83 ff.; Gerlach, *Morde*, 648.

47. Beer, 'Entwicklung', 408; 'Ermordung', 88 ff.; ZStL, 202 ARZ 152/159, testimony of Widmann, 11 January 1960, 33 ff. In addition, see the testimony of Georg Frentzel, 27 August 1970, and also Alexander N. Stepanow (at that time consultant in charge of the psychiatric hospital in Mogilew), 20 July 1944, both in a file (Central investigation 9 in the investigative files of the GDR Ministry of State Security) that I read in 1997 at the Department of Public Prosecutions in Munich.

48. Before Christmas 1941 further vehicles were driven from Berlin to Riga to Einsatzgruppe A; see Beer, 'Entwicklung', 413. On Sonderkommando 4a (Einsatzgruppe C) see ibid. 412. On Einsatzkommando 8 (Einsatzgruppe B) see Department of Public Prosecutions in Munich, central investigation 9 in the investigative files of the GDR Ministry of State Security, testimony of Otto Matonoga, 8–9 June 1945, to Soviet investigators. According to the testimony of a witness, Einsatzgruppe D used a gas van at the end of 1941; see Beer, 'Entwicklung', 413; regional court in Munich, 119 c Js 1/69, judgment; testimony of Jeckeln of 21 December 1945 (published in Wilhelm, 'Einsatzgruppe A', 548).

49. Alfred Gottwaldt and Diana Schulle, *Die 'Judendeportationen' aus dem Deutschen Reich 1941–1945. Eine kommentierte Chronologie* (Wiesbaden, 2005), 52 ff. Among the older research publications on the deportations from Germany, in addition to the indispensable study by Adler, *Mensch*, see in particular the contributions of Ino Arndt and Heinz Boberach on the Third Reich, of Ino Arndt on Luxembourg, of Jonny Moser on Austria, and of Eva Schmidt-Hartmann on Czechoslovakia, which are all in the volume edited by Wolfgang Benz, *Dimension des Völkermords. Die Zahl der jüdischen Opfer des Nationalsozialismus* (Munich, 1991). On the deportations to Riga see above all Buch der Erinnerung. *Die ins Baltikum deportierten deutschen, österreichischen und tschechoslowakischen Juden*, ed. Wolfgang Scheffler and Diana Schulle, 2 vols. (Munich, 2003); Gottwaldt and Schulle, 'Judendeportationen', 110 ff. On the deportation of the Gypsies of the Burgenland see Zimmermann, *Rassenutopie*, 223 ff.

50. *Nationalsozialistische Massentötungen*, 110 ff.

51. Regional court in Bonn, judgment of 23 July 1965, published in *Justiz und NS-Verbrechen*, vol. 21, no. 594; *Nationalsozialistische Massentötungen*, 110 ff.

52. IfZ, NO 365, also published in Helmut Krausnick, 'Judenverfolgung', in Hans Buchheim *et al.*, *Anatomie des SS-Staates*, 7th edn. (Munich, 1999), 545–678, here 649 f.

53. Andrej Angrick and Peter Klein, *Die 'Endlösung' in Riga. Ausbeutung und Vernichtung 1941–1944* (Darmstadt, 2006), 338 ff.

54. See above p. 547.

55. Patricia Heberer, 'Eine Kontinuität der Tötungsoperationen. T4-Täter und die "Aktion Reinhardt"', in Bogdan Musial (ed.), *'Aktion Reinhardt'. Der Völk-*

ermord an den Juden im Generalgouvernement 1941–1944 (Osnabrück, 2004), 285–308, at 295. The *Dienstkalender* for 14 December 1941 provides evidence of the meeting between Himmler and Brack, the word 'euthanasia' being noted in the entry. See also Brack's letter to Himmler, 23 June 1942, in which he declares himself willing to provide more staff and reminds Himmler of their earlier agreement (BAB, NS 19/1583).

56. Jean-Claude Pressac, *Die Krematorien von Auschwitz. Die Technik des Massenmordes* (Munich and Zurich, 1994), 19.

57. Stanislaw Klodzinski, 'Die erste Vergasung von Häftlingen und Kriegsgefangenen im Konzentrationslager Auschwitz', in *Die Auschwitz-Hefte*, ed. Hamburg Institute for Social Research (Weinheim and Basel, 1987), i. 261–75; Danuta Czech, *Kalendariumder Ereignisse im Konzentrationslager Auschwitz-Birkenau 1939–1945* (Reinbek bei Hamburg, 1989), 115 ff.; Jerzy Brandhuber, 'Die sowjetischen Kriegsgefangenen im Konzentrationslager Auschwitz', *Hefte von Auschwitz*, 4 (1961), 5–46, and Wojciech Barcz, 'Die erste Vergasung', in Hans G. Adler, *Auschwitz: Zeugnisse und Berichte*, 2nd edn. (Cologne and Frankfurt a. M., 1979), 17 f.

58. See Browning, *Entfesselung*, 13; Steinbacher, *'Musterstadt'*, 276 f.

59. See Aly, *'Endlösung'*, 342 ff.; Gerlach, 'Failure'.

60. Himmler expressed this intention in his letter to Greiser of 18 September 1941 (see above p. 542 f.).

61. This can be inferred from a note that Goebbels made about a discussion with Heydrich on 17 November (*Tagebücher Goebbels*, 18 November 1941).

62. This is clear from Leibrandt's message to Lohse of 4 December 1941, according to which Heydrich now intended to construct this camp near Pleskow (YIVO, Occ E 3–35, published in Gertrude Schneider, *Journey into Terror: Story of the Riga Ghetto*, new extended edn. (Newport, Conn., and London, 2001), 130).

63. IfZ, Fb 101/29, Jäger-Bericht. See Wolfgang Scheffler, 'Massenmord in Kowno', in *Buch der Erinnerung. Die ins Baltikum deportierten deutschen, österreichischen und tschechoslowakischen Juden*, ed. Scheffler and Diana Schulle, vol. 1 (Munich, 2003), 83–190.

64. Gerald Fleming, *Hitler und die Endlösung. 'Es ist des Führers Wunsch . . . '* (Wiesbaden and Munich, 1982), 87 ff.; EM 151 of 5 January 1942.

65. Testimony of 15 December 1945 to Soviet investigators, published in Wilhelm, 'Einsatzgruppe A', 566 f.

66. Published in *Dienstkalender*. The time was 13.30.

67. Angrick und Klein, *'Endlösung'*, 239 ff. The Jews arriving in the next 22 transports were as a rule brought to the Riga ghetto or to the two camps in Salaspils and Junfernhof. There were presumably two exceptions: the majority of the passengers on a transport of 19 January 1942 and a further 500 Jews from a transport at the end of January were evidently shot immediately after arrival.

68. *Dienstkalender*, 30 November and 4 December 1941; PRO, HW 16/32, telegrams from Himmler to Jeckeln, 1 and 4 December 1941.

69. Hitler, *Monologe*, 25 October 1941.
70. Draft of speech, cited in Hans-Heinrich Wilhelm, *Rassenpolitik und Kriegführung. Sicherheitspolizei und Wehrmacht in Polen und in der Sowjetunion 1939–1942* (Passau, 1991), 131 f., after PAA, Pol XIII, 25, VAA-Berichte; cf. notes by a press reporter, published in Hagemann, *Presselenkung*, 146.
71. Breitman, *Architekt*, 288 f.; BAB, R 43 II/684a, Brandt to Lammers, forwarding Himmler's notes for the file on the discussion, 25 November 1941.
72. *Dienstkalender*; Hitler, *Reden und Proklamationen* [Domarus], ii. 1794 ff.
73. *Tagebücher Goebbels*, 13 December 1941.
74. As Christian Gerlach argues, 'Die Wannsee-Konferenz, das Schicksal der deutschen Juden und Hitlers politische Grundentscheidung, alle Juden Europas zu ermorden', *Werkstatt Geschichte*, 6/18 (1997), 7–44.
75. *Dienstkalender*. According to Gerlach, 'Wannsee-Konferenz', 22 and 27, the expression 'partisan' refers to all European Jews; on the basis of his 'policy decision' of 12 December to murder the European Jews Hitler, he maintains, had therefore instructed Himmler in his new task. There is not sufficient evidence for this thesis: the contemporary use of the expression 'partisan' does not support it, nor does the casual manner in which this point is mentioned in Himmler's list of things to discuss.

CHAPTER 21

1. For all these dates see *Dienstkalender*.
2. PAA, Inland IIg 177, Heydrich to Luther, 29 November 1941; the meeting on 8 December 1941 was cancelled. On the Wannsee conference see Gerlach, 'Wannsee-Konferenz'; Eberhard Jäckel, 'On the Purpose of the Wannsee Conference', in James S. Pacy (ed.), *Perspectives on the Holocaust: Essays in Honor of Raul Hilberg* (Boulder, Colo., etc., 1995), 39–50; Peter Klein, *Die Wannsee-Konferenz vom 20. Januar 1942. Analyse und Dokumentation* (Berlin, [1995]); Peter Longerich, *Die Wannsee-Konferenz vom 20. Januar 1942. Planung und Beginn des Genozids an den europäischen Juden*, public lecture delivered at the Haus der Wannsee-Konferenz on 19 January 1998, with the addition of an annotated select bibliography on the Wannsee conference and the beginning of the genocide of the European Jews, with a facsimile of the conference minutes (Berlin, 1998); Kurt Pätzold and Erika Schwarz, *Tagesordnung: Judenmord. Die Wannsee-Konferenz am 20. Januar 1942. Eine Dokumentation zur Organisation der 'Endlösung'*, 3rd edn. (Berlin, 1992); Safrian, *Eichmann-Männer*, 171 ff.
3. See in particular Cornelia Essner, *Die 'Nürnberger Gesetze' oder die Verwaltung des Rassenwahns 1933–1945* (Paderborn, etc., 2002), 410 ff.; Jeremy Noakes, 'The Development of Nazi Policy towards the German-Jewish "Mischlinge", 1933–1945', *Leo Baeck Institute Year Book*, 34 (1989), 291–354; John A. S. Grenville, 'Die "Endlösung" und die "Judenmischlinge" im Dritten Reich',

in *Das Unrechtsregime. Internationale Forschung über den Nationalsozialismus*, ed. Ursula Büttner assisted by Werner Johe and Angelika Voss, vol. 2: *Verfolgung, Exil, belasteter Neubeginn* (Hamburg, 1986), 91–121.

4. PAA, Inland IIg 177, conference minutes.

5. Ibid. copy no. 16 of the minutes, published in Longerich, ed., *Ermordung*, 83 ff.

6. That at this stage deportation to the occupied Soviet territories really was still a serious option is shown not only by the forced-labour projects developed at the same time (which will be discussed in the next chapter) but is made clear also by the fact that on 12 January, only a few days before the Wannsee conference, the HSSPF Ukraine instructed the general commissars in Brest, Shitomir, Nikolajev, Dnjepropetrovsk, und Kiev to begin immediately to construct ghettos, so that 'in the course of 1942 Jews from the old Reich' could 'be accommodated' (Staatsarchiv Shitomir, P 1151-1-137). I am grateful to Wendy Lower for making me aware of this document.

7. Präg and Jacobmeyer (eds), *Diensttagebuch*, 16 December 1941.

8. 'We cannot shoot these 3.5 million Jews, nor can we poison them' (ibid.).

9. PAA, Inland IIg 177, copy of the minutes no. 16, published in Longerich (ed.), *Ermordung*, 83 ff.

10. Cf. Kaienburg, *'Vernichtung'*, 144 ff.; Schulte, *Zwangsarbeit*, 332 ff.

11. Schulte, *Zwangsarbeit*, 334 ff.

12. Ibid. 351 ff.; Christian Streit, *Keine Kameraden. Die Wehrmacht und die sowjetischen Kriegsgefangenen 1941–1945* (Bonn, 1997), 212 f.

13. Schulte, *Zwangsarbeit*, 208 f.

14. IfZ, NI 11086; Schulte, *Zwangsarbeit*, 209 f. On the Buna plant see Wagner, *IG Auschwitz*; Gottfried Plumpe, *Die I.G. Farbenindustrie AG. Wirtschaft, Technik und Politik 1904–1945* (Berlin, 1990), 382 ff.

15. Schulte, *Zwangsarbeit*, 211; Hans Mommsen and Manfred Grieger, *Das Volkswagenwerk und seine Arbeiter im Dritten Reich* (Düsseldorf, 1996), 496 ff.; Hitler's order is published in Klaus-Jörg Siegfried (ed.), *Rüstungsproduktion und Zwangsarbeit im Volkswagenwerk 1939–1945. Eine Dokumentation* (Frankfurt a. M., 1986), 61.

16. BAB, NS 19/2065; see also Schulte, *Zwangsarbeit*, 343 f.

17. *Faschismus, Ghetto, Massenmord*, 268. On this decision and its consequences see in particular Allen, *Business*, 48 ff., and also Schulte, *Zwangsarbeit*, 361. The day before this Himmler had given Heydrich the task of getting 'Jews into the concentration camps' (*Dienstkalender*, 25 January 1942). The decision to deport Jews en masse to the concentration camps and use them as slave labour was probably made at Himmler's meeting with the heads of the SS Main Offices on 14–15 January. A few days after this conference Pohl issued the order in Himmler's name to expand the Business and Administration Main Office (IfZ, NO 495). On 17 January 1942 the following telex was sent from the Reich Minister for the Occupied Eastern Territories to Reich Commissar Lohse, which made clear a fundamental change in the matter of how far Jewish

workers were to be kept alive: 'On the instructions of the leadership for Business East, Jewish skilled industrial workers and craftsmen, whose usefulness for the war economy must in isolated cases be regarded as particularly important, are to be preserved for work. The preservation of these workers must be negotiated with the local offices of the Reichsführer-SS' (BAB, R 92/1157, cf. Wolfgang Scheffler, 'Das Schicksal der in die baltischen Staaten deportierten deutschen, österreichischen und tschechoslowakischen Juden 1941–1945', in *Buch der Erinnerung. Die ins Baltikum deportierten deutschen, österreichischen und tschechoslowakischen Juden*, ed. Scheffler and Diana Schulle, vol. 1 (Munich, 2003), 1–78, here 6.) Only a few days later, on 20 January 1942, at the Wannsee conference Heydrich was to speak of the columns of Jewish slave workers who were to be taken to the east 'to build roads'.

18. See below p. 562.

19. Himmler's decision to amalgamate was presumably taken at a meeting on 15 January 1942 (*Dienstkalender*); the ensuing order from Pohl went out on 19 January 1942 (IfZ, NO 495); a facsimile of Pohl's order of 13 March 1942 about the incorporation of the inspectorate of concentration camps into the WVHA is published in Johannes Tuchel, *Die Inspektion der Konzentrationslager 1938–1945. Das System des Terrors* (Berlin, 1994), 88 f. For further details see Schulte, *Zwangsarbeit*, 197 ff. and 357.

20. Schulte, *Zwangsarbeit*, 344 ff.; IfZ, NO 3795, Himmler to Pohl, 31 January 1942; BAB, NS 19/2065, Kammler's extended proposal of 10 February 1942, forwarded on 5 March 1942 to Himmler.

21. BAB, NS 19/2065; see also Karl Heinz Roth, '"Generalplan Ost"—"Gesamtplan Ost". Forschungsstand, Quellenprobleme, neue Ergebnisse', in Mechthild Rössler (ed.), *Der 'Generalplan Ost'. Hauptlinien der nationalsozialistischen Planungs- und Vernichtungspolitik* (Berlin, 1993), 25–95, at 74 f.

22. BAB, NS 19/2065, 23 March 1942.

23. Doc. R-129, in *IMT*, vol.. 38, pp. 362 ff.; cf. Walter Naasner, *Neue Machtzentren in der deutschen Kriegswirtschaft 1942–1945. Die Wirtschaftsorganisation der SS, das Amt des Generalbevollmächtigten für den Arbeitseinsatz und das Reichsministerium für Bewaffnung und Munition, Reichsministerium für Rüstung und Kriegsproduktion im nationalsozialistischen Herrschaftssystem* (Boppard a. Rh., 1994), 269.

24. Doc.R-129, in *IMT*, vol. 38, pp. 365 ff.; Roth, '"Generalplan Ost"', 77.

25. Steinbacher, '*Musterstadt*', 276 f.; see also below p. 563.

26. See Hermann Kaienburg, 'Jüdische Arbeitslager an der "Straße der SS"', *1999*, 1(1996), 13–39. On the Galician section of Transit Road IV see Sandkühler, '*Endlösung*', 41 ff.; Pohl, *Ostgalizien*, 338 ff. Himmler inspected Transit Road IV in August 1942.

27. *Dienstkalender*.

28. See in particular, *Lublin*, 13 ff., and also David Silberklang, 'Die Juden und die ersten Deportationen aus dem Distrikt Lublin', in Bogdan Musial (ed.), '*Aktion*

Reinhardt'. Der Völkermord an den Juden im Generalgouvernement 1941–1944 (Osnabrück 2004), 41–164.

29. Pohl, *Lublin*, 18 ff.; Silberklang, 'Juden', 50 ff.; Musial, *Zivilverwaltung*, 254 ff.

30. *Tagebücher Goebbels*. A testimony by Eichmann reveals that at this point Globocnik's task was to murder the Jews of the district who were 'incapable of work'. According to Eichmann, after the mass murder had begun Globocnik sought permission from Heydrich to murder a further 150,000, probably 250,000 (*The Trial of Adolf Eichmann: Record of Proceedings in the District Court of Jerusalem*, vol. 7 (Jerusalem, 1995), 240). The testimony of Josef Oberhauser, the adjutant of the commandant of Belzec, Christian Wirth, of 10 November 1964 points in the same direction (StA München, I 110 Ks 3/64, vol. 14, pp. 2918 ff.); see Pohl, *Lublin*, 25 f.

31. Pohl, *Ostgalizien*, 79 ff.

32. On the third wave of deportations see in particular Eichmann's express letter of 31 January 1942 (doc. PS-1063, published in Longerich (ed.), *Ermordung*, 165 f.) and also the minutes of the meeting of 9 March 1943 (Eichmann trial, doc. no. 119, published in ibid. 167 f.).

33. Longerich, *Politik*, 485 f., also Gottwaldt and Schulle, *'Judendeportationen'*, 137 ff. Four transports ended in the Warsaw ghetto (ibid. 167 ff.).

34. *Dienstkalender*, 20 October 1941. The editors cite a declaration by Mach of 26 March 1942 to the Slovakian state council, from which the German offer is clear.

35. On this and on the sequence of the deportations see Ladislav Lipscher, *Die Juden im slowakischen Staat 1939–1945* (Munich and Vienna, 1980), 99 ff.; Raul Hilberg, *Die Vernichtung der europäischen Juden. Die Gesamtgeschichte des Holocaust* (Frankfurt a.M., 1990), 766; Yehoshua Büchler, 'The Deportation of Slovakian Jews to the Lublin District of Poland in 1942', *Holocaust and Genocide Studies*, 6 (1991), 151–66.

36. Robert-Jan van Pelt and Déborah Dwork, *Auschwitz. Von 1270 bis heute* (Zurich and Munich, 1998), 335 ff.; Czech, *Kalendarium*, for example, provides evidence for the gassing on 12 May 1942 of 1,500 Jewish men, women and children from Sosnowitz in Bunker I.

37. PAA, Büro StSekr, vol. 2, published in *ADAP*, Series E, vol. 2, no. 93.

38. Longerich, *Politik*, 496.

39. Büchler, 'Deportation', 153 and 166, also Czech, *Kalendarium*.

40. Büchler, 'Deportation', 155 ff.

41. The notes kept by the Personal Staff do not indicate what was discussed at these meetings. The only exception is Himmler's presentation to Hitler of 3 May: the notes by Himmler that survive lead one to infer that the Waffen-SS was discussed, but also other, non-military matters that Himmler did not note in detail (*Dienstkalender*, 415, note 6).

42. BAB, NS 19/3899, note by Himmler of the same day about this 'meeting' (also IfZ, NG 3333).

43. *VOGG* 1942, 263 f., Führer decree concerning the creation of a state secretariat for security in the General Government; Eisenblätter, 'Grundlinien', 247 ff.
44. *VOGG* 1942, 321 ff., decree concerning the transfer of responsibilities to the state secretary for security; cf. Pohl, *Ostgalizien*, 204 f. Krüger was already RKF appointee but had apparently had to share his powers with Frank.
45. Yitzhak Arad, *Belzec, Sobibor, Treblinka: The Operation Reinhard Death Camps* (Bloomington, 1987), 37 ff.
46. Pohl, *Lublin*, 20 ff. On Sobibor see Schelvis, *Sobibór*.
47. Steinbacher, *'Musterstadt'*, 285 f.
48. Arad, *Belzec*, 387 f.
49. Longerich, *Politik*, 48 ff.; Gottwaldt and Schulle, *'Judendeportationen'*, 237 ff.
50. On this the reports of a Sonderkommando for special tasks set up by a Waffen-SS battalion are available: *Unsere Ehre*, 236 ff.
51. Lucjan Dobroszycki (ed.), *The Chronicle of the Lodz Ghetto, 1941–1944* (New Haven, 1984), 53 f., 56 f., 59 ff., and 194.
52. This can certainly be assumed in the case of three transports that left the Reich between 13 and 15 June 1942; it is, however, possible that in the first half of the month several transports ended in the extermination camp (Gottwaldt and Schulle, *'Judendeportationen'*, 211 ff.).
53. On 18 May half of a group of about 800 people, who a few days before had been deported from Theresienstadt to Siedliszcze, were taken to Sobibor along with Polish Jews and murdered there; see Gottwaldt and Schulle, *'Judendeportationen'*, 206; Peter Witte, 'Letzte Nachrichten aus Siedliszce. Der Transport Ax aus Theresienstadt in den Distrikt Lublin', in *Theresienstädter Studien und Dokumente* (1996), 98–113.
54. Gottwaldt and Schulle, *'Judendeportationen'*, 215 ff., on three transports that arrived in Sobibor between 15 and 19 June. It is possible that the same happened to two further transports from Theresienstadt that reached the Lublin district on 15 and 16 (ibid. 211 ff.). In addition, the authors provide a series of indications, though not very solid ones, that three deportation trains from the Reich either went straight to Sobibor or that the passengers were finally murdered there after only a few days' stop on the way (ibid. 215 ff.).
55. Büchler, 'Deportation', 153 and 164.
56. ZStL, Dok.UdSSR 401, published in Klein (ed.), *Einsatzgruppen*, 410 f.
57. Dieter Wisliceny, one of Eichmann's closest colleagues, claimed on one occasion when questioned that he had seen a written order from Himmler to Heydrich in which Himmler, on Hitler's command, had ordered the total annihilation of all Jews unfit for work. This order—according to Wisliceny's recollection it dated from 1942—could be another version of the order of 18 May 1942 or it could be the 'general' order mentioned there that underlay Himmler's order of 18 May (*Trial*, vol. 9, Jerusalem, 1995, doc. no. 85, testimony by Wisliceny, 14 November 1945).
58. Gruner, *Arbeitseinsatz*, 291 ff.; Adler, *Mensch*, 216 ff.

59. *Tagebücher Goebbels*, 30 May 1942; see also Gruner, *Arbeitseinsatz*, 298 ff.

60. This visit was reconstructed by the court in the course of the Heuser trial, see *Justiz und NS-Verbrechen*, vol. 19 (Amsterdam, 1978), no. 552, judgment of 21 May 1963, p. 192; on the renewed escalation of the murders see the detailed description in Gerlach, *Morde*, 694 ff.

61. Pohl, 'Schauplatz'.

62. On the assassination of Heydrich see Brandes, *Tschechen*, 251 ff.; Guenter Deschner, *Reinhard Heydrich. Statthalter der totalen Macht* (Esslingen, 1977), 273 ff.; Edouard Calic, *Reinhard Heydrich. Schlüsselfigur des Dritten Reiches* (Düsseldorf, 1982), 476 ff.; Hellmut G. Haasis, *Tod in Prag. Das Attentat auf Reinhard Heydrich* (Reinbek beiHamburg, 2002).

63. Karl Hermann Frank's minutes of 27 May 1942, cited according to Brandes, *Tschechen*, 254.

64. Himmler's telex of 27 May 1942, cited according to ibid. 255.

65. Ibid. 256; Frank's notes, published in *Die Deutschen in der Tschechoslowakei*, 474 ff.

66. *Dienstkalender*, Deschner, *Heydrich*, 297.

67. Brandes, *Tschechen*, 260 f.; Frank's notes, published in *Die Deutschen in der Tschechoslowakei*, 474 ff.

68. On the Lidice massacre see Brandes, *Tschechen*, 262 ff.

69. Heinemann, 'Rasse', 515.

70. Gottwaldt and Schulle, 'Judendeportationen', 213.

71. On the meetings see *Dienstkalender*, 27, 28, 30, and 31 May, 3, 4, and 5 June 1942.

72. BAB, NS 19/4009.

73. Ibid.

74. The most common spelling Reinhardt (other versions are principally Reinhard and Reinhart) can be explained by the fact that Heydrich himself preferred the form Reinhardt for his first name. Himmler told this to his closest colleagues in a memorial speech for the former RSHA chief; see Richard Breitman and Shlomo Aronson, 'Eine unbekannte Himmler-Rede vom Januar 1943', *Vierteljahrshefte für Zeitgeschichte*, 38 (1990), 337–48. See also Peter Black, 'Die Trawniki-Männer und die Aktion Reinhard', in Bogdan Musial (ed.), *'Aktion Reinhardt'. Der Völkermord an den Juden im Generalgouvernement 1941–1944* (Osnabrück, 2004), 309–52, esp. 308 f.

75. On the details of the sequence of deportations see Gottwaldt and Schulle, 'Judendeportationen', 260 ff.

76. CDJC, RF-1217, note on the file, 15 June 1942, published in Klarsfeld, *Vichy*, 379 f.

77. CDJC, RF-1223, note on the file by Dannecker, 1 July 1942, published in Klarsfeld, *Vichy*, 390 f.

78. BAB, BDC, SS-O Oberg.

79. Juliane Wetzel, 'Frankreich und Belgien', in Wolfgang Benz (ed.), *Dimension des Völkermords. Die Zahl der jüdischen Opfer des Nationalsozialismus* (Munich, 1991), 105–35, 120 ff.

80. Klarsfeld, *Vichy*, 412. The quota of 10 per cent decreed by Himmler was in fact vastly exceeded in this first transport: 375 out of 1,000 people fell victim to the selections.

81. Czech, *Kalendarium*.

82. Gottwaldt and Schulle, *'Judendeportationen'*, 230 ff.

83. Pohl, *Lublin*, 27.

84. On the deportations from the individual districts see the lists in Arad, *Belzec*, 383 ff.

85. On this and on what follows see Pohl, *Lublin*, 27 f.

86. BAB, NS 19/2655, 29 July 1941; Himmler's letter of thanks of 13 August 1941 is also to be found here.

87. On 28 July 1942 Himmler wrote to the head of the SS Main Office, Gottlob Berger: 'The occupied eastern territories will become free of Jews. The Führer has laid on my shoulders the task of carrying out this very weighty order. It is a responsibility no one can relieve me of' (IfZ, NO 626).

88. *Dienstkalender*; Höss, *Kommandant*, 57 f. and 176 ff.

89. Christopher R. Browning, 'A Final Hitler Decision for the Final Solution? The RiegnerTelegram Reconsidered', *Holocaust and Genocide Studies*, 10 (1996), 3–10; Walter Laqueur and Richard Breitman, *Der Mann, der das Schweigen brach. Wie die Welt vom Holocaust erfuhr* (Frankfurt a. M., 1986); Höss, *Kommandant*, 78.

90. BAB, NS 19/1757, published in Longerich (ed.), *Ermordung*, 201. See also Pohl,*Lublin*, 28.

91. See the survey by Jace Andrzej Mlynarczyk, 'Treblinka—ein Todeslager der "Aktion Reinhard"', in Bogdan Musial (ed.), *'Aktion Reinhardt'. Der Völkermord an den Juden im Generalgouvernement 1941–1944* (Osnabrück, 2004), 257–81. On the construction see in addition Arad, *Belzec*, 37 ff.

92. Pohl, *Ostgalizien*, 215, and *Lublin*, 57 ff.; Sandkühler, *'Endlösung'*, 81 ff.

93. BAB, NS 19/1765, note by the chief of staff in the office of the SSPF Cracow, 27 July 1942, published in Longerich (ed.), *Ermordung*, 202 ff. Mention is made here of a 'new order' from Krüger. On Himmler's order of 18 May 1942 see above p. 567.

94. BAB, NS 19/2462.

CHAPTER 22

1. BAB, R 49/889, Himmler's order of 4 June 1941.

2. On the details see Stefan Karner, 'Die Aussiedlungen der Slowenen in der Untersteiermark. Ein Beispiel nationalsozialistischer Volkstumspolitik', *Österreich in Geschichte und Literatur*, 22 (1978), 154–74.

3. A collection of the relevant orders can be found in *Der Menscheneinsatz. Grundsätze, Anordnungen und Richtlinien*, ed. Hauptabteilung I des Stabshauptamtes des Reichskommissars für die Festigung deutschen Volkstums, I. Nachtrag (Berlin, 1941), 44 ff.

4. On the plans since 1939 see above pp. 441 ff.

5. *Dienstkalender*, accompanying letter from Meyer to the July version of the general plan (which has not been preserved), 15 July 1941, published in Czesław Madajczyk (ed.), *Vom Generalplan Ost zum Generalsiedlungsplan* (Munich, etc., 1994); see Heinemann, '*Rasse*', 362.

6. Heinemann, '*Rasse*', 363 f. The RHSA plan has not survived but there is a detailed assessment of it from the Reich Ministry for the East: IfZ, NG 2325, printed in Helmut Heiber, 'Generalplan Ost', *Vierteljahrshefte für Zeitgeschichte*, 6 (1958), 281–325, at 297 ff.

7. BAB, R 49/157a, General Plan East, legal, economic, and territorial foundations for the construction of the east, June 1942, and also R 49/985, short version of 28 May 1942, both printed in Madajczyk (ed.), *Generalplan Ost*, doc. no. 21 und no. 23; see also Heinemann, '*Rasse*', 368 ff.

8. IfZ, NO 2255, Himmler to Greifelt, 12 June 1942; see Heinemann, '*Rasse*', 370.

9. The documents and Greifelt's accompanying letter of 23 December 1942 are published in Madajczyk (ed.), *Generalplan Ost*, doc. no. 70 und no. 71. In the space of the twenty years Himmler envisaged as necessary for Germanization it was anticipated that 8 million people would be used as a 'pool of settlers'.

10. Letter of 12 January 1943, published in Madajczyk (ed.), *Generalplan Ost*, doc. no. 72.

11. Heinemann, '*Rasse*', 370.

12. BAB, NS 19/4009; see Heinemann, '*Rasse*', 371.

13. June–July issue, also published in Madajczyk (ed.), *Generalplan Ost*, doc. no. 21.

14. BAB, R 43 II/1411; see the introduction to the *Dienstkalender*, 81 f. (with incorrect signature).

15. Further detail on the 'racial inventory', which was disguised as an examination for tuberculosis, is contained in Heydrich's final report of 18 May 1942, published in *Deutsche Politik im 'Protektorat'*, 264 ff., quotation p. 272. On racial examination in the Protectorate see Heinemann, '*Rasse*', 158 ff.

16. The person in question was Ferdinand Fischer; see Heinemann, '*Rasse*', 151.

17. BAB, R 2/11402, Lammers to the Reich authorities, 14 November 1941. In fact Himmler made HSSPF Frank his appointee in the Protectorate but simultaneously gave instructions for Heydrich to deputize for him; see Brandes, *Tschechen*, 345.

18. Materials relating to the general settlement plan and sent by Griefelt to Himmler on 23 December 1942 are published in Madajczyk (ed.), *Generalplan Ost*, doc. no. 70 and no. 71.

19. Address of 4 February 1942, published in *Deutsche Politik im 'Protektorat'*, 221 ff., here 229.

20. Heinemann, *'Rasse'*, 377.

21. *Dienstkalender*, 20 July 1941; BAB, BDC, SS-O Globocnik, Himmler's note of 21 July 1941.

22. In the so-called SS Team House in Lublin, later renamed the research office for housing in the east, he had at his disposal a planning office for the restructuring of the district and beyond that of the General Government in line with population policy. He had obtained authorization from Himmler to establish this setup in October 1940 in Cracow (Heinemann, *'Rasse'*, 382 f.); Michael G. Esch, 'Das SS-Mannschaftshaus in Lublin und die Forschungsstelle für Ostunterkünfte', in Götz Aly (ed.), *Modelle für ein deutsches Europa. Ökonomie und Herrschaft im Großwirtschaftsraum* (Berlin, 1992), 206 f.

23. USHMM,RG 15.027M, Reel 1, file 4, speech at a leaders' conference in Lublin.

24. Heinemann, *'Rasse'*, 384 f.

25. Ibid. 386 ff.

26. Ibid. 398 ff.

27. Ibid. 402.

28. *Dienstkalender*; Heinemann, *'Rasse'*, 400 ff. Information on the visit is in BAB, R 69/601, examiner Bender, EWZ-Kommission XV Zamosc, to Dongus, the head of the external office for Race and Settlement in Litzmannstadt, 20 July 1942.

29. BAB, NS 19/1757.

30. On the Zamosc project see the survey in Heinemann, *'Rasse'*, 403 ff., the detailed account by Bruno Wasser, *Himmlers Raumplanung im Osten. Der Generalplan Ost in Polen 1940–1944* Basle, etc., 1993), esp. 133 ff., and also the document collection (including numerous German sources) by Czesław Madajczyk, *Zamojszczyzna—Sonderlaboratorium SS. Zbiór dokumentów polskich i niemieckich z okresu okupacji hitlerowskiej*, 2 vols. (Warsaw, 1977); see also IfZ, NO 2562, general instruction no. 17C from the RFSS as Settlement Commissar concerning the settlement of an initial settlement area in the General Government, signed by Himmler, 12 November 1940.

31. Schulte, *Zwangsarbeit*, 262 ff.

32. Heinemann, *'Rasse'*, 420 f.

33. Ibid. 422 f. On their deployment and activities see BAB, NS 2/116, head of RuSHA, letter of 4 October and 6 November 1941.

34. BAB, NS 19/1704 (also IfZ, NO 2703), note on the file by Berger on a meeting in the Führer headquarters on ethnic Germans; according to the

Dienstkalender, 527, this meeting took place on 10 August 1942 or a few days later.

35. BAB, NS 19/2837, Himmler to Koch; published in Madajczyk (ed.), *Generalplan Ost*, no. 47; see also Wendy Lower, *Nazi Empire-Building and the Holocaust in Ukraine* (Chapel Hill, NC, 2005), 174.

36. Heinemann, *'Rasse'*, 448 ff.

37. BAB, R 70 SU 35, final report of the Crimean Kommando, 31 May 1944; see Heinemann, *'Rasse'*, 464 ff.

38. Heinemann, *'Rasse'* , 453 ff; Lower, *Empire-Building*, 162 ff.

39. *Dienstkalender*, 20 October and 27 October–1 November 1942.

40. Heinemann, *'Rasse'*, 461 ff.

41. BAB, R 49/3537, 12 September 1941; Heinemann, *'Rasse'*, 312 f. Up to this point Berkelmann had been Bürckel's deputy with respect to the latter's responsibility for settlement matters.

42. Heinemann, *'Rasse'*, 314 ff.

43. *Dienstkalender*, 512.

44. BAB, NS 19/2747, Greifelt to Himmler and Himmler's reply of 7 September 1942, also printed in Madajczyk (ed.), *Generalplan Ost*, 485 ff.

45. BAB, NS 19/2747, transcript of a meeting between Himmler and Bürckel, signed by Himmler and undated. Brandt sent this set of minutes on 4 September to the RSHA, the Staff Main Office of the RKF, and other offices, indicating that that the agreement had been reached several days before. That was likely to have been 31 August, when Himmler met Bürckel in Wiesbaden (*Dienstkalender*).

46. BAB, R 49/2615, note by Stier of 3 May 1943; see Heinemann, *'Rasse'*, 317 ff. and 328 f.

47. Heinemann, *'Rasse'*, 319.

48. Ludwig Nestler (ed.), *Die faschistische Okkupationspolitik in Frankreich (1940–1944)* (Berlin, 1990), no. 103 (cites the former ZStA Potsdam, film no. 10,951).

49. Letter of 18 June 1942, published in Nestler (ed.), *Okkupationspolitik*, no. 117.

50. What is meant is the French underclass, identifiable by their use of dialect.

51. Doc. R-114, note of 7 August 1942, in *IMT*, vol. 38, pp. 330 ff.; cf. Heinemann, *'Rasse'*, 321. Contrary to Wagner's opinion, the conference attendees took the view that the 'displacement' of the 'patois' population should be postponed to the end of the war.

52. *Dienstkalender*; Heinemann, *'Rasse'*, 322.

53. Doc. R-114, note on the file by Hinrich of 29 August 1942, in *IMT*, vol. 38, pp. 334 ff.

54. Heinemann, *'Rasse'*, 322 ff.

55. Henry Picker (ed.), *Hitlers Tischgespräche im Führerhauptquartier* (Frankfurt a. M., 1989), 5 April 1942.

56. See Heinemann, *'Rasse'*, 331 ff., and Kettenacker, *Volkstumspolitik*, 255 ff.

57. Heinemann, 'Rasse', 331.
58. Ibid. 332; on Himmler's guidelines for the branch office and for the repatriation of those of German descent (sent with Greifelt's letter of 15 May 1941) see *Menscheneinsatz*, 39 ff.
59. BAB, R 69/650, 2 March 1942.
60. Heinemann, 'Rasse', 335 ff.; BAB, NS 47/49, transcript of the meeting on 12 March in VoMi about the granting of German nationality to the ethnic Germans registered in northern France; note on the file by the RKF, main office of VoMi, of 21 March 1943 about the granting of citizenship to the ethnic Germans in northern France; note by the head of the EWZ on the registration and granting of citizenship to those of German descent living in northern France (Volksdeutsche Kulturgemeinschaft Douai), 25 March 1943.
61. BAB, NS 2/153, instruction from the head of RuSHA, undated: 'The Reichsführer-SS has given instructions that the process of re-Germanization should be extended also to former Soviet Russian nationals (in other words, to eastern workers).' See Heinemann, 'Rasse', 486 f., which dates this instruction to January 1944.
62. BAB, NS 2/154, instruction from RuSHA, 29 September 1944.
63. BAB, NS 2/153, undated decree from RuSHA, cited from Heinemann, 'Rasse', 485, January 1944.
64. BAB, R 49/73, instruction no. 51 I, 1 October 1941.The precondition was acceptance into categories I and II.
65. BAB, NS 19/150, Himmler to the head of RSHA, RuSHA and the Staff Main Office, 10 July 1941.
66. Ibid. report from Creutz, Staff Main Office, 20 February 1942.
67. Heinemann, 'Rasse', 482 ff. See also Müller's decrees of 10 September 1942 (BAB, NS 47/31).
68. Heinemann, 'Rasse', 488 ff.
69. Ibid. 499 ff.
70. Ibid. 501 ff. The most important decrees on this matter came from the head of RSHA, 9 June 1942 (IfZ, NO 3520) and 27 July 1943 (NO 1383), and also from the head of RuSHA, 23 August 1943 (NO 933).
71. BAB, NS 19/3680, instruction no. 70 I of 23 March 1942; see Heinemann, 'Rasse', 476 f.
72. Heinemann, 'Rasse', 508 ff.
73. BAB, NS 2/58, instruction from Greifelt, 19 February 1942; see Heinemann, 'Rasse', 510 ff.
74. BAB, NS 19/2621.
75. IfZ, NO 3074, letter of 12 August 1941.
76. There are indications in Heinemann, 'Rasse', 510 ff.
77. His responsibilities related at first to the Volga region but were then extended to the entire European territories of the USSR (BAB, BDC, SS-O Pflaum, letter from Himmler, 11 July 1941 and 25 August 1941). On the placing of

predominantly Russian children in the home see IfZ, NO 5223, testimony of Willibald Zwirner, 19 June 1947, who as an SS doctor was in charge of the care of the children at various times.

78. BAB, NS 2/81, work report of the RuS leader Russia South for the period 1–15 October 1942, 25 October 1942. According to this the Staff Leader had a number of meetings with the commanding officer of the security police about orphan children who were to be assembled in camps by the SD; see Heinemann, 'Rasse', 514.

79. BAB, NS 19/2216, Staff Main Office to RFSS, 13 May 1942. Himmler renewed this instruction in January 1942 in relation to Lithuanian and Estonian children (ibid. Jeckeln to RFSS, 13 June 1942).

80. USHMM, RG 15.007 M/113, decree of 16 February 1942; see Heinemann, 'Rasse', 521 f.

81. Heinemann, 'Rasse', 522 f., based on statements made by the Polish historian Czesław Madajczyk.

82. BAB, NS 19/4009.

83. Doc. PS-1919, in *IMT*, vol. 29, pp. 110 ff., quotation p. 123.

84. Heinemann, 'Rasse', 515 ff.

85. Ibid. 515.

86. IfZ, NO 681; see Heinemann, 'Rasse', 519.

87. BAB, NS 19/1436, order from Himmler of 6 January 1943; see Gerlach, *Morde*, 1015 f.

88. See Heinemann, 'Rasse', 525 ff.

89. Ibid. 528 ff.

90. BAB, NS 2/82, report from Hauptsturmführer Dörhöfer on the tour of inspection in the Ukraine, 10–22 September 1942. As early as October 1942 the head of the SS Main Office discussed with Rosenberg the measures to be taken in this territory (NS 19/1976, report of 22 October 1942).

91. Heinemann, 'Rasse', 529; Gerlach, *Morde*, 1081.

92. Heinemann, 'Rasse', 530.

93. On the criteria see ibid. 50 ff., and for an illustration of a 'racial chart' see 64 f.

CHAPTER 23

1. Stein, *Geschichte*, 181 f.; *Dienstkalender*, 29 December 1942.

2. BAB, NS 19/2251, Himmler to Hitler, 12 December 1941.

3. For the first six months of 1942 see, for example, Himmler's *Dienstkalender*, 1 January, 17 February, 8 and 17 March, 3, 11, and 27 May 1942.

4. IfZ, NO 1087, note by Himmler of 29 June 1942; mentioned here are Norwegian, Croatian, Spanish, and Italian legions. Cf. Stein, *Geschichte*, 137.

5. Stein, *Geschichte*, 137.

6. Ibid. 138; Thomsen, *Besatzungspolitik*, 96 ff.

7. Stein, *Geschichte*, 138, instruction of 26 July 1941.

8. Ibid. instruction of 30 July 1941.

9. Ibid. 139.

10. IfZ, MA 109/263 3910, survey of the Germanic volunteers in the Waffen-SS as of 15 January 1942; Stein, *Geschichte*, 139 f.

11. NARA, T 175/109, Himmler's order concerning the creation and deployment of foreign volunteer units in countries of German and related blood of 6 November 1941.

12. Stein, *Geschichte*, 140 f.

13. NARA, T 175/109, note on the file by Gerlinger about a discussion with the head of the Finnish state police, Aaltonen, 8 January 1942.

14. Stein, *Geschichte*, 143 f.

15. Ibid. 142 ff.; NARA, T 1 175, 109, report by Berger about volunteers from Germanic countries, 9 February 1942.

16. IfZ, NO 1787, RFSS, duties of the head of the SS Main Office in the Germanic countries, 6 March 1942.

17. Stein, *Geschichte*, 145; order of 13 April 1942, published in *SS en Nederland*, doc. no. 144.

18. Stein, *Geschichte*, 146.

19. Picker (ed.), *Tischgespräche*, 5 April 1942; see Stein, *Geschichte*, 145.

20. Stein, *Geschichte*, 146.

21. Ibid. 147. The two units were constituted as the 28th SS Volunteer Grenadier Division 'Wallonia' (up to the autumn of 1944 Sturmbrigade Wallonia) and 33rd Armoured Grenadier Division 'Charlemagne'. After the retreat from France the French division was composed from, among others, members of Darnand's 'Milice' (see the correspondence in PAA, Inland IIg, R 101058, from the period September to December 1944).

22. Stein, *Geschichte*, 145 f.

23. BAB, NS 33/213, undated.

24. BAB, NS 2/79, letter from Hofmann to Lippert about the inspection of the Dutch volunteers, 4 April 1941. See Heinemann, *'Rasse'*, 341 f.

25. BAB, NS 2/82, order of 3 July 1942; Heinemann, *'Rasse'*, 344 ff. In Norway since the spring of 1942 and the Netherlands since July 1942 so-called SS leaders for race and settlement had been in place to monitor in particular the racial selection of SS recruits and compliance with the Marriage Order and to give SS 'ideological' guidance.

26. Stein, *Geschichte*, 124 f. The figures are based on estimates by the former Waffen-SS general Felix Steiner, *Die Freiwilligen. Idee und Opfergang* (Göttingen, 1958), 373. In his speech in Sonthofen to Wehrmacht generals on 21 June 1944 Himmler spoke of 30,000 Germanic volunteers; Steiner's figures refer to the total of all those recruited during the war. They may well still be somewhat exaggerated (BAB, NS 19/4014).

27. IfZ, Partei-Kanzlei, Anordnung A 54/42 of 12 August 1942.

28. Gerhard Hirschfeld, *Fremdherrschaft und Kollaboration. Die Niederlande unter deutscher Besatzung 1940–1945* (Stuttgart, 1984), 34; according to Hirschfeld the decree in question was that from the Reich Chancellery of 3 February 1943.

29. Thomsen, *Besatzungspolitik*, 138 ff.

30. Bohn, *Reichskommissariat*, 44 ff.

31. Kwiet, *Reichskommissariat*, 146 ff. See, for example, BAB, NS 19/3363, two letters from Himmler to Seyss-Inquart, 5 March 1942, also Himmler's letter to Rauter, 28 March 1942.

32. This attitude of resignation is clearly seen in his report of a discussion with Mussert on 8 July 1943, which he informed Rauter about (BAB, NS 19/3364). Himmler meanwhile confined himself to the hope 'that in this manner we shall be able to keep Mussert on board for the time being' (ibid.).

33. Meinoud Marinus Rost van Tonningen, *Correspondentie,* ed. and with an introduction by E. Fraenkel-Verkade in cooperation with A. J. van der Leuw, 2 vols. ('s-Gravenhage, 1967), i. 162 ff. and 912.

34. On Rost von Tonningen's withdrawal see Hirschfeld, *Fremdherrschaft*, 193.

35. Warmbrunn, *German Occupation*, 132 f.; on Himmler's support see his statements on 12 July 1944 (BAB, R 43 II/678a).

36. Warmbrunn, *German Occupation*, 135; Wagner, *Belgien*, 248. In total the SS was to recruit some 20,000 volunteers in Flanders and Wallonia up to the end of the war (Stein, *Geschichte*, 124 f.).

37. He made the speech in the Brussels Palais du Sport at a mass rally of Rexists in which many representatives of the occupying power also took part; see Martin Conway, *Collaboration in Belgium: Léon Degrelle and the Rexist Movement, 1940–1944* (New Haven and London, 1993), 173 ff.

38. BAB, NS 19/419, 20 January 1943; see Wagner, *Belgien*, 248.

39. Franz Petri, 'Die geschichtliche Stellung der Germanisch-Romanischen Grenzlande im Westen', in *Westland. Blätter für Landschaft, Geschichte und Kultur an Rhein, Mosel, Maas und Schelde,* ed. Reich Commissar for the Occupied Dutch Territories, 2nd series (1943), 66–72, extracts reprinted in Hans Derks, *Deutsche Westforschung. Ideologie und Praxis im 20. Jahrhundert* (Leipzig, 2001), 270 ff. An allusion to the continual 'incorporation' by the Reichsführer-SS of new territories on 'racial-biological' grounds can be found in a further article by Petri in the same journal, 1st series (1943), 61, reprinted in Derks, *Westforschung*, 267 ff. See also Wagner, *Belgien*, 249; Derks, *Westforschung*, esp. 85 ff., who engages critically with the older research literature, in particular with Karl Ditt, 'Die Kulturraumforschung zwischen Wissenschaft und Politik. Das Beispiel Karl Petri (1903–1993)', *Westfälische Forschungen*, 46 (1996), 73–176.

40. IfZ, NO 1469, Berger to Himmler, 27 October 1942. Hitler advocated the creation of two Reich Gaus on Belgian soil but his aim was annexation, as is clear from his comments at a meeting on 12 July 1944 on the inauguration of the civil administration in Belgium (BAB, R 43 II/678a).

41. Ibid. minutes of the meeting on the inauguration of the civil administration in Belgium of 12 July 1944.

42. See above p. 503.

43. BAB, NS 19/1846, Himmler to Berger, 29 October 1941; according to Himmler's *Dienstkalender* the meeting took place on 20 October 1941.

44. Kaiser, 'Politik', 549 ff.

45. Spannenberger, *Volksbund*, 310 ff.

46. Stein, *Geschichte*, 135; Casagrande, *'Prinz Eugen'*, 167; Shimizu, *Okkupation*, 223.

47. Holm Sundhaussen, 'Zur Geschichte der Waffen-SS in Kroatien 1941–1945', *Südost-Forschungen*, 30 (1971), 176–96, at 178.

48. PAA, Inland IIg 309. The agreement was confirmed by an exchange of notes of the foreign ministers (ibid.); see Sundhaussen, 'Geschichte', 180 f.; Casagrande, *'Prinz Eugen'*, 197 ff.

49. Sundhaussen, 'Geschichte', 179.

50. BAB, R 49/13, instruction from the RFSS on the expansion of the work on ethnic issues done by the party and the demarcation of the areas of responsibility of the SS Main Offices, 28 November 1941. According to Hess's instruction of 26 February 1941 Himmler had been appointed 'NSDAP expert responsible for all border and ethnic matters' (IfZ, Partei-Kanzlei, Anordnungen). See Lumans, *Auxiliaries*, 137; *Dienstkalender*, introduction, 54. The VoMi and Staff Main Office were raised in June 1941 to Main Offices (IfZ, NO 4047, Himmler's instruction of 11 June 1941).

51. See the *Dienstkalender* on the telephone conversation with Bormann, 13 November 1941.

52. Directive 2/42, published in *'Führer-Erlasse'*, no. 148.

53. *Dienstkalender*, 6 November 1941; Sepp Janko, *Weg und Ende der deutschen Volksgruppe in Jugoslawien* (Graz and Stuttgart, 1982), deals with this meeting (p. 214); see also Casagrande, *'Prinz Eugen'*, 185; Shimizu, *Okkupation*, 209.

54. BAB, NS 19/3519, Keitel to Himmler, 30 December 1941.

55. Shimizu, *Okkupation*, 148 ff.

56. Ibid. 152 ff. Under Meyszner a police command structure, with a commanding officer of the order police, of the security police, and of the SD, was established, that by September 1942 had taken over the police forces which up to that point had been under the command of the military: German police units, strengthened by ethnic Germans and also the 'Serbian Staff Guard'.

57. Ibid. 225; Führer decree of 22 January 1942 on the deployment of an HSSPF in the area of the military commander for Serbia, published in *'Führer-Erlasse'*, no. 139; see also BAB, NS 19/1728, Himmler to Werner Lorenz, who was originally to support recruitment on the spot, 24 January 1942.

58. Shimizu, *Okkupation*, 225 ff. He wrote the first draft of the call himself. After consultation with the Foreign Ministry the text was finally published in February 1942 (BAB, NS 19/1728, Himmler's draft call; text published in

Shimizu, *Okkupation*, p. 225f.; PAA, Inland IIg 323, draft by the Foreign Ministry). Casagrande, *'Prinz Eugen'*, 191 ff., compares the two versions.

59. Shimizu, *Okkupation*, 228 ff., Casagrande, *'Prinz Eugen'*, 188 ff.; Stein, *Geschichte*, 153 ff.

60. Casagrande, *'Prinz Eugen'*, 196.

61. Shimizu, *Okkupation*, 206 ff.

62. IfZ, NO 5901, Berger to Brandt, 16 June 1942.

63. Letter of 13 July 1942 to Lorenz, cited in Sundhaussen, 'Geschichte', 184, after a version commissioned by the German Protestant Church's relief organization at the end of 1951 (according to this the original document is in NARA, T 580/76/O345).

64. Casagrande, *'Prinz Eugen'*, 196.

65. Ibid. 233.

66. PAA, Inland IIg 305, note by Luther on a speech for Ribbentrop, 18 October 1941; Casagrande, *'Prinz Eugen'*, 197 f., also Sundhaussen, 'Geschichte', 181.

67. PAA, Inland IIg 309, letter from the German legation in Zagreb, 16 June 1942, quoting from a letter from a German general in Zagreb of 21 May 1942, according to which 'after a recent decision of the Wehrmacht High Command the registration, recruitment and training of ethnic Germans capable of military service' was 'to be carried out in the south-eastern area by the SS'; Casagrande, *'Prinz Eugen'*, 198, also Sundhaussen, 'Geschichte', 182.

68. In the Foreign Ministry the view was taken that the removal of the ethnic Germans would give a clear signal to the Italians, who occupied part of Croatia, that the Germans were prepared to cede the country to them. This can be read, for example, in PAA, Inland IIg 309, note by Luther on a speech for Ribbentrop, 12 June 1942.

69. See the material in PAA, Inland IIg 201; Sundhaussen, 'Geschichte', 183. See in addition the extensive material in the files PAA, Inland IIg 305 and 309. Berger's instruction to implement the inspection went out on 26 August 1942 (BAB, NS 19/319, letter to Nageler).

70. PAA, Inland IIg 309, note by SS Main Office, Amt VI, 24 July 1942, on the meeting on 23 July with Under-Secretary Luther about Hungary, Croatia, and Slovakia: 'As far as the outside world can tell the recruitment must seem to be voluntary but internally it must be pursued with vigour.' Cf. Sundhaussen, 'Geschichte', 184, also Casagrande, *'Prinz Eugen'*, 201. On 22 September the *German Newspaper in Croatia* published an order from the ethnic group leader which set out the rules for the call-up of ethnic Germans to the Waffen-SS (17 to 35 years) or to the squads of the 'German force' or the German units of the Croatian Home Guard.

71. PAA, Inland IIg 305, Berger and Lorenz signed a 'regulation of the recruitment procedure among ethnic Germans', 29 August 1942. See Casagrande, *'Prinz Eugen'*, 202 f.; Sundhaussen, 'Geschichte', 188 f.

72. Casagrande, *'Prinz Eugen'*, 201, and Sundhaussen, 'Geschichte', 191.

73. Sundhaussen, 'Geschichte', 188 and 191; Casagrande, 'Prinz Eugen', 204. PAA, Inland IIg 307, note on Croatia of 10 October 1942; a further note, in which the Croats declared their acceptance of the German measures, is referred to in the telegram from Kasche of 1 December 1943 (ibid.); Inland IIg 306, letter from Luther of 8 November 1942.

74. Valentin Oberkersch, Die Deutschen in Syrmien, Slawonien, Kroatien und Bosnien. Geschichte einer deutschen Volksgruppe in Südosteuropa (Munich, 1989), 387 f.

75. Spannenberger, Volksbund, 311 f.

76. Ibid. 314; Dienstkalender, 18 November 1941.

77. PAA, Inland IIg 305, draft by Rintelen for the Under-Secretary, 19 December 1941; see also Spannenberger, Volksbund, 315.

78. Spannenberger, Volksbund, 319 f.

79. See below p. 674.

80. See below p. 673.

81. BAB, R 49/2612, note by Stier of 3 September 1942 on a discussion with Himmler (of 1 September, Dienstkalender), in which the RFSS gave the instruction not to exert pressure on Hungary over this matter.

82. Gerhard Seewann and Norbert Spannenberger (eds), Akten des Volksgerichtsprozesses gegen Franz A. Basch, Volksgruppenführer der Deutschen in Ungarn, Budapest 1945/46 (Munich, 1999), 69.

83. PAA, Inland IIg 305, statement by Luther of 3(?) September 1942; Sundhaussen, 'Geschichte', 187. Luther makes a similar argument in Inland IIg 255, 5 November 1942, saying the resettlement would produce 'catastrophic psychological and also political consequences for the whole of the 2½ to 3 million Germans in the south east', and would 'prejudice' German policy with regard to these ethnic groups in an unacceptable way. See also Inland IIg 255, Rintelen to Ribbentrop, 27 September 1942, Foreign Ministry to VoMi, 4 November 1942, and also the note by the Under-Secretary on a speech of 5 December 1943; in addition Inland IIg 305, Berger to Triska, 2 September 1942.

84. PAA, Inland IIg 214, note by Triska, 7 January 1943.

85. The same is true of the small German minority in Danish North Schleswig. The German occupying powers used the ethnic group simply as a 'reservoir that it aimed to exploit for the German war effort' (Thomsen, Besatzungspolitik, 109)—by deploying it for the Waffen-SS, its own militia (the so-called temporary volunteer service), as well as for many ancillary services.

CHAPTER 24

1. For details see Himmler's office diary (Dienstkalender), 28 July to 6 August 1942.

2. Hannu Rautkallio, *Finland and the Holocaust: The Rescue of Finland's Jews* (New York, 1987), 163 ff. For a critical view of it see William B. Cohen and Jörgen Svensson, 'Finland and the Holocaust', *Holocaust and Genocide Studies*, 9/1 (1995), 70–92, esp. 82 f.

3. Hilberg, *Vernichtung*, 761 ff.; Holm Sundhaussen, 'Jugoslawien', in Wolfgang Benz, (ed.), *Dimension des Völkermords. Die Zahl der jüdischen Opfer des Nationalsozialismus* (Munich, 1991), 311–30, at 323.

4. Angrick, *Besatzungspolitik*, 131 ff.

5. PAA, Inland IIg 200, Killinger to the Foreign Ministry, 12 August 1942, and to Himmler, 26 July 1942; see Christopher R. Browning, *The Final Solution and the German Foreign Office: A Study of Referat D III of Abteilung Deutschland, 1940–1943* (New York and London, 1978), 115 ff.

6. This was Luther's assessment in PAA, Inland IIg 177, note of 21 August 1942.

7. PAA, Inland IIg 208, letter from the OKW, Armaments Office to the Foreign Ministry, 21 July 1942; see also Randolph L. Braham, *The Politics of Genocide: The Holocaust in Hungary*, 2 vols. (New York, 1994), 284 ff.

8. PAA, Inland IIg 208, Himmler to Ribbentrop, 30 November 1942.

9. Frederick B. Chary, *The Bulgarian Jews and the Final Solution 1940–1944* (Pittsburgh, 1972), 69 ff.

10. Daniel Carp, 'Notes on the History of the Jews in Greece during the Holocaust Period: The Attitude of the Italians (1941–1943)', in Michael R. Marrus (ed.), *The Nazi Holocaust: Historical Articles on the Destruction of European Jews*, vol. 5 (Westport, etc., 1989), 731–68, esp. 738 ff.; Browning, *Referat D III*, 136 f. and 140 f.

11. Klarsfeld, *Vichy*, 122.

12. Ibid. 122 and 434 ff.

13. Hirschfeld, *Fremdherrschaft*, 148 ff.

14. Office of the Foreign Ministry in Brussels, report of 24 September 1942, and Military Commander to Field and Higher Field Headquarters, 25 September 1942, both published in Serge Klarsfeld and Maxime Steinberg (eds), *Die Endlösung der Judenfrage in Belgien. Dokumente* (New York, 1980), 45 ff.

15. PAA, Inland IIg 182, report from the Brussels Office, 27 November 1942.

16. Pohl, *Ostgalizien*, 216 ff.

17. *Dienstkalender*; Pohl, *Ostgalizien*, 220.

18. *Dienstkalender*.

19. Ibid. 21 August 1942.

20. Between 31 August and 3 September 1942 he inspected in particular Wiesbaden, Mainz, Cologne, Düsseldorf, Münster, Osnabrück, Bremen, Hamburg, and Lübeck and conferred amongst others with Gauleiters Bürckel, Sprenger, Grohé, Florian, Wegener, and Kaufmann. On the three building brigades formed from KZ inmates originally envisaged for tasks in the east and on the manufacturing of door- and window-frames see BAB, NS 19/14, instruction to Pohl, 9 September 1942. On 30 September 1942 Himmler had already given

Daluege detailed instructions for the order police to remove air-raid damage, in order, for example, to prevent hoses icing up in the winter (NS 19/3165); see *Dienstkalender* and Karola Fings, *Krieg, Gesellschaft und KZ.Himmlers SS-Baubrigaden* (Paderborn, etc., 2005), 55 ff.

21. Willi A. Boelcke (ed.), *Deutschlands Rüstung im Zweiten Weltkrieg. Hitlers Konferenzen mit Albert Speer 1942–1945* (Frankfurt a. M., 1969).

22. See *Dienstkalender*, 22 September 1942, Interview with Hitler: 'Jewish emigration—how should we proceed further?' The next topic in Himmler's notes for the interview was: 'Settlement of Lublin—Lorrainers, Germans from Bosnia, Bessarabia' and 'Conditions in the Gen.Gov.—Globus [Globocnik's nickname]'. The fact that the 'emigration', that is, the murder, of the Jews from the district of Lublin could not be carried out at the speed envisaged by Himmler evidently had immediate repercussions for the settlement projects being pushed by Globocnik.

23. IfZ, NO 1611.

24. *VOGG* 1942, 665f., 1 November 1942, police decree of 28 October 1942, and 683 ff., 14 November 1942, police decree of 10 November 1942.

25. IfZ, NO 5194, Korherr report, 23 March 1943.

26. Doc. PS-3428, in *IMT*, vol. 32, pp. 279 ff., Kube report to the Reich Commissar Ostland, 31 July 1942. See Gerlach, *Morde*, 694 ff.

27. IfZ, NO 626.

28. Pohl, 'Schauplatz', 160 ff., and Gerlach, *Morde*, 709 ff.

29. *Reichsführer!*, no. 167.

30. Gerlach, *Morde*, 719 ff.

31. Pohl, 'Schauplatz'; Spector, *Holocaust*, 186.

32. IfZ, NO 3392, published in facsimile in the illustrations section of Fleming, *Hitler*.

33. Boelcke (ed.), *Deutschlands Rüstung*, 89.

34. *Tagebücher Goebbels*, 30 September 1942.

35. BAB, R 22/5029, report by the Justice Minister, 18 September 1942; see also doc. PS-654, in *IMT*, vol. 26, pp. 200 ff.

36. IfZ, NO 5522; see Orth, *System*, 173.

37. Klarsfeld, *Vichy*, 161 ff.

38. CDJC, XXVC-177, message from BdS Knochen to the RSHA, 23 September 1942, published in Klarsfeld, *Vichy*, 469.

39. Ibid. 474.

40. Samuel Abrahamsen, *Norway's Response to the Holocaust* (New York, 1991), 83 ff., Hilberg, *Vernichtung*, 582 ff.

41. Lipscher, *Juden*, 129 ff.

42. See various documents signed by Richter and Luther in PAA, Inland IIg 200.

43. Hilberg, *Vernichtung*, 851 f.

44. Chary, *Bulgarian Jews*, 72 ff.

45. See Braham, *Politics*, 287 ff., and Browning, *Referat D III*, 128 ff.

46. PAA, Inland IIg 208, Himmler to von Ribbentrop, 30 November 1942.

47. See PAA, Inland IIg 208, Note by Luther for Rademacher, 14 December 1942.

48. See the comprehensive correspondence between the Missions and Luther from October and November 1942 in PAA, Inland IIg 194 , plus further detail in Browning, *Referat D III*, 137 ff.

49. Himmler's notes from 11–14 October 1942, published in Helmut Krausnick, 'Himmler über seinen Besuch bei Mussolini', *Vierteljahrshefte für Zeitgeschichte*, 4 (1956), 423–6.

50. PAA, Inland IIg 194, report from the Zagreb embassy.

51. Keitel referred to this decision, which cannot be dated exactly in an order of 23 July 1942 (BAB, NS 19/1671). On the assignment of the 'combating of bandits' to Himmler in summer 1942 see Gerlach, *Morde*, 921 ff.

52. IFZ, NO 681, order of 25 June 1942.

53. Although no details could be gleaned about the carrying out of the 'action', the hostage shootings increased during July and August and the arrest of relatives of 'partisan suspects' and their subsequent consignment to KZs (or the compulsory adoption of 'racially valuable' children) reached a high point in August; see Milan Zevart, 'Geiselerschießungen im Besatzungsgebiet Untersteiermark (Spodnja Stajerska)', in Gerhard Jochem and Georg Seiderer (eds), *Entrechtung, Vertreibung, Mord. NS-Unrecht in Slowenien und seine Spuren in Bayern 1941–1945* (Berlin, 2005), 197–205.

54. BAB, NS 19/1671, Himmler's order of 28 July 1942. On the previous day, in response to a query, Himmler had told Daluege in telegram style who was responsible for combating bandits: 'I am myself. In the field the particular Higher SS and Police Leader. For the individual units the commanders who are already available' (BAB, NS 19/1432).

55. Himmler's order of 31 July 1942, published in Rürup (ed.), *Krieg*, 132.

56. Instruction No. 46, published in Hubatsch (ed.), *Hitlers Weisungen*, 232 ff. According to this, the RFSS was the 'central agency for the collection and evaluation of all experience acquired in the field of combating bandits'.

57. BAB, NS 19/1671, minute of 9 July 1942; on the impossibility of carrying it out see Gerlach, *Morde*, 924. On the meeting dealing with the combating of partisans see *Dienstkalender*, 9 July 1942.

58. Indispensable: anyone who counted as 'indispensable' (*unabkömmlich*) did not need to join the Wehrmacht (i.e. was in a reserved occupation).

59. BAB, NS 19/1671, order concerning an Increase in the Combat Strength of the SS and Police in the General Government and in the Occupied Eastern Territories, 17 August 1942.

60. Ibid. Himmler's order to suppress the bandit activity in White Ruthenia and in the district of Bialystok, 7 August 1942, which was based on his order for the crushing of bandit activity in the districts of Upper Carniola and Lower Styria of 25 June 1942 (ibid.).

61. On the course of the operations see Gerlach, *Morde*, 930 ff. Little is known about 'Wisent'.
62. BAB, NS 19/1671, von dem Bach-Zelewski to Himmler, 5 September 1942.
63. *Dienstkalender* 22 September 1942: 'task for von d. Bach.' Himmler had met von dem Bach-Zelewski on 9 September 1942 (ibid.).
64. BAB, NS 19/1671, contains all five edicts, which are dated 23 October 1942.
65. On von Gottberg see above pp. 346 and 420 f.
66. On Dirlewanger see above pp. 345 ff.
67. Gerlach, *Morde*, 928.
68. See the details of the figures in ibid. 900 f.
69. BAB, NS 19/1432.
70. Ibid. Himmler to Sauckel, 9 February 1943; see Gerlach, *Morde*, 996 ff.
71. Gerlach, *Morde*, 1055 f.
72. Ibid. 1058 ff.
73. Piper, *Rosenberg*, 547 f.
74. BAB, NS 19/1681, minute of 18 November 1942: 'We must never promise the Russians a nation state.'
75. *Der Untermensch*, ed. Reichsführer-SS and SS Main Office [Berlin, 1942], 2.
76. This is explored in detail in Piper, *Rosenberg*, esp. 562 ff. and 587 ff.
77. BAB, NS 19/1704, 9 April 1942.
78. Piper, *Rosenberg*, 563 f.
79. Bohn, *Reichskommissariat*, 113; however, in nineteen cases a pardon was issued.
80. Ibid. 84 f.
81. Weber, *Sicherheit*, 115.
82. Führer edict of 9 March 1942, published in *'Führer-Erlass'*, no. 147.
83. Kasten, *'Franzosen'*, 26 ff.
84. Ibid. 69 ff.
85. Meyer, *Besatzung*, 99 ff.
86. Brandes, *Tschechen*, vol. 2: *Besatzungspolitik, Kollaboration und Widerstand im Protektorat Böhmen und Mähren von Heydrichs Tod bis zum Prager Aufstand (1942–1945)* (Munich and Vienna, 1975), 21 ff.
87. Naasner, *Machtzentren*, 300 f. Rainer Fröbe, 'Der Arbeitseinsatz von KZ-Häftlingen und die Perspektive der Industrie 1943–1945', in Ulrich Herbert (ed.), *Europa und der "Reicheinsatz". Ausländische Zivilarbeiter, Kriegsgefangene und KZ-Häftlinge in Deutschland 1938–1945* (Essen, 1991), 351–83, shows that KZ prisoners during the whole of 1942 were used primarily for building-work, in part for the construction of industrial sites, but in general not yet for production in factories.
88. IfZ, NO 569, Saur Minutes; see Schulte, *Zwangsarbeit*, 213f.
89. BAB, NS 19/755, Schieber order of 17 March 1942; IfZ, NO 505, Glücks to RFSS, 2 April 1942, concerning the preparations for rifle production in Buchenwald; furthermore preparations for the production of parts for the Weser-Flug company and for Klöckner in Neuengamme were being discussed

(NO 1215, note of Amtsgruppe C concerning a conversation with Schieber on 16 May 1942). See Schulte, *Zwangsarbeit*, 214 f.

90. IfZ, NO 598, Himmler to Pohl, 7 July 1942; see also Schulte, *Zwangsarbeit*, 215.

91. On the failure of SS armaments production see Schulte, *Zwangsarbeit*, 216 ff. In August 1943 Speer tried to blame the Gustloff-Werke for the failure of rifle production at Buchenwald (BAB, NS 19/367, Brandt to Pohl, 17 August 1943).

92. Schulte, *Zwangsarbeit*, 224 and 231.

93. Himmler to Speer, 5 March 1943 (BAB, NS 19/3637).

94. Schulte, *Zwangsarbeit*, 218 f.; IfZ, NIK 15392, Pohl report to Himmler, 16 September 1942, published in Pingel, *Häftlinge*, 276 f.

95. Boelcke (ed.), *Deutschlands Rüstung*, 20–2 September 1942; Schulte, *Zwangsarbeit*, 220 f.

96. Orth, *System*, 169 ff; Mommsen and Grieger, *Volkswagenwerk*, 50 ff.

97. On the changes in the structure of criminality see Wagner, *Volksgemeinschaft*, 316 ff.

98. BAB, NS 19/219, published in Detlev Peukert, *Die Edelweißpiraten. Protestbewegungen jugendlicher Arbeiter im Dritten Reich. Eine Dokumentation* (Cologne, 1980), 156 f.

99. Picker (ed.), *Tischgespräche*, 7April 1942.

100. Wagner, *Volksgemeinschaft*, 314.

101. Herbert, *Fremdarbeiter*, 167, on the basis of a post-war statement by the responsible RSHA representative, Bernhard Baatz.

102. IfZ, PS-3040, contains the general regulations and the particular instruction to the security police and SD; see Herbert, *Fremdarbeiter*, 181 f.

103. Doc. PS-654, Thierack minute of 18 September 1942, published in *IMT*, vol. 26, pp. 200 ff.; *Dienstkalender*. It was already normal practice for prisoners in the judicial system who, in the view of the police, had been given too lenient sentences to be taken into 'preventive custody'. See Wagner, *Volksgemeinschaft*, 336.

104. Wagner, *Volksgemeinschaft*, 337.

105. The chief of the security police and SD laid down in an edict of 21 July 1942 that those considered unworthy of serving in the armed forces should be taken into preventive detention 'on the first occasion of their committing a breach of their conditions'. The Reich Criminal Police Office issued an instruction on 28 December 1942 that in cases involving 'those considered unworthy of serving in the armed forces', before the case was handed over to the public prosecutor consideration should be given as to whether police preventive measures should be imposed (both documents in IfZ, Dc 17.02, collection of edicts concerning the preventive combating of crime); see Wagner, *Volksgemeinschaft*, 338 f.

106. RSHA, 23 December 1942, published in Ifz, Dc 17.02, collection of edicts concerning the preventive combating of crime.
107. Wagner,*Volksgemeinschaft*, 342 f.
108. BAB, NS 19/4010, 14 October 1943, speech to the meeting of military commanders in Bad Schachen. It was printed under the title *Sicherheitsfragen. Vortrag, gehalten auf der Befehlshabertagung in Bad Schachen am 14. Oktober 1943*, ed. NS-Führungsstab des Oberkommandos der Wehrmacht (Berlin, 1943).
109. Broszat, *Polenpolitik*, 152 ff.

CHAPTER 25

1. In this context one should bear in mind Himmler's announcement in 1937 that, in the event of war, the SS had, apart from the three military fronts—on land, in the sea, and in the air—'the German homeland' as a 'fourth theatre of war' that it had to secure (doc. PS-1992 [A], Himmler's speech on the essential nature and tasks of the SS given to a Wehrmacht course on national politics, 15–23 January 1937, published in *IMT*, vol. 29, pp. 206 ff., 231).
2. BAB, NS 19/3402, 15 November 1942.
3. Ibid. 10 December 1942. This document, as was usual with documents given to Hitler to read, was typed in especially large letters and is minuted 'Abl. 10.12.'.
4. *Dienstkalender*, 10 December 1942; Himmler minute of 10 December 1942 (quoted in Ibid.) and Himmler to the RSHA (BAB, NS 19/1807).
5. BAB, NS 19/1929, Draft, signed Himmler, and minuted: 'Please submit to AH', 18 December 1942.
6. BAB, NS 19/120, Telex to Oberg, 30 December 1942. On the preparations for and implementation of the measures taken in Marseilles see Meyer, *Besatzung*, 115 ff.
7. BAB, NS 19/120, 4 January 1943.
8. Ibid. 5 January 1943.
9. BAB, NS 19/3402, message to Oberg, 5 January 1943.
10. BAB, BDC, SS-O Oberg, 6 January 1943.
11. BAB, NS 19/3401, message to Oberg, 11 January 1943.
12. BAB, NS 19/3402, 18 January 1943.
13. Meyer, *Besatzung*, 123 f.
14. BAB, NS 19/120, telex to Müller, 13 February 1943, and to Kaltenbrunner, 17 February 1943.
15. *Dienstkalender*, 25–30 December 1942 (in particular references to 25 December); Heinen, *Legion*, 460 f. On the conditions of Sima's internment see Heydrich's report of 8 January 1941 (BAB, NS 19/2863).
16. Kasten, 'Franzosen', 213.

17. PAA, state secretary France 15, Rudolf Schleier to Reich Foreign Minister about this meeting based on information that he had received from Laval, 6 April 1943; see Kasten, 'Franzosen', 205 ff. According to Schleier the meeting took place on 3 April 1943 in Paris; see also BAB, NS 19/1444 (Appointments).

18. Kasten, 'Franzosen', 208.

19. Ibid. 219 ff.

20. BAB, NS 19/1504, Berger to Oberg, 8 February 1944.

21. Ibid. Oberg to Himmler, 10 February 1944.

22. Ibid. telex Meine to Oberg, 18 February 1944.

23. BAB, NS 19/236, minute for RFSS on the meeting with SS-Obergruppenführer Berger, 11 April 1944.

24. Die Deutschen in der Tschechoslowakei, no. 407.

25. Brandes, Tschechen, ii. 22.

26. Die Deutschen in der Tschechoslowakei, no. 414a, 7 September 1944; on 3 January 1944, at the request of Frank, Himmler extended this authority, which had initially only be granted to 31 December 1943 (Ibid. no. 414b and c); see Brandes, Tschechen, ii. 23.

27. Thomsen, Besatzungspolitik, 130.

28. Ibid. 131 f., quotes in this context from the Danish national archive a message of 18 January 1943 from Himmler to Best.

29. BAB NS19/3473 Himmler to Berger, 15 July 1943.

30. Thomsen, Besatzungspolitik, 192; BAB, BDC, SS-O Best, message from Himmler of October 1943.

31. Thomsen, Besatzungspolitik, 201 f.

32. SS en Nederland, doc. no. 319, 6 February 1943, and doc. no. 320, Himmler's reply of 6 February 1943. On the repressive policy in the Netherlands see also Christoph Spieker, 'Enttäuschte Liebe. Funktionswandel der Ordnungspolizei in den Niederlanden', in Johannes Houwink ten Cate und Alfons Kenkmann (eds), Deutsche und holländische Polizei in den besetzten niederländischen Gebieten. Dokumentation einer Arbeitstagung (Münster, 2002), 67–95.

33. Telex, Himmler to Rauter, 10 February 1943 (SS en Nederland, doc. no. 328).

34. SS en Nederland, doc. no. 331, Himmler to Rauter, 11 February 1943.

35. Ibid. doc. no. 368, Himmler to Rauter, 31 March 1943.

36. Ibid. doc. no. 387, Message to Rauter, 9 May 1943; see Kwiet, Reichskommissariat, 150.

37. SS en Nederland, doc. no. 466, Himmler to Rauter, 24 September 1943.

38. Ibid. doc. no. 467, 27 September 1943.

39. Meershoek, 'Machtentfaltung', 400; Spieker, 'Liebe', 76.

40. Thomsen, Besatzungspolitik, 200 ff.; Herbert, Best, 373 ff.

41. Bohn, Reichskommissariat, 86.

42. Warmbrunn, German Occupation, 146 f.

43. IfZ, NO 2306, 10 November 1942.

44. BAB, NS 19/2648, order of 11 January 1943.

45. BAB, NS 19/2638, Krüger to Himmler, 16 February 1943.
46. Ibid. Himmler statement, 12 March 1943.
47. Madajczyk, *Okkupationspolitik*, 217.
48. BAB, NS 19/1432, Himmler note of 22 June 1943 about the meeting.
49. Ibid. various orders, 21 June 1943; see Gerlach, *Morde*, 952.
50. BAB, NS 19/1432, Himmler note about the interview with Hitler, 3 April 1944.
51. Madajczyk, *Okkupationspolitik*, 195 ff. and 191.
52. Gerlach, *Morde*, 1010.
53. BAB, NS 19/1432 (also IfZ, NO 2034), Himmler's order of 10 July 1943; see Gerlach, *Morde*, 1023 f.
54. Gerlach, *Morde*, 1010 ff.; for the areas concerned see p. 1034.
55. See ibid. 999 ff.
56. Ibid. 999.
57. BAB, NS 19/1681, 18 November 1942.
58. BAB, NS 19/4010, 4 October 1943, also published as doc. PS-1919, in *IMT*, vol. 29, pp. 110 ff., quotation 117 f.
59. Ibid. 122 f.
60. Peter Black, *Ernst Kaltenbrunner. Vasall Himmlers. Eine SS-Karriere* (Paderborn, etc., 1991), 143 ff. and 195 ff.
61. Thierack to Bormann, 16 November 1941, according to Herbert, *Fremdarbeiter*, 285; Broszat, *Polenpolitik*, 153.
62. Edict of 30 June 1943, quoted in Broszat, *Polenpolitik*, 154; Herbert, *Fremdarbeiter*, 286; Wagner, *Volksgemeinschaft*, 341.
63. Broszat, *Polenpolitik*, 154.
64. Edict of 10 August 1943; Kaltenbrunner quotes this order in an edict of 5 April 1944 (doc. PS-3855, in *IMT*, vol. 33, pp. 243 ff.); see Black, *Kaltenbrunner*, 152.
65. Doc. PS-1650, published in *IMT*, vol. 27, pp. 425 ff.; see Black, *Kaltenbrunner*, 152.
66. Michel Abitbol, *Les Juifs d'Afrique du Nord sous Vichy* (Paris. 1983); Klaus-Michael Mallmann and Martin Cüppers, *Halbmond und Hakenkreuz. Das Dritte Reich, die Araber und Palästina* (Darmstadt, 2006), 199 ff.
67. On Jewish persecution in France after the occupation of the southern zone see Klarsfeld, *Vichy*, 193 ff., and Susan Zuccotti, *The Holocaust, the French, and the Jews* (New York, 1993), 166 ff.
68. Klarsfeld, *Vichy*, 200 ff.
69. On the history of the Italian Jews under Fascism see Susan Zuccotti, *The Italians and the Holocaust: Persecution, Rescue, and Survival* (New York, 1987); Meir Michaelis, *Mussolini and the Jews: German–Italian Relations and the Jewish Question in Italy, 1922–1945* (Oxford, 1978).
70. Müller to Bergmann, Foreign Ministry, 25 February 1943, with a quote from Himmler's letter to Ribbentrop, 29 January 1943, published in Klarsfeld, *Vichy*, 495 ff.

71. IfZ, NG 4956, telex Special Train Westphalia to Wolff; German Department's reply of 24 February 1943.

72. Hagen Fleischer, *Im Kreuzschatten der Mächte: Griechenland 1941–1944*, 2 parts, (Frankfurt a. M., 1986), Part 1, p. 273.

73. Chary, *Bulgarian Jews*, 129 ff. See also Nir Baruch, *Der Freikauf. Zar Boris und das Schicksal der bulgarischen Juden* (Sofia, 1996), 103 ff., and Dieter Ruckhaberle and Christiane Ziesecke (eds), *Rettung der bulgarischen Juden—1943. Eine Dokumentation* (Berlin, 1984).

74. Chary, *Bulgarian Jews*, 178 ff., 197 ff., and 224 ff.

75. PAA, The office of the state secretary Bulgaria 5, Ribbentrop to Beckerle, 4 April 1943; see also Chary, *Bulgarian Jews*, 269 f.

76. Adler, *Mensch*, 224 ff.

77. IfZ, NO 1882, Himmler to Krüger, 11 January 1943.

78. BAB, NS 19/1740; see also Himmler's instruction to Krüger, 16 February 1943 (ibid.).

79. Arad, *Belzec*, 392; Yisrael Gutman, *The Jews of Warsaw, 1939–1943: Ghetto, Underground, Revolt* (Bloomington and Indianapolis, 1989), 307 ff.

80. Stroop gave Himmler a report illustrated with photographs in which he had proudly documented his destructive activities under the motto : 'A Jewish district in Warsaw no longer exists!' (Stroop Report, doc. PS-1061, published in *IMT*, vol. 30, pp. 357–472).

81. BAB, NS 19/2648, 12 May 1943; see also Himmler's minute of 10 May 1943, in which he emphasized that the 'evacuation of the remaining 300, 000 Jews in the General Government' must be carried out 'with the greatest speed' (published in *Faschismus, Ghetto, Massenmord*, 354 f.); see also Sandkühler, *'Endlösung'*, 197.

82. Präg and Jacobmeyer (eds), *Diensttagebuch*, 31 May 1943; see also Himmler's telephone notes of 20 May 1943: 'Jewish evacuation' (BAB, NS 19/1440).

83. Pohl, *Ostgalizien*, 246 ff.; Sandkühler, *'Endlösung'*, 194 ff.

84. Katzmann report to Krüger, 30 June 1943, published in *Faschismus, Ghetto, Massenmord*, 358 ff.

85. BAB, NS 19/1432, Himmler note of 22 June 1943 concerning the meeting.

86. BAB, NS 19/1740, Himmler to Pohl and Kaltenbrunner, 11 June 1943. 'A large park' was to be created on the land of the former ghetto.

87. BAB, NS 19/1571, Himmler order of 5 July 1943, which he withdrew on 20 July 1943 following objections from Pohl and Globocnik (ibid. message from Brandt of 20 July 1943); however, only four days later he renewed the order, see Schelvis, *Sobibór*, 173 f.

88. Pohl, *Lublin*, 160. Pohl, Krüger, and Globocnik agreed on the takeover of the camp on 7 September 1943 (Pohl note from the same date, IfZ, NO 599, published in *Faschismus, Ghetto, Massenmord*, 459 f.).

89. IfZ, NO 1036, minute concerning the transformation of the forced labour camps of the SSPF into KZ, 19 January 1944.

90. Steinbacher, '*Musterstadt*', 296.

91. Ibid. 300 ff.

92. In September 1943 Himmler distanced himself from this order but renewed it again in December.

93. *Faschismus, Ghetto, Massenmord*, 369 f., Greiser to Pohl, 14 February 1944. Here reference is also made to Himmler's order of 11 June 1944 to transform the ghettos, of which the original has not been found. See in detail Michael Alberti, *Die Verfolgung und Vernichtung der Juden im Reichsgau Wartheland 1939–1945* (Wiesbaden, 2006), 472 ff.

94. Alberti, *Verfolgung*, 473 f.

95. Arad, *Belzec*, 396; Sara Bender, 'The "Reinhardt Action" in the "Bialystok District"', in Freia Anders (ed.), *Bialystok in Bielefeld. Nationalsozialistische Verbrechen vor dem Landgericht Bielefeld 1958–1967* (Bielefeld, 2003), 186–208, at 204 ff.

96. *Enzyklopädie des Holocaust. Die Verfolgung und Ermordung der europäischen Juden*, 3 vols., edited under the auspices of Yad Vashem etc., main editor Israel Gutman; German edition ed. Eberhard Jäckel, Peter Longerich, and Julius H. Schoeps (Berlin, 1993), Bialystok article. On the background see Sara Bender, 'From Underground to Armed Struggle: The Resistance Movement in the Bialystok Ghetto', *Yad Vashem Studies*, 23 (1993), 145–71.

97. Gerlach, *Morde*, 739; Jakow Suchowolskij, 'Es gab weder Schutz noch Erlösung, weder Sicherheit noch Rettung. Jüdischer Widerstand und der Untergang des Ghettos Glubokoje', *Dachauer Hefte*, 20 (2004), 22–38.

98. On Treblinka and Sobibor see Reuben Ainsztein, *Jüdischer Widerstand im deutschbesetzten Osteuropa während des Zweiten Weltkrieges* (Oldenburg, 1993), 396 ff.

99. On the district of Lublin see Helge Grabitz and Wolfgang Scheffler (eds), *Letzte Spuren. Ghetto Warschau, SS-Arbeitslager Trawniki, Aktion Erntefest. Fotos und Dokumente über Opfer des Endlösungswahns im Spiegel der historischen Ereignisse*, 2nd rev. edn. (Berlin, 1993), 328 ff. In the district of Cracow the forced labour camps, Szebnie and Plaszow, were affected, on 19 November all the prisoners in the Lemberg camp, Janowska' in the district of Galicia were shot (on the district of Galicia see Jan Erik Schulte, 'Zwangsarbeit für die SS. Juden in der Ostindustrie GmbH', in Norbert Frei (ed.), *Ausbeutung, Vernichtung, Öffentlichkeit. Neue Studien zur nationalsozialistischen Lagerpolitik* (Munich, 2000), 43–74, 69).

100. The original order was dated 2 April and envisaged the retrospective establishment of a ghetto in Riga on 13 März (OA Moscow, 504-2-8). See in detail Angrick and Klein, '*Endlösung*', 382 ff.

101. IfZ, NO 2403. Apart from Bach-Zelewski, among others HSSP Russia-North, Prützmann, HSSPF East, Krüger, the head of the RSHA, Kaltenbrunner, the head of the WVHA, Pohl, and the head of the Commando Staff of the RFSS, Knoblauch, took part in the meeting.

102. On 13 August 1943 Himmler restricted the employment of Jews by an order
     that the OKH made 'binding for the whole of the Army in the field' (BAB,
     NS 2/83). It was not permitted to use Jews for office work or for 'personal
     service' (IfZ, NOKW 2368, Kriegstagebuch Oberkommando 3 Panzer-
     Army, Quartermaster 2, 4 November 1943); see also Gerlach, *Morde*, 739.
103. Avraham Tory, *Surviving the Holocaust: The Kovno Ghetto Diary*, edited and
     introduced by Martin Gilbert (Cambridge, Mass., and London, 1990); Alfred
     Streim, 'Konzentrationslager auf dem Gebiet der Sowjetunion', *Dachauer
     Hefte*, 5 (1989), 174–87, at 176; *Enzyklopädie*, 'Kowno' article.
104. Yitzhak Arad, *Ghetto in Flames: The Struggle and Destruction of the Jews in Vilna
     in the Holocaust* (Jerusalem, 1980), 401 ff.
105. Streim, 'Konzentrationslager', 177 f.; *Enzyklopädie*, 'Vaivara' article.
106. Gerlach, *Morde*, 739 ff.
107. PAA, Inland IIg 194, correspondence between the Foreign Ministry and the
     embassy, March–April; see also Hilberg, *Vernichtung*, 764; according to
     Czech, *Kalendarium*, the trains arrived in Auschwitz on 7 and 13 May.
108. IfZ, NG 4407, 29. June 1943. The ambassador, Hanns Elard Ludin, reported
     to the Foreign Ministry in June that 'the evacuation of the Jews from
     Slovakia' was 'at the moment at a standstill'.
109. Published in Klarsfeld and Steinberg (eds), *Endlösung*, 70.
110. Wetzel, 'Frankreich und Belgien', 30.
111. CDJC, XXVII–17, Hagen to Röthke, 16 June 1943, published in Klarsfeld,
     Vichy, 535.
112. Ibid. 256.
113. CDJC, XXVI–35, Hagen minute, 11 August 1943, published in ibid. 550 ff.;
     XXVI-36, Röthke minute, 15 August 1943, concerning the meeting on the
     previous day, published in ibid. 551 ff.; see also the account in ibid. 262 ff.
114. CDJC, XXVII-33, Office of the Head of State to Fernand de Brinon, the
     Vichy government's representative in Paris, 24 August 1943, published in
     ibid. 556; see also the account in ibid. 270.
115. Express letter from the RSHA dated 17 October 1939, published in IfZ, Dc
     17.02, collection of edicts concerning the preventive combating of crime; see
     Zimmermann, *Rassenutopie*, 167 ff.
116. Zimmermann, *Rassenutopie*, 168.
117. Express letter of 27 April 1940, signed Himmler, published in IfZ, Dc 17.02,
     collection of edicts concerning the preventive combating of crime. On the
     deportations in May see Zimmermann, *Rassenutopie*, 172 ff.
118. Zimmermann, *Rassenutopie*, 186, quoting in this context a letter from the
     office of the Governor-General of 3 August 1940, which is in the Lublin state
     archive.
119. Ibid. 186, based on the files in the Generallandesarchiv Karlsruhe.
120. On the details see ibid. 176 ff.

121. BAB, NS 19/2655, 10 October 1941, reply to the letter from Uebelhoer of 4 October (ibid.); see Zimmermann, *Rassenutopie*, 223 ff.

122. *Dienstkalender*.

123. Ibid. 20 April 1942, quoting a circular edict of the BdO in the General Government From the OA Moscow.

124. Zimmermann, *Rassenutopie*, 275 and 315, quoting the order of the BdS Ostland of 19 October 1942 and emphasizing Himmler's role in ordering this measure.

125. Ibid. 297 f.

126. IfZ, NO 1725, 16 September 1942; Zimmermann, *Rassenutopie*, 297

127. 13 October 1942, Edict of the Reich Criminal Police Office, published in IfZ, Dc 17.02, collection of edicts concerning the preventive combating of crime.

128. Minute of the Reich Ministry of Food, 14 November 1942, referred to in Martin Luchterhandt, *Der Weg nach Birkenau. Entstehung und Verlauf der nationalsozialistischen Verfolgung der 'Zigeuner'* (Lübeck, 2000), 239.

129. Himmler command of 16 November 1942, published in IfZ, Dc 17.02, collection of edicts concerning the preventive combating of crime.

130. Zimmermann, *Rassenutopie*, 305 ff.

131. BAB, NS 19/180, message from Bormann, 3 December 1942.

132. Zimmermann, *Rassenutopie*, 297.

133. The minutes are published in Joachim S. Hohmann, *Robert Ritter und die Erben der Kriminalbiologie. 'Zigeunerforschung' im Nationalsozialismus und in Westdeutschland im Zeichen des Rassismus* (Frankfurt a. M., etc., 1991), 75 ff., although without a source. See also Zimmermann, *Rassenutopie*, 302 f., and Karola Fings, 'Eine "Wannsee-Konferenz" über die Vernichtung der Zigeuner? Neue Forschungsergebnisse zum 15. Januar 1943 und dem "Auschwitz-Erlass"', *Jahrbuch für Antisemitismusforschung*, 15 (2006), 303–33.

134. IfZ, Dc 17.02, collection of edicts concerning the preventive combating of crime; see Zimmermann, *Rassenutopie*, 303 f.

135. Zimmermann, *Rassenutopie*, 305 ff., on the practice of selection.

136. Ibid. 326 ff.

137. Ibid. 375.

138. Ibid. 339 ff.

139. Ibid. 259 ff.

140. Ibid. 277 ff.

141. Ibid. 381 ff.

142. Ibid. 289 ff.

143. Ibid. 292.

144. Ibid. 235 ff.

145. Stein, *Geschichte*, 182 ff.

146. BAB, NS 19/4010, 6 October 1943, published in Himmler, *Geheimreden*, 162 ff., quotation p. 179.

147. Wegner, *Politische Soldaten*, 275 f.

148. IfZ, NO 2015, 'Volksdeutsche in der Waffen-SS', excerpt from Reichslei-terdienst, 28 December 1943; see Stein, *Geschichte*, 157.

149. *Das Schicksal der Deutschen in Rumänien*, ed. Bundesministerium für Vertrie-bene, Flüchtlinge und Kriegsgeschädigte (Berlin, 1957), Appendix 8, 147E; IfZ, NO 2236, Agreement of 12 May 1943.

150. Böhm, *Gleichschaltung*, 306 ff.; Casagrande, *'Prinz Eugen'*, 207 ff.

151. *Schicksal der Deutschen*, 56E.

152. IfZ, NO 2213.

153. Spannenberger, *Volksbund*, 389 ff.

154. PAA, Inland IIg 327, agreement of 22 May 1943.

155. Ibid. report on the II.Waffen-SS action, 8 June 1943.

156. Spannenberger, *Volksbund*, 400.

157. BAB, NS 19/2133, Himmler order of 29 March 1944.

158. Spannenberger, *Volksbund*, 412 ff.

159. Stein, *Geschichte*, 157.

160. Casagrande, *'Prinz Eugen'*, 204.

161. BAB, NS 19/319, Himmler to Phleps.

162. Stein, *Geschichte*, 162 ff.; BAB, NS 19/2601, Himmler to Phleps, 13 February 1943, re: the creation. For a detailed history of the division see George Lepre, *Himmler's Bosnian Division: The Waffen-SS Handschar Division, 1943–1945* (Atglen, 1997).

163. NARA, T 175/111, Himmler to Kammerhofer, 1 July 1943.

164. BAB, NS 19/2601, 6 August 1943; see the enquiry to Berger concerning the Grand Mufti's opinion on this matter, 2 July 1943, and Berger's reply of 26 July 1943 (ibid.).

165. Ibid. 26 November 1943.

166. Ibid. Himmler to Berger, 24 April 1943.

167. BAB, NS 19/4013, speech to the 13th SS Mountain Division, 11 January 1944.

168. BAB, NS 19/4013, 26 January 1944.

169. Stein, *Geschichte*, 164 f.

170. Ibid. 166.

171. BAB, NS 19/2601, Himmler to Phleps, 10 May 1944.

172. On the creation of the Baltic units see Stein, *Geschichte*, 157 ff.

173. IfZ, NO 3301, RFSS to SS Main Office and SS Leadership Main Office, 13 January 1943.

174. Ibid.

175. IfZ, NO 3300, Berger to Himmler, 11 December 1942.

176. IfZ, NO 3379, Berger to Himmler, 17 April 1943.

177. Stein, *Geschichte*, 160.

178. IfZ, NO 3044, Message from Jeckeln to the Reich Ministry for the Occupied Eastern Territories, 2 July 1944, that he had ordered the drafting of the 1925 age cohort in Latvia and the 1926 cohort in Estonia; NO 4884, Order

concerning the drafting of men born between the years 1904 and 1923 for military service, 30 January 1944 (Estonia); see Stein, *Geschichte*, 160.

179. Stein, *Geschichte*, 160.

180. Ibid. 167.

181. BAB, NS 19/4013, 16 May 1944.

182. Stein, *Geschichte*, 166 f.

183. Ibid. 168 f.

184. Helmut Heiber (ed.), *Hitlers Lagebesprechungen. Die Protokollfragmente seiner militärischen Konferenzen 1942–1945* (Stuttgart, 1962), 938 ff.

185. BAB, NS 19/4014, Speech to Wehrmacht generals on 24 May 1944 in Sonthofen, passage published in Himmler, *Geheimreden*, 208 f.; see Heinemann, 'Rasse', 540 f.

186. BAB, NS 2/19, 28 May 1944. See also BAB, NS 19/4014, speech in Kochem, 25 May 1944: '... the men involved are naturally not SS men'; NARA T-175/111, Himmler to Jüttner, 7 July 1942; Stein, *Geschichte*, 161.

187. BAB, NS 2/153, telex of 24 January 1944, quoted in circular from the head of RuSHA, Turner, 22 February 1944.

188. This could apply to the 'Prinz Eugene' and 'Horst Wessel' divisions and to the cavalry division; BAB, NS 2/154, SS Main Office to reinforcement agencies, 24 July 1944, with reference to Himmler's order of 27 June 1944.

189. *SS en Nederland*, doc. no. 349, Himmler note of 3 March 1943; see Wegner, *Politische Soldaten*, 313 ff.

190. NARA, T 175/74, Himmler note of 10 February 1943. The note is concerned with the establishment of another Germanic division, named 'Waräger'.

191. NARA, T 175/88, Brandt minute of 7 September 1943.

192. 'Himmler's speech to the Gauleiters on 3 August 1944', documented in *Vierteljahrshefte für Zeitgeschichte*, 1 (1953), 357–94, quotation p. 394.

193. References in *SS en Nederland*, doc. no. 604, Himmler to Jüttner and Berger, 4 December 1944, and doc. no. 434, Himmler note of 13 July 1943.

194. The precise official title in the document of appointment was 'Reich and Prussian Minister of the Interior'. This double title for the ministries, which had been combined in 1934, had not been used since 1938; the fact that the old title was now being reactivated can be seen as a gesture to Göring, who was still Prussian Prime Minister. On Himmler's appointment and activities see in particular Dieter Rebentisch, *Führerstaat und Verwaltung im Zweiten Weltkrieg. Verfassungsentwicklung und Verwaltungspolitik 1939–1945* (Stuttgart, 1989), 499 ff.; Stephan Lehnstaedt, 'Das Reichsministerium des Innern unter Heinrich Himmler 1943–1945', *Vierteljahrshefte für Zeitgeschichte*, 54 (2006), 639–72, and Birgit Schulze, 'Heinrich Himmler, das Reichsministerium des Innern und das Verhältnis von Staat und Partei, 1943–1945', in Klaus Mölltgen (ed.), *Kriegswirtschaft und öffentliche Verwaltung im Ruhrgebiet 1939–1945* (Gelsenkirchen, 1990), 9–33.

195. *Tagebücher Goebbels*, 10 August 1943.

196. Neliba, *Frick*, 354 ff.; BAB, R 43 II/136a, on the appointment process.
197. *Tagebücher Goebbels*, 21 August 1943. On 9 August 1943 Goebbels had proposed to Hitler that the Interior Ministry be split and Himmler appointed police minister (ibid. 10 August 1943).
198. See Rebentisch, *Führerstaat*, 502, with further details.
199. Michael Fahlbusch, *Wissenschaft im Dienst der nationalsozialistischen Politik? Die 'Volksdeutschen Forschungsgemeinschaften' von 1931–1945* (Baden-Baden, 1999), 738 ff.
200. On Himmler's leadership style as Reich Interior Minister see Rebentisch, *Führerstaat*, 508.
201. For example, he made this demand in his speeches of 4 and 6 October 1943 (BAB, NS 19/4010) and in his speech to the meeting of district governors (Regierungspräsidenten) in Breslau on 10 und 11 January 1944 (Note in R 43 II/425a); this was taken into account in a circular edict of 28 October 1943 (*MBliV* 1943, S. 1875); see Rebentisch, *Führerstaat*, 509.
202. Remark in the speech of 6 October 1943 (BAB, NS 19/4010); see Rebentisch, *Führerstaat*, 509 f.
203. Speeches of 4 and 6 October 1943 (BAB, NS 19/4010).
204. Hans Mommsen, 'Ein Erlass Himmlers zur Bekämpfung der Korruption in der inneren Verwaltung vom Dezember 1944', *Vierteljahrshefte für Zeitgeschichte*, 16 (1968), 295–309. Himmler had already referred to this in his speech of 6 October 1943.
205. BAB, NS 19/3280, speech at the meeting of Oberbürgermeisters and Landeshauptmänner on 12 and 13 February 1944 in Posen. See also NS 19/4010, speech of 4 October 1943, in which he declared 'getting rid of corruption and bad behaviour' to be one of his most important aims as Reich Interior Minister.
206. He had already made a note of this motto for his inaugural speech on 26 August 1943; see also BAB, NS 19/4010, Speech of 6 October 1943. For the following see Rebentisch, *Führerstaat*, 503 ff.
207. Ibid. 503 ff.; Longerich, *Stellvertreter*, 187 ff.
208. See his speeches of 4 and 6 October 1943 (BAB, NS 19/4010) and his address to the meeting of Oberbürgermeisters and Landeshauptmänner on 12 and 13 February 1944 in Posen (NS 19/3280); BAB, R 1501/1272, Stuckart to Kreiss, 14 February 1944. According to this Himmler intended to get the Ahnenerbe to publish monographs under the rubric 'German Mayors as Pillars of the Reich'.
209. Rebentisch, *Führerstaat*, 508.
210. Führer edicts of 1 April 1944, in *RGBl* 1944 I, 109 ff.
211. BAB, R 43 II/364a, Himmler to Lammers, 4 September 1944. Stuckart and Lammers agreed not to accept any closures, but to agree to Bormann's request to subordinate the Prussian district governors (Regierungspräsidenten) to the

provincial governors (Oberpräsidenten) (R 43II/656, especially the meeting of 27 September 1944).

212. BAB, NS 19/1272, Excerpt of the minutes concerning the 'Assembly' of the government of the General Government, 18 November 1943.

213. The district governors'meeting is dealt with in detail in Lehnstaedt, 'Reichsministerium', on the basis of a set of hitherto unknown minutes in the Archiwum Akt Nowych in Warsaw; a note of this speech is also in BAB, R 43 II/425a.

214. BAB, NS 19/3280.

215. Rebentisch, *Führerstaat*, 505 f.

216. *Tagebücher Goebbels*, 8 November 1943, also 31 January 1944.

217. Ibid. 25 and 29 February 1944.

218. Ibid. 20 December 1943. He was responding here to Himmler's alleged intention to subordinate the Education Ministry to himself.

219. Ibid. 25. January 1944. For Bormann's critical comments on Himmler's increase in power see also the entries for 13 March and 18 and 27 April 1944.

220. Ibid. 11 May 1944.

221. See above pp. 632 ff.

222. Schulte, *Zwangsarbeit*, 226.

223. The DEST produced aircraft parts: for Messerschmitt in Flossenbürg and Mauthausen, for Junkers in Natzweiler, and for a Luftwaffe plant in the Dutch KZ Herzogenbusch. In Oranienburg a large brick-factory was turned into a large foundry for producing shells; although Himmler requested Pohl to use 'Russian improvisation' in carrying out the changeover, production remained far below expectations (BAB, NS 19/443, Himmler to Pohl, 11 March 1944). The German Fine Furniture AG (Deutsche Edelmöbel AG) in Butschowitz and the German Master Workshops (Deutsche Meisterstätten) in Prague also produced aircraft parts. On armaments production in the plants see Schulte, *Zwangsarbeit*, 227 ff.

224. BAB, NS 19/4010, speech in Posen, 4 October 1943, also published as doc. PS-1919, in *IMT*, vol. 29, pp. 110 ff., quotation 144.

225. Schulte, *Zwangsarbeit*, 234; Kaienburg, *Wirtschaft*, 483 ff.

226. BAB, NS 19/1802, Report of the departmental head of W-5 in the WVHA on the experiments, countersigned by Himmler. On the Kok-Sagys project see Gerlach, *Morde*, 1023 ff.; Kaienburg, *Wirtschaft*, 847 ff.; Susanne Heim, *Kalorien, Kautschuk, Karrieren. Pflanzenzüchtung und landwirtschaftliche Forschung in Kaiser-Wilhelm-Instituten 1933–1945* (Göttingen, 2003), esp. 144 ff.

227. BAB, NS 19/1802, Himmler to Göring on the interview on 20 February 1943, 22 March 1943.

228. Ibid. and an undated note containing six points. On the institutions working on Kok-Sagys research see Heim, *Kalorien*, 131 ff.

229. BAB, NS 19/1802, minute of 15 April 1943; report on the workshop of those interested in Kok-Sagys rubber in the SS Main Office, 25 June 1943.

230. BAB, NS 19/1802, Göring, 9 July 1943.

231. Ibid. Himmler telex to the HSSPF, 21 July 1943; Himmler note of 7 July 1943 on the organization of the office of the representative for rubber plants; Himmler to Darré, 2 August 1943.

232. Heim, *Kalorien*, 172 ff.

233. BAB, NS 19/1802, minute of a meeting with Himmler on 24 July 1943.

234. During the summer and autumn 1943 he had a lengthy dispute with Governor-General Frank who eventually agreed to grant him 10,000 hectares. (BAB, NS 19/1802); see correspondence in the same file and Himmler's minute of 22 November 1943.

235. BAB, NS 19/1802, brief overview, 29 March 1944; according to that, in the winter of 1943–4 30,000 hectares were envisaged for Kok-Sagys.

236. Ibid. correspondence with the German ethnic group in Romania, State Peasant Office.

237. Ibid. Brandt to Winkelmann, 28 June 1944.

238. Ibid. Report of Corvette Captain Stahl about his official visit of 15–27 May 1944, 2 June 1944. Stahl refers to a meeting with Himmler on 20 May 1944.

239. BAB, NS 19/1802, Backe to Himmler, 20 December 1944. Backe asked Himmler to agree to reduce the amount of land, to which Brandt responded positively in his letter of 13 January 1945.

240. Ibid. Stahl, report on official visit to the west of Ukraine, 9 November 1943.

241. Ibid. Backe to Himmler, 20 December 1944.

242. Ibid. message of 14 March 1944. In the case of 10,000 hectares one could anticipate a yield of only 150 to 300 tons; originally it was assumed it would be more than 600 tons.

243. Ibid. 5 April 1944.

244. Schulte, *Zwangsarbeit*, 392 ff.; Orth, *System*, 175 ff.

245. IfZ, NO 1523.

246. Orth, *System*, 192.

247. Michael J. Neufeld, *Die Rakete und das Reich. Wernher von Braun, Peenemünde und der Beginn des Raketenzeitalters* (Berlin, 1997), 21 ff.; Heinz Dieter Hölsken, *Die V-Waffen. Entstehung, Propaganda, Kriegseinsatz* (Stuttgart, 1984), 40 f.

248. Neufeld, *Rakete*, 217 ff.

249. Ibid. 220; BAB, BDC, SS-O von Braun, who had joined the SS on 1 May 1940.

250. Neufeld, *Rakete*, 221 ff.

251. Ibid. 221 ff. The development work on the rockets was also moved underground in caves in the Austrian Alps, which were given the codename 'Cement' and were built by KZ prisoners under Kammler's direction. (ibid. 246 f.).

252. BAB, NS 19/1444; R 3/1583, Himmler to Speer, 21 August 1943. See also Neufeld, *Rakete*, 241 f.

253. Result of the Armaments' conference of 15–20 August 1943, published in Boelcke (ed.), *Deutschlands Rüstung*, 291.

254. Neufeld, *Rakete*, 258 f. The information is based on Braun's account. After the war he reported that he had been ordered to see Himmler, who offered to take over the development of the rocket programme. He had declined. The harassment that followed was, he said, intended to break his will.

255. Ibid. 260 ff.

256. See the overview in Rainer Fröbe, 'Hans Kammler—Technokrat der Vernichtung', in Ronald Smelser and Enrico Syring (eds), *Die SS. Elite unter dem Totenkopf. 30 Lebensläufe* (Paderborn, etc., 2000), 305–19.

257. BAB, NS 19/4010, speech in Posen, 4. October 1943, also published as doc. PS-1919, in *IMT*, vol. 29, pp. 110 ff., quotation p. 145 f.

258. BAB, NS 19/4010, published in Himmler, *Geheimreden*, 162 ff., quotation p. 169.

259. BAB, NS 19/2662.

260. Katrin Paehler, 'Ein Spiegel seiner selbst. Der SD-Ausland in Italien', in Michael Wildt, (ed.), *Nachrichtendienst, politische Elite, Mordeinheit. Der Sicherheitsdienst des Reichsführers-SS* (Hamburg, 2003), 241–66. On Himmler's prediction see already Josef Schröder, *Italiens Kriegsaustritt 1943. Die deutschen Gegenmaßnahmen im italienischen Raum: Fall 'Alarich' und 'Achse'* (Göttingen, etc., 1969), 196.

261. Stein, *Geschichte*, 192 f.

262. Querg, *Spionage*, 311 ff.

263. *ADAP*, Series E, vol. 6, no. 311, of 11 September 1943.

264. Lutz Klinkhammer, *Zwischen Bündnis und Besatzung. Das nationalsozialistische Deutschland und die Republik von Salò 1943–1945* (Tübingen, 1993), 117 f.

265. Ibid. 120 ff.

266. BAB, NS 19/1881, Order of 31 August 1943; see Klinkhammer, *Bündnis*, 356.

267. BAB, NS 19/1881, Himmler order of 2 October 1943; see Klinkhammer, *Bündnis*, 357.

268. BAB, R 70 Italien, vol. 5, minute for SS-Sturmbannführer Wenner of 13 February 1944; see Klinkhammer, *Bündnis*, 364. Stein, *Geschichte*, 270, mentions the creation of a Waffengrenadier division (ital. No. 1) in April 1945.

269. On the Jewish persecution in Italy from September 1943 see Liliana Picciotto Fargion, 'Italien', in Wolfgang Benz (ed.), *Dimension des Völkermords. Die Zahl der jüdischen Opfer des Nationalsozialismus* (Munich, 1991), 199–227; Michaelis, *Mussolini*, 342 ff.; Klinkhammer, *Bündnis*, 530 ff.

270. On Dannecker's activities in Italy see Steur, *Dannecker*, 113 ff.

271. PAA, Inland IIg 192, minute by Wagner of 4 December 1943, published in *ADAP*, Series E, vol. 7, 111.

272. Ibid.

273. Fargion, 'Italien', 215 ff.

274. Ibid. 206 and 222 f.

275. See Fleischer, *Griechenland*, 260 ff.

276. See the memoirs of Errikos Sevillias, *Athens—Auschwitz* (Athens, 1983). Moreover, in April there was a similar 'action' in Albania, during which around 300 Jews were arrested and transported to Bergen-Belsen via Belgrade (Gerhard Grimm, 'Albania', in Wolfgang Benz (ed.), *Dimension des Völkermords. Die Zahl der jüdischen Opfer des Nationalsozialismus* (Munich, 1991), 229–39, at 237).

277. Fleischer, *Griechenland*, 265 ff.

278. Sundhaussen, 'Jugoslawien', 325.

279. On German Jewish policy in France after the collapse of Italy see Klarsfeld, *Vichy*, 276 ff.; Jonathan Steinberg, *Deutsche, Italiener und Juden. Der italienische Widerstand gegen den Holocaust* (Göttingen, 1992), 206 ff.; Zuccotti, *Holocaust*, 180 ff.

280. Klarsfeld, *Vichy*, 278 ff.; Zuccotti, *Holocaust*, 181 ff.

281. See above p. 185.

282. Klarsfeld, *Vichy*, 289.

283. Ibid. 298 ff.; Zuccotti, *Holocaust*, 190 ff.

284. On the government reshuffle see Eberhard Jäckel, *Frankreich in Hitlers Europa. Die deutsche Frankreichpolitik im Zweiten Weltkrieg* (Stuttgart, 1966), 293 f.

285. CDJC,CXXXII-56, published in Klarsfeld, *Vichy*, 574 ff.; Zuccotti, *Holocaust*, 197 ff.

286. Klarsfeld, *Vichy*, 320. Somewhat different figures referred to in the literature are contained in Wetzel, 'Frankreich und Belgien', 132 f.

287. On the rescue of the Danish Jews see Herbert, *Best*, 360 ff.; Leni Yahil, *The Rescue of Danish Jewry: Test of a Democracy* (Philadelphia, 1969); Hans Kirchhoff, 'SS-Gruppenführer Werner Best and the Action Against the Danish Jews—October 1943', *Yad Vashem Studies*, 24 (1994), 195–222. On the passing on of the information about the impending deportations see Thomsen, *Besatzungspolitik*, 183 f.

288. Braham, *Politics*, 250 ff.

289. At the end of May 1943 Kállay made it clear in a speech that while he considered the 'complete de-settlement of the Jews' to be the 'final solution' of the 'Jewish question', this could only occur when the 'question of where the Jews were to be de-settled to had been resolved' (*Donauzeitung* 1 June 1943, see Hilberg, *Vernichtung*, 883 f.).

290. Braham, *Politics*, 381 ff.; on the organization of the occupation administration see ibid. 406 ff.

291. Ibid. 396 ff.

292. Christian Gerlach and Götz Aly, *Das letzte Kapitel. Realpolitik, Ideologie und der Mord an den ungarischen Juden 1944/1945* (Stuttgart and Zürich, 2002), 259.

293. Braham, *Politics*, 510 ff. and 446 ff.

294. Ibid. 674 ff.

295. Ibid. 850 ff.

296. Ibid. 1205 ff.
297. Telegram from Veesenmayer to Ribbentrop, 6 July 1944, published in *ADAP*, Series E, vol. 8, no. 101.
298. BAB, NS 19/4013.
299. BAB, NS 19/4014, passage published in Himmler, *Geheimreden*, 203.
300. Ibid.

CHAPTER 26

1. Bernhard Kroener, '*Der starke Mann im Heimatkriegsgebiet*'—*Generaloberst Friedrich Fromm. Eine Biographie* (Paderborn, etc., 2005), speaks of a 'monopoly of force on the home front' (p. 658).
2. In January 1944 the members of the Solf Circle and Count James von Moltke were arrested, in March 1944 Hartmut Plaas, and on 20 July 1944 the arrest of Goerdeler and Beck was imminent.
3. This is the thoroughly researched conclusion reached by Johannes Tuchel in his paper 'Heinrich Himmler und die Vorgeschichte des 20. Juli 1944' (manuscript), which the author kindly placed at my disposal. All assertions to the contrary in the literature are pure speculation; see e.g. Yehuda Bauer, *Freikauf von Juden? Verhandlungen zwischen dem nationalsozialistischen Deutschland und jüdischen Repräsentanten von 1933 bis 1945* (Frankfurt a. M., 1996), 173 ff.
4. BAB, NS 19/4015.
5. 'Die Rede Himmlers vor den Gauleitern am 3. August 1944', documented in *Vierteljahrshefte für Zeitgeschichte*, 1 (1953), 357–94, especially 375 f. Himmler also mentioned in his speech his conversation with Popitz of 26 August 1943. He emphasized that he had suspected Popitz of being a member of the conservative opposition and had therefore sought Hitler's permission to have the conversation.
6. On the conclusion of the attempted coup see Kroener, *Fromm*, 669 ff.; Peter Hoffmann, *Widerstand, Staatsstreich, Attentat. Der Kampf der Opposition gegen Hitler*, 3rd edn. (Munich, 1979), 627.
7. Ulrike Hett and Johannes Tuchel, 'Die Reaktionen des NS-Staates auf den Umsturzversuch vom 20. Juli 1944', in Peter Steinbach and Johannes Tuchel (eds), *Widerstand gegen den Nationalsozialismus* (Bonn, 1994), 377–89, at 378.
8. BAB, NS 19/1447.
9. Hett and Tuchel, 'Reaktionen', 379.
10. Ibid. 383 ff.
11. BAB, NS 6/3, Kaltenbrunner to Bormann.
12. BAB, R 58/1027.
13. BAB, NS 19/1447; Jürgen Zarusky, 'Von der Sondergerichtsbarkeit zum Endphasenterror. Loyalitätserzwingung und Rache am Widerstand im

Zusammenbruch des NS-Regimes', in Cord Arendes (ed.), *Terror nach innen. Verbrechen am Ende des Zweiten Weltkrieges* (Göttingen, 2006), 103–21.

14. Winfried Meyer, 'Aktion "Gewitter". Menschenopfer für Macht und Mythos der Gestapo', *Dachauer Hefte*, 21 (2005), 3–20, and Hett and Tuchel, 'Reaktionen', 382 f. The relevant orders issued by Müller are in BAB, R 58/775. Because of a typing error the action was sometimes called 'Aktion [Operation] Gitter'.

15. Zarusky, 'Sondergerichtsbarkeit', 113.

16. BAB, NS 33/7, note of the meeting of 15 July 1943. Two out of the three new General commandos, including troops subordinate to them, were established with the assistance of the army; see Andreas Kunz, *Wehrmacht und Niederlage. Die bewaffnete Macht in der Endphase der nationalsozialistischen Herrschaft 1944 bis 1945* (Munich, 2005), 123 f.

17. *RGBl* 1944 I, 161.

18. Second Edict Concerning the Exercise of Authority in an Area of Military Operations within the Borders of the Reich of 20 September 1944, published in *'Führer-Erlasse'*, no. 363. This decreed that the authority of the armed forces was confined to those areas directly involved in combat. The edict should be seen in the context of the Second Edict Concerning Cooperation between the Party and the Wehrmacht in an Area of Operations within the Borders of the Reich issued on the same day (ibid., no. 362) . On 13 July Hitler had already issued an edict increasing the responsibilities of the Gauleiters within an area involved in military operations but only with regard to party matters (ibid., no. 337).

19. Kroener, *Fromm*, 714.

20. BAB, NS 19/3910, 26 July 1944.

21. BAB, NS 19/4015.

22. Ibid. speech in Grafenwöhr, 25 July 1944, and speech at the Bitche military training area, 26 July 1944.

23. 'Die Rede Himmlers vor den Gauleitern am 3. August 1944', documented in *Vierteljahrshefte für Zeitgeschichte*, 1 (1953), 357–94, quotation p. 371.

24. BAB, NS 19/4043, 2 August 1944; see Kroener, *Fromm*, 712ff.; Kunz, *Wehrmacht*, 109.

25. BAB, NS 19/3191, Pohl to Himmler, 17 August 1944, and reply of 19 August 1944.

26. Ibid. 13 October 1944; see Kunz, *Wehrmacht*, 126 f.

27. Kunz, *Wehrmacht*, 122 ff.

28. BAB, NS 19/2409, Berger to Himmler, 1 August 1944.

29. Kunz, *Wehrmacht*, 125 f.

30. BAB, NS 19/4010, printed in Himmler, *Geheimreden*, 162 ff., quotation p. 164.

31. Matthias Schröder, *Deutschbaltische SS-Führer und Andrej Vlasov 1942–1945. 'Russland kann nur von Russen besiegt werden': Erhard Kroeger, Friedrich Buchardt und die 'Russische Befreiungsarmee'* (Paderborn, etc., 2001), 156. On the military

role of the Vlasov Army see Joachim Hoffmann, *Die Tragödie der 'Russischen Befreiungsarmee' 1944/45. Wlassow gegen Stalin* (Munich, 2003).

32. Schröder, *SS-Führer*, 192 ff.
33. Ibid. 198.
34. Ibid. 206 ff.
35. Norbert Haase, 'Justizterror in der Wehrmacht am Ende des Zweiten Weltkrieges', in Cord Arendes (ed.), *Terror nach innen. Verbrechen am Ende des Zweiten Weltkrieges* (Göttingen, 2006), 80–102.
36. Order of 5 September 1944, quoted in Haase, 'Justizterror', 81 (original in Bundesarchiv-Zentralnachweisstelle).
37. See Klaus-Dietmar Henke, *Die amerikanische Besetzung Deutschlands*, 2nd edn. (Munich, 1996), 812.
38. Neufeld, *Rakete*, 287 ff.; the directive is printed in facsimile (p. 289).
39. Ibid. 295.
40. See the statistics in Hölsken, *V-Waffen*, 163.
41. BAB, NS 19/4015, Speech to the officer corps of a Grenadier division at the Bitche military training ground on 26 July 1944, published in Himmler, *Geheimreden*, 215 ff., quotation pp. 231 f.
42. Churchill announced to the House of Commons that the number of those killed as a result of the bombardment was 2,752 at the beginning of July 1944 (ibid. 232, n. 44).
43. *Tagebücher Goebbels*, 24 August 1944.
44. Kunz, *Wehrmacht*, 129.
45. Doc. D-762, published (together with Keitel's edicts implementing it dated 18. August) in *IMT*, vol. 35, pp. 503 ff.).
46. Bohn, *Reichskommissariat*, 110 f.
47. Meershoek, 'Machtentfaltung', 401.
48. Hirschfeld, *Fremdherrschaft*, 38.
49. Thomsen, *Besatzungspolitik*, 206 ff.
50. Ibid. 193 and 210 f.
51. BAB, NS 19/4015.
52. Lipscher, *Juden*, 178 f.; Gila Fatran, 'Die Deportation der Juden aus der Slowakei 1944–1945', *Bohemia*, 37 (1996), 99–119, at 116 ff.
53. Braham, *Politics*, 890 ff.
54. PAA, Inland IIg 210, Budapest embassy to the Foreign Ministry, 19 August 1944, printed in *ADAP*, Series E, vol. 8, no. 167. On the August events see Braham, *Politics*, 911 ff.
55. PAA, Inland IIg 210, Veesenmayer to the Foreign Ministry, 24 August 1944.
56. 56 PAA, Inland IIg 209, Veesenmayer to Ribbentrop, 25 August 1944, published in Randolph L. Braham (ed.), *The Destruction of Hungarian Jewry: A Documentary Account*, 2 vols. (New York, 1963), no. 214.
57. Braham, *Politics*, 916.

58. Bauer's view in *Freikauf*, 347, that Himmler's halt order of 24 August 1944 was linked to the start of negotiations between Kurt Becher and Saly Mayer in Switzerland on 21 August, which were concerned with the possible liberation of Jews in return for foreign currency or deliveries of goods, cannot be proved.
59. Braham, *Politics*, 947 ff.
60. At this point the decision to dismantle the extermination facilities at Auschwitz had either already been or was about to be taken: Czech, *Kalendarium*, refers to 31 October 1944 (last murder with gas) and 25 November 1944 (the start of the demolition of the crematoria).
61. Veesenmayer report to the Foreign Ministry, 18. October 1941, published in *ADAP*, Series E, vol. 8, no. 275. Eichmann maintained this intention until at least the middle of November (PAA, Inland IIg 209, Veesenmayer report of 13 November 1944).
62. Braham, *Politics*, 957 ff.
63. Ibid. 976 ff.
64. Alexandra-Eileen Wenck, *Zwischen Menschenhandel und 'Endlösung'. Das Konzentrationslager Bergen-Belsen* (Paderborn, etc., 2000), 78 ff.
65. *Dienstkalender,* 10 December 1942, 637 ff. Himmler's entry read: '4. special camp for Jews with relatives in America. 5. Resettlement of the Jews—release in return for foreign currency—not in favour—more important as hostages.' To the phrase 'release in return for foreign currency' Himmler, plainly as a result of the discussion, later added the words 'from abroad'. In a note made the same day Himmler recorded that Hitler had given him permission for the 'release of Jews in return for foreign currency' if they 'bring in notable [*sic: namhaften*] amounts of foreign currency from abroad', quoted ibid. 639. On the building of the special camp: BAB, NS 19/2159, RFSS to Müller, December 1942.
66. Wenck, *Menschenhandel*, 102 ff.
67. Bauer, *Freikauf*, 149 ff.
68. Wenck, *Menschenhandel*, 289 ff.; Bauer, *Freikauf*, 231 ff.; Braham, *Politics*, 1069 ff.
69. Wenck, *Menschenhandel*, 294; Braham, *Politics*, 733 ff. and 1088 ff.; Bauer, *Freikauf*, 309 ff.
70. Bauer, *Freikauf*, 353 f.
71. This is what he said to Bernadotte (PRO, Prem 3/197/6, Ambassador Mallet to the Foreign Office concerning Bernadotte's confidential report, 13 April 1945) and to his Jewish interlocutor, Masur (see note 144). Before the meeting with Masur Schellenberg had advised him that it would be a good idea 'if he made it clear that he was disobeying Hitler and acting directly contrary to his wishes and those of his camarilla, but that was what he finally had to take it upon himself to do in recompense for his personal behaviour' (Ifz, Ed 90/7, Schellenberg-Manuscript, 51).
72. Orth, *System*, 272 f.

73. On the clearing of the concentration camps and the death marches see ibid. 270 ff.; Daniel Blatman, 'Die Todesmärsche—Entscheidungsträger, Mörder und Opfer', in Ulrich Herbert (ed.), *Die nationalsozialistischen Konzentrationslager. Entwicklung und Struktur*, vol. 2 (Göttingen, 1998), 1063–92; Yehuda Bauer, 'The Death Marches, January–May 1945', in Michael R. Marrus (ed.), *The Nazi Holocaust: Historical Articles on the Destruction of European Jews*, vol. 9: *The End of the Holocaust* (Westport, etc., 1989), 491–511.

74. Angrick and Klein, *'Endlösung'*, 419 ff.; Christoph Dieckmann, 'Das Ghetto und das Konzentrationslager in Kaunas 1941–1944', in Ulrich Herbert (ed.), *Die nationalsozialistischen Konzentrationslager. Entwicklung und Struktur*, vol. 1 (Göttingen, 1998), 439–71, at 458; Streim, 'Konzentrationslager', 184.

75. Angrick and Klein, *'Endlösung'*, 436 ff.

76. Orth, *System*, 282 ff.; Angrick and Klein, *'Endlösung'*, 442 ff.

77. Orth, *System*, 271 ff.

78. Ibid. 276 ff.; Andrzej Strzelecki, 'Der Todesmarsch der Häftlinge aus dem KL Auschwitz', in Ulrich Herbert (ed.), *Die nationalsozialistischen Konzentrationslager. Entwicklung und Struktur*, vol. 2 (Göttingen, 1998), 1093–1112.

79. *Tagebücher Goebbels*, 2, 3, and 4 September 1944.

80. BAB, NS 19/4015, 21 September 1944.

81. The Countryside Guard (Landwacht) was created by a RFSS edict of 17 January 1942, the Town Guard (Stadtwacht) by a RFSS edict of 9 November 1942 (BAB, NS 6/338, Party Chancellery circular of 9 December 1942, no. 192/42). See Rudolf Absolon, *Die Wehrmacht im Dritten Reich*, vol. 6: *19. Dezember 1941 bis 9. Mai 1945* (Boppard a. Rh., 1995), 72 f., and Klaus Mammach, *Der Volkssturm. Das letzte Aufgebot 1944/45* (Cologne, 1981), 31.

82. Mammach, *Volkssturm*, 32.

83. Published in ibid. 168 ff. The edict was dated 25 September 1944.

84. BAB, NS 19/4015, speech of 21 September 1944.

85. BAB, NS 19/4016.

86. Mammach, *Volkssturm*, 54.

87. See ibid. 56 f.; see also Franz W. Seidler, *'Deutscher Volkssturm'. Das letzte Aufgebot 1944/45* (Munich and Berlin, 1989), 56 ff.

88. Published in Mammach, *Volkssturm*, 60 f.

89. Ibid. 57 f.

90. Henke, *Besetzung*, 128 ff.; Mammach, *Volkssturm*, 134.

91. Mammach, *Volkssturm*, 62 ff.

92. Ibid. 63.

93. Ibid. 70 f. and 108 f.

94. Ibid. 72 f.

95. Ibid. 110 ff.

96. Henke, *Besetzung*, 131; Mammach, *Volkssturm*, 34 f.

97. BAB, NS 19/4016.

98. The older assessment is, for example, given in Henke, *Besetzung*, 943 ff. For a revision of this picture see in particular Perry Biddiscombe, *Werwolf! The History of the National Socialist Guerrilla Movement, 1944–1946* (Toronto, 1998); see also Cord Arendes, 'Schrecken aus dem Untergrund. Endphaseverbrechen des "Werwolf"', in id. (ed.), *Terror nach innen. Verbrechen am Ende des Zweiten Weltkrieges* (Göttingen, 2006), 149–71.

99. Aachen State Court, judgment of 22 October 1949, published in *Justiz und NS-Verbrechen*, vol. 5 (Amsterdam, 1970), no. 173.

100. Rainer Mennel, *Die Schlussphase des Zweiten Weltkrieges im Westen (1944/45). Eine Studie zur politischen Geographie* (Osnabrück, 1981), 317 ff.

101. Karl Volk, '"Gell, seller B'suech!" Heinrich Himmler in Triberg', in *Die Ortenau* (1997), 509–38; see also BAB, NS 19/1793, lists of appointments.

102. BAB, NS 19/1793, lists of appointments.

103. *Tagebücher Goebbels*, 20 January 1945.

104. Ibid. 22 January 1945.

105. Ibid. 23 January 1945.

106. BAM, N 265/127, notes of Colonel in the General Staff Eismann: as operations officer [Ia] of the Army Group 'Vistula', Historical Division, US Army. I am grateful to Andreas Kunz for alerting me to the existence of this document.

107. BAB, NS 19/4015, Grafenwöhr speech, 25 July 1944.

108. Kunz, *Wehrmacht*, 281, quoted telex Himmler to Fegelein, 30 January 1945.

109. Mammach, *Volkssturm*, 81.

110. *Tagebücher Goebbels*, 8 February 1942.

111. BAM, N 265/127, notes of Colonel in the General Staff Eismann.

112. Kunz, *Wehrmacht*, 236 ff.

113. Hans-Dieter Schmid, 'Die Geheime Staatspolizei in der Endphase des Krieges', *Geschichte in Wissenschaft und Unterricht*, 51/9 (2000), 528–39.

114. Kershaw, *Hitler*, vol. 2: *1936–1945* (Stuttgart, 2000), 948 f.; *Tagebücher Goebbels*, 20, 21, and 23 September (the text of the memorandum also bears this date).

115. Hansjakob Stehle, 'Deutsche Friedensfühler bei den Westmächten im Februar/März 1945', *Vierteljahrshefte für Zeitgeschichte*, 30 (1982), 538–55, here 538, based on Pierre Blet *et al.* (eds), *Actes et documents du Saint Siège relatifs à la Seconde Guerre mondiale*, vol. 11 (Vatican City, 1981), no. 371.

116. BAB, NS 19/1447.

117. PRO, HW 1/3196.

118. PAA, Inland IIg 6a, Kaltenbrunner to Wagner (AA), 9 May 1944. Kaltenbrunner provided Wagner with a copy of the letter, which had been written about three months before, so that 'if necessary it could be used for foreign policy purposes'.

119. It could refer to a telegram that was not sent to Churchill which the British bugging system may have picked up, in which case it is not clear why Churchill destroyed it.

120. *Tagebücher Goebbels*, 23, 26, and 28 January, 1, 12, and 13 February, 5, 12, and 22 March 1945.
121. Ibid. 5 March 1945.
122. Ibid. 8 March 1945.
123. Ibid. 12 March 1945.
124. Ibid. 15 and 16 March 1945.
125. Ibid. 14 March 1945.
126. Ibid. 15 April 1945.
127. Ibid. 16 March 1945.
128. Ibid. 22 March 1945.
129. BAM, N 265/127, notes of Colonel in the General Staff Eismann.
130. On the so-called armband order see *Tagebücher Goebbels*, 28 March 1945; Messenger, *Gladiator*, 168.
131. The original version of the Kersten–Himmler agreement no longer exists; it has only been recorded by Kersten (Kersten, *Totenkopf*, 343). Allegedly a document was signed on 12 March 1945. However, unlike other documents from his correspondence with Himmler, this one was not published as a facsimile. There is only (on pp. 353 f.) a facsimile of a letter from Kersten to Himmler of 20 March 1945 in which he lists the points in the agreement.
132. As he did to Bernadotte (transmitted by the head of the Secret Service, Walter Schellenberg), see Folke Bernadotte, *Das Ende. Meine Verhandlungen in Deutschland im Frühjahr 1945 und ihre politischen Folgen* (Zürich and New York, 1945), 71, as well as to the former Swiss president, Musy (IfZ, ED 90/7, Schellenberg Manuscript, 30). Schellenberg's statements are among the most important sources for this last phase. Schellenberg, who at the end became heavily involved in trying to rescue Scandinavian and other prisoners, initially remained in Sweden after the German capitulation and while there wrote a report on the events of the previous months. During this period he was in contact with Bernadotte; see the 'Final Report' on Schellenberg composed by the British Secret service in 1945, published in Reinhard R. Doerries, *Hitler's Last Chief of Foreign Intelligence: Allied Interrogations of Walter Schellenberg* (London, etc., 2003), 200 f. During his interrogations by the British Secret Service in London in 1945, after his stay in Sweden, Schellenberg based his recollections substantially on his original manuscript and appeared so plausible that the British 'Final Report' was largely shaped by his. While in prison—he was sentenced to six years imprisonment and was freed in 1951—he wrote his memoirs, which were published in English translation. The final chapter of these memoirs is in parts identical with the report he composed in 1945. In general, therefore, Schellenberg's statements are consistent. However, inevitably the question must be asked whether, in particular, he exaggerated his allegedly increasing attempts towards the end of the war to persuade Himmler to try to bring the war to an end, in order to provide himself with a strong defensive position for the future.

133. IfZ, NO 1210, Höss statement, 14 March 1946; Orth, *System*, 303.

134. As reported by the British embassy to the Foreign Office, despatch of 27 March 1945 (PRO, FO 188/526).

135. Bernadotte, *Ende*, 32 ff.; 'Final Report', published in Dörries, *Chief*, 167 ff.; IfZ, ED 90/7, Schellenberg Manuscript, 17 f. and 22 f.

136. Bauer, *Freikauf*, 380 ff.; on the problem posed by the variety of figures given in the literature for Jews who were rescued see Steven Koblik, *The Stones Cry Out: Sweden's Response to the Persecution of the Jews 1933–1945* (New York, 1988), 138 f.

137. Bernadotte, *Ende*, 33.

138. PRO, FO 188/526, Ambassador in Stockholm to the Foreign Office, 27 March 1945, with the letter enclosed. The letter is reproduced in facsimile in Kersten, *Totenkopf*, 358.

139. PRO, FO 954/23B, note for the Prime Minister, 14 April 1945. On the meeting see also Bernadotte, *Ende*, 66ff.; IfZ, ED 90/7, Schellenberg Manuscript, 35b.

140. PRO, Prem 3/197/6, Mallet to Foreign Office, 13 April 1945.

141. Bernadotte, *Ende*, 69 ff.; IfZ, ED 90/7, Schellenberg Manuscript, 56.

142. Lutz Graf Schwerin von Krosigk, *Memoiren* (Stuttgart, 1977), 239; 'Final Report', published in Doerries, *Chief*, 176.

143. Wenck, *Menschenhandel*, 374 ff.; on the assessment of the number of victims see Eberhard Kolb, *Bergen-Belsen. Geschichte des 'Aufenthaltslagers' 1943–1945* (Hanover, 1962), 308 ff.; from the extensive British literature on the liberation of Bergen-Belsen see Joanne Reilly, *Belsen: The Liberation of a Concentration Camp* (London and New York, 1998).

144. PRO, FO 188/526, Masur report. Masur published a longer version of the report, from which various details were taken, in Sweden in 1945 under the title: *En jude talar med Himmler*. A German manuscript version can be found in USHMM, A-000786, also in the translation by Hauke Siemen back into German as 'Ein Jude spricht mit Hitler', in Niklas Günther and Sönke Zankel (eds), *Abrahams Enkel. Juden, Christen, Muslime und die Schoa* (Stuttgart, 2006), 133–44. On the conversation see also IfZ, ED 90/7, 48 f.; 'Final Report', published in Doerries, *Chief*, 176 ff.; Kersten, *Totenkopf*, 371 ff.

145. Bernadotte, *Ende*, 76 f; IfZ, ED 90/7, Schellenberg Manuscript, 53 ff.; 'Final Report' published in Doerries, *Chief*, 179.

146. PRO, WO 208/4474, Report on Grothmann's interrogation, 13 June 1945.

147. PRO, FO 954/32, telegram from Churchill to Stalin, 25 April 1945, which reproduces the report of the British head of mission in Stockholm.

148. IfZ, ED 90/7, Schellenberg Manuscript, 63 ff.; 'Final Report', published in Doerries, *Chief*, 184 ff.; Bernadotte, *Ende*, 78 ff.

149. Karl Dönitz, *Zehn Jahre und zwanzig Tage* (Bonn, 1958), 431.

150. IfZ, ED 90/7, Schellenberg Manuscript, 73 ff.

151. Charles de Gaulle, *Memoiren 1942–46. Die Einheit, das Heil* (Düsseldorf, 1961), 456 f.

152. Hitler's political testament published in *Kriegstagebuch des Oberkommandos der Wehrmacht*, vol. 4: *1. Januar 1944–22. Mai 1945* (Frankfurt a. M., 1961), 1666 f., quotation 1667.

153. See the reflections of Reimer Hansen, *Das Ende des Dritten Reiches. Die deutsche Kapitulation 1945* (Stuttgart, 1966), 50 f.

154. Wenck, *Menschenhandel*, 374 ff.

155. On the liberations of the camps see the overview in Orth, *System*, 305 ff.

156. Ibid. 335.

157. Diary, USHMM, Archiv, Acc. 1999.A.0092, 16 January 1945.

158. Ibid. 2 February 1945.

159. Ibid. 21 February 1945.

160. PRO, Wo 204/12603; the exact location, as is clear from this file, was the 'R' Internee Camp, 334 PWE. See also the report of Major Wedekind, CSDIC Sub-Centre, 15th Army Group, 22 May 1945, in the same file. It is clear from an interview with Margarete Himmler, published on 13 July 1945 in *Giornale del Mattino,* that at this point she was living in a villa outside Rome. In September mother and daughter were flown back to Germany.

161. BAK, NL 1126/37, letter of 30 December 1944 and of 5, 11, and 12 January 1945.

162. PRO, HW 1/3741, Himmler to Kaltenbrunner, 30 April 1945.

163. Marlis G. Steinert, *Die 23 Tage der Regierung Dönitz* (Düsseldorf, 1967), 77; the information about this meeting is based on statements by Dönitz in *Zehn Jahre*, 432 f. On the visit see also 'Final Report', published in Doerries, *Chief,* 192.

164. Steinert, *23 Tage*, 141; Dönitz, *Zehn Jahre*, 435 ff.

165. Steinert, *23 Tage*, 143; Dönitz, *Zehn Jahre*, 461; in connection with this, Dönitz's adjutant quotes from a further note by the Grand Admiral: Walter Lüdde-Neurath, *Regierung Dönitz. Die letzten Tage des Dritten Reiches*, 3rd extended edn. (Göttingen, 1964), 89 f.

166. Lüdde-Neurath, *Regierung Dönitz*, 90 f. (among other things, about the plans to hide), Schwerin von Krosigk, *Memoiren*, 90 f.

167. Bernadotte, *Ende*, 76 f. and 80.

168. IfZ, ED 90/7, Schellenberg Manuscript, 68 and 78.

169. PRO, WO 208/4474, Report on Grothmann's interrogation, 13 June 1945.

Bibliography

ARCHIVAL DOCUMENTS

Archiv der deutschen Jugendbewegung, Witzenhausen
Dokumente zu den Artamanen

Bayerisches Hauptstaatsarchiv, München (BHStA)
StK Staatskanzlei
MA Ministerium des Äußeren
Reichsstatthalter Epp

Bundesarchiv, Abt. Berlin (BAB)
BDC Research
BDC SS-O-Akten, formerly Slg. Schumacher
NS 2 SS-Rasse- und Siedlungshauptamt
NS 3 SS-Wirtschaftsverwaltungs-Hauptamt
NS 6 Partei-Kanzlei der NSDAP
NS 7 SS- und Polizeigerichtsbarkeit
NS 10 Adjutantur des Führers
NS 15 Der Beauftragte für die gesamte weltanschauliche Erziehung der NSDAP
NS 18 Reichspropagandaleitung
NS 19 Persönlicher Stab Reichsführer-SS
NS 21 Ahnenerbe
NS 23 SA
NS 31 SS-Hauptamt
NS 33 SS-Führungshauptamt
NS 47 Allgemeine SS
R 2 Reichsfinanzministerium
R 3 Reichsministerium für Rüstung und Kriegsproduktion
R 6 Reichsministerium für die besetzten Ostgebiete
R 8 Reichsstellen für die gewerbliche Wirtschaft
R 18 Reichsinnenministerium
R 19 Ordnungspolizei
R 20 Einheiten der Ordnungspolizei
R 22 Reichsjustizministerium
R 43 II Reichskanzlei
R 49 Reichskommissar für die Festigung Deutschen Volkstums

R 58 Reichssicherheitshauptamt
R 69 Einwandererzentralstelle
R 70 Besetzte Gebiete
R 75 Umwandererzentrale Posen
R 92 Generalkommissariat Lettland
R 113 Reichsstelle für Raumordnung
R 1501 Reichsministerium des Innern
R 3001 Reichsjustizministerium

Bundesarchiv, Abt. Dahlwitz-Hoppegarten (BADH)
Sammlungen ZB, ZM, ZR

Bundesarchiv, Abt. Koblenz (BAK)
NL 1094 Nachlass Darré
NL 1126 Nachlass Himmler
NSD 41 NS-Drucksachen (SS)

Bundesarchiv/Militärarchiv, Freiburg (BAM)
M 806 Kopien Militärarchiv Prag
N 265 Aufzeichnungen Oberst i.G. Eismann
RH 2 OKH
RH 20-11 Armeeoberkommando 20
RH 22 Befehlshaber der rückwärtigen Hereresgebiete
RH 31-I Deutsche Heeresmission in Rumänien
RS 3 Divisionen der Waffen-SS
RS 4 Brigaden,Kampftruppen und Einheiten der Waffen-SS
RW 4 Wehrmachtführungsstab

Centre de Documentation Juive Contemporaine, Paris (CDJC)
Documents on German occupation policy in France (used as copies in Yad Vashem)

Geheimes Staatsarchiv, Berlin-Dahlem (GStA)
Rep 90 Preußisches Staatsministerium

Hoover Institution Archives, Stanford
Himmler Collection

Institut für Zeitgeschichte, Munich (IfZ)
Dc Drucksachen SS und Polizei
ED Nachlässe
Fb Gerichtsakten
Gm Gerichtsakten
Jahresbericht Amt V des RSHA
MA Microfilms
MB Microfilms of the Nuremberg trial
Nuremberg Documents from the seies NG, NI,NO,NOKW

Partei-Kanzlei: Anordnungen
Z S Zeugenschrifttum

Institute for Jewish Research, New York (YIVO)
Occ Berlin Collection

Kriegsarchiv Munich (KAM)
Personal file Heinrich Himmler

Osobyi Archiv Moskva (OA Moscow)
Himmler files
Fonds 500
Fonds 504
Fonds 1323

Politisches Archiv des Auswärtigen Amtes, Berlin (PAA)
Büro Staatssekretär
Handakten Luther
Inland IIg

Public Record Office, London (PRO) [now The National Archives]
FO Foreign Office
HW Government Code and Cypher School
Prem Prime Minister's Office
WO War Office

Staatsanwaltschaft bei dem Landgericht München I (StAnw München)
Trial files

Staatsarchiv Munich (StA Munich)
Polizeidirektion München
Staatsanwaltschaften
Amtsgerichte

Staatsarchiv Marburg (StA Marburg)
Landratsamt Eschwege

Stadtarchiv München
Rat Nr. 458/3 (Handakten Fiehler)

Universitätsarchiv München
Student files

US Holocaust Memorial Museum, Washington, DC (USHMM)
A.000786 Manuscript Masur
Acc. 1999.A.0092
Diary of Margarete Himmler

RG 15 Poland
RG 48 Czech Republic

US National Archives and Records Administration, Washington, DC (NARA)
T 580 Ahnenerbe
T 175 Reichsführer-SS

Yad Vashem Archives, Jerusalem (YV)
O 53 Gestapo Mährisch-Ostrau
M 12 Centre de Documentation Juive Contemporaine
M 36 Militärarchiv Prag
M 58 Staatsarchiv Prag

Zentrale Stelle Ludwigsburg (ZStL)
Trial files
Documentation

PUBLISHED DOCUMENTS

Akten zur deutschen auswärtigen Politik 1938–1945. Aus dem Archiv des Auswärtigen Amtes, Series D: *1937–1941* (Göttingen, 1950–61); Series E: *1941–1945* (Göttingen, 1969–79).

Bevölkerungsstruktur und Massenmord. Neue Dokumente zur deutschen Politik der Jahre 1938–1945, ed. Susanne Heim and Götz Aly (Berlin, 1991).

Boelcke, Willi A. (ed.), *Deutschlands Rüstung im Zweiten Weltkrieg. Hitlers Konferenzen mit Albert Speer 1942–1945* (Frankfurt a. M., 1969).

Braham, Randolph L. (ed.), *The Destruction of Hungarian Jewry: A Documentary Account*, 2 vols. (New York, 1963).

Bräutigam, Otto, 'Aus dem Kriegstagebuch des Diplomaten Otto Bräutigam', ed. H. D. Heilmann, *Beiträge zur nationalsozialistischen Gesundheits- und Sozialpolitik*, 4 (1989), 123–87.

Ciano, Galeazzo, *Tagebücher 1939–1943* (Bern, 1947) [*The Ciano Diaries 1939–1943* (London, 1947)].

Czech, Danuta, *Kalendarium der Ereignisse im Konzentrationslager Auschwitz-Birkenau 1939–1945* (Reinbek bei Hamburg, 1989).

Deutsche Politik im 'Protektorat Böhmen und Mähren' unter Reinhard Heydrich 1941–1942. Eine Dokumentation, ed. Miroslav Kárný´, Jaroslava Milotová and Margita Kárná (Berlin, 1997).

Die Deutschen in der Tschechoslowakei 1933–1947. Dokumentensammlung, ed. Václav Král (Prague, 1964).

Der Dienstkalender Heinrich Himmlers 1941/42, for the Forschungsstelle für Zeitgeschichte, ed. Peter Witte et al. (Hamburg, 1999).

Dobroszycki, Lucjan (ed.), *The Chronicle of the Lodz Ghetto, 1941–1944* (New Haven, 1984).

Documenta Occupationis, vol. 10: Praca przymusowa polaków pod panowaniem hitlerows-kim: 1939–1945 [*Polish forced labour under the Hitler regime*] (Posen, 1976).

Dokumentationsarchiv des österreichischen Widerstandes ed., *'Anschluß' 1938. Eine Dokumentation*, ed. Heinz Arnberger *et al.* (Vienna, 1988).

Dokumente über die Verfolgung der jüdischen Bürger in Baden-Württemberg durch das nationalsozialistische Regime, ed. Paul Sauer, vol. 2 (Stuttgart, 1966).

Dokumente zur Gleichschaltung des Landes Hamburg 1933, ed. Henning Timpke (Frankfurt a. M., 1964).

Engel, Gerhard, *Heeresadjutant bei Hitler 1938–1943. Aufzeichnungen des Majors Engel*, ed. Hildegard von Kotze (Stuttgart [1975]).

Die Erhebung der österreichischen Nationalsozialisten im Juli 1934. Akten der Historischen Kommission des Reichsführers SS (Vienna, etc., 1965).

'Die Ermordung psychisch kranker Menschen in der Sowjetunion. Dokumentation', ed. Angelika Ebbinghaus and Gerd Preissler, *Beiträge zur nationalsozialistischen Gesundheits- und Sozialpolitik*, 1 (1985), 75–107.

Faschismus, Ghetto, Massenmord. Dokumentation über Ausrottung und Widerstand der Juden in Polen während des 2. Weltkrieges, published by the Jüdische Historische Institut Warsaw, ed. Tatiana Berenstein, Artur Eisenbach, *et al.* (Frankfurt a. M., 1962).

Die faschistische Okkupationspolitik in Österreich und der Tschechoslowakei (1938–1945), ed. Helma Kaden (Berlin, 1988).

'*Führer-Erlasse' 1939–1945. Edition sämtlicher überlieferter, nicht im Reichsgesetzblatt abgedruckter, von Hitler während des Zweiten Weltkrieges schriftlich erteilter Direktiven aus den Bereichen Staat, Partei, Wirtschaft, Besatzungspolitik und Militärverwaltung*, ed. Martin Moll (Stuttgart, 1997).

Gestapa, 'Lagebericht für 1937', published in *Gestapo-Berichte über den antifaschistischen Widerstandskampf der KPD 1933–1939*, ed. Margot Pikarski and Elke Warning, vol. 1: *Anfang 1933 bis August 1939* (Berlin, 1989), doc. no. 16.

Gottwaldt, Alfred, and Diana Schulle, *Die 'Judendeportationen' aus dem Deutschen Reich 1941–1945. Eine kommentierte Chronologie* (Wiesbaden, 2005).

Grabitz, Helge, and Wolfgang Scheffle (eds), *Letzte Spuren. Ghetto Warschau, SS-Arbeitslager Trawniki, Aktion Erntefest. Fotos und Dokumente über Opfer des Endlösungswahns im Spiegel der historischen Ereignisse*, 2nd rev. edn. (Berlin, 1993).

Grau, Günter (ed.), *Homosexualität in der NS-Zeit. Dokumente einer Diskriminierung und Verfolgung*, 2nd rev. edn. (Frankfurt a. M., 2004).

Groscurth, Helmuth, *Tagebücher eines Abwehroffiziers 1938–1940. Mit weiteren Dokumenten zur Militäropposition gegen Hitler*, ed. Helmut Krausnick and Harold C. Deutsch (Stuttgart, 1970).

Halder, Franz, *Kriegstagebuch. Tägliche Aufzeichnungen des Chefs des Generalstabes des Heeres 1939–1942*, ed. Hans-Adolf Jacobsen and Alfred Philippi, 3 vols. (Stuttgart, 1962–4) [*The Halder War Diary 1939–1942*, ed. Charles Burdick and Hans-Adolf Jacobsen (Novato, Calif., 1988)].

Heiber, Helmut (ed.), *Hitlers Lagebesprechungen. Die Protokollfragmente seiner militärischen Konferenzen 1942–1945* (Stuttgart, 1962).

Hillgruber, Andreas (ed.), *Staatsmänner und Diplomaten bei Hitler. Vertrauliche Aufzeichnungen über Unterredungen mit Vertretern des Auslandes*, vol. 1: *1939–1941* (Frankfurt a. M., 1967).

Himmler, Heinrich, *Geheimreden 1933–1945*, ed. Bradley F. Smith and Agnes F. Peterson (Munich, 1974).

—— *Reichsführer!... Briefe an und von Himmler*, ed. Helmut Heiber (Stuttgart, 1968).

Hitler, Adolf, *Monologe im Führerhauptquartier 1941–1944. Die Aufzeichnungen Heinrich Heims*, ed. Werner Jochmann (Bindlach, 1988).

—— *Reden und Proklamationen 1932–1945. Kommentiert von einem deutschen Zeitgenossen*, 2 vols., ed. Max Domarus (Neustadt a. d. Aisch, 1963).

Der Hitler-Prozess 1924. Wortlaut der Hauptverhandlung vor dem Volksgericht München I, ed. Lothar Gruchmann and Reinhard Weber, 4 vols. (Munich, 1997–9).

Höss, Rudolf, *Kommandant in Auschwitz. Autobiographische Aufzeichnungen*, ed. Martin Broszat (Stuttgart, 1958) [*Commandant of Auschwitz: The Autobiography of Rudolf Hoess* (London, 1959)].

Hubatsch, Walther (ed.), *Hitlers Weisungen für die Kriegführung 1939–1945. Dokumente des Oberkommandos der Wehrmacht*, 2nd edn. (Koblenz, 1983) [*Hitler's War Directives 1939–1945*, ed. Hugh Trevor-Roper (London, 1964)].

International Military Tribunal: Der Prozess gegen die Hauptkriegsverbrecher vor dem Internationalen Militärgerichtshof, 14. Oktober 1945 bis 1. Oktober 1946, 42 vols. (Nuremberg, 1947–9).

Jacobsen, Hans-Adolf (ed.), *Hans Steinacher: Bundesleiter des VDA 1933–1937. Erinnerungen und Dokumente* (Boppard a. Rh., 1970).

Justiz und NS-Verbrechen. Sammlung deutscher Strafurteile wegen nationalsozialistischer Tötungsverbrechen 1945–1966, 39 vols. (Amsterdam, 1968–2007).

Klarsfeld, Serge, and Maxime Steinberg (eds), *Die Endlösung der Judenfrage in Belgien. Dokumente* (New York, 1980).

Koeppen, Werner, *Herbst 1941 im 'Führerhauptquartier'. Berichte Werner Koeppens an seinen Minister Alfred Rosenberg*, ed. Martin Vogt (Koblenz, 2002).

Kriegstagebuch des Oberkommandos der Wehrmacht 1940–1945, edited and with a commentary by Helmuth Greiner and Percy Ernst Schramm, vol 1: *1. August 1940–31. Dezember 1941* (Frankfurt a. M., 1965); vol. 4: *1. Januar 1944–22. Mai 1945* (Frankfurt a. M., 1961).

Kulka, Otto Dov, und Eberhard Jäckel (eds), *Die Juden in den geheimen NS-Stimmungsberichten 1933–1945* (Düsseldorf, 2004).

'Die letzten Tage von Heinrich Himmler. Neue Dokumente aus dem Archiv des Föderalen Sicherheitsdienstes', ed. Boris Chavkin and A. M. Kalganov, *Forum für osteuropäische Ideen- und Zeitgeschichte*, 4 (2000), 251–84.

Madajczyk, Czesław, *Zamojszczyzna—Sonderlaboratorium SS. Zbiór dokumentów polskichi niemieckich z okresu okupacji hitlerowskiej*, 2 vols. (Warsaw, 1977).

Maršálek, Hans, *Die Geschichte des Konzentrationslagers Mauthausen. Dokumentation*, 3rd edn. (Vienna, 1995).

Mason, Timothy W. (ed.), *Arbeiterklasse und Volksgemeinschaft. Dokumente und Materialien zur deutschen Arbeiterpolitik 1936–1939* (Opladen, 1975).

Meldungen aus dem Reich 1938–1945. Die geheimen Lageberichte des Sicherheitsdienstes der SS, ed. Heinz Boberach, 18 vols. (Herrsching, 1984–5).

Mollo, Andrew, *Uniforms of the SS, vol. 1: Allgemeine SS 1923–1945* (London, 1969).

Nationalsozialistische Massentötungen durch Giftgas. Eine Dokumentation, ed. Eugen Kogon, Hermann Langbein, and Adalbert Rückerl (Frankfurt a. M., 1986).

Nestler, Ludwig (ed.), *Die faschistische Okkupationspolitik in Frankreich (1940–1944)* (Berlin, 1990).

Der Nürnberger Ärazteprozess 1946/47. Wortprotokolle, Anklage- und Verteidigungsmaterial, Quellen zum Umfeld, im Auftrag der Stiftung für Sozialgeschichte des 20. Jahrhunderts, ed. Klaus Dörner et al. (Munich, 1999).

Die Okkupationspolitik des deutschen Faschismus in Dänemark und Norwegen (1940–1945), ed. Fritz Petrick (Berlin and Heidelberg, 1992).

Pätzold, Kurt, and Erika Schwarz, *Tagesordnung: Judenmord. Die Wannsee-Konferenz am 20. Januar 1942. Eine Dokumentation zur Organisation der "Endlösung"*, 3rd edn. (Berlin, 1992).

Picker, Henry, *Hitlers Tischgespräche im Führerhauptquartier* (Frankfurt a. M., 1989) [*Hitler's Table Talk 1941–1944*, with an introductory essay by Hugh Trevor-Roper (London, 1953)].

Das Protokoll.Die Autobiographie des Georg Elser (Königsbronn, 2006).

Recht, Verwaltung und Justiz im Nationalsozialismus. Ausgewählte Schriften, Gesetze und Gerichtsentscheidungen von 1933 bis 1945, ed. Martin Hirsch et al. (Cologne, 1984).

Rosenberg, Alfred, *Das politische Tagebuch Alfred Rosenbergs aus den Jahren 1934/1935 und 1939/1940*, ed. Hans-Günther Seraphim (Munich, 1964).

Rost van Tonningen, Meinoud Marinus, *Correspondentie*, ed. E. Fraenkel-Verkade and A. J. van der Leuw, 2 vols. ('s-Gravenhage, 1967).

Ruckhaberle, Dieter, and Christiane Ziesecke (eds), *Rettung der bulgarischen Juden— 1943. Eine Dokumentation* (Berlin, 1984).

Rürup, Reinhard (ed.), *Der Krieg gegen die Sowjetunion 1941–1945*. Eine Dokumentation (Berlin, 1991).

—— *Topographie des Terrors. Gestapo, SS und Reichssicherheitshauptamt auf dem 'Prinz-Albrecht-Gelände'. Eine Dokumentation* (Berlin, 1987).

Seewann, Gerhard, and Norbert Spannenberger (eds), *Akten des Volksgerichtsprozesses gegen Franz A. Basch, Volksgruppenführer der Deutschen in Ungarn, Budapest 1945/46*, (Munich, 1999).

Das Schicksal der Deutschen in Rumänien, published by the Bundesministerium für Vertriebene, Flüchtlinge, und Kriegsgeschädigte (Berlin, 1957).

'Schöne Zeiten'. Judenmord aus der Sicht der Täter und Gaffer, ed. Ernst Klee, Willi Dressen, and Volker Riess (Frankfurt a. M., 1988) [*The Good Old Days: The Holocaust as seen by its Perpetrators and Bystanders* (New York, 1996)].

Siegfried, Klaus-Jörg (ed.), *Rüstungsproduktion und Zwangsarbeit im Volkswagenwerk 1939–1945. Eine Dokumentation* (Frankfurt a. M., 1986).

De SS en Nederland. Documenten uit SS-Archieven 1933–1945, ed. K. C. A. in 't Veld, 2 vols. ('s Gravenhage, 1976).

Die Tagebücher von Joseph Goebbels, 2 parts, 9 and 15 vols, ed. Elke Fröhlich *et al.* (Munich, 1993–2006).

Tory, Avraham, *Surviving the Holocaust: The Kovno Ghetto Diary*, ed. Martin Gilbert (Cambridge, Mass. and London, 1990).

The Trial of Adolf Eichmann. Record of Proceedings in the District Court of Jerusalem, 8 vols. (Jerusalem, 1992–5).

Trials of War Criminals before the Nuernberg Military Tribunals under Control Council Law No. 10, vol. 1 (Nuremberg, 1949).

Unsere Ehre heißt Treue. Kriegstagebuch des Kommandostabes Reichsführer-SS, Tätigkeitsberichte der 1. und 2. SS-Infanterie-Brigade, der 1. SS-Kavallerie-Brigade und von Sonderkommandos der SS (Vienna, 1965).

Wagner, Gerhard (ed.), *Lagevorträge des Oberbefehlshabers der Kriegsmarine vor Hitler 1939–1945* (Munich, 1972).

Walk, Joseph (ed.), *Das Sonderrecht für die Juden im NS-Staat. Eine Sammlung der gesetzlichen Maßnahmen und Richtlinien. Inhalt und Bedeutung*, 2nd edn. (Heidelberg, 1996).

Widerstand und Verfolgung in Wien 1934–1945. Eine Dokumentation, published by the Dokumentationsarchiv des österreichischen Widerstandes, ed. Wolfgang Neugebauer, 3 vols. (Vienna, 1975).

Wildt, Michael (ed.), *Die Judenpolitik des SD 1935 bis 1938. Eine Dokumentation* (Munich, 1995).

CONTEMPORARY PUBLICATIONS

Best, Werner, *Die deutsche Polizei* (Darmstadt, 1940).

—— 'Kritik und Aporie des "Juristen"', *Deutsches Recht* 1939, 196–9.

—— 'Der Reichsführer SS und Chef der Deutschen Polizei', *Deutsches Recht* 1936, 257–8 (July 1936).

—— 'Die Geheime Staatspolizei', *Deutsches Recht* 1936, 125–8 (April 1936).

Corazza, Heinz, *Die Samurai. Ritter des Reiches in Ehre und Treue* (Berlin and Munich, 1937).

d'Alquen, Gunter, *Die SS. Geschichte, Aufgabe und Organisation der Schutzstaffeln der NSDAP* (Berlin, 1939).

Daluege, Kurt, 'Die Ordnungspolizei und ihre Entstehung im Dritten Reich', in Hans Pfundtner (ed.), *Dr. Wilhelm Frick und sein Ministerium. Aus Anlaß des 60. Geburtstages des Reichs- und preußischen Ministers des Innern Dr. Wilhelm Frick am 12. März 1937* (Munich, 1937), 133–5.

Disziplinar- und Beschwerdeordnung (Munich, 1933).

Eckhardt, Karl August, *Irdische Unsterblichkeit. Germanischer Glaube an die Wiederver-körperung in der Sippe* (Weimar, 1937).

Erzählte Geschichte. Arbeitsbuch für den Deutschunterricht, ed. Reichsführer-SS und SS-Hauptamt, Part 3 (Berlin, n.d).

Fahrenkamp, Karl, *Kreislauffürsorge und Gesundheitsführung* (Stuttgart, 1941).

Gründel, Günther, *Sendung der Jungen Generation. Versuch einer umfassenden revolu-tionären Sinndeutung der Krise* (Munich, 1932).

Grundfragen der deutschen Polizei. Bericht über die konstituierende Sitzung des Ausschusses für Polizeirecht der Akademie für Deutsches Recht am 11. Oktober 1936, ed. Hans Frank et al. (Hamburg, 1936).

Heydrich, Reinhard, 'Aufgaben und Aufbau der Sicherheitspolizei im Dritten Reich', in Hans Pfundtner (ed.), *Dr. Wilhem Frick und sein Ministerium. Aus Anlaß des 60. Geburtstages des Reichs- und preußischen Ministers des Innern Dr. Wilhelm Frick am 12 März 1937* (Munich, 1937), 149–53.

—— 'Die Bekämpfung der Staatsfeinde', *Deutsches Recht* 1936, 121–3 (April 1936).

Himmler, Heinrich, 'Aufgaben und Aufbau der Polizei des Dritten Reich', in Hans Pfundtner (ed.), *Dr. Wilhelm Frick und sein Ministerium. Aus Anlaß des 60. Geburts-tages des Reichs- und preußischen Ministers des Innern Dr. Wilhelm Frick am 12. März 1937* (Munich, 1937), 125–30.

—— *Rede des Reichsführers-SS im Dom zu Quedlinburg am 2. Juli 1936* (Magdeburg, 1936).

—— *Rede des Reichsführers-SS vor den Preußischen Staatsräten. 5. März 1936 im Haus der Flieger* (n.p., 1936).

—— *Die Schutzstaffel als antibolschewistische Kampforganisation* (Munich, 1936).

—— *Der Reichstag 1930. Das sterbende System und der Nationalsozialismus* (Munich, 1931).

Hoffmann, Heinrich, *Das Braune Heer. 100 Bilddokumente: Leben, Kampf und Sieg der SA und SS* (Berlin, 1932).

Jahrbuch Amt V (Reichskriminalpolizeiamt) des Reichssicherheitshauptamtes SS 1939/40 (Berlin, 1940).

Johst, Hanns, *Ruf des Reiches, Echo des Volkes! Eine Ostfahrt* (Munich, 1940).

Kiss, Edmund, *Das Sonnentor von Tihuanaku und Hörbigers Welteislehre* (Leipzig, 1937).

Der Menscheneinsatz. Grundsätze, Anordnungen und Richtlinien, published by the Hauptabteilung I des Stabshauptamts des Reichskommissars für die Festigung deutschen Volkstums, 1. Nachtrag (Berlin, 1941).

Meyer, Herbert, *Friedelehe und Mutterrecht* (Weimar, 1927).

Parteitag der Freiheit. Reden des Führers und ausgewählte Kongressreden am Reichsparteitag der NSDAP 1935 (Munich, 1935).

Reichspropagandaleitung (ed.), *Propaganda* (Munich, 1928).

Reichstags-Handbuch, IX. Wahlperiode 1933 (Berlin, 1934).

Schäfer, Ernst, *Geheimnis Tibet. Erster Bericht der deutschen Tibet-Expedition Ernst Schäfer 1938/39* (Munich, 1943).

Schäfer, *Dach der Erde. Durch das Wunderland Hochtibet. Tibetexpedition 1934/36* (Berlin, 1938).

—— *Unbekanntes Tibet. Durch die Wildnisse Osttibets zum Dach der Erde* (Berlin, 1937).

Schied- und Ehrengerichtsordnung der SS (Miesbach [*c.*1935]).

Sicherheitsfragen. Vortrag, gehalten auf der Befehlshabertagung in Bad Schachen am 14. Oktober 1943, published by the NS-Führungsstab des Oberkommandos der Wehrmacht (Berlin, 1943).

SS-Hauptamt (ed.), *Rassenpolitik* (Berlin, 1943).

Statistisches Jahrbuch der Schutzstaffel der NSDAP 1937 (Berlin, 1938).

Statistisches Jahrbuch der Schutzstaffel der NSDAP 1938 (Berlin, 1939).

Strasser, Gregor, *Kampf um Deutschland. Reden und Aufsätze eines Nationalsozialisten* (Munich, 1932).

Der Untermensch, published by the Reichsführer-SS und SS-Hauptamt [Berlin, 1942].

Verhandlungen des Reichstages. Stenographische Berichte, vol. 460 (Berlin 1939).

Wettenhovi-Aspa, Sigurd, *Fenno-Ägyptischer Kulturursprung der Alten Welt. Kommentare zu den vorhistorischen Völkerwanderungen* (Helsinki, 1942).

Wiligut, Karl Maria, 'Seyfrieds Runen (Rabensteinsage)' (Vienna, 1903), published in Winfried Katholing, *Die Sage von Ritter Seyfried und der Rabenstein bei Znaim* (Aschaffenburg, 2003), 73–115.

Zahlen zur Geldentwertung in Deutschland 1914 bis 1923, ed. Statistisches Reichsamt (Berlin, 1925).

Zipperer, Falk, 'Eschwege. Eine siedlungs- und verfassungsgeschichtliche Untersuchung', in *Festgabe für Heinrich Himmler* (Darmstadt, 1941), 215–92.

—— *Das Haberfeldtreiben. Seine Geschichte und seine Bedeutung* (Weimar, 1938).

MONOGRAPHS AND EDITED VOLUMES

Abitbol, Michel, *Les Juifs d'Afrique du Nord sous Vichy* (Paris, 1983).

Abrahamsen, Samuel, *Norway's Response to the Holocaust* (New York, 1991).

Absolon, Rudolf, *Die Wehrmacht im Dritten Reich*, vol. 6: *19. Dezember 1941 bis 9. Mai 1945* (Boppard a. Rh., 1995).

Ackermann, Josef, *Heinrich Himmler als Ideologe* (Göttingen, etc., 1970).

Adam, Uwe Dietrich, *Judenpolitik im Dritten Reich* (Düsseldorf, 1972).

Adler, Hans Günter, *Der verwaltete Mensch. Studien zur Deportation der Juden aus Deutschland* (Tübingen, 1974).

Ainsztein, Reuben, *Jüdischer Widerstand im deutschbesetzten Osteuropa während des Zweiten Weltkrieges* (Oldenburg, 1993).

Alberti, Michael, *Die Verfolgung und Vernichtung der Juden im Reichsgau Wartheland 1939–1945* (Wiesbaden, 2006).

Allen, Michael Thad, *The Business of Genocide: The SS, Slave Labor, and the Concentration Camps* (Chapel Hill, NC, 2002).

Aly, Götz, *Endlösung. Völkerverschiebung und der Mord an den europäischen Juden* (Frankfurt a. M., 1995) [*'Final Solution': Nazi Population Policy and the Murder of the European Jews* (London, 1999)].

Angrick, Andrej, *Besatzungspolitik und Massenmord. Die Einsatzgruppe D in der südlichen Sowjetunion 1941–1943* (Hamburg, 2003).

—— and Peter Klein, *Die 'Endlösung' in Riga. Ausbeutung und Vernichtung 1941–1944* (Darmstadt, 2006).

Anschluß 1938. Protokoll des Symposiums in Wien am 14. und 15. März 1978 (Vienna, 1981).

Arad, Yitzhak, *Belzec, Sobibor, Treblinka: The Operation Reinhard Death Camps* (Bloomington, Ind., 1987).

—— *Ghetto in Flames: The Struggle and Destruction of the Jews in Vilna in the Holocaust* (Jerusalem, 1980).

Aronson, Shlomo, *Reinhard Heydrich und die Frühgeschichte von SA und SD* (Stuttgart, 1971).

Baganz, Carina, *Erziehung zur 'Volksgemeinschaf'. Die frühen Konzentrationslager in Sachsen 1933–34/37* (Berlin, 2005).

Barkai, Avraham, *Vom Boykott zur 'Entjudung'. Der wirtschaftliche Existenzkampf der Juden im Dritten Reich 1933–1943* (Frankfurt a. M., 1987) [*From Boycott to Annihilation: The Economic Struggle of German Jews 1933–1941* (Hanover, 1989)].

Baruch, Nir, *Der Freikauf. Zar Boris und das Schicksal der bulgarischen Juden* (Sofia, 1996).

Bauer, Yehuda, *Freikauf von Juden? Verhandlungen zwischen dem nationalsozialistischen Deutschland und jüdischen Repräsentanten von 1933 bis 1945* (Frankfurt a. M., 1996) [*Jews for Sale? Nazi–Jewish Negotiations* (New Haven, 1994)].

Behrens, Beate, *Mit Hitler zur Macht. Aufstieg des Nationalsozialismus in Mecklenburg und Lübeck 1922–1933* (Rostock, 1998).

Benz, Wolfgang (ed.), *Dimension des Völkermords. Die Zahl der jüdischen Opfer des Nationalsozialismus* (Munich, 1991).

Bernadotte, Folke, *Das Ende. Meine Verhandlungen in Deutschland im Frühjahr 1945 und ihre politischen Folgen* (Zürich and New York, 1945).

Bernhardt, Heike, *Anstaltspsychiatrie und 'Euthanasie' in Pommern 1933–1945. Die Krankenmorde an Kindern und Erwachsenen am Beispiel der Landesheilanstalt Ueckermünde* (Frankfurt a. M., 1994).

Berschel, Holger, *Bürokratie und Terror. Das Judenreferat der Gestapo Düsseldorf 1933–1945* (Essen, 2001).

Bessel, Richard, *Political Violence and the Rise of Nazism: The Storm Troopers in Eastern Germany 1925–1934* (New Haven and London, 1984).

Biddiscombe, Perry, *Werwolf! The History of the National Socialist Guerrilla Movement, 1944–1946* (Toronto, 1998).

Birn, Ruth Bettina, *Die Höheren SS- und Polizeiführer. Himmlers Vertreter im Reich und in den besetzten Gebieten* (Düsseldorf, 1986).

Black, Peter, *Ernst Kaltenbrunner. Vasall Himmlers. Eine SS-Karriere* (Paderborn, etc., 1991) [*Ernst Kaltenbrunner: Ideological Sodier of the Third Reich* (Princeton, 1984)].

Böhler, Joachim, *Auftakt zum Vernichtungskrieg. Die Wehrmacht in Polen 1939* (Frankfurt a. M., 2006).

Böhm, Johann, *Die Gleichschaltung der deutschen Volksgruppe in Rumänien und das 'Dritte Reich' 1941–1944* (Frankfurt a. M., etc., 2003).

—— *Die Deutschen in Rumänien und das Dritte Reich 1933–1940* (Frankfurt a. M., 1999).

—— *Das nationalsozialistische Deutschland und die deutsche Volksgruppe in Rumänien 1936–1944. Das Verhältnis der deutschen Volksgruppe zum Dritten Reich und zum rumänischen Staat sowie der interne Widerstreit zwischen den politischen Gruppen* (Frankfurt a. M., etc., 1985).

Bohn, Robert, *Reichskommissariat Norwegen. 'Nationalsozialistische Neuordnung' und Kriegswirtschaft* (Munich, 2000).

Boog, Horst, *et al.*, *Der Angriff auf die Sowjetunion* (Frankfurt a. M., 1991) [*The Attack on the Soviet Union* (Oxford, 1998)].

Bosl, Karl (ed.), *Bayern im Umbruch. Die Revolution von 1918, ihre Voraussetzungen, ihr Verlauf und ihre Folgen* (Munich and Vienna, 1969).

Botz, Gerhard, *Die Eingliederung Österreichs in das Deutsche Reich. Planung und Verwirklichung des politisch-administrativen Anschlusses (1938–1940)*, 2nd edn. (Vienna, 1976).

—— *Wohnungspolitik und Judendeportation in Wien 1938. Zur Funktion des Antisemitismus als Ersatz nationalsozialistischer Sozialpolitik* (Vienna and Salzburg, 1975).

Bowlby, John, *Bindung und Verlust*, 3 vols. (Munich and Basle, 2006) [*Attachment and Loss*, 3 vols. (London, 1969, 1972, 1980)].

Braham, Randolph L., *The Politics of Genocide: The Holocaust in Hungary* (New York, 1994).

Bramwell, Anna, *Blood and Soil: Richard Walther Darré and Hitler's 'Green Party'* (Bourne End, 1985).

Brandes, Detlef, *Die Tschechen unter deutschem Protektorat*, 2 vols. (Munich and Vienna, 1969–75).

Brechtken, Magnus, *'Madagaskar für die Juden'. Antisemitische Idee und politische Praxis 1885–1945* (Munich, 1997).

Breitman, Richard, *Official Secrets: What the Nazis Planned, What the British and Americans Knew* (New York, 1998).

—— *Der Architekt der 'Endlösung'. Himmler und die Vernichtung der europäischen Juden* (Paderborn, 1996) [*The Architect of Genocide: Himmler and the 'Final Solution'* (New York, 1991)].

Broszat, Martin, *Nationalsozialistische Polenpolitik 1939–1945* (Stuttgart, 1961).

Browder, George C., *Hitler's Enforcers: The Gestapo and the SS Security Service in the Nazi Revolution* (New York, etc., 1996).

—— *Foundations of the Nazi Police State: The Formation of Sipo and SD* (Lexington, Ky., 1990).

Browning, Christopher R., *Die Entfesselung der 'Endlösung'. Nationalsozialistische Judenpolitik 1939–1942* (Berlin, 2006) [*The Origins of the Final Solution: The Evolution of Nazi Jewish Policy 1939–1942* (London, 2004)].

—— *Ganz normale Männer. Das Reserve-Polizeibataillon 101 und die 'Endlösung' in Polen* (Reinbek bei Hamburg, 1993) [*Ordinary Men: Reserve Police Batttalion 101 and the Final Solution in Poland* (New York, 1992)].

—— *The Final Solution and the German Foreign Office: A Study of Referat D III of Abteilung Deutschland, 1940–1943* (New York and London, 1978).

Brunck, Helma, *Die Deutsche Burschenschaft in der Weimarer Republik und im Nationalsozialismus* (Munich, 1999).

Buch der Erinnerung. Die ins Baltikum deportierten deutschen, österreichischen und tschechoslowakischen Juden, ed. Wolfgang Scheffler and Diana Schulle, 2 vols. (Munich, 2003).

Calic, Edouard, *Reinhard Heydrich. Schlüsselfigur des Dritten Reiches* (Düsseldorf, 1982).

Casagrande, Thomas, *Die volksdeutsche SS-Division 'Prinz Eugen'. Die Banater Schwaben und die nationalsozialistischen Kriegsverbrechen* (Frankfurt a. M. and New York, 2003).

Chary, Frederick B., *The Bulgarian Jews and the Final Solution, 1940–1944* (Pittsburgh, 1972).

Conway, Martin, *Collaboration in Belgium: Léon Degrelle and the Rexist Movement, 1940–1944* (New Haven and London, 1993).

Corni, Gustavo, und Horst Gies, *Brot—Butter—Kanonen. Die Ernährungswirtschaft in Deutschland unter der Diktatur Hitlers* (Berlin, 1997).

Cüppers, Martin, *Wegbereiter der Shoah. Die Waffen-SS, der Kommandostab Reichsführer-SS und die Judenvernichtung 1939–1945* (Darmstadt, 2005).

Derks, Hans, *Deutsche Westforschung. Ideologie und Praxis im 20. Jahrhundert* (Leipzig, 2001).

Deschner, Guenter, *Reinhard Heydrich. Statthalter der totalen Macht* (Esslingen, 1977).

Dierker, Wolfgang, *Himmlers Glaubenskrieger. Der Sicherheitsdienst der SS und seine Religionspolitik 1933–1941* (Paderborn, etc., 2002).

Dietrich, Otto, *12 Jahre mit Hitler* (Munich, 1955).

Distel, Barbara, und Ruth Jakusch, *Konzentrationslager Dachau 1933–1945* (Brussels, [1978]).

Doerries, Reinhard R., *Hitler's Last Chief of Foreign Intelligence: Allied Interrogations of Walter Schellenberg* (London, etc., 2003).

Dollmann, Eugen, *Dolmetscher der Diktatoren* (Bayreuth, 1963).

Domröse, Ortwin, *Der NS-Staat in Bayern von der Machtergreifung bis zum Röhm-Putsch* (Munich, 1974).

Dönitz, Karl, *Zehn Jahre und zwanzig Tage* (Bonn, 1958).

Dornberg, John, *Hitlers Marsch zur Feldherrnhalle. München, 8. und 9. November 1923* (Munich, 1983) [*The Putsch That Failed: Munich 1923. Hitler's Rehearsal for Power* (London, 1982)].

Döscher, Hans-Jürgen, *SS und Auswärtiges Amt im Dritten Reich. Diplomatie im Schatten der 'Endlösung'* (Berlin, 1991).

—— *'Reichskristallnacht'. Die Novemberpogrome 1938* (Frankfurt a. M., etc., 1988).

Drobisch, Klaus, und Günther Wieland, *System der NS-Konzentrationslager 1933–1939* (Berlin, 1993).

Duhnke, Horst, *Die KPD von 1933 bis 1945* (Cologne, 1972).

Düsterberg, Rolf, *Hanns Johst: 'Der Barde der SS'. Karrieren eines deutschen Dichters* (Paderborn, etc., 2004).

Enzyklopädie des Holocaust. Die Verfolgung und Ermordung der europäischen Juden, 3 vols., ed. Israel Gutman, German edition ed. Eberhard Jäckel, Peter Longerich, and Julius H. Schoeps (Berlin, 1993) [*Encyclopedia of the Holocaust*, 4 vols. (New York, 1990)].

Essner, Cornelia, *Die 'Nürnberger Gesetze' oder die Verwaltung des Rassenwahns 1933–1945* (Paderborn, etc., 2002).

Faatz, Martin, *Vom Staatsschutz zum Gestapo-Terror. Politische Polizei in Bayern in der Endphase der Weimarer Republik und der Anfangsphase der nationalsozialistischen Diktatur* (Würzburg, 1995).

Fahlbusch, Michael, *Wissenschaft im Dienst der nationalsozialistischen Politik? Die 'Volksdeutschen Forschungsgemeinschaften' von 1931–1945* (Baden-Baden, 1999).

Feldman, Gerald D., *The Great Disorder: Politics, Economics, and Society in the German Inflation, 1914–1924* (New York and Oxford, 1993).

Fenske, Hans, *Konservatismus und Rechtsradikalismus in Bayern nach 1918* (Bad Homburg v. d. H., etc., 1969).

Festschrift zur Vierhundert-Jahr-Feier des Wilhelms-Gymnasiums, 1559–1959 (Munich, 1959).

Fings, Karola, *Krieg, Gesellschaft und KZ. Himmlers SS-Baubrigaden* (Paderborn, etc., 2005).

Finn, Gerhard, *Sachsenhausen 1936–1950: Geschichte eines Lagers* (Berlin, 1988).

Fleischer, Hagen, *Im Kreuzschatten der Mächte: Griechenland 1941–1944*, 2 parts (Frankfurt a. M., 1986).

Fleming, Gerald, *Hitler und die Endlösung. 'Es ist des Führers Wunsch . . .'* (Wiesbaden and Munich, 1982) [*Hitler and the Final Solution* (London, 1985)].

Förster, Roland G. (ed.), *'Unternehmen Barbaross'. Zum historischen Ort der deutschsowjetischen Beziehungen von 1933 bis Herbst 1941* (Munich, 1993).

Frischauer, Willi, *Himmler: The Evil Genius of the Third Reich* (London, 1953).

Garbe, Detlef, *Zwischen Widerstand und Martyrium. Die Zeugen Jehovas im 'Dritten Reich'* (Munich, 1993).

Gaulle, Charles de, *Memoiren 1942–46. Die Einheit, das Heil* (Düsseldorf, 1961) [*The Complete War Memoirs of Charles de Gaulle* (London, 1964)].

Gellately, Robert, *Hingeschaut und weggesehen. Hitler und sein Volk* (Munich, 2002) [*Backing Hitler: Consent and Coercion in Nazi Germany* (Oxford, 2001)].

—— *Die Gestapo und die deutsche Gesellschaft. Die Durchsetzung der Rassenpolitik 1933–1945* (Paderborn, etc., 1993) [*The Gestapo and German Society* (Oxford, 1990)].

Georg, Enno, *Die wirtschaftlichen Unternehmungen der SS* (Stuttgart, 1963).

Gerlach, Christian, *Kalkulierte Morde. Die deutsche Wirtschafts- und Vernichtungspolitik in Weißrußland 1941 bis 1944* (Hamburg, 1999).

—— and Götz Aly, *Das letzte Kapitel. Realpolitik, Ideologie und der Mord an den ungarischen Juden 1944/1945* (Stuttgart and Zurich, 2002).

Geyer, Martin H., *Verkehrte Welt. Revolution, Inflation und Moderne, München 1914–1924* (Göttingen, 1998).

Gies, Horst, *R. Walther Darré und die nationalsozialistische Bauernpolitik in den Jahren 1930 bis 1933* (Frankfurt a. M., 1966).

Goldhagen, Daniel Jonah, *Hitlers willige Vollstrecker. Ganz gewöhnliche Deutsche und der Holocaust* (Berlin, 1996) [*Hitler's Willing Executioners: Ordinary Germans and the Holocaust* (New York, 1996)].

Golla, Karl-Heinz, *Der Fall Griechenlands 1941* (Hamburg, etc., 2007).

Goodrick-Clarke, Nicholas, *Die okkulten Wurzeln des Nationalsozialismus*, 2. edn. (Graz and Stuttgart, 2000) [*The Occult Roots of Nazism: The Ariosophists of Austria and Germany 1890–1935* (Wellingborough, 1985)].

Gordon, Harold J., *Hitlerputsch 1923. Machtkampf in Bayern 1923–1924* (Frankfurt a. M., 1971) [*Hitler and the Beer Hall Putsch* (Princeton, 1978)].

Goudsmit, Samuel A., *Alsos: The Failure in German Science* (London, 1947).

Graf, Christoph, *Politische Polizei zwischen Demokratie und Diktatur. Die Entwicklung der preußischen Politischen Polizei vom Staatsschutzorgan der Weimarer Republik zum Geheimen Staatspolizeiamt des Dritten Reiches* (Berlin, 1983).

Gruner, Wolf, *Der geschlossene Arbeitseinsatz deutscher Juden. Zur Zwangsarbeit als Element der Verfolgung 1938–1943* (Berlin, 1997).

Gutman, Yisrael, *The Jews of Warsaw, 1939–1943: Ghetto, Underground, Revolt* (Bloomington and Indianapolis, 1989).

Haasis, Hellmut G., *Tod in Prag. Das Attentat auf Reinhard Heydrich* (Reinbek bei Hamburg, 2002).

Hachmeister, Lutz, *Der Gegnerforscher. Die Karriere des SS-Führers Franz Alfred Six* (Munich, 1998).

Hagemann, Jürgen, *Die Presselenkung im Dritten Reich* (Bonn, 1970).

Hale, Christopher, *Himmler's Crusade: The True Story of the 1938 Nazi Expedition into Tibet* (London, 2003).

Hale, Oron J., *Presse in der Zwangsjacke, 1933–1945* (Düsseldorf, 1965) [*The Captive Press in the Third Reich* (Princeton, 1964)].

Halle, Uta, *'Die Externsteine sind bis auf weiteres germanisch!' Prähistorische Archäologie im Dritten Reich* (Bielefeld, 2002).

Hanfstaengl, Ernst, *Zwischen Weißem und Braunem Haus. Memoiren eines politischen Außenseiters* (Munich, 1970).

Hansen, Reimer, *Das Ende des Dritten Reiches. Die deutsche Kapitulation 1945* (Stuttgart, 1966).

Hausser, Paul, *Soldaten wie andere auch. Der Weg der Waffen-SS* (Osnabrück, 1967).

Hayes, Peter, *Industry and Ideology: IG Farben in the Nazi Era* (Cambridge, 2001).

Headland, Ronald, *Messages of Murder: A Study of the Reports of the Einsatzgruppen of the Security Police and the Security Service, 1941–1943* (Rutherford, 1992).

Heike, Otto, *Die deutsche Minderheit in Polen bis 1939. Ihr Leben und Wirken kulturell, gesellschaftlich, politisch. Eine historisch-dokumentarische Analyse* (Leverkusen, 1985).

Heim, Susanne, *Kalorien, Kautschuk, Karrieren. Pflanzenzüchtung und landwirtschaftliche Forschung in Kaiser-Wilhelm-Instituten 1933–1945* (Göttingen, 2003).

Heinemann, Isabel, *'Rasse, Siedlung, deutsches Blut'. Das Rasse- und Siedlungshauptamt der SS und die rassenpolitische Neuordnung Europas* (Göttingen, 2003).

Heinen, Armin, *Die Legion 'Erzengel Michael', in Rumänien. Soziale Bewegung und politische Organisation. Ein Beitrag zum Problem des internationalen Faschismus* (Munich, 1986).

Heinzle, Joachim, *Die Nibelungen. Lied und Sage* (Darmstadt, 2005).

Henke, Klaus-Dietmar, *Die amerikanische Besetzung Deutschlands*, 2nd edn. (Munich, 1996).

Herbert, Ulrich, *Fremdarbeiter. Politik und Praxis des 'Ausländer-Einsatzes' in der Kriegswirtschaft des Dritten Reiches*, 2nd edn (Bonn, 1999) [*Hitler's Foreign Workers: Enforced Foreign Labour in Germany under the Third Reich* (Cambridge, 1997)].

—— *Best. Biographische Studien über Radikalismus, Weltanschauung und Vernunft 1903–1989* (Bonn, 1996).

Heuer, Hans-Joachim, *Geheime Staatspolizei. Über das Töten und die Tendenzen der Entzivilisierung* (Berlin, 1995).

Hilberg, Raul, *Die Vernichtung der europäischen Juden. Die Gesamtgeschichte des Holocaust* (Frankfurt a. M., 1990) [*The Destruction of the European Jews*, 3 vols., rev. edn. (New York and London, 1985)]

Hildebrand, Klaus, *Das vergangene Reich. Deutsche Außenpolitik von Bismarck bis Hitler 1871–1945* (Stuttgart, 1995).

Hildesheimer, Esriel, *Jüdische Selbstverwaltung unter dem NS-Regime. Der Existenzkampf der Reichsvertretung und Reichsvereinigung der Juden in Deutschland* (Tübingen, 1994).

Hillgruber, Andreas, *Hitlers Strategie. Politik und Kriegführung 1940–1941*, 2nd edn. (Frankfurt a. M., 1982).

—— *Hitler, König Carol und Marschall Antonescu* (Mainz, 1954).

Hillmayr, Heinrich, *Roter und Weißer Terror in Bayern nach 1918. Ursachen, Erscheinungsformen und Folgen der Gewalttätigkeiten im Verlauf der revolutionären Ereignisse nach dem Ende des Ersten Weltkrieges* (Munich, 1974).

Himmler, Katrin, *Die Brüder Himmler. Eine deutsche Familiengeschichte* (Frankfurt a. M., 2005).

Himmlers Hexenkartothek. Das Interesse des Nationalsozialismus an der Hexenverfolgung, ed. Sönke Lorenz et al., 2nd edn. (Bielefeld, 2000).

Hirschfeld, Gerhard, *Fremdherrschaft und Kollaboration. Die Niederlande unter deutscher Besatzung 1940–1945* (Stuttgart, 1984).

Hoch, Anton, and Lothar Gruchmann, *Georg Elser. Der Attentäter aus dem Volke. Der Anschlag auf Hitler im Münchner Bürgerbräu 1939* (Frankfurt a. M., 1980).

Hockerts, Hans Günter, *Die Sittlichkeitsprozesse gegen katholische Ordensangehörige und Priester 1936/1937. Eine Studie zur nationalsozialistischen Herrschaftstechnik und zum Kirchenkampf* (Mainz, 1971).

Hoffmann, Joachim, *Die Tragödie der 'Russischen Befreiungsarmee' 1944/45. Wlassow gegen Stalin* (Munich, 2003).

Hoffmann, Peter, *Widerstand, Staatsstreich, Attentat. Der Kampf der Opposition gegen Hitler*, 3rd edn. (Munich, 1979).

—— *Die Sicherheit des Diktators. Hitlers Leibwachen, Schutzmaßnahmen, Residenzen, Hauptquartiere* (Munich, etc., 1975).

Hofmann, Hanns Hubert, *Der Hitlerputsch. Krisenjahre deutscher Geschichte, 1920–1924* (Munich, 1961).

Hohmann, Joachim S., *Robert Ritter und die Erben der Kriminalbiologie. 'Zigeunerforschung' im Nationalsozialismus und in Westdeutschland im Zeichen des Rassismus* (Frankfurt a. M., etc.,1991).

Höhne, Heinz, *Mordsache Röhm. Hitlers Durchbruch zur Alleinherrschaft 1933–1934* (Reinbek b. Hamburg, 1984).

—— *Der Orden unter dem Totenkopf. Die Geschichte der SS* (Gütersloh, 1967) [*The Order of the Death's Head: The Story of Hitler's SS* (London, 1969)].

Hölsken, Heinz Dieter, *Die V-Waffen. Entstehung, Propaganda, Kriegseinsatz* (Stuttgart, 1984).

Horn, Wolfgang, *Der Marsch zur Machtergreifung. Die NSDAP bis 1933* (Düsseldorf, 1972).

Howe, Ellic, *Uranias Children: The Strange World of the Astrologers* (London, 1967).

Huber, Ernst Rudolf, *Deutsche Verfassungsgeschichte seit 1789, vol. 7: Ausbau, Schutz und Untergang der Weimarer Republik* (Stuttgart, etc., 1984).

Huber, Gabriele, *Die Porzellan-Manufaktur Allach-München GmbH. Eine Wirtschaftsunternehmung der SS zum Schutz der 'deutschen Seele'* (Marburg, 1992).

Husemann, Friedrich, *Die guten Glaubens waren. Geschichte der SS-Polizeidivision. (4. SS Polizei-Panzer-Grenadier-Division), vol. 1: 1939–1942* (Osnabrück, 1971).

Hüser, Karl, *Wewelsburg 1933–1945. Kult- und Terrorstätte der SS. Eine Dokumentation* (Paderborn, 1982).

Hüttenberger, Peter, *Die Gauleiter. Studie zum Wandel des Machtgefüges in der NSDAP* (Stuttgart, 1969).

Jäckel, Eberhard, *Frankreich in Hitlers Europa. Die deutsche Frankreichpolitik im Zweiten Weltkrieg* (Stuttgart, 1966).

Jacobsen, Hans-Adolf, *Nationalsozialistische Außenpolitik 1933–1938* (Frankfurt a. M. and Berlin, 1968).

Jagschitz, Gerhard, *Der Putsch. Die Nationalsozialisten 1934 in Österreich* (Graz, etc., 1976).

Jahn, Peter, and Reinhard Rürup (eds), *Erobern und Vernichten. Der Krieg gegen die Sowjetunion 1941–1945. Essays* (Berlin, 1991).

Janka, Walter, *Spuren eines Lebens* (Berlin, 1991).

Janko, Sepp, *Weg und Ende der deutschen Volksgruppe in Jugoslawien* (Graz and Stuttgart, 1982).

Jansen, Christian, and Arno Weckbecker, *Der 'Volksdeutsche Selbstschutz' in Polen 1939/40* (Munich, 1992).

Jansen, Hans, *Der Madagaskar-Plan. Die beabsichtigte Deportation der europäischen Juden nach Madagaskar* (Munich, 1997).

Janssen, Karl-Heinz, and Fritz Tobias, *Der Sturz der Generäle. Hitler und die Blomberg-Fritsch-Krise 1938* (Munich, 1994).

Jastrzębski, Włodzimierz, *Der Bromberger Blutsonntag. Legende und Wirklichkeit* (Posen, 1990).

Jellonnek, Burkhard, *Homosexuelle unter dem Hakenkreuz. Die Verfolgung von Homosexuellen im Dritten Reich* (Paderborn, 1990).

Johnson, Eric A., *Der nationalsozialistische Terror. Gestapo, Juden und gewöhnliche Deutsche* (Berlin, 2001) [*The Nazi Terror: Gestapo, Jews and Ordinary Germans* (London, 1999)].

Jordan, Rudolf, *Erlebt und Erlitten.Weg eines Gauleiters von München bis Moskau* (Leoni and Starnb. See, 1971).

Kaienburg, Hermann, *Der Militär- und Wirtschaftskomplex der SS im KZ-Standort Sachsenhausen-Oranienburg. Schnittpunkt von KZ-System, Waffen-SS und Judenmord* (Berlin, 2006).

—— *Die Wirtschaft der SS* (Berlin, 2003).

—— *Das Konzentrationslager Neuengamme 1938–1945, published by the KZ-Gedenkstätte Neuengamme* (Berlin, 1997).

—— *'Vernichtung durch Arbeit'. Der Fall Neuengamme. Die Wirtschaftsbestrebungen der SS und ihre Auswirkungen auf die Existenzbedingungen der KZ-Gefangenen* (Bonn, 1990).

Kampe, Norbert, *Studenten und 'Judenfrage' im Deutschen Kaiserreich. Die Entstehung einer antisemitischen Trägerschicht des Antisemitismus* (Göttingen, 1988).

Kasten, Bernd, *'Gute Franzosen'. Die französische Polizei und die deutsche Besatzungsmacht im besetzten Frankreich 1940–1944* (Sigmaringen, 1993).

Kater, Michael H., *Das 'Ahnenerbe' der SS 1935–1945. Ein Beitrag zur Kulturpolitik des Dritten Reiches*, 4th enlarged edn. (Munich, 2006).

—— *Studentenschaft und Rechtsradikalismus in Deutschland 1918–1933. Eine sozialgeschichtliche Studie zur Bildungskrise in der Weimarer Republik* (Hamburg, 1975).

Kershaw, Ian, *Hitler*, 2 vols. (Stuttgart, 1998/2000) [*Hitler 1889–1936: Hubris* (London, 1998); *Hitler 1936–1945: Nemesis* (London, 2000)].

Kersten, Felix, *Totenkopf und Treue. Heinrich Himmler ohne Uniform. Aus den Tagebuchblättern des finnischen Medizinalrats Felix Kersten* (Hamburg, 1952) [*The Kersten Memoirs 1940–1945* (London, 1956)].

Kettenacker, Lothar, *Nationalsozialistische Volkstumspolitik im Elsaß* (Stuttgart, 1973).

Kipper, Rainer, *Der Germanenmythos im Deutschen Kaiserreich. Formen und Funktionen historischer Selbstthematisierung* (Göttingen, 2002).

Kissenkoetter, Udo, *Gregor Straßer und die NSDAP* (Stuttgart, 1978).

Klarsfeld, Serge, *Vichy—Auschwitz. Die Zusammenarbeit der deutschen und französischen Behörden bei der 'Endlösung der Judenfrage' in Frankreich* (Nördlingen, 1989).

—— *Die Endlösung der Judenfrage in Frankreich* (Paris, 1977).

Klausch, Hans-Peter, *Antifaschisten in SS-Uniform. Schicksal und Widerstand der deutschen politischen KZ-Häftlinge, Zuchthaus- und Wehrmachtstrafgefangenen in der SS Sonderformation Dirlewanger* (Bremen, 1993).

Klee, Ernst, *'Euthanasie' im NS-Staat. Die 'Vernichtung lebensunwerten Leben'* (Frankfurt a. M., 1983).

Klein, Pete (ed.), *Die Einsatzgruppen in der besetzten Sowjetunion 1941/42. Die Tätigkeits und Lageberichte des Chefs der Sicherheitspolizei und des SD* (Berlin, 1997).

—— *Die Wannsee-Konferenz vom 20. Januar 1942. Analyse und Dokumentation* (Berlin [1995]).

Klenner, Jochen, *Verhältnis von Partei und Staat 1933–1945, dargestellt am Beispiel Bayerns* (Munich, 1974).

Klinkhammer, Lutz, *Zwischen Bündnis und Besatzung. Das nationalsozialistische Deutschland und die Republik von Salò 1943–1945* (Tübingen, 1993).

Koblik, Steven, *The Stones Cry Out: Sweden's Response to the Persecution of the Jews 1933–1945* (New York, 1988).

Koch, Peter Ferdinand (ed.), *Himmlers graue Eminenz. Oswald Pohl und das Wirtschaftsverwaltungshauptamt der SS* (Hamburg, 1988).

Koehl, Robert Lewis, *The Black Corps: The Structure and Power Struggles of the Nazi SS* (Madison, Wisc., 1983).

Kolb, Eberhard, *Bergen-Belsen. Geschichte des 'Aufenthaltslagers' 1943–1945* (Hanover, 1962).

Krebs, Albert, *Tendenzen und Gestalten der NSDAP. Erinnerungen an die Frühzeit der Partei* (Stuttgart, 1959).

Kroener, Bernhard, *'Der starke Mann im Heimatkriegsgebiet'—Generaloberst Friedrich Fromm. Eine Biographie* (Paderborn, etc., 2005).

Kroll, Frank-Lothar, *Utopie als Ideologie. Geschichtsdenken und politisches Handeln im Dritten Reich* (Paderborn, 1998).

Kropat, Wolf-Arno, *Kristallnacht in Hessen. Der Judenpogrom vom November 1938. Eine Dokumentation* (Wiesbaden, 1988).

Kunz, Andreas, *Wehrmacht und Niederlage. Die bewaffnete Macht in der Endphase der nationalsozialistischen Herrschaft 1944 bis 1945* (Munich, 2005).

Kwiet, Konrad, *Reichskommissariat Niederlande. Versuch und Scheitern nationalsozialistischer Neuordnung* (Stuttgart, 1968).

Lang, Jochen von, *Der Adjutant. Karl Wolff, der Mann zwischen Hitler und Himmler* (Munich, 1985).

Lange, Hans-Jürgen, *Otto Rahn und die Suche nach dem Gral. Biografie und Quellen* (Engerda, 1999).

Lange, *Weisthor. Karl Maria Wiligut. Himmlers Rasputin und seine Erben* (Engerda, 1998).

—— *Otto Rahn. Leben & Werk* (Engerda, 1995).

Laqueur, Walter, and Richard Breitman, *Der Mann, der das Schweigen brach. Wie die Welt vom Holocaust erfuhr* (Frankfurt a. M., 1986) [*Breaking the Silence: The Secret Mission of Eduard Schulte Who Brought the World News of the Final Solution* (New York, 1986)].

Large, David Clay, *Hitlers München. Aufstieg und Fall der Hauptstadt der Bewegung* (Munich, 1998) [*Where Ghosts Walked: Munich's Road to the Third Reich* (New York and London, 1997)].

Latour, Conrad F., *Südtirol und die Achse Berlin–Rom 1938–1945* (Stuttgart, 1962).

Lepre, George, *Himmler's Bosnian Division: The Waffen-SS Handschar Division, 1943–1945* (Atglen, 1997).

Lethen, Helmut, *Verhaltenslehren der Kälte. Lebensversuche zwischen den Kriegen* (Frankfurt a. M., 1994).

Lewy, Guenter, *The Nazi Persecution of the Gypsies* (Oxford and New York, 2000).

Lichtenstein, Heiner, *Himmlers grüne Helfer. Die Schutz- und Ordnungspolizei im 'Dritten Reich'* (Cologne, 1990).

Lilienthal, Georg, *Der 'Lebensborn e.V.' Ein Instrument nationalsozialistischer Rassenpolitik* (Stuttgart and New York, 1985).

Linse, Ulrich, *Barfüßige Propheten. Erlöser der Zwanziger Jahre* (Berlin, 1983).

Lipscher, Ladislav, *Die Juden im slowakischen Staat 1939–1945* (Munich and Vienna, 1980).

Longerich, Peter *'Davon haben wir nichts gewusst!' Die Deutschen und die Judenverfolgung 1933–1945* (Munich, 2006).

—— *Geschichte der SA* (Munich, 2003).

—— *Der ungeschriebene Befehl. Hitler und der Weg zur 'Endlösung'* (Munich and Zurich, 2001).

—— *Politik der Vernichtung. Eine Gesamtdarstellung der nationalsozialistischen Judenverfolgung* (Munich and Zurich, 1998) [rev. edn., *Holocaust: The Nazi Persecution and Murder of the Jews* (Oxford, 2010)].

—— *Die Wannsee-Konferenz vom 20. Januar 1942. Planung und Beginn des Genozids an den europäischen Juden*, public lecture in the House of the Wannsee Conference on 19 January 1998, supplemented by a critical select bibliography of the Wannsee Conference and the start of the genocide of the European Jews with a facsimile of the minutes of the conference (Berlin, 1998).

—— *Hitlers Stellvertreter. Führung der Partei und Kontrolle des Staatsapparates durch den Stab Heß und die Partei-Kanzlei Bormann* (Munich, etc., 1992).

—— (ed.), *Die Ermordung der europäischen Juden. Eine umfassende Dokumentation des Holocaust 1941–1945* (Munich, 1989).

Loock, Hans-Dietrich, *Quisling, Rosenberg und Terboven. Zur Vorgeschichte und Geschichte der nationalsozialistischen Revolution in Norwegen* (Stuttgart, 1970).

Lower, Wendy, *Nazi Empire-Building and the Holocaust in Ukraine* (Chapel Hill, NC, 2005).

Luchterhandt, Martin, *Der Weg nach Birkenau. Entstehung und Verlauf der nationalsozialistischen Verfolgung der 'Zigeuner'* (Lübeck, 2000).

Lüdde-Neurath, Walter, *Regierung Dönitz. Die letzten Tage des Dritten Reiches*, 3rd edn. (Göttingen, 1964).

Lumans, Valdis O., *Himmler's Auxiliaries: The Volksdeutsche Mittelstelle and the German National Minorities of Europe, 1933–1945* (Chapel Hill and London, 1993).

Luther, Tammo, *Volkstumspolitik des Deutschen Reiches 1933–1938. Die Auslanddeutschen im Spannungsfeld zwischen Traditionalisten und Nationalsozialisten* (Stuttgart, 2004).

MacLean, French L., *The Cruel Hunters: SS-Sonder-Kommando Dirlewanger, Hitler's Most Notorious Anti-Partisan Unit* (Atglen, 1998).

Madajczyk, Czesław (ed.), *Vom Generalplan Ost zum Generalsiedlungsplan* (Munich, etc., 1994).

—— *Die Okkupationspolitik Nazideutschlands in Polen 1939–1945* (Cologne, 1988).

Mai, Uwe, *'Rasse und Raum'. Agrarpolitik, Sozial- und Raumplanung im NS-Staat* (Paderborn, etc., 2002).

Mallmann, Klaus-Michael, and Martin Cüppers, *Halbmond und Hakenkreuz. Das Dritte Reich, die Araber und Palästina* (Darmstadt, 2006).

Mammach, Klaus, *Widerstand 1933 bis 1945. Geschichte der deutschen antifaschistischen Widerstandsbewegung im Inland und in der Emigration* (Cologne, 1984).

—— *Der Volkssturm. Das letzte Aufgebot 1944/45* (Cologne, 1981).

Mann, Reinhard, *Protest und Kontrolle im Dritten Reich. Nationalsozialistische Herrschaft im Alltag einer rheinischen Großstadt* (Frankfurt a. M., etc., 1987).

Manoschek, Walter, *'Serbien ist judenfrei'. Militärische Besatzungspolitik und Judenvernichtung in Serbien 1941/42* (Munich, 1993).

Manvell, Roger, and Heinrich Fraenkel, *Himmler: Kleinbürger und Massenmörder* (Herrsching, 1981) [*Heinrich Himmler* (London, 1965)].

Marssolek, Inge, and René Ott, *Bremen im Dritten Reich. Anpassung—Widerstand—Verfolgung* (Bremen, 1986).

Matthäus, Jürgen, et al., *Ausbildungsziel Judenmord? 'Weltanschauliche Erziehung' von SS, Polizei und Waffen-SS im Rahmen der 'Endlösung'* (Frankfurt a. M., 2003).

Mennel, Rainer, *Die Schlussphase des Zweiten Weltkrieges im Westen (1944/45). Eine Studie zur politischen Geographie* (Osnabrück, 1981).

Merson, Allan, *Kommunistischer Widerstand in Nazideutschland* (Bonn, 1999) [*Communist Resistance in Nazi Germany* (London, 1985)].

Messenger, Charles, *Hitler's Gladiator: The Life and Times of Oberstgruppenführer and Panzergeneral-Oberst d. Waffen-SS Sepp Dietrich* (London, etc., 1988).

Meyer, Ahlrich, *Die deutsche Besatzung in Frankreich 1940–1944. Widerstandsbekämpfung und Judenverfolgung* (Darmstadt, 2000).

Michaelis, Meir, *Mussolini and the Jews: German–Italian Relations and the Jewish Question in Italy, 1922–1945* (Oxford, 1978).

Michaelis, Rolf, *Die Geschichte der SS-Heimwehr Danzig 1939* (Rodgau, 1990).

Mierau, Peter, *Nationalsozialistische Expeditionspolitik. Deutsche Asien-Expeditionen 1933–1945* (Munich, 2006).

Mitchell, Allan, *Revolution in Bayern 1918/1919. Die Eisner-Regierung und die Räterepublik* (Munich, 1967) [*Revolution in Bavaria: The Eisner Regime and the Soviet Republic* (Princeton, 1965)].

Möckl, Karl, *Die Prinzregentenzeit. Gesellschaft und Politik während der Ära des Prinzregenten Luitpold in Bayern* (Munich and Vienna, 1972).

Mommsen, Hans, and Manfred Grieger, *Das Volkswagenwerk und seine Arbeiter im Dritten Reich* (Düsseldorf, 1996).

Morsch, Günter (ed.), *Mord und Massenmord im Konzentrationslager Sachsenhausen 1936–1945* (Berlin, 2005).

Müller, Klaus-Jürgen, *General Ludwig Beck. Studien u. Dokumente zur politisch-militärischen Vorstellungswelt und Tätigkeit des Generalstabschefs des deutschen Heeres 1933–1938* (Boppard a. Rh., 1980).

—— *Das Heer und Hitler* (Stuttgart, 1968).

Müller, Rolf-Dieter, *Hitlers Ostkrieg und die deutsche Siedlungspolitik. Die Zusammenarbeit von Wehrmacht, Wirtschaft und SS* (Frankfurt a. M., 1991).

Mund, Rudolf J., *Der Rasputin Himmlers. Die Wiligut Saga* (Vienna, 1982).

Musial, Bogdan, *'Konterrevolutionäre Elemente sind zu erschießen'. Die Brutalisierung des deutsch–sowjetischen Krieges im Sommer 1941* (Berlin and Munich, 2000).

—— *Deutsche Zivilverwaltung und Judenverfolgung im Generalgouvernement. Eine Fallstudie zum Distrikt Lublin 1939–1944* (Wiesbaden, 1999).

Naasner, Walter, *Neue Machtzentren in der deutschen Kriegswirtschaft 1942–1945. Die Wirtschaftsorganisation der SS, das Amt des Generalbevollmächtigten für den Arbeitseinsatz und das Reichsministerium für Bewaffnung und Munition, Reichsministerium für Rüstung und Kriegsproduktion im nationalsozialistischen Herrschaftssystem* (Boppard a. Rh., 1994).

Nagel, Brigitte, *Die Welteislehre. Ihre Geschichte und ihre Rolle im 'Dritten Reich'* (Stuttgart, 1991).

Neliba, Günter, *Wilhelm Frick. Der Legalist des Unrechtsstaates. Eine politische Biographie* (Paderborn, etc., 1992).

Nesládková, Ludmila (ed.), *The Case Nisko in the History of the Final Solution of the Jewish Problem in Commemoration of the 55th Anniversary of the First Deportation of Jews in Europe* (Ostrava, 1995).

Neuberger, Helmut, *Freimaurerei und Nationalsozialismus. Die Verfolgung der deutschen Freimaurerei durch völkische Bewegung und Nationalsozialismus*, vol. 2: *Das Ende der deutschen Freimaurerei* (Hamburg, 1980).

Neufeld, Hans-Joachim, Jürgen Huck, and Georg Tessin, *Zur Geschichte der Ordnungspolizei 1936–1945* (Koblenz, 1957).

Neufeld, Michael J., *Die Rakete und das Reich. Wernher von Braun, Peenemünde und der Beginn des Raketenzeitalters* (Berlin, 1997).

Oberkersch, Valentin, *Die Deutschen in Syrmien, Slawonien, Kroatien und Bosnien. Geschichte einer deutschen Volksgruppe in Südosteuropa* (Munich, 1989).

Obst, Dieter, *'Reichskristallnacht'. Ursachen und Verlauf des antisemitischen Pogroms vom November 1938* (Frankfurt a. M., etc., 1991).

Ogorreck, Ralf, *Die Einsatzgruppen und die 'Genesis der Endlösung'* (Berlin, 1996).

Olshausen, Klaus, *Zwischenspiel auf dem Balkan. Die deutsche Politik gegenüber Jugoslawien und Griechenland von März bis Juli 1941* (Stuttgart, 1973).

Orb, Heinrich, *Nationalsozialismus: 13 Jahre Machtrausch*, 2nd edn. (Olten, 1945).

Orlow, Dietrich, *The History of the Nazi Party*, vol. 1: 1919–1933 (Newton Abbot, 1971).

Orth, Karin, *Das System der nationalsozialistischen Konzentrationslager. Eine politische Organisationsgeschichte* (Hamburg, 1999).

Osterloh, Jörg, *Nationalsozialistische Judenverfolgung im Reichsgau Sudetenland 1938–1945* (Munich, 2006).

Padfield, Peter, *Himmler: Reichsführer-SS* (London, 1990).

Patzwall, Klaus D., *Der SS-Totenkopfring. Seine illustrierte Geschichte 1933–1945*, 4th rev. edn. (Norderstedt, 2002).

Paul, Gerhard, *Aufstand der Bilder. Die NS-Propaganda vor 1933* (Bonn, 1990).

—— and Klaus-Michael Mallmann (eds), *Die Gestapo. Mythos und Realität* (Darmstadt, 1995).

Pelt, Robert-Jan van, and Déborah Dwork, *Auschwitz. Von 1270 bis heute* (Munich and Zurich, 1998).

Peukert, Detlev, *Die Edelweißpiraten. Protestbewegungen jugendlicher Arbeiter im Dritten Reich. Eine Dokumentation* (Cologne, 1980).

—— *Die KPD im Widerstand. Verfolgung und Untergrundarbeit an Rhein und Ruhr 1933–1945* (Wuppertal, 1980).

Pilichowski, Czesław, *Es gibt keine Verjährung* (Warsaw, 1980).

Pingel, Falk, *Häftlinge unter SS-Herrschaft. Widerstand, Selbstbehauptung und Vernichtung im Konzentrationslager* (Hamburg, 1978).

Piper, Ernst, *Alfred Rosenberg. Hitlers Chefideologe* (Munich, 2005).

Plant, Richard, *Rosa Winkel. Der Krieg der Nazis gegen die Homosexuellen* (Frankfurt a. M., etc., 1991).

Plumpe, Gottfried, *Die I. G. Farbenindustrie AG. Wirtschaft, Technik und Politik 1904–1945* (Berlin, 1990).

Pohl, Dieter, *Nationalsozialistische Judenverfolgung in Ostgalizien 1941–1944. Organisation und Durchführung eines staatlichen Massenverbrechens* (Vienna, 1996).

—— *Von der 'Judenpolitik' zum Judenmord. Der Distrikt Lublin des Generalgouvernements 1939–1944* (Frankfurt a. M., etc., 1993).

Präg, Werner, and Wolfgang Jacobmeyer (eds), *Das Diensttagebuch des deutschen Generalgouverneurs in Polen 1939–1945* (Stuttgart, 1975).

Pressac, Jean-Claude, *Die Krematorien von Auschwitz. Die Technik des Massenmordes* (Munich and Zurich, 1994).

Pringle, Heather, *The Master Plan: Himmler's Scholars and the Holocaust* (New York, 2006).

Prinz, Friedrich, und Marita Krauss (eds), *München—Musenstadt mit Hinterhöfen. Die Prinzregentenzeit 1886–1912* (Munich, 1988).

Pucher, Siegfried J., '... *in der Bewegung führend tätig'. Odilo Globocnik—Kämpfer für den 'Anschluß', Vollstrecker des Holocaust* (Klagenfurt, 1997).

Querg, Thorsten J., *Spionage und Terror. Das Amt VI des Reichssicherheitshauptamtes 1939–1945*, Phil. Diss. (Berlin, 1997) [Microfiche edition].

Rapp, Petra Madeleine, *Die Devisenprozesse gegen katholische Ordensangehörige und Geistliche im Dritten Reich. Eine Untersuchung zum Konflikt deutscher Orden und Klöster in Wirtschaftlicher Notlage, totalitärer Machtausübung des nationalsozialistischen Regimes und im Kirchenkampf 1935/1936* (Bonn, 1981).

Rautkallio, Hannu, *Finland and the Holocaust: The Rescue of Finland's Jews* (New York, 1987).

Rebentisch, Dieter (ed.), *Führerstaat und Verwaltung im Zweiten Weltkrieg. Verfassungsentwicklung und Verwaltungspolitik 1939–1945* (Stuttgart, 1989).

Reilly, Joanne, *Belsen: The Liberation of a Concentration Camp* (London and New York, 1998).

Ribbentrop, Joachim von, *Zwischen London und Moskau. Erinnerungen und letzte Aufzeichnungen*, aus dem Nachlass, ed. Annelies von Ribbentrop (Leoni and Starnb. See, 1953) [*The Ribbentrop Memoirs* (London, 1954)].

Richardi, Hans-Günter, *Schule der Gewalt. Die Anfänge des Konzentrationslagers Dachau 1933–1934. Ein dokumentarischer Bericht* (Munich, 1983).

Riess, Volker, *Die Anfänge der Vernichtung 'lebensunwerten Lebens' in den Reichsgauen Danzig-Westpreußen und Wartheland 1939/40* (Frankfurt a. M., etc., 1995).

Rösch, Mathias, *Die Münchner NSDAP 1925–1933. Eine Untersuchung zur inneren Struktur der NSDAP in der Weimarer Republik* (Munich, 2002).

Rosenkranz, Herbert, *Verfolgung und Selbstbehauptung. Die Juden in Österreich 1938–1945* (Vienna, 1978).

Rossino, Alexander B., *Hitler Strikes Poland: Blitzkrieg, Ideology, and Atrocity* (Lawrence, Kan., 2003).

Rother, Bernd, *Spanien und der Holocaust* (Tübingen, 2001).

Rusinek, Bernd-A., *Gesellschaft in der Katastrophe. Terror, Illegalität, Widerstand— Köln 1944/45* (Essen, 1989).

Safrian, Hans, *Die Eichmann-Männer* (Vienna and Zurich, 1993).

Sandkühler, Thomas, *'Endlösung' in Galizien. Der Judenmord in Ostpolen und die Rettungsinitiativen von Berthold Beitz 1941–1944* (Bonn, 1996).

Sauer, Paul, *Württemberg in der Zeit des Nationalsozialismus* (Ulm, 1975).

Schausberger, Norbert, *Der Griff nach Österreich. Der Anschluß* (Vienna and Munich, 1978).

Schellenberg, Walter, *The Schellenberg Memoirs*, ed. Louis Hagen (London, 1956).

Schelvis, Jules, *Vernichtungslager Sobibór* (Berlin, 1998).

Schenk, Dieter, *Hitlers Mann in Danzig. Albert Forster und die NS-Verbrechen in Danzig-Westpreußen* (Bonn, 2000).

—— *Die Post von Danzig. Geschichte eines deutschen Justizmords* (Reinbek bei Hamburg, 1995).

Schley, Jens, *Nachbar Buchenwald. Die Stadt Weimar und ihr Konzentrationslager 1937–1945* (Cologne, etc., 1999).

Schmeling, Anke, *Josias Erbprinz zu Waldeck und Pyrmont. Der politische Weg eines hohen SS-Führers* (Kassel, 1993).

Schmidt, Paul, *Statist auf diplomatischer Bühne 1923–1945. Erlebnisse des Chefdolmetschers im auswärtigen Amt mit den Staatsmännern Europas* (Bonn, 1949).

Schmidt, Rainer F., *Rudolf Heß—'Botengang eines Toren?' Der Flug nach Großbritannien vom 10. Mai 1941* (Düsseldorf, 1997).

Schmitz, Peter, *Die Artamanen. Landarbeit und Siedlung bündischer Jugend in Deutschland 1924–1935* (Bad Neustadt a.d. Saale, 1985).

Schneider, Gertrude, *Journey into Terror: Story of the Riga Ghetto*, enlarged new edn. (Newport, Conn., and London, 2001).

Schön, Eberhart, *Die Entstehung des Nationalsozialismus in Hessen* (Meisenheim a. Glan 1972).

Schröder, Josef, *Italiens Kriegsaustritt 1943. Die deutschen Gegenmaßnahmen im italienischen Raum: Fall 'Alarich' und 'Achse'* (Göttingen, etc., 1969).

Schröder, Matthias, *Deutschbaltische SS-Führer und Andrej Vlasov 1942–1945. 'Russland kann nur von Russen besiegt werde': Erhard Kroeger, Friedrich Buchardt und die 'Russische Befreiungsarmee'* (Paderborn, etc., 2001).

Schulte, Jan Erik, *Zwangsarbeit und Vernichtung. Das Wirtschaftsimperium der SS. Oswald Pohl und das SS-Wirtschafts-Verwaltungshauptamt 1933–1945* (Paderborn, etc., 2001).

Schulz, Gerhard, *Von Brüning zu Hitler. Der Wandel des politischen Systems in Deutschland 1930–1933* (Berlin and New York, 1992).

Schwarz, Gudrun, *Eine Frau an seiner Seite. Ehefrauen in der 'SS-Sippengemeinschaft'* (Hamburg, 1997).

Schwerin von Krosigk, Lutz Graf, *Memoiren* (Stuttgart, 1977).

See, Klausvon, *Deutsche Germanenideologie. Vom Humanismus bis zur Gegenwart* (Frankfurt a. M., 1970).

Seidler, Franz W., *'Deutscher Volkssturm'. Das letzte Aufgebot 1944/45* (Munich and Berlin, 1989).

Sevillias, Errikos, *Athens—Auschwitz* (Athens, 1983).

Shimizu, Akiko, *Die deutsche Okkupation des serbischen Banats 1941–1944 unter besonderer Berücksichtigung der deutschen Volksgruppe in Jugoslawien* (Münster, 2003).

Smelser, Ronald, *Das Sudetenproblem und das Dritte Reich (1933–1938). Von der Volkstumspolitik zur nationalsozialistischen Außenpolitik* (Munich, etc., 1980).

Smith, Bradley F., *Heinrich Himmler 1900–1926. Sein Weg in den deutschen Faschismus* (Munich, 1979) [*Heinrich Himmler: A Nazi in the Making, 1900–1926* (Stanford, Calif., 1971)].

Spangler, Gottfried, and Peter Zimmermann (eds), *Die Bindungstheorie. Grundlagen, Forschung und Anwendung* (Stuttgart, 1995).

Spannenberger, Norbert, *Der Volksbund der Deutschen in Ungarn 1938–1945 unter Horthy und Hitler*, 2nd edn. (Munich, 2005).

Spector, Shmuel, *The Holocaust of Volhynian Jews, 1941–1944* (Jerusalem, 1990).

Speer, Albert, *Erinnerungen* (Berlin, 1969) [*Inside the Third Reich: Memoirs by Albert Speer* (London and New York, 1970)].

Sprenger, Isabell, *Groß-Rosen. Ein Konzentrationslager in Schlesien* (Cologne, etc., 1996).

Stachura, Peter D., *Gregor Strasser and the Rise of Nazism* (London, 1983).

Stambolis, Barbara, *Der Mythos der jungen Generation. Ein Beitrag zur politischen Kultur der Weimarer Republik* (Bochum, 1982).

Stein, George H., *Geschichte der Waffen-SS* (Düsseldorf, 1967).

Stein, Harry, *Konzentrationslager Buchenwald 1937–1945. Begleitband zur ständigen historischen Ausstellung*, published by the Gedenkstätte Buchenwald (Göttingen, 1999).

Steinbacher, Sybille, *'Musterstadt' Auschwitz. Germanisierungspolitik und Judenmord in Ostoberschlesien* (Munich, 2000).

—— *Dachau—die Stadt und das Konzentrationslager in der NS-Zeit. Die Untersuchung einer Nachbarschaft* (Frankfurt a. M., 1993).

Steinberg, Jonathan, *Deutsche, Italiener und Juden. Der italienische Widerstand gegen den Holocaust* (Göttingen, 1992) [*All or Nothing: The Axis and the Holocaust 1941–43* (London and New York, 1990)].

Steiner, Felix, *Die Freiwilligen. Idee und Opfergang* (Göttingen, 1958).

Steinert, Marlis G., *Die 23 Tage der Regierung Dönitz* (Düsseldorf, 1967).

Steur, Claudia, *Theodor Dannecker. Ein Funktionär der 'Endlösung'* (Essen, 1997).

Steurer, Leopold, *Südtirol zwischen Rom und Berlin 1919–1939* (Vienna, etc., 1980).

Stolle, Michael, *Die Geheime Staatspolizei in Baden. Personal, Organisation, Wirkung und Nachwirken einer regionalen Verfolgungsbehörde im Dritten Reich* (Konstanz, 2001).

Strasser, Otto, *Hitler und ich* (Konstanz, 1948) [*Hitler and I* (London, 1940)].

Strebel, Bernhard, *Das KZ Ravensbrück. Geschichte eines Lagerkomplexes* (Paderborn, etc., 2003).

Streit, Christian, *Keine Kameraden. Die Wehrmacht und die sowjetischen Kriegsgefangenen 1941–1945* (Bonn, 1997).

Ströle-Bühle, Heike, *Studentischer Antisemitismus in der Weimarer Republik. Eine Analyse der burschenschaftlichen Blätter 1918 bis 1933* (Frankfurt a. M., etc., 1991).

Stuhlpfarrer, Karl, *Umsiedlung Südtirol 1939–1940* (Vienna, etc., 1985).

Stümke, Hans-Georg, *Homosexuelle in Deutschland. Eine politische Geschichte* (Munich, 1989).

Sydnor, Charles W., Jr. *Soldaten des Todes. Die 3. SS-Division 'Totenkopf' 1933–1945* (Paderborn, etc., 2002) [*Soldiers of Destruction: The SS Death's Head Division 1933–1945* (New York, 1977)].

Terhorst, Karl-Leo, *Polizeiliche planmäßige Überwachung und polizeiliche Vorbeugungshaft im Dritten Reich. Ein Beitrag zur Rechtsgeschichte vorbeugender Verbrechensbekämpfung* (Heidelberg, 1985).

Theweleit, Klaus, *Männerphantasien* (Munich and Zurich, 2000). (Original edition in two vols., Frankfurt a. M., 1977/8) [*Male Fantasies*, 2 vols. (Minneapolis, 1987)].

Thomsen, Erich, *Deutsche Besatzungspolitik in Dänemark 1940–1945* (Düsseldorf, 1971).

Tönsmeyer, Tatjana, *Das Dritte Reich und die Slowakei 1939–1945. Politischer Alltag zwischen Kooperation und Eigensinn* (Paderborn, etc., 2003).

Tuchel, Johannes, *Die Inspektion der Konzentrationslager 1938–1945. Das System des Terrors* (Berlin, 1994).

——*Konzentrationslager. Organisationsgeschichte und Funktion der 'Inspektion der Konzentrationslager' 1934–1938* (Boppard a. Rh., 1991).

Turner, Henry, *Hitlers Weg zur Macht. Der Januar 1933* (Munich, 1997) [*Hitler's 30 Days to Power: January 1933* (London, 1996)].

Tyrell, Albrecht, *Führer befiehl... Selbstzeugnisse aus der 'Kampfzeit' der NSDAP. Dokumentation und Analyse* (Düsseldorf, 1969).

Ueberschär, Gerd R., und Wolfram Wette (eds), *Der deutsche Überfall auf die Sowjetunion. 'Unternehmen Barbarossa' 1941*, rev. edn. (Frankfurt a. M., 1991).

Vieregge, Bianca, *Die Gerichtsbarkeit einer 'Elite'. Nationalsozialistische Rechtsprechung am Beispiel der SS- und Polizeigerichtsbarkeit* (Baden-Baden and Berlin, 2002).

Vogelsang, Reinhard, *Der Freundeskreis Heinrich Himmler* (Göttingen, etc., 1972).

Wagener, Otto, *Hitler aus nächster Nähe. Aufzeichnungen eines Vertrauten 1929–1932* (Frankfurt a. M., etc., 1978).

Wagner, Bernd C., *IG Auschwitz. Zwangsarbeit und Vernichtung von Häftlingen des Lagers Monowitz 1941–1945* (Munich, 2000).

Wagner, Patrick, *Volksgemeinschaft ohne Verbrecher. Konzeptionen und Praxis der Kriminalpolizei in der Zeit der Weimarer Republik und des Nationalsozialismus* (Hamburg, 1996).

Wagner, Wilfried, *Belgien in der deutschen Politik während des Zweiten Weltkrieges* (Boppard a. Rh., 1974).

Warmbrunn, Werner, *The German Occupation of Belgium, 1940–1944* (New York, 1993).

Wasser, Bruno, *Himmlers Raumplanung im Osten. Der Generalplan Ost in Polen 1940–1944* (Basle, etc., 1993).

Weber, Wolfram, *Die innere Sicherheit im besetzten Belgien und Nordfrankreich 1940–44. Ein Beitrag zur Geschichte der Besatzungsverwaltungen* (Düsseldorf, 1978).

Wegner, Bernd, *Hitlers Politische Soldaten. Die Waffen-SS 1933–1945: Leitbild, Struktur und Funktion einer nationalsozialistischen Elite*, 5th edn. (Paderborn, 1997).

—— *Zwei Wege nach Moskau. Vom Hitler–Stalin-Pakt bis zum 'Unternehmen Barbarossa'* (Munich and Zurich, 1991).

Weidinger, Otto, *Division Das Reich. Der Weg der 2. SS-Panzer-Division 'Das Reich'. Die Geschichte der Stammdivision der Waffen-SS*, vol. 1 (Osnabrück, 1967).

Weingarten, Ralph, *Die Hilfeleistungen der westlichen Welt bei der Endlösung der deutschen Judenfrage. Das 'Intergovernmental Committee on Political Refugees' IGC 1938–1939* (Bern, Frankfurt a. M., and Las Vegas, 1981).

Weingartner, James J., *Hitler's Guard: The Story of the Leibstandarte SS Adolf Hitler, 1933–1945* (Carbondale, Ill., etc., 1974).

Wenck, Alexandra-Eileen, *Zwischen Menschenhandel und 'Endlösung'. Das Konzentrationslager Bergen-Belsen* (Paderborn, etc., 2000).

Westenrieder, Norbert, *'Deutsche Frauen und Mädchen!' Vom Alltagsleben 1933–1945* (Düsseldorf, 1984).

Westermann, Edward B., *Hitler's Police Battalions: Enforcing Racial War in the East* (Lawrence, Kansas, 2005).

Weyrauch, Walter Otto, *Gestapo V-Leute. Tatsachen und Theorie des Geheimdienstes. Untersuchungen zur Geheimen Staatspolizei während der nationalsozialistischen Herrschaft* (Frankfurt a. M., 1989).

Wiehn, Erhard Roy (ed.), *Die Schoáh von Babij Jar. Das Massaker deutscher Sonderkommandos an der jüdischen Bevölkerung von Kiew 1941 fünfzig Jahre danach zum Gedenken* (Konstanz, 1991).

Wildt, Michael, *Generation des Unbedingten. Das Führungskorps des Reichssicherheitshauptamtes* (Hamburg, 2003).

Wilhelm, Friedrich, *Die Polizei im NS-Staat. Die Geschichte ihrer Organisation im Überblick* (Paderborn, etc., 1997).

Wilhelm, Hans-Heinrich, *Die Einsatzgruppe A der Sicherheitspolizei und des SD 1941/42* (Frankfurt a. M., etc., 1996).

—— *Rassenpolitik und Kriegführung. Sicherheitspolizei und Wehrmacht in Polen und in der Sowjetunion 1939–1942* (Passau, 1991).

Winkler, Heinrich August, *Weimar 1918–1933. Die Geschichte der ersten deutschen Demokratie* (Munich, 1993).

—— *Von der Revolution zur Stabilisierung. Arbeiter und Arbeiterbewegung in der Weimarer Republik 1918 bis 1924*, 2nd edn. (Berlin and Bonn, 1985).

Wulff, Wilhelm, *Tierkreis und Hakenkreuz. Als Astrologe an Himmlers Hof* (Gütersloh, 1968).

Wysocki, Gerhard, *Die Geheime Staatspolizei im Land Braunschweig. Polizeirecht und Polizeipraxis im Nationalsozialismus* (Frankfurt a. M. and New York, 1997).

Zámeaník, Stanislav, *Das war Dachau* (Luxembourg, 2002).

Zimmermann, Michael, *Rassenutopie und Genozid. Die nationalsozialistische 'Lösung der Zigeunerfrage'* (Hamburg, 1996).

Zipfel, Friedrich, *Kirchenkampf in Deutschland 1933–1945. Religionsverfolgung und Selbstbehauptung der Kirchen in der nationalsozialistischen Zeit* (Berlin, 1965).

Zirlewagen, Marc, *Der Kyffhäuser-Verband der Vereine Deutscher Studenten in der Weimarer Republik* (Cologne, 1999).

Zuccotti, Susan, *The Holocaust, the French, and the Jews* (New York, 1993).

—— *The Italians and the Holocaust: Persecution: Rescue, and Survival* (New York, 1987).

ARTICLES AND CHAPTERS IN BOOKS

Aly, Götz, and Susanne Heim, 'Staatliche Ordnung und "organische Lösung". Die Rede Hermann Görings "über die Judenfrage" vom 6. Dezember 1938', *Jahrbuch für Antisemitismusforschung*, 2 (1993), 378–404.

Angrick, Andrej, et al., '"Da hätte man schon ein Tagebuch führen müssen". Das Polizeibataillon 322 und die Judenmorde im Bereich der Heeresgruppe Mitte während des Sommers und Herbstes 1941. Miteiner Auseinandersetzung über die rechtlichen Konsequenzen', in Helge Grabitz (ed.), *Die Normalität des Verbrechens. Bilanz und Perspektiven der Forschung zu den nationalsozialistischen Gewaltverbrechen*, Festschrift für Wolfgang Scheffler zum 65.Geburtstag (Berlin, 1994), 325–84.

Arad, Yitzhak, 'Alfred Rosenberg and the "Final Solution" in the Occupied Soviet Territories', *Yad Vashem Studies*, 13 (1979), 263–86.

Arendes, Cord, 'Schrecken aus dem Untergrund. Endphaseverbrechen des "Werwolf"', in id. (ed.), *Terror nach innen. Verbrechen am Ende des Zweiten Weltkrieges* (Göttingen, 200), 149–71.

Arnold, Klaus Jochen, 'Die Eroberung und Behandlung der Stadt Kiew durch die Wehrmacht im September 1941. Zur Radikalisierung der Besatzungspolitik', *Militärgeschichtliche Mitteilungen*, 58/1 (1999), 23–63.

Auerbach, Hellmuth, 'Der Begriff "Sonderbehandlung" im Sprachgebrauch der SS', in *Gutachten des Instituts für Zeitgeschichte*, vol. 2 (Stuttgart, 1966), 182–9.

——— 'Die Einheit Dirlewanger', *Vierteljahrshefte für Zeitgeschichte*, 10 (1962), 250–63.

Ayass, Wolfgang, '"Ein Gebot der nationalen Arbeitsdisziplin": Die Aktion "Arbeitsscheu Reich" 1938', in *Feindererklärung und Prävention. Kriminalbiologie, Zigeunerforschung und Asozialenpolitik* (Berlin, 1988), 43–74.

Barcz, Wojciech, 'Die erste Vergasung', in Hans G. Adler (ed.), *Auschwitz: Zeugnisse und Berichte*, 2nd edn. (Cologne and Frankfurt a. M., 1979), 17 f.

Bauer, Yehuda, 'The Death Marches, January–May 1945', in Michael R. Marrus (ed.), *The Nazi Holocaust: Historical Articles on the Destruction of European Jews*, vol. 9: *The End of the Holocaust* (Westport, Conn., etc., 1989), 491–511.

Baumgart, Winfried, 'Zur Ansprache Hitlers vor den Führern der Wehrmacht am 22.8.1939: eine quellenkritische Untersuchung', *Vierteljahrshefte für Zeitgeschichte*, 16 (1968), 120–49.

Beckenbauer, Alfons, 'Eine Landshuter Jugendfreundschaft und ihre Verwicklung in die NS-Politik. Der Arzt Dr. Karl Gebhardt und der Reichsführer-SS Heinrich Himmler', *Verhandlungen des Historischen Vereins für Niederbayern*, 100 (1974), 5–22.

——— 'Musterschüler und Massenmörder. Heinrich Himmlers Landshuter Jugendjahre', *Verhandlungen des Historischen Vereins für Niederbayern*, 95 (1969), 93–106.

Beer, Mathias, 'Die Entwicklung der Gaswagen beim Mord an den Juden', *Vierteljahrshefte für Zeitgeschichte*, 35/3 (1987), 403–17.

Bender, Sara, 'The "Reinhardt Action" in the "Bialystok District"', in Freia Anders (ed.), *Bialystok in Bielefeld. Nationalsozialistische Verbrechen vor dem Landgericht Bielefeld 1958–1967* (Bielefeld, 2003), 186–208.

—— 'From Underground to Armed Struggle: The Resistance Movement in the Bialystok Ghetto', *Yad Vashem Studies*, 23 (1993), 145–71.

Black, Peter, 'Die Trawniki-Männer und die Aktion Reinhard', in Bogdan Musial (ed.), *'Aktion Reinhardt'. Der Völkermord an den Juden im Generalgouvernement 1941–1944* (Osnabrück, 2004), 309–52.

Blatman, Daniel, 'Die Todesmärsche—Entscheidungsträger, Mörder und Opfer', in Ulrich Herbert (ed.), *Die nationalsozialistischen Konzentrationslager. Entwicklung und Struktur*, vol. 2 (Göttingen, 1998), 1063–92.

Böhler, Joachim, '"Tragische Verstrickung" oder Auftakt zum Vernichtungskrieg? Die Wehrmacht in Polen 1939', in Klaus-Michael Mallmann and Bogdan Musial (eds), *Genesis des Genozids. Polen 1939–1941* (Darmstadt, 2004), 36–57.

Boll, Bernd, '"Aktionen nach Kriegausbruch". Wehrmacht und 1. SS-Infanteriebrigade 1941', *Zeitschrift für Geschichtswissenschaft*, 48/9 (2000), 775–88.

Braham, Randolph L., 'The Kamenets-Podolsk and Délvidék Massacres: Prelude to the Holocaust in Hungary', *Yad Vashem Studies*, 9 (1973), 133–56.

Brandhuber, Jerzy, 'Die sowjetischen Kriegsgefangenen im Konzentrationslager Auschwitz', in *Hefte von Auschwitz*, 4 (1961), 5–46.

Breitman, Richard, 'Friedrich Jeckeln, Spezialist für die "Endlösung" im Osten', in Ronald Smelser und Enrico Syring (eds), *Die SS. Elite unter dem Totenkopf. 30 Lebensläufe* (Paderborn, etc., 2000), 267–75.

—— 'Mein Kampf and the Himmler Family: Two Generations React to Hitler's Ideas', *Holocaust and Genocide Studies*, 13 (1999), 90–7.

—— and Shlomo Aronson, 'Eine unbekannte Himmler-Rede vom Januar 1943', *Vierteljahrshefte für Zeitgeschichte*, 38 (1990), 337–48.

Broszat, Martin, 'Nationalsozialistische Konzentrationslager 1933–1945', in Hans Buchheim *et al.*, *Anatomie des SS-Staates*, 7th edn. (Munich, 1999), 321–445.

—— 'Heranziehung von slowakischen Staatsbürgern deutscher Volkszugehörigkeit zum Dienst in der Waffen-SS', in *Gutachten des Instituts für Zeitgeschichte*, vol. 1 (Munich, 1958), 412–17.

—— 'Zur Perversion der Strafjustiz im Dritten Reich', with a documentary appendix, *Vierteljahrshefte für Zeitgeschichte*, 6 (1958), 390–443.

Browder, George C., 'Schellenberg—Eine Geheimdienst-Phantasie', in Ronald Smelser and Enrico Syring (eds), *Die SS. Elite unter dem Totenkopf. 30 Lebensläufe* (Paderborn, etc., 2000), 418–30.

Browning, Christopher R., 'Die nationalsozialistische Umsiedlungspolitik und die Suche nach einer "Lösung der Judenfrage" 1939–1941', in id., *Der Weg zur 'Endlösung'. Entscheidungen und Täter* (Bonn, 1998), 13–36.

—— 'A Final Hitler Decision for the Final Solution? The Riegner Telegram Reconsidered', *Holocaust and Genocide Studies*, 10 (1996), 3–10.

—— 'The Decision Concerning the Final Solution', in id., *Fateful Months: Essays on the Emergence of the Final Solution* (New York and London, 1985), 8–38.

Buchheim, Hans, 'Befehl und Gehorsam', in id. *et al.*, *Anatomie des SS-Staates*, 7th edn. (Munich, 1999), 213–320.

—— 'Die SS—Das Herrschaftsinstrument', in id. *et al.*, *Anatomie des SS-Staates*, 7th edn. (Munich, 1999), 13–212.

Büchler, Yehoshua, 'The Deportation of Slovakian Jews to the Lublin District of Poland in 1942', *Holocaust and Genocide Studies*, 6 (1991), 151–66.

—— 'Kommandostab Reichsführer-SS: Himmler's Personal Murder Brigades in 1941', *Holocaust and Genocide Studies*, 1/1 (1986), 11–25.

Bussmann, Walter, 'Zur Entstehung und Überlieferung der "Hoßbach-Niederschrift"', *Vierteljahrshefte für Zeitgeschichte*, 16 (1968), 373–84.

Carpi, Daniel, 'Notes on the History of the Jews in Greece during the Holocaust Period: The Attitude of the Italians (1941–1943)', in Michael R. Marrus (ed.), *The Nazi Holocaust: Historical Articles on the Destruction of European Jews*, vol. 5 (Westport, Conn., etc., 1989), 731–68.

Clark, Christopher, 'Josef "Sepp" Dietrich. Landsknecht im Dienste Hitlers', in Ronald Smelser und Enrico Syring (eds), *Die SS. Elite unter dem Totenkopf. 30 Lebensläufe* (Paderborn, etc., 2000), 119–33.

Cohen, William B., and Jörgen Svensson, 'Finland and the Holocaust', *Holocaust and Genocide Studies* 9/1 (1995), 70–92.

D'Onofrio, Andrea, 'Rassenzucht und Lebensraum: Zwei Grundlagen im Blut- und Boden-Gedanken von Richard Walther Darré', *Zeitschrift für Geschichtswissenschaft* 'Berlin', 49 (2001), 140–57.

Deichmann, Hans, and Peter Hayes, 'Standort Auschwitz. Eine Kontroverse über die Entscheidungsgründe für den Bau des I.G. Farben-Werks in Auschwitz', *1999*, 11/1 (1996), 73–101.

Dieckmann, Christoph, 'Das Ghetto und das Konzentrationslager in Kaunas 1941–1944', in Ulrich Herbert (ed.), *Die nationalsozialistischen Konzentrationslager. Entwicklung und Struktur*, vol. 1 (Göttingen, 1998), 439–71.

Ditt, Karl, 'Die Kulturraumforschung zwischen Wissenschaft und Politik. Das Beispiel Karl Petri (1903–1993)', *Westfälische Forschungen*, 46 (1996), 73–176.

Eiber, Ludwig, 'Polizei, Justiz und Verfolgung in München 1933 bis 1945', in Richard Bauer *et al.* (eds), *München—'Hauptstadt der Bewegung'. Bayerns Metropole und der Nationalsozialismus*, new edn. (Munich, 2002), 235–43.

—— 'Unter Führung des NSDAP-Gauleiters. Die Hamburger Staatspolizei (1933–1937)', in Gerhard Paul and Klaus-Michael Mallmann (eds), *Die Gestapo. Mythos und Realität* (Darmstadt, 1995), 101–17.

Endlich, Stefanie, 'Die Lichtenburg 1933–1939. Haftort politischer Prominenz und Frauen-KZ', in Wolfgang Benz and Barbara Distel (eds), *Herrschaft und Gewalt. Frühe Konzentrationslager 1933–1939* (Berlin, 2002), 11–64.

Engelmann, Roger, 'Öffentlichkeit and Zensur. Literatur und Theater als Provoka-tion', in Friedrich Prinz and Marita Krauss (eds), *München—Musenstadt mit Hinterhöfen. Die Prinzregentenzeit 1886–1912* (Munich, 1988), 267–76.

Esch, Michael G., 'Das SS-Mannschaftshaus in Lublin und die Forschungsstelle für Ostunterkünfte', in Götz Aly (ed.), *Modelle für ein deutsches Europa. Ökonomie und Herrschaft im Großwirtschaftsraum* (Berlin, 1992), 206 f.

Fargion, Liliana Picciotto, 'Italien', in Wolfgang Benz (ed.), *Dimension des Völker-mords. Die Zahl der jüdischen Opfer des Nationalsozialismus* (Munich, 1991), 199–227.

Fatran, Gila, 'Die Deportation der Juden aus der Slowakei 1944–1945', *Bohemia*, 37 (1996), 99–119.

Fings, Karola, 'Eine "Wannsee-Konferenz" über die Vernichtung der Zigeuner? Neue Forschungsergebnisse zum 15. Januar 1943 und dem "Auschwitz-Erlass" ', *Jahrbuch für Antisemitismusforschung*, 15 (2006), 303–33.

Foedrowitz, Michael, 'Auf der Suche nach einer besatzungspolitischen Konzeption. Der Befehlshaber der Sicherheitspolizei und des SD im Generalgouvernement', in Gerhard Paul and Klaus-Michael Mallmann (eds), *Die Gestapo im Zweiten Weltkrieg. 'Heimatfront' und besetztes Europa* (Darmstadt, 2000), 340–61.

Freund, Florian, and Bertrand Perz, 'Mauthausen-Stammlager', in Wolfgang Benz and Barbara Distel (eds), *Der Ort des Terrors. Geschichte der nationalsozialistischen Konzentrationslager*, vol. 4: *Flossenbürg, Mauthausen, Ravensbrück* (Munich, 2006), 293–346.

Fröbe, Rainer, 'Hans Kammler—Technokrat der Vernichtung', in Ronald Smelser and Enrico Syring (eds), *Die SS. Elite unter dem Totenkopf. 30 Lebensläufe* (Pader-born, etc., 2000), 305–19.

—— 'Der Arbeitseinsatz von KZ-Häftlingen und die Perspektive der Industrie 1943–1945', in Ulrich Herbert (ed.), *Europa und der 'Reichseinsatz'. Ausländische Zivilarbeiter, Kriegsgefangene und KZ-Häftlinge in Deutschland 1938–1945* (Essen, 1991), 351–83.

Gellately, Robert, 'Allwissend und allgegenwärtig? Entstehung, Funktion und Wandel des Gestapo-Mythos', in Gerhard Paul and Klaus-Michael Mallmann (eds), *Die Gestapo. Mythos und Realität* (Darmstadt, 1995), 47–70.

Gerlach, Christian, 'Failure of Plans for an SS Extermination Camp in Mogilev, Belorussia', *Holocaust and Genocide Studies*, 11/1 (1997), 60–78.

—— 'Die Wannsee-Konferenz, das Schicksal der deutschen Juden und Hitlers politische Grundentscheidung, alle Juden Europas zu ermorden', *Werkstatt Geschichte*, 6/18 (1997), 7–44.

Giles, Geoffrey, 'The Denial of Homosexuality: Same-Sex Incidents in Himmler's SS and Police', *Journal of the History of Sexuality* (2002), 256–90.

—— 'The Institutionalization of Homosexual Panic in the Third Reich', in Robert Gellately and Nathan Stoltzfus (eds), *Social Outsiders in Nazi Germany* (Princeton, etc., 2001), 233–55.

Goshen, Seev, 'Nisko. Ein Ausnahmefall unter den Judenlagern der SS', *Vierteljahrs-hefte für Zeitgeschichte*, 40/1 (1992), 95–106.

—— 'Eichmann und die Nisko-Aktion im Oktober 1939. Eine Fallstudie zur NS-Judenpolitik in der letzten Etappe vor der "Endlösung"', *Vierteljahrshefte für Zeitgeschichte*, 29/1 (1981), 74–96.

Grenville, John A. S., 'Die "Endlösung" und die "Judenmischlinge" im "Dritten Reich"', in Ursula Büttner, Werner Johe, and Angelika Voss (eds), *Das Unrechtsregime. Internationale Forschung über den Nationalsozialismus*, vol. 2: *Verfolgung, Exil, belasteter Neubeginn* (Hamburg, 1986), 91–121.

Greve, Reinhard, 'Tibetforschung im SS-Ahnenerbe', in Thomas Hauschild (ed.), *Lebenslust und Fremdenfurcht. Ethnologie im Dritten Reich* (Frankfurt a. M., 1995), 168–99.

Grill, Johnpeter Horst, 'The Nazi Party's Rural Propaganda before 1928', *Central European History*, 15 (1982), 149–85.

Grimm, Gerhard, 'Albanien', in Wolfgang Benz (ed.), *Dimension des Völkermords. Die Zahl der jüdischen Opfer des Nationalsozialismus* (Munich, 1991), 229–39.

Gruchmann, Lothar, 'Die bayerische Justiz im politischen Machtkampf 1933/34. Ihr Scheitern bei der Strafverfolgung von Mordfällen in Dachau', in Martin Broszat and Elke Fröhlich (eds), *Bayern in der NS-Zeit*, vol. 2: *Herrschaft und Gesellschaft im Konflikt*. Part *A* (Munich, 1979), 415–28.

Gruner, Wolf, 'Von der Kollektivausweisung zur Deportation der Juden aus Deutschland (1938–1945). Neue Perspektiven und Dokumente', *Beiträge zur Geschichte des Nationalsozialismus*, 20 (2004), 21–62.

—— 'Poverty and Persecution: the Reichsvereinigung, the Jewish Population, and Anti-Jewish Policy in the Nazi State, 1939–1945', *Yad Vashem Studies*, 27 (1999), 23–60.

Haase, Norbert, 'Justizterror in der Wehrmacht am Ende des Zweiten Weltkrieges', in Cord Arendes (ed.), *Terror nach innen. Verbrechen am Ende des Zweiten Weltkrieges* (Göttingen, 2006), 80–102.

Hallgarten, George W. F., 'Mein Mitschüler Heinrich Himmler', *Germanica Judaica*, 1/2 (1960/1).

Heberer, Patricia, 'Eine Kontinuität der Tötungsoperationen. T4-Täter und die "Aktion Reinhardt"', in Bogdan Musial (ed.), *'Aktion Reinhardt'. Der Völkermord an den Juden im Generalgouvernement 1941–1944* (Osnabrück, 2004), 285–308.

Heiber, Helmut, 'Generalplan Ost', *Vierteljahrshefte für Zeitgeschichte*, 6 (1958), 281–325.

Henke, Josef, 'Von den Grenzen der SS-Macht. Eine Fallstudie zur Tätigkeit des SS-Wirtschafts-Verwaltungshauptamtes', in Dieter Rebentisch and Karl Teppe (eds), *Verwaltung contra Menschenführung im Staat Hitlers. Studien zum politisch-administrativen System* (Göttingen, 1986), 255–77.

Herbert, Ulrich, 'Die deutsche Militärverwaltung in Paris und die Deportation der französischen Juden', in Christian Jansen (ed.), *Von der Aufgabe der Freiheit. Politische Verantwortung und bürgerliche Gesellschaft im 19. und 20. Jahrhundert. Festschrift für Hans Mommsen zum 5. November 1995* (Berlin, 1995), 427–50.

Hesse, Klaus, ' "... Gefangenenlager, Exekution,... Irrenanstalt... "'. Walter Frentz' Reise nach Minsk im Gefolge Heinrich Himmlers im August 1941', in Hans Georg Hiller von Gaertringen (ed.), *Das Auge des Dritten Reiches. Hitlers Kameramann und Fotograf Walter Frentz* (Munich and Berlin, 2006), 176–94.

Hett, Ulrike, and Johannes Tuchel, 'Die Reaktionen des NS-Staates auf den Umsturzversuch vom 20. Juli 1944', in Peter Steinbach and Johannes Tuchel (eds), *Widerstand gegen den Nationalsozialismus* (Bonn, 1994), 377–89.

Hochberger, Ernst, 'Die Deutschen in der Slowakei', in id., Anton Scherer, and Friedrich Spiegel-Schmidt, *Die Deutschen zwischen Karpaten und Krain* (Munich, 1994), 12–78.

Hölzl, Martin, 'Grüner Rock und Weiße Weste. Adolf von Bomhard und die Legende von der sauberen Ordnungspolizei', *Zeitschrift für Geschichtswissenschaft*, 50 (2002), 22–43.

Jäckel, Eberhard, 'On the Purpose of the Wannsee Conference', in James S. Pacy (ed.), *Perspectives on the Holocaust: Essays in Honor of Raul Hilberg* (Boulder, Colo., etc., 1995), 39–50.

Jacobsen, Hans-Adolf, 'Kommissarbefehl und Massenexekutionen sowjetischer Kriegsgefangener', in Hans Buchheim *et al.*, *Anatomie des SS-Staates*, 7th edn. (Munich, 1999), 449–544.

Jellonnek, Burkhard, 'Staatspolizeiliche Fahndungs- und Ermittlungsmethoden gegen Homosexuelle. Regionale Differenzen und Gemeinsamkeiten', in Gerhard Paul and Klaus-Michael Mallmann (eds), *Die Gestapo. Mythos und Realität* (Darmstadt, 1995), 343–56.

Kaienburg, Hermann, 'Sachsenhausen–Stammlager', in Wolfgang Benz und Barbara Distel (eds), *Der Ort des Terrors. Geschichte der nationalsozialistischen Konzentrationslager*, vol. 3: *Sachsenhausen, Buchenwald* (Munich, 2006).

——'Jüdische Arbeitslager an der "Straße der SS" ', *1999*, 1 (1996), 13–39.

Karner, Stefan, 'Die Aussiedlungen der Slowenen in der Untersteiermark. Ein Beispiel nationalsozialistischer Volkstumspolitik', *Österreich in Geschichte und Literatur*, 22 (1978), 154–74.

Kárny, Miroslav, 'Nisko in der Geschichte der Endlösung', *Judaica Bohemiae*, 23 (1987), 69–84.

Kater, Michael H., 'Zum gegenseitigen Verhältnis von SA und SS in der Sozialgeschichte des Nationalsozialismus von 1925 bis 1939', *Vierteljahrsschrift für Sozial- und Wirtschaftsgeschichte*, 62/3 (1975), 339–79.

—— 'Die Artamanen. Völkische Jugend in der Weimarer Republik', *Historische Zeitschrift*, 213 (1971), 577–683.

Kellerhoff, Sven Felix, 'Schüsse am Ballhausplatz. Der Putsch gegen Österreichs Kanzler Dollfuß 1934', in Alexander Demandt (ed.), *Das Attentat in der Geschichte* (Cologne, etc., 1996), 345–60.

Kimmel, Günther, 'Das Konzentrationslager Dachau. Eine Studie zu den natio-nalsozialistischen Gewaltverbrechen', in Martin Broszat and Elke Fröhlich (eds),

Bayern in der NS-Zeit, vol. 2: *Herrschaft und Gesellschaft im Konflikt*. Part A (Munich, 1979), 349–413.

Kinder, Elisabeth, 'Der Persönliche Stab Reichsführer-SS. Geschichte, Aufgaben und Überlieferung', in Heinz Boberach und Hans Booms (eds), *Aus der Arbeit des Bundesarchivs. Beiträge zum Archivwesen, zur Quellenkunde und Zeitgeschichte* (Boppard a. Rh., 1977), 379–97.

Kirchhoff, Hans, 'SS-Gruppenführer Werner Best and the Action against the Danish Jews—October 1943', *Yad Vashem Studies*, 24 (1994), 195–222.

Klein, Peter, 'Curt von Gottberg—Siedlungsfunktionär und Massenmörder', in Klaus-Michael Mallmann and Gerhard Paul (eds), *Karrieren der Gewalt. Nationalsozialistische Täterbiographien* (Darmstadt, 2004), 95–103.

—— 'Die Rolle der Vernichtungslager Kulmhof (Chełmno), Belzec (Bełżec) und Auschwitz-Birkenau in den frühen Deportationsvorbereitungen', in Dittmar Dahlmann (ed.), *Lager, Zwangsarbeit, Vertreibung und Deportation. Dimensionen der Massenverbrechen in der Sowjetunion und in Deutschland 1933 bis 1945* (Essen, 1999), 459–81.

Klodzinski, Stanislaw, 'Die erste Vergasung von Häftlingen und Kriegsgefangenen im Konzentrationslager Auschwitz', in *Die Auschwitz-Hefte*, published by the Hamburg Institut für Sozialforschung (Weinheim and Basle, 1987), i. 261–75.

Knoll, Albert, 'Die Porzellanmanufaktur München-Allach. Das Lieblingskind von Heinrich Himmler', in *KZ-Außenlager. Geschichte und Erinnerung, Dachauer Hefte*, 15 (Dachau, 1999), 116–33.

Kohlhaas, Elisabeth, 'Die Mitarbeiter der regionalen Staatspolizeistellen. Quantitative und qualitative Befunde zur Personalausstattung der Gestapo', in Gerhard Paul and Klaus-Michael Mallmann (eds), *Die Gestapo. Mythos und Realität* (Darmstadt, 1995), 219–35.

Krausnick, Helmut, 'Judenverfolgung', in Hans Buchheim *et al.*, *Anatomie des SS-Staates*, 7th edn. (Munich, 1999), 545–678.

—— 'Die Einsatzgruppen vom Anschluß Österreichs bis zum Feldzug gegen die Sowjetunion. Entwicklung und Verhältnis zur Wehrmacht', in id. and Hans-Heinrich Wilhelm, *Die Truppe des Weltanschauungskrieges. Die Einsatzgruppen der Sicherheitspolizei und des SD 1938–1942* (Stuttgart, 1981), 13–278.

—— 'Hitler und die Morde in Polen. Ein Beitrag zum Konflikt zwischen Heer und SS um die Verwaltung der besetzten Gebiete', *Vierteljahrshefte für Zeitgeschichte*, 11/2 (1963), 196–209.

—— 'Himmler über seinen Besuch bei Mussolini', *Vierteljahrshefte für Zeitgeschichte*, 4 (1956), 423–6.

Kwiet, Konrad, 'Auftakt zum Holocaust. Ein Polizeibataillon im Osteinsatz', in Bundeszentrale für politische Bildung (ed.), *Der Nationalsozialismus* (Frankfurt a. M., 1993), 191–208.

—— 'Nach dem Pogrom. Stufen der Ausgrenzung', in Wolfgang Benz (ed.), *Die Juden in Deutschland 1933–1945. Leben unter nationalsozialistischer Herrschaft* (Munich, 1989), 545–659.

Lehnstaedt, Stephan, 'Das Reichsministerium des Innern unter Heinrich Himmler 1943–1945', *Vierteljahrshefte für Zeitgeschichte*, 54 (2006), 639–72.

Leo, Annette, 'Ravensbrück-Stammlager', in Wolfgang Benz and Barbara Distel (eds), *Der Ort des Terrors. Geschichte der nationalsozialistischen Konzentrationslager*, vol. 4: *Flossenbürg, Mauthausen, Ravensbrück* (Munich, 2006), 473–520.

Lüerssen, Dirk, ' "Moorsoldaten" in Esterwegen, Bürgermoor, Neusustrum. Die frühen Konzentrationslager im Emsland 1933 bis 1936', in Wolfgang Benz and Barbara Distel (eds), *Herrschaft und Gewalt. Frühe Konzentrationslager 1933–1939* (Berlin, 2002), 157–210.

Mallmann, Klaus-Michael, 'Der qualitative Sprung im Vernichtungsprozess. Das Massaker von Kamenez-Podolsk Ende August 1941', *Jahrbuch für Antisemitismusforschung*, 10 (2001), 239–64.

—— 'Vom Fußvolk der "Endlösung". Ordnungspolizei, Ostkrieg und Judenmord', *Tel Aviver Jahrbuch für Deutsche Geschichte*, 26 (1997), 355–91.

—— 'Die V-Leute der Gestapo. Umrisse einer kollektiven Biographie', in Gerhard Paul and Klaus-Michael Mallmann (eds), *Die Gestapo. Mythos und Realität* (Darmstadt, 1995), 268–87.

Masur, Norbert, 'Ein Jude spricht mit Hitler', in Niklas Günther and Sönke Zankel (eds), *Abrahams Enkel. Juden, Christen, Muslime und die Schoa* (Stuttgart, 2006), 133–44.

Matthäus, Jürgen, 'Die "Judenfrage" als Schulungsthema von SS und Polizei. "Inneres Erlebnis" und Handlungslegitimation', in id. et al., *Ausbildungsziel Judenmord? 'Weltanschauliche Erziehung' von SS, Polizei und Waffen-SS im Rahmen der 'Endlösung'* (Frankfurt a. M., 2003), 35–86.

—— ' "Weltanschauliche Forschung und Auswertung". Aus den Akten des Amtes VII im Reichssicherheitshauptamt', *Jahrbuch für Antisemitismusforschung*, 5 (1996), 287–330.

—— 'What about the "Ordinary Men"? The German Order Police and the Holocaust in the Occupied Soviet Union', *Holocaust and Genocide Studies*, 10/2 (1996), 134–50.

Maurer, Trude, 'Abschiebung und Attentat. Die Ausweisung der polnischen Juden und der Vorwand für die "Kristallnacht" ', in Walter H. Pehle (ed.), *Der Judenpogrom 1938. Von der 'Reichskristallnacht' zum Völkermord* (Frankfurt a. M., 1988), 52–73.

Meershoek, Guus, 'Machtentfaltung und Scheitern. Sicherheitspolizei und SD in den Niederlanden', in Gerhard Paul and Michael Mallmann (eds), *Die Gestapo im Zweiten Weltkrieg. 'Heimatfront' und besetztes Europa* (Darmstadt, 2000), 383–402.

Mehringer, Hartmut, 'Die bayerische Sozialdemokratie bis zum Ende des NS-Regimes. Vorgeschichte, Verfolgung und Widerstand', in id., Anton Grossmann, and Klaus Schoenhoven (eds), *Bayern in der NS-Zeit*, vol. 5: *Die Parteien KPD, SPD, BVP in Verfolgung und Widerstand* (Munich, 1983), 287–432.

—— 'Die KPD in Bayern 1919–1945. Vorgeschichte, Verfolgung und Widerstand', in id., Anton Grossmann, und Klaus Schoenhoven (eds), *Bayern in der NS-Zeit*, vol. 5: *Die Parteien KPD, SPD, BVP in Verfolgung und Widerstand* (Munich, 1983), 1–286.

Meyer, Ahlrich, ' "... daß französische Verhältnisse anders sind als polnische". Die Bekämpfung des Widerstands durch die deutsche Militärverwaltung in Frankreich 1941', in Guus Meershoek *et al.*, *Repression und Kriegsverbrechen. Die Bekämpfung von Widerstands- und Partisanenbewegungen gegen die deutsche Besatzung in West und Südosteuropa* (Berlin and Göttingen, 1997), 43–91.

Meyer, Winfried, 'Aktion "Gewitter". Menschenopfer für Macht und Mythos der Gestapo', *Dachauer Hefte*, 21 (2005), 3–20.

Michman, Dan, 'Why Did Heydrich Write the "Schnellbrief"? A Remark on the Reason and on its Significance', *Yad Vashem Studies*, 32 (2004), 433–47.

Mlynarczyk, Jace Andrzej, 'Treblinka—ein Todeslager der "Aktion Reinhard" ', in Bogdan Musial (ed.), *'Aktion Reinhardt'. Der Völkermord an den Juden im General- gouvernement 1941–1944* (Osnabrück, 2004), 257–81.

Mommsen, Hans, 'Ein Erlass Himmlers zur Bekämpfung der Korruption in der inneren Verwaltung vom Dezember 1944', *Vierteljahrshefte für Zeitgeschichte*, 16 (1968), 295–309.

Moser, Jonny, 'Nisko: The First Experiment in Deportation', *Simon Wiesenthal Center Annual*, 2/1 (1985), 1–30.

Mühldorfer, Friedbert, 'Fridolfing', in Wolfgang Benz and Barbara Distel (eds), *Der Ort des Terrors. Geschichte der nationalsozialistischen Konzentrationslager*, vol. 2: *Frühe Lager, Dachau, Emslandlager* (Munich, 2005), 327.

Mühleisen, Horst, 'Die Fritsch-Krise im Frühjahr 1938. Neun Dokumente aus dem Nachlaß des Generalobersten', *Militärgeschichtliche Mitteilungen*, 56/2 (1997), 471–508.

Noakes, Jeremy, 'The Development of Nazi Policy towards the German-Jewish "Mischlinge" 1933–1945', *Leo Baeck Institute Year Book*, 34 (1989), 291–354.

Paehler, Katrin, 'Ein Spiegel seiner selbst. Der SD-Ausland in Italien', in Michael Wildt (ed.), *Nachrichtendienst, politische Elite, Mordeinheit. Der Sicherheitsdienst des Reichsführers-SS* (Hamburg, 2003), 241–66.

Plum, Günter, 'Staatspolizei und innere Verwaltung 1934–1936', *Vierteljahrshefte für Zeitgeschichte*, 13 (1965), 191–224.

Pohl, Dieter, 'Schauplatz Ukraine. Der Massenmord an den Juden im Militärver- waltungsgebiet und im Reichskommissariat 1941–1943', in Norbert Frei (ed.), *Ausbeutung, Vernichtung, Öffentlichkeit. Neue Studien zur nationalsozialistischen Lagerpolitik* (Munich, 2000), 135–73.

—— 'Die Einsatzgruppe C 1941/42', in Peter Klein (ed.), *Die Einsatzgruppen in der besetzten Sowjetunion 1941/42. Die Tätigkeits- und Lageberichte des Chefs der Sicherheitspolizei und des SD* (Berlin, 1997), 71–87.

Pollmeier, Heiko, 'Inhaftierung und Lagererfahrung deutscher Juden im November 1938', *Jahrbuch für Antisemitismusforschung*, 8 (1999), 107–30.

Přibyl, Lukáš, 'Das Schicksal des dritten Transports aus dem Protektorat nach Nisko', in *Theresienstädter Studien und Dokumente* (2000), 297–342.

Reinerth, Karl M., 'Zu den innenpolitischen Auseinandersetzungen unter den Deutschen in Rumänien zwischen den beiden Weltkriegen', in Walter König (ed.), *Siebenbürgen zwischen den beiden Weltkriegen* (Cologne, Weimar, and Vienna, 1994), 149–67.

Richardi, Hans-Günter, 'Der gerade Weg. Der Dachauer Häftling Karl Wagner', *Dachauer Hefte*, 7 (1991), 52–101.

Rohde, Horst, 'Hitlers erster "Blitzkrieg" und seine Auswirkungen auf Nordosteuropa', in Klaus A. Maier *et al.*, *Die Errichtung der Hegemonie auf dem europäischen Kontinent* (Stuttgart, 1979), 79–156.

Röhr, Werner, 'Das Sudetendeutsche Freikorps—Diversionsinstrument der Hitler-Regierung bei der Zerschlagung der Tschechoslowakei', *Militärgeschichtliche Mitteilungen*, 52 (1993), 35–66.

Rönn, Peter von, 'Politische und psychiatrische Homosexualitätskonstruktion im NS Staat', Part I: 'Die politische Genese des Homosexuellen als Staatsfeind', Part II: 'Die soziale Genese der Homosexualität als defizitäre Heterosexualität', *Zeitschrift für Sexualforschung*, 11 (1998), 99–129 and 220–60.

Rossino, Alexander B., 'Nazi Anti-Jewish Policy during the Polish Campaign: The Case of the Einsatzgruppe von Woyrsch', *German Studies Review*, 24/1 (2001), 35–53.

Roth, Karl Heinz, ' "Generalplan Ost"—"Gesamtplan Ost". Forschungsstand, Quellenprobleme, neue Ergebnisse', in Mechthild Rössler (ed.), *Der 'Generalplan Ost'. Hauptlinien der nationalsozialistischen Planungs- und Vernichtungspolitik* (Berlin, 1993), 25–95.

Rudolph, Jörg, ' "Geheime Reichskommando-Sache!" Hexenjäger im Schwarzen Orden. Der H-Sonderauftrag des Reichsführers-SS, 1935–1944', in Sönke Lorenz *et al.* (eds), *Himmlers Hexenkartothek. Das Interesse des Nationalsozialismus an der Hexenverfolgung*, 2nd edn. (Bielefeld, 2000), 47–97.

Runzheimer, Jürgen, 'Die Grenzzwischenfälle am Abend vor dem deutschen Angriff auf Polen', in Wolfgang Benz and Hermann Graml (eds), *Sommer 1939. Die Großmächte und der Europäische Krieg* (Stuttgart, 1979), 107–47.

—— 'Der Überfall auf den Sender Gleiwitz im Jahre 1939', *Vierteljahrshefte für Zeitgeschichte*, 10 (1962), 408–26.

Rüss, Hartmut, 'Wer war verantwortlich für das Massaker von Babij Jar?', *MilitärgeschichtlicheMitteilungen*, 57/2 (1998), 483–508.

Sauer, Wolfgang, 'Die Mobilmachung der Gewalt', in Karl Dietrich Bracher *et al.*, *Die nationalsozialistische Machtergreifung. Studien zur Geschichte des totalitären Herrschaftssystems in Deutschland 1933/34* (Cologne and Opladen, 1960), 685–972.

Scheffler, Wolfgang, 'Massenmord in Kowno', in id. and Diana Schulle (eds), *Buch der Erinnerung. Die ins Baltikum deportierten deutschen, österreichischen und tschechoslowakischen Juden*, vol. 1 (Munich, 2003), 83–190.

—— 'Das Schicksal der in die baltischen Staaten deportierten deutschen, österreichischen und tschechoslowakischen Juden 1941–1945', in id. and Diana Schulle (eds), *Buch der Erinnerung. Die ins Baltikum deportierten deutschen, österreichischen und tschechoslowakischen Juden*, vol. 1 (Munich, 2003), 1–78.

'Das Schicksal der Juden im Saarland 1920–1945', ed. Hans-Walter Herrmann, in *Dokumentation zur Geschichte der jüdischen Bevölkerung in Rheinland-Pfalz und im Saarland von 1800–1945*, published by the Landesarchivverwaltung Rheinland-Pfalz and the Landesarchiv Saarbrücken (Koblenz, 1974), 257–491.

Schilde, Kurt, 'Vom Tempelhofer Feld-Gefängnis zum Schutzhaftlager: Das "Columbia-Haus" in Berlin', in Wolfgang Benz and Barbara Distel (eds), *Herrschaft und Gewalt. Frühe Konzentrationslager 1933–1939* (Berlin, 2002), 65–81.

Schmid, Hans-Dieter, 'Die Geheime Staatspolizei in der Endphase des Krieges', *Geschichte in Wissenschaft und Unterricht*, 51/9 (2000), 528–39.

Schmuhl, Hans-Walter, 'Philipp Bouhler—Ein Voreiter des Massenmordes', in Ronald Smelser, Enrico Syring, and Rainer Zitelmann (eds), *Die Braune Elite II. 21 weitere biographische Skizzen* (Darmstadt, 1993), 39–50.

Schuhladen-Krämer, Jürgen, 'Die Exekutoren des Terrors. Herrmann Mattheiss, Walther Stahlecker, Friedrich Mussgay, Leiter der Geheimen Staatspolizeistelle Stuttgart', in Michael Kissener and Joachim Scholtyseck (eds), *Die Führer der Provinz. NS-Biographien aus Baden und Württemberg* (Konstanz, 1997).

Schulte, Jan Erik, 'Zwangsarbeit für die SS. Juden in der Ostindustrie GmbH', in Norbert Frei (ed.), *Ausbeutung, Vernichtung, Öffentlichkeit. Neue Studien zur nationalsozialistischen Lagerpolitik* (Munich, 2000), 43–74.

Schulze, Birgit, 'Heinrich Himmler, das Reichsministerium des Innern und das Verhältnis von Staat und Partei, 1943–1945', in Klaus Möltgen (ed.), *Kriegswirtschaft und öffentliche Verwaltung im Ruhrgebiet 1939–1945* (Gelsenkirchen, 1990), 9–33.

Silberklang, David, 'Die Juden und die ersten Deportationen aus dem Distrikt Lublin', in Bogdan Musial (ed.), *'Aktion Reinhardt'. Der Völkermord an den Juden im Generalgouvernement 1941–1944* (Osnabrück, 2004), 41–164.

Skriebeleit, Jörg, 'Flossenbürg-Stammlager', in Wolfgang Benz and Barbara Distel (eds), *Der Ort des Terrors. Geschichte der nationalsozialistischen Konzentrationslager*, vol. 4: *Flossenbürg, Mauthausen, Ravensbrück* (Munich, 2006), 17–66.

Sládek, Oldrich, 'Standrecht and Standgericht. Die Gestapo in Böhmen und Mähren', in Gerhard Paul and Michael Mallmann (eds), *Die Gestapo im Zweiten Weltkrieg. 'Heimatfront' und besetztes Europa* (Darmstadt, 2000), 317–39.

Smith, Bradley F., 'Die Überlieferung der Hoßbach-Niederschrift im Lichte neuer Quellen', *Vierteljahrshefte für Zeitgeschichte*, 38 (1990), 329–36.

Sowade, Hanno, 'Otto Ohlendorf—Nonkonformist, SS-Führer und Wirtschaftsfunktionär', in Ronald Smelser and Rainer Zitelmann (eds), *Die braune Elite. 22 biographische Skizzen* (Darmstadt, 1989), 188–200.

Spieker, Christoph, 'Enttäuschte Liebe. Funktionswandel der Ordnungspolizei in den Niederlanden', in Johannes Houwink ten Cate and Alfons Kenkmann (eds),

Deutsche und holländische Polizei in den besetzten niederländischen Gebieten. Doku-mentation einer Arbeitstagung (Münster, 2002), 67–95.

Stachura, Peter D., 'Der kritische Wendepunkt? Die NSDAP und die Reichstags-wahlen vom 20. Mai 1928', *Vierteljahrshefte für Zeitgeschichte*, 26 (1978), 66–99.

Stang, Knut, 'Dr. Oskar Dirlewanger—Protagonist der Terrorkriegführung', in Klaus-Michael Mallmann and Gerhard Paul (eds), *Karrieren der Gewalt. Natio-nalsozialistische Täterbiographien* (Darmstadt, 2004), 66–75.

Stehle, Hansjakob, 'Deutsche Friedensfühler bei den Westmächten im Februar/ März 1945', *Vierteljahrshefte für Zeitgeschichte*, 30 (1982), 538–55.

Stein, Harry, 'Buchenwald–Stammlager', in Wolfgang Benz and Barbara Distel (eds), *Der Ort des Terrors. Geschichte der nationalsozialistischen Konzentrationslager*, vol. 3: *Sachsenhausen, Buchenwald* (Munich, 2006), 301–56.

—— 'Das Sonderlager im Konzentrationslager Buchenwald nach den Pogromen 1938', in Monica Kingreen (ed.), *Nach der Kristallnacht. Jüdisches Leben und antijüdische Politik in Frankfurt am Main 1938–1945* (Frankfurt a. M., 1999), 19–54.

Strauss, Herbert A., 'Jewish Emigration from Germany: Nazi Policies and Jewish Response', *Leo Baeck Institute Yearbook*, 25 (1980), 313–61 (I), and 26 (1981), 343–409.

Strauss, Walter, 'Das Reichsministerium des Inneren und die Judengesetzgebung. Die Aufzeichnungen von Dr. Bernhard Lösener: Als Rassereferent im Reichs-ministerium des Inneren', *Vierteljahrshefte für Zeitgeschichte*, 9 (1961), 262–313.

Streim, Alfred, 'Konzentrationslager auf dem Gebiet der Sowjetunion', *Dachauer Hefte*, 5 (1989), 174–87.

Strzelecki, Andrzej, 'Der Todesmarsch der Häftlinge aus dem KL Auschwitz', in Ulrich Herbert (ed.), *Die nationalsozialistischen Konzentrationslager. Entwicklung und Struktur*, vol. 2 (Göttingen, 1998), 1093–1112.

Suchowolskij, Jakow, 'Es gab weder Schutz noch Erlösung, weder Sicherheit noch Rettung. Jüdischer Widerstand und der Untergang des Ghettos Glubokoje', *Dachauer Hefte*, 20 (2004), 22–38.

Sundhaussen, Holm, 'Jugoslawien', in Wolfgang Benz (ed.), *Dimension des Völkermords. Die Zahl der jüdischen Opfer des Nationalsozialismus* (Munich, 1991), 31–330.

—— 'Zur Geschichte der Waffen-SS in Kroatien 1941–1945', *Südost-Forschungen*, 30 (1971), 176–96.

'Tätigkeit der Zeugen Jehovas in der Neuzeit: Deutschland', *Jahrbuch der Zeugen Jehovas* (1974), 66–253.

Tregenza, Michael, 'Belzec Death Camp', *Wiener Library Bulletin*, 30 (1977), 8–25.

Tuchel, Johannes, 'Gestapa und Reichssicherheitshauptamt. Die Berliner Zentral-institutionen der Gestapo', in Gerhard Paul and Klaus-Michael Mallmann (eds), *Die Gestapo. Mythos und Realität* (Darmstadt, 1995), 84–100.

Ulbricht, Justus H., ' "Heil Dir,Wittekinds Stamm".Verden, der "Sachsenhain" und die Geschichte völkischer Religiosität in Deutschland', *Heimatkalender für den Landkreis Verden* (1995), 69–123, and (1996), 224–67.

Volk, Karl, '"Gell, seller B'suech!" Heinrich Himmler in Triberg', *Die Ortenau* (1997), 509–38.

Weiss, Aharon, 'The Holocaust and the Ukrainian Victims', in Michael Berenbaum (ed.), *A Mosaic of Victims: Non-Jews Persecuted and Murdered by the Nazis* (New York, 1990), 109–15.

Weisz, Franz, 'Personell vor allem ein "ständestaatlicher" Polizeikörper. Die Gestapo in Österreich', in Gerhard Paul and Klaus-Michael Mallmann (eds), *Die Gestapo. Mythos und Realität* (Darmstadt, 1995), 439–62.

Weitbrecht, Dorothee, 'Ermächtigung zur Vernichtung. Die Einsatzgruppen in Polen im Herbst 1939', in Klaus-Peter Mallmann and Bogdan Musial (eds), *Genesis des Genozids. Polen 1939–1941* (Darmstadt, 2004), 57–70.

Wetzel, Juliane, 'Frankreich und Belgien', in Wolfgang Benz (ed.), *Dimension des Völkermords. Die Zahl der jüdischen Opfer des Nationalsozialismus* (Munich, 1991), 105–35.

Wildt, Michael, 'Himmlers Terminkalender aus dem Jahr 1937', *Vierteljahrshefte für Zeitgeschichte*, 52 (2004), 671–91.

—— 'Der Hamburger Gestapochef Bruno Streckenbach. Eine nationalsozialistische Karriere', in Frank Bajohr and Joachim Szodrzynski (eds), *Hamburg in der NS-Zeit. Ergebnisse neuerer Forschungen* (Hamburg, 1995), 93–123.

Wilhelm, Hans-Heinrich, 'Die Einsatzgruppe A der Sicherheitspolizei und des SD 1941/42—eine exemplarische Studie', in Helmut Krausnick and Hans-Heinrich Wilhelm, *Die Truppe des Weltanschauungskrieges. Die Einsatzgruppen der Sicherheitspolizei und des SD 1938–1942* (Stuttgart, 1981), 281–636.

Witte, Peter, 'Letzte Nachrichten aus Siedliszce. Der Transport Ax aus Theresienstadt in den Distrikt Lublin', *Theresienstädter Studien und Dokumente* (1996), 98–113.

Wiwjorra, Ingo, 'Hermann Wirth—Ein gescheiterter Ideologe zwischen "Ahnenerbe" und Atlantis', in Barbara Danckwortt *et al.*, *Historische Rassismusforschung. Ideologen, Täter, Opfer* (Hamburg and Berlin, 1995), 91–112.

Wohlfeld, Udo, 'Im Hotel "Zum Großherzog". Das Konzentrationslager Bad Sulza 1933–1937', in Wolfgang Benz and Barbara Distel (eds), *Instrumentarium der Macht. Frühe Konzentrationslager 1933–1937* (Berlin, 2003), 263–75.

Wrobel, Johannes, 'Valepp/Schliersee (Bauer Marx)', in Wolfgang Benz and Barbara Distel (eds), *Der Ort des Terrors. Geschichte der nationalsozialistischen Konzentrationslager*, vol. 2: *Frühe Lager, Dachau, Emslandlager* (Munich, 2005), 522 f.

Wysocki, Gerd, 'Lizenz zum Töten. Die "Sonderbehandlungs"-Praxis der Stapo-Stelle Braunschweig', in Gerhard Paul and Michael Mallmann (eds), *Die Gestapo im Zweiten Weltkrieg. 'Heimatfront' und besetztes Europa* (Darmstadt, 2000), 237–54.

Yahil, Leni, 'Madagascar, Phantom of a Solution for the Jewish Question', in Bela Vago and George L. Mosse (eds), *Jews and Non-Jews in Eastern Europe, 1918–1945* (New York, 1974), 315–34.

Zámečník, Stanislav, 'Dachau-Stammlager', in Wolfgang Benz and Barbara Distel (eds), *Der Ort des Terrors. Geschichte der nationalsozialistischen Konzentrationslager*, vol. 2: *Frühe Lager, Dachau, Emslandlager* (Munich, 2005), 233–74.

—— 'Das frühe Konzentrationslager Dachau', in Wolfgang Benz and Barbara Distel (eds), *Terror ohne System. Die ersten Konzentrationslager im Nationalsozialismus 1933–1935* (Berlin, 2001), 13–39.

Zarusky, Jürgen, 'Von der Sondergerichtsbarkeit zum Endphasenterror. Loyalitätserzwingung und Rache am Widerstand im Zusammenbruch des NS-Regimes', in Cord Arendes (ed.), *Terror nach innen. Verbrechen am Ende des Zweiten Weltkrieges* (Göttingen, 2006), 103–21.

Zbikowski, Andrzej, 'Local Anti-Jewish Pogroms in the Occupied Territories of Eastern Poland, June–July 1941', in Lucjan Dobroszycki and Jeffrey S. Gurock (eds), *The Holocaust in the Soviet Union: Studies and Sources on the Destruction of the Jews in the Nazi Occupied Territories of the USSR, 1941–1945* (Armonk and London, 1993), 173–9.

Zevart, Milan, 'Geiselerschießungen im Besatzungsgebiet Untersteiermark (Spodnja Stajerska)', in Gerhard Jochem and Georg Seiderer (eds), *Entrechtung, Vertreibung, Mord. NS-Unrecht in Slowenien und seine Spuren in Bayern 1941–1945* (Berlin, 2005), 197–205.

NEWSPAPERS AND PERIODICALS

Bayerische Staatszeitung und Bayerischer Staatsanzeiger
Berliner Börsenzeitung
Biuletyn Głównej Komisji Badania Zbrodni Niemieckich w Polsce
Blätter für das Gymnasial-Schulwesen
Deutsche Allgemeine Zeitung
Die Deutsche Polizei
Deutsche Zeitung in Kroatien
Donauzeitung
Frankfurter Zeitung
Germanien
Il Giornale del Mattino
Kurier von Niederbayern
Langquaider Zeitung
Ministerialblatt des Reichs- und Preußischen Ministeriums des Innern
Münchner Neueste Nachrichten
Neue Zürcher Zeitung
New York Times
Nordwestdeutsche Hefte
NS-Kurier (Stuttgart)
Preußische Gesetzsammlung
Reichsgesetzblatt

Das Schwarze Korps
SS-Leitheft
Süddeutsche Zeitung
Volk und Rasse
Völkischer Beobachter
Westdeutscher Beobachter

UNPUBLISHED THESES AND MANUSCRIPTS

Cradle, Caron, ' "My Honor is Loyalty": The Biography of General Kurt Daluege', diss., Princeton (1979).

Eisenblätter, Gerhard, 'Grundlinien der Politik des Reichs gegenüber dem Generalgouvernement, 1939–1945' (MS) Phil. diss., Frankfurt (1969).

Kaiser, Johann, 'Die Politik des Dritten Reiches gegenüber der Slowakei 1939–1945. Ein Beitrag zur Erforschung der nationalsozialistischen Satellitenpolitik in Südosteuropa', diss., Bochum (1970).

Materne, Barbara, 'Die Germanische Leitstelle der SS 1940–1945. Entstehung, Aufgabenbereiche und Bedeutung in der Machtstruktur des Dritten Reiches', Magisterarbeit, Düsseldorf (2000).

Tuchel, Johannes, 'Heinrich Himmler und die Vorgeschichte des 20. Juli 1944' (manuscript).

Index

Bold entries refer to illustrations.